Econometric
Analysis

ECONOMETRIC ANALYSIS

Second Edition

William H. Greene
New York University

Macmillan Publishing Company
NEW YORK

Maxwell Macmillan Canada
TORONTO

Maxwell Macmillan International Publishing Group
NEW YORK   OXFORD   SINGAPORE   SYDNEY

Editor: Jill Lectka
Marketing Manager: Dave Borkowsky
Production Supervisor: Ron Harris
Production Manager: Su Levine
Text Designer: Jane Edelstein
Cover Designer: Tom Mack

This book was set in Times Roman by York Graphic Services, Inc.
printed by Quinn Woodbine, and bound by Quinn Woodbine.
The cover was printed by PHEONIX COLOR CORP.

Macmillan Publishing Company
866 Third Avenue, New York, New York 10022

Macmillan Publishing Company is part
of the Maxwell Communication Group of Companies.

Maxwell Macmillan Canada, Inc.
1200 Eglinton Avenue East
Suite 200
Don Mills, Ontario M3C 3N1

Library of Congress Cataloging in Publication Data

Greene, William H.
  Econometric analysis / William H. Greene.—2nd ed.
    p. cm.
  Includes bibliographical references and indexes.
  ISBN 0-02-346391-0
  1. Econometrics. I. Title.
HB139.G74 1993
330′.01′5195—dc20   92-219
                                                                      CIP

Printing: 2 3 4 5 6 7 8   Year: 3 4 5 6 7 8 9 0 1

For Lesley, Elizabeth, Allison, and Juliana

PREFACE

This book is intended for a one-year graduate course in econometrics. The prerequisites for that course would include calculus, basic mathematical statistics, and an introduction to econometrics at the level of, say, Gujarati's *Basic Econometrics* (McGraw-Hill, 1988) or Maddala's *Introduction to Econometrics* (Macmillan, 1992). I have included in Chapters 2 through 4 self-contained summaries of the matrix algebra and statistical theory used later in the book. The remainder of the book is intended to provide an up-to-date summary of econometric methods. This includes the traditional treatment of the multiple linear regression model as well as some recent developments in estimation and hypothesis testing. The latter include GMM estimation, Lagrange multiplier and conditional moment tests, testing for unit roots in macroeconomic data, the analysis of panel data, and limited dependent variables.

Readers may wonder what has motivated a second edition so soon (three years) after the first. One consideration was some second thoughts about some of the presentations. But with this edition I hope to offer students an accessible treatment of some important topics which, surprisingly, still remain absent from even the most recently published texts. These include estimation by the method of moments (GMM), conditional moment testing, and models of duration. The latter was deliberately and, I now believe, mistakenly omitted from my first edition. The former has simply become too widespread to neglect. Also, my earlier disclaimer notwithstanding, I hope that Chapter 19 has satisfactorily updated the treatment of at least some topics in time-series analysis.

I have attempted to keep the mathematical level consistent throughout. This has meant liberal use of matrix algebra but has required relatively little advanced distribution theory. Still, purists may prefer more in the way of detailed mathematical proofs. I give formal proofs only when they are particularly revealing about some underlying principle that will reappear in other contexts or provide students with a useful tool for their work. White's proof of the limiting distribution of the Wald statistic in Chapter 10 is an example. In contrast, a proof of the central limit theorem, while obviously of great utility on its own, is a one-shot deal. For those who are teaching at a relatively high level and who desire more of the theorem/proof format, I would suggest Peter Schmidt's *Econometrics* (Marcel Dekker, 1976) as a very handy adjunct.

One feature that distinguishes this work from its predecessors is its greater attention to nonlinear models, including full chapters on nonlinear regression and nonlinear optimization. Computer software now in wide use has made estimation of nonlinear models as simple as estimation of linear ones, and the recent literature reflects that progression. The purpose of these chapters is to bring the textbook treatment up to the level of common practice. I have also included two long chapters on limited dependent-variable models. These models are becoming ever more common in the applied literature. I have written these chapters because there is no other source that presents these topics at a level elementary enough to initiate the newcomer but complete enough to enable a diligent student to use the information to undertake a serious piece of empirical analysis.

It is now generally accepted that training in econometrics must include some exposure to the mechanics of computation. This, it seems to me, should be self-evident. Computers and computer software have come a long way from the days when one trudged across campus in the snow to hand a deck of cards to the operator of a hostile mainframe (only to find out the next day that the entire job had aborted because of a comma punched in the wrong column). The greatest advance has been the appearance of microcomputers, which have changed both teaching and research. One now has on a desktop as much computer power as was once contained in a room-sized mainframe. What this means for teaching is that students can be given realistic data sets and challenging empirical analyses as routinely as theoretical exercises. To this end, I have included in this book a large number of data sets, many of which have been used in studies already in the literature. In addition, the appendix to Chapter 20 contains a yearly data set on a number of macroeconomic variables. (Quarterly data are available from the same sources.) These could be used, for example, to update Klein's model I or, for the more ambitious, to estimate a new model.

There are many computer programs that students can use in an econometrics course. Their most important features are ease of use and flexibility; the same program can easily be used for many different types of analyses. A partial list of the general econometrics programs now in use is as follows:

ET*   Econometric Software, Bellport, New York (general econometrics, tobit, probit, matrix algebra)

GAUSS*   Aptech Systems, Kent, Washington (matrix programming language, maximum likelihood)

LIMDEP   Econometric Software, Bellport, New York (limited and qualitative dependent variables and general econometrics)

MicroTSP*   Quantitative Micro Software, Irvine, California (forecasting and time-series models, nonlinear regression)

RATS   VAR Econometrics, Minneapolis, Minnesota (regression analysis of time series)

SAS   SAS Institute, Cary, North Carolina (general econometrics and modeling)

SHAZAM   Professor Ken White, University of British Columbia (general econometrics, multiple-equations models, tobit, probit)

SORITEC   Sorites Group, Springfield, Virginia (large-scale multiple-equation modeling)

SPSS   SPSS, Inc., Chicago, Illinois (general statistical analysis for social scientists)

SST   Dubin Rivers Research, Pasadena, California (regression, maximum likelihood, limited dependent variables)

TSP   TSP International, Palo Alto, California (general econometrics, linear and nonlinear multiple-equation models, time-series analysis)

Most of these programs are available in both mainframe and microcomputer versions. Those marked with an asterisk were written especially for personal computers. All are general-purpose programs. Their primary differences (apart from price) are their range of techniques (suggested in the listing), the amount of programming required of the user, and the level of difficulty of command entry. For the last of these, programs vary from those with commands that are very low level, such as Gauss, which is a programming language, to those that use powerful single commands to invoke large processors that automate many complex computations, such as TSP's LSQ procedures. Since the tastes and needs of users will vary, prospective users should contact the authors for information about the programs. Journals such as *The American Statistician* and the *Journal of Applied Econometrics* also publish reviews of particular programs. Finally, a clearing house for information about software is the Centre for Computing in Economics at the University of Bristol in the United Kingdom.

It is a pleasure to express my appreciation to those who have influenced this work (some inadvertently). I would add my name to the long list of practitioners, teachers, and authors who have thanked Arthur Goldberger for his contribution to their education. Dennis Aigner and Laurits Christensen were also influential in shaping my views on econometrics. The number of students and colleagues whose input has helped produce what you find here is far too large to allow me to thank them individually. I do owe a debt to Aline Quester, whose persistent questioning and encouragement strongly influenced Chapters 21 and 22, to David Hensher and Donald Waldman, who allowed me to cite their unpublished work in these chapters, and to Martin Evans and Paul Wachtel, whose suggestions helped to shape Chapter 19.

This book has benefited at several stages from the careful reading of many reviewers, including Badi H. Baltagi, University of Houston; Leonard A. Carlson, Emory University; Chris Cornwell, University of Georgia; Michael Ellis, Wesleyan University; K. Rao Kadiyala, Purdue University; William Lott, University of Connecticut; Edward J. Mathis, Villanova University; Thad Mirer, State University of New York at Albany; Peter J. Schmidt, Michigan State University; Terry G. Seaks, University of North Carolina at Greensboro; Donald Snyder, California State University, Los Angeles; Houston H. Stokes, University of Illinois at Chicago; Mark Watson, Harvard University; and Kenneth D. West, Princeton University. The empirical work has been improved by a thorough review by Ken White of the University of British Columbia. This edition will also reflect many of the suggestions of those too numerous to thank individually who wrote, called, and e-mailed (a new verb?) to comment on the first edition. I would also like to thank Jack Repcheck, who initiated my first edition; Ron Harris and Jill Lectka, of Macmillan; and Diane Belleville, of NYU, for their contribution to the completion of this book. I owe special thanks to Terry Seaks, whose painstaking review went far beyond the call of duty. I owe my greatest debt to my wife, Lynne, and to my daughters, Lesley, Allison, Elizabeth, and Juliana.

W. H. G.

CONTENTS

3 PROBABILITY AND DISTRIBUTION THEORY 53

9   DATA PROBLEMS   266

10   LARGE-SAMPLE RESULTS FOR THE
CLASSICAL REGRESSION MODEL   292

16 MODELS THAT USE BOTH CROSS-SECTION AND TIME-SERIES DATA   444

17 SYSTEMS OF REGRESSION EQUATIONS   486

CHAPTER 1

Introduction

1.1. Econometrics

In the first issue of *Econometrica,* the Econometric Society stated that

> its main object shall be to promote studies that aim at a unification of the theoretical-quantita-
> tive and the empirical-quantitative approach to economic problems and that are penetrated by
> constructive and rigorous thinking similar to that which has come to dominate the natural
> sciences.
>
> But there are several aspects of the quantitative approach to economics, and no single one
> of these aspects, taken by itself, should be confounded with econometrics. Thus, econome-
> trics is by no means the same as economic statistics. Nor is it identical with what we call
> general economic theory, although a considerable portion of this theory has a definitely
> quantitative character. Nor should econometrics be taken as synonomous [sic] with the appli-
> cation of mathematics to economics. Experience has shown that each of these three view-
> points, that of statistics, economic theory, and mathematics, is a necessary, but not by itself a
> sufficient, condition for a real understanding of the quantitative relations in modern economic
> life. It is the *unification* of all three that is powerful. And it is this unification that constitutes
> econometrics.[1]

Frisch and his society responded to an unprecedented accumulation of statistical information. They saw a need to establish a body of principles that could organize what would
otherwise become a bewildering mass of data. Neither the pillars nor the objectives of
econometrics have changed in the half century since this editorial appeared. Econometrics
is the field of economics that concerns itself with the application of mathematical statistics
and the tools of statistical inference to the empirical measurement of relationships postu-
lated by economic theory.

1.2. Econometric Modeling

Economic theory is typically crisp and unambiguous. Models of demand, production, and
aggregate consumption all postulate precise, *deterministic* relationships. Dependent and
independent variables are identified, a functional form is specified, and, in most cases, at
least a qualitative statement is made about effects that occur when independent variables
in the model change. Of course, the model is only a simplification of reality. It will

---

[1] Frish (1933).

include the salient features of the relationship of interest, but will leave unaccounted for influences that might well be present but are, for our purposes, unimportant. Naturally, people may differ on just how minimal some influences really are, and in the end, this may be yet another empirical question. Still, only the most optimistic analyst would expect to find an exact correspondence between his or her model and its real-world counterpart.

No model could hope to encompass the myriad essentially random aspects of economic life. For example, no matter how elegant or complete a model of production might be, it has no way of coping with the possibility that a snowy day might necessitate a plant closing and show up as an outlier in an otherwise immaculately constructed body of data on production costs. It is thus necessary to incorporate stochastic elements in our empirical models. As a consequence, observations on the dependent variable will display variation attributable not only to differences in variables we have explicitly accounted for, but also to the randomness of human behavior and the interaction of countless minor influences that we have not. It is understood that the introduction of a random "disturbance" into a deterministic model is not intended merely to paper over its inadequacies. It is essential to examine the results of the study, in a sort of post mortem, to ensure that the allegedly random, unexplained factor is truly unexplainable. If it is not, the model is, in fact, inadequate. To pursue our example, ignoring (or being unaware of) a snowstorm is one thing; neglecting regional differences in the unit prices of the factors of production is quite another. Without such omissions, the stochastic element endows the model with its statistical properties. Observations on the variable(s) under study are thus taken to be the outcomes of a random process. With a sufficiently detailed stochastic structure and adequate data, our analysis will become a matter of deducing the properties of a probability distribution. The tools and methods of mathematical statistics will provide the operating principles.

A model (or theory) can never truly be confirmed unless it is made so broad as to include every possibility. But we may subject it to ever more rigorous scrutiny and, in the face of contradictory evidence, refute it. A deterministic theory will be invalidated by a single errant observation. The introduction of stochastic elements into the model changes it from an exact statement to a probabilistic description about expected outcomes and carries with it an important implication. Only a preponderance of contradictory evidence can convincingly invalidate the probabilistic model, and what constitutes a "preponderance of evidence" is a matter of interpretation. Thus, the probabilistic model is both less precise and, perhaps not necessarily to the good, more robust.

The role of theory in econometrics cannot be overstated. The belief that we may scrutinize a set of nonexperimental data and expect some complex truth to be revealed to us if we only spend enough time manipulating the numbers is hopelessly optimistic. In an experimental setting, we are free to choose the values of the stimuli and move them in whatever way we wish to elicit a change in the response variable. What remains is only to quantify the observed relationship. In the realm of economics, we are only passive observers of the economy. The notion of a controlled experiment is almost unheard of. At best, we can expect to sample observations from a large population and to assume that the conditions needed to employ our tools of statistical inference are met. Theory plays the role of organizer of the data. With no theoretical basis, the result of the exercise is most likely to be an ambiguous catalog of possibilities.

The process of econometric analysis departs from the specification of a theoretical relationship. We initially proceed on the optimistic assumption that we can obtain precise measurements on all of the variables in our correctly specified model. If the ideal conditions are met at every step, the subsequent analysis will probably be routine. Unfortunately, they rarely are. Some of the difficulties one can expect to encounter are the following:

1. The data may be badly measured or may correspond only vaguely to the variables in the model. ''The interest rate'' is one example.
2. Some of the variables may be inherently unmeasurable. ''Expectations'' are a case in point.
3. The theory may make only a rough guess as to the correct functional form, if it makes any at all, and we may be forced to choose from an embarrassingly long menu of possibilities.
4. The assumed stochastic properties of the random terms in the model may be demonstrably violated. This may call into question the methods of estimation and inference procedures we have used.
5. Some relevant variables may be missing from the model.

And so on. The ensuing steps of the analysis consist of coping with these problems and attempting to cull whatever information is likely to be present in such obviously imperfect data. The methodology is that of mathematical statistics and econometric theory. The product is an econometric model.

1.3. Theoretical and Applied Econometrics

A distinction is usually made between theoretical and applied econometrics. A rough line can be drawn between the development of techniques and the application of those techniques in a particular setting. Theorists also analyze the consequences of applying particular methods when the assumptions that justify them are not met. But the distinction is often artificial. It is common for new techniques to be developed in the field, in response to a particular problem in a specific study, rather than in the laboratory.[2] This book is oriented to techniques that are usable (and used) in the field. Still, the emphasis is on methods, rather than on specific results.[3] The numerous examples are presented to illustrate techniques rather than to produce new empirical evidence. In a few instances, we have attempted to replicate (sometimes without success) earlier studies, while in others we have repeated studies already in the literature with more recent data. The interested reader may wish to extend these studies with newer or different data sets.

1.4. Plan of the Book

This book is organized into four parts.

The first three chapters survey the tools used in econometrics: Chapter 2 on matrix algebra, Chapter 3 on probability and distribution theory, and Chapter 4 on statistical inference. Since it is assumed that the reader has some previous training in each of these topics, these summaries are fairly brief and are included primarily for those who desire a refresher or a convenient reference.

---

[2] In the abstract, there is an intellectual appeal to a technique that is developed in order to solve a particular problem, as opposed to one that is devised and then sent off to find a problem to solve.

[3] There are a number of excellent works devoted to applied econometrics, among them Bridge (1971), Desai (1976), and Berndt (1990).

Chapters 5, 6, and 7 present the basic results of the classical linear regression model. Chapter 8 discusses extensions of the classical model that show, among other things, that the linear model is not nearly so restrictive as its appearance might suggest. Chapter 9, on multicollinearity, measurement error, and missing data, raises some issues that impede the simple, mechanical application of the theoretical model to real-world data. Chapters 10, 11, and 12 present somewhat more advanced topics. The large-sample results used throughout the subsequent chapters are discussed in Chapter 10. Chapter 11 is devoted to nonlinear regression models. Chapter 12 introduces some of the technical aspects of nonlinear optimization.

From Chapter 13 onward, the restrictions of the classical model are progressively relaxed. Chapter 13 presents some general theoretical results for the model. These principles are then used in two standard applications: heteroscedasticity in Chapter 14 and autocorrelation in Chapter 15. The combination of these two phenomena is discussed in Chapter 16 under the heading "Time Series–Cross-Section Data."

The remaining chapters survey more or less advanced topics in econometrics. (I hesitate to use that term, since most of the methods discussed there are, in fact, widely used by practitioners throughout the profession. Perhaps *further* topics would be a better name.) Chapter 17 discusses the multivariate regression model and the estimation of systems of demand equations. Chapters 18 and 19 present topics in time-series analysis and distributed lag models. Chapter 20 discusses simultaneous equations models. Interest in this topic is marked by an ebb and flow. Empirical applications of simultaneous equations models, for example as envisioned by the Cowles Commission, have received progressively less emphasis and far less attention in the applied econometrics literature in recent years. Interestingly enough, theoretical research on the topic continues unabated and regularly produces important insights, which are often more useful in other frameworks. Chapters 21 and 22 present three relatively new areas in econometrics: models with discrete dependent variables, limited dependent variable models, and models of duration.

CHAPTER 2

Matrix Algebra

2.1. Introduction

This is the first of three chapters devoted to mathematical and statistical tools used in econometrics. This chapter presents most of the matrix results used in this book; the few additional results that become necessary later will be developed in passing. By using matrix algebra, the fundamental results in econometrics can be presented in an elegant, compact, and uncluttered format. But, more important, we find that many diverse and seemingly complex results have a common structure and a surprising simplicity. The set of theorems and techniques we require are collected here, in one place, so that later in the book we can use them without interrupting the discussion to derive them. For those students who have not used matrix algebra for a while (or have not yet encountered the subject), this chapter also provides a reasonably concise summary.[1]

2.2. Some Terminology

A **matrix** is a rectangular array of numbers, denoted

$$\mathbf{A} = [a_{ik}] \qquad \text{or} \qquad [\mathbf{A}]_{ik}$$

$$= \begin{bmatrix} a_{11} & a_{12} & \cdots & a_{1K} \\ a_{21} & a_{22} & \cdots & a_{2K} \\ & & \vdots & \\ a_{n1} & a_{n2} & \cdots & a_{nK} \end{bmatrix}. \tag{2-1}$$

Note, in the first line, how the typical element is used to denote the matrix. A subscripted element of a matrix is always read as $a_{\text{row, column}}$. An example is given in Table 2.1. In these data, the rows are identified with years and the columns with particular variables.

A **vector** is an ordered set of numbers arranged in either a row or a column. In view of the preceding, a **row vector** is also a matrix with one row, while a **column vector** is a matrix with one column. Thus, the five variables observed for 1972 constitute a row vector, while the time series of values for consumption is a column vector.

A matrix can also be viewed as a set of column vectors, which would be a natural interpretation of the sample data set, or, of course, as a set of row vectors.[2] The **dimen-**

---

[1] For a more complete description of the topic, some sources to consider are Dhrymes (1974), Bellman (1970), Hadley (1961), Strang (1976), and for a large collection of useful results, Rao (1965).

[2] Henceforth, we shall denote a matrix by a boldfaced capital letter, as in (2–1), and a vector as a boldfaced lowercase letter, as in **a**. Unless otherwise noted, a vector will always be assumed to be a *column vector*.

TABLE 2.1

			Column		
	1	**2**	**3**	**4**	**5**
		Consumption	**GNP (billions**	**GNP**	**Discount Rate**
Row	**Year**	**(billions of dollars)**	**of dollars)**	**Deflator**	**(N.Y. Fed, avg.)**
1	1972	737.1	1185.9	1.0000	4.50
2	1973	812.0	1326.4	1.0575	6.44
3	1974	808.1	1434.2	1.1508	7.83
4	1975	976.4	1549.2	1.2579	6.25
5	1976	1084.3	1718.0	1.3234	5.50
6	1977	1204.4	1918.3	1.4005	5.46
7	1978	1346.5	2163.9	1.5042	7.46
8	1979	1507.2	2417.8	1.6342	10.28
9	1980	1667.2	2633.1	1.7864	11.77

Source: Data from the *Economic Report of the President,* U.S. Government Printing Office, Washington, D.C., 1983.

sions of a matrix are the numbers of rows and columns it contains. "**A** is an $n \times K$ matrix" (read "n by K") will always mean that **A** has n rows and K columns. If n equals K, then **A** is a **square matrix.** There are several particular types of square matrices that occur frequently in econometrics.

1. A **symmetric matrix,** **A**, is one in which $a_{ik} = a_{ki}$ for all i and k. For example,

$$\mathbf{A} = \begin{bmatrix} 1 & 3 & 7 \\ 3 & 5 & 2 \\ 7 & 2 & 1 \end{bmatrix}.$$

2. A **diagonal matrix** is a square matrix whose only nonzero elements appear on the main diagonal, moving from upper left to lower right.

3. A **scalar matrix** is a diagonal matrix with the same value in all diagonal elements.

4. An **identity matrix** is a scalar matrix with ones on the diagonal. This is always denoted **I.** A subscript is sometimes included to indicate its size, or **order.** For example,

$$\mathbf{I}_3 = \begin{bmatrix} 1 & 0 & 0 \\ 0 & 1 & 0 \\ 0 & 0 & 1 \end{bmatrix}. \tag{2-2}$$

5. A **triangular matrix** is one that has only zeros either above or below the main diagonal. If the zeros are above the diagonal, the matrix is lower triangular.

2.3. Algebraic Manipulation of Matrices

Matrices provide a convenient way of collecting sets of equations and equations involving sums of values. This section outlines some of the basic arithmetic operations of matrix algebra.

2.3.1. Equality of Matrices

Matrices (or vectors) **A** and **B** are equal if and only if they have the same dimensions and each element of **A** equals the corresponding element of **B**.

$$\mathbf{A} = \mathbf{B} \text{ if and only if } a_{ik} = b_{ik} \text{ for all } i \text{ and } k.$$

2.3.2. Transposition

The **transpose** of a matrix **A,** denoted **A′**, is obtained by creating the matrix whose kth row is the kth column of the original matrix. Thus, if **B** = **A′**, each column of **A** will appear as the corresponding row of **B**. If **A** is $n \times K$, **A′** is $K \times n$. For example,

$$\mathbf{A} = \begin{bmatrix} 1 & 2 & 3 \\ 5 & 1 & 5 \\ 6 & 4 & 5 \\ 3 & 1 & 4 \end{bmatrix}, \quad \mathbf{A'} = \begin{bmatrix} 1 & 5 & 6 & 3 \\ 2 & 1 & 4 & 1 \\ 3 & 5 & 5 & 4 \end{bmatrix}.$$

An equivalent definition of the transpose of a matrix is

$$\mathbf{B} = \mathbf{A'} \Leftrightarrow b_{ik} = a_{ki} \qquad \text{for all } i \text{ and } k. \tag{2–3}$$

The definition of a symmetric matrix implies that

$$\text{if } \mathbf{A} \text{ is symmetric, } \mathbf{A} = \mathbf{A'}. \tag{2–4}$$

For any **A**,

$$(\mathbf{A'})' = \mathbf{A}. \tag{2–5}$$

Finally, the transpose of a column vector, **a**, is a row vector:

$$\mathbf{a'} = [a_1 \quad a_2 \quad \cdots \quad a_n].$$

2.3.3. Matrix Addition

The operation of addition is extended to matrices by defining

$$\mathbf{C} = \mathbf{A} + \mathbf{B} = [a_{ik} + b_{ik}]. \tag{2–6}$$

Matrices cannot be added unless they have the same dimensions, in which case they are said to be **conformable for addition. A zero matrix** or **null matrix** is one whose elements are all zero. In the addition of matrices, it plays the same role as the scalar 0 in scalar addition, that is,

$$\mathbf{A} + \mathbf{0} = \mathbf{A}. \tag{2–7}$$

We also extend the operation of subtraction to matrices precisely as if they were scalars by performing the operation element by element. Thus,

$$\mathbf{A} - \mathbf{B} = [a_{ik} - b_{ik}]. \tag{2–8}$$

It follows that matrix addition is commutative

$$\mathbf{A} + \mathbf{B} = \mathbf{B} + \mathbf{A} \tag{2–9}$$

and associative

$$(\mathbf{A} + \mathbf{B}) + \mathbf{C} = \mathbf{A} + (\mathbf{B} + \mathbf{C}) \tag{2–10}$$

and that

$$(\mathbf{A} + \mathbf{B})' = \mathbf{A'} + \mathbf{B'}. \tag{2–11}$$

2.3.4. Matrix Multiplication

Matrices are multiplied by using the **inner product.** The inner product (or **dot product**) of two vectors, **a** and **b**, is a scalar, and is written

$$\mathbf{a'b} = a_1 b_1 + a_2 b_2 + \cdots + a_n b_n. \tag{2–12}$$

Note that the inner product is written as the transpose of vector **a** times vector **b**, a row vector times a column vector. For example,

$$\mathbf{a'b} = [1 \quad 3 \quad 4] \begin{bmatrix} 3 \\ 8 \\ 2 \end{bmatrix} = 1(3) + 3(8) + 4(2) = 35.$$

In (2–12), each term $a_j b_j$ equals $b_j a_j$; hence

$$\mathbf{a'b} = \mathbf{b'a}. \tag{2–13}$$

For an $n \times K$ matrix **A** and a $K \times T$ matrix **B**, the product matrix

$$\mathbf{C} = \mathbf{AB} \tag{2–14}$$

is an $n \times T$ matrix whose ikth element is the inner product of row i of **A** and column k of **B**. We need a notation for the ith row of a matrix. In nearly all of what follows, we will use $\mathbf{a}_i$ to denote the ith column. To avoid confusion, we'll use $\mathbf{a}^i$ to denote the ith row of **A**. Thus,

$$\mathbf{C} = \mathbf{AB} \Rightarrow c_{ik} = \mathbf{a}^i \mathbf{b}_k. \tag{2–15}$$

In order to multiply two matrices, the number of columns in the first must be the same as the number of rows in the second, in which case, they are **conformable for multiplication.**[3] For example,

$$\mathbf{AB} = \begin{bmatrix} 1 & 3 & 2 \\ 4 & 5 & -1 \end{bmatrix} \begin{bmatrix} 2 & 4 \\ 1 & 6 \\ 0 & 5 \end{bmatrix}$$

$$= \begin{bmatrix} 1(2) + 3(1) + 2(0) & 1(4) + 3(6) + 2(5) \\ 4(2) + 5(1) + (-1)(0) & 4(4) + 5(6) + (-1)(5) \end{bmatrix}$$

$$= \begin{bmatrix} 5 & 32 \\ 13 & 41 \end{bmatrix}.$$

Multiplication of matrices is generally not commutative. For example, in the preceding calculation, **AB** is a 2×2 matrix, while

$$\mathbf{BA} = \begin{bmatrix} 2(1) + 4(4) & 2(3) + 4(5) & 2(2) + 4(-1) \\ 1(1) + 6(4) & 1(3) + 6(5) & 1(2) + 6(-1) \\ 0(1) + 5(4) & 0(3) + 5(5) & 0(2) + 5(-1) \end{bmatrix}$$

$$= \begin{bmatrix} 18 & 26 & 0 \\ 25 & 33 & -4 \\ 20 & 25 & -5 \end{bmatrix}.$$

[3] A simple way to check the conformability of two matrices for multiplication is to write down the dimensions of the operation, for example, $(n \times K)$ times $(K \times T)$. The inner dimensions must be equal; the result has dimensions equal to the outer values.

In other cases, **AB** may exist, but **BA** may be undefined or, if it does exist, may have different dimensions, as in the preceding example. However, in general, even if **AB** and **BA** do have the same dimensions, they will not be equal. In view of this, we define **premultiplication** and **postmultiplication** of matrices. In the product **AB**, **B** is *premultiplied by* **A**, while **A** is *postmultiplied* by **B**.

The product of a matrix and a vector is written

$$\mathbf{c} = \mathbf{Ab}.$$

The number of elements in **b** must equal the number of columns in **A**; the result is a vector with a number of elements equal to the number of rows in **A**. For example,

$$\begin{bmatrix} 5 \\ 4 \\ 1 \end{bmatrix} = \begin{bmatrix} 4 & 2 & 1 \\ 2 & 6 & 1 \\ 1 & 1 & 0 \end{bmatrix} \begin{bmatrix} a \\ b \\ c \end{bmatrix}.$$

We can interpret this in two ways. First, it is a compact way of writing the three equations

$$5 = 4a + 2b + 1c,$$

$$4 = 2a + 6b + 1c,$$

$$1 = 1a + 1b + 0c.$$

Second, by writing the set of equations as

$$\begin{bmatrix} 5 \\ 4 \\ 1 \end{bmatrix} = a\begin{bmatrix} 4 \\ 2 \\ 1 \end{bmatrix} + b\begin{bmatrix} 2 \\ 6 \\ 1 \end{bmatrix} + c\begin{bmatrix} 1 \\ 1 \\ 0 \end{bmatrix},$$

we see that the right-hand side is a **linear combination** of the columns of the matrix where the coefficients are the elements of the vector. For the general case,

$$\begin{aligned} \mathbf{c} &= \mathbf{Ab} \\ &= b_1\mathbf{a}_1 + b_2\mathbf{a}_2 + \cdots + b_K\mathbf{a}_K. \end{aligned} \tag{2-16}$$

In the calculation of a matrix product $\mathbf{C} = \mathbf{AB}$, each column of **C** is a linear combination of the columns of **A**, where the coefficients are the elements in the corresponding column of **B**. That is,

$$\mathbf{C} = \mathbf{AB} \Leftrightarrow \mathbf{c}_k = \mathbf{Ab}_k. \tag{2-17}$$

Let $\mathbf{e}_k$ be a column vector that has 0s everywhere except for a 1 in the kth position. Then $\mathbf{Ae}_k$ is a linear combination of the columns of **A** in which the coefficient on every column but the kth is 0, while that on the kth is 1. The result is

$$\mathbf{a}_k = \mathbf{Ae}_k. \tag{2-18}$$

Combining this result with (2–17) produces

$$(\mathbf{a}_1 \quad \mathbf{a}_2 \quad \cdots \quad \mathbf{a}_n) = \mathbf{A}(\mathbf{e}_1 \quad \mathbf{e}_2 \quad \cdots \quad \mathbf{e}_n)$$

$$= \mathbf{A}\begin{bmatrix} 1 & 0 & 0 & \cdots & 0 \\ 0 & 1 & 0 & \cdots & 0 \\ & & & \vdots & \\ 0 & 0 & 0 & \cdots & 1 \end{bmatrix} \tag{2-19}$$

$$= \mathbf{AI} = \mathbf{A}.$$

In connection with matrix multiplication, the identity matrix is analogous to the scalar 1. For any matrix or vector, **A**, **AI** = **A**. In addition, **IA** = **A**, though if **A** is not a square matrix, the two identity matrices are of different orders.

A conformable matrix of zeros produces the expected result: **A0** = **0**.

Some general rules for matrix multiplication are as follows:

$$\text{\textbf{Associative law:}} \qquad (\mathbf{AB})\mathbf{C} = \mathbf{A}(\mathbf{BC}), \qquad (2\text{--}20)$$

$$\text{\textbf{Distributive law:}} \qquad \mathbf{A}(\mathbf{B} + \mathbf{C}) = \mathbf{AB} + \mathbf{AC}. \qquad (2\text{--}21)$$

(Note the order of multiplication of the matrices in the second rule: **BA** and **CA** may not be defined.)

$$\text{\textbf{Transpose of a product:}} \qquad (\mathbf{AB})' = \mathbf{B'A'}. \qquad (2\text{--}22)$$

By direct extension,

$$(\mathbf{ABC})' = \mathbf{C'B'A'}. \qquad (2\text{--}23)$$

Finally, **scalar multiplication** of a matrix is the operation of multiplying every element of the matrix by a given scalar. For scalar c and matrix **A**,

$$c\mathbf{A} = [ca_{ik}]. \qquad (2\text{--}24)$$

Note how this operation is used in (2–16).

2.3.5. Sums of Values

Matrices and vectors provide a particularly convenient way to represent sums of values. A useful device is the vector **i**, which contains a column of 1s. The sum of the elements in any vector **x** is

$$\sum_{i=1}^{n} x_i = x_1 + x_2 + \cdots + x_n = \mathbf{i'x}. \qquad (2\text{--}25)$$

If all elements in **x** are equal to the same constant, a, then $\mathbf{x} = a\mathbf{i}$ and

$$\sum_i x_i = \mathbf{i'}(a\mathbf{i}) = a(\mathbf{i'i}) = na. \qquad (2\text{--}26)$$

For any constant, a, and vector, **x**,

$$\sum_i ax_i = a \sum_i x_i = a\mathbf{i'x}. \qquad (2\text{--}27)$$

If $a = 1/n$, we obtain the arithmetic mean,

$$\bar{x} = \frac{1}{n} \sum_i x_i = \frac{1}{n}\mathbf{i'x}, \qquad (2\text{--}28)$$

from which it follows that

$$\sum_i x_i = \mathbf{i'x} = n\bar{x}.$$

Sums of squares and cross products are obtained easily with the inner product operation. The sum of squares of the elements in a vector $\mathbf{x}$ is

$$\sum_i x_i^2 = \mathbf{x}'\mathbf{x}; \tag{2-29}$$

the sum of the products of the elements in vectors $\mathbf{x}$ and $\mathbf{y}$ is

$$\sum_i x_i y_i = \mathbf{x}'\mathbf{y}. \tag{2-30}$$

By the definition of matrix multiplication,

$$[\mathbf{X}'\mathbf{X}]_{ij} = [\mathbf{x}_i'\mathbf{x}_j] \tag{2-31}$$

is the inner product of the ith and jth columns of $\mathbf{X}$. Thus, for example, for the data set given in Table 2.1, if we define $\mathbf{X}$ as the 9×3 matrix containing (year, consumption, GNP), then

$$[\mathbf{X}'\mathbf{X}]_{23} = \sum_{i=1}^{9} \text{consumption}_i \text{GNP}_i$$

$$= 737.1(1185.9) + \cdots + 1667.2(2633.1) = 19{,}743{,}711.34.$$

If $\mathbf{X}$ is $n \times K$,

$$\mathbf{X}'\mathbf{X} = \sum_{i=1}^{n} \mathbf{x}^{i'}\mathbf{x}^{i},$$

where $\mathbf{x}^{i'}$ is the transpose of the ith row of $\mathbf{X}$.[4] This form shows that the $K \times K$ matrix $\mathbf{X}'\mathbf{X}$ is the sum of n $K \times K$ matrices, each formed from a single row (year) of $\mathbf{X}$. For the example given earlier, this is the sum of nine 3×3 matrices, each formed from one row (year) of the original data matrix. Suppose that $\mathbf{X}'\mathbf{X}$ for the nine years of data was already in hand, and a tenth year of data was obtained. The matrix of sums of squares and cross products can be updated just by adding a 3×3 matrix to the $\mathbf{X}'\mathbf{X}$ already computed.

2.3.6. A Useful Idempotent Matrix

A fundamental matrix in statistics is the one that is used to transform data to deviations from their mean. First,

$$\mathbf{i}\bar{x} = \mathbf{i}\frac{1}{n}\mathbf{i}'\mathbf{x}$$

$$= \begin{bmatrix} \bar{x} \\ \bar{x} \\ \vdots \\ \bar{x} \end{bmatrix} = \frac{1}{n}\mathbf{i}\mathbf{i}'\mathbf{x}. \tag{2-32}$$

The matrix $(1/n)\mathbf{i}\mathbf{i}'$ is an $n \times n$ matrix with every element equal to $1/n$. The set of values in deviations form is thus

$$\begin{bmatrix} x_1 - \bar{x} \\ x_2 - \bar{x} \\ \vdots \\ x_n - \bar{x} \end{bmatrix} = [\mathbf{x} - \mathbf{i}\bar{x}] = \left[\mathbf{x} - \frac{1}{n}\mathbf{i}\mathbf{i}'\mathbf{x}\right]. \tag{2-33}$$

---

[4] Later, for example in Chapter 10, when there is no possible ambiguity regarding rows and columns, we will switch to the conventional notation $\mathbf{X}'\mathbf{X} = \Sigma_i \mathbf{x}_i\mathbf{x}_i'$.

Since $\mathbf{x} = \mathbf{Ix}$,

$$\left[\mathbf{x} - \frac{1}{n}\mathbf{ii'x} \right] = \left[\mathbf{Ix} - \frac{1}{n}\mathbf{ii'x} \right]$$

$$= \left[\mathbf{I} - \frac{1}{n}\mathbf{ii'} \right]\mathbf{x} \qquad (2\text{–}34)$$

$$= \mathbf{M}^0\mathbf{x}.$$

Henceforth, the symbol $\mathbf{M}^0$ will be used only for this matrix. Its diagonal elements are all $1 - 1/n$, and its off-diagonal elements are $-1/n$.

The matrix $\mathbf{M}^0$ is primarily useful in computing sums of squared deviations. Some computations are simplified by the result

$$\mathbf{M}^0\mathbf{i} = \left[\mathbf{I} - \frac{1}{n}\mathbf{ii'} \right]\mathbf{i}$$

$$= \mathbf{i} - \frac{1}{n}\mathbf{i}(\mathbf{i'i})$$

$$= \mathbf{0}.$$

This implies that $\mathbf{i'M}^0 = \mathbf{0'}$. The sum of deviations about the mean is then

$$\sum_i (x_i - \bar{x}) = \mathbf{i'}[\mathbf{M}^0\mathbf{x}] = \mathbf{0'x} = 0. \qquad (2\text{–}35)$$

For a single variable, $\mathbf{x}$, the sum of squared deviations about the mean is

$$\sum_i (x_i - \bar{x})^2 = \sum_i (x_i^2 - 2\bar{x}x_i + \bar{x}^2)$$

$$= \left(\sum_i x_i^2 \right) - n\bar{x}^2. \qquad (2\text{–}36)$$

In matrix terms,

$$\sum_i (x_i - \bar{x})^2 = (\mathbf{x} - \bar{x}\mathbf{i})'(\mathbf{x} - \bar{x}\mathbf{i})$$

$$= (\mathbf{M}^0\mathbf{x})'(\mathbf{M}^0\mathbf{x})$$

$$= \mathbf{x'M}^{0\prime}\mathbf{M}^0\mathbf{x}.$$

Two properties of $\mathbf{M}^0$ are useful at this point. First, since all off-diagonal elements of $\mathbf{M}^0$ equal $-1/n$, $\mathbf{M}^0$ is symmetric. Second, as can easily be verified by multiplication, $\mathbf{M}^0$ is equal to its square; $\mathbf{M}^0\mathbf{M}^0 = \mathbf{M}^0$.

Definition. An **idempotent** matrix is one that is equal to its square, that is, $\mathbf{M}^2 = \mathbf{MM} = \mathbf{M}$. If $\mathbf{M}$ is a symmetric idempotent matrix—most of the idempotent matrices we shall encounter are—then $\mathbf{M'M} = \mathbf{M}$.

Thus, $\mathbf{M}^0$ is an idempotent matrix. Combining results, we obtain

$$\sum_i (x_i - \bar{x})^2 = \mathbf{x'M}^0\mathbf{x}. \qquad (2\text{–}37)$$

Consider constructing a matrix of sums of squares and cross products in deviations from the column means. For two vectors **x** and **y**,

$$\sum_i (x_i - \bar{x})(y_i - \bar{y}) = (\mathbf{M}^0\mathbf{x})'(\mathbf{M}^0\mathbf{y}), \tag{2-38}$$

so,

$$\begin{bmatrix} \Sigma_i(x_i - \bar{x})^2 & \Sigma_i(x_i - \bar{x})(y_i - \bar{y}) \\ \Sigma_i(y_i - \bar{y})(x_i - \bar{x}) & \Sigma_i(y_i - \bar{y})^2 \end{bmatrix} = \begin{bmatrix} \mathbf{x}'\mathbf{M}^0\mathbf{x} & \mathbf{x}'\mathbf{M}^0\mathbf{y} \\ \mathbf{y}'\mathbf{M}^0\mathbf{x} & \mathbf{y}'\mathbf{M}^0\mathbf{y} \end{bmatrix}. \tag{2-39}$$

If we put the two column vectors, **x** and **y**, in an $n \times 2$ matrix $\mathbf{Z} = [\mathbf{x}, \mathbf{y}]$, then $\mathbf{M}^0\mathbf{Z}$ is the $n \times 2$ matrix in which the two columns of data are in mean deviation form. Then

$$(\mathbf{M}^0\mathbf{Z})'(\mathbf{M}^0\mathbf{Z}) = \mathbf{Z}'\mathbf{M}^0\mathbf{M}^0\mathbf{Z} = \mathbf{Z}'\mathbf{M}^0\mathbf{Z}.$$

2.4. Geometry of Matrices

Matrix algebra is extremely useful in the formulation and solution of sets of linear equations. At the same time, the algebraic results have a geometrical basis that is very helpful in understanding the calculations. Before developing the mathematical results, it will be useful to digress to a geometric treatment of matrices and vectors.

2.4.1. Vector Spaces

The K elements of a column vector

$$\mathbf{a} = \begin{bmatrix} a_1 \\ a_2 \\ a_3 \\ \vdots \\ a_K \end{bmatrix}$$

can be viewed as the coordinates of a point in a K-dimensional space, as shown in Figure 2.1 for two dimensions, or as the definition of the line segment connecting the origin and this point.

Two basic operations are defined for vectors, **scalar multiplication** and **addition.** A scalar multiple of a vector, **a**, is another vector, say **a***, whose coordinates are the scalar multiple of **a**'s coordinates. Thus, in Figure 2.1,

$$\mathbf{a} = \begin{bmatrix} 1 \\ 2 \end{bmatrix}, \qquad \mathbf{a}^* = 2\mathbf{a} = \begin{bmatrix} 2 \\ 4 \end{bmatrix}, \qquad \text{and} \qquad \mathbf{a}^{**} = -\tfrac{1}{2}\mathbf{a} = \begin{bmatrix} -\tfrac{1}{2} \\ -1 \end{bmatrix}.$$

The set of all possible scalar multiples of **a** is the line through **0** and **a**. Any scalar multiple of **a** is a segment of this line. The sum of two vectors, **a** and **b**, is a third vector whose coordinates are the sums of the corresponding coordinates of **a** and **b**. For example,

$$\mathbf{c} = \mathbf{a} + \mathbf{b} = \begin{bmatrix} 1 \\ 2 \end{bmatrix} + \begin{bmatrix} 2 \\ 1 \end{bmatrix} = \begin{bmatrix} 3 \\ 3 \end{bmatrix}.$$

Geometrically, **c** is obtained by moving in the distance and direction defined by **b** from the tip of **a** or, because addition is commutative, from the tip of **b** in the distance and direction of **a**. This is a geometric interpretation of the operations of scalar multiplication and addition of matrices applied to vectors.

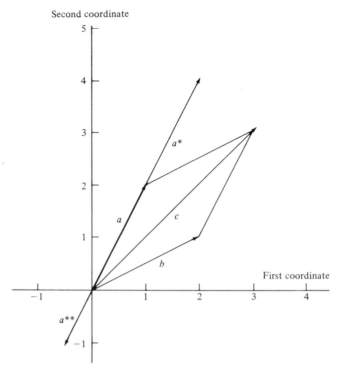

FIGURE 2.1 Vector space.

The two-dimensional plane is the set of all vectors with two real-valued coordinates. We label this set $\mathbb{R}^2$. It has two important properties.

1. $\mathbb{R}^2$ *is closed under scalar multiplication;* every scalar multiple of a vector in the plane is also in the plane.
2. $\mathbb{R}^2$ *is closed under addition;* the sum of any two vectors is always a vector in the plane.

Definition. A **vector space** is any set of vectors that is closed under scalar multiplication and addition.

Another example is the set of all real numbers, that is $\mathbb{R}^1$, the set of vectors with one real element. In general, that set of K-element vectors all of whose elements are real numbers is a K-dimensional vector space, denoted $\mathbb{R}^K$. The preceding examples are drawn in $\mathbb{R}^2$.[5]

2.4.2. Linear Combinations of Vectors and Basis Vectors

In Figure 2.2, $\mathbf{c} = \mathbf{a} + \mathbf{b}$ and $\mathbf{d} = \mathbf{a}^* + \mathbf{b}$. But since $\mathbf{a}^* = 2\mathbf{a}$, $\mathbf{d} = 2\mathbf{a} + \mathbf{b}$. Also, $\mathbf{e} = \mathbf{a} + 2\mathbf{b}$ and $\mathbf{f} = \mathbf{b} + (-\mathbf{a}) = \mathbf{b} - \mathbf{a}$. As this exercise suggests, any vector in $\mathbb{R}^2$ could be obtained as a **linear combination** of $\mathbf{a}$ and $\mathbf{b}$.

Definition. A set of vectors in a vector space is a **basis** for that vector space if any vector in the vector space can be written as a linear combination of them.

---

[5] The definition extends to $\mathbb{C}^K$, the set of vectors whose elements are complex pairs. We shall not require complex vectors in this book.

As is clear from Figure 2.2, any pair of two-element vectors, including **a** and **b**, that point in different directions will form a basis for $\mathbb{R}^2$. Consider an arbitrary set of vectors in $\mathbb{R}^2$, **a**, **b**, and **c**. If **a** and **b** are a basis, we can find numbers α_1 and α_2 such that $\mathbf{c} = \alpha_1\mathbf{a} + \alpha_2\mathbf{b}$. Let

$$\mathbf{a} = \begin{bmatrix} a_1 \\ a_2 \end{bmatrix}, \qquad \mathbf{b} = \begin{bmatrix} b_1 \\ b_2 \end{bmatrix}, \qquad \text{and} \qquad \mathbf{c} = \begin{bmatrix} c_1 \\ c_2 \end{bmatrix}.$$

Then

$$\begin{aligned} c_1 &= \alpha_1 a_1 + \alpha_2 b_1, \\ c_2 &= \alpha_1 a_2 + \alpha_2 b_2. \end{aligned} \tag{2-40}$$

The solutions to this pair of equations are

$$\begin{aligned} \alpha_1 &= \frac{b_2 c_1 - b_1 c_2}{a_1 b_2 - b_1 a_2}, \\ \alpha_2 &= \frac{a_1 c_2 - a_2 c_1}{a_1 b_2 - b_1 a_2}. \end{aligned} \tag{2-41}$$

This gives a unique solution unless $(a_1 b_2 - b_1 a_2) = 0$. If $(a_1 b_2 - b_1 a_2) = 0$, then $a_1/a_2 = b_1/b_2$, which means that **b** is just a multiple of **a**. This returns us to our original

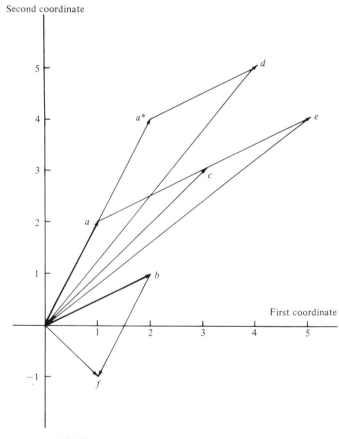

FIGURE 2.2 Linear combinations of vectors.

condition, that **a** and **b** point in different directions. The implication is that if **a** and **b** are any pair of vectors for which the denominator in (2–41) is not zero, then any other vector, **c,** can be formed as a *unique* linear combination of **a** and **b**. The basis of a vector space is not unique, since any set of vectors that satisfy the definition will do. But for any particular basis, there is only one linear combination of them that will produce another particular vector in the vector space.

2.4.3. Linear Dependence

As the preceding should suggest, K vectors are required to form a basis for $\mathbb{R}^K$. Although the basis for a vector space is not unique, not every set of K vectors will suffice. In Figure 2.2, **a** and **b** form a basis for $\mathbb{R}^2$, but **a** and **a*** do not. The difference between these two pairs is that **a** and **b** are linearly independent while **a** and **a*** are linearly dependent.

> **Definition.** A set of vectors is **linearly dependent** if any one of the vectors in the set can be written as a linear combination of the others.

Since **a*** is a multiple of **a**, **a** and **a*** are linearly dependent. For another example, if

$$\mathbf{a} = \begin{bmatrix} 1 \\ 2 \end{bmatrix}, \qquad \mathbf{b} = \begin{bmatrix} 3 \\ 3 \end{bmatrix}, \qquad \mathbf{c} = \begin{bmatrix} 10 \\ 14 \end{bmatrix},$$

then

$$2\mathbf{a} + \mathbf{b} - (\tfrac{1}{2})\mathbf{c} = \mathbf{0},$$

so **a**, **b**, and **c** are linearly dependent. However, any of the three possible pairs of them are linearly independent.

> **Definition.** A set of vectors is **linearly independent** if and only if the only solution to
>
> $$\alpha_1 \mathbf{a}_1 + \alpha_2 \mathbf{a}_2 + \cdots + \alpha_K \mathbf{a}_K = \mathbf{0}$$
>
> is
>
> $$\alpha_1 = \alpha_2 = \cdots = \alpha_K = 0.$$

The preceding implies the following equivalent definition of a basis:

> **Definition.** A basis for a vector space of K dimensions is any set of K linearly independent vectors in that space.

Since any $(K + 1)$st vector can be written as a linear combination of the K basis vectors, it follows that any set of more than K vectors in $\mathbb{R}^K$ must be linearly dependent.

2.4.4. Subspaces

> **Definition.** The set of all linear combinations of a set of vectors is the vector space that is **spanned** by those vectors.

For example, by definition, the space spanned by a basis for $\mathbb{R}^K$ is $\mathbb{R}^K$. An implication of this is that if **a** and **b** are a basis for $\mathbb{R}^2$ and **c** is another vector in $\mathbb{R}^2$, the space spanned by [**a**, **b**, **c**] is, again, $\mathbb{R}^2$. Of course, **c** is superfluous. Nonetheless, any vector in $\mathbb{R}^2$ can be expressed as a linear combination of **a**, **b**, and **c**. (The linear combination will not be unique. Suppose, for example that **a** and **c** are also a basis for $\mathbb{R}^2$.)

Consider the set of three coordinate vectors whose third element is zero. In particular,

$$\mathbf{a}' = [a_1 \quad a_2 \quad 0] \qquad \text{and} \qquad \mathbf{b}' = [b_1 \quad b_2 \quad 0].$$

Vectors **a** and **b** do not span the three-dimensional space $\mathbb{R}^3$. Every linear combination of **a** and **b** has a third coordinate equal to zero, so, for instance, $\mathbf{c}' = [1, 2, 3]$ could not be written as a linear combination of **a** and **b**. However, if $(a_1b_2 - a_2b_1)$ is not equal to zero [see (2–41)], then *any vector whose third element is zero can be expressed as a linear combination of* **a** *and* **b**. So, while **a** and **b** do not span $\mathbb{R}^3$, they do span something, the set of vectors in $\mathbb{R}^3$ whose third element is zero. This is a plane (the ''floor'' of the box in a three-dimensional figure). This plane in $\mathbb{R}^3$ is a **subspace,** in this instance, a two-dimensional subspace. Note that *it is not* $\mathbb{R}^2$. It is the set of vectors in $\mathbb{R}^3$ whose third coordinate is 0. Any plane in $\mathbb{R}^3$, regardless of how it is oriented, forms a two-dimensional subspace. Any two independent vectors that lie in that subspace will span it. But without a third vector that points in some other direction, we cannot span any more of $\mathbb{R}^3$ than this two-dimensional part of it. By the same logic, any line in $\mathbb{R}^3$ is a one-dimensional subspace, in this case, the set of all vectors in $\mathbb{R}^3$ whose coordinates are multiples of those of the vector that define the line. A subspace is a vector space in all of the respects in which we have defined it. We emphasize that it is *not* a vector space of lower dimension. For example, $\mathbb{R}^2$ is not a subspace of $\mathbb{R}^3$. The essential difference is the number of dimensions in the vectors. The vectors in $\mathbb{R}^3$ that form a two-dimensional subspace are still three-element vectors; they all just happen to lie in the same plane.

The space spanned by a set of vectors in $\mathbb{R}^K$ has at most K dimensions. If this space has fewer than K dimensions, it is a subspace, or **hyperplane.** But the important point in the preceding discussion is that *every set of vectors spans some space;* it may be the entire space in which the vectors reside, or some subspace of it.

2.4.5. Rank of a Matrix

We view a matrix as a set of column vectors. The number of columns in the matrix equals the number of vectors in the set, and the number of rows equals the number of coordinates in each column vector.

Definition. The **column space** of a matrix is the vector space that is spanned by its column vectors.

If the matrix contains K rows, its column space might have K dimensions. But, as we have seen, it might have fewer dimensions; the column vectors might be linearly dependent, or there might be fewer than K of them. Consider the matrix

$$\mathbf{A} = \begin{bmatrix} 1 & 5 & 6 \\ 2 & 6 & 8 \\ 7 & 1 & 8 \end{bmatrix}.$$

It contains three vectors from $\mathbb{R}^3$, but the third is the sum of the first two, so the column space of this matrix cannot have three dimensions. Nor does it have only one, since the three columns are not all scalar multiples of one another. Hence it has two, and the column space of this matrix is a two-dimensional subspace of $\mathbb{R}^3$.

Definition. The **column rank** of a matrix is the dimension of the vector space that is spanned by its columns.

It follows that the column rank of a matrix is equal to the largest number of linearly independent column vectors it contains. The column rank of **A** is 2. For another specific example, consider

$$\mathbf{B} = \begin{bmatrix} 1 & 2 & 3 \\ 5 & 1 & 5 \\ 6 & 4 & 5 \\ 3 & 1 & 4 \end{bmatrix}.$$

It can be shown (we shall see how later) that this matrix has a column rank equal to 3. Since each column of **B** is a vector in $\mathbb{R}^4$, the column space of **B** is a three-dimensional subspace of $\mathbb{R}^4$.

Consider, instead, the set of vectors obtained by using the *rows* of **B** instead of the columns. The new matrix would be

$$\mathbf{C} = \begin{bmatrix} 1 & 5 & 6 & 3 \\ 2 & 1 & 4 & 1 \\ 3 & 5 & 5 & 4 \end{bmatrix}.$$

This matrix is composed of four column vectors from $\mathbb{R}^3$. (Note that **C** is **B**′.) The column space of **C** is at most $\mathbb{R}^3$, since four vectors in $\mathbb{R}^3$ must be linearly dependent. In fact, the column space of **C** *is* $\mathbb{R}^3$. Although this is not the same as the column space of **B**, it does have the same dimension. Thus, the column rank of **C** and the column rank of **B** are the same. But the columns of **C** are the rows of **B**. Thus, the column rank of **C** equals the **row rank** of **B**. The fact that the column and row ranks of **B** are the same is not a coincidence. The general results (which are equivalent) are

1. The **column rank** and **row rank** of a matrix are equal.
2. The **row space** and **column space** of a matrix have the same dimension.   (2–42)

The two propositions hold regardless of the actual row and column rank. If the column rank of a matrix happens to equal the number of columns it contains, the matrix is said to have **full column rank. Full row rank** is defined likewise. Since the row and column ranks of a matrix are always equal, we can speak unambiguously of the **rank of a matrix.** For either the row rank or the column rank (and, at this point, we shall drop the distinction),

$$\text{rank}(\mathbf{A}) = \text{rank}(\mathbf{A}') \leq \min(\#\text{rows}, \#\text{columns}). \qquad (2–43)$$

In most contexts, we shall be interested in the columns of the matrices we manipulate. We shall use the term **full rank** to describe a matrix whose rank is equal to the number of columns it contains.

Of particular interest will be the distinction between **full rank** and **short rank matrices.** The distinction turns on the solutions to $\mathbf{Ax} = \mathbf{0}$. If a nonzero **x** for which $\mathbf{Ax} = \mathbf{0}$ exists, **A** does not have full rank. Equivalently, if the nonzero **x** exists, the columns of **A** are linearly dependent, and at least one of them can be expressed as a linear combination of the others. For example, a nonzero set of solutions to

$$\begin{bmatrix} 1 & 3 & 10 \\ 2 & 3 & 14 \end{bmatrix} \begin{bmatrix} x_1 \\ x_2 \\ x_3 \end{bmatrix} = \begin{bmatrix} 0 \\ 0 \end{bmatrix}$$

is any multiple of $\mathbf{x}' = (2, 1, -\frac{1}{2})$.

In a product matrix, $\mathbf{C} = \mathbf{AB}$, every column of **C** is a linear combination of the columns of **A**, so each column of **C** is in the column space of **A**. It is possible that the set of columns in **C** could span this space, but it is not possible for them to span a higher dimensional space. At best, they could be a full set of linearly independent vectors in **A**'s column space. We conclude that the column rank of **C** could not be greater than that of **A**. Now, apply the same logic to the rows of **C**, which are all linear combinations of the rows of **B**. For the same reason that the column rank of **C** cannot exceed the column rank of **A**, the row rank of **C** cannot exceed the row rank of **B**. Since row and column ranks are always equal, we conclude that

$$\text{rank}(\mathbf{AB}) \leq \min(\text{rank}(\mathbf{A}), \text{rank}(\mathbf{B})). \qquad (2–44)$$

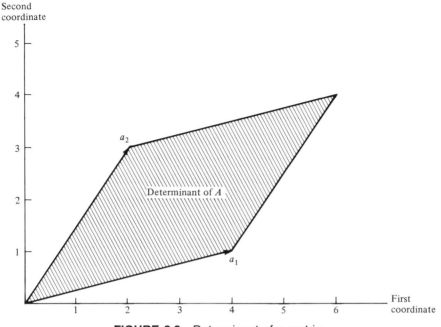

FIGURE 2.3   Determinant of a matrix.

A useful corollary of (2–44) is

If **A** is $M \times n$ and **B** is a square matrix of rank n, rank(**AB**) = rank(**A**). (2–45)

The proof is left as an exercise.

Another application that plays a central role in the development of regression analysis is, for any **A**,

$$\text{rank}(\mathbf{A}) = \text{rank}(\mathbf{A'A}) = \text{rank}(\mathbf{AA'}). \tag{2–46}$$

2.4.6. Determinant of a Matrix

The vectors of the matrix

$$\mathbf{A} = [\mathbf{a}, \mathbf{b}]$$

$$= \begin{bmatrix} 4 & 2 \\ 1 & 3 \end{bmatrix}$$

are shown in Figure 2.3. The area of the parallelogram formed by the columns of **A** can be obtained by manipulating congruent triangles. The result is $4(3) - 1(2) = 10$. This area is the **determinant** of **A**.[6] If the columns of **A** were linearly dependent, that is, if one were a scalar multiple of the other, the two vectors would lie on the same line. The "parallelogram" would collapse to a line and would have zero area. This implies that *if the columns of a matrix are linearly dependent, its determinant is zero*. Recalling our earlier discussion of linear dependence in $\mathbb{R}^2$, we see that this is the case of $(a_1 b_2 - a_2 b_1) = 0$ in (2–41). (The determinant of **A** is, in fact, $a_1 b_2 - a_2 b_1$.)

---

[6] Strictly speaking, the area is the absolute value of the determinant. Since we are concerned with geometric results at this point, we shall neglect the sign. Later, in an algebraic context, the sign of the determinant will be important. Note that *the determinant is defined only for square matrices*.

Consider the same exercise in $\mathbb{R}^3$. If we complete the parallelograms in all dimensions for a set of three-dimensional vectors, we shall form a solid, that is, a parallelotope. The determinant will be the volume of this solid. But if the columns of the matrix are linearly dependent, the columns will all lie in the same plane (or on the same line). The "solid" thus formed will collapse to a plane or a line and will have no volume; again, the determinant will be zero. This general result carries over to higher dimensions as well.

Proposition. The determinant of a matrix is nonzero if and only if it has full rank.

Full rank and short rank matrices can be distinguished by whether their determinants are nonzero or not. There are some settings in which the value of the determinant is also of interest, so we now consider some algebraic results.

It is most convenient to begin with a diagonal matrix,

$$\mathbf{D} = \begin{bmatrix} d_1 & 0 & 0 & \cdots & 0 \\ 0 & d_2 & 0 & \cdots & 0 \\ & & & \vdots & \\ 0 & 0 & 0 & \cdots & d_K \end{bmatrix}.$$

The column vectors of $\mathbf{D}$ define a "box" in $\mathbb{R}^K$ whose sides are all at right angles to one another.[7] Its "volume," or determinant, is simply the product of the lengths of the sides, which we denote

$$|\mathbf{D}| = d_1 d_2 \cdots d_K = \prod_{i=1}^{K} d_i. \tag{2-47}$$

A special case is the identity matrix, which has, regardless of K, $|\mathbf{I}_K| = 1$. Multiplying $\mathbf{D}$ by a scalar, c, is equivalent to multiplying the length of each side of the box by c, which would multiply its volume by c^K. Thus,

$$|c\mathbf{D}| = c^K |\mathbf{D}|. \tag{2-48}$$

Continuing with this admittedly special case, we suppose that only one column of $\mathbf{D}$ is multiplied by c. In two dimensions, this would make the box wider, but not higher, or vice versa. Hence, the "volume" (area) would also be multiplied by c. Now suppose that each side of the box were multiplied by a different c, the first by c_1, the second by c_2, and so on. The volume would, by an obvious extension, now be $c_1 c_2 \cdots c_K |\mathbf{D}|$. The matrix with columns defined by $[c_1\mathbf{d}_1, c_2\mathbf{d}_2, \ldots]$ is just $\mathbf{DC}$, where $\mathbf{C}$ is a diagonal matrix with c_i as its ith diagonal element. The computation just described is, therefore,

$$|\mathbf{DC}| = |\mathbf{D}| \cdot |\mathbf{C}|. \tag{2-49}$$

(The determinant of $\mathbf{C}$ is the product of the c_i's since $\mathbf{C}$, like $\mathbf{D}$, is a diagonal matrix.) Note, in particular, what happens to the whole thing if one of the c_i's is zero.

Thus far, we have considered only diagonal matrices. We now consider the general case. The absolute value of a determinant is still the volume of the parallelotope built up from the columns of the matrix. We have already seen the result for 2×2 matrices:

$$\begin{vmatrix} a & c \\ b & d \end{vmatrix} = (ad - bc). \tag{2-50}$$

Notice that it is a function of all of the elements of the matrix. This will be true, in general. For more than two dimensions, the determinant can be obtained by using an

---

[7] Each column vector defines a segment on one of the axes.

expansion by cofactors. Using *any* row, say i, we obtain

$$|\mathbf{A}| = \sum_{j=1}^{K} a_{ij}(-1)^{i+j}|\mathbf{A}_{ij}|, \tag{2–51}$$

where $\mathbf{A}_{ij}$ is the matrix obtained from $\mathbf{A}$ by deleting row i and column j. The determinant of $\mathbf{A}_{ij}$ is called a **minor** of $\mathbf{A}$.[8] When the correct sign, $(-1)^{i+j}$, is added, it becomes a **cofactor.** This operation can be done using any column as well. For example, a 4×4 determinant becomes a sum of four 3×3s while a 5×5 is a sum of five 4×4s, each of which is a sum of four 3×3s, and so on. Obviously, it is a good idea, if possible, to base (2–51) on a row or column with many zeros in it. In practice, this rapidly becomes a heavy burden. It is unlikely, though, that you will ever calculate any determinants over 3×3 without a computer. You might, however, compute a 3×3 determinant on occasion; if so, the following shortcut will prove useful:

$$\begin{vmatrix} a_{11} & a_{12} & a_{13} \\ a_{21} & a_{22} & a_{23} \\ a_{31} & a_{32} & a_{33} \end{vmatrix} = \begin{aligned} &a_{11}a_{22}a_{33} + a_{12}a_{23}a_{31} + a_{13}a_{32}a_{21} \\ &-a_{31}a_{22}a_{13} - a_{21}a_{12}a_{33} - a_{11}a_{23}a_{32}. \end{aligned}$$

Although (2–48) and (2–49) were given for diagonal matrices, they hold for general matrices $\mathbf{C}$ and $\mathbf{D}$. One special case of (2–48) to note is that of $c = -1$. Multiplying a matrix by -1 does not necessarily change the sign of its determinant. It does so only if the order of the matrix is odd. By using the expansion by cofactors formula, an additional result can be shown:

$$|\mathbf{A}| = |\mathbf{A}'|. \tag{2–52}$$

2.4.7. A Least Squares Problem

Given a vector, $\mathbf{y}$, and a matrix, $\mathbf{X}$, we are interested in expressing $\mathbf{y}$ as a linear combination of the columns of $\mathbf{X}$. There are two possibilities. If $\mathbf{y}$ lies in the column space of $\mathbf{X}$, we shall be able to find a $\mathbf{b}$ such that

$$\mathbf{y} = \mathbf{Xb}. \tag{2–53}$$

Figure 2.4 illustrates such a case for three dimensions in which the two columns of $\mathbf{X}$ both have a third coordinate equal to zero. Only $\mathbf{y}$s whose third coordinate is zero, such as $\mathbf{y}^0$ in the figure, can be expressed as $\mathbf{Xb}$ for some $\mathbf{b}$. For the general case, assuming that $\mathbf{y}$ is, indeed, in the column space of $\mathbf{X}$, we can find the coefficients $\mathbf{b}$ by solving the set of equations in (2–53). Procedures for doing so are discussed in the next section.

Suppose, however, that $\mathbf{y}$ is not in the column space of $\mathbf{X}$. In the context of our example, suppose that $\mathbf{y}$'s third component is not zero. Then there is no $\mathbf{b}$ such that (2–53) holds. We can, however, write

$$\mathbf{y} = \mathbf{Xb} + \mathbf{e}, \tag{2–54}$$

where $\mathbf{e}$ is the difference between $\mathbf{y}$ and $\mathbf{Xb}$. By this construction, we find an $\mathbf{Xb}$ that is in the column space of $\mathbf{X}$, and $\mathbf{e}$ is the difference, or "residual." The figure shows two examples, $\mathbf{y}$ and $\mathbf{y}^*$. For the present, we consider only $\mathbf{y}$. We are interested in finding the $\mathbf{b}$ such that $\mathbf{y}$ is as close as possible to $\mathbf{Xb}$ in the sense that $\mathbf{e}$ is as short as possible.

---

[8] If i equals j, the determinant is a **principal minor**.

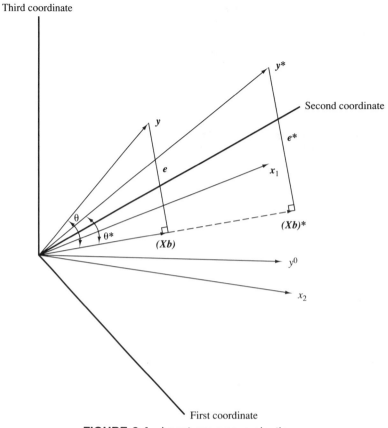

FIGURE 2.4 Least squares projections.

Definition. The length, or **norm,** of a vector **e** is

$$\|\mathbf{e}\| = \sqrt{\mathbf{e}'\mathbf{e}}.\tag{2-55}$$

The problem is to find the **b** for which

$$\|\mathbf{e}\| = \|\mathbf{y} - \mathbf{Xb}\|$$

is as small as possible. The solution is that **b** that makes **e** perpendicular, or orthogonal, to **Xb.**

Definition. Two vectors, **a** and **b,** are **orthogonal,** written **a** ⊥ **b,** if and only if

$$\mathbf{a}'\mathbf{b} = \mathbf{b}'\mathbf{a} = 0.$$

Returning once again to our fitting problem, we find that the **b** we seek is that for which

$$\mathbf{e} \perp \mathbf{Xb.}$$

Expanding this set of equations gives the requirement

$$(\mathbf{Xb})'\mathbf{e} = \mathbf{0}$$

$$= \mathbf{b}'\mathbf{X}'\mathbf{y} - \mathbf{b}'\mathbf{X}'\mathbf{Xb}$$

$$= \mathbf{b}'[\mathbf{X}'\mathbf{y} - \mathbf{X}'\mathbf{Xb}]$$

or, since **b** is not **0**, the set of equations

$$\mathbf{X'y} = \mathbf{X'Xb}.$$

The means of solving such a set of equations is the subject of the next section.

In Figure 2.4, the linear combination **Xb** is called the **projection** of **y** into the space of **X**. The figure is drawn so that although **y** and **y*** are different, they have the same projection. The question we wish to pursue here is, which vector, **y** or **y***, is closer to its projection in the space of **X**? Superficially, it would appear that **y** is closer, since **e** is shorter than **e***. However, **y*** is much more nearly parallel to its projection than **y**; the only reason that its residual vector is longer is that **y*** is so long compared to **y**. A measure of comparison that would be unaffected by the length of the vectors is the angle between the vector and its projection. By this measure, θ^* is considerably smaller than θ, which would reverse the earlier conclusion.

THEOREM. *The angle θ between two vectors, **a** and **b**, satisfies*

$$\cos \theta = \frac{\mathbf{a'b}}{\|\mathbf{a}\| \cdot \|\mathbf{b}\|}.$$

The two vectors in the calculation would be **y** or **y*** and **Xb.** A zero cosine implies that the vectors are orthogonal. If the cosine is one, the angle is zero, which means that the vectors are the same. (They would be if **y** were in the column space of **X**.) By dividing by the lengths, we automatically compensate for the length of **y**. By this measure, we would find that **y*** is closer to its projection than **y**.

2.5. Solution of a System of Equations

Consider the set of n linear equations

$$\mathbf{Ax} = \mathbf{b}, \tag{2–56}$$

in which the K elements of **x** constitute the unknowns. **A** is a known matrix of coefficients, and **b** is a specified vector of values. We are interested in knowing whether a solution exists; if so, how to obtain it; and, finally, if it does exist, whether it is unique.

2.5.1. Systems of Linear Equations

For most of our applications, we shall consider only square systems of equations, that is, those in which **A** is a square matrix. In what follows, therefore, we take n to equal K. Since the number of rows in **A** is the number of equations, while the number of columns in **A** is the number of variables, this is the familiar case of "n equations in n unknowns." There are two types of systems:

1. Homogeneous system: $\mathbf{Ax} = \mathbf{0}$.

By definition, a nonzero solution to such a system will exist if and only if **A** does not have full rank. If so, then for at least one column of **A**, we can write the preceding as

$$\mathbf{a}_j = -\sum_{i \neq j} \frac{x_i}{x_j} \mathbf{a}_i.$$

This means, as we know, that the columns of **A** are linearly dependent and that $|\mathbf{A}| = 0$.

2. Nonhomogeneous system: $\mathbf{Ax} = \mathbf{b}$.

The vector $\mathbf{b}$ is chosen arbitrarily and is to be expressed as a linear combination of the columns of $\mathbf{A}$. Since $\mathbf{b}$ has K elements, this will be possible only if the columns of $\mathbf{A}$ span the entire K-dimensional space, $\mathbb{R}^K$.[9] Equivalently, we shall require that the columns of $\mathbf{A}$ be linearly independent, or that $|\mathbf{A}|$ not be equal to zero.

2.5.2. Inverse Matrices

To solve the system $\mathbf{Ax} = \mathbf{b}$ for $\mathbf{x}$, something akin to division by a matrix is called for. Suppose we could find a square matrix, $\mathbf{B}$, such that $\mathbf{BA} = \mathbf{I}$. If the equation system is premultiplied by this $\mathbf{B}$, the following would be obtained:

$$\mathbf{BAx} = \mathbf{Ix} = \mathbf{x} = \mathbf{Bb}. \tag{2-57}$$

If the matrix $\mathbf{B}$ exists, it is the **inverse** of $\mathbf{A}$, denoted

$$\mathbf{B} = \mathbf{A}^{-1}.$$

From the definition,

$$\mathbf{A}^{-1}\mathbf{A} = \mathbf{I}.$$

In addition, by premultiplying by $\mathbf{A}$ and postmultiplying by $\mathbf{A}^{-1}$, then canceling terms, we find

$$\mathbf{AA}^{-1} = \mathbf{I}$$

as well.

If the inverse exists, it must be unique. Suppose that it is not, and that $\mathbf{C}$ is a different inverse of $\mathbf{A}$. Then $\mathbf{CAB} = \mathbf{CAB}$, but $(\mathbf{CA})\mathbf{B} = \mathbf{IB} = \mathbf{B}$ and $\mathbf{C}(\mathbf{AB}) = \mathbf{C}$, which would be a contradiction if $\mathbf{C}$ did not equal $\mathbf{B}$. Since, by (2–57), the solution is $\mathbf{x} = \mathbf{A}^{-1}\mathbf{b}$, the solution to the equation system is unique as well.

We now consider the calculation of the inverse matrix. For a 2×2 matrix,

$$\mathbf{AB} = \mathbf{I}$$

implies

$$\begin{bmatrix} a_{11} & a_{12} \\ a_{21} & a_{22} \end{bmatrix} \begin{bmatrix} b_{11} & b_{12} \\ b_{21} & b_{22} \end{bmatrix} = \begin{bmatrix} 1 & 0 \\ 0 & 1 \end{bmatrix}$$

or

$$a_{11}b_{11} + a_{12}b_{21} = 1$$
$$a_{11}b_{12} + a_{12}b_{22} = 0$$
$$a_{21}b_{11} + a_{22}b_{21} = 0$$
$$a_{21}b_{12} + a_{22}b_{22} = 1.$$

The solutions are

$$\begin{bmatrix} b_{11} & b_{12} \\ b_{21} & b_{22} \end{bmatrix} = \frac{1}{a_{11}a_{22} - a_{12}a_{21}} \begin{bmatrix} a_{22} & -a_{12} \\ -a_{21} & a_{11} \end{bmatrix}$$

$$= \frac{1}{|\mathbf{A}|} \begin{bmatrix} a_{22} & -a_{12} \\ -a_{21} & a_{11} \end{bmatrix}. \tag{2-58}$$

---

[9] If $\mathbf{A}$ does not have full rank, the nonhomogeneous system will have solutions for *some* vectors, $\mathbf{b}$, namely, any $\mathbf{b}$ in the column space of $\mathbf{A}$. But we are interested in the case in which there are solutions for *all* nonzero vectors, $\mathbf{b}$, which requires $\mathbf{A}$ to have full rank.

Notice the presence of the reciprocal of $|\mathbf{A}|$ in $\mathbf{A}^{-1}$. This is not specific to the 2×2 case. We infer from it that if the determinant is zero, the inverse does not exist.

Definition. A matrix whose inverse exists is **nonsingular.**

The simplest inverse matrix to compute is that of a diagonal matrix. If

$$\mathbf{D} = \begin{bmatrix} d_1 & 0 & 0 & \cdots & 0 \\ 0 & d_2 & 0 & \cdots & 0 \\ & & \vdots & & \\ 0 & 0 & 0 & & d_K \end{bmatrix}, \quad \mathbf{D}^{-1} = \begin{bmatrix} 1/d_1 & 0 & 0 & \cdots & 0 \\ 0 & 1/d_2 & 0 & \cdots & 0 \\ & & \vdots & & \\ 0 & 0 & 0 & \cdots & 1/d_K \end{bmatrix},$$

which shows, incidentally, that $\mathbf{I}^{-1} = \mathbf{I}$.

We shall use a^{ij} to indicate the ijth element of $\mathbf{A}^{-1}$. The general formula for computing an inverse matrix is

$$a^{ij} = \frac{|\mathbf{C}_{ji}|}{|\mathbf{A}|}, \tag{2-59}$$

where $|\mathbf{C}_{ji}|$ is the jith cofactor of $\mathbf{A}$. It follows, therefore, that for $\mathbf{A}$ to be nonsingular, $|\mathbf{A}|$ must be nonzero. Notice the reversal of the subscripts. For anything larger than a 3×3 matrix, (2–59) represents a formidable computation. But that is why we have computers.

Some computational results involving inverses are[10]

$$|\mathbf{A}^{-1}| = \frac{1}{|\mathbf{A}|}, \tag{2-60}$$

$$(\mathbf{A}^{-1})^{-1} = \mathbf{A}, \tag{2-61}$$

$$(\mathbf{A}^{-1})' = (\mathbf{A}')^{-1}. \tag{2-62}$$

If $\mathbf{A}$ is symmetric, $\mathbf{A}^{-1}$ is symmetric. (2-63)

When both inverse matrices exist,

$$(\mathbf{AB})^{-1} = \mathbf{B}^{-1}\mathbf{A}^{-1}. \tag{2-64}$$

Note the condition preceding (2–64). It may be that $\mathbf{AB}$ is a square, nonsingular matrix when neither $\mathbf{A}$ nor $\mathbf{B}$ are even square. (Consider, for example, $\mathbf{A}'\mathbf{A}$.) Extending (2–64), we have

$$(\mathbf{ABC})^{-1} = \mathbf{C}^{-1}(\mathbf{AB})^{-1} = \mathbf{C}^{-1}\mathbf{B}^{-1}\mathbf{A}^{-1}. \tag{2-65}$$

Recall that for a data matrix $\mathbf{X}$, $\mathbf{X}'\mathbf{X}$ is the sum of the *outer products* of the rows $\mathbf{X}$. Suppose we have already computed $\mathbf{S} = (\mathbf{X}'\mathbf{X})^{-1}$ for a number of years of data, such as those given at the beginning of this chapter. The following result, which is called an **updating formula,** shows how to compute the new $\mathbf{S}$ that would result when a new row is added to $\mathbf{X}$:

$$[\mathbf{A} \pm \mathbf{bb}'] = \mathbf{A}^{-1} \mp \left[\frac{1}{1 \pm \mathbf{b}'\mathbf{A}^{-1}\mathbf{b}}\right]\mathbf{A}^{-1}\mathbf{bb}'\mathbf{A}^{-1}. \tag{2-66}$$

Note the reversal of the sign in the inverse. Two more general forms of (2–66) that are occasionally useful are

$$[\mathbf{A} \pm \mathbf{bc}']^{-1} = \mathbf{A}^{-1} \mp \left[\frac{1}{1 \pm \mathbf{c}'\mathbf{A}^{-1}\mathbf{b}}\right]\mathbf{A}^{-1}\mathbf{bc}'\mathbf{A}^{-1}, \tag{2-66'}$$

$$[\mathbf{A} \pm \mathbf{BCB}']^{-1} = \mathbf{A}^{-1} \mp \mathbf{A}^{-1}\mathbf{B}[\mathbf{C}^{-1} \pm \mathbf{B}'\mathbf{A}^{-1}\mathbf{B}]^{-1}\mathbf{B}'\mathbf{A}^{-1}. \tag{2-66''}$$

---

[10] The proofs of most of these results are obvious and are left as exercises.

2.5.3. Nonhomogeneous Systems of Equations

For the nonhomogeneous system,

$$\mathbf{Ax} = \mathbf{b},$$

if $\mathbf{A}$ is nonsingular, the unique solution is[11]

$$\mathbf{x} = \mathbf{A}^{-1}\mathbf{b}.$$

2.6. Partitioned Matrices

In formulating the elements of a matrix—for example, in structuring sets of equations—it is sometimes useful to group some of the elements in **submatrices.** For example, we might write

$$\mathbf{A} = \begin{bmatrix} 1 & 4 & \vdots & 5 \\ 2 & 9 & \vdots & 3 \\ \cdots & \cdots & \cdots & \cdots \\ 8 & 9 & \vdots & 6 \end{bmatrix}$$

$$= \begin{bmatrix} \mathbf{A}_{11} & \mathbf{A}_{12} \\ \mathbf{A}_{21} & \mathbf{A}_{22} \end{bmatrix}.$$

$\mathbf{A}$ is a **partitioned matrix.** The subscripts of the submatrices are defined in the same fashion as those for the elements of a matrix. A common special case is the **block diagonal matrix.**

$$\mathbf{A} = \begin{bmatrix} \mathbf{A}_{11} & \mathbf{0} \\ \mathbf{0} & \mathbf{A}_{22} \end{bmatrix},$$

where $\mathbf{A}_{11}$ and $\mathbf{A}_{22}$ are square matrices.

2.6.1. Addition and Multiplication of Partitioned Matrices

Addition and multiplication extend to partitioned matrices. For conformably partitioned matrices $\mathbf{A}$ and $\mathbf{B}$,

$$\mathbf{A} + \mathbf{B} = \begin{bmatrix} \mathbf{A}_{11} + \mathbf{B}_{11} & \mathbf{A}_{12} + \mathbf{B}_{12} \\ \mathbf{A}_{21} + \mathbf{B}_{21} & \mathbf{A}_{22} + \mathbf{B}_{22} \end{bmatrix} \tag{2-67}$$

and

$$\mathbf{AB} = \begin{bmatrix} \mathbf{A}_{11} & \mathbf{A}_{12} \\ \mathbf{A}_{21} & \mathbf{A}_{22} \end{bmatrix} \begin{bmatrix} \mathbf{B}_{11} & \mathbf{B}_{12} \\ \mathbf{B}_{21} & \mathbf{B}_{22} \end{bmatrix}$$

$$= \begin{bmatrix} \mathbf{A}_{11}\mathbf{B}_{11} + \mathbf{A}_{12}\mathbf{B}_{21} & \mathbf{A}_{11}\mathbf{B}_{12} + \mathbf{A}_{12}\mathbf{B}_{22} \\ \mathbf{A}_{21}\mathbf{B}_{11} + \mathbf{A}_{22}\mathbf{B}_{21} & \mathbf{A}_{21}\mathbf{B}_{12} + \mathbf{A}_{22}\mathbf{B}_{22} \end{bmatrix}. \tag{2-68}$$

In all of these, the matrices must be conformable for the operations involved. With respect to addition, the dimensions of $\mathbf{A}_{ij}$ and $\mathbf{B}_{ij}$ must be the same. For multiplication, the

---

[11] Computationally, there are simpler (albeit equivalent) ways of obtaining $\mathbf{x}$ that do not require explicit computation of $\mathbf{A}^{-1}$. See Johnston (1984, pp. 138–140) or Strang (1976).

number of columns in $\mathbf{A}_{ij}$ must equal the number of rows in $\mathbf{B}_{jk}$ for all pairs i and j. That is, all of the necessary matrix products of the submatrices must be defined.

Two cases frequently encountered are of the form

$$\begin{bmatrix} \mathbf{A}_1 \\ \mathbf{A}_2 \end{bmatrix}' \begin{bmatrix} \mathbf{A}_1 \\ \mathbf{A}_2 \end{bmatrix} = [\mathbf{A}_1' \quad \mathbf{A}_2'] \begin{bmatrix} \mathbf{A}_1 \\ \mathbf{A}_2 \end{bmatrix}$$
$$= [\mathbf{A}_1'\mathbf{A}_1 + \mathbf{A}_2'\mathbf{A}_2] \qquad (2\text{-}69)$$

and

$$\begin{bmatrix} \mathbf{A}_{11} & \mathbf{0} \\ \mathbf{0} & \mathbf{A}_{22} \end{bmatrix}' \begin{bmatrix} \mathbf{A}_{11} & \mathbf{0} \\ \mathbf{0} & \mathbf{A}_{22} \end{bmatrix} = \begin{bmatrix} \mathbf{A}_{11}'\mathbf{A}_{11} & \mathbf{0} \\ \mathbf{0} & \mathbf{A}_{22}'\mathbf{A}_{22} \end{bmatrix}. \qquad (2\text{-}70)$$

2.6.2. Determinants of Partitioned Matrices

The determinant of a block diagonal matrix is obtained analogously to that of a diagonal matrix.

$$\begin{vmatrix} \mathbf{A}_{11} & \mathbf{0} \\ \mathbf{0} & \mathbf{A}_{22} \end{vmatrix} = |\mathbf{A}_{11}| \cdot |\mathbf{A}_{22}|. \qquad (2\text{-}71)$$

The result for a general 2×2 partitioned matrix is

$$\begin{vmatrix} \mathbf{A}_{11} & \mathbf{A}_{12} \\ \mathbf{A}_{21} & \mathbf{A}_{22} \end{vmatrix} = |\mathbf{A}_{22}| \cdot |\mathbf{A}_{11} - \mathbf{A}_{12}\mathbf{A}_{22}^{-1}\mathbf{A}_{21}|$$
$$= |\mathbf{A}_{11}| \cdot |\mathbf{A}_{22} - \mathbf{A}_{21}\mathbf{A}_{11}^{-1}\mathbf{A}_{12}|. \qquad (2\text{-}72)$$

The result for matrices larger than 2×2 is extremely cumbersome but will not be necessary for our work.

2.6.3. Inverses of Partitioned Matrices

The inverse of a block diagonal matrix is

$$\begin{bmatrix} \mathbf{A}_{11} & \mathbf{0} \\ \mathbf{0} & \mathbf{A}_{22} \end{bmatrix}^{-1} = \begin{bmatrix} \mathbf{A}_{11}^{-1} & \mathbf{0} \\ \mathbf{0} & \mathbf{A}_{22}^{-1} \end{bmatrix}, \qquad (2\text{-}73)$$

which can be verified by direct multiplication.

For the general 2×2 partitioned matrix, one form of the **partitioned inverse** is

$$\begin{bmatrix} \mathbf{A}_{11} & \mathbf{A}_{12} \\ \mathbf{A}_{21} & \mathbf{A}_{22} \end{bmatrix}^{-1} = \begin{bmatrix} \mathbf{A}_{11}^{-1}(\mathbf{I} + \mathbf{A}_{12}\mathbf{F}_2\mathbf{A}_{21}\mathbf{A}_{11}^{-1}) & -\mathbf{A}_{11}^{-1}\mathbf{A}_{12}\mathbf{F}_2 \\ -\mathbf{F}_2\mathbf{A}_{21}\mathbf{A}_{11}^{-1} & \mathbf{F}_2 \end{bmatrix}, \qquad (2\text{-}74)$$

where

$$\mathbf{F}_2 = (\mathbf{A}_{22} - \mathbf{A}_{21}\mathbf{A}_{11}^{-1}\mathbf{A}_{12})^{-1}.$$

This can be checked most easily by postmultiplying $\mathbf{A}$ by the inverse. In view of the symmetry of the calculation, the upper left block could also be written as

$$\mathbf{F}_1 = (\mathbf{A}_{11} - \mathbf{A}_{12}\mathbf{A}_{22}^{-1}\mathbf{A}_{21})^{-1}.$$

2.6.4. Deviations from Means

A useful application of the preceding is the following calculation: Suppose that we begin with a column vector of n values, $\mathbf{x}$, and let

$$\mathbf{A} = \begin{bmatrix} n & \Sigma_i x_i \\ \Sigma_i x_i & \Sigma_i x_i^2 \end{bmatrix}$$

$$= \begin{bmatrix} \mathbf{i'i} & \mathbf{i'x} \\ \mathbf{x'i} & \mathbf{x'x} \end{bmatrix}.$$

We are interested in the lower right-hand element of $\mathbf{A}^{-1}$. Upon using the definition of $\mathbf{F}_2$ in (2–74), this will be

$$\mathbf{F}_2 = [\mathbf{x'x} - (\mathbf{x'i})(\mathbf{i'i})^{-1}(\mathbf{i'x})]^{-1}$$

$$= \left\{ \mathbf{x'} \left[\mathbf{Ix} - \mathbf{i}\left(\frac{1}{n}\right)\mathbf{i'x} \right] \right\}^{-1}$$

$$= \left\{ \mathbf{x'} \left[\mathbf{I} - \left(\frac{1}{n}\right)\mathbf{ii'} \right]\mathbf{x} \right\}^{-1}$$

$$= [\mathbf{x'M^0x}]^{-1}.$$

Therefore, the lower right-hand value in the inverse matrix is

$$(\mathbf{x'M^0x})^{-1} = \frac{1}{\Sigma_i(x_i - \bar{x})^2} = a^{22}.$$

Now, suppose that instead of only a single column, $\mathbf{x}$ were $\mathbf{X}$, a matrix with several columns. We seek the lower right block of $[\mathbf{Z'Z}]^{-1}$ where $\mathbf{Z} = [\mathbf{i}, \mathbf{X}]$. The analogous result is

$$(\mathbf{Z'Z})^{22} = [\mathbf{X'X} - \mathbf{X'i}(\mathbf{i'i})^{-1}\mathbf{i'X}]^{-1}$$

$$= [\mathbf{X'M^0X}]^{-1},$$

which implies that the $K \times K$ matrix in the lower right of $(\mathbf{Z'Z})^{-1}$ is the inverse of the $K \times K$ matrix whose jkth element is $\Sigma_i(x_{ij} - \bar{x}_j)(x_{ik} - \bar{x}_k)$. Thus, when a data matrix contains a column of 1s, the elements of the inverse of the matrix of sums of squares and cross products will be computed from the original data in the form of deviations from the respective column means.

2.6.5. Kronecker Products

A calculation that helps to condense the notation when dealing with sets of regression models (see Chapter 17) is the **Kronecker product.** For general matrices $\mathbf{A}$ and $\mathbf{B}$,

$$\mathbf{A} \otimes \mathbf{B} = \begin{bmatrix} a_{11}\mathbf{B} & a_{12}\mathbf{B} & \cdots & a_{1K}\mathbf{B} \\ a_{21}\mathbf{B} & a_{22}\mathbf{B} & \cdots & a_{2K}\mathbf{B} \\ & & \vdots & \\ a_{n1}\mathbf{B} & a_{n2}\mathbf{B} & \cdots & a_{nK}\mathbf{B} \end{bmatrix}. \tag{2–75}$$

For example,

$$\begin{bmatrix} 3 & 0 \\ 5 & 2 \end{bmatrix} \otimes \begin{bmatrix} 1 & 4 \\ 4 & 7 \end{bmatrix} = \begin{bmatrix} 3\begin{bmatrix} 1 & 4 \\ 4 & 7 \end{bmatrix} & 0\begin{bmatrix} 1 & 4 \\ 4 & 7 \end{bmatrix} \\ 5\begin{bmatrix} 1 & 4 \\ 4 & 7 \end{bmatrix} & 2\begin{bmatrix} 1 & 4 \\ 4 & 7 \end{bmatrix} \end{bmatrix}.$$

Notice that there is no requirement for conformability in this operation. The Kronecker product can be computed for any pair of matrices. If $\mathbf{A}$ is $K \times L$ and $\mathbf{B}$ is $m \times n$, then $\mathbf{A} \otimes \mathbf{B}$ is $(Km) \times (Ln)$.

For the Kronecker product,

$$[\mathbf{A} \otimes \mathbf{B}]^{-1} = [\mathbf{A}^{-1} \otimes \mathbf{B}^{-1}], \tag{2–76}$$

which can be verified by direct multiplication. If $\mathbf{A}$ is $M \times M$ and $\mathbf{B}$ is $n \times n$, then

$$|\mathbf{A} \otimes \mathbf{B}| = |\mathbf{A}|^M |\mathbf{B}|^n, \qquad (\mathbf{A} \otimes \mathbf{B})' = \mathbf{A}' \otimes \mathbf{B}'$$

and (see Section 2.7.7)

$$\text{tr}(\mathbf{A} \otimes \mathbf{B}) = \text{tr}(\mathbf{A})\text{tr}(\mathbf{B}).$$

2.7. Characteristic Roots and Vectors

A useful set of results for analyzing a square matrix, $\mathbf{A}$, arises from the solutions to the set of equations

$$\mathbf{Ac} = \lambda\mathbf{c}. \tag{2–77}$$

The pairs of solutions are the **characteristic vectors**, $\mathbf{c}$, and characteristic roots, λ. If $\mathbf{c}$ is any solution vector, $k\mathbf{c}$ is also for any value of k. To remove the indeterminacy, $\mathbf{c}$ is **normalized** so that

$$\mathbf{c}'\mathbf{c} = 1.$$

The solution then consists of λ and the $n - 1$ unknown elements in $\mathbf{c}$.

2.7.1. The Characteristic Equation

Solving (2–77) can, in principle, proceed as follows: First, (2–77) implies that

$$\mathbf{Ac} = \lambda\mathbf{Ic}$$

or that

$$(\mathbf{A} - \lambda\mathbf{I})\mathbf{c} = \mathbf{0}.$$

This is a homogeneous system that has a nonzero solution only if the matrix $(\mathbf{A} - \lambda\mathbf{I})$ is singular or has a zero determinant. Therefore, if λ is a solution,

$$|\mathbf{A} - \lambda\mathbf{I}| = \mathbf{0}. \tag{2–78}$$

This polynomial in λ is the **characteristic equation** of $\mathbf{A}$. For example, if

$$\mathbf{A} = \begin{bmatrix} 5 & 1 \\ 2 & 4 \end{bmatrix},$$

then

$$\begin{aligned} |\mathbf{A} - \lambda\mathbf{I}| &= \begin{vmatrix} 5 - \lambda & 1 \\ 2 & 4 - \lambda \end{vmatrix} \\ &= (5 - \lambda)(4 - \lambda) - 2(1) \\ &= \lambda^2 - 9\lambda + 18. \end{aligned}$$

The two solutions are $\lambda = 6$ and $\lambda = 3$.

In solving the characteristic equation, there is no guarantee that the characteristic roots will be real. In the preceding example, if the 2 in the lower left-hand corner of the matrix were -2 instead, the solution would be a pair of complex values. The same problem can emerge in the general $n \times n$ case. The characteristic roots of a symmetric matrix are real, however.[12] This result will be convenient, as most of our applications will involve the characteristic roots and vectors of symmetric matrices.

For an $n \times n$ matrix, the characteristic equation is an nth-order polynomial in λ. Its solutions may be n distinct values, as in the preceding example, or may contain repeated values of λ, as in

$$\begin{vmatrix} 2 - \lambda & 6 \\ 6 & 2 - \lambda \end{vmatrix} = 0 = (2 - \lambda)^2 - 36$$

$$\Rightarrow \lambda_1 = \lambda_2 = 8,$$

and may, as well, contain some zeros, as in

$$\begin{vmatrix} 1 - \lambda & 2 \\ 2 & 4 - \lambda \end{vmatrix} = \lambda^2 - 5\lambda = 0$$

$$\Rightarrow \lambda_1 = 5 \quad \text{and} \quad \lambda_2 = 0.$$

2.7.2. Characteristic Vectors

With λ in hand, the characteristic vectors are derived from the original problem,

$$\mathbf{Ac} = \lambda \mathbf{c}$$

or

$$(\mathbf{A} - \lambda \mathbf{I})\mathbf{c} = \mathbf{0}.$$

For the first example, we have

$$\begin{bmatrix} 5 - \lambda & 1 \\ 2 & 4 - \lambda \end{bmatrix} \begin{bmatrix} c_1 \\ c_2 \end{bmatrix} = \begin{bmatrix} 0 \\ 0 \end{bmatrix}. \tag{2-79}$$

The two values for λ are 6 and 3. Inserting these values in (2–41) yields:

1. For $\lambda = 6$, $-c_1 + c_2 = 0$ and $2c_1 - 2c_2 = 0$, or $c_1 = c_2$.
2. For $\lambda = 3$, $2c_1 + c_2 = 0$ and $2c_1 + c_2 = 0$, or $c_1 = (-\frac{1}{2})c_2$.

Neither pair determines the values of c_1 and c_2. But this was to be expected; it was the reason $\mathbf{c}'\mathbf{c} = 1$ was specified at the outset. So, for example, if $\lambda = 6$, any vector $\mathbf{c}$ with equal elements will satisfy (2–79). However, the additional equation $\mathbf{c}'\mathbf{c} = 1$ produces complete solutions for both vectors:

1. For $\lambda = 6$, $\mathbf{c} = \begin{bmatrix} 1/\sqrt{2} \\ 1/\sqrt{2} \end{bmatrix}$.

2. For $\lambda = 3$, $\mathbf{c} = \begin{bmatrix} 1/5 \\ -2/5 \end{bmatrix}$.

These are the only vectors that satisfy both (2–79) and $\mathbf{c}'\mathbf{c} = 1$.

---

[12] A proof may be found in Theil (1971).

2.7.3. General Results for Characteristic Roots and Vectors

A $K \times K$ symmetric matrix has K distinct characteristic vectors, $c_1, c_2, \ldots, c_K$. The corresponding characteristic roots, $\lambda_1, \lambda_2, \ldots, \lambda_K$, while real, need not be distinct. The characteristic vectors of a symmetric matrix are orthogonal.[13] This implies that for every $i \neq j$, $c_i'c_j = 0$.[14] It is convenient to collect the K-characteristic vectors in a $K \times K$ matrix whose ith column is the c_i corresponding to λ_i,

$$C = [c_1 \quad c_2 \quad \cdots \quad c_K],$$

and the K-characteristic roots in the same order, in a diagonal matrix,

$$\Lambda = \begin{bmatrix} \lambda_1 & 0 & 0 & \cdots & 0 \\ 0 & \lambda_2 & 0 & \cdots & 0 \\ & & & \vdots & \\ 0 & 0 & 0 & \cdots & \lambda_K \end{bmatrix}.$$

Then, the full set of equations,

$$Ac_i = \lambda_i c_i,$$

is contained in

$$AC = C\Lambda. \tag{2-80}$$

Since the vectors are orthogonal and $c_i'c_i = 1$, we have

$$C'C = \begin{bmatrix} c_1'c_1 & c_1'c_2 & \cdots & c_1'c_K \\ c_2'c_1 & c_2'c_2 & \cdots & c_2'c_K \\ & & \vdots & \\ c_K'c_1 & c_K'c_2 & \cdots & c_K'c_K \end{bmatrix} \tag{2-81}$$

$$= I.$$

Result (2–81) implies that

$$C' = C^{-1}. \tag{2-82}$$

Consequently,

$$CC' = CC^{-1} = I \tag{2-83}$$

as well; the rows of C are also orthogonal.

2.7.4. Diagonalization of a Matrix

By premultiplying (2–80) by C' and using (2–81), we obtain the **diagonalization** of A;

$$C'AC = C'C\Lambda = I\Lambda = \Lambda. \tag{2-84}$$

---

[13] For proofs of these propositions, see Hadley (1961) or Strang (1976).

[14] This is not true if the matrix is not symmetric. For instance, it does not hold for the characteristic vectors computed in the first example. For nonsymmetric matrices, there is also a distinction between "right" characteristic vectors, $Ac = \lambda c$, and "left" characteristic vectors, $d'A = \lambda d'$, which may not be equal.

2.7.5. Rank of a Matrix

The diagonalization theorem enables us to obtain the rank of a matrix very easily.[15] To do so, we use can use the following result:

(Rank of a product) For any matrix $\mathbf{A}$ and nonsingular matrices $\mathbf{B}$ and $\mathbf{C}$, the rank of $\mathbf{BAC}$ is equal to the rank of $\mathbf{A}$. The proof is simple. By (2–45), $\text{rank}(\mathbf{BAC}) = \text{rank}[(\mathbf{BA})\mathbf{C}] = \text{rank}(\mathbf{BA})$. By (2–43), $\text{rank}(\mathbf{BA}) = \text{rank}(\mathbf{A}'\mathbf{B}')$, and, applying (2–45) again, $\text{rank}(\mathbf{A}'\mathbf{B}') = \text{rank}(\mathbf{A}')$ since $\mathbf{B}'$ is nonsingular if $\mathbf{B}$ is (once again, by 2–43). Finally, applying (2–43) again to obtain $\text{rank}(\mathbf{A}') = \text{rank}(\mathbf{A})$ gives the result.

Since $\mathbf{C}$ and $\mathbf{C}'$ are nonsingular, we can use them to apply this result to (2–84). By an obvious substitution,

$$\text{rank}(\mathbf{A}) = \text{rank}(\mathbf{\Lambda}).$$

Finding the rank of $\mathbf{\Lambda}$ is trivial. Since $\mathbf{\Lambda}$ is a diagonal matrix, its rank is just the number of nonzero values on its diagonal. The general result, then, is the following:

$$\begin{array}{cc} \text{The rank of a symmetric matrix is the number of} \\ \text{nonzero characteristic roots it contains.} \end{array} \qquad (2\text{–}85)$$

It would appear that this simple rule will not be useful if $\mathbf{A}$ is not square. But recall that

$$\text{rank}(\mathbf{A}) = \text{rank}(\mathbf{A}'\mathbf{A}).$$

Since $\mathbf{A}'\mathbf{A}$ is always square, we can use it instead of $\mathbf{A}$. Indeed, we can use it even if $\mathbf{A}$ is square, which leads to a fully general result:

$$\begin{array}{cc} \text{The rank of } any \text{ matrix, } \mathbf{A}, \text{ equals the number} \\ \text{of nonzero characteristic roots in } \mathbf{A}'\mathbf{A}. \end{array} \qquad (2\text{–}86)$$

This result is useful because it provides a simple way to find the rank of a nonsymmetric matrix. Computationally, finding the characteristic roots of nonsymmetric matrices is rather difficult and involves complex arithmetic. But symmetric matrices, because of their real roots, are much simpler to analyze.

Since the row rank and column rank of a matrix are equal, we should be able to apply (2–86) to $\mathbf{AA}'$ as well. This requires, however, an additional result:

$$\begin{array}{cc} \text{The nonzero characteristic roots of } \mathbf{AA}' \text{ are} \\ \text{the same as those of } \mathbf{A}'\mathbf{A}. \end{array} \qquad (2\text{–}87)$$

The proof is left as an exercise. A useful special case for you to examine is the characteristic roots of $\mathbf{aa}'$ and $\mathbf{a}'\mathbf{a}$, where $\mathbf{a}$ is an $n \times 1$ vector.

If a characteristic root of a matrix is zero, then we have $\mathbf{Ac} = \mathbf{0}$. This means that if the matrix has a zero root, it must be singular. Otherwise, no nonzero $\mathbf{c}$ would exist. In general, therefore, a matrix is singular, that is, it does not have full rank if and only if it has at least one zero root.

2.7.6. Condition Number of a Matrix

As the preceding might suggest, there is a discrete difference between full rank and short rank matrices. However, in analyzing data matrices such as the one in Section 2.2, we

---

[15] Recall that when we last considered this problem, we had to try to identify the largest set of linearly independent columns. This might be hopelessly cumbersome if $\mathbf{A}$ has, say, 20 columns, which would be common in regression analysis.

shall often encounter cases in which a matrix is not quite short ranked, as it has all nonzero roots, but it is close. That is, by some measure, we can come very close to being able to write one column as a linear combination of the others. This is an important case; we shall examine it at length in our discussion of multicollinearity. Our definitions of rank and determinant will fail to indicate this possibility, but an alternative measure, the **condition number,** is designed for that purpose. Formally, the condition number for a square matrix, **A**, is

$$\gamma = \left[\frac{\text{maximum root}}{\text{minimum root}} \right]^{1/2}.$$

For nonsquare matrices, **X**, such as the data matrix in the example, we use $\mathbf{A} = \mathbf{X'X}$. As a further refinement, because the characteristic roots are affected by the scaling of the columns of **X**, we scale the columns to have length 1 by dividing each column by its norm [see (2–55).] For the **X** in Section 2.2, the largest characteristic root of **A** is 4.9255 and the smallest is 0.0001543. Therefore, the condition number is 178.67, which is extremely large. (Values larger than 20 are large.) The fact that the smallest root is close to zero compared to the largest means that this matrix is nearly singular. Matrices with large condition numbers are difficult to invert accurately.

2.7.7. Trace of a Matrix

The **trace** of a square matrix is the sum of its diagonal elements:

$$\text{tr}(\mathbf{A}) = \sum_i a_{ii}. \tag{2–88}$$

Some easily proven results are

$$\text{tr}(c\mathbf{A}) = c(\text{tr}(\mathbf{A})), \tag{2–89}$$

$$\text{tr}(\mathbf{A}') = \text{tr}(\mathbf{A}), \tag{2–90}$$

$$\text{tr}(\mathbf{A} + \mathbf{B}) = \text{tr}(\mathbf{A}) + \text{tr}(\mathbf{B}), \tag{2–91}$$

and

$$\text{tr}(\mathbf{I}_K) = K. \tag{2–92}$$

A particularly useful result is the trace of a product matrix:

$$\text{tr}(\mathbf{AB}) = \text{tr}(\mathbf{BA}). \tag{2–93}$$

See, for example, the two product matrices after (2–15). Two useful applications of (2–93) are

$$\mathbf{a'a} = \text{tr}(\mathbf{a'a}) = \text{tr}(\mathbf{aa'})$$

and

$$\text{tr}(\mathbf{A'A}) = \sum_i \mathbf{a}_i'\mathbf{a}_i = \sum_i \sum_j a_{ij}^2.$$

The permutation rule can be extended to any *cyclic* permutation in a product:

$$\text{tr}(\mathbf{ABCD}) = \text{tr}(\mathbf{BCDA}) = \text{tr}(\mathbf{CDAB}) = \text{tr}(\mathbf{DABC}). \tag{2–94}$$

By using (2–84), we obtain

$$\text{tr}(\mathbf{C}'\mathbf{AC}) = \text{tr}(\mathbf{ACC}') = \text{tr}(\mathbf{AI})$$
$$= \text{tr}(\mathbf{A}) = \text{tr}(\boldsymbol{\Lambda}). \tag{2–95}$$

Since $\boldsymbol{\Lambda}$ is diagonal with the roots of $\mathbf{A}$ on its diagonal, the general result is:

> The trace of a matrix equals the sum of its characteristic roots. (2–96)

2.7.8. Determinant of a Matrix

Recalling how tedious the calculation of a determinant promised to be, we find that the following is particularly useful. Since

$$\mathbf{C}'\mathbf{AC} = \boldsymbol{\Lambda},$$
$$|\mathbf{C}'\mathbf{AC}| = |\boldsymbol{\Lambda}|.$$

Using a number of earlier results, we have, for orthogonal matrix, $\mathbf{C}$,

$$|\mathbf{C}'\mathbf{AC}| = |\mathbf{C}'| \cdot |\mathbf{A}| \cdot |\mathbf{C}| = |\mathbf{C}'| \cdot |\mathbf{C}| \cdot |\mathbf{A}| = |\mathbf{C}'\mathbf{C}| \cdot |\mathbf{A}|$$
$$= |\mathbf{I}| \cdot |\mathbf{A}| = 1 \cdot |\mathbf{A}|$$
$$= |\mathbf{A}|$$
$$= |\boldsymbol{\Lambda}|.$$

Since $|\boldsymbol{\Lambda}|$ is just the product of its diagonal elements, this implies:

> The determinant of a matrix equals the product of its characteristic roots. (2–97)

Notice that we get the expected result if any of these roots is zero. Since the determinant is the product of the roots, it follows that a matrix is singular if and only if its determinant is zero, and, in turn, if and only if it has at least one zero characteristic root.

2.7.9. Spectral Decomposition of a Matrix

Starting once more with $\mathbf{AC} = \mathbf{C}\boldsymbol{\Lambda}$, we have $\mathbf{ACC}' = \mathbf{C}\boldsymbol{\Lambda}\mathbf{C}'$, or

$$\mathbf{A} = \mathbf{C}\boldsymbol{\Lambda}\mathbf{C}'. \tag{2–98}$$

This is called the **spectral** or **eigenvalue decomposition** of matrix $\mathbf{A}$. We can write this as a sum of outer products:

$$\mathbf{A} = \sum_{i=1}^{n} \lambda_i \mathbf{c}_i \mathbf{c}_i'. \tag{2–99}$$

2.7.10. Powers of a Matrix

We often use expressions involving powers of matrices, such as $\mathbf{AA} = \mathbf{A}^2$. For positive-integer powers, this can be computed by repeated multiplication. But this does not show how to handle a problem such as finding a $\mathbf{B}$ such that $\mathbf{B}^2 = \mathbf{A}$, that is, the square root of a matrix. The characteristic roots and vectors provide a simple solution.

Consider, first,

$$\mathbf{AA} = \mathbf{A}^2$$

$$= (\mathbf{C\Lambda C'})(\mathbf{C\Lambda C'}) = \mathbf{C\Lambda C'C\Lambda C'} \qquad (2\text{--}100)$$

$$= \mathbf{C\Lambda I\Lambda C'} = \mathbf{C\Lambda\Lambda C'} = \mathbf{C\Lambda^2 C'}.$$

Two results follow immediately. Since $\mathbf{\Lambda}^2$ is a diagonal matrix whose nonzero elements are the squares of those in $\mathbf{\Lambda}$, this implies the following:

> For any symmetric matrix, $\mathbf{A}$, the characteristic
> roots of $\mathbf{A}^2$ are the squares of those of $\mathbf{A}$ and $\qquad (2\text{--}101)$
> the characteristic vectors are the same.

The proof is obtained by observing that the last line in (2–100) is the eigenvalue decomposition of the matrix $\mathbf{B} = \mathbf{AA}$. Since $\mathbf{A}^3 = \mathbf{AA}^2$, and so on, (2–101) extends to any positive integer. By convention, for any $\mathbf{A}$, $\mathbf{A}^0 = \mathbf{I}$. Thus, for any symmetric matrix, $\mathbf{A}$, $\mathbf{A}^K = \mathbf{C\Lambda^K C'}$, $K = 0, 1, \ldots$. Hence the characteristic roots of $\mathbf{A}^K$ are λ^K, while the characteristic vectors are the same as those of $\mathbf{A}$. If $\mathbf{A}$ is nonsingular, so that all of its roots, λ_i, are nonzero, this can be extended to negative powers as well. If $\mathbf{A}^{-1}$ exists, then

$$\mathbf{A}^{-1} = (\mathbf{C\Lambda C'})^{-1}$$

$$= (\mathbf{C'})^{-1}\mathbf{\Lambda}^{-1}\mathbf{C}^{-1} \qquad (2\text{--}102)$$

$$= \mathbf{C\Lambda^{-1}C'},$$

where we have used the earlier result, $\mathbf{C'} = \mathbf{C}^{-1}$. If $\mathbf{A}^{-1}$ exists, the characteristic roots of $\mathbf{A}^{-1}$ are the reciprocals of those of $\mathbf{A}$ and the characteristic vectors are the same. By extending the notion of repeated multiplication, we have:

> For any *nonsingular* symmetric matrix, $\mathbf{A}$,
> $\mathbf{A}^K = \mathbf{C\Lambda^K C'}$, $\qquad K = \cdots, -2, -1, 0, 1, 2, \ldots$. $\qquad (2\text{--}103)$

We now turn to the general problem of how to compute the square root of a matrix. In the scalar case, the value would have to be nonnegative. The matrix analog to this requirement is that all of the characteristic roots are nonnegative. Consider, then, the candidate,

$$\mathbf{A}^{1/2} = \mathbf{C\Lambda^{1/2}C'}$$

$$= \mathbf{C}\begin{bmatrix} \sqrt{\lambda_1} & 0 & \cdots & 0 \\ 0 & \sqrt{\lambda_2} & \cdots & 0 \\ & & \vdots & \\ 0 & 0 & \cdots & \sqrt{\lambda_n} \end{bmatrix}\mathbf{C'}. \qquad (2\text{--}104)$$

This satisfies the requirement for a square root, since

$$\mathbf{A}^{1/2}\mathbf{A}^{1/2} = \mathbf{C\Lambda^{1/2}C'C\Lambda^{1/2}C'} = \mathbf{C\Lambda C'}$$

$$= \mathbf{A}.$$

If we continue in this fashion, we can define the powers of a matrix more generally, still assuming that all of the characteristic roots are nonnegative. For example, $\mathbf{A}^{1/3} = \mathbf{C\Lambda^{1/3}C'}$. If all of the roots are strictly positive, we can go one step further and extend the result to any real power. For reasons that will be made clear in the next section, we say that a matrix with positive characteristic roots is **positive definite.** It is the matrix analog to a positive number.

> For a *positive definite matrix*, $\mathbf{A}$, $\mathbf{A}^r = \mathbf{C\Lambda^r C'}$ $\qquad (2\text{--}105)$

for any real number, r. The characteristic roots of $\mathbf{A}^r$ are the rth power of those of $\mathbf{A}$, and the characteristic vectors are the same.

If $\mathbf{A}$ is only **nonnegative definite,** that is, has roots that are either zero or positive, (2–105) holds only for nonnegative r.

2.7.11. Idempotent Matrices

Idempotent matrices are equal to their squares. [See (2–37) to (2–39).] In view of their importance in econometrics, we collect a few results related to idempotent matrices at this point. First, (2–101) implies that if λ is a characteristic root of an idempotent matrix, $\lambda = \lambda^K$ for all nonnegative integers K. As such, if $\mathbf{A}$ is a symmetric idempotent matrix, all of its roots are 1 or 0. Assume that all of the roots of $\mathbf{A}$ are 1. Then $\mathbf{\Lambda} = \mathbf{I}$, and $\mathbf{A} = \mathbf{C\Lambda C'} = \mathbf{CIC'} = \mathbf{CC'} = \mathbf{I}$. If the roots are not all 1, one or more are 0. Consequently, we have the following results for symmetric idempotent matrices:[16]

> The only full rank, symmetric idempotent matrix is the identity matrix, $\mathbf{I}$. $\qquad$ (2–106)

> All symmetric idempotent matrices except the identity matrix are singular. $\qquad$ (2–107)

The final result on idempotent matrices is obtained by observing that the count of the nonzero roots of $\mathbf{A}$ is also equal to their sum. Hence

> The rank of a symmetric idempotent matrix is equal to its trace. $\qquad$ (2–108)

2.7.12. Factoring a Matrix

In some applications, we shall require a matrix $\mathbf{P}$ such that

$$\mathbf{P'P} = \mathbf{A}^{-1}.$$

One choice is

$$\mathbf{P} = \mathbf{\Lambda}^{-1/2}\mathbf{C'},$$

hence

$$\mathbf{P'P} = (\mathbf{C'})'(\mathbf{\Lambda}^{-1/2})'\mathbf{\Lambda}^{-1/2}\mathbf{C'}$$

$$= \mathbf{C\Lambda}^{-1}\mathbf{C'},$$

as desired.[17]

The **Cholesky factorization** of a symmetric positive definite matrix is an alternative representation that is useful in regression analysis. Any symmetric positive definite matrix, $\mathbf{A}$, may be written as the product of a **lower triangular** matrix, $\mathbf{L}$, and its transpose (which is an **upper triangular matrix**), $\mathbf{L'} = \mathbf{U}$. Thus, $\mathbf{A} = \mathbf{LU}$. This is the Cholesky decomposition of $\mathbf{A}$. The square roots of the squares of the diagonal elements of $\mathbf{L}$, d_i, are the Cholesky values of $\mathbf{A}$. By arraying these in a diagonal matrix, $\mathbf{D}$, we may also write $\mathbf{A} = \mathbf{LD}^{-1}\mathbf{D}^2\mathbf{D}^{-1}\mathbf{U} = \mathbf{L^*DU^*}$. This is similar to the spectral decomposition in (2–99). The usefulness of this formulation arises when the inverse of $\mathbf{A}$ is required. Once $\mathbf{L}$ is

---

[16] Not all idempotent matrices are symmetric. However, we shall not encounter any asymmetric ones in our work.

[17] We say that this is "one" choice because if $\mathbf{A}$ is symmetric, as it will be in all of our applications, there are other candidates. You can easily verify that $\mathbf{C\Lambda}^{-1/2}\mathbf{C'} = \mathbf{A}^{-1/2}$ works as well.

computed, finding $\mathbf{A}^{-1} = \mathbf{U}^{-1}\mathbf{L}^{-1}$ is also straightforward, as well as extremely fast and accurate. Most recently developed econometric software uses this technique for inverting positive definite matrices.

2.7.13. The Generalized Inverse of a Matrix

The inverse matrix is fundamental in econometrics. Although we shall not require them much in our treatment in this book, there are more general forms of inverse matrices than we have considered thus far. A generalized inverse of a matrix, $\mathbf{A}$, is another matrix, $\mathbf{A}^+$, that satisfies the following requirements:

1. $\mathbf{A}\mathbf{A}^+\mathbf{A} = \mathbf{A}$.
2. $\mathbf{A}^+\mathbf{A}\mathbf{A}^+ = \mathbf{A}^+$.
3. $\mathbf{A}^+\mathbf{A}$ is symmetric.
4. $\mathbf{A}\mathbf{A}^+$ is symmetric.

A unique $\mathbf{A}^+$ can be found for any matrix, whether $\mathbf{A}$ is singular or not, or even if $\mathbf{A}$ is not square.[18] The unique matrix that satisfies all four requirements is called the **Moore–Penrose inverse** or **pseudoinverse** of $\mathbf{A}$. If $\mathbf{A}$ happens to be square and nonsingular, the generalized inverse will be the familiar ordinary inverse. But if $\mathbf{A}^{-1}$ does not exist, $\mathbf{A}^+$ can still be computed.

An important special case is the overdetermined system of equations

$$\mathbf{A}\mathbf{b} = \mathbf{y},$$

where $\mathbf{A}$ has n rows, $K < n$ columns, and column rank equal to $R \leq K$. Suppose that R equals K, so that $(\mathbf{A}'\mathbf{A})^{-1}$ exists. Then the Moore–Penrose inverse of $\mathbf{A}$ is

$$\mathbf{A}^+ = (\mathbf{A}'\mathbf{A})^{-1}\mathbf{A}',$$

which can be verified by multiplication. A solution to the system of equations can be written

$$\mathbf{b} = \mathbf{A}^+\mathbf{y}.$$

Readers familiar with regression will recognize this as the least squares solution.

Now suppose that $\mathbf{A}$ does not have full rank. The previous solution cannot be computed. However, an alternative solution can be obtained. We continue to use the matrix $\mathbf{A}'\mathbf{A}$. In the spectral decomposition of section 2.7.9, if $\mathbf{A}$ has rank R, there are R terms in the summation in (2–99). In (2–102), the spectral decomposition using the reciprocals of the characteristic roots is used to compute the inverse. To compute the Moore–Penrose inverse, we apply this calculation to $\mathbf{A}'\mathbf{A}$, using only the nonzero roots, then postmultiply the result by $\mathbf{A}'$. Let $\mathbf{C}_1$ be the R characteristic vectors corresponding to the nonzero roots, which we array in the diagonal matrix, $\mathbf{\Lambda}_1$. Then the Moore–Penrose inverse is

$$\mathbf{A}^+ = \mathbf{C}_1\mathbf{\Lambda}_1^{-1}\mathbf{C}_1'\mathbf{A}',$$

which is very similar to the previous solution.

If $\mathbf{A}$ is a square matrix with rank $R \leq K$, the Moore–Penrose inverse is computed precisely as in the preceding equation without postmultiplying by $\mathbf{A}'$. Thus, for a symmetric matrix, $\mathbf{A}$,

$$\mathbf{A}^+ = \mathbf{C}_1\mathbf{\Lambda}_1^{-1}\mathbf{C}_1',$$

where $\mathbf{\Lambda}_1$ is a diagonal matrix containing the reciprocals of the *nonzero* roots of $\mathbf{A}$.

---

[18] A proof of uniqueness, with several other results, may be found in Theil (1983).

2.8. Quadratic Forms and Definite Matrices

Many optimization problems involve double sums of the form

$$q = \sum_{i=1}^{n} \sum_{j=1}^{n} x_i x_j a_{ij}. \tag{2-109}$$

This **quadratic form** can be written

$$q = \mathbf{x}'\mathbf{A}\mathbf{x},$$

where $\mathbf{A}$ is a symmetric matrix. In general, q may be positive, negative, or zero; it depends on $\mathbf{A}$ and $\mathbf{x}$. However, there are some matrices for which q will be positive regardless of $\mathbf{x}$, and others for which q will always be negative (or nonnegative or nonpositive). For a given matrix, $\mathbf{A}$,

1. If $\mathbf{x}'\mathbf{A}\mathbf{x} > (<)\mathbf{0}$ for all nonzero $\mathbf{x}$, then $\mathbf{A}$ is **positive (negative) definite**.
2. If $\mathbf{x}'\mathbf{A}\mathbf{x} \geq (\leq)\mathbf{0}$ for all nonzero $\mathbf{x}$, then $\mathbf{A}$ is **nonnegative definite** or **positive semidefinite** (nonpositive definite).

It might seem that it would be impossible to check a matrix for definiteness, since $\mathbf{x}$ can be chosen arbitrarily. But we have already used the set of results necessary to do so. Recall that a symmetric matrix can be decomposed into

$$\mathbf{A} = \mathbf{C}\mathbf{\Lambda}\mathbf{C}'.$$

Therefore, the quadratic form can be written as

$$\mathbf{x}'\mathbf{A}\mathbf{x} = \mathbf{x}'\mathbf{C}\mathbf{\Lambda}\mathbf{C}'\mathbf{x}.$$

Let $\mathbf{y} = \mathbf{C}'\mathbf{x}$. Then

$$\mathbf{x}'\mathbf{A}\mathbf{x} = \mathbf{y}'\mathbf{\Lambda}\mathbf{y} \tag{2-110}$$

$$= \sum_{i=1}^{n} \lambda_i y_i^2.$$

If λ_i is positive for all i, then regardless of $\mathbf{y}$, that is, regardless of $\mathbf{x}$, q will be positive. This was the case identified earlier as a positive definite matrix. Continuing this line of reasoning, if all of the characteristic roots of $\mathbf{A}$ are negative, we find that $\mathbf{A}$ is **negative definite**. If some of the roots are zero, then $\mathbf{A}$ is **nonnegative definite** if the remainder are positive and **nonpositive definite** if they are negative. If $\mathbf{A}$ has both negative and positive roots, then $\mathbf{A}$ is **indefinite**. (The preceding give, in each case, the "if" part of the theorem. To establish the "only if" part, assume that the condition on the roots does not hold. This must lead to a contradiction. For example, if some λ can be negative, then $\mathbf{y}'\mathbf{\Lambda}\mathbf{y}$ could be negative for some $\mathbf{y}$, so $\mathbf{A}$ cannot be positive definite.)

2.8.1. Nonnegative Definite Matrices

A case of particular interest is that of nonnegative definite matrices. The previous theorem implies a number of related results.

$$\text{If } \mathbf{A} \text{ is nonnegative definite, then } |\mathbf{A}| \geq 0. \tag{2-111}$$

The proof follows from the fact that the determinant is the product of the roots.

The converse, however, is not true. For example, a 2×2 matrix with two negative roots is clearly not positive definite, but it does have a positive determinant.

$$\text{If } \mathbf{A} \text{ is positive definite, so is } \mathbf{A}^{-1}. \tag{2-112}$$

Proof: The roots are the reciprocals of those of $\mathbf{A}$, which are, therefore, positive.

$$\text{The identity matrix, } \mathbf{I}, \text{ is positive definite.} \tag{2-113}$$

Proof: $\mathbf{x}'\mathbf{I}\mathbf{x} = \mathbf{x}'\mathbf{x} > 0$ if $\mathbf{x} \neq \mathbf{0}$.

A very important result for regression analysis is

$$\text{If } \mathbf{A} \text{ is } n \times K \text{ with full rank and } n > K, \text{ then } \mathbf{A}'\mathbf{A} \text{ is} \atop \text{positive definite and } \mathbf{A}\mathbf{A}' \text{ is nonnegative definite.} \tag{2-114}$$

Proof: By assumption, $\mathbf{A}\mathbf{x} \neq \mathbf{0}$. So $\mathbf{x}'\mathbf{A}'\mathbf{A}\mathbf{x} = (\mathbf{A}\mathbf{x})'(\mathbf{A}\mathbf{x}) = \mathbf{y}'\mathbf{y} = \sum_i y_i^2 > 0$.

A similar proof establishes the nonnegative definiteness of $\mathbf{A}\mathbf{A}'$. The difference in the latter case is that because $\mathbf{A}$ has more rows than columns, there is an $\mathbf{x}$ such that $\mathbf{A}'\mathbf{x} = \mathbf{0}$. Thus, in the proof, we only have $\mathbf{y}'\mathbf{y} \geq 0$. The case in which $\mathbf{A}$ does not have full column rank is the same as that of $\mathbf{A}\mathbf{A}'$.

$$\text{If } \mathbf{A} \text{ is positive definite and } \mathbf{B} \text{ is a nonsingular matrix,} \atop \text{then } \mathbf{B}'\mathbf{A}\mathbf{B} \text{ is positive definite.} \tag{2-115}$$

Proof: $\mathbf{x}'\mathbf{B}'\mathbf{A}\mathbf{B}\mathbf{x} = \mathbf{y}'\mathbf{A}\mathbf{y} > 0$, where $\mathbf{y} = \mathbf{B}\mathbf{x}$. But, $\mathbf{y}$ cannot be $\mathbf{0}$ because $\mathbf{B}$ is nonsingular.

Note, finally, that for $\mathbf{A}$ to be negative definite, all of $\mathbf{A}$'s characteristic roots must be negative. But, in this case, $|\mathbf{A}|$ is positive if $\mathbf{A}$ is of even order and negative if $\mathbf{A}$ is of odd order.

2.8.2. Idempotent Quadratic Forms

Quadratic forms in idempotent matrices play an important role in the distributions of many test statistics. As such, we shall encounter them fairly often. There are two central results that will be of interest.

$$\text{Every symmetric idempotent matrix is nonnegative definite.} \tag{2-116}$$

Proof: All roots are 1 or 0; hence, the matrix is nonnegative definite by definition.

Combining this with some earlier results yields a result used in determining the sampling distribution of most of the standard test statistics.

$$\text{If } \mathbf{A} \text{ is symmetric and idempotent, } n \times n \text{ with rank } J, \atop \text{then every quadratic form in } \mathbf{A} \text{ can be written} \tag{2-117}$$

$$\mathbf{x}'\mathbf{A}\mathbf{x} = \sum_{i=1}^{J} y_i^2.$$

Proof: This is (2–110) with $\lambda = 1$ or 0.

2.8.3. Ranking Matrices

It is not obvious how one can compare two matrices. As a starting point, of course, the matrices must be of the same dimensions. A useful, although not always conclusive comparison is based on

$$d = \mathbf{x}'\mathbf{A}\mathbf{x} - \mathbf{x}'\mathbf{B}\mathbf{x}.$$

If this is always positive, regardless of the choice of $\mathbf{x}$, then, at least by this criterion, we could say that

$$\mathbf{A} > \mathbf{B}. \tag{2-118}$$

The reverse would apply if d is always negative. For some matrices, the result might be ambiguous. It follows from the definition that

$$d > 0 \text{ implies that } \mathbf{A} - \mathbf{B} \text{ is positive definite,}$$

as

$$d = \mathbf{x}'(\mathbf{A} - \mathbf{B})\mathbf{x}.$$

For example,

$$\mathbf{A} = \begin{bmatrix} 3 & -1 \\ -1 & 49 \end{bmatrix} \quad \text{and} \quad \mathbf{B} = \begin{bmatrix} 2 & 5 \\ 5 & 13 \end{bmatrix}.$$

Is $\mathbf{A} > \mathbf{B}$?

$$\mathbf{A} - \mathbf{B} = \begin{bmatrix} 1 & -6 \\ -6 & 36 \end{bmatrix}.$$

The characteristic roots of this rank 1 matrix are 37 and 0. Therefore, $\mathbf{A} - \mathbf{B}$ is nonnegative definite. For this $\mathbf{A}$ and $\mathbf{B}$, a quadratic form in $\mathbf{A}$ will always be at least as large as the one in $\mathbf{B}$ that uses the same $\mathbf{x}$.

A particular case of the general result is

$$\text{If } \mathbf{A} \text{ is positive definite and } \mathbf{B} \text{ is}$$
$$\text{nonnegative definite, then } \mathbf{A} + \mathbf{B} > \mathbf{A}. \tag{2-119}$$

Consider, for example, the "updating formula" introduced in (2–66). This uses a matrix

$$\mathbf{A} = \mathbf{B}'\mathbf{B} + \mathbf{bb}' > \mathbf{B}'\mathbf{B}.[19]$$

Finally, in comparing matrices, it may be more convenient to compare their inverses. The result analogous to a familiar result for scalars is

$$\text{If } \mathbf{A} > \mathbf{B}, \text{ then } \mathbf{B}^{-1} > \mathbf{A}^{-1}. \tag{2-120}$$

[See Goldberger (1964, Chapter 2).]

2.9. Calculus and Matrix Algebra

Many problems in econometrics involve the extension of some familiar results from calculus to a multivariate setting. Examples include the formulation of approximating functions, maximization or minimization of a function of many variables, and the analysis of transformations from one set of variables to another. This section presents the basic set of results used later in the book in the discussion of these problems.[20] Each of the three parts begins with the basic result from the univariate calculus and then proceeds to the extension to the multivariate case.

[19] The earlier example is constructed using this result.

[20] For a complete exposition, see Magnus and Neudecker (1988).

2.9.1. Differentiation and the Taylor Series

A variable, y, is a function of another variable, x, written

$$y = f(x), \qquad y = g(x), \qquad y = y(x), \qquad \text{and so on}$$

if each value of x is associated with a single value of y. In this relationship, y and x are sometimes labeled the **dependent variable** and the **independent variable,** respectively. Assuming that the function $f(x)$ is continuous and differentiable, we obtain the following derivatives:

$$f'(x) = \frac{dy}{dx},$$

$$f''(x) = \frac{d^2y}{dx^2},$$

and so on.

A frequent use of the derivatives of $f(x)$ is in the **Taylor series approximation.** A Taylor series is a polynomial approximation to $f(x)$. Letting x^0 be an arbitrarily chosen expansion point,

$$f(x) \simeq f(x^0) + \sum_{i=1}^{P} \frac{1}{i!} \left. \frac{d^i f(x)}{dx^i} \right|_{x=x^0} \cdot (x - x^0)^i. \tag{2--121}$$

The choice of the number of terms is arbitrary; the more that are used, the more accurate will be the approximation. The approximations used most frequently in econometrics are the **linear approximation,**

$$
\begin{aligned}
f(x) &\simeq [f(x^0) - f'(x^0)x^0] + f'(x^0)x \\
&= \beta_1 + \beta_2 x
\end{aligned}
\tag{2--122}
$$

and the **quadratic approximation,**

$$
\begin{aligned}
f(x) &\simeq [f^0 - f'^0 x^0 + \tfrac{1}{2}f''^0(x^0)^2] + [f'^0 - f''^0 x^0]x + \tfrac{1}{2}f''^0 x^2 \\
&= \beta_1 + \beta_2 x + \beta_3 x^2,
\end{aligned}
\tag{2--123}
$$

where the superscript indicates that the function is evaluated at x^0.

We can regard a function $y = f(x_1, x_2, \ldots x_n)$ as a **scalar-valued function** of a vector, that is, $y = f(\mathbf{x})$. The vector of partial derivatives, or **gradient vector** (or simply **gradient**) is

$$\frac{\partial f(\mathbf{x})}{\partial \mathbf{x}} = \begin{bmatrix} \partial y/\partial x_1 \\ \partial y/\partial x_2 \\ \vdots \\ \partial y/\partial x_n \end{bmatrix} = \begin{bmatrix} f_1 \\ f_2 \\ \vdots \\ f_n \end{bmatrix}. \tag{2--124}$$

The vector $\mathbf{g}(\mathbf{x})$ or $\mathbf{g}$ is used to represent the gradient vector. Notice that it is a column vector. The shape of the derivative is determined by the denominator of the derivative.

A **second derivatives matrix** or **Hessian matrix** is computed as

$$
\begin{aligned}
\mathbf{H} &= \begin{bmatrix} \partial^2 y/\partial x_1 \partial x_1 & \partial^2 y/\partial x_1 \partial x_2 & \cdots & \partial^2 y/\partial x_1 \partial x_n \\ \partial^2 y/\partial x_2 \partial x_1 & \partial^2 y/\partial x_2 \partial x_2 & \cdots & \partial^2 y/\partial x_2 \partial x_n \\ \vdots & \vdots & \vdots & \vdots \\ \partial^2 y/\partial x_n \partial x_1 & \partial^2 y/\partial x_n \partial x_2 & \cdots & \partial^2 y/\partial x_n \partial x_n \end{bmatrix} \\
&= [f_{ij}].
\end{aligned}
\tag{2--125}
$$

In general, $\mathbf{H}$ is a square, symmetric matrix. Each row and column of $\mathbf{H}$ is the derivative of the gradient vector with respect to one of the variables. Therefore,

$$\mathbf{H} = \left[\frac{\partial[\partial y/\partial \mathbf{x}]}{\partial x_1} \quad \frac{\partial[\partial y/\partial \mathbf{x}]}{\partial x_2} \quad \cdots \quad \frac{\partial[\partial y/\partial \mathbf{x}]}{\partial x_n} \right]$$

$$= \frac{\partial[\partial y/\partial \mathbf{x}]}{\partial(x_1 \quad x_2 \quad \cdots \quad x_n)}$$

$$= \frac{\partial[\partial y/\partial \mathbf{x}]}{\partial \mathbf{x}'}$$

$$= \frac{\partial^2 y}{\partial \mathbf{x} \partial \mathbf{x}'}.$$

The first-order, or linear Taylor series, approximation is

$$y \simeq f(\mathbf{x}^0) + \sum_i f_i(\mathbf{x}^0)(x_i - x_i^0)$$

$$= f(\mathbf{x}^0) + \left[\frac{\partial f(\mathbf{x}^0)}{\partial \mathbf{x}^0} \right]'(\mathbf{x} - \mathbf{x}^0)$$

$$= f(\mathbf{x}^0) + \mathbf{g}(\mathbf{x}^0)'(\mathbf{x} - \mathbf{x}^0) \tag{2-126}$$

$$= [f(\mathbf{x}^0) - \mathbf{g}(\mathbf{x}^0)'\mathbf{x}^0] + \mathbf{g}(\mathbf{x}^0)'\mathbf{x}$$

$$= [f^0 - \mathbf{g}^{0'}\mathbf{x}^0] + \mathbf{g}^{0'}\mathbf{x}$$

$$= \beta_1 + \boldsymbol{\beta}_2'\mathbf{x}.$$

The second-order, or quadratic, approximation adds the second-order terms in the approximation,

$$\tfrac{1}{2} \sum_i \sum_j f_{ij}^0(x_i - x_i^0)(x_j - x_j^0) = \tfrac{1}{2}(\mathbf{x} - \mathbf{x}^0)'\mathbf{H}^0(\mathbf{x} - \mathbf{x}^0)$$

to the preceding one. Collecting terms in the same manner as in (2–126), we have

$$y \simeq \beta_1 + \boldsymbol{\beta}_2'\mathbf{x} + \tfrac{1}{2}\mathbf{x}'\boldsymbol{\Gamma}_3\mathbf{x}, \tag{2-127}$$

where

$$\beta_1 = f^0 - \mathbf{g}^{0'}\mathbf{x}^0 + \tfrac{1}{2}\mathbf{x}^{0'}\mathbf{H}^0\mathbf{x}^0,$$

$$\boldsymbol{\beta}_2 = -\mathbf{g}^0 + \mathbf{H}^0\mathbf{x}^0,$$

and

$$\boldsymbol{\Gamma}_3 = \mathbf{H}^0.$$

A linear function can be written

$$y = \mathbf{a}'\mathbf{x} = \mathbf{x}'\mathbf{a} = \sum_i a_i x_i.$$

Hence

$$\frac{\partial(\mathbf{a}'\mathbf{x})}{\partial \mathbf{x}} = \mathbf{a}. \tag{2-128}$$

Note, in particular, that $\partial(\mathbf{a}'\mathbf{x})/\partial\mathbf{x} = \mathbf{a}$, not $\mathbf{a}'$. In a set of linear functions,

$$\mathbf{y} = \mathbf{Ax},$$

each element y_i of $\mathbf{y}$ is

$$y_i = \mathbf{a}^i\mathbf{x},$$

where $\mathbf{a}^i$ is the ith row of $\mathbf{A}$. Therefore,

$$\frac{\partial y_i}{\partial\mathbf{x}} = \mathbf{a}^{i\prime}$$

$$= \text{transpose of } i\text{th row of } \mathbf{A}$$

and

$$\begin{bmatrix} \partial y_1/\partial\mathbf{x}' \\ \partial y_2/\partial\mathbf{x}' \\ \vdots \\ \partial y_n/\partial\mathbf{x}' \end{bmatrix} = \begin{bmatrix} \mathbf{a}^1 \\ \mathbf{a}^2 \\ \vdots \\ \mathbf{a}^n \end{bmatrix}.$$

Collecting all terms, we find that $\partial\mathbf{Ax}/\partial\mathbf{x}' = \mathbf{A}$, while the more familiar form will be

$$\frac{\partial\mathbf{Ax}}{\partial\mathbf{x}} = \mathbf{A}'. \tag{2-129}$$

A quadratic form is written

$$\mathbf{x}'\mathbf{Ax} = \sum_i \sum_j x_i x_j a_{ij}. \tag{2-130}$$

For example,

$$\mathbf{A} = \begin{bmatrix} 1 & 3 \\ 3 & 4 \end{bmatrix},$$

so that

$$\mathbf{x}'\mathbf{Ax} = 1x_1^2 + 4x_2^2 + 6x_1x_2.$$

Then

$$\frac{\partial\mathbf{x}'\mathbf{Ax}}{\partial\mathbf{x}} = \begin{bmatrix} 2x_1 + 6x_2 \\ 6x_1 + 8x_2 \end{bmatrix}$$

$$= \begin{bmatrix} 2 & 6 \\ 6 & 8 \end{bmatrix}\begin{bmatrix} x_1 \\ x_2 \end{bmatrix} = 2\mathbf{Ax}, \tag{2-131}$$

which is the general result when $\mathbf{A}$ is a symmetric matrix. If $\mathbf{A}$ is not symmetric, then

$$\frac{\partial(\mathbf{x}'\mathbf{Ax})}{\partial\mathbf{x}} = (\mathbf{A} + \mathbf{A}')\mathbf{x}. \tag{2-132}$$

Referring to the preceding double summation, we find that for each term, the coefficient on a_{ij} is $x_i x_j$. Therefore,

$$\frac{\partial(\mathbf{x}'\mathbf{Ax})}{\partial a_{ij}} = x_i x_j.$$

The square matrix whose ijth element is $x_i x_j$ is $\mathbf{xx'}$, so

$$\frac{\partial(\mathbf{x'Ax})}{\partial \mathbf{A}} = \mathbf{xx'}. \tag{2-133}$$

Derivatives involving determinants appear in maximum likelihood estimation. From the cofactor expansion in (2–51),

$$\frac{\partial|\mathbf{A}|}{\partial a_{ij}} = (-1)^{i+j}|\mathbf{C}_{ji}|,$$

where $|\mathbf{C}_{ij}|$ is the ijth cofactor in $\mathbf{A}$. The inverse of $\mathbf{A}$ can be computed using

$$\mathbf{A}_{ij}^{-1} = \frac{(-1)^{i+j}|\mathbf{C}_{ij}|}{|\mathbf{A}|}$$

—note the reversal of the subscripts—which implies that

$$\frac{\partial\ln|\mathbf{A}|}{\partial a_{ij}} = \frac{(-1)^{i+j}|\mathbf{C}_{ij}|}{|\mathbf{A}|}$$

or, collecting terms,

$$\frac{\partial\ln|\mathbf{A}|}{\partial \mathbf{A}} = \mathbf{A}^{-1'}.$$

Since the matrices for which we shall make use of this calculation will be symmetric in our applications, the transposition will be unnecessary.

2.9.2. Optimization

Many problems involve finding the x where $f(x)$ is maximized or minimized. Since $f'(x)$ is the slope of $f(x)$, either optimum must occur where $f'(x) = 0$. Otherwise, the function will be increasing or decreasing at x. This implies the **first-order** or

necessary condition for an optimum:

$$\frac{dy}{dx} = 0. \tag{2-134}$$

The same condition is necessary for both a maximum and a minimum. For a maximum, the function must be concave; for a minimum, it must be convex. This leads to a

sufficient condition for an optimum:

$$\text{For a maximum, } \frac{d^2y}{dx^2} < 0;$$

$$\text{For a minimum, } \frac{d^2y}{dx^2} > 0. \tag{2-135}$$

Some functions, such as the sine and cosine functions, have many **local optima,** that is, many minima and maxima. A function such as $\sin x/|x|$, which is a damped sine wave, does as well but differs in that although it has many local maxima, it has one, at $x = 0$, at which $f(x)$ is greater than it is at any other point. Thus, $x = 0$ is the **global maximum,** while the other maxima are only **local maxima.** Certain functions, such as a quadratic, have only a single optimum. These functions are **globally concave** if the optimum is a maximum and **globally convex** if it is a minimum.

For maximizing or minimizing a function of several variables, the first-order conditions are

$$\frac{\partial f(\mathbf{x})}{\partial \mathbf{x}} = \mathbf{0}. \tag{2-136}$$

This is interpreted in the same manner as the necessary condition in the univariate case. At the optimum, it must be true that no small change in any variable leads to an improvement in the function value. In the single-variable case, d^2y/dx^2 must be positive for a minimum and negative for a maximum. In the multivariate case, we attach a similar condition to the second derivatives matrix of the objective function. In particular, the second-order conditions for an optimum are that at the optimizing value,

$$\mathbf{H} = \frac{\partial^2 f(\mathbf{x})}{\partial \mathbf{x} \partial \mathbf{x}'} \tag{2-137}$$

must be positive definite for a minimum and negative definite for a maximum.

In a single-variable problem, the second-order condition can usually be verified by inspection. This will not generally be true in the multivariate case. As discussed earlier, checking the definiteness of a matrix is, in general, a relatively difficult problem. For most of the problems encountered in econometrics, however, the second-order condition will be implied by the structure of the problem. That is, the matrix $\mathbf{H}$ will usually be of such a form that it is always definite.

For an example of the preceding, consider the problem

$$\text{Maximize}_{\mathbf{x}} \; R = \mathbf{a}'\mathbf{x} - \mathbf{x}'\mathbf{A}\mathbf{x},$$

where

$$\mathbf{a}' = (5 \quad 4 \quad 2)$$

and

$$\mathbf{A} = \begin{bmatrix} 2 & 1 & 3 \\ 1 & 3 & 2 \\ 3 & 2 & 5 \end{bmatrix}.$$

Using some now familiar results, we obtain

$$\frac{\partial R}{\partial \mathbf{x}} = \mathbf{a} - 2\mathbf{A}\mathbf{x}$$

$$= \begin{bmatrix} 5 \\ 4 \\ 2 \end{bmatrix} - \begin{bmatrix} 4 & 2 & 6 \\ 2 & 6 & 4 \\ 6 & 4 & 10 \end{bmatrix} \begin{bmatrix} x_1 \\ x_2 \\ x_3 \end{bmatrix} = \mathbf{0}. \tag{2-138}$$

The solutions are

$$\begin{bmatrix} x_1 \\ x_2 \\ x_3 \end{bmatrix} = \begin{bmatrix} 4 & 2 & 6 \\ 2 & 6 & 4 \\ 6 & 4 & 10 \end{bmatrix}^{-1} \begin{bmatrix} 5 \\ 4 \\ 2 \end{bmatrix} = \begin{bmatrix} 11.25 \\ 1.75 \\ -7.25 \end{bmatrix}.$$

The sufficient condition is that

$$\frac{\partial^2 R(\mathbf{x})}{\partial \mathbf{x} \, \partial \mathbf{x}'} = -2\mathbf{A} = \begin{bmatrix} -4 & -2 & -6 \\ -2 & -6 & -4 \\ -6 & -4 & -10 \end{bmatrix} \tag{2-139}$$

must be negative definite. The three characteristic roots of this matrix are -15.776, -4, and -0.25403. Since all three roots are negative, the matrix is negative definite, as required.

In the preceding, it was necessary to compute the characteristic roots of the Hessian to verify the sufficient condition. For a general matrix of order larger than 2, this will normally require a computer. However, suppose that $\mathbf{A}$ is of the form

$$\mathbf{A} = \mathbf{B}'\mathbf{B},$$

where $\mathbf{B}$ is some known matrix. Then, as shown earlier, we know that $\mathbf{A}$ will always be positive definite (assuming that $\mathbf{B}$ has full rank). It is not necessary to calculate the characteristic roots of $\mathbf{A}$ to verify the sufficient conditions.

2.9.3. Constrained Optimization

It is often necessary to solve an optimization problem subject to some constraints on the solution. One method is merely to "solve out" the constraints. For example, in the maximization problem considered earlier, suppose that the constraint $x_1 = x_2 - x_3$ is imposed on the solution. For a single constraint such as this one, it is possible merely to substitute the right-hand side of this equation for x_1 in the objective function and solve the resulting problem as a function of the remaining two variables. However, for more general constraints, or when there is more than one constraint, the method of Lagrange multipliers provides a more straightforward method of solving the problem. We

$$\text{Maximize}_\mathbf{x} \, f(\mathbf{x}) \text{ subject to } c_1(\mathbf{x}) = 0$$

$$c_2(\mathbf{x}) = 0$$
$$\vdots \qquad\qquad (2\text{--}140)$$
$$c_J(\mathbf{x}) = 0.$$

The Lagrangean formulation is

$$\text{Maximize}_{\mathbf{x}, \, \boldsymbol{\lambda}} \, L^*(\mathbf{x}, \boldsymbol{\lambda}) = f(\mathbf{x}) + \sum_{j=1}^{J} \lambda_j c_j(\mathbf{x}), \qquad (2\text{--}141)$$

where $c_1(\cdot)$, . . . , $c_J(\cdot)$ are the J constraints and λ_j are the Lagrange multipliers. Define a vector of Lagrange multipliers, $\boldsymbol{\lambda}$, and arrange the constraints in a vector, $\mathbf{c}(\mathbf{x})$. Then the Lagrangean formula is

$$L^*(\mathbf{x}, \boldsymbol{\lambda}) = f(\mathbf{x}) + \boldsymbol{\lambda}'\mathbf{c}(\mathbf{x}). \qquad (2\text{--}142)$$

The first-order conditions are

$$\frac{\partial L^*}{\partial \mathbf{x}} = \frac{\partial f(\mathbf{x})}{\partial \mathbf{x}} + \frac{\partial \boldsymbol{\lambda}'\mathbf{c}(\mathbf{x})}{\partial \mathbf{x}} = \mathbf{0}(n \times 1)$$

$$\qquad\qquad (2\text{--}143)$$

$$\frac{\partial L^*}{\partial \boldsymbol{\lambda}} = \mathbf{c}(\mathbf{x}) = \mathbf{0}(J \times 1).$$

The second term in $\partial L^*/\partial \mathbf{x}$ is

$$\frac{\partial \boldsymbol{\lambda}'\mathbf{c}(\mathbf{x})}{\partial \mathbf{x}} = \frac{\partial \mathbf{c}(\mathbf{x})'\boldsymbol{\lambda}}{\partial \mathbf{x}}$$

$$= \left[\frac{\partial \mathbf{c}(\mathbf{x})'}{\partial \mathbf{x}} \right] \boldsymbol{\lambda} \qquad (2\text{--}144)$$

$$= \mathbf{C}'\boldsymbol{\lambda},$$

where $\mathbf{C}$ is the derivatives of the constraints with respect to $\mathbf{x}$. The jth row of the $J \times n$ matrix $\mathbf{C}$ is the vector of derivatives of the jth constraint, $c_j(\mathbf{x})$, with respect to $\mathbf{x}'$. Upon collecting terms, the first-order conditions are

$$\frac{\partial L^*}{\partial \mathbf{x}} = \frac{\partial f(\mathbf{x})}{\partial \mathbf{x}} + \mathbf{C}'\boldsymbol{\lambda} = \mathbf{0}$$

$$\frac{\partial L^*}{\partial \boldsymbol{\lambda}} = \mathbf{c}(\mathbf{x}) = \mathbf{0}.$$

(2–145)

There is one very important aspect of the constrained solution to consider. In the unconstrained solution, we have $\partial f(\mathbf{x})/\partial \mathbf{x} = \mathbf{0}$. From (2–145), we obtain for a constrained solution,

$$\frac{\partial f(\mathbf{x})}{\partial \mathbf{x}} = -\mathbf{C}'\boldsymbol{\lambda},$$

which will not equal $\mathbf{0}$ unless $\boldsymbol{\lambda} = \mathbf{0}$. This has two important implications:

1. The constrained solution *must* be inferior to the unconstrained solution. This is implied by the nonzero gradient at the constrained solution.
2. If the Lagrange multipliers are zero, then the constrained solution will equal the unconstrained solution.

To continue the example begun earlier, suppose that we add the following conditions:

$$x_1 - x_2 + x_3 = 0,$$

$$x_1 + x_2 + x_3 = 0.$$

To put this in the format of the general problem, write the constraints as

$$\mathbf{c}(\mathbf{x}) = \mathbf{Cx} = \mathbf{0},$$

where

$$\mathbf{C} = \begin{bmatrix} 1 & -1 & 1 \\ 1 & 1 & 1 \end{bmatrix}.$$

The Lagrangean problem is

$$R^*(\mathbf{x}, \boldsymbol{\lambda}) = \mathbf{a}'\mathbf{x} - \mathbf{x}'\mathbf{A}\mathbf{x} + \boldsymbol{\lambda}'\mathbf{C}\mathbf{x}.$$

Note the dimensions and arrangement of the various parts. In particular, $\mathbf{C}$ is a 2×3 matrix, with one row for each constraint and one column for each variable in the objective function. The vector of Lagrange multipliers thus has two elements, one for each constraint. The first-order conditions are

$$\mathbf{a} - 2\mathbf{A}\mathbf{x} + \mathbf{C}'\boldsymbol{\lambda} = \mathbf{0} \qquad \text{(three equations)}$$

and

$$\mathbf{Cx} = \mathbf{0} \qquad \text{(two equations)}$$

(2–146)

These may be combined in the single equation

$$\begin{bmatrix} -2\mathbf{A} & \mathbf{C}' \\ \mathbf{C} & \mathbf{0} \end{bmatrix}\begin{bmatrix} \mathbf{x} \\ \boldsymbol{\lambda} \end{bmatrix} = \begin{bmatrix} -\mathbf{a} \\ \mathbf{0} \end{bmatrix}.$$

Using the partitioned inverse of (2–74) produces the solution

$$\boldsymbol{\lambda} = -[\mathbf{C}\mathbf{A}^{-1}\mathbf{C}']\mathbf{C}\mathbf{A}^{-1}\mathbf{a}$$

(2–147)

and

$$\mathbf{x} = \tfrac{1}{2}\mathbf{A}^{-1}[\mathbf{I} - \mathbf{C}'(\mathbf{CA}^{-1}\mathbf{C}')^{-1}\mathbf{CA}^{-1}]\mathbf{a}. \tag{2-148}$$

The two results, (2–147) and (2–148), yield analytic solutions for $\boldsymbol{\lambda}$ and $\mathbf{x}$. For the specific matrices and vectors of the example, these are $\boldsymbol{\lambda} = [-0.5 \quad -7.5]'$ and the constrained solution vector is $x^* = [1.5 \quad 0 \quad -1.5]'$. Note that in computing the solution to this sort of problem, it is not necessary to use the rather cumbersome form of (2–148). Once $\boldsymbol{\lambda}$ is obtained from (2–147), the solution can be inserted in (2–146) for a much simpler computation. The solution

$$\mathbf{x} = \tfrac{1}{2}\mathbf{A}^{-1}\mathbf{a} + \tfrac{1}{2}\mathbf{A}^{-1}\mathbf{C}'\boldsymbol{\lambda}$$

suggests a useful result for the constrained optimum:

$$\text{constrained solution} = \text{unconstrained solution} + [2\mathbf{A}]^{-1}\mathbf{C}'\boldsymbol{\lambda}. \tag{2-149}$$

Finally, inserting the two solutions in the original function, we find that $R = 24.375$ and $R^* = 2.25$, which illustrates again that the constrained solution (in this *maximization* problem) is inferior to the unconstrained solution.

2.9.4. Transformations

If a function is strictly monotonic, then it is **one-to-one.** Each y is associated with exactly one value of x, and vice versa. In this case, an **inverse function** exists, which expresses x as a function of y, written

$$y = f(x) \qquad \text{and} \qquad x = f^{-1}(y). \tag{2-150}$$

An example is the inverse relationship between the log and the exponential functions.

The slope of the inverse function,

$$\frac{dx}{dy} = \frac{df^{-1}(y)}{dy} = f^{-1\prime}(y) \tag{2-151}$$

is the **Jacobian** of the transformation from x to y. For example, if

$$y = a + bx, \tag{2-152}$$

then

$$x = -\frac{a}{b} + \left(\frac{1}{b}\right)y \tag{2-153}$$

is the inverse transformation and

$$J = \frac{dx}{dy} = \frac{1}{b}. \tag{2-154}$$

Looking ahead to the statistical application of this concept, we observe that if $y = f(x)$ were *vertical,* then this would no longer be a functional relationship. The same x would be associated with more than one value of y. In this case, at this value of x, we would find that $J = 0$, indicating a singularity in the function.

If $\mathbf{y}$ is a column vector of functions, $\mathbf{y} = \mathbf{f}(\mathbf{x})$, then

$$\mathbf{J} = \frac{\partial \mathbf{x}}{\partial \mathbf{y}'}$$

$$\begin{bmatrix} \partial x_1/\partial y_1 & \partial x_1/\partial y_2 & \cdots & \partial x_1/\partial y_n \\ \partial x_2/\partial y_1 & \partial x_2/\partial y_2 & \cdots & \partial x_2/\partial y_n \\ & & \vdots & \\ \partial x_n/\partial y_1 & \partial x_n/\partial y_2 & \cdots & \partial x_n/\partial y_n \end{bmatrix}. \tag{2-155}$$

Consider the set of linear functions $\mathbf{y} = \mathbf{A}\mathbf{x} = \mathbf{f}(\mathbf{x})$. The inverse transformation is $\mathbf{x} = \mathbf{f}^{-1}(\mathbf{y})$, which will be either

$$\mathbf{x} = \mathbf{A}^{-1}\mathbf{y}$$

if $\mathbf{A}$ is nonsingular or

$$\mathbf{x} = \mathbf{0}$$

if $\mathbf{A}$ is singular. Let $\mathbf{J}$ be the matrix of partial derivatives of the inverse functions;

$$\mathbf{J} = \left[\frac{\partial x_i}{\partial y_j}\right]. \tag{2-156}$$

The absolute value of the determinant of $\mathbf{J}$,

$$\text{abs}(|\mathbf{J}|) = \left|\frac{\partial \mathbf{x}}{\partial \mathbf{y}'}\right|, \tag{2-157}$$

is the **Jacobian** of the transformation from $\mathbf{x}$ to $\mathbf{y}$. In the nonsingular case,

$$\text{abs}(|\mathbf{J}|) = \text{abs}(|\mathbf{A}^{-1}|) = \frac{1}{\text{abs}(|\mathbf{A}|)}. \tag{2-158}$$

In the singular case, all of the partial derivatives will be zero, as will the Jacobian. In this instance, a zero Jacobian implies that $\mathbf{A}$ is singular, or equivalently, that the transformations from $\mathbf{x}$ to $\mathbf{y}$ are functionally dependent. The singular case is analogous to the single-variable case.

Clearly, if the vector $\mathbf{x}$ is given, then $\mathbf{y} = \mathbf{A}\mathbf{x}$ can be computed from $\mathbf{x}$. Whether $\mathbf{x}$ can be deduced from $\mathbf{y}$ is another question. Evidently, it depends on the Jacobian. If the Jacobian is not zero, then the inverse transformations exist, and we can obtain $\mathbf{x}$. If not, then we cannot obtain $\mathbf{x}$.

EXERCISES

1. For the matrices

$$\mathbf{A} = \begin{bmatrix} 1 & 3 & 3 \\ 2 & 4 & 1 \end{bmatrix}, \qquad \mathbf{B} = \begin{bmatrix} 2 & 4 \\ 1 & 5 \\ 6 & 2 \end{bmatrix},$$

compute $\mathbf{AB}$, $\mathbf{A'B'}$, and $\mathbf{BA}$.

2. Prove that $\text{tr}(\mathbf{AB}) = \text{tr}(\mathbf{BA})$, where $\mathbf{A}$ and $\mathbf{B}$ are any two matrices that are conformable for both multiplications. They need not be square.

3. Prove that $\text{tr}(\mathbf{A'A}) = \Sigma_i\Sigma_j a_{ij}^2$.

4. Expand the matrix product

$$\mathbf{X} = ([\mathbf{AB} + (\mathbf{CD})'][(\mathbf{EF})^{-1} + \mathbf{GH}])'.$$

Assume that all matrices are square and $\mathbf{E}$ and $\mathbf{F}$ are nonsingular.

5. Prove that for n $K \times 1$ column vectors $\mathbf{x}_i$, $i = 1, \ldots, n$, and some nonzero vector $\mathbf{a}$,

$$\sum_i (\mathbf{x}_i - \mathbf{a})(\mathbf{x}_i - \mathbf{a})' = \mathbf{X}'\mathbf{M}^0\mathbf{X} + n(\bar{\mathbf{x}} - \mathbf{a})(\bar{\mathbf{x}} - \mathbf{a})',$$

where the ith row of $\mathbf{X}$ is $\mathbf{x}_i'$ and $\mathbf{M}^0$ is defined in (2-34).

6. Let $\mathbf{A}$ be any square matrix whose columns are $[\mathbf{a}_1, \mathbf{a}_2, \ldots, \mathbf{a}_M]$, and let $\mathbf{B}$ be any rearrangement of the columns of the $M \times M$ identity matrix. What operation is performed by the multiplication $\mathbf{AB}$? By the multiplication $\mathbf{BA}$?

7. Consider the 3×3 case of the matrix $\mathbf{B}$ in Exercise 6. For example,

$$\mathbf{B} = \begin{bmatrix} 0 & 1 & 0 \\ 0 & 0 & 1 \\ 1 & 0 & 0 \end{bmatrix}.$$

   Compute $\mathbf{B}^2$ and $\mathbf{B}^3$. Repeat for a 4×4 matrix. Can you generalize your finding?

8. Calculate $|\mathbf{A}|$, $\mathrm{tr}(\mathbf{A})$, and $\mathbf{A}^{-1}$ for

$$\mathbf{A} = \begin{bmatrix} 1 & 4 & 7 \\ 3 & 2 & 5 \\ 5 & 2 & 8 \end{bmatrix}.$$

9. Obtain the Cholesky decomposition of the matrix

$$\mathbf{A} = \begin{bmatrix} 25 & 7 \\ 7 & 13 \end{bmatrix}.$$

   Recall that the Cholesky decomposition of a matrix, $\mathbf{A}$, is the matrix product $\mathbf{LU} = \mathbf{A}$, where $\mathbf{L}$ is a lower triangular matrix and $\mathbf{U} = \mathbf{L}'$.

10. A symmetric positive definite matrix, $\mathbf{A}$, can also be written as $\mathbf{A} = \mathbf{UL}$, where $\mathbf{U}$ is an upper triangular matrix and $\mathbf{L} = \mathbf{U}'$. This is not the Cholesky decomposition, however. Obtain this decomposition of the matrix in Exercise 9.

11. What operation is performed by postmultiplying a matrix by a diagonal matrix? What about premultiplication?

12. Are the following quadratic forms positive for all values of $\mathbf{x}$?
    (a) $y = x_1^2 - 28x_1x_2 + (11x_2)^2$.
    (b) $y = 5x_1^2 + x_2^2 + 7x_3^2 + 4x_1x_2 + 6x_1x_3 + 8x_2x_3$.

13. Prove that $\mathrm{tr}(\mathbf{A} \otimes \mathbf{B}) = \mathrm{tr}(\mathbf{A})\,\mathrm{tr}(\mathbf{B})$.

14. A matrix, $\mathbf{A}$, is **nilpotent** if $\lim_{K \to \infty} \mathbf{A}^K = \mathbf{0}$. Prove that a necessary and sufficient condition for a symmetric matrix to be nilpotent is that all of its characteristic roots be less than 1 in absolute value. (For an application, see Section 18.6.3.)

15. Compute the characteristic roots of

$$\mathbf{A} = \begin{bmatrix} 2 & 4 & 3 \\ 4 & 8 & 6 \\ 3 & 6 & 5 \end{bmatrix}.$$

16. Suppose that $\mathbf{A} = \mathbf{A}(z)$, where z is a scalar. What is $\partial(\mathbf{x}'\mathbf{Ax})/\partial z$? Suppose that each element of $\mathbf{x}$ is also a function of z. Once again, what is $\partial(\mathbf{x}'\mathbf{Ax})/\partial z$?

17. Show that the solutions to the determinantal equations

$$|\mathbf{B} - \lambda\mathbf{A}| = 0 \quad \text{and} \quad |\mathbf{A}^{-1}\mathbf{B} - \lambda\mathbf{I}| = 0$$

   are the same. How do the solutions to this equation relate to those of the equation $|\mathbf{B}^{-1}\mathbf{A} - \mu\mathbf{I}| = 0$? (For an application of the first of these equations, see Section 20.4.4c.)

18. Using matrix **A** in Exercise 9, find the vector **x** that minimizes $y = \mathbf{x'Ax} + 2x_1 + 3x_2 - 10$. What is the value of y at the minimum? Now minimize y subject to the constraint $x_1 + x_2 = 1$. Compare the two solutions.

19. What is the Jacobian for the following transformations?

$$y_1 = \frac{x_1}{x_2},$$

$$\ln y_2 = \ln x_1 - \ln x_2 + \ln x_3,$$

and

$$y_3 = x_1 x_2 x_3.$$

20. Prove that exchanging two columns of a square matrix reverses the sign of its determinant. (**Hint:** Use a permutation matrix. See Exercise 6.)

21. Suppose that $\mathbf{x} = \mathbf{x}(z)$, where z is a scalar. What is

$$\frac{\partial[\mathbf{x'Ax}/\mathbf{x'Bx}]}{\partial z}?$$

22. Suppose that **y** is an $n \times 1$ vector and **X** is an $n \times K$ matrix. The projection of **y** into the column space of **X** is defined earlier after (2–55), $\hat{\mathbf{y}} = \mathbf{Xb}$. Now consider the projection of $\mathbf{y}^* = c\mathbf{y}$ into the column space of $\mathbf{X}^* = \mathbf{XP}$, where c is a scalar and **P** is a nonsingular $K \times K$ matrix. Find the projection of $\mathbf{y}^*$ into the column space of $\mathbf{X}^*$. Prove that the cosine of the angle between $\mathbf{y}^*$ and its projection into the column space of $\mathbf{X}^*$ is the same as that between **y** and its projection into the column space of **X**. How do you interpret this result?

23. For the matrix

$$\mathbf{X'} = \begin{bmatrix} 1 & 1 & 1 & 1 \\ 4 & -2 & 3 & -5 \end{bmatrix}$$

compute $\mathbf{P} = \mathbf{X(X'X)}^{-1}\mathbf{X'}$ and $\mathbf{M} = (\mathbf{I} - \mathbf{P})$. Verify that $\mathbf{MP} = \mathbf{0}$. Let

$$\mathbf{Q} = \begin{bmatrix} 1 & 3 \\ 2 & 8 \end{bmatrix}.$$

(**Hint:** Show that **M** and **P** are idempotent.)
(a) Compute **P** and **M** based on **XQ** instead of **X**.
(b) What are the characteristic roots of **M** and **P**?

24. Suppose that **A** is an $n \times n$ matrix of the form

$$\mathbf{A} = (1 - \rho)\mathbf{I} + \rho\mathbf{ii'},$$

where **i** is a column of 1s and $0 < \rho < 1$. Write the format of **A** explicitly for $n = 4$. Find all of the characteristic roots and vectors of **A**. (**Hint:** There are only two distinct characteristic roots, which occur with multiplicity 1 and $n - 1$. Every **c** of a certain type is a characteristic vector of **A**.) For an application that uses a matrix of this type, see Section 16.4.3 on the random effects model.

25. Find the inverse of the matrix in Exercise 24. [**Hint:** Use (2–66).]

26. Prove that every matrix in the sequence of matrices

$$\mathbf{H}_{i+1} = \mathbf{H}_i + \mathbf{d}_i\mathbf{d}'_i,$$

where

$$\mathbf{H}_0 = \mathbf{I},$$

is positive definite. For an application, see Section 12.5.5. For an extension, prove that every matrix in the sequence of matrices defined in (12–28) is positive definite if $\mathbf{H}_0 = \mathbf{I}$.

27. What is the inverse matrix of

$$\mathbf{P} = \begin{bmatrix} \cos(x) & \sin(x) \\ -\sin(x) & \cos(x) \end{bmatrix}?$$

What are the characteristic roots of **P**?

28. Derive the off-diagonal block of $\mathbf{A}^{-1}$ in Section 2.6.4.

29. (This requires a computer.) For the $\mathbf{X'X}$ matrix at the end of Section 6.3.2:
   (a) Compute the characteristic roots of $\mathbf{X'X}$.
   (b) Compute the condition number of $\mathbf{X'X}$. (Do not forget to scale the columns of the matrix, so that the diagonal elements are 1.)

CHAPTER 3

Probability and Distribution Theory

3.1. Introduction

This chapter reviews the distribution theory used later in the book. Since a previous course in statistics is assumed, most of the results will be stated without proof. The more advanced results in the later sections will be developed in greater detail.

3.2. Random Variables

We view our observation on some aspect of the economy as the **outcome** of a random experiment. The outcomes of the experiment are assigned unique numeric values. The assignment is one-to-one; each outcome gets one value, and no two distinct outcomes receive the same value. This outcome variable, X, is a **random variable** because, until the experiment is performed, it is uncertain what value X will take. Probabilities are associated with outcomes to quantify this uncertainty. We usually use capital letters for the ''name'' of a random variable and lowercase letters for the values it takes. Thus, the probability that X takes a particular value, x, might be denoted $\text{Prob}(X = x)$.

A random variable is **discrete** if the set of outcomes is either finite in number or countably infinite. The random variable is **continuous** if the set of outcomes is infinitely divisible and, hence, not countable. These definitions will correspond to the sorts of data we observe in practice. Counts of occurrences will provide observations on discrete random variables, while measurements such as time or income will give observations on continuous random variables.

3.2.1. Probability Distributions

A listing of the values, x, taken by a random variable, X, and their associated probabilities is a **probability distribution,** $f(x)$. For a discrete random variable,

$$f(x) = \text{Prob}(X = x). \tag{3–1}$$

The axioms of probability require that:

$$1. \ \ 0 \le \text{Prob}(X = x) \le 1.$$
$$\tag{3–2}$$
$$2. \ \ \sum_x f(x_i) = 1.$$

EXAMPLE 3.1 _____

X = number of customers to arrive at a teller's window at a bank in a randomly chosen time span of given length. A frequently used model is the **Poisson distribution:**

$$f(x) = \frac{e^{-\lambda}\lambda^x}{x!}, \qquad x = 0, 1, 2, \ldots, \tag{3-3}$$

where λ is the average number of persons to arrive in a given time span. Note that regardless of the value of λ, the probability model is, in fact, at odds with the physical phenomenon being described. The number of persons must, of course, be finite. But, for large values of x, the probabilities assigned by this model become arbitrarily small.

_____

For the continuous case, the probability associated with any particular point is zero, and we can only assign positive probabilities to intervals in the range of x. The **probability density function (pdf)** is defined so that $f(x) \geq 0$ and

$$1. \ \text{Prob}(a \leq x \leq b) = \int_a^b f(x) \, dx \geq 0. \tag{3-4}$$

This is the area under $f(x)$ in the range from a to b. For a continuous variable,

$$2. \ \int_{-\infty}^{+\infty} f(x) \, dx = 1. \tag{3-5}$$

If the range of x is not infinite, it is understood that $f(x) = 0$ anywhere outside the appropriate range. Since the probability associated with any individual point is 0,

$$\text{Prob}(a \leq x \leq b) = \text{Prob}(a \leq x < b)$$
$$= \text{Prob}(a < x \leq b)$$
$$= \text{Prob}(a < x < b).$$

3.2.2. Cumulative Distribution Function

For any random variable x, the probability that x is less than or equal to a is denoted $F(a)$. $F(x)$ is the **cumulative distribution function (cdf).** For a discrete random variable,

$$F(x) = \sum_{X \leq x} f(x)$$
$$= \text{Prob}(X \leq x). \tag{3-6}$$

In view of the definition of $f(x)$,

$$f(x_i) = F(x_i) - F(x_{i-1}). \tag{3-7}$$

For a continuous random variable

$$F(x) = \int_{-\infty}^x f(t) \, dt \tag{3-8}$$

and

$$f(x) = \frac{dF(x)}{dx}. \tag{3-9}$$

In both the continuous and discrete cases, $F(x)$ must satisfy the following properties:

1. $0 \le F(x) \le 1$.
2. If $x > y$, $F(x) \ge F(y)$.
3. $F(+\infty) = 1$.
4. $F(-\infty) = 0$.

From the definition of the cdf,

$$\text{Prob}(a < x \le b) = F(b) - F(a). \tag{3-10}$$

Any valid pdf will imply a valid cdf, so there is no need to verify these conditions separately.

3.3. Expectations of a Random Variable

Definition. The **mean,** or **expected value,** of a random variable is

$$E[x] = \begin{cases} \sum_x xf(x) & \text{if } x \text{ is discrete,} \\[2mm] \int_x xf(x) \, dx & \text{if } x \text{ is continuous.} \end{cases} \tag{3-11}$$

(The notation $\sum_x$ or $\int_x$, used henceforth, means the sum or integral over the entire range of values of x.) The mean is usually denoted μ. It is a weighted average of the values taken by x, where the weights are the respective probabilities. It is not necessarily a value actually taken by the random variable. For example, the expected number of heads in one toss of a coin is $\frac{1}{2}$.

Other **measures of central tendency** are the **median,** which is the value m such that $\text{Prob}(X \le m) \ge \frac{1}{2}$ and $\text{Prob}(X \ge m) \le \frac{1}{2}$, and the **mode,** which is the value of x at which $f(x)$ takes its maximum. The first of these measures is more frequently used. Loosely speaking, the median corresponds more closely than the mean to the middle of a distribution. It is unaffected by extreme values. In the discrete case, the modal value of x has the highest probability of occurring.

Let $g(x)$ be a function of x. The function that gives the expected value of $g(x)$ is denoted

$$E[g(x)] = \begin{cases} \sum_i g(x_i) \, \text{Prob}(X = x_i) & \text{if } X \text{ is discrete,} \\[2mm] \int_{-\infty}^{+\infty} g(x)f(x) \, dx & \text{if } X \text{ is continuous.} \end{cases} \tag{3-12}$$

If $g(x) = a + bx$ for constants a and b,

$$E[a + bx] = a + bE[x].$$

One important case is the expected value of a constant, a, which is just a.

Definition. The **variance** of a random variable is

$$\text{Var}[x] = E[(x - \mu)^2]$$

$$= \begin{cases} \sum_x (x - \mu)^2 f(x) & \text{if } x \text{ is discrete,} \\ \int_x (x - \mu)^2 f(x) \, dx & \text{if } x \text{ is continuous.} \end{cases} \tag{3-13}$$

$\text{Var}[x]$, which must be positive, is usually denoted σ^2. This is a measure of the dispersion of a distribution. Computation of the variance is simplified by using the following important result:

$$\text{Var}[x] = E[x^2] - \mu^2. \tag{3-14}$$

A convenient corollary to (3–14) is

$$E[x^2] = \sigma^2 + \mu^2. \tag{3-15}$$

By inserting $y = a + bx$ in (3–13) and expanding, we find that

$$\text{Var}[a + bx] = b^2 \, \text{Var}[x], \tag{3-16}$$

which implies, for any constant, a, that

$$\text{Var}[a] = 0. \tag{3-17}$$

To describe a distribution, we usually use σ, the positive square root, which is the **standard deviation** of x. The standard deviation can be interpreted as having the same units of measurement as x and μ. For any random variable x and any positive constant k, the **Chebyshev inequality** states that

$$\text{Prob}(\mu - k\sigma \leq x \leq \mu + k\sigma) \geq 1 - \frac{1}{k^2}. \tag{3-18}$$

[A proof appears in Goldberger (1964).]

Two other measures often used to describe a probability distribution are

$$\text{skewness} = E[(x - \mu)^3]$$

and

$$\text{kurtosis} = E[(x - \mu)^4].$$

Skewness is a measure of the asymmetry of a distribution. For symmetric distributions,

$$f(\mu - x) = f(\mu + x)$$

and

$$\text{skewness} = 0.$$

For asymmetric distributions, the skewness will be positive if the "long tail" is in the positive direction. Kurtosis is a measure of the thickness of the tails of the distribution. A shorthand expression for other **central moments** is

$$\mu_r = E[(x - \mu)^r].$$

Since μ_r tends to explode as r grows, the normalized measure, μ_r/σ^r, is often used for description. Two common measures are

$$\text{skewness coefficient} = \frac{\mu_3}{\sigma^3}$$

and

$$\text{degree of excess} = \frac{\mu_4}{\sigma^4} - 3.$$

The second is based on the normal distribution, which has excess of zero.

For any two functions $g_1(x)$ and $g_2(x)$,

$$E[g_1(x) + g_2(x)] = E[g_1(x)] + E[g_2(x)]. \qquad (3-19)$$

For the general case of a possibly nonlinear $g(x)$,

$$E[g(x)] = \int_x g(x)f(x)\ dx \qquad (3-20)$$

and

$$\text{Var}[g(x)] = \int_x (g(x) - E[g(x)])^2 f(x)\ dx. \qquad (3-21)$$

(For convenience, we shall omit the equivalent definitions for discrete variables in the following discussion and use the integral to mean either integration or summation, whichever is appropriate.)

A device used to approximate $E[g(x)]$ and $\text{Var}[g(x)]$ is the linear Taylor series approximation:

$$\begin{aligned} g(x) &\simeq [g(x^0) - g'(x^0)x^0] + g'(x^0)x \\ &= \beta_1 + \beta_2 x \qquad (3-22) \\ &= g^*(x). \end{aligned}$$

If the approximation is reasonably accurate, the mean and variance of $g^*(x)$ will be approximately equal to the mean and variance of $g(x)$. A natural choice for the expansion point is $x^0 = \mu = E(x)$. Inserting this in (3-22) gives

$$g(x) \simeq [g(\mu) - g'(\mu)\mu] + g'(\mu)x, \qquad (3-23)$$

so that

$$E[g(x)] \simeq g(\mu) \qquad (3-24)$$

and

$$\text{Var}[g(x)] \simeq [g'(\mu)]^2 \text{Var}[x]. \qquad (3-25)$$

A point to note in view of (3-22) to (3-24) is that $E[g(x)]$ will generally not equal $g(E[x])$.

3.4. Some Specific Probability Distributions

Certain experimental situations give rise naturally to specific probability distributions. In the majority of cases in economics, however, the distributions used are merely models of the observed phenomena. Although the normal distribution, which we shall discuss at length, is the mainstay of econometric research, economists have used a wide variety of other distributions. A few are discussed here.[1]

---

[1] A much more complete listing appears in Maddala (1977, Chaps. 3 and 18) and in most mathematical statistics textbooks.

3.4.1. The Normal Distribution

The general form of a normal distribution with mean μ and standard deviation σ is

$$f(x \mid \mu, \sigma) = \frac{1}{\sqrt{2\pi}\,\sigma} e^{-(x-\mu)^2/(2\sigma^2)}. \tag{3-26}$$

This is usually denoted $x \sim N[\mu, \sigma^2]$. The standard notation $x \sim f(x)$ is used to state that "x has probability distribution $f(x)$." Among the most useful properties of the normal distribution is its preservation under linear transformation.

$$\text{If } x \sim N[\mu, \sigma^2], \ (a + bx) \sim N[a + b\mu, b^2\sigma^2]. \tag{3-27}$$

One particularly convenient transformation is $a = -\mu/\sigma$ and $b = 1/\sigma$. The resulting variable,

$$z = \frac{x - \mu}{\sigma},$$

has the **standard normal distribution,** denoted $N[0, 1]$, with density

$$\phi(z) = \frac{1}{\sqrt{2\pi}} e^{-z^2/2}. \tag{3-28}$$

The specific notation, $\phi(z)$, is often used for this distribution and $\Phi(z)$ for its cdf.

Tables of the standard normal cdf appear in most statistics and econometrics textbooks. Because the form of the distribution does not change under a linear transformation, it is not necessary to tabulate the distribution for other values of μ and σ. For any normally distributed variable,

$$\text{Prob}(a < x < b) = \text{Prob}\left(\frac{a - \mu}{\sigma} < \frac{x - \mu}{\sigma} < \frac{b - \mu}{\sigma}\right), \tag{3-29}$$

which can always be read from a table of the standard normal distribution. In addition, because the distribution is symmetric, $\Phi(-z) = 1 - \Phi(z)$. Hence, it is not necessary to tabulate both the negative and positive halves of the distribution.

3.4.2. The Chi-Squared, t, and F Distributions

The chi-squared, t, and F distributions are derived from the normal distribution. They arise in econometrics as sums of n or n_1 and n_2 other variables. These three distributions have associated with them one or two "degrees of freedom" parameters, which for our purposes, will be the number of variables in the relevant sum.

The first of the essential results is

If $z \sim N[0, 1]$, $x = z^2 \sim$ chi-squared[1], that is,
chi-squared with one degree of freedom, denoted

$$z^2 \sim \chi^2[1]. \tag{3-30}$$

This is a skewed distribution with mean 1 and variance 2. The second is

If $x_1, \ldots, x_n$ are n *independent* chi-squared[1]
variables, then $\Sigma_i x_i \sim$ chi-squared[n]. \hfill (3-31)

The mean and variance of a chi-squared variable with n degrees of freedom are n and $2n$, respectively. A number of useful corollaries can be derived using (3-30) and (3-31).

If z_i, $i = 1, \ldots, n$ are independent $N[0, 1]$ variables,

$$\sum_{i=1}^{n} z_i^2 \sim \chi^2[n]. \tag{3-32}$$

If z_i, $i = 1, \ldots, n$ are independent $N[0, \sigma^2]$ variables,

$$\sum_{i=1}^{n} \left(\frac{z_i}{\sigma}\right)^2 \sim \chi^2[n]. \tag{3-33}$$

If x_1 and x_2 are independent chi-squared variables
with n_1 and n_2 degrees of freedom, respectively,

$$x_1 + x_2 \sim \chi^2[n_1 + n_2]. \tag{3-34}$$

This can be generalized to the sum of an arbitrary number of independent chi-squared variables.

Unlike the normal distribution, a separate table is required for the chi-squared distribution for each value of n. Typically, only a few percentage points of the distribution are tabulated for each n. Table 4 in the appendix of this book gives upper (right) tail areas for a number of values.

If x_1 and x_2 are two *independent* chi-squared variables with degrees of freedom parameters n_1 and n_2, respectively, the ratio

$$F[n_1, n_2] = \frac{x_1/n_1}{x_2/n_2} \tag{3-35}$$

has the **F distribution**. The two degrees of freedom parameters n_1 and n_2 are the numerator and denominator degrees of freedom, respectively. Tables of the F distribution must be computed for each pair of values of (n_1, n_2). As such, only one or two specific values, such as the 95 percent and 99 percent upper tail values, are tabulated in most cases.

If z is an $N[0, 1]$ variable and x is $\chi^2[n]$ and is independent of z, the ratio

$$t[n] = \frac{z}{\sqrt{x/n}} \tag{3-36}$$

is distributed as t with n degrees of freedom. The t distribution has the same shape as the normal distribution but has thicker tails.[2] This distribution is tabulated in the same manner as the chi-squared distribution, with several specific cutoff points corresponding to specified tail areas for various values of the degrees of freedom parameter.

Comparing (3–35) with $n_1 = 1$ and (3–36), we see the useful relationship between the t and F distributions:

$$\text{If } t \sim t[n], \quad t^2 \sim F[1, n].$$

3.4.3. Distributions with Large Degrees of Freedom

The chi-squared, t, and F distributions usually arise in connection with sums of sample observations. The degrees of freedom parameter in each case grows with the number of observations. We often deal with larger degrees of freedom than are shown in the tables.

---

[2] The special case of $t[1]$, which is the ratio of two standard normal variables, is the Cauchy distribution.

Thus, the standard tables are often inadequate. However, in all cases, there are **limiting distributions** that we can use when the degrees of freedom parameter grows large. The simplest case is the t distribution. The t distribution with infinite degrees of freedom is equivalent to the standard normal distribution. Beyond about 100 degrees of freedom, they are almost indistinguishable.

For degrees of freedom greater than 30, a commonly used approximation for the distribution of the chi-squared variable, x, is

$$z = \sqrt{2x} - \sqrt{2n - 1}, \tag{3-37}$$

which is approximately standard normally distributed. Thus,

$$\text{Prob}(\chi^2[n] < a) \simeq \Phi(\sqrt{2a} - \sqrt{2n - 1}).$$

EXAMPLE 3.2 _____

If x is chi-squared with 70 degrees of freedom,

$$\text{Prob}(x < 85) \simeq \text{Prob}(z < \sqrt{170} - \sqrt{139})$$

$$= \text{Prob}(z < 1.249) = 0.8942.$$

The correct value from the chi-squared distribution is 0.89409.

_____

As used in econometrics, the F distribution with a large-denominator degrees of freedom is common. As n_2 becomes infinite, the denominator of F converges identically to 1, so we can treat the variable

$$x = n_1 F \tag{3-38}$$

as a chi-squared variable with n_1 degrees of freedom. Since the numerator degrees of freedom will typically be small, this approximation will suffice for the types of applications we are likely to encounter.[3] If not, the approximation given earlier for the chi-squared distribution can be applied to $n_1 F$.

3.4.4. Size Distributions—The Lognormal Distribution

In modeling size distributions, such as the distribution of firm sizes in an industry or the distribution of income in a country, the lognormal distribution has been particularly useful:[4]

$$f(x) = \frac{1}{\sqrt{2\pi}\,\sigma x} e^{-[(\ln x - \mu)^2]/(2\sigma^2)}, \qquad x \geq 0.$$

A lognormal variable has a mean equal to $e^{\mu + \sigma^2/2}$ and a variance equal to $e^{2\mu + \sigma^2}$ $(e^{\sigma^2} - 1)$. If $y \sim \text{lognormal}[\mu, \sigma^2]$, $\ln y \sim N[\mu, \sigma^2]$. If x has a lognormal distribution with mean θ and variance λ^2, $\ln x \sim N(\mu, \sigma^2)$, where $\mu = \ln \theta^2 - \frac{1}{2} \ln(\theta^2 + \lambda^2)$ and $\sigma^2 = \ln(1 + \lambda^2/\theta^2)$.

_____

[3] See Johnson and Kotz (1970) for other approximations.

[4] A study of applications of the lognormal distribution appears in Aitchison and Brown (1969).

3.4.5. The Gamma Distribution

The **gamma distribution** has been used in a variety of settings, including the study of income distribution[5] and production functions.[6] The general form of the distribution is

$$f(x) = \frac{\lambda^P}{\Gamma(P)} e^{-\lambda x} x^{P-1}, \qquad x \geq 0. \tag{3-39}$$

Many familiar distributions are special cases, including the exponential ($P = 1$) and chi-squared ($\lambda = 1/2$, $P = n/2$). The mean is P/λ and the variance is P/λ^2.

3.4.6. The Beta Distribution

Distributions are often chosen on the basis of the range within which the random variable is constrained to vary. The lognormal distribution, for example, is sometimes used to model a variable that is always nonnegative. For a variable constrained between 0 and $c > 0$, the **beta distribution** has proved useful. Its density is

$$f(x) = \frac{\Gamma(\alpha + \beta)}{\Gamma(\alpha)\Gamma(\beta)} \left(\frac{x}{c}\right)^{\alpha-1} \left(1 - \frac{x}{c}\right)^{\beta-1} \left(\frac{1}{c}\right). \tag{3-40}$$

This functional form is extremely flexible in the shapes it will accommodate. It is symmetric if $\alpha = \beta$, asymmetric otherwise, and can be hump-shaped or U-shaped. The mean is $\alpha/(\alpha + \beta)$ and the variance is $\alpha\beta/(\alpha + \beta)^2$. The beta distribution has been applied in the study of labor force participation rates.[7]

3.5. The Distribution of a Function of a Random Variable

We considered finding the expected value of a function of a random variable. It is fairly common to analyze the random variable itself, which results when we compute a function of some random variable. There are three types of transformation to consider. One discrete random variable may be transformed into another; a continuous variable may be transformed into a discrete one; and one continuous variable may be transformed into another.

The simplest case is the first one. The probabilities associated with the new variable are computed according to the laws of probability. If y is derived from x and the function is one to one, then the probability that $Y = y(x)$ equals the probability that $X = x$. If several values of x yield the same value of y, then Prob($Y = y$) is the sum of the corresponding probabilities for x.

The second type of transformation is illustrated by the way individual data on income are typically obtained in a survey. Income in the population can be expected to be distributed according to some skewed, continuous distribution such as the one shown in Figure 3.1.

Data are normally reported categorically, as shown in the lower part of the figure. Thus, the random variable corresponding to observed income is a discrete transformation

---

[5] Salem and Mount (1974).

[6] Greene (1980a).

[7] Heckman and Willis (1975).

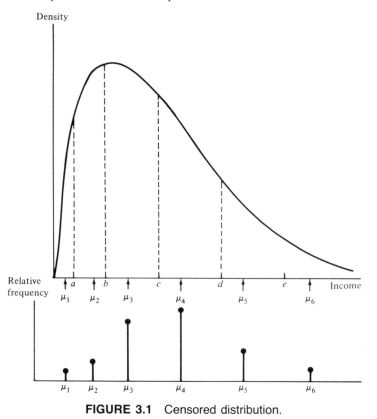

FIGURE 3.1 Censored distribution.

of the actual underlying continuous random variable. Suppose, for example, that the transformed variable, y, is the mean income in the respective interval. Then

$$\text{Prob}(Y = \mu_1) = P(-\infty < X \le a),$$

$$\text{Prob}(Y = \mu_2) = P(a < X \le b),$$

$$\text{Prob}(Y = \mu_3) = P(b < X \le c),$$

and so on, which illustrates the general procedure.

If x is a continuous random variable with pdf $f_x(x)$ and $y = g(x)$ is a continuous monotonic function of x, the density of y is obtained by using the change of variable technique to find the cdf of y.

$$\text{Prob}(y \le b) = \int_{-\infty}^{b} f_x(g^{-1}(y))|g^{-1\prime}(y)|dy.$$

This can now be written as

$$\text{Prob}(y \le b) = \int_{-\infty}^{b} f_y(y)\ dy.$$

Hence

$$f_y(y) = f_x(g^{-1}(y))|g^{-1\prime}(y)|. \tag{3-41}$$

To avoid the possibility of a negative pdf if $g(x)$ is decreasing, we use the absolute value of the derivative in the previous expression. The term $|g^{-1\prime}(y)|$ is the Jacobian of the transformation from x to y. The Jacobian must be nonzero for the density of y to be nonzero. In words, the probabilities associated with intervals in the range of y must be associated with intervals in the range of x. If the Jacobian is zero, the function $y = g(x)$ is vertical, and hence all values of y in the given range are associated with the same value of x. This single point must have probability zero.

EXAMPLE 3.3

If $x \sim N[\mu, \sigma^2]$, what is the distribution of $y = x/\sigma - \mu/\sigma$?

$$y = \frac{x}{\sigma} - \frac{\mu}{\sigma} \Rightarrow x = \sigma y + \mu \Rightarrow f^{-1\prime}(y) = \frac{dx}{dy} = \sigma.$$

Thus,

$$f_y(y) = \frac{1}{\sqrt{2\pi}\,\sigma} e^{-[(\sigma y + \mu) - \mu]^2/(2\sigma^2)}|\sigma| = \frac{1}{\sqrt{2\pi}} e^{-y^2/2},$$

which is the density of a normally distributed variable with mean 0 and standard deviation 1.

3.6. Joint Distributions

The **joint density function** for two random variables, X and Y, denoted $f(x,y)$, is defined so that

$$\text{Prob}(a \le x \le b, c \le y \le d) = \int_a^b \int_c^d f(x, y)\, dy\, dx \tag{3–42}$$

or

$$= \sum_{a \le x \le b} \sum_{c \le x \le d} f(x, y).$$

The counterparts of the requirements for a univariate probability density are

$$f(x, y) \ge 0$$

and

$$\sum_x \sum_y f(x, y) = 1 \qquad \text{if } x \text{ and } y \text{ are discrete,}$$

$$\int_x \int_y f(x, y)\, dy\, dx = 1 \qquad \text{if } x \text{ and } y \text{ are continuous.} \tag{3–43}$$

The cumulative probability is likewise the probability of a joint event:

$$F(x, y) = \text{Prob}(X \le x, Y \le y)$$

$$= \begin{cases} \sum_{X \le x} \sum_{Y \le y} f(x, y) & \text{in the discrete case,} \\[2ex] \int_{-\infty}^x \int_{-\infty}^y f(t, s)\, ds\, dt & \text{in the continuous case.} \end{cases} \tag{3–44}$$

3.6.1. Marginal Distributions

A **marginal probability density** or marginal probability distribution is defined with respect to an individual variable. To obtain the marginal distributions from the joint density, it is necessary to sum or integrate out the other variable:

$$f_x(x) = \begin{cases} \int_y f(x, y)\, dy & \text{if } y \text{ is continuous,} \\ \\ \sum_y f(x, y) & \text{if } y \text{ is discrete,} \end{cases}$$

(3–45)

and similarly for $f_y(y)$.

Two random variables are **statistically independent** if and only if their joint density is the product of the marginal densities:

$$f(x, y) = f_x(x)f_y(y) \Leftrightarrow x \text{ and } y \text{ are independent.}$$

(3–46)

If (and only if) x and y are independent, then the cdf factors as well as the pdf:

$$F(x, y) = F_x(x)F_y(y)$$

(3–47)

or

$$\text{Prob}(X \le x, Y \le y) = \text{Prob}(X \le x)\ \text{Prob}(Y \le y).$$

3.6.2. Expectations in a Joint Distribution

The means, variances, and higher moments of the variables in a joint distribution are defined with respect to the marginal distributions. For the mean of x in a discrete distribution,

$$E[x] = \sum_x xf_x(x)$$

$$= \sum_x x\left[\sum_y f(x, y)\right]$$

(3–48)

$$= \sum_x \sum_y xf(x, y).$$

The means of the variables in a continuous distribution are defined likewise, using integration instead of summation:

$$E[x] = \int_x xf_x(x)\, dx.$$

$$= \int_x \int_y xf(x, y)\, dy\, dx.$$

(3–49)

Variances are computed in the same manner:

$$\text{Var}[x] = \sum_x (x - E[x])^2 f_x(x)$$

$$= \sum_x \sum_y (x - E[x])^2 f(x, y).$$

(3–50)

3.6.3. Covariance and Correlation

For any function $g(x, y)$,

$$E[g(x, y)] = \sum_x \sum_y g(x, y)f(x, y)$$

or $\qquad\qquad\qquad\qquad\qquad\qquad\qquad\qquad\qquad\qquad\qquad\qquad$ (3–51)

$$\int_x \int_y g(x, y)f(x, y) \, dy \, dx.$$

The **covariance** of x and y is a special case:

$$\begin{aligned}
\text{Cov}[x, y] &= E[(x - \mu_x)(y - \mu_y)] \\
&= E[xy] - \mu_x\mu_y \\
&= \sigma_{xy}.
\end{aligned}$$
$\qquad\qquad\qquad\qquad\qquad\qquad\qquad\qquad$ (3–52)

If x and y are independent, $f(x, y) = f_x(x)f_y(y)$ and

$$\begin{aligned}
\sigma_{xy} &= \sum_x \sum_y f_x(x)f_y(y)(x - \mu_x)(y - \mu_y) \\
&= \sum_x [x - \mu_x]f_x(x) \sum_y [y - \mu_y]f_y(y) \\
&= E[x - \mu_x]E[y - \mu_y] \\
&= 0.
\end{aligned}$$

The sign of the covariance will indicate the direction of covariation of X and Y. However, its magnitude depends on the scales of measurement. In view of this, a preferable measure is the **correlation coefficient**:

$$\begin{aligned}
r[x, y] &= \rho_{xy} \\
&= \frac{\sigma_{xy}}{\sigma_x\sigma_y},
\end{aligned}$$
$\qquad\qquad\qquad\qquad\qquad\qquad\qquad\qquad$ (3–53)

where σ_x and σ_y are the standard deviations of x and y, respectively. The correlation coefficient has the same sign as the covariance but is always between -1 and 1, and is thus unaffected by any scaling of the variables.

Variables that are uncorrelated are not necessarily independent. For example, in the discrete distribution $f(-1, 1) = f(0, 0) = f(1, 1) = \frac{1}{3}$, the correlation is zero, but $f(1, 1)$ does not equal $f_x(1)f_y(1) = (\frac{1}{3})(\frac{2}{3})$. An important exception is the joint normal distribution discussed subsequently, in which lack of correlation does imply independence.

Some general results regarding expectations in a joint distribution, which can be verified by applying the appropriate definition, are

$$E[ax + by + c] = aE[x] + bE[y] + c, \qquad\qquad (3\text{–}54)$$

$$\begin{aligned}
\text{Var}[ax + by + c] &= a^2\text{Var}[x] + b^2\text{Var}[y] + 2ab\,\text{Cov}[x, y] \\
&= \text{Var}[ax + by],
\end{aligned}$$
$\qquad\qquad\qquad\qquad\qquad\qquad$ (3–55)

and

$$\text{Cov}[ax + by, cx + dy] = ac\text{Var}[x] + bd\,\text{Var}[y] + (ad + bc)\text{Cov}[x, y]. \quad (3\text{–}56)$$

If X and Y are uncorrelated,

$$\text{Var}[x + y] = \text{Var}[x - y]$$
$$= \text{Var}[x] + \text{Var}[y]. \tag{3-57}$$

For any two functions, $g_1(x)$ and $g_2(y)$, if x and y are independent,

$$E[g_1(x)g_2(y)] = E[g_1(x)]E[g_2(y)]. \tag{3-58}$$

3.6.4. Distribution of Functions of Bivariate Random Variables

The result for a function of a random variable in (3–41) must be modified for a joint distribution. Suppose that x_1 and x_2 have a joint distribution $f_x(x_1, x_2)$ and that y_1 and y_2 are two monotonic functions of x_1 and x_2:

$$y_1 = y_1(x_1, x_2)$$

and

$$y_2 = y_2(x_1, x_2).$$

Since the functions are monotonic, the inverse transformations,

$$x_1 = x_1(y_1, y_2)$$

and

$$x_2 = x_2(y_1, y_2),$$

exist. The Jacobian of the transformations is the absolute value of the determinant of the matrix of partial derivatives,

$$\mathbf{J} = \text{abs} \begin{vmatrix} \partial x_1/\partial y_1 & \partial x_1/\partial y_2 \\ \partial x_2/\partial y_1 & \partial x_2/\partial y_2 \end{vmatrix} = \text{abs} \left| \frac{\partial \mathbf{x}}{\partial \mathbf{y}'} \right|.$$

Then the joint distribution of y_1 and y_2 is

$$f_y(y_1, y_2) = f_x[x_1(y_1, y_2), x_2(y_1, y_2)] \text{ abs} \mid \mathbf{J} \mid.$$

The Jacobian must be nonzero for the transformation to exist. A zero Jacobian implies that the two transformations are functionally dependent.

EXAMPLE 3.4 _____

Suppose that x_1 and x_2 are independently distributed $N[0, 1]$, and the transformations are

$$y_1 = \alpha_1 + \beta_{11}x_1 + \beta_{12}x_2,$$
$$y_2 = \alpha_2 + \beta_{21}x_1 + \beta_{22}x_2.$$

What is the joint distribution of y_1 and y_2? It is simpler to write the transformations as

$$\mathbf{y} = \mathbf{a} + \mathbf{Bx}.$$

The inverse transformation is

$$\mathbf{x} = \mathbf{B}^{-1}(\mathbf{y} - \mathbf{a}),$$

so the Jacobian is

$$J = \text{abs} \mid \mathbf{B}^{-1} \mid = \frac{1}{\text{abs} \mid \mathbf{B} \mid}.$$

The joint distribution of $\mathbf{x}$ is the product of the marginal distributions since they are independent. Thus,

$$f_\mathbf{x}(\mathbf{x}) = (2\pi)^{-1}e^{-(x_1^2+x_2^2)/2} = (2\pi)^{-1}e^{-\mathbf{x}'\mathbf{x}/2}.$$

Inserting the results for $\mathbf{x}(\mathbf{y})$ and J into $f_y(y_1, y_2)$ gives

$$f_{\mathbf{y}}(\mathbf{y}) = (2\pi)^{-1} \frac{1}{\text{abs} \mid \mathbf{B} \mid} e^{-(\mathbf{y}-\mathbf{a})'(\mathbf{B}'\mathbf{B})^{-1}(\mathbf{y}-\mathbf{a})/2}.$$

This **joint normal distribution** is the subject of Section 3.8.

3.7. Conditioning in a Bivariate Distribution

Conditioning and the use of conditional distributions play a pivotal role in econometric modeling. We consider some general results for a bivariate distribution. (All of these results will carry over directly to the multivariate case.)

In a bivariate distribution, there is a **conditional distribution** over y for each value of x. The conditional densities are

$$f(y \mid x) = \frac{f(x, y)}{f_x(x)} \tag{3-59}$$

and

$$f(x \mid y) = \frac{f(x, y)}{f_y(y)}.$$

It follows from (3-46) that:

$$\text{If } x \text{ and } y \text{ are independent,}$$
$$f(y \mid x) = f_y(y) \text{ and } f(x \mid y) = f_x(x). \tag{3-60}$$

The interpretation is that if the variables are independent, the probabilities of events relating to one variable are unrelated to the other. The definition of conditional densities implies the important result

$$f(x, y) = f(y \mid x) f_x(x) \tag{3-61}$$
$$= f(x \mid y) f_y(y).$$

3.7.1. Regression—The Conditional Mean

A **conditional mean** is the mean of the conditional distribution and is defined by

$$E[y \mid x] = \begin{cases} \displaystyle\int_y y f(y \mid x) \, dy & \text{if } y \text{ is continuous,} \\[2em] \displaystyle\sum_y y f(y \mid x) & \text{if } y \text{ is discrete.} \end{cases} \tag{3-62}$$

The conditional mean function $E[y \mid x]$ is called the **regression of y on x.**

EXAMPLE 3.5 —————————————————————————

Consider the conditional distribution:

$$f(y \mid x) = \frac{1}{\alpha + \beta x} e^{-y/(\alpha + \beta x)}, \qquad y \geq 0, \qquad 0 \leq x \leq 1.$$

Note that the conditional density of y is a function of x. The conditional mean can be derived by integration by parts or by noting that this is an exponential distribution with $\lambda = 1/(\alpha + \beta x)$. The mean of an exponential distribution with parameter λ is $1/\lambda$. Therefore,

$$E[y|x] = \alpha + \beta x.$$

A random variable may always be written as

$$y = E[y|x] + (y - E[y|x])$$
$$= E[y|x] + \varepsilon.$$

EXAMPLE 3.6

In a recent study, Hausman et al. (1984) suggest that the Poisson distribution (see Example 3.1) is a reasonable model for the distribution of the number of patents granted to firms in any given year (P):

$$f(P) = \frac{\lambda^P e^{-\lambda}}{P!}, \qquad P = 0, 1, 2, \ldots .$$

However, it is known that the more is spent on research and development (R), the greater, on average, is the number of patents received. This interaction should affect the distribution of P. How R is distributed across firms is a side issue that may or may not be of any interest. But we are interested in how R and the average number of patents interact. Since the mean value of patents received is λ, suppose we make the preceding a conditional distribution, and specify that

$$\lambda = \alpha + \beta R = E[P|R].$$

We would expect β to be positive. Thus,

$$f(P|R) = \frac{(\alpha + \beta R)^P e^{-(\alpha + \beta R)}}{P!},$$

which captures the effect we sought. The observation of a large number of patents may reflect a high value from the Poisson process or may follow from an unusually high value of R.

3.7.2. Conditional Variance

A conditional variance is the variance of the conditional distribution:

$$\text{Var}[y|x] = E[(y - E[y|x])^2 | x]$$

(3–63)

$$= \int_y (y - E[y|x])^2 f(y|x) \, dy$$

or

$$\sum_y (y - E[y|x])^2 f(y|x).$$

The computation can be simplified by using

$$\text{Var}[y|x] = E[y^2|x] - (E[y|x])^2. \tag{3–64}$$

EXAMPLE 3.7

The Poisson distribution of Example 3.6 illustrates a pitfall that occasionally arises in specifying an econometric model. In a Poisson distribution, the mean is equal to the variance. We have not ruled out the possibility that $\alpha + \beta R$ could be negative for some values of α and β. Not only is this an invalid parameter for the Poisson distribution in any event, but beyond this, it allows a negative variance. This is a common error of specification.[8]

The conditional variance is called the **scedastic function,** and, like the regression, is generally a function of x. Unlike the conditional mean function, however, it is common for the conditional variance not to vary with x. We shall examine a particular case. This does not imply, however, that $\text{Var}[y|x]$ equals $\text{Var}[y]$, which will usually not be the case. It implies only that the conditional variance is a constant. The case in which the conditional variance does not vary with x is called **homoscedasticity** (same variance).

3.7.3. Relationships Among Marginal and Conditional Moments

Some useful results for the moments of a conditional distribution are as follows:

$$E[y] = E_x[E[y|x]]. \tag{3–65}$$

The notation $E_x[\cdot]$ indicates the expectation over the values of x. This is sometimes labeled the **law of iterated expectations.**

EXAMPLE 3.8

In the distribution of Example 3.5, assume that x is uniformly distributed between 0 and 1. Then the marginal distribution of x is $f(x) = 1$ and the joint distribution is

$$f(x, y) = f(y|x)f(x).$$

Then

$$E[y] = \int_0^\infty \int_0^1 y\left(\frac{1}{\alpha + \beta x}\right)e^{-y/(\alpha+\beta x)} \, dx \, dy.$$

But $E[y|x] = \alpha + \beta x$, so

$$E[y] = E_x[E[y|x]]$$
$$= E[\alpha + \beta x] \tag{3–66}$$
$$= \alpha + \beta E[x].$$

Since x has a uniform distribution between 0 and 1, $E[x] = \frac{1}{2}$. Therefore,

$$E[y] = \alpha + \beta(\tfrac{1}{2}).$$

---

[8] See Section 21.8 for an alternative specification.

In any bivariate distribution,

$$Cov[x, y] = Cov[x, E[y|x]]$$

$$= \int_x (x - E[x])E[y|x]f_x(x) \, dx.$$

EXAMPLE 3.9 _____

To continue Example 3.8,

$$Cov[x, y] = \int_0^\infty \int_0^1 \frac{(x - \frac{1}{2})[y - (\alpha + (\beta/2))]}{\alpha + \beta x} e^{-y/(\alpha+\beta x)} \, dx \, dy,$$

which can, in principle, be computed directly. However,

$$Cov[x, y] = Cov[x, E[y|x]]$$

$$= Cov[x, \alpha + \beta x] \qquad (3\text{--}67)$$

$$= \beta \, Var[x] = \beta(\tfrac{1}{12}).$$

_____

The preceding examples provide an additional result for the special case in which the conditional mean function is linear in x.

Moments in a Linear Regression

If $E[y|x] = \alpha + \beta x$, then

$$\alpha = E[y] - \beta E[x] \qquad (3\text{--}68)$$

and

$$\beta = \frac{Cov[x, y]}{Var[x]}. \qquad (3\text{--}69)$$

The proof follows from (3–66) and (3–67).

The following also appears in various forms in regression analysis:

Decomposition of Variance

$$Var[y] = Var_x[E[y|x]] + E_x[Var[y|x]]. \qquad (3\text{--}70)$$

The notation $Var_x[\cdot]$ indicates the variance over the distribution of x. This states that in a bivariate distribution, the variance of y decomposes into the variance of the conditional mean function plus the expected variance around the conditional mean. For an application, see the proof of Theorem 22.3 in Section 22.3.

EXAMPLE 3.10 _____

The variance of y in Example 3.5 remains to be derived. As before, the direct integration of the joint distribution is somewhat difficult. However,

$$Var_x[E[y|x]] = Var[\alpha + \beta x] = \beta^2 \, Var[x]$$

$$= \frac{\beta^2}{12}$$

and since the variance of the exponential variable is $1/\lambda^2$,

$$E_x[\text{Var}[y|x]] = E[[\alpha + \beta x]^2]$$
$$= \alpha^2 + \beta^2 E[x^2] + 2\alpha\beta E[x]$$
$$= \alpha^2 + \beta^2(\tfrac{1}{3}) + 2\alpha\beta(\tfrac{1}{2}).$$

The unconditional variance is the sum of the two parts:

$$\text{Var}[y] = \alpha(\alpha + \beta) + \frac{5\beta^2}{12}.$$

By rearranging (3–70), we obtain the following important result:

Residual Variance in a Regression

$$E_x[\text{Var}[y|x]] = \text{Var}[y] - \text{Var}_x[E[y|x]]. \qquad (3\text{--}71)$$

On average, conditioning reduces the variance of the variable subject to the conditioning. For example, if y is homoscedastic, we have the unambiguous result that the variance of the conditional distribution(s) is less than or equal to the unconditional variance of y.

EXAMPLE 3.11 _____

For the patents–R&D relationship in Example 3.6, suppose that R is a constant fraction of firm size and that firm sizes have a lognormal distribution. Then R will have a lognormal distribution as well. The density, mean, and variance of the distribution are given in Section 3.4.4. Assume that $\mu = 0$ and $\sigma = 1$. Then

$$E[R] = \sqrt{e} = 1.65 \qquad \text{and} \qquad \text{Var}[R] = 4.65.$$

Assume, as well, that $\alpha = 1$ and $\beta = 2$. Then

$$E[P|R] = 1 + 2R,$$
$$E[P] = 1 + 2E[R] = 4.30,$$
$$\text{Var}_R[E[P|R]] = 4\,\text{Var}[R] = 18.6,$$
$$\text{Var}[P|R] = 1 + 2R,$$
$$E_R[\text{Var}[P|R]] = 4.30,$$
$$\text{Var}(P) = 18.6 + 4.30 = 22.9.$$

Note that $\text{Var}[P]$ is substantially greater than $E[\text{Var}[P|R]]$.

3.7.4. The Analysis of Variance

The variance decomposition result implies that in a bivariate distribution, variation in y arises from two sources:

1. Variation due to the fact that $E[y|x]$ varies with x:

$$\textbf{regression variance} = \text{Var}_x[E[y|x]]. \qquad (3\text{--}72)$$

2. Variation that arises because, in each conditional distribution, y varies around the conditional mean:

$$\textbf{residual variance} = E_x[\text{Var}[y|x]]. \qquad (3\text{--}73)$$

Thus,

$$\text{Var}[y] = \text{regression variance} + \text{residual variance}. \tag{3-74}$$

In analyzing a regression, we shall usually be interested in which of the two parts of the **total variance**, $\text{Var}[y]$, is the larger one. For example, in the patents–R&D relationship, which explains more of the variance in the number of patents received, variation in the amount of R&D (regression variance) or random variation in patents received within the Poisson distribution (residual variance)? A natural measure is the ratio

$$\textbf{coefficient of determination} = \frac{\text{regression variance}}{\text{total variance}}. \tag{3-75}$$

EXAMPLE 3.12 _____

For the decomposition in Example 3.11,

$$\text{coefficient of determination} = \frac{18.6}{22.9} = 0.812.$$

In the setting of a linear regression, (3–75) arises from another relationship that emphasizes the interpretation of the correlation coefficient.

If $E[y|x] = \alpha + \beta x$, then

$$\text{coefficient of determination} = \text{COD} = \rho^2, \tag{3-76}$$

where ρ^2 is the squared correlation between x and y. We conclude that the correlation coefficient (squared) is a measure of the proportion of the variance of y accounted for by variation in the mean of y given x. It is in this sense that correlation can be interpreted as a **measure of linear association** between two variables.

3.8. The Bivariate Normal Distribution

A bivariate distribution that embodies many of the features described earlier is the bivariate normal. This is the joint distribution of two normally distributed variables. The density is

$$f(x, y) = \frac{1}{2\pi\sigma_x\sigma_y\sqrt{1 - \rho^2}} e^{-(\varepsilon_x^2 + \varepsilon_y^2 - 2\rho\varepsilon_x\varepsilon_y)/(2(1 - \rho^2))}$$

$$\varepsilon_x = \frac{x - \mu_x}{\sigma_x} \tag{3-77}$$

$$\varepsilon_y = \frac{y - \mu_y}{\sigma_y}.$$

The parameters μ_x, σ_x, μ_y, and σ_y are the means and standard deviations of the marginal distributions of x and y, respectively. The additional parameter, ρ, is the correlation between x and y. The covariance is

$$\sigma_{xy} = \rho\sigma_x\sigma_y. \tag{3-78}$$

The density is defined only if ρ is not 1 or -1. This, in turn, requires that the two variables not be linearly related.

If x and y have a bivariate normal distribution, denoted

$$(x, y) \sim N_2[\mu_x, \mu_y, \sigma_x^2, \sigma_y^2, \rho],$$

1. The marginal distributions are normal;

$$f_x(x) = N[\mu_x, \sigma_x^2]$$
$$f_y(y) = N[\mu_y, \sigma_y^2], \tag{3-79}$$

2. The conditional distributions are normal;

$$f(y|x) = N[\alpha + \beta x, \sigma_y^2 (1 - \rho^2)]$$
$$\alpha = \mu_y - \beta \mu_x \tag{3-80}$$
$$\beta = \frac{\sigma_{xy}}{\sigma_x^2},$$

and likewise for $f(x|y)$; and
3. x and y are independent if and only if $\rho = 0$. The density factors into the product of the two marginal normal distributions if $\rho = 0$.

Two things to note about the conditional distributions beyond their normality are their linear regression functions and their constant conditional variances. The conditional variance is less than the unconditional variance, which is consistent with the results of the previous section.

3.9. Multivariate Distributions

The extension of the results for bivariate distributions to more than two variables is direct. It is made much more convenient by using matrices and vectors. The term **random vector** applies to a vector whose elements are random variables. The joint density is $f(\mathbf{x})$, while the cdf is

$$F(\mathbf{x}) = \int_{-\infty}^{x_n} \int_{-\infty}^{x_{n-1}} \cdots \int_{-\infty}^{x_1} f(\mathbf{x}) \, dx_1 \cdots dx_{n-1} \, dx_n. \tag{3-81}$$

Note that the cdf is an n-fold integral. The marginal distribution of any one (or more) of the n variables is obtained by integrating or summing over the other variables.

3.9.1. Moments

The expected value of a vector or matrix is the vector or matrix of expected values. A mean vector is defined as

$$\boldsymbol{\mu} = \begin{bmatrix} \mu_1 \\ \mu_2 \\ \vdots \\ \mu_n \end{bmatrix} = \begin{bmatrix} E[x_1] \\ E[x_2] \\ \vdots \\ E[x_n] \end{bmatrix} = E[\mathbf{x}]. \tag{3-82}$$

Define the matrix

$$(\mathbf{x} - \boldsymbol{\mu})(\mathbf{x} - \boldsymbol{\mu})' = \begin{bmatrix} (x_1 - \mu_1)(x_1 - \mu_1) & (x_1 - \mu_1)(x_2 - \mu_2) & \cdots & (x_1 - \mu_1)(x_n - \mu_n) \\ (x_2 - \mu_2)(x_1 - \mu_1) & (x_2 - \mu_2)(x_2 - \mu_2) & \cdots & (x_2 - \mu_2)(x_n - \mu_n) \\ \vdots & & & \\ (x_n - \mu_n)(x_1 - \mu_1) & (x_n - \mu_n)(x_2 - \mu_2) & \cdots & (x_n - \mu_n)(x_n - \mu_n) \end{bmatrix}.$$

The expected value of each element in the matrix is the covariance of the two variables in the product. (The covariance of a variable with itself is its variance.) Thus,

$$E[(\mathbf{x} - \boldsymbol{\mu})(\mathbf{x} - \boldsymbol{\mu})'] = \boldsymbol{\Sigma}$$

$$= \begin{bmatrix} \sigma_{11} & \sigma_{12} & \cdots & \sigma_{1n} \\ \sigma_{21} & \sigma_{22} & \cdots & \sigma_{2n} \\ \vdots & \vdots & & \\ \sigma_{n1} & \sigma_{n2} & \cdots & \sigma_{nn} \end{bmatrix} \qquad (3\text{--}83)$$

$$= E[\mathbf{x}\mathbf{x}'] - \boldsymbol{\mu}\boldsymbol{\mu}',$$

which is the **covariance matrix** of the random vector $\mathbf{x}$. Henceforth, we shall denote the covariance matrix of a random vector in boldface, as in

$$\text{Var}[\mathbf{x}] = \boldsymbol{\Sigma}.$$

By dividing σ_{ij} by $\sigma_i \sigma_j$, we obtain the **correlation matrix:**

$$\mathbf{R} = \begin{bmatrix} 1 & \rho_{12} & \rho_{13} & \cdots & \rho_{1n} \\ \rho_{21} & 1 & \rho_{23} & \cdots & \rho_{2n} \\ \vdots & \vdots & \vdots & & \vdots \\ \rho_{n1} & \rho_{n2} & \rho_{n3} & \cdots & 1 \end{bmatrix}.$$

3.9.2. Sets of Linear Functions

Our earlier results for the mean and variance of a linear function can be extended directly to the multivariate case. For the mean,

$$E[a_1 x_1 + a_2 x_2 + \cdots + a_n x_n] = E[\mathbf{a}'\mathbf{x}]$$

$$= a_1 E[x_1] + a_2 E[x_2] + \cdots + a_n E[x_n]$$

$$= a_1 \mu_1 + a_2 \mu_2 + \cdots + a_n \mu_n \qquad (3\text{--}84)$$

$$= \mathbf{a}'\boldsymbol{\mu}.$$

For the variance,

$$\text{Var}[\mathbf{a}'\mathbf{x}] = E[(\mathbf{a}'\mathbf{x} - E[\mathbf{a}'\mathbf{x}])^2]$$

$$= E[\{\mathbf{a}'(\mathbf{x} - E[\mathbf{x}])\}^2]$$

$$= E[\mathbf{a}'(\mathbf{x} - \boldsymbol{\mu})(\mathbf{x} - \boldsymbol{\mu})'\mathbf{a}]$$

as $E[\mathbf{x}] = \boldsymbol{\mu}$ and $\mathbf{a}'(\mathbf{x} - \boldsymbol{\mu}) = (\mathbf{x} - \boldsymbol{\mu})'\,\mathbf{a}$. Since $\mathbf{a}$ is a vector of constants,

$$\text{Var}[\mathbf{a}'\mathbf{x}] = \mathbf{a}'E[(\mathbf{x} - \boldsymbol{\mu})(\mathbf{x} - \boldsymbol{\mu})']\mathbf{a}$$

$$= \mathbf{a}'\boldsymbol{\Sigma}\mathbf{a} \qquad (3\text{--}85)$$

$$= \sum_i \sum_j a_i a_j \sigma_{ij}.$$

Since it is the expected value of a square, we know that a variance cannot be negative. As such, the preceding quadratic form is nonnegative, and the symmetric matrix, $\boldsymbol{\Sigma}$, must be nonnegative definite.

In the set of linear functions $\mathbf{y} = \mathbf{A}\mathbf{x}$, the ith element of $\mathbf{y}$ is $y_i = \mathbf{a}^i\mathbf{x}$, where $\mathbf{a}^i$ is the ith row of $\mathbf{A}$. Therefore,

$$E[y_i] = \mathbf{a}^i\boldsymbol{\mu}.$$

Collecting the results in a vector, we have

$$E[\mathbf{Ax}] = \mathbf{A}\boldsymbol{\mu}. \tag{3-86}$$

For two row vectors, $\mathbf{a}^i$ and $\mathbf{a}^j$,

$$\text{Cov}[\mathbf{a}^i\mathbf{x}, \mathbf{a}^j\mathbf{x}] = \mathbf{a}^i\boldsymbol{\Sigma}\mathbf{a}^{j\prime}.$$

Since $\mathbf{a}^i\boldsymbol{\Sigma}\mathbf{a}^j$ is the ijth element of $\mathbf{A}\boldsymbol{\Sigma}\mathbf{A}'$,

$$\text{Var}[\mathbf{Ax}] = \mathbf{A}\boldsymbol{\Sigma}\mathbf{A}'. \tag{3-87}$$

This will be either nonnegative definite or positive definite, depending on the column rank of $\mathbf{A}$.

3.9.3. Nonlinear Functions

Consider a set of possibly nonlinear functions of $\mathbf{x}$, $\mathbf{y} = \mathbf{g}(\mathbf{x})$. Each element of $\mathbf{y}$ can be approximated with a linear Taylor series. Let $\mathbf{j}^i$ be the row vector of partial derivatives of the ith function with respect to the n elements of $\mathbf{x}$:

$$\mathbf{j}^i = \frac{\partial g_i(\mathbf{x})}{\partial \mathbf{x}'} = \frac{\partial y_i}{\partial \mathbf{x}'}. \tag{3-88}$$

Then, proceeding in the now familiar way, we use $\boldsymbol{\mu}$, the mean vector of $\mathbf{x}$, as the expansion point, so that $\mathbf{j}^i$ is the row vector of partial derivatives evaluated at $\boldsymbol{\mu}$. Then

$$g_i(\mathbf{x}) \simeq g_i(\boldsymbol{\mu}) + \mathbf{j}^i(\mathbf{x} - \boldsymbol{\mu}). \tag{3-89}$$

From this we obtain

$$E[g_i(\mathbf{x})] \simeq g_i(\boldsymbol{\mu}), \tag{3-90}$$

$$\text{Var}[g_i(\mathbf{x})] \simeq \mathbf{j}^i\boldsymbol{\Sigma}\mathbf{j}^{i\prime}, \tag{3-91}$$

and

$$\text{Cov}[g_i(\mathbf{x}), g_j(\mathbf{x})] \simeq \mathbf{j}^i\boldsymbol{\Sigma}\mathbf{j}^{\prime j}. \tag{3-92}$$

These can be collected in a convenient form by arranging the row vectors $\mathbf{j}^i$ in a matrix $\mathbf{J}$. Then, corresponding to the preceding equations, we have

$$E[\mathbf{g}(\mathbf{x})] \simeq \mathbf{g}(\boldsymbol{\mu}) \tag{3-93}$$

$$\mathbf{Var}[\mathbf{g}(\mathbf{x})] \simeq \mathbf{J}\boldsymbol{\Sigma}\mathbf{J}'. \tag{3-94}$$

The matrix $\mathbf{J}$ in the last preceding line is $\partial \mathbf{y}/\partial \mathbf{x}'$.

3.10. The Multivariate Normal Distribution

The foundation of most multivariate analysis in econometrics is the multivariate normal distribution. Let the vector $(x_1, x_2, \ldots, x_n)' = \mathbf{x}$ be the set of n random variables, $\boldsymbol{\mu}$ their mean vector, and $\boldsymbol{\Sigma}$ their covariance matrix. The general form of the joint density is

$$f(\mathbf{x}) = (2\pi)^{-n/2} |\boldsymbol{\Sigma}|^{-1/2} e^{(-1/2)(\mathbf{x}-\boldsymbol{\mu})'\boldsymbol{\Sigma}^{-1}(\mathbf{x}-\boldsymbol{\mu})}. \tag{3-95}$$

If $\mathbf{R}$ is the correlation matrix of the variables and $R_{ij} = \sigma_{ij}/(\sigma_i \sigma_j)$,

$$f(\mathbf{x}) = (2\pi)^{-n/2}(\sigma_1 \sigma_2 \cdots \sigma_n)^{-1} |\mathbf{R}|^{(-1/2)} e^{(-1/2)\boldsymbol{\epsilon}' \mathbf{R}^{-1} \boldsymbol{\epsilon}}, \tag{3–96}$$

where $\epsilon_i = (x_i - \mu_i)/\sigma_i$.[9]

Two special cases are of interest. If all of the variables are uncorrelated, $\rho_{ij} = 0$ for $i \neq j$. Thus, $\mathbf{R} = \mathbf{I}$ and the density becomes

$$f(\mathbf{x}) = (2\pi)^{-n/2}(\sigma_1 \sigma_2 \cdots \sigma_n)^{-1} e^{-\boldsymbol{\epsilon}' \boldsymbol{\epsilon}/2}$$

$$= f(x_1) f(x_2) \cdots f(x_n) = \prod_{i=1}^{n} f(x_i). \tag{3–97}$$

As in the bivariate case, if normally distributed variables are uncorrelated, they are independent. If $\sigma_i = \sigma$ and $\boldsymbol{\mu} = \mathbf{0}$, $x_i \sim N[0, \sigma^2]$, $\epsilon_i = x_i/\sigma$, and the density becomes

$$f(\mathbf{x}) = (2\pi)^{-n/2}(\sigma^2)^{-n/2} e^{-\mathbf{x}'\mathbf{x}/(2\sigma^2)}. \tag{3–98}$$

Finally, if $\sigma = 1$,

$$f(\mathbf{x}) = (2\pi)^{-n/2} e^{-\mathbf{x}'\mathbf{x}/2}. \tag{3–99}$$

This is the multivariate standard normal, or spherical normal distribution.

3.10.1. Marginal and Conditional Distributions

Let $\mathbf{x}_1$ be any subset of the variables, including a single variable, and let $\mathbf{x}_2$ be the remaining variables. Partition $\boldsymbol{\mu}$ and $\boldsymbol{\Sigma}$ likewise, so that

$$\boldsymbol{\mu} = \begin{bmatrix} \boldsymbol{\mu}_1 \\ \boldsymbol{\mu}_2 \end{bmatrix} \quad \text{and} \quad \boldsymbol{\Sigma} = \begin{bmatrix} \boldsymbol{\Sigma}_{11} & \boldsymbol{\Sigma}_{12} \\ \boldsymbol{\Sigma}_{21} & \boldsymbol{\Sigma}_{22} \end{bmatrix}.$$

Then the marginal distributions are also normal. In particular,

$$\mathbf{x}_1 \sim N(\boldsymbol{\mu}_1, \boldsymbol{\Sigma}_{11}) \tag{3–100}$$

and

$$\mathbf{x}_2 \sim N(\boldsymbol{\mu}_2, \boldsymbol{\Sigma}_{22}). \tag{3–101}$$

The conditional distribution of $\mathbf{x}_1$ given $\mathbf{x}_2$ is normal as well:

$$\mathbf{x}_1 \,|\, \mathbf{x}_2 \sim N(\boldsymbol{\mu}_{1.2}, \boldsymbol{\Sigma}_{11.2}), \tag{3–102}$$

where

$$\boldsymbol{\mu}_{1.2} = \boldsymbol{\mu}_1 + \boldsymbol{\Sigma}_{12} \boldsymbol{\Sigma}_{22}^{-1}(\mathbf{x}_2 - \boldsymbol{\mu}_2) \tag{3–102a}$$

$$\boldsymbol{\Sigma}_{11.2} = \boldsymbol{\Sigma}_{11} - \boldsymbol{\Sigma}_{12} \boldsymbol{\Sigma}_{22}^{-1} \boldsymbol{\Sigma}_{21}. \tag{3–102b}$$

Proof: We partition $\boldsymbol{\mu}$ and $\boldsymbol{\Sigma}$ as shown above and insert the parts in (3–95). To construct the density, we require the partitioning of the determinant,

$$|\boldsymbol{\Sigma}| = |\boldsymbol{\Sigma}_{22}| \, |\boldsymbol{\Sigma}_{11} - \boldsymbol{\Sigma}_{12} \boldsymbol{\Sigma}_{22}^{-1} \boldsymbol{\Sigma}_{21}|,$$

and the inverse,

$$\begin{bmatrix} \boldsymbol{\Sigma}_{11} & \boldsymbol{\Sigma}_{12} \\ \boldsymbol{\Sigma}_{21} & \boldsymbol{\Sigma}_{22} \end{bmatrix}^{-1} = \begin{bmatrix} \boldsymbol{\Sigma}_{11.2}^{-1} & -\boldsymbol{\Sigma}_{11.2}^{-1}\mathbf{B} \\ -\mathbf{B}'\boldsymbol{\Sigma}_{11.2}^{-1} & \boldsymbol{\Sigma}_{22}^{-1} + \mathbf{B}'\boldsymbol{\Sigma}_{11.2}^{-1}\mathbf{B} \end{bmatrix}.$$

---

[9]This result is obtained by constructing $\boldsymbol{\Delta}$, the diagonal matrix with σ_i as its ith diagonal element. Then, $\mathbf{R} = \boldsymbol{\Delta}^{-1}\boldsymbol{\Sigma}\boldsymbol{\Delta}^{-1}$, which implies that $\boldsymbol{\Sigma}^{-1} = \boldsymbol{\Delta}^{-1}\mathbf{R}^{-1}\boldsymbol{\Delta}^{-1}$. Inserting this in (3–95) yields (3–96). Note that the ith element of $\boldsymbol{\Delta}^{-1}(\mathbf{x} - \boldsymbol{\mu})$ is $(x_i - \mu_i)/\sigma_i$.

For simplicity, we let

$$\mathbf{B} = \mathbf{\Sigma}_{12}\,\mathbf{\Sigma}_{22}^{-1}.$$

Inserting these in (3–95) and collecting terms produces the joint density as a product of two terms:

$$f(\mathbf{x}_1, \mathbf{x}_2) = f_{1.2}(\mathbf{x}_1 \,|\, \mathbf{x}_2)f_2(\mathbf{x}_2).$$

The first of these is a normal distribution with mean $\boldsymbol{\mu}_{1.2}$ and variance $\mathbf{\Sigma}_{11.2}$, while the second is the marginal distribution of $\mathbf{x}_2$. The conditional mean vector is a linear function of the unconditional mean and the conditioning variables, and the conditional variance matrix is constant and is smaller (in the sense discussed in Section 2.8.3) than the unconditional variance matrix. Notice that the conditional variance matrix is the inverse of the upper left block of $\mathbf{\Sigma}^{-1}$. [That is, this is of the form shown in (2–74) for the partitioned inverse of a matrix.] An important special case is that in which $\mathbf{x}_1$ is a single variable, y, and $\mathbf{x}_2$ is K variables. Then the conditional distribution is a multivariate version of that in (3–80) with $\boldsymbol{\beta} = \mathbf{\Sigma}_{\mathbf{xx}}^{-1}\,\boldsymbol{\sigma}_{xy}$ where $\boldsymbol{\sigma}_{xy}$ is the vector of covariances of y with $\mathbf{x}_2$.

3.10.2. Linear Functions of a Normal Vector

Any linear function of a vector of joint normally distributed variables is also normally distributed. The mean vector and covariance matrix of $\mathbf{Ax,}$ where $\mathbf{x}$ is normally distributed, follow the general pattern given earlier. Thus,

$$\text{If } \mathbf{x} \sim N[\boldsymbol{\mu}, \mathbf{\Sigma}], \ \mathbf{Ax} + \mathbf{b} \sim N[\mathbf{A}\boldsymbol{\mu} + \mathbf{b}, \mathbf{A}\mathbf{\Sigma}\mathbf{A}'], \qquad (3–103)$$

assuming that $\mathbf{A}$ has full rank. If $\mathbf{A}$ does not have full rank, $\mathbf{A}\mathbf{\Sigma}\mathbf{A}'$ is singular and the density does not exist. Nonetheless, even in this case, the individual elements of $\mathbf{Ax}$ will still be normally distributed.

3.10.3. Quadratic Forms in a Standard Normal Vector

The earlier discussion of the chi-squared distribution gives the distribution of $\mathbf{x}'\mathbf{x}$ if $\mathbf{x}$ has a standard normal distribution. It follows from (2–36) that

$$\mathbf{x}'\mathbf{x} = \sum_i x_i^2 = \sum_i (x_i - \bar{x})^2 + n\bar{x}^2. \qquad (3–104)$$

We know from (3–32) that $\mathbf{x}'\mathbf{x}$ has a chi-squared distribution. It seems natural, therefore, to invoke (3–34) for the two parts on the right-hand side of (3–104). However, it is not yet obvious that either of the two terms has a chi-squared distribution or that the two terms are independent, as required. To show these conditions, it is necessary to derive the distributions of **idempotent quadratic forms** and to show when they are independent.

To begin, the second term is the square of $(\sqrt{n})\bar{x}$, which can easily be shown to have a standard normal distribution. Thus, the second term is the square of a standard normal variable and has chi-squared distribution with one degree of freedom. But the first term is the sum of n nonindependent variables, and it remains to be shown that the two terms are independent.

3.10.3a. Idempotent Quadratic Forms. A particular case of (3–103) is

If $\mathbf{x} \sim N(\mathbf{0}, \mathbf{I})$ and $\mathbf{C}$ is a square matrix
such that $\mathbf{C}'\mathbf{C} = \mathbf{I}$, then $\mathbf{C}'\mathbf{x} \sim N[\mathbf{0}, \mathbf{I}]$.

Consider, then, a quadratic form in a standard normal vector, **x:**

$$q = \mathbf{x'Ax}. \tag{3-105}$$

Let the characteristic roots and vectors of **A** be arranged in a diagonal matrix, **Λ,** and an orthogonal matrix, **C,** as in Section 2.7.3. Then

$$q = \mathbf{x'C\Lambda C'x}. \tag{3-106}$$

By definition, **C** satisfies the requirement that $\mathbf{C'C} = \mathbf{I}$. Thus, the vector $\mathbf{y} = \mathbf{C'x}$ has a standard normal distribution. Consequently,

$$q = \mathbf{y'\Lambda y}$$
$$= \sum_i \lambda_i y_i^2. \tag{3-107}$$

If λ_i is always 1 or 0,

$$q = \sum_i y_i^2, \tag{3-108}$$

which has a chi-squared distribution. The sum is taken over the $j = 1, \ldots, J$ elements associated with the roots that are equal to 1. A matrix whose characteristic roots are all 0 or 1 is idempotent. Therefore, we have proved the result that

> If $\mathbf{x} \sim N[\mathbf{0}, \mathbf{I}]$ and **A** is idempotent, then $\mathbf{x'Ax}$ has a chi-squared distribution with degrees of freedom equal to the number of unit roots of **A.**

The rank of a matrix is equal to the number of nonzero characteristic roots it has. Therefore, the degrees of freedom in the preceding chi-squared distribution equals J, the rank of **A.**

We can apply this result directly to the earlier sum of squares. The first term is

$$\sum_i (x_i - \bar{x})^2 = \mathbf{x'M^0x},$$

where $\mathbf{M}^0$ was defined in (2–34) as the matrix that transforms data to mean deviation form:

$$\mathbf{M}^0 = \left[\mathbf{I} - \frac{1}{n}\mathbf{ii'}\right].$$

Since $\mathbf{M}^0$ is idempotent, the sum of squared deviations from the mean has a chi-squared distribution. The degrees of freedom equals the rank of $\mathbf{M}^0$, which is not obvious except for the useful result in (2–108), that

> The rank of an idempotent matrix is equal to its trace. (3–109)

Each diagonal element of $\mathbf{M}^0$ is $1 - (1/n)$; hence, the trace is $n(1 - (1/n)) = n - 1$. Therefore,

$$\text{If } \mathbf{x} \sim N[\mathbf{0}, \mathbf{I}], \sum_i (x_i - \bar{x})^2 \sim \chi^2[n - 1]. \tag{3-110}$$

We have already shown that the second term in (3–110) has a chi-squared distribution with one degree of freedom. It is instructive to set this up as a quadratic form:

$$n\bar{x}^2 = \mathbf{x'}\left[\frac{1}{n}\mathbf{ii'}\right]\mathbf{x}$$
$$= \mathbf{x'[jj']x}. \tag{3-111}$$

where

$$\mathbf{j} = \left(\frac{1}{\sqrt{n}}\right)\mathbf{i}.$$

The matrix in brackets is the outer product of a nonzero vector, which always has rank one. You can verify that it is idempotent by multiplication. Thus, $\mathbf{x}'\mathbf{x}$ is the sum of two chi-squared variables, one with $n - 1$ degrees of freedom and the other with one. It is now necessary to show that the two terms are independent.

3.10.3b. Independence of Idempotent Quadratic Forms. As before, we show the result for the general case and then specialize it for the example. The general result is

If $\mathbf{x} \sim N[\mathbf{0}, \mathbf{I}]$ and $\mathbf{x}'\mathbf{A}\mathbf{x}$ and $\mathbf{x}'\mathbf{B}\mathbf{x}$ are two idempotent quadratic forms in $\mathbf{x}$, $\mathbf{x}'\mathbf{A}\mathbf{x}$ and $\mathbf{x}'\mathbf{B}\mathbf{x}$ are independent if $\mathbf{A}\mathbf{B} = \mathbf{0}$. $\qquad$ (3–112)

Since both $\mathbf{A}$ and $\mathbf{B}$ are symmetric and idempotent, $\mathbf{A} = \mathbf{A}'\mathbf{A}$ and $\mathbf{B} = \mathbf{B}'\mathbf{B}$. The quadratic forms are therefore

$$\mathbf{x}'\mathbf{A}\mathbf{x} = \mathbf{x}'\mathbf{A}'\mathbf{A}\mathbf{x} = \mathbf{x}_1'\mathbf{x}_1 \qquad \text{where } \mathbf{x}_1 = \mathbf{A}\mathbf{x}$$

and

$$\mathbf{x}'\mathbf{B}\mathbf{x} = \mathbf{x}_2'\mathbf{x}_2 \qquad \text{where } \mathbf{x}_2 = \mathbf{B}\mathbf{x}. \qquad (3–113)$$

Both vectors have zero mean vectors, so the covariance matrix of $\mathbf{x}_1$ and $\mathbf{x}_2$ is

$$E(\mathbf{x}_1\mathbf{x}_2') = \mathbf{A}\mathbf{I}\mathbf{B}' = \mathbf{A}\mathbf{B} = \mathbf{0}.$$

Since $\mathbf{A}\mathbf{x}$ and $\mathbf{B}\mathbf{x}$ are linear functions of a normally distributed random vector, they are, in turn, normally distributed. Their zero covariance matrix implies that they are statistically independent.[10] This establishes the independence of the two quadratic forms. For the case of $\mathbf{x}'\mathbf{x}$, the two matrices are $\mathbf{M}^0$ and $[\mathbf{I} - \mathbf{M}^0]$. You can show that $\mathbf{M}^0[\mathbf{I} - \mathbf{M}^0] = \mathbf{0}$ just by multiplying it out.

3.10.4. The *F* Distribution

The normal family of distributions (chi-squared, F, and t) can all be derived as functions of idempotent quadratic forms in a standard normal vector. The F distribution is the ratio of two independent chi-squared variables, each divided by its respective degrees of freedom. Let $\mathbf{A}$ and $\mathbf{B}$ be two idempotent matrices with ranks r_a and r_b, and let $\mathbf{A}\mathbf{B} = \mathbf{0}$. Then

$$\frac{\mathbf{x}'\mathbf{A}\mathbf{x}/r_a}{\mathbf{x}'\mathbf{B}\mathbf{x}/r_b} \sim F[r_a, r_b]. \qquad (3–114)$$

If $\text{Var}[\mathbf{x}] = \sigma^2\mathbf{I}$ instead, this is modified to

$$\frac{(\mathbf{x}'\mathbf{A}\mathbf{x}/\sigma^2)/r_a}{(\mathbf{x}'\mathbf{B}\mathbf{x}/\sigma^2)/r_b} \sim F[r_a, r_b]. \qquad (3–115)$$

3.10.5. A Full Rank Quadratic Form

Finally, consider the general case,

$$\mathbf{x} \sim N[\boldsymbol{\mu}, \boldsymbol{\Sigma}].$$

---

[10] Note that both $\mathbf{x}_1 = \mathbf{A}\mathbf{x}$ and $\mathbf{x}_2 = \mathbf{B}\mathbf{x}$ have singular covariance matrices. Nonetheless, every element of $\mathbf{x}_1$ is independent of every element of $\mathbf{x}_2$, so the vectors are independent.

We are interested in the distribution of

$$q = (\mathbf{x} - \boldsymbol{\mu})'\boldsymbol{\Sigma}^{-1}(\mathbf{x} - \boldsymbol{\mu}). \tag{3-116}$$

First, the vector can be written as $\mathbf{z} = \mathbf{x} - \boldsymbol{\mu}$, and $\boldsymbol{\Sigma}$ is the variance matrix of $\mathbf{z}$ as well as of $\mathbf{x}$. Therefore, we seek the distribution of

$$q = \mathbf{z}'\boldsymbol{\Sigma}^{-1}\mathbf{z} = \mathbf{z}'(\mathbf{Var}[\mathbf{z}])^{-1}\mathbf{z}, \tag{3-117}$$

where $\mathbf{z}$ is normally distributed with mean $\mathbf{0}$. This is a quadratic form, but not necessarily in an idempotent matrix.[11] Since $\boldsymbol{\Sigma}$ is positive definite, it has a square root. Define the symmetric matrix, $\boldsymbol{\Sigma}^{1/2}$, so that $\boldsymbol{\Sigma}^{1/2}\boldsymbol{\Sigma}^{1/2} = \boldsymbol{\Sigma}$. Then

$$\boldsymbol{\Sigma}^{-1} = \boldsymbol{\Sigma}^{-1/2}\boldsymbol{\Sigma}^{-1/2}$$

and

$$\begin{aligned}
\mathbf{z}'\boldsymbol{\Sigma}^{-1}\mathbf{z} &= \mathbf{z}'\boldsymbol{\Sigma}^{-1/2'}\boldsymbol{\Sigma}^{-1/2}\mathbf{z} \\
&= (\boldsymbol{\Sigma}^{-1/2}\mathbf{z})'(\boldsymbol{\Sigma}^{-1/2}\mathbf{z}) \\
&= \mathbf{w}'\mathbf{w}.
\end{aligned}$$

Now $\mathbf{w} = \mathbf{A}\mathbf{z}$, so

$$E(\mathbf{w}) = \mathbf{A}E[\mathbf{z}] = \mathbf{0}$$

and

$$\mathbf{Var}[\mathbf{w}] = \mathbf{A}\boldsymbol{\Sigma}\mathbf{A}' = \boldsymbol{\Sigma}^{-1/2}\boldsymbol{\Sigma}\boldsymbol{\Sigma}^{-1/2} = \boldsymbol{\Sigma}^0 = \mathbf{I}.$$

This provides two results:

1. If $\mathbf{x} \sim N[\boldsymbol{\mu}, \boldsymbol{\Sigma}]$, then $\boldsymbol{\Sigma}^{-1/2}(\mathbf{x} - \boldsymbol{\mu}) \sim N[\mathbf{0}, \mathbf{I}]$.

The simplest special case is that in which $\mathbf{x}$ has only one variable, so that the transformation is just $(x - \mu)/\sigma$. Combining this with (3–32) concerning the sum of squares of standard normals, we have:

2. If $\mathbf{x} \sim N[\boldsymbol{\mu}, \boldsymbol{\Sigma}]$, then $(\mathbf{x} - \boldsymbol{\mu})'\boldsymbol{\Sigma}^{-1}(\mathbf{x} - \boldsymbol{\mu}) \sim \chi^2[n]$.

3.10.6. Independence of a Linear and a Quadratic Form

The t distribution is used in many forms of hypothesis tests. In some situations, it arises as the ratio of a linear to a quadratic form in a normal vector. To establish the distribution of these statistics, we use the following result:

> A linear function, $\mathbf{L}\mathbf{x}$, and an idempotent quadratic form, $\mathbf{x}'\mathbf{A}\mathbf{x}$, in a standard normal vector are statistically independent if $\mathbf{L}\mathbf{A} = \mathbf{0}$.

The proof follows the same logic as that for two quadratic forms. Write $\mathbf{x}'\mathbf{A}\mathbf{x}$ as $\mathbf{x}'\mathbf{A}'\mathbf{A}\mathbf{x} = (\mathbf{A}\mathbf{x})'(\mathbf{A}\mathbf{x})$. The covariance matrix of the variables $\mathbf{L}\mathbf{x}$ and $\mathbf{A}\mathbf{x}$ is $\mathbf{L}\mathbf{A} = \mathbf{0}$, which establishes the independence of these two random vectors. The independence of the linear function and the quadratic form follows immediately.

The t distribution is defined as the ratio of a standard normal variable to the square root of a chi-squared variable divided by its degrees of freedom:

$$t[J] = \frac{N[0, 1]}{\{\chi^2[J]/J\}^{1/2}}.$$

---

[11] It will be idempotent only in the special case of $\boldsymbol{\Sigma} = \mathbf{I}$.

A particular case is

$$t[n - 1] = \frac{\sqrt{n}\,\bar{x}}{[(\Sigma_i\,(x_i - \bar{x})^2)/(n - 1)]^{1/2}}$$

$$= \frac{\sqrt{n}\,\bar{x}}{s},$$

where s is the standard deviation of the values in $\mathbf{x}$. the distribution of the two variables in $t[n - 1]$ was shown earlier; we need only show that they are independent. But

$$\sqrt{n}\,\bar{x} = \frac{1}{\sqrt{n}}\mathbf{i}'\mathbf{x} = \mathbf{j}'\mathbf{x}$$

and

$$s^2 = \frac{\mathbf{x}'\mathbf{M}^0\mathbf{x}}{n - 1}.$$

It suffices to show that $\mathbf{M}^0\mathbf{j} = \mathbf{0}$, which follows from

$$\mathbf{M}^0\mathbf{i} = [\mathbf{I} - \mathbf{i}(\mathbf{i}'\mathbf{i})^{-1}\mathbf{i}']\mathbf{i}$$

$$= \mathbf{i} - \mathbf{i}(\mathbf{i}'\mathbf{i})^{-1}(\mathbf{i}'\mathbf{i})$$

$$= \mathbf{0}.$$

EXERCISES

1. How many different five-card poker hands can be dealt from a deck of 52 cards?

2. Compute the probability of being dealt four of a kind in a poker hand.

3. Suppose that a lottery ticket costs $1 per play. The game is played by drawing six numbers without replacement from the numbers 1 to 48. If you guess all six numbers, you win the prize. Now suppose that N = the number of tickets sold and P = the size of the prize. N and P are related by

$$N = 5 + 1.2P,$$

$$P = 1 + 0.4N.$$

N and P are in millions. What is the expected value of a ticket in this game? (Don't forget that you may have to share the prize with other winners.)

4. If x has a normal distribution with mean 1 and standard deviation 3, what are the following?
   (a) $\text{Prob}(|x| > 2)$.
   (b) $\text{Prob}(x > -1 \,|\, x < 1.5)$.

5. Approximately what is the probability that a random variable with chi-squared distribution with 264 degrees of freedom is less than 297?

6. *Chebyshev inequality:* For the following two probability distributions, find the lower limit of the probability of the indicated event, using the Chebyshev inequality (3–18), and the exact probability, using the appropriate table:
   (a) $x \sim \text{normal}(0, 3^2)$ and $-4 < x < 4$.
   (b) $x \sim$ chi-squared, eight degrees of freedom, $0 < x < 16$.

7. Given the following joint probability distribution

		X		
		0	1	2
	0	0.05	0.1	0.03
Y	1	0.21	0.11	0.19
	2	0.08	0.15	0.08

(a) Compute the following probabilities:

$$\text{Prob}(Y < 2),$$
$$\text{Prob}(Y < 2, X > 0),$$
$$\text{Prob}(Y = 1, X \geq 1).$$

(b) Find the marginal distributions of X and Y.

(c) Calculate $E[X]$, $E[Y]$, $\text{Var}[X]$, $\text{Var}[Y]$, $\text{Cov}[X, Y]$, and $E[X^2 Y^3]$.

(d) Calculate $\text{Cov}[Y, X^2]$.

(e) What is the conditional distribution of Y given $X = 2$? What is the conditional distribution of X given $Y > 0$?

(f) Find $E[Y|X]$ and $\text{Var}[Y|X]$. Obtain the two parts of the variance decomposition

$$\text{Var}[Y] = E_x[\text{Var}[Y \mid X]] + \text{Var}_x[E[Y|X]].$$

8. *Minimum mean-squared-error predictor:* For the joint distribution in Exercise 7, compute $E[y - E[y|x]]^2$. Now find the a and b that minimize the function $E[y - a - bx]^2$. Given the solutions, verify that

$$E[y - E[y|x]]^2 \leq E[y - a - bx]^2.$$

The result is fundamental in least squares theory. Verify that the a and b that you found satisfy (3–68) and (3–69).

9. Suppose that x has an exponential distribution,

$$f(x) = \theta e^{-\theta x}, \qquad x \geq 0.$$

(For an application, see Examples 3.5, 3.8, and 3.10.) Find the mean, variance, skewness, and kurtosis of x. [**Hints:** The latter two are defined in Section 3.3. The gamma integral in the appendix to this chapter will be useful for finding the raw moments.]

10. For the random variable in Exercise 9, what is the probability distribution of the random variable $y = e^{-x}$? What is $E[y]$? Prove that the distribution of this y is a special case of the beta distribution in (3–40).

11. If the probability density of y is $\alpha y^2 (1 - y)^3$ for y between 0 and 1, what is α? What is the probability that y is between 0.25 and 0.75?

12. Suppose that x has the discrete probability distribution

X	1	2	3	4
Prob($X = x$)	0.1	0.2	0.4	0.3

Find the exact mean and variance of X. Now suppose that $Y = 1/X$. Find the exact mean and variance of Y. Find the mean and variance of the linear and quadratic approximations to $Y = f(X)$. Are the mean and variance of the quadratic approximation closer to the true mean than those of the linear approximation?

13. *Interpolation in the chi-squared table:* In order to find a percentage point in the chi-squared table that is between two values, we interpolate linearly between the *reciprocals* of the degrees of freedom. The chi-squared distribution is defined for noninteger values of the degrees of freedom parameter [see (3–39)], but your table does not contain critical values for noninteger values. Using linear interpolation, find the 99 percent critical value for a chi-squared variable with degrees of freedom parameter 11.3. (For an application of this calculation, see Section 8.5.1 and Example 8.6.)

14. Suppose that x has a standard normal distribution. What is the pdf of the following random variable?

$$y = \frac{1}{\sqrt{2\pi}} e^{-x^2/2}.$$

[**Hints:** You know the distribution of $z = x^2$ from (3–30). The density of this z is given in (3–39). Solve the problem in terms of $y = g(z)$.]

15. *The fundamental probability transformation:* Suppose that the continuous random variable x has cumulative distribution $F(x)$. What is the probability distribution of the random variable $y = F(x)$? (**Observation:** This result forms the basis of the simulation of draws from many continuous distributions.)

16. *Random number generators:* Suppose that x is distributed uniformly between 0 and 1, so $f(x) = 1$, $0 \le x \le 1$. Let θ be some positive constant. What is the pdf of $y = -(1/\theta) \ln x$? (**Hint:** See Section 3.5.) Does this suggest a means of simulating draws from this distribution if one has a random number generator that will produce draws from the uniform distribution? To continue, suggest a means of simulating draws from a logistic distribution, $f(x) = e^{-x}/(1 + e^{-x})^2$.

17. Suppose that x_1 and x_2 are distributed as independent standard normal. What is the joint distribution of $y_1 = 2 + 3x_1 + 2x_2$ and $y_2 = 4 + 5x_1$? Suppose that you were able to obtain two samples of observations from independent standard normal distributions. How would you obtain a sample from the bivariate normal distribution with means 1 and 2, variances 4 and 9, and covariance 3?

18. The density of the standard normal distribution, denoted $\phi(x)$, is given in (3–28). The function based on the ith derivative of the density given by

$$H_i = \frac{(-1)^i d^i \phi(x)/dx^i}{\phi(x)}, \qquad i = 0, 1, 2, \ldots$$

is called a **hermite polynomial.** By definition, $H_0 = 1$.
(a) Find the next three hermite polynomials.
(b) A useful device in this context is the differential equation

$$\frac{d^r \phi(x)}{dx^r} + \frac{x d^{r-1}\phi(x)}{dx^{r-1}} + \frac{(r-1)d^{r-2}\phi(x)}{dx^{r-2}} = 0.$$

Use this result and the results of part (a) to find H_4 and H_5.

19. Continuation: *orthogonal polynomials:* The hermite polynomials are orthogonal if x has a standard normal distribution. That is, $E[H_i H_j] = 0$. Prove this for the H_1, H_2, and H_3 that you just obtained.

20. If x and y have means μ_x and μ_y, variances σ_x^2 and σ_y^2, and covariance σ_{xy}, what is the approximation of the covariance matrix of the two random variables $f_1 = x/y$ and $f_2 = xy$?

21. *Factorial moments:* For finding the moments of a distribution such as the Poisson, a useful device is the factorial moment. (The Poisson distribution is given in Example 3.1.) The density is

$$f(x) = \frac{e^{-\lambda}\lambda^x}{x!}, \qquad x = 0, 1, 2, \ldots .$$

To find the mean, we can use

$$E[x] = \sum_{x=0}^{\infty} xf(x) = \sum_{x=0}^{\infty} \frac{xe^{-\lambda}\lambda^x}{x!}$$

$$= \lambda \sum_{x=1}^{\infty} \frac{e^{-\lambda}\lambda^{x-1}}{(x-1)!}$$

$$= \lambda \sum_{y=0}^{\infty} \frac{e^{-\lambda}\lambda^y}{y!}$$

$$= \lambda,$$

since the probabilities sum to 1. To find the variance, we can extend this method by finding $E[x(x - 1)]$, and likewise for other moments. Use this method to find the variance and third central moment of the Poisson distribution. (Note that this device is used to transform the factorial in the denominator in the probability.)

22. If x has a normal distribution with mean μ and standard deviation σ, what is the probability distribution of $y = e^x$?

23. If y has a lognormal distribution, what is the probability distribution of y^2?

24. Suppose that y, x_1, and x_2 have a joint normal distribution with parameters

$$\boldsymbol{\mu}' = [1 \quad 2 \quad 4]$$

and covariance matrix

$$\Sigma = \begin{bmatrix} 2 & 3 & 1 \\ 3 & 5 & 2 \\ 1 & 2 & 6 \end{bmatrix}.$$

(a) Compute the intercept and slope in the function $E[y|x_1]$, $\text{Var}[y|x_1]$ and the coefficient of determination in this regression. (**Hint:** See Section 3.10.1.)
(b) Compute the intercept and slopes in the conditional mean function, $E[y|x_1, x_2]$. What is $E[y|x_1 = 2.5, x_2 = 3.3]$? What is $\text{Var}[y|x_1 = 2.5, x_2 = 3.3]$?

25. What is the density of $y = 1/x$ if x has a chi-squared distribution?

26. *Probability generating function:* For a discrete random variable, x, the function

$$E[t^x] = \sum_{x=0}^{\infty} t^x \, \text{Prob}(X = x)$$

is called the **probability generating function** because in the function the coefficient on t^i is $\text{Prob}(X = i)$. Suppose that x is the number of the repetitions of an experiment with probability π of success upon which the first success occurs. The density of x is the **geometric distribution:**

$$\text{Prob}(X = x) = (1 - \pi)^{x-1}\pi.$$

What is the probability generating function?

27. *Moment generating function:* For the random variable X with pdf $f(x)$, if the function

$$M(t) = E[e^{tx}]$$

exists, it is the moment generating function (MGF). Assuming that the function exists, it can be shown that

$$\frac{d^r M(t)}{dt^r}\bigg|_{t=0} = E[x^r].$$

Find the MGFs for
(a) The exponential distribution of Exercise 9.
(b) The Poisson distribution of Exercise 21.
The moment generating function need not exist for some values of t. We are interested in convergence of the Taylor series expansion in the neighborhood of $t = 0$, so the nonconvergence need not be a problem. But for some distributions, such as $f(x) = \exp(-x^2)$, the moment generating function does not exist for any t. A companion function for which convergence is not a problem is the **characteristic function**, $E[\exp(itx)]$, where $i^2 = -1$. We shall not require the characteristic function in this book, but it is an important tool in more advanced treatments, for example, in proofs of variants of the central limit theorem.

28. *Moment generating function for a sum of variables:* When it exists, the moment generating function has a one-to-one correspondence with the distribution. Thus, for example, if we begin with some random variable and find that a transformation of it has a particular familiar MGF, we may infer that the function of the random variable has the distribution associated with that MGF. A useful application is the following:

If x and y are independent, the MGF of $x + y$ is $M_x(t)M_y(t)$.

(a) Use this result to prove that the sum of Poisson random variables has a Poisson distribution.
(b) Use this result to prove that the sum of chi-squared variables has a chi-squared distribution. [*Note:* you must first find the MGF for a chi-squared variate. The density is given in (3–39).]
(c) The MGF for the standard normal distribution is

$$M_z = e^{-t^2/2}.$$

Find the MGF for the $N[\mu, \sigma^2]$ distribution; then find the distribution of a sum of normally distributed variables.

Appendix: Integration—The Gamma Function

For any positive constant, p, the gamma function is

$$\Gamma(p) = \int_0^\infty t^{p-1}e^{-t}\, dt.$$

For an integer p,

$$\Gamma(p) = (p - 1)!, \qquad p = 1, 2, \ldots ,$$

which follows from the recursion

$$\Gamma(p) = (p - 1)\Gamma(p - 1).$$

For p greater than 1, the gamma function may be regarded as a generalization of the factorial operation for noninteger values of p. In addition,

$$\Gamma(\tfrac{1}{2}) = \sqrt{\pi}.$$

For integer values of p,

$$\Gamma(p + \tfrac{1}{2}) = (p - \tfrac{1}{2})\Gamma(p - \tfrac{1}{2}).$$

For positive constants a, p, and c,

$$\int_0^\infty x^{p-1} e^{-ax^c}\, dx = \int_0^\infty x^{-(p+1)} e^{-a/x^c}\, dx = \left(\frac{1}{c}\right) a^{-p/c} \Gamma\left(\frac{p}{c}\right).$$

The derivatives of the gamma function are

$$\frac{d^r \Gamma(p)}{dp^r} = \int_0^\infty (\ln p)^r x^{p-1} e^{-x}\, dx.$$

For values of p that are not multiples of 0.5, the gamma function must be numerically approximated. The derivatives must be approximated for all values of p. The first two derivatives of $\ln \Gamma(p)$ are denoted $\Psi(p) = \Gamma'/\Gamma$ and $\Psi'(p) = (\Gamma\Gamma'' - \Gamma'^2)/\Gamma^2$. Many sources, such as Abramovitz and Stegun (1977), provide tables of Ψ and Ψ' for values of p.

CHAPTER 4

Statistical Inference

4.1. Introduction

The probability distributions discussed in Chapter 3 serve as models for the underlying processes that produce our observed data. The goal of statistical inference in econometrics is to use the principles of mathematical statistics to combine these theoretical distributions and the observed data into an empirical model of the economy. This analysis takes place in one of two frameworks, classical or Bayesian. The overwhelming majority of empirical study in econometrics has been done in the classical framework. Our focus, therefore, will be on classical methods of inference. Bayesian methods will be discussed briefly in Chapter 8.[1]

4.2. Samples and Sampling Distributions

The classical theory of statistical inference centers on rules for using the sampled data effectively. These rules, in turn, are based on the properties of samples and sampling distributions.

4.2.1. Random Sampling

A sample of n observations on one or more variables, denoted $\mathbf{x}_1$, $\mathbf{x}_2$, . . . , $\mathbf{x}_n$ is a **random sample** if the n observations are drawn independently from the same population, or probability distribution, $f(\mathbf{x}_i, \boldsymbol{\theta})$. The sample may be univariate if $\mathbf{x}_i$ is a single random variable or multivariate if each observation contains several variables. The vector $\boldsymbol{\theta}$ contains one or more unknown parameters. Data are generally drawn in one of two settings. A **cross section** is a sample of a number of observational units all drawn at the same point in time. A **time series** is a set of observations drawn on the same observational unit at a number of (usually evenly spaced) points in time. Many recent studies have been based on time-series cross sections, which generally consist of the same cross section observed at several points in time. Since the typical data set of this sort consists of a large number of cross-sectional units observed at a few points in time, the common term **panel data set** is usually more fitting for this sort of study.

---

[1] An excellent reference is Leamer (1978). A summary of the results as they apply to econometrics is contained in Zellner (1971). For some recent applications, see Poirier (1991).

4.2.2. Descriptive Statistics

Before attempting to estimate parameters of a population or fit models to data, we normally examine the data themselves. One place to begin is with a **scatter diagram,** which is useful in a bivariate sample if the sample contains a reasonable number of observations. Figure 4.1 shows an example for a small data set. However, in most cases, and particularly if the number of observations in the sample is large, we shall use some summary statistics to describe the sample data. Of most interest are measures of **location,** that is, the center of the data, and **scale,** or the dispersion of the data. If the sample contains data on more than one variable, we are also interested in measures of association among the variables.

A few measures of central tendency are as follows:

$$\textbf{Mean: } \bar{x} = \frac{\Sigma_i x_i}{n}.$$

Median: m = the middle ranked observation. $\hfill$ (4–1)

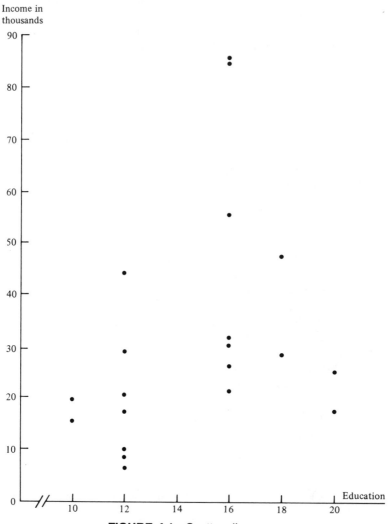

FIGURE 4.1 Scatter diagram.

Sample midrange: $\text{midrange} = \dfrac{\text{maximum} - \text{minimum}}{2}$.

The dispersion of the sample observations is usually measured by the

$$\textbf{Standard deviation: } s_x = \left[\frac{\Sigma_i(x_i - \bar{x})^2}{n - 1} \right]^{1/2}. \tag{4-2}$$

Other measures, such as the average absolute deviation from the sample mean, are used as well, though less frequently. If the sample is a multivariate one, the degree of linear association among the variables can be measured by the pairwise measures

$$\textbf{Covariance: } s_{xy} = \frac{\Sigma_i(x_i - \bar{x})(y_i - \bar{y})}{n - 1} \tag{4-3}$$

and

$$\textbf{Correlation: } r_{xy} = \frac{s_{xy}}{s_x s_y}.$$

If the sample contains data on several variables, it is sometimes convenient to arrange the covariances or correlations in a

$$\textbf{Covariance matrix: } \mathbf{S} = [s_{ij}] \tag{4-4}$$

or

$$\textbf{Correlation matrix: } \mathbf{R} = [r_{ij}].$$

Some useful algebraic results for any two variables, (x_i, y_i), $i = 1, \ldots, n$, and constants, a and b, are

$$s_x^2 = \frac{\Sigma_i x_i^2 - n\bar{x}^2}{n - 1}, \tag{4-5}$$

$$s_{xy} = \frac{\Sigma_i x_i y_i - n\bar{x}\bar{y}}{n - 1}, \tag{4-6}$$

$$-1 \le r_{xy} \le 1,$$

$$r_{ax,by} = \frac{ab}{|ab|} r_{xy} \qquad \text{for } a, b \ne 0, \tag{4-7}$$

$$s_{ax} = |a| s_x,$$

$$s_{ax,by} = ab s_{xy}. \tag{4-8}$$

Note that these algebraic results parallel the theoretical results for bivariate probability distributions.

EXAMPLE 4.1

Table 4.1 is a (hypothetical) sample of observations on income and education. A scatter diagram appears in Figure 4.1. It suggests a weak positive association between income and education in these data.

Means:

$$\bar{I} = \tfrac{1}{20}(20.5 + \cdots + 84.9) = 31.28,$$

$$\bar{E} = \tfrac{1}{20}(12 + \cdots + 16) = 14.6.$$

TABLE 4.1. Observations on Income and Education[a]

Observation	Income	Education	Observation	Income	Education
1	20.5	12	11	55.8	16
2	31.5	16	12	25.2	20
3	47.7	18	13	29.0	12
4	26.2	16	14	85.5	16
5	44.0	12	15	15.1	10
6	8.28	12	16	28.5	18
7	30.8	16	17	21.4	16
8	17.2	12	18	17.7	20
9	19.9	10	19	6.42	12
10	9.96	12	20	84.9	16

[a] Income in thousands, education in years.

Standard deviations:

$$s_I = \sqrt{\tfrac{1}{19}[(20.5 - 31.28)^2 + \cdots + (84.9 - 31.28)^2]} = 22.37,$$

$$s_E = \sqrt{\tfrac{1}{19}[(12 - 14.6)^2 + \cdots + (16 - 14.6)^2]} = 3.119.$$

Covariance:

$$\tfrac{1}{19}[20.5(12) + \cdots + 84.9(16) - 20(31.28)(14.6)] = 23.59.$$

Correlation:

$$\frac{23.59}{(22.37)(3.19)} = 0.338.$$

The positive correlation is consistent with our observation of the scatter diagram.

4.2.3. Sampling Distributions

The measures described in the preceding section summarize the data in a random sample. Each measure has a counterpart in the population, that is, the distribution from which the data were drawn. Sample quantities such as the means and the correlation coefficient correspond to population expectations, while the values in Table 4.2 parallel the population pdf and cdf. In the setting of a random sample, we expect these quantities to mimic the population, though not perfectly. The precise manner in which these quantities reflect the population values defines the sampling distribution of a sample statistic.

Definition. A statistic is any function computed from the data in a sample.

TABLE 4.2. Income Distribution

Range	Relative Frequency	Cumulative Frequency
<$10,000	0.15	0.15
10,000–25,000	0.30	0.45
25,000–50,000	0.40	0.85
>50,000	0.15	1.00

If another sample were drawn under identical conditions, different values would be obtained for the observations, as each one is a random variable. Consequently, the statistic is also a random variable with a probability distribution called a **sampling distribution**. For example, the following shows an exact result for the sampling behavior of a widely used statistic:

THEOREM 4.1. SAMPLING DISTRIBUTION OF THE SAMPLE MEAN: *If* $x_1, \ldots, x_n$ *are a random sample from a population with mean* μ *and variance* σ^2, *then* $\bar{x}$ *is a random variable with mean* μ *and variance* σ^2/n.

Proof: $\bar{x} = (1/n)\Sigma_i x_i$. $E[\bar{x}] = (1/n)\Sigma_i \mu = \mu$. The observations are independent, so $\mathrm{Var}[\bar{x}] = (1/n)^2 \mathrm{Var}[\Sigma_i x_i] = (1/n^2)\Sigma_i \sigma^2 = \sigma^2/n$.

Notice that the fundamental result in Theorem 4.1 does not assume a distribution for x_i.

EXAMPLE 4.2 ────────────────────────────────

Figure 4.2 shows a frequency plot of the means of 1000 random samples of four observations drawn from a chi-squared distribution with one degree of freedom, which has mean 1 and variance 2.

──

We are often interested in how a statistic behaves in a large sample or as the sample size increases. The following illustrates one such case.

EXAMPLE 4.3 ────────────────────────────────

If $x_1, \ldots, x_n$ are a random sample from an exponential distribution with $f(x) = \theta e^{-\theta x}$, the sampling distribution of the sample minimum in a sample of n observations, denoted $x_{(1)}$, is

$$f(x_{(1)}) = (n\theta)e^{-(n\theta)x_{(1)}}.$$

The proof is considered in the exercises. Since $E[x] = 1/\theta$ and $\mathrm{Var}[x] = 1/\theta^2$, by analogy $E[x_{(1)}] = 1/(n\theta)$ and $\mathrm{Var}[x_{(1)}] = 1/(n\theta)^2$. Thus, in increasingly larger samples, the minimum will be arbitrarily close to 0. (The Chebyshev inequality in (4–17) can be used to prove this intuitively appealing result.)

──

Sampling distributions are used to make inferences about the population. To consider a perhaps obvious example, since the sampling distribution of the mean of a set of normally distributed observations has mean μ, the sample mean is a natural candidate for an estimate of μ. The observation that the sample "mimics" the population is a statement about the sampling distributions of the sample statistics. Consider, for example, the sample data collected in Figure 4.2. The sample mean of four observations clearly has a sampling distribution, which appears to have a mean roughly equal to the population mean. This is the departure point for our theory of parameter estimation.

4.3. Point Estimation of Parameters

Our objective is to use the sample data to infer the value of a parameter or set of parameters, which we denote θ. A **point estimate** is a statistic computed from a sample that gives a single value for θ. The **standard error** of the estimate is the standard deviation of the

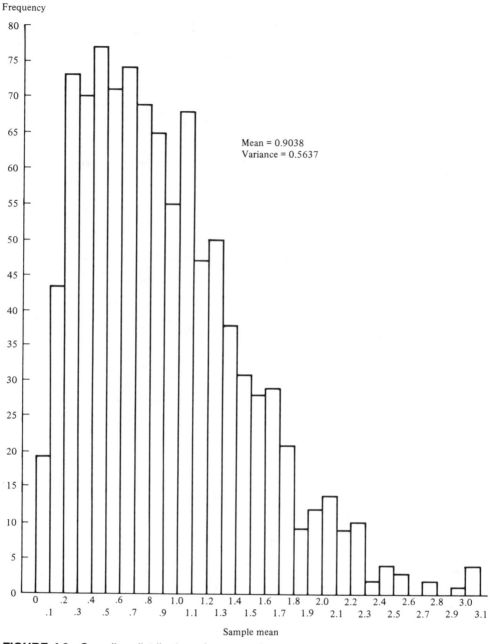

FIGURE 4.2 Sampling distribution of means of 1000 samples of size 4 from chi-squared (1).

sampling distribution of the statistic; the square of this quantity is the **sampling variance.** An **interval estimate** is a range of values that will contain the true parameter with a preassigned probability. There will be a connection between the two types of estimates; generally, if $\hat{\theta}$ is the point estimate, the interval estimate will be $\hat{\theta} \pm$ a measure of sampling error.

An **estimator** is a rule or strategy for using the data to estimate the parameter. It is defined before the data are drawn. Obviously, some estimators are better than others. To take a simple example, your intuition should convince you that the sample mean would be a better estimator of the population mean than the sample minimum; the minimum is almost certain to underestimate the mean. Nonetheless, the minimum is not entirely without virtue; it is easy to compute, and ease of computation is occasionally a relevant criterion. The search for good estimators constitutes much of econometrics. Estimators are compared on the basis of a variety of attributes. **Finite sample properties** of estimators are those attributes that can be compared regardless of the sample size. Some estimation problems involve characteristics that are not known in finite samples. In these instances, estimators are compared on the basis of their large sample, or **asymptotic properties.** We consider these in turn.

4.3.1. Estimation in a Finite Sample

The following are some finite sample estimation criteria for estimating a single parameter. The extensions to the multiparameter case are direct. We shall consider them in passing where necessary.

Definition. An estimator of a parameter, θ, is **unbiased** if the mean of its sampling distribution is θ. Formally,

$$E[\hat{\theta}] = \theta$$

or

$$E[\hat{\theta} - \theta] = \text{Bias}[\hat{\theta} \mid \theta] = 0$$

implies that $\hat{\theta}$ is unbiased. Note that this implies that the expected sampling error is zero. If $\boldsymbol{\theta}$ is a vector of parameters, the estimator is unbiased if the expected value of every element of $\hat{\boldsymbol{\theta}}$ equals the corresponding element of $\boldsymbol{\theta}$.

If samples of size n are drawn repeatedly and $\hat{\theta}$ is computed for each one, the average value of these estimates will tend to equal θ. For example, the average of the 1000 sample means underlying Figure 4.2 is 0.9038, which is reasonably close to the population mean of 1. The sample minimum is clearly a biased estimator of the mean; it will almost always underestimate the mean, so it will do so on average as well.

Unbiasedness is a desirable attribute, but it is rarely used by itself as an estimation criterion. One reason is that there are many unbiased estimators that are obviously poor uses of the data. For example, in a sample of size n, the first observation drawn is an unbiased estimator of the mean that clearly wastes a great deal of information. A second criterion used to choose among unbiased estimators is efficiency.

Definition. An unbiased estimator $\hat{\theta}_1$ is more **efficient** than another unbiased estimator, $\hat{\theta}_2$, if the sampling variance of $\hat{\theta}_1$ is less than that of $\hat{\theta}_2$. That is,

$$\text{Var}[\hat{\theta}_1] < \text{Var}[\hat{\theta}_2].$$

In the multiparameter case, the comparison is based on the covariance matrices of the two estimators; $\hat{\boldsymbol{\theta}}_1$ is more efficient than $\hat{\boldsymbol{\theta}}_2$ if $\text{Var}[\hat{\boldsymbol{\theta}}_2] - \text{Var}[\hat{\boldsymbol{\theta}}_1]$ is a nonnegative definite matrix.

By this criterion, the sample mean is obviously to be preferred to the first observation as an estimator of the population mean. If σ^2 is the population variance,

$$\text{Var}[x_1] = \sigma^2 > \text{Var}[\bar{x}] = \frac{\sigma^2}{n}.$$

In discussing efficiency, we have restricted the discussion to unbiased estimators. Clearly, there are biased estimators that have smaller variances than the unbiased ones we have considered. Any constant has a variance of zero. Of course, using a constant as an estimator is not likely to be an effective use of the sample data. However, focusing on unbiasedness may still preclude a *tolerably* biased estimator with a much smaller variance. A criterion that recognizes this possible tradeoff is the mean-squared error.

Definition. The **mean-squared error** of an estimator is

$$\text{MSE}[\hat{\theta}] = E[(\hat{\theta} - \theta)^2]$$

$$= \text{Var}[\hat{\theta}] + (\text{Bias}[\hat{\theta}])^2 \qquad \text{if } \theta \text{ is a scalar} \qquad (4\text{-}9)$$

$$= \text{Var}[\hat{\boldsymbol{\theta}}] + \text{Bias}[\hat{\boldsymbol{\theta}}]\text{Bias}[\hat{\boldsymbol{\theta}}]' \qquad \text{if } \boldsymbol{\theta} \text{ is a vector.}$$

Figure 4.3 illustrates the effect. On average, the biased estimator will be closer to the true parameter than will the unbiased estimator.

EXAMPLE 4.4 _____

In sampling from a normal distribution, the most frequently used estimator for σ^2 is

$$s^2 = \frac{\Sigma_i(x_i - \bar{x})^2}{n - 1}.$$

It is straightforward to show that s^2 is unbiased, so

$$\text{Var}[s^2] = \frac{2\sigma^4}{n - 1} = \text{MSE}[s^2].$$

(A proof is based on the distribution of the idempotent quadratic form $(\mathbf{x} - \mathbf{i}\mu)'\mathbf{M}^0$ $(\mathbf{x} - \mathbf{i}\mu)$, which we discussed in Section 3.10.3.) A less frequently used estimator is

$$\hat{\sigma}^2 = \frac{\Sigma_i(x_i - \bar{x})^2}{n} = \frac{(n - 1)s^2}{n}.$$

This estimator is slightly biased downward:

$$E[\hat{\sigma}^2] = \frac{(n - 1)E(s^2)}{n} = \frac{(n - 1)\sigma^2}{n},$$

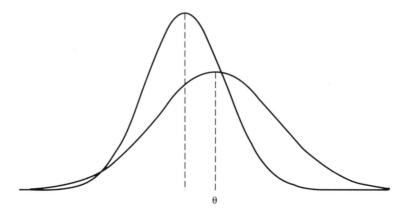

FIGURE 4.3 Sampling distributions.

so its bias is

$$E[\hat{\sigma}^2 - \sigma^2] = \text{Bias}[\hat{\sigma}^2] = \frac{-1}{n}\sigma^2,$$

But it has a smaller variance than s^2:

$$\text{Var}[\hat{\sigma}^2] = \left[\frac{n-1}{n}\right]^2 \frac{2\sigma^4}{n-1} < \text{Var}[s^2].$$

To compare the two estimators, we can use the difference in their mean-squared errors:

$$\text{MSE}[\hat{\sigma}^2] - \text{MSE}[s^2] = \sigma^4\left[\frac{2n-1}{n^2} - \frac{2}{n-1}\right] < 0.$$

The biased estimator is a bit more precise. The difference will obviously be negligible in a large sample, but, for example, it is about 10 percent in a sample of 16.

Which of these criteria should be used in a given situation depends on the particulars of that setting and our objectives in the study.

EXAMPLE 4.5 _____

In a **decision theoretic** setting, the purpose of estimating the parameter is to use the data to formulate a decision. The decision depends on the estimated parameter and will be erroneous if $\hat{\theta}$ does not equal the true parameter. The cost of the decision, or **loss,** will depend on the estimate and the true value of θ. Since $\hat{\theta}$ is random, so is the loss. Suppose that the cost associated with a decision is proportional to the square of the difference between the estimate and the true parameter. To minimize the expected loss, we would choose the estimator with the minimum mean-squared error.

Unfortunately, the MSE criterion is rarely operational; minimum mean-squared error estimators, when they exist at all, usually depend upon unknown parameters. Thus, we are usually less demanding. A commonly used criterion is **minimum variance unbiasedness.**

4.3.2. Efficient Unbiased Estimation

In a random sample of n observations, the density of each observation is $f(x_i, \theta)$. Since the n observations are independent, their joint density is

$$f(x_1, x_2, \ldots, x_n, \boldsymbol{\theta}) = f(x_1, \boldsymbol{\theta})f(x_2, \boldsymbol{\theta}) \cdots f(x_n, \boldsymbol{\theta})$$

$$= \Pi_{i=1}^n f(x_i, \boldsymbol{\theta}) = L(\boldsymbol{\theta}|x_1, x_2, \ldots, x_n). \tag{4-10}$$

The function $L(\boldsymbol{\theta}|\mathbf{X})$ is the likelihood function for $\boldsymbol{\theta}$ given the data, $\mathbf{x}$. It is frequently abbreviated to $L(\boldsymbol{\theta})$. Where no ambiguity can arise, we shall abbreviate it further to L.

EXAMPLE 4.6 _____

If $x_1, \ldots, x_n$ are a sample of n observations from an exponential distribution with parameter θ,

$$L(\theta) = \Pi_i \theta e^{-\theta x_i}$$

$$= \theta^n e^{-\theta\Sigma_i x_i}.$$

EXAMPLE 4.7

If $x_1, \ldots, x_n$ are a sample of n observations from a normal distribution with mean μ and standard deviation σ,

$$L(\mu, \sigma) = \Pi_i (2\pi\sigma^2)^{-1/2} e^{-(1/(2\sigma^2))(x_i - \mu)^2}$$

$$= (2\pi\sigma^2)^{-n/2} e^{-(1/(2\sigma^2))\Sigma_i(x_i - \mu)^2}. \tag{4-11}$$

The likelihood function is the cornerstone for most of our theory of parameter estimation. An important result for efficient estimation is the following:

Cramér–Rao Lower Bound. Assuming that the density of x satisfies certain regularity conditions, the variance of an unbiased estimator of a parameter, θ, will always be at least as large as

$$[I(\theta)]^{-1} = \left(-E\left[\frac{\partial^2 \ln L(\theta)}{\partial\theta^2} \right] \right)^{-1}$$

$$= \left(E\left[\left(\frac{\partial \ln L(\theta)}{\partial\theta} \right)^2 \right] \right)^{-1}. \tag{4-12}$$

The quantity $I(\theta)$ is the **information number** for the sample.

The regularity conditions are quite technical in nature. [See Theil (1971, Chap. 8).] Loosely, they are conditions imposed on the density of the random variable which appears in the likelihood function which will ensure that the Lindberg–Levy central limit theorem will apply to the sample of observations on the random vector $\mathbf{y} = \partial \ln f(x|\boldsymbol{\theta})/\partial\boldsymbol{\theta}$. Among the conditions are finite moments of x up to order 3. An additional condition normally included in the set is that the range of the random variable be independent of the parameters.[2]

In some cases, the second derivative of the log likelihood is a constant, so the Cramér–Rao bound is simple to obtain. For instance, in sampling from an exponential distribution, from Example 4.6,

$$\ln L = n \ln \theta - \theta \sum_i x_i,$$

$$\frac{\partial \ln L}{\partial\theta} = \frac{n}{\theta} - \sum_i x_i,$$

$$\frac{\partial^2 \ln L}{\partial\theta^2} = -\frac{n}{\theta^2}.$$

Therefore, the variance bound is

$$[I(\theta)]^{-1} = \frac{\theta^2}{n}.$$

In most situations, the second derivative is a random variable with a distribution of its own. The following examples show two such cases.

---

[2] A discussion of these conditions can be found in Theil (1971, Chap. 8). They are rarely violated in the models analyzed by econometricians. For a case in which they are, see Greene (1980a).

EXAMPLE 4.8

For the Poisson distribution,

$$f(x) = \frac{e^{-\theta}\theta^x}{x!},$$

$$\ln L = -n\theta + \left(\sum_i x_i\right) \ln \theta - \sum_i \ln (x_i!),$$

$$\frac{\partial \ln L}{\partial \theta} = -n + \frac{\Sigma_i x_i}{\theta},$$

$$\frac{\partial^2 \ln L}{\partial \theta^2} = -\frac{\Sigma_i x_i}{\theta^2}.$$

The sum of n identical Poisson variables has a Poisson distribution. We have seen that the actual distribution of the first derivative will be that of a linear function of a Poisson distributed variable. Since

$$E\left[\sum_i x_i\right] = nE[x_i] = n\theta,$$

the variance bound for the Poisson distribution is

$$[I(\theta)]^{-1} = \frac{\theta}{n}.$$

Consider, finally, a multivariate case. If $\boldsymbol{\theta}$ is a vector of parameters, $\mathbf{I}(\boldsymbol{\theta})$ is the **information matrix.** The Cramér–Rao theorem states that the difference between the variance matrix of any unbiased estimator and the inverse of the information matrix,

$$[\mathbf{I}(\boldsymbol{\theta})]^{-1} = \left\{-E\left[\frac{\partial^2 \ln L(\boldsymbol{\theta})}{\partial\boldsymbol{\theta}\partial\boldsymbol{\theta}'}\right]\right\}^{-1}$$

$$= \left\{E\left[\left(\frac{\partial \ln L(\boldsymbol{\theta})}{\partial\boldsymbol{\theta}}\right)\left(\frac{\partial \ln L(\boldsymbol{\theta})}{\partial\boldsymbol{\theta}'}\right)\right]\right\}^{-1}$$

will be a nonnegative definite matrix.

EXAMPLE 4.9

For random sampling from a normal distribution, the log-likelihood and its derivatives are

$$\ln L(\mu, \sigma^2) = -\frac{n}{2} \ln (2\pi) - \frac{n}{2} \ln \sigma^2 - \frac{1}{2\sigma^2} \sum_i (x_i - \mu)^2,$$

$$\frac{\partial \ln L}{\partial \mu} = \frac{1}{\sigma^2} \sum_i (x_i - \mu),$$

$$\frac{\partial \ln L}{\partial \sigma^2} = -\frac{n}{2\sigma^2} + \frac{1}{2\sigma^4} \sum_i (x_i - \mu)^2, \tag{4–13}$$

$$\frac{\partial^2 \ln L}{\partial \mu^2} = -\frac{n}{\sigma^2},$$

$$\frac{\partial^2 \ln L}{\partial (\sigma^2)^2} = \frac{n}{2\sigma^4} - \frac{1}{\sigma^6} \sum_i (x_i - \mu)^2,$$

$$\frac{\partial^2 \ln L}{\partial \mu \partial \sigma^2} = -\frac{1}{\sigma^4} \sum_i (x_i - \mu).$$

The information matrix contains the negatives of the expected values of the second derivatives:

$$\mathbf{I}(\mu, \sigma^2) = \begin{bmatrix} n/\sigma^2 & 0 \\ 0 & n/2\sigma^4 \end{bmatrix}.$$

The inverse is the variance bound for unbiased estimation of μ and σ^2 of a normal distribution:

$$[\mathbf{I}(\mu, \sigma^2)]^{-1} = \begin{bmatrix} \sigma^2/n & 0 \\ 0 & 2\sigma^4/n \end{bmatrix}. \tag{4-14}$$

The normal distribution is somewhat unusual in its diagonal information matrix.

If $\hat{\mu}$ and $\hat{\sigma}^2$ are any pair of unbiased estimators for μ and σ^2, and $\mathbf{V}$ is their 2×2 covariance matrix, then $\mathbf{V} - [\mathbf{I}(\mu, \sigma^2)]^{-1}$ is a nonnegative definite matrix. Consider the two unbiased estimators

$$\hat{\mu} = \bar{x} = \frac{1}{n} \, \mathbf{i}'\mathbf{x},$$

$$\hat{\sigma}^2 = s^2 = \frac{\Sigma_i (x_i - \bar{x})^2}{n - 1} = \frac{\mathbf{x}'\mathbf{M}^0\mathbf{x}}{n - 1}.$$

The mean and variance of $\bar{x}$ were given in Theorem 4.1. The independence of $\bar{x}$ and s^2 was shown in Section 3.10.6. Thus, their covariance is 0. Therefore,

$$\text{Var}[\bar{x}, s^2] - [\mathbf{I}(\mu, \sigma^2)]^{-1} = \begin{bmatrix} \sigma^2/n & 0 \\ 0 & 2\sigma^4/(n - 1) \end{bmatrix} - \begin{bmatrix} \sigma^2/n & 0 \\ 0 & 2\sigma^4/n \end{bmatrix}$$

$$= \begin{bmatrix} 0 & 0 \\ 0 & 2\sigma^4/(n(n - 1)) \end{bmatrix}, \tag{4-15}$$

which is a nonnegative definite matrix. Note that the mean attains the variance bound, while the variance estimator does not.

In most settings, there are numerous estimators available for the parameters of a distribution. The usefulness of the Cramér-Rao bound is that if one of these is known to attain the variance bound, there is no need to consider any other in order to seek a more efficient estimator. Regarding the use of the variance bound, we emphasize that if an unbiased estimator attains it, that estimator is efficient. However, if a given estimator does not attain the variance bound, we do not know, except in a few special cases, whether this estimator is efficient or not. It may be that no unbiased estimator can attain the Cramér-Rao bound, which can leave the question of whether a given unbiased estimator is efficient or not unanswered.

We note, finally, that in some cases we further restrict the set of estimators to linear functions of the data.

Definition. An estimator is **minimum variance linear unbiased (MVLUE)** or **best linear unbiased (BLUE)** if it is a linear function of the data and has minimum variance among linear unbiased estimators.

In a few instances, such as the normal mean, there will be an efficient linear unbiased estimator; $\bar{x}$ is efficient among all unbiased estimators, both linear and nonlinear. In other cases, such as the normal variance, there is no linear unbiased estimator. This criterion is useful because we can sometimes find an MVLU estimator without having to specify the distribution at all. Thus, by limiting ourselves to a somewhat restricted class of estimators, we free ourselves from having to assume a particular distribution.

4.4. Large-Sample Distribution Theory[3]

In most cases, whether an estimator is exactly unbiased, or what its exact sampling variance is in samples of a given size, will be unknown. But we may be able to obtain approximate results about the behavior of the distribution of an estimator as the sample becomes large. For example, it is well known that the distribution of the mean of a sample tends to approximate normality as the sample size grows, regardless of the distribution of the individual observations. Knowledge about the limiting behavior of the distribution of an estimator can be used to infer an approximate distribution for the estimator in a finite sample. In order to describe how this is done, it is necessary, first, to present some results on convergence of random variables.

4.4.1. Convergence in Probability

Limiting arguments in this discussion will be with respect to the sample size, n. Let x_n be a random variable indexed by the size of a sample.

Definition. x_n **converges in probability** to a constant, c, if $\lim_{n \to \infty} \text{Prob}(|x_n - c| > \varepsilon) = 0$ for any positive ε.

Convergence in probability implies that the values that the variable may take that are not close to c become increasingly unlikely. To consider one example, suppose that the random variable x_n takes two values, 0 and n, with probabilities $1 - (1/n)$ and $(1/n)$, respectively. As n increases, the second point will become ever more remote from any constant but, at the same time, will become increasingly less probable. In this example, x_n converges in probability to 0. The crux of this form of convergence is that all of the probability of the distribution becomes concentrated at points close to c. If x_n converges in probability to c, we write

$$\text{plim } x_n = c. \tag{4-16}$$

A special case of convergence in probability is **convergence in mean square** or **convergence in quadratic mean.**

---

[3] An up-to-date summary of many recent developments in large-sample theory appears in White (1984).

THEOREM 4.2: *If x_n has mean μ_n and variance σ_n^2 such that the ordinary limits of μ_n and σ_n^2 are c and 0, respectively, then x_n converges in mean square to c, and*

$$\text{plim } x_n = c.$$

The **Chebyshev inequality** states that for *any* random variable,

$$\text{Prob}(|x_n - \mu_n| > \varepsilon) \le \frac{\sigma_n^2}{\varepsilon^2}. \tag{4-17}$$

Taking the limits of μ_n and σ_n^2 in this expression, we see that if

$$\lim_{n \to \infty} E[x_n] = c \qquad \text{and} \qquad \lim_{n \to \infty} \text{Var}[x_n] = 0, \tag{4-18}$$

then

$$\text{plim } x_n = c.$$

As we have shown, convergence in mean square implies convergence in probability. Mean-square convergence implies that the distribution of x_n collapses to a spike at plim x_n, as shown in Figure 4.4.

EXAMPLE 4.10

As noted in Example 4.3, in sampling from an exponential distribution, for the sample minimum, $x_{(1)}$,

$$\lim_{n \to \infty} E[x_{(1)}] = \lim_{n \to \infty} \frac{1}{n\theta} = 0,$$

$$\lim_{n \to \infty} \text{Var}[x_{(1)}] = \lim_{n \to \infty} \frac{1}{(n\theta)^2} = 0.$$

Therefore,

$$\text{plim } x_{(1)} = 0.$$

Note, in particular, that the variance is divided by n^2. Thus, this estimator converges very rapidly to 0.

Convergence in probability does not imply convergence in mean square. Consider the simple example given earlier in which x_n equals either 0 or n with probabilities $1 - (1/n)$ and $(1/n)$. The exact expected value of x_n is 1 for all n, which is not the probability limit. Indeed, if we let $\text{Prob}(x_n = n^2) = (1/n)$ instead, the mean of the distribution explodes, but the probability limit is still zero. Again, the point $x_n = n^2$ becomes ever more extreme but, at the same time, becomes ever less likely. The conditions for convergence in mean square are usually easier to verify than those for the more general form. Fortunately, we shall rarely encounter circumstances in which it will be necessary to show convergence in probability in which we cannot rely upon convergence in mean square. Our most frequent use of this concept will be in formulating consistent estimators.

Definition. An estimator $\hat{\theta}$ of a parameter θ is a **consistent** estimator of θ if and only if

$$\text{plim } \hat{\theta} = \theta. \tag{4-19}$$

THEOREM 4.3: *The mean of a random sample from* any *population with finite mean μ and finite variance σ^2 is a consistent estimator of μ.*

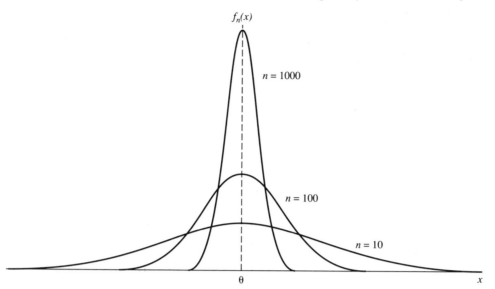

FIGURE 4.4   Quadratic convergence to a constant, θ.

Proof: $E[\bar{x}] = \mu$ and $\text{Var}[\bar{x}] = \sigma^2/n$. Therefore, $\bar{x}$ converges in mean square to μ, or plim $\bar{x} = \mu$.

This theorem is broader than it might appear at first.

Corollary. In random sampling, for any function $g(x)$, if $E[g(x)]$ and $\text{Var}[g(x)]$ are finite constants,

$$\text{plim} \frac{1}{n} \sum_i g(x_i) = E[g(x)]. \qquad (4\text{--}20)$$

The proof follows from Theorem 4.3 by defining $y_i = g(x_i)$.

EXAMPLE 4.11 _____

In sampling from a normal distribution with mean μ and variance 1,

$$E[e^x] = e^{\mu + 1/2} \qquad \text{and} \qquad \text{Var}[e^x] = e^{2\mu + 2} - e^{2\mu + 1}.$$

Hence,

$$\text{plim} \frac{1}{n} \sum_i e^{x_i} = e^{\mu + 1/2}.$$

A particularly convenient result is the

SLUTSKY THEOREM: *For a continuous function $g(x_n)$ that is not a function of n,*

$$\text{plim}\, g(x_n) = g(\text{plim}\, x_n). \qquad (4\text{--}21)$$

The generalization to a function of several random variables is direct, as illustrated in the next example.

EXAMPLE 4.12 _____

In random sampling from a population with mean μ and variance σ^2, the exact expected value of $\bar{x}^2/s^2$ will be difficult, if not impossible, to derive. But, by the Slutsky theorem,

$$\text{plim}\ \frac{\bar{x}^2}{s^2} = \frac{\mu^2}{\sigma^2}.$$

_____

If $\text{plim}\ x_n = c$ and $\text{plim}\ y_n = d$, a few implications of the Slutsky theorem are as follows:

$$\text{plim}(x_n + y_n) = c + d, \tag{4-22}$$

$$\text{plim}\ x_n y_n = cd, \tag{4-23}$$

$$\text{plim}\ \frac{x_n}{y_n} = \frac{c}{d} \qquad \text{as long as } d \neq 0, \tag{4-24}$$

and so on. The Slutsky theorem applies to functions of random vectors and matrices as well. For example, suppose that $\mathbf{W}_n$ is a random matrix (i.e., a matrix whose elements are random variables). Then,

$$\text{If plim}\ \mathbf{W}_n = \mathbf{\Omega},\ \text{plim}\ \mathbf{W}_n^{-1} = \mathbf{\Omega}^{-1}. \tag{4-25}$$

Also,

$$\text{If plim}\ \mathbf{X}_n = \mathbf{A} \text{ and plim}\ \mathbf{Y}_n = \mathbf{B},\ \text{plim}\ \mathbf{X}_n\mathbf{Y}_n = \mathbf{AB}. \tag{4-26}$$

4.4.2. Convergence in Distribution—Limiting Distributions

A second form of convergence is **convergence in distribution.** Let x_n be a sequence of random variables indexed by the sample size, and assume that x_n has cdf $F_n(x)$.

Definition. x_n converges in distribution to a random variable x with cdf $F(x)$ if $\lim_{n \to \infty} |F_n(x) - F(x)| = 0$ at all continuity points of $F(x)$.

Note that this is a statement about the probability distribution associated with x_n; it does not imply that x_n converges at all. To take a trivial example, suppose that the exact distribution of the random variable x_n is

$$\text{Prob}(x_n = 1) = \frac{1}{2} + \frac{1}{n+1},$$

$$\text{Prob}(x_n = 2) = \frac{1}{2} - \frac{1}{n+1}.$$

As n increases without bound, the two probabilities converge to $\frac{1}{2}$, but x_n obviously does not converge to a constant.

Definition. If x_n converges in distribution to x, where $F(x)$ is the cdf of x, then $F(x)$ is the **limiting distribution** of x. This is written

$$x_n \xrightarrow{d} x.$$

The limiting distribution is often given in terms of the pdf, or simply the parametric family. For example, "the limiting distribution of x_n is standard normal."

EXAMPLE 4.13

Consider a sample of size n from a standard normal distribution. A familiar inference problem is the test of the hypothesis that the population mean is zero. The test statistic usually used is the t statistic:

$$t_{n-1} = \frac{\bar{x}}{s/\sqrt{n}},$$

where

$$s^2 = \frac{\Sigma_i(x_i - \bar{x})^2}{n - 1}.$$

The exact distribution of the random variable t_{n-1} is t with $n - 1$ degrees of freedom. The density is different for every n:

$$f(t_{n-1}) = \frac{\Gamma(n/2)}{\Gamma((n-1)/2)}((n-1)\pi)^{-1/2}\left[1 + \frac{t_{n-1}^2}{n-1}\right]^{-n/2} \qquad (4\text{-}27)$$

as is the cdf, $F_{n-1}(t) = \int_{-\infty}^{t} f_{n-1}(x)dx$. This distribution has mean 0 and variance $(n - 1)/(n - 3)$. As n grows to infinity, t_{n-1} converges to the standard normal, which is written

$$t_{n-1} \overset{d}{\to} N[0, 1].$$

Definition. The **limiting mean** and **variance** of a random variable are the mean and variance of the limiting distribution, assuming that the limiting distribution and its moments exist.

For the random variable with $t[n]$ distribution, the exact mean and variance are 0 and $n/(n - 2)$, while the limiting mean and variance are 0 and 1. The example might suggest that the moments of the limiting distribution are the ordinary limits of the moments of the finite sample distributions. This is almost always true. However, it need not be the case. It is possible to construct examples in which the exact moments do not even exist, even though the moments of the limiting distribution are well defined.[4] Even in such cases, we can usually derive the mean and variance of the limiting distribution.

Limiting distributions, like probability limits, can greatly simplify the analysis of a problem. Some results that combine the two concepts are as follows:[5]

1. If $x_n \overset{d}{\to} x$ and   plim $y_n = c$, then

$$x_n y_n \overset{d}{\to} cx, \qquad (4\text{-}28)$$

which means that the limiting distribution of $x_n y_n$ is the distribution of cx:

$$x_n + y_n \overset{d}{\to} x + c, \qquad (4\text{-}29)$$

$$\frac{x_n}{y_n} \overset{d}{\to} \frac{x}{c} \quad \text{if } c \neq 0. \qquad (4\text{-}30)$$

2. If $x_n \overset{d}{\to} x$ and $g(x_n)$ is a continuous function,

$$g(x_n) \overset{d}{\to} g(x). \qquad (4\text{-}31)$$

---

[4] See, for example, Maddala (1977, p. 150).

[5] For proofs and further discussion, see, for example, Greenberg and Webster (1983).

The second of these results is analogous to the Slutsky theorem for probability limits. For an example, consider the t_n random variable discussed earlier. The *exact* distribution of t_n^2 is $F[1, n]$. But as n increases, t_n converges to a standard normal variable. According to the previous result, the limiting distribution of t_n^2 will be that of the square of a standard normal, which is chi-squared with one degree of freedom. We conclude, therefore, that

$$F[1, n] \xrightarrow{d} \text{chi-squared}(1). \qquad (4\text{–}32)$$

We encountered this result in our earlier discussion of limiting forms of the standard normal family of distributions.

3. A result that combines convergence in distribution and in probability is

> If y_n has a limiting distribution and $\text{plim}(x_n - y_n) = 0$,
> then x_n has the same limiting distribution as y_n.

It may be possible to establish this property by using mean-square convergence.[6]

We are ultimately interested in finding a way to describe the statistical properties of estimators when their exact distributions are unknown. The concepts of consistency and convergence in probability are obviously important. But the theory of limiting distributions given earlier is not yet adequate. We rarely deal with estimators that are not consistent for something, though perhaps not always the parameter we are trying to estimate. As such, if

$$\text{plim } \hat{\theta}_n = \theta, \qquad \text{then} \qquad \hat{\theta}_n \xrightarrow{d} \theta.$$

That is, the limiting distribution of $\hat{\theta}_n$ is a spike. This is not very informative, nor is it at all what we have in mind when we speak of the statistical properties of an estimator. (To endow our finite sample estimator, $\hat{\theta}_n$, with the zero sampling variance of the spike at θ would be optimistic in the extreme.)

As an intermediate step, then, to a more reasonable description of the statistical properties of an estimator, we use a **stabilizing transformation** of the random variable to one that does have a well-defined limiting distribution. To jump to the most common application, whereas

$$\text{plim } \hat{\theta}_n = \theta,$$

we often find that

$$z = \sqrt{n}\,(\hat{\theta} - \theta) \xrightarrow{d} f(z),$$

where $f(z)$ is a well-defined distribution with a mean and a positive variance. The single most important theorem in econometrics provides an application of this proposition.

CENTRAL LIMIT THEOREM: *If $x_1, \ldots, x_n$ are a random sample from any probability distribution with finite mean μ and finite variance σ^2 and $\bar{x}_n = (1/n)\Sigma_i x_i$,*

$$\sqrt{n}\,(\bar{x}_n - \mu) \xrightarrow{d} N[0, \sigma^2].$$

Notice that the central limit theorem holds regardless of the form of the parent distribution. For a striking example, return to Figure 4.2. The distribution from which the data were drawn in that figure does not even remotely resemble a normal distribution. How-

---

[6]Lucid discussion of this topic may be found in Greenberg and Webster (1983, pp. 12–13).

ever, in samples of only four observations, the force of the central limit theorem is clearly visible in the sampling distribution of the means.

The preceding is one of several forms of this extremely powerful result.[7] For our purposes, an important extension allows us to relax the assumption of equal variances. Let μ be the common mean of the x's, but suppose that they are drawn from distributions with different positive variances. Let

$$\bar{\sigma}_n^2 = \frac{1}{n} (\sigma_1^2 + \sigma_2^2 + \cdots).$$

As long as no single term dominates the average variance and the average converges to a finite constant, then

$$\sqrt{n} \, (\bar{x}_n - \mu) \xrightarrow{d} N[0, \bar{\sigma}^2] \qquad \text{where} \quad \bar{\sigma}^2 = \lim_{n \to \infty} \bar{\sigma}_n^2 .^{[8]}$$

In practical terms, the theorem states that sums of random variables, regardless of their form, will tend to be normally distributed. Since nearly all of the estimators we construct in econometrics fall under the purview of the central limit theorem, it is obviously an important result.

For later purposes (e.g., in Chapter 10), we will require multivariate versions of these theorems. Proofs of the following may be found, for example, in Greenberg and Webster (1983).

THEOREM 4.4. LINDBERG–LEVY CENTRAL LIMIT THEOREM: *If* $x_1, \ldots, x_n$ *are a random sample from a multivariate distribution with finite mean vector* μ *and finite positive definite covariance matrix,* $\mathbf{Q}$, *then*

$$\sqrt{n} \, (\bar{\mathbf{x}}_n - \mu) \xrightarrow{d} N[\mathbf{0}, \mathbf{Q}],$$

where

$$\bar{\mathbf{x}}_n = \frac{1}{n} \sum_i \mathbf{x}_i.$$

The extension of this result to unequal covariance matrices requires some intricate mathematics. The following is an informal statement of the relevant conditions. Further discussion and references appear in Fomby et al. (1984) and Greenberg and Webster (1983).

LINDBERG–FELLER CENTRAL LIMIT THEOREM: *Suppose that* $x_1, \ldots, x_n$ *are a sample of random vectors such that*

$$E[\mathbf{x}_i] = \mu,$$

$$\text{Var}[\mathbf{x}_i] = \mathbf{Q}_i,$$

and all third moments of the multivariate distribution are finite. Let

$$\bar{\mathbf{Q}}_n = \frac{1}{n} \sum_i \mathbf{Q}_i.$$

[7] See, for example, Greenberg and Webster (1983).

[8] The result also requires that the third moment of x_i be finite. See Greenberg and Webster (1983).

We assume that

$$\lim_{n\to\infty} \overline{\mathbf{Q}}_n = \mathbf{Q},$$

where $\mathbf{Q}$ is a positive definite matrix, and that for every i,

$$\lim_{n\to\infty} (n\overline{\mathbf{Q}}_n^{-1})\mathbf{Q}_i = \lim_{n\to\infty} \left(\sum_i \mathbf{Q}_i\right)^{-1} \mathbf{Q}_i = \mathbf{0}.$$

The second assumption states that individual components of the sum must diminish in significance. (There is also an implicit assumption that the sum of matrices is nonsingular. Since the limiting matrix is nonsingular, the assumption must hold for large enough n, which is all that concerns us here.) With these in place, the result is

$$\sqrt{n}\,(\overline{\mathbf{x}}_n - \boldsymbol{\mu}) \xrightarrow{d} N[\mathbf{0},\,\mathbf{Q}].$$

4.4.3. Asymptotic Distributions

The theory of limiting distributions is only a means to an end. We are interested in the behavior of the estimators themselves. The limiting distributions obtained through the central limit theorem all involve unknown parameters, generally the ones we are trying to estimate. Moreover, our samples are always finite. Thus, we depart from the limiting distributions to derive the asymptotic distributions of the estimators.

Definition. An **asymptotic distribution** is a distribution that is used to approximate the true finite sample distribution of a random variable.

By far the most common means of formulating an asymptotic distribution (at least by econometricians) is to construct it from the known limiting distribution of a function of the random variable. If

$$\frac{\sqrt{n}\,(\overline{x}_n - \mu)}{\sigma} \xrightarrow{d} N[0,\,1], \tag{4-33}$$

then approximately, or asymptotically,

$$\overline{x}_n \sim N\left[\mu,\,\frac{\sigma^2}{n}\right],$$

which we write

$$\overline{x}_n \xrightarrow{a} N\left[\mu,\,\frac{\sigma^2}{n}\right]. \tag{4-34}$$

The statement that $\overline{x}_n$ is asymptotically normally distributed with mean μ and variance σ^2/n says only that this normal distribution provides an approximation to the true distribution, not that the true distribution is exactly normal.

EXAMPLE 4.14 _____

In sampling from an exponential distribution with parameter θ, the *exact* distribution of $\overline{x}$ is that of $\theta/(2n)$ times a chi-squared variable with $2n$ degrees of freedom. The *asymptotic* distribution is $N[\theta,\,\theta^2/n]$. The exact and asymptotic distributions are shown in Figure 4.5 for the case of $\theta = 1$ and $n = 16$.

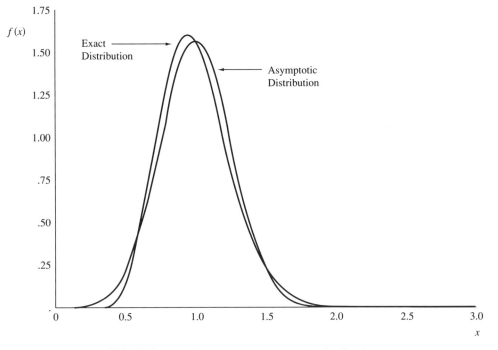

FIGURE 4.5   True versus asymptotic distribution.

Extending the definition, suppose that $\hat{\boldsymbol{\theta}}$ is an estimate of the parameter vector $\boldsymbol{\theta}$. The asymptotic distribution of the vector $\hat{\boldsymbol{\theta}}$ is obtained from the limiting distribution:

$$\sqrt{n}\,(\hat{\boldsymbol{\theta}} - \boldsymbol{\theta}) \xrightarrow{d} N[\mathbf{0}, \mathbf{V}] \qquad (4\text{--}35)$$

implies that

$$\hat{\boldsymbol{\theta}} \xrightarrow{a} N\left[\boldsymbol{\theta}, \frac{1}{n}\,\mathbf{V}\right]. \qquad (4\text{--}36)$$

This is read "$\hat{\boldsymbol{\theta}}$ is asymptotically normally distributed, with mean vector $\boldsymbol{\theta}$ and covariance matrix $(1/n)\mathbf{V}$." The covariance matrix of the asymptotic distribution is the **asymptotic covariance matrix** and is denoted

$$\text{Asy.Var}[\hat{\boldsymbol{\theta}}] = \frac{1}{n}\mathbf{V}.$$

Note, once again, the logic used to reach the result; (4–35) holds exactly as $n \to \infty$. We assume that it holds approximately for finite n, which leads to (4–36).

Definition. An estimator $\hat{\boldsymbol{\theta}}$ is **asymptotically normal** if (4–35) holds. The estimator is **asymptotically efficient** if the variance matrix of any other consistent, asymptotically normally distributed estimator exceeds $(1/n)\mathbf{V}$ by a nonnegative definite matrix.

For most estimation problems, these are the criteria used to choose an estimator.

EXAMPLE 4.15 _____

In sampling from a normal distribution with mean μ and variance σ^2, both the mean and the median of the sample are consistent estimators of μ. Since the limiting distributions of both estimators are spikes at μ, they can only be compared on the basis of their asymptotic properties. The necessary results are

$$\bar{x} \overset{a}{\rightarrow} N\left[\mu, \frac{\sigma^2}{n}\right] \quad \text{and} \quad M \overset{a}{\rightarrow} N\left[\mu, \frac{\pi\sigma^2}{2n}\right].$$

Therefore, the mean is more efficient by a factor of $\pi/2$.

4.4.4. Asymptotic Distribution of a Nonlinear Function

At several points in Chapter 3, we used a linear Taylor series approximation to analyze the distribution and moments of a random variable. We are now able to justify this usage.

THEOREM 4.5: *If $\sqrt{n}(\hat{\theta} - \theta) \overset{d}{\rightarrow} N[0, \sigma^2]$, and if $g(\theta)$ is a continuous function,*

$$\sqrt{n}(g(\hat{\theta}) - g(\theta)) \overset{d}{\rightarrow} N[0, \{g'(\theta)\}^2\sigma^2] \tag{4–37}$$

and

$$g(\hat{\theta}) \overset{a}{\rightarrow} N\left[g(\theta), \frac{\{g'(\theta)\}^2\sigma^2}{n}\right].$$

Notice that the mean and variance of the asymptotic distribution are the mean and variance of the linear approximation:

$$g(\hat{\theta}) \simeq g(\theta) + g'(\theta)(\hat{\theta} - \theta). \tag{4–38}$$

The generalization to a multivariate setting is direct, as the following example illustrates.

EXAMPLE 4.16

Suppose that b and t are estimates of parameters β and θ, such that

$$\begin{bmatrix} b \\ t \end{bmatrix} \overset{a}{\rightarrow} N\left[\begin{bmatrix} \beta \\ \theta \end{bmatrix}, \begin{bmatrix} \sigma_{\beta\beta} & \sigma_{\beta\theta} \\ \sigma_{\theta\beta} & \sigma_{\theta\theta} \end{bmatrix}\right].$$

Find the asymptotic distribution of $c = b/(1 - t)$. Let $\gamma = \beta/(1 - \theta)$. By the Slutsky theorem, c is consistent for γ. We shall require

$$\frac{\partial\gamma}{\partial\beta} = \frac{1}{1 - \theta} = \gamma_\beta$$

and

$$\frac{\partial\gamma}{\partial\theta} = \frac{\beta}{(1 - \theta)^2} = \gamma_\theta.$$

Let Σ be the 2×2 asymptotic covariance matrix given previously. Then, the asymptotic variance of c is

$$(\gamma_\beta \quad \gamma_\theta)\Sigma\begin{bmatrix} \gamma_\beta \\ \gamma_\theta \end{bmatrix} = \gamma_\beta^2\sigma_{\beta\beta} + \gamma_\theta^2\sigma_{\theta\theta} + 2\gamma_\beta\gamma_\theta\sigma_{\beta\theta}.$$

This is the variance of the linear approximation:

$$\hat{\gamma} \simeq \gamma + \gamma_\beta(b - \beta) + \gamma_\theta(t - \theta).$$

4.4.5. Asymptotic Expectations

The asymptotic mean and variance of a random variable are usually the mean and variance of the asymptotic distribution. Thus, for an estimator with the limiting distribution defined in

$$\sqrt{n}(\hat{\boldsymbol{\theta}} - \boldsymbol{\theta}) \xrightarrow{d} N[\mathbf{0}, \mathbf{V}],$$

the asymptotic expectation is $\boldsymbol{\theta}$ and the asymptotic variance is $(1/n)\mathbf{V}$. This implies, among other things, that the estimator is "asymptotically unbiased."

At the risk of clouding the issue a bit, it is necessary to reconsider one aspect of the previous description. We have deliberately avoided the use of consistency in spite of the fact that, in most instances, that is what we have in mind. The description thus far might suggest that consistency and asymptotic unbiasedness are the same. Unfortunately (because it is a source of some confusion), they are not. They are if the estimator is consistent and asymptotically normally distributed, or CAN. However, they may differ in other settings. There are at least three possible definitions of asymptotic unbiasedness:

1. The mean of the limiting distribution of $\sqrt{n}(\hat{\theta} - \theta)$ is 0.
2. $\mathrm{Lim}_{n\to\infty} E[\hat{\theta}] = \theta$.
3. Plim $\hat{\theta} = \theta$.

In most cases encountered in practice, the estimator in hand will have all three properties, so there is no ambiguity. However, it is not difficult to construct cases in which the left-hand sides of all three definitions are different.[9] There is no general agreement among authors as to the precise meaning of asymptotic unbiasedness, perhaps because the term is misleading at the outset; *asymptotic* refers to an approximation, while *unbiasedness* is an exact result.[10] Nonetheless, the majority view seems to be that (2) is the proper definition of asymptotic unbiasedness.[11] Note, though, that this definition relies upon quantities that are generally unknown and that may not exist.

A similar problem arises in the definition of the asymptotic variance of an estimator. One common definition is

$$\text{Asy. Var}[\hat{\theta}] = \frac{1}{n} \lim_{n\to\infty} E\left[\left\{\sqrt{n}\left(\hat{\theta} - \lim_{n\to\infty} E[\hat{\theta}]\right)\right\}^2\right].[12] \qquad (4\text{--}39)$$

This is a **leading term approximation,** and it will be sufficient for nearly all applications. Note, however, that like definition (2) of asymptotic unbiasedness, it relies on unknown and possibly nonexistent quantities.

EXAMPLE 4.17 ─────────────────────────────

In any population, the exact expected value and variance of the variance estimator

$$m_2 = \frac{1}{n} \sum_i (x_i - \bar{x})^2 \qquad (4\text{--}40)$$

---

[9] See, for example, Maddala (1977, p. 150).

[10] See, for example, Theil (1971, p. 377).

[11] Many studies of estimators analyze the "asymptotic bias" of, say, $\hat{\theta}$ as an estimator of a parameter, θ. In most cases, the quantity of interest is actually plim$[\hat{\theta} - \theta]$. See, for example, Greene (1980b) and another example in Johnston (1984, p. 312).

[12] Kmenta (1986, p. 165).

are

$$E[m_2] = \frac{(n-1)\sigma^2}{n} \tag{4-41}$$

and

$$\text{Var}[m_2] = \frac{\mu_4 - \sigma^4}{n} - \frac{2(\mu_4 - 2\sigma^4)}{n^2} + \frac{\mu_4 - 3\sigma^4}{n^3}, \tag{4-42}$$

where

$$\mu_4 = E[(x-\mu)^4].^{13}$$

The leading term approximation would be

$$\text{Asy. Var}[m_2] = \frac{\mu_4 - \sigma^4}{n}.$$

The formal definition given in (4–39) is adequate if the exact variance is "of order $1/n$."

Definition. c_n is of order $1/n$, denoted $O(1/n)$, if plim nc_n is a nonzero constant.

Definition. c_n is of order less than $1/n$, denoted $o(1/n)$, if plim nc_n equals 0.

For example, the variance of the sample minimum in Example 4.3 is $o(1/n)$ because n times this variance still converges to zero. In sampling from an exponential distribution, the variance of the sample minimum is $O(1/n^2)$. If we use the definition just given, the asymptotic variance is 0, which would be a poor approximation to the variance in a finite sample.

The point of this discussion is to emphasize the need for care and precision in formulating asymptotic distributions. The central limit theorem and the surrounding results allow the simple formulation of the correct asymptotic distribution in the vast majority of cases encountered in econometrics. However, there are relatively common situations, particularly in theoretical econometrics, in which some caution is warranted.

4.5. Efficient Estimation—Maximum Likelihood

The principle of **maximum likelihood** provides a means of choosing an asymptotically efficient estimator for a parameter or a set of parameters. The logic of the technique is best illustrated in the setting of a discrete distribution. Consider a random sample of 10 observations from a Poisson distribution: 5, 0, 1, 1, 0, 3, 2, 3, 4, and 1. The density for each observation is

$$f(x_i, \theta) = \frac{e^{-\theta}\theta^{x_i}}{x_i!}.$$

Since the observations are independent, their joint density, which was identified earlier as the **likelihood** for the sample, is

---

[13] A proof appears in Goldberger (1964, pp. 97–99).

$$f(x_{i1}, x_2, \ldots, x_{10} | \theta) = \Pi_{i=1}^{10} f(x_i, \theta)$$

$$= \frac{e^{-10\theta}\theta^{\Sigma_i x_i}}{\Pi x_i!}$$

$$= \frac{e^{-10\theta}\theta^{20}}{207,360}.$$

The last line gives the probability of observing *this particular sample*, assuming that a Poisson distribution with as yet unknown parameter θ generated the data. What value of θ would make this sample most probable? Figure 4.6 plots this function for various values of θ. It has a single mode at $\theta = 2$, which would be the maximum likelihood estimate, or MLE, of θ.

Consider maximizing the function directly. Since the log function is monotonically increasing and easier to work with, we usually maximize $\ln L(\theta)$ instead:

$$\ln L(\theta) = -10\theta + 20 \ln \theta - 12.242,$$

$$\frac{d \ln L(\theta)}{d\theta} = -10 + \frac{20}{\theta} = 0 \Rightarrow \hat{\theta} = 2,$$

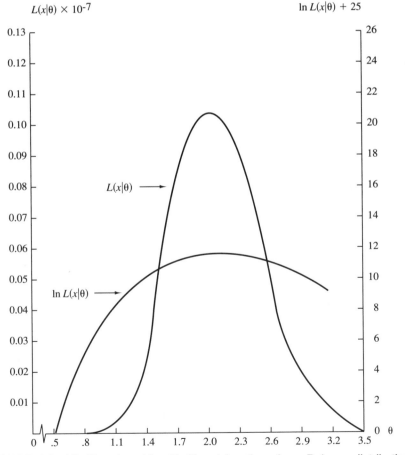

FIGURE 4.6 Likelihood and log likelihood functions for a Poisson distribution.

and

$$\frac{d^2 \ln L(\theta)}{d\theta^2} = \frac{-20}{\theta^2} < 0 \Rightarrow \text{ this is a maximum.}$$

Of course, the solution is the same as before. Figure 4.6 also plots the log of L to illustrate the result.

In a continuous distribution, the analogy to the probability of observing the given sample is not exact, since a particular sample has probability zero. However, the principle is the same for either. The joint density of the n observations, which may be univariate (x_i) or multivariate ($\mathbf{x}_i$), is the product of the individual densities. This joint density is the **likelihood function,** defined as a function of the unknown parameter vector, $\boldsymbol{\theta}$:

$$f(\mathbf{x}_1, \ldots, \mathbf{x}_n, \boldsymbol{\theta}) = \Pi_i f(\mathbf{x}_i, \boldsymbol{\theta})$$
$$= L(\boldsymbol{\theta} | \mathbf{X}), \tag{4–43}$$

where $\mathbf{X}$ is used to indicate the sample data. It is usually simpler to work with the log of the likelihood function:

$$\ln L(\boldsymbol{\theta} | \mathbf{X}) = \sum_i \ln f(\mathbf{x}_i, \boldsymbol{\theta}). \tag{4–44}$$

The values of the parameters that maximize this function are the maximum likelihood estimates, generally denoted $\hat{\boldsymbol{\theta}}$. Since the logarithm is a monotonic function, the values that maximize L are the same as those that maximize $\ln L$. The likelihood function and its logarithm, evaluated at $\hat{\boldsymbol{\theta}}$, are usually denoted $\hat{L}$ and $\ln \hat{L}$, respectively. The necessary condition for maximizing $\ln L(\boldsymbol{\theta})$ is

$$\frac{\partial \ln L(\boldsymbol{\theta})}{\partial \boldsymbol{\theta}} = \mathbf{0}, \tag{4–45}$$

which is called the **likelihood equation.**

EXAMPLE 4.18 _____

In sampling from a Poisson population,

$$\ln L(\theta) = -n\theta + (\ln \theta) \sum_i x_i - \sum_i \ln (x_i!),$$

$$\frac{d \ln L(\theta)}{d\theta} = -n + \frac{1}{\theta} \sum_i x_i = 0 \Rightarrow \hat{\theta} = \bar{x}.$$

EXAMPLE 4.19 _____

In sampling from a normal distribution with mean μ and variance σ^2, the log-likelihood function and the likelihood equations for μ and σ^2 are

$$\ln L(\mu, \sigma^2) = -\frac{n}{2} \ln (2\pi) - \frac{n}{2} \ln \sigma^2 - \frac{1}{2} \sum_i \left[\frac{(x_i - \mu)^2}{\sigma^2} \right], \tag{4–46}$$

$$\frac{\partial \ln L}{\partial \mu} = \frac{1}{\sigma^2} \sum_i (x_i - \mu) = 0, \tag{4–47}$$

and

$$\frac{\partial \ln L}{\partial \sigma^2} = -\frac{n}{2\sigma^2} + \frac{1}{2\sigma^4} \sum_i (x_i - \mu)^2 = 0. \qquad (4\text{--}48)$$

To solve the likelihood equations, multiply (4–47) by σ^2 and solve for $\hat{\mu}$; then insert this solution in (4–48) and solve for σ^2. The solutions are

$$\hat{\mu} = \frac{1}{n} \sum_i x_i = \bar{x} \qquad (4\text{--}49)$$

and

$$\hat{\sigma}^2 = \frac{1}{n} \sum_i (x_i - \bar{x})^2.$$

Note that this is the biased estimator discussed in Example 4.4. MLEs are consistent but not necessarily unbiased.

EXAMPLE 4.20. Multivariate Normal Mean Vector

Consider, finally, sampling from a multivariate normal distribution with mean vector $\boldsymbol{\mu} = (\mu_1, \mu_2, \ldots, \mu_M)$ and variance matrix $\sigma^2 \mathbf{I}$. (The M random variables each have a different mean but a common variance, σ^2, and they are uncorrelated.) The sample consists of n multivariate observations, $\mathbf{x}_1, \ldots, \mathbf{x}_n$. The density for each observation, from (3–95), is

$$f(\mathbf{x}_i) = (2\pi)^{-M/2} |\sigma^2 \mathbf{I}|^{-1/2} e^{-1/2(\mathbf{x}_i - \boldsymbol{\mu})'[\sigma^2 \mathbf{I}]^{-1}(\mathbf{x}_i - \boldsymbol{\mu})}$$

$$= (2\pi)^{-M/2} (\sigma^2)^{-M/2} e^{-(1/2\sigma^2)(\mathbf{x}_i - \boldsymbol{\mu})'(\mathbf{x}_i - \boldsymbol{\mu})}.$$

Taking logs and summing over the sample gives the log-likelihood for n observations:

$$\ln L = -\frac{nM}{2} \ln (2\pi) - \frac{nM}{2} \ln \sigma^2 - \frac{1}{2\sigma^2} \sum_i (\mathbf{x}_i - \boldsymbol{\mu})'(\mathbf{x}_i - \boldsymbol{\mu}).$$

To obtain the maximum likelihood estimators, we require

$$\frac{\partial \ln L}{\partial \boldsymbol{\mu}} = \frac{1}{\sigma^2} \sum_i (\mathbf{x}_i - \boldsymbol{\mu}) = \mathbf{0}$$

and

$$\frac{\partial \ln L}{\partial \sigma^2} = -\frac{nM}{2\sigma^2} + \frac{1}{2\sigma^4} \sum_i (\mathbf{x}_i - \boldsymbol{\mu})'(\mathbf{x}_i - \boldsymbol{\mu}).$$

Solving the first set of equations gives, as might be expected,

$$\hat{\mu}_i = \bar{x}_i.$$

Inserting this solution in the second condition gives

$$\hat{\sigma}^2 = \frac{\Sigma_i \Sigma_j (x_{ij} - \bar{x}_j)^2}{nM}.$$

4.5.1. Properties of Maximum Likelihood Estimators

Maximum likelihood estimators are most attractive because of their large-sample or a-symptotic properties. If we assume that the regularity conditions stated earlier are met by $f(\mathbf{x}, \boldsymbol{\theta})$,[14] the maximum likelihood estimator will have the following **asymptotic properties:**

1. It is consistent:[15]

$$\text{plim } \hat{\boldsymbol{\theta}}_{\text{ML}} = \boldsymbol{\theta}.$$

2. It is asymptotically normally distributed:[16]

$$\hat{\boldsymbol{\theta}} \xrightarrow{a} N[\boldsymbol{\theta}, \{\mathbf{I}(\boldsymbol{\theta})\}^{-1}].$$

3. It is asymptotically efficient and achieves the Cramér-Rao lower bound for consistent estimators:

$$\text{Asy. Var}[\hat{\boldsymbol{\theta}}_{\text{ML}}] = \left\{ -E\left[\frac{\partial^2 \ln L(\boldsymbol{\theta})}{\partial \boldsymbol{\theta}\, \partial \boldsymbol{\theta}'} \right] \right\}^{-1}$$

$$= \left\{ E\left[\left(\frac{\partial \ln L(\boldsymbol{\theta})}{\partial \boldsymbol{\theta}} \right) \left(\frac{\partial \ln L(\boldsymbol{\theta})}{\partial \boldsymbol{\theta}'} \right) \right] \right\}^{-1}.$$

These three properties explain the prevalence of the maximum likelihood technique in econometrics. The second one greatly facilitates hypothesis testing and the construction of interval estimates. The third one is a particularly powerful result. The MLE has the minimum variance achievable by a consistent estimator. It is important to note, however, that these are asymptotic properties. The finite sample properties of the MLE are usually unknown. When they are known, we sometimes find that the MLE is not the best estimator in a small sample.

EXAMPLE 4.21 _____

For the likelihood function in Example 4.20, the second derivatives are

$$\frac{\partial^2 \ln L}{\partial \boldsymbol{\mu}\, \partial \boldsymbol{\mu}'} = -\frac{n}{\sigma^2}\mathbf{I},$$

$$\frac{\partial^2 \ln L}{\partial (\sigma^2)^2} = \frac{nM}{2\sigma^4} - \frac{1}{\sigma^6} \sum_i (\mathbf{x}_i - \boldsymbol{\mu})'(\mathbf{x}_i - \boldsymbol{\mu}),$$

$$\frac{\partial^2 \ln L}{\partial \boldsymbol{\mu}\, \partial \sigma^2} = -\frac{1}{\sigma^4} \sum_i (\mathbf{x}_i - \boldsymbol{\mu}).$$

For the asymptotic variance of the maximum likelihood estimator, we need the expectations of these derivatives. The first is nonstochastic, and the third has expectation **0**, as $E[\mathbf{x}_i] = \boldsymbol{\mu}.$ That leaves the second, which you can verify has expectation $-nM/(2\sigma^4)$ because each of the n terms $(\mathbf{x}_i - \boldsymbol{\mu})'(\mathbf{x}_i - \boldsymbol{\mu})$ has expected value $M\sigma^2$. Collecting these

---

[14] Discussions of these conditions can be found in Theil (1971) and Greenberg and Webster (1983).

[15] It may, however, be biased. For example, the MLE of σ^2 in a normal distribution is biased downward. See (4–49) and Example 4.4.

[16] A proof of this, which is based on the central limit theorem, may be found in Theil (1971) or in Norden (1972). Another extensive source on the theory of maximum likelihood estimation is Stuart and Ord (1989).

in the information matrix, reversing the sign, and inverting the matrix gives the asymptotic covariance matrix for the maximum likelihood estimators:

$$\left\{-E\left[\frac{\partial^2 \ln L}{\partial \boldsymbol{\theta} \, \partial \boldsymbol{\theta}'}\right]\right\}^{-1} = \begin{bmatrix} \sigma^2 \mathbf{I}/n & \mathbf{0} \\ \mathbf{0}' & 2\sigma^4/(nM) \end{bmatrix}.$$

The asymptotic covariance matrix for estimating a single mean and the variance of a normal distribution is given in (4–14) in Example 4.9. Notice that the preceding expression is analogous for the means but differs in the divisor for the variance. In this case, instead of one estimator of σ^2, we have M, which explains the difference.

Finally, maximum likelihood estimators have a very useful feature.

Invariance. If $\hat{\boldsymbol{\theta}}_{\text{ML}}$ is the maximum likelihood estimate of $\boldsymbol{\theta}$ and if $g(\boldsymbol{\theta})$ is a continuous function, the maximum likelihood estimate of $g(\boldsymbol{\theta})$ is $g(\hat{\boldsymbol{\theta}}_{\text{ML}})$.

For the asymptotic distribution of $g(\hat{\boldsymbol{\theta}})$, we refer to our earlier general set of results. The invariance property has two useful practical implications. First, if estimates have already been obtained for a set of parameters, and estimates are desired for a function of them, there is no need to reestimate the model. For example, to estimate σ from a normal distribution, we may simply use the square root of $\hat{\sigma}^2$. Second, the invariance principle implies that we are free to **reparameterize** a likelihood function in any way we like, which may simplify estimation. For an application, see Section 22.3.3.

4.5.2. Estimating the Variance of the Maximum Likelihood Estimator

The asymptotic covariance matrix of the maximum likelihood estimator is a matrix of parameters that must be estimated. (That is, it is a function of the $\boldsymbol{\theta}$ that is being estimated.) If the form of the expected values of the second derivatives of the log likelihood is known,

$$[\mathbf{I}(\boldsymbol{\theta})]^{-1} = \left\{-E\left[\frac{\partial^2 \ln L(\boldsymbol{\theta})}{\partial \boldsymbol{\theta} \, \partial \boldsymbol{\theta}'}\right]\right\}^{-1} \tag{4–50}$$

can be evaluated at $\hat{\boldsymbol{\theta}}$ to estimate the variance matrix for the MLE. This estimator will rarely be available. The second derivatives of the log likelihood will almost always be complicated nonlinear functions of the data, whose exact expected values will be unknown. There are, however, two alternatives. A second estimator is

$$[\hat{\mathbf{I}}(\hat{\boldsymbol{\theta}})]^{-1} = \left(-\frac{\partial^2 \ln L(\hat{\boldsymbol{\theta}})}{\partial \hat{\boldsymbol{\theta}} \, \partial \hat{\boldsymbol{\theta}}'}\right)^{-1}. \tag{4–51}$$

This is computed simply by evaluating the actual (not expected) second derivatives matrix of the log-likelihood function at the maximum likelihood estimates. It is straightforward to show that this amounts to estimating the expected second derivatives of the density with the sample mean of this quantity. Result (4–20) can be used to justify the computation. The only shortcoming of this estimator is that the second derivatives can be complicated to derive and program for a computer. A third estimator based on the result that the expected second derivatives matrix is the variance matrix of the first derivatives vector[17] is

$$[\hat{\hat{\mathbf{I}}}(\hat{\boldsymbol{\theta}})]^{-1} = \left[\sum_i \hat{\mathbf{g}}_i \hat{\mathbf{g}}_i'\right]^{-1}, \tag{4–52}$$

---

[17] See, for example, Theil (1971, Chap. 8).

where

$$\hat{\mathbf{g}}_i = \frac{\partial \ln f(\mathbf{x}_i, \hat{\boldsymbol{\theta}})}{\partial \hat{\boldsymbol{\theta}}}.$$

For a single parameter, this is just the reciprocal of the sum of squares of the first derivatives. This estimator is extremely convenient, in most cases, because it does not require any computations beyond those required to solve the likelihood equation.[18]

EXAMPLE 4.22

The sample data in Table 4.1 are generated by a model of the form

$$f(y_i, \beta) = \frac{1}{\beta + x_i} \, e^{-y_i/(\beta + x_i)},$$

where y = income and x = education. To find the maximum likelihood estimate of β, we maximize

$$\ln L(\beta) = -\sum_i \ln(\beta + x_i) - \sum_i \frac{y_i}{\beta + x_i}.$$

The likelihood equation is

$$\frac{\partial \ln L(\beta)}{\partial \beta} = -\sum_i \frac{1}{\beta + x_i} + \sum_i \frac{y_i}{(\beta + x_i)^2} = 0, \qquad (4\text{--}53)$$

which has the solution $\hat{\beta} = 15.60275$. To compute the asymptotic variance of the MLE, we require

$$\frac{\partial^2 \ln L(\beta)}{\partial \beta^2} = \sum_i \frac{1}{(\beta + x_i)^2} - 2\sum_i \frac{y_i}{(\beta + x_i)^3}. \qquad (4\text{--}54)$$

Since $E(y_i) = \beta + x_i$ is known, the exact form of the expected value in (4–54) is known. Inserting $\beta + x_i$ for y_i in (4–54) and taking the reciprocal yields the first variance estimate, 44.255. Simply inserting $\hat{\beta} = 15.60275$ in (4–54) and taking the reciprocal gives the second estimate, 46.164. Finally, by computing the reciprocal of the sum of squares of first derivatives of the densities evaluated at $\hat{\beta}$,

$$[\hat{\hat{I}}(\hat{\beta})]^{-1} = \frac{1}{\sum_i [-1/(\hat{\beta} + x_i) + y_i/(\hat{\beta} + x_i)^2]^2},$$

we obtain the Berndt et al. estimate, 100.512.

None of the three estimators given previously is preferable to the others on statistical grounds; all are asymptotically equivalent. In most cases, the third will be easiest to compute. One caution is in order. As the example illustrates, they can give different results in a finite sample. This is an unavoidable finite sample problem that can, in some cases, lead to different statistical conclusions. The example is a case in point. Using the usual procedures, we would reject the hypothesis that $\beta = 0$ if either of the first two variance estimators were used, but not if the third were used.

[18] It appears to have been advocated first in the econometrics literature in Berndt et al. (1974).

4.6. Consistent Estimation—The Method of Moments[19]

There are situations in which all that is required is a consistent estimator of a parameter; efficiency is secondary. Examples include the correlation coefficient in the AR(1) regression model, the disturbance covariance matrix in a multiple equation model, the correlation coefficient in the sample selection model, and the disturbance variances in some heteroskedastic regressions.

A technique used in many such cases is the **method of moments.** The basis of this method is as follows: In random sampling, a sample statistic will converge in probability to some constant. For example, $(1/n)\Sigma_i x_i^2$ will converge in mean square to the variance plus the square of the mean of the distribution of x_i. This constant will, in turn, be a function of the unknown parameters of the distribution. To estimate K parameters, θ_1, . . . , θ_K, we compute K statistics, m_1, . . . , m_K, whose probability limits are known functions of the parameters. These K moments are equated to the K functions, and the functions are inverted to express the parameters as functions of the moments. The estimators are consistent by virtue of the Slutsky theorem [(4–21) and Theorem 4.3].

This section will develop this technique in some detail, partly to present it in its own right, and partly as a prelude to the discussion of the generalized method of moments, or GMM, estimation technique discussed in Section 13.5. The results in this section have been applied in standard problems in estimating the parameters of distributions. Recent econometric applications have extended the method of moments to problems involving regressions and much more involved models than we will consider here. The extension to GMM estimation is treated in Chapter 13.

4.6.1. Random Sampling and Estimating the Parameters of Distributions

Consider random sampling from a distribution $f(x \mid \theta_1, \ldots, \theta_K)$ with finite moments, $E[x^k]$. The sample consists of n observations, $x_1, \ldots, x_n$. The kth "raw" or **uncentered moment** is

$$m_k' = \frac{1}{n} \sum_i x_i^k.$$

By substituting $z_i = x_i^k$, we obtain the following results: By (3–14) and Theorem 4.1,

$$E[m_k'] = \mu_k' = E[x_i^k]$$

and

$$\mathrm{Var}[m_k'] = \frac{1}{n} \mathrm{Var}[x_i^k] = \frac{1}{n} (\mu_{2k}' - \mu_k'^2).$$

By Theorem 4.3,

$$\mathrm{plim}\ m_k' = \mu_k' = E[x_i^k].$$

Finally, by Theorem 4.4,

$$\sqrt{n}\ (m_k' - \mu_k') \xrightarrow{d} N[0, \mu_{2k}' - \mu_k'^2].$$

---

[19] The material of this section is relatively advanced. It may be skipped without loss of continuity.

By convention,

$$\mu_1' = E[x_i] = \mu.$$

In general, μ_k' will be a function of the underlying parameters. By computing K raw moments and equating them to these functions, we obtain K equations which can be solved to provide estimates of the K unknown parameters.

EXAMPLE 4.23 _____

In random sampling from $N[\mu, \sigma^2]$,

$$\text{plim} \frac{1}{n} \sum_i x_i = \text{plim } m_1' = E[x_i] = \mu$$

and

$$\text{plim} \frac{1}{n} \sum_i x_i^2 = \text{plim } m_2' = \text{Var}[x_i] + \mu^2 = \sigma^2 + \mu^2.$$

Equating the right- and left-hand sides of the probability limits gives moment estimators

$$\hat{\mu} = m_1' = \bar{x}$$

and

$$\hat{\sigma}^2 = m_2' - m_1'^2 = \frac{1}{n} \sum_i (x_i - \bar{x})^2.$$

Note that $\hat{\sigma}^2$ is biased, although both estimators are consistent.

_____

EXAMPLE 4.24 _____

Quandt and Ramsey (1978) analyzed the problem of estimating the parameters of a mixture of normal distributions. Suppose that each observation in a random sample is drawn from one of two different normal distributions. The probability that the observation is drawn from the first distribution, $N[\mu_1, \sigma_1^2]$, is λ and the probability that it is drawn from the second is $(1 - \lambda)$. The density is

$$f(x) = \lambda N[\mu_1, \sigma_1^2] + (1 - \lambda)N[\mu_2, \sigma_2^2], \qquad 0 \le \lambda \le 1$$

$$= \frac{\lambda}{(2\pi\sigma_1^2)^{1/2}} e^{-1/2[(x - \mu_1)/\sigma_1]^2} + \frac{1 - \lambda}{(2\pi\sigma_2^2)^{1/2}} e^{-1/2[(x - \mu_2)/\sigma_2]^2}.$$

The sample mean and second through fifth **central moments,**

$$m_k = \frac{1}{n} \sum_i (x_i - \bar{x})^k, \qquad k = 2, 3, 4, 5,$$

provide five equations in five unknowns that can be solved (via a ninth-order polynomial) for consistent estimators of the five parameters. Note that $m_1 = 0$ and $m_2 = \hat{\sigma}^2$. Because $\bar{x}$ converges in probability to μ, the theorems given above for m_k' as an estimator of μ_k' apply as well to m_k as an estimator of

$$\mu_k = E[(x_i - \mu)^k].$$

Although the moments based on powers of x provide a natural source of information about the parameters, other functions of the data may also be useful. Let $g_k(\cdot)$ be any continuous function not involving the sample size, n, and let

$$\bar{g}_k = \frac{1}{n} \sum_i g_k(x_i), \qquad k = 1, 2, \ldots, K.$$

These are also "moments" of the data. It follows from Theorem 4.3 that

$$\text{plim } \bar{g}_k = E[g_k(x)] = \gamma_k(\theta_1, \ldots, \theta_K).$$

We assume that $\gamma_k(\cdot)$ involves some or all of the parameters of the distribution. With K parameters to be estimated, the K **moment equations,**

$$\bar{g}_1 - \gamma_1(\theta_1, \ldots, \theta_K) = 0$$
$$\vdots$$
$$\bar{g}_K - \gamma_K(\theta_1, \ldots, \theta_K) = 0,$$

provide K equations in K unknowns, $\theta_1, \ldots, \theta_K$. If they are independent, **method of moments estimators** are obtained by solving the system of equations for

$$\hat{\theta}_k = \hat{\theta}_k[\bar{g}_1, \ldots, \bar{g}_K].$$

EXAMPLE 4.24 (Continued) _____

For the mixed normal distribution,

$$E[e^{tx_i}] = \lambda e^{t\mu_1 + t^2 \sigma_1^2/2} + (1 - \lambda)e^{t\mu_2 + t^2 \sigma_2^2/2} = \Lambda_t,$$

where t is any value not necessarily an integer. Quandt and Ramsey suggest choosing five values of t that are not too close together, and using the statistics

$$M_t = \frac{1}{n} \sum_i e^{tx_i}$$

to estimate the parameters. The moment equations are $M_t = \Lambda_t$. They label this the "method of moment generating functions." (See Exercise 27 in Chapter 3.)

_____

As Example 4.24 suggests, there may be more than one set of moments that one can use for estimating the parameters, or there may be more moment equations available than are necessary.

EXAMPLE 4.25 _____

In sampling from the gamma distribution (see Section 3.4.5),

$$f(x) = \frac{\lambda^P}{\Gamma(P)} e^{-\lambda x} x^{P-1}, \qquad x > 0, \quad P > 0, \quad \lambda > 0,$$

$$\text{plim } \frac{1}{n} \sum_i x_i = \frac{P}{\lambda},$$

$$\text{plim } \frac{1}{n} \sum_i x_i^2 = \frac{P(P + 1)}{\lambda^2},$$

$$\text{plim} \frac{1}{n} \sum_i \ln x_i = \frac{\text{d} \ln \Gamma(P)}{\text{d}P} - \ln \lambda = \Psi(P) - \ln \lambda,$$

$$\text{plim} \frac{1}{n} \sum_i \frac{1}{x_i} = \frac{\lambda}{P - 1}.$$

[The functions $\Gamma(P)$ and $\Psi(P)$ are discussed in the appendix to Chapter 3.] Any two of these could be used to estimate λ and P. The set could be expanded, since plim $m'_k = \lambda^{-k}\Gamma(P + k)/\Gamma(P)$ for $k = 1, 2, \ldots$.

In most cases, method of moments estimators are not efficient. The exception is in random sampling from **exponential families** of distributions.

Definition. An exponential (parametric) family of distributions is one whose log-likelihood is of the form

$$\ln L(\boldsymbol{\theta}|\mathbf{X}) = a(\mathbf{X}) + b(\boldsymbol{\theta}) + \sum_j c_j(\mathbf{X})s_j(\boldsymbol{\theta}),$$

where $a(\cdot)$, $b(\cdot)$, $c(\cdot)$, and $s(\cdot)$ are functions. (The members of the "family" are distinguished by the different parameter values.) If the log-likelihood function is of this form, then the functions $c_j(\cdot)$ are called **sufficient statistics.**[20] When sufficient statistics exist, the method of moments estimator(s) will be functions of them. Also, in this case, the method of moments estimators will be the maximum likelihood estimators, so, of course, they will be efficient, at least asymptotically.

EXAMPLE 4.25 (Continued)

The log-likelihood function for the gamma distribution is

$$\ln L = n(P \ln \lambda - \ln \Gamma(P)) - \lambda \sum_i x_i + (P - 1) \sum_i \ln x_i.$$

This is an exponential family with $a(\mathbf{X}) = 0$, $b(\boldsymbol{\theta}) = n(P \ln \lambda - \ln \Gamma(P))$, and two sufficient statistics, $\Sigma_i x_i$ and $\Sigma_i \ln x_i$. The method of moments estimators based on $\Sigma_i x_i$ and $\Sigma_i \ln x_i$ would be the maximum likelihood estimators.

For the income data in Table 4.1, the four moments listed above are

$$\frac{1}{n} \left[\sum_i x_i, \sum_i x_i^2, \sum_i \ln x_i, \sum_i \frac{1}{x_i} \right] = [31.278, 1453.957, 3.221387, 0.0500141]$$

$$= (m'_1, m'_2, m'_*, m'_{-1}).$$

Denote the estimated parameters as $\boldsymbol{\theta} = (P, \lambda)$. The method of moments estimators of P and λ based on pairs of these moments are as follows:

$$\hat{\boldsymbol{\theta}}(m'_1, m'_2) = (2.05682, 0.065759), \qquad \hat{\boldsymbol{\theta}}(m'_1, m'_*) = (2.4106, 0.077707),$$

$$\hat{\boldsymbol{\theta}}(m'_1, m'_{-1}) = (2.7714, 0.088605), \qquad \hat{\boldsymbol{\theta}}(m'_2, m'_*) = (2.2644, 0.071302),$$

$$\hat{\boldsymbol{\theta}}(m'_{-1}, m'_2) = (2.3952, 0.074797), \qquad \hat{\boldsymbol{\theta}}(m'_{-1}, m'_*) = (3.0358, 0.101782).$$

The maximum likelihood estimates are $\hat{\boldsymbol{\theta}}(m'_1, m'_*) = (2.4106, 0.077707)$.

---

[20] Stuart and Ord (1989, pp. 1–29) give a discussion of sufficient statistics and exponential families of distributions.

4.6.2. Computing the Variance of a Method of Moments Estimator

In a few cases, the exact variance of the method of moments estimator can be obtained. For example, in sampling from the normal distribution, the variance of $\hat{\mu}$ is σ^2/n while the variance of $\hat{\sigma}^2$ is $[(n-1)/n]^2 2\sigma^4/(n-1)$. (See Example 4.4.) If sampling is not from the normal distribution, the exact variance of the sample mean will still be σ^2/n, while an asymptotic variance for the moment estimator of the population variance can be based on the leading term in (4–42). But these are particularly simple cases. Method of moments estimators are usually more complicated than simple sums and sums of squares.

EXAMPLE 4.26

Characterizing the "Normality" of a Distribution. Two useful parameters are

$$\theta_1 = \text{skewness coefficient} = \frac{E[(x-\mu)^3]}{(\text{Var}[x])^{3/2}} = \frac{\mu_3}{\sigma^3}$$

and

$$\theta_2 = \text{kurtosis coefficient} = \frac{E[(x-\mu)^4]}{(\text{Var}[x])^2} = \frac{\mu_4}{\sigma^4}.$$

The sample values of $c_1 = m_3/m_2^{3/2}$ and $c_2 = m_4/m_2^2$ are often compared to the population values for the normal distribution, 0 and 3, respectively, to characterize departure from normality. (The quantity $\theta_2 - 3$ is called the "degree of excess"; see Section 10.5.4.) These statistics are based on three central moments (see Example 4.24), m_2, m_3, and m_4. To obtain an asymptotic covariance matrix for $[c_1, c_2]$, we can proceed as follows: First obtain the asymptotic covariance matrix for the three sample moments. Second, use result (3–94) of Section 3.9.3 and Section 4.4.4 on nonlinear functions to obtain the appropriate asymptotic covariance. The following result from Kendall and Stuart (1969, p. 230) will be useful:

$$n\,(\text{Asy.Cov}[m_j, m_k]) = \lim_{n\to\infty} n\text{Cov}[m_j, m_k]$$

$$= \mu_{j+k} - \mu_j\mu_k + jk\mu_2\mu_{j-1}\mu_{k-1} - j\mu_{j-1}\mu_{k+1} - k\mu_{j+1}\mu_{k-1}.$$

Since these are central moments, $m_1 = \mu_1 = 0$. For the six terms for $j, k = 2, 3, 4$, this formula gives

$$\text{Asy.Var}[m_2] = \frac{1}{n}[\mu_4 - \mu_2^2],$$

$$\text{Asy.Var}[m_3] = \frac{1}{n}[\mu_6 - \mu_3^2 - 6\mu_4\mu_2 + 9\mu_2^3],$$

$$\text{Asy.Var}[m_4] = \frac{1}{n}[\mu_8 - \mu_4^2 - 8\mu_5\mu_3 + 16\mu_2\mu_3^2],$$

$$\text{Asy.Cov}[m_2, m_3] = \frac{1}{n}[\mu_5 - 4\mu_3\mu_2],$$

$$\text{Asy.Cov}[m_2, m_4] = \frac{1}{n}[\mu_6 - \mu_2\mu_4 - 4\mu_3^2],$$

$$\text{Asy.Cov}[m_3, m_4] = \frac{1}{n}[\mu_7 - \mu_3\mu_4 + 12\mu_2^2\mu_3 - 3\mu_2\mu_5 - \mu_4\mu_3].$$

We would estimate these with the sample moments $m_2, \ldots, m_8$ and collect them in a 3×3 matrix,

$$\mathbf{V} = \text{Est.Asy.Cov}[m_2, m_3, m_4].$$

The necessary matrix of derivatives is

$$\mathbf{J} = \begin{bmatrix} \partial\theta_1/\partial m_2 & \partial\theta_1/\partial m_3 & \partial\theta_1/\partial m_4 \\ \partial\theta_2/\partial m_2 & \partial\theta_2/\partial m_3 & \partial\theta_2/\partial m_4 \end{bmatrix} = \begin{bmatrix} -\frac{3}{2}\mu_2^{-5/2}\mu_3 & \mu_2^{-3/2} & 0 \\ -2\mu_2^{-3}\mu_4 & 0 & \mu_2^{-2} \end{bmatrix}.$$

Then the estimate of the asymptotic covariance matrix for the estimators of θ_1 and θ_2 would be $\mathbf{JVJ'}$.

There will be cases in which there is no explicit expression available for the variance of the underlying sample moment. For instance, in Example 4.24, the underlying sample statistic is

$$M_t = \frac{1}{n} \sum_i e^{tx_i}.$$

The exact variance of M_t is known only if t is an integer. But if sampling is random, a consistent estimator for the variance of M_t can easily be computed since M_t is a sample mean,

$$M_t = \frac{1}{n}\sum_i z_i = \bar{z}.$$

Therefore, we can estimate the variance of M_t with $1/n$ times the sample variance of the observations on z. We can also obtain an estimate of the covariance of M_t and M_s with $1/n$ times the sample covariance of the individual terms. In particular,

$$\text{Est.Asy.Cov}[M_t, M_s] = \frac{1}{n}\frac{1}{n-1}\sum_i [(e^{tx_i} - M_t)(e^{sx_i} - M_s)].$$

More generally, when the moments are computed as

$$\bar{g}_k = \frac{1}{n}\sum_i g_k(\mathbf{x}_i), \qquad k = 1, \ldots, K,$$

where $\mathbf{x}_i$ may be an observation on a vector of variables, an appropriate estimate of the asymptotic covariance matrix for $[g_1, \ldots, g_K]$ can be computed using

$$\mathbf{V} = \frac{1}{n}\frac{1}{n-1}\sum_i [(g_j(\mathbf{x}_i) - \bar{g}_j)(g_k(\mathbf{x}_i) - \bar{g}_k)], \qquad j, k = 1, \ldots, K. \quad (4\text{--}55)$$

This provides the asymptotic covariance matrix for the moments used in computing the estimated parameters. Note that this estimator could have been used in Example 4.26. We would have computed $\mathbf{V}$ equal to $(1/n)$ times the sample covariance matrix of x^2, x^3, and x^4.

To complete the computation, refer back to the moment equations

$$\bar{m}_k = \bar{g}_k - \gamma_k(\theta_1, \theta_2, \ldots, \theta_k) = 0, \qquad k = 1, \ldots, K.$$

Let $\mathbf{G}$ be the $K \times K$ matrix whose kth row is the vector of partial derivatives

$$\mathbf{G}^k = \frac{\partial\bar{g}_k}{\partial\boldsymbol{\theta}'}.$$

Now expand the set of solved moment equations around the true values of the parameters, $\boldsymbol{\theta}$, in a linear Taylor series. The linear approximation is

$$\overline{\mathbf{g}} \approx \boldsymbol{\gamma}(\boldsymbol{\theta}) + \mathbf{G}(\boldsymbol{\theta})(\hat{\boldsymbol{\theta}} - \boldsymbol{\theta}).$$

Therefore,

$$(\hat{\boldsymbol{\theta}} - \boldsymbol{\theta}) \approx \mathbf{G}(\boldsymbol{\theta})^{-1}(\overline{\mathbf{g}} - \boldsymbol{\gamma}(\boldsymbol{\theta})) = \mathbf{G}(\boldsymbol{\theta})^{-1}\overline{\mathbf{m}}.$$

The arguments needed to characterize the large sample behavior of the estimator of $\hat{\boldsymbol{\theta}}$ are discussed in Chapter 10. We have from Theorem 4.4 (the central limit theorem) that $\overline{\mathbf{g}} - \boldsymbol{\gamma}(\boldsymbol{\theta})$ is asymptotically normally distributed with mean vector $\mathbf{0}$ and asymptotic covariance matrix equal to $1/n$ times $\text{plim}(n\mathbf{V})$. Under fairly general conditions, we can use (3–87) for the variance of a set of linear functions. Thus, the asymptotic covariance matrix for the method of moments estimator may be estimated with

$$\text{Est.Asy.Var}[\hat{\boldsymbol{\theta}}] = (\hat{\mathbf{G}}^{-1})\mathbf{V}(\hat{\mathbf{G}}^{-1})'. \tag{4–56}$$

EXAMPLE 4.25 (Continued) _____

Using the estimates $\hat{\boldsymbol{\theta}}(m_1', m_*') = (2.4106, 0.077707)$,

$$\hat{\mathbf{G}} = \begin{bmatrix} -1/\hat{\lambda} & \hat{P}/\hat{\lambda}^2 \\ -\hat{\Psi}' & 1/\hat{\lambda} \end{bmatrix} = \begin{bmatrix} -12.97522 & 405.8396 \\ 0.51444 & 12.97522 \end{bmatrix}.$$

[The function Ψ' is $d^2 \ln \Gamma(P)/dP^2 = (\Gamma\Gamma'' - \Gamma'^2)/\Gamma^2$. With $\hat{P} = 2.4027$, $\hat{\Gamma} = 1.244389$, $\hat{\Psi} = 0.6543072$, and $\hat{\Psi}' = 0.5144425$.] The matrix $\mathbf{V}$ is $1/n$ times the sample covariance matrix of x and $\ln x$:

$$\mathbf{V} = \begin{bmatrix} 25.034 & 0.7155 \\ 0.7155 & 0.023873 \end{bmatrix}.$$

The product in (4–56) is

$$\hat{\mathbf{G}}^{-1}\mathbf{V}(\hat{\mathbf{G}}')^{-1} = \begin{bmatrix} 0.38974 & 0.014411 \\ 0.014603 & 0.0006874 \end{bmatrix}.$$

_____

For the maximum likelihood estimators of (P, λ) in the gamma distribution, the asymptotic covariance matrix can also be based on (4–51) or (4–52). Using the first of these, the Hessian would simply be $\mathbf{G}$ with the rows interchanged, then the signs reversed in the second row. (This occurs because we chose to use the sufficient statistics for the moment estimators, so the moment equations that we differentiated are, apart from a sign change, also the derivatives of the log likelihood.) Differentiating again produces the Hessian. Based on the Hessian, $(1/n)\mathbf{H}^{-1}$, the estimates of the two variances are 0.51243 and 0.00064699, respectively, which agrees reasonably well with the estimates above. The difference would be due to sampling variability in a finite sample.

4.7. Interval Estimation

Regardless of the properties of an estimator, the estimate obtained will vary from sample to sample, and there is some probability that it will be quite erroneous. A point estimate will not provide any information on the likely range of error. The logic behind an **interval estimate** is that we use the sample data to construct an interval, [lower($\mathbf{X}$), upper($\mathbf{X}$)], such that we can expect this interval to contain the true parameter in some specified proportion of samples, or equivalently, with some desired level of confidence. Clearly, the wider the interval, the more confident we can be that it will, in any given sample, contain the parameter being estimated.

The theory of interval estimation is based on a **pivotal quantity,** which is a function of both the parameter and a point estimate that has a known distribution. Consider the following examples.

EXAMPLE 4.27

In sampling from a normal distribution with mean μ and standard deviation σ,

$$z = \frac{\sqrt{n}(\bar{x} - \mu)}{s} \sim t[n - 1],$$

$$c = \frac{(n - 1)s^2}{\sigma^2} \sim \chi^2[n - 1].$$

Given the pivotal quantity, we can make probability statements about events involving the parameter and the estimate. Let $p(g, \theta)$ be the constructed random variable, for example, z or c. Given a prespecified **confidence level,** $1 - \alpha$, we can state that

$$\text{Prob}(\text{lower} < p(g, \theta) < \text{upper}) = 1 - \alpha, \tag{4-57}$$

where lower and upper are obtained from the appropriate table. This statement is then manipulated to make equivalent statements about the endpoints of the intervals. For example, the following statements are equivalent:

$$\text{Prob}\left(-z < \frac{\sqrt{n}(\bar{x} - \mu)}{s} < z\right) = 1 - \alpha,$$

$$\text{Prob}\left(\bar{x} - \frac{zs}{\sqrt{n}} < \mu < \bar{x} + \frac{zs}{\sqrt{n}}\right) = 1 - \alpha.$$

Note that the second of these is a statement about the interval, not the parameter; that is, it is the interval that is random, not the parameter. We attach a probability, or $100(1 - \alpha)$ percent confidence level, to the interval itself; in repeated sampling, an interval constructed in this fashion will contain the true parameter $100(1 - \alpha)$ percent of the time.

In general, the interval constructed by this method will be of the form

$$\text{Lower}(\mathbf{X}) = \hat{\theta} - e_1,$$

$$\text{Upper}(\mathbf{X}) = \hat{\theta} + e_2,$$

where $\mathbf{X}$ is the sample data, e_1 and e_2 are sampling errors, and $\hat{\theta}$ is a point estimate of θ. It is clear from the preceding example that if the sampling distribution of the pivotal quantity is either t or standard normal, which will be true in the vast majority of cases we encounter in practice, then the confidence interval will be

$$\hat{\theta} \pm C_{1-\alpha/2}[\text{se}(\hat{\theta})], \tag{4-58}$$

where $\text{se}(\cdot)$ is the (known or estimated) standard error of the parameter estimate and $C_{1-\alpha/2}$ is the value from the t or standard normal distribution that is exceeded with probability $1 - \alpha/2$. The usual values for α are 0.10, 0.05, or 0.01.

EXAMPLE 4.28

In a sample of 25,

$$\bar{x} = 1.63 \qquad \text{and} \qquad s = 0.51.$$

Construct a 95 percent confidence interval for μ. Assuming that the sample of 25 is from a normal distribution,

$$\text{Prob}\left(-2.064 < \frac{5(\bar{x} - \mu)}{s} < 2.064\right) = 0.95,$$

where 2.064 is the critical value from a t distribution with 24 degrees of freedom. Thus, the confidence interval is

$$1.63 \pm \frac{2.064(0.51)}{5} \qquad \text{or} \qquad [1.4195, \ 1.8405].$$

Remark. Had the parent distribution not been specified, it would have been natural to use the standard normal distribution instead, perhaps relying on the central limit theorem. But a sample size of 25 is small enough that the more conservative t distribution might still be preferable.

The theory does not prescribe exactly how to choose the endpoints for the confidence interval. An obvious criterion is to minimize the width of the interval. If the sampling distribution is symmetric, the symmetric interval is the best one. If the sampling distribution is not symmetric, however, this procedure will not be optimal.

EXAMPLE 4.29

The chi-squared distribution is used to construct a confidence interval for the variance of a normal distribution. Using the data from Example 4.28, we find that the usual procedure would use

$$\text{Prob}\left(12.4 < \frac{24s^2}{\sigma^2} < 39.4\right) = 0.95,$$

where 12.4 and 39.4 are the 0.025 and 0.975 cutoff points from the chi-squared(24) distribution. This leads to the 95 percent confidence interval [0.1581, 0.5032]. By making use of the asymmetry of the distribution, a narrower interval can be constructed. Allocating 4 percent to the left-hand tail and 1 percent to the right instead of 2.5 percent to each, the two cutoff points are 13.4 and 42.9, and the resulting 95 percent confidence interval is [0.1455, 0.4659].[21]

Finally, the confidence interval can be manipulated to obtain a confidence interval for a function of a parameter. For example, based on the preceding, a 95 percent confidence interval for σ would be $[\sqrt{0.1581}, \ \sqrt{0.5032}] = [0.3976, 0.7094]$.

4.8. Hypothesis Testing

The second major group of statistical inference procedures is hypothesis tests. The classical testing procedures are based on constructing a statistic from a random sample that will enable the analyst to decide, with reasonable confidence, whether or not the data in the sample would have been generated by a hypothesized population. The formal procedure involves a statement of the hypothesis, usually in terms of a "null" or maintained hypothesis and an alternative, conventionally denoted H_0 and H_1, respectively. The procedure

---

[21] Formal conditions for finding the narrowest interval are considered in Exercise 19.

itself is a rule, stated in terms of the data, that dictates whether the null hypothesis should be rejected or not. For example, the hypothesis might state that a parameter is equal to a specified value. The decision rule might state that the hypothesis should be rejected if a sample estimate of that parameter is too far away from that value (where "far" remains to be defined). More generally, the classical, or Neyman–Pearson, methodology involves partitioning the sample space into two regions. If the observed data (i.e., the test statistic) fall in the **rejection region** (sometimes called the **critical region**), the null hypothesis is rejected; if they fall in the **acceptance region,** it is not.

4.8.1. Testing Procedures

Since the sample is random, the test statistic, however defined, is also random. The same test procedure can lead to different conclusions in different samples. As such, there are two ways such a procedure can be in error:

1. **Type I error.** The procedure may lead to rejection of the null hypothesis when it is true.
2. **Type II error.** The procedure may fail to reject the null hypothesis when it is false.

To continue the previous example, there is some probability that the estimate of the parameter will be quite far from the hypothesized value, even if the hypothesis is true. This might cause a type I error.

Definition. The probability of a type I error is the **size** of the test. This is conventionally denoted α and is also called the **significance level.**

The size of the test is under the control of the analyst. It can be changed just by changing the decision rule. Indeed, the type I error could be eliminated altogether just by making the rejection region very small. But this would come at a cost. By eliminating the probability of a type I error, that is, by making it unlikely that the hypothesis is rejected, we must increase the probability of a type II error. Ideally, we would like both probabilities to be as small as possible. However, it is clear that there is a tradeoff between the two. The best we can hope for is that for a given probability of type I error, the procedure we choose will have as small a probability of type II error as possible.

Definition. The **power** of a test is the probability that it will correctly lead to rejection of a false null hypothesis:

$$\text{power} = 1 - \beta = 1 - \text{Prob(type II error)}. \qquad (4\text{--}59)$$

For a given significance level, α, we would like β to be as small as possible. Since β is defined in terms of the alternative hypothesis, it depends on the true value of the parameter.

EXAMPLE 4.30 _____

For testing $H_0 : \mu = \mu^0$ in a normal distribution with known variance, σ^2, the decision rule is to reject the hypothesis if the absolute value of the z statistic, $\sqrt{n}(\bar{x} - \mu^0)/\sigma$, exceeds the predetermined critical value. For a test at the 5 percent significance level, we set the critical value at 1.96. The power of the test is, therefore, the probability that the absolute value of the test statistic will exceed 1.96 given that the true value of μ is, in fact, not μ^0. This depends on the alternative value of μ, as shown in Figure 4.7. Notice that for this test the power is equal to the size at the point where μ equals μ^0. As might be expected, the test becomes more powerful the farther the true mean is from the hypothesized value.

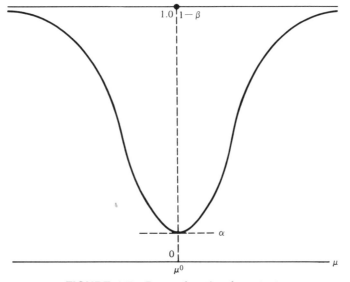

FIGURE 4.7 Power function for a test.

Testing procedures, like estimators, can be compared using a number of criteria.

Definition. A test is **most powerful** if it has greater power than any other test of the same size.

This is a very strong requirement. Since the power depends on the alternative hypothesis, we might require that the test be **uniformly most powerful (UMP),** that is, have greater power than any other test of the same size for all admissable values of the parameter. There are few situations in which a UMP test is available. We usually must be less stringent in our requirements. Nonetheless, the criteria for comparing hypothesis testing procedures are generally based on their respective power functions. A common and very modest requirement is that the test be unbiased.

Definition. A test is **unbiased** if its power $(1 - \beta)$ is greater than or equal to its size α for all values of the parameter.

If a test is **biased,** then for some values of the parameter, we are more likely to accept the null hypothesis when it is false than when it is true.

The use of the term *unbiased* here is unrelated to the concept of an unbiased estimator. Fortunately, there is little chance of confusion. However, tests and estimators are clearly connected. The following criterion derives, in general, from the corresponding attribute of a parameter estimate.

Definition. A test is **consistent** if its power goes to one as the sample size grows to infinity.

EXAMPLE 4.31 _____

A confidence interval for the mean of a normal distribution is $\bar{x} \pm t_{1-\alpha/2}(s/\sqrt{n})$, where $\bar{x}$ and s are the usual consistent estimators for μ and σ, n is the sample size, and $t_{1-\alpha/2}$ is the correct critical value from the t distribution with $n - 1$ degrees of freedom. For testing $H_0{:}\mu = \mu_0$ versus $H_1{:}\mu \neq \mu_0$, let the procedure be to reject H_0 if the confidence interval does not contain μ_0. Since $\bar{x}$ is consistent for μ, if H_0 is false, as $n \to \infty$, this will be discernible with probability 1, as $\bar{x}$ will be arbitrarily close to the true μ. Therefore, this test is consistent.

As a general rule, a test will be consistent if it is based on a consistent estimator of the parameter.

4.8.2. Tests Based on Confidence Intervals

There is an obvious link between interval estimation and the sorts of hypothesis tests we have been discussing here. The confidence interval gives a range of plausible values for the parameter. Therefore, it stands to reason that if a hypothesized value of the parameter does not fall in this range of plausible values, the data are not consistent with the hypothesis, and it should be rejected. Consider, then, testing

$$H_0{:}\theta = \theta_0,$$

$$H_1{:}\theta \neq \theta_0.$$

We form a confidence interval based on $\hat{\theta}$ as described earlier;

$$\hat{\theta} - C_{1-\alpha/2}[\text{se}(\hat{\theta})] < \theta < \hat{\theta} + C_{1-\alpha/2}[\text{se}(\hat{\theta})].$$

H_0 is rejected if θ_0 exceeds the upper limit or is less than the lower limit. Equivalently, H_0 is rejected if

$$\left| \frac{\hat{\theta} - \theta_0}{\text{se}(\hat{\theta})} \right| > C_{1-\alpha/2}.$$

In words, the hypothesis is rejected if the estimate is too far from θ_0, where the distance is measured in standard error units. The critical value is taken from the t or standard normal distribution, whichever is appropriate.

EXAMPLE 4.32 _____

For the results in Example 4.28, test $H_0{:}\mu = 1.98$ versus $H_1{:}\mu \neq 1.98$, assuming sampling from a normal distribution.

$$t = \left| \frac{\bar{x} - 1.98}{s/\sqrt{n}} \right| = \left| \frac{1.63 - 1.98}{0.102} \right| = 3.43.$$

The 95 percent critical value for $t(24)$ is 2.064. Therefore, reject H_0. If the critical value from the standard normal table of 1.96 is used instead, the same result is obtained.

If the test is one-sided, as in

$$H_0{:}\theta \geq \theta_0,$$

$$H_1{:}\theta < \theta_0,$$

the critical region must be adjusted. Thus, for this test, H_0 will be rejected if a point estimate of θ falls sufficiently below θ_0. (Tests can usually be set up by departing from the decision criterion "What sample results are inconsistent with the hypothesis?")

EXAMPLE 4.33 _____

A sample of 25 from a normal distribution yields $\bar{x} = 1.63$ and $s = 0.51$. Test

$$H_0: \mu \le 1.5,$$

$$H_1: \mu > 1.5.$$

Obviously, no observed $\bar{x}$ less than or equal to 1.5 will lead to rejection of H_0. Using the borderline value of 1.5 for μ, we obtain

$$\text{Prob}\left(\frac{\sqrt{n}(\bar{x} - 1.5)}{s} > \frac{5(1.63 - 1.5)}{0.51}\right) = \text{Prob}(t_{24} > 1.27).$$

This is approximately 0.11. This is not unlikely by the usual standards. Hence, at a significance level of 0.11, we would not reject the hypothesis.

_____

4.8.3. Three Asymptotically Equivalent Test Procedures

The next several sections will discuss the most commonly used test procedures, the likelihood ratio, Wald, and Lagrange multiplier tests. We consider maximum likelihood estimation of a parameter, θ, and a test of the hypothesis $H_0: c(\theta) = 0$. The logic of the tests can be seen in Figure 4.8.[22] The figure plots the log-likelihood function, $\ln L(\theta)$, its derivative with respect to θ, $d \ln L(\theta)/d\theta$, and the constraint, $c(\theta)$. There are three approaches to testing the hypothesis suggested in the figure:

- **Likelihood ratio test.** If the restriction, $c(\theta) = 0$, is valid, imposing it should not lead to a large reduction in the log-likelihood function. Therefore, we base the test on the difference, $\ln L - \ln L_R$, where L is the value of the likelihood function at the unconstrained value of θ and L_R is the value of the likelihood function at the restricted estimate.
- **Wald test.** If the restriction is valid, $c(\hat{\theta}_{MLE})$ should be close to zero, since the MLE is consistent. Therefore, the test is based on $c(\hat{\theta}_{MLE})$. We reject the hypothesis if this is significantly different from zero.
- **Lagrange multiplier test.** If the restriction is valid, the restricted estimator should be near the point that maximizes the log likelihood. Therefore, the slope of the log-likelihood function should be near zero at the restricted estimator. The test is based on the slope of the log likelihood at the point where the function is maximized subject to the restriction.

These three tests are asymptotically equivalent, but they can behave rather differently in a small sample. Unfortunately, their small-sample properties are unknown, except in a few special cases. As a consequence, the choice among them is typically made on the basis of ease of computation. The likelihood ratio test requires calculation of both restricted and unrestricted estimators. If both are simple to compute, this will be a convenient way to proceed. The Wald test requires only the unrestricted estimator, and the Lagrange multiplier test requires only the restricted estimator. In some problems, one of these estimators may be much easier to compute than the other. For example, a linear model is simple to estimate but becomes nonlinear and cumbersome if a nonlinear constraint is imposed. In this case, the Wald statistic would be preferable. Alternatively,

_____

[22] See Buse (1982). Note that the scale of the vertical axis would be different for each curve. As such, the points of intersection have no significance.

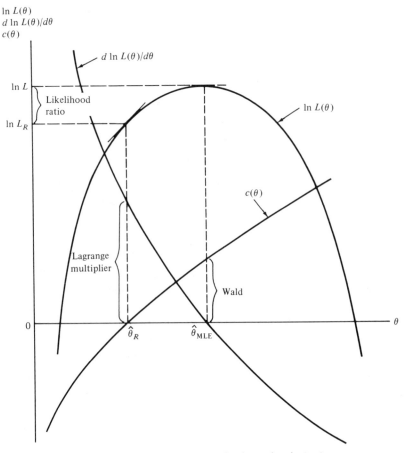

FIGURE 4.8 Three bases for hypothesis tests.

restrictions sometimes amount to the removal of nonlinearities, which would make the Lagrange multiplier test the simpler procedure.

4.8.3a. The Likelihood Ratio Test. Let θ be a vector of parameters to be estimated, and let H_0 specify some sort of restriction on these parameters. Let $\hat{\theta}_U$ be the maximum likelihood estimate of θ obtained without regard to the constraints, and let $\hat{\theta}_R$ be the constrained maximum likelihood estimator. If $\hat{L}_U$ and $\hat{L}_R$ are the likelihood functions evaluated at these two estimates, then the **likelihood ratio** is

$$\lambda = \frac{\hat{L}_R}{\hat{L}_U}. \tag{4–60}$$

This function must be between 0 and 1. Both likelihoods are positive, and $\hat{L}_R$ cannot be larger than $\hat{L}_U$. (A restricted optimum is never superior to an unrestricted one.) If λ is too small, doubt is cast on the restrictions.

An example from a discrete distribution helps to fix these ideas. In estimating from a sample of 10 from a Poisson distribution at the beginning of Section 4.5, we found the MLE of the parameter θ to be 2. At this value, the likelihood, which is the probability of observing the sample we did, is 0.104×10^{-8}. Are these data consistent with H_0 $\theta = 1.8$? $L_R = 0.0936 \times 10^{-8}$, which is, as expected, smaller. This particular sample is somewhat less probable under the hypothesis.

The formal test procedure is based on the following result:

Likelihood Ratio Test Statistic. Under regularity, the large sample distribution of $-2 \ln \lambda$ is chi-squared, with degrees of freedom equal to the number of restrictions imposed.

The null hypothesis is rejected if this value exceeds the appropriate critical value from the chi-squared tables. Thus, for the Poisson example,

$$-2 \ln \lambda = -2 \ln \left(\frac{0.0936}{0.104} \right) = 0.21072.$$

This chi-squared statistic with one degree of freedom is not significant at any conventional level, so we would not reject the hypothesis that $\theta = 1.8$ on the basis of this test.[23]

It is tempting to use the likelihood ratio test to test a simple null hypothesis against a simple alternative. For example, we might be interested in the Poisson setting in testing $H_0: \theta = 1.8$ against $H_1: \theta = 2.2$. Unfortunately, the test cannot be used in this fashion. The degrees of freedom of the chi-squared statistic for the likelihood ratio test equals the reduction in the number of dimensions in the parameter space that results from imposing the restrictions. In testing a single null hypothesis against a single alternative, this is zero.[24] Second, one sometimes encounters an attempt to test one distributional assumption against another with a likelihood ratio test; for example, a certain model will be estimated assuming a normal distribution and then assuming a t distribution. The ratio of the two likelihoods is then compared to determine which distribution is preferred. This is also inappropriate. The parameter spaces, and hence the likelihood functions of the two cases, are unrelated.

4.8.3b. The Wald Test. A practical shortcoming of the likelihood ratio test is that it requires estimation of both the restricted and unrestricted parameter vectors. In complex models, one or the other of these estimates may be very difficult to compute. Fortunately, there are two alternative testing procedures, the Wald test and the Lagrange multiplier test, which circumvent this problem. Both tests are based on an estimator that is asymptotically normally distributed.

These two tests are based on the distribution of the full rank quadratic form considered at the end of the previous chapter. Specifically,

$$\text{If } \mathbf{x} \sim N_J[\boldsymbol{\mu}, \boldsymbol{\Sigma}], \quad (\mathbf{x} - \boldsymbol{\mu})' \boldsymbol{\Sigma}^{-1} (\mathbf{x} - \boldsymbol{\mu}) \sim \text{chi-squared}[J]. \tag{4-61}$$

In the setting of a hypothesis test, under the hypothesis that $E(\mathbf{x}) = \boldsymbol{\mu}$, the quadratic form has the chi-squared distribution. However, if the hypothesis that $E(\mathbf{x}) = \boldsymbol{\mu}$ is false, the quadratic form just given will, on average, be larger than it would be if the hypothesis were true.[25] This condition forms the basis for the test statistics discussed in this and the next section.

Let $\hat{\boldsymbol{\theta}}$ be the vector of parameter estimates obtained without restrictions. We hypothesize a set of restrictions

$$H_0: \mathbf{c}(\boldsymbol{\theta}) = \mathbf{q}.$$

---

[23] Of course, our use of the large-sample result in a sample of 10 might be questionable.

[24] Note that because both likelihoods are restricted in this instance, there is nothing to prevent $-2 \ln \lambda$ from being negative.

[25] If the mean is not $\boldsymbol{\mu}$, the statistic in (4–61) will have a **noncentral chi-squared distribution.** This distribution has the same basic shape as the central chi-squared distribution, with the same degrees of freedom, but lies to the right of it. Thus, a random draw from the noncentral distribution will tend, on average, to be larger than a random observation from the central distribution.

If the restrictions are valid, then at least approximately, $\hat{\boldsymbol{\theta}}$ should satisfy them. However, if the hypothesis is erroneous, $\mathbf{c}(\hat{\boldsymbol{\theta}}) - \mathbf{q}$ should be farther from $\mathbf{0}$ than would be explained by sampling variability alone. The device we use to formalize this notion is the Wald test.

Wald Test Statistic

$$W = (\mathbf{c}(\hat{\boldsymbol{\theta}}) - \mathbf{q})'(\mathrm{Var}[\mathbf{c}(\hat{\boldsymbol{\theta}}) - \mathbf{q}])^{-1}(\mathbf{c}(\hat{\boldsymbol{\theta}}) - \mathbf{q}). \tag{4–62}$$

Under H_0, W has a chi-squared distribution with degrees of freedom equal to the number of restrictions [i.e., the number of equations in $\mathbf{c}(\hat{\boldsymbol{\theta}}) = \mathbf{q}$].

This test is analogous to the chi-squared statistic in (4–61) if $\mathbf{c}(\hat{\boldsymbol{\theta}}) - \mathbf{q}$ is normally distributed, with a hypothesized mean of $\mathbf{0}$. A large value of W leads to rejection of the hypothesis. Note, finally, that W only requires computation of the unrestricted model. One must still compute the variance matrix appearing in the preceding quadratic form. This is the variance of a possibly nonlinear function, which we treated earlier.

$$\mathrm{Var}[\mathbf{c}(\hat{\boldsymbol{\theta}}) - \mathbf{q}] = \mathbf{C} \ \mathrm{Var}[\hat{\boldsymbol{\theta}}]\mathbf{C}',$$

$$\mathbf{C} = \left[\frac{\partial \mathbf{c}(\hat{\boldsymbol{\theta}})}{\partial \hat{\boldsymbol{\theta}}'} \right]. \tag{4–63}$$

That is, $\mathbf{C}$ is the $J \times K$ matrix whose jth row is the derivatives of the jth constraint with respect to the K elements of $\boldsymbol{\theta}$. A common application occurs in testing a set of linear restrcitions.

For testing a set of linear restrictions, $\mathbf{R}\boldsymbol{\theta} = \mathbf{q}$, the Wald test would be based on

$$H_0\text{:}\mathbf{c}(\boldsymbol{\theta}) - \mathbf{q} = \mathbf{R}\boldsymbol{\theta} - \mathbf{q} = \mathbf{0},$$

$$\mathbf{C} = \left[\frac{\partial \mathbf{c}(\hat{\boldsymbol{\theta}})}{\partial \hat{\boldsymbol{\theta}}'} \right] = \mathbf{R}, \tag{4–64}$$

$$\mathrm{Var}[\mathbf{c}(\hat{\boldsymbol{\theta}}) - \mathbf{q}] = \mathbf{R} \ \mathrm{Var}[\hat{\boldsymbol{\theta}}]\mathbf{R}'$$

and

$$W = [\mathbf{R}\hat{\boldsymbol{\theta}} - \mathbf{q}]'[\mathbf{R} \ \mathrm{Var}(\hat{\boldsymbol{\theta}})\mathbf{R}']^{-1}[\mathbf{R}\hat{\boldsymbol{\theta}} - \mathbf{q}].$$

The degrees of freedom is the number of rows in $\mathbf{R}$.

EXAMPLE 4.34 _____

If $\mathbf{c}(\boldsymbol{\theta}) - \mathbf{q}$ is a single restriction, the Wald test will be the same as the test based on the confidence interval developed previously. If the test is

$$H_0\text{:}\theta = \theta_0 \qquad \text{vs.} \qquad H_1\text{:}\theta \neq \theta_0,$$

then the earlier test is based on

$$z = \frac{|\hat{\theta} - \theta_0|}{s(\hat{\theta})}, \tag{4–65}$$

where s is the estimated asymptotic standard error. The test statistic is compared to the appropriate value from the standard normal table. The Wald test will be based on

$$W = [(\hat{\theta} - \theta_0) - 0](\mathrm{Var}[(\hat{\theta} - \theta_0) - 0])^{-1}[(\hat{\theta} - \theta_0) - 0]$$

$$= \frac{(\hat{\theta} - \theta_0)^2}{\mathrm{Var}[\hat{\theta}]} \tag{4–66}$$

$$= z^2.$$

Here W has a chi-squared distribution with one degree of freedom, which is, of course, the distribution of the square of the standard normal test statistic in (4–65).

EXAMPLE 4.35. Testing a Hypothesis About a Mean

For sampling from a normal distribution, the Wald statistic for testing the hypothesis that the mean takes a particular value is simply the square of the t statistic in Example 4.32 or the t ratio, which uses s^2 instead of σ^2 if σ^2 is unknown. Consider the multivariate example in Example 4.20, in which we obtained the maximum likelihood estimate of a vector of means. Suppose that we wished to test the hypothesis that the means of the M distributions were all equal. There are two cases to consider. First, we might have a particular value, μ^0, in mind. Using the results from that example and the variance matrix we derived in Example 4.21, we find that the Wald statistic would be

$$W = (\bar{\mathbf{x}} - \mu^0 \mathbf{i})' \left(\frac{\hat{\sigma}^2}{n} \mathbf{I} \right)^{-1} (\bar{\mathbf{x}} - \mu^0 \mathbf{i})$$

$$= \frac{n}{s^2} (\bar{\mathbf{x}} - \mu^0 \mathbf{i})' (\bar{\mathbf{x}} - \mu^0 \mathbf{i})$$

where $\bar{\mathbf{x}}$ is the vector of sample means. This statistic would be asymptotically distributed as chi-squared with M degrees of freedom. A slightly less restrictive hypothesis is that the means are equal, but we do not have a specific value in mind. This imposes only $M - 1$ restrictions. The statistic is the same one, except that μ^0 must be replaced with a consistent estimator of the common mean, for which we can use $\bar{\bar{x}} = (1/(nM))\Sigma_i \Sigma_j x_{ij}$.

To summarize, then, the Wald test is based on measuring the extent to which the unrestricted estimates fail to satisfy the hypothesized restrictions.

4.8.3c. The Lagrange Multiplier Test. The third test procedure is the **Lagrange multiplier (LM)** or **efficient score** test. It is based on the restricted model instead of the unrestricted model. Suppose that we maximize the log-likelihood subject to the set of constraints $\mathbf{c}(\boldsymbol{\theta}) - \mathbf{q} = \mathbf{0}$. Let $\boldsymbol{\lambda}$ be a vector of Lagrange multipliers. The necessary conditions for maximizing the Lagrangean function, $\ln L^*$, are

$$\frac{\partial \ln L^*}{\partial \boldsymbol{\theta}} = \frac{\partial \ln L(\boldsymbol{\theta})}{\partial \boldsymbol{\theta}} + \mathbf{C}' \boldsymbol{\lambda} = \mathbf{0},$$

$$\frac{\partial \ln L^*}{\partial \boldsymbol{\lambda}} = \mathbf{0},$$

(4–67)

where $\mathbf{C}'$ is the transpose of the matrix in the second line of (4–63). If the restrictions are valid, imposing them will not lead to a significant difference in the maximized value of the likelihood function. In the first-order conditions, this will mean that the second term in the derivative vector will be small. In particular, $\boldsymbol{\lambda}$ will be small. We could test this directly; that is, test $H_0 : \boldsymbol{\lambda} = \mathbf{0}$, which leads to the Lagrange multiplier test. However, there is an equivalent simpler formulation. At the restricted maximum, the derivatives of the unrestricted log likelihood are

$$\frac{\partial \ln L(\boldsymbol{\theta})}{\partial \boldsymbol{\theta}} = -\mathbf{C}' \boldsymbol{\lambda}.$$

(4–68)

If the restrictions are valid, at least within the range of sampling variability,

$$\frac{\partial \ln L(\hat{\boldsymbol{\theta}}_R)}{\partial \hat{\boldsymbol{\theta}}_R} \simeq \mathbf{0}.$$

That is, the derivatives of the log likelihood evaluated at the **restricted** parameter vector will be approximately zero. The vector of first derivatives of the log likelihood is the vector of **efficient scores.** Since the test is based on this vector, it is called the **score test** as well as the Lagrange multiplier test. The variance of the first derivative vector is the information matrix, which we have used to compute the asymptotic variance matrix of the MLE. Therefore, the test statistic, based on reasoning analogous to that behind the Wald test statistic, is

Lagrange Multiplier Test Statistic

$$\text{LM} = \left(\frac{\partial \ln L(\hat{\boldsymbol{\theta}}_R)}{\partial \hat{\boldsymbol{\theta}}_R}\right)' [\mathbf{I}(\hat{\boldsymbol{\theta}}_R)]^{-1} \left(\frac{\partial \ln L(\hat{\boldsymbol{\theta}}_R)}{\partial \hat{\boldsymbol{\theta}}_R}\right). \tag{4-69}$$

LM has a chi-squared distribution with degrees of freedom equal to the number of restrictions. All terms are computed at the restricted estimator.

4.8.4. An Example of the Test Procedures

Consider, again, the data in Table 4.1. In Example 4.22, the parameter β in the model

$$f(y_i, \beta) = \frac{1}{\beta + x_i} e^{-y_i/(\beta + x_i)} \tag{4-70}$$

was estimated by maximum likelihood. This exponential density is a restricted form of the more general gamma distribution:

$$f(y_i, \beta, \rho) = \frac{(\beta + x_i)^{-\rho}}{\Gamma(\rho)} y_i^{\rho-1} e^{-y_i/(\beta + x_i)}. \tag{4-71}$$

The restriction is $\rho = 1$.[26] We consider testing

$$H_0 : \rho = 1 \qquad \text{versus} \qquad H_1 : \rho \neq 1,$$

using the various procedures developed previously.

The log likelihood and its derivatives are

(a) $\ln L(\beta, \rho) = -\rho \sum_i \ln (\beta + x_i) - n \ln \Gamma(\rho) - \sum_i \frac{y_i}{\beta + x_i} + (\rho - 1) \sum_i \ln y_i,$

(b) $\dfrac{\partial \ln L}{\partial \beta} = -\rho \sum_i \dfrac{1}{\beta + x_i} + \sum_i \dfrac{y_i}{(\beta + x_i)^2},$

(c) $\dfrac{\partial \ln L}{\partial \rho} = -\sum_i \ln (\beta + x_i) - \dfrac{n\Gamma'(\rho)}{\Gamma(\rho)} + \sum_i \ln y_i,$

$$\tag{4-72}$$

(d) $\dfrac{\partial^2 \ln L}{\partial \beta^2} = \rho \sum_i \dfrac{1}{(\beta + x_i)^2} - 2\sum_i \dfrac{y_i}{(\beta + x_i)^3},$

---

[26] The gamma function, $\Gamma(\rho)$, and the gamma distribution are described in Section 3.4.5 and the appendix to Chapter 3.

(e) $\quad \dfrac{\partial^2 \ln L}{\partial \rho^2} = -\dfrac{n[\Gamma(\rho)\Gamma''(\rho) - \Gamma'(\rho)^2]}{\Gamma(\rho)^2},$

(f) $\quad \dfrac{\partial^2 \ln L}{\partial \beta \partial \rho} = -\displaystyle\sum_i \dfrac{1}{\beta + x_i}.$

Maximum likelihood estimates are obtained by equating the two first derivatives to zero, with and without the restriction. The results are shown in Table 4.3.

4.8.4a. Confidence Interval Test. A 95 percent confidence interval for ρ based on the unrestricted estimates is

$$3.151 \pm 1.96\sqrt{0.6625} = [1.556, 4.746].$$

This does not contain $\rho = 1$; therefore, the hypothesis is rejected.

4.8.4b. Likelihood Ratio Test. The likelihood ratio test statistic is

$$\lambda = -2[-88.436 - (-82.916)] = 11.04.$$

The table value for the test, with one degree of freedom, is 3.842. The hypothesis is again rejected.

4.8.4c. Wald Test. The Wald test is based on the unrestricted estimates. For this restriction,

$$c(\theta) - q = \rho - 1,$$

$$\frac{dc(\hat{\rho})}{d\hat{\rho}} = 1,$$

$$\widehat{\text{Var}}[c(\hat{\rho}) - q] = \widehat{\text{Var}}[\hat{\rho}] = 0.6625,$$

$$W = (3.151 - 1)[0.6625]^{-1}(3.151 - 1) = 6.984.$$

TABLE 4.3. Maximum Likelihood Estimates

Quantity	Unrestricted	Restricted
$\hat{\beta}$	−4.719	15.603
$\hat{\rho}$	3.151	1.000
$\ln \hat{L}$	−82.916	−88.436
$\dfrac{\partial \ln \hat{L}}{\partial \hat{\beta}}$	0.000	0.000
$\dfrac{\partial \ln \hat{L}}{\partial \hat{\rho}}$	0.000	7.914
$\dfrac{\partial^2 \ln \hat{L}}{\partial \hat{\beta}^2}$	−0.8534	−0.02166
$\dfrac{\partial^2 \ln \hat{L}}{\partial \hat{\rho}^2}$	−7.436	−32.894
$\dfrac{\partial^2 \ln \hat{L}}{\partial \hat{\beta} \partial \hat{\rho}}$	−2.242	−0.6689
$\widehat{\text{Var}}(\hat{\beta})$	5.773	46.164
$\widehat{\text{Var}}(\hat{\rho})$	0.6625	0.000
$\widehat{\text{Cov}}(\hat{\beta},\hat{\rho})$	−1.746	0.000

The critical value is the same as the previous one; hence, H_0 is again rejected. Note that the Wald test statistic is the square of the corresponding test statistic that would be used in the confidence interval test:

$$\frac{|3.151 - 1|}{\sqrt{0.6625}} = 2.626.$$

4.8.4d. Lagrange Multiplier Test. The Lagrange multiplier test is based on the restricted estimates:

$$LM = [0.000 \quad 7.914] \begin{bmatrix} 0.02166 & 0.6689 \\ 0.6689 & 32.894 \end{bmatrix}^{-1} \begin{bmatrix} 0.000 \\ 7.914 \end{bmatrix} = 5.120.$$

The conclusion is the same as before.

Note that the latter three test statistics have substantially different values. It is possible to reach different conclusions depending upon which one is used. For example, if the test had been carried out at the 1 percent significance level instead of the 5 percent level, the critical value from the chi-squared table would be 6.635. The hypothesis would then have been rejected if the test were based on the likelihood ratio or the Wald test statistics, but not if it were based on the LM statistic. Asymptotically, all three tests are equivalent. However, in a finite sample, differences such as these are to be expected, particularly in a small sample such as ours.[27] Unfortunately, there is no clear rule for how to proceed in such a case. Its possibility, however, does highlight the problem of relying upon a particular significance level and drawing a firm reject/accept conclusion based on sample evidence.

EXERCISES

1. The following sample is drawn from a normal distribution with mean μ and standard deviation σ:

$$x = 1.3, \quad 2.1, \quad 0.4, \quad 1.3, \quad 0.5, \quad 0.2, \quad 1.8, \quad 2.5, \quad 1.9, \quad 3.2.$$

Compute the mean, median, variance, and standard deviation of the sample.

2. Using the data in Exercise 1, test the following hypotheses:

$$\mu \geq 2.$$
$$\mu \leq 0.7.$$
$$\sigma^2 = 0.5.$$

Using a likelihood ratio test, test the following hypothesis:

$$\mu = 1.8, \qquad \sigma^2 = 0.8.$$

3. Suppose that the following sample is drawn from a normal distribution with mean μ and standard deviation σ:

$$y = 3.1, \quad -0.1, \quad 0.3, \quad 1.4, \quad 2.9, \quad 0.3, \quad 2.2, \quad 1.5, \quad 4.2, \quad 0.4.$$

Test the hypothesis that the mean of the distribution that produced these data is the same as the one that produced the data in Exercise 1. Test the hypothesis assuming

---

[27] For further discussion of this problem, see Berndt and Savin (1977).

that the variances are the same. Test the hypothesis that the variances are the same using an F test and using a likelihood ratio test. (Do not assume that the means are the same.)

4. A common method of simulating random draws from the standard normal distribution is to compute the sum of 12 draws from the uniform [0, 1] distribution and subtract 6. Can you justify this procedure?

5. Using the data in Exercise 1, form confidence intervals for the mean and standard deviation.

6. Based on a sample of 65 observations from a normal distribution, you obtain a *median* of 34 and a standard deviation of 13.3. Form a confidence interval for the mean. (**Hint:** Use the asymptotic distribution; see Example 4.15.) Compare your confidence interval to the one you would have obtained had the estimate of 34 been the sample mean instead of the sample median.

7. The random variable x has a continuous distribution $f(x)$ and a cumulative distribution function $F(x)$. What is the probability distribution of the sample maximum? (**Hint:** In a random sample of n observations, $x_1, x_2, \ldots, x_n$, if z is the maximum, every observation in the sample is less than or equal to z. Use the cdf.)

8. Assume that the distribution of x is

$$f(x) = \frac{1}{\theta}, \qquad 0 \le x \le \theta.$$

In random sampling from this distribution, prove that the sample maximum is a consistent estimator of θ. *Note:* You can prove that the maximum is the maximum likelihood estimator of θ. But the usual properties do not apply here. Why not? (**Hint:** Attempt to verify that the expected first derivative of the log likelihood with respect to θ is zero.)

9. In random sampling from the exponential distribution,

$$f(x) = \frac{1}{\theta}e^{-x/\theta}, \qquad x > 0, \qquad \theta > 0,$$

find the maximum likelihood estimator of θ and obtain the asymptotic distribution of this estimator.

10. Suppose that in a sample of 500 observations from a normal distribution with mean μ and standard deviation σ, you are told that 35 percent of the observations are less than 2.1 and 55 percent are less than 3.6. Estimate μ and σ.

11. For random sampling from a normal distribution with nonzero mean μ and standard deviation σ, find the asymptotic joint distribution of the maximum likelihood estimators of μ/σ and μ^2/σ^2.

12. The random variable x has the following distribution:

$$f(x) = \frac{e^{-\lambda}\lambda^x}{x!}, \qquad x = 0, 1, 2, \ldots.$$

The following random sample is drawn:

$$1, \quad 1, \quad 4, \quad 2, \quad 0, \quad 0, \quad 3, \quad 2, \quad 3, \quad 5, \quad 1, \quad 2, \quad 1, \quad 0, \quad 0.$$

Carry out a Wald test of the hypothesis that $\lambda = 2$.

13. Based on random sampling of 16 observations from the exponential distribution of Exercise 9, we wish to test the hypothesis that $\theta = 1$. We will reject the hypothesis if $\bar{x}$ is greater than 1.2 or less than 0.8. We are interested in the power of this test.

    (a) Using the asymptotic distribution of $\bar{x}$, graph the asymptotic approximation to the true power function.

    (b) Using the result discussed in Example 4.14, describe how to obtain the true power function for this test.

14. For the normal distribution, $\mu_{2k} = \sigma^{2k}(2k)!/(k!\, 2^k)$ and $\mu_{2k+1} = 0$, $k = 0, 1, \ldots$. Use this result to show that in Example 4.26, $\theta_1 = 0$, $\theta_2 = 3$, and

$$\mathbf{JVJ'} = \begin{bmatrix} 6 & 0 \\ 0 & 24 \end{bmatrix}$$

15. *Testing for normality:* One method that has been suggested for testing whether the distribution underlying a sample is normal is to refer the statistic

$$L = n\left[\frac{\text{skewness}^2}{6} + \frac{(\text{kurtosis} - 3)^2}{24}\right]$$

to the chi-squared distribution with two degrees of freedom. Using the data in Exercise 1, carry out the test.

16. Suppose that the joint distribution of the two random variables x and y is

$$f(x, y) = \frac{\theta e^{-(\beta+\theta)y}(\beta y)^x}{x!} \qquad \beta, \theta > 0, \qquad y \geq 0, \qquad x = 0, 1, 2, \ldots.$$

    (a) Find the maximum likelihood estimators of β and θ and their asymptotic joint distribution.

    (b) Find the maximum likelihood estimator of $\theta/(\beta + \theta)$ and its asymptotic distribution.

    (c) Prove that $f(x)$ is of the form

$$f(x) = \gamma(1 - \gamma)^x, \qquad x = 0, 1, 2, \ldots.$$

    Then find the maximum likelihood estimator of γ and its asymptotic distribution.

    (d) Prove that $f(y|x)$ is of the form

$$\frac{\lambda e^{-\lambda y}(\lambda y)^x}{x!}.$$

    Prove that $f(y|x)$ integrates to 1. Find the maximum likelihood estimator of λ and its asymptotic distribution. (**Hint:** In the conditional distribution, just carry the x's along as constants.)

    (e) Prove that

$$f(y) = \theta e^{-\theta y}.$$

    Then find the maximum likelihood estimator of θ and its asymptotic variance.

    (f) Prove that

$$f(x|y) = \frac{e^{-\beta y}(\beta y)^x}{x!}.$$

    Based on this distribution, what is the maximum likelihood estimator of β?

17. Suppose that x has the Weibull distribution:

$$f(x) = \alpha\beta x^{\beta-1}e^{-\alpha x^{\beta}}, \qquad x > 0, \qquad \alpha, \beta > 0.$$

(a) Obtain the log-likelihood function for a random sample of n observations.

(b) Obtain the likelihood equations for maximum likelihood estimation of α and β. Note that the first provides an explicit solution for α in terms of the data and β. But after inserting this in the second, we obtain only an implicit solution for β. How would you obtain the maximum likelihood estimators?

(c) Obtain the second derivatives matrix of the log likelihood with respect to α and β. The exact expectations of the elements involving β include the derivatives of the gamma function and are quite messy analytically. Of course, your exact result provides an empirical estimator. How would you estimate the asymptotic covariance matrix for your estimators in part (b)?

(d) Prove that $\alpha\beta\text{Cov}(\ln x, x^{\beta}) = 1$. (**Hint:** Use the fact that the expected first derivatives of the log-likelihood function are zero.)

18. The following data were generated by the Weibull distribution of Exercise 17:

1.3043	0.49254	1.2742	1.4019	0.32556	0.29965	0.26423
1.0878	1.9461	0.47615	3.6454	0.15344	1.2357	0.96381
0.33453	1.1227	2.0296	1.2797	0.96080	2.0070	

(a) Obtain the maximum likelihood estimates of α and β, and give the asymptotic covariance matrix for the estimates.

(b) Carry out a Wald test of the hypothesis that $\beta = 1$.

(c) Obtain the maximum likelihood estimate of α under the hypothesis that $\beta = 1$.

(d) Using the results of parts (a) and (c), carry out a likelihood ratio test of the hypothesis that $\beta = 1$.

(e) Carry out a Lagrange multiplier test of the hypothesis that $\beta = 1$.

19. We consider forming a confidence interval for the variance of a normal distribution. As shown in Example 4.29, the interval is formed by finding c_{lower} and c_{upper} such that

$$\text{Prob}(c_{\text{lower}} < \chi^2(n-1) < c_{\text{upper}}) = 1 - \alpha.$$

The endpoints of the confidence interval are then $(n-1)s^2/c_{\text{upper}}$ and $(n-1)s^2/c_{\text{lower}}$. How do we find the narrowest interval? Consider simply minimizing the width of the interval $c_{\text{upper}} - c_{\text{lower}}$, subject to the constraint that the probability contained in the interval is $(1 - \alpha)$. Prove that for symmetric and asymmetric distributions alike, the narrowest interval will be such that the density is the same at the two endpoints.

20. Using the results in Example 4.25 and Section 4.6.2, estimate the asymptotic covariance matrix of the method of moments estimators of P and λ based on m'_{-1} and m'_2. (**Note:** You will need to use the data in Table 4.1 to estimate **V**.)

CHAPTER 5

The Classical Linear Regression Model

5.1. Introduction

An econometric study begins with a set of theoretical propositions about some aspect of the economy. The theory specifies a set of relationships among variables. Familiar examples are demand equations, production functions, and macroeconomic models. The empirical investigation provides estimates of unknown parameters in the model, such as elasticities or the marginal propensity to consume, and often attempts to measure the validity of the propositions against the behavior of observable data. This and the next several chapters develop a number of techniques used in this context. We begin with the simplest case of a linear equation linking two variables. Subsequent chapters are devoted to more elaborate specifications and to various complications that arise in the application of these techniques.

5.2. Specifying the Regression Model—An Example

Consider the following propositions from Keynes's (1936) *General Theory:*

> We shall therefore define what we shall call the propensity to consume as the functional relationship f between X, a given level of income and C the expenditure on consumption out of that level of income, so that $C = f(X)$.[1]
>
> The amount that the community spends on consumption depends (i) partly on the amount of its income, (ii) partly on other objective attendant circumstances, and (iii) partly on the subjective needs and the psychological propensities and habits of the individuals composing it. . . .
>
> The fundamental psychological law upon which we are entitled to depend with great confidence, both a priori from our knowledge of human nature and from the detailed facts of experience, is that men are disposed, as a rule and on the average, to increase their consumption as their income increases, but not by as much as the increase in their income.[2] That is . . . dC/dX is positive and less than unity.
>
> But, apart from short-period changes in the level of income, it is also obvious that a higher absolute level of income will tend as a rule to widen the gap between income and consumption. . . . These reasons will lead, as a rule, to a greater proportion of income being saved as real income increases.

---

[1] Keynes's original text denoted the function X, not f, and income Y, not X. We have changed the notation to avoid confusion with the later discussion.

[2] Modern economists are rarely this confident about their theories.

The theory posits a stable relationship between consumption and income:

$$C = f(X)$$

and claims in the third paragraph that the marginal propensity to consume (MPC) is between 0 and 1:

$$0 < \frac{dC}{dX} < 1.$$

The final paragraph asserts that the average propensity to consume (APC), that is, the ratio of consumption to income, falls as income rises, or

$$\frac{d(\text{APC})}{dX} = \frac{d(C/X)}{dX} = \frac{(\text{MPC} - \text{APC})}{X} < 0.$$

It follows that MPC < APC. The most common formulation of the consumption function is a linear relationship

$$C = \alpha + \beta X \qquad (5\text{--}1)$$

that satisfies Keynes's "laws" if β lies between 0 and 1 and α is greater than 0.[3]

These theoretical results provide the basis for an empirical study. In particular, given an appropriate data set, we could investigate whether the linear function just given is a satisfactory description of the relation between consumption and income, and, if so, whether α is positive and β is between 0 and 1.

Figure 5.1 and Table 5.1 present aggregate consumption and personal income in constant dollars for the U.S. economy for the 10 years 1970–1979.

It is apparent from the figure that, at least superficially, the data are consistent with the theory. But the linear function is only approximate; in fact, it is unlikely that consumption and income can be connected by any simple relationship. The **deterministic** relationship in (5–1) is clearly inadequate. (Recall the list of three explanations in the second paragraph of the excerpt.) The model is intended only to represent the salient features of this part of the economy. We are not so ambitious as to attempt to capture every influence in our relationship, but only those that are substantial enough to model directly.

Our next step is to incorporate in the model the inherent randomness in its real-world counterpart. Thus, we write

$$C = f(X, \varepsilon),$$

where ε is the stochastic element. It is important not to view the disturbance ε as a catchall for the inadequacies of the model. For example, Figure 5.2 shows the same measured variables as 5.1 for the years 1940 to 1950. The same moderate lack of fit appears. But for the years 1942–1945, something is obviously missing. These differences are not the result of random variation; 1942–1945 were years of wartime rationing, which prevented consumption from rising to rates historically consistent with these levels of income. This fact would be incorporated in the model if one intended to apply it to this earlier period. It remains to establish how the stochastic element will be incorporated in the regression equation. The most frequent approach is to assume that it is *additive*. Thus, we can recast the equation in **stochastic** terms:

$$C = \alpha + \beta X + \varepsilon, \qquad (5\text{--}2)$$

where ε is a random **disturbance.**

---

[3] For analysis of nonlinear models, see Chapter 11 and, for example, Husby (1971).

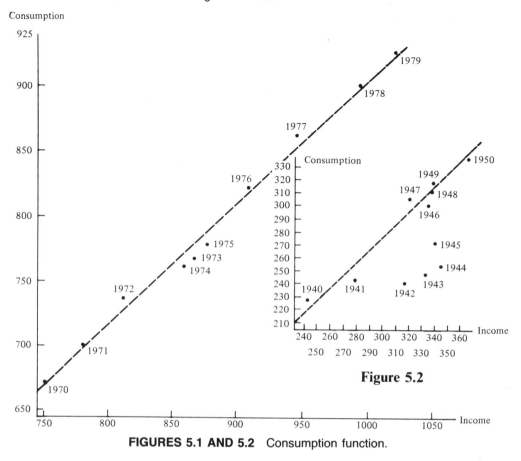

FIGURES 5.1 AND 5.2 Consumption function.

Equation (5–2) is the empirical counterpart to the theoretical model in (5–1). The disturbance (so named because it "disturbs" an otherwise stable relationship) arises for several reasons. The primary reason is that we cannot hope to capture every influence on consumption, such as expectations, seasonal factors, fads, and all of the inherent random-

TABLE 5.1. Disposable Personal Income and Personal Consumption Expenditures[a]

Year	Disposable Income	Personal Consumption
1970	751.6	672.1
1971	779.2	696.8
1972	810.3	737.1
1973	864.7	767.9
1974	857.5	762.8
1975	874.9	779.4
1976	906.8	823.1
1977	942.9	864.3
1978	988.8	903.2
1979	1015.7	927.6

Source: Data from the *Economic Report of the President,* U.S. Government Printing Office, Washington, D.C., 1984.
[a]Income and expenditures are in billions of 1972 dollars.

ness in human behavior, in a model, no matter how elaborate. The net effect, which can be positive or negative, of these omitted factors is captured in the disturbance. There are many other contributors to the disturbance in an empirical model. Probably the most significant is errors of measurement. It is easy to theorize about the relationships among precisely defined variables; it is quite another to obtain accurate measures of these variables. For example, the difficulty of obtaining reasonable measures of profits, interest rates, capital stocks, or, worse yet, flows of services from capital stocks is a recurrent theme in the empirical literature. At the extreme, there may be no observable counterpart to the theoretical variable. The literature on the permanent income model of consumption [e.g., Friedman (1957)] provides an interesting example.

We assume that each observation in our sample, (C_i, X_i), $i = 1, \ldots , n$, is generated by an underlying process described by

$$C_i = \alpha + \beta X_i + \varepsilon_i, \qquad i = 1, \ldots , n. \tag{5-3}$$

Observed consumption is the sum of two parts, a deterministic part, $\alpha + \beta X$, and the random component, ε. Our objective is to estimate the unknown parameters of the model, use the data to study the validity of the theoretical propositions, and perhaps use the estimated model to predict the value of consumption. How we proceed from here depends crucially on what we assume about the stochastic process that has led to our observations of the data in hand.

5.3. The Assumptions of the Linear Regression Model

In general terms, the model to be estimated is of the form

$$y_i = \alpha + \beta x_i + \varepsilon_i, \qquad i = 1, \ldots , n, \tag{5-4}$$

where y is the **dependent** or explained variable, x is the **independent** or explanatory variable, and i indexes the n sample observations. This is commonly called the **population linear regression equation** of y on x. In this setting, y is the **regressand** and x is the **regressor**.

The basic set of assumptions that comprise the **classical linear regression model** are as follows:

1. *Functional form:* $y_i = \alpha + \beta x_i + \varepsilon_i$, $i = 1, \ldots , n$.
2. *Zero mean of the disturbance:* $E[\varepsilon_i] = 0$ for all i.
3. *Homoscedasticity:* $\mathrm{Var}[\varepsilon_i] = \sigma^2$, a constant, for all i.
4. *Nonautocorrelation:* $\mathrm{Cov}[\varepsilon_i, \varepsilon_j] = 0$ if $i \neq j$.
5. *Uncorrelatedness of regressor and disturbance:* $\mathrm{Cov}[x_i, \varepsilon_j] = 0$ for all i and j.[4]

Figure 5.3 summarizes these assumptions. The disturbance is assumed to be the sum of many small, individually unimportant effects, some positive and others negative. Thus, it is common to appeal to the central limit theorem and add an additional assumption to the list:

6. *Normality:* $\varepsilon_i \sim N[0, \sigma^2]$.

If the disturbances are normally distributed, then assumption 4 implies that they are independent as well. The normality assumption is useful for making exact statements

---

[4] Keynes's consumption function provides the basis for a convenient illustration of the principles of regression analysis. But we should note that because consumption is a major determinant of national income, high values of X will be associated with high values of ε *through* C, in violation of assumption 5.

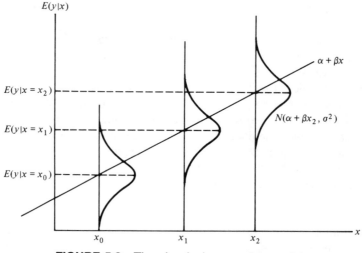

FIGURE 5.3 The classical regression model.

about the behavior of estimators and hypothesis testing procedures, but it is worth noting that most of the results we shall obtain in this chapter require only assumptions 1 to 5.

5.3.1. Functional Form and Nonlinear Models

For the present, we shall focus on the deterministic part of (5–4), $\alpha + \beta x$. The stochastic element is reconsidered in the next section. Linearity of the regression model implies that apart from the random disturbances, the observations on x and y will be scattered about a straight line in the x–y plane. The linearity assumption is not so narrow as it might at first appear. In the regression context, *linearity* refers to the manner in which the parameters enter the equation, not necessarily to the relationship between variables x and y. For example, only one of the four relations shown in Figure 5.4 is linear in the familiar sense. However, by letting z equal e^x, $r = (1/x)$, and $q = \ln x$, we obtain

$$y = a + bx, \quad y = a + bz, \quad y = a + br, \quad y = a + bq,$$

all of which are linear by the definition we shall use here. The variety of functional forms that can be transformed to linearity is substantial. All that is required is that we be able to specify the model as a linear relationship between y and x or some functions of them. In the examples, only x has been transformed, but y could have been as well, and there are many other functions that could have been used.

A commonly used functional form is the **log-linear** model:

$$y = Ax^\beta.$$

In logs,

$$\ln y = \alpha + \beta \ln x.$$

This is also known as the *constant elasticity form,* as in this equation, the elasticity of y with respect to changes in x is

$$\eta = \frac{dy/y}{dx/x} = \frac{d \ln y}{d \ln x} = \beta,$$

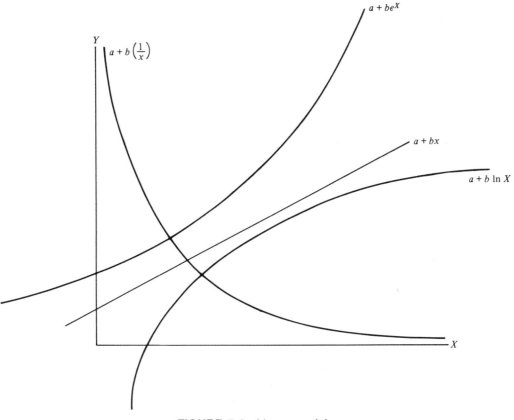

FIGURE 5.4 Linear models.

which does not vary with x. In contrast, the elasticity in the linear (in x) model is

$$\eta = \left(\frac{dy}{dx} \middle/ \frac{y}{x}\right) = \left(\frac{x}{\alpha + \beta x}\right)\left(\frac{dy}{dx}\right)$$

$$= \frac{\beta x}{\alpha + \beta x}.$$

The log-linear model is often used in the estimation of demand equations and production functions. Different values of β produce widely varying functions.

Other variations of the general form

$$f(y_i) = \alpha + \beta g(x_i) + \varepsilon_i$$

will allow a tremendous variety of functional forms, all of which fit into our definition of a linear model. In spite of its great flexibility, the linear model does not include all of the situations we encounter in practice. For example, there is no transformation that will reduce

$$y = \alpha + \frac{1}{\beta + x}$$

to linearity. The methods we consider in this chapter are not appropriate for estimating the parameters of such a model. However, relatively straightforward techniques have been developed for inherently nonlinear models. We shall treat them in detail in Chapter 11.

5.3.2. The Regressor

It is common to assume that x_i is nonstochastic, as it would be in an experimental situation. Here the analyst chooses the values of the regressor x_i and then observes y_i. This would apply, for example, in an agricultural experiment in which y_i is yield and x_i is fertilizer concentration. As a point of departure, we will make that assumption here.

  7. *Nonstochastic regressor:* The value of x_i is a known constant in the probability distribution of y_i.

The implication is that each value of y_i is a realization from a probability distribution with mean

$$E[y_i|x_i] = E[\alpha + \beta x_i + \varepsilon_i] = \alpha + \beta x_i + E[\varepsilon_i] = \alpha + \beta x_i$$

and variance

$$\text{Var}[y_i|x_i] = \text{Var}[\alpha + \beta x_i + \varepsilon_i] = \text{Var}[\varepsilon_i] = \sigma^2.$$

In addition, it is necessary to assume that for any n greater than 1,

$$\left(\frac{1}{n}\right)S_{xx} = \left(\frac{1}{n}\right)\sum_i (x_i - \bar{x})^2$$

is a finite positive number. This assumption is known as an **identification condition.** If there is no variation in x_i, all of our observations will lie on a vertical line, for example, above x_2 in Figure 5.3. This does not invalidate the other assumptions of the model; presumably, it is a flaw in the data set. But if all of our observations lie on a vertical line, our observed data will not permit us to infer anything about the regression, $\alpha + \beta x$.

The assumption of a nonstochastic regressor at this point is largely a convenience. With it, we shall be able to use the results of elementary statistics to obtain our results, as we did in deriving $\text{Var}[y_i]$. However, social scientists are rarely able to analyze experimental data, and relatively few of their models are built around nonrandom regressors. Clearly, for example, in the consumption function, it would be difficult to defend such an asymmetric treatment of aggregate consumption and aggregate income. Since some of our results rely on the assumption that x_i is a known constant, it is important to consider the implications of a random regressor.

If x is taken to be a random variable, Assumption 1 becomes a statement about the joint distribution of y and x. The development of Section 3.7 would apply. It is common in social science research to take the alternative view that the observations of x are "fixed in repeated samples," which is equivalent to doing the statistical analysis conditionally on the sample we have observed. Thus, we would only assume that the regression model and its assumptions apply to the particular set of x's we have observed. This treatment allows us to disregard the ultimate source of variation in x and concentrate on the relationship between y and x. The precise nature of the regressor and how we view the sampling process will be a major determinant of our derivation of the statistical properties of our estimators and test statistics. As we shall see in Chapter 10, we can relax the assumption of fixed regressors at almost no cost. In the end, the crucial assumption is Assumption 5, the uncorrelatedness of x and ε.

5.3.3. The Disturbance

The assumption of linearity of the regression model includes the additive disturbance. For the regression to be linear in the sense described here, it must be of the form

$$y = \alpha + \beta x + \varepsilon$$

either in the original variables or after some suitable transformation. For example, the model

$$y = Ax^\beta e^\varepsilon$$

is linear, while

$$y = Ax^\beta + \varepsilon$$

is not. The observed dependent variable is thus the sum of two components, a nonstochastic element, $\alpha + \beta x$, and a random variable, ε. It is worth emphasizing that neither of the two parts is directly observed because α and β are unknown.

The assumption of a zero mean for the disturbance,

$$E[\varepsilon_i] = 0 \qquad \text{for all } i, \tag{5-5}$$

is natural. Since ε is usually viewed as the sum of many individual effects, the sign of each of which is unknown, there is no reason to expect any other value. Arguably, if we have reason to specify that the mean of the disturbance is something other than zero, we shall build it into the systematic part of our regression, leaving in the disturbance only the unknown part of ε.[5]

Each disturbance is a realization of a random variable with a continuous probability distribution. We assume at this point that these all have the same variance:

$$\text{Var}[\varepsilon_i] = \sigma^2 \qquad \text{for all } i. \tag{5-6}$$

This is termed **homoscedasticity.** Consider a model that describes the profits of firms in an industry as a function of, say, size. Even accounting for size, measured in dollar terms, the profits of large firms will exhibit much greater variation than those of smaller firms. The homoscedasticity assumption would be inappropriate here. Also, survey data on household expenditure patterns often display marked **heteroscedasticity,** even after accounting for income and household size. In contrast, the data in Figure 5.1 appear consistent with this assumption; the variance of consumption does not appear to be changing over time or with different values of income.

The random components of the observations are assumed to be uncorrelated:

$$E[\varepsilon_i \varepsilon_j] = 0 \qquad \text{for all } i \text{ not equal to } j. \tag{5-7}$$

This is also called **nonautocorrelation.** Note that this does not imply that observations y_i and y_j are uncorrelated. The assumption is that *deviations* of observations from their expected values are uncorrelated.

In Figure 5.1, there is some suggestion that the disturbances might not be truly independent across observations. Although the number of observations is limited, it does appear that, on average, each disturbance tends to be followed by one with the same sign. This "inertia" is precisely what is meant by autocorrelation, and it is assumed away at this point. Methods of handling autocorrelation in economic data occupy a large proportion of the literature and will be treated at length in Chapter 15.

It is convenient to assume that the disturbances are independent and **normally distributed,** with zero mean and constant variance. This will enable us to obtain several exact statistical results. In view of our description of the source of ϵ, the conditions of the central limit theorem will generally apply, at least approximately, and the normality assumption will be reasonable in most settings. Later, it will be possible to relax this assumption and retain most of the statistical results we obtain here.

---

[5] Suppose that the mean of ε is μ. Then $\alpha + \beta x + \varepsilon$ is the same as $(\alpha + \mu) + \beta x + (\varepsilon - \mu)$. Letting $\alpha' = \alpha + \mu$ and $\varepsilon' = \varepsilon - \mu$ produces the original model. For an application, see the discussion of frontier production functions in Example 10.4.

5.4. Least Squares

The unknown parameters of the stochastic reaction

$$y_i = \alpha + \beta x_i + \varepsilon_i = E[y_i|x_i] + \varepsilon_i \qquad (5\text{–}8)$$

are the objects of estimation. It is necessary to distinguish between population quantities, such as α and β, and our sample estimates of them, denoted a and b. The population regression is $E[y_i|x_i] = \alpha + \beta x_i$, while our estimate of $E[y_i|x_i]$ is denoted

$$\hat{y}_i = a + bx_i.$$

The disturbance associated with the ith data point is

$$\varepsilon_i = y_i - \alpha - \beta x_i.$$

For any values of a and b, we shall estimate ε_i with the **residual,**

$$e_i = y_i - a - bx_i.$$

From the definitions,

$$y_i = \alpha + \beta x_i + \varepsilon_i$$
$$= a + bx_i + e_i.$$

These are summarized in Figure 5.5.

5.4.1. The Least Squares Coefficients

The population quantities α and β are unknown parameters of the probability distribution of y_i whose values we hope to estimate with our sample data. This is a problem of

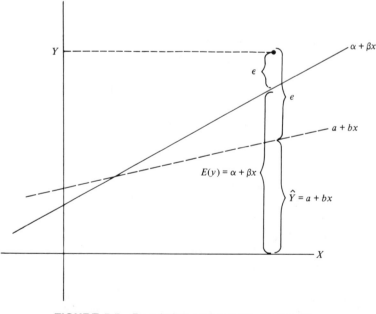

FIGURE 5.5 Population and sample regression.

statistical inference. It is instructive, however, to begin by considering the purely algebraic problem of choosing an a and a b so that the fitted line, $a + bx$, is close to the data points. The scatter of points in Figure 5.1 provides a good illustration. The measure of closeness constitutes a **fitting criterion.** Although numerous candidates have been suggested, the one used most frequently is **least squares.**[6]

For any pair of values, a and b, the **sum of squared residuals** is

$$\sum_i e_i^2 = \sum_i (y_i - a - bx_i)^2. \tag{5-9}$$

The least squares coefficients are the values of a and b that minimize this fitting criterion. The first-order conditions for a minimum are

$$\frac{\partial(\Sigma_i e_i^2)}{\partial a} = \sum_i 2(y_i - a - bx_i)(-1)$$

$$= -2\sum_i (y_i - a - bx_i) = 0,$$

or, equivalently,

$$\sum_i e_i = 0 \tag{5-10}$$

and

$$\frac{\partial(\Sigma_i e_i^2)}{\partial b} = \sum_i 2(y_i - a - bx_i)(-x_i) = 0$$

$$= -2\sum_i x_i(y_i - a - bx_i) = 0,$$

which implies that

$$\sum_i x_i e_i = 0. \tag{5-11}$$

Expanding these and collecting terms yields the **normal equations**

$$\sum_i y_i = na + \left(\sum_i x_i\right)b, \tag{5-12}$$

$$\sum_i x_i y_i = \left(\sum_i x_i\right)a + \left(\sum_i x_i^2\right)b. \tag{5-13}$$

To obtain a solution, we first divide (5-12) by n. The result is

$$\bar{y} = a + b\bar{x}.$$

The least squares regression line passes through the point of means. (If there is no intercept term, this will not be true. This is considered in the exercises.) Now isolate a:

$$a = \bar{y} - b\bar{x}. \tag{5-14}$$

---

[6]We shall have to establish that the practical criterion of fitting the line as closely as possible to the data by least squares leads to estimates with good statistical properties. This makes intuitive sense and is, indeed, the case.

With a in hand, we can solve (5–13) for b. First, $\Sigma_i x_i = n\bar{x}$. Insert this and (5–14) in (5–13) and rearrange the terms:

$$\sum_i x_i y_i - n\overline{xy} = b\left(\sum_i x_i^2 - n\bar{x}^2\right)$$

or

$$b = \frac{\Sigma_i x_i y_i - n\overline{xy}}{\Sigma_i x_i^2 - n\bar{x}^2}$$

$$= \frac{\Sigma_i(x_i - \bar{x})(y_i - \bar{y})}{\Sigma_i(x_i - \bar{x})^2}. \tag{5–15}$$

The solution is given only in terms of the sample means, sums of squares, and cross products, so b may be computed independently of a. Once this explicit solution for b is computed, the value of a may be obtained from (5–14).

EXAMPLE 5.1

For the consumption data in Table 5.1, the normal equations are

$$7934.3 \quad = \quad 10a + \quad 8792.4b,$$

$$7041953.27 = 8792.4a + 7797822.22b.$$

The solutions are

$$a = -67.5806 \quad \text{and} \quad b = 0.979267.$$

This is the line plotted in Figure 5.1.

It remains to verify that we have, indeed, found a minimum of the sum of squared residuals. The matrix of second derivatives with respect to a and b is

$$\begin{bmatrix} \partial^2(\Sigma_i e_i^2)/\partial a^2 & \partial^2(\Sigma_i e_i^2)/\partial a \partial b \\ \partial^2(\Sigma_i e_i^2)/\partial b \partial a & \partial^2(\Sigma_i e_i^2)/\partial b^2 \end{bmatrix} = \begin{bmatrix} 2n & 2\Sigma_i x_i \\ 2\Sigma_i x_i & 2\Sigma_i x_i^2 \end{bmatrix}.$$

We must show that this matrix is positive definite. The two diagonal elements are always positive, so it is only necessary to verify that the determinant is positive. This is $(4n)\Sigma_i x_i^2 - 4(\Sigma_i x_i)^2$. But $\Sigma_i x_i = n\bar{x}$, so the determinant is

$$4n\left(\sum_i x_i^2 - n\bar{x}^2\right) = 4n\left(\sum_i (x_i - \bar{x})^2\right),$$

which is positive. Thus, a and b are the minimizers of the sum of squares.[7]

5.4.2. Evaluating the Fit of the Regression

The original fitting criterion, the sum of squared residuals, also provides a measure of the fit of the regression line to the data. Unfortunately, as can easily be verified, the sum of squared residuals can be scaled arbitrarily just by multiplying the values of y by the desired scale factor. Since the fitted values from the regression are based on the value of

---

[7] The second-order condition fails if $\Sigma_i(x_i - \bar{x})^2$ is zero. But this is the case in which all of the values of x are the same. This was ruled out earlier.

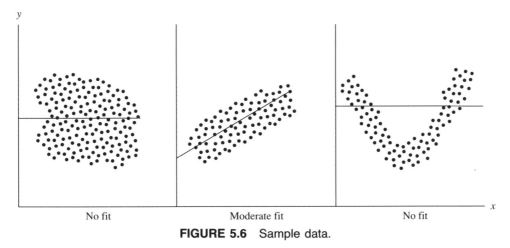

FIGURE 5.6 Sample data.

x, we might ask, instead, whether variation in x is a good predictor of variation in y. Figure 5.6 shows several possible cases. The measure of fit described here embodies both of these considerations.

Variation of the dependent variable is defined in terms of deviations from its mean $(y_i - \bar{y})$. The **total variation** in y is the sum of squared deviations:

$$\text{SST} = \sum_i (y_i - \bar{y})^2.$$

The squares are used because the sum of deviations is always zero. In terms of the regression equation, we may write

$$y_i = \hat{y}_i + e_i$$
$$= a + bx_i + e_i$$
$$= \bar{y} - b\bar{x} + bx_i + e_i.$$

Subtracting $\bar{y}$ from both sides gives

$$(y_i - \bar{y}) = \hat{y} - \bar{y} + e_i = b(x_i - \bar{x}) + e_i. \tag{5-16}$$

Figure 5.7 illustrates the computation. Intuitively, the regression would appear to fit well if the deviations of y from its mean are more largely accounted for by deviations of x from its mean than by the residuals. However, since both terms in (5–16) sum to zero, we use the sums of squares instead. It follows from (5–10) and (5–11) that the cross-product term in the sum of squares of the deviations in (5–16) is zero, and

$$\sum_i (y_i - \bar{y})^2 = \sum_i (\hat{y}_i - \bar{y})^2 + \sum_i e_i^2$$
$$= b^2 \sum_i (x_i - \bar{x})^2 + \sum_i e_i^2. \tag{5-17}$$

We write this as

total sum of squares = regression sum of squares + error sum of squares

or

$$\text{SST} = \text{SSR} + \text{SSE}. \tag{5-18}$$

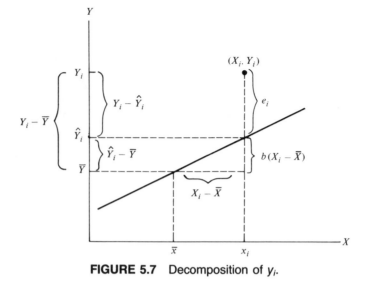

FIGURE 5.7 Decomposition of y_i.

Returning to the original question, we can obtain a measure of how well the regression line fits the data by using the

$$\text{coefficient of determination} = \frac{\text{SSR}}{\text{SSE}}. \tag{5-19}$$

As we have shown, this must be between 0 and 1. It is denoted R^2. It takes the value of zero if the regression is a horizontal line. In this case, the predicted values of y are always $\bar{y}$, so deviations of x from its mean do not translate into different predictions for y. As such, x has no explanatory power. The other extreme, R^2 equals 1, occurs if the values of x and y all lie on a straight line, so that the residuals are zero. If all of the values of y_i lie on a vertical line, R^2 has no meaning and cannot be computed.

There are some useful shortcuts for the computation of this **variance decomposition.** For convenience, define the sample quantities

$$S_{xx} = \sum_i (x_i - \bar{x})^2, \qquad S_x = \sqrt{S_{xx}},$$

$$S_{yy} = \sum_i (y_i - \bar{y})^2, \qquad S_y = \sqrt{S_{yy}},$$

and

$$S_{xy} = \sum_i (x_i - \bar{x})(y_i - \bar{y}).$$

The sample correlation between x and y is $r_{xy} = S_{xy}/(S_x S_y)$. By using $b = S_{xy}/S_{xx}$, we obtain $r_{xy} = b(S_x/S_y)$, which shows that the slope of the regression has the same sign as the correlation between x and y. Therefore,

$$R^2 = \frac{\text{SSR}}{\text{SST}} = \frac{b^2 S_{xx}}{S_{yy}} = r_{xy}^2. \tag{5-20}$$

A result that will be useful in cases in which we have more than one explanatory variable is obtained by computing the squared correlation between the actual and fitted values of y:

$$r_{xy}^2 = \frac{[\Sigma_i(\hat{y}_i - \bar{y})(y_i - \bar{y})]^2}{\text{SSR } S_{yy}}.$$

But $(\hat{y}_i - \bar{y}) = b(x_i - \bar{x})$. So, the numerator is $b^2 S_{xy}^2$ and the denominator is $b^2 S_{xx} S_{yy}$. Collecting terms, we have shown that the coefficient of determination is the squared correlation between the actual and fitted values of the dependent variable. This further justifies our use of R^2 as a measure of goodness of fit of the regression model.

EXAMPLE 5.2 —————————————————————————————————

Continuing the example of the consumption function, where C is consumption and X is income, we find that

$$\bar{C} = 793.43, \qquad \bar{X} = 879.24,$$

$$S_{CC} = 64{,}972.12, \qquad S_{XX} = 67{,}192.44,$$

$$S_{XC} = 65{,}799.34.$$

The components of the total sum of squares are

$$\text{total sum of squares} = 64{,}972.12$$

$$\text{regression sum of squares} = 64{,}435.13$$

$$\text{error sum of squares} = 537.00$$

$$R^2 = \frac{64{,}435.13}{64{,}972.12} = 0.99173.$$

Apparently (as can be seen in Figure 5.1), the regression provides quite a good fit.

A convenient way to summarize these calculations is the **analysis of variance table.** The general form of this table for a simple regression is as shown in Table 5.2.

TABLE 5.2. Analysis of Variance Table

Source of Variation	Variation	Degrees of Freedom	Mean Square
Regression	$\text{SSR} = b^2 S_{xx}$	1	$\dfrac{\text{SSR}}{1}$
Residual	$\text{SSE} = \Sigma_i e_i^2$	$n - 2$	$\dfrac{\text{SSE}}{n - 2}$
Total	$\text{SST} = S_{yy}$	$n - 1$	$\dfrac{S_{yy}}{n - 1}$
	$F[1, n - 2] = \dfrac{\text{SSR}/1}{\text{SSE}/(n - 2)}$		

EXAMPLE 5.3

For the consumption and income data, the analysis of variance table would be as shown in Table 5.3.

TABLE 5.3. Analysis of Variance Table for the Data in Example 5.2

Source of Variation	Variation	Degrees of Freedom	Mean Square
Regression	64,435.13	1	64,435.13
Residual	537.00	8	67.124
Total	64,972.12	9	7,219.12

$$F[1, 8] = \frac{64,435.13}{67.124} = 959.94$$

The value of R^2 we obtained for the consumption function seems high in an absolute sense. Is it? Unfortunately, there is no absolute basis for comparison. In fact, in using aggregate time-series data, coefficients of determination this high are routine. In terms of the values one normally encounters in cross sections, an R^2 of 0.5 is relatively high. Still, it is much lower than the one obtained for the consumption function. Coefficients of determination in cross sections of individual data as high as 0.2 are sometimes noteworthy. The point of this discussion is that whether a regression line provides a good fit to a body of data depends on the setting.

Little can be said about the relative quality of fits of regression lines in different contexts. One must be careful, however, even in a single context, to be sure to use the same basis for comparison for competing models. Usually, this concerns how the dependent variable is computed. For example, a perennial question concerns whether a linear or log-linear model fits the data better. Unfortunately, the question cannot be answered with a direct comparison. An R^2 for the linear regression model is different from an R^2 for the log-linear model. Variation in y is different from variation in $\ln y$. To continue the example, the R^2 in the regression of $\ln C$ on $\ln X$ is 0.99154, which suggests that (albeit only trivially) the linear model fits slightly better. However, it is often useful to compute an analog to the usual R^2 that can be used to compare models:

$$R^2 = 1 - \frac{\Sigma_i e_i^2}{S_{yy}}.$$

The residuals can be computed as $y_i - \hat{y}_i$ from any model. To continue the example, if we compute the predicted values from the log-linear model, and then use for the fitted values

$$\hat{C} = e^{\ln C},$$

the R^2 for this "regression," computed as previously, is 0.991956, which is a slight improvement over the linear model.

It is worth emphasizing that R^2 is a measure of *linear* association between x and y. For example, the third panel of Figure 5.6 shows data that might arise from the model

$$y_i = \alpha + \beta(x_i - c)^2 + \varepsilon_i.$$

(The constant, c, allows x to be distributed about some value other than zero.) The relationship between y and x in this model is nonlinear, and a linear regression would find no fit.

A final word of caution is in order. The interpretation of R^2 as a proportion of variation explained is dependent on the use of least squares to compute the fitted values. It is always correct to write

$$y_i - \bar{y} = (\hat{y}_i - \bar{y}) + e_i.$$

However, in computing the sum of squares on the two sides, the cross-product term vanishes only if least squares is used to compute the fitted values and if the model contains a constant term.[8] Thus, in our previous example, it is not unambiguous that the log-linear model fits better; the cross-product term has been ignored in computing R^2 for the log-linear model. Thus, it is only in the case of least squares applied to a linear equation that R^2 can be interpreted as the proportion of variation in y explained by variation in x.

5.5. Statistical Properties of the Least Squares Estimator

The preceding discussion treated the fitting of the regression to the data as a purely algebraic problem. We can now treat the results as parameter estimates and assess the virtues of least squares on a statistical basis. There are other candidates for estimating α and β. We might, for example, just find the slope of the line between the points with the largest and smallest values of x or (which would be more difficult) find the a and b that minimize the sum of absolute values of the residuals. The question of which estimator to choose is usually based on the statistical properties of the candidates, such as unbiasedness, efficiency, and precision.[9] These, in turn, frequently depend on the particular distribution that we assume produced the data. It is interesting that a number of desirable properties can be obtained for the least squares estimator without even specifying a particular distribution for the disturbances in the regression.

Recall that the statistical model underlying the observed data is

$$y_i = \alpha + \beta x_i + \varepsilon_i.$$

The least squares estimator of β is

$$b = \frac{S_{xy}}{S_{xx}} = \frac{\Sigma_i(x_i - \bar{x})y_i}{S_{xx}}$$

$$= \sum_i c_i y_i.$$

(5–21)

The weight in the sum

$$c_i = \frac{x_i - \bar{x}}{S_{xx}}$$

---

[8] An analogous computation can be done without computing deviations from means if the regression does not contain a constant term. However, other purely algebraic artifacts will crop up in regressions without a constant. For example, the value of R^2 will change when the same constant is added to each observation on y, but it is obvious that nothing fundamental has changed in the regression relationship. One should be wary (even skeptical) in the calculation and interpretation of fit measures for regressions without constant terms.

[9] See Section 4.3.

is a function of only $x_1, \ldots, x_n$. Inserting $y_i = \alpha + \beta x_i + \varepsilon_i$ in (5–21), we obtain

$$b = \frac{\Sigma_i(x_i - \bar{x})(\alpha + \beta x_i + \varepsilon_i)}{S_{xx}}$$

$$= \frac{\alpha\Sigma_i(x_i - \bar{x})}{S_{xx}} + \frac{\beta\Sigma_i(x_i - \bar{x})x_i}{S_{xx}} + \frac{\Sigma_i(x_i - \bar{x})\varepsilon_i}{S_{xx}} \qquad (5–22)$$

$$= \beta + \sum_i c_i\varepsilon_i$$

because $S_{xx} = \Sigma_i(x_i - \bar{x})^2 = \Sigma_i(x_i - \bar{x})x_i$ and $\Sigma_i(x_i - \bar{x}) = 0$. Therefore,

$$E[b] = \beta + E\left[\sum_i c_i\varepsilon_i\right]$$

$$= \beta, \qquad (5–23)$$

since $E[\varepsilon_i] = 0$. *Regardless of the distribution of ε, under our other assumptions, b is an unbiased estimator of β.* The sampling variance of b is derived by using (5–23).

$$\text{Var}[b] = \text{Var}[b - \beta] = \text{Var}\left[\sum_i c_i\varepsilon_i\right].$$

Assumption 4 of the linear regression model (Section 5.3) implies that the covariance terms in the variance of this sum are zero, which leaves

$$\text{Var}[b] = \sum_i \text{Var}[c_i\varepsilon_i] = \sum_i \sigma^2 c_i^2 = \frac{\sigma^2}{S_{xx}}. \qquad (5–24)$$

Note, in particular, the denominator of the variance of b. The greater the variation in x, the smaller this variance will be. For example, consider the problem of estimating the slopes of the two regressions in Figure 5.8. Obviously, a more precise result will be obtained for the data in panel 2 of the figure. This does not necessarily argue that one should always attempt, if possible, to maximize the variation in x. The greater the range of variation we consider, the more likely it becomes that our assumption of linearity of the regression becomes suspect. This notwithstanding, greater variation in the explanatory variable is to be preferred.

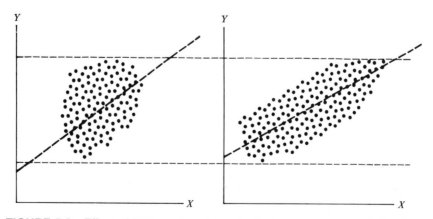

FIGURE 5.8 Effect of increased variation in X given the same variation in Y.

By similar reasoning, we can write the least squares intercept, a, as

$$a = \bar{y} - b\bar{x}$$

$$= \frac{1}{n} \sum_i y_i - b\bar{x}$$

$$= \frac{1}{n} \sum_i (\alpha + \beta x_i + \varepsilon_i) - b\bar{x}.$$

Collecting terms, we have

$$a - \alpha = \sum_i d_i \varepsilon_i,$$

where

$$d_i = \left(\frac{1}{n} - \bar{x} c_i\right).$$

Therefore, since each term in the sum has expectation 0, a is also unbiased. The sampling variance of a is the variance of $\sum_i d_i \varepsilon_i$, which by independence is

$$\text{Var}[a] = \sum_i \sigma^2 d_i^2 = \sigma^2 \left(\frac{1}{n} + \bar{x}^2 \sum_i c_i^2\right) \qquad (5\text{--}25)$$

(The latter result is obtained by squaring the term in parentheses and using the result that $\sum_i c_i = 0$.) From the earlier results,

$$\text{Var}[a] = \sigma^2 \left[\frac{1}{n} + \frac{\bar{x}^2}{S_{xx}}\right].$$

The covariance of the two estimators is

$$\text{Cov}[a, b] = E[(a - \alpha)(b - \beta)] = E\left[\left(\sum_i d_i \varepsilon_i\right)\left(\sum_i c_i \varepsilon_i\right)\right]$$

$$= \sigma^2 \sum_i c_i d_i \qquad (5\text{--}26)$$

$$= \frac{-\bar{x}\sigma^2}{S_{xx}}.$$

Both a and b are of the form $\sum_i w_i y_i$; thus, they are **linear** estimators. The preceding gives the sampling mean and variance of both and establishes that they are **unbiased.** As noted, there are other ways one might use the data to estimate α and β. However, in the context of **linear unbiased estimators,** no estimator has a smaller sampling variance than least squares. This is the **Gauss–Markov theorem,** which we shall prove for the slope estimator. The proof for the intercept is left as an exercise. Recall that the least squares slope is $b = \sum c_i y_i$. Let a competing estimator be

$$b' = \sum_i q_i y_i = \alpha \sum_i q_i + \beta \sum_i q_i x_i + \sum_i q_i \varepsilon_i.$$

Taking expectations on both sides of the equation, we see that for b' to be unbiased, we must have $\Sigma_i q_i = 0$ and $\Sigma_i q_i x_i = 1$. (You should verify that these are true for c_i.) Thus, $b' = \beta + \Sigma_i q_i \varepsilon_i$. The variance of b' is

$$\text{Var}[b'] = \sigma^2 \sum_i q_i^2.$$

Let $v_i = q_i - c_i$. Then $q_i = c_i + v_i$ and

$$\text{Var}[b'] = \sigma^2 \sum_i (c_i + v_i)^2$$

$$= \sigma^2 \left(\sum_i c_i^2 + \sum_i v_i^2 + 2 \sum_i c_i v_i \right).$$

But $\Sigma_i c_i v_i = 0$. This leaves only the two sums of squares in the variance of b', which means that $\text{Var}[b']$ must be greater than $\text{Var}[b]$. A similar proof establishes the result for a.

The Gauss–Markov theorem is a powerful result. It is remarkable that we are able to establish such a strong result for least squares without any assumption about the disturbances beyond their zero mean, independence, and constant variance. Note, in particular that we have not used the assumption of normality in the proof. This follows because we have restricted ourselves to a relatively small class of estimators, namely, those that are both linear and unbiased. There may be (indeed, we know that there are) more precise estimators than least squares in the broader classes that allow for small amounts of bias or, possibly in some settings, nonlinear estimators.

When the assumption of normally distributed disturbances is added to the preceding, we obtain a complete result for the distributions of the estimators. Because they are linear functions of normally distributed variables, a and b are also normally distributed, with the means and variances derived earlier. To summarize, under the assumption of normality,

$$\begin{bmatrix} a \\ b \end{bmatrix} \sim N\left[\begin{bmatrix} \alpha \\ \beta \end{bmatrix}, \quad \sigma^2 \begin{bmatrix} 1/n + \bar{x}^2/S_{xx} & -\bar{x}/S_{xx} \\ -\bar{x}/S_{xx} & 1/S_{xx} \end{bmatrix} \right]. \tag{5-27}$$

We obtained the Gauss–Markov result as a characterization of the least squares estimator. That is, we began with a particular estimator in mind and assessed its statistical properties. An alternative approach would have been to pose the general problem of finding the estimator with the smallest variance, subject to the constraint that it be linear and unbiased. Of course, we would have been led, once again, to least squares. Suppose that we drop the assumption of linearity and seek only the minimum variance unbiased estimator? This is a far more difficult problem that requires us to specify a particular distribution for the disturbance. Under normality, linearity is, in fact, superfluous. The least squares estimator has minimum variance among *all* unbiased estimators. However, as we shall show in Chapter 9, there *are* biased estimators with smaller *mean squared errors* than least squares.[10] If we drop the assumption of normality, many of these results no longer hold. The Gauss–Markov theorem is intact, but without normality, the class of **linear unbiased estimators** becomes a bit restrictive. Other ''robust'' estimators, which may outperform least squares in some circumstances, have been proposed. The conclusion is that least squares is a powerful technique that produces an estimator with desirable

---

[10] See Judge et al. (1985) for an extensive discussion.

statistical properties in many cases. However, in more general cases than we consider here, the field is much broader and there is room for other estimators to compete quite favorably with least squares.

5.6. Statistical Inference

The preceding section presented the exact sampling distribution of the least squares estimators, a and b, under two specific assumptions: that the disturbances are normally distributed and that the sample $x_1, \ldots, x_n$ may taken as fixed and nonstochastic (or fixed in repeated samples). The usual procedures in parameter estimation will involve forming confidence intervals and testing hypotheses about the values of α and β. In order to do so, we need estimates of the true sampling variances of the parameters, which will require an estimate of the unknown σ^2.

5.6.1. Estimating the Sampling Distribution

Since σ^2 is the expected value of ε_i^2 and e_i is an estimate of ε_i,

$$\hat{\sigma}^2 = \frac{1}{n} \sum_i e_i^2 \tag{5-28}$$

would seem to be a natural estimator. By writing $e_i = y_i - a - bx_i$, and substituting $y_i = \alpha + \beta x_i + \varepsilon_i$, $\alpha = \bar{y} - \beta\bar{x} - \bar{\varepsilon}$, and $a = \bar{y} - b\bar{x}$, we obtain

$$e_i = \varepsilon_i - \bar{\varepsilon} - (x_i - \bar{x})(b - \beta)$$
$$= \varepsilon_i - \bar{\varepsilon} - (x_i - \bar{x})\left(\sum_j c_j\varepsilon_j\right). \tag{5-29}$$

Our estimate of an individual disturbance, ε_i, is distorted by two elements: the *sample average* of all the disturbances and an effect that we can attribute to the fact that β is not estimated perfectly. Recall that all disturbances are independent, so $E(\varepsilon_i\varepsilon_j) = 0$ if $i \neq j$. Now we square both sides of (5–29) and take expected values, which yields

$$E[e_i^2] = \sigma^2 + \frac{\sigma^2}{n} + \sigma^2(x_i - \bar{x})^2\left(\sum_j c_j^2\right) - \frac{2\sigma^2}{n} - 2\sigma^2(x_i - \bar{x})c_i$$

$$+ \frac{2\sigma^2}{n}(x_i - \bar{x})\left(\sum_j c_j\right).$$

In summing these terms, we use $\Sigma_i c_i = 0$, $\Sigma_i(x_i - \bar{x})c_i = 1$, and $\Sigma_i c_i^2 = 1/S_{xx}$. Collecting terms, we have

$$E\left[\sum_i e_i^2\right] = (n - 2)\sigma^2.$$

This implies that an unbiased estimator of σ^2 is

$$s^2 = \frac{\Sigma_i e_i^2}{n - 2}. \tag{5-30}$$

Thus, we can obtain an estimate of the sampling variance of b with

$$\text{Est. Var}[b] = \frac{s^2}{S_{xx}}.$$

(Henceforth, we shall use the notation Est. Var[·] to indicate a sample estimate of the sampling variance of an estimator.) The square root of this quantity,

$$s_b = \frac{s}{\sqrt{S_{xx}}},$$

is the "standard error" of the estimate, b. This is often denoted simply "the standard error of b."

Based on (5–27), the exact distribution of

$$z = \frac{b - \beta}{\sqrt{\sigma^2/S_{xx}}} \tag{5–31}$$

is standard normal. We defer until Chapter 6 (where it will be much simpler, using the tools of matrix algebra) a proof of the following:

$$\frac{(n-2)s^2}{\sigma^2} \sim \text{chi-squared } [n-2], \tag{5–32}$$

which is independent of b (and z). Consider, then, replacing the unknown value of σ^2 in (5–31) with s^2, our unbiased estimate. The result,

$$t = \frac{b - \beta}{\sqrt{s^2/S_{xx}}},$$

is the ratio of a standard normal variable to the square root of a chi-squared variable divided by its degrees of freedom, which has a t distribution with $(n-2)$ degrees of freedom. Thus, the ratio

$$\frac{b - \beta}{s_b} \sim t[n-2] \tag{5–33}$$

can form the basis of statistical inference.

5.6.2. Testing a Hypothesis About β

A confidence interval for β would be based on (5–33). In particular, we could say that

$$\text{Prob}(b - t_{\lambda/2}s_b \le \beta \le b + t_{\lambda/2}s_b) = 1 - \lambda,$$

where $1 - \lambda$ is the desired level of confidence and $t_{\lambda/2}$ is the appropriate critical value from the t distribution with $(n-2)$ degrees of freedom. A confidence interval for α would be constructed likewise, using a and its estimated variance.

EXAMPLE 5.4 ─────────────────────────────────

In the earlier regression, we obtained

$$a = -67.5806 \quad \text{and} \quad b = 0.9793.$$

To compute the standard errors, we need

$$s^2 = \frac{537.00}{8} = 67.125,$$

$$S_{xx} = 67,192.45,$$

and

$$\bar{x} = 879.24.$$

Inserting these in (5–24) and (5–25), using s^2 instead of σ^2, the estimated variances are

$$\text{Est. Var}[a] = 778.96 \qquad \text{or} \qquad s_a = 27.91$$

and

$$\text{Est. Var}[b] = 0.0009992 \qquad \text{or} \qquad s_b = 0.03161.$$

For a t distribution with $n - 2 = 8$ degrees of freedom, the 95 percent critical value is 2.306. Therefore, 95 percent confidence intervals for α and β are

$$-67.5806 \pm 2.306(27.91) \qquad \text{or} \qquad -131.94 \text{ to } -3.22 \text{ for } \alpha$$

and

$$0.9793 \pm 2.306(0.03161) \qquad \text{or} \qquad 0.90641 \text{ to } 1.0522 \text{ for } \beta.$$

We can also form a confidence interval for the disturbance variance, σ^2. Using (5–32) and the same reasoning we used previously, we find that a 95 percent confidence interval for σ^2 would be

$$\frac{(n-2)s^2}{\chi^2_{0.975}} \qquad \text{to} \qquad \frac{(n-2)s^2}{\chi^2_{0.025}}. \tag{5–34}$$

EXAMPLE 5.5

Continuing Example 5.4, we obtain a confidence interval for σ^2 that would be based on the chi-squared distribution with $(10 - 2) = 8$ degrees of freedom. The appropriate critical values are 2.18 and 15.5, so that the interval is

$$(10 - 2)\frac{67.125}{17.54} < \sigma^2 < (10 - 2)\frac{67.125}{2.18}$$

or

$$30.62 < \sigma^2 < 246.33.$$

This might seem to be rather wide. However, we are usually more interested in the standard deviation rather than the variance of ε. A 95 percent confidence interval for σ, based on these same results, would be 5.89 to 15.69.[11]

A related procedure is to test whether the parameter takes a given value. To test the hypothesis

$$H_0 : \beta = \beta^0 \qquad \text{versus} \qquad H_1 : \beta \neq \beta^0,$$

the simplest procedure is to appeal to our confidence interval. The confidence interval gives a set of plausible values of β, given our sample data. If this set does not include β^0, the null hypothesis should be rejected. Formally, under the null hypothesis, the ratio

$$t = \frac{b - \beta^0}{s_b} \tag{5–35}$$

has a t distribution with $(n - 2)$ degrees of freedom, which has a mean of zero. Extreme values of this ratio, in either tail of the distribution, cast doubt on the hypothesis. Thus, in general, we reject H_0 if

$$\frac{|b - \beta^0|}{s_b} \geq t_{\lambda/2},$$

---

[11] It is also not the narrowest possible confidence interval for σ^2 because of the asymmetry of the chi-squared distribution. See Exercise 19 in Chapter 4.

where $t_{\lambda/2}$ is the $100(1 - \lambda/2)$ percent critical value from the t distribution with $(n - 2)$ degrees of freedom. For a one-sided test, we adjust the critical region and use the t_λ critical point from the distribution. Again, values of the sample estimate that are greatly inconsistent with the hypothesis cast doubt upon it.

EXAMPLE 5.6 _____

Recall Keynes's fundamental principle that the marginal propensity to consume is less than 1. Are the data consistent with the hypothesis that β is less than 1? Consider testing the alternative,

$$H_0:\beta \geq 1 \quad \text{versus} \quad H_1:\beta < 1.$$

The appropriate test statistic is

$$t = \frac{0.9793 - 1}{0.03161} = -0.655.$$

This is well above the 0.05 critical point of -2.306. We conclude that H_0 should not be rejected. The data are consistent with the hypothesis that $\beta \geq 1$. They are also consistent with the hypothesis that $\beta < 1$. That is, the estimate is not *significantly* different from 1.

_____

A common test is whether a parameter, β, is significantly different from zero. The appropriate test statistic,

$$t = \frac{b}{s_b}, \tag{5–36}$$

is presented as standard output with the other results by most computer programs. The test is done in the usual way. This is usually labeled the *t ratio* for the estimate, b. If $|b/s_b| > t_{\lambda/2}$, the hypothesis is rejected and the coefficient is said to be "statistically significant." The value of 1.96, which would apply for the 5 percent significance level in a large sample, is often used as a benchmark value when a table of critical values is not immediately available.

5.6.3. Tests Based on the Fit of the Regression

A different type of hypothesis test focuses on the fit of the regression. Recall that the least squares value of b was chosen to minimize the sum of squared deviations. Since $R^2 = 1 - \text{SSE}/S_{yy}$, it follows that the value of b is chosen to maximize R^2. One might ask whether choosing some other value for the slope of the line leads to a significant loss of fit. For example, for the consumption function, one might be interested in whether a value of 0.8 as opposed to the least squares value of 0.9793 leads to a substantially worse fit.

It is clear that if b equals zero, R^2 equals zero as well. Thus, the t ratio in (5–36) can be construed as a test of whether choosing $b = 0$ would lead to a significant loss of fit. Formally, consider the square of the t ratio in (5–36):

$$t^2 = \frac{b^2 S_{xx}}{s^2} = \frac{(S_{xy}^2/S_{xx}^2)S_{xx}}{S_{yy}(1 - R^2)/(n - 2)}$$

$$= \frac{R^2/1}{(1 - R^2)/(n - 2)}$$

$$= F[1, n - 2].$$

(The division by one in the numerator is included to maintain consistency with several results that we will derive later.) The square of a variable with a t distribution with $(n - 2)$ degrees of freedom has an F distribution with one and $(n - 2)$ degrees of freedom.[12] Thus, this provides an alternative test of the hypothesis that $\beta = 0$.

EXAMPLE 5.7 _____

In the consumption function, the t ratio for testing

$$H_0 : \beta = 0$$

is 0.97927/0.031608, or 30.982. (This is, of course, significant by any standard.) The F ratio for the same hypothesis is

$$F[1, 8] = \frac{0.991735/1}{(1 - 0.991735)/8} = 959.93.$$

This equals the square of the t ratio. The critical value from the table of $F -$ ratios is $5.32 = 2.306^2$, as expected. Obviously, the hypothesis should be rejected.

_____

The two tests we have considered are equivalent. Not only is the F statistic shown in the table of Example 5.7 equal to the square of the t ratio (that is how it was derived), but the critical values of F and t in the tables have the same relationship. If the t ratio is large in absolute value, the F statistic will be large as well.

Consider, then, how the fit of the line to our data changes if we use, say, b_* for the slope rather than b, the least squares value. If we use a different slope, a different intercept will result as well; that is, if we minimize

$$\sum_i e_{i*}^2 = \Sigma(y_i - a_* - b_* x_i)^2 \tag{5-37}$$

with respect to a_* with the given value of b_*, the result is

$$a_* = \bar{y} - b_* \bar{x}.$$

The resulting sum of squares when we use a_* and b_* is given in (5–37). Using a well-known trick, we first note that we can write

$$a_* = a + (b - b_*)\bar{x},$$

where a is the original least squares value given in (5–14). Now

$$\sum_i e_{i*}^2 = \sum_i [y_i - a - (b - b_*)\bar{x} - bx_i + bx_i - b_* x_i]^2$$

$$= \sum_i [e_i + (b - b_*)(x_i - \bar{x})]^2 \tag{5-38}$$

$$= \sum_i e_i^2 + (b - b_*)^2 S_{xx},$$

where e_i is the original least squares residual. This new sum of squares is larger than the one that uses b. We define R_*^2 to be the coefficient of determination when we use this alternative estimate:

$$R_*^2 = 1 - \frac{\Sigma_i e_{i*}^2}{S_{yy}}.$$

_____

[12] See Section 3.4.2.

From before, $R^2 = 1 - (\Sigma_i e_i^2)/S_{yy}$. Therefore, the difference between these two values is

$$R^2 - R_*^2 = \frac{(b - b_*)^2 S_{xx}}{S_{yy}},$$

which is, of course, positive.[13]

The alternative regression line will not fit as well as the least squares regression line. To test this statistically, recall that the earlier test of $H_0: \beta = \beta^0$ was based on the test statistic

$$t(n - 2) = \left| \frac{b - \beta_0}{s_b} \right|.$$

Suppose that we use b_* for β^0. Squaring this and inserting the previous result, we have

$$
\begin{aligned}
t^2 &= \frac{(b - b_*)^2 S_{xx}/S_{yy}}{(1 - R^2)/(n - 2)} \\
&= \frac{(R^2 - R_*^2)/1}{(1 - R^2)/(n - 2)}.
\end{aligned}
\tag{5-39}
$$

Thus, the test statistic is based on the difference in the two coefficients of determination. Again, the test is precisely equivalent to the earlier t test. The test statistic is just the square of the t statistic (by definition) and the critical value used as the benchmark will be the square of the t value found in the tables.

The preceding has shown that we may test a hypothesis about the slope in our regression from either of two points of view. Our first test, the t test, is based on the difference between our least squares estimate of a parameter and a hypothesized value. The principle involved is that if the hypothesis is correct, the least squares estimate will satisfy it within the range of sampling variation (i.e., we measure the distance of b from β_0 in standard error units). The second equivalent test is based on the principle that if a hypothesis is correct, assuming it is true will not significantly degrade the fit of the regression. It is thus based on the difference between a measure of goodness of fit computed for the least squares value and for the hypothesized one.

5.7. Prediction

Aside from the estimation of parameters, the most common use of regression is for prediction. Suppose that x^0 is a known value of the regressor, and we are interested in predicting y^0, the value of y associated with x^0. At the outset, we must reconcile ourselves to at least two sources of error. We shall attempt to predict the true value of y^0:

$$y^0 = \alpha + \beta x^0 + \varepsilon^0.$$

Since we have only our sample estimates of α and β, one source of error will be the sampling error in our parameter estimates. But regardless of the precision of our parameter estimates, we will never be able to forecast ε^0 perfectly. The forecast will be

$$\hat{y}^0 = a + bx^0. \tag{5-40}$$

The prediction error is

$$
\begin{aligned}
e^0 &= y^0 - \hat{y}^0 \\
&= \alpha + \beta x^0 + \varepsilon^0 - a - bx^0 \\
&= (\alpha - a) + (\beta - b)x^0 + \varepsilon^0.
\end{aligned}
$$

[13] Note that R_*^2 might be negative.

By taking expectations on both sides, we see that $E(e^0) = 0$. Therefore, the least squares forecast is **unbiased** in the sense that the forecast error has a mean of zero. The variance of the prediction error is

$$\text{Var}[e^0] = \text{Var}[a] + (x^0)^2 \text{Var}[b] + 2x^0 \text{Cov}[a,b] + \text{Var}[\varepsilon^0]$$

$$= \sigma^2 \left[1 + \frac{1}{n} + \frac{\bar{x}^2}{S_{xx}} + \frac{(x^0)^2}{S_{xx}} - \frac{2\bar{x}x^0}{S_{xx}} \right] \tag{5-41}$$

$$= \sigma^2 \left[1 + \frac{1}{n} + \frac{(x^0 - \bar{x})^2}{S_{xx}} \right].$$

By inserting the sample estimate of s^2 for σ^2, we can construct a **prediction interval** for y^0 in the same fashion as we did for the individual parameters. In particular, our forecast interval will be

$$(a + bx^0) \pm t_{\lambda/2} \sqrt{ s^2 \left[1 + \frac{1}{n} + \frac{(x^0 - \bar{x})^2}{S_{xx}} \right] }. \tag{5-42}$$

EXAMPLE 5.8.

Suppose, using the consumption data of Example 5.1, that 1980 disposable income were forecasted to be $1030 billion. To compute a forecast interval, we require

$$a = -67.5806,$$

$$b = 0.9793,$$

$$s^2 = 67.125,$$

$$\bar{x} = 879.24,$$

$$S_{xx} = 67,192.44,$$

$$n = 10.$$

The critical value from the t distribution is 2.306. Inserting these in (5–42) produces a forecast interval of

$$-67.5806 + 0.9793(1030) \pm 2.306(9.8256)$$

or

$$941.1 \pm 22.658.^{[14]}$$

Figure 5.9 shows the computation for the data we have been using in our example of the consumption function. There are two important features of the prediction interval. First, note that its width is a function of $(x^0 - \bar{x})^2$. Thus, the farther x^0 is from $\bar{x}$, the wider will be the forecast interval. This reflects the intuitively appealing result that forecasting is more difficult the further we go outside the range of our experience (in either direction). Second, note that the forecast variance in (5–41) is composed of three parts. The second and third become progressively smaller as we accumulate more data (i.e., as n increases). But the first term, σ^2, is constant, which implies that no matter how much data we have, we can never predict perfectly.

---

[14] The actual outcomes were disposable income of $1021.6 billion and consumption of $931.8 billion. Based on knowledge of the figure of 1021.6, our forecast of consumption would have been 932.9, with an ex post forecast error of 0.12 percent.

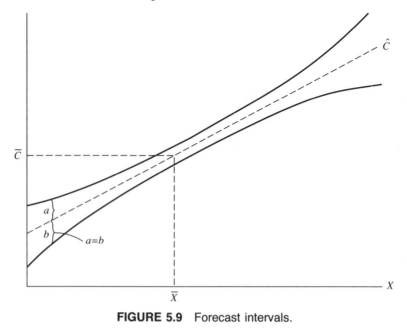

FIGURE 5.9 Forecast intervals.

EXERCISES

1. Production data for 22 firms in a certain industry produce the following, where $y = \ln$ output and $x = \ln$ labor hours input:

$$\bar{y} = 20 \qquad \sum_i (y_i - \bar{y})^2 = 100,$$

$$\bar{x} = 10 \qquad \sum_i (x_i - \bar{x})^2 = 60$$

$$\sum_i (x_i - \bar{x})(y_i - \bar{y}) = 30.$$

  (a) Compute the least squares estimates of α and β in the model
$$y = \alpha + \beta x + \varepsilon.$$
  (b) Test the hypothesis that $\beta = 1$.
  (c) Form a 99 percent confidence interval for σ^2, the variance of ε.

2. Data from a different industry are used to obtain the following estimated regression:
$$\hat{y} = 25 + 0.4x, \quad R^2 = 0.2, \ \bar{y} = 35, \ n = 12,$$

$$\sum_i (x_i - \bar{x})^2 = 100.$$

Test the hypothesis that the slopes are the same in this regression and the one in the previous problem, assuming that the disturbance variances are the same. [**Hint:** For independent samples, there are two approaches. If it can be assumed that the disturbance variances in the two models are equal, the two samples can be pooled to estimate the common σ^2. Determine the pooled moments by manipulating the previous results. Then the statistic $(b_1 - b_2)/\{s^2[(1/(\mathbf{x}_1'\mathbf{M}^0\mathbf{x}_1)) + (1/(\mathbf{x}_2'\mathbf{M}^0\mathbf{x}_2))]\}^{1/2}$ may be referred to the t distribution with $n_1 + n_2 - 4$ degrees of freedom. If the assumption of equal variances is untenable, the statistic $(b_1 - b_2)/\{\text{Est. Var}[b_1] + \text{Est. Var}[b_2]\}^{1/2}$ will be approximately distributed as standard normal. Carry out the test, using both methods.]

3. Suppose that you have two independent unbiased estimators of the same parameter, θ, say $\hat{\theta}_1$ and $\hat{\theta}_2$, with different variances, v_1 and v_2. What linear combination, $\hat{\theta} = c_1\hat{\theta}_1 + c_2\hat{\theta}_2$, is the minimum variance unbiased estimator of θ? Use your result to compute the minimum variance unbiased estimator of the common slope in the two regressions in Exercises 1 and 2.

4. For the data in Exercise 1, what is the R^2 in the regression of y on x? Now suppose that the regression is fit without a constant term and the computer program computes the R^2 using

$$R^2 = 1 - \frac{\mathbf{e}'\mathbf{e}}{\Sigma_i(y_i - \bar{y})^2}.$$

What value will be reported? What if it uses

$$R^2 = \frac{b^2\Sigma_i(x_i - \bar{x})^2}{\Sigma_i(y_i - \bar{y})^2}$$

instead? What value will be reported? What is the appropriate value to report?

5. We are interested in studying salary differences between two professions. Our sample consists of 60 individuals from profession A and 40 from profession B. The average salary in B is 1. The average salary in the entire sample is 0.85. If we compute a least squares regression of salaries on a constant and a variable that is simply 0 for all individuals in A and 1 for those in B, what will be the constant and the slope? If the standard deviations of the two samples are 0.2 for profession A and 0.3 for profession B, what are the estimates of the variances and covariance of the two estimates? What is the R^2 in the regression? (For further applications, see Section 8.2.)

6. Suppose that a regression of the balance of trade with a particular country gives results

$$Y = 100{,}000 + 0.6X + e, \qquad R^2 = 0.4,$$

using yearly observations quoted in 1972 dollars. Suppose that the figures were rescaled to 1982 dollars by multiplying by 0.74. What would have been obtained for the constant and slope? Based on the previous figures, would you be able to determine the least squares results if the figures were quoted in the currency of the other country instead if you knew the exchange rates?

7. Three variables, N, D, and Y, all have zero means and unit variances. A fourth variable is $C = N + D$. In the regression of C on Y, the slope is 0.8. In the regression of C on N, the slope is 0.5. In the regression of D on Y, the slope is 0.4. What is the sum of squared residuals in the regression of C on D? There are 21 observations, and all moments are computed using $1/(n - 1)$ as the divisor.

8. Prove that the least squares intercept estimator in the classical regression model is the minimum variance linear unbiased estimator.

9. Suppose that the data for a regression are given in terms of deviations from the sample means. What is the expected value of the slope in the regression of $(y_i - \bar{y})$ on $(x_i - \bar{x})$ if it is computed without a constant term? Suppose that only the data on x are in mean deviation form. Now what is the expected value of the slope estimator? Finally, suppose that only y is in mean deviation form. What is the expected value of the slope estimator in the regression of the centered y's on the uncentered x's, assuming that the true value of the intercept is not zero?

10. Consider the simple regression

$$y_i = \beta x_i + \varepsilon_i.$$

(a) What is the minimum mean-squared error linear estimator of β? [**Hint:** Let the estimator be $\hat{\beta} = \mathbf{c}'\mathbf{y}$. Choose $\mathbf{c}$ to minimize $\text{Var}[\hat{\beta}] + (E[\hat{\beta} - \beta])^2$. The answer is a function of the unknown parameters.]

(b) For the estimator in part (a), show that the ratio of the mean-squared error of $\hat{\beta}$ to that of the ordinary least squares estimator, b, is

$$\frac{\text{MSE}[\hat{\beta}]}{\text{MSE}[b]} = \frac{\tau^2}{(1 + \tau^2)},$$

where

$$\tau^2 = \frac{\beta^2}{\sigma^2/\mathbf{x}'\mathbf{x}}.$$

Note that τ is the square of the population analog to the t ratio for testing the hypothesis that $\beta = 0$, which is given in (5–33). How do you interpret the behavior of this ratio as $\tau \rightarrow \infty$? (For some further discussion of this result and some related issues, see Section 8.5.)

11. Suppose that the classical regression model applies, but the true value of the constant is zero. Compare the variance of the least squares slope estimator computed without a constant term to that of the estimator computed with an unnecessary constant term.

12. The next year's data for the consumption data given in Table 5.1 appear in a footnote to Example 5.8. Reestimate the regression with this new information; then use the updated regression to compute a 95 percent forecast interval for 1981 consumption, assuming that disposable income is forecasted to be $1037.4 billion.

13. Suppose that the regression model is

$$y_i = \alpha + \beta x_i - \varepsilon_i,$$

$$f(\varepsilon_i) = \left(\frac{1}{\lambda}\right)e^{-\varepsilon_i/\lambda}, \qquad \varepsilon_i \geq 0.$$

This is a rather peculiar model in that all of the disturbances are assumed to be positive. Note that the disturbances have $E[\varepsilon_i] = \lambda$. Show that the least squares slope is unbiased but that the intercept is biased.

14. For the regression model without a constant term in Exercise 10, prove that the estimator $\bar{y}/\bar{x}$ is unbiased and show that its variance is greater than that of the ordinary least squares estimator.

15. As a profit-maximizing monopolist, you face the demand curve

$$Q = \alpha + \beta P + \varepsilon.$$

In the past, you have set the following prices and sold the accompanying quantities:

Q	3	3	7	6	10	15	16	13	9	15	9	15	12	18	21
P	18	16	17	12	15	15	4	13	11	6	8	10	7	7	7

Suppose that your marginal cost is 10. Based on the least squares regression, compute a 95 percent confidence interval for the profit-maximizing output.

16. For the bivariate distribution in Exercise 16 of Chapter 4, it is shown (claimed) in part (f) that

$$f(x|y) = \frac{e^{-\beta y}(\beta y)^x}{x!}.$$

It follows that

$$E[x|y] = \beta y.$$

(a) Does this suggest an alternative estimator for β to the maximum likelihood estimator of part (a) of that exercise?

(b) It can also be shown (can you do it?) that in the conditional distribution in part (d),

$$E[y|x] = \alpha(x + 1) \qquad \text{where} \qquad \alpha = \frac{1}{\beta + \theta}.$$

Does this suggest an alternative estimator to the maximum likelihood estimator of α implied by part (a) of that exercise? What is the MLE of α for that bivariate distribution? What is its asymptotic distribution?

6

Multiple Regression

6.1. Introduction

The regression model developed in Chapter 5 is flexible enough to accommodate a variety of settings. But it is inadequate when we can identify more than one independent influence on the dependent variable. The **multiple regression model** allows us to study the relationship between a dependent variable and several independent variables.

EXAMPLE 6.1

A number of recent studies have analyzed the relationship between income and education. We would expect, on average, higher levels of education to be associated with higher incomes. However, the simple regression model

$$\text{income} = \beta_1 + \beta_2 \, \text{education} + \varepsilon$$

neglects the fact that most people have a higher income when they are older than when they are young, regardless of their education. This means that β_2 will overstate the marginal impact of education. If age and education are positively correlated, it will associate all of the observed increases in income with increases in education. A better specification would account for the effect of age, as in

$$\text{income} = \beta_1 + \beta_2 \, \text{education} + \beta_3 \, \text{age} + \varepsilon.$$

It is often observed that income tends to rise less rapidly in the later earning years than in the early ones. To accommodate this possibility, we might extend the model to

$$\text{income} = \beta_1 + \beta_2 \, \text{education} + \beta_3 \, \text{age} + \beta_4 \, \text{age}^2 + \varepsilon.$$

We would expect β_3 to be positive and β_4 to be negative.

6.2. Assumptions of the Linear Model

The general form of the multiple linear regression model is

$$y_i = \beta_1 x_{i1} + \beta_2 x_{i2} + \cdots + \beta_K x_{iK} + \varepsilon_i. \tag{6-1}$$

The nature and sources of the disturbance were discussed in Chapter 5. The only difference here is the number of right-hand variables in the model. The model is linear in the variables x_k and has an additive disturbance. (Of course, this does not restrict us to simple linear equations, however. Consider, for instance, the quadratic function of age in the model discussed in the Introduction.)

Let the column vector $\mathbf{x}_k$ be the n observations on variable x_k, $k = 1, \ldots, K$ and assemble these data in an $n \times K$ data matrix, $\mathbf{X}$. In most contexts, the first column of $\mathbf{X}$ is assumed to be a column of ones, so that β_1 is the constant term in the model. Finally, let $\mathbf{y}$ be the n observations, $y_1, \ldots, y_n$. The model can now be written

$$\mathbf{y} = \mathbf{x}_1\beta_1 + \cdots + \mathbf{x}_K\beta_K + \boldsymbol{\varepsilon} \tag{6–2}$$

or

Assumption 1. $\mathbf{y} = \mathbf{X}\boldsymbol{\beta} + \boldsymbol{\varepsilon}.$ $\tag{6–3}$

As before, our primary interest is in estimation and inference about the parameter vector $\boldsymbol{\beta}$. Note that the simple regression model of Chapter 5 is a special case in which $\mathbf{X}$ has only two columns.

It is convenient to reformulate our earlier assumptions about the disturbance in matrix notation.

$$E[\varepsilon_i] = 0$$

or

Assumption 2. $E[\boldsymbol{\varepsilon}] = \begin{bmatrix} E[\varepsilon_1] \\ E[\varepsilon_2] \\ \vdots \\ E[\varepsilon_n] \end{bmatrix} = \mathbf{0},$ $\tag{6–4}$

which implies that

$$E[\mathbf{y}] = \mathbf{X}\boldsymbol{\beta}.$$

The assumptions of constant variance, or homoscedasticity, and uncorrelatedness across observations imply that

$$
E[\boldsymbol{\varepsilon}\boldsymbol{\varepsilon}'] = \begin{bmatrix} E[\varepsilon_1\varepsilon_1] & E[\varepsilon_1\varepsilon_2] & \cdots & E[\varepsilon_1\varepsilon_n] \\ E[\varepsilon_2\varepsilon_1] & E[\varepsilon_2\varepsilon_2] & \cdots & E[\varepsilon_2\varepsilon_n] \\ \vdots & \vdots & \vdots & \vdots \\ E[\varepsilon_n\varepsilon_1] & E[\varepsilon_n\varepsilon_2] & \cdots & E[\varepsilon_n\varepsilon_n] \end{bmatrix}
$$

$$
= \begin{bmatrix} \sigma^2 & 0 & \cdots & 0 \\ 0 & \sigma^2 & \cdots & 0 \\ & & \vdots & \\ 0 & 0 & \cdots & \sigma^2 \end{bmatrix}.
$$

Assumption 3. $E[\boldsymbol{\varepsilon}\boldsymbol{\varepsilon}'] = \sigma^2\mathbf{I}.$ $\tag{6–5}$

This is equivalent to Assumptions 3 and 4 in Chapter 5.

Assumption 4. $E[\boldsymbol{\varepsilon}|\mathbf{X}] = \mathbf{0}.$

As before, we assume that there is no information about $\boldsymbol{\varepsilon}$ embodied in $\mathbf{X}$. Note that since

$$\text{Cov}[\mathbf{x}, \boldsymbol{\varepsilon}] = \text{Cov}[\mathbf{x}, E(\boldsymbol{\varepsilon}|\mathbf{X})],$$

Assumption 4 implies that $\text{Cov}[\mathbf{X}, \boldsymbol{\varepsilon}] = 0$.

Another very important assumption must be made about the regressors. We assume that there are no exact linear relationships among the variables.

Assumption 5. $\mathbf{X}$ is a nonstochastic $n \times k$ matrix with rank K. $\tag{6–6}$

This means that $\mathbf{X}$ has full column rank; the columns of $\mathbf{X}$ are linearly independent. The counterpart in the simple model of the previous chapter was the assumption that $\Sigma_i(x_i - \bar{x})^2$ is greater than zero. If not, all values are the same and the second column of $\mathbf{X}$ is a multiple of the first. Among other things, this implies that we must have at least K observations. To see the need for this assumption, consider an example.

EXAMPLE 6.2 _____

Suppose that a cross-section model specifies $C = \beta_1 + \beta_2$ nonlabor income $+ \beta_3$ salary $+ \beta_4$ income $+ \varepsilon$, where income is exactly equal to salary plus nonlabor income. Clearly, there is an exact linear dependency in the model. Now let

$$\beta_2' = \beta_2 + a,$$

$$\beta_3' = \beta_3 + a,$$

and

$$\beta_4' = \beta_4 - a,$$

where a is any number. Then the exact same value appears on the right-hand side of C if we substitute β_2', β_3', and β_4' for β_2, β_3, and β_4. Obviously, there is no way to estimate the parameters of this model. There are certain functions of the parameters that can be estimated in a case such as this. For instance, regardless of the value of a,

$$\beta_2 + \beta_4 = \beta_2' + \beta_4'$$

and

$$\beta_3 + \beta_4 = \beta_3' + \beta_4'.$$

We should be able to estimate a model that is a function of $\gamma_1 = \beta_2 + \beta_4$ and $\gamma_2 = \beta_3 + \beta_4$. By substituting income = nonlabor income + salary in the previous equation, we obtain precisely

$$C = \beta_1 + \gamma_1 \text{ nonlabor income} + \gamma_2 \text{ salary} + \varepsilon.$$

The assumption that $\mathbf{X}$ is nonstochastic is, in fact, unessential. We examine the implications of dropping the assumption in Section 6.4.2 and again in Section 10.4.

In Section 6.5, we will add the assumption that the disturbances are independently and identically normally distributed:

Assumption 6. $\varepsilon \sim N[\mathbf{0}, \sigma^2\mathbf{I}]$. (6–7)

The assumption of normality of the disturbances is not necessary to obtain the statistical results we use in multiple regression analysis. However, except in those cases in which some alternative distribution is explicitly assumed,[1] the normality assumption is probably quite reasonable. It does prove useful in constructing test statistics, as shown in Section 6.5.[2]

6.3. Least Squares Regression

As before, we consider the most common method of estimating the parameters of the linear regression model, least squares.

_____

[1] See Example 10.3.

[2] But see also Section 10.3.

A Notational Convention. Henceforth, to avoid a possibly confusing and cumbersome notation, we use a boldface **x** to denote a column or a row of **X**. Which applies should be obvious from the context. Also, subscripts j and k will be used to denote columns (variables) and i and t will be used to denote rows (observations).

6.3.1. The Least Squares Coefficient Vector

The least squares coefficient vector minimizes the sum of squared residuals:

$$\sum_i \tilde{\varepsilon}_i^2 = \sum_i (y_i - \tilde{\boldsymbol{\beta}}' \mathbf{x}_i)^2, \tag{6-8}$$

where $\tilde{\boldsymbol{\beta}}$ is the arbitrary choice for the coefficient vector. The minimization problem, then, is to choose $\tilde{\boldsymbol{\beta}}$ to

$$\text{Minimize }_{\tilde{\boldsymbol{\beta}}}\; S(\tilde{\boldsymbol{\beta}}) = \tilde{\boldsymbol{\varepsilon}}'\tilde{\boldsymbol{\varepsilon}} = (\mathbf{y} - \mathbf{X}\tilde{\boldsymbol{\beta}})'(\mathbf{y} - \mathbf{X}\tilde{\boldsymbol{\beta}}). \tag{6-9}$$

Expanding this, we have

$$\tilde{\boldsymbol{\varepsilon}}'\tilde{\boldsymbol{\varepsilon}} = \mathbf{y}'\mathbf{y} - \tilde{\boldsymbol{\beta}}'\mathbf{X}'\mathbf{y} - \mathbf{y}'\mathbf{X}\tilde{\boldsymbol{\beta}} + \tilde{\boldsymbol{\beta}}'\mathbf{X}'\mathbf{X}\tilde{\boldsymbol{\beta}} \tag{6-10}$$

or

$$S(\tilde{\boldsymbol{\beta}}) = \mathbf{y}'\mathbf{y} - 2\tilde{\boldsymbol{\beta}}'\mathbf{X}'\mathbf{y} + \tilde{\boldsymbol{\beta}}'\mathbf{X}'\mathbf{X}\tilde{\boldsymbol{\beta}}.$$

The necessary condition for a minimum is

$$\frac{\partial S(\tilde{\boldsymbol{\beta}})}{\partial \tilde{\boldsymbol{\beta}}} = -2\mathbf{X}'\mathbf{y} + 2\mathbf{X}'\mathbf{X}\tilde{\boldsymbol{\beta}} = \mathbf{0}. \tag{6-11}$$

Let **b** be the solution. Then **b** satisfies the normal equations

$$\mathbf{X}'\mathbf{X}\mathbf{b} = \mathbf{X}'\mathbf{y}.$$

These are the least squares normal equations that we analyzed earlier. Assuming that the inverse of $\mathbf{X}'\mathbf{X}$ exists, which follows from the full rank assumption,[3] we find that the solution is

$$\mathbf{b} = (\mathbf{X}'\mathbf{X})^{-1}\mathbf{X}'\mathbf{y}. \tag{6-12}$$

In order to verify that this is indeed a minimum, we require

$$\frac{\partial^2 S(\mathbf{b})}{\partial \mathbf{b}\, \partial \mathbf{b}'} = 2\mathbf{X}'\mathbf{X} \tag{6-13}$$

to be a positive definite matrix. Let $q = \mathbf{c}'\mathbf{X}'\mathbf{X}\mathbf{c}$ for some arbitrary nonzero vector, **c.** Then

$$q = \mathbf{v}'\mathbf{v} = \sum_i v_i^2, \quad \text{where } \mathbf{v} = \mathbf{X}\mathbf{c}.$$

Unless every element of **v** is zero, q is positive. But if **v** could be zero, **v** would be a linear combination of the columns of **X** that equals **0.** This contradicts the assumption that **X** has full rank.

---

[3] The condition assumed in Chapter 5 that $\Sigma(x_i - \bar{x})^2$ is positive is the equivalent in the two-variable case.

6.3.2 Some Examples

EXAMPLE 6.3 ────────────────────────────────

To illustrate the computations, we consider an example based on macroeconomic data (see Table 6.1).

In order to estimate an investment equation, we first convert the Investment and GNP series to real terms by dividing them by the CPI[4] and then scale the two series so that they are measured in trillions of dollars. The other variables in the regression are a time trend $(1, 2, \ldots)$, the interest rate, and the rate of inflation, computed as the percentage change in the CPI.[5] These produce the data matrices listed in Table 6.2.

Consider first a regression of real investment on a constant, a time trend, and real GNP, which correspond to x_1, x_2, and x_3. The normal equations are

$$\begin{bmatrix} \Sigma_i x_{i1} x_{i1} & \Sigma_i x_{i1} x_{i2} & \Sigma_i x_{i1} x_{i3} \\ \Sigma_i x_{i2} x_{i1} & \Sigma_i x_{i2} x_{i2} & \Sigma_i x_{i2} x_{i3} \\ \Sigma_i x_{i3} x_{i1} & \Sigma_i x_{i3} x_{i2} & \Sigma_i x_{i3} x_{i3} \end{bmatrix} \begin{bmatrix} b_1 \\ b_2 \\ b_3 \end{bmatrix} = \begin{bmatrix} \Sigma_i x_{i1} y_i \\ \Sigma_i x_{i2} y_i \\ \Sigma_i x_{i3} y_i \end{bmatrix}.$$

Inserting the specific variables of the example, we have

$$b_1 n \quad\;\; + b_2 \sum T \;\; + b_3 \sum G \;\; = \sum Y,$$

$$b_1 \sum T + b_2 \sum T^2 \; + b_3 \sum TG = \sum TY,$$

$$b_1 \sum G + b_2 \sum TG + b_3 \sum G^2 = \sum GY.$$

A solution can be obtained by first dividing the first equation by n to obtain

$$b_1 = \overline{Y} - b_2 \overline{T} - b_3 \overline{G}.$$

Insert this in the second and third equations, and rearrange terms to yield a set of two equations:

$$b_2 \sum (T - \overline{T})^2 \qquad\;\; + b_3 \sum (T - \overline{T})(G - \overline{G}) = \sum (T - \overline{T})(Y - \overline{Y}),$$

$$b_2 \sum (T - \overline{T})(G - \overline{G}) + b_3 \sum (G - \overline{G})^2 \qquad\;\; = \sum (G - \overline{G})(Y - \overline{Y}).$$

This shows the nature of the solution for the slopes, which will be computed from the sums of squared deviations and cross products of the variables. Letting lowercase letters indicate variables measured as deviations from the sample means, we find that the least squares solutions for b_2 and b_3 are

$$b_2 = \frac{\sum ty \sum g^2 - \sum gy \sum tg}{\sum t^2 \sum g^2 - \left(\sum gt\right)^2},$$

$$b_3 = \frac{\sum gy \sum t^2 - \sum ty \sum tg}{\sum t^2 \sum g^2 - \left(\sum gt\right)^2}.$$

────────────────

[4] Arguably, one might choose a better deflator.

[5] The 1967 figure for the CPI is 79.06.

TABLE 6.1

Year	Nominal GNP	Nominal Investment	CPI	Interest Rate[a]
1968	873.4	133.3	82.54	5.16
1969	944.0	149.3	86.79	5.87
1970	992.7	144.2	91.45	5.95
1971	1077.6	166.4	96.01	4.88
1972	1185.9	195.0	100.00	4.50
1973	1326.4	229.8	105.75	6.44
1974	1434.2	228.7	115.08	7.83
1975	1549.2	206.1	125.79	6.25
1976	1718.0	257.9	132.34	5.50
1977	1918.3	324.1	140.05	5.46
1978	2163.9	386.6	150.42	7.46
1979	2417.8	423.0	163.42	10.28
1980	2633.1	402.3	178.64	11.77
1981	2937.7	471.5	195.51	13.42
1982	3057.5	421.9	207.23	11.02

Source: Data from the *Economic Report of the President,* Government Printing Office, Washington, D.C., 1983. CPI 1967 is 79.06.
[a] Average yearly discount rate at the New York Federal Reserve Bank.

With these solutions in hand, the intercept can now be computed. The sample sums for the variables of this regression are

$$\bar{Y} = 0.20333 \qquad \sum y^2 = 0.016353 \qquad \sum ty = 1.60400,$$

$$\bar{T} = 8 \qquad \sum t^2 = 280 \qquad \sum gy = 0.066196,$$

$$\bar{G} = 1.2873 \qquad \sum g^2 = 0.359609 \qquad \sum tg = 9.82000.$$

TABLE 6.2[a]

Real Investment (Y)	Constant (1)	Trend (T)	Real GNP (G)	Interest Rate (R)	Inflation Rate (P)
0.161	1	1	1.058	5.16	4.40
0.172	1	2	1.088	5.87	5.15
0.158	1	3	1.086	5.95	5.37
0.173	1	4	1.122	4.88	4.99
0.195	1	5	1.186	4.50	4.16
0.217	1	6	1.254	6.44	5.75
0.199	1	7	1.246	7.83	8.82
y = 0.163	X = 1	8	1.232	6.25	9.31
0.195	1	9	1.298	5.50	5.21
0.231	1	10	1.370	5.46	5.83
0.257	1	11	1.439	7.46	7.40
0.259	1	12	1.479	10.28	8.64
0.225	1	13	1.474	11.77	9.31
0.241	1	14	1.503	13.42	9.44
0.204	1	15	1.475	11.02	5.99

[a] Subsequent results are based on these values.

Therefore, the least squares slopes and intercept in the regression of Y on a constant, T and G, are

$$b_1 = -0.500639,$$

$$b_2 = -0.0171984,$$

$$b_3 = 0.653716.$$

Some additional insight is provided by manipulating the solution for, say b_3, the slope on GNP. Suppose that we just regressed investment on GNP, neglecting the time trend. At least some of the correlation we observe will be explainable by the fact that both investment and real GNP have an obvious time trend. The slope in this regression would be

$$b_{yg} = \frac{\sum gy}{\sum g^2} = 0.184078.$$

Now divide the preceding expression for b_3 by $\Sigma t^2 \Sigma g^2$. By manipulating it a bit and using the definition of the sample correlation between G and T, $r_{gt}^2 = (\Sigma gt)^2/(\Sigma g^2 \Sigma t^2)$, we obtain

$$b_{yg.t} = \frac{b_{yg}}{1 - r_{gt}^2} - \frac{b_{yt} b_{tg}}{1 - r_{gt}^2} = 0.653791.$$

(The notation used on the left-hand side is interpreted to mean the slope in the regression of y on g "in the presence of t.") The slope in the multiple regression embodies a correction to the slope in the simple regression that accounts for the influence of the additional variable, T, on both Y and G. For an explicit example of this effect, note what we get in the simple regression of real investment on a time trend: $b_{yt} = 1.604/280 = 0.057286$, a positive number that reflects the upward trend apparent in the preceding data. But in the multiple regression, after we account for the influence of GNP on real investment, the slope on the time trend, as we have seen, is -0.0171984, indicating instead a downward trend. This simple example illustrates the considerable danger of drawing conclusions from a badly specified regression model. The general result for a three-variable regression in which x_1 is a constant term is

$$b_{y2.3} = \frac{b_{y2} - b_{y3} b_{32}}{1 - r_{23}^2}. \tag{6-14}$$

It is clear from this expression that the magnitudes of $b_{y2.3}$ and b_{y2} can be quite different. They need not even have the same sign. The omission of important variables can be particularly serious.

As a final observation, note what becomes of $b_{yg.t}$ if r_{gt}^2 equals zero. The first term becomes b_{yg}, while the second becomes zero. (If G and T are not correlated, the slope in the regression of G on T, b_{gt}, is zero.) Therefore, we conclude the following:

> If the variables in a multiple regression are
> not correlated (i.e., are orthogonal), the
> multiple regression slopes are the same as the
> slopes in the individual simple regressions.

In practice, you will rarely compute a multiple regression by hand or with a calculator. Computers and easy-to-use software have greatly simplified the process. Still, it helps to see the nature of the calculations involved. For a regression with more than three variables, the calculations proceed along similar lines but are extremely cumbersome. The tools of matrix algebra rapidly become indispensable (as does a computer). Consider, for example, an enlarged model of investment that includes, in addition to the constant, time trend, and GNP, an interest rate and the rate of inflation. Least squares requires the simultaneous solution of five normal equations. Letting $\mathbf{X}$ and $\mathbf{y}$ denote the full data matrices shown previously, the normal equations are

$$(\mathbf{X}'\mathbf{X})\mathbf{b} = \mathbf{X}'\mathbf{y}$$

or

$$\begin{bmatrix} 15.000 & 120.00 & 19.310 & 111.79 & 99.770 \\ 120.000 & 1240.0 & 164.30 & 1035.9 & 875.60 \\ 19.310 & 164.30 & 25.218 & 148.98 & 131.22 \\ 111.79 & 1035.9 & 148.98 & 953.86 & 799.02 \\ 99.770 & 875.60 & 131.22 & 799.02 & 716.67 \end{bmatrix} \begin{bmatrix} b_1 \\ b_2 \\ b_3 \\ b_4 \\ b_5 \end{bmatrix} = \begin{bmatrix} 3.0500 \\ 26.004 \\ 3.9926 \\ 23.521 \\ 20.732 \end{bmatrix}.$$

The solution is

$$\mathbf{b} = (\mathbf{X}'\mathbf{X})^{-1}\mathbf{X}'\mathbf{y}$$

or

$$\begin{bmatrix} b_1 \\ b_2 \\ b_3 \\ b_4 \\ b_5 \end{bmatrix} = \begin{bmatrix} -0.5090 \\ -0.0166 \\ 0.6704 \\ -0.0023 \\ -0.0001 \end{bmatrix}$$

$$= \begin{bmatrix} 67.41 & 2.270 & -66.77 & 0.1242 & -0.0711 \\ 2.270 & 0.08624 & -2.257 & -0.0064 & -0.0009 \\ -66.77 & -2.257 & 67.09 & -0.1614 & -0.0506 \\ 0.1242 & -0.0064 & -0.1614 & 0.03295 & -0.01665 \\ -0.0711 & -0.0009 & -0.0506 & -0.01665 & 0.04028 \end{bmatrix} \begin{bmatrix} 3.050 \\ 26.004 \\ 3.993 \\ 23.521 \\ 20.732 \end{bmatrix}.$$

6.3.3. Algebraic Aspects of the Solution

As a prelude to some later results, it is useful to examine some algebraic aspects of the least squares solution. The normal equations are

$$\mathbf{X}'\mathbf{X}\mathbf{b} - \mathbf{X}'\mathbf{y} = -\mathbf{X}'(\mathbf{y} - \mathbf{X}\mathbf{b}) = -\mathbf{X}'\mathbf{e}$$

$$= \mathbf{0}.$$

This means that for every column $\mathbf{x}_k$ of $\mathbf{X}$,

$$\mathbf{x}_k'\mathbf{e} = 0.$$

In particular, if the first column of $\mathbf{X}$ is a column of ones, the least squares residuals sum to zero. Two implications of this are as follows:

1. The regression hyperplane passes through the point of means of the data. The first normal equal implies that

$$\bar{y} = \mathbf{b}'\bar{\mathbf{x}},$$

where $\bar{\mathbf{x}}$ is the vector of means of the regressors.

2. The mean of the fitted values from the regression equals the mean of the actual values. This follows from (1) because the fitted values are just

$$\hat{\mathbf{y}} = \mathbf{Xb}.$$

It is important to note that neither of these results need hold if the regression does not contain a constant term.

By definition, the vector of least squares residuals is

$$\mathbf{e} = \mathbf{y} - \mathbf{Xb}. \tag{6-15}$$

Inserting (6–12) for **b** gives

$$\begin{aligned}
\mathbf{e} &= \mathbf{y} - \mathbf{X(X'X)}^{-1}\mathbf{X'y} \\
&= (\mathbf{I} - \mathbf{X(X'X)}^{-1}\mathbf{X'})\mathbf{y} \\
&= \mathbf{My}.
\end{aligned} \tag{6-16}$$

The $n \times n$ matrix, **M,** is fundamental in regression analysis. You can easily show that **M** is both symmetric ($\mathbf{M} = \mathbf{M'}$) and idempotent ($\mathbf{M} = \mathbf{M}^2$). In view of (6–16), we can interpret **M** as a matrix that, when it premultiplies any vector **y,** produces the vector of least squares residuals in the regression of **y** on **X.** It follows immediately that

$$\mathbf{MX} = \mathbf{0}.$$

One way to interpret this result is that if **X** is regressed on **X,** a perfect fit will result and the residuals will be zero.

Finally, (6–15) implies that

$$\mathbf{y} = \mathbf{Xb} + \mathbf{e},$$

which is the sample analog to (6–3). Our least squares results partition **y** into two parts, the fitted values, $\hat{\mathbf{y}} = \mathbf{Xb}$, and the residuals, **e.** We see from $\mathbf{MX} = \mathbf{0}$ that these two parts are orthogonal. Now, given (6–16),

$$\hat{\mathbf{y}} = \mathbf{y} - \mathbf{e} = [\mathbf{I} - \mathbf{M}]\mathbf{y} = \mathbf{Py}.$$

The matrix **P,** which is also symmetric and idempotent, is a **projection matrix.** It is the matrix formed from **X** such that when a vector, **y,** is premultiplied by **P,** the result is the fitted values in the least squares regression of **y** on **X.**[6] Given the earlier results,

$$\mathbf{PX} = \mathbf{X}$$

and

$$\mathbf{PM} = \mathbf{MP} = \mathbf{0}.$$

In manipulating equations involving least squares results, the following equivalent expressions for the sum of squared residuals are often useful:

$$\mathbf{e'e} = \mathbf{y'M'My} = \mathbf{y'My} = \mathbf{y'e} = \mathbf{e'y},$$

$$\mathbf{e'e} = \mathbf{y'y} - \mathbf{b'X'Xb},$$

and

$$\mathbf{e'e} = \mathbf{y'y} - \mathbf{b'X'y} = \mathbf{y'y} - \mathbf{y'Xb}.$$

---

[6] It creates the projection of the vector **y** in the column space of **X.** This is the problem analyzed in Section 2.4.7.

6.3.4. Partitioned Regression and Partial Regression

It is common to specify a multiple regression model when, in fact, interest centers on only one or a subset of the full set of variables. Consider, for example, the income equation discussed in the Introduction. Although we are primarily interested in the association of income and education, age is, of necessity, included in the model. We have already established that it would be erroneous to omit age from the equation. The question we consider here is what computations are involved in obtaining, in isolation, the coefficients of a subset of the variables in a multiple regression, for example, the coefficient of education in the aforementioned regression.

In general terms, suppose that the regression involves two sets of variables, X_1 and X_2. Thus,

$$y = X\beta + \varepsilon = X_1\beta_1 + X_2\beta_2 + \varepsilon.$$

What is the algebraic solution for b_2? The normal equations are

$$\begin{matrix}(1) \\ (2)\end{matrix} \begin{bmatrix} X_1'X_1 & X_1'X_2 \\ X_2'X_1 & X_2'X_2 \end{bmatrix} \begin{bmatrix} b_1 \\ b_2 \end{bmatrix} = \begin{bmatrix} X_1'y \\ X_2'y \end{bmatrix}.$$

A solution can be obtained by using the partitioned inverse matrix of Section 2.6.3 in the result

$$\begin{bmatrix} X_1'X_1 & X_1'X_2 \\ X_2'X_1 & X_2'X_2 \end{bmatrix}^{-1} \begin{bmatrix} X_1'y \\ X_2'y \end{bmatrix} = \begin{bmatrix} b_1 \\ b_2 \end{bmatrix}.$$

Alternatively, (1) and (2) can be manipulated directly to solve for b_2. We first solve (1) for b_1:

$$\begin{aligned} b_1 &= (X_1'X_1)^{-1}X_1'y - (X_1'X_1)^{-1}X_1'X_2b_2 \\ &= (X_1'X_1)^{-1}X_1'(y - X_2b_2). \end{aligned} \qquad (6\text{--}17)$$

(Note that this solution states that b_1 is the set of coefficients in the regression of y on X_1, minus a correction vector.) Then, inserting this in (2) produces

$$X_2'X_1(X_1'X_1)^{-1}X_1'y - X_2'X_1(X_1'X_1)^{-1}X_1'X_2b_2 + X_2'X_2b_2 = X_2'y.$$

After collecting terms,

$$X_2'(I - X_1(X_1'X_1)^{-1}X_1')X_2b_2 = X_2'(I - X_1(X_1'X_1)^{-1}X_1')y.$$

The solution is

$$\begin{aligned} b_2 &= [X_2'(I - X_1(X_1'X_1)^{-1}X_1')X_2]^{-1}[X_2'(I - X_1(X_1'X_1)^{-1}X_1')y] \\ &= (X_2'M_1X_2)^{-1}(X_2'M_1y). \end{aligned} \qquad (6\text{--}18)$$

Notice that the matrix appearing in parentheses inside each set of square brackets is the "residual maker" discussed earlier, in this case for a regression on the columns of X_1. Thus, M_1X_2 is a matrix of residuals; each column of M_1X_2 is a vector of residuals in the regression of the corresponding column of X_2 on the variables in X_1. By exploiting the fact that M_1, like M, is idempotent, we can rewrite (6–18) as

$$b_2 = (X_2^{*\prime}X_2^*)^{-1}X_2^{*\prime}y^*, \qquad (6\text{--}19)$$

where

$$X_2^* = M_1X_2 \qquad \text{and} \qquad y^* = M_1y.$$

Therefore, b_2 is the set of coefficients obtained when the residuals from a regression of y on X_1 alone are regressed on the set of residuals obtained when each column of X_2 is regressed on X_1. This process is commonly called *partialing out* or *netting out* the effect of X_1. It is partly for this reason that the coefficients in a multiple regression are often called the *partial regression coefficients*.

In terms of our first example, we could obtain the coefficient on education in the least squares regression by first regressing income and education on age (or age and age squared) and then using the residuals from these regressions in a simple regression. In a classic application of this latter observation, Frisch and Waugh (1933) noted that in a time series setting, the same results were obtained whether a regression was fitted with a time trend variable or the data were first "detrended" by netting out the effect of time, as noted earlier, and using just the detrended data in a simple regression.[7]

6.3.5 Partial Regression and Partial Correlation Coefficients

The use of multiple regression involves a conceptual experiment that we might not be able to carry out in practice, the *ceteris paribus* analysis familiar in economics. To pursue an example considered in the Introduction, a regression equation relating income to age and education enables us to do the conceptual experiment of comparing the incomes of two individuals of the same age with different education levels, *even if the sample contains no such pair of individuals*. It is this characteristic of the regression that is implied by the term *partial regression coefficients*. The way we obtain this result, as we have seen, is first to regress income and education on age and then to compute the residuals from this regression. By construction, age will not have any power in explaining variation in these residuals. Therefore, any correlation between income and education after this "purging" is independent of (or after netting out the effect of) age.

The same principle can be applied to the correlation between two variables. To continue our example, when we observe a correlation of, say, 0.7 between income and education in our sample, to what extent can we assume that this correlation is due to any direct relationship, as opposed to being due to the fact that as individuals become older, both income and education tend, on average, to rise? To find out, we would use a **partial correlation coefficient,** which is computed along the same lines as the partial regression coefficient. In the context of our example, the partial correlation coefficient between income and education, controlling for the effect of age, is obtained as follows:

1. Y^* = the residuals in a regression of income on age.
2. E^* = the residuals in a regression of education on age.
3. The partial correlation r_{YE}^*, is the simple correlation between Y^* and E^*.

This might seem to be a formidable amount of computation. There is, however, a convenient shortcut. Once the multiple regression is computed, the t ratio in (6–31) for testing the hypothesis that the coefficient equals zero (e.g., the last column of Table 6.5) can be used to compute

$$r_{yk}^{*2} = \frac{t_k^2}{t_k^2 + \text{degrees of freedom}}. \qquad (6\text{–}20)$$

EXAMPLE 6.4. Partial Correlations ─────────────────────

For the data of Example 6.3, the simple correlations between investment and the regressors r_{yk}, and partial correlations (given the other variables), r_{yk}^*, between investment and the four regressors are listed in Table 6.3.

───────────────

[7] Recall our earlier investment example.

TABLE 6.3

	Simple Correlation	Partial Correlation
Time	0.7496	−0.9360
GNP	0.8632	0.9680
Interest	0.5871	−0.5166
Inflation	0.4777	−0.0253

As is clear from the figures, there is no necessary relation between the simple and partial correlation coefficients. One thing worth noting is the signs of the coefficients. The signs of the partial correlation coefficients are the same as the signs of the respective regression coefficients, three of which are negative. All of the simple correlation coefficients are positive because of the latent "effect" of time.

6.3.6. Deviations from Means—Regression on a Constant

As an application of the results in the preceding section, consider the case in which $\mathbf{X}_1$ is just the first column of $\mathbf{X}$, the column of ones. The solution for $\mathbf{b}_2$ in this case will then be the slopes in a regression with a constant term. Let $\mathbf{i}$ be the column of ones. The coefficient in a regression of any variable, $\mathbf{z}$, on $\mathbf{i}$ is $[\mathbf{i}'\mathbf{i}]^{-1}\mathbf{i}'\mathbf{z} = \bar{z}$, the fitted values are $\mathbf{i}\bar{z}$, and the residuals are $z_i - \bar{z}$. Therefore, when we apply this to our previous results, we find the following:

> The slopes in a multiple regression that contains a constant term are obtained by transforming the data to deviations from their means, then regressing the variable y in deviation form on the explanatory variables, also in deviation form.

(We obtained this result for a specific case, $K = 3$, earlier.)

Exercise. What happens in the preceding regression if we neglect to transform $\mathbf{y}$ to deviations from $\bar{y}$ before we compute the slopes?

Having obtained the coefficients on $\mathbf{X}_2$, how can we recover the coefficients on $\mathbf{X}_1$? One way, of course, is to repeat the exercise of the previous section while reversing the roles of $\mathbf{X}_1$ and $\mathbf{X}_2$. But there is an easier way. For the general case, the first of the two normal equations is

$$\mathbf{X}_1'\mathbf{X}_1\mathbf{b}_1 + \mathbf{X}_1'\mathbf{X}_2\mathbf{b}_2 = \mathbf{X}_1'\mathbf{y}.$$

We have already solved for $\mathbf{b}_2$. Therefore, we can use this in a solution for $\mathbf{b}_1$:

$$\mathbf{b}_1 = (\mathbf{X}_1'\mathbf{X}_1)^{-1}\mathbf{X}_1'\mathbf{y} - (\mathbf{X}_1'\mathbf{X}_1)^{-1}\mathbf{X}_1'\mathbf{X}_2\mathbf{b}_2 = (\mathbf{X}_1'\mathbf{X}_1)^{-1}\mathbf{X}_1'(\mathbf{y} - \mathbf{X}_2\mathbf{b}_2). \quad (6\text{--}21)$$

If $\mathbf{X}_1$ is just a column of ones, the first of these produces the result

$$\mathbf{b}_1 = \bar{y} - \bar{x}_2 b_2 - \cdots - \bar{x}_K b_K, \quad (6\text{--}22)$$

which we have seen before.

6.4. Statistical Properties of the Least Squares Estimator

In Chapter 5, we showed that the least squares estimator was the best linear unbiased estimator of β under the classical assumptions. Since that model is just a special case of the one considered here, we should expect these results to carry over to this more general case.

6.4.1. Nonstochastic Regressors

If the regressors can be treated as nonstochastic, as they would be in an experimental situation in which the analyst chooses the values in $\mathbf{X}$, then the properties of the least squares estimator can be derived by treating $\mathbf{X}$ as a matrix of constants. Insert (6–3) in (6–12) to obtain

$$\mathbf{b} = (\mathbf{X'X})^{-1}\mathbf{X'}(\mathbf{X}\beta + \varepsilon) = \beta + (\mathbf{X'X})^{-1}\mathbf{X'}\varepsilon. \tag{6–23}$$

If $\mathbf{X}$ is nonstochastic, or if $E(\mathbf{X'}\varepsilon) = \mathbf{0}$, the expected value of the second term in (6–23) is $\mathbf{0}$. The least squares estimator is, therefore, unbiased. Its covariance matrix is

$$
\begin{aligned}
\text{Var}[\mathbf{b}] &= E[(\mathbf{b} - \beta)(\mathbf{b} - \beta)'] \\
&= E[(\mathbf{X'X})^{-1}\mathbf{X'}\varepsilon\varepsilon'\mathbf{X}(\mathbf{X'X})^{-1}] \\
&= (\mathbf{X'X})^{-1}\mathbf{X'}E[\varepsilon\varepsilon']\mathbf{X}(\mathbf{X'X})^{-1} \\
&= (\mathbf{X'X})^{-1}\mathbf{X'}(\sigma^2\mathbf{I})\mathbf{X}(\mathbf{X'X})^{-1} \\
&= \sigma^2(\mathbf{X'X})^{-1}.
\end{aligned}
\tag{6–24}
$$

The Gauss–Markov theorem derived in Chapter 5 implies that for a special case ($K = 2$), $\mathbf{b}$ is the most efficient linear unbiased estimator of β. We now give a more general proof of this fundamental result. Let $\tilde{\mathbf{b}} = \mathbf{Cy}$ be another linear unbiased estimator of β, where $\mathbf{C}$ is a $K \times n$ matrix. If $\tilde{\mathbf{b}}$ is unbiased,

$$E[\mathbf{Cy}] = E[\mathbf{CX}\beta + \mathbf{C}\varepsilon] = \beta,$$

which implies that $\mathbf{CX} = \mathbf{I}$. The covariance matrix of $\tilde{\mathbf{b}}$ can be found by replacing $(\mathbf{X'X})^{-1}\mathbf{X'}$ with $\mathbf{C}$ in (6–24); the result is

$$\text{Var}[\tilde{\mathbf{b}}] = \sigma^2\mathbf{CC'}.$$

Now let $\mathbf{D} = \mathbf{C} - (\mathbf{X'X})^{-1}\mathbf{X'}.$[8] Then

$$\text{Var}[\tilde{\mathbf{b}}] = \sigma^2[(\mathbf{D} + (\mathbf{X'X})^{-1}\mathbf{X'})(\mathbf{D} + (\mathbf{X'X})^{-1}\mathbf{X'})'].$$

Before expanding this sum of four terms, we note that

$$\mathbf{CX} = \mathbf{I} = \mathbf{DX} + (\mathbf{X'X})^{-1}(\mathbf{X'X}).$$

Since the last preceding term is $\mathbf{I}$, $\mathbf{DX} = \mathbf{0}.$ Therefore,

$$
\begin{aligned}
\text{Var}[\tilde{\mathbf{b}}] &= \sigma^2\mathbf{DD'} + \sigma^2(\mathbf{X'X})^{-1} \\
&= \text{Var}[\mathbf{b}] + \sigma^2\mathbf{DD'}.
\end{aligned}
$$

---

[8] Thus, $\mathbf{Dy}$ is just $\tilde{\mathbf{b}} - \mathbf{b}$.

The variance matrix of $\tilde{\mathbf{b}}$ equals that of $\mathbf{b}$ plus a nonnegative definite matrix.[9] Therefore, every quadratic form in $\mathrm{Var}[\tilde{\mathbf{b}}]$ is larger than the corresponding quadratic form in $\mathrm{Var}[\mathbf{b}]$. This implies the

GAUSS–MARKOV THEOREM: *For any vector of constants,* $\mathbf{w}$, *the minimum variance linear unbiased estimator of* $\mathbf{w}'\boldsymbol{\beta}$ *in the classical regression model is* $\mathbf{w}'\mathbf{b}$, *where* $\mathbf{b}$ *is the least squares estimator. The proof follows from the previous derivation, since the variance of* $\mathbf{w}'\mathbf{b}$ *is a quadratic form in* $\mathrm{Var}[\mathbf{b}]$, *and likewise for any* $\tilde{\mathbf{b}}$.

This proves that each estimator, b_k, is the best linear unbiased estimator of β_k. (Let $\mathbf{w}$ be all zeros except for a one in the kth position.) However, the theorem is much broader than this, since the result also applies to every other linear combination of the elements of $\boldsymbol{\beta}$.

6.4.2. Stochastic Regressors

Social scientists are rarely able to analyze experimental data. As such, in order to achieve much generality for the properties of the least squares estimator, it is necessary to extend the results of the preceding section to cases in which some or all of the independent variables are randomly drawn from some probability distribution. A convenient method of obtaining the statistical properties of $\mathbf{b}$ is to obtain first the desired results conditioned on $\mathbf{X}$. This is equivalent to the nonstochastic regressors case. We then find the unconditional result by ''averaging'' (e.g., by integrating over) the conditional distributions. The crux of the argument is that if we can establish unbiasedness conditionally on an arbitrary $\mathbf{X}$, we can average over $\mathbf{X}$'s to obtain an unconditional result.

As before,

$$\mathbf{b} = \boldsymbol{\beta} + (\mathbf{X}'\mathbf{X})^{-1}\mathbf{X}'\boldsymbol{\varepsilon}.$$

So, conditioned on the observed $\mathbf{X}$,

$$E[\mathbf{b}|\mathbf{X}] = \boldsymbol{\beta} + (\mathbf{X}'\mathbf{X})^{-1}\mathbf{X}'E[\boldsymbol{\varepsilon}|\mathbf{X}] = \boldsymbol{\beta} + (\mathbf{X}'\mathbf{X})^{-1}\mathbf{X}'\mathbf{0} = \boldsymbol{\beta}.$$

A useful device is the law of iterated expectations:

$$E[\mathbf{b}] = E_{\mathbf{x}}[E[\mathbf{b}|\mathbf{X}]]$$
$$= \boldsymbol{\beta} + E_{\mathbf{x}}[(\mathbf{X}'\mathbf{X})^{-1}\mathbf{X}'E[\boldsymbol{\varepsilon}|\mathbf{X}]].$$

Since $E[\boldsymbol{\varepsilon}|\mathbf{X}] = \mathbf{0}$ by assumption 4, $\mathbf{b}$ is unbiased unconditionally as well. Thus,

$$E[\mathbf{b}] = E_{\mathbf{x}}[E[\mathbf{b}|\mathbf{X}]] = E_{\mathbf{x}}[\boldsymbol{\beta}] = \boldsymbol{\beta}.$$

The unbiasedness of OLS is robust to assumptions about the $\mathbf{X}$ matrix; it rests only on assumption 4.

The variance of $\mathbf{b}$, again conditional on $\mathbf{X}$, is

$$\mathrm{Var}[\mathbf{b}|\mathbf{X}] = \sigma^2(\mathbf{X}'\mathbf{X})^{-1}.$$

For the exact variance, we use the decomposition of variance of (3–70):

$$\mathrm{Var}[\mathbf{b}] = E_{\mathbf{x}}[\mathrm{Var}[\mathbf{b}|\mathbf{X}]] + \mathrm{Var}_{\mathbf{x}}[E[\mathbf{b}|\mathbf{X}]].$$

The second term is zero since $E[\mathbf{b}|\mathbf{X}] = \boldsymbol{\beta}$ for all $\mathbf{X}$, so

$$\mathrm{Var}[\mathbf{b}] = E[\sigma^2(\mathbf{X}'\mathbf{X})^{-1}] = \sigma^2 E[(\mathbf{X}'\mathbf{X})^{-1}].$$

---

[9] A quadratic form in $\mathbf{DD}'$ is $\mathbf{q}'\mathbf{DD}'\mathbf{q} = \mathbf{z}'\mathbf{z} \geq 0$.

Our earlier conclusion is altered slightly. We must replace $(\mathbf{X'X})^{-1}$ with its expected value to get the appropriate covariance matrix.

The Gauss–Markov theorem can be established logically from the results of the preceding paragraph. We showed in Section 6.4.1 that

$$\text{Var}[\mathbf{b}|\mathbf{X}] \le \text{Var}[\tilde{\boldsymbol{\beta}}|\mathbf{X}]$$

for any $\tilde{\boldsymbol{\beta}} \ne \mathbf{b}$. But if this inequality holds for a particular $\mathbf{X}$, it must hold for

$$\text{Var}[\mathbf{b}] = E_x[\text{Var}[\mathbf{b}|\mathbf{X}]].$$

That is, if it holds for every particular $\mathbf{X}$, it must hold over the average value(s) of $\mathbf{X}$.

The conclusion, therefore, is that the important results that we have obtained thus far for the least squares estimator, unbiasedness and the Gauss–Markov theorem, hold whether or not we regard $\mathbf{X}$ as stochastic.

6.5. Statistical Inference

Thus far, we have not made any use of assumption 6, normality of $\boldsymbol{\epsilon}$, in any of our results. The assumption is useful for constructing statistics for testing hypotheses. For the moment, we continue to assume that the regressors are nonstochastic. The assumption will be reconsidered in Section 6.5.3.

6.5.1. Testing a Hypothesis About a Coefficient

In (6–23), $\mathbf{b}$ is a linear function of the disturbance vector $\boldsymbol{\epsilon}$. If we assume that $\boldsymbol{\epsilon}$ has a multivariate normal distribution, we may use the results of Section 3.10.2 and the mean vector and covariance matrix derived earlier to state that

$$\mathbf{b} \sim N[\boldsymbol{\beta}, \sigma^2(\mathbf{X'X})^{-1}]. \tag{6–25}$$

This is a multivariate normal distribution, so each element of $\mathbf{b}$ is normally distributed:

$$b_k \sim N[\beta_k, \sigma^2(\mathbf{X'X})_{kk}^{-1}]. \tag{6–26}$$

Let S^{kk} be the kth diagonal element of $(\mathbf{X'X})^{-1}$. Then

$$z_k = \frac{b_k - \beta_k}{\sqrt{\sigma^2 S^{kk}}} \tag{6–27}$$

has a standard normal distribution. If σ^2 were known, statistical inference about β_k could be based on z_k. However, σ^2 remains to be estimated, so (6–27) is not usable.

The least squares residuals are

$$\mathbf{e} = \mathbf{My} = \mathbf{M}[\mathbf{X}\boldsymbol{\beta} + \boldsymbol{\varepsilon}] = \mathbf{M}\boldsymbol{\varepsilon},$$

as $\mathbf{MX} = \mathbf{0}$. An estimator of σ^2 will be based on the sum of squared residuals:

$$\mathbf{e'e} = \boldsymbol{\varepsilon'}\mathbf{M}\boldsymbol{\varepsilon}.$$

The expected value of this quadratic form is

$$E[\mathbf{e'e}] = E[\boldsymbol{\varepsilon'}\mathbf{M}\boldsymbol{\varepsilon}].$$

By using the result on cyclic permutations (2–94),

$$E[\text{tr}(\boldsymbol{\varepsilon'}\mathbf{M}\boldsymbol{\varepsilon})] = E[\text{tr}(\mathbf{M}\boldsymbol{\varepsilon}\boldsymbol{\varepsilon'})].$$

Since $\mathbf{M}$ is fixed, this is

$$\text{tr}(\mathbf{M}E[\boldsymbol{\varepsilon}\boldsymbol{\varepsilon}']) = \text{tr}(\mathbf{M}\sigma^2\mathbf{I}) = \sigma^2\text{tr}(\mathbf{M}).$$

The trace of $\mathbf{M}$ is

$$\text{tr}[\mathbf{I}_n - \mathbf{X}(\mathbf{X}'\mathbf{X})^{-1}\mathbf{X}'] = \text{tr}(\mathbf{I}_n) - \text{tr}((\mathbf{X}'\mathbf{X})^{-1}\mathbf{X}'\mathbf{X})$$

$$= \text{tr}(\mathbf{I}_n) - \text{tr}(\mathbf{I}_K) = n - K.$$

Therefore,

$$E[\mathbf{e}'\mathbf{e}] = (n - K)\sigma^2,$$

and an unbiased estimator of σ^2 is

$$s^2 = \frac{\mathbf{e}'\mathbf{e}}{n - K}. \tag{6–28}$$

The **standard error of the regression** is s, the square root of s^2. With s^2, we can then compute

$$\text{Est. Var}[\mathbf{b}] = s^2(\mathbf{X}'\mathbf{X})^{-1}.$$

By using s^2 instead of σ^2, we can derive a statistic to use in place of z_k in (6–27). The quantity

$$\frac{(n - K)s^2}{\sigma^2} = \frac{\mathbf{e}'\mathbf{e}}{\sigma^2} = \left(\frac{\boldsymbol{\varepsilon}}{\sigma}\right)'\mathbf{M}\left(\frac{\boldsymbol{\varepsilon}}{\sigma}\right) \tag{6–29}$$

is an idempotent quadratic form in a standard normal vector $(\boldsymbol{\varepsilon}/\sigma)$. Therefore, it has a chi-squared distribution with $\text{rank}(\mathbf{M}) = \text{trace}(\mathbf{M}) = n - K$ degrees of freedom.[10] The chi-squared variable in (6–29) is independent of the standard normal variable in (6–27). To prove this, it suffices to show that

$$\frac{\mathbf{b} - \boldsymbol{\beta}}{\sigma} = (\mathbf{X}'\mathbf{X})^{-1}\mathbf{X}'\left(\frac{\boldsymbol{\varepsilon}}{\sigma}\right) \tag{6–30}$$

is independent of $(n - K)s^2/\sigma^2$. In Section 3.10.6, we found that a sufficient condition for the independence of a linear form, $\mathbf{L}\mathbf{x}$, and an idempotent quadratic form, $\mathbf{x}'\mathbf{A}\mathbf{x}$, in a standard normal vector, $\mathbf{x}$, is that $\mathbf{L}\mathbf{A} = \mathbf{0}$. Letting $\boldsymbol{\varepsilon}/\sigma$ equal $\mathbf{x}$, we find that the requirement here would be that $(\mathbf{X}'\mathbf{X})^{-1}\mathbf{X}'\mathbf{M} = \mathbf{0}$. It does, as can be verified by multiplying it out. The general result is central in the derivation of many test statistics in regression analysis:

> If $\boldsymbol{\varepsilon}$ is normally distributed, the least squares coefficient estimator, $\mathbf{b}$, is statistically independent of the residual vector, $\mathbf{e}$, and therefore, all functions of $\mathbf{e}$, including s^2.

Therefore, the ratio

$$t_k = \frac{(b_k - \beta_k)/\sqrt{\sigma^2 S^{kk}}}{\{[(n - K)s^2/\sigma^2]/(n - K)\}^{1/2}}$$

$$= \frac{b_k - \beta_k}{\sqrt{s^2 S^{kk}}} \tag{6–31}$$

---

[10]This was proved in Section 3.10.3a.

has a t distribution with $(n - K)$ degress of freedom.[11] We can use t_k in the same fashion as in Chapter 5 to test hypotheses or form confidence intervals about the individual elements of $\boldsymbol{\beta}$. For example, the t ratio for the test of the hypothesis that a coefficient equals zero is a standard part of the regression output of most computer programs.

EXAMPLE 6.5

To continue the earlier investment example, the matrix $(\mathbf{X'X})^{-1}$ for the five-variable regression has been given. The sum of squared residuals from that regression is 0.0004507, so the estimate of σ^2 is $s^2 = 0.0004507/(15 - 5) = 0.00004507$. Multiplying $(\mathbf{X'X})^{-1}$ by this yields the estimated covariance matrix for the least squares slopes shown in Table 6.4.

A summary of the regression results is presented in Table 6.5.

There are 15 observations and 5 coefficients, so the t statistics have 10 degrees of freedom. The 5 percent critical value for a t distribution with 10 degrees of freedom is 2.228. Thus, the individual hypotheses that the first 3 coefficients are zero are rejected. The last 2 are not significantly different from zero by this test. Testing a hypothesis about a particular value of a coefficient other than zero proceeds along the lines developed in Chapter 5. For example, are these data consistent with the hypothesis that each \$1 billion increase in GNP will be associated with an equal increase in investment? The t ratio for testing this hypothesis is $(0.67038 - 1)/0.05499 = -5.994$, which indicates that the slope on GNP is significantly less than 1.

TABLE 6.4

Constant	Time	Real GNP	Interest	Inflation
0.00304				
0.000102	0.0000039			
−0.00301	−0.000102	0.00302		
0.0000056	−0.0000003	−0.000007	0.0000015	
−0.0000032	−0.00000004	−0.0000022	−0.0000008	0.0000018

TABLE 6.5. Regression Results for an Investment Equation

Sum of squared residuals:	0.0004507
Standard error of the regression:	0.006713

Variable	Coefficient	Standard Error	t ratio
Constant	−0.50907	0.0551	−9.23
Time	−0.01658	0.001972	−8.41
Real GNP	0.67038	0.05499	12.19
Interest	−0.00232	0.001219	1.91
Inflation	−0.00009	0.001347	−0.070

[11] See (3–36) in Section 3.4.2. It is the ratio of a standard normal variable to the square root of a chi-squared variable divided by its degrees of freedom.

6.5.2. Testing a Linear Restriction

We shall often be interested in testing hypotheses involving more than one coefficient. We can use a test statistic similar to the one in (6–31). Suppose that the hypothesis is

$$H_0: r_1\beta_1 + r_2\beta_2 + \cdots + r_K\beta_K = \mathbf{r}'\boldsymbol{\beta} = q.$$

(Usually some of the r's will be zero.) The sample estimate of the left-hand side is

$$r_1 b_1 + r_2 b_2 + \cdots + r_K b_K = \mathbf{r}'\mathbf{b} = \hat{q}.$$

If $\hat{q}$ differs significantly from q, we conclude that the sample data are not consistent with the hypothesis. Consistent with (6–31), it is natural to base the test on

$$t = \frac{\hat{q} - q}{\text{se}(\hat{q})}. \tag{6–32}$$

We require an estimate of the standard error of $\hat{q}$. Since $\hat{q}$ is a linear function of $\mathbf{b}$ and we have an estimate of the variance matrix of $\mathbf{b}$, $s^2(\mathbf{X}'\mathbf{X})^{-1}$, we can estimate the variance of $\hat{q}$ with

$$\text{Est.Var}[\hat{q}] = \mathbf{r}'[s^2(\mathbf{X}'\mathbf{X})^{-1}]\mathbf{r}.$$

The denominator in (6–32) is the square root of this quantity.[12] In words, (6–32) is the distance between the hypothesized function of the true coefficients and the same function of our estimates of them. If the hypothesis is true, our estimates should reflect that fact, at least within the range of sampling variability. Thus, if the absolute value of the preceding t ratio is larger than the appropriate critical value, doubt is cast on the hypothesis.

EXAMPLE 6.6. Linear Combination of Coefficients ──────────────

In Example 6.5, we might ask whether it is more appropriate to formulate the regression in terms of the real interest rate, rather than to treat the interest rate and the rate of inflation separately.[13] If investors were only interested in the real rate of interest, equal increases in interest rates and the rate of inflation would have no effect on investment. The hypothesis is

$$H_0: \beta_4 + \beta_5 = 0.$$

To form the appropriate test statistic, we require the standard error of $\hat{q} = b_4 + b_5$, which is

$$\text{se}(\hat{q}) = [0.15 \times 10^{-5} + 0.18 \times 10^{-5} + 2(-0.8 \times 10^{-6})]^{1/2} = 0.001303.$$

The t ratio for the test is, therefore,

$$t = \frac{-0.00232 + (-0.00009)}{0.001303} = -1.8496.$$

Using the same critical value as before, we conclude that the sum of the two coefficients is not significantly different from zero.

──

[12] This is a special case of the more general result to be proven, so we need not derive the distribution separately.

[13] Once again, the use of the CPI and, here, an ex post rate of inflation is questionable. We retain these variables purely for the sake of a reasonably uncomplicated example.

Finally, we consider a set of J linear restrictions of the form

$$H_0 : \mathbf{R}\boldsymbol{\beta} = \mathbf{q}.$$

Each row of $\mathbf{R}$ is a single linear restriction on the coefficient vector. Typically, $\mathbf{R}$ will have only a few rows and numerous zeros in each row. Some examples are as follows.

1. One of the coefficients is zero; $\beta_j = 0$,

  $\mathbf{R} = [0 \quad 0 \quad \cdots \quad 1 \quad 0 \quad \cdots \quad 0]$ and $\mathbf{q} = 0.$

2. Two of the coefficients are equal; $\beta_k = \beta_j$,

  $\mathbf{R} = [0 \quad 0 \quad 1 \quad \cdots \quad -1 \quad \cdots \quad 0]$ and $\mathbf{q} = 0.$

3. A set of the coefficients sum to one; $\beta_2 + \beta_3 + \beta_4 = 1$,

  $\mathbf{R} = [0 \quad 1 \quad 1 \quad 1 \quad 0 \quad \cdots]$ and $\mathbf{q} = 1.$

4. A subset of the coefficients are all zero; $\beta_1 = 0$, $\beta_2 = 0$, and $\beta_3 = 0$,

$$\mathbf{R} = \begin{bmatrix} 1 & 0 & 0 & 0 & \cdots & 0 \\ 0 & 1 & 0 & 0 & \cdots & 0 \\ 0 & 0 & 1 & 0 & \cdots & 0 \end{bmatrix} \quad \text{and} \quad \mathbf{q} = \begin{bmatrix} 0 \\ 0 \\ 0 \end{bmatrix}$$

or, equivalently,

$$[\mathbf{I}:\mathbf{0}]\boldsymbol{\beta} = \mathbf{0}.$$

5. Several constraints hold simultaneously:

$$\beta_2 + \beta_3 = 1, \; \beta_4 + \beta_6 = 0, \text{ and } \beta_5 + \beta_6 = 0,$$

$$\begin{bmatrix} 0 & 1 & 1 & 0 & 0 & 0 \\ 0 & 0 & 0 & 1 & 0 & 1 \\ 0 & 0 & 0 & 0 & 1 & 1 \end{bmatrix} \begin{bmatrix} \beta_1 \\ \beta_2 \\ \beta_3 \\ \beta_4 \\ \beta_5 \\ \beta_6 \end{bmatrix} = \begin{bmatrix} 1 \\ 0 \\ 0 \end{bmatrix}.$$

Given the least squares estimator, $\mathbf{b}$, our interest centers on the "discrepancy," vector $\mathbf{d} = \mathbf{Rb} - \mathbf{q}$. It is unlikely that $\mathbf{d}$ will be exactly $\mathbf{0}$. The statistical question is whether the deviation of $\mathbf{d}$ from $\mathbf{0}$ can be attributed to sampling error or whether it is significant. Since $\mathbf{b}$ is normally distributed and $\mathbf{d}$ is a linear function of $\mathbf{b}$, $\mathbf{d}$ is also normally distributed. If the null hypothesis is true, $\mathbf{d}$ has mean vector $\mathbf{0}$ and variance

$$\text{Var}[\mathbf{d}] = \text{Var}[\mathbf{Rb} - \mathbf{q}] = \mathbf{R}(\text{Var}[\mathbf{b}])\mathbf{R}' = \sigma^2 \mathbf{R}(\mathbf{X}'\mathbf{X})^{-1}\mathbf{R}'. \tag{6-33}$$

We can base a test of H_0 on the *Wald criterion:*

$$W = \chi^2(J) = \mathbf{d}'(\text{Var}[\mathbf{d}])^{-1}\mathbf{d}. \tag{6-34}$$

This has a chi-squared distribution with J degrees of freedom if the hypothesis is correct.[14] Intuitively, the larger is $\mathbf{d}$, that is, the worse is the failure of least squares to satisfy the restrictions, the larger will be the chi-squared statistic. Therefore, a large chi-squared value will weigh against the hypothesis.

---

[14] This is an application of the "full rank quadratic form" of Section 3.10.5.

The chi-squared statistic in (6–34) is not usable because of the unknown σ^2. We can derive a usable sample statistic similar to the t ratio in (6–31) by using s^2 instead of σ^2. Let

$$F = \frac{(\mathbf{Rb} - \mathbf{q})'[\sigma^2 \mathbf{R}(\mathbf{X}'\mathbf{X})^{-1}\mathbf{R}']^{-1}(\mathbf{Rb} - \mathbf{q})/J}{[(n - K)s^2/\sigma^2]/(n - K)}. \tag{6–35}$$

The numerator is $(1/J)$ times W in (6–34). The denominator is $1/(n - K)$ times the idempotent quadratic form in (6–29). Therefore, F is the ratio of two chi-squared variates, each divided by its degrees of freedom. If they are independent, F is distributed as $F[J, (n - K)]$. We found earlier that $\mathbf{b}$ is distributed independently of s^2, so the condition is met. It is instructive, however, to verify it directly. By using (6–29) and the fact that $\mathbf{M}$ is idempotent, we may write F as

$$F = \frac{\{\mathbf{R}(\mathbf{b} - \boldsymbol{\beta})/\sigma\}'[\mathbf{R}(\mathbf{X}'\mathbf{X})^{-1}\mathbf{R}']^{-1}\{\mathbf{R}(\mathbf{b} - \boldsymbol{\beta})/\sigma\}/J}{[\mathbf{M}(\boldsymbol{\varepsilon}/\sigma)]'[\mathbf{M}(\boldsymbol{\varepsilon}/\sigma)]/(n - K)}. \tag{6–36}$$

Since

$$\frac{\mathbf{R}(\mathbf{b} - \boldsymbol{\beta})}{\sigma} = \mathbf{R}(\mathbf{X}'\mathbf{X})^{-1}\mathbf{X}'\left(\frac{\boldsymbol{\varepsilon}}{\sigma}\right) = \mathbf{T}\left(\frac{\boldsymbol{\varepsilon}}{\sigma}\right),$$

the F statistic is the ratio of two quadratic forms in $(\boldsymbol{\varepsilon}/\sigma)$. Since $\mathbf{M}(\boldsymbol{\varepsilon}/\sigma)$ and $\mathbf{T}(\boldsymbol{\varepsilon}/\sigma)$ are normally distributed and their covariance, $\mathbf{TM}$, is $\mathbf{0}$, the vectors of the quadratic forms are independent. The numerator and denominator of F are functions of independent random vectors and are, therefore, independent. This completes the proof.

Canceling the two appearances of σ^2 in (6–35) leaves the F statistic for testing a linear hypothesis:

$$\begin{aligned} F &= \frac{(\mathbf{Rb} - \mathbf{q})'[\mathbf{R}(\mathbf{X}'\mathbf{X})^{-1}\mathbf{R}']^{-1}(\mathbf{Rb} - \mathbf{q})/J}{\mathbf{e}'\mathbf{e}/(n - K)}, \\[2mm] &= \frac{(\mathbf{Rb} - \mathbf{q})'[s^2\mathbf{R}(\mathbf{X}'\mathbf{X})^{-1}\mathbf{R}']^{-1}(\mathbf{Rb} - \mathbf{q})}{J}. \end{aligned} \tag{6–37}$$

EXAMPLE 6.7 _____

In the investment equation estimated earlier, consider a test of the joint hypothesis

$$\beta_2 = 0 \quad \text{(there is no time trend)}$$

$$\beta_3 = 1 \quad \text{(the marginal propensity to invest} = 1)$$

$$\beta_4 + \beta_5 = 0 \quad \text{(investors consider the real interest rate)}$$

Then

$$\mathbf{R} = \begin{bmatrix} 0 & 1 & 0 & 0 & 0 \\ 0 & 0 & 1 & 0 & 0 \\ 0 & 0 & 0 & 1 & 1 \end{bmatrix} \quad \text{and} \quad \mathbf{q} = \begin{bmatrix} 0 \\ 1 \\ 0 \end{bmatrix}.$$

Based on the sample estimates, we obtain

$$\mathbf{RB} - \mathbf{q} = \begin{bmatrix} -0.0166 \\ -0.3296 \\ -0.0024 \end{bmatrix}.$$

The covariance matrix was given in Example 6.5. Inserting these values in (6–37) yields

$$F = 1266.35$$

The 5 percent critical value for $F[3, 10]$ from the table is 3.71. We conclude, therefore, that these data are not consistent with the hypothesis. This gives no hint as to which of the restrictions is particularly problematic. However, based on the individual test statistics, we would expect both the first and second hypotheses to be rejected.

A confidence interval for a single coefficient is based on a set of values for which the t ratio in (6–31) is less than a specified critical value. It is the set of values for which, at a given level of significance, we would not reject the hypothesis that β equals this value. In a multiple regression model, a joint confidence region for a set of coefficients would be the set of values for which the hypothesis that the set of true coefficients simultaneously equal these values would not be rejected. The test statistic is the F ratio in (6–37). For two coefficients, this would be

$$F[2, n - K] = \tfrac{1}{2}(\mathbf{b} - \boldsymbol{\beta})'(\text{Est. Var}[\mathbf{b}])^{-1}(\mathbf{b} - \boldsymbol{\beta}). \tag{6–38}$$

(For convenience, we assume that only the two coefficients of interest appear in the vectors in (6–38) and that the estimated variance matrix is a 2×2 submatrix of the full covariance matrix.) The set of values of β_1 and β_2 for which this quadratic form is less than a tabulated critical value form a joint confidence region for β_1 and β_2.

EXAMPLE 6.8 Joint Confidence Region ———————————————

Figure 6.1 shows a confidence region for β_2 and β_3 for the investment equation. It is the set of values for which the quadratic form

$$\tfrac{1}{2}\begin{bmatrix} -0.01658 - \beta_1 \\ 0.67038 - \beta_2 \end{bmatrix}'\begin{bmatrix} 0.389 \times 10^{-5} & -0.102 \times 10^{-3} \\ -0.102 \times 10^{-3} & 0.302 \times 10^{-2} \end{bmatrix}^{-1}\begin{bmatrix} -0.01658 - \beta_1 \\ 0.67038 - \beta_2 \end{bmatrix}$$

is less than or equal to the critical $F[2, 10]$ of 4.1. The individual confidence intervals for the coefficients are shown on the axes. Note how the interaction of the two coefficients affects the joint confidence region.

The calculation of the confidence ellipse can be a bit tedious. It can be shown that the simple rectangle formed by the two individual confidence intervals provides a confidence region with probability at least $1 - \alpha_1 - \alpha_2$.[15] Thus, for example, the rectangle in Figure 6.1 contains at least 90 percent of the probability in the estimate of the joint distribution of b_2 and b_3.

6.5.3. Test Statistics with Stochastic **X** and Normal ε

Finally, we consider the validity of our sample test statistics and inference procedures when $\mathbf{X}$ is stochastic. Consider, first, the conventional t statistic in (6–31) for testing $H_0 : \beta_k = \beta_k^0$:

$$t|\mathbf{X} = \frac{(b_k - \beta_k^0)}{[s^2(\mathbf{X}'\mathbf{X})_{kk}^{-1}]^{1/2}}.$$

---

[15] See Theil (1971, p. 132). The confidence levels chosen for the individual estimates are α_1 and α_2.

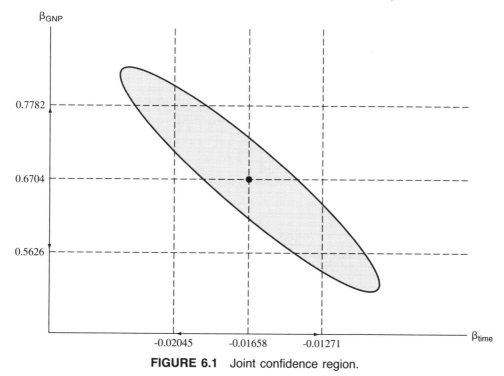

FIGURE 6.1   Joint confidence region.

Conditional on $\mathbf{X}$, $t\,|\,\mathbf{X}$ has a t distribution with $(n - K)$ degrees of freedom. However, what interests us is the marginal, that is, the unconditional, distribution of t. As we saw, $\mathbf{b}$ is only normally distributed conditionally on $\mathbf{X}$; the marginal distribution is not normal. Similarly because of the presence of the stochastic $\mathbf{X}$, the denominator of the t statistic is not the square root of a chi-square divided by its degrees of freedom, again, except conditional on this $\mathbf{X}$. The surprising result, however, is that *in spite of these complications,*

> The *marginal* distribution of t is still t, with $(n - K)$ degrees of freedom, regardless of the distribution of $\mathbf{X}$ or even of whether $\mathbf{X}$ is stochastic or nonstochastic!

This intriguing result follows from the fact that $f(t\,|\,\mathbf{X})$ is not a function of $\mathbf{X}$. The same reasoning can be used to deduce that the usual F ratio used for testing linear restrictions is valid whether $\mathbf{X}$ is stochastic or not. This is a quite powerful result. Its upshot is that

> If the disturbances are normally distributed, we may carry out tests and construct confidence intervals for the parameters without making any change in our procedures, regardless of whether the regressors are stochastic, nonstochastic, or some mix of the two.

6.6. Goodness of Fit and the Analysis of Variance

Regression analysis is primarily used for two purposes: for estimating coefficients of interest and testing hypotheses about them, and for forecasting. For the second, we are interested in how well the regression model predicts movements in the dependent variable. The **coefficient of determination,** R^2, is a measure of the fit of the model. Two equivalent ways to compute R^2 are

$$R^2 = 1 - \frac{\mathbf{e'e}}{\mathbf{y'M^0y}}$$

$$= 1 - \frac{\text{residual sum of squares}}{\text{total sum of squares}} \quad (6\text{–}39)$$

$$= \frac{\text{regression sum of squares}}{\text{total sum of squares}}$$

and

$$R^2 = \frac{\left[\sum_i (y_i - \bar{y})(\hat{y}_i - \hat{\bar{y}})\right]^2}{\left[\sum_i (y_i - \bar{y})^2\right]\left[\sum_i (\hat{y}_i - \hat{\bar{y}})^2\right]}.$$

The first of these methods measures the proportion of the total variation in $\mathbf{y}$ that is accounted for by variation in the regressors. The second is the squared correlation between the observed values of y and the predictions produced by the estimated regression equation.

If $\mathbf{X}$ contains a constant term, R^2 is constrained to lie between 0 and 1. We start from

$$\mathbf{y} = \mathbf{Xb} + \mathbf{e}$$

and then put all variables in deviation form by writing

$$\mathbf{M^0y} = \mathbf{M^0Xb} + \mathbf{M^0e.}$$

(See Section 2.3.6.) Note that the column of $\mathbf{M^0X}$ corresponding to the constant term is zero and, since the residuals already have mean zero, $\mathbf{M^0e} = \mathbf{e}$. Then

$$\mathbf{y'M^0y} = \mathbf{b'X'M^0Xb} + \mathbf{e'e,}$$

as $\mathbf{e'M^0X} = \mathbf{e'X} = \mathbf{0}$. Both terms on the right-hand side are positive. Dividing both sides by $\mathbf{y'M^0y}$ and rearranging gives the result. We can summarize the calculation of R^2 in an analysis of variance table, which might appear as shown in Table 6.6.[16]

TABLE 6.6. Analysis of Variance

	Source	Degrees of Freedom	Mean Square
Regression	$\mathbf{b'X'y} - n\bar{y}^2$	$K - 1$[16]	
Residual	$\mathbf{e'e}$	$n - K$	s^2
Total	$\mathbf{y'y} - n\bar{y}^2$	$n - 1$	S_{yy}

[16]This assumes that there is a constant term in the equation.

EXAMPLE 6.9 _____

The analysis of variance table for the investment equation is given in Table 6.7.

TABLE 6.7. Analysis of Variance for the Investment Equation

	Source	Degrees of Freedom	Mean Square
Regression	0.0159023	4	0.003976
Residual	0.0004507	10	0.00004507
Total	0.016353	14	0.0011681

$R^2 = 0.0159023/0.016353 = 0.97244$.

There are two problems with the use of R^2 in analyzing goodness of fit. The first concerns the number of degrees of freedom used up in estimating the parameters. It can be shown algebraically that R^2 will never decrease when another variable is added to a regression equation. (The proof appears in Chapter 7.) It is tempting to exploit this fact by just adding variables to the model; R^2 will continue to rise to its limit of 1.[17] In view of this, we sometimes report an *adjusted* (for degrees of freedom) R^2, which is computed as follows:[18]

$$\bar{R}^2 = 1 - \frac{\mathbf{e}'\mathbf{e}/(n - K)}{\mathbf{y}'\mathbf{M}^0\mathbf{y}/(n - 1)}.$$

For computational purposes, the connection between R^2 and $\bar{R}^2$ is

$$\bar{R}^2 = 1 - \frac{n - 1}{n - K}(1 - R^2). \tag{6–40}$$

The essential point to observe about this measure is that it may decline when a variable is added to the set of independent variables. Indeed, $\bar{R}^2$ may even be negative. To consider an admittedly extreme case, suppose that $\mathbf{x}$ and $\mathbf{y}$ have a sample correlation of zero. Then the adjusted R^2 will be $-1/(n - 2)$. Whether $\bar{R}^2$ rises or falls depends on whether the contribution of the new variable to the fit of the regression more than offsets the correction for the loss of an additional degree of freedom. The general result (the proof of which is left as an exercise) is as follows:

> In a multiple regression, $\bar{R}^2$ will fall (rise) when the variable x is deleted from the regression if the t ratio associated with this variable is greater (less) than 1.

A second difficulty with R^2 concerns the constant term in the model. The proof that $0 \le R^2 \le 1$ requires $\mathbf{X}$ to contain a column of 1s. If not, then (1) $\mathbf{M}^0\mathbf{e} \ne \mathbf{e}$ and

---

[17] This comes at a cost, however. The parameter estimates become progressively less precise as we do so.

[18] This measure is sometimes advocated on the basis of the unbiasedness of the two quantities in the fraction. Since the ratio is not an unbiased estimator of any population quantity, it is difficult to justify the adjustment on this basis.

(2) $e'M^0X \neq 0$, and the third term in the preceding expansion will not drop out. Consequently, when we compute

$$R^2 = 1 - \frac{e'e}{y'M^0y},$$

the result is unpredictable. It may be higher or lower than the same figure computed for the regression with a constant term included. It can even be negative. Computer packages differ on the computation of R^2. An alternative computation,

$$R^2 = \frac{b'X'y}{y'M^0y},$$

is equally problematic. Again, this calculation will differ from the one obtained with the constant term included; this time, R^2 may be larger than 1.

This might suggest that we can produce a higher R^2 simply by choosing whether or not to include a constant term in the model. One ought not to view the inclusion of a constant as an option. Certain models specify that the equation should not contain an intercept. But estimating a model without a constant term amounts to imposing a linear restriction, that is, that the constant term is zero. Arbitrarily assuming that the intercept is zero is no less restrictive than arbitrarily imposing some other linear restriction on the coefficients.

6.7. Testing the Significance of the Regression

A hypothesis that is often tested is the significance of the regression equation as a whole. This is a joint test of the hypothesis that *all* of the coefficients except the constant term are zero. If all of the coefficients are zero, the multiple correlation is zero as well, so we can base a test of this hypothesis on the value of R^2. The central result needed to carry out the test was presented in Chapter 5. The statistic

$$F[K - 1, n - K] = \frac{R^2/(K - 1)}{(1 - R^2)/(n - K)}$$

has an F distribution with $K - 1$ and $n - K$ degrees of freedom. The logic of the test is that the F statistic is a measure of the loss of fit (namely, all of R^2) that results when we impose the restriction that all of the slopes are zero. If F is large, the hypothesis is rejected.

EXAMPLE 6.10 ──────────────────────────────

The F ratio for testing the hypothesis that the four slopes in the investment equation are all zero is

$$F[4, 10] = \frac{0.97244/4}{(1 - 0.97244)/10} = 88.211,$$

which is far larger than the critical value of 3.48.

───

We might have expected the preceding result, given the substantial t ratios presented earlier. Unfortunately, this need not always be the case. Examples can be constructed in which the individual coefficients are statistically significant, while jointly they are not.[19]

[19] See, Maddala (1977, pp. 123–124).

This can be regarded as a pathological case, but the opposite one, in which none of the coefficients are significantly different from zero while R^2 is highly significant, is relatively common. The problem is that the interaction among the variables may serve to obscure their individual contribution to the fit of the regression, while their joint effect may still be significant. We will return to this point in Chapter 9 in our discussion of multicollinearity.

6.8. Prediction

The results for forecasting in the multiple regression setting are essentially the same as those discussed in Chapter 5. Suppose that we wish to predict the value y^0 associated with a regressor vector $\mathbf{x}^0$. This would be

$$y^0 = \boldsymbol{\beta}'\mathbf{x}^0 + \varepsilon^0.$$

If follows from the Gauss–Markov theorem that

$$\hat{y}^0 = \mathbf{b}'\mathbf{x}^0 \tag{6-41}$$

is the minimum variance linear unbiased estimator of $E[y^0]$. The forecast error is

$$e^0 = y^0 - \hat{y}^0 = (\boldsymbol{\beta} - \mathbf{b})'\mathbf{x}^0 + \varepsilon^0.$$

Using the results of Chapter 5, the forecast variance to be applied to this estimate is

$$\begin{aligned} \mathrm{Var}[e^0] &= \sigma^2 + \mathrm{Var}[(\boldsymbol{\beta} - \mathbf{b})'\mathbf{x}^0] \\ &= \sigma^2 + \mathbf{x}^{0\prime}[\sigma^2(\mathbf{X}'\mathbf{X})^{-1}]\mathbf{x}^0. \end{aligned} \tag{6-42}$$

If the regression contains a constant term, an equivalent expression is

$$\mathrm{Var}[e^0] = \sigma^2 + \frac{\sigma^2}{n} + \sigma^2\left\{\sum_{j=2}^{K}\sum_{k=2}^{K}(x_j^0 - \bar{x}_j)(x_k^0 - \bar{x}_k)(\underline{\mathbf{X}}'\mathbf{M}^0\underline{\mathbf{X}})^{jk}\right\},$$

where $\underline{\mathbf{X}}$ is the last $K - 1$ columns of $\mathbf{X}$ not including the column of 1s. This shows, as before, that the width of the interval depends on the distance of the elements of $\mathbf{x}^0$ from the center of the data.

The forecast variance can be estimated by using s^2 in place of σ^2. A confidence interval for y^0 would be formed using

$$\text{forecast interval} = \hat{y}^0 \pm t_{\lambda/2}\mathrm{se}(\hat{y}^0).$$

EXAMPLE 6.11 _____

Suppose that we wish to forecast the 1983 value of real investment based on forecasts of (1) real GNP = 1.5 trillion, (2) a discount rate of 10 percent, and (3) inflation of 4 percent, using the regression results in Example 6.5. The forecast is $\mathbf{x}^0\mathbf{b}$:

$$(1,\ 16,\ 1.5,\ 10,\ 4)(-0.509,\ -0.017,\ 0.670,\ -0.002,\ -0.0001)' = 0.2036.$$

The estimated variance of this forecast is

$$s^2(1 + \mathbf{x}^{0\prime}(\mathbf{X}'\mathbf{X})^{-1}\mathbf{x}^0) = 0.00009772113.$$

Using the square root of this result, we obtain the forecast interval:

$$0.2036 \pm 2.228(0.009885) = \langle 0.1811,\ 0.2262\rangle.$$

6.8.1. A Convenient Method of Computing the Forecasts

The preceding would suggest that two sets of computations are necessary in order to obtain the predictions (6–41) and the associated standard errors (6–42): first, the least squares estimates, and second, the forecasts and the forecast variances. Salkever (1976) has suggested a convenient method of combining the computations by using an expanded regression. Suppose that the estimation is based on n observations, and we desire to forecast n^0 observations:

$$\mathbf{y}^0 = \mathbf{X}^0\boldsymbol{\beta} + \boldsymbol{\varepsilon}^0.$$

We first construct an augmented regression:

$$\begin{bmatrix} \mathbf{y} \\ \mathbf{0} \end{bmatrix} = \begin{bmatrix} \mathbf{X} & \mathbf{0} \\ \mathbf{X}^0 & -\mathbf{I} \end{bmatrix}\begin{bmatrix} \boldsymbol{\beta} \\ \boldsymbol{\gamma} \end{bmatrix} + \begin{bmatrix} \boldsymbol{\varepsilon} \\ \boldsymbol{\varepsilon}^0 \end{bmatrix} \tag{6–43}$$

or

$$\mathbf{y}^* = \mathbf{X}^*\boldsymbol{\beta}^* + \boldsymbol{\varepsilon}^*.$$

In (6–43) there are n^0 new observations added and a set of n^0 new variables. Each column in the second part of $\mathbf{X}^*$ is a **dummy variable** that takes the value one only for that observation and zero for all others. (Note that the new parameter vector, $\boldsymbol{\gamma}$, is $\mathbf{y}^0$.)

Based on the expanded regression model, we obtain the following results:

1. The least squares regression of $\mathbf{y}^*$ on $\mathbf{X}^*$ produces the coefficient vector $[\mathbf{b}, \mathbf{c}]$, where $\mathbf{b}$ is the original OLS coefficient vector and $\mathbf{c}$ is the predictions for $\mathbf{y}^0$.

   Proof:

   $$\mathbf{X}^{*\prime}\mathbf{X}^* = \begin{bmatrix} \mathbf{X}'\mathbf{X} + \mathbf{X}^{0\prime}\mathbf{X}^0 & -\mathbf{X}^{0\prime} \\ -\mathbf{X}^0 & \mathbf{I} \end{bmatrix} \quad \text{and} \quad \mathbf{X}^{*\prime}\mathbf{y}^* = \begin{bmatrix} \mathbf{X}'\mathbf{y} \\ \mathbf{0} \end{bmatrix}.$$

   Using the partitioned inverse formula from Chapter 2, we obtain

   $$(\mathbf{X}^{*\prime}\mathbf{X}^*)^{-1} = \begin{bmatrix} (\mathbf{X}'\mathbf{X})^{-1} & (\mathbf{X}'\mathbf{X})^{-1}\mathbf{X}^{0\prime} \\ \mathbf{X}^0(\mathbf{X}'\mathbf{X})^{-1} & \mathbf{I} + \mathbf{X}^{0\prime}(\mathbf{X}'\mathbf{X})^{-1}\mathbf{X}^0 \end{bmatrix}.$$

   Postmultiplying $(\mathbf{X}^{*\prime}\mathbf{X}^*)^{-1}$ by $\mathbf{X}^{*\prime}\mathbf{y}^*$ produces the result.

2. The residuals from this regression are, for the first T observations, the original least squares residuals, and for the last T^0, zero. The first part is obvious, since the coefficient vector is the same. Multiplying it out produces

   $$\mathbf{y}^* - \mathbf{X}^*\mathbf{b}^* = \begin{bmatrix} \mathbf{e} \\ \mathbf{0} \end{bmatrix}.$$

3. The estimated covariance matrix for the expanded vector of coefficient estimates contains, in its upper left block, the covariance matrix for the least squares estimates of $\boldsymbol{\beta}$ and, in its lower right block, the covariance matrix for the forecasts.
   Proof:

   $$s^{2*} = \mathbf{e}^{*\prime}\mathbf{e}^* = \frac{\mathbf{e}'\mathbf{e} + \mathbf{0}'\mathbf{0}}{n + n^0 - (K + n^0)} = s^2.$$

   Therefore,

   $$s^{2*}(\mathbf{X}^{*\prime}\mathbf{X}^*)^{-1} = \begin{bmatrix} s^2(\mathbf{X}'\mathbf{X})^{-1} & * \\ * & s^2[\mathbf{I} + \mathbf{X}^{0\prime}(\mathbf{X}'\mathbf{X})^{-1}\mathbf{X}^0] \end{bmatrix},$$

where * indicates a submatrix for which we have no convenient interpretation. The upper matrix is familiar. The ith diagonal element of the lower matrix is

$$\text{Est. Var}[c_i] = \text{Est. Var}[\hat{y}_i^0] = s^2(1 + \mathbf{x}_i^{0\prime}(\mathbf{X}'\mathbf{X})^{-1}\mathbf{x}_i^0),$$

which is (6–42). This completes the proof.

These results imply that the standard computer output from this expanded regression will contain, in addition to the usual least squares results, the forecasts and estimated forecast variances or standard errors. One thing to note is that the R^2 in the expanded regression will be incorrect. The total sum of squares will be computed using an expanded $\mathbf{y}$ vector containing a set of zeros. It would be possible to patch this up by replacing the zeros in $\mathbf{y}^*$ with $\bar{y}$ from the original data, but then the lower subvector of the coefficient vector would no longer be the least squares predictions.

There is an interesting corollary that follows from result 2. It is not uncommon for researchers to include a dummy variable in a regression to account for something that applies only to a single observation. For example, in time series studies, an occasional study includes a dummy variable that is one only in a single unusual year, such as the year of a major strike. Result 2 shows clearly what the effect of this variable will be

A dummy variable that takes the value 1
only for one observation has the effect of deleting
that observation from the least squares computations.

6.8.2. Measuring the Accuracy of Forecasts

Various measures have been proposed for assessing the predictive accuracy of forecasting models.[20] Most of these measures are designed to evaluate ex post forecasts, that is, forecasts for which the exogenous variables do not have to be forecasted. Two that are based on the residuals from the forecasts are

$$\text{root mean-squared error} = \text{RMSE} = \sqrt{\frac{1}{n^0} \sum_i (y_i - \hat{y}_i)^2}$$

and

$$\text{mean absolute error} = \text{MAE} = \frac{1}{n^0} \sum_i |y_i - \hat{y}_i|,$$

where n^0 is the number of periods being forecasted. These have an obvious scaling problem. Several that do not are based on the Theil U statistic:[21]

$$U = \sqrt{\frac{(1/n^0) \sum_i (y_i - \hat{y}_i)^2}{(1/n^0) \sum_i y_i^2}}.$$

This measure is related to R^2 but is not bounded by zero and one. Large values indicate a poor forecasting performance. An alternative is to compute the measure in terms of the changes in y:

$$U_\Delta = \sqrt{\frac{(1/n^0) \sum_i (\Delta y_i - \Delta \hat{y}_i)^2}{(1/n^0) \sum_i (\Delta y_i)^2}},$$

[20] See Theil (1961) and Fair (1984).

[21] Ibid.

where

$$\Delta y_i = y_i - y_{i-1} \quad \text{and} \quad \Delta \hat{y}_i = \hat{y}_i - y_{i-1},$$

or, in percentage changes,

$$\Delta y_i = \frac{y_i - y_{i-1}}{y_{i-1}} \quad \text{and} \quad \Delta \hat{y}_i = \frac{\hat{y}_i - y_{i-1}}{y_{i-1}}.$$

These measures will reflect the model's ability to track turning points in the data.

EXAMPLE 6.12

Most of the cyclical variation in the investment data we have analyzed is picked up by GNP. Consider a comparison of the predictions of two models, one that includes GNP and one that does not. For these two candidates, the results are listed in Table 6.8. The last of these is particularly pronounced. In a forecasting model, the ability to predict turning points is obviously important. The actual values and predictions from the two competing models presented are shown in Table 6.9. There were declines in real investment in 1970, 1973, 1974, 1980, and 1982. The model including GNP predicted all five turning points. The one omitting GNP missed all five. Figure 6.2 shows the effect.

TABLE 6.8

	With GNP	Without GNP
RMSE	0.005482	0.02183
MAE	0.004227	0.01692
U	0.02661	0.10559
$U_\Delta{}^a$	0.19727	0.89600

[a] U_Δ is computed using the absolute rather than the percentage changes.

TABLE 6.9

	1968	1969	1970	1971	1972	1973	1974	1975
Actual	0.161	0.172	0.158	0.173	0.195	0.217	0.199	0.163
With GNP	0.171	0.173	0.155	0.165	0.192	0.217	0.191	0.187
Without GNP	0.162	0.168	0.174	0.181	0.187	0.192	0.198	0.205

	1976	1977	1978	1979	1980	1981	1982
Actual	0.195	0.231	0.257	0.259	0.225	0.241	0.204
With GNP	0.199	0.230	0.255	0.259	0.234	0.234	0.205
Without GNP	0.210	0.216	0.222	0.226	0.231	0.236	0.243

EXERCISES

1. Using the matrices of sums of squares and cross products immediately preceding Section 6.3.3, compute the coefficients in the multiple regression of real investment on a constant, real GNP, and the interest rate. The sum of squares of real investment is 0.63652. Compute R^2 and the estimate of the covariance matrix of the estimated

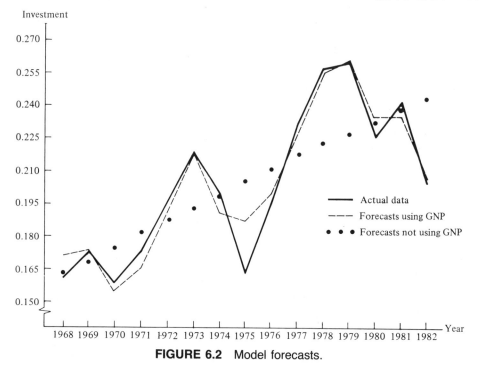

FIGURE 6.2 Model forecasts.

slopes and constant term. Test the individual hypotheses that the two slopes are zero. Test the joint hypothesis that both slopes are zero.

2. The following matrix gives the slope in the simple regression of the column variable on the row variable:

$$\mathbf{A} = \begin{bmatrix} & y & x_1 & x_2 \\ 1 & 0.03 & 0.36 \\ 0.4 & 1 & 0.3 \\ 1.25 & 0.075 & 1 \end{bmatrix} \begin{matrix} y \\ x_1 \\ x_2 \end{matrix}$$

For example, if y is regressed on x_1, the slope is 0.4, but if x_1 is regressed on y, the slope is 0.03. All variables have zero means, so the constant terms in all regressions are zero. What are the two slope coefficients in the multiple regression of y on x_1 and x_2?

3. Assuming that x_1 and x_2 have zero sample means and zero sample correlation, where is the inconsistency in the following results? (Estimated standard errors of the parameter estimates are given in parentheses.)

$$\hat{y} = 3 + 2x_1 + 1x_2, \qquad R^2 = 0.77$$

$$(0.25) \qquad (0.25) \qquad n = 23$$

Analysis of Variance

	Variation	Degrees of Freedom	Mean Square
Regression	68	2	34
Residual	20	20	1
Total	88	22	4

4. If the interest rate were added to the regression of investment on a constant, the time trend, and GNP that is given after Example 6.3, what would be its coefficient in the multiple regression? (**Hint:** You will find the necessary sums in the matrix you used for Exercise 1.)

5. For the regression in the previous problem, what is the new value of R^2 after you add the interest rate to the regression?

6. The following data relate to gasoline consumption in the United States in the years 1960 to 1986:

TABLE 6.10. Data on U.S. Gasoline Market

Year	G	P_g	Y	P_{nc}	P_{uc}	P_{pt}	P_d	P_n	P_s
1960	129.7	0.925	6036	1.045	0.836	0.810	0.444	0.331	0.302
1961	131.3	0.914	6113	1.045	0.869	0.846	0.448	0.335	0.307
1962	137.1	0.919	6271	1.041	0.948	0.874	0.457	0.338	0.314
1963	141.6	0.918	6378	1.035	0.960	0.885	0.463	0.343	0.320
1964	148.8	0.914	6727	1.032	1.001	0.901	0.470	0.347	0.325
1965	155.9	0.949	7027	1.009	0.994	0.919	0.471	0.353	0.332
1966	164.9	0.970	7280	0.991	0.970	0.952	0.475	0.366	0.342
1967	171.0	1.000	7513	1.000	1.000	1.000	0.483	0.375	0.353
1968	183.4	1.014	7728	1.028	1.028	1.046	0.501	0.390	0.368
1969	195.8	1.047	7891	1.044	1.031	1.127	0.514	0.409	0.386
1970	207.4	1.056	8134	1.076	1.043	1.285	0.527	0.427	0.407
1971	218.3	1.063	8322	1.120	1.102	1.377	0.547	0.442	0.431
1972	226.8	1.076	8562	1.110	1.105	1.434	0.555	0.458	0.451
1973	237.9	1.181	9042	1.111	1.176	1.448	0.566	0.497	0.474
1974	225.8	1.599	8867	1.175	1.226	1.480	0.604	0.572	0.513
1975	232.4	1.708	8944	1.276	1.464	1.586	0.659	0.615	0.556
1976	241.7	1.779	9175	1.357	1.679	1.742	0.695	0.638	0.598
1977	249.2	1.882	9381	1.429	1.828	1.824	0.727	0.671	0.648
1978	261.3	1.963	9735	1.538	1.865	1.878	0.769	0.719	0.698
1979	248.9	2.656	9829	1.660	2.010	2.003	0.821	0.800	0.756
1980	226.8	3.691	9722	1.793	2.081	2.516	0.892	0.894	0.839
1981	225.6	4.109	9769	1.902	2.569	3.120	0.957	0.969	0.926
1982	228.8	3.894	9725	1.976	2.964	3.460	1.000	1.000	1.000
1983	239.6	3.764	9930	2.026	3.297	3.626	1.041	1.021	1.062
1984	244.7	3.707	10421	2.085	3.757	3.852	1.038	1.050	1.117
1985	245.8	3.738	10563	2.152	3.797	4.028	1.045	1.075	1.173
1986	269.4	2.921	10780	2.240	3.632	4.264	1.053	1.069	1.224

The variables are

G = total gasoline consumption, computed as current dollar expenditure divided by the price index

P_g = price index for gasoline

Y = per capita real disposable income

P_{nc} = price index for new cars

P_{uc} = price index used cars

P_{pt} = price index for public transportation

P_d = aggregate price index for consumer durable goods

P_n = aggregate price index for consumer nondurable goods

P_s = aggregate price index for consumer services.

[All data are from the *Economic Report of the President, 1987,* (Council of Economic Advisors,1987).]

(a) Compute the multiple regression of G on all of the other explanatory variables, including the time trend, and report all results. Do the signs of the estimates agree with your expectations?

(b) Test the hypothesis that at least in regard to demand for gasoline, consumers do not differentiate between changes in the prices of new and used cars.

(c) Estimate the own price elasticity of demand, the income elasticity, and the cross-price elasticity with respect to changes in the price of public transportation.

(d) Reestimate the regression in logarithms so that the coefficients are direct estimates of the elasticities. (Do not use the log of the time trend). How do your estimates compare to the results in the previous question? Which specification do you prefer?

(e) Notice that the price indices for the automobile market are normalized to 1967, while the aggregate price indices are anchored at 1982. Does this discrepancy affect the results? How? If you were to renormalize the indices so that they were all 1.000 in 1982, how would your results change? Note that this would be an application of the principle in Exercise 12. What is the **P** matrix?

7. Suppose, for purposes of this exercise, that the variable Y in the previous exercise is total expenditure on consumer durables, nondurables, and services, rather than total income (which includes savings as well). Suppose, as well, that E_d, E_n, and E_s are the expenditures on the three categories. As defined,

$$Y = E_d + E_n + E_s.$$

Now consider the expenditure system

$$E_d = \alpha_d + \beta_d Y + \gamma_{dd} P_d + \gamma_{dn} P_n + \gamma_{ds} P_s + \varepsilon_d$$

$$E_n = \alpha_n + \beta_n Y + \gamma_{nd} P_d + \gamma_{nn} P_n + \gamma_{ns} P_s + \varepsilon_n$$

$$E_s = \alpha_s + \beta_s Y + \gamma_{sd} P_d + \gamma_{sn} P_n + \gamma_{ss} P_s + \varepsilon_s.$$

If all equations are estimated by ordinary least squares, prove that the sum of the income coefficients will be one and the other four column sums in the preceding model will be zero. (Some applications of demand systems such as this are discussed in Section 17.4)

8. Prove the result in (6–20).

9. Prove that the adjusted R^2 in (6–40) rises (falls) when variable x_k is deleted from the regression if the square of the t ratio on x_k in the multiple regression is less (greater) than one.

10. Consider the multiple regression of **y** on K variables, **X,** and an additional variable, **z.** Prove that the true variance of the least squares estimator of the slopes on **X** is larger when **z** is included in the regression than when it is not. Does the same hold for the sample estimate of this covariance matrix? Why or why not?

11. An estimate of a Cobb–Douglas production function is given in the discussion preceding Example 7.1 in the next chapter. The basic equation is of the form

$$\ln Y = \alpha + \beta_k \ln K + \beta_l \ln L + \varepsilon.$$

We are interested in the issue of constant returns to scale, which is implied by $\beta_k + \beta_l = 1$. This hypothesis is tested in Example 7.2. For present purposes, construct a confidence region for these two parameters in the manner of Example 6.8. On the same figure, draw the line that represents the set of points for which $\beta_k + \beta_l = 1$.

12. Consider the least squares regression of y on K variables (with a constant), X. Consider an alternative set of regressors, $Z = XP$, where P is a nonsingular matrix. Thus, each column of Z is a mixture of some of the columns of X. Prove that the residual vectors in the regressions of y on X and y on Z are identical. What relevance does this have to the question of changing the fit of a regression by changing the units of measurement of the independent variables?

13. Suppose b is the least squares coefficient vector in the regression of y on X and c is any other $K \times 1$ vector. Prove that the difference in the two sums of squared residuals is

$$(y - Xc)'(y - Xc) - (y - Xb)'(y - Xb) = (c - b)'X'X(c - b).$$

Prove that this difference is positive.

14. (Once again . . .) Suppose that you estimate a multiple regression first with and then without a constant. Whether the R^2 is higher in the second case than the first will depend in part on how it is computed. Upon using the (relatively) standard method,

$$R^2 = 1 - \frac{e'e}{y'M^0y},$$

which regression will have a higher R^2? (**Hint:** Consider Exercise 13.)

15. In the least squares regression of y on a constant and X, in order to compute the regression coefficients on X, we can first transform y to deviations from the mean, $\bar{y}$, and transform each column of X to deviations from the respective column mean; second, we can regress the transformed y on the transformed X without a constant. Do we get the same result if we transform only y? What if we transform only X?

16. What is the result of the matrix product M_1M, where M_1 is defined in (6–18) and M is defined in (6–16)?

17. Using the results of Example 6.5, compute a 95 percent forecast interval for real investment for 1983, assuming forecasts of 3100 for nominal GNP, 212 for the CPI, and 10.0 for the interest rate.

CHAPTER 7

Hypothesis Tests with the Multiple Regression Model

7.1. Introduction

In this chapter, we examine some applications of hypothesis tests using the classical model. The basic statistical theory was developed in Section 6.5. This chapter also presents additional statistical results for some tests that do not fit into the framework of Chapter 6.

7.2. Testing Restrictions

Our approach to testing a hypothesis will be to formulate a statistical model that contains the hypothesis as a restriction on its parameters. A theory is said to have *testable implications* if it implies some testable restrictions on the model. Consider, for example, a simple model of investment,

$$\text{investment} = \beta_1 + \beta_2 \text{interest} + \beta_3 \text{inflation} + \varepsilon,$$

which states that investors are sensitive to nominal interest rates and the rate of inflation. An alternative theory states that "investors care about real interest rates." The alternative model is

$$\text{investment} = \beta_1 + \beta_2(\text{interest-inflation}) + \beta_3 \text{inflation} + \varepsilon.$$

Although this new model does embody the theory, the equation still contains both nominal interest and inflation. The theory has no testable implication for our model. However, consider the stronger hypothesis, "investors care *only* about real interest rates." The resulting equation,

$$\text{investment} = \beta_1 + \beta_2(\text{interest-inflation}) + \varepsilon,$$

is now restricted; in the context of the first one, the implication is that $\beta_2 + \beta_3 = 0$. The stronger statement implies something very specific about the parameters in the equation that may or may not be supported by the empirical evidence.

7.2.1. Two Approaches to Testing Hypotheses

Hypothesis testing can be approached from two viewpoints. First, having computed a set of parameter estimates, we can ask whether the estimates come reasonably close to satisfying the restrictions implied by the hypothesis. More formally, we can ascertain whether the failure of the estimates to satisfy the restrictions is simply the result of sampling error or is, instead, systematic. An alternative view of the testing procedure might proceed as follows: Suppose that we impose the restrictions implied by the theory. Since unrestricted least squares is, by definition, "least squares," this imposition must lead to a loss of fit. We can then ascertain whether this loss of fit results merely from sampling error or whether it is so large as to cast doubt on the validity of the restrictions.

7.2.2. Testing a Set of Linear Restrictions

Beginning with the linear regression model,

$$\mathbf{y} = \mathbf{X}\boldsymbol{\beta} + \boldsymbol{\varepsilon}, \tag{7-1}$$

we consider a set of linear restrictions of the form

$$r_{11}\beta_1 + r_{12}\beta_2 + \cdots + r_{1K}\beta_K = q_1$$
$$r_{21}\beta_1 + r_{22}\beta_2 + \cdots + r_{2K}\beta_K = q_2$$
$$\vdots$$
$$r_{J1}\beta_1 + r_{J2}\beta_2 + \cdots + r_{JK}\beta_K = q_J.$$

These can be combined into the single equation

$$\mathbf{R}\boldsymbol{\beta} = \mathbf{q}. \tag{7-2}$$

Each row of $\mathbf{R}$ is the coefficients in one of the restrictions.[1] The matrix $\mathbf{R}$ has K columns to be conformable with $\boldsymbol{\beta}$, J rows for a total of J restrictions, and full row rank, so J must be less than or equal to K. The rows of $\mathbf{R}$ must be linearly independent. Although it does not violate the condition, the case of $J = K$ must also be ruled out.[2]

The restriction $\mathbf{R}\boldsymbol{\beta} = \mathbf{q}$ imposes J restrictions on K otherwise free parameters. This means that with the restrictions imposed, there are, in principle, only $K - J$ free parameters remaining. One way to view this is to partition $\mathbf{R}$ into two groups of columns, one with J and one with $K - J$, so that the first set are linearly independent. (There are many ways to do so; any one will do for the present.) Then, with $\boldsymbol{\beta}$ likewise partitioned and its elements reordered in whatever way is needed, we may write

$$\mathbf{R}\boldsymbol{\beta} = \mathbf{R}_1\boldsymbol{\beta}_1 + \mathbf{R}_2\boldsymbol{\beta}_2 = \mathbf{q}.$$

If the J columns of $\mathbf{R}_1$ are independent,

$$\boldsymbol{\beta}_1 = \mathbf{R}_1^{-1}[\mathbf{q} - \mathbf{R}_2\boldsymbol{\beta}_2]. \tag{7-3}$$

The implication is that although $\boldsymbol{\beta}_2$ is free to vary, once $\boldsymbol{\beta}_2$ is determined, $\boldsymbol{\beta}_1$ is determined by (7–3). Thus, only the $K - J$ elements of $\boldsymbol{\beta}_2$ are free parameters in the model.

The sample statistic used for testing

$$H_0 : \mathbf{R}\boldsymbol{\beta} = \mathbf{q} \tag{7-4}$$

was derived in Section 6.5. To reiterate, we compare the test statistic

$$F[J, n - K] = \frac{(\mathbf{R}\mathbf{b} - \mathbf{q})'\{\mathbf{R}[s^2(\mathbf{X}'\mathbf{X})^{-1}]\mathbf{R}'\}^{-1}(\mathbf{R}\mathbf{b} - \mathbf{q})}{J} \tag{7-5}$$

to the critical value in the standard F table. A large value of F is evidence against the hypothesis.

---

[1] Several examples are given in Section 6.5.

[2] If the K slopes satisfy $J = K$ restrictions, $\mathbf{R}$ is square and nonsingular and $\boldsymbol{\beta} = \mathbf{R}^{-1}\mathbf{q}$. There is no estimation or inference problem.

7.2.3. The Restricted Least Squares Estimator

Suppose, instead, that we explicitly impose the restrictions of the hypothesis in the regression. The restricted least squares estimator is obtained as the solution to

$$\text{Minimize}_{\tilde{\beta}} S(\tilde{\beta}) = (\mathbf{y} - \mathbf{X}\tilde{\beta})'(\mathbf{y} - \mathbf{X}\tilde{\beta}) \text{ subject to } \mathbf{R}\tilde{\beta} = \mathbf{q}. \tag{7-6}$$

A Lagrangean solution for this problem can be written

$$\mathbf{b}_* = \text{Min}_{\tilde{\beta}, \lambda} S^*(\tilde{\beta}) = (\mathbf{y} - \mathbf{X}\tilde{\beta})'(\mathbf{y} - \mathbf{X}\tilde{\beta}) + 2\lambda'(\mathbf{R}\tilde{\beta} - \mathbf{q}).^3 \tag{7-7}$$

The solutions $\mathbf{b}_*$ and λ will satisfy the necessary conditions

$$\frac{\partial S^*}{\partial \mathbf{b}*} = -2\mathbf{X}'(\mathbf{y} - \mathbf{X}\mathbf{b}_*) + 2\mathbf{R}'\lambda = 0, \tag{7-8}$$

$$\frac{\partial S^*}{\partial \lambda} = 2(\mathbf{R}\mathbf{b}_* - \mathbf{q}) = 0. \tag{7-9}$$

Dividing through by 2 and expanding terms produces the partitioned matrix equation

$$\begin{bmatrix} \mathbf{X}'\mathbf{X} & \mathbf{R}' \\ \mathbf{R} & \mathbf{0} \end{bmatrix} \begin{bmatrix} \mathbf{b}_* \\ \lambda \end{bmatrix} = \begin{bmatrix} \mathbf{X}'\mathbf{y} \\ \mathbf{q} \end{bmatrix} \tag{7-10}$$

or

$$\mathbf{W}\mathbf{d}_* = \mathbf{v}.$$

Assuming that the partitioned matrix in brackets is nonsingular, the restricted least squares estimator is the solution

$$\mathbf{d}_* = \mathbf{W}^{-1}\mathbf{v}$$

$$= \begin{bmatrix} \mathbf{b}_* \\ \lambda \end{bmatrix}. \tag{7-11}$$

If, in addition, $\mathbf{X}'\mathbf{X}$ is nonsingular, then explicit solutions for $\mathbf{b}_*$ and λ may be obtained by using the formula for the partitioned inverse (2–74),[4]

$$\mathbf{b}_* = \mathbf{b} - (\mathbf{X}'\mathbf{X})^{-1}\mathbf{R}'[\mathbf{R}(\mathbf{X}'\mathbf{X})^{-1}\mathbf{R}']^{-1}(\mathbf{R}\mathbf{b} - \mathbf{q})$$

and

$$\lambda = [\mathbf{R}(\mathbf{X}'\mathbf{X})^{-1}\mathbf{R}']^{-1}(\mathbf{R}\mathbf{b} - \mathbf{q}). \tag{7-12}$$

Greene and Seaks (1991) show that the covariance matrix for $\mathbf{b}_*$ is simply σ^2 times the upper left block of $\mathbf{W}^{-1}$. Once again, in the usual case in which $\mathbf{X}'\mathbf{X}$ is nonsingular, an explicit formulation may be obtained,

$$\text{Var}[\mathbf{b}_*] = \sigma^2(\mathbf{X}'\mathbf{X})^{-1} - \sigma^2(\mathbf{X}'\mathbf{X})^{-1}\mathbf{R}'[\mathbf{R}(\mathbf{X}'\mathbf{X})^{-1}\mathbf{R}']^{-1}\mathbf{R}(\mathbf{X}'\mathbf{X})^{-1}.$$

Thus,

$$\text{Var}[\mathbf{b}_*] = \text{Var}[\mathbf{b}] - \text{a positive definite matrix}.$$

---

[3] The value of λ will be obtained subsequently. Since λ is not restricted, we can formulate the constraints in terms of 2λ. It will be clear shortly why this is convenient.

[4] The general solution given for $\mathbf{d}_*$ may be usable even if $\mathbf{X}'\mathbf{X}$ is singular. Suppose, for example, that $\mathbf{X}'\mathbf{X}$ is 4×4 with rank 3. Then $\mathbf{X}'\mathbf{X}$ is singular. But if there is a parametric restriction on β, the 5×5 matrix in brackets may still have rank 5. Whether or not $\mathbf{X}'\mathbf{X}$ is singular, (7–10) and (7–11) are likely to be simpler to program for a computer than (7–12). This formulation and a number of related results are given in Greene and Seaks (1991).

One way to interpret this reduction in variance is as the value of the information contained in the restrictions.

Note that the explicit solution for λ involves the discrepancy vector, $\mathbf{Rb} - \mathbf{q}$. If the unrestricted least squares estimator satisfied the restrictions, the Lagrangean multipliers would equal zero and $\mathbf{b}_*$ would equal $\mathbf{b}$. Of course, this is unlikely. The constrained solution $\mathbf{b}_*$ is equal to the unconstrained solution, $\mathbf{b}$, plus a term that accounts for the failure of the unrestricted solution to satisfy the constraints.

7.2.4. Testing the Restrictions

We know from several earlier results that the fit of the restricted least squares coefficients will be worse than that of the unrestricted solution. Let $\mathbf{e}_*$ equal $\mathbf{y} - \mathbf{Xb}_*$. Then, using a familiar device,

$$\mathbf{e}_* = \mathbf{y} - \mathbf{Xb} - \mathbf{X}(\mathbf{b}_* - \mathbf{b}) = \mathbf{e} - \mathbf{X}(\mathbf{b}_* - \mathbf{b}).$$

The new sum of squared deviations is

$$\mathbf{e}_*'\mathbf{e}_* = \mathbf{e}'\mathbf{e} + (\mathbf{b}_* - \mathbf{b})'\mathbf{X}'\mathbf{X}(\mathbf{b}_* - \mathbf{b}) \geq \mathbf{e}'\mathbf{e}.^5$$

(The middle term in the expression involves $\mathbf{X}'\mathbf{e}$, which is zero.) As an alternative approach, then, we could base a test of the restrictions on the loss of fit, which is

$$\mathbf{e}_*'\mathbf{e}_* - \mathbf{e}'\mathbf{e} = (\mathbf{Rb} - \mathbf{q})'[\mathbf{R}(\mathbf{X}'\mathbf{X})^{-1}\mathbf{R}']^{-1}(\mathbf{Rb} - \mathbf{q}). \tag{7-13}$$

This appears in the numerator of the F statistic derived earlier. Inserting the remaining parts, we obtain an alternative form,

$$F[J, n - K] = \frac{(\mathbf{e}_*'\mathbf{e}_* - \mathbf{e}'\mathbf{e})/J}{\mathbf{e}'\mathbf{e}/(n - K)}. \tag{7-14}$$

Finally, by dividing the numerator and denominator of F by $\Sigma(y - \bar{y})^2$, we obtain a third form,

$$F[J, n - K] = \frac{(R^2 - R_*^2)/J}{(1 - R^2)/(n - K)}. \tag{7-15}$$

This form has some intuitive appeal in that the difference in the fits of the two models is directly incorporated in the test statistic. As an example of this approach, consider the earlier joint test that all of the slopes in the model are zero. This is the overall F ratio discussed in Section 6.7, where $R_*^2 = 0$.

7.2.5. Examples and Some General Procedures

The data in Table 7.1 have been used in several studies of production functions.[6]

Least squares regression of log output (value added) on a constant and the logs of labor and capital produce the estimates of a Cobb–Douglas production function shown in Table 7.2.

---

[5] An interesting variation is $\mathbf{e}_*'\mathbf{e}_* = \mathbf{e}'\mathbf{e} + \Sigma_j \lambda_j(\mathbf{R}^j\boldsymbol{\beta} - \mathbf{q}_j)$, where $\mathbf{R}^j$ is the jth row of $\mathbf{R}$ (i.e., the coefficients in the jth restriction). This decomposes the increase in the sum of squares into the contributions of the individual discrepancies.

[6] The data are statewide observations on SIC 33, the primary metals industry. They were originally constructed by Hildebrand and Liu (1957) and have subsequently been used by a number of authors, notably Aigner et al. (1977). The 28th data point used in the original study is incomplete; we have used only the remaining 27.

TABLE 7.1. Production Data for SIC 33: Primary Metals[a]

Observation	Value Added	Labor	Capital
1	657.29	162.31	279.99
2	935.93	214.43	542.50
3	1110.65	186.44	721.51
4	1200.89	245.83	1,167.68
5	1052.68	211.40	811.77
6	3406.02	690.61	4,558.02
7	2427.89	452.79	3,069.91
8	4257.46	714.20	5,585.01
9	1625.19	320.54	1,618.75
10	1272.05	253.17	1,562.08
11	1004.45	236.44	662.04
12	598.87	140.73	875.37
13	853.10	145.04	1,696.98
14	1165.63	240.27	1,078.79
15	1917.55	536.73	2,109.34
16	9849.17	1564.83	13,989.55
17	1088.27	214.62	884.24
18	8095.63	1083.10	9,119.70
19	3175.39	521.74	5,686.99
20	1653.38	304.85	1,701.06
21	5159.31	835.69	5,206.36
22	3378.40	284.00	3,288.72
23	592.85	150.77	357.32
24	1601.98	259.91	2,031.93
25	2065.85	497.60	2,492.98
26	2293.87	275.20	1,711.74
27	745.67	137.00	768.59

[a] Data are per establishment; labor is a measure of labor input; and capital is the gross value of plant and equipment. A scale factor used to normalize the capital figure in the original study has been omitted.

TABLE 7.2

Number of observations	27
Standard error of regression	0.18840
Sum of squared residuals	0.85163
R-squared	0.94346
Adjusted R-squared	0.93875

Variable	Coefficient	Std. Error	t ratio
Constant	1.171	0.3268	3.583
ln labor	0.6030	0.1260	4.787
ln capital	0.3757	0.0853	4.402

Estimated Covariance Matrix of the Estimates

	Constant	ln labor	ln capital
Constant	0.1068		
ln labor	−0.01984	0.01586	
ln capital	0.00189	−0.00961	0.00728

EXAMPLE 7.1 _____

For testing the hypothesis that the jth coefficient is equal to a particular value, $\mathbf{R}$ has a single row with a one in the jth position. Thus, $\mathbf{R}(\mathbf{X}'\mathbf{X})^{-1}\mathbf{R}'$ is the jth diagonal element of the inverse matrix, and $\mathbf{Rb} - \mathbf{q}$ is $(b_j - q)$. The F statistic is

$$F[1, n - K] = \frac{(b_j - q)^2}{\text{Var}[b_j]}, \tag{7-16}$$

which is the square of the t statistic formulated in Chapter 6. For the preceding data, the hypothesis $H_0: \beta_2 = 1$ is rejected on the basis of an F statistic of

$$F[1, 24] = \frac{(0.6030 - 1)^2}{0.01586} = 9.937.$$

The 5 percent critical value from the F table is 4.26.

_____

For testing a single linear restriction of the form

$$H_0: \mathbf{r}'\boldsymbol{\beta} = q,$$

The F statistic is

$$F[1, n - K] = \frac{(\sum_j r_j b_j - q)^2}{\sum_j \sum_k r_j r_k \, \text{Cov}[b_j, b_k]}. \tag{7-17}$$

EXAMPLE 7.2 Constant Returns to Scale _____

The hypothesis that the two coefficients of the production function sum to one is equivalent to one of constant returns to scale. This is often tested in studies of production. For the preceding data,

$$F[1, 24] = \frac{(0.6030 + 0.3757 - 1)^2}{0.01586 + 0.00728 - 2(0.00961)}$$

$$= 0.1157.$$

This is substantially less than the critical value given earlier. We would not reject the hypothesis; the data are consistent with the hypothesis of constant returns to scale.

_____

In most cases encountered in practice, it is possible to incorporate the restrictions of a hypothesis directly on the regression and estimate a restricted model.[7] For example, to impose the constraint $\beta_2 = 1$ on the model, we would write

$$\ln Y = \beta_1 + 1.0 \ln L + \beta_3 \ln K + \varepsilon$$

or

$$\ln Y - \ln L = \beta_1 + \beta_3 \ln K + \varepsilon.$$

Thus, the restricted model is estimated by regressing $\ln Y - \ln L$ on a constant and $\ln K$. Some care is needed if this regression is to be used to compute an F statistic. If the F statistic is computed using the sum of squared residuals [i.e., using (7–14)], no problem

_____

[7] This is not the case when the restrictions are nonlinear. We consider this issue in Chapter 12.

will arise. However, if (7–15) is used instead, it may be necessary to account for the fact that the restricted regression has a different dependent variable from the unrestricted one. In the example just given, the dependent variable in the unrestricted regression is $\ln Y$, while in the restricted regression it is $\ln Y - \ln L$. The R^2 from the restricted regression is only 0.26979, which would imply an F statistic of 285.96, while the correct value is, as we saw earlier, 9.375. However, if we compute the appropriate R_*^2 using the correct denominator, its value is 0.94339 and the correct F value results.

For imposing a set of exclusion restrictions such as $\beta_k = 0$, for one or more coefficients, the obvious approach is simply to omit the variables from the regression and base the test on the sums of squared residuals from the restricted and unrestricted regressions.

EXAMPLE 7.3 Translog Production Function

A generalization of the Cobb–Douglas model used earlier is the *translog* model,[8] which is

$$\ln Y = \beta_1 + \beta_2 \ln L + \beta_3 \ln K + \beta_4 \frac{\ln^2 L}{2} + \beta_5 \frac{\ln^2 K}{2} + \beta_6 \ln L \ln K + \varepsilon.$$

As we shall analyze further in Chapter 17, this model differs from the Cobb–Douglas model in that it relaxes the Cobb–Douglas's assumption of a unitary elasticity of substitution. The Cobb–Douglas model is obtained by the restriction $\beta_4 = \beta_5 = \beta_6 = 0$. Thus, the restricted regression is simply the one we computed earlier. The results for the unrestricted regression are given in Table 7.3.

TABLE 7.3

Standard error of regression	0.17994
Sum of squared residuals	0.67993
R-squared	0.95486
Adjusted R-squared	0.94411

Variable	Coefficient	Standard Error	t ratio
Constant	0.944216	2.911	0.324
$\ln L$	3.61363	1.548	2.334
$\ln K$	−1.89311	1.016	−1.863
$\frac{1}{2} \ln^2 L$	−0.96406	0.7074	−1.363
$\frac{1}{2} \ln^2 K$	0.08529	0.2926	0.291
$\ln L \times \ln K$	0.31239	0.4389	0.712

Estimated Covariance Matrix for Coefficient Estimates

	Constant	$\ln L$	$\ln K$	$\ln^2 L/2$	$\ln^2 K/2$	$\ln L \times \ln K$
Constant	8.472					
$\ln L$	−2.388	2.397				
$\ln K$	−0.3313	−1.231	1.033			
$\frac{1}{2} \ln^2 L$	−0.08760	−0.6658	0.5231	0.5004		
$\frac{1}{2} \ln^2 K$	0.2332	0.03477	0.02637	0.1467	0.08562	
$\ln L \times \ln K$	0.3635	0.1831	−0.2255	−0.2880	−0.1160	0.1927

---

[8] Berndt and Christensen (1972).

The F statistic for the hypothesis of a Cobb–Douglas model is

$$F[3, 21] = \frac{(0.85163 - 0.67993)/3}{0.67993/21}$$

$$= 1.768.$$

The critical value from the F table is 3.07, so we would not reject the hypothesis that a Cobb–Doublas model is appropriate.

Note that the coefficient on ln K is now negative. We might conclude that the estimated output elasticity with respect to capital now has the wrong sign. However, this would be incorrect. In the translog model, the capital elasticity of output is

$$\frac{\partial \ln Y}{\partial \ln K} = \beta_3 + \beta_5 \ln K + \beta_6 \ln L.$$

If we insert the coefficient estimates and the mean values for ln K and ln L (not the logs of the means) of 7.44592 and 5.7637, respectively, the result is 0.5425, which is quite in line with our expectations and is fairly close to the value of 0.3757 obtained earlier. The estimated standard error for this linear combination of the least squares estimates is computed as the square root of

$$\text{Est. Var}[b_3 + b_5 \ln K + b_6 \ln L] = \mathbf{w}'(\text{Est. Var}[\mathbf{b}])\mathbf{w}$$

where

$$\mathbf{w} = (0, 0, 1, 0, \overline{\ln K}, \overline{\ln L})'$$

and $\mathbf{b}$ is the full 6×1 least squares coefficient vector. This is 0.1122, which is reasonably close to the earlier estimate of 0.0854.

The F statistic for testing the hypothesis that a subset, say $\boldsymbol{\beta}_2$, of the coefficients are all zero is constructed using

$$\mathbf{R} = (\mathbf{0}:\mathbf{I}), \qquad \mathbf{q} = \mathbf{0},$$

and

$$J = K_2 = \text{the number of elements in } \boldsymbol{\beta}_2.$$

The matrix $\mathbf{R}(\mathbf{X}'\mathbf{X})^{-1}\mathbf{R}'$ is the $K_2 \times K_2$ lower right block of the full inverse matrix. Using our earlier results for partitioned inverses and the results of Section 6.3.4, we have

$$\mathbf{R}(\mathbf{X}'\mathbf{X})^{-1}\mathbf{R}' = (\mathbf{X}_2'\mathbf{M}_1\mathbf{X}_2)^{-1}$$

and

$$\mathbf{Rb} - \mathbf{q} = \mathbf{b}_2.$$

Inserting these in (7–13), we have the loss of fit that results when we drop a subset of the variables from the regression,

$$\mathbf{e}_*'\mathbf{e}_* - \mathbf{e}'\mathbf{e} = \mathbf{b}_2'\mathbf{X}_2'\mathbf{M}_1\mathbf{X}_2\mathbf{b}_2. \tag{7–18}$$

The procedure for computing the appropriate F statistic amounts simply to comparing the sums of squared deviations from the "short" and "long" regressions, which we saw earlier.

7.3. Tests of Structural Change

One of the more common applications of the F test is in tests of structural change.[9] In specifying a regression model, we assume that its assumptions apply to all of the observations in our sample. It is, however, straightforward to test the hypothesis that some or all of the regression coefficients are different in subsets of the data. To analyze a number of examples, we use the *Longley data,* a data set that is widely used to calibrate regression programs.[10] (See Table 7.4.)

The dependent variable in the regression models will be employment, either total or in one of the two sectors given. The regressors will be a constant and the set of four variables listed at the left of the table.

7.3.1. Different Parameter Vectors

The preceding data span the years of the Korean conflict, which ended in 1953. Note the considerable change in the size of the armed forces during the period of this war. It is possible that the relationship between total employment and the variables in **X** changed after the war. To test this as a hypothesis, we can proceed as follows: Denote the first 7 years of the data in **y** and **X** as $\mathbf{y}_1$ and $\mathbf{X}_1$. An unrestricted regression which allows the coefficients to be different in the two periods is

$$\begin{bmatrix} \mathbf{y}_1 \\ \mathbf{y}_2 \end{bmatrix} = \begin{bmatrix} \mathbf{X}_1 & \mathbf{0} \\ \mathbf{0} & \mathbf{X}_2 \end{bmatrix}\begin{bmatrix} \boldsymbol{\beta}_1 \\ \boldsymbol{\beta}_2 \end{bmatrix} + \begin{bmatrix} \boldsymbol{\varepsilon}_1 \\ \boldsymbol{\varepsilon}_2 \end{bmatrix}. \tag{7-19}$$

[9]This test is often labeled a *Chow test,* in reference to Chow (1960).

[10]These data are unusual in that the exact results of the least squares computation are known. They are from Longley (1967). Note that the total employment is not the sum of the two sectors given; several sectors from the original data set have been omitted.

TABLE 7.4. The Longley Data

Year	GNP Deflator	GNP (mil.)	Armed Forces	Employment (thou.)		
				Total	Agr.	Nonagr.
1947	83.0	234,289	1590	60,323	8256	38,407
1948	88.5	259,426	1456	61,122	7960	39,241
1949	88.2	258,054	1616	60,171	8017	37,922
1950	89.5	284,599	1650	61,187	7497	39,196
1951	96.2	328,975	3099	63,221	7048	41,460
1952	98.1	346,999	3594	63,639	6792	42,216
1953	99.0	365,385	3547	64,989	6555	43,587
1954	100.0	363,112	3350	63,761	6495	42,271
1955	101.2	397,469	3048	66,019	6718	43,761
1956	104.6	419,180	2857	67,857	6572	45,131
1957	108.4	442,769	2798	68,169	6222	45,278
1958	110.8	444,546	2637	66,513	5844	43,530
1959	112.6	482,704	2552	68,655	5836	45,214
1960	114.2	502,601	2514	69,564	5723	45,850
1961	115.7	518,173	2572	69,331	5463	45,397
1962	116.9	554,894	2827	70,551	5190	46,652

Denoting the data matrices as $\mathbf{y}$ and $\mathbf{X}$, we find that the unrestricted least squares estimator is

$$\mathbf{b} = (\mathbf{X}'\mathbf{X})^{-1}\mathbf{X}'\mathbf{y}$$

$$= \begin{bmatrix} \mathbf{X}_1'\mathbf{X}_1 & \mathbf{0} \\ \mathbf{0} & \mathbf{X}_2'\mathbf{X}_2 \end{bmatrix}^{-1} \begin{bmatrix} \mathbf{X}_1'\mathbf{y}_1 \\ \mathbf{X}_2'\mathbf{y}_2 \end{bmatrix} = \begin{bmatrix} \mathbf{b}_1 \\ \mathbf{b}_2 \end{bmatrix}, \tag{7-20}$$

which is least squares applied to the two equations separately. Therefore, the total sum of squared residuals from this regression will be the sum of the two residual sums of squares from the two separate regressions,

$$\mathbf{e}'\mathbf{e} = \mathbf{e}_1'\mathbf{e}_1 + \mathbf{e}_2'\mathbf{e}_2.$$

The restricted coefficient vector can be obtained in two ways. Formally, the restriction $\boldsymbol{\beta}_1 = \boldsymbol{\beta}_2$ is $\mathbf{R}\boldsymbol{\beta} = \mathbf{q}$, where $\mathbf{R} = [\mathbf{I}: -\mathbf{I}]$ and $\mathbf{q} = \mathbf{0}$. The general result given earlier can be applied directly. An easier way to proceed is to build the restriction directly into the model. If the two coefficient vectors are the same, (7-19) may be written

$$\begin{bmatrix} \mathbf{y}_1 \\ \mathbf{y}_2 \end{bmatrix} = \begin{bmatrix} \mathbf{X}_1 \\ \mathbf{X}_2 \end{bmatrix} \boldsymbol{\beta} + \begin{bmatrix} \boldsymbol{\varepsilon}_1 \\ \boldsymbol{\varepsilon}_2 \end{bmatrix}$$

and the restricted estimator can be obtained simply by stacking the data and estimating a single regression. The residual sum of squares from this regression then forms the basis for the test.

EXAMPLE 7.4 Separate Regressions

Using the data on total employment for this example, we obtain the three estimated regression equations shown in Table 7.5.

TABLE 7.5

Coefficients	1947–1962	1947–1953	1954–1962
Constant	1,169,090	1,678,148	3,776,130
Year	−576.464	−835.193	−1914.17
Deflator	−19.7681	−163.292	−42.4647
GNP	0.0643940	0.0948082	0.11233
Armed forces	−0.0101452	−0.246697	−2.57928
Standard error	667.328	415.459	447.28
Sum of squares	4,898,596	345,212	800,244

The F statistic for testing the restriction that the coefficients in the two equations are the same is

$$F[5, 6] = \frac{(4,898,596 - 345,212 - 800,244)/5}{(345,212 + 800,244)/(7 + 9 - 10)} = 3.932.$$

The tabled critical value is 4.39 for 5 percent significance, so we would not reject the hypothesis that the coefficient vectors are the same in the two periods.

7.3.2. Different Constant Terms

The general formulation previously suggested lends itself to many variations that allow a wide range of possible tests. Some important particular cases are suggested by our test data. We might consider the difference between employment in the agricultural and non-agricultural sectors. However, the figures for the two dependent variables are of a different order of magnitude. There are various ways to deal with this problem. One crude way would be to allow for different intercepts in the equations while stacking only the regressors in the restricted equation. Thus, the unrestricted equation is based on least squares regression of each category of employment on a constant and the four regressors, while the restricted regression is a pooled one with 32 observations. The restricted model has a regressor matrix of the form

$$X = \begin{bmatrix} i & 0 & W \\ 0 & i & W \end{bmatrix}.$$

The first two columns of X are **dummy variables** that indicate which sector the observation falls in. (This device was used in Section 6.8.1 in Salkever's formulation of the computation of least squares forecasts.)

EXAMPLE 7.5 Change in Slope Coefficients _____

Using the 16 observations on the two dependent variables for the test, we obtain the results shown in Table 7.6. The F statistic is

$$F[4, 22] = \frac{(107,780,171 - 241,184 - 5,037,866)/4}{(241,184 + 5,037,866)/22}$$

$$= 106.79.$$

This is extremely large and leads to rejection of the hypothesis at any significance level.

TABLE 7.6

Coefficients	Agricultural	Nonagricultural	Pooled
Constant			
Agr.	201,828	—	626,192
Nonagr.	—	1,086,740	662,375
Year	−97.5838	−544.519	−321.051
Deflator	−40.5182	−23.3502	−31.9342
GNP	0.000513124	0.0534508	0.026982
Armed forces	−0.208122	0.764720	0.278299
Standard error	148.074	676.748	2036.024
Sum of squares	241,184	5,037,866	107,780,171

7.3.3. Change in a Subset of Coefficients

One factor that might have a strong influence in Example 7.5 is the clear secular trend in the dependent variables. In the cases of agricultural and nonagricultural employment, they are in opposite directions. It might have been more reasonable to allow both the constant term and the time trend (coefficient on "Year") to differ across the two equations. Once again, the unrestricted coefficient vector is the earlier one. The restricted coefficients are computed using a regressor matrix of the form

$$X = \begin{bmatrix} i & Year & 0 & 0 & W \\ 0 & 0 & i & Year & W \end{bmatrix}, \tag{7-21}$$

where **W** contains (replicated for both data series) the last three columns of the original data matrix.

EXAMPLE 7.6 _____

The F ratio that results from estimating the model in (7–21) is

$$F[3, 22] = \frac{(11{,}917{,}648 - 5{,}279{,}050)/3}{5{,}279{,}050/22} = 9.221.$$

The critical value from the F table is 3.05, so we would still reject the hypothesis. However, the sample value is substantially reduced. Apparently, the difference in the secular trends accounted for much of the difference in the coefficient vectors.

_____

7.3.4. Insufficient Observations

There are circumstances in which the data series are not long enough to estimate one or the other of the separate regressions for a test of structural change. For example, the data presented earlier on the armed forces series suggests that the major employment change, if there was one, occurred in 1951, not 1954. We might naturally consider the same test we did earlier, using the two subperiods 1947–1950 and 1951–1962. However, there are five parameters to estimate and only four observations in the first data set. Fisher (1970) has shown that in such a circumstance, a valid way to proceed is as follows:

1. Estimate the regression, using the full data set, and compute the restricted residual sum of squared residuals, $\mathbf{e}'_*\mathbf{e}_*$.
2. Use the longer (adequate) subperiod to estimate the regression, and compute the unrestricted sum of squares, $\mathbf{e}'\mathbf{e}$. This latter computation is done under the assumption that with only $n_1 < K$ observations, we could obtain a perfect fit and thus contribute zero to the sum of squares.
3. The F statistic is then computed, using

$$F[n_1, n_2 - K] = \frac{(\mathbf{e}'_*\mathbf{e}_* - \mathbf{e}'\mathbf{e})/n_1}{\mathbf{e}'\mathbf{e}/(n_2 - K)}. \tag{7–22}$$

Note that the numerator degrees of freedom is n_1, not K.[11] This test has been labeled the Chow *predictive test,* as it is equivalent to extending the restricted model to the shorter subperiod and basing the test on the prediction errors of the model in this period.

EXAMPLE 7.7 Inadequate Degrees of Freedom _____

Using the total employment series as an example, we find that the F test for stability of the coefficients in the equation across the two subperiods is

$$F[4, 7] = \frac{(4{,}898{,}726 - 3{,}394{,}431)/4}{3{,}394{,}431/(12 - 5)} = 0.776$$

This is not larger than the critical value of 4.12. Hence, the hypothesis of stability would not be rejected.

_____

[11] One way to view this is that only $n_1 < K$ coefficients are needed to obtain this perfect fit.

7.4. Tests of Structural Change with Unequal Variances

An important assumption made in using the Chow test is that the disturbance variance is the same in both (or all) regressions. In the restricted model, if this is not true, the first n_1 elements of ε have variance σ_1^2, while the next n_2 have variance σ_2^2, and so on. The restricted model is, therefore, heteroscedastic, and our results for the classical regression model no longer apply. As analyzed by Schmidt and Sickles (1977), Ohtani and Toyoda (1985), and Toyoda and Ohtani (1986), it is quite likely that we shall overestimate the significance level of our test statistic. (That is, we shall regard as large an F statistic that is actually less than the *appropriate* table value.) Precisely how severe this effect is going to be will depend on the data and the extent to which the variances differ, in ways that are not likely to be obvious.

There are direct ways to deal with this problem. Assuming that we can estimate both (all) of the separate regressions, we can examine our estimates of the disturbance variances. With these in hand, for instance, we can test directly for significant differences.[12] Without any significant difference, we can proceed as described. If, however, there is evidence to suggest that the variances actually are different, there are still simple and appropriate ways to carry out the analysis by explicitly estimating the model, accounting for the heteroscedasticity. This relies on some results that we develop more fully in Section 16.3.1, so we defer until that point a more complete discussion of the procedure.[13]

If the sample is reasonably large, we have a test that is valid whether or not the disturbance variances are the same. To set up the test, we shall use some general results presented in Chapter 4. Suppose that $\hat{\boldsymbol{\theta}}_1$ and $\hat{\boldsymbol{\theta}}_2$ are two normally distributed estimators of a parameter based on independent samples,[14] with variance matrices $\mathbf{V}_1$ and $\mathbf{V}_2$. Then, under the null hypothesis that the two estimates have the same expected value,

$$\hat{\boldsymbol{\theta}}_1 - \hat{\boldsymbol{\theta}}_2 \text{ has mean } \mathbf{0} \text{ and variance } \mathbf{V}_1 + \mathbf{V}_2.$$

Thus, the Wald statistic,

$$W = (\hat{\boldsymbol{\theta}}_1 - \hat{\boldsymbol{\theta}}_2)'(\mathbf{V}_1 + \mathbf{V}_2)^{-1}(\hat{\boldsymbol{\theta}}_1 - \hat{\boldsymbol{\theta}}_2), \tag{7-23}$$

has a chi-squared distribution with K degrees of freedom. A test that the difference between the parameters is zero can be based on this statistic. It is straightforward to apply this to our test of common parameter vectors in our regressions. Large values of the statistic lead us to reject the hypothesis. What remains for us to resolve is whether it is valid to base such a test on *estimates* of $\mathbf{V}_1$ and $\mathbf{V}_2$. Looking ahead to our results in Chapter 14, the test is indeed valid in large samples, so we may use our least squares estimates of the two covariance matrices to compute W.

EXAMPLE 7.8 Wald Test for Structural Change

The test statistic in (7-23) for the regression results in Table 7.5 gives a value of 13.895. The 5 percent critical value from the chi-squared table for 5 degrees of freedom is 11.075.

---

[12] We consider this more fully in the discussion of the Goldfeld–Quandt test in Section 14.3.2.

[13] Since the initial test will have some probability of a type II error, there is that probability that we will fail to pick up an actual difference in the disturbance variances, and incorrectly estimate the model as if there were none. This potential is a contributor to *pretest bias* and is discussed more fully for this model in Toyoda and Ohtani (1986).

[14] Without the required independence, this test and several similar ones will fail completely. The problem becomes a variant of the famous Behrens–Fisher problem.

So, on the basis of the Wald test, we would reject the hypothesis that the same coefficient vector applies in the two subperiods 1947–1953 and 1954–1962. We should note that the Wald statistic is valid only in large samples, and our samples of seven and nine observations hardly meet that standard.

In a small or moderate-sized sample, the Wald test has the unfortunate property that the probability of a type I error is persistently larger than the critical level we use to carry it out. (That is, we shall too frequently reject the null hypothesis that the parameters are the same in the subsamples.) We should be using a larger critical value. Ohtani and Kobiyashi (1986) have devised a "bounds" test that gives a partial remedy for the problem.[15]

7.5. Alternative Tests of Model Stability

Example 7.7 shows a test of structural change based essentially on the model's ability to predict correctly outside the range of the observations used to estimate it. A similar logic underlies an alternative test of model stability proposed by Brown, Durbin, and Evans (1975) based on **recursive residuals.** The technique is appropriate for time-series data, and might be used if one is uncertain about when a structural change might have taken place. The null hypothesis is that the coefficient vector, $\boldsymbol{\beta}$, is the same in every period; the alternative is simply that it (or the disturbance variance) is not. The test is quite general in that it does not require a prior specification of when the structural change takes place. The cost, however, is that the power of the test is rather limited compared to that of the Chow test.[16]

Suppose that the sample contains a total of T observations.[17] The tth recursive residual is the ex post prediction error for y_t when the regression is estimated using only the first $t - 1$ observations:

$$e_t = y_t - \mathbf{x}_t'\mathbf{b}_{t-1},$$

where $\mathbf{x}_t$ is the vector of regressors associated with observation y_t and $\mathbf{b}_{t-1}$ is the least squares coefficients computed using the first $t - 1$ observations.[18] The forecast variance of this residual is

$$\sigma_{ft}^2 = \sigma^2[1 + \mathbf{x}_t'(\mathbf{X}_{t-1}'\mathbf{X}_{t-1})^{-1}\mathbf{x}_t]. \tag{7-24}$$

Let the rth scaled residual be

$$w_r = \frac{e_r}{\sqrt{1 + \mathbf{x}_r'(\mathbf{X}_{r-1}'\mathbf{X}_{r-1})^{-1}\mathbf{x}_r}}. \tag{7-25}$$

---

[15] See also Kobiyashi (1986). An alternative, somewhat more cumbersome test is proposed by Jayatissa (1977). Further discussion is given in Thursby (1982).

[16] The test is frequently criticized on this basis. However, the Chow test is based on a rather definite piece of information, namely, when the structural change takes place. If this is not known or must be estimated, the advantage of the Chow test diminishes considerably.

[17] Since we are dealing explicitly with time-series data at this point, it is convenient to use T instead of n for the sample size and t instead of i to index observations.

[18] In principle, this requires the computation of $T - K$ regressions. The difficult part of the computation is $(\mathbf{X}_t'\mathbf{X}_t)^{-1}$. However, since $\mathbf{X}_t'\mathbf{X}_t = \mathbf{X}_{t-1}'\mathbf{X}_{t-1} + \mathbf{x}_t\mathbf{x}_t'$, the rank one updating formula of Section 2.5.2, equation (2–66) can be applied, beginning with an initial regression based on K observations. The result is useful and does provide insight into the calculation. [Discussion can be found in Johnston (1984, p. 387).] However, using an electronic computer, it is unlikely that using the updating formula instead of actually computing the regression will save a noticeable amount of time. It is also possible, depending on how the accumulation is programmed, that this will introduce a new source of accumulated rounding error into the calculations. This may be a problem in a badly conditioned data set such as the Longley data used earlier.

Under the hypothesis that the coefficients remain constant during the full sample period, $w_r \sim N[0, \sigma^2]$ and is independent of w_s for all $s \neq r$. Evidence that the distribution of w_r is changing over time weighs against the hypothesis of model stability.

Brown et al. suggest two tests based on w_r. The CUSUM test is based on the cumulated sum of the residuals:

$$W_t = \sum_{r=K+1}^{r=t} \frac{w_r}{\hat{\sigma}}, \tag{7–26}$$

where

$$\hat{\sigma}^2 = \frac{1}{T-K-1} \sum_{r=K+1}^{T} (w_r - \overline{w})^2$$

and

$$\overline{w} = \frac{1}{T-K} \sum_{r=K+1}^{r=T} w_r.$$

Under the null hypothesis, W_t has a mean of zero and a variance of approximately the number of residuals being summed (as each term has variance 1 and they are independent). The test is performed by plotting W_t against t. Confidence bounds for the sum are obtained by plotting the two lines that connect the points $(K, \pm a\sqrt{T-K})$ and $(T, \pm 3a\sqrt{T-K})$. Values of a that correspond to various significance levels can be found in their paper. Those corresponding to 95 percent and 99 percent are 0.948 and 1.143, respectively. The hypothesis is rejected if W_t strays outside the boundaries.

An alternative similar test is based on the squares of the recursive residuals. The CUSUM of squares (CUSUMSQ) test uses

$$S_t = \frac{\sum_{r=K+1}^{r=t} w_r^2}{\sum_{r=K+1}^{r=T} w_r^2}. \tag{7–27}$$

Since the residuals are independent, each of the two terms is approximately a sum of chi-squared variables each with one degree of freedom. Therefore, $E[S_t]$ is approximately $(t-K)/(T-K)$. The test is carried out by constructing confidence bounds for $E[S_t]$ at the values of t and plotting S_t and these bounds against t. The appropriate bounds are $E(S) \pm c_0$, where c_0 depends on both $(T-K)$ and the significance level desired.[19] As before, if the cumulated sum strays outside the confidence bounds, doubt is cast on the hypothesis of parameter stability.

A related test proposed by Harvey and Collier (1977) is based directly on the mean. Under the hypothesis of model stability, $\overline{w}$ is normally distributed, with mean zero and variance $\sigma^2/(T-K)$. The test is a familiar t test of the hypothesis that the mean of w_t is zero. The procedure uses

$$t[T-K-1] = \frac{(\sqrt{T-K})\overline{w}}{s}, \tag{7–28}$$

where

$$s^2 = \frac{1}{T-K-1} \sum_{r=K+1}^{r=T} (w_r - \overline{w})^2. \tag{7–29}$$

The statistic is compared to the t distribution with $T-K-1$ degrees of freedom.

---

[19] Tables may be found in Harvey (1990) and Johnston (1984). For an application, see Galpin and Hawkins (1984).

EXAMPLE 7.9 Tests of Model Stability ——————————————————————

Example 11.4 presents estimates of a model of the demand for money, using aggregate U.S. data for 1966 through 1985. Applying the previous tests to the data given in the example, we find the evidence mixed on whether the underlying parameter vector is unchanged for the 20 years.

				CUSUM					
0	0	0	−0.002	0.25	0.48	0.40	0.36	0.83	1.99
2.77	3.06	3.20	3.86	5.03	6.07	8.87	12.41	14.28	15.96

				CUSUM of Squares					
0	0	0	0.000	0.002	0.004	0.004	0.004	0.011	0.053
0.072	0.074	0.075	0.089	0.131	0.165	0.410	0.830	0.912	1.000

Figure 7.1 shows the CUSUM and CUSUMSQ tests based on these data. The CUSUM strays outside the boundaries for the last four observations. The CUSUM of squares is smaller than would be expected for most of the sample. Both tests suggest that the model is not stable over time. The Harvey–Collier test is based on

$$\overline{w} = 120.26$$

and

$$s = 132.08,$$

which gives

$$t[16] = 3.75.$$

This test agrees with the CUSUM test in suggesting that the parameters are not constant across the full 20 years. The CUSUM series suggests that the source of the instability, such as it is, is the last four observations. As a final check, we compute the Chow test of Example 7.7 for these four observations The results are

$$F[3, 17] = \frac{[525,006.1 - (86,545.6 + 1330.8)]/3}{(86,545.6 + 1330.8)/(20 - 3 - 3)} = 23.21.$$

This is quite large, and agrees with the CUSUM and Harvey–Collier tests.

7.6. Testing Nonlinear Restrictions

The preceding discussion has relied heavily on the linearity of the regression model. Most of the distributional results, for example, follow either from the normality of a linear function of normally distributed variables or from the F and chi-squared distributions derived from the normal distribution. When we analyze nonlinear functions of the parameters and nonlinear regression models, most of these exact distributional results no longer hold. We shall consider the appropriate asymptotic results in more detail in Chapter 10. However, there are some fairly straightforward results we can obtain now.

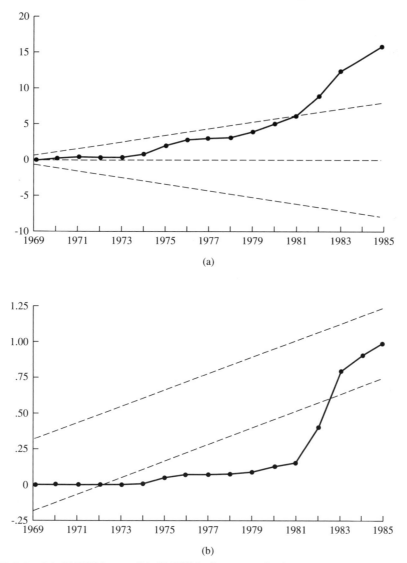

FIGURE 7.1 (a) CUSUM test; (b) CUSUM of squares test.

The general problem is that of testing a hypothesis that involves a nonlinear function of the regression coefficients:

$$H_0 : f(\boldsymbol{\beta}) = q.$$

We shall look at the case of a single restriction. However, the more general one, in which $\mathbf{f}(\boldsymbol{\beta}) = \mathbf{q}$ is a set of restrictions, is a simple extension. The counterpart to the test statistic we used earlier would be

$$z = \frac{f(\hat{\boldsymbol{\beta}}) - q}{\text{estimated standard error}} \tag{7–30}$$

or its square, which in the preceding were distributed as $t[n - K]$ and $F[1, n - K]$, respectively. The discrepancy in the numerator presents no difficulty. However, obtaining an estimate of the sampling variance of $f(\hat{\boldsymbol{\beta}}) - q$ involves the variance of a nonlinear function of $\hat{\boldsymbol{\beta}}$.

An approach that uses the large-sample properties of the estimates and provides an approximation to the variances we need is based on a linear Taylor series approximation. A linear Taylor series approximation to $f(\hat{\boldsymbol{\beta}})$ around the true parameter vector, $\boldsymbol{\beta}$, is

$$f(\hat{\boldsymbol{\beta}}) \simeq f(\boldsymbol{\beta}) + \left(\frac{\partial f(\boldsymbol{\beta})}{\partial \boldsymbol{\beta}}\right)' (\hat{\boldsymbol{\beta}} - \boldsymbol{\beta}). \tag{7–31}$$

We must rely on consistency rather than unbiasedness here, since, in general, the expected value of a nonlinear function is not equal to the function of the expected value. Thus, in view of the approximation, and assuming that $\text{plim}(\hat{\boldsymbol{\beta}}) = \boldsymbol{\beta}$, we are justified in using $f(\hat{\boldsymbol{\beta}})$ as an estimate of $f(\boldsymbol{\beta})$. (The relevant result is the Slutsky theorem.) Assuming that our use of this approximation is appropriate, the variance of the nonlinear function is approximately equal to the variance of the right-hand side, which is, then,

$$\text{Var}[f(\hat{\boldsymbol{\beta}})] \simeq \mathbf{g}'\text{Var}[\hat{\boldsymbol{\beta}} - \boldsymbol{\beta}]\mathbf{g}$$
$$\mathbf{g} = \frac{\partial f(\boldsymbol{\beta})}{\partial \boldsymbol{\beta}}. \tag{7–32}$$

The derivatives in the expression for the variance are functions of the unknown parameters. Since these are being estimated, we use our sample estimates in computing the derivatives. To estimate the variance of the estimator, we can use $s^2(\mathbf{X}'\mathbf{X})^{-1}$, as is familiar. Finally, we rely on results to be treated in more detail in Chapter 10 and use the standard normal distribution instead of the t distribution for the test statistic. Using $f(\hat{\boldsymbol{\beta}})$ to estimate $f(\boldsymbol{\beta})$, we can now test a hypothesis in the same fashion we did earlier.

EXAMPLE 7.10 A Long-Run Marginal Propensity to Consume

A consumption function that has different short- and long-run marginal propensities to consume can be written in the form

$$C_t = \alpha + \beta Y_t + \gamma C_{t-1} + \varepsilon_t.$$

(This is a *distributed lag* model. We consider these models in more detail in Chapter 18.) In this model, the short-run marginal propensity to consume is β, while the long-run marginal propensity to consume is $\delta = \beta/(1 - \gamma)$. Consider testing the hypothesis that $\delta = 1$.[20]

The data in Table 7.7 are aggregate data on real consumption and GNP (deflated by the CPI) from the 1983 *Economic Report of the President*.

Least squares regression of consumption on a constant, GNP, and lagged consumption produces the results in Table 7.8.

The estimate of the long-run marginal propensity to consume is

$$d = \frac{b}{1 - c} = \frac{0.400147}{1 - 0.380728} = 0.6461.$$

To compute the estimated variance of d, we require

$$\frac{\partial \delta}{\partial \beta} = \frac{1}{1 - \gamma} = 1.6149,$$

$$\frac{\partial \delta}{\partial \gamma} = \frac{\beta}{(1 - \gamma)^2} = 1.0434$$

---

[20] The observant reader will notice that this is equivalent to $\beta = 1 - \gamma$, which is linear. However, it is instructive to pursue it as a nonlinear restriction.

TABLE 7.7

Year	Consumption	GNP	Year	Consumption	GNP
1963	522.67	832.57	1973	767.85	1254.28
1964	550.36	876.32	1974	771.72	1246.26
1965	578.81	929.40	1975	776.21	1231.58
1966	605.92	984.89	1976	819.93	1298.17
1967	620.16	1011.38	1977	859.98	1369.73
1968	650.47	1058.15	1978	895.16	1438.57
1969	670.35	1087.68	1979	922.29	1479.50
1970	679.83	1085.51	1980	933.27	1473.97
1971	700.14	1122.38	1981	942.77	1502.58
1972	737.10	1185.90	1982	951.60	1475.41

TABLE 7.8

R-squared   0.99758

Variable	Coefficient	Standard Error	t ratio
Constant	−7.69575	11.44	−0.672
Real GNP	0.400147	0.06272	6.380
Cons. $(t-1)$	0.380728	0.09479	4.017

Estimated Covariance Matrix of Estimates			
	Constant	**Real GNP**	**Cons. $(t-1)$**
Constant	130.972		
Real GNP	−0.43868	0.00393	
Cons. $(t-1)$	0.54959	−0.005590	0.00898

when evaluated at our estimates. The estimated variance is

$$\text{Est. Var}[\hat{\delta}] = 1.6149^2(0.00393) + 1.0434^2(0.00898) - 2(1.6149)(1.0434)0.00559$$
$$= 0.00118728.$$

The square root is 0.034457. To test the hypothesis that the long-run marginal propensity to consume is greater than or equal to one, we would use

$$z = \frac{0.6461 - 1}{0.034457} = -10.271.$$

Because we are using a large-sample approximation, we refer this to a standard normal table instead of the usual t distribution. Obviously, the hypothesis should be rejected.[21]

The generalization to more than one function of the parameters proceeds along similar lines. Let $\mathbf{f}(\hat{\boldsymbol{\beta}})$ be a set of J functions of the estimated parameter vector. The estimate of the sampling covariance matrix of these functions is

$$\text{Est. Var}[\hat{\mathbf{f}}] = \hat{\mathbf{G}}\{\text{Est. Var}[\hat{\boldsymbol{\beta}}]\}\hat{\mathbf{G}}', \qquad (7\text{--}33)$$

---

[21] The t test of the equivalent restriction noted in the previous footnote produces a test statistic of −5.268, which also leads to rejection of the hypothesis.

where $\hat{\mathbf{G}}$ is a $J \times K$ matrix of derivatives:

$$\hat{\mathbf{G}} = \frac{\partial \mathbf{f}(\hat{\boldsymbol{\beta}})}{\partial \hat{\boldsymbol{\beta}}'}. \tag{7-34}$$

The jth row of $\mathbf{G}$ is the K derivatives of f_j with respect to the K elements of $\hat{\boldsymbol{\beta}}$. For example, the variance matrix for estimates of the short- and long-run marginal propensity to consume would be obtained using

$$\mathbf{G} = \begin{bmatrix} 0 & 1 & 0 \\ 0 & 1/(1 - \gamma) & \beta/(1 - \gamma)^2 \end{bmatrix}.$$

The statistic for testing the J hypotheses $\mathbf{f}(\boldsymbol{\beta}) = \mathbf{q}$, which in large samples has a chi-squared distribution with degrees of freedom equal to the number of restrictions, is

$$c = (\hat{\mathbf{f}} - \mathbf{q})'\{\text{Est. Var}[\hat{\mathbf{f}}]\}^{-1}(\hat{\mathbf{f}} - \mathbf{q}). \tag{7-35}$$

Note that for a single restriction, this is the square of the statistic in (7–30).

The preceding analysis is based on the unrestricted least squares estimates. In the same way that we approached this problem before, we might have examined the loss of fit that results when the restrictions are imposed. But in this case, that would have involved fitting the regression subject to a set of nonlinear restrictions. Although straightforward in principle, this procedure is a bit more difficult in practice. It is taken up in Chapter 11.

7.7. Choosing Between Nonnested Models

The classical testing procedures that we have been using have been shown to be quite powerful for the types of hypotheses we have considered.[22] Although this is clearly desirable, the requirement that we be able to express the hypotheses in the form of restrictions on the model $\mathbf{y} = \mathbf{X}\boldsymbol{\beta} + \boldsymbol{\varepsilon}$,

$$H_0 : \mathbf{R}\boldsymbol{\beta} = \mathbf{q},$$

versus

$$H_1 : \mathbf{R}\boldsymbol{\beta} \neq \mathbf{q},$$

can be limiting. Two common exceptions are the general problem of determining which of two possible sets of regressors is more appropriate and whether a linear or log-linear model is more appropriate for a given analysis.

For the present, we restrict our attention to two competing linear models:

$$H_0 : \mathbf{y} = \mathbf{X}\boldsymbol{\beta} + \boldsymbol{\varepsilon}_0 \tag{7-36a}$$

and

$$H_1 : \mathbf{y} = \mathbf{Z}\boldsymbol{\gamma} + \boldsymbol{\varepsilon}_1. \tag{7-36b}$$

We shall consider nonlinear models and the question of linear versus log-linear models in Chapter 11.

Since H_1 cannot be written as a restriction on H_0, none of the procedures we have considered thus far are appropriate. One possibility is an artificial nesting of the two models. Let $\overline{\mathbf{X}}$ be the set of variables in $\mathbf{X}$ that are not in $\mathbf{Z}$, define $\overline{\mathbf{Z}}$ likewise with respect

---

[22] See, for example, Stuart and Ord (1989, Chapter 27).

to **X,** and let **W** be the variables that the models have in common. Then H_0 and H_1 could be combined in a "super model."

$$\mathbf{y} = \overline{\mathbf{X}\boldsymbol{\beta}} + \overline{\mathbf{Z}\boldsymbol{\gamma}} + \mathbf{W}\boldsymbol{\delta} + \boldsymbol{\varepsilon}.$$

In principle, H_1 is rejected if it is found that $\overline{\boldsymbol{\gamma}} = \mathbf{0}$ by a conventional F test, while H_0 is rejected if it is found that $\overline{\boldsymbol{\beta}} = \mathbf{0}.$ There are two problems with this approach. First, $\boldsymbol{\delta}$ remains a mixture of parts of $\boldsymbol{\beta}$ and $\boldsymbol{\gamma}$, and it is not established by the F test that either of these parts is zero. Hence, this test does not really distinguish between H_0 and H_1; it distinguishes between H_1 and a hybrid model. Second, this compound model may have an extremely large number of regressors. In a time-series setting, the problem of collinearity may be severe.

The J test proposed by Davidson and MacKinnon (1981) is similar in spirit to the nesting strategy but overcomes its practical problems. An alternative to the preceding compound model is

$$\mathbf{y} = (1 - \alpha)\mathbf{X}\boldsymbol{\beta} + \alpha(\mathbf{Z}\boldsymbol{\gamma}) + \boldsymbol{\varepsilon}.$$

As written, a test of $\alpha = 0$ would be a test against H_1. The problem is that α cannot be estimated in this model. Davidson and MacKinnon's J test consists of estimating $\boldsymbol{\gamma}$ by a least squares regression and then regressing $\mathbf{y}$ on $\mathbf{X}$ and $\mathbf{Z}\boldsymbol{\gamma}$, the fitted values in this regression. A valid test, at least asymptotically, of H_1 is to test $H_0: \alpha = 0$. If H_0 is true,

$$\text{plim } \hat{\alpha} = 0.$$

Asymptotically, the ratio $\hat{\alpha}/se(\hat{\alpha})$ (i.e., the usual t ratio) is distributed as standard normal and may be referred to the standard tables to carry out the test. Unfortunately, in testing H_0 versus H_1 and vice versa, all four possibilities (reject both, neither, or either one of the two hypotheses) could occur. This is, however, a finite sample problem. Davidson and MacKinnon show that as $n \rightarrow \infty$, if H_1 is true, the probability that $\hat{\alpha}$ will differ significantly from zero approaches 1.

EXAMPLE 7.11 J Test for a Consumption Function

Gaver and Geisel (1974) propose two forms of a consumption function:

$$H_0: C_t = \beta_1 + \beta_2 Y_t + \beta_3 Y_{t-1} + \varepsilon_{0t}$$

and

$$H_1: C_t = \gamma_1 + \gamma_2 Y_t + \gamma_3 C_{t-1} + \varepsilon_{1t}.$$

The first implies that consumption responds to changes in income over two periods, while the second implies that the effects of changes in income on consumption persist for many periods. (These models are examined further in Chapter 18.) Data on aggregate U.S. consumption and income are given in Example 7.10. Here we apply the J test to these data and the previous two specifications. First, the two models are estimated separately. The least squares regression of C on a constant, Y, lagged Y, and the fitted values from the second model produces an estimate of α of 2.74 with a t ratio of 5.21. Thus, H_0 should be rejected in favor of H_1. But reversing the roles of H_0 and H_1, we obtain an estimate of α of -2.70 with a t ratio of -3.55. Thus, H_1 is rejected as well.[23]

A related set of procedures based on the likelihood ratio test has been devised by Cox (1961, 1962). The versions of the Cox test appropriate for the linear and nonlinear regression models have been derived by Pesaran (1974) and Pesaran and Deaton (1978). The

---

[23] For related discussion of this possibility, see McAleer et al. (1982).

latter present a test statistic for testing linear versus log-linear models that is extended in Aneuryn-Evans and Deaton (1980). Since, in the classical regression model, the least squares estimator is also the maximum likelihood estimator, it is perhaps not suprising that Davidson and MacKinnon (1981, p. 789) find that their test statistic is asymptotically equal to the negative of the Cox–Pesaran and Deaton statistic. The Cox statistic for testing the hypothesis that $\mathbf{X}$ is the correct set of regressors and $\mathbf{Z}$ is not is

$$c_{12} = \frac{n}{2} \ln \left[\frac{s_z^2}{s_x^2 + (1/n)\mathbf{b}'\mathbf{X}'\mathbf{M}_z\mathbf{X}\mathbf{b}} \right]$$

$$= \frac{n}{2} \ln \left[\frac{s_z^2}{s_{zx}^2} \right],$$

(7–37)

where $\mathbf{M}_z = \mathbf{I} - \mathbf{Z}(\mathbf{Z}'\mathbf{Z})^{-1}\mathbf{Z}'$ and $\mathbf{b} = (\mathbf{X}'\mathbf{X})^{-1}\mathbf{X}'\mathbf{y}$.

The hypothesis is tested by taking

$$q = \frac{c_{12}}{(\text{Est.Var}[c_{12}])^{1/2}} = \frac{c_{12}}{[(s_x^2/s_{zx}^4)\mathbf{b}'\mathbf{X}'\mathbf{M}_z\mathbf{M}_x\mathbf{M}_z\mathbf{X}\mathbf{b}]^{1/2}},$$

(7–38)

where $\mathbf{M}_x = \mathbf{I} - \mathbf{X}(\mathbf{X}'\mathbf{X})^{-1}\mathbf{X}'$, into a standard normal table. A large value of q is evidence against the hypothesis. Although this involves a substantial amount of matrix algebra, there are several shortcuts that will simplify the result. First,

$$s_z^2 = \frac{\mathbf{e}_z'\mathbf{e}_z}{n} = \text{mean-squared residual in the regression of } \mathbf{y} \text{ on } \mathbf{Z},$$

$$s_x^2 = \frac{\mathbf{e}_x'\mathbf{e}_x}{n} = \text{mean-squared residual in the regression of } \mathbf{y} \text{ on } \mathbf{X},$$

$$\mathbf{X}\mathbf{b} = \text{fitted values in the regression of } \mathbf{y} \text{ on } \mathbf{X},$$

$$\mathbf{M}_z\mathbf{X}\mathbf{b} = \text{residuals in a regression of } \mathbf{X}\mathbf{b} \text{ on } \mathbf{Z},$$

$$\mathbf{b}'\mathbf{X}'\mathbf{M}_z\mathbf{X}\mathbf{b} = \text{sum of squared residuals in the regression of } \mathbf{X}\mathbf{b} \text{ on } \mathbf{Z},$$

$$s_{zx}^2 = s_x^2 + \frac{1}{n}\mathbf{b}'\mathbf{X}'\mathbf{M}_z\mathbf{X}\mathbf{b},$$

$$(\mathbf{b}'\mathbf{X}'\mathbf{M}_z)\mathbf{M}_x(\mathbf{M}_z\mathbf{X}\mathbf{b}) = \text{sum of squared residuals in the regression of } \mathbf{M}_z\mathbf{X}\mathbf{b} \text{ on } \mathbf{X}.$$

Therefore, the Cox statistic can be computed simply by computing a set of least squares regressions.

EXAMPLE 7.12 Cox Test for a Consumption Function

We continue the previous example by applying the Cox test to the data of Example 7.10. For purposes of the test, let

$$\mathbf{X} = [\mathbf{i} \quad \mathbf{y} \quad \mathbf{y}_{-1}] \quad \text{and} \quad \mathbf{Z} = [\mathbf{i} \quad \mathbf{y} \quad \mathbf{c}_{-1}].$$

Using the notation of (7–37) and (7–38), we find that

$$s_x^2 = 60.09631 \quad \text{and} \quad s_z^2 = 39.36133,$$

$$\mathbf{b}'\mathbf{X}'\mathbf{M}_z\mathbf{X}\mathbf{b} = 46.630105 \quad \text{and} \quad \mathbf{b}'\mathbf{X}'\mathbf{M}_z\mathbf{M}_x\mathbf{M}_z\mathbf{X}\mathbf{b} = 40.592986,$$

so that

$$s_{zx}^2 = 60.09631 + \frac{46.630105}{19} = 62.50527.$$

Thus,

$$c_{12} = \frac{19}{2} \ln \left(\frac{39.36133}{62.50527} \right) = -4.4003$$

and

$$\text{Est. Var}[c_{12}] = \frac{60.09631(40.592986)}{62.50527^2} = 0.62441$$

Thus, $q = -5.569$. On this basis, we reject the hypothesis that $\mathbf{X}$ is the correct set of regressors. Note, in the previous example, that we reached the same conclusion based on a t ratio of 5.21. As expected, the result has the opposite sign from the corresponding J statistic in the previous example. Now we reverse the roles of $\mathbf{X}$ and $\mathbf{Z}$ in our calculations. Letting $\mathbf{d}$ denote the least squares coefficients in the regression of consumption on $\mathbf{Z}$, we find

$$\mathbf{d}'\mathbf{Z}'\mathbf{M}_x\mathbf{Z}\mathbf{d} = 97.63601 \qquad \text{and} \qquad \mathbf{d}'\mathbf{Z}'\mathbf{M}_x\mathbf{M}_z\mathbf{M}_x\mathbf{Z}\mathbf{d} = 84.99524,$$

so that

$$s_{xz}^2 = 39.36133 + \frac{97.63601}{19} = 44.50007.$$

Thus,

$$c_{12} = \left(\frac{19}{2} \right) \ln \left(\frac{60.09631}{44.50007} \right) = 2.8543$$

and

$$\text{Est. Var}[c_{12}] = \frac{39.36133(84.99524)}{44.50007^2} = 1.6894.$$

This produces a value of $q = 2.196$, which is considerably smaller (in absolute value) than its counterpart in Example 7.11, -3.55. Since 2.196 is greater than the 5 percent critical value of 1.96, we would once again reject the hypothesis that $\mathbf{Z}$ is the preferred set of regressors.

The two approaches to nonnested models, Davidson and MacKinnon's J test and Cox's extension of the likelihood ratio test, have been analyzed in a large amount of recent research.[24]

EXERCISES

1. A multiple regression of y on a constant, x_1, and x_2 produces the following results:

$$\hat{y} = 4 + 0.4x_1 + 0.9x_2, \qquad R^2 = \tfrac{8}{60},$$

$$\mathbf{e}'\mathbf{e} = 520, \qquad n = 29,$$

$$\mathbf{X}'\mathbf{X} = \begin{bmatrix} 29 & 0 & 0 \\ 0 & 50 & 10 \\ 0 & 10 & 80 \end{bmatrix}$$

Test the hypothesis that the two slopes sum to 1.

---

[24] See, for example, two symposia in the *Journal of Econometrics* by White (1982b, 1983). The Cox and J tests are extended to nonnested restricted regressions in Pesaran and Hall (1989). See also Greene (1991).

2. Using the results in Exercise 1, test the hypothesis that the slope on x_1 is zero by running the restricted regression and comparing the two sums of squared deviations.

3. The translog production function in Example 7.3 has constant returns to scale if

$$\frac{\partial \ln Y}{\partial \ln L} + \frac{\partial \ln Y}{\partial \ln K} = 1$$

for all values of K and L. (This model is analyzed in some detail in Chapter 17.)

   (a) What restrictions on the coefficients produce constant returns to scale? How would you estimate the restricted model? A Cobb–Douglas production function with constant returns to scale is a restriction on the translog model with constant returns to scale. What is the restriction? How would you test the restriction as a hypothesis?

   (b) Using the data given in Table 7.1, estimate the translog model subject to the restrictions of constant returns to scale and test the hypothesis. Carry out a test of the hypothesis of a Cobb–Douglas technology, assuming constant returns to scale.

4. The gasoline data of Exercise 6 in Chapter 6 span the years of the oil embargo of 1973 and the tumultuous period thereafter. Did the market change sufficiently in 1973 that it is inappropriate to pool the data? The results of that example notwithstanding, regressions of G on a constant, P_g, Y, and P_{pt} produce the following residual sums of squares:

1960–1986	1960–1973	1974–1986
841.3	40.57	246.51

   (a) Carry out a Chow test of the hypothesis that the coefficient vectors are the same in the two subperiods. What are you assuming in making this test?

   (b) An alternative hypothesis is that the year 1973 and the few (say, four) subsequent years that it took to return to normalcy in the market were aberrations. How would you test this hypothesis in the context of the full regression estimated in Exercise 6 of Chapter 6?

   (c) Carry out the test in part (b).

5. Two samples of 50 observations each produce the following moment matrices (in each case, **X** is a constant and one variable):

	Sample 1	Sample 2
X'X	$\begin{bmatrix} 50 & 300 \\ 300 & 2100 \end{bmatrix}$	$\begin{bmatrix} 50 & 300 \\ 300 & 2100 \end{bmatrix}$
y'X	[300 2000]	[300 2200]
y'y	2100	2500

   (a) Test the hypothesis that the same regression coefficients apply in both data sets, assuming that the disturbance variances are the same.

   (b) Use a Wald test to test the hypothesis that the two coefficient vectors are the same without assuming that the disturbance variances are the same.

6. The regression model to be analyzed is

$$\mathbf{y} = \mathbf{X}_1\boldsymbol{\beta}_1 + \mathbf{X}_2\boldsymbol{\beta}_2 + \boldsymbol{\varepsilon},$$

where $\mathbf{X}_1$ and $\mathbf{X}_2$ have K_1 and K_2 columns, respectively. The restriction is $\boldsymbol{\beta}_2 = \mathbf{0}.$

(a) Using (7–12), prove that the restricted estimator is simply $[\mathbf{b}_1, \mathbf{0}]$, where $\mathbf{b}_1$ is the least squares coefficient vector in the regression of $\mathbf{y}$ on $\mathbf{X}_1$.

(b) Prove that if the restriction is $\boldsymbol{\beta}_2 = \boldsymbol{\beta}_2^0$ for a nonzero $\boldsymbol{\beta}_2^0$, the restricted estimator of $\boldsymbol{\beta}_1$ is

$$\mathbf{b}_{1*} = (\mathbf{X}_1'\mathbf{X}_1)^{-1}\mathbf{X}_1'(\mathbf{y} - \mathbf{X}_2\boldsymbol{\beta}_2^0).$$

7. The expression for the restricted coefficient vector in (7–12) may be written in the form

$$\mathbf{b}_* = [\mathbf{I} - \mathbf{CR}]\mathbf{b} + \mathbf{w},$$

where $\mathbf{w}$ does not involve $\mathbf{b}$. What is $\mathbf{C}$? Show that the covariance matrix of the restricted least squares estimator is

$$\sigma^2(\mathbf{X}'\mathbf{X})^{-1} - \sigma^2(\mathbf{X}'\mathbf{X})^{-1}\mathbf{R}'[\mathbf{R}(\mathbf{X}'\mathbf{X})^{-1}\mathbf{R}']^{-1}\mathbf{R}(\mathbf{X}'\mathbf{X})^{-1}$$

and that this matrix may be written as

$$\text{Var}(\mathbf{b})[\{\text{Var}(\mathbf{b})\}^{-1} - \mathbf{R}'\{\text{Var}(\mathbf{Rb})\}^{-1}\mathbf{R}]\text{Var}(\mathbf{b}).$$

8. Prove the result that the restricted least squares estimator never has a larger variance matrix than the unrestricted least squares estimator.

9. Prove the result that the R^2 associated with a restricted least squares estimator is never larger than that associated with the unrestricted least squares estimator. Conclude that imposing restrictions never improves the fit of the regression.

10. What is the vector $\mathbf{w}$ in Exercise 7?

11. The Lagrange multiplier test of the hypothesis in (7–4) is equivalent to a Wald test of the hypothesis that $\boldsymbol{\lambda} = \mathbf{0},$ where $\boldsymbol{\lambda}$ is defined in (7–12). Prove that

$$\chi^2 = \boldsymbol{\lambda}'\{\text{Est. Var}[\boldsymbol{\lambda}]^{-1}\}\boldsymbol{\lambda} = (n - K)\left[\frac{\mathbf{e}_*'\mathbf{e}_*}{\mathbf{e}'\mathbf{e}} - 1\right].$$

Note that the fraction in brackets is the ratio of two estimators of σ^2. By virtue of (7–13) and the preceding discussion, we know that this is greater than 1. [For some applications that reach a similar result, see (14–13) and especially Example 16.3 and (16–64).] Finally, prove that the Lagrange multiplier statistic is simply $JF,$ where J is the number of restrictions being tested and F is the conventional F statistic given in (7–14).

12. Use the Lagrange multiplier test to test the hypothesis in Exercise 1.

13. Using the data and model of Exercise 6 in Chapter 6, carry out a test of the hypothesis that the three aggregate price indices are not significant determinants of the demand for gasoline.

14. Suppose that there are two competing models for the gasoline market of Exercise 6 in Chapter 6. Both models include the constant, time trend, price of gasoline, and income. Model 1 includes the three microeconomic price indices, P_{nc}, P_{uc}, and P_{pt}. Model 2 argues that these are just components of the broader categories. Thus, Model 2 includes P_d, P_n, and P_s instead. Use the J or Cox tests to determine which theory is

better. [**Hint:** The results of Exercise 6(a) in Chapter 6 should give you an idea of what to expect.]

15. The model of Exercise 6 in Chapter 6 may be written in logarithmic terms as

$$\ln G = \alpha + \beta_p \ln P_g + \beta_y \ln Y + \gamma_{nc} \ln P_{nc} + \gamma_{uc} \ln P_{uc} + \gamma_{pt} \ln P_{pt}$$
$$+ \beta_t \text{year} + \delta_d \ln P_d + \delta_n \ln P_n + \delta_s \ln P_s + \varepsilon.$$

Consider the hypothesis that the "micro" elasticities are a constant proportion of the elasticity with respect to their corresponding aggregate. Thus, for some positive θ (presumably between zero and 1),

$$\gamma_{nc} = \theta\delta_d,$$

$$\gamma_{uc} = \theta\delta_d,$$

$$\gamma_{pt} = \theta\delta_s.$$

The first two imply the simple linear restriction $\gamma_{nc} = \gamma_{uc}$. By taking ratios, the first (or second) and third imply the nonlinear restriction

$$\frac{\gamma_{nc}}{\gamma_{pt}} = \frac{\delta_d}{\delta_s} \qquad \text{or} \qquad \gamma_{nc}\delta_s - \gamma_{pt}\delta_d = 0.$$

(a) Describe in detail how you would test the validity of the restriction.
(b) Using the data in Exercise 6 in Chapter 6, test the restrictions separately and jointly.

16. Prove that under the hypothesis $\mathbf{R}\beta = \mathbf{q}$, the estimator

$$s_*^2 = \frac{(\mathbf{y} - \mathbf{Xb}_*)'(\mathbf{y} - \mathbf{Xb}_*)}{n - K + J},$$

where J is the number of restrictions, is unbiased for σ^2.

17. Show that in the multiple regression of $\mathbf{y}$ on a constant, $\mathbf{x}_1$, and $\mathbf{x}_2$, using (7–3) to impose the restriction $\beta_1 + \beta_2 = 1$ leads to the regression of $\mathbf{y} - \mathbf{x}_1$ on a constant and $\mathbf{x}_2 - \mathbf{x}_1$.

CHAPTER 8

Functional Form, Nonlinearity, and Specification

8.1. Introduction

In this chapter we are concerned with the functional form of the regression model. There are many different types of functions that are "linear" by our definition. By using dummy variables and different arrangements of functions of variables, we can produce an impressive variety of models. Sections 8.2 and 8.3 examine some of the devices used in constructing regression models. Sections 8.4 and 8.5 consider some questions concerning errors in the specification of the model and the dangers of using the same data both to estimate parameters and to determine what form the model will take.

8.2. Dummy Variables

One of the most useful devices in regression analysis is the binary, or *dummy,* variable. We have used it in two previous applications: in Section 6.8.1 in computing forecasts and in Chapter 7 in constructing Chow tests for structural change. In both cases, these variables were only computational devices. But binary variables are also a convenient means of building discrete shifts of the function into a regression model.

8.2.1. Comparing Two Means

A comparison of the means of a variable in two groups might be formulated as follows:

$$\text{Group 1: } y_i = \mu + \varepsilon_i,$$
$$\text{Group 2: } y_i = \mu + \delta + \varepsilon_i.$$

The parameter δ is of particular interest. By defining the variable, d, as

$$d_i = 0 \text{ if group 1} \quad \text{and} \quad d_i = 1 \text{ if group 2,}[1]$$

these may be combined into the single equation

$$y_i = \mu + \delta d_i + \varepsilon_i.$$

If, for example, y_i is income and d_i indicates whether or not the individual attended college,

$$E[\text{income}|\text{did not attend college}] = \mu$$

and

$$E[\text{income}|\text{attended college}] = \mu + \delta.$$

---

[1] The choice of zero and one for the two values is purely for convenience. Any other two values could be used; however, the interpretation of the equation is simplest when we use zero and one.

In this model, δ is the difference between the expected incomes of the two groups. A test of whether δ is zero is equivalent to a test that this difference is zero or that the means are the same. An alternative model is

$$y_i = \mu_N + \varepsilon_i \qquad \text{for those who did not attend college,}$$

and

$$y_i = \mu_C + \varepsilon_i \qquad \text{for those who attended college.}$$

By defining $h_i = 1$ if individual i did not attend college and $h_i = 0$ otherwise, so that h_i equals $1 - d_i$, we can combine these equations in

$$y_i = \mu_N h_i + \mu_C d_i + \varepsilon_i.$$

Of course, these are the same; in the first formulation,

$$\delta = \mu_C - \mu_N.$$

There is a difference in interpretation, however. A test of $\mu_N = 0$ or $\mu_C = 0$ makes little sense, but the test of $\delta = 0$ is equivalent to a test of $\mu_C = \mu_N$.[2]

Aside from the special nature of the independent variables, there are multiple regression models that we can estimate by least squares. We arrange the observations so that the first n_1 are the individuals who did not attend college and the remaining n_2 are those who did. Denote by $\mathbf{i}_g$ a column of ones with n_g elements, either n_1 or n_2. Then the first model is

$$\mathbf{y} = \begin{bmatrix} \mathbf{i}_1 & \mathbf{0} \\ \mathbf{i}_2 & \mathbf{i}_2 \end{bmatrix} \begin{bmatrix} \mu \\ \delta \end{bmatrix} + \boldsymbol{\varepsilon}.$$

Least squares produces

$$\begin{bmatrix} m \\ d \end{bmatrix} = \begin{bmatrix} n_1 + n_2 & n_2 \\ n_2 & n_2 \end{bmatrix}^{-1} \begin{bmatrix} n_1 \bar{y}_1 + n_2 \bar{y}_2 \\ n_2 \bar{y}_2 \end{bmatrix} = \begin{bmatrix} \bar{y}_1 \\ \bar{y}_2 - \bar{y}_1 \end{bmatrix}.$$

For the second model,

$$\mathbf{y} = \begin{bmatrix} \mathbf{i}_1 & \mathbf{0} \\ \mathbf{0} & \mathbf{i}_2 \end{bmatrix} \begin{bmatrix} \mu_N \\ \mu_C \end{bmatrix} + \boldsymbol{\varepsilon}$$

and

$$\mathbf{m} = (\mathbf{X}'\mathbf{X})^{-1}\mathbf{X}'\mathbf{y} = \begin{bmatrix} 1/n_1 & 0 \\ 0 & 1/n_2 \end{bmatrix} \begin{bmatrix} n_1 \bar{y}_1 \\ n_2 \bar{y}_2 \end{bmatrix} = \begin{bmatrix} \bar{y}_1 \\ \bar{y}_2 \end{bmatrix}.$$

The equation may be written either with an overall intercept and a dummy variable for the effect being analyzed or with no constant term and two dummy variables. What might seem like a third possibility, an overall constant term and separate dummy variables for each group, leads to the *dummy variable trap*, a case of perfect collinearity. If the first model shown were written

$$\text{income}_i = \mu + \delta_N h_i + \delta_C d_i + \varepsilon_i,$$

the matrix of independent variables would be

$$\mathbf{X} = \begin{bmatrix} \mathbf{i}_1 & \mathbf{i}_1 & \mathbf{0} \\ \mathbf{i}_2 & \mathbf{0} & \mathbf{i}_2 \end{bmatrix}.$$

The second and third columns sum to the first, which makes least squares estimation of the three parameters impossible.

[2] See Suits (1984).

8.2.2. Binary Variables in Regression

Dummy variables are most frequently used in regression equations that also contain other quantitative variables. Recall the consumption data discussed in Chapter 5 and shown in Figure 5.2. There are four data points, the years 1942–1945, that lie conspicuously below the regression line for the remaining data. Figure 8.1 suggests a means of treating this effect.

EXAMPLE 8.1

Consumption and income data for the years 1940 to 1950 are listed in Table 8.1. The regression model is

$$C_t = \beta_1 + \beta_2 x_t + \beta_3 W_t + \varepsilon_t,$$

where x_t is disposable income and W_t is the wartime dummy variable, which takes the value one in the years 1942–1945 and zero in the other years. (The subscript t is used here to indicate the observation at time t.) The regression results are given in Table 8.2. The regression results confirm that consumption during World War II was significantly below what would have been expected, given income.

In more recent applications, researchers in many fields often study the effects of *treatments* on some kind of *response*. Examples include the effect of college on income, as in the preceding example, cross-sex differences in labor supply behavior and in salary structures in industries, and in pre- versus postregime shifts in macroeconomic models, to

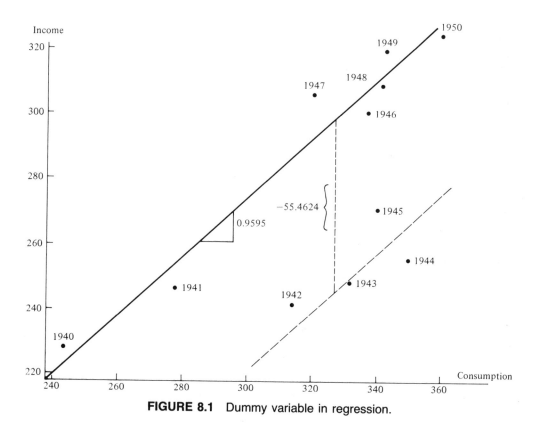

FIGURE 8.1 Dummy variable in regression.

TABLE 8.1 Consumption Expenditures[a]

Year	Disposable Income	Personal Consumption
1940	244.0	229.9
1941	277.9	243.6
1942	317.5	241.1
1943	332.1	248.2
1944	343.6	255.2
1945	338.1	270.9
1946	332.7	301.0
1947	318.8	305.8
1948	335.8	312.2
1949	336.8	319.3
1950	362.8	337.3

[a]Income and consumption are in billions of 1972 dollars.

TABLE 8.2

Number of observations	11
Standard error of regression	9.088
R-squared	0.95283

Variable	Coefficient	Standard Error	t ratio
Constant	-10.065	28.44	-0.354
x	0.959595	0.0895	10.724
W	-55.4624	5.902	-9.397

name but a few. These can all be formulated in regression models involving a single dummy variable:

$$y_i = \boldsymbol{\beta}' \mathbf{x}_i + \delta d_i + \varepsilon_i.$$

8.2.3. Several Categories

When there are several categories, a set of binary variables is necessary. Correcting for seasonal factors in macroeconomic data is a common application. Extending the device used earlier, we could write a consumption function for quarterly data as

$$C_t = \beta_1 + \beta_2 x_t + \delta_1 D_{t1} + \delta_2 D_{t2} + \delta_3 D_{t3} + \varepsilon_t,$$

where x_t is disposable income. Once again, to avoid the dummy variable trap, we drop the dummy variable for the fourth quarter. (Depending on the application, it might be preferable to have four separate dummy variables and drop the overall constant.)[3] Any of the four quarters (or 12 months) can be used as the base period. The matrix of independent variables for this model is

$$\mathbf{X} = \begin{bmatrix} 1 & 0 & 0 & 0 & x_1 \\ 1 & 1 & 0 & 0 & x_2 \\ 1 & 0 & 1 & 0 & x_3 \\ 1 & 0 & 0 & 1 & x_4 \\ 1 & 0 & 0 & 0 & x_5 \\ \vdots & \vdots & \vdots & \vdots & \vdots \\ 1 & 0 & 0 & 1 & x_T \end{bmatrix}.$$

[3] See Suits (1984) and Greene and Seaks (1991).

The preceding is a means of *deseasonalizing* the data. Consider the alternative formulation:

$$C_t = \beta x_t + \delta_1 D_{t1} + \delta_2 D_{t2} + \delta_3 D_{t3} + \delta_4 D_{t4} + \varepsilon_t. \tag{8-1}$$

Using the results from Chapter 6 on partitioned regression, we know that the preceding multiple regression is equivalent to first regressing $\mathbf{C}$ and $\mathbf{x}$ on the four dummies and then using the residuals from these regressions in the subsequent regression of deseasonalized consumption on deseasonalized income. Clearly, deseasonalizing in this fashion prior to computing the simple regression of consumption on income is the same as including the set of dummy variables in the regression.

8.2.4. Several Groupings

The case in which several sets of dummy variables are needed is much the same as those we have already considered, with one important exception. Consider a model of statewide per capita expenditure, y, as a function of statewide per capita income, x. Suppose that we have observations on all $n = 50$ states for $T = 10$ years. A regression model that allows the expected expenditure to change over time, as well as across states would be

$$y_{it} = \alpha + \beta x_{it} + \delta_i + \theta_t + \varepsilon_{it}. \tag{8-2}$$

This is essentially the same as the earlier regression model. As before, it is necessary to drop one of the variables in the set of dummy variables to avoid the dummy variable trap. This is necessary even if the overall constant term is dropped. For our example, if the overall constant term is omitted and a total of 50 state dummies and 10 time dummies is retained, a problem of perfect multicollinearity remains; the sum of the 50 state dummies and the 10 time dummies are the same, that is, one. One of the variables in one of the sets must be omitted.

EXAMPLE 8.2 Analysis of Variance ⎯⎯⎯⎯⎯⎯⎯⎯⎯⎯⎯⎯⎯⎯⎯⎯⎯⎯⎯⎯⎯

The number of incidents of damage to a sample of ships, with the type of ship and the period when it was constructed, is shown in Table 8.3. There are five types of ships and four different periods of construction. On inspection, it seems clear that the means will differ across ship types. Whether they will differ across periods is less clear. The regression results are shown in Table 8.4 (we report only the regression coefficients).

According to the full model, the expected number of incidents for a ship of the base type, A, built in the base period, 1960–1964, is 3.4. The other 19 predicted values follow from the previous results and are left as an exercise. The relevant test statistics for differences across ship type and year are as follows:

$$\text{Type: } F[4,\ 12] = \frac{(3925.2 - 660.9)/4}{660.9/12} = 14.82,$$

$$\text{Year: } F[3,\ 12] = \frac{(1090.3 - 660.9)/3}{660.9/12} = 2.60.$$

The 5 percent critical values from the F table with these degrees of freedom are 3.26 and 3.49, respectively, so we would conclude that the average number of incidents varies significantly across ship types but not across years.

TABLE 8.3

Ship Type	Period Constructed			
	1960–1964	**1965–1969**	**1970–1974**	**1975–1979**
A	0	4	18	11
B	29	53	44	18
C	1	1	2	1
D	0	0	11	4
E	0	7	12	1

Source: Data from McCullagh and Nelder (1983, p. 137).

TABLE 8.4

	Full Model	**Time Effects**	**Type Effects**	**No Effects**
Constant	3.4	6.0	8.25	10.85
B	27.75	0	27.75	0
C	−7.0	0	−7.0	0
D	−4.5	0	−4.5	0
E	−3.25	0	−3.25	0
65–69	7.0	7.0	0	0
70–74	11.4	11.4	0	0
75–79	1.0	1.0	0	0
R^2	0.84823	0.0986	0.74963	0
$e'e$	660.9	3925.2	1090.2	4354.5

8.2.5. Threshold Effects

In most applications, we use dummy variables to account for purely qualitative factors, such as membership in a group, or to represent a particular time period. There are cases, however, in which the dummy variable(s) represent levels of some underlying factor that might have been measured directly if this were possible. For example, education is a case in which we typically observe certain thresholds rather than, say, years of education[4]. Suppose, for example, our interest is in a regression of the form

$$\text{income} = \beta_1 + \beta_2 \text{age} + \text{effect of education} + \varepsilon.$$

The data on education might consist of the highest level of education attained, for example, high school, undergraduate, masters, or Ph.D. An obviously unsatisfactory way to proceed is to use a variable, E, that is 0 for the first group, 1 for the second, 2 for the third, and 3 for the fourth. That is,

$$\text{income} = \beta_1 + \beta_2 \text{age} + \beta_3 E + \varepsilon.$$

The difficulty with this approach is that it assumes that the increment in income at each threshold is the same; β_3 is the difference between income with a Ph.D. and a master's and between a master's and a bachelor's degree. This is unlikely and unduly restricts the regression. A more flexible model would use three (or four) binary variables, one for each level of education. Thus, we would write

$$\text{income} = \beta_1 + \beta_2 \text{age} + \delta_1 \text{BA} + \delta_2 \text{MA} + \delta_3 \text{PhD} + \varepsilon.$$

---

[4]Even this quantitative measure is only a crude measure of amount of education.

The correspondence between the coefficients and income for a given age is

High school: Income $= \beta_1 + \beta_2 \text{age}$,
B.A.:   Income $= \beta_1 + \beta_2 \text{age} + \delta_1$,
M.A.:   Income $= \beta_1 + \beta_2 \text{age} + \delta_2$,
Ph.D.:   Income $= \alpha_1 + \beta_2 \text{age} + \delta_3$.

The differences between, say, δ_3 and δ_2 and between δ_2 and δ_1 are of interest. Obviously, these are simple to compute. An alternative way to formulate the equation that reveals these differences directly is to redefine the dummy variables to be 1 if the individual has the degree, rather than whether the degree is the highest degree obtained. Thus, for someone with a Ph.D., all three binary variables are 1, and so on. The independent variables appear as follows, where individuals with only a high school education are grouped first, and those with higher degrees are arranged in order below them:

$$\mathbf{X} = \begin{bmatrix} \mathbf{i}_h & \mathbf{0} & \mathbf{0} & \mathbf{0} & \mathbf{Age}_h \\ \mathbf{i}_b & \mathbf{i}_b & \mathbf{0} & \mathbf{0} & \mathbf{Age}_b \\ \mathbf{i}_m & \mathbf{i}_m & \mathbf{i}_m & \mathbf{0} & \mathbf{Age}_m \\ \mathbf{i}_p & \mathbf{i}_p & \mathbf{i}_p & \mathbf{i}_p & \mathbf{Age}_p \end{bmatrix}$$

By defining the variables in this fashion, the regression is

High school: Income $= \alpha + \beta \text{age}$,

B.A.:   Income $= \alpha + \beta \text{age} + \delta_1$,

M.A.:   Income $= \alpha + \beta \text{age} + \delta_1 + \delta_2$,

Ph.D.:   Income $= \alpha + \beta \text{age} + \delta_1 + \delta_2 + \delta_3$.

Instead of the difference between a Ph.D. and the base case, in this model δ_3 is the marginal value of the Ph.D. How equations with dummy variables are formulated is a matter of convenience. All of the results can be obtained from a basic equation.[5]

8.2.6. Interactions and Spline Regression

The tests of structural change analyzed earlier illustrate another common use of dummy variables. Recall that the data matrix for that model could be formulated as

$$\mathbf{X} = \begin{bmatrix} \mathbf{i}_1 & \mathbf{0} & \mathbf{X}_1 & \mathbf{0} \\ \mathbf{i}_2 & \mathbf{i}_2 & \mathbf{X}_2 & \mathbf{X}_2 \end{bmatrix}.$$

If we let **d** be the second column of this matrix and **i** be a full column of 1's, this data matrix is of the form

$$\mathbf{Z} = [\mathbf{i} \quad \mathbf{d} \quad \mathbf{X} \quad \mathbf{dX}].$$

The last column is just the product of the dummy variable and the other regressors. Consider, for example, a regression model that embodies the proposition that "not only are the salaries of college graduates higher than those of noncollege graduates at any given age, but they rise faster as the individuals grow older."[6] The regression would appear as in Figure 8.2 and could be written

$$S = \beta_1 + \beta_2 \text{age} + \beta_3 d + \beta_4 d\text{age} + \varepsilon.$$

[5] See Suits (1984).

[6] The first of these propositions may, in fact, be inappropriate. In the earliest earning years, those who go to college are foregoing the income being earned by those of like age who are not in school.

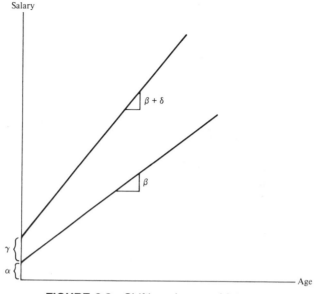

FIGURE 8.2 Shifting slope and intercept.

Estimating the parameters is a straightforward application of multiple regression. It is simple to show (we leave it as an exercise) that this is the same as computing two separate regressions. One ambiguity does arise in the estimation of the disturbance variance. If we assume that the two groups have equal disturbance variances, then

$$E[\varepsilon^2|d = 0] = \sigma^2$$

and

$$E[\varepsilon^2|d = 1] = \sigma^2.$$

In this case, it is most efficient to pool the observations and estimate a single parameter. However, if the variances differ across groups, then pooling the observations will result in one biased estimate of both disturbance variances. In addition, the usual estimate of the variance matrix of the coefficients will be incorrect. In this instance, the proper approach is to disaggregate the data and use the subsamples separately.

If one is examining income data for a large cross section of individuals of varying ages in a population, certain patterns with regard to some age thresholds will be clearly evident. In particular, throughout the range of values of age, income will be rising, but the slope might change at some distinct milestones, for example, at age 18, when the typical individual graduates from high school, and at age 22, when he or she graduates from college. The *time profile* of income for the typical individual in this population might appear as in Figure 8.3. Based on the discussion in the preceding paragraph, we could fit such a regression model just by dividing the sample into three subsamples. However, this would neglect the continuity of the preceding function; the result would appear more like the dotted figure than the continuous function we had in mind. Restricted regression, and what is known as a **spline** function, can be used to achieve the desired effect.[7]

---

[7] An important reference on this subject is Poirier (1974). An often cited application appears in Garber and Poirier (1974).

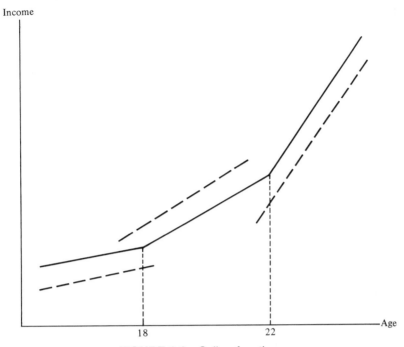

Income

Age

18   22

FIGURE 8.3 Spline function.

The function we wish to estimate is

$$\text{Income} = \alpha^0 + \beta^0 \text{age} \qquad \text{if age} < 18,$$
$$\alpha^1 + \beta^1 \text{age} \qquad \text{if age} \geq 18 \text{ and } < 22,$$
$$\alpha^2 + \beta^2 \text{age} \qquad \text{if age} \geq 22.$$

The specific values for the thresholds, 18 and 22, are called *knots*. The function is simple enough to specify using dummy variables, as we have done. In particular, let

$$d_1 = 1 \text{ if age} \geq t_1^*,$$
$$d_2 = 1 \text{ if age} \geq t_2^*,$$

where $t_1^* = 18$ and $t_2^* = 22$. To combine all three equations, we use

$$\text{Income} = \beta_1 + \beta_2 \text{age} + \gamma_1 d_1 + \delta_1 d_1 \text{age} + \gamma_2 d_2 + \delta_2 d_2 \text{age} + \varepsilon. \qquad (8\text{--}3)$$

This is the dashed function in Figure 8.3. The slopes in the three segments are β_2, $\beta_2 + \delta_1$, and $\beta_2 + \delta_1 + \delta_2$. To make the figure continuous, we require that the segments join at the knots, that is,

$$\beta_1 + \beta_2 t_1^* = (\beta_1 + \gamma_1) + (\beta_2 + \delta_1)t_1^*$$

and

$$(\beta_1 + \gamma_1) + (\beta_2 + \delta_1)t_2^* = (\beta_1 + \gamma_1 + \gamma_2) + (\beta_2 + \delta_1 + \delta_2)t_2^*.$$

These are linear restrictions on the coefficients. Collecting terms, the first one is

$$\gamma_1 + \delta_1 t_1^* = 0 \qquad \text{or} \qquad \gamma_1 = -\delta_1 t_1^*.$$

Doing likewise for the second and inserting these in (8–3), we obtain

$$\text{income} = \beta_1 + \beta_2 \text{age} + \delta_1 d_1(\text{age} - t_1^*) + \delta_2 d_2(\text{age} - t_2^*).$$

Constrained least squares estimates are obtainable by multiple regression, using the variables

$$x_1 = \text{age},$$

$$x_2 = \text{age} - 18 \text{ if age is} \geq 18 \text{ and 0 otherwise,}$$

and

$$x_3 = \text{age} - 22 \text{ if age is} \geq 22 \text{ and 0 otherwise.}$$

We can test the hypothesis that the slope of the function is constant with the joint test of $\delta_1 = 0$ and $\delta_2 = 0$. Whether the individual tests, $\delta_1 = 0$ or $\delta_2 = 0$, are meaningful will depend on the context. In our example, the first of these is a test that graduating from high school (actually, reaching 18) does not carry with it any increase in the slope of the earnings function until age 22 is reached.

8.3. Nonlinearity in the Variables

It is useful at this point to write the linear regression model in a very general form: Let $\mathbf{z} = z_1, z_2, \ldots, z_L$ be a set of L independent variables; let $f_1, f_2, \ldots, f_K$ be K independent functions of $\mathbf{z}$; let $g(y)$ be an observable function of y; and retain the usual assumptions about the disturbance. The linear regression model is

$$\begin{aligned} g(y) &= \beta_1 f_1(\mathbf{z}) + \beta_2 f_2(\mathbf{z}) + \cdots + \beta_K f_K(\mathbf{z}) + \varepsilon \\ &= \beta_1 x_1 + \beta_2 x_2 + \cdots + \beta_K x_K + \varepsilon \qquad (8\text{--}4) \\ &= \mathbf{x}'\boldsymbol{\beta} + \varepsilon. \end{aligned}$$

By using logarithms, exponentials, reciprocals, transcendental functions, polynomials, products, ratios, and so on, this "linear" model can be tailored to any number of situations.

8.3.1. Functional Forms

A commonly used form of regression model is the log-linear model

$$y = \alpha \prod_k X_k^{\beta_k} e^{\varepsilon}$$

or

$$\ln y = \ln \alpha + \sum_k \beta_k \ln X_k + \varepsilon$$

$$= \beta_1 + \sum_k \beta_k x_k + \varepsilon.$$

In this model, the coefficients are elasticities:

$$\left(\frac{\partial y}{\partial x_k}\right)\left(\frac{x_k}{y}\right) = \frac{\partial \ln y}{\partial \ln X_k} = \beta_k. \qquad (8\text{--}5)$$

This formulation is particularly useful in studies of demand and production.

A hybrid of the linear and log-linear models is the semilog equation

$$y = e^{\beta_1 + \beta_2 x + \varepsilon}$$

or

$$\ln y = \beta_1 + \beta_2 x + \varepsilon.$$

A common use of semilog formulation is in exponential growth curves. If x is "time," t, then

$$\frac{d \ln y}{dt} = \beta_2$$

$$= \text{average rate of growth of } y.$$

Macroeconomic models are often formulated with autonomous time trends. For example, aggregate models of productivity will usually include a trend variable, as in

$$\ln \left(\frac{Q}{L} \right)_t = \beta_1 + \beta_2 \ln \left(\frac{K}{L} \right)_t + \delta t + \varepsilon_t.$$

This provides an estimate of the "autonomous growth in productivity," usually attributed to technical change. In this equation, δ is the rate of growth of average product not attributable to increases in the use of capital.

Another useful formulation of the regression model is one with **interaction terms.** For example, a model relating braking distance, D, to speed, S, and road wetness, W, might be

$$D = \beta_1 + \beta_2 S + \beta_3 W + \beta_4 SW + \varepsilon.$$

In this model,

$$\frac{\partial E[D]}{\partial S} = \beta_2 + \beta_4 W$$

$$\frac{\partial E[D]}{\partial W} = \beta_3 + \beta_4 S,$$

which implies that the marginal effect of higher speed on braking distance is increased when the road is wetter (assuming that β_4 is positive).

A form of the linear model

$$y = \alpha + \beta g(x) + \varepsilon$$

that has appeared in a number of recent studies is the **Box–Cox transformation,**[8]

$$g^{(\lambda)}(x) = \frac{x^\lambda - 1}{\lambda}. \tag{8–6}$$

The linear model results if λ equals 1, while a log-linear or semilog model (depending on how y is measured) results if λ equals 0.[9] Other values of λ produce many different functional forms. For example, if λ equals -1, then the equation will involve the reciprocal of x. The Box–Cox model is a useful formulation that embodies many of the models

---

[8] See Box and Cox (1964) and Zarembka (1974). A survey of the properties of this model appears in Spitzer (1982b). Some further results on estimation appear in Spitzer (1982a).

[9] For λ equal to zero, L'Hôpital's rule can be used to obtain the result of the transformation; $g^{(0)}(x) = [\lim_{\lambda \to 0} d(x^\lambda - 1)/d\lambda]/[\lim_{\lambda \to 0} d\lambda/d\lambda] = \ln x$.

we have considered as special cases. Of course, in itself, this is only a minor virtue; if λ is known, we merely insert the known value and obtain a model linear in the transformed variables. But except for the polar cases of λ equal to -1, 0, or 1, it is hard to conceive of situations in which a particular value would be specified a priori. By treating λ as an additional unknown parameter in the equation, we obtain a tremendous amount of flexibility.[10] The cost of doing so is that the model then becomes nonlinear in its parameters. We shall study the model in detail in Chapter 11.

In spite of their very complex functional forms, these models are **intrinsically linear** because they can be placed directly in the form of (8–4). As discussed in Chapter 5, the distinguishing feature of the linear model is not the relationship among the variables as such but the way the parameters enter the equation.

8.3.2. Identifying Nonlinearity

If the functional form is not known a priori, there are a few approaches that might help at least to identify any nonlinearity and to provide some information about it from the sample. For example, if the suspected nonlinearity is with respect to a single regressor in the equation, fitting a quadratic or cubic polynomial rather than a linear function may capture some of the nonlinearity. By choosing several ranges for the regressor in question and allowing the slope of the function to be different in each range, a piecewise linear approximation to the nonlinear function can be fit.

EXAMPLE 8.3 Nonlinear Regression _____

In a celebrated study of the U.S. electric power industry, Nerlove (1963) analyzed the production costs of 145 American electric generating companies. At the outset of the study, he fit a Cobb–Douglas cost function of the form

$$\log C = \beta_1 + \beta_q \log Q + \sum_k \beta_k \log P_k + \varepsilon, \qquad (8-7)$$

where C is total cost, Q is output, and P_k is the unit price of the kth factor of production (k = labor, fuel, capital). The underlying theory implies that $\Sigma_k \beta_k = 1$. This is imposed by regressing $\log C - \log P_F$ on a constant, $\log Q$, $\log P_L - \log P_F$, and $\log P_K - \log P_F$. This first set of results appears at the top of Table 8.5.

The implied total and average cost functions for these results are shown in Figure 8.4. The striking pattern of the residuals (sketched in the figure) and some thought about the implied form of production suggested that something was missing from the model.[11] In theory, the estimated model implies a continually declining average cost curve, which, in turn, implies pervasive economies of scale at all levels of output. This conflicts with the textbook notion of a U-shaped average cost curve and appears implausible for the data. Two approaches were used to analyze the model.[12]

---

[10] In principle, y could be modified by the Box − Cox transformation as well. However, some important issues of specification will arise. (That is, is the model linear or log-linear? What is the allowable range of the dependent variable?) We defer until Chapter 11 a detailed treatment of the Box − Cox transformation applied to the dependent variable.

[11] A Durbin–Watson test of correlation among the residuals (see Section 15.5.1) revealed substantial autocorrelation. This is to be expected, given the pattern in the figure.

[12] A third approach based on a model of the production function appears in Example 11.5.

TABLE 8.5. Cobb–Douglas Cost Function (Standard Errors in Parentheses)

	$\log Q$	$\log P_L - \log P_F$	$\log P_K - \log P_F$	R^2
All firms	0.721	0.562	−0.003	0.931
	(0.175)	(0.198)	(0.192)	
Group 1	0.398	0.641	−0.093	0.512
	(0.079)	(0.691)	(0.669)	
Group 2	0.668	0.105	0.364	0.635
	(0.116)	(0.275)	(0.277)	
Group 3	0.931	0.408	0.249	0.571
	(0.198)	(0.199)	(0.189)	
Group 4	0.915	0.472	0.133	0.871
	(0.108)	(0.174)	(0.157)	
Group 5	1.045	0.604	−0.295	0.920
	(0.065)	(0.197)	(0.175)	

By sorting his sample into five groups on the basis of output and fitting separate regressions to each group, Nerlove fit a piecewise linear model. The results are given in the lower rows of the table, where the firms in the successive groups are progressively larger. The results are persuasive that the (log)-linear cost function is inadequate. The output coefficient that rises toward and then crosses 1 is consistent with a U-shaped cost curve as surmised earlier. (See Exercise 3 in Chapter 10.)

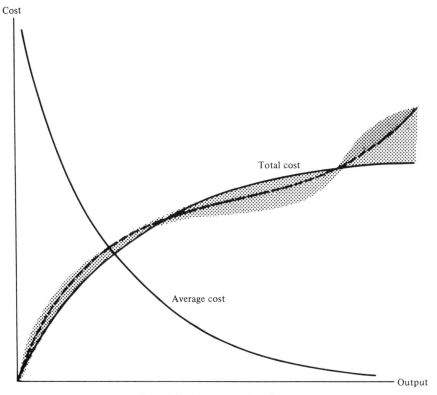

FIGURE 8.4 Cost functions.

TABLE 8.6. Log-Quadratic Cost Function (Standard Errors in Parentheses)

	$\log Q$	$\log^2 Q$	$\log P_L - \log P_F$	$\log P_K - \log P_F$	R^2
All firms	0.151	0.117	0.498	0.062	0.958
	(0.062)	(0.012)	(0.161)	(0.151)	

A second approach was to expand the cost function to include a quadratic term in log output. This corresponds to a much more general model (the dashed cost curve shown in Figure 8.4) and produced the results given in Table 8.6. Again, a simple t test strongly suggests that increased generality is called for.[13]

The preceding illustrates three useful tools in identifying and dealing with unspecified nonlinearity: analysis of residuals, the use of piecewise linear regression,[14] and the use of polynomials to approximate the unknown regression function.

8.3.3. Intrinsic Linearity and Identification

The log-linear model illustrates an intermediate case of a nonlinear regression model. The equation is intrinsically linear by our definition; by taking logs of

$$Y_i = \alpha X_i^{\beta_2} e^{\varepsilon_i},$$

we obtain

$$\ln Y_i = \ln \alpha + \beta_2 \ln X_i + \varepsilon_i. \qquad (8\text{--}8)$$

or

$$y_i = \beta_1 + \beta_2 x_i + \varepsilon_i.$$

Although this equation is linear in most respects, something has changed in that it is no longer linear in α. Written in terms of β_1, we obtain a fully linear model. However, this may not be the form of interest. Nothing is lost, of course, since β_1 is just $\ln \alpha$. If β_1 can be estimated, an obvious estimate of α is suggested.[15] This leads us to a second aspect of intrinsically linear models.

Maximum likelihood estimators have an invariance property. In the classical normal regression model, the maximum likelihood estimator of σ is the square root of the maximum likelihood estimator of σ^2. Under some conditions, least squares estimates have the same property. By exploiting this fact, we can broaden the definition of linearity and include some additional cases that might otherwise be quite complex.

Definition. In the classical regression model, if the K parameters, $\beta_1, \beta_2, \ldots, \beta_K$ can be written as K one-to-one possibly nonlinear functions of a set of K underlying parameters, $\theta_1, \theta_2, \ldots, \theta_K$, then the model is intrinsically linear in $\boldsymbol{\theta}$.

---

[13] Nerlove inadvertently measured economies of scale from this function as $1/(\beta_q + \delta \log Q)$, where β_q and δ are the coefficients on $\log Q$ and $\log^2 Q$. The correct expression would have been $1/[\partial \log C/\partial \log Q] = 1/[\beta_q + 2\delta \log Q]$. This slip was periodically rediscovered in several later papers.

[14] It might seem that a spline regression might be useful here. However, there is no theoretical basis for the choice of output knots. In fact, they were chosen simply to have 29 firms in each group.

[15] See Example 10.2 for some related results.

The emphasis here is on "one-to-one." If the conditions are met, the model can be estimated in terms of the functions, $\beta_1, \ldots, \beta_K$, and the underlying parameters derived after these are estimated. The one-to-one correspondence is an **identification condition.** If the condition is met, the underlying parameters of the regression (θ) are said to be **exactly identified** in terms of the parameters of the linear model, β. An excellent example is provided by Kmenta (1986, p. 515).[16]

EXAMPLE 8.4 CES Production Function

The constant elasticity of substitution production function may be written

$$\ln Y = \ln \gamma - \frac{v}{\rho}\ln[\delta K^{-\rho} + (1 - \delta)L^{-\rho}] + \varepsilon. \tag{8-9}$$

A Taylor series approximation to this function around the point $\rho = 0$ is

$$\ln Y = \ln \gamma + v\delta \ln K + v(1 - \delta) \ln L - \tfrac{1}{2}\rho v\delta(1 - \delta)[\ln K - \ln L]^2 + \varepsilon$$
$$= \beta_1 + \beta_2 x_1 + \beta_3 x_2 + \beta_4 x_3 + \varepsilon, \tag{8-10}$$

where $x_1 = \ln K$, $x_2 = \ln L$, $x_3 = \ln^2(K/L)$, and

$$\beta_1 = \ln \gamma \qquad\qquad \gamma = e^{\beta_1}$$

$$\beta_2 = v\delta \qquad\qquad \delta = \frac{\beta_2}{\beta_2 + \beta_3}$$

$$\beta_3 = v(1 - \delta) \qquad\qquad v = \beta_2 + \beta_3 \tag{8-11}$$

$$\beta_4 = -\frac{\rho v\delta(1 - \delta)}{2} \qquad\qquad \rho = -\frac{2\beta_4(\beta_2 + \beta_3)}{\beta_2\beta_3}.$$

Estimates of β_1, β_2, β_3, and β_4 can be computed by least squares. The estimates of γ, δ, v, and ρ obtained by the second column of (8-11) are the same as those we would obtain had we found the nonlinear least squares estimates of (8-10) directly. [As Kmenta shows, they are not the same as the nonlinear least squares estimates of (8-9) due to the use of the Taylor series approximation to get to (8-10).]

Not all models of the form

$$y_i = \beta_1(\theta)x_{i1} + \beta_2(\theta)x_{i2} + \cdots + \beta_K(\theta)x_{iK} + \varepsilon_i \tag{8-12}$$

are intrinsically linear. Recall that the condition that the functions be one-to-one (i.e., that the parameters be exactly identified) was required. For example,

$$y_i = \alpha + \beta x_{i1} + \gamma x_{i2} + \beta\gamma x_{i3} + \varepsilon_i$$

is nonlinear. The reason is that if we write it in the form of (8-12), we fail to account for the condition that β_4 equals $\beta_2\beta_3$, which is a nonlinear restriction. In this model, the three parameters α, β, and γ are said to be **overidentified** in terms of the four parameters β_1, β_2, β_3, and β_4. Unrestricted least squares estimates of β_2, β_3, and β_4 can be used to obtain two estimates of each of the underlying parameters, and there is no assurance that these will be the same.

---

[16] A second example appears in Example 11.5.

8.4. Specification Analysis

Our analysis has been based on the assumption that the correct specification of the regression model is known to be

$$y = X\beta + \varepsilon.$$

There are numerous types of errors that one might make in the specification of the estimated equation. Perhaps the most common ones are the omission of relevant variables and the inclusion of superfluous variables.

8.4.1. Selection of Variables

Consider an initial model, which we assume contains a constant term and several independent variables:

$$y = X_1\beta_1 + \varepsilon. \tag{8--13}$$

It is not unusual to begin with some formulation and then contemplate adding more variables to the model. As shown earlier, the effects of a new variable on the coefficients on X_1 are uncertain. However, the effect on R^2 is unambiguous. The change in the residual sum of squares when a set of variables, X_2, is added to the regression is

$$e'_{1,2}e_{1,2} = e'_1e_1 - b'_2X'_2M_1X_2b_2,$$

where we use subscript 1 to indicate the regression based on (8--13) and 1,2 to indicate the use of both X_1 and X_2. The coefficient vector b_2 is the coefficients on X_2 in the multiple regression of y on X_1 and X_2. [See (6--18) for definitions of b_2 and M_1.] Therefore,

$$R^2_{1,2} = 1 - \frac{e'_1e_1 - b'_2X'_2M_1X_2b_2}{y'M^0y}$$

$$= R^2_1 + \frac{b'_2X'_2M_1X_2b_2}{y'M^0y}.$$

This is greater than R^2_1 unless b_2 equals zero. (M_1X_2 could not be zero unless X_2 was a linear function of X_1, in which case the regression could not be computed.) This can be manipulated a bit further to obtain

$$R^2_{1,2} = R^2_1 + \frac{y'M_1y}{y'M^0y} \frac{b'_2X'_2M_1X_2b_2}{y'M_1y}.$$

But $y'M_1y = e'_1e_1$, so the first term in the product is $1 - R^2_1$. The second is the multiple correlation in the regression of M_1y on M_1X_2, or the **partial correlation** (after the effect of X_1 is removed) in the regression of y on X_2.[17] Collecting terms, we have

$$R^2_{1,2} = R^2_1 + (1 - R^2_1)r^2_{y2.1}.[18]$$

Clearly, it would be possible to push R^2 as high as desired just by adding regressors. It is this problem that motivates the use of the **adjusted R squared,**

$$\bar{R}^2 = 1 - \frac{n-1}{n-K}(1 - R^2),$$

---

[17] Partial correlation is discussed in Section 6.3.5.

[18] The interpretation of $r^2_{y2.1}$ as a multiple correlation coefficient requires x_1 to contain a constant term.

instead of R^2 as a method of choosing among alternative models.[19] Since $\overline{R}^2$ incorporates a penalty for reducing the degrees of freedom while still revealing an improvement in fit, one possibility is to choose the specification that maximizes $\overline{R}^2$. It can be shown that this is equivalent to minimizing the variance estimator, $\mathbf{e}'\mathbf{e}/(n - K)$. It has been suggested that the adjusted R-squared does not penalize the loss of degrees of freedom heavily enough.[20] Two alternatives that have been proposed for comparing models (which we index by j) are

$$\widetilde{R}_j^2 = \frac{n + K_j}{n - K_j}(1 - R_j^2),$$

which minimizes Amemiya's **prediction criterion**,[21]

$$\text{PC} = \frac{\mathbf{e}_j'\mathbf{e}_j}{n - K_j}\left(1 + \frac{K_j}{n}\right) = s_j^2\left(1 + \frac{K_j}{n}\right),$$

and Akaike's (1973) **information criterion,**

$$\text{AIC}_j = \ln\left(\frac{\mathbf{e}_j'\mathbf{e}_j}{n}\right) + \frac{2K_j}{n} = \ln \widehat{\sigma}_j^2 + \frac{2K_j}{n}.$$

Although intuitively appealing, these measures are a bit unorthodox in that they have no firm basis in theory.[22] Perhaps a somewhat more palatable alternative is the method of stepwise regression.[23] This procedure evaluates each variable in turn on the basis of its significance level and accumulates the model by adding or deleting variables sequentially. At the second step, to say nothing of the latter steps of this procedure, the classical inference procedures break down. Suppose, for example (as is common), that the method is used to ensure that all of the variables ultimately included have F statistics (the square of the conventional t ratio) larger than four. It is hardly appropriate to call these F statistics and base inference on them as if they were drawn from an F distribution; it is known a priori that all of them will be larger than four. For this reason, economists have tended to avoid stepwise regression methods.

The preceding creates a bit of a methodological dilemma for researchers using the classical procedures. On the one hand, there is a presumption that there is a "true model" known a priori. If so, orthodoxy dictates that the researcher will compute only a single regression and report the results. Of course, this is hardly likely, and in practice, some exploratory work is always necessary. There is, however, good reason to be skeptical of a "model" that is constructed entirely by mechanical means.

8.4.2. Omission of Relevant Variables

Suppose that a correctly specified regression model would be

$$\mathbf{y} = \mathbf{X}_1\boldsymbol{\beta}_1 + \mathbf{X}_2\boldsymbol{\beta}_2 + \boldsymbol{\varepsilon}, \tag{8-14}$$

[19] See Section 6.6.

[20] See, for example, Amemiya (1985, pp. 50–51).

[21] Ibid.

[22] There is a computer program that will automatically do the complete search among the 2^{K-1} specifications to find the maximum $\overline{R}^2$. In the interest of conserving resources, we leave the readers to their own devices to locate it.

[23] See Draper and Smith (1980) and Maddala (1977, pp. 124–127) for discussion.

where the two parts of $\mathbf{X}$ have K_1 and K_2 columns, respectively. If we regress $\mathbf{y}$ on $\mathbf{X}_1$ without including $\mathbf{X}_2$, the estimator is

$$\mathbf{b}_1 = (\mathbf{X}_1'\mathbf{X}_1)^{-1}\mathbf{X}_1'\mathbf{y}$$
$$= \boldsymbol{\beta}_1 + (\mathbf{X}_1'\mathbf{X}_1)^{-1}\mathbf{X}_1'\mathbf{X}_2\boldsymbol{\beta}_2 + (\mathbf{X}_1'\mathbf{X}_1)^{-1}\mathbf{X}_1'\boldsymbol{\varepsilon}. \tag{8-15}$$

Taking the expectation, we see that unless $\mathbf{X}_1'\mathbf{X}_2 = \mathbf{0}$, $\mathbf{b}_1$ is biased:

$$E[\mathbf{b}_1] = \boldsymbol{\beta}_1 + \mathbf{P}_{1.2}\boldsymbol{\beta}_2, \tag{8-16}$$

where

$$\mathbf{P}_{1.2} = (\mathbf{X}_1'\mathbf{X}_1)^{-1}\mathbf{X}_1'\mathbf{X}_2. \tag{8-17}$$

Each column of the $K_1 \times K_2$ matrix $\mathbf{P}_{1.2}$ is the column of slopes in the least squares regression of the corresponding column of $\mathbf{X}_2$ on the columns of $\mathbf{X}_1$.

EXAMPLES 8.5 Omitted Variable

If a demand equation is estimated without the relevant income variable, (8–16) shows how the estimated price elasticity will be biased. Letting b be the estimate, we obtain

$$E[b] = \beta + \frac{\text{Cov}[\text{price},\text{income}]}{\text{Var}[\text{price}]}\gamma,$$

where γ is the income coefficient. In aggregate data, it is unclear whether the missing covariance would be positive or negative. However, the sign of the bias in b would be the same as this covariance, because $\text{Var}[\text{price}]$ and γ would be positive.

In this development, it is straightforward to deduce the directions of bias when there is a single included variable and one omitted variable. However, it is important to note that if more than one variable is included, the terms in the **omitted variable formula** involve multiple regression coefficients, which themselves have the sign of partial, not simple, correlations. For example, in the demand equation, if the price of a closely related product had been included as well, then the simple correlation between price and income would be insufficient to determine the direction of the bias in the price elasticity. What would be required would be the sign of the correlation between price and income net of the effect of the other price. This might not be obvious, and it would become even less so as more regressors were added to the equation.

The variance of $\mathbf{b}_1$ is that of the third term in (8–15), which is

$$\text{Var}[\mathbf{b}_1] = \sigma^2(\mathbf{X}_1'\mathbf{X}_1)^{-1}. \tag{8-18}$$

If we had computed the correct regression, including $\mathbf{X}_2$, the slopes on $\mathbf{X}_1$ would have been unbiased and would have had a variance matrix equal to the upper left block of $\sigma^2(\mathbf{X}'\mathbf{X})^{-1}$. This is

$$\text{Var}[\mathbf{b}_{1.2}] = \sigma^2(\mathbf{X}_1'\mathbf{M}_2\mathbf{X}_1)^{-1} \tag{8-19}$$

where

$$\mathbf{M}_2 = \mathbf{I} - \mathbf{X}_2(\mathbf{X}_2'\mathbf{X}_2)^{-1}\mathbf{X}_2',$$

or

$$\text{Var}[\mathbf{b}_{1.2}] = \sigma^2[\mathbf{X}_1'\mathbf{X}_1 - \mathbf{X}_1'\mathbf{X}_2(\mathbf{X}_2'\mathbf{X}_2)^{-1}\mathbf{X}_2'\mathbf{X}_1]^{-1}.$$

We can compare the variance matrices of $\mathbf{b}_1$ and $\mathbf{b}_{1.2}$ more easily by comparing their inverses [see result (2–120)]:

$$\text{Var}[\mathbf{b}_1]^{-1} - \text{Var}[\mathbf{b}_{1.2}]^{-1} = \sigma^2 \mathbf{X}_1' \mathbf{X}_2 (\mathbf{X}_2' \mathbf{X}_2)^{-1} \mathbf{X}_2' \mathbf{X}_1,$$

which is positive definite. We conclude that although $\mathbf{b}_1$ is biased, it has a smaller variance than $\mathbf{b}_{1.2}$ (since the inverse of its variance is larger).

Suppose, for instance, that $\mathbf{X}_1$ and $\mathbf{X}_2$ are each a single column and that the variables are measured as deviations from their respective means. Then

$$\text{Var}[b_1] = \frac{\sigma^2}{s_{11}}, \qquad \text{where} \quad s_{11} = \Sigma(x_1 - \bar{x}_1)^2,$$

while

$$\text{Var}[b_{1.2}] = \sigma^2 (\mathbf{x}_1' \mathbf{x}_1 - \mathbf{x}_1' \mathbf{x}_2 (\mathbf{x}_2' \mathbf{x}_2)^{-1} \mathbf{x}_2' \mathbf{x}_1)^{-1}$$

$$= \frac{\sigma^2}{s_{11}(1 - r_{12}^2)}, \tag{8–20}$$

where

$$r_{12}^2 = \frac{(\mathbf{x}_1' \mathbf{x}_2)^2}{\mathbf{x}_1' \mathbf{x}_1 \mathbf{x}_2' \mathbf{x}_2}$$

is the squared sample correlation between $\mathbf{x}_1$ and $\mathbf{x}_2$. The more highly correlated are $\mathbf{x}_1$ and $\mathbf{x}_2$, the larger will be the variance of $b_{1.2}$ compared to that of b_1. Therefore, it is possible that b_1 is a more precise estimator based on the **mean-squared-error** criterion.

For statistical inference, it would be necessary to estimate σ^2. Proceeding as usual, we would use

$$s^2 = \frac{\mathbf{e}_1' \mathbf{e}_1}{n - K_1}.$$

But,

$$\mathbf{e}_1 = \mathbf{M}_1 \mathbf{y} = \mathbf{M}_1 (\mathbf{X}_1 \boldsymbol{\beta}_1 + \mathbf{X}_2 \boldsymbol{\beta}_2 + \boldsymbol{\varepsilon}) = \mathbf{M}_1 \mathbf{X}_2 \boldsymbol{\beta}_2 + \mathbf{M}_1 \boldsymbol{\varepsilon}.$$

In order to find the expected value of $\mathbf{e}_1' \mathbf{e}_1$, we use the same approach we used in Section 6.5.1 and the fact that $E[\mathbf{X}_1' \boldsymbol{\varepsilon}] = \mathbf{0}$ to drop the middle term in the quadratic form. Thus,

$$E[\mathbf{e}_1' \mathbf{e}_1] = \boldsymbol{\beta}_2' \mathbf{X}_2' \mathbf{M}_1 \mathbf{X}_2 \boldsymbol{\beta}_2 + \sigma^2 tr(\mathbf{M}_1)$$

$$= \boldsymbol{\beta}_2' \mathbf{X}_2' \mathbf{M}_1 \mathbf{X}_2 \boldsymbol{\beta}_2 + (n - K_1)\sigma^2. \tag{8–21}$$

The first term in the expectation is the population counterpart to the increase in the residual sum of squares that results when $\mathbf{X}_2$ is dropped from the regression. It is simple to show that the first term is positive, so that s^2 is biased upward. Unfortunately, to take any account of this bias, we would require an estimate of $\boldsymbol{\beta}_2$.

The conclusion from this is that if we omit relevant variables from the regression, our estimates of both $\boldsymbol{\beta}_1$ and σ^2 are biased. It is possible for $\mathbf{b}_1$ to be more precise than $\mathbf{b}_{1.2}$. But even this should be of limited comfort. Since we cannot estimate σ^2, we cannot test hypotheses about $\boldsymbol{\beta}_1$. To make matters worse, even if we had an estimate of σ^2, we could only test hypotheses about $\boldsymbol{\beta}_1 + \mathbf{P}_{1.2} \boldsymbol{\beta}_2$, which is unlikely to be of much interest. As a final observation, note that when the regressors are orthogonal, $(\mathbf{X}_1' \mathbf{X}_2) = \mathbf{0}$, the estimator in the short regression is unbiased. But the estimator of σ^2 is *still* biased upward, so we are still precluded from drawing valid inferences about $\boldsymbol{\beta}_1$. Of course, it is unlikely that in practice the regressors would be orthogonal.

8.4.3. Inclusion of Irrelevant Variables

If the regression model is correctly given by

$$\mathbf{y} = \mathbf{X}_1\boldsymbol{\beta}_1 = \boldsymbol{\varepsilon} \tag{8-22}$$

and we estimate it as if (8–14) were correct (i.e., we include some extra variables), it might seem that the same sorts of problems considered earlier would arise. In fact, this is not the case. We can view the omission of a set of relevant variables as equivalent to imposing an incorrect restriction on (8–14). In particular, omitting $\mathbf{X}_2$ is equivalent to *incorrectly* estimating (8–14) subject to the restriction

$$\boldsymbol{\beta}_2 = \mathbf{0}. \tag{8-23}$$

As we discovered, incorrectly imposing a restriction leads to a number of biases. Another way to view this error is to note that it amounts to incorporating incorrect information in our estimation. Suppose, however, that our error is simply a failure to use some information that *is correct*.

The inclusion of the irrelevant variables $\mathbf{X}_2$ in the regression is equivalent to failing to impose (8–23) on (8–14) in estimation. However, (8–14) is not incorrect; it simply fails to incorporate (8–23). Therefore, we do not need to prove formally that the least squares estimator of $\boldsymbol{\beta}$ in (8–14) is unbiased *even given* (8–23); we have already proved it. We can assert on the basis of all of our earlier results that

$$E[\mathbf{b}] = \begin{bmatrix} \boldsymbol{\beta}_1 \\ \boldsymbol{\beta}_2 \end{bmatrix} = \begin{bmatrix} \boldsymbol{\beta}_1 \\ \mathbf{0} \end{bmatrix}. \tag{8-24}$$

By the same reasoning, s^2 is also unbiased:

$$E\left[\frac{\mathbf{e}'\mathbf{e}}{n - K_1 - K_2}\right] = \sigma^2.$$

Then where is the problem? It would seem that one would generally want to "overfit" the model. From a theoretical standpoint, the difficulty with this view is that the failure to use correct information is always costly. In this instance, the cost is reduced precision of the estimates. As we have shown, the variance matrix in the short regression (omitting $\mathbf{X}_2$) is never larger than the variance matrix for the estimator obtained in the presence of the superfluous variables.[24] Consider again the single-variable comparison given earlier. If $\mathbf{x}_2$ is highly correlated with $\mathbf{x}_1$, incorrectly including it in the regression will greatly inflate the variance of the estimator.

8.5. Biased Estimators and Pretest Estimators

Our focus on unbiased estimators parallels the general attraction among economists for them. However, it has been amply demonstrated that this approach will almost surely bypass estimators that though biased, are more precise in an expected squared error sense.[25] Indeed, the famous result of James and Stein (1961) shows that by a squared error loss criterion, there is always a feasible estimator that dominates least squares for every value of $\boldsymbol{\beta}$.[26] From our point of view, the importance of this result will lie in how we can

---

[24] There is no loss if $\mathbf{X}_1'\mathbf{X}_2 = 0$, which makes sense in terms of the information about $\mathbf{X}_1$ contained in $\mathbf{X}_2$ (here, none). However, this is not likely to occur in practice.

[25] See, for example, Judge et al. (1985) and the many references cited therein.

[26] See, as well, the discussions in Judge et al. (1985, pp. 82–92) and Amemiya (1985, pp. 61–63).

use information drawn from outside the sample data to sharpen our parameter estimates. At several points, we have invoked the general proposition that increased information, good or bad, reduces variance. However, we have also found that *incorrect* information will induce biases.[27] Here we shall explore further the possibility that when our out-of-sample information is sufficiently close to the truth, the induced bias will be offset by the improvement in the variance of the estimator in its expected squared error.

8.5.1. The Mean-Squared-Error Test

Suppose that we incorporate a set of restrictions, $\mathbf{R}\boldsymbol{\beta} = \mathbf{q}$, on the least squares estimator of $\boldsymbol{\beta}$ in the model $\mathbf{y} = \mathbf{X}\boldsymbol{\beta} + \boldsymbol{\varepsilon}$. The restricted least squares estimator is

$$\mathbf{b}_* = \mathbf{b} - (\mathbf{X'X})^{-1}\mathbf{R'}[\mathbf{R}(\mathbf{X'X})^{-1}\mathbf{R'}]^{-1}(\mathbf{Rb} - \mathbf{q}) = \mathbf{b} - \mathbf{W}(\mathbf{Rb} - \mathbf{q}) \quad (8\text{--}25)$$

and its variance matrix is

$$\text{Var}[\mathbf{b}_*] = \sigma^2[(\mathbf{X'X})^{-1} - (\mathbf{X'X})^{-1}\mathbf{R'}(\mathbf{R}(\mathbf{X'X})^{-1}\mathbf{R'})^{-1}\mathbf{R}(\mathbf{X'X})^{-1}]. \quad (8\text{--}26)$$

The variance matrix of $\mathbf{b}_*$ is equal to that of $\mathbf{b}$ minus a positive definite matrix, so it is smaller in the sense defined in Chapter 2. However, unless the restrictions are correct in the population, $\mathbf{b}_*$ is biased; $E[\mathbf{b}_*] = \boldsymbol{\beta} - \mathbf{W}(\mathbf{R}\boldsymbol{\beta} - \mathbf{q})$. It is still possible that the mean-squared error of $\mathbf{b}_*$ is smaller than that of $\mathbf{b}$.

Since $\mathbf{b}$ is unbiased, its mean-squared-error matrix is its variance matrix:

$$\text{MSE}[\mathbf{b}\,|\,\boldsymbol{\beta}] = \sigma^2(\mathbf{X'X})^{-1}.$$

To obtain the mean-squared-error matrix for $\mathbf{b}_*$, we can use (8–26) and the result preceding it:

$$\begin{aligned}\text{MSE}[\mathbf{b}_*\,|\,\boldsymbol{\beta}] &= \text{Var}[\mathbf{b}_*] + E[\mathbf{b}_* - \boldsymbol{\beta}]E[\mathbf{b}_* - \boldsymbol{\beta}]' \\ &= \sigma^2(\mathbf{I} - \mathbf{WR})(\mathbf{X'X})^{-1}(\mathbf{I} - \mathbf{WR})' + \mathbf{W}(\mathbf{R}\boldsymbol{\beta} - \mathbf{q})(\mathbf{R}\boldsymbol{\beta} - \mathbf{q})'\mathbf{W}'.\end{aligned}$$

It has been shown that $\mathbf{b}_*$ will be more precise in the sense that $\text{MSE}[\mathbf{b}\,|\,\boldsymbol{\beta}] - \text{MSE}[\mathbf{b}_*\,|\,\boldsymbol{\beta}]$ is a positive definite matrix if[28]

$$\lambda = \frac{(\mathbf{R}\boldsymbol{\beta} - \mathbf{q})'[\mathbf{R}(\mathbf{X'X})^{-1}\mathbf{R'}]^{-1}(\mathbf{R}\boldsymbol{\beta} - \mathbf{q})}{2\sigma^2} < \frac{1}{2}. \quad (8\text{--}27)$$

This is $J/2$ times the population analog to the F statistic that would be used to test the validity of the restrictions. *This implies that if the failure of the true parameters to satisfy the restrictions is not too severe, the biased estimator will be more precise in spite of its bias.*

Since λ depends on the unknown parameters we are trying to estimate, (8–27) cannot be computed. It is possible to test the inequality in (8–27) as a hypothesis, but not with the procedures we have used thus far. Under the hypothesis that $(\mathbf{R}\boldsymbol{\beta} - \mathbf{q}) = \mathbf{0}$,

$$\frac{2\hat{\lambda}}{J} = F = \frac{(\mathbf{Rb} - \mathbf{q})'[\mathbf{R}(\mathbf{X'X})^{-1}\mathbf{R'}]^{-1}(\mathbf{Rb} - \mathbf{q})/\sigma^2}{Js^2/\sigma^2} \quad (8\text{--}28)$$

has the familiar F distribution. But if the hypothesis is incorrect, the F distribution no longer applies. The difference arises because the numerator of (8–28) has a chi-squared distribution with J degrees of freedom only if $E[\mathbf{Rb} - \mathbf{q}] = \mathbf{0}$. If not, the numerator has a

---

[27] See the discussion of specification errors in Section 8.4.

[28] See, for example, Fomby et al. (1984, pp. 98–100).

noncentral chi-squared distribution, and the ratio has a **noncentral F** distribution. These distributions arise as follows:

1. *Noncentral chi-squared distribution.* If z has a normal distribution with mean μ and standard deviation 1, the distribution of z^2 is *noncentral* chi-squared with parameters 1 and $\mu^2/2$. If μ equals zero, the familiar *central* chi-squared distribution results. The extensions that will enable us to deduce the distribution of F when the restrictions do not hold in the population are

   a. If $z \sim N[\mu, \Sigma]$, with J elements, $z'\Sigma^{-1}z$ has a noncentral chi-squared distribution with J degrees of freedom and noncentrality parameter $\mu'\Sigma^{-1}\mu/2$, which we denote $\chi_*^2[J, \mu'\Sigma^{-1}\mu/2]$.

   b. If $z \sim N[\mu, I]$ and M is an idempotent matrix with rank J, then $z'Mz \sim \chi_*^2[J, \mu'M\mu/2]$.

2. *Noncentral F distribution.* If X_1 has a noncentral chi-squared distribution with noncentrality parameter λ and degrees of freedom n_1, and X_2 has a central chi-squared distribution with degrees of freedom n_2 and is independent of X_1,

$$F_* = \frac{X_1/n_1}{X_2/n_2}$$

has a noncentral F distribution with parameters n_1, n_2, and λ.[29] Note that in each of these cases the statistic and the distribution are the familiar ones, except that the effect of the nonzero mean, which induces the noncentrality, is to push the distribution to the right.

Thus, the distribution of the sample F statistic in (8–28) is noncentral F with degrees of freedom J and $n - K$ and noncentrality parameter λ, as given in (8–27). If the restrictions are valid, λ will be zero and the familiar central F distribution will result.

A test of the hypothesis that the mean-squared error of the restricted estimator is smaller than that of the unrestricted one can now be constructed. The test of $H_0: \lambda \leq \frac{1}{2}$ can be carried out by referring the sample F ratio to the noncentral F distribution with parameters J, $n - K$, and $\frac{1}{2}$. A value of F larger than the critical value in the table is taken as evidence that $\lambda > \frac{1}{2}$. Critical values for the noncentral F distribution have been tabulated by Wallace and Toro-Vizcarrondo (1969). Since this is a three-parameter distribution, the complete tabulation is a bit cumbersome. There is, however, a very simple and accurate approximation that requires only the central F tables given in the appendixes of most textbooks (including this one).

For degrees of freedom J and T, we can approximate the noncentral F critical values by using

$$C_* \simeq \left(1 + \frac{1}{J}\right)C,$$

where

$$\text{Prob}\left(F\left[J + \frac{1}{J+2}, T\right] > C\right) = 0.05.$$

To find the critical value for noninteger degrees of freedom, it is necessary to interpolate in the F table, which is done using the reciprocals of the degrees of freedom.

---

[29]The denominator chi-squared could also be noncentral, but we shall not use any statistics with doubly noncentral distributions.

EXAMPLE 8.6 Mean-Squared-Error Test (Hypothetical) ——————————

A Cobb–Douglas cost function of the form

$$\ln\left(\frac{C}{P_m}\right) = \beta_1 + \beta_2 \ln Q + \beta_3 \ln\left(\frac{P_k}{P_m}\right) + \beta_4 \ln\left(\frac{P_l}{P_m}\right) + \beta_5 \ln\left(\frac{P_e}{P_m}\right)$$

is estimated using 20 observations, where C is cost, Q is output, and P_k, P_l, P_e, and P_m are the unit prices of four factors of production: capital, labor, energy, and materials. The restriction that the function be homogeneous of degree zero in the prices is already imposed. The parameter β_2 is of primary interest. The F statistic for testing the hypothesis that $\beta_3 = \beta_4 = \beta_5 = 0$ is 4.17. Will the estimate of β_2 be improved by imposing the restriction? First, the critical value from the central F distribution for 5 percent significance is 3.29; so, outright, the restrictions are rejected by the familiar standard. But, for this test, we require the 5 percent critical value from the noncentral F distribution. This is C^* such that

$$\text{Prob}(F_*[3, 15, \tfrac{1}{2}] > C_*) = 0.05.$$

The neighboring values to the critical value for $F[3.2, 15]$ are 3.29 for $F[3, 15]$ and 3.06 for $F[4, 15]$. Therefore,

$$C = 3.29 - (3.29 - 3.06)\frac{(1/3.2 - 1/3)}{(1/4 - 1/3)} = 3.233,$$

so,

$$C_* = (1 + \tfrac{1}{3})3.233 = 4.310.$$

(The corresponding value from the Toro-Vizcarrondo and Wallace tables is 4.315.) Since the test statistic was 4.17, we would conclude that the restricted estimator is more precise, in spite of the earlier finding.

———

Because the critical points of the noncentral distribution are always to the right of those for the central distribution, it is worth emphasizing that this test can lead to retention of a set of restrictions when we might reject the restrictions themselves.

Should we use the restricted or the unrestricted estimator? This question is relevant in all of the settings we have considered thus far in this chapter. (That is, having tested a set of restrictions and failed to reject them, should we then impose them on the model and reestimate?) It is clear from the preceding that the answer depends on the precision of the estimator in a way that depends on some unknown parameters. Obviously, if we are sure that the restrictions are correct, we should impose them a priori and not concern ourselves with the unrestricted model. If we are sure that the restrictions are incorrect, it is unlikely that the earlier mean-squared-error test would favor the restricted estimator. It is the intermediate case, in which we are uncertain, that is at issue. Unfortunately, the problem becomes yet more complicated, because the process of sequential estimation implied here calls into question any further statistical inference that might be done.

8.5.2. Pretest Estimators

In dealing with the problem of multicollinearity,[30] one of the most tempting (and commonly used) strategies is simply to drop the variable(s) suspected of causing the problem.

———

[30] This is the subject of Section 9.2 of the next chapter. For the present, we may view it as an imprecision in the estimation of the parameters that is caused by correlation between the independent variables in a multiple regression.

Consider the simplest case: that of a regression with two independent variables and no constant term. The regression is

$$\mathbf{y} = \beta_1\mathbf{x}_1 + \beta_2\mathbf{x}_2 + \boldsymbol{\varepsilon}.$$

Two competing estimators are the *short regression,*

$$b_1 = (\mathbf{x}_1'\mathbf{x})^{-1}\mathbf{x}_1'\mathbf{y}$$

and the *long regression,*

$$b_{1.2} = (\mathbf{x}_1'\mathbf{M}_2\mathbf{x}_1)^{-1}\mathbf{x}_1'\mathbf{M}_2\mathbf{y}.$$

From our earlier results,

$$E[b_1] = \beta_1 + \beta_2\frac{\mathbf{x}_1'\mathbf{x}_2}{\mathbf{x}_1'\mathbf{x}_1}$$

and

$$\mathrm{Var}[b_1] = \frac{\sigma^2}{\mathbf{x}_1'\mathbf{x}_1},$$

while

$$E[b_{1.2}] = \beta_1$$

and

$$\mathrm{Var}[b_{1.2}] = \frac{\sigma^2}{\mathbf{x}_1'\mathbf{x}_1(1 - r_{12}^2)}.$$

Therefore, b_1 is biased but has a smaller variance. The estimators can be compared on the basis of their mean squared errors. Using the results of the previous section, we find that the short regression estimator is more precise if the population analog to the F statistic for testing $H_0: \beta_2 = 0$ is less than one. Since this is the square of the usual t ratio for this simple hypothesis, the basis for the mean-squared-error test of (8–27) is

$$\tau^2 = \frac{\beta_2^2}{\sigma^2/(S_{22}(1 - r_{12}^2))}. \tag{8–29}$$

The larger is β_2, the worse is the bias in b_1 and the less likely it is that λ will be less than $\frac{1}{2}$. Thus, b_1 will be a preferable estimator only if this bias is small, as measured by the earlier population t ratio. The test itself can be carried out by referring the square of the t ratio associated with b_2 to $F_*[1, n - K, \frac{1}{2}]$.

There are a few ways in which one might proceed at this point. If it is strongly believed that τ is close to zero, it makes sense to omit x_2 from the regression at the outset and use b_1. On the other hand, if one is convinced that x_2 is a significant influence in the regression, it makes little sense even to consider b_1; $b_{1.2}$ is the better estimator. Unfortunately, most of the time, we shall be in neither situation. A third possibility (probably the one used most often) is to use a *sequential estimator.* We first compute the long regression and then choose the estimator on the basis of the t test, where we use t, the sample analog to τ, in

$$b_1^* = \begin{array}{ll} b_1 & \text{if } t^2 < 1 \\ b_{1.2} & \text{if } t^2 \geq 1. \end{array} \tag{8–30}$$

This is a "pretest" estimator because it is based on the preliminary regression. It has been analyzed extensively, with some striking results.[31] Remember that b_1^* is a function not of

---

[31] Pretest estimators are examined at length in Judge and Bock (1978, 1983) and Feldstein (1973).

the true τ but of the sample statistic, t. Therefore, its mean and variance depend on the value of t that is "drawn" in the sample. In particular,

$$E[b_1^*] = E[b_{1.2}]\text{Prob}(t^2 \geq 1) + E[b_1]\text{Prob}(t^2 < 1).$$

(Of course, t^2 can be less than 1 even if τ^2 is greater than 1.) Since b_1^* is a weighted average of an unbiased estimator and a biased one, it must be biased. The larger is τ^2, the less likely it is that t^2 will be less than 1, so this bias is a decreasing function of τ^2. The variance of b_1^* behaves similarly. The important thing to note is that this variance will not equal either of the variances of the two competing estimators unless τ^2 is zero or infinity.[32]

8.5.3. Inequality Restrictions

In many instances, prior information about the regression parameters is in the form of inequality restrictions. For example:

1. The price elasticities in a demand equation must be negative.
2. The marginal propensity to consume is between zero and 1.
3. To rule out decreasing returns to scale, we would require that the sum of the output elasticities in a production function be greater than or equal to 1.

Estimation subject to inequality restrictions can be formulated as a quadratic programming problem in the framework of the Kuhn–Tucker problem:

$$\text{Minimize}_{\hat{\beta}} \tilde{L} = (\mathbf{y} - \mathbf{X}\hat{\boldsymbol{\beta}})'(\mathbf{y} - \mathbf{X}\hat{\boldsymbol{\beta}}) + \boldsymbol{\lambda}'(\mathbf{R}\hat{\boldsymbol{\beta}} - \mathbf{q}).$$

The necessary conditions, in which we let $\tilde{\mathbf{b}}$ be the solution, are

$$\frac{\partial \tilde{L}}{\partial \tilde{\mathbf{b}}} = 2\mathbf{X}'\mathbf{X}\tilde{\mathbf{b}} - 2\tilde{\mathbf{b}}'\mathbf{X}'\mathbf{y} + \mathbf{R}'\boldsymbol{\lambda} = 0$$

$$\frac{\partial \tilde{L}}{\partial \boldsymbol{\lambda}} = \mathbf{R}\tilde{\mathbf{b}} - \mathbf{q} \geq 0$$

$$\boldsymbol{\lambda}'(\mathbf{R}\tilde{\mathbf{b}} - \mathbf{q}) = 0$$

$$\boldsymbol{\lambda} \leq 0.$$

As we have seen before, if $\mathbf{Rb} - \mathbf{q} = 0$, where $\mathbf{b} = (\mathbf{X}'\mathbf{X})^{-1}\mathbf{X}'\mathbf{y}$, then $\boldsymbol{\lambda}$ will equal zero, and this will be a solution. If not, some other solution will be required. Standard algorithms exist for solving the problem, and the computational aspects, while not simple, are at least straightforward.[33] The very difficult matter concerns the sampling properties of the estimator.[34] The following generalities have been obtained:

1. $\tilde{\mathbf{b}}$ is biased. It is, as always, a mix of an unbiased and a biased estimator.
2. $\text{Var}[\tilde{\mathbf{b}}]$ is always less than that of $\mathbf{b}$. This follows the arguments we have seen before; it is the value of the prior information.
3. $\text{MSE}[\tilde{\mathbf{b}} \mid \boldsymbol{\beta}]$ can be less than that of $\mathbf{b}$ but will sometimes be larger.

---

[32] It is a weighted average of the estimators plus a term that arises out of the noncentral distribution. See Bock et al. (1972).

[33] See, for example, Fletcher (1980) and Bazaraa and Shetty (1979).

[34] An illustrative case in a relatively simple setting is analyzed by Thomson (1982). A recent study that employs some of these results is Goldberger (1986).

There will be some cases in which the solution can be written

$$\tilde{\mathbf{b}} = \mathbf{b} \qquad \text{if } \mathbf{Rb} - \mathbf{q} \geq \mathbf{0},$$

$$\tilde{\mathbf{b}} = \mathbf{b}_* \qquad \text{if } \mathbf{Rb} - \mathbf{q} < \mathbf{0},$$

where $\mathbf{b}_*$ is the equality restricted least squares estimator in (8–25). This will always be the case if there is only one constraint, which will be true in most instances analyzed in practice.[35] The estimator $\mathbf{b}$ fits directly into the pretest estimators we have discussed. The sampling distribution of the inequality restricted estimator is quite complicated, but it has been derived from some cases.[36]

EXAMPLE 8.7 Restricting a Coefficient to Be Positive

Suppose that the regression model is of the form[37]

$$y = \beta_1 + \beta_2 x + \varepsilon,$$

and the constraint is

$$\beta_2 \geq 0.$$

The inequality-constrained least squares estimator is

$$\tilde{b}_2 = 0 \qquad \text{if } b_2 < 0,$$

$$\tilde{b}_2 = b_2 \qquad \text{if } b_2 \geq 0.$$

Without restrictions, b_2 has the familiar normal distribution with mean β_2 and variance σ^2/S_{xx}, which, for convenience, we denote θ^2. Then $\tilde{b}_2$ is biased unless β_2 equals zero:

$$E[\tilde{b}_2] = 0 \ \text{Prob}(b_2 < 0) + \beta_2 \ \text{Prob}(b_2 \geq 0),$$

which is between β_2 and 0. Let τ equal β_2/θ. This is the population t ratio that appeared earlier in (8–29), although here there is no other regressor. Since b_2 is normally distributed, we can use the standard normal distribution to obtain $\text{Prob}(b_2 \geq 0) = \Phi(-\tau)$. Let the density of the standard normal distribution evaluated at $-\tau$ be $\phi(-\tau)$, and denote $\phi(-\tau)/\Phi(-\tau) = \lambda(\tau)$. Thomson (1982) gives the following:[38]

$$\text{Bias}[\tilde{b}_2] = \beta_2 \Phi(-\tau)[\lambda(\tau) - \tau]$$

$$\text{MSE}[\tilde{b}_2] = \theta^2 + \theta^2 \Phi(-\tau)[\tau - 1 + \tau\lambda(\tau)].$$

The bias, as we have seen, is toward zero. The mean-squared error may be greater than or less than θ^2. Note the presence of $\tau - 1$ in the mean-squared error. If τ is greater than 1, the mean-squared error of b_2 is greater than that of $b_{2.1}$, which is what we found earlier in a different problem. If $\tau < 1$, this mixed estimator may have a smaller mean-squared error than that of least squares.

---

[35] If there are several constraints, it is still possible that the solution will appear as given earlier. However, it is also possible that only some of the constraints will be violated by the least squares estimator. Imposing only these particular constraints may induce failure of the other constraints, which previously were not violated. This complicates the analysis substantially. See Fomby et al. (1984, pp. 104–105) for a discussion.

[36] See Judge and Bock (1978) and Judge and Yancey (1981).

[37] Adding a set of additional regressors would complicate the algebra but would not materially change the solution we shall obtain.

[38] Ibid. We have simplified Thomson's results a bit.

8.6. Bayesian Estimation

The results of Section 8.5 present a bit of a methodological dilemma. They would seem to straightjacket the researcher into a fixed and immutable specification of the model. But, of course, in any analysis, there is uncertainty as to the magnitudes and even on occasion the signs of coefficients. It is rare that the presentation of a set of empirical results has not been preceded by at least some exploratory analysis. Proponents of the Bayesian methodology argue that the process of estimation is not one of deducing the values of fixed parameters, but rather of continually updating and sharpening our subjective beliefs about the state of the world.[39] Assembled in the Bayesian methodology, these aspects of the theory come together in an appealing format.

The centerpiece of the Bayesian methodology is Bayes' theorem:

$$P(A|B) = \frac{P(B|A)P(A)}{P(B)}. \tag{8-31}$$

Paraphrased for our applications here, we should write this as

$$P(\text{parameters}|\text{data}) = \frac{P(\text{data}|\text{parameters})P(\text{parameters})}{P(\text{data})}. \tag{8-32}$$

In this setting, the data are viewed as constants whose distribution does not involve the parameters of interest. For the purpose of the study, we treat the data as only a fixed set of additional information to be used in updating our beliefs about the parameters. Thus, we write

$$P(\text{parameters}|\text{data}) \propto P(\text{data}|\text{parameters})P(\text{parameters}).$$

The symbol $\propto$ means "is proportional to." In the preceding, we have dropped the density of the data, so what remains is not a proper density until it is scaled by what will be an inessential proportionality constant. The first term on the right is the joint distribution of the observed random variables, $\mathbf{y}$, given the parameters. As we shall analyze it here, this is the normal distribution we have used in all of our previous analysis. The second term is the "prior" beliefs of the analyst. The left-hand side is the "posterior" density of the parameters, given the current body of data, or our revised beliefs about the distribution of the parameters. The posterior is a mixture of the prior information and the "current information," that is, the data. Once obtained, this posterior density is available to be the prior density function when the next body of data or other usable information becomes available. The principle involved, which appears nowhere in the classical analysis, is one of continual accretion of knowledge about the parameters.

8.6.1. Bayesian Analysis of the Classical Regression Model

The complexity of the algebra involved in Bayesian analysis is extremely burdensome. However, for the classical regression model, many fairly straightforward results have been obtained. To provide some of the flavor of the techniques, we present the full derivation only for the simplest case. In the interest of brevity, and to avoid the burden of

---

[39] Indeed, they take as evidence of this the fact the researchers do such exploratory analysis. Consider, for example, "Personally, I find the Bayesian philosophy compelling [see Poirier (1988)]. While I believe that *everyone is a Bayesian deep down inside,* I realize that relatively few researchers are 'out-of-the-closet'" [Poirier (1991, p. 1), emphasis added].

excessive algebra, we refer the reader to one of the several sources that present the full derivation of the more complex cases.[40]

The classical normal regression model we have analyzed thus far is constructed around the conditional distribution

$$f(\mathbf{y} \mid \boldsymbol{\beta}, \sigma, \mathbf{X}) = N[\mathbf{X}\boldsymbol{\beta}, \sigma^2 \mathbf{I}],$$
$$= (2\pi\sigma^2)^{-n/2} e^{-(1/(2\sigma^2))(\mathbf{y} - \mathbf{X}\boldsymbol{\beta})'(\mathbf{y} - \mathbf{X}\boldsymbol{\beta})}. \tag{8-33}$$

The departure point for the Bayesian analysis of this model is the specification of a prior distribution. This reflects the analyst's prior beliefs about the parameters of the model. One of two approaches is taken. If no prior information is known about the parameters, we can specify a "noninformative" prior that reflects that fact. We do this by specifying a flat prior for the parameter in question:[41]

$$f(\text{parameter}) \propto \text{constant}.$$

The second possibility, an "informative prior," is treated in the next section.

To begin, we analyze the case in which σ is assumed to be known. This is obviously unrealistic, and we do so only to establish a point of departure. Using (8–32), we construct

$$f(\boldsymbol{\beta} \mid \mathbf{y}, \mathbf{X}, \sigma) = \frac{f(\mathbf{y} \mid \boldsymbol{\beta}, \sigma, \mathbf{X}) f(\boldsymbol{\beta} \mid \sigma, \mathbf{X})}{f(\mathbf{y})}$$

$$\propto f(\mathbf{y} \mid \boldsymbol{\beta}, \sigma, \mathbf{X}) f(\boldsymbol{\beta}),$$

assuming that the distribution of $\boldsymbol{\beta}$ does not depend on σ or $\mathbf{X}$. Since $f(\boldsymbol{\beta}) \propto$ a constant, this is the density in (8–33). By substituting

$$\mathbf{y} - \mathbf{X}\boldsymbol{\beta} = \mathbf{y} - \mathbf{X}\mathbf{b} - \mathbf{X}(\boldsymbol{\beta} - \mathbf{b}),$$

where $\mathbf{b} = (\mathbf{X}'\mathbf{X})^{-1}\mathbf{X}'\mathbf{y}$, we may write the exponent in (8–33) as

$$\left(\frac{-1}{2\sigma^2}\right)(\mathbf{y} - \mathbf{X}\mathbf{b})'(\mathbf{y} - \mathbf{X}\mathbf{b}) - \left(\frac{1}{2\sigma^2}\right)(\boldsymbol{\beta} - \mathbf{b})'\mathbf{X}'\mathbf{X}(\boldsymbol{\beta} - \mathbf{b})$$

$$= -\left(\frac{1}{2}\right)\left(\frac{vs^2}{\sigma^2}\right) - \left(\frac{1}{2}\right)(\boldsymbol{\beta} - \mathbf{b})'[\sigma^2(\mathbf{X}'\mathbf{X})^{-1}]^{-1}(\boldsymbol{\beta} - \mathbf{b}),$$

where v is the degrees of freedom, $n - K$, and $s^2 = \mathbf{e}'\mathbf{e}/v$. We may also write

$$(\sigma^2)^{-n/2} = \sigma^{-v}(\sigma^2)^{-K/2}$$

and

$$(2\pi)^{-n/2} = (2\pi)^{-v/2}(2\pi)^{-K/2}.$$

Using these three results, we can factor the density in (8–33) into two parts:

$$f(\boldsymbol{\beta} \mid \mathbf{y}, \mathbf{X}, \sigma) \quad \propto$$
$$h(\sigma) \times (2\pi\sigma^2)^{-K/2} e^{(-1/2)(\boldsymbol{\beta} - \mathbf{b})'[\sigma^2(\mathbf{X}'\mathbf{X})^{-1}]^{-1}(\boldsymbol{\beta} - \mathbf{b})}, \tag{8-34}$$

---

[40] These include Judge et al. (1982, 1985), Maddala (1977), and the canonical reference for econometricians, Zellner (1971).

[41] The fact that this "improper" density does not integrate to one is only a minor difficulty. Any constant of integration would ultimately drop out of the final result. See Zellner (1971, pp. 41–53) for a discussion of noninformative priors.

where

$$h(\sigma) = \sigma^{-\nu}(2\pi)^{-\nu/2}e^{-(1/2)(\nu s^2/\sigma^2)}. \tag{8-35}$$

For the present, we treat $h(\sigma)$ simply as a constant that involves σ, not as a probability density; (8–34) is *conditional* on σ. Since σ^2 and $\mathbf{X'X}$ are being treated as known constants, we may multiply the latter part of (8–34) by $|\mathbf{X'X}|^{-1/2}$, and since $h(\sigma)$ does not involve $\boldsymbol{\beta}$, drop it. (The density $f(\boldsymbol{\beta}|\mathbf{y}, \mathbf{X}, \sigma)$ is only *proportional* to the result we obtain here.) Moving σ^2 inside the K-order determinant, we obtain

$$f(\boldsymbol{\beta}|\mathbf{y}, \mathbf{X}, \sigma) \quad \propto$$
$$(2\pi)^{-K/2}|\sigma^2(\mathbf{X'X})^{-1}|^{-1/2}e^{(-1/2)(\boldsymbol{\beta}-\mathbf{b})'[\sigma^2(\mathbf{X'X})^{-1}]^{-1}(\boldsymbol{\beta}-\mathbf{b})}. \tag{8-36}$$

This is the density of the multivariate normal distribution with mean $\mathbf{b}$ and variance matrix $\sigma^2(\mathbf{X'X})^{-1}$.

This is a familiar result, but it is interpreted differently in this setting. First, we have combined our prior information about $\boldsymbol{\beta}$ (in this case, no information) and the sample information to obtain a posterior distribution. Thus, on the basis of the sample data in hand, we obtain a distribution for $\boldsymbol{\beta}$ with mean $\mathbf{b}$ and variance matrix $\sigma^2(\mathbf{X'X})^{-1}$. There are two things to note. First, the result is dominated by the sample information, as it should be if there is no prior information. Second, in the absence of any prior information, the mean of the posterior distribution, which is our Bayesian point estimate, is the sampling theory estimator.

In order to generalize the preceding to an unknown σ, we specify a noninformative prior distribution for $\ln \sigma$ over the entire real line.[42] By the change of variable formula, if $f(\ln \sigma)$ is constant, $f(\sigma)$ is proportional to $1/\sigma$. Assuming that $\boldsymbol{\beta}$ and σ are independent, this gives the noninformative joint prior distribution:

$$f(\boldsymbol{\beta}, \sigma) \quad \propto \quad \frac{1}{\sigma}.$$

We can obtain the joint posterior distribution for $\boldsymbol{\beta}$ and σ by using

$$f(\boldsymbol{\beta}, \sigma|\mathbf{y}, \mathbf{X}) = f(\boldsymbol{\beta}|\mathbf{y}, \mathbf{X}, \sigma)f(\sigma|\mathbf{y}, \mathbf{X})$$
$$= f(\boldsymbol{\beta}|\mathbf{y}, \mathbf{X}, \sigma)f(\sigma) \tag{8-37}$$
$$\propto f(\boldsymbol{\beta}|\mathbf{y}, \mathbf{X}, \sigma) \times \frac{1}{\sigma}.$$

Multiplying (8–36) by $1/\sigma$, therefore, gives the joint posterior for $\boldsymbol{\beta}$ and σ, given $\mathbf{y}$ and $\mathbf{X}$. In order to obtain the marginal posterior distribution for $\boldsymbol{\beta}$, it is now necessary to integrate σ out of the joint distribution (and vice versa to obtain the marginal distribution for σ.) Doing so for $\boldsymbol{\beta}$ produces what is known as a **multivariate t distribution.**[43] This is a generalization of the familiar univariate distribution we have used at various points. This distribution has a degrees of freedom parameter, $\nu = n - K$, mean $\mathbf{b}$, and variance matrix $(\nu/(\nu - 2))[s^2(\mathbf{X'X})^{-1}]$. Each element of the K-element vector $\boldsymbol{\beta}$ has a marginal distribution that is the univariate t distribution with degrees of freedom $n - K$, mean b_k, and variance equal to the kth diagonal element of the variance matrix given earlier. Once again, this is the same as our sampling theory result. The difference is a matter of interpretation. In the current context, the estimated distribution is for $\boldsymbol{\beta}$ and is centered at $\mathbf{b}$.

---

[42] See Zellner (1971) for justification of this prior distribution.

[43] See, for example, Judge et al. (1985) for details.

The counterpart to a confidence interval in this setting is an interval of the posterior distribution that contains a specified probability. Clearly, it is desirable to have this interval be as narrow as possible. For a unimodal density, this corresponds to an interval within which the density function is higher than any points outside it, which justifies the term **highest posterior density (HPD) interval.** For the case we have analyzed, which involves a symmetric distribution, we would form the HPD interval for β around the least squares estimate, **b,** with terminal values taken from the standard t tables.

One might ask at this point, why bother? The Bayesian point estimates are identical to the sampling theory estimates, and the HPD interval for a parameter is exactly the same as the usual confidence interval. All that has changed is our interpretation of the results. This is, however, exactly the way it should be. Remember that we entered this analysis with noninformative priors for β and σ. Therefore, the only information brought to bear on estimation is the sample data, and it would be peculiar if anything other than the sampling theory estimates emerged at the end. The results do change when our prior brings data out of the sample information into the estimates.

8.6.2. Estimation with an Informative Prior Density

Once we leave the simple case of noninformative priors, matters become quite complicated, both at a practical level and, methodologically, in terms of just where the prior comes from. The integration of σ out of the joint posterior in (8–36) is complicated by itself. It is made much more so if the prior distribution of β is at all involved. Partly to offset these difficulties, we often use what is called a **conjugate prior,** which is one that has the same form as the conditional density and is, therefore, amenable to the integration needed to obtain the marginal distributions.[44]

Suppose that we assume that the prior beliefs about β may be summarized in a K-variate normal distribution with mean β^0 and variance matrix Σ^0. Once again, it is illuminating to begin with the case in which σ is assumed to be known. Proceeding in exactly the same fashion as before, we would obtain the following result: The posterior density of β conditioned on σ and the data will be normal with

$$E[\beta \,|\, \mathbf{y},\, \mathbf{X},\, \sigma] = \{\Sigma^{0-1} + [\sigma^2(\mathbf{X'X})^{-1}]^{-1}\}^{-1}\{\Sigma^{0-1}\beta^0 + [\sigma^2(\mathbf{X'X})^{-1}]^{-1}\mathbf{b}\}$$
$$= \mathbf{F}\beta^0 + (\mathbf{I} - \mathbf{F})\mathbf{b}, \tag{8–38}$$

where

$$\mathbf{F} = \{\Sigma^{0-1} + [\sigma^2(\mathbf{X'X})^{-1}]^{-1}\}^{-1}\Sigma^{0-1}$$
$$= \{\mathrm{Var}[\beta^0]^{-1} + \mathrm{Var}[\mathbf{b}\,|\,\mathbf{y},\,\mathbf{X},\,\sigma]^{-1}\}^{-1}\,\mathrm{Var}[\beta^0]^{-1}.$$

This is a weighted average of the prior and the least squares coefficients, where the weights are the inverses of the prior and the conditional covariance matrices. The smaller the variance of the estimator, the larger its weight, which makes sense. Also, still taking σ as known, we can write the variance of the posterior normal distribution as

$$\mathrm{Var}[\beta \,|\, \mathbf{y},\, \mathbf{X},\, \sigma] = \{\Sigma^{0-1} + [\sigma^2(\mathbf{X'X})^{-1}]^{-1}\}^{-1}. \tag{8–39}$$

(Notice that the posterior variance combines the prior and conditional variances on the basis of their inverses.) We may interpret the noninformative prior as having infinite elements in Σ^0, which would reduce this to the earlier case.

---

[44] The idea that the prior can be specified arbitrarily in whatever form is mathematically convenient is very troubling in view of the fact that it is supposed to represent the accumulated prior belief about the parameter. On the other hand, it could be argued that the conjugate prior is the posterior of a previous analysis, which could justify its form.

Once again, it is necessary to account for the unknown σ. If our prior over σ is to be informative as well, the resulting distribution will be extremely cumbersome. A conjugate prior for $\boldsymbol{\beta}$ and σ that has been used is

$$f(\boldsymbol{\beta}, \sigma) = f(\boldsymbol{\beta} \mid \sigma)f(\sigma), \tag{8-40}$$

where $f(\boldsymbol{\beta} \mid \sigma)$ is normal, with mean $\boldsymbol{\beta}^0$ and variance $\sigma^2 \mathbf{A}^{-1}$, and $f(\sigma)$ is of the form $h(\sigma)$ in (8–35).[45] This distribution is an *inverted gamma* distribution. It implies that $1/\sigma$ has a gamma distribution.[46] The product in (8–40) produces what is called a *normal gamma prior*, which is the natural conjugate prior for this form of the model. By integrating out σ, we would obtain the prior marginal for $\boldsymbol{\beta}$ alone, which would be a multivariate t distribution. Combining (8–40) with (8–33) produces the joint posterior distribution for $\boldsymbol{\beta}$ and σ. Finally, the marginal posterior distribution for $\boldsymbol{\beta}$ is obtained by integrating out σ. It has been shown that this posterior distribution is multivariate t with

$$E[\boldsymbol{\beta} \mid \mathbf{y}, \mathbf{X}] = \{\boldsymbol{\Sigma}^{0-1} + [\bar{s}^2(\mathbf{X}'\mathbf{X})^{-1}]^{-1}\}^{-1}\{\boldsymbol{\Sigma}^{0-1}\boldsymbol{\beta}^0 + [\bar{s}^2(\mathbf{X}'\mathbf{X})^{-1}]^{-1}\mathbf{b}\} \tag{8-41}$$

and

$$\text{Var}[\boldsymbol{\beta} \mid \mathbf{y}, \mathbf{X}] = \left(\frac{m}{(m-2)}\right)\{\boldsymbol{\Sigma}^{0-1} + [\bar{s}^2(\mathbf{X}'\mathbf{X})^{-1}]^{-1}\}^{-1}, \tag{8-42}$$

where m is a degrees of freedom parameter

$$m = n - K + d \tag{8-43}$$

and $\bar{s}^2$ is the Bayesian estimate of σ^2, the posterior mean of the distribution of σ.[47] The prior degrees of freedom, d, is a parameter of the prior distribution for σ that would have been determined at the outset. (See the following example.) Once again, it is clear that as the amount of data increases, the posterior density, and the estimates thereof, converge to the sampling theory results.

EXAMPLE 8.8 Bayesian Estimates of a Consumption Function _____

In Example 5.1, an estimate of the marginal propensity to consume is obtained using 10 observations from 1970 to 1979, with the following results:

Estimated MPC:	0.9793
Variance of b:	$0.0316^2 = 0.0009989$
Degrees of freedom:	$10 - 2 = 8$
Estimated σ:	8.192

A classical 95 percent confidence interval for β based on these estimates is $\langle 0.90641, 1.1251 \rangle$, as given earlier. Based on noninformative priors for β and σ, we would estimate the posterior density for β to be univariate t with eight degrees of freedom, with mean 0.9793 and variance $(8/6)0.0009989 = 0.0013319$. An HPD interval for β would coincide with the confidence interval.

---

[45] A constant of integration is needed to make it a proper prior, and instead of s^2, we would have a prior estimate of σ^2, that is, $\bar{\sigma}^2$.

[46] See Maddala (1977, pp. 406–412) for details.

[47] This is a bit more complicated to compute. See Judge et al. (1985) for details.

An alternative estimate of β is obtained in Example 8.1, based on 11 observations from 1940 to 1950, with the following results:

Estimated MPC:	0.9596
Variance of b:	$0.0895^2 = 0.0081025$
Degrees of freedom:	$11 - 3 = 8$
Estimated σ:	9.0088

We take the earlier estimate and its estimated distribution as our prior for β and obtain a posterior density for β based on an informative prior instead. We assume for this exercise that σ may be taken as known at the sample value of 8.192. Then

$$\bar{b} = \left\{ \frac{1}{0.0081025} + \frac{1}{0.0009989} \right\}^{-1} \left\{ \frac{0.9596}{0.0081025} + \frac{0.9793}{0.0009989} \right\}.$$

The weights in the average are 0.1109 and 0.8891, which gives an estimated posterior mean of 0.9771. The posterior variance is the inverse in brackets, which is 0.0008881. Since σ is assumed to be known, the posterior distribution is normal with this mean and variance. An HPD interval can be formed in the familiar fashion. Using the posterior standard deviation of 0.0298, we find that a 95 percent HPD interval for β is 0.9771 ± 1.96(0.0298) = $\langle 0.9187, 1.0355 \rangle$. Note that this is narrower than the earlier interval; this is the value of the prior information.

EXERCISES

1. Using the data in Table 7.1 (Section 7.2.5) to estimate the CES production function in Example 8.4, we obtain the following ordinary least squares regression results:[48]

$$\ln Y = 1.4677 - 0.1115 \ln K + 1.1002 \ln L + 0.1522 \ln^2\!\left(\frac{K}{L}\right),$$

$$R^2 = 0.94677, \qquad \mathbf{e}'\mathbf{e} = 0.8018, \qquad n = 27,$$

$$\text{Est. Var } [\mathbf{b}] = \begin{matrix} 0.1665 & & & \\ -0.1009 & 0.1732 & & \\ 0.08385 & -0.1789 & 0.1885 & \\ 0.03164 & -0.05192 & 0.05296 & 0.1622. \end{matrix}$$

(a) Compute the implied estimates of the underlying parameters.
(b) Estimate the standard error of the estimate of ρ.
(c) Test the hypothesis that the coefficients on $\ln K$ and $\ln L$ sum to 1.
(d) Test the hypothesis that ρ is zero. [**Hint:** Look closely at (8–11).]

2. Use (8–16) to derive the bias that results when the constant term in a regression is inappropriately omitted.

---

[48] Note that the functional form would be the same as that for the translog model, with constant returns to scale imposed if the second and third coefficients were made to sum to 1. (See Exercise 3 in Chapter 7.) This function, proposed by Kmenta (1967), is a precursor to the translog models that appeared in great number a few years later. The original source of the CES production function is Arrow et al. (1961). The paper is also reprinted in Zellner (1968).

3. In Solow's classic (1957) study of technical change in the U.S. economy, he suggests the aggregate production function

$$q(t) = A(t)f[k(t)],$$

where $q(t)$ is aggregate output per worker-hour, $k(t)$ is the aggregate capital/labor ratio, and $A(t)$ is the technology index. Solow considered four static models:

$$\frac{q}{A} = \alpha + \beta \ln k,$$

$$\frac{q}{A} = \alpha - \frac{\beta}{k},$$

$$\ln\left(\frac{q}{A}\right) = \alpha + \beta \ln k,$$

$$\ln\left(\frac{q}{A}\right) = \alpha - \frac{\beta}{k}.$$

[He also estimated a dynamic model, $q(t)/A(t) - q(t-1)/A(t-1) = \alpha + \beta k$.]
(a) Sketch the four functions.
(b) Solow's data for the years 1909–1949 are listed here:

Year	q	k	A	Year	q	k	A	Year	q	k	A
1909	0.623	2.06	1.000	1923	0.809	2.61	1.196	1937	0.971	2.71	1.415
1910	0.616	2.10	0.983	1924	0.836	2.74	1.215	1938	1.000	2.78	1.445
1911	0.647	2.17	1.021	1925	0.872	2.81	1.254	1939	1.034	2.66	1.514
1912	0.652	2.21	1.023	1926	0.869	2.87	1.241	1940	1.082	2.63	1.590
1913	0.680	2.23	1.064	1927	0.871	2.93	1.235	1941	1.122	2.58	1.660
1914	0.682	2.20	1.071	1928	0.874	3.02	1.226	1942	1.136	2.64	1.665
1915	0.669	2.26	1.041	1929	0.895	3.06	1.251	1943	1.180	2.62	1.692
1916	0.700	2.34	1.076	1930	0.880	3.30	1.197	1944	1.265	2.63	1.812
1917	0.679	2.21	1.065	1931	0.904	3.33	1.226	1945	1.296	2.66	1.850
1918	0.729	2.22	1.142	1932	0.879	3.28	1.198	1946	1.215	2.50	1.769
1919	0.767	2.47	1.157	1933	0.869	3.10	1.211	1947	1.194	2.50	1.739
1920	0.721	2.58	1.069	1934	0.921	3.00	1.298	1948	1.221	2.55	1.767
1921	0.770	2.55	1.146	1935	0.943	2.87	1.349	1949	1.275	2.70	1.809
1922	0.788	2.49	1.183	1936	0.982	2.72	1.429				

(Op. cit., p. 314. Several variables are omitted.) Use these data to estimate the α and β of the four functions listed earlier. (Note that your results will not quite match Solow's. See Exercise 4 for resolution of the discrepancy.) Sketch the functions, using your particular estimates of the parameters.

4. In the aforementioned study, Solow states:

A scatter of q/A against k is shown in Chart 4. Considering the amount of a priori doctoring which the raw figures have undergone, the fit is remarkably tight. Except, that is, for the layer of points which are obviously too high. These maverick observations relate to the seven last years of the period, 1943–1949. From the way they lie almost exactly parallel to the main scatter, one is tempted to conclude that in 1943 the aggregate production function simply shifted.

(a) Draw a scatter diagram of q/A against k. [Or, obtain Solow's original study and examine his. An alternative source of the original paper is the volume edited by Zellner (1968).]

(b) Estimate the four models you estimated in the previous exercise, including a dummy variable for the years 1943–1949. How do your results change? (Note that these results match those reported by Solow, though he did not report the coefficient on the dummy variable.)

(c) Solow went on to surmise that, in fact, the data were fundamentally different in the years before 1943 than during and after. If so, one would guess that the regression should be different as well (though whether the change is merely in the data or in the underlying production function is not settled). Use a Chow test to examine the difference in the two subperiods, using your four functional forms. Note that with the dummy variable, you can do the test by introducing an interaction term between the dummy and whichever function of k appears in the regression. Use an F test to test the hypothesis.

5. Consider the two alternative regressions

$$(1) \quad y = \alpha_1 D_1 + \alpha_2 D_2 + \alpha_3 D_3 + \alpha_4 D_4 + \varepsilon,$$
$$(2) \quad y = \alpha + \alpha_2 D_2 + \alpha_3 D_3 + \alpha_4 D_4 + \varepsilon.$$

The variables are quarterly dummy variables [see (8–1)]. There are equal numbers of observations in each quarter. By computing $(\mathbf{X}'\mathbf{X})^{-1}\mathbf{X}'\mathbf{y}$ for the two models, obtain the precise formulas for the least squares coefficients in the two cases. Prove that if there were a term βx in the two equations, the least squares estimates of β would be identical.

6. What restriction on the parameters of (8–1) leads to the model

$$C_t = \beta_1 + \beta_2 X_t + \delta q_t + \varepsilon_t$$

where $q_t = 1, 2, 3$ in the second, third, and fourth quarters, respectively? How would you test the restriction?

7. In a widely cited study of the American automobile market, Griliches (1961b) reports the following regression results:

$\ln$ price $= 6.4 + 0.056H + 0.249W + 0.023L + 0.010V$

$\qquad\qquad + 0.023T + 0.090A + 0.088P + 0.109B + 0.157C$

$\qquad\qquad - 0.044D_1 - 0.015D_2 + 0.019D_3 + 0.44D_4 + 0.044D_5 + 0.023D_6,$

where $\qquad$ H = advertised horsepower, in hundreds

$\qquad\qquad\quad$ W = shipping weight, in thousands of pounds

$\qquad\qquad\quad$ L = overall length, in tens of inches

$\qquad\qquad\quad$ V = 1 if the car has a V8 engine, 0 otherwise

$\qquad\qquad\quad$ T = 1 if the car is a hard top, 0 if a convertible

$\qquad\qquad\quad$ A = 1 if it has an automatic transmission, 0 if not

$\qquad\qquad\quad$ P = 1 if power steering is standard, 0 if not

$\qquad\qquad\quad$ B = 1 if power brakes are standard, 0 if not

$\qquad\qquad\quad$ C = 1 if the car is a compact, 0 if not

$D_1 = 1$ for 1955 model car, 0 otherwise

$D_2 = 1$ for 1956 model car, 0 otherwise

$D_3 = 1$ for 1957 model car, 0 otherwise

$D_4 = 1$ for 1958 model car, 0 otherwise

$D_5 = 1$ for 1959 model car, 0 otherwise

$D_6 = 1$ for 1960 model car, 0 otherwise
1954 is the base year.

(The value of 6.4 for the constant term is assumed here. The author did not report the constant terms in his results.)

The regression is estimated using a large sample of prices of cars for the years 1954–1960. Since the dependent variable is in logarithms and the coefficients are close to zero, they may be treated as percentage changes. For example, the model predicts that everything else held constant, an increase of 100 horsepower increased the cost of a car by 5.6 percent, while from 1954 to 1956, the price of a particular car fell by 1.5 percent.

(a) As a benchmark, suppose that an average car in 1954 had 141 horsepower, weighed 3452 pounds, and was 205 inches long (from Griliches, Table 1). Suppose, as well, that in 1954, 25 percent of the cars had V8's, 75 percent were hard tops, 20 percent had automatic transmission, 10 percent had power steering, 5 percent had power brakes, and 10 percent of the cars sold could be called compact. (All of these data are hypothetical; Griliches gives no figures for them.) What does the model predict for the median price of a car? Griliches reports a *geometric* mean of all prices for 1954 of $2360.

(b) Everything else held constant, how much more would it cost to buy a car with a V8 and power steering in 1955 than without these two features in 1954?

(c) Everything else held constant, how much did the price of a car rise from 1956 to 1957? From 1956 to 1959?

(d) Suppose that putting a hard top on a car instead of manufacturing a convertible always added exactly 100 pounds to the weight of the car. How would this affect the interpretation of the coefficients on W and T in the regression?

(e) The R^2 in the previous regression was 0.922, using 570 observations. If the R^2 in the regression without $D_1, \ldots$ were 0.919, would the results support the hypothesis that variation in the mix of options and other features was entirely responsible for the variation in car prices in the 7-year period?

(f) Suppose that the preceding data had also been used to compute seven separate regressions, one for each year, with the following results:

	1954	1955	1956	1957	1958	1959	1960	All
Observations	65	55	87	95	103	87	78	570
$e'e$	104	88	206	144	199	308	211	1425

Test the hypothesis that the same coefficients apply in each year. (Note that the model with the pooled data allows a separate constant for each year. Note as well that you may need an approximate value for the F distribution with large degrees of freedom.)

8. Suppose that estimation of the model in (8–6) produced estimates of 0.34 for β and 0.1 for λ. The means of y and x are one and two respectively. What is the estimate of the elasticity, $(x/y)\partial E[y]/\partial x$? (For applications of the Box–Cox regression, see Section 11.4.)

9. Let $\mathbf{b}_* = [\mathbf{X}'\mathbf{X} + k\mathbf{I}]^{-1}\mathbf{X}'\mathbf{y}$. Prove that this is a biased estimator of $\boldsymbol{\beta}$ in the classical regression model. What is its mean squared error matrix? (This is a *ridge regression* estimator.)

10. Given the results in part (e) of Exercise 7, would the estimates of the other parameters in the model be sharpened if the six yearly dummy variables were dropped? Use the noncentral F test (see Example 8.6) to find out. Do this first assuming that there are 30 observations in total. Then use the chi-squared approximation to the distribution of JF.

11. *Reverse regression:* A common method of analyzing statistical data to detect discrimination in the workplace is to fit the following regression:

$$y = \alpha + \boldsymbol{\beta}'\mathbf{x} + \gamma d + \varepsilon, \tag{1}$$

where y is the wage rate and d is a dummy variable indicating either membership ($d = 1$) or nonmembership ($d = 0$) in the class toward which it is suggested the discrimination is directed. The regressors, $\mathbf{x}$, include factors specific to the particular type of job, as well as indicators of the qualifications of the individual. The hypothesis of interest is $H_0: \gamma < 0$ versus $H_1: \gamma = 0$. The regression seeks to answer the question "In a given job, are individuals in the class ($d = 1$) paid less than equally qualified individuals not in the class ($d = 0$)?" Consider, however, the alternative possibility. Do individuals in the class in the same job as others, and receiving the same wage, uniformly have higher qualifications? If so, this might also be viewed as a form of discrimination. To analyze this question, Conway and Roberts (1983) suggested the following procedure:
(a) Fit (1) by ordinary least squares. Denote the estimates a, $\mathbf{b}$, and c.
(b) Compute the set of *qualification indices,*

$$\mathbf{q} = a\mathbf{i} + \mathbf{Xb}. \tag{2}$$

(Note the omission of $c\mathbf{d}$ from the fitted value.)
(c) Regress $\mathbf{q}$ on a constant, $\mathbf{y}$, and $\mathbf{d}$. The equation is

$$\mathbf{q} = \alpha^*\mathbf{i} + \beta^*\mathbf{y} + \gamma^*\mathbf{d} + \boldsymbol{\varepsilon}^*. \tag{3}$$

The analysis suggests that if $\gamma < 0$, $\gamma^* > 0$.
(1) Prove that the theory notwithstanding, the least squares estimates, c and c^*, are related by

$$c^* = \frac{(\bar{y}_1 - \bar{y})(1 - R^2)}{(1 - P)(1 - r_{yd}^2)} - c, \tag{4}$$

where $\bar{y}_1 = $ mean of y for observations with $d = 1$

$\bar{y} = $ mean of y for all observations

$P = $ mean of d

$R^2 = $ coefficient of determination for (1)

$r_{yd}^2 = $ squared correlation between y and d.

[**Hint:** The model contains a constant term. Thus, to simplify the algebra, assume that all variables are measured as deviations from the overall sample means and use a partitioned regression to compute the coefficients in (3). Second, in (2), use the fact that, based on the least squares results,

$$\mathbf{y} = a\mathbf{i} + \mathbf{Xb} + c\mathbf{d} + \mathbf{e},$$

so

$$\mathbf{q} = \mathbf{y} - c\mathbf{d} - \mathbf{e}.$$

From here on, we drop the constant term.] Thus, in the regression in (**c**), you are regressing $[\mathbf{y} - c\mathbf{d} - \mathbf{e}]$ on $\mathbf{y}$ and $\mathbf{d}$. Remember, all variables are in deviation form.

(2) Will the sample evidence necessarily be consistent with the theory? (**Hint:** Suppose that $c = 0$?)

A symposium on the Conway and Roberts paper appeared in the *Journal of Business and Economic Statistics* in April 1984.

12. For the aforementioned study preceding Example 7.1, suppose that an earlier study had produced the following estimated production function:

$$\ln Q = 1.2 + 0.65 \ln L + 0.31 \ln K$$
$$\quad\quad\quad (0.09) \quad\quad\quad (0.16)$$

$$\text{Est. Cov}[b_k, b_l] = 0.1$$

Using these estimates and the estimates of Example 7.1, form the Bayesian estimate of the posterior joint distribution, assuming a normal distribution for the prior. Assume that σ^2 is known.

CHAPTER 9

Data Problems

9.1. Introduction

It is rare that the data one has in hand for estimating a regression model conform exactly to the theory underlying the model. Any number of problems will arise, even in the most carefully designed survey. The most prevalent of these are the following:

1. *Multicollinearity.* The measured variables are too highly intercorrelated to allow precise analysis of their individual effects.
2. *Missing data.* There are gaps in the data set.
3. *Grouped data.* The information contained in the original data has been masked by averaging or some other kind of data aggregation.
4. *Measurement error.* The measured data do not conform to the variables in the model, either because of poor measurement or because the variables in the model are inherently unmeasurable.

All of these factors cause problems in estimating and interpreting regression models. This chapter will survey some results in detecting and solving these problems.

9.2. Multicollinearity

In our analysis of the classical regression model, we have assumed that the matrix of independent variables, $\mathbf{X}$, has full rank, that is, there is no exact linear relationship among the independent variables. In order for $(\mathbf{X'X})^{-1}$ to exist, $\mathbf{X}$ must have full column rank. Consider the case of just two explanatory variables and a constant. For either slope coefficient,

$$\text{Var}[b_k] = \frac{\sigma^2}{(1 - r_{12}^2)\Sigma_i(x_{ik} - \bar{x}_k)^2} = \frac{\sigma^2}{(1 - r_{12}^2)S_{kk}}, \qquad k = 1, 2. \qquad (9\text{--}1)$$

If the two variables are perfectly correlated, the variance is infinite. The case of an exact linear relationship among the regressors is a serious failure of the assumptions of the model, not of the data. The more common case is one in which the variables are highly but not perfectly correlated. In this instance, the regression model retains all of its assumed properties, although potentially severe statistical problems arise. We consider the two cases in turn.

9.2.1. Perfect Collinearity

We first considered the possibility of perfect collinearity when we laid out the assumptions of the regression model. In a consumption function,

$$C = \beta_1 + \beta_2 \text{ nonlabor income} + \beta_3 \text{ salary} + \beta_4 \text{ income} + \varepsilon, \qquad (9\text{--}2)$$

it is not possible to separate individual effects of the components of income and total income. In particular, if we let N be nonlabor income, S be salary, and T be total income, then $T = N + S$ for every individual. According to the model,

$$E[C] = \beta_1 + \beta_2 N + \beta_3 S + \beta_4 T.$$

But if we let q be any nonzero value and let $\beta_2' = \beta_2 + q$, $\beta_3' = \beta_3 + q$, and $\beta_4' = \beta_4 - q$,

$$E[C] = \beta_1 + \beta_2' N + \beta_3' S + \beta_4' T$$

as well for a different set of parameters. Unlike the full rank case, this one allows the same value of $E[C]$ for many different values of the parameters.

It is worth emphasizing that this is a badly specified model, and its failure has nothing to do with the quality of the data involved. The parameters of this regression model are said to be **unidentified.** We shall return to this subject at several points later. In this example we see the hallmark of what is known as the **identification problem.** For this model, as it is specified, there are an infinite number of possible parameter vectors that are consistent with the same expected value. Thus, no matter how much data we are able to obtain, we cannot estimate the parameters. The full rank assumption can be viewed as an identification assumption; it means that for a given vector $\mathbf{x}$, there is only one set of parameters consistent with a given value of $E(y)$.[1]

9.2.2. Near Multicollinearity

In the short-rank case, the regressor matrix has K columns but only rank $L < K$. It follows from the result given earlier that only L functions of the parameters can be estimated. The significance of this is that in the K columns of $\mathbf{X}$, there are only L independent sources of variation. Hence, the data permit only L estimable functions of the parameters. It is much more common for the variables to be correlated, but not perfectly so. The case of near collinearity or high intercorrelation among the variables is, in contrast, a statistical problem. The difficulty in estimation is not one of identification but of precision. The higher the correlation between the regressors becomes, the less precise our estimates will be.

9.2.3. The Symptoms of Multicollinearity

When the regressors are highly correlated, we often observe the following problems:

1. Small changes in the data can produce wide swings in the parameter estimates.
2. Coefficients may have very high standard errors and low significance levels in spite of the fact that they are jointly highly significant and the R^2 in the regression is quite high.
3. Coefficients will have the wrong sign or an implausible magnitude.

---

[1] See Theil (1971) and Schmidt (1976, pp. 43–44) for further discussion.

EXAMPLE 9.1

The Longley data analyzed in Section 7.3 are notorious for severe multicollinearity. Look, for example, at the last year of the data set. The last observation does not appear to be unusual. However, the results listed in Table 9.1, in which the earlier regression is reestimated without the last year of the data, suggest how severe the multicollinearity problem is in these data. The change in the results that occurs when one year of the data is dropped is dramatic. The last coefficient rises by 600 percent and the third rises by 800 percent. One might reach very different conclusions, depending on when the data were drawn.

TABLE 9.1. Dependent Variable: Total Employment

	1947–1961	1947–1962
Constant	1,459,400	1,169,090
Year	−721.76	−576.464
GNP deflator	−181.12	−19.761
GNP	0.091068	0.064394
Armed forces	−0.074937	−0.010145

In the inverse matrix, $(\mathbf{X'X})^{-1}$, the kth diagonal element (where we let k equal one for convenience) is

$$(\mathbf{x}_1'\mathbf{M}_2\mathbf{x}_1)^{-1} = (\mathbf{x}_1'\mathbf{x}_1 - \mathbf{x}_1'\mathbf{X}_2(\mathbf{X}_2'\mathbf{X}_2)^{-1}\mathbf{X}_2'\mathbf{x}_1)^{-1}$$

$$= \left(\mathbf{x}_1'\mathbf{x}_1\left(1 - \frac{\mathbf{x}_1'\mathbf{X}_2(\mathbf{X}_2'\mathbf{X}_2)^{-1}\mathbf{X}_2'\mathbf{x}_1}{\mathbf{x}_1'\mathbf{x}_1}\right)\right)^{-1} \tag{9-3}$$

$$= \frac{1}{S_{11}(1 - R_{1.}^2)}.$$

$R_{1.}^2$ is the R^2 in the regression of $\mathbf{x}_1$ on the other independent variables in the regression. Therefore, in the multiple regression, the variance of b_1 is

$$\text{Var}[b_1] = \frac{\sigma^2}{(1 - R_{1.}^2)S_{11}}. \tag{9-4}$$

We can envision a case in which we add a variable to the regression that is highly correlated with $\mathbf{x}_1$. S_{11} will not change at all, while R_1^2 will rise and $\text{Var}[b_1]$ will rise correspondingly.

The role of these $R_{k.}^2$'s is considerable. The simple correlations among the variables may not give an adequate indication of the problem. For a particular variable, Leamer (1978, p. 179) suggests the following measure of the effect of multicollinearity:

$$c_2(b_k) = \left\{\frac{[\Sigma_i(x_{ik} - \bar{x}_k)^2]^{-1}}{[(\mathbf{X'X})_{kk}^{-1}]}\right\}^{1/2}. \tag{9-5}$$

This measure is the square root of the ratio of the true variances of b_k when estimated with and without the other variables. If $\mathbf{x}_k$ were uncorrelated with the other variables, $c_2(b_k)$ would be 1. Otherwise, $c_2(b_k)$ is equivalent to $(1 - R_{k.}^2)^{1/2}$, which again suggests the usefulness of the auxiliary coefficients of determination. For example, our results thus far suggest that the coefficient on "armed forces" is being adversely affected by multicollinearity. However, the three simple correlations of this variable with "Year," "GNP deflator,'' and ''GNP'' are 0.417, 0.465, and 0.446, which are not particularly high. But, the corresponding R^2 in the regression of ''armed forces'' on these three variables is only 0.3562, so, evidently, yet more analysis is called for.[2]

Our primary concern might be the imprecision of our estimates. One rule of thumb that has been suggested is that we should be concerned about multicollinearity if the overall R^2 in the regression is less than any of the individual R_i^2's we have been considering.[3] The *estimated* variance of the kth coefficient (assuming that the constant term is the first) is

$$\text{Est. Var}[b_k] = \frac{s^2}{(1 - R_k^2)S_{kk}} = \frac{(1 - R^2)S_{yy}}{(n - K)(1 - R_k^2)S_{kk}}, \qquad k = 2, \ldots, K. \quad (9\text{–}6)$$

This shows the interaction of the two coefficients of determination. For our sample data, the overall R^2 is 0.97352, while the four coefficients of determination for the regressions of each independent variable on the other regressors are 0.99303, 0.98679, 0.99245, and 0.35616. On the basis of this criterion, we conclude that multicollinearity in these data is, indeed, a problem. The auxiliary R^2s of 0.99 for the first three variables are extremely high. Of course, this rule is only suggestive. It gives no indication of how to proceed. The second most volatile of the coefficients was that on ''armed forces.'' But the R_k^2 for the ''armed forces'' variable is only 0.35616, so in spite of the obvious problem with this coefficient, the rule of thumb appears not to pick it up.

An alternative measure of multicollinearity has been suggested by Belsley et al. (1980). The **condition number** of a matrix is the square root of the ratio of the largest to the smallest characteristic root:

$$\gamma = \left(\frac{\lambda_{\max}}{\lambda_{\min}}\right)^{1/2}. \qquad (9\text{–}7)$$

Belsley et al. suggest computing this ratio for the moment matrix, $\mathbf{X'X}$. Since the roots are dependent on the scaling of the data, we first normalize the data by dividing each column in $\mathbf{X}$ by $\sqrt{\mathbf{x}_k'\mathbf{x}_k}$.[4] If the regressors are orthogonal (so that R_k^2 will be zero for all k), γ will be one. The greater the intercorrelation among the variables, the higher will be the condition number. Belsley et al. suggest that values in excess of 20 suggest potential problems.

EXAMPLE 9.2 Condition Number

The largest and smallest characteristic roots of the normalized 5×5 matrix for the Longley data are 4.91993902 and $0.399295027 \times 10^{-7}$. Thus, the condition number for these data is 11,100.25. This confirms what we have already suspected.

___

The results thus far suggest that the coefficient on ''armed forces'' is adversely affected by multicollinearity. But in the regression on the full data set (all 16 observations), the t ratio on the ''armed forces'' coefficient is -0.033, indicating that this coefficient is not significantly different from zero by any standard. A 95 percent confidence interval for the coefficient would be $[-0.6794, 0.6691]$, which is quite wide. Apparently, the range of variation we observed in this coefficient was simply due to the fact that it does not really have much explanatory power in the regression, and we merely observed sampling variation.

___

[2] The *multiple correlation* is the square root of this value, 0.5968.

[3] See, for example Klein (1962).

[4] For computational purposes, the correct matrix is obtained by the product $\mathbf{S(X'X)S}$, where $\mathbf{S}$ is a diagonal matrix with $1/\sqrt{\mathbf{x}_k'\mathbf{x}_k}$ on the diagonals.

The point just noted has been the source of some confusion in the literature. It is tempting to conclude that a variable has a low t ratio, or is insignificant, because of multicollinearity. One might (some authors have) then conclude that if the data were not collinear, the coefficient would be significantly different from zero. Of course, this is not necessarily true. Sometimes a coefficient turns out to be insignificant because the variable does not have any explanatory power in the model. Moreover, in nonexperimental data, the suggestion that the results might be different if the data were not collinear has little practical value.

9.2.4. Suggested Remedies for the Multicollinearity Problem

Several methods have been proposed for coping with multicollinearity. The obvious remedy (and surely the most frequently used) is to drop variables suspected of causing the problem from the regression. Of course, in so doing, one encounters the problems of specification analyzed in Section 8.4. A number of other approaches have been suggested. Before considering them, it is worth making a few observations about our predicament. Under the assumptions of the regression model, the least squares estimator (assuming that it exists) is the best unbiased estimator of the parameters. The problem with multicollinearity is that "best" is not very good.

One approach to the problem involves the incorporation of additional information. One might argue, however, that if such information were available at the outset, we ought to have used it before discovering the problem of multicollinearity. The situations in which such useful outside information is available are, unfortunately, rare in any event.

Another possibility for improvement within the confines of the model is to find a slightly biased estimator with a much smaller variance, that is, one with a smaller mean-squared error. Unfortunately, the distributions of such estimators, at least the ones that have been devised thus far, depend on unknown parameters. This puts us back where we started. The other "solutions" we shall discuss involve trading our unbiased estimator for a biased one about which our ability to make statistical inferences will be limited.[5]

Two purely mechanical solutions have been proposed for dealing with the most obvious problem of multicollinearity, the large standard errors of the estimates. The **ridge regression estimator** is

$$\mathbf{b}_r = [\mathbf{X'X} + r\mathbf{D}]^{-1}\mathbf{X'y}, \tag{9-8}$$

where $\mathbf{D}$ is a diagonal matrix containing the diagonal elements of $\mathbf{X'X}$ and the scalar r is chosen arbitrarily.[6] In application, r is to be chosen in such a way that the resulting estimates are "stable" with respect to small variations in r. The authors of the technique suggest that a small value be chosen at the outset, say 0.01, and then that successively larger values be tried until the coefficients stabilize.[7] In its favor, it is easily shown that although the ridge estimator is biased,

$$E[\mathbf{b}_r] = [\mathbf{X'X} + r\mathbf{D}]^{-1}\mathbf{X'X}\boldsymbol{\beta},$$

its covariance matrix,

$$\text{Var}[\mathbf{b}_r] = \sigma^2[\mathbf{X'X} + r\mathbf{D}]^{-1}\mathbf{X'X}[\mathbf{X'X} + r\mathbf{D}]^{-1}, \tag{9-9}$$

is smaller than that of the ordinary least squares estimator.[8]

---

[5]Nonetheless, this idea has produced a large and insightful literature. A recent summary for econometrics appears in Judge et al. (1985).

[6]See Hoerl and Kennard (1970) and extensive discussion in Judge et al. (1985, pp. 912–922).

[7]The ridge estimator for the Longley data is extremely volatile. With $r = 0.01$, it bears little resemblance to the least squares estimator. With $r = 0.75, 1.0, \ldots$ the estimator continues to change rapidly.

[8]The proof is left as an exercise.

The ridge estimator may have a smaller mean-squared error than ordinary least squares.[9] Unfortunately, this mean-squared error is a function of the unknown parameters that we are trying to estimate (here, with a clear bias). Thus, this is unlikely to be a useful criterion. Economists have avoided use of this estimator, perhaps because of their aversion to biased estimators and partly because of the difficulty it presents for statistical inference. Unlike our earlier case of omitted variables, in this case, we have an unbiased estimate of σ^2, that obtained from the OLS regression with r equal to zero. Still, it is difficult to attach much meaning to hypothesis tests about an estimator that is biased in an unknown direction.

A second approach that offers somewhat more intuitive appeal is that of principal components. Referring back to our discussion of exact collinearity, we considered the problem that although the data matrix has K columns, it may have fewer than K truly independent sources of information, that is, variation. We can carry the same reasoning over to the full rank case. Even though the $\mathbf{X}$ matrix may have full rank, if there is substantial collinearity, we may still believe that there is only a limited number of independent sources of variation. The use of principal components is an attempt to extract from the $\mathbf{X}$ matrix a small number of variables that, in some sense, account for most or all of the variation in $\mathbf{X}$.

Algebraically, we may approach the calculation of principal components as a regression problem. What linear combination of the columns of $\mathbf{X}$ provides the best fit to all of the columns of $\mathbf{X}$? The linear combination will be

$$\mathbf{z}_1 = \mathbf{X}\mathbf{c}_1.$$

Since the R^2 in the regression of any column of $\mathbf{X}$ on $\mathbf{z}_1$ will be the same for any scalar multiple of $\mathbf{c}_1$, we remove the indeterminacy by imposing

$$\mathbf{z}_1'\mathbf{z}_1 = 1.^{[10]}$$

For each column of $\mathbf{X}$, $\mathbf{x}_k$, the sum of squared residuals will be

$$\mathbf{e}_k'\mathbf{e}_k = \mathbf{x}_k'[\mathbf{I} - \mathbf{z}_1(\mathbf{z}_1'\mathbf{z}_1)^{-1}\mathbf{z}_1']\mathbf{x}_k = \mathbf{x}_k'[\mathbf{I} - \mathbf{z}_1\mathbf{z}_1']\mathbf{x}_k.$$

Taking all of the $\mathbf{x}_k$s simultaneously, we seek to minimize

$$\sum_k \mathbf{e}_k'\mathbf{e}_k = \text{tr}(\mathbf{X}'[\mathbf{I} - \mathbf{z}_1\mathbf{z}_1']\mathbf{X})$$

subject to $\mathbf{z}_1'\mathbf{z}_1 = 1$. This is the same as maximizing the second part of the trace since $\mathbf{X}'\mathbf{X}$ does not involve $\mathbf{c}_1$. We can set this up as a Lagrangean problem,

$$\text{Max}_{\mathbf{c}_1, \lambda}\ \ell = \text{tr}(\mathbf{X}'\mathbf{z}_1\mathbf{z}_1'\mathbf{X}) + \lambda(1 - \mathbf{z}_1'\mathbf{z}_1).$$

By permuting in the trace and substituting $\mathbf{z}_1 = \mathbf{X}\mathbf{c}_1$, we obtain the equivalent problem,

$$\text{Max}_{\mathbf{c}_1, \lambda}\ \ell = \mathbf{c}_1'(\mathbf{X}'\mathbf{X})^2\mathbf{c}_1 + \lambda(1 - \mathbf{c}_1'(\mathbf{X}'\mathbf{X})\mathbf{c}_1).$$

The first order condition for $\mathbf{c}_1$ is

$$\frac{\partial \ell}{\partial \mathbf{c}_1} = 2(\mathbf{X}'\mathbf{X})^2\mathbf{c}_1 - 2\lambda(\mathbf{X}'\mathbf{X})\mathbf{c}_1 = \mathbf{0}.$$

---

[9] Schmidt (1976, pp. 48–55) proves that there is always a r such that the trace of the mean-squared-error matrix for the ridge estimator is smaller than that for least squares. Since this r depends on both β and σ^2, it is unlikely to be of much practical use.

[10] Since principal components are very sensitive to the scaling of the data, the columns of $\mathbf{X}$ should also be normalized so that $\mathbf{x}_k'\mathbf{x}_k = 1$. This can be done without modifying the original data just by pre- and postmultiplying $\mathbf{X}'\mathbf{X}$ by $[\text{diag}(\mathbf{X}'\mathbf{X})]^{-1/2}$.

Now, premultiply both sides of the equation by $\frac{1}{2}(\mathbf{X}'\mathbf{X})^{-1}$ to obtain the result for $\mathbf{c}_1$,

$$(\mathbf{X}'\mathbf{X})\mathbf{c}_1 - \lambda\mathbf{c}_1 = \mathbf{0}.$$

Therefore, $\mathbf{c}_1$ is a characteristic vector of $\mathbf{X}'\mathbf{X}$. Which one? The criterion is

$$\mathbf{c}_1'(\mathbf{X}'\mathbf{X})^2\mathbf{c}_1 = \lambda^2\mathbf{c}_1'\mathbf{c}_1 = \lambda^2$$

since $\mathbf{c}_1'\mathbf{c}_1$ must equal 1. Therefore, in order to maximize the criterion, we choose the characteristic vector associated with the largest characteristic root. If the total variation in $\mathbf{X}$ is defined to be the trace of $\mathbf{X}'\mathbf{X}$, the proportion of the variation in $\mathbf{X}'\mathbf{X}$ explained by this variable is

$$w_1 = \frac{\lambda_1}{\Sigma_k \lambda_k}.$$

This exercise can be repeated by seeking a second linear combination of the columns of $\mathbf{X}$ with the same criterion, subject to the condition that this second variable be orthogonal to the first. There are K such variables, the kth computed using the characteristic vector corresponding to the kth largest characteristic root.

If we use all K principal components, we end up exactly where we started. This would amount to regressing $\mathbf{y}$ on K linear combinations of the columns of $\mathbf{X}$. The point of the exercise is to use a small number of principal components, so that the sum of their contributions is satisfactorily close to one.

Suppose that of the K columns of $\mathbf{X}$, we use $L < K$ principal components. Thus, we regress $\mathbf{y}$ on $\mathbf{XC}_L$, where $\mathbf{C}_L$ is a $K \times L$ matrix containing L characteristic vectors of $\mathbf{X}'\mathbf{X}$. The estimator is

$$\mathbf{d} = (\mathbf{Z}'\mathbf{Z})^{-1}\mathbf{Z}'\mathbf{y}. \tag{9--10}$$

From the definitions of characteristic roots and vectors,

$$\mathbf{Z}'\mathbf{Z} = \mathbf{C}_L'\mathbf{X}'\mathbf{XC}_L = \mathbf{\Lambda}_L,$$

where $\mathbf{\Lambda}_L$ is the $L \times L$ matrix that contains the L largest characteristic roots of $\mathbf{X}'\mathbf{X}$ on its diagonal. Also,

$$\mathbf{Z}'\mathbf{y} = \mathbf{C}_L'\mathbf{X}'\mathbf{y} = \mathbf{C}_L'\mathbf{X}'\mathbf{Xb},$$

but

$$\mathbf{C}_L'\mathbf{X}'\mathbf{X} = \mathbf{\Lambda}_L\mathbf{C}_L'.$$

By making the preceding substitutions,

$$\mathbf{d} = \mathbf{C}_L'\mathbf{b}. \tag{9--11}$$

Therefore, if we use L principal components the resulting coefficient vector in the regression of $\mathbf{y}$ on $\mathbf{Z}$ is a simple function of the ordinary least squares coefficients in the regression of $\mathbf{y}$ on $\mathbf{X}$.

Like the ridge estimator, the principal components estimator is a biased estimator that may be more precise than its OLS counterpart. If we insert our estimate, $\mathbf{d}$, in the original formulation, we obtain the fitted values

$$\hat{\mathbf{y}} = \mathbf{Zd} = \mathbf{XC}_L\mathbf{d},$$

so we may view the principal components estimator of the full coefficient vector as

$$\mathbf{b}_p = \mathbf{C}_L\mathbf{d} = \mathbf{C}_L\mathbf{C}_L'\mathbf{b},$$

where **b** is the original OLS estimator. Since **b** is unbiased, this competing estimator is clearly biased.[11] However, its variance matrix is unambiguously smaller than the variance of **b**.[12]

There are three problems with using this estimator. First, the results are quite sensitive to the scale of measurement in the variables. The obvious remedy is to standardize the variables, but, unfortunately, this has substantial effects on the computed results. Second, the principal components are not chosen on the basis of any relationship of the regressors to **y**, the variable we are attempting to explain. Lastly, the calculation makes ambiguous the interpretation of the results. The principal components estimator is a mixture of all of the original coefficients. It is unlikely that we shall be able to interpret these combinations in any meaningful way.

9.3. Missing Observations

It is fairly common for a data set to have gaps, for a variety of reasons. Perhaps the most common occurrence of this problem is in survey data, in which it often happens that respondents simply fail to answer the questions. In a time series, the data may be missing because they do not exist at the frequency we wish to observe them; the model may specify monthly relationships, but some variables are observed only on a quarterly basis.

There are two possible cases to consider, depending on why the data are missing. One is that the data are simply unavailable, for reasons unknown to the analyst and unrelated to the fact that other observations in the sample are complete. If this is the case, the complete observations in the sample constitute a usable data set, and the only issue is what possibly helpful information could be salvaged from the incomplete observations. Griliches (1986) calls this the *ignorable case* in that, for purposes of estimation, if we are not concerned with efficiency, we may simply ignore the problem. A second case, which has recently attracted a great deal of attention in the econometrics literature, is that in which the gaps in the data set are not benign but are systematically related to the phenomenon being modeled. This happens most often in surveys when the data are self-selected.[13] For example, if a survey were designed to study expenditure patterns and high-income individuals tended to withhold information about their income, the gaps in the data set would represent more than just missing information. In this case, the complete observations would be qualitatively different. We treat this second case in Chapter 22, so we shall defer our discussion until later.

The early work on the subject of missing data concentrated primarily on the ignorable case.[14] The data in this instance may usefully be partitioned into three subsets:

$$\mathbf{y} = \mathbf{X}\boldsymbol{\beta} + \boldsymbol{\varepsilon}$$

[11] It is not biased if $\mathbf{C}_L\mathbf{C}_L' = \mathbf{I}$. Could this happen?

[12] Fomby et al. (1978) show that we can view the principal components estimator as a restricted least squares estimator with the property that its variance matrix has a smaller trace than that of any other restricted least squares estimator with the same number of restrictions. The small variance is, of course, a virtue, but because the estimator is biased, the relative size of its mean-squared error remains ambiguous.

[13] The vast surveys of Americans' opinions about sex by Ann Landers (*Chicago Tribune*, 1984, passim) and Shere Hite (1987) constitute two celebrated studies that were surely tainted by a heavy dose of self-selection bias. The latter was pilloried in numerous publications for purporting to represent the population at large instead of the opinions of those strongly enough inclined to respond to the survey. The first was presented with much greater modesty.

[14] Afifi and Elashoff (1966, 1967), Haitovsky (1968), Anderson (1957), and Kelejian (1969) are a few of the major works.

for all observations, but the data are

$$y_A \ \mathbf{X}_A \cdots n_A \text{ complete observations,}$$
$$-\mathbf{X}_B \cdots n_B \text{ observations missing } y_B,$$

and

$$y_C - \cdots n_C \text{ observations missing } \mathbf{X}_C.$$

In the third case, if $\mathbf{X}_C$ contains multiple regressors, we suppose that only some of the observations on some of the variables are missing. As noted, since this case is ignorable, the least squares regression of y_A on $\mathbf{X}_A$ produces estimates of $\boldsymbol{\beta}$ that have all of the usual properties. The various schemes for dealing with missing data concern how to fill the gaps in some way in order to use whatever information may be contained in the latter two sets. The question is solely one of efficiency and lost information.

Consider, first, case B, in which data on y are missing. Any method devised to utilize $\mathbf{X}_B$ will have to employ some predictor of y_B, so let $\hat{y}_B$ be that predictor. At this point, we leave unspecified just what that might be; some possibilities will be noted. The least squares slope vector in this "filled" data set is

$$\mathbf{b} = \left[\begin{bmatrix} \mathbf{X}_A \\ \mathbf{X}_B \end{bmatrix}' \begin{bmatrix} \mathbf{X}_A \\ \mathbf{X}_B \end{bmatrix} \right]^{-1} \begin{bmatrix} \mathbf{X}_A \\ \mathbf{X}_B \end{bmatrix}' \begin{bmatrix} y_A \\ y_B \end{bmatrix}.$$

We can write this as

$$\mathbf{b}_f = [\mathbf{X}_A'\mathbf{X}_A + \mathbf{X}_B'\mathbf{X}_B]^{-1}[\mathbf{X}_A'y_A + \mathbf{X}_B'\hat{y}_B].$$

Recall the normal equation for the multiple regression model,

$$\mathbf{X}'\mathbf{X}\mathbf{b} = \mathbf{X}'\mathbf{y}.$$

Let $\mathbf{b}_A$ be the least squares slope in a regression that uses only the observations in group A, and define $\mathbf{b}_B$ likewise for the group B, using $\hat{y}_B$. Then we may write

$$\mathbf{b}_f = [\mathbf{X}_A'\mathbf{X}_A + \mathbf{X}_B'\mathbf{X}_B]^{-1}[\mathbf{X}_A'\mathbf{X}_A\mathbf{b}_A + \mathbf{X}_B'\mathbf{X}_B\mathbf{b}_B]$$
$$= \mathbf{F}\mathbf{b}_A + (\mathbf{I} - \mathbf{F})\mathbf{b}_B, \tag{9-12}$$

where

$$\mathbf{F} = [\mathbf{X}_A'\mathbf{X}_A + \mathbf{X}_B'\mathbf{X}_B]^{-1}\mathbf{X}_A'\mathbf{X}_A.$$

This is a *matrix weighted average* of two least squares estimators. Now

$$E[\mathbf{b}_f] = \mathbf{F}\boldsymbol{\beta} + (\mathbf{I} - \mathbf{F})E[\mathbf{b}_B], \tag{9-13}$$

which will equal $\boldsymbol{\beta}$ only if $\mathbf{b}_B$ is unbiased. A weighted average of an unbiased estimator and some other estimator can be unbiased only if the other estimator is unbiased as well. Therefore, we can draw a conclusion:

> Any scheme that purports to obtain an unbiased estimate by filling in missing values of the dependent variable must do so in such a way that a regression using only the filled observations would produce an unbiased estimator.[15]

---

[15] If there are too few incomplete observations to compute the regression, it suffices for the expected value of each y_{Bi} to be $\mathbf{x}_i'\boldsymbol{\beta}$.

This may be a tall order. Two schemes that have been suggested are as follows:

1. *Zero-order regression.* Replace the missing values in $\mathbf{y}_B$ with the mean of the complete observations in $\mathbf{y}_A$. Then the estimator using only the filled observations will be

$$\mathbf{b}_B = [\mathbf{X}'_B\mathbf{X}_B]^{-1}\mathbf{X}'_B\mathbf{i}\bar{y}_A,$$

where $\mathbf{i}$ is a column of n_B ones. But

$$\bar{y}_A = \bar{\mathbf{x}}'_A\boldsymbol{\beta} + \bar{\varepsilon}_A,$$

so

$$\mathbf{b}_B = [\mathbf{X}'_B\mathbf{X}_B]^{-1}\mathbf{X}'_B[\mathbf{i}\bar{\mathbf{x}}'_A\boldsymbol{\beta} + \bar{\varepsilon}_A\mathbf{i}].$$

The expected value of $\bar{\varepsilon}_A$ is zero. Also,

$$\mathbf{X}'_B\mathbf{i} = n_B\bar{\mathbf{x}}_B.$$

But

$$n_B[\mathbf{X}'_B\mathbf{X}_B]^{-1}\bar{\mathbf{x}}_B\bar{\mathbf{x}}'_A \neq \mathbf{I},$$

so this estimator fails the test.[16] There is another, perhaps more intuitive reason for this finding. Consider a simple regression with only a single regressor. If β is not zero, there is some covariation between y and x. Suppose that it is positive. Then high values of x are associated with high values of y. But if we replace every missing y_B with $\bar{y}_A$, high values of x_B do not imply higher values of these $\bar{y}$'s, even in expectation. Therefore, the higher the value of x_B, the larger is the disturbance at this observation. The regressor and the disturbance are, therefore, not independent for these observations. When this is the case, the least squares estimator is biased, which is what we found earlier.

2. *First-order regression.* Use the A group to estimate $\boldsymbol{\beta}$; then estimate $\mathbf{y}_B$ with $=\mathbf{X}_B\mathbf{b}_A$. This method passes the test of unbiasedness and appears to bring a gain in efficiency. But the gain in efficiency from using these fitted values may be illusory.[17] In finding the variance of the "mixed" estimator, we must account for the additional variation present in the predicted values.

Other suggestions have been made. In general, not much is known about the properties of estimators based on predicted values of y. Those results we do have are largely from simulation studies based on a particular data set or pattern of missing data. The results of these *Monte Carlo studies* are usually difficult to generalize. The overall conclusion seems to be that in a single-equation regression context, filling in missing values of y is not a good idea.

For the case of missing data in the regressors, it helps to consider the simple regression and multiple regression cases separately. In the first instance, $\mathbf{X}_C$ has two columns: the column of ones for the constant and a column of blanks where the missing data would be if we had them. As before, several schemes have been suggested for filling the blanks. The zero-order method of replacing each missing x in group C with $\bar{x}_A$ results in no changes and is equivalent to dropping the incomplete data. There are several ways

---

[16] The conclusion to the contrary drawn by Kmenta (1986, p. 385) is in error. In his ratio, even if the means are the same, there are different numbers of observations in the numerator and denominator. What he does show is that the estimator is biased toward zero, which makes sense in view of the next result.

[17] See Kosobud (1963) and Kelejian (1969).

to prove this, but the simplest is to observe that if each of the missing observations is equal to $\bar{x}_A$, then $\bar{x}$ for the full sample is equal to $\bar{x}_A$, and each term in $\Sigma(x - \bar{x})^2$ and $\Sigma(x - \bar{x})(y - \bar{y})$ that corresponds to one of these constructed observations is a zero. Therefore, the sample moments upon which the regression is computed are unchanged. Unfortunately, the R^2 will be lower, since even though the numerator in $b^2 S_{xx}/S_{yy}$ is unchanged, the denominator is increased by the new observations that have been brought into the sum. We conclude that there is no gain in the estimation of $\boldsymbol{\beta}$, and the cost is to bring a poor fit for the constructed data. An alternative, *modified zero-order regression,* is to fill the second column of $\mathbf{X}_C$ with zeros and add a dummy variable that takes the value one for missing observations and zero for complete ones.[18] We leave it as an exercise to show that this is algebraically identical to simply filling the gaps with $\bar{x}_A$. Lastly, there is the possibility of computing fitted values for the missing x's by a regression of x on y in the complete data. The sampling properties of the resulting estimator are largely unknown, but what evidence there is suggests that this is not a beneficial way to proceed.[19]

Thus far, the picture is quite pessimistic. The best we have done is to present a case in which no harm was done. However, in a multiple regression, there is scope for culling some useful information from the incomplete observations. Consider a regression with just two regressors to illustrate the point.[20] The model is

$$\mathbf{y} = \beta\mathbf{x} + \gamma\mathbf{z} + \boldsymbol{\varepsilon}.$$

Suppose that it were valid to posit a linear relationship between $\mathbf{x}$ and $\mathbf{z}$.[21] Then if, in addition

$$\mathbf{x} = \delta\mathbf{z} + \mathbf{u},$$

the model may be written in three equations:

$$\mathbf{y}_A = \beta\mathbf{x}_A + \gamma\mathbf{z}_A + \boldsymbol{\varepsilon}_A,$$

$$\mathbf{x}_A = \delta\mathbf{z}_A + \mathbf{u}_A,$$

$$\mathbf{y}_C = (\beta + \gamma\delta)\mathbf{z}_C + \boldsymbol{\varepsilon}_C + \beta\mathbf{u}_C.$$

Each of the first two can be estimated by ordinary least squares. Let $\hat{\mathbf{x}}_C$ be the predicted values of the missing x's obtained by using $\hat{\delta}$ and $\mathbf{z}_C$. Consider combining the two data sets in one regression model:

$$\begin{bmatrix} \mathbf{y}_A - \hat{\beta}\mathbf{x}_A \\ \mathbf{y}_C - \hat{\beta}\hat{\mathbf{x}}_C \end{bmatrix} = \gamma \begin{bmatrix} \mathbf{z}_A \\ \mathbf{z}_C \end{bmatrix} + \mathbf{v}.$$

The compound disturbance, $\mathbf{v}$, is a hodgepodge of the original disturbances and the sampling errors in estimation of β, γ, and δ. Assuming (correctly) that $\mathbf{v}$ and $\mathbf{z}$ are uncorrelated (at least asymptotically), γ can be estimated by least squares. At this point, the important thing to note is that although we have done nothing to the original estimate of β, some new information is being used to estimate γ in the second regression, which can be expected to provide added efficiency. Griliches provides additional results. The overall conclusion is that even though there may be a still more efficient way to use the same data, *there is some possibility that this estimator may outperform least squares, omitting group C.* In a multiple regression, there is information about the covariation between the regres-

---

[18] See Maddala (1977, p. 202).

[19] Afifi and Elashoff (1966) and Haitovsky (1968).

[20] This set of results is presented in much greater detail in Griliches (1986).

[21] In the case of nonstochastic regressors, this will only be descriptive; if the regressors are stochastic, it characterizes their joint distribution.

sors with complete data and the dependent variable that is not used if these observations are discarded. The problem is to use that information in such a way that the influence of the other variables is partialed out. The preceding illustrates one possibility.

9.4. Grouped Data

Reporting agencies often release only group mean data to preserve the anonymity of the constituents. Data are *censored* when a range of values that contains the actual value rather than the value itself is given. For example, rather than ask for income, surveys often request only the income category in which respondent falls. As a practical matter, to ease the burden of computation, it may make sense to analyze group means even if the original ungrouped data are available. There are two changes that generally occur as a result of this form of data aggregation:

1. The parameter estimates are less efficient, due to the loss of information.
2. The fit of the regression improves, sometimes dramatically.

Suppose that the usual regression model,

$$\mathbf{y} = \mathbf{X}\boldsymbol{\beta} + \boldsymbol{\varepsilon}, \tag{9–14}$$

applies to a full data set and that a preassigned grouping allocates the n observations into G groups, with $n_1, n_2, \ldots, n_G$ observations in them. For the n_g observations in group g, the same model applies, so for them, that is, for these particular rows of (9–14),

$$\mathbf{y}_g = \mathbf{X}_g\boldsymbol{\beta} + \boldsymbol{\varepsilon}_g. \tag{9–15}$$

These n_g observations are collapsed into a single observation, $[\bar{y}_g, \bar{x}_{1g}, \ldots, \bar{x}_{Kg}]$ by premultiplying by the $n_g \times 1$ vector, $(1/n_g)\mathbf{i}'$. Applying this to (9–15), we obtain

$$\frac{1}{n_g}\mathbf{i}'\mathbf{y}_g = \frac{1}{n_g}\mathbf{i}'\mathbf{X}_g\boldsymbol{\beta} + \frac{1}{n_g}\mathbf{i}'\boldsymbol{\varepsilon}_g,$$

which implies that

$$\bar{y}_g = \bar{\mathbf{x}}_g'\boldsymbol{\beta} + \bar{\varepsilon}_g. \tag{9–16}$$

The same regression model applies to each group mean as well. Assuming that G is larger than K, we can stack these observations in G rows in

$$\bar{\mathbf{y}} = \bar{\mathbf{X}}\boldsymbol{\beta} + \bar{\boldsymbol{\varepsilon}}.$$

Each element of $\bar{\boldsymbol{\varepsilon}}$ has mean zero, and it is easy to verify that the conditions necessary for least squares to be unbiased are met here. In principle, we need go no further. Least squares continues to be unbiased. Given the convenience of using the smaller number of observations, why not do this routinely?

Each element of $\bar{\boldsymbol{\varepsilon}}$ is $\bar{\varepsilon}_g = (1/n_g)(\varepsilon_{g1} + \varepsilon_{g2} + \cdots + \varepsilon_{gn_g})$, which has mean zero and variance σ^2/n_g. Therefore, one of the conditions of the classical regression model, equal variances across the disturbances, is not met here unless all of the groups have the same number of members. However, if we just multiply both sides of (9–16) by $\sqrt{n_g}$, the disturbance, say $\bar{\varepsilon}^* = \sqrt{n_g}\bar{\varepsilon}_g$, has variance σ^2 for all g. Therefore, a slightly modified model,

$$\bar{y}_g^* = \bar{\mathbf{x}}_g^{*\prime}\boldsymbol{\beta} + \bar{\varepsilon}_g^*, \tag{9–16'}$$

fits all of the assumptions of the classical regression model. Least squares regression of $\bar{y}_g^*$ on $\bar{\mathbf{x}}_g^*$ gives the best linear unbiased estimate of $\boldsymbol{\beta}$, given the data (i.e., the group means) in hand.[22] (We emphasize the qualification because, as we will show, we would do better yet if we had the original data.) Collecting the G observations in $\overline{\mathbf{X}}^*$ and $\overline{\mathbf{y}}^*$, the least squares estimator is

$$\mathbf{b}^* = [\overline{\mathbf{X}}^{*\prime}\overline{\mathbf{X}}^*]^{-1}[\overline{\mathbf{X}}^{*\prime}\overline{\mathbf{y}}^*] = \left[\sum_g n_g\overline{\mathbf{x}}_g\overline{\mathbf{x}}_g'\right]^{-1}\left[\sum_g n_g\overline{\mathbf{x}}_g\overline{y}_g\right]. \tag{9-17}$$

Note that the efficient estimator is obtained by multiplying each ''observation'' (i.e., group mean) by the respective group size. In effect, this replicates each group mean observation n_g times.

Obviously, the estimator in (9–17) is different from the one that would result if the original data were used. But it remains to be shown that any loss in efficiency has occurred. Let $\mathbf{H}$ be the $G \times n$ matrix that transforms the entire sample to $\overline{y}_g^*$ and $\overline{\mathbf{x}}_g^*$. $\mathbf{H}$ would appear

$$\mathbf{H} = \begin{bmatrix} \dfrac{1}{\sqrt{n_1}}(1 \ \ 1 \ \ \cdots \ \ 1) & (0 \ \ 0 \ \ \cdots \ \ 0) & \cdots & (0 \ \ 0 \ \ \cdots \ \ 0) \\ (0 \ \ 0 \ \ \cdots \ \ 0) & \dfrac{1}{\sqrt{n_2}}(1 \ \ 1 \ \ \cdots \ \ 1) & \cdots & (0 \ \ 0 \ \ \cdots \ \ 0) \\ & \vdots & & \\ (0 \ \ 0 \ \ \cdots \ \ 0) & (0 \ \ 0 \ \ \cdots \ \ 0) & \cdots & \dfrac{1}{\sqrt{n_G}}(1 \ \ 1 \ \ \cdots \ \ 1) \end{bmatrix}.$$

Since $\overline{\mathbf{X}}^* = \mathbf{H}\mathbf{X}$ and the classical regression model applies to (9–16′), the variance matrix of $\mathbf{b}^*$ in (9–17) is

$$\text{Var}[\mathbf{b}^*] = \sigma^2[\mathbf{X}'\mathbf{H}'\mathbf{H}\mathbf{X}]^{-1}. \tag{9-18}$$

To show that this is no smaller than $\sigma^2(\mathbf{X}'\mathbf{X})^{-1}$, the variance matrix of the estimator for the ungrouped data, it is much easier to show that the inverse of the matrix in (9–18) is *no larger* than $\mathbf{X}'\mathbf{X}$. The difference is

$$\mathbf{X}'\mathbf{X} - \mathbf{X}'\mathbf{H}'\mathbf{H}\mathbf{X} = \mathbf{X}'(\mathbf{I} - \mathbf{H}'\mathbf{H})\mathbf{X}. \tag{9-19}$$

All that must be shown is that $(\mathbf{I} - \mathbf{H}'\mathbf{H})$ is positive semidefinite, which can easily be done by showing that $(\mathbf{I} - \mathbf{H}'\mathbf{H})$ is idempotent.[23] You can do this just by multiplying it out. The conclusion is that the best use of the group means will never be better than using the original data and may be worse.

The larger is the difference matrix in (9–19), the greater is the information loss in the grouped data. The kmth element of this difference matrix is

$$(\mathbf{X}'(\mathbf{I} - \mathbf{H}'\mathbf{H})\mathbf{X})_{km} = \sum_{g=1}^{G}\left[\left(\sum_{i=1}^{n_g} x_{ik}x_{im}\right) - n_g\overline{x}_k\overline{x}_m\right]. \tag{9-20}$$

This is the within-groups variation in the language of the analysis of variance. It is no surprise that this is the result that emerges. The greater the variation within the groups that is discarded by replacing individual elements with group means, the greater will be the information loss.

---

[22] This is an example of weighted least squares in a heteroscedastic regression model. The model is analyzed in greater detail in Chapter 14. This particular application is somewhat different from the usual case of heteroscedasticity in that the unequal variances arise as a consequence of the data construction rather than as a part of the structure of the model.

[23] See result (2–116).

Although grouping results in a loss of information in the regressors, it often brings a striking increase in the fit of the regression. Cramer's classic (1964) study on the subject provides a good example. A subset of his results is given in Example 9.3.

EXAMPLE 9.3 Regressions Based on Group Mean Data ———————————————

The results shown in Table 9.2 are reported in Cramer (op. cit.). The slope estimate is on income in an Engle curve. Essentially, the averaging has the additional effect of averaging out the disturbance variation.[24]

TABLE 9.2

Observations   278
Groups   Six of 5, 26, 73, 106, 52, and 16 observations

Commodity	Slope		R^2	
	Ungrouped	**Grouped**	**Ungrouped**	**Grouped**
Oranges	16.87	16.84	0.242	0.968
Eggs	139.20	142.06	0.234	0.972
Apples	21.35	21.47	0.165	0.924
Butter	39.14	38.21	0.116	0.784
Cheese	29.01	30.00	0.105	0.876
Soap	3.73	3.55	0.099	0.949
Fish	14.31	15.40	0.036	0.868

9.5. Measurement Error and Proxy Variables

Thus far, it has been assumed (at least implicitly) that the data used to estimate the parameters of our models are true measurements on their theoretical counterparts. In practice, this happens only in the best of circumstances. All sorts of measurement problems creep into the data that must be used in our analyses. Even carefully constructed survey data do not always conform exactly to the variables the analysts have in mind for their regressions. Aggregate statistics such as GNP are only estimates of their theoretical counterparts, and some variables, such as depreciation, the services of capital, and the interest rate, do not even exist in an agreed-upon theory. At worst, there may be no physical measure corresponding to the variable in our model; intelligence, education, and permanent income are but a few examples. Nonetheless, all of them have appeared in very precisely defined regression models.

In this section, we examine some of the received results on regression analysis with badly measured data. The general assessment of the problem is not particularly optimistic. The biases introduced by measurement error can be rather severe. There are almost no known finite sample results for the models of measurement error; nearly all of the results that have been developed are asymptotic. The following presentation will use a few simple asymptotic results for the classical regression model. These are discussed in detail in the next chapter.[25] For purposes of the discussion, it is useful to summarize the essential result before proceeding.

---

[24] Cramer (1964) contains further discussion of this issue.

[25] It may be useful to review the general results in Section 4.4 as well.

The properties of the least squares estimator derived in the previous chapters have been obtained by analyzing the identity

$$\mathbf{b} = \boldsymbol{\beta} + [\mathbf{X'X}]^{-1}\mathbf{X'\varepsilon}. \tag{9-21}$$

The unbiasedness property follows from the assumption that

$$\text{Cov}[\mathbf{X}, \boldsymbol{\varepsilon}] = \mathbf{0}.$$

When this assumption is not met, it is clear that the second term in the previous equation will not be zero, and **b** will no longer estimate $\boldsymbol{\beta}$. We have seen this at several points in our analysis. For example:

1. In the analysis of specification errors in Section 8.4, the bias due to left-out variables can be cast in the framework of correlation between the included $\mathbf{X}_1$ and a disturbance consisting of $\boldsymbol{\varepsilon} + \mathbf{X}_2\boldsymbol{\beta}_2$.
2. The problem with certain schemes to fill in missing data on a regressor is that the filled-in data are correlated with the disturbance.

We may write (9–21) as

$$\mathbf{b} - \boldsymbol{\beta} = \left[\frac{\mathbf{X'X}}{n}\right]^{-1}\left[\frac{\mathbf{X'\varepsilon}}{n}\right].$$

Under most conditions, it will follow that

$$\text{plim}[\mathbf{b} - \boldsymbol{\beta}] = \boldsymbol{\Sigma}_{xx}\boldsymbol{\sigma}_{x\varepsilon},$$

where $\boldsymbol{\Sigma}_{xx}$ is a positive definite matrix and $\boldsymbol{\sigma}_{x\varepsilon}$ is a vector of covariances. If these covariances are not zero, least squares is inconsistent. The topics considered in this section are concerned with situations in which these covariances do not vanish even as $n \to \infty$. In the discussion, since only large-sample results are known, we assume that sample moments such as $\mathbf{X'X}/n$ will converge in probability to population parameters such as $\boldsymbol{\Sigma}_{xx}$. For convenience, results are cast in terms of the probability limits of sample moments. For example, we shall usually write "Cov[x, y]" when "the parameter estimated by $(1/n)\Sigma_i x_i y_i$" would be appropriate.

9.5.1. One Badly Measured Variable

The simplest case to analyze is that of a regression model with a single regressor and no constant term. Although this is admittedly unrealistic, it illustrates the essential concepts, and we shall generalize it presently. Assume that the model

$$y^* = \beta x^* + \varepsilon \tag{9-22}$$

conforms to all of the assumptions of the classical normal regression model. If data on y^* and x^* were available, all of the apparatus of the classical model would apply. Suppose, however, that our observed data are only imperfectly measured versions of y^* and x^*. To put this in the context of an example, suppose that y^* is ln(output/labor) and x^* is ln(capital/labor). Neither factor input can be measured with precision, so the observed y and x contain errors of measurement. We assume that

$$y = y^* + v \qquad \text{with } v \sim N[0, \sigma_v^2] \tag{9-23a}$$

and

$$x = x^* + u \qquad \text{with } u \sim N[0, \sigma_u^2]. \tag{9-23b}$$

(We adhere to the widely used conventions of using *s to indicate unobserved variables and omitting them on the measured variables.) Assume, as well, that u and v are independent of each other and of $y*$ and $x*$. (As we shall see, adding these restrictions is not sufficient to rescue a bad situation.)

As a first step, insert (9–23a) in (9–22), assuming for the moment that only $y*$ is measured with error:

$$y = \beta x* + \varepsilon + v$$
$$= \beta x* + \varepsilon*.$$

This conforms completely to the assumptions of the classical regression model. As long as the regressor is measured properly, measurement error on the dependent variable can be absorbed in the disturbance of the regression and ignored. To save some cumbersome notation, therefore, we shall henceforth assume that our measurement error problems concern only the independent variables in the model.

Consider, then, the regression of y on the observed x. By substituting (9–23b) in (9–22), we obtain

$$y = \beta x + [\varepsilon - \beta u] = \beta x + w. \tag{9–24}$$

Since x equals $x* + u$, the regressor in (9–24) is correlated with the disturbance:

$$\text{Cov}[x, w] = \text{Cov}[x* + u, \varepsilon - \beta u] = -\beta \sigma_u^2. \tag{9–25}$$

This violates one of the central assumptions of the classical model, so we can expect the least squares estimator,

$$b = \frac{(1/n) \, \Sigma \, xy}{(1/n) \, \Sigma \, x^2},$$

to be inconsistent. To find the probability limits, insert (9–22) and (9–23b) and use the Slutsky theorem:

$$\text{plim } b = \frac{\text{plim}(1/n) \, \Sigma \, (x* + u)(\beta x* + \varepsilon)}{\text{plim}(1/n) \, \Sigma \, (x* + u)^2}.$$

Since $x*$, ε, and u are mutually independent, this reduces to

$$\text{plim } b = \frac{\beta Q*}{Q* + \sigma_u^2} = \frac{\beta}{1 + \sigma_u^2/Q*}, \tag{9–26}$$

where $Q* = \text{plim}(1/n)\Sigma x*^2$. As long as σ_u^2 is positive, b is inconsistent, with a persistent bias toward zero. Clearly, the greater the variability in the measurement error, the worse the bias. The effect of biasing the coefficient toward zero is called **attenuation.**

The result makes some sense in view of (9–24). In regressing y on x, we have omitted a variable, u, from the regression. Write (9–24) in a slightly different form:

$$y = \beta x + \theta u + \varepsilon. \tag{9–24'}$$

It so happens that θ equals $-\beta$, but neglect that for the moment. Were u an observed variable, the *multiple* regression of y on x and u would produce unbiased estimates of β and θ.[26] The important thing to note is that both x and u appear in the regression, and both affect y when they vary. In a model that contains only x, the effect of variation of u on y must be transmitted through variation in x. Viewed in this light, the omitted variable

---

[26]They would not be efficient, as they neglect the constraint, $\theta = -\beta$, but they *are* unbiased nonetheless.

formula (8–16) applies directly. In regressing y only on x, the coefficient we obtain is a mixture of that on x, that is, β, and that on u, that is, $-\beta$.

To this point, we have been unable to estimate β. The problem is one of identification. There are four "parameters" in the model—β, σ_ε^2, σ_u^2, and Q*—and only three pieces of information:

$$S_{yy}, \text{ which estimates plim } S_{yy} = \beta^2 Q^* + \sigma_\varepsilon^2,$$
$$S_{xx}, \text{ which estimates plim } S_{xx} = Q^* + \sigma_u^2,$$
$$S_{xy}, \text{ which estimates plim } S_{xy} = \beta Q^*.$$

Using the Slutsky theorem (i.e., the method of moments), we could, at this point, only manipulate our three estimators. As it stands, none of the parameters can be estimated. One approach to estimation is based on assuming that there is an additional known quantity or restriction. For example:

1. If σ_ε^2 were known, $(S_{yy} - \sigma_\varepsilon^2)/S_{xy}$ would be a consistent estimator of β, and the rest of the puzzle would unfold.
2. If σ_u^2 were known, $S_{xy}/(S_{xx} - \sigma_u^2)$ would be a consistent estimator of β.
3. If $\lambda = \sigma_u^2/Q^*$ were known, $(S_{xy}/S_{xx})(1 + \lambda)$ would be a consistent estimator of β.

Other combinations are possible; the logic is that any known function of the underlying parameters raises the number of known estimators to the number of unknown parameters. However, assuming that the unknown parameters are known is a bit utopian. Perhaps the third suggestion offers some hope; it is not unusual to have at least some information about the degree of error in a measured variable. Government statistics are often released with a range of error. Otherwise, the appeal of this approach is largely intellectual.

It has been pointed out that the preceding trap was set by locking ourselves into the normal distribution at the outset. If, for example, some other distribution were specified for ε and u, perhaps some higher moments, that is, the third moment of y or the product of y^2 and x, could be used to provide additional information about the parameters. It is known that this approach will be fruitless for the normal distribution, but almost any other symmetric distribution solves the identification problem.[27] Of course, assuming that some other particular distribution applies is also somewhat optimistic.

The approach stated in the preceding paragraph does, however, suggest a possibility in a time-series setting. The difficulty we face is that there is not enough information in the contemporaneous variances and covariances of the observed variables to identify the parameters of the model. To take a simple example, suppose that we add to the basic model of (9–22) and (9–23b) that x is a time series characterized by

$$x_t = x_t^* + u_t, \tag{9–23b$'$}$$

and

$$x_t^* = \rho x_{t-1}^* + v_t.$$

Then, because the disturbances and measurement errors are uncorrelated across observations, that is, across time,

$$\text{plim } \frac{1}{n} \sum x_{t-1} y_t = \text{plim } \frac{1}{n} \sum (\beta \rho x_{t-1}^* + \beta v_t + \varepsilon_t)(x_{t-1}^* + u_{t-1})$$
$$= \beta \rho Q^* \tag{9–27}$$

---

[27] See Pal (1980). In a much earlier analysis, Riersol (1950) showed that the fundamental problem of identification in this model is peculiar to the bivariate normal distribution.

and

$$\text{plim} \ \frac{1}{n} \sum x_{t-1} x_t = \text{plim} \ \frac{1}{n} \sum (x_{t-1}^* + v_{t-1})(\rho x_{t-1}^* + v_t + u_t)$$

$$= \rho Q^*.$$

The ratio $\hat{\beta} = (\Sigma x_{t-1} y_t)/(\Sigma_t x_{t-1} x_t)$ provides a consistent estimator of β, after which the remaining parameters can be derived.

9.5.2. Multiple Regression with Measurement Error

In a multiple regression model, matters only get worse. Suppose, to begin, we assume that

$$\mathbf{y} = \mathbf{X}^* \boldsymbol{\beta} + \boldsymbol{\varepsilon}$$

and

$$\mathbf{X} = \mathbf{X}^* + \mathbf{U},$$

allowing every observation on every variable to be measured with error. The extension of our earlier results is direct:

$$\text{plim} \ \frac{\mathbf{X}'\mathbf{X}}{n} = \mathbf{Q}^* + \boldsymbol{\Sigma}_{uu},$$

$$\text{plim} \ \frac{\mathbf{X}'\mathbf{y}}{n} = \mathbf{Q}^* \boldsymbol{\beta}.$$

Hence,

$$\text{plim} \ \mathbf{b} = [\mathbf{Q}^* + \boldsymbol{\Sigma}_{uu}]^{-1} \mathbf{Q}^* \boldsymbol{\beta} = \boldsymbol{\beta} - [\mathbf{Q}^* + \boldsymbol{\Sigma}_{uu}]^{-1} \boldsymbol{\Sigma}_{uu} \boldsymbol{\beta}. \qquad (9\text{--}28)$$

This is a mixture of all of the parameters in the model. In the same fashion as before, bringing in outside information could lead to identification; however, the amount of information necessary is extremely large, and this approach is not particularly promising.

There are some particular cases of interest. It is common for only a single variable to be measured with error, and one might speculate that the problems would be isolated to the single coefficient. Unfortunately, this is not the case. For a single bad variable—assume that it is the first—the matrix $\boldsymbol{\Sigma}_{uu}$ is of the form

$$\boldsymbol{\Sigma}_{uu} = \begin{bmatrix} \sigma_u^2 & 0 & \cdots & 0 \\ 0 & 0 & \cdots & 0 \\ & & \vdots & \\ 0 & 0 & \cdots & 0 \end{bmatrix}.$$

It can be shown that for this special case

$$\text{plim} \ b_1 = \frac{\beta_1}{1 + \sigma_u^2 q^{*11}} \qquad (9\text{--}29\text{a})$$

(note the similarity of this result to the earlier one) and, for $k \neq 1$,

$$\text{plim} \ b_k = \beta_k - \beta_1 \left[\frac{\sigma_u^2 q^{*k1}}{1 + \sigma_u^2 q^{*11}} \right], \qquad (9\text{--}29\text{b})$$

where q^{*k1} is the $(k, 1)$th element in $\mathbf{Q}^{*-1}$.[28] This depends on several unknowns and cannot be estimated. The coefficient on the badly measured variable is still biased toward zero. The other coefficients are all biased as well, though in unknown directions. A badly measured variable contaminates all of the least squares estimates.[29]

If more than one variable is measured with error, there is very little that can be said.[30] Although expressions can be derived for the biases in a few of these cases, they generally depend on numerous parameters whose signs and magnitudes are unknown and, presumably, unknowable.

9.5.3. The Method of Instrumental Variables

An alternative set of results for estimation in this model (and numerous others) is built around the method of instrumental variables. To introduce it, consider once again the errors in variables model

$$y = \beta x^* + \varepsilon, \qquad x = x^* + u.$$

The parameters, β, σ_ε^2, q^*, and σ_u^2, are not identified in terms of the moments of x and y. Suppose, however, that there exists a variable, z, such that z is correlated with x^* but not with u. For example, in surveys of families, income is notoriously badly reported, partly deliberately and partly because the respondent often neglects some minor sources. In fitting consumption functions based on these data, the regressor is thus subject to measurement error. Suppose, however, that one could determine the total amount of checks written by the head(s) of the household. It is quite likely that this z would be highly correlated with both consumption and income, but perhaps not significantly correlated with the errors of measurement. If $\text{Cov}[x^*, z]$ is not zero, the parameters of the model become estimable, as

$$\text{plim} \frac{(1/n) \Sigma yz}{(1/n) \Sigma xz} = \frac{\beta \, \text{Cov}[x^*, z]}{\text{Cov}[x^*, z]} = \beta. \tag{9-30}$$

It is not always clear where instrumental variables are to be found. For the simple errors in variables model we have discussed here, a few instruments have been devised based only on the data in hand:

$$z = 1 \text{ if } x > \text{median } x \text{ and } -1 \text{ if } x < \text{median } x$$
$$\text{(if } n \text{ is even, the middle observation is discarded)}[31]$$

or

$$z = \text{rank of } x.[32]$$

[28] Use (2–66) to invert $[\mathbf{Q}^* + \mathbf{\Sigma}_{uu}] = [\mathbf{Q}^* + (\sigma_u \mathbf{e}_1)(\sigma_u \mathbf{e}_1)']$, where $\mathbf{e}_1$ is the first column of a $K \times K$ identity matrix. The remaining results are then straightforward.

[29] This point is important to remember when the presence of measurement error is suspected. For example, notice that the marginal product of capital estimated in Example 8.3 is negative, which contradicts a firm theoretical result. Nerlove (1963) attributed this finding largely to measurement error in the variable used for the price of capital, but made no note of the likely effects on the other coefficients in the model.

[30] Some firm analytic results have been obtained by Levi (1973), Theil (1961), Klepper and Leamer (1983), Garber and Klepper (1980), and Griliches (1986).

[31] This is sometimes called the *method of group averages*, as it amounts to passing a line between the group means of two groups of observations, one with small values of x and one with large values.

[32] To the extent that the ranking of x is determined by the size of the measurement error rather than by x^*, this instrument, like the one before it, will fail to satisfy the requirement that it be uncorrelated with the measurement error. The relevant quantity, as we have seen before, is σ_u^2/Q^*.

Notice, for instance, that in the time-series example of (9–23b'), the variable x_{t-1} is being used as an instrumental variable.

In a multiple regression framework, if only a single variable is measured with error, the preceding can be applied to that variable and the remaining variables can serve as their own instruments. If more than one variable is measured with error, the first preceding proposal will be cumbersome at best, while the second can be applied to each.

The preceding describes the application of the technique of instrumental variables to a particular problem. However, the technique is quite general and is used in numerous settings. Here we consider some general results. The consistency of least squares in the classical regression model,

$$\mathbf{y} = \mathbf{X}\boldsymbol{\beta} + \boldsymbol{\varepsilon},$$

hinges on

$$\text{plim } \frac{1}{n}\mathbf{X}'\boldsymbol{\varepsilon} = \mathbf{0}.$$

If this does not hold, least squares is not a consistent estimator of $\boldsymbol{\beta}$. Suppose, however, that there exists a matrix of K variables $\mathbf{Z}$ such that

$$\text{plim } \frac{1}{n}\mathbf{Z}'\boldsymbol{\varepsilon} = \mathbf{0}, \qquad \text{plim } \frac{1}{n}\mathbf{Z}'\mathbf{X} \neq \mathbf{0}.$$

Then the instrumental variable estimator

$$\mathbf{b}_{\text{IV}} = [\mathbf{Z}'\mathbf{X}]^{-1}\mathbf{Z}'\mathbf{y} \tag{9–31}$$

has

$$\text{plim } \mathbf{b}_{\text{IV}} = \text{plim } \left[\frac{1}{n}\mathbf{Z}'\mathbf{X}\right]^{-1} \text{plim } \left[\frac{1}{n}\mathbf{Z}'(\mathbf{X}\boldsymbol{\beta} + \boldsymbol{\varepsilon})\right]$$

$$= \boldsymbol{\beta} + \text{plim } \left[\frac{1}{n}\mathbf{Z}'\mathbf{X}\right]^{-1}\left[\frac{1}{n}\mathbf{Z}'\boldsymbol{\varepsilon}\right]$$

$$= \boldsymbol{\beta}.$$

To obtain the asymptotic covariance matrix for this estimator, we require

$$(\mathbf{b}_{\text{IV}} - \boldsymbol{\beta})(\mathbf{b}_{\text{IV}} - \boldsymbol{\beta})' = (\mathbf{Z}'\mathbf{X})^{-1}\mathbf{Z}'\boldsymbol{\varepsilon}\boldsymbol{\varepsilon}'\mathbf{Z}(\mathbf{X}'\mathbf{Z})^{-1},$$

from which it follows that the asymptotic covariance matrix is

$$\text{Asy. Var}[\mathbf{b}_{\text{IV}}] = \sigma^2[\mathbf{Z}'\mathbf{X}]^{-1}[\mathbf{Z}'\mathbf{Z}][\mathbf{X}'\mathbf{Z}]^{-1}. \tag{9–32}$$

Asymptotic normality of the estimator can be shown if some additional conditions are attached to the behavior of the columns of $\mathbf{Z}$. In general, if they are as well behaved as those of $\mathbf{X}$, which is likely, all of the necessary results can be obtained.[33]

It should be noted that the asymptotic variance of this estimator can be rather large if $\mathbf{Z}$ is not highly correlated with $\mathbf{X}$. Unfortunately, in most cases, there will not be much freedom in the choice of instruments. For any variables that are not correlated with the disturbances, as in the previous discussion, the column of $\mathbf{Z}$ can be the corresponding variable in $\mathbf{X}$. For the others, the choice of $\mathbf{Z}$ will usually be ad hoc.[34]

---

[33] White (1984) presents an extensive analysis.

[34] Results on "optimal instruments" appear in White (1984) and Hansen (1982).

There will be cases in which several variables are available to serve as instruments. Suppose, for example, that only one variable, x_j, is measured with error, and there are a set of L instrumental variables, $z_1, \ldots, z_L$ available. Another way to apply (9–31) is to use $Z = \hat{X}$, where the columns of $\hat{X}$ are the fitted values in a regression of all of the columns of X on all of the columns in X *excluding* X_j plus all of the z's that are not already in X. In this case, each of the included columns of X is replicated exactly, and x_j is replaced with the fitted value in the regression.[35] We can show that this procedure will satisfy the requirements for an instrumental variable estimator, provided that plim $z_l'\varepsilon/n = 0$ for all l.

9.5.4. Proxy Variables

There are situations in which the variable in a model simply has no observable counterpart. Education, intelligence, and like factors are perhaps the most common examples. In this instance, unless there is some observable indicator for the variable, the model will have to be treated in the framework of missing variables. Usually, however, such an indicator can be obtained; for the factors just given, years of schooling and test scores of various sorts are familiar examples. The usual treatment of such variables is in the measurement error framework. If, for example,

$$\text{income} = \beta_1 + \beta_2 \text{ education} + \varepsilon$$

and

$$\text{years of schooling} = \text{education} + u,$$

then the model of Section 9.5.1 applies directly. The only difference here is that the true variable in the model is "latent." No amount of improvement in reporting or measurement would bring the proxy closer to the variable for which it is proxying.

It is to be emphasized that a proxy variable is not an instrument (or the reverse). In the instrumental variables framework, this implies that we do not regress y on Z to obtain the estimates. To take an extreme example, suppose that the full model was

$$y = X^*\beta + \varepsilon,$$

$$X = X^* + U,$$

$$Z = X^* + W.$$

That is, we happen to have two badly measured estimates of X^*. The parameters of this model can be estimated without difficulty if W is uncorrelated with U and X^*, *but not by regressing* y on Z. The instrumental variables technique is called for.

When the model contains a variable such as education, the question naturally arises if interest centers on the other coefficients in the model, why not just discard the problem variable?[36] This produces the familiar problem of an omitted variable, compounded by the fact that the least squares estimator in the full model is inconsistent. Which estimator is worse? McCallum (1972) and Wickens (1972) show that the asymptotic bias (actually, degree of inconsistency) is worse if the proxy is omitted, even if it is a bad one (has a high proportion of measurement error). This neglects, however, the precision of the estimates. Aigner (1974) analyzed this aspect of the problem and found, as might be expected, that it could go either way. He concluded, however, that "there is evidence to broadly support use of the proxy."

---

[35] This is the method of two-stage least squares, which is discussed in Chapter 20.

[36] This discussion applies to the measurement error and latent variable problems equally.

9.5.5. A Specification Test for Measurement Error

Hausman (1978) has devised a test for the presence of errors of measurement. Under the hypothesis of no measurement error, both **b,** the least squares estimator, and $\mathbf{b}_{IV}$, the instrumental variables estimator, are consistent estimators of $\boldsymbol{\beta}$, although least squares is efficient, while the IV estimator is inefficient. But if the hypothesis is false, only $\mathbf{b}_{IV}$ is consistent. The test, then, examines the difference between **b** and $\mathbf{b}_{IV}$. Under the hypothesis of no measurement error, $\text{plim}(\mathbf{b} - \mathbf{b}_{IV}) = \mathbf{0}$, while if there is measurement error, this plim will be nonzero. We have done similar tests at many points before, using the Wald statistic, which is what Hausman suggests. The innovation of his study is to determine the appropriate covariance matrix to use. Let $\mathbf{V}_1$ be the estimated asymptotic covariance matrix for the IV estimator, and let $\mathbf{V}_0$ be $s^2(\mathbf{X}'\mathbf{X})^{-1}$, where s^2 is the estimate of σ^2 obtained using the IV estimator. We know that $\mathbf{V}_1$ is larger than $\mathbf{V}_0$ asymptotically, and our use of the same estimate of σ^2 will ensure this algebraically as well. Then the Wald statistic is simply

$$W = (\mathbf{b} - \mathbf{b}_{IV})'[\mathbf{V}_1 - \mathbf{V}_0]^{-1}(\mathbf{b} - \mathbf{b}_{IV}) \sim \chi^2[K]. \tag{9-33}$$

As Hausman then shows, this may be referred to a chi-squared table.

The algebra simplifies a bit because the same estimate of σ^2 is used for both matrices. Inserting (9–32) and using $\mathbf{q} = \mathbf{b} - \mathbf{b}_{IV}$ reduces (9–33) to

$$\begin{aligned}
W &= \frac{\mathbf{q}'\{[\mathbf{X}'\mathbf{Z}(\mathbf{Z}'\mathbf{Z})^{-1}\mathbf{Z}'\mathbf{X}]^{-1} - (\mathbf{X}'\mathbf{X})^{-1}\}^{-1}\mathbf{q}}{s^2} \\
&= \frac{\mathbf{q}'\{(\hat{\mathbf{X}}'\hat{\mathbf{X}})^{-1} - (\mathbf{X}'\mathbf{X})^{-1}\}^{-1}\mathbf{q}}{s^2}.
\end{aligned} \tag{9-34}$$

Each column of $\hat{\mathbf{X}}$ is the set of fitted values when the corresponding column of **X** is regressed on all of the columns of **Z**.

For the simple regression model with only a single regressor, the algebra simplifies even further. It can be shown that the test is equivalent to applying a standard test of significance to the coefficient on $\hat{\mathbf{u}}$ in the least squares regression,

$$\mathbf{y} = \beta_1 + \beta_2\mathbf{x} + \gamma\hat{\mathbf{u}} + \tilde{\boldsymbol{\varepsilon}},$$

where $\hat{\mathbf{u}}$ is the vector of residuals obtained by regressing **x** on the instrumental variable, **z.** The results are valid only asymptotically, so the standard normal table is used instead of the t table.

9.6. Regression Diagnostics and Influential Data Points

Even in the absence of multicollinearity or other data problems, it is worthwhile to examine one's data and regression results closely for two reasons. First, the identification of outliers in the data is useful, particularly in relatively small cross sections in which the identity and perhaps even the ultimate source of the data point may be known. Second, it is possible to ascertain which, if any, particular observations are especially influential in the results obtained. As such, the identification of these data points may call for further study. It is worth emphasizing, though, that there is a certain danger in singling out particular observations for scrutiny or even elimination from the sample on the basis of statistical results that are based on those data. At the extreme, this may invalidate the usual inference procedures.[37]

---

[37] See the discussion of pretest estimators in Chapter 8.

Of particular importance in this analysis is the *hat matrix:*

$$\mathbf{H} = \mathbf{X(X'X)}^{-1}\mathbf{X'}. \qquad (9\text{--}35)$$

This matrix appeared earlier as the matrix that projects any $n \times 1$ vector into the column space of $\mathbf{X}$; for any vector $\mathbf{y}$, $\mathbf{Hy}$ is the set of fitted values in the least squares regression of $\mathbf{y}$ on $\mathbf{X}$. The least squares residuals are

$$\mathbf{e} = \mathbf{My} = \mathbf{M}\boldsymbol{\varepsilon} = (\mathbf{I} - \mathbf{H})\boldsymbol{\varepsilon},$$

so the variance matrix for the OLS residuals is

$$E[\mathbf{ee'}] = \sigma^2\mathbf{M} = \sigma^2(\mathbf{I} - \mathbf{H}).$$

If one desires to identify which residuals are significantly large, they should be standardized by dividing by the appropriate standard error for that particular residual. Thus, we would use

$$\hat{e}_i = \frac{e_i}{(s^2(1 - h_{ii}))^{1/2}} = \frac{e_i}{(s^2 M_{ii})^{1/2}}. \qquad (9\text{--}36)$$

As a diagnostic tool, Belsley et al.[38] suggest going one step further. If the regression were estimated without the ith observation, the least squares coefficients would be

$$\mathbf{b}(i) = [\mathbf{X}(i)'\mathbf{X}(i)]^{-1}\mathbf{X}(i)'\mathbf{y}(i),$$

where the (i) notation indicates that the ith observation has been omitted. Using these coefficients, the modified residual would be

$$e_i(i) = y_i - \mathbf{b}(i)'\mathbf{x}_i$$
$$= \varepsilon_i + [\boldsymbol{\beta} - \mathbf{b}(i)]'\mathbf{x}_i.$$

Since the ith observation is not used in computing $\mathbf{b}(i)$, these two terms are independent. The appropriate variance is, therefore,

$$\text{Var}[e_i(i)] = \sigma^2[1 + \mathbf{x}_i'(\mathbf{X}(i)'\mathbf{X}(i))^{-1}\mathbf{x}_i]$$
$$= \sigma^2[1 + h_{ii}(i)]. \qquad (9\text{--}37)$$

The estimate of σ^2 is $s^2(i)$. The standardized residual is approximately distributed as standard normal.[39] Values in excess of two suggest observations that deserve closer scrutiny. The calculation is repeated for each observation.[40]

This approach has some intuitive appeal. If the observation conforms to the model that is estimated with the other observations, this standardized residual should be small. If not, the particular observation may deserve scrutiny as perhaps not conforming to the model. It is worth emphasizing, though, that this interpretation is likely to be a bit problematic in a time-series setting unless one is aware of some unusual event taking place at the time the observation in question was generated. The set of calculations is similar in spirit to the CUSUM and CUSUM of squares tests discussed earlier.

---

[38] Op. cit.

[39] $e_i(i)$ is normally distributed, but in using s^2 instead of σ^2, we lose the normal distribution of the ratio. Nor is this distributed as t, since $e_i(i)$ is not independent of s^2.

[40] This does not require that the regression be recomputed n times. The rank one update formula can be used to do the computation recursively if desired. For each observation, the matrix $\mathbf{X'X}$ is "updated" by subtracting an observation. If this exercise is to be performed on a large cross section involving many regressors, the economy provided by the updating formula may be worth exploiting.

EXERCISES

1. The following sample moments were computed from 100 observations produced using a random number generator.

$$
\mathbf{X'X} = \begin{array}{cccc} \mathbf{one} & \mathbf{x1} & \mathbf{x2} & \mathbf{x3} \end{array} \\
\begin{bmatrix} 100 & 123 & 96 & 109 \\ 123 & 252 & 125 & 189 \\ 96 & 125 & 167 & 146 \\ 109 & 189 & 146 & 168 \end{bmatrix}, \quad
\mathbf{X'y} = \begin{bmatrix} 460 \\ 810 \\ 615 \\ 712 \end{bmatrix}, \quad \mathbf{y'y} = 3924,
$$

$$
(\mathbf{X'X})^{-1} = \begin{bmatrix} 0.03767 & & & \\ -0.06263 & 1.129 & & \\ -0.06247 & 1.107 & 1.110 & \\ 0.1003 & -2.192 & -2.170 & 4.292 \end{bmatrix}.
$$

The true model underlying these data is $y = x_1 + x_2 + x_3 + \varepsilon$.

(a) Compute the simple correlations among the regressors.

(b) Compute the ordinary least squares coefficients in the regression of y on a constant, x_1, x_2, and x_3.

(c) Compute the ordinary least squares coefficients in the regression of y on a constant, x_1, and x_2, on a constant, x_1, and x_3, and on a constant, x_2, and x_3.

(d) Compute Leamer's magnification factor [see (9–5)] associated with each variable.

(e) The regressors are obviously collinear. Which is the problem variable?

2. For the data in Exercise 1, compute the condition number for the moment matrix based on the constant, x_1, and x_2.

3. Prove that

$$
E[\mathbf{b'b}] = \boldsymbol{\beta'\beta} + \sigma^2 \sum_k \frac{1}{\lambda_k},
$$

where $\mathbf{b}$ is the ordinary least squares estimator and λ_k is a characteristic root of $\mathbf{X'X}$.

4. Prove that the covariance matrix of the principal components estimator $\mathbf{b}_p = \mathbf{C}_L \mathbf{C}_L' \mathbf{b}$ (defined at the end of Section 9.2) is smaller than that of $\mathbf{b}$.

5. Suppose that instead of choosing the principal components in (9–10) on the basis of the variation in $\mathbf{X}$, we compute all of the principal components and choose the one that is most highly correlated with $\mathbf{y}$. Show that the principal component, $\mathbf{z}_j = \mathbf{Xc}_j$, which is most highly correlated with $\mathbf{y}$, is the one that maximizes $\sqrt{\lambda_j} \mathbf{b'c}_j$, where $\mathbf{b}$ is the OLS estimator of $\boldsymbol{\beta}$, $\mathbf{c}_j$ is a characteristic vector of $\mathbf{X'X}$, and λ_j is the associated characteristic root.

6. Consider the simple regression $y = \alpha + \beta x + \varepsilon$. Assume that some of the observations on x are missing. Prove that filling these observations with zeros and adding a dummy variable to the regression that is one for each missing observation and zero otherwise is equivalent to dropping the incomplete observations.

7. The simple regression model

$$y_{ig} = \beta x_{ig} + \varepsilon_{ig},$$

$$E[\varepsilon_{ig}] = 0, \qquad \text{Var}[\varepsilon_{ig}] = \sigma^2$$

applies to observation i in group g. The observed data consist of group means. The following data are obtained from five groups:

Group	1	2	3	4	5	All
n_g	10	20	15	30	25	100
$\bar{y}_g$	2	4	3	1	5	—
$\bar{x}_g$	1	4	2	1	6	—

The following are three possible estimators of β:

$$\frac{\bar{y}}{\bar{x}} = \frac{\Sigma_g n_g \bar{y}_g / \Sigma_g n_g}{\Sigma_g n_g \bar{x}_g / \Sigma_g n_g},$$

$$\frac{\Sigma_g \bar{y}_g \bar{x}_g}{\Sigma_g \bar{x}_g^2} = \text{least squares},$$

and

$$\frac{\Sigma_g n_g \bar{x}_g \bar{y}_g}{\Sigma_g n_g \bar{x}_g^2} = \text{estimator in (9–17)}.$$

(a) Prove that all three estimators are unbiased.
(b) Derive the expression for the sampling variance of each estimator.
(c) Using the previous sample data, compute the three estimators and their sampling variances. Assume that $\sigma^2 = 1$. Which is the most efficient? The least efficient? (The difference you observe between the second and third estimators is that between the ordinary and generalized least squares estimator. This is the subject of Chapter 14.)
(d) Prove that the sampling variance of the third estimator is always less than that of the second.

8. For the model in (9–22) and (9–23), prove that when only x^* is measured with error, the squared correlation between y and x is less than that between y^* and x^*. (Note the assumption that $y^* = y$.) Does the same hold true if y^* is also measured with error?

9. *Reverse regression:* This and the next exercise continue the analysis of Exercise 11, Chapter 8. In the earlier exercise, interest centered on a particular dummy variable in which the regressors were accurately measured. Here we consider the case in which the crucial regressor in the model is measured with error. The paper by Kamlich and Polachek (1982) is directed to this issue.
   Consider the simple errors in the variables model

$$y = \alpha + \beta x^* + \varepsilon,$$

$$x = x^* + u,$$

where u and ε are uncorrelated and x is the erroneously measured, observed counterpart to x^*.

(a) Assume that x^*, u, and ε are all normally distributed, with means μ^*, 0, and 0, variances σ_*^2, σ_u^2, and σ_ε^2, and zero covariances. Obtain the probability limits of the least squares estimates of α and β.

(b) As an alternative, consider regressing x on a constant and y, and then computing the reciprocal of the estimate. Obtain the probability limit of this estimate.

(c) Do the "direct" and "reverse" estimators bound the true coefficient?

10. *Reverse regression continued:* Suppose that the model in Exercise 9 is extended to

$$y = \beta x^* + \gamma d + \varepsilon,$$

$$x = x^* + u.$$

For convenience, we drop the constant term. Assume that x^*, ε, and u are independent and normally distributed, with zero means. Suppose that d is a random variable that takes the values one and zero, with probabilities π and $1 - \pi$ in the population, and is independent of all other variables in the model. To put this in context, the preceding model (and variants of it) have appeared in the literature on discrimination. We view y as a "wage" variable, x^* as "qualifications," and x as some imperfect measure such as education. The dummy variable, d, is membership ($d = 1$) or non-membership ($d = 0$) in some protected class. The hypothesis of discrimination turns on $\gamma < 0$ versus $\gamma = 0$.

(a) What is the probability limit of c, the least squares estimator of γ, in the least squares regression of y on x and d? [**Hints:** The independence of x^* and d is important. Also, plim $\mathbf{d}'\mathbf{d}/n = \text{Var}[d] + E^2[d] = \pi(1 - \pi) + \pi^2 = \pi$. This minor modification does not affect the model substantively, but it greatly simplifies the algebra.] Now, suppose that x^* and d are not independent. In particular, suppose that $E[x^* | d = 1] = \mu^1$ and $E[x^* | d = 0] = \mu^0$. Repeat the derivation with this assumption.

(b) Consider, instead, a regression of x on y and d. What is the probability limit of the coefficient on d in this regression? Assume that x^* and d are independent.

(c) Suppose that x^* and d are not independent, but γ is, in fact, less than zero. Assuming that both preceding equations still hold, what is estimated by $(\bar{y} | d = 1) - (\bar{y} | d = 0)$? What does this quantity estimate if γ does equal zero?

11. A data set consists of n observations in $\mathbf{X}_n$ and $\mathbf{y}_n$. The least squares estimator based on these n observations is

$$\mathbf{b}_n = (\mathbf{X}_n'\mathbf{X}_n)^{-1}\mathbf{X}_n'\mathbf{y}_n.$$

Another observation, $\mathbf{x}_s$ and y_s, becomes available. Prove that the least squares estimator computed using this additional observation is

$$\mathbf{b}_{n,s} = \mathbf{b}_n + \frac{1}{1 + \mathbf{x}_s'(\mathbf{X}_n'\mathbf{X}_n)^{-1}\mathbf{x}_s}(\mathbf{X}_n'\mathbf{X}_n)^{-1}\mathbf{x}_s(y_s - \mathbf{x}_s'\mathbf{b}_n).$$

Note that the last term is e_s, the residual from the prediction of y_s, using the coefficients based on $\mathbf{X}_n$ and $\mathbf{y}_n$. Conclude that the new data change the results of least squares only if the new observation on y cannot be perfectly predicted using the information already in hand.

10

Large-Sample Results for the Classical Regression Model

10.1. Introduction

The discussion thus far has concerned *finite sample* properties of the least squares estimator. Under the two assumptions of nonstochastic regressors and normally distributed disturbances, we know the exact distribution of the least squares estimator and several test statistics, regardless of the sample size. However, the classical normal regression with nonstochastic regressors is a special case and does not include many of the most common applications, for example, time series models with lagged dependent variables. This chapter will generalize the classical regression model by relaxing these two important assumptions.[1]

10.2. The Finite-Sample Properties of Least Squares

The basic assumptions of the classical regression model are

    I. $\mathbf{y} = \mathbf{X}\boldsymbol{\beta} + \boldsymbol{\varepsilon}$.
   II. $\mathbf{X}$ is a nonstochastic $n \times K$ matrix of rank K.
  III. $E[\boldsymbol{\varepsilon}] = \mathbf{0}$.
  IV. $E[\boldsymbol{\varepsilon}\boldsymbol{\varepsilon}'] = \sigma^2 \mathbf{I}$.

The least squares estimators of the unknown parameters, $\boldsymbol{\beta}$ and σ^2, are

$$\mathbf{b} = (\mathbf{X}'\mathbf{X})^{-1}\mathbf{X}'\mathbf{y}$$

and

$$s^2 = \frac{\mathbf{e}'\mathbf{e}}{n - K}.$$

By analyzing

$$\mathbf{b} = \boldsymbol{\beta} + (\mathbf{X}'\mathbf{X})^{-1}\mathbf{X}'\boldsymbol{\varepsilon}$$

and

$$s^2 = \frac{\boldsymbol{\varepsilon}'\mathbf{M}\boldsymbol{\varepsilon}}{n - K},$$

we obtained the following exact, *finite sample* results:

    1. $E[\mathbf{b}] = \boldsymbol{\beta}$. (Least squares is unbiased.)
    2. $\text{Var}[\mathbf{b}] = \sigma^2(\mathbf{X}'\mathbf{X})^{-1}$.

---

[1] Most of this discussion will use standard results on asymptotic and limiting distributions. It may be helpful to review the related sections in Chapter 4 before proceeding.

3. The minimum variance linear unbiased estimator of any function $\mathbf{r'\beta}$ is $\mathbf{r'b}$. (This is the Gauss–Markov theorem.)
4. $E[s^2] = \sigma^2$.
5. $\text{Cov}[\mathbf{b}, \mathbf{e}] = \mathbf{0}$.

For constructing confidence intervals and testing hypotheses, we derived additional results based on the normality assumption,

V. $\boldsymbol{\varepsilon} \sim N[\mathbf{0}, \sigma^2\mathbf{I}]$.

These are:

6. $\mathbf{b}$ and $\mathbf{e}$ are statistically independent. It follows that $\mathbf{b}$ and s^2 are uncorrelated and statistically independent.
7. The exact distribution of $\mathbf{b}$, conditioned on $\mathbf{X}$, is $N[\boldsymbol{\beta}, \sigma^2(\mathbf{X'X})^{-1}]$.
8. $(n - K)s^2/\sigma^2$ is distributed as $\chi^2[n - K]$. s^2 has mean σ^2 and variance $2\sigma^4/ (n - K)$.
9. Based on results **6** through **8**, the statistic

$$t[n - K] = \frac{b_k - \beta_k}{s^2(\mathbf{X'X})_{kk}^{-1}}$$

has a t distribution with $n - K$ degrees of freedom.
10. The test statistic for testing a set of J linear restrictions, $\mathbf{R}\boldsymbol{\beta} = \mathbf{q}$,

$$\frac{(\mathbf{Rb} - \mathbf{q})'[\mathbf{R}(\mathbf{X'X})^{-1}\mathbf{R'}]^{-1}(\mathbf{Rb} - \mathbf{q})/J}{\mathbf{e'e}/(n - K)} =$$

$$\frac{(\mathbf{Rb} - \mathbf{q})'[\mathbf{R}s^2(\mathbf{X'X})^{-1}\mathbf{R'}]^{-1}(\mathbf{Rb} - \mathbf{q})}{J}$$

has an F distribution with J and $n - K$ degrees of freedom.

Note the distinction between the properties of $\mathbf{b}$ established using **I** through **IV** and the additional inference results that are obtained with the further assumption of normality of the disturbances. The primary result in the first set is the Gauss–Markov theorem, which holds regardless of the distribution of the disturbances. The important additional result brought by the normality assumption is 10 (and result 9, which is a special case). Normality does not produce any additional finite sample optimality results.

10.3. Asymptotic Distribution Theory for the Classical Regression Model

For the basic model of assumptions I through IV, it is straightforward to derive the large-sample properties of the least squares estimator. We shall continue to assume that $\mathbf{X}$ is nonstochastic until Section 10.4. The normality assumption is inessential at this point. We examine its implications in Section 10.5.

10.3.1. Consistency of the Least Squares Coefficient Vector

We begin by assuming that

$$\lim_{n\to\infty} \frac{1}{n} \mathbf{X'X} = \mathbf{Q} \qquad \text{a positive definite matrix.} \qquad (10\text{--}1)$$

If $\mathbf{X}$ is taken to be "fixed in repeated samples," or equivalently, if the assumptions of this regression model are meant to apply only to the $\mathbf{X}$ matrix in hand, then (10–1) leads to $\mathbf{Q} = (1/n)\mathbf{X'X}$. If, instead, $\mathbf{X}$ is taken to be nonstochastic, but not constant in repeated samples, then (10–1) is a statement about the means of choosing the sample data. The least squares estimator may be written

$$\mathbf{b} = \boldsymbol{\beta} + \left(\frac{1}{n}\,\mathbf{X'X}\right)^{-1}\!\left(\frac{1}{n}\,\mathbf{X'}\boldsymbol{\varepsilon}\right). \tag{10-2}$$

Assuming that $\mathbf{Q}^{-1}$ exists, since the inverse is a continuous function of the original matrix, we obtain

$$\text{plim }\mathbf{b} = \boldsymbol{\beta} + \mathbf{Q}^{-1}\,\text{plim}\left(\frac{1}{n}\,\mathbf{X'}\boldsymbol{\varepsilon}\right).$$

[We have invoked result (4–23).] We now require the probability limit of the last term. Let

$$\overline{\mathbf{w}} = \frac{1}{n}\,\mathbf{X'}\boldsymbol{\varepsilon}$$

$$= \frac{1}{n}\sum_i \mathbf{x}_i\varepsilon_i = \frac{1}{n}\sum_i \mathbf{w}_i.$$

Then

$$\mathbf{b} = \boldsymbol{\beta} + \left(\frac{1}{n}\,\mathbf{X'X}\right)^{-1}\overline{\mathbf{w}}$$

and

$$\text{plim }\mathbf{b} = \boldsymbol{\beta} + \mathbf{Q}^{-1}\,\text{plim }\overline{\mathbf{w}}.$$

Because $\mathbf{X}$ is a nonstochastic matrix,

$$E[\overline{\mathbf{w}}] = \frac{1}{n}\,\mathbf{X'}E[\boldsymbol{\varepsilon}] = \mathbf{0} \tag{10-3}$$

and

$$\text{Var}[\overline{\mathbf{w}}] = E[\overline{\mathbf{w}}\,\overline{\mathbf{w}}'] = \frac{1}{n}\,\mathbf{X'}E[\boldsymbol{\varepsilon}\boldsymbol{\varepsilon}']\mathbf{X}\frac{1}{n} = \frac{\sigma^2}{n}\left(\frac{\mathbf{X'X}}{n}\right).$$

It follows, then, that

$$\lim_{n\to\infty}\text{Var}[\overline{\mathbf{w}}] = 0\cdot\mathbf{Q} = \mathbf{0}.$$

Since the mean of $\overline{\mathbf{w}}$ is identically zero and its variance converges to zero, $\overline{\mathbf{w}}$ converges in mean square to zero, and plim $\overline{\mathbf{w}} = \mathbf{0}$. Therefore,

$$\text{plim}\left(\frac{1}{n}\,\mathbf{X'}\boldsymbol{\varepsilon}\right) = \mathbf{0}. \tag{10-4}$$

Consequently,

$$\text{plim }\mathbf{b} = \boldsymbol{\beta} + \mathbf{Q}^{-1}\cdot\mathbf{0} = \boldsymbol{\beta}. \tag{10-5}$$

This establishes that $\mathbf{b}$ is a consistent estimator of $\boldsymbol{\beta}$ in the classical regression model.

This way of proceeding is useful in order to set the stage for the results derived in the next section. It is worth noting, though, that although (10–1) is a conventional assumption, it is a bit stronger than necessary and excludes one very common case. If $\mathbf{X}$ contains a time trend, $(1/n)\mathbf{X}'\mathbf{X}$ will explode as n goes to infinity, not converge to a positive definite matrix. In this case, it would follow from the exact results

$$E[\mathbf{b}] = \boldsymbol{\beta}, \qquad \text{hence,} \quad \lim_{n \to \infty} E[\mathbf{b}] = \boldsymbol{\beta}$$

and

$$\text{Var}[\mathbf{b}] = \sigma^2(\mathbf{X}'\mathbf{X})^{-1}, \qquad \text{hence,} \quad \lim_{n \to \infty} \text{Var}[\mathbf{b}] = \mathbf{0}$$

that $\mathbf{b}$ converges in mean square to $\boldsymbol{\beta}$. Indeed, this case is particularly favorable in that the sampling difference between $\mathbf{b}$ and $\boldsymbol{\beta}$ converges to zero more rapidly than in the conventional case.[2]

Time series settings that involve time trends, polynomial time series, and trending variables often pose cases in which the preceding assumptions are too restrictive.[3] A somewhat weaker set of assumptions about $\mathbf{X}$ that is broad enough to include most of these is the **Grenander conditions:**[4]

1. For each column of $\mathbf{X}$, $\mathbf{x}_k$, if $d_{nk}^2 = \mathbf{x}_k'\mathbf{x}_k$, $\lim_{n \to \infty} d_{nk}^2 = +\infty$. This means that $\mathbf{x}_k$ does not degenerate to a sequence of zeroes.[5]
2. $\text{Lim}_{n \to \infty} x_{ik}^2/d_{nk}^2 = 0$ for all $i = 1, \ldots, n$. This implies that no single observation will ever dominate $\mathbf{x}_k'\mathbf{x}_k$, and as $n \to \infty$, individual observations will become less important.
3. Let $\mathbf{R}_n$ be the sample correlation matrix of the columns of $\mathbf{X}$, excluding the constant term if there is one. Then $\lim_{n \to \infty} \mathbf{R}_n = \mathbf{C}$, a positive definite matrix. This implies that the full rank condition will always be met.[6] We have already assumed that $\mathbf{X}$ has full rank in a finite sample, so this assumption ensures that the condition will never be violated.

The conditions ensure that the data matrix is "well behaved" in large samples in that no single observation dominates the sum of squares and that sums of squares continue to grow as the sample size grows, but at a reasonable rate. This is a very weak assumption and is likely to be satisfied by almost any data set encountered in practice.[7]

10.3.2. Asymptotic Normality of the Least Squares Estimator

In order to derive the asymptotic distribution of the least squares estimator, we shall use the results of Section 4.4.2. First, it follows from (10–2) that

$$\sqrt{n}(\mathbf{b} - \boldsymbol{\beta}) = \left(\frac{\mathbf{X}'\mathbf{X}}{n}\right)^{-1}\left(\frac{1}{\sqrt{n}}\right)\mathbf{X}'\boldsymbol{\varepsilon}. \tag{10–6}$$

---

[2]Further discussion of this case and several others is given in Schmidt (1976, pp. 85–88). White (1984) examines a number of other cases. It is more difficult to establish consistency of s^2 when $\mathbf{X}$ contains a time trend. See Schmidt (1975) and Theil (1971) for discussion.

[3]These are sometimes labeled *asymptotically uncooperative regressors*. See, for example, Schmidt (1976, p. 85). An example is a regressor of the form λ^t, where t indexes the time series observations. A variable of precisely this form will figure prominently in our analysis of the geometric distributed lag model in Chapter 18. It turns out that consistency *cannot* be established in the presence of this type of variable unless $|\lambda| > 1$, which will cause other problems.

[4]Judge et al. (1985, p. 162).

[5]The regressor λ^t described earlier violates this assumption.

[6]The formal statement of this condition, for example, in Judge et al. (1985), is a bit more involved. The preceding is equivalent.

[7]White (1984) continues this line of analysis. He also provides additional results on conditions that must be attached to *stochastic* regressors in order to establish the asymptotic properties of least squares. We turn to this subject in Section 10.4.

Since the inverse matrix is a continuous function of the original matrix, $\lim_{n \to \infty} (\mathbf{X'X}/n)^{-1} = \mathbf{Q}^{-1}$. Therefore, if the limiting distribution exists, the limiting distribution of the statistic in (10–6) is the same as that of

$$\left[\lim_{n \to \infty} \left(\frac{\mathbf{X'X}}{n} \right)^{-1} \right] \left(\frac{1}{\sqrt{n}} \right) \mathbf{X'\varepsilon} = \mathbf{Q}^{-1} \left(\frac{1}{\sqrt{n}} \right) \mathbf{X'\varepsilon}.^{8} \tag{10–7}$$

Thus, we must establish the limiting distribution of

$$\frac{1}{\sqrt{n}} \mathbf{X'\varepsilon} = \sqrt{n}(\overline{\mathbf{w}} - E[\overline{\mathbf{w}}]), \tag{10–8}$$

where $E[\overline{\mathbf{w}}] = \mathbf{0}$. [See (10–3).] We can use the Lindberg–Feller version of the central limit theorem given in Section 4.4.2 to obtain the limiting distribution of $\sqrt{n}\,\overline{\mathbf{w}}$. Using that formulation,

$$\overline{\mathbf{w}} = \frac{1}{n} \sum_i \mathbf{x}_i \varepsilon_i$$

is the average of n independent random vectors, $\mathbf{x}_i \varepsilon_i$, with means $\mathbf{0}$ and variances

$$\text{Var}[\mathbf{x}_i \varepsilon_i] = \sigma^2 \mathbf{x}_i \mathbf{x}_i' = \sigma^2 \mathbf{Q}_i. \tag{10–9}$$

The variance of $\sqrt{n}\,\overline{\mathbf{w}}$ is

$$\sigma^2 \overline{\mathbf{Q}}_n = \sigma^2 \left(\frac{1}{n} \right) [\mathbf{Q}_1 + \mathbf{Q}_2 + \cdots + \mathbf{Q}_n]$$

$$= \sigma^2 \left(\frac{1}{n} \right) \sum_i \mathbf{x}_i \mathbf{x}_i' \tag{10–10}$$

$$= \sigma^2 \left(\frac{\mathbf{X'X}}{n} \right).$$

As long as the sum is not dominated by any particular term and the regressors are well behaved, which in this case means that (10–1) holds,

$$\lim_{n \to \infty} \sigma^2 \overline{\mathbf{Q}}_n = \sigma^2 \mathbf{Q}. \tag{10–11}$$

Therefore, we may apply the central limit theorem to the vector $\sqrt{n}\,\overline{\mathbf{w}}$, as we did in Section 4.4.2 for the univariate case, $\sqrt{n}\,\overline{x}$.

Formal proofs of the following result, which is based on the Lindberg–Feller variant of the central limit theorem, are given in Schmidt (1976) and White (1984). If

1. The disturbances all have the same distribution, with zero mean and finite variance, σ^2,
2. The elements of $\mathbf{X}$ are bounded such that $|x_{tk}|$ is finite and $\lim(\mathbf{X'X}/n) = \mathbf{Q}$, a finite positive definite matrix, then

$$\left(\frac{1}{\sqrt{n}} \right) \mathbf{X'\varepsilon} \xrightarrow{d} N[\mathbf{0}, \sigma^2 \mathbf{Q}]. \tag{10–12}$$

It follows, then, that

$$\mathbf{Q}^{-1} \left(\frac{1}{\sqrt{n}} \right) \mathbf{X'\varepsilon} \xrightarrow{d} N[\mathbf{Q}^{-1}\mathbf{0}, \mathbf{Q}^{-1}(\sigma^2 \mathbf{Q})\mathbf{Q}^{-1}] \tag{10–13}$$

---

[8] This is a multivariate version of result (4–28).

or, combining terms,

$$\sqrt{n}\,(\mathbf{b} - \boldsymbol{\beta}) \xrightarrow{d} N[\mathbf{0},\,\sigma^2\mathbf{Q}^{-1}]. \tag{10-14}$$

Using the technique of Section 4.4.3, we then obtain the asymptotic distribution for **b**:

$$\mathbf{b} \xrightarrow{a} N\left[\boldsymbol{\beta},\,\frac{\sigma^2}{n}\,\mathbf{Q}^{-1}\right]. \tag{10-15}$$

In practice, it is necessary to estimate $(1/n)\mathbf{Q}^{-1}$ with $(\mathbf{X'X})^{-1}$ and σ^2 with $\mathbf{e'e}/(n - K)$.

If $\boldsymbol{\varepsilon}$ is normally distributed, result 7 given in Section 10.2 holds in every sample, so it holds asymptotically as well. The important implication of the derivation above is that if the regressors are well behaved, the asymptotic normality of the least squares estimator does not depend on normality of the disturbances; it is a consequence of the central limit theorem.

10.3.3. Asymptotic Distribution of a Function of **b**—The Delta Method

To complete the derivation, we can extend Theorem 4.4 directly to functions of the least squares estimator. Let $\mathbf{f(b)}$ be a set of J continuous, linear or nonlinear functions of the least squares estimators and let

$$\mathbf{G} = \frac{\partial \mathbf{f(b)}}{\partial \mathbf{b'}}.$$

G is the $J \times K$ matrix whose jth row is the vector of derivatives of the jth function with respect to **b.** By the Slutsky theorem (4–21),

$$\text{plim } \mathbf{f(b)} = \mathbf{f(\boldsymbol{\beta})}$$

and

$$\text{plim } \mathbf{G} = \frac{\partial \mathbf{f(\boldsymbol{\beta})}}{\partial \boldsymbol{\beta'}} = \boldsymbol{\Gamma}.$$

Then

$$\mathbf{f(b)} \xrightarrow{a} N\left[\mathbf{f(\boldsymbol{\beta})},\,\boldsymbol{\Gamma}\left(\frac{\sigma^2}{n}\,\mathbf{Q}^{-1}\right)\boldsymbol{\Gamma'}\right]. \tag{10-16}$$

In practice, the estimator of the asymptotic covariance matrix would be

$$\text{Est. Asy. Var}[\mathbf{f(b)}] = \mathbf{G}[s^2(\mathbf{X'X})^{-1}]\mathbf{G'}.$$

If any of the functions are nonlinear, the property of unbiasedness that holds for **b** may not carry over to $\mathbf{f(b)}$. Nonetheless, it follows from (10–14) that $\mathbf{f(b)}$ is a consistent estimator of $\mathbf{f(\boldsymbol{\beta})}$, and the asymptotic covariance matrix is readily available.

EXAMPLE 10.1 Estimating an Elasticity ─────────────────────────────

In the linear model,

$$y = \boldsymbol{\beta'}\mathbf{x} + \boldsymbol{\varepsilon},$$

the elasticity of y with respect to changes in x_k is

$$\eta_k = \frac{\partial \ln y}{\partial \ln x_k} = \beta_k\left(\frac{x_k}{y}\right).$$

This value is often estimated by computing it at the sample means as

$$h_k = b_k \frac{\bar{x}_k}{\mathbf{b'\bar{x}}}.$$

The denominator is the estimate of $E[y]$ using the mean values of the regressors. (If the model contains a constant term, this will equal $\bar{y}$.) What are the asymptotic properties of h_k? The finite sample properties of h_k are not likely to be tractable because of the division by $\mathbf{b'\bar{x}}$. But with (10–16), the large-sample properties should be straightforward. First,

$$\text{plim } \mathbf{b} = \boldsymbol{\beta}.$$

If (10–1) is met, then $\bar{x}$ will converge to a finite vector, say $\mathbf{q}$. As such, it follows from the Slutsky theorem that

$$\text{plim } h_k = \eta_{k|\mathbf{x}=\mathbf{q}}.$$

That is, the sample estimate will converge to the true elasticity, evaluated at the limiting values of the sample means of the regressors. To find the asymptotic distribution, we use the delta method of the preceding section. The vector of derivatives is

$$\boldsymbol{\gamma} = \frac{\partial \eta}{\partial \boldsymbol{\beta}}$$

$$= \frac{(\boldsymbol{\beta'q})q_k\mathbf{e}_k - (\beta_k q_k)\mathbf{q}}{(\boldsymbol{\beta'q})^2}$$

$$= \frac{q_k\mathbf{e}_k - \eta_k\mathbf{q}}{\boldsymbol{\beta'q}},$$

where $\mathbf{e}_k$ is the kth column of a $K \times K$ identity matrix. (It is a column vector with 1 in the kth position and zeros elsewhere.) The asymptotic distribution would be normal with mean η_k and variance

$$\text{Asy. Var}[h_k] = \boldsymbol{\gamma'}\left[\left(\frac{\sigma^2}{n}\right)\mathbf{Q}^{-1}\right]\boldsymbol{\gamma}.$$

In practice, $(\sigma^2/n)\mathbf{Q}^{-1}$ is estimated with $s^2(\mathbf{X'X})^{-1}$ and $\mathbf{g}$ can be computed by adding $\bar{x}_k/\bar{y}$ to the kth element of $(-h_k/\bar{y})\bar{\mathbf{x}}$.

EXAMPLE 10.2 Asymptotic Distribution of the Constant in a Log-linear Model

To estimate a log-linear model,

$$Y = AX^\beta e^\varepsilon$$

we first write

$$\ln Y = \ln A + \beta \ln X + \varepsilon$$

$$= \alpha + \beta x + \varepsilon$$

and then estimate the parameters by ordinary least squares. Assume for the moment that ε has a normal distribution. Then, from (5–27), the exact finite sample distribution of a, the estimator of α, is

$$a \sim N\left[\alpha, \sigma^2\left\{\frac{1}{n} + \frac{\bar{x}^2}{\Sigma_i(x_i - \bar{x})^2}\right\}\right].$$

For estimating $A = e^{\alpha}$, the usual estimator will be e^a. The exact distribution, mean, and variance of e^a can be found by using the result:

$$\text{If } a \sim N[\alpha, \gamma^2], \text{ then } e^a \sim \textit{lognormal} \text{ with} \quad\quad (10\text{–}17)$$
$$\text{mean } e^{\alpha + \gamma^2/2} \text{ and variance } e^{2\alpha + \gamma^2} (e^{\gamma^2} - 1).$$

By inserting the expression for the variance of a, we obtain the *exact*, lognormal distribution with mean

$$E[e^a] = e^{\alpha} \times e^{\sigma^2[1/n + \bar{x}^2/\Sigma_i(x_i - \bar{x})^2]/2}$$

and

$$\text{Var}[e^a] = e^{2\alpha} \times e^{\sigma^2[1/n + \bar{x}^2/\Sigma_i(x_i - \bar{x})^2]} \times (e^{\sigma^2[1/n + \bar{x}^2/\Sigma_i(x_i - \bar{x})^2]} - 1).$$

Clearly, e^a is a biased estimator of A, since $E[e^a]$ is greater than e^{α}. But since the second term in $E[e^a]$ will converge to 1 as $n \to \infty$, $E[e^a] \to e^{\alpha}$. (The exponent converges to zero from above.) Likewise, the second and third terms in $\text{Var}[e^a]$ converge to 1 and zero, respectively, as $n \to \infty$, so the variance converges to zero. Therefore, e^a converges in mean square to e^{α}.

Based on (10–16), the *asymptotic* distribution of e^a will be normal (not lognormal) with mean A. The asymptotic variance of a is

$$\theta^2 = \frac{1}{n} \lim_{n \to \infty} n \times \sigma^2 \left\{ \frac{1}{n} + \frac{\bar{x}^2}{\Sigma_i(x_i - \bar{x})^2} \right\}.$$

So, using (10–16), the asymptotic variance of e^a is

$$(dA/d\alpha)^2 \text{ Asy. Var}[a] = (e^{\alpha})^2 \theta^2 = e^{2\alpha}\theta^2.$$

Note the difference between the exact variance given earlier and the variance of the asymptotic normal distribution. We would estimate the asymptotic variance with

$$T^2 = e^{2a}s^2 \left[\frac{1}{n} + \frac{\bar{x}^2}{\Sigma_i(x_i - \bar{x})^2} \right]$$

$$= e^{2a} \times \text{Est. Var}[a].$$

The comparison between the true and asymptotic distributions would be similar to that in Figure 4.5.

10.3.4. Asymptotic Behavior of the Standard Test Statistics

Without normality of ε, the t, F, and chi-squared statistics given earlier do not have these distributions. We can appeal instead to the results of Section 4.4.3. We have shown that

$$\mathbf{b} \xrightarrow{a} N\left[\boldsymbol{\beta}, \frac{\sigma^2}{n} \mathbf{Q}^{-1} \right].$$

It follows that the asymptotic distribution of

$$\theta_k = \frac{b_k - \beta_k}{[(\sigma^2/n) \mathbf{Q}_{kk}^{-1}]^{1/2}}$$

is standard normal. Since plim $s^2(\mathbf{X'X}/n)^{-1} = \sigma^2\mathbf{Q}^{-1}$,

$$t_k = \frac{b_k - \beta_k}{[s^2(\mathbf{X'X})_{kk}^{-1}]^{1/2}}$$

will have the same asymptotic distribution as θ_k. So, instead of the t distribution, we can refer the usual statistic for a hypothesis about an element of $\boldsymbol{\beta}$ to the standard normal distribution.

The F statistic for testing a set of linear restrictions,

$$F = \frac{(\mathbf{e}'_*\mathbf{e}_* - \mathbf{e}'\mathbf{e})/J}{\mathbf{e}'\mathbf{e}/(n - K)} = \frac{(\mathbf{Rb} - \mathbf{q})'[\mathbf{R}(s^2(\mathbf{X}'\mathbf{X})^{-1})\mathbf{R}']^{-1}(\mathbf{Rb} - \mathbf{q})}{J},$$

is no longer distributed as F because neither the numerator nor the denominator has the necessary chi-squared distribution. However, the Wald statistic, $JF[J, n - K]$, does have a chi-squared distribution asymptotically and can be used instead. This is the same result we have for the case of normally distributed disturbances. Under the usual assumptions, the Wald statistic may be used whether or not the disturbances are normally distributed. A proof of this important conclusion will be instructive.[9]

THEOREM 10.1: LIMITING DISTRIBUTION OF THE WALD STATISTIC: *If* $\sqrt{n}(\mathbf{b} - \boldsymbol{\beta}) \xrightarrow{d} N[\mathbf{0}, \sigma^2\mathbf{Q}^{-1}]$, *and if* $H_0: \mathbf{R}\boldsymbol{\beta} - \mathbf{q} = \mathbf{0}$ *is true, then*

$$W = (\mathbf{Rb} - \mathbf{q})'[\mathbf{R}(s^2(\mathbf{X}'\mathbf{X})^{-1})\mathbf{R}']^{-1}(\mathbf{Rb} - \mathbf{q}) = JF$$

converges in distribution to a chi-squared variate with J degrees of freedom.

Proof: Since $\mathbf{R}$ is a matrix of constants,

$$\sqrt{n}\mathbf{R}(\mathbf{b} - \boldsymbol{\beta}) \xrightarrow{d} N[\mathbf{0}, \mathbf{R}(\sigma^2\mathbf{Q}^{-1})\mathbf{R}']. \tag{1}$$

But $\mathbf{R}\boldsymbol{\beta} = \mathbf{q}$, so

$$\sqrt{n}(\mathbf{Rb} - \mathbf{q}) \xrightarrow{d} N[\mathbf{0}, \mathbf{R}(\sigma^2\mathbf{Q}^{-1})\mathbf{R}']. \tag{2}$$

For convenience, write this as

$$\mathbf{z} \xrightarrow{d} N[\mathbf{0}, \mathbf{P}]. \tag{2'}$$

In Section 2.7.12, we defined the inverse square root of a positive definite matrix, $\mathbf{P}$, as another matrix, say, $\mathbf{T}$ such that $\mathbf{T}^2 = \mathbf{P}^{-1}$, and denoted $\mathbf{T}$ as $\mathbf{P}^{-1/2}$. Let $\mathbf{T}$ be the inverse square root of $\mathbf{P}$. Then, by the same reasoning as in (1) and (2),

$$\text{If } \mathbf{z} \xrightarrow{d} N[\mathbf{0}, \mathbf{P}], \ \mathbf{P}^{-1/2}\mathbf{z} \xrightarrow{d} N[\mathbf{0}, \mathbf{P}^{-1/2}\mathbf{P}\mathbf{P}^{-1/2}] = N[\mathbf{0}, \mathbf{I}]. \tag{3}$$

We now invoke (4–31) for the limiting distribution of a function of a random variable. The sum of squares of uncorrelated (i.e., independent) standard normal variables is distributed as chi-squared. Thus, the limiting distribution of

$$(\mathbf{P}^{-1/2}\mathbf{z})'(\mathbf{P}^{-1/2}\mathbf{z}) = \mathbf{z}'\mathbf{P}^{-1}\mathbf{z} \xrightarrow{d} \chi^2(J). \tag{4}$$

Reassembling the parts from before, we have shown that the limiting distribution of

$$n(\mathbf{Rb} - \mathbf{q})'[\mathbf{R}(\sigma^2\mathbf{Q}^{-1})\mathbf{R}']^{-1}(\mathbf{Rb} - \mathbf{q}) \tag{5}$$

is chi-squared, with J degrees of freedom. Note the similarity of this to the results of Section 3.10.5. Finally, if

$$\text{plim } s^2\left(\frac{1}{n}\mathbf{X}'\mathbf{X}\right)^{-1} = \sigma^2\mathbf{Q}^{-1}, \tag{6}$$

---

[9] See White (1984, p. 71).

the statistic obtained by replacing $\sigma^2\mathbf{Q}^{-1}$ by $s^2(\mathbf{X}'\mathbf{X}/n)^{-1}$ in (5) has the same limiting distribution.[10] The n's cancel, and we are left with the Wald statistic from before. This completes the proof. The Wald statistic can be computed as J times the usual F statistic.

The implication of these asymptotic results is that if the normality assumption of the classical model with normal disturbances is not met, the significance levels assigned to the familiar test statistics will be inappropriate. The exact finite sample distribution of, for example, a t statistic will almost surely be intractable. But the same statistic will be asymptotically distributed as standard normal. Unfortunately, this leaves open the question of how to proceed in a moderately sized sample. If the sample is not large, the limiting distributions (e.g., standard normal instead of t) are likely to be overly optimistic. Conservativism may still argue in favor of using the finite sample distributions, t, F, or chi-squared.

10.3.5. Consistency of s^2 and the Estimator of Asy. Var[b]

The proof in the preceding section relied on an assumption that $s^2(\mathbf{X}'\mathbf{X}/n)^{-1} \to \sigma^2\mathbf{Q}^{-1}$. This section will obtain conditions under which the assumption is valid. With (10–1) it is sufficient to restrict attention to s^2, so the purpose here is to assess the consistency of s^2 for σ^2. Expanding

$$s^2 = \frac{1}{n-K}\, \boldsymbol{\varepsilon}'\mathbf{M}\boldsymbol{\varepsilon}$$

produces

$$s^2 = \frac{1}{n-K}\,[\boldsymbol{\varepsilon}'\boldsymbol{\varepsilon} - \boldsymbol{\varepsilon}'\mathbf{X}(\mathbf{X}'\mathbf{X})^{-1}\mathbf{X}'\boldsymbol{\varepsilon}].$$

$$= \frac{n}{n-K}\left[\frac{\boldsymbol{\varepsilon}'\boldsymbol{\varepsilon}}{n} - \left(\frac{\boldsymbol{\varepsilon}'\mathbf{X}}{n}\right)\left(\frac{\mathbf{X}'\mathbf{X}}{n}\right)^{-1}\left(\frac{\mathbf{X}'\boldsymbol{\varepsilon}}{n}\right)\right].$$

The leading constant obviously converges to 1, and by Theorem 4.4, the first term in brackets converges in probability to σ^2. This implies that

$$\text{plim } s^2 = \sigma^2 - \text{plim}\left(\frac{\boldsymbol{\varepsilon}'\mathbf{X}}{n}\right)\left(\frac{\mathbf{X}'\mathbf{X}}{n}\right)^{-1}\left(\frac{\mathbf{X}'\boldsymbol{\varepsilon}}{n}\right).$$

It is tempting to apply (10–1), (10–4) (twice) and the product rule for probability limits, (4–23), to assert that the second term converges to zero, but this oversimplifies the problem a bit and neglects an important aspect of the result.

Taking the second term in plim s^2 in isolation, and rearranging it slightly, we have

$$\left(\frac{\boldsymbol{\varepsilon}'\mathbf{X}}{n}\right)\left(\frac{\mathbf{X}'\mathbf{X}}{n}\right)^{-1}\left(\frac{\mathbf{X}'\boldsymbol{\varepsilon}}{n}\right) = \left(\frac{1}{n}\right)\left(\frac{\boldsymbol{\varepsilon}'\mathbf{X}}{\sqrt{n}}\right)\left(\frac{\mathbf{X}'\mathbf{X}}{n}\right)^{-1}\left(\frac{\mathbf{X}'\boldsymbol{\varepsilon}}{\sqrt{n}}\right).$$

The large-sample behavior of this statistic is the same as that of

$$q = \left(\frac{1}{n}\right)\left(\frac{\boldsymbol{\varepsilon}'\mathbf{X}}{\sqrt{n}}\right)\mathbf{Q}^{-1}\left(\frac{\mathbf{X}'\boldsymbol{\varepsilon}}{\sqrt{n}}\right).$$

Now, note that q equals $1/n$ times a quadratic form in the normally distributed vector which appears in (10–12). Moreover, the asymptotic covariance matrix of that vector is

---

[10] Consistency of s^2 is discussed in the next section.

Q. Therefore, using the results of the proof of Theorem 10.1, we find that q may be written as

$$q = \left(\frac{1}{n}\right)\mathbf{z}'\mathbf{z}, \quad \text{where} \quad \mathbf{z} \xrightarrow{d} N[\mathbf{0},\,\mathbf{I}].$$

Thus,

$$nq \xrightarrow{d} \chi^2[K].$$

It follows, therefore, that q itself converges in mean square to 0. This establishes the consistency of s^2 for σ^2. The end result is that (10–1) and (10–12) are sufficient for consistency of s^2. But as noted, (10–4) will suffice. It follows that the appropriate estimator for the asymptotic covariance matrix of $\mathbf{b}$ is, as expected,

$$\text{Est. Asy. Var}[\mathbf{b}] = \left(\frac{1}{n}\right)s^2\left(\frac{\mathbf{X}'\mathbf{X}}{n}\right)^{-1} = s^2(\mathbf{X}'\mathbf{X})^{-1}.$$

10.4. Stochastic Regressors and Lagged Dependent Variables

The assumption of nonstochastic regressors simplifies the derivation of the statistical properties of the least squares estimator. But as we saw in Sections 6.4 and 6.5, the important finite sample results (unbiasedness and the Gauss–Markov theorem) do not depend on it, nor do the distributions of the conventional test statistics (t, F, and chi-squared) that are based on normality of the disturbances. (See Section 6.5.) For practical purposes, at least as regards the finite sample results, the assumption of nonstochastic regressors is inessential. This section will continue the analysis to determine whether any of the asymptotic results in Section 10.3 must be revised to accommodate stochastic regressors.

The crucial results needed to establish the consistency and asymptotic normality of $\mathbf{b}$ with nonstochastic regressors are (10–1), (10–4), and (10–12). If we assume that the regressors are stochastic and replace the ordinary limit in (10–1) with

$$\text{plim}\,\frac{1}{n}\,\mathbf{X}'\mathbf{X} = \mathbf{Q}, \quad \text{a positive definite matrix,} \tag{10–18}$$

then the consistency of $\mathbf{b}$ can be established using the same line of argument as that used in Section 10.3.1. If, in addition, (10–12) continues to hold, then the asymptotic normality of $\mathbf{b}$ can be shown as well. What remains, then, is to consider the more general conditions under which (10–18), (10–12), and by implication, (10–4) will hold.

To begin, assume that the rows of $\mathbf{X}$ are random and independent draws from a multivariate distribution with mean vector $\boldsymbol{\mu}_x$, finite, positive definite covariance matrix $\boldsymbol{\Sigma}_{xx}$, and finite fourth moments, $\phi_{jklm} = E[x_j x_k x_l x_m]$.[11] Then (10–18) can be established by using a mean-squared convergence argument for random sampling from a distribution. The matrix $\mathbf{Q}_n$ of (10–10) is the mean of a random sample;

$$\overline{\mathbf{Q}}_n = \frac{1}{n}\sum_i \mathbf{x}_i\mathbf{x}_i' = \frac{1}{n}\sum_i \mathbf{Q}_i.$$

[11] This is general enough to include any nonstochastic elements in $\mathbf{x}$, such as the constant term.

The population counterpart to $\overline{\mathbf{Q}}_n$ is

$$E[\mathbf{x}_i\mathbf{x}_i'] = \mathbf{Q} = \mathbf{\Sigma}_{xx} + \boldsymbol{\mu}_x\boldsymbol{\mu}_x'.$$

A multivariate generalization of Theorem 4.3 and (4–20) can be used to assert that plim $\overline{\mathbf{Q}}_n = \mathbf{Q}$. The jkth element of $\overline{\mathbf{Q}}_n$, which we denote $\overline{\mathbf{Q}}_{n,jk}$, is an unbiased estimator of that element of $\mathbf{Q}$ (i.e., $\mathbf{Q}_{jk}$). (This follows just by applying Theorem 4.1 element by element.) Each pair of elements $(\overline{\mathbf{Q}}_{n,jk}, \overline{\mathbf{Q}}_{n,lm})$ in $\overline{\mathbf{Q}}_n$ will have

$$\text{Cov}[\overline{\mathbf{Q}}_{n,jk}, \overline{\mathbf{Q}}_{n,lm}] = \frac{1}{n}[\phi_{jklm} - \mathbf{Q}_{jk}\mathbf{Q}_{lm}], \qquad (10\text{--}19)$$

which converges to zero. This establishes (10–18) for the assumption of random sampling of the rows of $\mathbf{X}$.

Now, assume that the observations ε_i are a random sample from a distribution, with mean 0 and constant variance σ^2 and zero covariance with every observation $\mathbf{x}_s$. The observations in

$$\overline{\mathbf{w}} = \frac{1}{n}\mathbf{X}'\boldsymbol{\varepsilon}$$

are

$$\mathbf{w}_i = \mathbf{x}_i\varepsilon_i.$$

It follows from our assumptions that the observations $\mathbf{w}_i$ are independent and identically distributed with mean

$$E[\mathbf{w}_i] = E[\mathbf{x}_i]E[\varepsilon_i] = \boldsymbol{\mu}_x \times 0 = \mathbf{0}$$

and covariance matrix

$$\text{Var}[\mathbf{w}_i] = E[\mathbf{w}_i\mathbf{w}_i'] = E[\varepsilon_i^2\mathbf{x}_i\mathbf{x}_i'] = E[\varepsilon_i^2]E[\mathbf{x}_i\mathbf{x}_i'] = \sigma^2\mathbf{Q}.$$

Thus, the Lindberg–Levy variant of the central limit theorem (Theorem 4.4) can be applied. This establishes (10–12) and (10–14). Therefore,

> if the rows of $\mathbf{X}$ are a random sample from a distribution with finite fourth moments and the observations on ε are random observations from a distribution with zero mean and constant variance, σ^2, and are independent of all observations in $\mathbf{X}$, then $\mathbf{b}$ is consistent and asymptotically normally distributed as shown in (10–15).[12]

The preceding arguments are general enough to accommodate cases in which the rows of $\mathbf{X}$ are independent. Exceptions to the simple set of assumptions made above are likely to arise in two settings. In a **panel data set,** the sample will consist of multiple observations on each of many observational units. For example, a study might consist of a set of observations made at different points in time on a large number of families. In this case, the $\mathbf{x}$'s will surely be correlated across observations, at least within observational units. They might even be the same for all of the observations on a single family. They are also likely to be a mixture of random variables, such as family income, and nonstochastic regressors, such as a fixed "family effect" represented by a dummy variable. The second case would be that of a time series model, in which lagged values of the dependent variable appear on the right-hand side of the model.

---

[12] If some columns of $\mathbf{X}$ are nonstochastic, a mix of the results here and in Section 10.3 is easily constructed.

The panel data set can be handled as follows: Assume for the moment that the data consist of a fixed number of observations, say, T, on a set of N families, so that the total number of rows in $\mathbf{X}$ is NT. The matrix

$$\overline{\mathbf{Q}}_n = \frac{1}{n} \sum_i \mathbf{Q}_i$$

[see (10–10)], in which n is all of the observations in the sample, could be viewed as

$$\overline{\mathbf{Q}}_n = \frac{1}{N} \sum_i \frac{1}{T} \sum_{\substack{\text{observations} \\ \text{for family } i}} \mathbf{Q}_{ij}$$

$$= \frac{1}{N} \sum_i \tilde{\mathbf{Q}}_i, \qquad \text{where } \tilde{\mathbf{Q}}_i = \text{average } \mathbf{Q}_{ij} \text{ for family } i.$$

We might then view the set of observations on the ith unit as if they were a single observation and apply our convergence arguments to the number of families increasing without bound. The point is that the conditions that are needed to establish convergence will apply with respect to the number of observational units. The number of observations taken for each observation unit might be fixed and could be quite small. Extensions to the case of unequal-sized groups and other configurations of the data are considered in Chapter 16.

The second difficult case is that in which there are lagged dependent variables among the right-hand-side variables. Suppose that the model may be written

$$y_t = \boldsymbol{\beta}'\mathbf{x}_t + \gamma_1 y_{t-1} + \cdots + \gamma_p y_{t-p} + \varepsilon_t.$$

(Once again, since this is a time series setting, we use t to index the observations.) We assume that the disturbances are uncorrelated across observations and have constant variance and finite moments of all orders. To establish counterparts to (10–12) and (10–18), it is necessary to make additional assumptions about the regressors. In particular, we replace (10–18) with the assumption

$$\text{plim} \frac{1}{T - s} \sum_{t=s+1}^{T} \mathbf{x}_t \mathbf{x}_{t-s}' = \mathbf{Q}(s), \qquad \text{a finite matrix, } s \geq 0 \tag{10–20}$$

and $\mathbf{Q}(0)$ is nonsingular if $T \geq K$.

[Note that $\mathbf{Q} = \mathbf{Q}(0)$.] This is the matrix of cross products of the elements of $\mathbf{x}$ with lagged values of $\mathbf{x}$. The assumption that the sum converges to a finite matrix is a **stationarity** assumption. Heuristically, it says that the correlation between values of the $\mathbf{x}$'s at different points in time varies only with how far apart in time they are, not specifically with the points in time at which observations are made. An additional implication of the assumption is that the distribution or process generating the $\mathbf{x}$'s is such that the means of the *nonrandom* samples (the observations are correlated across time) converge to population quantities in the same fashion that means of independent and identically distributed samples do. Second, we assume that the roots of the polynomial

$$1 - \gamma_1 L - \gamma_2 L^2 - \cdots - \gamma_P L^P = 0 \tag{10–21}$$

are all outside the unit circle. (See Section 18.6.3 for further details.[13])

These conditions are sufficient to yield

$$\text{plim} \frac{1}{T - P} \sum_t \mathbf{z}_t \mathbf{z}_t' = \mathbf{Q}, \qquad \text{a finite, positive definite matrix,} \tag{10–22}$$

---

[13] More detailed treatments of this issue appear in Chapters 15 and 19 and in Goldberger (1990, Chap. 27).

where

$$\mathbf{z}_t = [\mathbf{x}_t, y_{t-1}, y_{t-2}, \cdots, y_{t-P}].$$

The results of Mann and Wald (1943) provide the basis for the asymptotic normal distribution in (10–12). This, then, produces the asymptotic distribution of the least squares estimator. We should note that the conditions needed for the finite sample results we had earlier no longer hold. Although $E[\varepsilon_t, y_{t-1}, \cdots, y_{t-p}] = 0$ for each observation, it is clear that $E[\boldsymbol{\varepsilon} \mid \mathbf{Z}]$, where the columns of $\mathbf{Z}$ include the $\mathbf{x}$'s and the lagged values of y, is not zero. For example, $E[\varepsilon_t \mid x_t, y_{t+1}]$ is clearly not zero since ε_t appears on the right-hand side of y_t. Without unbiasedness, the Gauss–Markov theorem no longer applies, and we are left only with our asymptotic results for this case.

In sum, the important properties of consistency and asymptotic normality of the least squares estimator are preserved under the assumption of stochastic regressors, provided that additional assumptions are made. In most cases, these assumptions are quite benign, so we conclude that the two asymptotic properties of least squares considered here, consistency and asymptotic normality, are quite robust to different specifications of the regressors.

10.5. Normally Distributed Disturbances

The results in Sections 10.3 and 10.4 were established under minimal assumptions about the distribution of ε, only zero mean, constant variance, finite higher moments, and independence of $\mathbf{x}$ and ε. It would appear that as far as the asymptotic results are concerned, the assumption of normally distributed disturbances would be entirely superfluous. However, we have not established any large-sample counterpart to the Gauss–Markov theorem. That is, it remains to establish whether the large-sample properties of the least squares estimator are optimal by any measure. At the end of Section 10.4 we broadened the class of estimators under consideration to those which are consistent and asymptotically normally distributed, but are not necessarily unbiased. Moreover, linearity may also prove unduly restrictive. In this section we will examine the implications of the normality assumption for the asymptotic properties of least squares. As should be clear from the preceding, the only remaining issue is efficiency, and it will turn out that normality plays a crucial role in this regard.

10.5.1. Asymptotic Efficiency—Maximum Likelihood Estimation

Definition. An estimator is asymptotically efficient if it is consistent, asymptotically normally distributed, and has an asymptotic covariance matrix that is not larger than the asymptotic covariance matrix of any other consistent, asymptotically normally distributed estimator.[14]

Taken directly, asymptotic efficiency is likely to be extremely difficult to verify. There is, however, an indirect strategy. In any regular problem, the maximum likelihood estimator is asymptotically efficient by the previous definition.[15] Therefore, in order to establish that an estimator is asymptotically efficient, one need only show that the estimator in question either (1) *is* the maximum likelihood estimator or (2) has the same asymptotic

[14] *Smaller* is defined in the sense of (2–118): The covariance matrix of the less efficient estimator equals that of the efficient estimator plus a nonnegative definite matrix.

[15] By *regular*, we mean a likelihood function that satisfies the regularity conditions discussed in Section 4.3.2.

properties as the maximum likelihood estimator. We shall use both of these approaches here, the first for the least squares estimator of $\boldsymbol{\beta}$ and the second for the least squares estimator of σ^2. As such, least squares has all of the desirable properties of maximum likelihood estimators, including asymptotic efficiency.[16]

The likelihood function for a sample of n independent, identically and normally distributed disturbances is

$$L = (2\pi\sigma^2)^{-n/2} e^{-\boldsymbol{\varepsilon}'\boldsymbol{\varepsilon}/(2\sigma^2)}. \tag{10-23}$$

The transformation from ε_i to y_i is $\varepsilon_i = y_i - \boldsymbol{\beta}'\mathbf{x}_i$, so the Jacobian for each observation, $|\partial\varepsilon_i/\partial y_i|$, is one.[17] Making the transformation, we find that the likelihood function for the n observations on the observed random variables is[18]

$$
\begin{aligned}
L &= (2\pi\sigma^2)^{-n/2} e^{(-1/(2\sigma^2))\Sigma_i(y_i - \boldsymbol{\beta}'\mathbf{x}_i)^2} \\
&= (2\pi\sigma^2)^{-n/2} e^{(-1/(2\sigma^2))(\mathbf{y} - \mathbf{X}\boldsymbol{\beta})'(\mathbf{y} - \mathbf{X}\boldsymbol{\beta})}.
\end{aligned} \tag{10-24}
$$

It is clear that to maximize this function with respect to $\boldsymbol{\beta}$, it will be necessary to maximize the exponent or minimize the familiar sum of squares. Taking logs in (10–24), we obtain the log-likelihood function for the classical regression model:

$$\ln L = -\frac{n}{2}\ln 2\pi - \frac{n}{2}\ln\sigma^2 - \frac{1}{2\sigma^2}(\mathbf{y} - \mathbf{X}\boldsymbol{\beta})'(\mathbf{y} - \mathbf{X}\boldsymbol{\beta}).$$

The necessary conditions for maximizing this log-likelihood are

$$
\begin{aligned}
\frac{\partial\ln L}{\partial\boldsymbol{\beta}} &= \frac{1}{\sigma^2}\mathbf{X}'(\mathbf{y} - \mathbf{X}\boldsymbol{\beta}) = \mathbf{0}, \\
\frac{\partial\ln L}{\partial\sigma^2} &= -\frac{n}{2\sigma^2} + \frac{1}{2\sigma^4}(\mathbf{y} - \mathbf{X}\boldsymbol{\beta})'(\mathbf{y} - \mathbf{X}\boldsymbol{\beta}) = 0.
\end{aligned} \tag{10-25}
$$

The values that satisfy these equations are

$$\hat{\boldsymbol{\beta}}_{ML} = (\mathbf{X}'\mathbf{X})^{-1}\mathbf{X}'\mathbf{y} = \mathbf{b} \tag{10-26}$$

and

$$\hat{\sigma}^2_{ML} = \frac{\mathbf{e}'\mathbf{e}}{n}.$$

The slope estimator is the familiar one, while the variance estimator differs from the least squares value by the divisor of n instead of $n - K$.[19]

The Cramér–Rao bound for the variance of an unbiased estimator is the negative inverse of the expectation of

$$
\begin{bmatrix}
\partial^2\ln L/\partial\boldsymbol{\beta}\,\partial\boldsymbol{\beta}' & \partial^2\ln L/\partial\boldsymbol{\beta}\,\partial\sigma^2 \\
\partial^2\ln L/\partial\sigma^2\,\partial\boldsymbol{\beta}' & \partial^2\ln L/\partial(\sigma^2)^2
\end{bmatrix} =
\begin{bmatrix}
-(1/\sigma^2)\mathbf{X}'\mathbf{X} & -(1/(2\sigma^4))\mathbf{X}'\boldsymbol{\varepsilon} \\
-(1/(2\sigma^4))\boldsymbol{\varepsilon}'\mathbf{X} & n/(2\sigma^4) - \boldsymbol{\varepsilon}'\boldsymbol{\varepsilon}/\sigma^6
\end{bmatrix}.
\tag{10-27}
$$

---

[16] The general results are presented in Section 4.5.

[17] See (3–41) in Section 3.5.

[18] The analysis is conditioned on $\mathbf{X}$. For now, we take $\mathbf{X}$ to be nonstochastic. For stochastic regressors, the analysis is the same as long as the distribution of $\mathbf{X}$ does not involve $\boldsymbol{\beta}$ or σ^2.

[19] As a general rule, maximum likelihood estimators do not make corrections for degrees of freedom.

In taking expected values, the off diagonal term vanishes. Thus, the Cramér–Rao variance bound is

$$[-\mathbf{I}(\boldsymbol{\beta}, \sigma^2)]^{-1} = \begin{bmatrix} \sigma^2(\mathbf{X'X})^{-1} & \mathbf{0} \\ \mathbf{0'} & 2\sigma^4/n \end{bmatrix}. \tag{10–28}$$

The least squares slope estimator coincides with the maximum likelihood estimator for this problem. Therefore, it inherits all of the desirable *asymptotic* properties of maximum likelihood estimators. To reiterate:

1. It is *consistent,* which we showed earlier.
2. It is *asymptotically normally distributed,* with an asymptotic variance matrix equal to the Cramér–Rao bound for efficient estimation.
3. It is *asymptotically efficient.* No other consistent and asymptotically normally distributed estimator has a smaller asymptotic covariance matrix.
4. Maximum likelihood estimators are also *invariant.* The maximum likelihood estimator of any continuous function of $\boldsymbol{\beta}$ is that function of the maximum likelihood estimator. Whereas, by the Gauss–Markov theorem, we could assert that the most efficient linear unbiased estimator of $\mathbf{r'\boldsymbol{\beta}}$ is $\mathbf{r'b,}$ we now have a much broader result. At least asymptotically, the most efficient estimator of $\mathbf{f}(\boldsymbol{\beta})$, where $\mathbf{f}(\boldsymbol{\beta})$ is any set of continuous functions, is $\mathbf{f}(\mathbf{b})$. The asymptotic distribution of this continuous function of the maximum likelihood estimator is given by (10–16).

We showed earlier that $s^2 = \mathbf{e'e}/(n - K)$ is an unbiased estimator of σ^2. Therefore, the maximum likelihood estimator is biased toward zero:

$$E[\hat{\sigma}^2] = \frac{n - K}{n} \sigma^2 = \left(1 - \frac{K}{n}\right)\sigma^2 < \sigma^2. \tag{10–29}$$

In spite of its small-sample bias, the maximum likelihood estimator of σ^2 has all of the desirable asymptotic properties. We see in (10–29) that s^2 and $\hat{\sigma}^2$ differ only by a factor $-K/n$, which vanishes in large samples. Nonetheless, it is instructive to formalize the asymptotic equivalence of the two. From (10–26) and (10–28), we know that

$$\sqrt{n}(\hat{\sigma}^2 - \sigma^2) \xrightarrow{d} N[0, 2\sigma^4].$$

It follows that the limiting distribution of

$$z_n = \left(1 - \frac{K}{n}\right)\sqrt{n}(\hat{\sigma}^2 - \sigma^2) + \frac{K}{\sqrt{n}}\sigma^2$$

is that of

$$\left(1 - \frac{K}{n}\right)N[0, 2\sigma^4] + \frac{K}{\sqrt{n}}\sigma^2.$$

But $K/\sqrt{n}$ and K/n vanish as $n \to \infty$, so the limiting distribution of z_n is also $N[0, 2\sigma^4]$. Since

$$z_n = \sqrt{n}(s^2 - \sigma^2),$$

we have shown that the asymptotic distribution of s^2 is the same as that of the maximum likelihood estimator.

10.5.2. Cases in Which Least Squares Is Inefficient

The result in Section 10.5.1 is useful insofar as it establishes conditions under which least squares is optimal. On the other hand, there is an opposite and much less pleasing conclusion to be drawn. That is, since maximum likelihood estimators are asymptotically efficient, the optimality of least squares in large samples depends on the assumption of normality. More to the point, if any other distribution is specified for ε and it emerges that **b** is not the maximum likelihood estimator, it follows directly that least squares is not efficient. In the absence of a specific model, it is rarely appropriate to specify a particular, nonnormal distribution for the disturbance in a regression model. But there are many applications that do specify other distributions.

EXAMPLE 10.3 The Gamma Regression Model _____

Greene (1980a) considers estimation in a regression model with an asymmetrically distributed disturbance,

$$
\cdot \, y = \left(\alpha - \frac{\sqrt{P}}{\sigma} \right) + \beta'\mathbf{x} - \left(\varepsilon - \frac{\sqrt{P}}{\sigma} \right)
$$
$$
= \alpha^* + \beta'\mathbf{x} + \varepsilon^*, \tag{10--30}
$$

where ε has the gamma distribution in Section 3.4.5 [see (3--39)] and $\sigma = \sqrt{P}/\lambda$ is the standard deviation of the disturbance. He shows that the covariance matrix of the least squares estimator of the slope coefficients (not including the constant term) is, as always,

$$
\mathrm{Var}[\mathbf{b}] = \sigma^2(\mathbf{X}'\mathbf{M}^0\mathbf{X})^{-1},
$$

while for the maximum likelihood estimator (which is not the OLS estimator),

$$
\mathrm{Asy.\ Var}[\hat{\beta}_{ML}] \simeq \left[\frac{P-2}{P} \right] \sigma^2(\mathbf{X}'\mathbf{M}^0\mathbf{X})^{-1}.^{[20]}
$$

But for the asymmetry parameter, this would be the same as the least squares estimator. We conclude that the estimator that accounts for the asymmetric disturbance distribution is more efficient asymptotically.

_____

10.5.3. Alternative Estimation Criteria

As a general rule, least squares treats negative and positive observations symmetrically and involves sums of observations that weight all observations equally. Maximum likelihood estimators make more explicit use of information about the shape of the disturbance distribution and, when appropriate, weight observations according to a more appropriate weighting scheme. To consider another example, if the disturbances were distributed according to the Laplace distribution,

$$
f(\varepsilon) = \frac{1}{2\sigma} e^{-|\varepsilon|/2\sigma},
$$

the maximum likelihood estimator of β would minimize the sum of absolute values of the residuals instead of the sum of squares.[21] The least squares estimator can be seriously distorted by outlying observations in a relatively small sample, while the minimum absolute deviations (MAD) estimator will be considerably less so.

_____

[20] The matrix $\mathbf{M}^0$ produces data in the form of deviations from sample means. (See Section 2.3.6.) In Greene's model, P must be strictly greater than 2.

[21] See L. Taylor (1974).

The possibility of disturbance distributions with thicker tails than the normal, particularly in microeconomic data and in applications in finance, has led to the proposal of numerous robust estimators.[22] Most of these can be written in the form

$$S(\mathbf{b}) = \sum \eta \left[\frac{y - \mathbf{b}'\mathbf{x}}{s} \right],$$

where $\eta[\cdot]$ is a weighting function designed to reduce the weight attached to extreme observations. Least squares and MAD are two we have already considered. Alternatives that have been suggested include $\eta(z) = |z|^p$ for alternative values of p between one and two and some discontinuous ones such as $\eta(z) = -\cos(z) - 1$ if $|z| \le \pi$ and zero otherwise.[23] Koenkar and Bassett (1978) have proposed the following criterion function:

$$S(\mathbf{b}) = t \sum_{+} |y - \mathbf{b}'\mathbf{x}| + (1 - t) \sum_{-} |y - \mathbf{b}'\mathbf{x}|,$$

where t is a predetermined proportion. For certain thick-tailed distributions, this estimator has performed well in Monte Carlo studies. However, in practice, the choice of t is likely to be a problem. These estimators have found little use in econometrics, primarily because of the difficulty in implementing them and their largely ad hoc nature. Tinkering with the outlying observations amounts to letting the computer be the ultimate judge of the estimated relationship and diminishes the role of the underlying theory. Least squares remains by far the estimator of choice for the linear regression model.

10.5.4. Detecting Departures from Normality

This section considers the general problem of using the moments of the least squares residuals to make inference about the distribution of the true disturbances.

The natural estimator of

$$\mu_r = E[\varepsilon^r]$$

would be

$$m_r = \left(\frac{1}{n} \right) \sum_i e_i^r.$$

However, the least squares residuals are only imperfect estimates of the true disturbances:

$$e_i = \varepsilon_i - \mathbf{x}_i'(\mathbf{b} - \boldsymbol{\beta}).$$

Since plim $\mathbf{b} = \boldsymbol{\beta}$, the larger the sample, the better an estimate this becomes. This is sometimes labeled **pointwise consistency.** It can be shown that the sample of least squares residuals converges to the sample of true disturbances.[24] This implies that if

$$\hat{\mu}_r = \frac{1}{n} \sum_i \varepsilon_i^r$$

is a consistent estimator of μ_r, then

$$m_r = \frac{1}{n} \sum_i e_i^r$$

is also.

---

[22] An extensive survey may be found in Amemiya (1985, pp. 70–80).

[23] Andrews (1974).

[24] See Theil (1971).

The foregoing has been used to devise a test of normality.[25] The normal distribution is symmetric and **mesokurtic.** The symmetry implies that the third moment, $E[\varepsilon^3]$, is zero. The standard measure of symmetry of a distribution is the skewness coefficient,

$$\sqrt{\beta_1} = \frac{E[\varepsilon^3]}{(\sigma^2)^{3/2}}.$$

Kurtosis is a measure of the thickness of the tails of a distribution. The measure is

$$\beta_2 = \frac{E[\varepsilon^4]}{(\sigma^2)^2}.$$

The normal distribution is the usual yardstick for this; the mesokurtic value is the kurtosis of the normal distribution, which is 3. Therefore, we might compare a distribution to the normal distribution by comparing this skewness to zero and its kurtosis to three. In practice, the usual measure is the **degree of excess,** $(\beta_2 - 3)$. The device we shall use is a Wald statistic. Under the hypothesis of normality, the test statistic would be

$$W = n\left[\frac{b_1}{6} + \frac{(b_2 - 3)^2}{24}\right] \sim \chi^2(2).$$

This is asymptotically distributed as chi-squared with two degrees of freedom. Feasible estimators of these parameters are computed using the least squares residuals.[26] The statistic can be referred to the standard chi-squared tables.

This test statistic has been derived as a Lagrange multiplier test in the context of the Pearson distributions by Bera and Jarque (1980a, 1980b).[27] It should be noted that the test is essentially nonconstructive. A finding of nonnormality does not necessarily suggest what to do next.[28] Note, also, that failing to reject normality does not confirm it. This remains only a test of symmetry and mesokurtosis.

EXAMPLE 10.4 A Model with a Nonnormal Disturbance

The data listed in Table 7.1 were used by Aigner, Lovell, and Schmidt (1977) to estimate a **stochastic frontier** model. Their model may be written

$$y_i = \alpha + \boldsymbol{\beta}'\mathbf{x}_i + \varepsilon_i$$

$$\varepsilon_i = v_i - |u_i|$$

where v_i and u_i are normally distributed with zero means and constant variances σ_v^2 and σ_u^2. The distribution of the absolute value of a normally distributed variable is shown in Figure 22.1; it is clearly nonnormal. The difference of the two variables is asymmetric and nonnormal.[29] The asymmetry of the distribution of ε_i is a central feature of the model. The degree of asymmetry can be characterized by the parameter $\lambda = \sigma_u/\sigma_v$. The larger is

---

[25] Kiefer and Salmon (1983).

[26] It is sometimes suggested that the residuals be transformed to remove their finite sample covariance before these testing procedures are performed. See, for example, Judge et al. (1985, p. 826). Since the tests are valid only asymptotically, when the residuals are uncorrelated anyway, this would not add to the validity of the test procedures. There is some evidence, for example, by Ramsey (1974), that using uncorrelated BLUS residuals [see Theil (1971)] makes matters worse instead of better.

[27] Additional results appear in Kiefer and Salmon (1983).

[28] Proceeding with estimation of Bera and Jarque's more general Pearson type 7 distribution is so cumbersome that empirical implementation is likely to be exceedingly difficult.

[29] The density of ε is $(2/\pi)^{1/2}\Phi(-\varepsilon\lambda/\sigma)(1/\sigma)\phi(\varepsilon/\sigma)$, where $\sigma = (\sigma_v^2 + \sigma_u^2)^{1/2}$.

λ, the more pronounced will be the asymmetry. Conversely, if λ equals zero, then $\varepsilon_i = v_i$, which has a normal distribution. The expected value of ε_i is

$$E[v_i - |u_i|] = \mu_\varepsilon = -\left(\frac{2}{\pi}\right)^{1/2} \sigma_u.$$

As such, the model can be written

$$y_i = (\alpha + \mu_\varepsilon) + \boldsymbol{\beta}'\mathbf{x}_i + (\varepsilon_i - \mu_\varepsilon)$$
$$= \alpha^* + \boldsymbol{\beta}'\mathbf{x}_i + \varepsilon_i^*,$$

where ε_i^* has zero mean, constant variance, but a nonnormal and asymmetric distribution. A test of the model can be based on the least squares residuals.

The results of least squares regression of the log of output (value added) on the logs of capital and labor are given in Table 7.2. Although the least squares estimator is inefficient—it is not the maximum likelihood estimator for this model—it is consistent. The moments of the residuals are

$$m_2 = 0.03154199,$$

$$m_3 = 0.004741061,$$

$$m_4 = 0.00410284.$$

The skewness and excess coefficients are

$$\frac{m_3}{(m_2)^{3/2}} = 0.846334$$

$$\frac{m_4}{(m_2)^2} - 3 = 1.12388.$$

With 27 observations, the chi-squared statistic is 4.6443. The 5 percent critical value from the chi-squared table for two degrees of freedom is 5.99, so we conclude that the residuals do not depart significantly from normality. As an indirect test of the same hypothesis, Aigner et al.'s estimate of λ is only 0.1, with an asymptotic t ratio of 0.05. Therefore, their results are consistent with these.

EXERCISES

1. Let e_i be the ith residual in the ordinary least squares regression of $\mathbf{y}$ on $\mathbf{X}$ in the classical regression model, and let ε_i be the corresponding true disturbance. Prove that $\text{plim}(e_i - \varepsilon_i) = 0$.

2. For the simple regression model,

$$y_i = \mu + \varepsilon_i, \qquad \varepsilon_i \sim N[0, \sigma^2],$$

prove that the sample mean is consistent and asymptotically normally distributed. Now consider the alternative estimator

$$\hat{\mu} = \sum_i w_i y_i,$$

$$w_i = \frac{i}{(n(n + 1)/2)} = \frac{i}{\Sigma_i \, i}.$$

Note that $\Sigma_i w_i = 1$. Prove that this is a consistent estimator of μ and obtain its asymptotic variance. [**Hint:** $\Sigma_i i^2 = n(n + 1)(2n + 1)/6$.]

3. Example 8.3 presents Nerlove's estimates of a generalized Cobb–Douglas cost function:

$$\log\left(\frac{C}{P_f}\right) = \alpha + \beta \log Q + \gamma \log^2 Y + \delta_k \log\left(\frac{P_k}{P_f}\right) + \delta_l \log\left(\frac{P_l}{P_f}\right) + \varepsilon.$$

(Nerlove used common, not natural, logarithms.) The purpose of the generalization was to produce a U-shaped average total cost curve. We are interested in the output at which the cost curve reaches its minimum. That is the point at which

$$\left.\frac{\partial \log C}{\partial \log Q}\right|_{Q=Q^*} = 1$$

or

$$Q^* = 10^{[(1-\beta)/(2\gamma)]}.$$

(You can simplify the analysis a bit by using the fact that $10^x = \exp(2.3026x)$. Thus,

$$Q^* = \exp\left(2.3026\left[\frac{1-\beta}{2\gamma}\right]\right).$$

Using the estimates given in the example, compute the estimate of this *efficient scale*. Estimate the asymptotic distribution of this estimate, assuming that the estimate of the asymptotic covariance of $\hat{\beta}$ and $\hat{\gamma}$ is -0.00008.

4. Suppose that y_i is a discrete random variable whose distribution, given x_i, is

$$\text{Prob}(Y_i = y_i) = \frac{e^{-\beta x_i}(\beta x_i)^{y_i}}{y_i!}, \qquad y_i = 0, 1, \ldots$$

Thus, y_i has a Poisson distribution. We also assume that $x_i > 0$ for all i.
(a) Compute the maximum likelihood estimator of β and its asymptotic distribution. Using the result that the sum of Poisson variables y_i with parameters λ_i is distributed as Poisson with parameter $\Sigma_i \lambda_i$, it is possible to obtain the exact distribution of the maximum likelihood estimator. What is this?
(b) As shown in Chapter 3, $E[y_i|x_i] = \beta x_i$. Therefore, this is a linear regression model. It does not satisfy the assumptions of the classical model, however, since $\text{Var}[y_i|x_i] = \beta x_i$. Nonetheless, it can be shown that the OLS estimator is consistent. Do so. Obtain the asymptotic distribution of the estimator. What assumptions are necessary to ensure your result?
(c) Prove that the asymptotic variance of the maximum likelihood estimator is smaller than that of the OLS estimator. (**Hint:** The proof will hinge upon the assumption that x_i is strictly positive.)

5. For the principal components estimator in (9–10), prove that the variance estimator,

$$q^2 = \frac{(\mathbf{y} - \mathbf{Zd})'(\mathbf{y} - \mathbf{Zd})}{n},$$

is not a consistent estimator of σ^2. Obtain the probability limit of q^2. (**Hint:** $\mathbf{I} - \mathbf{C}_L\mathbf{C}_L' = \mathbf{C}_M\mathbf{C}_M'$, where $\mathbf{C}_M$ is the matrix of the other $K - L$ characteristic vectors of $\mathbf{X}'\mathbf{X}$.)

6. For the classical regression model $y = X\beta + \varepsilon$ with no constant term and K regressors, what is

$$\text{plim } F[K, n - K] = \text{plim } \frac{R^2/K}{(1 - R^2)/(n - K)},$$

assuming that the true value of β is zero? What is the exact expected value?

7. For the instrumental variables estimator of (9–31), prove that

$$\hat{\sigma}^2 = \frac{(y - Xb_{IV})'(y - Xb_{IV})}{n}$$

is a consistent estimator of σ^2.

8. The density function for the compound disturbance in the stochastic frontier model is given in a footnote at the end of Section 10.5.4.
   (a) Derive the log-likelihood function and its first derivatives to define the maximum likelihood estimators of β, σ, and λ. Note that a useful shortcut is $d\phi(x)/dx = -x\phi(x)$, and $d\Phi(x)/dx = \phi(x)$.
   (b) Show how you would obtain estimates and standard errors for the underlying parameters, σ_v^2 and σ_u^2, given estimates of σ and λ and the appropriate estimate of their asymptotic covariance matrix.

11

Nonlinear Regression Models

11.1. Introduction

To this point, we have considered only linear models that can be estimated by ordinary least squares. Although the linear model is flexible enough to allow great variety in the shape of the regression, it still rules out many useful functional forms. In this chapter we shall examine models that are intrinsically nonlinear in their parameters. Although these models are often difficult to estimate, with the development of easy-to-use software, they have become quite common.

11.2. Nonlinear Regression Models

A general form of the regression model is

$$y_i = h(\mathbf{x}_i, \boldsymbol{\beta}) + \varepsilon_i.^1 \tag{11–1}$$

The linear model is obviously a special case, but this includes far more possibilities. For example,

$$y = \beta_1 + \beta_2 e^{\beta_3 x} + \varepsilon \tag{11–2}$$

cannot be transformed to linearity. It would appear that

$$y = \beta_1 x_1{}^{\beta_2} x_2{}^{\beta_3} e^{\varepsilon}$$

is also nonlinear, but for the purposes of our discussion, this is a linear regression model, while the first is not. The second can be transformed to linearity by taking logarithms on both sides of the equation.

We shall require an operational definition to distinguish these cases. In the context of regression analysis, what will characterize (11–1) as a **nonlinear regression model** is the method used to estimate the parameters. In particular, we take as our benchmark the case in which ε is normally distributed. Then, using the argument of Chapter 10, the values of the parameters that minimize the sum of squared deviations,

$$S(\widetilde{\boldsymbol{\beta}}) = \sum_i \varepsilon_i^2 = \sum_i [y_i - h(\mathbf{x}_i, \widetilde{\boldsymbol{\beta}})]^2 \tag{11–3}$$

---

[1] In principle, it could be written in terms of $g(Y_i)$. But unless $g(Y_i)$ introduces new unknown parameters, as in the Box–Cox model, we can view this as determining the units of measurement of Y and retain the less cumbersome notation.

will be the maximum likelihood estimators, as well as the **nonlinear least squares** estimators. The first-order conditions for minimization of $S(\tilde{\boldsymbol{\beta}})$ are

$$\frac{\partial S(\tilde{\boldsymbol{\beta}})}{\partial \tilde{\boldsymbol{\beta}}} = -2 \sum_i [y_i - h(\mathbf{x}_i, \tilde{\boldsymbol{\beta}})] \frac{\partial h(\mathbf{x}_i, \tilde{\boldsymbol{\beta}})}{\partial \tilde{\boldsymbol{\beta}}} = \mathbf{0}. \qquad (11\text{--}4)$$

In the linear model of Chapter 6, this will be a set of linear equations, that is, the normal equations (6–11). But in this more general case, this will be a set of nonlinear equations that do not have an explicit solution. This will typically require an iterative procedure for solution.

EXAMPLE 11.1 _____

The first-order conditions for estimating the parameters of (11–2) by least squares are

$$\frac{\partial S(\boldsymbol{\beta})}{\partial \beta_1} = -2 \sum_i [y_i - \beta_1 - \beta_2 e^{\beta_3 x_i}] \qquad = 0,$$

$$\frac{\partial S(\boldsymbol{\beta})}{\partial \beta_2} = -2 \sum_i [y_i - \beta_1 - \beta_2 e^{\beta_3 x_i}] e^{\beta_3 x_i} \qquad = 0,$$

$$\frac{\partial S(\boldsymbol{\beta})}{\partial \beta_3} = -2 \sum_i [y_i - \beta_1 - \beta_2 e^{\beta_3 x_i}] \beta_2 x_i e^{\beta_3 x_i} = 0.$$

These equations do not have an explicit solution.

_____

Conceding the potential for ambiguity, we define a nonlinear regression model at this point as follows:

> **Definition.** A **nonlinear regression model** is one for which the first-order conditions for least squares estimation of the parameters are nonlinear functions of the parameters.[2]

Thus, nonlinearity is defined in terms of the techniques needed to estimate the parameters, not the shape of the regression function. Later, we shall broaden our definition to include other techniques besides least squares.

11.2.1. The Linearized Regression

The nonlinear regression model is

$$y = h(\mathbf{x}, \boldsymbol{\beta}) + \varepsilon.$$

(To save some notation, we have dropped the observation subscript.) Many of the results that have been obtained for nonlinear regression models are based on a linear Taylor series approximation to $h(\mathbf{x}, \boldsymbol{\beta})$ at a particular value for the parameter vector, $\boldsymbol{\beta}^0$:

$$h(\mathbf{x}, \boldsymbol{\beta}) \simeq h(\mathbf{x}, \boldsymbol{\beta}^0) + \sum_k \frac{\partial h(\mathbf{x}, \boldsymbol{\beta})}{\partial \beta_k}\bigg|_{\boldsymbol{\beta}=\boldsymbol{\beta}^0} (\beta_k - \beta_k^0). \qquad (11\text{--}5)$$

---

[2] Judge et al. (1985, pp. 195–196) adopt a similar approach but take a somewhat broader view of estimation. In their framework, the nonlinearity of the model is defined by the optimization criterion used to define the estimator. Thus, least squares is but one of the possibilities they would consider. The broader definition will be useful when we analyze models for which maximum likelihood techniques are indispensable. But in this chapter, least squares will provide a satisfactory benchmark.

This is called the **linearized regression model.** By collecting terms, we obtain

$$h(\mathbf{x}, \boldsymbol{\beta}) \simeq h(\mathbf{x}, \boldsymbol{\beta}^0) - \sum_k \beta_k^0 \frac{\partial h(\mathbf{x}, \boldsymbol{\beta})}{\partial \beta_k}\bigg|_{\boldsymbol{\beta}=\boldsymbol{\beta}^0} + \sum_k \beta_k \frac{\partial h(\mathbf{x}, \boldsymbol{\beta})}{\partial \beta_k}\bigg|_{\boldsymbol{\beta}=\boldsymbol{\beta}^0}. \quad (11\text{-}6)$$

Let $\tilde{x}_k^0$ equal the kth partial derivative,[3] $\partial h(\mathbf{x}, \boldsymbol{\beta}^0)/\partial \beta_k^0$. For a given value of $\boldsymbol{\beta}^0$, this is a function only of the data, not of the unknown parameters. We now have

$$h(\mathbf{x}, \boldsymbol{\beta}) \simeq [h^0 - \sum_k \tilde{x}_k^0 \beta_k^0] + \sum \tilde{x}_k^0 \beta_k \quad (11\text{-}7)$$

$$= h^0 - \tilde{\mathbf{x}}^{0\prime} \boldsymbol{\beta}^0 + \tilde{\mathbf{x}}^{0\prime} \boldsymbol{\beta}$$

or

$$y \simeq h^0 - \tilde{\mathbf{x}}^{0\prime} \boldsymbol{\beta}^0 + \tilde{\mathbf{x}}^{0\prime} \boldsymbol{\beta} + \varepsilon.$$

By placing the known terms on the left-hand side of the equation, we obtain a regression model:

$$\tilde{y}^0 = y - h^0 + \tilde{\mathbf{x}}^{0\prime} \boldsymbol{\beta}^0 = \tilde{\mathbf{x}}^{0\prime} \boldsymbol{\beta} + \varepsilon^0. \quad (11\text{-}8)$$

With a value of $\boldsymbol{\beta}^0$ in hand, we could compute $\tilde{y}^0$ and $\tilde{\mathbf{x}}^0$ and estimate the parameters of (11-8) by linear least squares.

EXAMPLE 11.2 _____

For the example given in (11-2), the regressors in the linearized equation would be

$$\tilde{x}_1^0 = \frac{\partial h(.)}{\partial \beta_1} = 1,$$

$$\tilde{x}_2^0 = \frac{\partial h(.)}{\partial \beta_2} = e^{\beta_3^0 x},$$

$$\tilde{x}_3^0 = \frac{\partial h(.)}{\partial \beta_3} = \beta_2^0 x e^{\beta_3^0 x}.$$

With a set of values of the parameters, $\boldsymbol{\beta}^0$,

$$\tilde{y}^0 = y - h(x, \beta_1^0, \beta_2^0, \beta_3^0) + \beta_1^0 \tilde{x}_1^0 + \beta_2^0 \tilde{x}_2^0 + \beta_3^0 \tilde{x}_3^0$$

could be regressed on the three variables previously defined to estimate β_1, β_2, and β_3.

11.2.2. Nonlinear Least Squares Estimation

Least squares remains an attractive way to proceed for estimating the parameters. Numerous analytical results have been obtained for the estimator, for example, consistency and asymptotic normality.[4] However, we cannot be sure that nonlinear least squares is the most efficient estimator, except in the case of normally distributed disturbances. (This is the same conclusion we drew for the linear model.) Some examples that follow will illustrate the point.

---

[3] You should verify that for the linear regression model, these derivatives are the independent variables.

[4] A complete discussion of the subject can be found in Amemiya (1985). Other important references are Jennrich (1969) and Malinvaud (1970), and, especially, Goldfeld and Quandt (1972).

Before continuing, it is necessary to make some assumptions about the regressors. The precise requirements are discussed in some detail in Judge et al. (1985) and Amemiya (1985). In the classical regression model, in order to obtain our asymptotic results, we assumed that the sample moment matrix, $(1/n)\mathbf{X'X}$, converged to a positive definite matrix, $\mathbf{Q}$. By analogy, we impose the same condition on the "regressors" in the linearized model *when they are computed at the true parameter values*. Therefore, for the nonlinear regression model, the analog to (10–18) is

$$\text{plim}\left(\frac{1}{n}\right)\widetilde{\mathbf{X}}'\widetilde{\mathbf{X}} = \text{plim}\left(\frac{1}{n}\right)\sum_i \left[\frac{\partial h(\mathbf{x}_i, \boldsymbol{\beta}^0)}{\partial \boldsymbol{\beta}^0}\right]\left[\frac{\partial h(\mathbf{x}_i, \boldsymbol{\beta}^0)}{\partial \boldsymbol{\beta}^{0\prime}}\right] = \widetilde{\mathbf{Q}}, \qquad (11-9)$$

where $\widetilde{\mathbf{Q}}$ is a positive definite matrix. With this in hand, the asymptotic properties of the nonlinear least squares estimator have been derived. They are, in fact, much like those we have already seen for the linear model, except that in this case we place the derivatives in $\widetilde{\mathbf{X}}$ in the role of the regressors.[5]

The requirement that the matrix in (11–9) converge to a positive definite matrix carries with it the condition that the columns of the regressor matrix, $\widetilde{\mathbf{X}}$, be linearly independent. This is an identification condition analogous to the requirement that the independent variables in the linear model be linearly independent.

The nonlinear least squares criterion function is

$$S(\mathbf{b}) = \sum_i [y_i - h(\mathbf{x}_i, \mathbf{b})]^2 = \sum_i e_i^2, \qquad (11-10)$$

where we have inserted what will be the solution value, $\mathbf{b}$. The first-order conditions for a minimum are

$$\mathbf{g}(\mathbf{b}) = -2\sum_i [y_i - h(\mathbf{x}_i, \mathbf{b})]\frac{\partial h(\mathbf{x}_i, \mathbf{b})}{\partial \mathbf{b}} = \mathbf{0}. \qquad (11-11)$$

Notice that

$$\mathbf{g}(\mathbf{b}) = -2\widetilde{\mathbf{X}}'\mathbf{e},$$

which is the same as (6–11) for the linear model. This is a standard problem in nonlinear optimization, which can be solved by a number of methods.[6] The method of Gauss–Newton is often used in this setting. Recall that in our discussion of the linearized regression model, if a value of $\boldsymbol{\beta}_0$ were available, the linear regression model shown there could be estimated by ordinary least squares. Once a parameter vector is obtained, it can play the role of a new $\boldsymbol{\beta}_0$ and the computation can be done again. The iteration can continue until the difference between successive parameter vectors is small enough to assume convergence. One of the main virtues of this method is that at the last iteration the estimate of $\widetilde{\mathbf{Q}}^{-1}$ will, apart from the scale factor $\hat{\sigma}^2$, provide the correct estimate of the asymptotic covariance matrix for the parameter estimates.[7] A consistent estimate of σ^2 can be computed using the residuals:

$$\hat{\sigma}^2 = \left(\frac{1}{n}\right)\sum_i [y_i - h(\mathbf{x}_i, \mathbf{b})]^2. \qquad (11-12)$$

---

[5] This description is a bit informal. The specific results, and additional assumptions necessary to reach these conclusions, are spelled out in detail in Amemiya (1985). However, the overall assessment of that study is as follows: "[T]he practical consequence . . . is that all of the results for the linear regression model are asymptotically valid for the nonlinear regression model if we treat $\mathbf{G}$ as the regressor matrix" (p. 136). His $\mathbf{G}$ is our $\widetilde{\mathbf{X}}$.

[6] Chapter 12 includes some of these methods.

[7] There are some drawbacks to this method, including the possibility that the process may not converge at all. These problems are discussed in Chapter 12.

(A degrees of freedom correction, $1/(n - K)$, would have no virtue here, as all results are asymptotic in any event. The estimator in (11–12) is the maximum likelihood estimator.)

It has been shown[8] that

$$\mathbf{b} \xrightarrow{a} N\left[\boldsymbol{\beta}, \frac{\sigma^2}{n}\mathbf{Q}^{-1}\right],$$

where

$$\mathbf{Q} = \text{plim}\left(\frac{\tilde{\mathbf{X}}'\tilde{\mathbf{X}}}{n}\right).$$

The sample estimate of the asymptotic covariance matrix is

$$\text{Est.Asy.Var}[\mathbf{b}] = \hat{\sigma}^2(\tilde{\mathbf{X}}'\tilde{\mathbf{X}})^{-1}. \tag{11–13}$$

Once these are in hand, inference and hypothesis tests can proceed in the same fashion as prescribed in Chapter 7. A minor problem can arise in evaluating the fit of the regression in that

$$R^2 = 1 - \frac{\sum e_i^2}{\sum (y_i - \bar{y})^2} \tag{11–14}$$

is no longer guaranteed to be in the range of zero to one. It does, however, provide a useful descriptive measure.

EXAMPLE 11.3 A Nonlinear Consumption Function _____

The linear consumption function analyzed at the beginning of Chapter 5 is a restricted version of the more general consumption function

$$C = \alpha + \beta Y^\gamma + \varepsilon,$$

in which γ equals one. With this restriction, the model is linear. However, if γ is free to vary, this becomes a nonlinear regression. The linearized model is

$$C - (\alpha^0 + \beta^0 Y^{\gamma^0}) + \alpha^0(1) + \beta^0(Y^{\gamma^0}) + \gamma^0(\beta^0 Y^{\gamma^0} \ln Y) =$$
$$\alpha + \beta(Y^{\gamma^0}) + \gamma(\beta^0 Y^{\gamma^0} \ln Y) + \varepsilon.$$

After a bit of manipulation, the nonlinear least squares procedure reduced to iterated regression of

$$C^0 = C + \gamma^0\beta^0 Y^{\gamma^0} \ln Y$$

on

$$\frac{\partial h(.)}{\partial \alpha} = 1,$$

$$\frac{\partial h(.)}{\partial \beta} = Y^{\gamma^0},$$

$$\frac{\partial h(.)}{\partial \gamma} = \beta^0 Y^{\gamma^0} \ln Y.$$

The data on consumption and income listed in Table 11.1 are used to fit the consumption function.

---

[8] A comprehensive discussion may be found in Amemiya (1985).

TABLE 11.1   Aggregate Income, *Y* and Consumption, *C*

	1950	1951	1952	1953	1954	1955	1956	1957	1958
Y	791.8	819.0	844.3	880.0	894.0	944.5	989.4	1012.1	1028.8
C	733.2	748.7	771.4	802.5	822.7	873.8	899.8	919.7	932.9
	1959	**1960**	**1961**	**1962**	**1963**	**1964**	**1965**	**1966**	**1967**
Y	1067.2	1091.1	1123.2	1170.2	1207.3	1291.0	1365.7	1431.3	1493.2
C	979.4	1005.1	1025.2	1069.0	1108.4	1170.6	1236.4	1298.9	1337.7
	1968	**1969**	**1970**	**1971**	**1972**	**1973**	**1974**	**1975**	**1976**
Y	1551.3	1599.8	1688.1	1728.4	1797.4	1916.3	1896.6	1931.7	2001.0
C	1405.9	1456.7	1492.0	1538.8	1621.9	1689.6	1674.0	1711.9	1803.9
	1977	**1978**	**1979**	**1980**	**1981**	**1982**	**1983**	**1984**	**1985**
Y	2066.6	2167.4	2212.6	2214.3	2248.6	2261.5	2334.6	2468.4	2509.0
C	1883.8	1961.0	2004.4	2000.4	2024.2	2050.7	2145.9	2239.9	2312.6

Source: Data from the *Economic Report of the President,* U.S. Government Printing Office, Washington, D.C., 1986.

In general, finding the initial values for a nonlinear procedure can be a problem.[9] Simply trying a convenient set of values can be unproductive. Unfortunately, there are no good rules for starting values, except that they should be as close to the final values as possible (not particularly helpful). When it is possible, an initial consistent estimator of $\boldsymbol{\beta}$ will be a good starting value. However, in many cases, the only consistent estimator available is the one we are trying to compute by least squares. For better or worse, trial and error is the most frequently used procedure. For the present model, a natural set of values can be obtained because a simple linear model is a special case. Thus, we can start α and β at the linear least squares values that would result in the special case of $\gamma = 1$ and use 1 for the starting value for γ.

The parameter estimates are stable to five digits after only six iterations (see Table 11.2).

The procedures outlined earlier are used at the last iteration to obtain asymptotic standard errors and an estimate of σ^2. It is illustrative to compare these to the estimates for the linear consumption function, as shown in Table 11.3.

For hypothesis testing and confidence intervals, the usual procedures can be used, with the proviso that all results are only asymptotic. As such, for testing a restriction, the chi-squared statistic rather than the *F* ratio is likely to be more appropriate. For example, for testing the hypothesis that γ is different from one, an asymptotic *t* test, based on the standard normal distribution, is carried out, using

$$z = \frac{1.1564 - 1}{0.03927} = 3.983$$

This is larger than the critical values of 1.96 for the 5 percent significance level, and we thus reject the linear model in favor of the nonlinear regression. We are also interested in the marginal propensity to consume. In this expanded model, $H_0: \gamma = 1$ is a test that the

---

[9] A lengthy discussion may be found in Draper and Smith (1980, pp. 473–474).

TABLE 11.2

	Iterations		
	$\hat{\alpha}$	$\hat{\beta}$	$\hat{\gamma}$
1	11.1458	0.898534	1.0
2	209.825	−0.237125	1.15139
3	187.786	0.246078	1.14613
4	187.710	0.245692	1.15699
5	187.915	0.245968	1.15641
6	187.899	0.246004	1.15640

TABLE 11.3

	Linear		Nonlinear	
	Estimate	Std. Error	Estimate	Std. Error
α	11.1458	9.64	187.899	38.946
β	0.898530	0.00586	0.246004	0.07947
γ	1.00000	—	1.15640	0.03927
$e'e$	12,068		8420	
σ	18.309		15.294	
R^2	0.99856		0.99899	

Estimated Asymptotic Covariance Matrix

	$\hat{\alpha}$	$\hat{\beta}$	$\hat{\gamma}$
$\hat{\alpha}$	1516.8		
$\hat{\beta}$	−3.0533	0.006315	
$\hat{\gamma}$	1.5045	−0.003120	0.001542

marginal propensity to consume is constant, not that it is one. (That would be a joint test of both $\gamma = 1$ and $\beta = 1$.) In this model, the marginal propensity to consume is

$$\text{MPC} = \frac{dc}{dY} = \beta\gamma Y^{\gamma-1},$$

which varies with Y. To test the hypothesis that this is one, we require a particular value of Y. Since it is the most recent value, we choose $Y_{1985} = 2509$. At this value, MPC is estimated as 0.9676. We estimate its standard error as the square root of

$$[\partial\text{MPC}/\partial b \quad \partial\text{MPC}/\partial c]\begin{bmatrix} \text{Var}(b) & \text{Cov}(b, c) \\ \text{Cov}(b, c) & \text{Var}(c) \end{bmatrix}\begin{bmatrix} \partial\text{MPC}/\partial b \\ \partial\text{MPC}/\partial c \end{bmatrix}$$

$$= [cY^{c-1} \quad bY^{c-1}(1 + c \ln Y)]\begin{bmatrix} 0.006315 & -0.00312 \\ -0.00312 & 0.001542 \end{bmatrix}\begin{bmatrix} cY^{c-1} \\ bY^{c-1}(1 + c \ln Y) \end{bmatrix}$$

$$= 0.00033939$$

which gives a standard error of 0.018423. For testing the hypothesis that in 1985 the MPC was equal to 1.0, we would refer

$$z = \frac{0.9676 - 1}{0.018423} = 1.7587.$$

to a standard normal table. This is not statistically significant, so we would not reject the hypothesis.

11.2.3. A Specification Test for Nonlinear Regressions: Testing for Linear Versus Log-Linear Specification

MacKinnon et al. (1983) have extended the J test discussed in Section 7.7 to nonlinear regressions. One result of this analysis is a simple test for linearity versus log linearity.

The specific hypotheses to be tested are:

$$H_0: y = h^0(\mathbf{x}, \boldsymbol{\beta}) + \varepsilon_0,$$

versus

$$H_1: g(y) = h^1(\mathbf{z}, \boldsymbol{\gamma}) + \varepsilon_1,$$

where $\mathbf{x}$ and $\mathbf{z}$ are regressor vectors and $\boldsymbol{\beta}$ and $\boldsymbol{\gamma}$ are the parameters. As the authors note, using y instead of, say $j(y)$ in the first function is nothing more than an implicit definition of the units of measurement of the dependent variable.

An intermediate case is useful. If we assume that $g(y)$ is equal to y, but allow $h^0(.)$ and $h^1(.)$ to be nonlinear, the necessary modification of the J test is straightforward, albeit perhaps a bit more difficult to carry out. For this case, we form the compound model

$$\begin{aligned} y &= (1 - \alpha)h^0(\mathbf{x}, \boldsymbol{\beta}) + \alpha h^1(\mathbf{z}, \boldsymbol{\gamma}) + \varepsilon \\ &= h^0(\mathbf{x}, \boldsymbol{\beta}) + \alpha(h^1(\mathbf{z}, \boldsymbol{\gamma}) - h^0(\mathbf{x}, \boldsymbol{\beta})) + \varepsilon. \end{aligned} \tag{11-15}$$

Presumably, both $\boldsymbol{\beta}$ and $\boldsymbol{\gamma}$ could be estimated in isolation by nonlinear least squares. Suppose a nonlinear least squares estimate of $\boldsymbol{\gamma}$ has been obtained. One approach is to insert this in (11–15) and then estimate $\boldsymbol{\beta}$ and α by nonlinear least squares. The J test amounts to testing the significance of the estimate of α. Of course, the model is symmetric in $h^0(.)$ and $h^1(.)$, so their roles could be reversed. The same conclusions drawn earlier would apply here.

Davidson and MacKinnon (1981) propose what may be a simpler alternative. Given an estimate of $\boldsymbol{\beta}$, say $\hat{\boldsymbol{\beta}}$, approximate $h^0(\mathbf{x}, \boldsymbol{\beta})$ with a linear Taylor series at this point. The result is

$$h^0(\mathbf{x}, \boldsymbol{\beta}) \simeq h^0(\mathbf{x}, \hat{\boldsymbol{\beta}}) + \left[\frac{\partial h^0(.)}{\partial \hat{\boldsymbol{\beta}}'}\right]\hat{\boldsymbol{\beta}} \tag{11-16}$$

$$= \tilde{h}^0 + \hat{\mathbf{H}}^0\mathbf{b}.$$

Using this device, they replace (11–15) with

$$y - \hat{h}^0 = \hat{\mathbf{H}}^0\mathbf{b} + \alpha(h^1(\mathbf{z}, \hat{\boldsymbol{\gamma}}) - h^0(\mathbf{x}, \hat{\boldsymbol{\beta}})) + \varepsilon,$$

in which $\mathbf{b}$ and α can be estimated by linear least squares. As before, the J test amounts to testing the significance of $\hat{\alpha}$. If it is found that $\hat{\alpha}$ is significantly different from zero, H_0 is rejected. For the authors' asymptotic results to hold, any consistent estimate of $\mathbf{b}$ will suffice for $\hat{\boldsymbol{\beta}}$; the nonlinear least squares estimator that they suggest seems a natural choice.[10]

Now we can generalize the test to allow a nonlinear function $g(y)$, in H_1. Davidson and MacKinnon require $g(y)$ to be monotonic, continuous, continuously differentiable, and

---

[10]This assumes that H_0 is correct, of course.

not introduce any new parameters. (This excludes the Box–Cox model, which is considered in Section 11.4.) The compound model that forms the basis of the test is

$$(1 - \alpha)(y - h^0(\mathbf{x}, \boldsymbol{\beta})) + \alpha(g(y) - h^1(\mathbf{z}, \boldsymbol{\gamma})) = \varepsilon. \qquad (11\text{--}17)$$

Again, there are two approaches. As before, if $\hat{\boldsymbol{\gamma}}$ is an estimate of $\boldsymbol{\gamma}$, $\boldsymbol{\beta}$ and α can be estimated by maximum likelihood conditional on this estimate.[11] This promises to be extremely messy, and an alternative is proposed. Rewrite (11–17) as

$$y - h^0(\mathbf{x}, \boldsymbol{\beta}) = \alpha(\mathrm{h}^1(\mathbf{z}, \boldsymbol{\gamma}) - g(y)) + \alpha(y - h^0(\mathbf{x}, \boldsymbol{\beta})) + \varepsilon.$$

Now utilize the same linear Taylor series expansion for $h^0(\mathbf{x}, \boldsymbol{\beta})$ on the left-hand side, and replace both y and $h^0(\mathbf{x}, \boldsymbol{\beta})$ with h^0 on the right. The resulting model is

$$y - \widehat{h^0} = \widehat{\mathbf{H}}^0\mathbf{b} + \alpha(\widehat{h^1} - g(\widehat{h^0})) + e. \qquad (11\text{--}18)$$

As before, with an estimate of $\boldsymbol{\beta}$, this can be estimated by least squares.

This modified form of the J test is labeled the P_E *test*. As the authors discuss, it is probably not as powerful as any of the Wald, Lagrange multiplier, or likelihood ratio tests that we have considered. However, in their experience, it has sufficient power for applied research and is clearly simple to carry out.

The P_E test can be used to test a linear specification against a log-linear model. For this test, both $h^0(.)$ and $h^1(.)$ are linear, while $g(y) = \ln y$. Let the two competing models be denoted

$$H_0 : y = \mathbf{x}'\boldsymbol{\beta} + \varepsilon,$$

and

$$H_1 : \ln y = \ln(\mathbf{x})'\boldsymbol{\gamma} + \varepsilon.$$

[We stretch the usual notational conventions by using $\ln(\mathbf{x})$ for $(\ln x_1, \ldots, \ln x_k)$.] Now let $\mathbf{b}$ and $\mathbf{c}$ be the two linear least squares estimates of the parameters vectors. The P_E test for H_1 as an alternative to H_0 is carried out by testing the significance of the coefficient $\hat{\alpha}$ in the model

$$y = \mathbf{x}'\boldsymbol{\beta} + \alpha[\widehat{\ln} \, y - \ln(\mathbf{x}'\mathbf{b})] + \varepsilon. \qquad (11\text{--}19)$$

The second term is the difference between predictions of y obtained directly from the log-linear model and obtained as the log of the prediction from the linear model. We can also reverse the roles of the two formulas and test H_0 as the alternative. The compound regression is

$$\ln y = \ln(\mathbf{x})'\boldsymbol{\gamma} + \alpha(\hat{y} - e^{\ln(\mathbf{x})'\mathbf{c}}) + \varepsilon. \qquad (11\text{--}20)$$

EXAMPLE 11.4 Money Demand

A large number of studies have estimated money demand equations, some linear and some log linear.[12] Yearly data for estimation of a money demand equation are given in Table 11.4. The data are taken from the 1986 *Economic Report of the President*. The interest rate is the end of December value of the discount rate at the New York Federal Reserve Bank. The money stock is M2. The GNP is seasonally adjusted and stated in 1982 constant dollars. Results of the P_E test of the linear versus the log-linear model are shown in Table 11.5.

---

[11] Least squares will be inappropriate because of the transformation of y, which will translate to a Jacobian term in the log likelihood. See the later discussion of the Box–Cox model.

[12] A comprehensive survey appears in Goldfeld (1973).

TABLE 11.4

Year	Interest r	Money M	GNP Y	Year	Interest r	Money M	GNP Y
1966	4.50	480.0	2208.3	1976	5.50	1163.6	2826.7
1967	4.19	524.3	2271.4	1977	5.46	1286.6	2958.6
1968	5.16	566.3	2365.6	1978	7.46	1388.9	3115.2
1969	5.87	589.5	2423.3	1979	10.28	1497.9	3192.4
1970	5.95	628.2	2416.2	1980	11.77	1631.4	3187.1
1971	4.88	712.8	2484.8	1981	13.42	1794.4	3248.8
1972	4.50	805.2	2608.5	1982	11.02	1954.9	3166.0
1973	6.44	861.0	2744.1	1983	8.50	2188.8	3277.7
1974	7.83	908.4	2729.3	1984	8.80	2371.7	3492.0
1975	6.25	1023.1	2695.0	1985	7.69	2563.6	3573.5

TABLE 11.5   Estimates of α

	Estimate	Standard Error	t ratio
Linear	−751.21	242.21	−3.102
Log linear	−0.0001363	0.0002067	−0.659

Regressions of M on a constant, r, and Y, and $\ln M$ on a constant, $\ln r$, and $\ln Y$, produce the following results (standard errors are given in parentheses):

$$\text{linear } R^2 = 0.93526$$

$$\text{standard error} = 175.73$$

$$M = \quad a \quad + \quad b_r r \quad + \quad c_Y Y$$

$$-3169.42 \quad -14.9223 \quad 1.58815$$

$$(310.8) \quad (22.59) \quad (0.1434)$$

$$\text{log-linear } R^2 = 0.97578$$

$$\text{standard error} = 0.0881$$

$$\ln M = \quad a' \quad + \quad b_{\ln r} \ln r \quad + c_{\ln Y} \ln Y$$

$$-21.992 \quad -0.03157 \quad 3.65628$$

$$(1.648) \quad (0.0969) \quad (0.2255)$$

Both models appear to fit quite well,[13] and the pattern of significance of the coefficients is the same in both equations. After computing fitted values from the two equations, the estimates of α from the two models are as shown in Table 11.5. Referring these to a standard normal table, we reject the linear model in favor of the log-linear model.

The test of linearity vs. loglinearity has been the subject of a number of studies. Godfrey and Wickens (1981) discuss several approaches.

[13] The interest elasticity is in line with the received results. The income elasticity is quite a bit larger.

11.3. Parametric Transformations of the Dependent Variable

Thus far, we have considered models in which the nonlinearity in the parameters was entirely on the right-hand side of the equation. There are models in which parameters appear nonlinearly in functions of the dependent variable as well. The Box–Cox transformation considered in the next section is one example. Another is given here.

EXAMPLE 11.5 A Generalized Production Function _____

The Cobb–Douglas production function has often been used to study production. Among the assumptions of this model is that the average cost of production increases or decreases monotonically with increases in output. This is in direct contrast to the standard textbook treatment of a U-shaped average cost curve, as well as to a large amount of empirical evidence. In order to relax this assumption, Zellner and Revankar (1970) proposed a generalization of the Cobb–Douglas production function.[14] Their model allows economies of scale to vary output, and to increase and then decrease as output rises:

$$\ln y + \theta y = \ln \gamma + \alpha(1 - \delta) \ln K + \alpha\delta \ln L + \varepsilon.$$

Note that the right-hand side of their model is intrinsically linear according to the results of Section 8.3.3. However, the model as a whole is intrinsically nonlinear due to the transformation of y appearing on the left.

_____

Suppose that, in general, the model is

$$g(y_i, \boldsymbol{\theta}) = h(\mathbf{x}_i, \boldsymbol{\beta}) + \varepsilon_i. \tag{11-21}$$

One approach to estimation would be least squares, minimizing

$$S(\boldsymbol{\theta}, \boldsymbol{\beta}) = \sum_i [g(y_i, \boldsymbol{\theta}) - h(\mathbf{x}_i, \boldsymbol{\beta})]^2.$$

However, for this kind of regression model, maximum likelihood estimation is more efficient and generally not appreciably more difficult. For normally distributed disturbances, the density of y_i is

$$f(y_i) = \left| \frac{\partial \varepsilon_i}{\partial y_i} \right| (2\pi\sigma^2)^{-1/2} e^{-(g(y_i, \boldsymbol{\theta}) - h(\mathbf{x}_i, \boldsymbol{\beta}))^2/(2\sigma^2)}.$$

The Jacobian of the transformation [see (3–41)] is

$$J(y_i, \boldsymbol{\theta}) = \left| \frac{\partial \varepsilon_i}{\partial y_i} \right| = \left| \frac{\partial g(y_i, \boldsymbol{\theta})}{\partial y_i} \right| = J_i.$$

Upon collecting terms, the log-likelihood function will be

$$\ln L = -\frac{n}{2}\ln 2\pi - \frac{n}{2} \ln \sigma^2 + \sum_i \ln J(y_i, \boldsymbol{\theta}) - \frac{1}{2\sigma^2} \sum_i [g(y_i, \boldsymbol{\theta}) - h(\mathbf{x}_i, \boldsymbol{\beta})]^2. \tag{11-22}$$

[14] An alternative approach is to model costs directly with a flexible functional form such as the translog model. This is examined in detail in Chapter 17.

Before proceeding, two aspects of the log likelihood should be noted. First, it is obvious that but for the Jacobians, nonlinear least squares would be maximum likelihood. However, if the Jacobian terms involve $\boldsymbol{\theta}$, *least squares is not maximum likelihood*. Second, as regards σ^2, this likelihood function is essentially the same as that for the simpler nonlinear regression model of (11–1). The maximum likelihood estimator of σ^2 will be

$$\hat{\sigma}^2 = \frac{1}{n} \sum_i [g(y_i, \hat{\boldsymbol{\theta}}) - h(\mathbf{x}_i, \hat{\boldsymbol{\beta}})]^2$$

$$= \frac{1}{n} \sum_i e_i^2.$$

$(11–23)$

The likelihood equations for the unknown parameters are

$$\frac{\partial \ln L}{\partial \boldsymbol{\beta}} = \frac{1}{\sigma^2} \sum_i \varepsilon_i \frac{\partial h(\mathbf{x}_i, \boldsymbol{\beta})}{\partial \boldsymbol{\beta}} = \mathbf{0},$$

$$\frac{\partial \ln L}{\partial \boldsymbol{\theta}} = \sum_i \frac{1}{J_i} \left(\frac{\partial J_i}{\partial \boldsymbol{\theta}} \right) - \left(\frac{1}{\sigma^2} \right) \sum_i \varepsilon_i \frac{\partial g(y_i, \boldsymbol{\theta})}{\partial \boldsymbol{\theta}} = \mathbf{0}, \qquad (11–24)$$

$$\frac{\partial \ln L}{\partial \sigma^2} = -\frac{n}{2\sigma^2} + \frac{1}{2\sigma^4} \sum_i \varepsilon_i^2 = 0.$$

These will usually be nonlinear, so a solution must be obtained iteratively. One special case that is common is a model in which $\boldsymbol{\theta}$ is a single parameter. Given a particular value of θ, we would maximize (11–22) with respect to $\boldsymbol{\beta}$ by using nonlinear least squares. (It would be simpler yet if, in addition, $h(\mathbf{x}_i, \boldsymbol{\beta})$ were linear, so that we could use ordinary linear least squares. See the following example.) Therefore, a way to maximize L for all of the parameters is to scan over values of θ for the one that, with the associated least squares estimates of $\boldsymbol{\beta}$ and σ^2, gives the highest value of L. (This requires, of course, that we know roughly what values of θ to examine.)

For more general models, a similar method could be used, but this will probably be much more difficult. If $\boldsymbol{\theta}$ is a vector of parameters, direct maximization of L with respect to the full set of parameters may be preferable. (Methods of maximization are discussed in the next chapter.) There is an additional simplification that may be useful. Whatever values are ultimately obtained for the estimates of $\boldsymbol{\theta}$ and $\boldsymbol{\beta}$, the estimate of σ^2 will be given by (11–23). If we insert this solution in (11–22), we obtain the **concentrated log likelihood**,

$$\ln L_c = \sum_i \ln J(y_i, \boldsymbol{\theta}) - \frac{n}{2}(1 + \ln(2\pi)) - \frac{n}{2}\ln\left[\frac{1}{n} \sum_i \varepsilon_i^2 \right].$$

This is a function only of $\boldsymbol{\theta}$ and $\boldsymbol{\beta}$. We can maximize it with respect to $\boldsymbol{\theta}$ and $\boldsymbol{\beta}$, and obtain the estimate of σ^2 as a by-product.[15]

An estimate of the asymptotic covariance matrix of the maximum likelihood estimators can be obtained by inverting the estimated information matrix. However, it is quite likely that the Berndt et al. (1974) estimator will be much easier to compute. The log of the density for the ith observation is

$$\ln L_i = \ln J_i - \frac{1}{2}(\ln(2\pi) + \ln \sigma^2) - \frac{1}{2\sigma^2}[g(y_i, \boldsymbol{\theta}) - h(\mathbf{x}_i, \boldsymbol{\beta})]^2.$$

---

[15] A formal proof that this is a valid way to proceed is given by Amemiya (1985, pp. 125–127).

The derivatives of $\ln L_i$ with respect to the unknown parameters are

$$\mathbf{w}_i = \begin{bmatrix} \partial \ln L_i / \partial \boldsymbol{\beta} \\ \partial \ln L_i / \partial \boldsymbol{\theta} \\ \partial \ln L_i / \partial \sigma^2 \end{bmatrix} = \begin{bmatrix} (\varepsilon_i / \sigma^2)[\partial h(\mathbf{x}_i, \boldsymbol{\beta}) / \partial \boldsymbol{\beta}] \\ (1/J_i)[\partial J_i / \partial \boldsymbol{\theta}] - (\varepsilon_i / \sigma^2)[\partial g(y_i, \boldsymbol{\theta}) / \partial \boldsymbol{\theta}] \\ (1/(2\sigma^2))[\varepsilon_i^2 / \sigma^2 - 1] \end{bmatrix} \quad (11\text{–}25)$$

The covariance matrix for the maximum likelihood estimators is consistently estimated, using

$$\text{Est.Asy.Var[MLE]} = \left[\sum_i \hat{\mathbf{w}}_i \hat{\mathbf{w}}_i' \right]^{-1}.$$

EXAMPLE 11.5 Continued

For Zellner and Revankar's production function, the Jacobian of the transformation from ε_i to y_i is $\partial \varepsilon_i / \partial y_i = (\theta + 1/y_i)$. Some simplification is achieved by writing this as $(1 + \theta y_i)/y_i$. The log likelihood is, then,

$$\ln L = \sum_i \ln(1 + \theta y_i) - \sum_i \ln y_i - \frac{n}{2}\ln(2\pi) - \frac{n}{2}\ln \sigma^2 - \frac{1}{2\sigma^2} \sum_i \varepsilon_i^2,$$

where

$$\varepsilon_i = (\ln y_i + \theta y_i - \beta_1 - \beta_2 \ln \text{Capital}_i - \beta_3 \ln \text{Labor}_i).$$

Estimation of this model is straightforward. For a given value of θ, $\boldsymbol{\beta}$ and σ^2 are estimated by ordinary least squares. Therefore, to estimate the full set of parameters, we can scan over the range of zero to one for θ. The value of θ that, with its associated least squares estimates of $\boldsymbol{\beta}$ and σ^2, maximizes the log-likelihood function provides the desired estimate. This is the procedure used by Zellner and Revankar. The data used for the study are listed in Table 11.6.[16]

In their model, Zellner and Revankar report the maximum likelihood estimates of the parameters listed in Table 11.7. For each estimate, three estimates of the asymptotic standard error are given. The authors report asymptotic standard errors based on the information matrix (1) and the (inappropriate) OLS standard errors (2). The third estimate is that obtained using the Berndt et al. estimator based on (11–25) instead of the second derivatives.

As usual, there is a problem in interpreting the coefficients in this nonlinear regression model. The slope coefficients of the regression are not the marginal effects. An approximation to the appropriate value can be obtained with

$$\frac{\partial E[y]}{\partial x_j} \simeq \left[\frac{\partial h(\mathbf{x}, \boldsymbol{\beta})}{\partial x_j} \right] \frac{1}{g'(y)}. \quad (11\text{–}26)$$

The authors do not report the estimate of σ^2. The one in Table 11.7 was computed using their data and estimates. The maximum likelihood estimates of the slope parameters are obtained by least squares regression of $\ln y + \theta y$ on a constant, $\ln K$, and $\ln L$. Using the preceding data and their estimate of θ, we find the OLS slope estimates are, however, 3.0741, 0.36828, and 1.13455. There is no obvious reason for the discrepancy.[17]

Elasticities are computed using

$$\frac{\partial \ln y}{\partial \ln x_j} \simeq \left[\frac{\partial h(\mathbf{x}, \boldsymbol{\beta})}{\partial x_j} \right] \left[\frac{x_j}{yg'(y)} \right]. \quad (11\text{–}27)$$

---

[16] Zellner and Revankar (1979, p. 249). Full descriptions of the variables are given in the study.

[17] The values shown in the table are those reported in the original study.

TABLE 11.6 U.S. Annual Survey of Manufactures Data for the Transportation Equipment Industry, 1957[a]

State	Value Added	Capital	Labor	Establishments
Ala.	126.148	3.804	31.551	68
Calif.	3201.486	185.446	452.844	1372
Conn.	690.670	39.712	124.074	154
Fla.	56.296	6.547	19.181	292
Ga.	304.531	11.530	45.534	71
Ill.	723.028	58.987	88.391	275
Ind.	992.169	112.884	148.530	260
Iowa	35.796	2.698	8.017	75
Kans.	494.515	10.360	86.189	76
Ky.	124.948	5.213	12.000	31
La.	73.328	3.763	15.900	115
Maine	29.467	1.967	6.470	81
Md.	415.262	17.546	69.342	129
Mass.	241.530	15.347	39.416	172
Mich.	4079.554	435.105	490.384	568
Mo.	652.085	32.840	84.831	125
N.J.	667.113	33.292	83.033	247
N.Y.	940.430	72.974	190.094	461
Ohio	1611.899	157.978	259.916	363
Pa.	617.579	34.324	98.152	233
Tex.	527.413	22.736	109.728	308
Va.	174.394	7.173	31.301	85
Wash.	636.948	30.807	87.963	179
W. Va.	22.700	1.543	4.063	15
Wis.	349.711	22.001	52.818	142

Source: A. Zellner and N. Revankar, "Generalized Production Functions," *Review of Economic Studies, Ltd.,* 37, 1970, p. 249.

[a]"Value Added," "Capital," and "Labor" are in millions of dollars. Data used for the regressions are per establishment.

TABLE 11.7 Maximum Likelihood Estimates

	Estimate	SE(1)	SE(2)	SE(3)
β_1	3.0129	0.3854	0.1343	0.3438
β_2	0.333	0.1023	0.1022	0.1004
β_3	1.1551	0.1564	0.1228	0.1402
θ	0.134	0.0638	—	0.0609
σ^2	0.0485	0.0137	—	—

(Note the similarity to the form for the log-linear model. If $g(y) = \ln y$, then $yg'(y) = 1$ and we get the familiar result. These functions will vary with the data, so they must be computed at a particular data point. The predicted values and functions of them can be used in place of y and $g'(y)$ on the right-hand side of (11–26) and (11–27).

EXAMPLE 11.5 Continued _____

For Zellner and Revankar's generalized Cobb–Douglas production function, the elasticities are simple to compute using (11–27). First, we use the result

$$x_j \left[\frac{\partial h(\mathbf{x}, \boldsymbol{\beta})}{\partial x_j} \right] = \frac{\partial h(\mathbf{x}, \boldsymbol{\beta})}{\partial \ln x_j}.$$

Since $h(\mathbf{x}, \boldsymbol{\beta}) = \beta_1 + \beta_2 \ln K + \beta_3 \ln L$, these derivatives are the slope coefficients, β_2 and β_3. To compute a value for y, we insert the means of $\ln K$ and $\ln L$ on the right-hand side to obtain a prediction for $\ln y + \theta y = 1.1478$. The value of y for which $\ln y + 0.134y = 1.1478$ is 2.31. Finally, for this model,

$$g'(y) = \frac{1}{y} + \theta.$$

So,

$$\frac{\partial \ln y}{\partial \ln x_j} = \frac{\beta_j}{1 + \theta y}.$$

Assembling the terms, we obtain estimates of the output elasticities of

$$\text{Capital:} \quad \frac{0.333}{1 + 0.134(2.31)} = 0.254,$$

$$\text{Labor:} \quad \frac{1.551}{1 + 0.134(2.31)} = 0.882.$$

As a rough check on these values, consider a simple Cobb–Douglas function, which has $\theta = 0$. This can be efficiently estimated by ordinary least squares regression of $\ln y$ on a constant, $\ln K$, and $\ln L$. The slope coefficients in this regression, using the preceding data, are 0.279 and 0.927. Once again, the linear regression approximates the nonlinear regression surprisingly closely.

In this study, the parameter θ was of primary interest, so the result in the preceding paragraph is not necessarily a virtue. In the Cobb-Douglas model, the economies of scale parameter is the sum of the output elasticities. For these data, that would be 1.136, indicating a fair degree of economies of scale. (It can be shown that this parameter also corresponds to the ratio of average to marginal cost on the cost side, which indicates that average costs are declining throughout the range of y.) For the previous generalized production function, the economies of scale parameter is

$$\alpha = \frac{\beta_K + \beta_L}{1 + \theta y}.$$

Some representative values for their sample are listed in Table 11.8.

TABLE 11.8

State	Output	Economies of Scale
Florida	0.193	1.45
Louisiana	0.638	1.37
California	2.333	1.13
Maryland	3.219	1.04
Ohio	4.440	0.93
Michigan	7.182	0.76

11.4. The Box–Cox Transformation

The Box–Cox transformation was introduced in Chapters 5 and 8 as a method of generalizing the linear model. The transformation is[18]

$$x^{(\lambda)} = \frac{x^\lambda - 1}{\lambda}.$$

As noted earlier, in a regression model the analysis could be done *conditionally*. For a given value of λ, the model

$$y = \alpha + \sum \beta_k x_k^{(\lambda)} + \varepsilon \tag{11–28}$$

is a linear regression that can be estimated by least squares.[19] Save for the complexity of the calculations, in principle, each regressor could be transformed by a different value of λ. In most applications, this level of generality becomes excessively cumbersome, and λ is assumed to be the same for all of the variables in the model.[20] At the same time, it is also possible to transform y by $y^{(\theta)}$.

EXAMPLE 11.6 Flexible Cost Function _____

Caves et al. (1980) analyzed the costs of production for railroads providing freight and passenger service. Continuing a long line of literature on the costs of production in regulated industries, a translog cost function (see Example 7.3) would be a natural choice for modeling this multiple-output technology. However, several of the firms in the study produced no passenger service, which would preclude the use of the translog model. (This would require the log of zero.) An alternative is the Box–Cox transformation, which is computable for zero output levels. A constraint must still be placed on λ in their model, as $0^{(\lambda)}$ is defined only if λ is strictly positive. As shown in Example 11.8, a positive value of λ is not assured. A question does arise in this context (and other similar ones) as to whether zero outputs should be treated the same as nonzero outputs or whether an output of zero represents a discrete corporate decision distinct from other variation in the output levels. In addition, this is only a partial solution. The zero values of the regressors preclude computation of appropriate standard errors.

11.4.1. Transforming the Independent Variables

If λ in (11–28) is taken to be an unknown parameter, the regression becomes nonlinear in the parameters. While no transformation will reduce it to linearity, nonlinear least squares is straightforward. In most instances, we can expect to find the least squares value of λ between -2 and 2. Typically, then, λ is estimated by scanning this range in increments of 0.1.

When λ equals zero, the transformation is, by L'Hôspital's rule,

$$\lim_{\lambda \to 0} \frac{x^\lambda - 1}{\lambda} = \lim_{\lambda \to 0} \frac{d(x^\lambda - 1)/d\lambda}{1}$$

$$= \lim_{\lambda \to 0} x^\lambda \times \ln x = \ln x.$$

---

[18] Box and Cox (1964). To be defined for all values of λ, x must be strictly positive.

[19] In most applications, some of the regressors will not be transformed, for example, dummy variables. For such a variable, say v_k, $v_k^{(\lambda)} = v_k$ and the relevant derivatives in (11–29) and (11–38) will be zero.

[20] See, for example, Seaks and Layson (1983).

If a minimum is found and greater precision is desired, the area to the right and left of the current optimum can be searched in increments of 0.01, and so on. Once the optimum value of λ is located, the least squares estimates, the mean squared residual, and this value of λ constitute the nonlinear least squares (and maximum likelihood) estimates of the parameters.

After determining the optimal value of λ, it is sometimes treated as if it were a *known* value in the least squares results. However, λ is an estimate of an unknown parameter. It is not hard to show that the least squares standard errors will always underestimate the correct asymptotic standard errors.[21] To get the appropriate values, we need the derivatives of the right-hand side of (11–28) with respect to α, $\boldsymbol{\beta}$, and λ. In the notation of (11–1), these are

$$\frac{\partial h(.)}{\partial \alpha} = 1,$$

$$\frac{\partial h(.)}{\partial \beta_k} = x_k^{(\lambda)},$$

$$\frac{\partial h(.)}{\partial \lambda} = \sum_k \beta_k \frac{\partial x_k^{(\lambda)}}{\partial \lambda},$$

$$= \sum_k \beta_k \left[\frac{1}{\lambda}(x_k^\lambda \ln x_k - x_k^{(\lambda)}) \right].$$

(11–29)

We can now use (11–13) to estimate the asymptotic covariance matrix of the parameter estimates. Note that $\ln x_k$ appears in $\partial h(.)/\partial \lambda$. If $x_k = 0$, this cannot be computed.

EXAMPLE 11.7 A More General Money Demand Equation _____

The estimates of the log-linear money demand equation in Example 11.4 are implicitly a Box–Cox model:

$$\ln M = \alpha + \beta_r r^{(\lambda)} + \beta_Y Y^{(\lambda)} + \varepsilon,$$

(11–30)

with λ equal to zero. Here we will allow λ to be a free parameter. For a given value of λ, the Box–Cox model is a linear regression model; we can compute $r^{(\lambda)}$ and $Y^{(\lambda)}$ and then obtain the remaining parameters by least squares. Maximum likelihood estimates of all of the parameters in the model are obtained by scanning over the range of λ from minus one to one. The sums of squared deviations, which we denote $S(\boldsymbol{\beta})$, for a range of values of λ are shown in Table 11.9.

TABLE 11.9 Sums of Squared Deviations for Given λ

λ	$S(\boldsymbol{\beta})$	λ	$S(\boldsymbol{\beta})$	λ	$S(\boldsymbol{\beta})$
0.3	0.13016	0.44	0.12723	0.49	0.12721
0.4	0.12732	0.45	0.12721	0.50	0.12721
0.41	0.12729	0.46	0.12721	0.60	0.12753
0.42	0.12726	0.47	0.12720		
0.43	0.12724	0.48	0.12721		

[21] See Fomby et al. (1984, pp. 426–431).

TABLE 11.10

Variable	Coefficient	Standard Error	t ratio	Alternative Standard Errors		
				OLS	ML/BHHH	ML/Hessian
Constant	−0.543	8.048	−0.067	0.3614	15.38	7.713
$r^{(0.47)}$	−0.00607	0.0344	−0.177	0.0352	0.0480	0.0344
$\gamma^{(0.47)}$	0.0867	0.3804	0.228	0.00505	0.7221	0.5303
λ	0.47	0.5510	0.853	0	1.044	1.016

At the optimal value of 0.47, the least squares results with the appropriate standard errors are as listed in Table 11.10. The standard errors are computed using the nonlinear least squares results, (11–29) and (11–13). Table 11.10 contains three alternative estimates of the set of standard errors. The OLS standard errors are computed by ignoring the variation in the estimate of λ. These are the standard errors that the least squares regression produces automatically when $\ln M$ is regressed on a constant, $r^{(\lambda)}$ and $Y^{(\lambda)}$. Obviously, they would be seriously misleading. The standard errors denoted ML/BHHH are computed according to (11–38) and (11–39) without a transformation of the dependent variable. The change to (11–38) is that the Jacobian term, $\ln y_i$, and the first term in the parentheses in $\partial \ln f(y_i)/\partial \lambda$ are omitted. Note that (11–39) also produces an estimated standard error for the estimate of σ^2. This is omitted from Table 11.10. The last column gives the standard errors computed using the actual second derivatives of the log-likelihood function. For this problem, that would be (11–34) without the term $(\lambda − 1) \Sigma_i \ln y_i$ and without the transformation of y_i in the sum of squares. With the exception of the OLS column, the estimators are all appropriate, and all would be the same asymptotically. The differences that are evident are small sample variation—we have used only 20 observations. There is no obvious answer to which is right; all are. The choice is usually based on ease of computation, which would generally favor the one we used originally.

It is important to remember that the coefficients in a nonlinear model are not equal to the slopes (i.e., here, the demand elasticities) with respect to the variables. In the simple Box–Cox model,[22]

$$\ln Y = \alpha + \beta \left[\frac{X^\lambda − 1}{\lambda} \right],$$

$$\frac{d \ln Y}{d \ln X} = \beta X^\lambda. \tag{11-31}$$

Inserting the means for r (7.273) and Y (2849.23), we obtain elasticities of −0.0154 and 3.6454, respectively. These are quite similar to the estimates for the log-linear model in Example 11.4. Standard errors for these estimates could be obtained using (10–16). In the interest of brevity, the calculation is omitted here.

11.4.2. Transforming the Model

It seems a natural generalization at this point to extend (11–28) to

$$y^{(\theta)} = \alpha + \sum \beta_k x_k^{(\lambda)} + \varepsilon \tag{11-32}$$

---

[22] We have used the result $d \ln Y/d \ln X = X d \ln Y/dX$.

or

$$y^{(\theta)} = \beta' \mathbf{x}^{(\lambda)} + \varepsilon.$$

This includes the linear and log-linear models as special cases.

Allowing θ to differ from λ is usually taken to be more cumbersome than necessary. The computational burden increases greatly with this level of generality. We shall assume that they are equal. If $\varepsilon \sim N[0, \sigma^2]$, the log-likelihood for a sample of n observation is

$$\ln L = -\frac{n}{2}\ln(2\pi) - \frac{n}{2}\ln \sigma^2 - \frac{1}{2\sigma^2} \sum_i \varepsilon_i^2. [23]$$

Transforming from the distribution ε to that of y, we use the change of variable result

$$f_y(y) = \left| \frac{d\varepsilon}{dy} \right| f_\varepsilon(y).$$

From (11–32),

$$\varepsilon = y^{(\lambda)} - \mathbf{x}^{(\lambda)'}\boldsymbol{\beta}, \qquad (11\text{–}33)$$

so the Jacobian is

$$\left| \frac{d\varepsilon}{dy} \right| = y^{\lambda - 1}.$$

Making the substitution and multiplying by the Jacobian, we obtain the log-likelihood function for the Box–Cox model:

$$\ln L = -\frac{n}{2}\ln(2\pi) - \frac{n}{2}\ln \sigma^2 + (\lambda - 1) \sum_i \ln y_i - \frac{1}{2\sigma^2} \sum_i (y_i^{(\lambda)} - \boldsymbol{\beta}'\mathbf{x}_i^{(\lambda)})^2. \qquad (11\text{–}34)$$

As a first step, we "concentrate" the log likelihood. The maximum likelihood estimator of σ^2 will be the average squared residual. By inserting this result in (11–34), we see that at the maximum of the log likelihood, the last term will be $-n/2$. So the log likelihood will collapse to

$$\ln L_c = (\lambda - 1) \sum_i \ln y_i - \frac{n}{2}(\ln(2\pi) + 1) - \frac{n}{2}\ln \hat{\sigma}^2. \qquad (11\text{–}35)$$

The maximum likelihood estimates of λ and $\boldsymbol{\beta}$ are computed by maximizing this function. The estimate of σ^2 will be a by-product and need not be considered separately. Now since there is still only one value of λ to be found, we can use the same one-dimensional grid search used in Examples 11.5 and 11.7. However, it must be remembered that the criterion function is not $S(\boldsymbol{\beta}|\lambda)$ but

$$\ln L_c = (\lambda - 1) \sum_i \ln y_i - \frac{n}{2}(\ln(2\pi) + 1) - \frac{n}{2}\ln\left(\frac{S(\boldsymbol{\beta}, \lambda)}{n}\right). [24] \qquad (11\text{–}36)$$

After searching for the appropriate λ, it is necessary to correct the least squares standard errors. The appropriate estimate of the asymptotic covariance matrix for the maximum likelihood estimates was presented in Chapter 4. For this model, the second deriva-

---

[23] Two useful references on this form of the model are Spitzer (1982a, 1982b). See also Poirier (1978b), Poirier and Melino (1978), and Draper and Cox (1969) for discussion of the implications of this more general model for the allowable values of y. Note that in view of (11–29), y must be positive, and, as such, the normality assumption cannot hold exactly. See Poirier and Melino (1978).

[24] A method of simplifying the search is suggested by Zarembka (1968).

tives of the log likelihood are quite cumbersome.[25] The estimator of the asymptotic covariance matrix for the maximum likelihood presented by Berndt et al. (1974) is much more convenient. The advantage of this estimator is that it only requires us to compute the first derivatives.[26] For the Box–Cox model,

$$\ln f(y_i, \theta) = (\lambda - 1) \ln y_i - \frac{1}{2} \ln 2\pi - \frac{1}{2} \ln \sigma^2 - \frac{1}{2\sigma^2} (y_i^{(\lambda)} - \boldsymbol{\beta}' \mathbf{x}_i^{(\lambda)})^2. \quad (11-37)$$

Upon using

$$\varepsilon_i = y_i^{(\lambda)} - \boldsymbol{\beta}' \mathbf{x}_i^{(\lambda)},$$

the derivatives are

$$\frac{\partial \ln f(y_i)}{\partial \boldsymbol{\beta}} = \frac{\varepsilon_i}{\sigma^2} \mathbf{x}_i^{(\lambda)},$$

$$\frac{\partial \ln f(y_i)}{\partial \lambda} = \ln y_i - \frac{\varepsilon_i}{\sigma^2} \left(\frac{\partial y_i^{(\lambda)}}{\partial \lambda} - \sum_k \beta_k \frac{\partial x_k^{(\lambda)}}{\partial \lambda} \right), \quad (11-38)$$

$$\frac{\partial \ln f(y_i)}{\partial \sigma^2} = \frac{1}{2\sigma^2} \left(\frac{\varepsilon_i^2}{\sigma^2} - 1 \right).$$

For the second of these,

$$\frac{\partial([z^\lambda - 1]/\lambda)}{\partial \lambda} = \frac{\lambda z^\lambda \ln z - (z^\lambda - 1)}{\lambda^2} = \frac{1}{\lambda} (z^\lambda \ln z - z^{(\lambda)}).$$

(See Exercise 8.) The various parts are reasonably simple to compute. If we then let

$$\mathbf{w}_i = \begin{bmatrix} \partial \ln f(y_i)/\partial \hat{\boldsymbol{\beta}} \\ \partial \ln f(y_i)/\partial \hat{\lambda} \\ \partial \ln f(y_i)/\partial \hat{\sigma}^2 \end{bmatrix}, \quad (11-39)$$

the estimator of the asymptotic variance matrix for the maximum likelihood estimator is

$$\text{Est.Asy.Var}[\hat{\boldsymbol{\theta}}] = \left[\sum_i \hat{\mathbf{w}}_i \hat{\mathbf{w}}_i' \right]^{-1} = (\mathbf{W}'\mathbf{W})^{-1}, \quad (11-40)$$

where each row of $\mathbf{W}$ is an observation $\mathbf{w}_i'$ and $\boldsymbol{\theta}$ is the full parameter vector.

Note that the preceding differs from the procedure suggested in (11–29) in the inclusion of a row and a column for σ^2 in the covariance matrix. The difference arises because in the model that transforms y as well as $\mathbf{x}$ [i.e., (11–32) versus (11–28)], the Hessian of the log likelihood is not block diagonal with respect to λ and σ^2. When y is transformed, the maximum likelihood estimates of λ and σ^2 are positively correlated, as both parameters reflect the scaling of the dependent variable in the model. This may seem a counterintuitive result. Consider the difference in the variance estimators that arises when a linear and a log-linear model are estimated. The variance of $\ln y$ around its mean is obviously different from that of y around its mean. These two models arise with different values of λ. By contrast, consider what happens when only the independent variables are transformed. The slope estimators vary accordingly, but in such a way that the variance of y around its conditional mean will stay constant.[27]

---

[25] They are presented in full in Fomby et al. (1984, p. 429) and Greene (1991).

[26] See also Spitzer (1984) and Blackley et al. (1984).

[27] See Seaks and Layson (1983).

EXAMPLE 11.8 Money Demand Equation Continued _____

The model of Example 11.7 treats y and $\mathbf{x}$ asymmetrically in that there $\theta = 0$, while the estimate of λ that was used was 0.45. By using the criterion in (11–36) instead and scanning over the range of minus two to plus two, we find the maximum likelihood estimate of λ to be -0.35. At this estimate, least squares regression gives the results shown in Table 11.11. The standard errors are computed using the Berndt et al. estimator.[28] For illustration, those computed (incorrectly) by least squares are also shown in parentheses.

In the more general model, the analog to the elasticity computed in Example 11.7 is

$$\frac{d \ln y}{d \ln x} = \beta \left(\frac{x}{y} \right)^{\lambda}. \tag{11–41}$$

In order to compute these values, we once again use the mean values of the regressors. For the values of y, we must compute a fitted value at these means. Assuming $\varepsilon = E(\varepsilon) = 0$,

$$\mathbf{b}' \overline{\mathbf{x}}^{(\lambda)} = \hat{y}^{(\lambda)} = \frac{\hat{y}^{\lambda} - 1}{\lambda},$$

we can then obtain the predicted value by inverting this function:

$$\hat{y} = [\lambda \{ \mathbf{b}' \overline{\mathbf{x}}^{(\lambda)} \} + 1]^{1/\lambda}. \tag{11–42}$$

At the means of the independent variables, the two elasticities are -0.03289 for r and 3.6769 for Y, which, once again, are quite comparable to those obtained with the log-linear model.

TABLE 11.11   Estimated Money Demand Equation

	Estimate	**Standard Error**		*t* **ratio**
Constant	-11.170	3.1515	(0.7830)	-3.177
r	-0.005689	0.021017	(0.0159)	-0.271
Y	5.1437	1.1260	(0.2988)	4.568

11.4.3. A Test for (Log-) Linearity

Given the unrestricted estimates of $\boldsymbol{\beta}$, λ, and σ^2, a model that is linear ($\lambda = 1$) or log linear ($\lambda = 0$) is a simple parametric restriction and can be tested with a likelihood ratio statistic. The test statistic, as usual, is

$$\text{chi-squared}(1) = -2[\ln L(\lambda = 1 \text{ or } 0) - \ln L(\lambda = \text{MLE})]. \tag{11–43}$$

This will have a chi-squared distribution with one degree of freedom and can be referred to the standard table. Using the estimate of λ and its standard error, we could also carry out a t test (actually, a Wald test) of the hypothesis that $\lambda = 0$. An alternative Lagrange multiplier test is derived in Example 11.10.

It is not appropriate to test the linear model as an alternative to the log-linear model in this fashion. The models are not nested and neither estimate (zero or one) is an MLE. As

---

[28] Spitzer (1984) discusses using BHHH versus the Hessian to estimate the asymptotic covariance matrix. His main conclusion (which is, fortunately, incorrect) is that the Hessian is more "accurate." He also neglects to include $\hat{\sigma}^2$ among the estimated parameters.

such, this test is not a likelihood ratio test. (There is nothing to prevent the chi-squared statistic from being negative, which should suggest that there is something amiss with this "test.") It is tempting to use the two log likelihoods in a heuristic fashion to choose between them, but it should be remembered that except for the classical regression model, maximum likelihood is not a fitting criterion, that is, it doesn't maximize the fit. As such, choosing between estimators on this basis will not necessarily improve the model.

EXAMPLE 11.9 Test for Linearity ─────────────────────────────

For the money demand data, the three relevant log-likelihood values are

$$\ln L(-0.35) = -116.51,$$

$$\ln L(0) = -118.073,$$

$$\ln L(1) = -130.133.$$

With 20 observations, the two chi-squared test statistics are

Linearity: $\quad -2[-130.133 - (-116.51)] = 27.25,$

Log linearity: $\quad -2[-118.073 - (-116.51)] = 3.13.$

Linearity is rejected, but the log linear model is not rejected as the 5 percent significance level. The critical value from the table is 3.84.

11.5. Hypothesis Testing and Parametric Restrictions

In most cases, the sorts of hypotheses one would test in this context will involve fairly simple linear restrictions. The tests can be carried out using the usual formulas discussed in Chapter 7 and the asymptotic covariance matrix presented earlier. For more involved hypotheses and for nonlinear restrictions, the procedures are a bit less clear-cut. Three principal testing procedures were discussed in Chapter 4: the Wald, likelihood ratio, and Lagrange multiplier tests. In the linear model, it is simple to show that these are identical. In the nonlinear case, they are equivalent only asymptotically. We will work through each of these tests for the general case and then apply them to the example of the previous section.

The hypothesis to be tested is

$$H_0 : \mathbf{R}(\boldsymbol{\beta}) = \mathbf{q}. \tag{11-44}$$

These may be any kind of restrictions, linear or nonlinear. It is necessary, however, that they be **overidentifying restrictions.** This means, in formal terms, that if the original parameter vector has K free elements, the hypothesis $\mathbf{R}(\boldsymbol{\beta}) = \mathbf{q}$ must impose at least one functional relationship on the parameters. If there is more than one restriction, they must be functionally independent. These two conditions imply that the $J \times K$ matrix

$$\mathbf{G} = \frac{\partial \mathbf{R}(\boldsymbol{\beta})}{\partial \boldsymbol{\beta}'} \tag{11-45}$$

must have full row rank and that J, the number of restrictions, must be strictly less than K. (This is analogous to the linear model, in which $\mathbf{G}$ would be the matrix of coefficients in the restrictions.)

Let **b** be the unrestricted, nonlinear least squares estimator, and let **b**$_*$ be the estimator obtained when the constraints of the hypothesis are imposed.[29] All of the test statistics to be considered here are the same asymptotically. Therefore, which test statistic one uses depends on how difficult the computations are. Unlike the linear model, the various testing procedures vary in complexity. For instance, in our example, the Lagrange multiplier is by far the simplest to compute. Of the four methods we will consider, only this test does not require us to compute a nonlinear regression.

11.5.1. An Asymptotically Valid *F* Test

The nonlinear analog to the familiar *F* statistic based on the fit of the regression (i.e., the sum of squared residuals) would be

$$F[J, n - K] = \frac{[S(\mathbf{b}_*) - S(\mathbf{b})]/J}{S(\mathbf{b})/(n - K)}. \tag{11–46}$$

This has the appearance of our earlier *F* ratio. However, in the nonlinear setting, neither the numerator nor the denominator has exactly the necessary chi-squared distribution, so the *F* distribution is only approximate. Note that this *F* statistic requires that both the restricted and unrestricted models be estimated.

11.5.2. Wald Test

The Wald test is based on the distance between **R(b)** and **q.** If the unrestricted estimates fail to satisfy the restrictions, doubt is cast on the validity of the restrictions. The statistic is

$$W = (\mathbf{R}(\mathbf{b}) - \mathbf{q})'\{\text{Est.Asy.Var}[\mathbf{R}(\mathbf{b}) - \mathbf{q}]\}^{-1}(\mathbf{R}(\mathbf{b}) - \mathbf{q})$$
$$= (\mathbf{R}(\mathbf{b}) - \mathbf{q})'\{\mathbf{G}\hat{\mathbf{V}}\mathbf{G}'\}^{-1}(\mathbf{R}(\mathbf{b}) - \mathbf{q}), \tag{11–47}$$

where

$$\hat{\mathbf{V}} = \text{Est.Asy.Var}[\mathbf{b}].$$

This is a chi-squared statistic with *J* degrees of freedom. Under the null hypothesis that the restrictions are correct, the Wald statistic and *J* times the *F* statistic are asymptotically equivalent. The Wald statistic can be based on the estimated covariance matrix obtained earlier using the unrestricted estimates. This may provide a large saving in computing effort if the restrictions are nonlinear.

11.5.3. Likelihood Ratio Test

The log likelihood for a sample of *n* observations, assuming normally distributed disturbances, is

$$\ln L = \text{Jacobian} - \frac{n}{2}\ln(2\pi\sigma^2) - \frac{\varepsilon'\varepsilon}{2\sigma^2}. \tag{11–48}$$

Letting ln *L** be the log likelihood evaluated at the restricted estimates, the likelihood ratio statistic for testing the restrictions is

$$\lambda = -2(\ln L^* - \ln L). \tag{11–49}$$

---

[29] This may be an extremely difficult computational problem in its own right, especially if the constraints are nonlinear. We defer until later consideration of this issue and assume here that the estimator has been obtained by whatever means is necessary.

This statistic is asymptotically distributed as chi-squared with J degrees of freedom. For the present, assume that there is no Jacobian term in L. In each case, the maximum likelihood estimate of σ^2 is $\mathbf{e'e}/n$, so the log likelihood computed at the least squares estimates is

$$\ln L = -\frac{n}{2}\left[1 + \ln(2\pi) + \ln\left(\frac{\mathbf{e'e}}{n}\right)\right].\tag{11-50}$$

and likewise for the restricted estimates.[30] This is easily computed using only the sum of squared residuals. After collecting terms, the likelihood ratio statistic for a classical regression model (linear or nonlinear) is

$$\begin{aligned}
\lambda &= n(\ln\hat{\sigma}_*^2 - \ln\hat{\sigma}^2)\\
&= n\ln\left(\frac{\hat{\sigma}_*^2}{\hat{\sigma}^2}\right).
\end{aligned}\tag{11-51}$$

Like the earlier F statistic, the likelihood ratio statistic requires both restricted and unrestricted estimates.

11.5.4. Lagrange Multiplier Test

The Lagrange multiplier test is based on the decrease in the sum of squared residuals that would result if the restrictions in the restricted model were released. The formalities of the test are given in Section 4.8.3c. For the nonlinear regression model, the test has a particularly appealing form.[31] Let $\mathbf{e}_*$ be the vector of residuals, $y_i - h(\mathbf{x}_i, \mathbf{b}_*)$, computed using the restricted estimates. Recall that we defined $\widetilde{\mathbf{X}}$ as an $n \times K$ matrix of derivatives, computed at a particular parameter vector in (11–9). Let $\widetilde{\mathbf{X}}^*$ be this matrix *computed at the restricted estimates*. Then the Lagrange multiplier statistic for the nonlinear regression model is

$$\text{LM} = \frac{\mathbf{e}_*'\widetilde{\mathbf{X}}^*[\widetilde{\mathbf{X}}^{*\prime}\widetilde{\mathbf{X}}^*]^{-1}\widetilde{\mathbf{X}}^{*\prime}\mathbf{e}_*}{\mathbf{e}_*'\mathbf{e}_*/n} = n\widetilde{R}_*^2.\tag{11-52}$$

This is asymptotically distributed as a chi-squared statistic with J degrees of freedom. What is especially appealing about this approach is that it requires only the restricted estimates. This may provide some savings in computing effort if, as in our example, the restrictions result in a linear model. Note, also, that the Lagrange multiplier statistic is n times the uncentered R^2 in the regression of $\mathbf{e}_*$ on $\widetilde{\mathbf{x}}^*$. Many Lagrange multiplier statistics are computed in this fashion.

EXAMPLE 11.10 Lagrange Multiplier Tests for the Box–Cox Model _____

For simplicity, we first consider the basic model

$$\begin{aligned}
y &= \beta_1 + \beta_2\frac{x^\lambda - 1}{\lambda} + \varepsilon\\
&= f(x, \beta_1, \beta_2, \lambda) + \varepsilon.
\end{aligned}$$

---

[30] This applies for all cases, both linear and nonlinear.

[31] This is derived in Judge et al. (1985).

(For convenience, we have dropped the observation subscript.) We consider a Lagrange multiplier test of the hypothesis that λ equals zero. The *pseudo-regressors* are

$$x_1^* = \frac{\partial f(.)}{\partial \beta_1} = 1,$$

$$x_2^* = \frac{\partial f(.)}{\partial \beta_2} = \frac{x^\lambda - 1}{\lambda},$$

$$x_3^* = \frac{\partial f(.)}{\partial \lambda} = \beta_2 \frac{\lambda(\ln x)x^\lambda - x^\lambda + 1}{\lambda^2}.$$

The test is carried out by first regressing y on a constant and $\ln x$ (i.e., the regressor evaluated at $\lambda = 0$) and then computing nR_*^2 in the regression of the residuals from this first regression on x_1^*, x_2^*, and x_3^*, also evaluated at $\lambda = 0$. The first and second of these are 1 and $\ln x$. To obtain the third, we use the following approach: We require

$$x_{3|\lambda=0}^* = \beta_2 \lim_{\lambda \to 0} \frac{\partial x^{(\lambda)}}{\partial \lambda}.$$

The limit can be obtained thus:

$$\lim_{\lambda \to 0} \frac{\partial x^{(\lambda)}}{\partial \lambda} = \lim_{\lambda \to 0} \left[\frac{x^\lambda \ln x - x^{(\lambda)}}{\lambda} \right].$$

Now applying l'Hôspital's rule to the right-hand side, differentiate numerator and denominator with respect to λ:

$$\lim_{\lambda \to 0} \frac{\partial x^{(\lambda)}}{\partial \lambda} = \lim_{\lambda \to 0} \left[x^\lambda (\ln x)^2 - \frac{\partial x^{(\lambda)}}{\partial \lambda} \right].$$

The limit of the derivative appears on both sides of the equals sign. Collect the two on the left, then divide by 2, to obtain

$$\lim_{\lambda \to 0} \frac{\partial x^{(\lambda)}}{\partial \lambda} = \frac{1}{2} \lim_{\lambda \to 0} x^\lambda (\ln x)^2 = \frac{1}{2} (\ln x)^2.[32]$$

Therefore,

$$\lim_{\lambda \to 0} x_3^* = \beta_2 [\tfrac{1}{2}(\ln x)^2].$$

Therefore, the Lagrange multiplier test is carried out in two steps. First we regress $\ln y$ on a constant and $\ln x$ and compute the residuals. Second, we regress these residuals on a constant, $\ln x$, and $(b_2/2)(\ln x)^2$, where b_2 is the coefficient on $\ln x$ in the first regression. The Lagrange multiplier is nR^2 from the second regression. The generalization to several regressors is immediate. In the first regression, we would use the logs of all of the regressors. The additional regressor for the second regression would be

$$x_\lambda^* = \left(\frac{1}{2} \right) \sum_k b_k (\ln x_k)^2,$$

where the sum is taken over all of the variables that are transformed in the original model and the b_k's are the least squares coefficients in the first regression.

---

[32] See Exercise 8 for an extension to higher derivatives.

For an example, consider the Box–Cox model of Example 11.7. The model is

$$\ln M = \alpha + \beta_r r^{(\lambda)} + \beta_Y Y^{(\lambda)} + \varepsilon.$$

To carry out the Wald test, we use the square of the ratio of $\hat{\lambda}$ to its estimated standard error as a chi-squared statistic with one degree of freedom. This is $(0.47/0.5467)^2 = 0.7391$. For the likelihood ratio test, we use (11–51). With $\lambda = 0.47$, the sum of squared residuals is 0.1272. With $\lambda = 0$, we obtain the sum of squared residuals in the regression of $\ln M$ on a constant, $\ln r$, and $\ln Y$, which is 0.13196. Therefore, the likelihood ratio statistic is $20 \ln\{(0.13196/20)/(0.1272/20)\} = 0.7342$. Finally, for the Lagrange multiplier test, we first regress $\ln M$ on a constant, $\ln r$, and $\ln Y$ and compute the residuals, $\mathbf{e}_*$. The R^2 in the regression of $\mathbf{e}_*$ on one, $\ln r$, $\ln Y$, and $(1/2)(b_r(\ln r)^2 + b_Y(\ln Y)^2)$, is 0.03613, so the Lagrange multiplier test statistic is $20(0.03613) = 0.7226$. None of these are larger than the tabled critical value, so the hypothesis that $\lambda = 0$ is not rejected.

By extending this to the model of (11–32), we can devise a bona fide test of log linearity (against the more general model, not linearity).[33] The log likelihood for the model

$$\frac{y^\lambda - 1}{\lambda} = \beta_1 + \beta_2 \frac{x^\lambda - 1}{\lambda} + \varepsilon$$

is given in (11–34). The first derivatives are obtained in (11–37) to (11–39). Using the Berndt et al. estimator given in (11–40), we could construct the Lagrange multiplier statistic as

$$\text{LM} = \chi^2[1] = \left(\sum_i \mathbf{w}_i\right)' \left\{\sum_i \mathbf{w}_i \mathbf{w}_i'\right\}^{-1} \left(\sum_i \mathbf{w}_i\right),$$

where, for the preceding model, we would compute the various terms at $\lambda = 0$. Thus,

$$\hat{\varepsilon}_i = \ln y_i - \hat{\beta}_1 - \hat{\beta}_2 \ln x_i,$$

$\hat{\beta}_1$ and $\hat{\beta}_2$ computed by the OLS regression of y on a constant and x, and

$$\hat{\sigma}^2 = \frac{1}{n} \sum_i \hat{\varepsilon}_i^2.$$

Let

$$\hat{\varepsilon}_i^* = \frac{1}{2}(\ln y_i)^2 - \frac{\hat{\beta}_2}{2}(\ln x_i)^2.$$

[See (11–38).] Then

$$\mathbf{w}_i = \begin{bmatrix} \hat{\varepsilon}_i/\hat{\sigma}^2 \\ (\ln x_i)\hat{\varepsilon}_i/\hat{\sigma}^2 \\ \ln y_i - \hat{\varepsilon}_i\hat{\varepsilon}_i^*/\hat{\sigma}^2 \\ (\hat{\varepsilon}_i^2/\hat{\sigma}^2 - 1)/(2\hat{\sigma}^2) \end{bmatrix}.$$

(If there are k regressors in the model, the second component in $\mathbf{w}_i$ will be a vector containing the logs of the variables, while $\hat{\varepsilon}_i^*$ in the third becomes

$$\hat{\varepsilon}_i^* = \frac{1}{2}(\ln y_i)^2 - \sum_k \frac{\hat{\beta}_k}{2}(\ln x_{ik})^2.$$

---

[33] This test was proposed by Davidson and MacKinnon (1985). They also suggested a test of a linearity based on the same methodology by using $\lambda = 1$ instead of $\lambda = 0$ in the computations just described.

The usefulness of this approach for either of the models we have examined is that in testing the hypothesis, it is not necessary to compute the nonlinear, unrestricted, Box–Cox regression.

EXAMPLE 11.11 Hypotheses Tests in a Nonlinear Regression Model _____

For a second example, we test the hypothesis

$$H_0 : \gamma = 1$$

in the consumption function of Example 11.3.

    1. *F statistic*

$$F[1, 36 - 3] = \frac{(12{,}068 - 8420)/1}{8420/(36 - 3)}$$

$$= 14.297.$$

The critical value from the tables is 4.18, so the hypothesis is rejected.

    2. *Wald statistic.* For our example, this is based on the distance of $\hat{\gamma}$ from one, and is simply the square of the asymptotic t ratio we computed at the end of the example.

$$W = \frac{(1.1564 - 1)^2}{0.001681} = 14.551.$$

The critical value from the chi-squared table is 3.84.

    3. *Likelihood ratio.* For the example, $\mathbf{e}'\mathbf{e}$ is 8,420, while $\mathbf{e}'_* \mathbf{e}_*$ is 12,068. With $n = 36$, this yields

$$\lambda = 36(5.8147 - 5.4548) = 12.9548.$$

This is also larger than the tabled critical value. Note, however, that it is noticeably less than the Wald statistic. It is possible that the two different statistics could lead to different inferences. Unfortunately, this is a problem that can arise in a finite sample, and there is no formal result that mandates which is the better to choose.[34]

    4. *Lagrange multiplier.* For our example, the elements in $\tilde{\mathbf{x}}_i$ are

$$\tilde{\mathbf{x}}_i = [1, Y^\gamma, \beta \gamma Y^\gamma \ln Y].$$

To compute this at the restricted estimates, we use the ordinary least squares estimates for α and β, and one for γ, so that

$$\tilde{\mathbf{x}}_i^* = [1, Y, \beta Y \ln Y].$$

The residuals are the ordinary least squares residuals computed from the linear regression. Inserting the values given earlier, we have

$$LM = \frac{3547.3}{12{,}068/36} = 10.582.$$

As expected, this statistic is also larger than the critical value from chi-squared table.

___

There is a large and growing literature on the use of these tests in econometrics. The emerging results have documented many ways to extend beyond the conventional t and F tests, particularly in the area of nonnested models. The Lagrange multiplier test has been

___

[34] There is some evidence, though no prescription, on this problem in Berndt and Savin (1977).

shown to be especially convenient in gathering under a broad umbrella an impressive variety of already familiar tests.[35]

EXERCISES

1. Describe how to obtain nonlinear least squares estimates of the parameters of the model

$$y = \alpha x^\beta + \varepsilon.$$

2. Use MacKinnon et al.'s P_E test to determine whether a linear or log-linear production model is more appropriate for the data in Table 7.1. (The test is described in Section 11.2.3 and Example 11.4.)

3. Example 8.4 discusses a method of estimating the parameters of the CES production function based on a linearization of the model around $\rho = 0$. An alternative way to proceed is by direct nonlinear least squares. For the model

$$\ln Y = \ln \gamma - \left(\frac{v}{\rho}\right) \ln [\delta K^{-\rho} + (1 - \delta)L^{-\rho}] + \varepsilon,$$

derive the linearized model shown in (11–8). Describe in full how to obtain the nonlinear least squares estimates and how to compute the estimate of the asymptotic covariance matrix of these estimates.

4. Using the Box–Cox transformation, we may specify an alternative to the Cobb–Douglas model as

$$\ln Y = \alpha + \frac{\beta_k(K^\lambda - 1)}{\lambda} + \frac{\beta_l(L^\lambda - 1)}{\lambda} + \varepsilon.$$

Using Zellner and Revankar's data in Table 11.6, estimate α, β_k, β_l, and λ, using the scanning method suggested in Section 11.4.1. (Do not forget to scale Y, K, and L by the number of establishments.) Use (11–29) to compute the appropriate asymptotic standard errors for your estimates. Compute the two output elasticities, $\partial \ln Y / \partial \ln K$ and $\partial \ln Y / \partial \ln L$ at the sample means of K and L. (**Hint:** $\partial \ln Y / \partial \ln K = K\partial \ln Y/\partial K$.) How do these estimates compare to the values given in Example 11.5? Finally, compute the estimates of economies of scale for the states shown in Example 11.5 and compare your estimates to the values given there.

5. For the model in the previous exercise, test the hypothesis that $\lambda = 0$, using a Wald test, a likelihood ratio test, and a Lagrange multiplier test. Note that the restricted model is the Cobb–Douglas log-linear model.

6. To extend Zellner and Revankar's model in a fashion similar to theirs, we can use the Box–Cox transformation for the dependent variable as well. Use the method of Section 11.4.2 (with $\theta = \lambda$) to repeat the study of the preceding two exercises. How do your results change?

7. Suppose that we wished to test the specification of Exercise 6 against that of Exercise 4. The models are not nested, so there is no obvious test. Indeed, they both use exactly the same parameters. One possibility is the following: Both models are special cases of

---

[35] Some useful references are Buse (1982), Pagan and Hall (1983), Engle (1984), Breusch and Pagan (1980), and Godfrey (1988).

(11–32). In Exercise 4 we assume that $\theta = 0$ while in Exercise 6 we impose $\theta = \lambda$. Thus, although it might seem otherwise, it is not obvious that Exercise 6 is a less restrictive or preferable model. One way to determine which model is preferable (albeit not a formal test) is to compare the log likelihoods under the two specifications. This can be done directly, using the results already obtained. Somewhat more evidence can be obtained by estimating the unrestricted model. This requires a two-dimensional search for θ and λ. Estimate the unrestricted model; then carry out an analysis of the sort done in Example 11.9.

8. Verify the following differential equation, which applies to the Box–Cox transformation:

$$\frac{d^i x^{(\lambda)}}{d\lambda^i} = \left(\frac{1}{\lambda}\right)\left[x^\lambda (\ln x)^i - \frac{i\, d^{i-1} x^{(\lambda)}}{d\lambda^{i-1}}\right].$$

Show that the limiting sequence for $\lambda = 0$ is

$$\frac{d^i x^{(\lambda)}}{d\lambda^i}\bigg|_{\lambda=0} = \frac{(\ln x)^{i+1}}{i+1}.$$

(These results can be used to great advantage in deriving the actual second derivatives of the log-likelihood function for the Box–Cox model. **Hint:** See Example 11.10.)

9. How would you estimate the asymptotic standard error of the estimator of the elasticity in (11–41) and (11–42)? If you have access to the necessary software, do this computation for the money demand equation.

CHAPTER 12

An Introduction to Nonlinear Optimization[1]

12.1. Introduction

The nonlinear least squares regression discussed in Chapter 11 is an example of a nonlinear optimization problem. With the exception of the normal linear regression model, maximum likelihood estimation usually involves the solution of nonlinear equations as well. Nonlinear optimization is an intriguing practical problem. The theory provides few hard and fast rules, and there are relatively few cases in which it is obvious how to proceed. This chapter introduces some of the terminology and underlying theory of nonlinear optimization.[2] We begin with some general discussion on how to search for a solution to a nonlinear optimization problem and describe some specific commonly used methods. We then consider some practical problems that arise in optimization. An example is given in the final section.

12.2. Optimization Problems

Consider maximizing the quadratic function

$$F(\boldsymbol{\theta}) = a + \mathbf{b}'\boldsymbol{\theta} - \tfrac{1}{2}\boldsymbol{\theta}'\mathbf{C}\boldsymbol{\theta}, \tag{12-1}$$

where $\mathbf{C}$ is a positive definite matrix. The first-order condition for a maximum is

$$\frac{\partial F(\boldsymbol{\theta})}{\partial \boldsymbol{\theta}} = \mathbf{b} - \mathbf{C}\boldsymbol{\theta} = \mathbf{0}. \tag{12-2}$$

This set of *linear* equations has unique solution

$$\boldsymbol{\theta} = \mathbf{C}^{-1}\mathbf{b}. \tag{12-3}$$

This is a linear optimization problem. Note that it has a **closed-form solution;** for any a, $\mathbf{b}$, and $\mathbf{C}$, the solution can be computed directly.[3] In the more typical situation,

$$\frac{\partial F(\boldsymbol{\theta})}{\partial \boldsymbol{\theta}} = \mathbf{0} \tag{12-4}$$

---

[1] The material of this chapter is somewhat advanced and may be skipped with no loss of continuity.

[2] There are numerous excellent references that offer a more complete exposition. Among these are Quandt (1983), Bazaraa and Shetty (1979), and Fletcher (1980).

[3] Notice that the constant, a, is irrelevant to the solution. Many maximum likelihood problems are presented with the preface "neglecting an irrelevant constant." For example, the log likelihood for the normal linear regression model contains a term, $-(n/2)\ln(2\pi)$, that can be discarded.

is a set of nonlinear equations that cannot be solved explicitly for $\boldsymbol{\theta}$.[4] The techniques considered in this chapter provide systematic means of searching for a solution.

We consider the general problem of maximizing a function of several variables:

$$\text{Maximize}_{\boldsymbol{\theta}} \, F(\boldsymbol{\theta}), \tag{12-5}$$

where $F(\boldsymbol{\theta})$ may be a log likelihood or some other function. Minimization of $F(\boldsymbol{\theta})$ is handled by maximizing $-F(\boldsymbol{\theta})$. Two special cases are

$$F(\boldsymbol{\theta}) = \sum_i f_i(\boldsymbol{\theta}), \tag{12-6}$$

which is typical for maximum likelihood problems, and the **least squares problem**,[5]

$$f_i(\boldsymbol{\theta}) = -(y_i - f(\mathbf{x}_i, \, \boldsymbol{\theta}))^2. \tag{12-7}$$

12.3. Grid Search

An obvious way to search for the $\boldsymbol{\theta}$ that maximizes $F(\boldsymbol{\theta})$ is by trial and error. If $\boldsymbol{\theta}$ has only a single element and it is known approximately where the optimum will be found, a **grid search** will be a feasible strategy. The Box–Cox model of Section 11.4 is usually estimated by scanning the range of -2 to 2 for the optimal value of λ.[6] Another example is a common time series problem, in which a one-dimensional search for a correlation coefficient is made in the interval $(-1, 1)$. The grid search can proceed in the obvious fashion, that is, . . . , $-0.1, 0, 0.1, 0.2, . . .$, then $\hat{\theta}_{\max} - 0.1$ to $\hat{\theta}_{\max} + 0.1$ in increments of 0.01, and so on, until the desired precision is achieved. If $\boldsymbol{\theta}$ contains more than one parameter, a grid search is likely to be extremely costly, particularly if little is known about the parameter vector at the outset. Nonetheless, relatively efficient methods have been devised. Quandt (1983) and Fletcher (1980) contain further details.

12.4. General Characteristics of Algorithms

A more effective means of solving most nonlinear maximization problems is by an **iterative algorithm:**

> Beginning from initial value $\boldsymbol{\theta}_0$, at entry to iteration t, if $\boldsymbol{\theta}_t$ is not the optimal value for $\boldsymbol{\theta}$, compute direction vector, $\boldsymbol{\Delta}_t$, step size λ_t, then
>
> $$\boldsymbol{\theta}_{t+1} = \boldsymbol{\theta}_t + \lambda_t \, \boldsymbol{\Delta}_t. \tag{12-8}$$

Figure 12.1 illustrates the structure of an iteration for a hypothetical function of two variables. The direction vector, $\boldsymbol{\Delta}_t$, is shown in the figure with $\boldsymbol{\theta}_t$. The dashed line is the set of points $\boldsymbol{\theta}_t + \lambda_t \, \boldsymbol{\Delta}_t$. Different values of λ_t lead to different contours; for this $\boldsymbol{\theta}_t$ and $\boldsymbol{\Delta}_t$, the best value of λ_t is about 0.5.

Notice in Figure 12.1 that for a given direction vector, $\boldsymbol{\Delta}_t$, and current parameter vector, $\boldsymbol{\theta}_t$, a secondary optimization is required to find the best λ_t. Translating from Figure 12.1, we obtain the form of this problem as shown in Figure 12.2. This subsidiary

---

[4] See, for example, the normal equations for the nonlinear least squares estimators of the previous chapter.

[5] Least squares is, of course, a minimizing problem. The negative of the criterion is used to maintain consistency with the general formulation.

[6] It should be remembered, however, that nothing prevents λ from being outside this range. For example, if a Box–Cox model is fit to the production data of Example 7.1, two minima of the sum of squares can be found: a local minimum at 0.29 and a global minimum at 1.7.

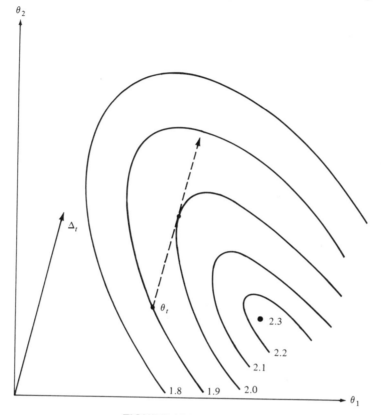

FIGURE 12.1 Iteration.

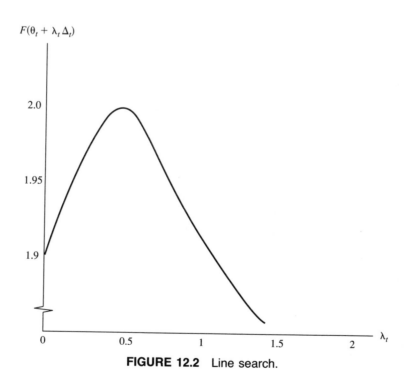

FIGURE 12.2 Line search.

search is called a **line search,** as we search along the line $\boldsymbol{\theta}_t + \lambda_t \, \boldsymbol{\Delta}_t$ for the optimal value of $F(.)$. The formal solution to the line search problem would be the λ_t that satisfies

$$\frac{\partial F(\boldsymbol{\theta}_t + \lambda_t \, \boldsymbol{\Delta}_t)}{\partial \lambda_t} = \mathbf{g}(\boldsymbol{\theta}_t + \lambda_t \, \boldsymbol{\Delta}_t)' \boldsymbol{\Delta}_t$$

$$= 0, \tag{12–9}$$

where $\mathbf{g}$ is the vector of partial derivatives of $F(.)$ evaluated at $\boldsymbol{\theta}_t + \lambda_t \, \boldsymbol{\Delta}_t$. In general, this will also be a nonlinear problem. In most cases, adding a formal search for λ_t will be too expensive, as well as unnecessary. Some approximate or ad hoc method will usually be chosen. It is worth emphasizing that finding the λ_t that maximizes $F(\boldsymbol{\theta}_t + \lambda_t \, \boldsymbol{\Delta}_t)$ at a given iteration does not generally lead to the overall solution in that iteration. This is clear in Figure 12.1, where the optimal value of λ_t leads to $F(.) = 2.0$, at which point we reenter the iteration.

12.5. Gradient Methods

The most commonly used algorithms are **gradient methods,** in which

$$\boldsymbol{\Delta}_t = \mathbf{H}_t \mathbf{g}_t, \tag{12–10}$$

where $\mathbf{H}_t$ is a positive definite matrix and $\mathbf{g}_t$ is the **gradient** of $F(\boldsymbol{\theta}_t)$:

$$\mathbf{g}_t = \mathbf{g}(\boldsymbol{\theta}_t) = \frac{\partial F(\boldsymbol{\theta}_t)}{\partial \boldsymbol{\theta}}. \tag{12–11}$$

These methods are motivated partly by the following: Consider a linear Taylor series approximation to $F(\boldsymbol{\theta}_t + \lambda_t \, \boldsymbol{\Delta}_t)$ around $\lambda = 0$:

$$F(\boldsymbol{\theta}_t + \lambda_t \, \boldsymbol{\Delta}_t) \simeq F(\boldsymbol{\theta}_t) + \lambda_t \mathbf{g}(\boldsymbol{\theta}_t)' \, \boldsymbol{\Delta}_t. \tag{12–12}$$

Let $F(\boldsymbol{\theta}_t + \lambda_t \, \boldsymbol{\Delta}_t)$ equal F_{t+1}. Then

$$F_{t+1} - F_t \simeq \lambda_t \mathbf{g}_t' \, \boldsymbol{\Delta}_t.$$

If $\boldsymbol{\Delta}_t = \mathbf{H}_t \mathbf{g}_t$,

$$F_{t+1} - F_t \simeq \lambda_t \mathbf{g}_t' \mathbf{H}_t \mathbf{g}_t.$$

If $\mathbf{g}_t$ is not $\mathbf{0}$ and λ_t is small enough, $F_{t+1} - F_t$ must be positive. This means that if $F(\boldsymbol{\theta})$ is not already at its maximum, we can always find a stepsize such that a gradient-type iteration will lead to an increase in the function. (Recall that $\mathbf{H}_t$ is assumed to be positive definite.)

In the following, we will omit the iteration index, t, except where it is necessary to distinguish one vector from another. The following are some commonly used algorithms.[7]

12.5.1. Steepest Ascent

The simplest algorithm to employ is the **steepest ascent** method, which uses

$$\mathbf{H} = \mathbf{I} \quad \text{so that} \quad \boldsymbol{\Delta} = \mathbf{g}. \tag{12–13}$$

---

[7] A more extensive catalog may be found in Judge et al. (1985, Appendix B). Those mentioned here are some of the more commonly used ones and are chosen primarily because they illustrate many of the important aspects of nonlinear optimization.

As its name implies, the direction is the one of greatest increase of $F(.)$. Another virtue is that the line search has a straightforward solution; at least near the maximum, the optimal λ is

$$\lambda = \frac{-\mathbf{g}'\mathbf{g}}{\mathbf{g}'\mathbf{G}\mathbf{g}}, \tag{12–14}$$

where

$$\mathbf{G} = \frac{\partial^2 F(\boldsymbol{\theta})}{\partial \boldsymbol{\theta} \partial \boldsymbol{\theta}'}.$$

Therefore, the steepest ascent iteration is

$$\boldsymbol{\theta}_{t+1} = \boldsymbol{\theta}_t - \left(\frac{\mathbf{g}_t'\mathbf{g}_t}{\mathbf{g}_t'\mathbf{G}_t\mathbf{g}_t}\right)\mathbf{g}_t. \tag{12–15}$$

Computation of the second derivatives matrix may be extremely burdensome. Also, if $\mathbf{G}_t$ is not negative definite, which is likely if $\boldsymbol{\theta}_t$ is far from the maximum, the iteration may diverge. A systematic line search can bypass this problem. This algorithm usually converges very slowly, however, so other techniques are usually used.

12.5.2. Newton's Method

The basis for **Newton's method** is a linear Taylor series approximation. Expanding the first-order conditions (equation by equation)

$$\frac{\partial F(\boldsymbol{\theta})}{\partial \boldsymbol{\theta}} = \mathbf{0}$$

in a linear Taylor series around an arbitrary $\boldsymbol{\theta}^0$ yields

$$\frac{\partial F(\boldsymbol{\theta})}{\partial \boldsymbol{\theta}} \simeq \mathbf{g}^0 + \mathbf{G}^0(\boldsymbol{\theta} - \boldsymbol{\theta}^0) = \mathbf{0}, \tag{12–16}$$

where the superscript indicates that the term is evaluated at $\boldsymbol{\theta}^0$. Solving for $\boldsymbol{\theta}$ and then equating $\boldsymbol{\theta}$ to $\boldsymbol{\theta}_{t+1}$ and $\boldsymbol{\theta}^0$ to $\boldsymbol{\theta}_t$, we obtain the iteration

$$\boldsymbol{\theta}_{t+1} = \boldsymbol{\theta}_t - \mathbf{G}_t^{-1}\mathbf{g}_t. \tag{12–17}$$

Thus, for Newton's method,

$$\mathbf{H} = -\mathbf{G}^{-1}, \qquad \boldsymbol{\Delta} = -\mathbf{G}^{-1}\mathbf{g}, \qquad \text{and } \lambda = 1. \tag{12–18}$$

Newton's method will converge very rapidly in many problems. If the function is quadratic, this method will reach the optimum in one iteration from any starting point. [Consider, for example, the optimization problem posed in (12–1).] If the criterion function is globally concave, as it is in a number of problems that we shall examine later, it is probably the best algorithm available. This method is very well suited to maximum likelihood estimation.

12.5.3. Maximum Likelihood Estimation

For solving a maximum likelihood problem, the **method of scoring** replaces $\mathbf{H}$ with

$$\overline{\mathbf{H}} = (-E[\mathbf{G}(\boldsymbol{\theta})])^{-1}, \tag{12–19}$$

which will be recognized as the asymptotic variance of $\sqrt{n}$ times the maximum likelihood estimator. There is some evidence that where it can be used, this method performs better than Newton's method. However, the exact form of the expectation of the Hessian of the log likelihood is rarely known.[8] Newton's method, which uses actual instead of expected second derivatives, is generally used instead.

A particularly convenient variant of Newton's method is the **one-step maximum likelihood estimator.** It has been shown that if θ^0 is *any* consistent initial estimator of θ and **H*** is **H** or $\overline{\mathbf{H}}$, or any other asymptotically equivalent estimator of $\text{Var}[\sqrt{n}(\hat{\theta}_{MLE} - \theta)]$,

$$\theta^1 = \theta^0 + H^{*-1}g^0 \qquad (12\text{--}20)$$

is an estimator of θ that has the same asymptotic properties as the maximum likelihood estimator.[9] (Note that it is *not* the maximum likelihood estimator. As such, for example, it should not be used as the basis for likelihood ratio tests.)

12.5.4. Alternatives to Newton's Method

Newton's method is very effective in some settings, but it can perform very poorly in others. If the function is not approximately quadratic or the current estimate is very far from the maximum, it can cause wide swings in the estimates and even fail to converge at all. A number of means have been devised to improve upon Newton's method. An obvious one is to include a line search at each iteration rather than use $\lambda = 1$. However, two problems remain. At points distant from the optimum, the second derivatives matrix may not be negative definite, and, in any event, the computational burden of computing **G** may be excessive.

The **quadratic hill-climbing method** proposed by Goldfeld et al. (1966) deals directly with the first of these problems. In any iteration, if **G** is not negative definite, it is replaced with

$$\mathbf{G}_\alpha = \mathbf{G} - \alpha\mathbf{I}, \qquad (12\text{--}21)$$

where α is a positive number chosen large enough to ensure the negative definiteness of $\mathbf{G}_\alpha$. Another suggestion is that of Greenstadt (1967), which uses, at every iteration,

$$\mathbf{G}_\pi = -\sum_i |\pi_i|\mathbf{c}_i\mathbf{c}_i', \qquad (12\text{--}22)$$

where π_i is the ith characteristic root of **G** and $\mathbf{c}_i$ is its associated characteristic vector. Other proposals have been made to ensure the negative definiteness of the required matrix at each iteration.[10] However, the computational complexity of these methods remains a problem.

Two commonly used methods simultaneously simplify the calculation of **H** and solve the problem of definiteness. For maximum likelihood problems, the method of Berndt et al. (1974) replaces **H** with

$$\hat{\mathbf{H}} = \left[\sum_i \mathbf{g}_i\mathbf{g}_i'\right]^{-1}, \qquad (12\text{--}23)$$

where

$$\mathbf{g}_i = \frac{\partial \ln f(\mathbf{x}_i, \theta)}{\partial \theta}.$$

---

[8] Amemiya (1981) provides a number of examples.

[9] See, for example, Rao (1965).

[10] See, for example, Goldfeld and Quandt (1971).

This is the third estimator for the variance of the maximum likelihood estimator that we considered in Chapter 4.[11] While $\hat{\mathbf{H}}$ and a consistent estimator of $-\mathbf{G}$ are asymptotically equivalent, $\hat{\mathbf{H}}$ has the additional virtues that it is always positive definite, and it is only necessary to differentiate the log likelihood once in order to compute it.

For the nonlinear least squares problem, the correct second derivatives matrix is

$$\mathbf{G} = -2\sum_i [\mathbf{g}_i\mathbf{g}_i' - (y_i - f_i)\mathbf{G}_i], \tag{12-24}$$

where $f_i = f(\mathbf{x}_i, \boldsymbol{\theta})$ and $\mathbf{g}_i$ and $\mathbf{G}_i$ are its first and second derivatives, respectively. This matrix can also fail to be positive definite at points different from the minimum. The **Gauss–Newton method** amounts simply to dropping the second term, which leaves a matrix that is always negative definite. Recall the linearized regression of Section 11.2.1:

$$f_i \simeq f_i^0 + \mathbf{g}_i^{0\prime}(\boldsymbol{\theta} - \boldsymbol{\theta}^0).$$

Inserting this in the sum of squares yields

$$F(\boldsymbol{\theta}) \simeq \sum_i [(y_i - f_i^0 + \mathbf{g}_i^{0\prime}\boldsymbol{\theta}^0) - \mathbf{g}_i^{0\prime}\boldsymbol{\theta}]^2 \tag{12-25}$$

$$= \sum_i [y_i^0 - \mathbf{g}_i^{0\prime}\boldsymbol{\theta}]^2.$$

For a given value of $\boldsymbol{\theta}^0$, this is the linear least squares problem. The iterative solution to the minimization problem is, then,

$$\boldsymbol{\theta}_{t+1} = \left[\sum_i \mathbf{g}_i\mathbf{g}_i'\right]^{-1}\left[\sum_i \mathbf{g}_i(y_i - f_i + \mathbf{g}_i'\boldsymbol{\theta}_t)\right] \tag{12-26}$$

$$= \boldsymbol{\theta}_t + \left[\sum_i \mathbf{g}_i\mathbf{g}_i'\right]^{-1}\left[\sum_i \mathbf{g}_i(y_i - f_i)\right],$$

where all terms on the right-hand side are evaluated at $\boldsymbol{\theta}_t$.

This particular algorithm has some intuitive appeal. For each iteration, we update the previous parameter estimate by regressing the nonlinear least squares residuals, $(y_i - f_i)$, on the derivatives of the regression functions. As discussed in Chapter 11, the derivatives, $\mathbf{g}_i$, are in some respects analogous to the regressors, $\mathbf{x}_i$, in the linear model. Let $\tilde{\mathbf{X}}$ be the $n \times K$ matrix of derivatives and let $\tilde{\mathbf{e}}$ be the $n \times 1$ vector of residuals. Then the iteration in (12–26) is equivalent to

$$\boldsymbol{\theta}_{t+1} - \boldsymbol{\theta}_t = [\tilde{\mathbf{X}}'\tilde{\mathbf{X}}]^{-1}\tilde{\mathbf{X}}'\tilde{\mathbf{e}}.$$

The process will have converged (i.e., the update will be $\mathbf{0}$) when $\tilde{\mathbf{X}}'\tilde{\mathbf{e}}$ is close enough to $\mathbf{0}$.[12] This has a direct counterpart in the normal equations for the linear model,

$$\mathbf{X}'\mathbf{e} = \mathbf{0}.$$

---

[11] This is the estimator of the asymptotic covariance matrix used for the Box–Cox model in Example 11.8.

[12] It will not be exactly zero. See Section 12.6 for a discussion of convergence of nonlinear optimization algorithms.

12.5.5. Quasi-Newton Methods—Davidon–Fletcher–Powell

A very effective class of algorithms has been developed that eliminates second derivatives altogether and has excellent convergence properties, even for ill-behaved problems. These are the **quasi-Newton methods,** which form

$$\mathbf{H}_{t+1} = \mathbf{H}_t + \mathbf{E}_t,$$

where $\mathbf{E}_t$ is a positive definite matrix.[13] As long as $\mathbf{H}_0$ is positive definite—$\mathbf{I}$ is commonly used—$\mathbf{H}_t$ will be positive definite at every iteration. In the **Davidon–Fletcher–Powell (DFP) method,** after a sufficient number of iterations, $\mathbf{H}_{t+1}$ will be an approximation to $-\mathbf{G}^{-1}$. Let

$$\boldsymbol{\delta}_t = \lambda_t \boldsymbol{\Delta}_t \qquad \text{and} \qquad \boldsymbol{\gamma}_t = \mathbf{g}(\boldsymbol{\theta}_{t+1}) - \mathbf{g}(\boldsymbol{\theta}_t). \tag{12–27}$$

The DFP **variable metric algorithm** uses

$$\mathbf{H}_{t+1} = \mathbf{H}_t + \frac{\boldsymbol{\delta}_t \boldsymbol{\delta}_t'}{\boldsymbol{\delta}_t' \boldsymbol{\gamma}_t} + \frac{\mathbf{H}_t \boldsymbol{\gamma}_t \boldsymbol{\gamma}_t' \mathbf{H}_t}{\boldsymbol{\gamma}_t' \mathbf{H}_t \boldsymbol{\gamma}_t}. \tag{12–28}$$

Notice that in the DFP algorithm, the change in the first derivative vector is used in $\mathbf{H}$; an estimate of the inverse of the second derivatives matrix is being accumulated.

The variable metric algorithms are those that update $\mathbf{H}$ at each iteration while preserving its definiteness. For the DFP method, the accumulation of $\mathbf{H}_{t+1}$ is of the form

$$\mathbf{H}_{t+1} = \mathbf{H}_t + \mathbf{aa}' + \mathbf{bb}' = \mathbf{H}_t + [\mathbf{a}, \mathbf{b}][\mathbf{a}, \mathbf{b}]'$$

The two-column matrix $[\mathbf{a}, \mathbf{b}]$ will have rank two; hence this is called a **rank two update** or **rank two correction.** Other methods, such as **Broyden's method,** involve a rank one correction instead. Any method that is of the form

$$\mathbf{H}_{t+1} = \mathbf{H}_t + \mathbf{QQ}'$$

will preserve the definiteness of $\mathbf{H}$, regardless of the number of columns in $\mathbf{Q}$.

The DFP algorithm is extremely effective and is among the most widely used gradient methods. An important practical consideration to keep in mind is that although $\mathbf{H}_t$ accumulates an estimate of the negative inverse of the second derivatives matrix, in maximum likelihood problems it rarely converges to a very good estimate of the variance matrix of the estimator and should generally not be used as one.

12.6. Some Practical Considerations

The reasons for the good performance of many algorithms, including DFP, are unknown. Moreover, different algorithms may perform differently in given settings. Indeed, for some problems, one algorithm may fail to converge, while another will succeed in finding a solution without great difficulty. In view of this, computer programs such as GQOPT[14] and Gauss[15] that offer a menu of different preprogrammed algorithms can be particularly useful. It is sometimes worth the effort to try more than one algorithm on a given problem.

Except for the steepest ascent case, an optimal line search is likely to be infeasible or to require more effort than it is worth in view of the potentially large number of function

---

[13] See Fletcher (1980).

[14] Goldfeld and Quandt (1972).

[15] Edlefson and Jones (1985).

evaluations required. In most cases, the choice of a stepsize is likely to be rather ad hoc. But within limits, the most widely used algorithms appear to be robust to inaccurate line searches. For example, one method used by the widely used TSP computer program[16] is the method of *squeezing,* which tries $\lambda = 1, \frac{1}{2}, \frac{1}{4}$, and so on, until an improvement in the function results. Although this is obviously a bit unorthodox, it appears to be quite effective when used with the Gauss–Newton method. A somewhat more elaborate rule is suggested by Berndt et al.[17] Choose an ε between 0 and $\frac{1}{2}$; then find a λ such that

$$\varepsilon < \frac{F(\boldsymbol{\theta} + \lambda\boldsymbol{\Delta}) - F(\boldsymbol{\theta})}{\lambda \mathbf{g}' \boldsymbol{\Delta}} < 1 - \varepsilon. \tag{12–29}$$

Of course, which value of ε to choose is still open, so the choice of λ remains ad hoc. Moreover, in neither of these cases is there any optimality to the choice; we merely find a λ that leads to a function improvement. Other authors have devised relatively efficient means of searching for a stepsize without doing the full optimization at each iteration.[18]

For certain functions, the programming of derivatives may be quite difficult. Numerical approximations can be used, although it should be borne in mind that analytic derivatives obtained by formally differentiating the functions involved are to be preferred. First derivatives can be approximated by using

$$\frac{\partial F(\boldsymbol{\theta})}{\partial \theta_i} \simeq \frac{F(\cdots \theta_i + \varepsilon \cdots) - F(\cdots \theta_i - \varepsilon \cdots)}{2\varepsilon} \tag{12–30}$$

The choice of ε is a remaining problem. Extensive discussion may be found in Quandt (1983).

There are three drawbacks to this means of computing derivatives compared to using the analytic derivatives. A possibly major consideration is that it may substantially increase the amount of computation needed to obtain a function and its gradient. In particular, $K + 1$ function evaluations (the criterion and K derivatives) are replaced with $2K + 1$ functions. The latter may be more burdensome than the former, depending on the complexity of the partial derivatives compared to the function, itself. The comparison will depend on the application. But, in most settings, careful programming which avoids superfluous or redundant calculation can make the advantage of the analytic derivatives substantial. Second, the choice of ε can be problematic. If it is chosen too large, the approximation will be inaccurate. If it is chosen too small, there may be insufficient variation in the function to produce a good estimate of the derivative. A compromise which is likely to be effective is to compute ε_i separately for each parameter, as in

$$\varepsilon_i = \text{Max}[\alpha|\theta_i|, \gamma]$$

[see Goldfeld and Quandt (1972)]. The values α and γ should be relatively small, such as 10^{-5}. Third, though numerical derivatives computed in this fashion are likely to be reasonably accurate, in a sum of a large number of terms, say several thousand, enough approximation error can accumulate to cause the numerical derivatives to differ significantly from their analytic counterparts. Second derivatives can also be computed numerically; however, in addition to the preceding problems, it is generally not possible to ensure negative definiteness of a Hessian computed in this manner. Unless the choice of ε is made extremely carefully, an indefinite matrix is a possibility. As a general proposi-

[16] Hall (1982, p. 147).

[17] Op. cit.

[18] See, for example, Joreskog and Gruvaeus (1970), Powell (1964), Quandt (1983), and Hall (1982).

tion, the use of numerical derivatives should be avoided if the analytic derivatives are available.

Ideally, the iterative procedure should terminate when the gradient vector is zero. In practice, this will not be possible, primarily because of accumulated rounding error in the computation of the function and its derivatives. In view of this, a number of alternative convergence criteria are used. Most of them are based on the relative changes in the function or the parameters. There is considerable variation in those used in different computer programs. There are some pitfalls that should be avoided. A critical absolute value for the elements of the gradient vector or its norm will be affected by any scaling of the function, such as normalizing it by the sample size. Similarly, stopping on the basis of small absolute changes in the parameters can lead to premature convergence when the parameter vector approaches the maximum. It is probably best to use several criteria simultaneously, such as the change in both the function and the parameters. Belsley (1980) discusses a number of possible stopping rules. One that has proved useful and is immune to the scaling problem is to base convergence on $\mathbf{g'G^{-1}g}$.

It is possible for a function to have several local extrema. Obviously, it is difficult to know a priori whether this is true of the one at hand. But if the function is not globally concave, it may be a good idea to attempt to maximize it from several starting points in order to ensure that the maximum obtained is the global one. Ideally, a starting value near the optimum can facilitate matters; in some settings, this can be obtained by using a consistent estimate of the parameter for the starting point. The method of moments, if available, is sometimes a convenient device for doing so.

Finally, it should be noted that in a nonlinear setting the iterative algorithm can break down, even in the absence of constraints, for at least two reasons. The first is that the problem being solved may be so numerically complex as to defy solution. The second possibility, which is often neglected, is that the proposed model may simply be inappropriate for the data. In a linear setting, a low R^2 or some other diagnostic test may suggest that the model and data are mismatched, but as long as the full rank condition is met by the regressor matrix, a linear regression can *always* be computed. Nonlinear models are not so forgiving. The failure of an iterative algorithm to find a maximum of the criterion function may be a warning that the model is not appropriate for this body of data.

12.7. Examples

To illustrate the use of gradient methods, we consider two simple problems.

EXAMPLE 12.1 Function of One Parameter _____

Consider, first, maximizing a function of a single variable,

$$f(\theta) = \ln(\theta) - \theta^2.$$

The first and second derivatives are

$$f'(\theta) = \frac{1}{\theta} - 2\theta$$

and

$$f''(\theta) = \frac{-1}{\theta^2} - 2$$

Equating f' to zero yields the simple solution $\theta = \sqrt{0.5} = 0.7071$. At the solution, $f'' = -4$, so this is indeed a maximum. To demonstrate the use of an iterative method, we solve this problem using Newton's method. Observe, first, that the second derivative is always negative for any admissible (positive) θ.[19] (The function resembles a parabola.) Therefore, it will not matter where we start the iterations; we shall eventually find the maximum. For a single parameter, Newton's method is

$$\theta_{t+1} = \theta_t - \frac{f'}{f''}$$

The sequence of values that results when 5 is used as the starting value is given in Table 12.1.

TABLE 12.1

Iteration	θ	$f(\theta)$	$f'(\theta)$	$f''(\theta)$
0	5	-23.39	-9.80	-2.04
1	0.1961	-1.67	4.71	-28.01
2	0.3642	-1.14	2.02	-9.54
3	0.5746	-0.88	0.59	-5.02
4	0.6924	-0.85	0.06	-4.08
5	0.7070	-0.85	0.00	-4.00
6	0.7071			

If we begin from the starting values of 1, 25, and 0.001, the method requires 3, 8, and 12 iterations, respectively, to reach the same solution.

EXAMPLE 12.2 Function of Two Parameters—The Gamma Distribution _____

For random sampling from the gamma distribution,

$$f(y_i, \beta, \rho) = \left[\frac{\beta^\rho}{\Gamma(\rho)}\right]e^{-\beta y_i}y_i^{\rho-1}.$$

The log likelihood is

$$\ln L(\beta, \rho) = n\rho \ln \beta - n \ln \Gamma(\rho) - \beta \sum_i y_i + (\rho - 1) \sum_i \ln y_i.$$

It is often convenient to scale the log likelihood by the sample size. Suppose, as well, that we have a sample with

$$\bar{y} = 3,$$
$$\overline{\log y} = 1.$$

Then the function to be maximized is

$$F(\beta, \rho) = \rho \ln \beta - \ln \Gamma(\rho) - 3\beta + \rho - 1.$$

The derivatives are

$$\frac{\partial F}{\partial \beta} = \frac{\rho}{\beta} - 3,$$

---

[19] This is a problem in which an inequality restriction, $\theta > 0$, is required. However, as is common, for our first attempt we shall neglect the constraint.

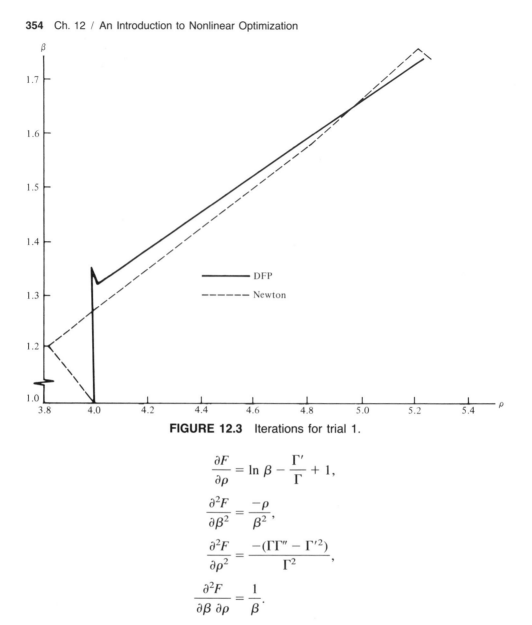

FIGURE 12.3 Iterations for trial 1.

$$\frac{\partial F}{\partial \rho} = \ln \beta - \frac{\Gamma'}{\Gamma} + 1,$$

$$\frac{\partial^2 F}{\partial \beta^2} = \frac{-\rho}{\beta^2},$$

$$\frac{\partial^2 F}{\partial \rho^2} = \frac{-(\Gamma \Gamma'' - \Gamma'^2)}{\Gamma^2},$$

$$\frac{\partial^2 F}{\partial \beta \, \partial \rho} = \frac{1}{\beta}.$$

Finding a good set of starting values is often a difficult problem. Here we choose three starting points somewhat arbitrarily:

	Trial			Correct
	1	2	3	Solution
ρ^0	4	8	2	5.233
β^0	1	3	7	1.7438

Two commonly used methods are Newton's method and DFP. For the DFP method, we include a line search;[20] for Newton's method, $\lambda = 1$. The results for trials 1 and 2 are shown in Figures 12.3 and 12.4. Note the similarity between the two methods when

---

[20]The one used is described in Joreskog and Gruvaeus (1970).

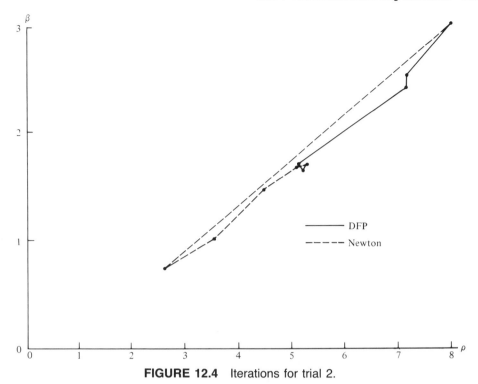

FIGURE 12.4   Iterations for trial 2.

beginning from a relatively good starting value, in trial 1, and the substantial difference between them when beginning from a somewhat poorer one. The third starting point shows the value of a line search. At this starting value, the Hessian is extremely large. The second value for the parameter vector with Newton's method is

$$\begin{bmatrix} \rho \\ \beta \end{bmatrix} = \begin{bmatrix} 2 \\ 7 \end{bmatrix} - \begin{bmatrix} 49.671 \\ 240.35 \end{bmatrix} = \begin{bmatrix} -47.671 \\ -233.35 \end{bmatrix},$$

at which point F cannot be computed and this method must be abandoned. Beginning with $\mathbf{H} = \mathbf{I}$ and using a line search, DFP reaches the point $(6.53, 2.14)$ at the first iteration, after which convergence occurs routinely in three more iterations.

12.8. The Concentrated Log Likelihood

There is another way that the problem in Section 12.7 might have been solved. The first of the necessary conditions implies that at the joint solution for (ρ, β), β will equal $\rho/3$. Suppose that we impose this requirement on the function we are maximizing. This produces the **concentrated** (over β) **log-likelihood function:**

$$F_c(\rho) = \rho \ln\left(\frac{\rho}{3}\right) - \ln \Gamma(\rho) - 3\left(\frac{\rho}{3}\right) + \rho - 1$$

$$= \rho \ln\left(\frac{\rho}{3}\right) - \ln \Gamma(\rho) - 1.$$

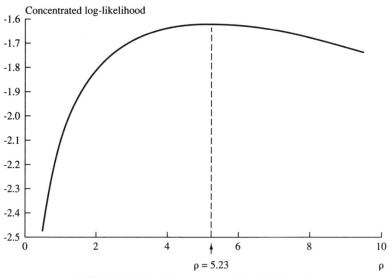

FIGURE 12.5 Concentrated log likelihood.

This function could be maximized by an iterative search or by a simple one-dimensional grid search. Figure 12.5 shows the behavior of this function. As expected, the maximum occurs at $\rho = 5.23$. The value of β is found as $5.23/3 = 1.743$.[21]

The concentrated log-likelihood is a useful device in many problems. Note the interpretation of the function plotted in Figure 12.5. The original function of ρ and β is a surface in three dimensions. The curve in Figure 12.5 is a projection of that function; it is a plot of the function values above the line $\beta = \rho/3$. By virtue of the first-order condition, we know that one of these points will be the maximizer of the function. Therefore, we may restrict our search for the overall maximum of $F(\beta, \rho)$ to the points on this line.

EXERCISES

1. Show how to maximize the function

$$f(\beta) = \frac{1}{\sqrt{2\pi}} e^{-(\beta - c)^2/2}$$

with respect to β for a constant, c, using Newton's method. Show that maximizing $\ln f(\beta)$ leads to the same solution. Plot $f(\beta)$ and $\ln f(\beta)$.

2. Prove that Newton's method for the minimizing the sum of squared residuals in the linear regression model will converge to the minimum in one iteration.

3. For the Poisson regression model,

$$\text{Prob}(Y_i = y_i | \mathbf{x}_i) = \frac{e^{-\lambda_i} \lambda_i^{y_i}}{y_i!},$$

where

$$\lambda_i = e^{\boldsymbol{\beta}' \mathbf{x}_i},$$

---

[21] Another application of this method appears in Section 11.2.1.

the log-likelihood function is

$$\ln L = \sum_i \ln \text{Prob}(Y_i = y_i | \mathbf{x}_i).$$

(a) Insert the expression for λ_i to obtain the log-likelihood function in terms of the observed data.

(b) Derive the first-order conditions for maximizing this function with respect to $\boldsymbol{\beta}$.

(c) Derive the second derivatives matrix of this criterion function with respect to $\boldsymbol{\beta}$. Is this matrix negative definite?

(d) Define the computations for using Newton's method to obtain estimates of the unknown parameters.

(e) Write out the full set of steps in an algorithm for obtaining the estimates of the parameters of this model. Include in your algorithm a test for convergence of the estimates based on Belsley's suggested criterion.

(f) How would you obtain starting values for your iterations?

(g) The following data are generated by the Poisson regression model with

$$\ln \lambda = \alpha + \beta x:$$

y	6	7	4	10	10	6	4	7
x	1.5	1.8	1.8	2.0	1.3	1.6	1.2	1.9

y	2	3	6	5	3	3	4
x	1.8	1.0	1.4	0.5	0.8	1.1	0.7

Use your results from parts (a) to (f) to compute the maximum likelihood estimates of α and β. Also, obtain estimates of the asymptotic covariance matrix of your estimates.

13

Nonspherical Disturbances

13.1. Introduction

In this chapter we extend the multiple regression model to disturbances that violate the classical assumptions. The **generalized regression model** is

$$y = X\beta + \varepsilon,$$

$$E[\varepsilon] = 0, \qquad\qquad (13\text{--}1)$$

$$E[\varepsilon\varepsilon'] = \sigma^2\Omega,$$

where Ω is a positive definite matrix.

Two cases we shall consider in detail are **heteroscedasticity** and **autocorrelation.** Disturbances are heteroscedastic when they have different variances. Heteroscedasticity usually arises in cross-section data where the scale of the dependent variable and the explanatory power of the model tend to vary across observations. Microeconomic data such as expenditure surveys are typical. The disturbances are still assumed to be uncorrelated across observations, so $\sigma^2\Omega$ would be

$$\sigma^2\Omega = \begin{bmatrix} \sigma_1^2 & 0 & \cdots & 0 \\ 0 & \sigma_2^2 & \cdots & 0 \\ & & \vdots & \\ 0 & 0 & \cdots & \sigma_n^2 \end{bmatrix}.$$

Autocorrelation is usually found in time-series data. Economic time series often display a "memory" in that variation is not independent from one period to the next. The seasonally adjusted price and quantity series published by government agencies are examples. The adjustment is done in order to smooth out unusual movements in the data, and, as such, makes the current observation dependent on what was typical in the past. But a series of unusually high or low values will be carried forward to the adjustment of later data points as well. Time-series data are usually homoscedastic, so $\sigma^2\Omega$ might be

$$\sigma^2\Omega = \sigma^2 \begin{bmatrix} 1 & \rho_1 & \cdots & \rho_{n-1} \\ \rho_1 & 1 & \cdots & \rho_{n-2} \\ & & \vdots & \\ \rho_{n-1} & \rho_{n-2} & & 1 \end{bmatrix}.$$

The values that appear off the diagonal depend on the model used for the disturbance. In most cases, consistent with the notion of a fading memory, the values decline as we move away from the diagonal.

In recent studies, **panel data** sets, consisting of cross sections observed at several points in time, have exhibited both characteristics. We shall consider them in Chapter 16. This chapter presents some general results for this extended model. The next three chapters examine in detail specific types of generalized regression models.

Our earlier results for the classical model will have to be modified. We first consider the consequences of this more general formula for the least squares estimator. In subsequent sections, we will be interested in both appropriate estimation techniques and procedures for testing for the failure of the classical assumptions. We shall consider their general theoretical aspects in this chapter and then examine each topic in detail in Chapters 14 through 16.

13.2. Consequences for Ordinary Least Squares

The essential results for the classical model with **spherical** disturbances,

$$E[\boldsymbol{\varepsilon}] = \mathbf{0}$$

and

$$E[\boldsymbol{\varepsilon}\boldsymbol{\varepsilon}'] = \sigma^2 \mathbf{I}, \tag{13-2}$$

are presented in Chapters 5 through 10. To reiterate, we found that the ordinary least squares estimator,

$$\begin{aligned}
\mathbf{b} &= (\mathbf{X}'\mathbf{X})^{-1}\mathbf{X}'\mathbf{y} \\
&= \boldsymbol{\beta} + (\mathbf{X}'\mathbf{X})^{-1}\mathbf{X}'\boldsymbol{\varepsilon},
\end{aligned} \tag{13-3}$$

is best linear unbiased, consistent and asymptotically normally distributed (CAN), and, if the disturbances are normally distributed, asymptotically efficient among all CAN estimators. We now consider which of these properties continue to hold in the model of (13–1).

13.2.1. Finite-Sample Properties

By taking expectations on both sides of (13–3), we find that if $E[\boldsymbol{\varepsilon}|\mathbf{X}] = \mathbf{0}$, then

$$E[\mathbf{b}] = E_\mathbf{x}[E[\mathbf{b}|\mathbf{X}]] = \boldsymbol{\beta}. \tag{13-4}$$

> If the regressors and disturbances are uncorrelated, the unbiasedness of least squares is unaffected by violations of assumption (13–2).

The sampling variance of the least squares estimator is

$$\begin{aligned}
\text{Var}[\mathbf{b} - \boldsymbol{\beta}] &= E[(\mathbf{b} - \boldsymbol{\beta})(\mathbf{b} - \boldsymbol{\beta})'] \\
&= E[(\mathbf{X}'\mathbf{X})^{-1}\mathbf{X}'\boldsymbol{\varepsilon}\boldsymbol{\varepsilon}'\mathbf{X}(\mathbf{X}'\mathbf{X})^{-1}] \\
&= (\mathbf{X}'\mathbf{X})^{-1}\mathbf{X}'(\sigma^2\boldsymbol{\Omega})\mathbf{X}(\mathbf{X}'\mathbf{X})^{-1} \\
&= \frac{\sigma^2}{n}\left(\frac{\mathbf{X}'\mathbf{X}}{n}\right)^{-1}\left(\frac{\mathbf{X}'\boldsymbol{\Omega}\mathbf{X}}{n}\right)\left(\frac{\mathbf{X}'\mathbf{X}}{n}\right)^{-1}
\end{aligned} \tag{13-5}$$

In (13–3), $\mathbf{b}$ is a linear function of $\boldsymbol{\varepsilon}$. Therefore, if $\boldsymbol{\varepsilon}$ is normally distributed,

$$\mathbf{b} \sim N[\boldsymbol{\beta},\, \sigma^2(\mathbf{X}'\mathbf{X})^{-1}(\mathbf{X}'\boldsymbol{\Omega}\mathbf{X})(\mathbf{X}'\mathbf{X})^{-1}].$$

Since the variance of the least squares estimator is not $\sigma^2(\mathbf{X}'\mathbf{X})^{-1}$, any inference based on $s^2(\mathbf{X}'\mathbf{X})^{-1}$ is likely to be misleading. Not only is this the wrong matrix to be used, but s^2

may be a biased estimator of σ^2. There is usually no way to know whether $\sigma^2(\mathbf{X}'\mathbf{X})^{-1}$ is larger or smaller than the true variance of $\mathbf{b}$, so even with a good estimate of σ^2, the conventional estimator of Var[$\mathbf{b}$] may not be particularly useful. Finally, since we have dispensed with the fundamental underlying assumption, the familiar inference procedures based on the F and t distributions will no longer be appropriate.

13.2.2. Asymptotic Properties of Least Squares

If Var[$\mathbf{b}$] converges to zero, $\mathbf{b}$ is consistent. With well-behaved regressors, $(\mathbf{X}'\mathbf{X}/n)^{-1}$ will converge to a constant matrix (perhaps $\mathbf{0}$), and the leading scalar, σ^2/n, will converge to 0. But $\mathbf{X}'\mathbf{\Omega}\mathbf{X}/n$ need not converge at all. If it does, ordinary least squares is consistent as well as unbiased. Therefore,

$$\text{If plim } (\mathbf{X}'\mathbf{X}/n) \text{ and plim } (\mathbf{X}'\mathbf{\Omega}\mathbf{X}/n) \text{ are both} \atop \text{finite positive definite matrices, } \mathbf{b} \text{ is} \qquad (13\text{--}6) \atop \text{consistent for } \boldsymbol{\beta}.$$

The conditions in (13–6) depend on both $\mathbf{X}$ and $\mathbf{\Omega}$. An alternative formula[1] that separates the two components is: Ordinary least squares is consistent in the generalized regression model if

1. The smallest characteristic root of $\mathbf{X}'\mathbf{X}$ increases without bound as $n \to \infty$. This implies that plim$(\mathbf{X}'\mathbf{X})^{-1} = \mathbf{0}$. If the regressors satisfy the Grenander conditions of Section 10.3.1, they will meet this requirement.
2. The largest characteristic root of $\mathbf{\Omega}$ is finite for all n. For the heteroscedastic model, the variances are the characteristic roots, so this requires them to be finite. For models with autocorrelation, this requires that the elements of $\mathbf{\Omega}$ be finite and that the off-diagonal elements not be too large relative to the diagonal elements.

EXAMPLE 13.1 A Model in Which Ordinary Least Squares Is Inconsistent ____

Suppose that the regression model is $y = \mu + \varepsilon$, where ε has a zero mean, constant variance, and equal correlation ρ across observations. Then

$$\mathbf{\Omega} = \begin{bmatrix} 1 & \rho & \rho & \cdots & \rho \\ \rho & 1 & \rho & \cdots & \rho \\ \rho & \rho & 1 & \cdots & \rho \\ & & & \vdots & \\ \rho & \rho & \rho & \cdots & 1 \end{bmatrix}.$$

The matrix $\mathbf{X}$ is a column of ones. The ordinary least squares estimator of μ is $\bar{y}$. Inserting this $\mathbf{\Omega}$ into (13–5), we obtain

$$\text{Var}[\bar{y}] = \frac{\sigma^2}{n}(1 - \rho + n\rho). \qquad (13\text{--}7)$$

The limit of this expression is $\rho\sigma^2$, not zero. Although ordinary least squares is unbiased, it is not consistent. For this model, $\mathbf{X}'\mathbf{\Omega}\mathbf{X}/n = 1 + \rho(n - 1)$, which does not converge. Using (13–7) instead, $\mathbf{X}$ is a column of ones, so $\mathbf{X}'\mathbf{X} = n$, a scalar, which satisfies condition (1). But the characteristic roots of $\mathbf{\Omega}$ are $(1 - \rho)$ with multiplicity $n - 1$ and $(1 - \rho + n\rho)$, which does not satisfy condition (2). The difficulty with the model in this example is essentially that there is too much correlation across observations. In time-series settings, we shall generally require that the timewise correlation of observations

[1] Amemiya (1985, p. 184).

fade as the distance between them grows. That condition is not met here. This gives some suggestion of what sort of requirement we shall have to place upon the covariance matrix for autocorrelated disturbances discussed in the Introduction.

The OLS estimator is asymptotically normally distributed if the limiting distribution of

$$\sqrt{n}\,(\mathbf{b} - \boldsymbol{\beta}) = \left(\frac{\mathbf{X'X}}{n}\right)^{-1} \frac{1}{\sqrt{n}} \mathbf{X'}\boldsymbol{\varepsilon} \qquad (13\text{--}8)$$

is normal. If $\text{plim}(\mathbf{X'X}/n) = \mathbf{Q}$, the limiting distribution of the right-hand side is the same as that of

$$\mathbf{v} = \mathbf{Q}^{-1} \frac{1}{\sqrt{n}} \mathbf{X'}\boldsymbol{\varepsilon}$$

$$= \mathbf{Q}^{-1} \frac{1}{\sqrt{n}} \sum_i \mathbf{x}_i \varepsilon_i, \qquad (13\text{--}9)$$

where $\mathbf{x}_i'$ is a row of $\mathbf{X}$ (assuming, of course, that the limiting distribution exists at all). The question now is whether a central limit theorem can be applied directly to $\mathbf{v}$. If the disturbances are merely heteroscedastic and still uncorrelated, the answer is generally yes. In this case, it can easily be shown that as long as $\mathbf{X}$ is well behaved and the diagonal elements of $\boldsymbol{\Omega}$ are finite, the least squares estimator is asymptotically normally distributed, with the variance matrix given in (13–5).[2] For the most general case, the answer is no because the sums in (13–9) are not necessarily sums of independent or even uncorrelated random variables. Nonetheless, Amemiya (1985, p. 187) and Anderson (1971) have shown the asymptotic normality of $\mathbf{b}$ in a model of autocorrelated disturbances general enough to include most of the settings we are likely to meet in practice. We can conclude that, except in particularly unfavorable cases,

$$\begin{array}{l} \mathbf{b} \text{ is asymptotically normally distributed with} \\ \text{mean } \boldsymbol{\beta} \text{ and covariance matrix given in (13--5).} \end{array} \qquad (13\text{--}10)$$

To summarize, ordinary least squares retains only some of its desirable properties in this model. It is unbiased, consistent, and asymptotically normally distributed. However, it will no longer be efficient—this remains to be verified—and the usual inference procedures are no longer appropriate.

13.3. Efficient Estimation

Efficient estimation of $\boldsymbol{\beta}$ in the general regression model requires knowledge of $\boldsymbol{\Omega}$. To begin, it is useful to consider cases in which $\boldsymbol{\Omega}$ is a known, symmetric, positive definite matrix. This will occasionally be true, but in most models $\boldsymbol{\Omega}$ will contain unknown parameters that must also be estimated. We shall examine this problem in Section 13.4.

13.3.1. Generalized Least Squares

Since $\boldsymbol{\Omega}$ is a positive definite symmetric matrix, it can be factored into

$$\boldsymbol{\Omega} = \mathbf{C}\boldsymbol{\Lambda}\mathbf{C'}, \qquad (13\text{--}11)$$

---

[2] The Lindeberg–Feller variant of the central limit theorem can be applied. See, for example, Schmidt (1976, pp. 57–65) or Greenberg and Webster (1983, pp. 17–22).

where the columns of $\mathbf{C}$ are the characteristic vectors of $\boldsymbol{\Omega}$ and the characteristic roots of $\boldsymbol{\Omega}$ are arrayed in the diagonal matrix, $\boldsymbol{\Lambda}$. Let $\boldsymbol{\Lambda}^{1/2}$ be the diagonal matrix with ith diagonal element $\sqrt{\lambda_i}$, and let $\mathbf{T} = \mathbf{C}\boldsymbol{\Lambda}^{1/2}$. Then $\boldsymbol{\Omega} = \mathbf{TT}'$. Also, let $\mathbf{P} = \mathbf{C}\boldsymbol{\Lambda}^{-1/2}$, so

$$\boldsymbol{\Omega}^{-1} = \mathbf{PP}'.$$

It is useful to denote

$$\mathbf{P} = \boldsymbol{\Omega}^{-1/2}.$$

Premultiply the model in (13–1) by $\mathbf{P}$ to obtain

$$\mathbf{Py} = \mathbf{PX}\boldsymbol{\beta} + \mathbf{P}\boldsymbol{\varepsilon},$$

or

$$\mathbf{y}_* = \mathbf{X}_*\boldsymbol{\beta} + \boldsymbol{\varepsilon}_*. \tag{13–12}$$

The variance of $\boldsymbol{\varepsilon}_*$ is

$$E[\boldsymbol{\varepsilon}_*\boldsymbol{\varepsilon}_*'] = \mathbf{P}\sigma^2\boldsymbol{\Omega}\mathbf{P}' = \sigma^2\mathbf{I},$$

so that the classical regression model of Chapter 6 applies to this transformed model. Since $\boldsymbol{\Omega}$ is known, $\mathbf{y}_*$ and $\mathbf{X}_*$ are observed data. In the classical model, ordinary least squares is efficient; hence

$$\hat{\boldsymbol{\beta}} = (\mathbf{X}_*'\mathbf{X}_*)^{-1}\mathbf{X}_*'\mathbf{y}_* = (\mathbf{X}'\mathbf{P}'\mathbf{PX})^{-1} \mathbf{X}'\mathbf{P}'\mathbf{Py} = (\mathbf{X}'\boldsymbol{\Omega}^{-1}\mathbf{X})^{-1}\mathbf{X}'\boldsymbol{\Omega}^{-1}\mathbf{y}$$

is the efficient estimator of $\boldsymbol{\beta}$. This is the **generalized least squares (GLS)** estimator of $\boldsymbol{\beta}$. By appealing to the classical regression model in (13–12), we have the following, which are the generalized regression model analogs to our results of Chapter 6:

> *The GLS estimator $\hat{\boldsymbol{\beta}}$ is unbiased* if $E[\boldsymbol{\varepsilon}_* | \mathbf{X}_*] = \mathbf{0}$. This is equivalent to $E[\mathbf{P}\boldsymbol{\varepsilon} | \mathbf{PX}] = \mathbf{0}$, but since $\mathbf{P}$ is a matrix of known constants, we return to the familiar requirement $E[\boldsymbol{\varepsilon} | \mathbf{X}] = \mathbf{0}$. The requirement that the regressors and disturbances be uncorrelated is unchanged. $\tag{13–13}$

> *The GLS estimator is consistent* if

$$\text{plim}\left(\frac{\mathbf{X}_*'\mathbf{X}_*}{n}\right) = \mathbf{Q}_*,$$

where $\mathbf{Q}_*$ is a finite positive definite matrix. Making the substitution, we see that this is

$$\text{plim}\left(\frac{\mathbf{X}'\boldsymbol{\Omega}^{-1}\mathbf{X}}{n}\right)^{-1} = \mathbf{Q}_*^{-1}. \tag{13–14}$$

We require the transformed data, $\mathbf{X}_* = \mathbf{PX}$, not the original data, $\mathbf{X}$, to be well behaved.[3]

Under the assumption in (13–14), *the GLS estimator is asymptotically normally distributed*, with mean $\boldsymbol{\beta}$ and sampling variance

$$\text{Var}[\hat{\boldsymbol{\beta}}] = \sigma^2(\mathbf{X}_*'\mathbf{X}_*)^{-1} = \sigma^2(\mathbf{X}'\boldsymbol{\Omega}^{-1}\mathbf{X})^{-1}. \tag{13–15}$$

> *The GLS estimator $\hat{\boldsymbol{\beta}}$ is the minimum variance linear unbiased estimator in the generalized regression model.* $\tag{13–16}$

---

[3] Once again, in order to allow a time trend, we could weaken this assumption a bit.

This follows by applying the Gauss–Markov theorem to the model in (13–12). The result in (13–16) is Aitken's (1935) theorem, and $\hat{\boldsymbol{\beta}}$ is sometimes called the *Aitken estimator*. This is a broad result that includes the Gauss–Markov theorem as a special case when $\boldsymbol{\Omega} = \mathbf{I}$.

For testing hypotheses, we can apply the full set of results in Chapter 7 to the transformed model in (13–12). For testing the J linear restrictions, $\mathbf{R}\boldsymbol{\beta} = \mathbf{q}$, the appropriate statistic is

$$F[J, n - K] = \frac{(\mathbf{R}\hat{\boldsymbol{\beta}} - \mathbf{q})'[\mathbf{R}(\hat{\sigma}^2(\mathbf{X}'_*\mathbf{X}_*)^{-1})\mathbf{R}']^{-1}(\mathbf{R}\hat{\boldsymbol{\beta}} - \mathbf{q})}{J}$$

$$= \frac{(\hat{\boldsymbol{\varepsilon}}'_c\hat{\boldsymbol{\varepsilon}}_c - \hat{\boldsymbol{\varepsilon}}'\hat{\boldsymbol{\varepsilon}})/J}{\sigma^2}, \tag{13–17}$$

where the residual vector is

$$\hat{\boldsymbol{\varepsilon}} = \mathbf{y}_* - \mathbf{X}_*\hat{\boldsymbol{\beta}}$$

and

$$\hat{\sigma}^2 = \frac{\hat{\boldsymbol{\varepsilon}}'\hat{\boldsymbol{\varepsilon}}}{n - K} = \frac{(\mathbf{y} - \mathbf{X}\hat{\boldsymbol{\beta}})'\boldsymbol{\Omega}^{-1}(\mathbf{y} - \mathbf{X}\hat{\boldsymbol{\beta}})}{n - K}.$$

The constrained GLS residuals, $\hat{\boldsymbol{\varepsilon}}_c = \mathbf{y}_* - \mathbf{X}_*\hat{\boldsymbol{\beta}}_c$, are based on

$$\hat{\boldsymbol{\beta}}_c = \hat{\boldsymbol{\beta}} - [\mathbf{X}'\boldsymbol{\Omega}^{-1}\mathbf{X}]^{-1}\mathbf{R}'[\mathbf{R}(\mathbf{X}'\boldsymbol{\Omega}^{-1}\mathbf{X})^{-1}\mathbf{R}']^{-1}(\mathbf{R}\hat{\boldsymbol{\beta}} - \mathbf{q}).^4 \tag{13–18}$$

To summarize, all of the results for the classical model, including the usual inference procedures, apply to the model in (13–12).

There is no precise counterpart to R^2 in the generalized regression model. Alternatives have been proposed, but care must be taken when using them. For example, one choice is the R^2 in the transformed regression, (13–12). But this regression need not have a constant term, so the R^2 is not bounded by zero and one. Even if there is a constant term, the transformed regression is a computational device, not the model of interest. The fact that a good (or bad) fit is obtained in the model in (13–12) may be of no interest; the dependent variable in that model, y_*, is different from the one in the model as originally specified. The usual R^2 often suggests that the fit of the model is improved by a correction for heteroscedasticity and degraded by a correction for autocorrelation, but both changes can often be attributed to the computation of y_*. A more appealing fit measure might be based on the residuals from the original model once the GLS estimator is in hand, for example,

$$\tilde{R}^2 = 1 - \frac{(\mathbf{y} - \mathbf{X}\hat{\boldsymbol{\beta}})'(\mathbf{y} - \mathbf{X}\hat{\boldsymbol{\beta}})}{\Sigma_i(y_i - \overline{y})^2}.$$

However, like the earlier contender, this measure is not bounded in the unit interval. In addition, this measure cannot be reliably used to compare models. The generalized least squares estimator minimizes the generalized sum of squares,

$$\boldsymbol{\varepsilon}'_*\boldsymbol{\varepsilon}_* = (\mathbf{y} - \mathbf{X}\boldsymbol{\beta})'\boldsymbol{\Omega}^{-1}(\mathbf{y} - \mathbf{X}\boldsymbol{\beta}),$$

not $\boldsymbol{\varepsilon}'\boldsymbol{\varepsilon}$. As such, there is no assurance, for example, that dropping a variable from the model will result in a decrease in $\tilde{R}^2$, as it will in R^2. Other goodness of fit measures, designed primarily to be a function of the sum of squared residuals (raw or weighted by

---

[4] Note that this is the constrained OLS estimator using the transformed data.

Ω^{-1}) and to be bounded by zero and one, have been proposed.[5] Unfortunately, all of them suffer from at least one of the previously noted shortcomings. The R^2-like measures in this setting are purely descriptive.

13.3.2. Maximum Likelihood Estimation

If the disturbances are multivariate normally distributed, the log-likelihood function for the sample is

$$\ln L = -\frac{n}{2} \ln (2\pi) - \frac{1}{2} \ln |\sigma^2 \Omega| - \frac{1}{2} \varepsilon'(\sigma^2 \Omega)^{-1} \varepsilon.$$

Making the change of variable to $\mathbf{y} - \mathbf{X}\boldsymbol{\beta} = \boldsymbol{\varepsilon}$, we obtain

$$\ln L = -\frac{n}{2} \ln (2\pi) - \frac{n}{2} \ln \sigma^2 - \frac{1}{2\sigma^2} (\mathbf{y} - \mathbf{X}\boldsymbol{\beta})'\Omega^{-1}(\mathbf{y} - \mathbf{X}\boldsymbol{\beta}) - \frac{1}{2} \ln |\Omega|.$$

$$(13\text{--}19)$$

Since Ω is a matrix of known constants, the maximum likelihood estimator of $\boldsymbol{\beta}$ is the vector that minimizes the **generalized sum of squares,**

$$S_*(\boldsymbol{\beta}) = (\mathbf{y} - \mathbf{X}\boldsymbol{\beta})'\Omega^{-1}(\mathbf{y} - \mathbf{X}\boldsymbol{\beta}) \qquad (13\text{--}20)$$

(hence the name *generalized least squares*). The necessary conditions for maximizing L are

$$\frac{\partial \ln L}{\partial \boldsymbol{\beta}} = \frac{1}{\sigma^2} \mathbf{X}'\Omega^{-1}(\mathbf{y} - \mathbf{X}\boldsymbol{\beta}) = \frac{1}{\sigma^2} \mathbf{X}'_*(\mathbf{y}_* - \mathbf{X}_*\boldsymbol{\beta}) = \mathbf{0} \qquad (13\text{--}21)$$

and

$$\frac{\partial \ln L}{\partial \sigma^2} = -\frac{n}{2\sigma^2} + \frac{1}{2\sigma^4} (\mathbf{y} - \mathbf{X}\boldsymbol{\beta})'\Omega^{-1}(\mathbf{y} - \mathbf{X}\boldsymbol{\beta})$$

$$(13\text{--}22)$$

$$= -\frac{n}{2\sigma^2} + \frac{1}{2\sigma^4} (\mathbf{y}_* - \mathbf{X}_*\boldsymbol{\beta})'(\mathbf{y}_* - \mathbf{X}_*\boldsymbol{\beta}) = 0.$$

The solutions are the OLS estimators using the transformed data:

$$\hat{\boldsymbol{\beta}}_{\text{ML}} = (\mathbf{X}'_*\mathbf{X}_*)^{-1}\mathbf{X}'_*\mathbf{y}_* = (\mathbf{X}'\Omega^{-1}\mathbf{X})^{-1}\mathbf{X}'\Omega^{-1}\mathbf{y} \qquad (13\text{--}23)$$

$$\hat{\sigma}^2_{\text{ML}} = \frac{(\mathbf{y}_* - \mathbf{X}_*\hat{\boldsymbol{\beta}})'(\mathbf{y}_* - \mathbf{X}_*\hat{\boldsymbol{\beta}})}{n}$$

$$(13\text{--}24)$$

$$= \frac{(\mathbf{y} - \mathbf{X}\hat{\boldsymbol{\beta}})'\Omega^{-1}(\mathbf{y} - \mathbf{X}\hat{\boldsymbol{\beta}})}{n}.$$

This implies that with normally distributed disturbances, generalized least squares is also maximum likelihood. As in the classical regression model, the maximum likelihood estimator of σ^2 is biased. An unbiased estimator is

$$s^2 = \frac{(\mathbf{y} - \mathbf{X}\hat{\boldsymbol{\beta}})'\Omega^{-1}(\mathbf{y} - \mathbf{X}\hat{\boldsymbol{\beta}})}{n - K}. \qquad (13\text{--}25)$$

---

[5] See, for example, Judge et al. (1985, p. 32) and Buse (1973).

In order to obtain the asymptotic distribution for the maximum likelihood estimators, we can apply the results of Section 10.3.2 to the transformed model. The asymptotic distribution of $[\hat{\boldsymbol{\beta}}_{ML}, \hat{\sigma}^2_{ML}]$ is, therefore,

$$\begin{bmatrix} \hat{\boldsymbol{\beta}}_{ML} \\ \hat{\sigma}^2_{ML} \end{bmatrix} \overset{a}{\to} N\left[\begin{bmatrix} \boldsymbol{\beta} \\ \sigma^2 \end{bmatrix}, \begin{bmatrix} \sigma^2(\mathbf{X}'\boldsymbol{\Omega}^{-1}\mathbf{X})^{-1} & \mathbf{0} \\ \mathbf{0}' & 2\sigma^4/n \end{bmatrix} \right]. \tag{13-26}$$

An alternative to (13–17) for testing a hypothesis about $\boldsymbol{\beta}$ is the likelihood ratio statistic. If we insert (13–23) and (13–24) in (13–19), we find, at the maximum likelihood estimators,

$$\ln \hat{L} = -\frac{n}{2} (1 + \ln (2\pi) + \ln \hat{\sigma}^2) - \frac{1}{2} \ln |\boldsymbol{\Omega}|.$$

Therefore, the likelihood ratio test is based on

$$\lambda = -2(\ln \hat{L}_c - \ln \hat{L}) = n(\ln \hat{\sigma}^2_c - \ln \hat{\sigma}^2)$$

$$= n \ln \left(\frac{\hat{\sigma}^2_c}{\hat{\sigma}^2} \right).$$

The statistic is asymptotically distributed as chi-squared with J degrees of freedom, where J is the number of restrictions.

13.4. Estimation When Ω Is Unknown

In order to use the results of Section 13.3, Ω must be known. If Ω contains unknown parameters that must be estimated, generalized least squares is not feasible. But with an unrestricted Ω, there are $n(n + 1)/2$ additional parameters in $\sigma^2\Omega$. This is far too many to estimate with n observations. Obviously, some structure must be imposed on the model if we are to proceed.

13.4.1. Feasible Generalized Least Squares

The typical problem involves a small set of parameters, $\boldsymbol{\theta}$, such that $\Omega = \Omega(\boldsymbol{\theta})$. For example, the Ω in Example 13.1 has only one unknown parameter, ρ. Another commonly used formula is

$$\Omega = \begin{bmatrix} 1 & \rho & \rho^2 & \rho^3 & \cdots & \rho^{n-1} \\ \rho & 1 & \rho & \rho^2 & \cdots & \rho^{n-2} \\ & & & & \vdots & \\ \rho^{n-1} & \rho^{n-2} & & & \cdots & 1 \end{bmatrix},$$

which also involves only one additional unknown parameter. A model of heteroscedasticity that also has only one new parameter is

$$\sigma_i^2 = \sigma^2 z_i^\alpha.$$

Suppose, then, that $\hat{\boldsymbol{\theta}}$ is a consistent estimator of $\boldsymbol{\theta}$. (We consider later how such an estimator might be obtained.) In order to make GLS estimation feasible, we shall use

$$\hat{\boldsymbol{\Omega}} = \Omega(\hat{\boldsymbol{\theta}})$$

instead of the true Ω. The issue we consider here is whether using $\Omega(\hat{\boldsymbol{\theta}})$ requires us to change any of the results of Section 13.3.

It would seem that if plim $\hat{\boldsymbol{\theta}} = \boldsymbol{\theta}$, using $\hat{\boldsymbol{\Omega}}$ is asymptotically equivalent to using the true $\boldsymbol{\Omega}$.[6] However, this need not be the case.[7] Let the **feasible generalized least squares** or **(FGLS)** estimator be denoted

$$\hat{\hat{\boldsymbol{\beta}}} = (\mathbf{X}'\hat{\boldsymbol{\Omega}}^{-1}\mathbf{X})^{-1}\mathbf{X}'\hat{\boldsymbol{\Omega}}^{-1}\mathbf{y}.$$

Conditions that imply that $\hat{\hat{\boldsymbol{\beta}}}$ is asymptotically equivalent to $\hat{\boldsymbol{\beta}}$ are

$$\text{plim} \frac{\mathbf{X}'\hat{\boldsymbol{\Omega}}^{-1}\mathbf{X}}{n} = \text{plim} \frac{\mathbf{X}'\boldsymbol{\Omega}^{-1}\mathbf{X}}{n} \tag{13-27}$$

and

$$\text{plim} \frac{1}{\sqrt{n}}\mathbf{X}'\hat{\boldsymbol{\Omega}}^{-1}\boldsymbol{\varepsilon} = \text{plim} \frac{1}{\sqrt{n}}\mathbf{X}'\boldsymbol{\Omega}^{-1}\boldsymbol{\varepsilon}. \tag{13-28}$$

If the transformed regressors in (13–12) are well behaved, the right-hand side of (13–28) has a limiting normal distribution. This is exactly the condition we used in Chapter 10 to obtain the asymptotic distribution of the least squares estimator. Therefore, (13–28) requires the same condition to hold when $\boldsymbol{\Omega}$ is replaced with $\hat{\boldsymbol{\Omega}}$.

These are conditions that must be verified on a case-by-case basis. Fortunately, in most familiar settings, they are met. If we assume that they are, the FGLS estimator based on $\hat{\boldsymbol{\theta}}$ has the same asymptotic properties as the GLS estimator. This is an extremely useful result. Note, especially, the following:

> An asymptotically efficient FGLS estimator
> does not require that we have an efficient estimator
> of $\boldsymbol{\theta}$, only a consistent one.

Except for the simplest cases, the finite sample properties and exact distributions of FGLS estimators are unknown.[8] The asymptotic efficiency of FGLS estimators may not carry over to small samples because of the variability introduced by the estimated $\boldsymbol{\Omega}$. Some analyses for the case of heteroscedasticity are given by Taylor (1977). A model of autocorrelation is analyzed by Griliches and Rao (1969). In both studies, the authors find that over a broad range of parameters, FGLS is more efficient than least squares. But if the departure from the classical assumptions is not too severe, least squares may be more efficient than FGLS in a small sample.

13.4.2. Maximum Likelihood Estimation

For the moment, it is useful to treat $\boldsymbol{\Omega}$ as an unrestricted matrix of unknown parameters. We shall impose the restrictions $\boldsymbol{\Omega} = \boldsymbol{\Omega}(\boldsymbol{\theta})$ later. It will simplify the computations if we estimate $\boldsymbol{\Gamma} = \boldsymbol{\Omega}^{-1}$ instead of $\boldsymbol{\Omega}$. Given the MLE of $\boldsymbol{\Gamma}$, the MLE of $\boldsymbol{\Omega}$ is $\hat{\boldsymbol{\Gamma}}_{\text{ML}}^{-1}$.[9] We shall

---

[6] This is sometimes denoted plim $\hat{\boldsymbol{\Omega}} = \boldsymbol{\Omega}$. Since $\boldsymbol{\Omega}$ is $n \times n$, it cannot have a probability limit. We use this term to indicate convergence element by element.

[7] Schmidt (1976, p. 69) constructs a counterexample.

[8] The difficult part of most derivations is determining the exact distribution of functions of $\hat{\boldsymbol{\Omega}}^{-1}$. There is one general, exact result that applies in several settings. If $\hat{\boldsymbol{\theta}}$ is an *even function* of the true disturbances, the FGLS estimator is unbiased. The estimator, $\hat{\boldsymbol{\theta}}$, is an even function of $\boldsymbol{\varepsilon}$ if the same numerical value would be obtained using $-\boldsymbol{\varepsilon}$ instead. Consider, for example, the OLS estimator, $\mathbf{e}'\mathbf{e}/(n - K) = \boldsymbol{\varepsilon}'\mathbf{M}\boldsymbol{\varepsilon}/(n - K) = (-\boldsymbol{\varepsilon})'\mathbf{M}(-\boldsymbol{\varepsilon})/(n - K)$. The result was first reported by Kakwani (1967) for a multiple equation model. But it is straightforward to broaden the result to encompass the fuller generalized regression model we consider here. See, for example, Schmidt (1976, p. 72). Different conditions for the unbiasedness of the FGLS estimator are presented by Don and Magnus (1980) and Magnus (1978).

[9] The invariance principle is discussed in Section 4.5.1.

also use the results

$$\log|\boldsymbol{\Gamma}| = -\log|\boldsymbol{\Omega}|,^{10}$$

$$\frac{\partial \log|\boldsymbol{\Gamma}|}{\partial \boldsymbol{\Gamma}} = \boldsymbol{\Gamma}^{-1},$$

and

$$\frac{\partial \boldsymbol{\varepsilon}'\boldsymbol{\Gamma}\boldsymbol{\varepsilon}}{\partial \boldsymbol{\Gamma}} = \boldsymbol{\varepsilon}\boldsymbol{\varepsilon}'.^{11}$$

Substituting $\boldsymbol{\Gamma}$ for $\boldsymbol{\Omega}^{-1}$ in L, we obtain

$$\ln L = -\frac{n}{2}(\ln (2\pi) + \ln \sigma^2) - \frac{1}{2\sigma^2}\boldsymbol{\varepsilon}'\boldsymbol{\Gamma}\boldsymbol{\varepsilon} + \frac{1}{2}\ln |\boldsymbol{\Gamma}|$$

$$\frac{\partial \ln L}{\partial \boldsymbol{\beta}} = \frac{1}{\sigma^2}\mathbf{X}'\boldsymbol{\Gamma}(\mathbf{y} - \mathbf{X}\boldsymbol{\beta}) \tag{13-29}$$

$$\frac{\partial \ln L}{\partial \sigma^2} = -\frac{n}{2\sigma^2} + \frac{1}{2\sigma^4}(\mathbf{y} - \mathbf{X}\boldsymbol{\beta})'\boldsymbol{\Gamma}(\mathbf{y} - \mathbf{X}\boldsymbol{\beta}) \tag{13-30}$$

$$\frac{\partial \ln L}{\partial \boldsymbol{\Gamma}} = \frac{1}{2}\left[\boldsymbol{\Gamma}^{-1} - \left(\frac{1}{\sigma^2}\right)\boldsymbol{\varepsilon}\boldsymbol{\varepsilon}'\right]$$

$$= \frac{1}{2\sigma^2}[\sigma^2\boldsymbol{\Omega} - \boldsymbol{\varepsilon}\boldsymbol{\varepsilon}']. \tag{13-31}$$

At the maximum of the likelihood function, the following are apparent:

1. We would use FGLS to obtain the MLE of $\boldsymbol{\beta}$, using the maximum likelihood estimate of $\boldsymbol{\Omega}$.
2. Given the MLEs of $\boldsymbol{\beta}$ and $\boldsymbol{\Omega}$, the MLE of σ^2 would be $(1/n)(\mathbf{y} - \mathbf{X}\hat{\boldsymbol{\beta}}_{\text{ML}})'\hat{\boldsymbol{\Omega}}_{\text{ML}}^{-1} \times (\mathbf{y} - \mathbf{X}\hat{\boldsymbol{\beta}}_{\text{ML}})$.

The problem of too many parameters can be seen in the likelihood equation for $\boldsymbol{\Gamma}$. At the solution, we would require the rank one matrix $\hat{\boldsymbol{\varepsilon}}\hat{\boldsymbol{\varepsilon}}'$ to equal the positive definite matrix $\hat{\sigma}^2\hat{\boldsymbol{\Omega}}$, which is a contradiction. It might seem that we could simply use $\mathbf{e}\mathbf{e}'$ to estimate $\sigma^2\boldsymbol{\Omega}$, as prescribed by (13–31), but this matrix is singular and could not be used in (13–29) or (13–30).

Since $\boldsymbol{\Omega}$ must be restricted in some way to make the estimation problem tractable, let us assume, once again, that $\boldsymbol{\Omega} = \boldsymbol{\Omega}(\boldsymbol{\theta})$, where $\boldsymbol{\theta}$ is a vector of a small number of parameters and $\boldsymbol{\theta}$ *is not a function of any elements of $\boldsymbol{\beta}$.* With this assumption, there are two methods of obtaining estimates of the full set of parameters.

If it is straightforward to obtain estimates of $\boldsymbol{\theta}$ that satisfy (13–31) for a given set of estimates of $\boldsymbol{\beta}$ and σ^2, the iterative two-step method proposed by Oberhofer and Kmenta (1974) will usually be the easiest way to proceed. Since the MLEs of $\boldsymbol{\beta}$ and σ^2 are the GLS estimates using the MLE of $\boldsymbol{\Omega}$, given an estimate $\hat{\boldsymbol{\theta}}$, we use points 1 and 2 above to estimate $\boldsymbol{\beta}$ and σ^2. With the new estimates of $\boldsymbol{\beta}$ and σ^2, we then reestimate $\boldsymbol{\theta}$. Thereafter we repeat the iteration until satisfactory convergence has been achieved. If the initial $\hat{\boldsymbol{\theta}}$ is a consistent estimator of $\boldsymbol{\theta}$, this estimator will be asymptotically efficient at every step.

---

[10]The characteristic roots of $\boldsymbol{\Gamma}$ are the reciprocals of those of $\boldsymbol{\Omega}$. The determinants are the products of the characteristic roots, so the result follows immediately.

[11] See Section 2.9.1 for derivations of these results.

However, under certain conditions, the values to which $\boldsymbol{\beta}$, σ^2, and $\boldsymbol{\Omega}$ converge will also be the maximum likelihood estimates.[12] These include

1. The information matrix must be block diagonal. That is, $\boldsymbol{\Omega}$ must not be a function of $\boldsymbol{\beta}$.
2. The initial estimate of $\boldsymbol{\theta}$ must be consistent.
3. At each step, the updated estimate of $\boldsymbol{\theta}$ must be obtained by solving the first-order conditions for maximum likelihood estimates, given the present estimate of $\boldsymbol{\beta}$.

The third condition is important to remember. There are cases, including one that we shall examine in detail in Section 15.7, in which there is more than one consistent estimate of $\boldsymbol{\theta}$ given the current estimate of $\boldsymbol{\beta}$.

If the method of Oberhofer and Kmenta is not usable, it may be necessary to maximize the log likelihood directly, for example, using one of the gradient methods described in Chapter 12. At the solution, regardless of how it is obtained, the MLEs of $\boldsymbol{\beta}$ and σ^2 will be the FGLS estimators. The difficult part of the problem is estimating $\boldsymbol{\theta}$. A complete analysis, including several applications, is presented by Magnus (1978). We shall examine some specific cases in the chapters to follow.

The information matrix for the maximum likelihood estimators of $\boldsymbol{\beta}$, σ^2, and $\boldsymbol{\theta}$ will be block diagonal of the form

$$-E\left[\frac{\partial^2 \ln L}{\partial \boldsymbol{\gamma}\, \partial \boldsymbol{\gamma}'}\right] = \begin{array}{c} \\ \boldsymbol{\beta} \\ \sigma^2 \\ \boldsymbol{\theta} \end{array}\begin{array}{c} \overset{\boldsymbol{\beta}'}{} \quad\overset{\sigma^2}{} \quad\overset{\boldsymbol{\theta}'}{} \\ \left[\begin{array}{c|cc} (1/\sigma^2)\mathbf{X}'\boldsymbol{\Omega}^{-1}\mathbf{X} & \mathbf{0} & \mathbf{0}' \\ \hline \mathbf{0}' & n/(2\sigma^4) & \boldsymbol{\delta}' \\ \mathbf{0} & \boldsymbol{\delta} & \mathbf{C} \end{array}\right] \end{array}, \tag{13–32}$$

where $\boldsymbol{\gamma}$ is the full set of parameters. The inverse matrix will be block diagonal as well. Therefore, the asymptotic variance matrix of the maximum likelihood estimator is

$$\text{Asy.Var}[\hat{\boldsymbol{\beta}}_{\text{ML}}] = \sigma^2(\mathbf{X}'\boldsymbol{\Omega}^{-1}\mathbf{X})^{-1}.$$

This is the same as that of the FGLS estimator. We conclude, therefore, that as long as the information matrix is block diagonal, the GLS, FGLS, and ML estimators of $\boldsymbol{\beta}$ have the same asymptotic distributions. It follows that

> Exact knowledge of $\boldsymbol{\Omega}$ brings no gain in
> asymptotic efficiency in the estimation of $\boldsymbol{\beta}$.

This is not true if the information matrix is not block diagonal.

It is important to note that in this and many cases we shall examine later, having the same properties as the maximum likelihood estimator does not imply that the FGLS estimator *is* the maximum likelihood estimator. This means that likelihood ratio tests and Lagrange multiplier tests based on the FGLS estimator are only approximate at best. By exploiting the asymptotic normality of the estimator, we can use the usual F statistic or an asymptotically equivalent chi-squared statistic to test a hypothesis about $\boldsymbol{\beta}$.

EXAMPLE 13.2 Groupwise Heteroscedasticity ————

A groupwise heteroscedastic regression is based on

$$y_i = \boldsymbol{\beta}'\mathbf{x}_i + \varepsilon_i, \qquad i = 1, \ldots, n$$

$$E[\varepsilon_i] = 0, \qquad i = 1, \ldots, n.$$

---

[12]Note that the divisor in the estimator of σ^2 must be n, not $n - K$.

The n observations are grouped into G groups, each with n_g observations. The slope vector is the same in all groups, but within group g,

$$\text{Var}[\varepsilon_{ig}] = \sigma_g^2, \qquad i = 1, \ldots, n_g.$$

The log-likelihood function is

$$\ln L = -\frac{n}{2} \ln (2\pi) - \frac{1}{2} \sum_g n_g \ln \sigma_g^2 - \frac{1}{2} \sum_g \sum_{i=1}^{n_g} \frac{\varepsilon_{ig}^2}{\sigma_g^2}.$$

The MLE for $\boldsymbol{\beta}$ is generalized least squares, using the MLEs for σ_g^2. The **weighting matrix** is

$$\sigma^2\boldsymbol{\Omega} = \begin{bmatrix} \sigma_1^2\mathbf{I} & \mathbf{0} & \cdots & \mathbf{0} \\ \mathbf{0} & \sigma_2^2\mathbf{I} & \cdots & \mathbf{0} \\ & & \vdots & \\ \mathbf{0} & \mathbf{0} & \cdots & \sigma_G^2\mathbf{I} \end{bmatrix},$$

so the GLS estimator is

$$\hat{\boldsymbol{\beta}} = \left[\sum_g \frac{1}{\sigma_g^2}\mathbf{X}_g'\mathbf{X}_g \right]^{-1} \left[\sum_g \frac{1}{\sigma_g^2} \mathbf{X}_g'\mathbf{y}_g \right]. \tag{13–33}$$

For each variance parameter, σ_g^2, the likelihood equation is

$$\frac{\partial \ln L}{\partial \sigma_g^2} = 0 = -\frac{n_g}{2\sigma_g^2} + \frac{1}{2\sigma_g^4} \sum_i \varepsilon_{ig}^2,$$

so that given the current value of $\hat{\boldsymbol{\beta}}$,

$$\hat{\sigma}_g^2 = \frac{\mathbf{e}_g'\mathbf{e}_g}{n_g}.$$

To obtain this maximum likelihood estimator, a simple iterative procedure that satisfies the Oberhofer–Kmenta requirements is as follows:

1. Pool the data and estimate $\boldsymbol{\beta}$ by OLS.
2. Estimate the disturbance variances separately with $\mathbf{e}_g'\mathbf{e}_g/n_g$, where $\mathbf{e}_g = \mathbf{y}_g - \mathbf{X}_g\mathbf{b}$.
3. Compute $\hat{\boldsymbol{\beta}}$ according to (13–33).
4. If $\hat{\boldsymbol{\beta}}$ has not converged, go to step 2; otherwise, exit.

The likelihood ratio test of Section 13.3.2 can be used to test a hypothesis about $\boldsymbol{\beta}$ or $\boldsymbol{\Omega}$. Once again, we insert the MLE for σ^2 in (13–24) in the likelihood function. At the maximum, we have

$$\ln \hat{L} = -\frac{n}{2}(1 + \ln(2\pi) + \ln \hat{\sigma}^2) - \frac{1}{2} \log|\hat{\boldsymbol{\Omega}}|$$

$$= -\frac{n}{2} (1 + \ln(2\pi)) - \frac{1}{2} \ln|\hat{\sigma}^2\hat{\boldsymbol{\Omega}}|.$$

Therefore, for testing constraints on $\boldsymbol{\beta}$ and/or $\boldsymbol{\Omega}$, the likelihood ratio statistic is

$$\lambda = \log|(\hat{\sigma}^2\hat{\boldsymbol{\Omega}})_c| - \log|\hat{\sigma}^2\hat{\boldsymbol{\Omega}}|.$$

The degrees of freedom for the chi-squared test is the number of parametric restrictions imposed. For the groupwise heteroscedastic model of Example 13.2, a likelihood ratio test of the hypothesis of homoscedasticity would be based on

$$\lambda = n \ln s^2 - \sum_g n_g \ln s_g^2,$$

where $n = \Sigma_g n_g$, s^2 is the pooled, least squares residual variance, $\mathbf{e'e}/n$ (not $n - K$), and s_g^2 is defined in Example 13.2.

In general, maximum likelihood estimation of an unknown $\mathbf{\Omega}$ greatly complicates the estimation problem. The likelihood equations for the unknown parameters in $\mathbf{\Omega}$ are usually extremely involved and difficult to solve. In most cases, the asymptotically equivalent procedure of finding a consistent estimator for $\mathbf{\Omega}$ and using FGLS is used instead. (Where it is convenient, analysts often use the Oberhofer–Kmenta procedure.) If $\boldsymbol{\theta}$ contains any of the parameters in $\boldsymbol{\beta}$, neither FGLS nor GLS is efficient. Full maximum likelihood estimation is likely to be extremely difficult in this case, but the maximum likelihood estimator that makes use of the information that $\boldsymbol{\beta}$ enters $\mathbf{\Omega}$ as well as the regression will necessarily be more efficient.

13.5. The Generalized Method of Moments (GMM) Estimator

A large proportion of the recent empirical work in econometrics, particularly in macroeconomics and finance, has employed what have come to be called GMM estimators. As we shall see, this is a broad class of estimators that, in fact, includes almost all of the estimators discussed elsewhere in this book. But recent extensions of the technique have greatly added to the stock of tools available to the applied econometrician.

This section of the text is actually out of order. We will require parts of several chapters that follow this one. But, short of including another chapter at the end of the book, this is the logical place for it. Before continuing, it will be useful for you to read (or reread) the following sections:

1. *The method of moments:* Section 4.6.
2. *Instrumental variable estimation:* Sections 9.5.3, 18.5.4b, and, especially, 20.4.3.
3. *Nonlinear regression models:* Chapter 11.
4. *Nonlinear optimization:* Chapter 12.
5. *Robust estimation of covariance matrices:* Sections 14.2.3 and, especially, 15.4.3.
6. *The Wald statistic:* Sections 10.3.4 and 22.3.4c.

The GMM estimation technique is a direct extension of the method of moments technique described in Section 4.6.[13]

13.5.1. Method of Moments Estimators

Estimation by the method of moments proceeds as follows: The model specified for the random variable y_i implies certain expectations, for example,

$$E[y_i] = \mu,$$

[13] This section will give a largely heuristic development of the GMM estimator. Formal presentation of the results required for this analysis are given by Hansen (1982), Hansen and Singleton (1988), Chamberlain (1987), Cumby et al. (1983), Newey (1984, 1985a, 1985b), and Davidson and MacKinnon (1993). A useful recent summary of GMM estimation and other developments in econometrics is Pagan and Wickens (1989). An application of some of these techniques that contains useful summaries is Pagan and Vella (1989).

where μ is the mean of the distribution of y_i. Estimation of μ then proceeds by forming a sample analog to the "moment condition":

$$E[y_i - \mu] = 0.$$

The sample counterpart to the expectation is

$$\frac{1}{n} \sum_i (y_i - \hat{\mu}) = 0.$$

The estimator is the value of $\hat{\mu}$ that satisfies the sample moment condition. The example given is, of course, a trivial one. Example 4.25 gives the much more elaborate case of sampling from a Gamma distribution. The moment conditions used for estimation in that example (taken two at a time from a set of four) include

$$E\left[x_i - \frac{P}{\lambda}\right] = 0$$

and

$$E\left[\frac{1}{x_i} - \frac{\lambda}{P-1}\right] = 0.$$

Inserting the sample data into the sample analogs produce the moment equations for estimation.

Now, consider the apparently different case of the ordinary least squares estimator of the parameters in the classical linear regression model. Among the assumptions of the model is

$$E[\mathbf{x}_i \varepsilon_i] = \mathbf{0}.$$

The sample analog is

$$\frac{1}{n} \sum_i \mathbf{x}_i e_i = \frac{1}{n} \sum_i \mathbf{x}_i (y_i - \mathbf{x}_i' \hat{\boldsymbol{\beta}}) = \mathbf{0}.$$

The estimator of $\boldsymbol{\beta}$ is the one that satisfies these moment equations. Of course, this is just the normal equations for the least squares estimator, so we see that the OLS estimator is a method of moments estimator. Indeed, by this construction, nearly all of the estimators defined in this book are method of moments estimators. The GLS estimator is defined by

$$E[\mathbf{X}' \boldsymbol{\Omega}^{-1} \boldsymbol{\varepsilon}] = \mathbf{0},$$

which we could rewrite as

$$E[\mathbf{X}_*' \boldsymbol{\varepsilon}] = \mathbf{0},$$

or

$$E[\mathbf{x}_i^* \varepsilon_i] = \mathbf{0}.$$

All of the maximum likelihood estimators that we have looked at thus far and will encounter later are obtained by equating the derivatives of a log likelihood to zero. The operating principle is that

$$\ln L = \Sigma_i \ln f(y_i, \mathbf{x}_i \mid \boldsymbol{\theta}),$$

where $f(\cdot)$ is the density function and $\boldsymbol{\theta}$ is the parameter vector. Underlying the theory of maximum likelihood estimation is the result that for regular problems [see Section 4.5.2 and (4–52)],

$$E\left[\frac{\partial \ln f(y_i, \mathbf{x}_i \mid \boldsymbol{\theta})}{\partial \boldsymbol{\theta}}\right] = \mathbf{0}.$$

The maximum likelihood estimator is obtained by equating the sample analog to zero:

$$\frac{1}{n}\frac{\partial \ln L}{\partial \boldsymbol{\theta}} = \frac{1}{n}\sum_i \frac{\partial \ln f(y_i, \mathbf{x}_i \mid \boldsymbol{\theta})}{\partial \boldsymbol{\theta}} = \mathbf{0}.$$

(Dividing by n to make this comparable to our earlier results does not change the solution.) The upshot is that nearly all of the estimators we have discussed and will encounter later can be construed as method of moments estimators.

13.5.2. Generalizing the Method of Moments

The preceding examples all have a common aspect. In every case listed, there are exactly as many moment equations as there are parameters to be estimated. Thus, each of these are *exactly identified* cases. There will be a single solution to the moment equations, and at the solution, the equations will be exactly satisfied. (That is, of course if there is *any* solution—in the regression model with collinearity, there are K parameters, but less than K independent moment equations.) But there are cases in which there are more moment equations than parameters, so the system is overdetermined.

EXAMPLE 13.3 (Example 4.25 Continued) ───────────────────

In Example 4.25 we computed four sample moments,

$$\bar{\mathbf{g}} = \frac{1}{n}\sum_i \left[x_i,\ x_i^2,\ \frac{1}{x_i},\ \ln x_i \right]$$

with probability limits P/λ, $P(P + 1)/\lambda^2$, $\lambda/(P - 1)$, and $\Psi(P) - \ln \lambda$, respectively. Any pair could be used to estimate the two parameters, but as shown in the earlier example, the six pairs produce six somewhat different estimates of (P, λ).

──

In such a case, in order to use all of the information in the sample, it is necessary to devise a way to reconcile the conflicting estimates that will emerge from the overdetermined system. More generally, suppose that the model involves K parameters, $\boldsymbol{\theta} = (\theta_1, \theta_2, \ldots, \theta_K)$, and that it implies a set of $J > K$ moment conditions,

$$E[m_j(y_i, \mathbf{x}_i, \mathbf{z}_i, \boldsymbol{\theta})] = 0, \qquad j = 1, \ldots, J,$$

where y_i, $\mathbf{x}_i$, and $\mathbf{z}_i$ are variables that appear in the model. Denote the corresponding sample sums as

$$\bar{m}_j(\mathbf{y}, \mathbf{X}, \mathbf{Z}, \boldsymbol{\theta}) = \frac{1}{n}\sum_i m_j(y_i, \mathbf{x}_i, \mathbf{z}_i, \boldsymbol{\theta}).$$

Unless the equations are functionally dependent, the system of J equations in K unknown parameters,

$$\bar{m}_j = \frac{1}{n}\sum_i m_j(y_i, \mathbf{x}_i, \mathbf{z}_i, \boldsymbol{\theta}) = 0, \qquad j = 1, \ldots, J,$$

will not have a unique solution. It will be necessary to reconcile the $\binom{J}{K}$ different sets of estimates that can be produced. One possibility would be to minimize a criterion function, such as the sum of squares,

$$q = \sum_j \bar{m}_j^2 = \bar{\mathbf{m}}(\boldsymbol{\theta})'\bar{\mathbf{m}}(\boldsymbol{\theta}).^{14} \qquad (13\text{--}34)$$

─────────

[14] This is one of the approaches that Quandt and Ramsey (1978) suggested for the problem in Example 4.24.

The preceding is an ordinary least squares approach. Since the moments are sums of the observations, they are, in fact, random variables whose variances are estimable. [See (4–55).] As such, by the same logic that makes GLS preferable to OLS, it should be beneficial to use a weighted procedure, in which the weights are inversely proportional to the variances of the moments. Let $\mathbf{W}$ be a diagonal matrix whose diagonal elements are

$$w_{jj} = \text{Asy.Var}[\overline{m}_j].$$

Then, a *weighted least squares* procedure would minimize

$$q = \overline{\mathbf{m}}'\mathbf{W}^{-1}\overline{\mathbf{m}}. \tag{13–35}$$

In general, the J elements of $\overline{\mathbf{m}}$ are freely correlated, whereas in (13–35) we have used a diagonal $\mathbf{W}$ which ignores this correlation. To use GLS, we should define

$$\mathbf{W} = \text{Asy.Var}[\overline{\mathbf{m}}]. \tag{13–36}$$

The estimators defined by choosing $\boldsymbol{\theta}$ to minimize

$$q = \overline{\mathbf{m}}(\boldsymbol{\theta})'\mathbf{W}^{-1}\overline{\mathbf{m}}(\boldsymbol{\theta})$$

are *minimum distance estimators*. If $\mathbf{W}$ is a positive definite matrix and

$$\text{plim } \overline{\mathbf{m}} = \mathbf{0},$$

then the estimator of $\boldsymbol{\theta}$ is consistent.[15] Since the OLS criterion in (13–34) uses $\mathbf{I}$, this produces a consistent estimator, as does the weighted least squares estimator and the full GLS estimator. What remains to be decided is the best $\mathbf{W}$ to use. Intuition might suggest (correctly) that the one defined in (13–36) would be optimal, once again based on the logic that motivates generalized least squares. This is the now celebrated result of Hansen (1982). The asymptotic covariance matrix of this *generalized method of moments* estimator is

$$\boldsymbol{\Sigma} = [\mathbf{G}'\mathbf{W}^{-1}\mathbf{G}]^{-1} \tag{13–37}$$

where $\mathbf{G}$ is a matrix of derivatives whose jth row is

$$\mathbf{G}^j = \frac{\partial \overline{m}_j}{\partial \boldsymbol{\theta}'}. \tag{13–38}$$

Finally, by virtue of the central limit theorem applied to the sample moments and the Slutsky theorem applied to this manipulation, we can assert that

$$\hat{\boldsymbol{\theta}} \xrightarrow{a} N[\boldsymbol{\theta}, \boldsymbol{\Sigma}]. \tag{13–39}$$

EXAMPLE 13.4 (Example 4.25 Continued)

GMM Estimation for the Gamma Distribution. Referring once again to our earlier results, we consider how to use all four of our sample moments to estimate the parameters of the gamma distribution. The four moment equations are

$$E\left[x_i - \frac{P}{\lambda}\right] = 0,$$

---

[15] In the most general cases, there are a number of other subtle conditions that must be met in order to assert consistency and the other properties we discuss. For our purposes, the conditions given will suffice. Minimum distance estimators are discussed in Malinvaud (1970), Hansen (1982), and Amemiya (1985).

$$E\left[x_i^2 - \frac{P(P+1)}{\lambda^2}\right] = 0,$$

$$E\left[\frac{1}{x_i} - \frac{\lambda}{P-1)}\right] = 0,$$

$$E[\ln x_i - \Psi(P) + \ln \lambda] = 0.$$

The sample means of these will provide our moment equations for estimation. As before, we denote by m_1', m_2', m_{-1}', m_*' the sample means of x, x^2, $1/x$, and $\ln x$, respectively. It turns out that for purposes of the nonlinear optimization procedure, a rescaling of the moment conditions greatly eases convergence. (See Chapter 12 for discussion.) By multiplying the first three equations by λ, λ^2, and $(P-1)$, respectively, we obtain a much more convenient system of equations. Thus, our four moment equations for estimation are

$$m_1 = \lambda m_1' - P$$

$$m_2 = \lambda^2 m_2' - P(P+1)$$

$$m_3 = (P-1)m_{-1}' - \lambda$$

$$m_4 = m_*' - \Psi(P) - \ln \lambda.$$

To compute **W**, we require an estimate of the asymptotic covariance matrix of

$$\mathbf{m} = (m_1, m_2, m_3, m_4).$$

We can obtain this as **JVJ**, where **V** is the estimated asymptotic covariance matrix for $(m_1', m_2', m_{-1}', m_*')$ and **J** is a diagonal matrix with $(\lambda, \lambda^2, (P-1), 1)$ on the diagonals. Of course, this requires estimates of P and λ, which we are now trying to obtain. But we do have our consistent maximum likelihood estimates. Indeed, we can choose among the six pairs of estimates, all of which are consistent. The following is based on the MLEs. We can estimate **V** with $1/n$ times the sample covariance matrix of $(x, x^2, 1/x, \ln x)$. Then the values of (P, λ) that minimize

$$q = \mathbf{m}'\mathbf{W}^{-1}\mathbf{m}$$

are $(2.5655, 0.081854)$. The value of q with these estimates is 44.58023. To compute the asymptotic covariance matrix, we require

$$\mathbf{G}' = \begin{bmatrix} \partial m_1/\partial P & \partial m_2/\partial P & \partial m_3/\partial P & \partial m_4/\partial P \\ \partial m_1/\partial \lambda & \partial m_2/\partial \lambda & \partial m_3/\partial \lambda & \partial m_4/\partial \lambda \end{bmatrix} = \begin{bmatrix} -1 & -2P-1 & m_{-1}' & -\Psi'(P) \\ m_1' & 2\lambda m_2' & -1 & -1/2\lambda \end{bmatrix}.$$

This produces an estimated asymptotic covariance matrix whose two diagonal elements are $(0.012251, 0.0001109)$. Recall that the counterparts for the maximum likelihood estimator were $(0.51243, 0.00064699)$, so it appears that there is a large payoff to using the additional moments. (The appearance is illusory, as we discuss in Example 13.5.)

13.5.3. Testing the Validity of the Moment Restrictions

In the exactly identified cases we examined earlier, the criterion for GMM estimation,

$$q = \mathbf{m}'\mathbf{W}^{-1}\mathbf{m}$$

would be exactly zero because we can find a set of estimates for which **m** is exactly zero. This means, of course, that in the exactly identified case, when there are the same number of moment equations as there are parameters to estimate, the weighting matrix, **W** is irrelevant. But if the parameters are overidentified by the moment equation, these equations imply substantive restrictions. As such, if the hypothesis of the model that led to the moment equations in the first place is incorrect, at least some of the sample moment restrictions will be systematically violated. This provides the basis for a test of the overidentifying restrictions. In particular, we note that by construction,

$$q = \mathbf{m}'\{\text{Est.Asy.Var}[\mathbf{m}]\}^{-1}\mathbf{m},$$

and, as such, q is a Wald statistic. (See Sections 10.3.4 and 22.3.4c.) Therefore,

$$q \xrightarrow{d} \chi^2[J - K].$$

(For the exactly identified case, there are zero degrees of freedom, and $q = 0$.)

EXAMPLE 13.5 (Example 4.25 Concluded) ──────────────────

In Example 13.4, we found that the value of q for our data was 44.58. This far exceeds the critical value from the table, of 5.99. As such, the hypothesis that all four moment equations are satisfied is rejected. This should have been expected. In point of fact, for random sampling from the gamma distribution, the maximum likelihood estimators are efficient among all consistent estimators. As such, there is surely an inconsistency in the fact that the standard errors for the GMM estimator appear to be far smaller than those for the MLE. The conflict is resolved by the hypothesis test, which implies that the restrictions should be rejected. The implications of this for estimation in this context are that, first, the hypothesis that the data were drawn from an underlying gamma population should be rejected. (They were not; they were chosen at random by the author.) Second, given this, the method used to compute the asymptotic covariance matrix for the MLE is incorrect. Finally, the moment equations themselves should be deemed invalid. You should note that it is not possible to do this sort of analysis based on only two of the moments, regardless of which two are chosen. In an exactly identified case, all of the information in the sample is consumed in estimation of the parameters. It is only when the restrictions overidentify the parameters that q can be used to make inference about the specification of the model.

13.5.4. GMM Estimation of Econometric Models

The preceding has developed the method of moments largely in the context of estimation of the parameters of a distribution using a random sample. The extension to estimation of the parameters of econometric models is fairly straightforward. For purposes of an uncomplicated introduction, we will consider the problem of estimation of the parameters in a single equation, but recent applications have extended the technique to multiple equations models as well.

Suppose that the theory specifies a relationship

$$y_i = h(\mathbf{x}_i, \boldsymbol{\theta}) + \varepsilon_i,$$

where $\boldsymbol{\theta}$ is a $K \times 1$ parameter vector that we wish to estimate. This might not be a regression relationship, since it is possible that

$$\text{Cov}[\varepsilon_i, h(\mathbf{x}_i, \boldsymbol{\theta})] \neq 0,$$

or even

$$\text{Cov}[\varepsilon_i, \mathbf{x}_j] \neq \mathbf{0} \qquad \text{for all } i \text{ and } j.$$

Consider, for example, a model that contains lagged dependent variables and autocorrelated disturbances. (See Sections 15.4.1, 18.5.4, 18.6, and 19.2.1.) We assume that

$$E[\boldsymbol{\varepsilon}] = \mathbf{0}$$

and

$$E[\boldsymbol{\varepsilon}\boldsymbol{\varepsilon}'] = \boldsymbol{\Omega},$$

where $\boldsymbol{\Omega}$ is unrestricted. The disturbances may be both heteroscedastic and/or autocorrelated. But for the possibility of correlation between regressors and disturbances, this would be a generalized, possibly nonlinear regression model. Suppose that at each observation, i, we observe a vector of J variables, $\mathbf{z}_i$, such that $\mathbf{z}_i$ is uncorrelated with ε_i. You will recognize $\mathbf{z}$ as a set of *instrumental variables*. The assumptions thus far have implied a set of **orthogonality conditions,**

$$E[\mathbf{z}_i \, \varepsilon_i] = \mathbf{0},$$

which may be sufficient to identify (if $J = K$) or even overidentify (if $J > K$) the parameters of the model.

For convenience, define

$$\mathbf{e}(\mathbf{X}, \hat{\boldsymbol{\theta}}) = y_i - h(\mathbf{x}_i, \hat{\boldsymbol{\theta}}), \qquad i = 1, \ldots, n,$$

and

$$\mathbf{Z} = n \times J \text{ matrix whose } i\text{th row is } \mathbf{z}_i'.$$

By a straightforward extension of our earlier results, we can produce a GMM estimator of $\boldsymbol{\theta}$. The sample moments will be

$$\mathbf{m} = \frac{1}{n} \sum_i \mathbf{z}_i e(\mathbf{x}_i, \boldsymbol{\theta}) = \frac{1}{n}\mathbf{Z}'\mathbf{e}(\mathbf{X}, \boldsymbol{\theta}) = \mathbf{m}(\boldsymbol{\theta}).$$

The minimum distance estimator will be the $\hat{\boldsymbol{\theta}}$ that minimizes

$$
\begin{aligned}
q &= \mathbf{m}(\hat{\boldsymbol{\theta}})'\mathbf{W}^{-1}\mathbf{m}(\hat{\boldsymbol{\theta}}) \\
&= (1/n^2)[\mathbf{e}(\mathbf{X}, \hat{\boldsymbol{\theta}})'\mathbf{Z}]\mathbf{W}^{-1}[\mathbf{Z}'\mathbf{e}(\mathbf{X}, \hat{\boldsymbol{\theta}})].
\end{aligned}
\tag{13–40}
$$

for some choice of $\mathbf{W}$ that we have yet to determine. The criterion given above produces the *nonlinear instrumental variable estimator*. Of course, the linear IV estimator is a special case. For any given choice of $\mathbf{W}$, as long as there are enough orthogonality conditions to identify the parameters, estimation by minimizing q is, at least in principle, a straightforward problem in nonlinear optimization. Hansen (1982) showed that the optimal choice of $\mathbf{W}$ for this estimator is

$$
\begin{aligned}
\mathbf{W}_{\text{GMM}} &= \text{Asy.Var}[\mathbf{m}(\boldsymbol{\theta})] \\
&= \text{Asy.Var}\left[\frac{1}{n}\sum_i \mathbf{z}_i\varepsilon_i\right] \\
&= \text{Asy.Var}\left[\frac{1}{n}\mathbf{Z}'\mathbf{e}(\mathbf{X}, \boldsymbol{\theta})\right].
\end{aligned}
\tag{13–41}
$$

For our model, this is

$$\mathbf{W} = \frac{1}{n^2} \sum_i \sum_j \text{Cov}[\mathbf{z}_i \varepsilon_i, \mathbf{z}_j \varepsilon_j]$$

$$= \frac{1}{n^2} \sum_i \sum_j \omega_{ij} \mathbf{z}_i \mathbf{z}_j'$$

$$= \left(\frac{1}{n^2}\right) \mathbf{Z}' \mathbf{\Omega} \mathbf{Z}.$$

If we insert this in (13–40), we obtain the criterion for the GMM estimator,

$$q = \left[\left(\frac{1}{n}\right) \mathbf{e}(\mathbf{X}, \hat{\boldsymbol{\theta}})' \mathbf{Z}\right] \left(\frac{\mathbf{Z}' \mathbf{\Omega} \mathbf{Z}}{n^2}\right)^{-1} \left[\left(\frac{1}{n}\right) \mathbf{Z}' \mathbf{e}(\mathbf{X}, \hat{\boldsymbol{\theta}})\right].$$

There is a possibly difficult detail to be considered. The GMM estimator involves

$$\left(\frac{1}{n^2}\right) \mathbf{Z}' \mathbf{\Omega} \mathbf{Z} = \frac{1}{n^2} \sum_i \sum_j \mathbf{z}_i \mathbf{z}_j' \, \text{Cov}[\varepsilon_i \varepsilon_j]$$

$$= \frac{1}{n^2} \sum_i \sum_j \mathbf{z}_i \mathbf{z}_j' \, \text{Cov}[y_i - h(\mathbf{x}_i, \boldsymbol{\theta}))(y_j - h(\mathbf{x}_j, \boldsymbol{\theta}))].$$

The conditions under which such a double sum might converge to a positive definite matrix are sketched in Section 10.4. Assuming that they hold, estimation appears to require that an estimate of $\boldsymbol{\theta}$ be in hand already, even though it is the target of estimation.[16] It may be that a consistent but inefficient estimate of $\boldsymbol{\theta}$ is available. Suppose for the present that one is. If observations are independent, the cross terms may be omitted, and what is required is

$$\left(\frac{1}{n^2}\right) \mathbf{Z}' \mathbf{\Omega} \mathbf{Z} = \frac{1}{n^2} \sum_i \mathbf{z}_i \mathbf{z}_i' \text{Var}[(y_i - h(\mathbf{x}_i, \boldsymbol{\theta}))].$$

White (1980) has shown that this matrix can be estimated by using

$$\left(\frac{1}{n}\right) \mathbf{S}_0 = \frac{1}{n} \left[\frac{1}{n} \sum_i \mathbf{z}_i \mathbf{z}_i' (y_i - h(\mathbf{x}_i, \hat{\boldsymbol{\theta}}))^2\right]. \tag{13–42}$$

(Further discussion appears in Section 14.2.3.) If the disturbances are autocorrelated, Newey and West's (1987) estimator is available,

$$\left(\frac{1}{n}\right) \mathbf{S} = \frac{1}{n} \left[\mathbf{S}_0 + \frac{1}{n} \sum_{\ell=1}^{L} w(\ell) \sum_{i=\ell+1}^{n} e_i e_{i-\ell} [\mathbf{z}_i \mathbf{z}_{i-\ell}' + \mathbf{z}_{i-\ell} \mathbf{z}_i']\right]$$

$$\tag{13–43}$$

$$= \frac{1}{n} \sum_{\ell=0}^{L} w(\ell) \mathbf{S}_\ell,$$

---

[16] This suggests that an estimate of $\mathbf{\Omega}$, itself, is needed. The logic of the White (1980) and Newey–West (1987a) estimators is such that, in fact, this is not precisely correct. The matrix product $\mathbf{Z}' \mathbf{\Omega} \mathbf{Z}$, which in turn involves expected squares and cross products of disturbances, is all that is needed. The distinction is discussed in Sections 14.2.3 and 15.4.3.

where

$$w(\ell) = 1 - \frac{\ell}{L + 1}.$$

The maximum lag length, L, must be decided upon in advance. (This is discussed in Section 15.4.3.) As we saw in Chapter 10, we will require that observations which are far apart in time, that is, for which $|i - \ell|$ is large, must have increasingly small covariances in order for us to establish the convergence results that justify OLS, GLS, and now GMM estimation. The choice of L is a reflection of how far back in time one must go to consider the autocorrelation negligible for purposes of estimating $(1/n^2)\mathbf{Z}'\mathbf{\Omega}\mathbf{Z}$.

This leaves open the question of where the initial consistent estimator should be obtained. One possibility is to obtain an inefficient but consistent GMM estimator by using $\mathbf{W} = \mathbf{I}$ in (13–40). That is, use a nonlinear (or linear, if the equation is linear) instrumental variables estimator. This first step estimator can then be used to construct $\mathbf{W}$, which, in turn, can then be used in the GMM estimator. Another possibility is that $\boldsymbol{\theta}$ may be consistently estimable by some straightforward procedure other than GMM. We will consider a case in one of the examples below.

Once the GMM estimator has been computed, its asymptotic covariance matrix and asymptotic distribution can be estimated based on (13–37) to (13–39). Recall that

$$\mathbf{m}(\boldsymbol{\theta}) = \frac{1}{n} \sum_i \mathbf{z}_i \varepsilon_i,$$

which is a sum of $J \times 1$ vectors. The derivative, $\partial \mathbf{m}(\boldsymbol{\theta})/\partial \boldsymbol{\theta}'$ is a sum of n $K \times J$ matrices,

$$\mathbf{G}_i(\boldsymbol{\theta}) = \left[\frac{\partial \varepsilon_i}{\partial \boldsymbol{\theta}}\right]\mathbf{z}_i',$$

so

$$\mathbf{G}(\boldsymbol{\theta}) = \frac{\partial \mathbf{m}(\boldsymbol{\theta})}{\partial \boldsymbol{\theta}} = \frac{1}{n} \sum_i \mathbf{G}_i. \tag{13–44}$$

In the model we are considering here,

$$\frac{\partial \varepsilon_i}{\partial \boldsymbol{\theta}} = \frac{-\partial h(\mathbf{x}_i, \boldsymbol{\theta})}{\partial \boldsymbol{\theta}}.$$

The derivatives are the "regressors" in the linearized regression model that we examined in Section 11.2.1. Using the notation defined there,

$$\frac{\partial \varepsilon_i}{\partial \boldsymbol{\theta}} = -\tilde{\mathbf{x}}_i,$$

so

$$\mathbf{G}_i(\boldsymbol{\theta}) = -\tilde{\mathbf{x}}_i \mathbf{z}_i'.$$

The sum would be

$$\mathbf{G}(\boldsymbol{\theta}) = \frac{1}{n} \sum_i \mathbf{G}_i = \frac{-1}{n} \tilde{\mathbf{X}}'\mathbf{Z}. \tag{13–44'}$$

With this in hand, the estimated asymptotic covariance matrix for the GMM estimator is

$$\text{Est.Asy.Var}[\hat{\boldsymbol{\theta}}] = \left[\mathbf{G}(\hat{\boldsymbol{\theta}}) \left(\frac{\mathbf{Z}'\hat{\boldsymbol{\Omega}}\mathbf{Z}}{n^2} \right)^{-1} \mathbf{G}(\hat{\boldsymbol{\theta}})' \right]^{-1}$$

$$= [(\tilde{\mathbf{X}}'\mathbf{Z})(\mathbf{Z}'\hat{\boldsymbol{\Omega}}\mathbf{Z})^{-1}(\mathbf{Z}'\tilde{\mathbf{X}})]^{-1}. \tag{13-45}$$

(The two minus signs, a $1/n^2$ and an n^2, all fall out of the result.)

EXAMPLE 13.6 Linear Models —————————————————————————

You should be able to prove the following: For the class of linear models,

$$y_i = \boldsymbol{\beta}'\mathbf{x}_i + \varepsilon_i,$$

GMM estimation can be based on the orthogonality conditions

$$E[\mathbf{z}_i(y_i - \mathbf{x}_i'\boldsymbol{\beta})].$$

If the disturbances are uncorrelated and homoscedastic and $\mathbf{z} = \mathbf{x}$, this is obviously just the OLS estimator. On the other hand, if we allow for correlation between $\mathbf{x}$ and ε, and $\mathbf{z}$ is a set of K instrumental variables that satisfy the requirements in Section 9.5.3, then the IV estimator in (9–31) emerges. If $\mathbf{z}$ is $J > K$ instrumental variables but we maintain the assumptions about the disturbances, then the 2SLS estimator in (20–23) is the resulting GMM estimator. (This requires a slight change in notation.) If we continue to assume that $\mathbf{z}$ equals $\mathbf{x}$, but that the disturbances are heteroscedastic, then the GMM estimator will be OLS. But the estimated asymptotic covariance matrix will be the White estimator given in (14–8) and (14–9). If $\mathbf{z} = \mathbf{x}$, but we allow for autocorrelation of the disturbances, the GMM estimator will, once again, be OLS, but the estimated asymptotic covariance matrix will be the Newey–West estimator defined by (14–8), (14–9), (15–24), and (15–25).

In two of the cases in Example 13.6, the GMM estimator is inefficient. This is a function of the orthogonality conditions. The GMM estimator is efficient in the class of instrumental variable estimators *defined by the orthogonality conditions*.

EXAMPLE 13.7 A Two-Step Approach —————————————————————

Avery, Hansen, and Hotz (1981) have devised an estimator for the model

$$y_{it}^* = \boldsymbol{\beta}_i'\mathbf{x}_{it} + \varepsilon_{it}, \qquad i = 1, \ldots, n, \quad t = 1, \ldots, T$$

$$y_{it} = 1 \quad \text{if } y_{it}^* > 0, \quad \text{else } y_{it} = 0.$$

This is a "probit model" for panel data. (The probit model is discussed in Section 21.3.) The disturbances are assumed to be independent across groups ($i \neq j$) but freely correlated across time ($s \neq t$) for a given i. Maximum likelihood estimation of the model for T greater than 2 is nearly intractable. The authors devised a GMM estimator for more than 2 periods. The method requires an initial consistent estimator for the set of slope vectors in order to compute the counterpart to our $\mathbf{Z}'\boldsymbol{\Omega}\mathbf{Z}$. The consistent estimator is easily computed because the T cross sections can be analyzed one at a time using conventional maximum likelihood procedures.

13.5.5. Testing Restrictions

Section 4.8.3 describes a trio of testing procedures that can be applied to a hypothesis in the context of maximum likelihood estimation. To reiterate, let the hypothesis to be tested be a set of J possibly nonlinear restrictions on K parameters, $\boldsymbol{\theta}$, in the form $H_0:\mathbf{R}(\boldsymbol{\theta}) - \mathbf{r} = \mathbf{0}$, where $\boldsymbol{\theta}$ is the parameter vector being estimated. Let $\mathbf{c}_1$ be the maximum likelihood estimates of $\boldsymbol{\theta}$ estimated without the restrictions, and let $\mathbf{c}_0$ denote the restricted maximum likelihood estimates, that is, the estimates obtained while imposing the null hypothesis. The three statistics, which are asymptotically equivalent, are obtained as follows:

$$\text{LR} = \text{likelihood ratio} = \chi^2[J] = -2(\ln L_0 - \ln L_1), \tag{13-46}$$

where

$$\ln L_j = \log = \text{likelihood function evaluated at } \mathbf{c}_j, \ j = 0, 1.$$

The likelihood ratio statistic requires that both estimates be computed. The Wald statistic is

$$W = \text{Wald} = \chi^2[J] = [\mathbf{R}(\mathbf{c}_1) - \mathbf{r}]'\{\text{Est.Asy.Var}[\mathbf{R}(\mathbf{c}_1) - \mathbf{r}]\}^{-1}[\mathbf{R}(\mathbf{c}_1) - \mathbf{r}]. \tag{13-47}$$

The Wald statistic is the distance measure for the degree to which the unrestricted estimator fails to satisfy the restrictions. The usual estimator for the asymptotic covariance matrix would be

$$\text{Est.Asy.Var}[\mathbf{R}(\mathbf{c}_1) - \mathbf{r}] = \mathbf{A}_1 \{\text{Est.Asy.Var}[\mathbf{c}_1]\}\mathbf{A}_1', \tag{13-48}$$

where

$$\mathbf{A}_1 = \frac{\partial \mathbf{R}(\boldsymbol{\theta})}{\partial \boldsymbol{\theta}'} \Big| \boldsymbol{\theta} = \mathbf{c}_1 \qquad (\mathbf{A}_1 \text{ is a } J \times K \text{ matrix}).$$

The Wald statistic can be computed using only the unrestricted estimate. The LM statistic is

$$\text{LM} = \text{Lagrange multiplier} = \chi^2[J] = \mathbf{g}_0'\{\text{Est.Asy.Var}[\mathbf{g}_0]\}^{-1}\mathbf{g}_0, \tag{13-49}$$

where

$$\mathbf{g}_0 = \frac{\partial \ln L}{\partial \boldsymbol{\theta}} \Big| \boldsymbol{\theta} = \mathbf{c}_0,$$

that is, the first derivatives of the log likelihood computed at the restricted estimates. The Est.Asy.Var$[\mathbf{g}_0]$ is any of the usual estimators of the asymptotic covariance matrix of the maximum likelihood estimators of the parameters, computed using the restricted estimates. The most convenient choice is often the BHHH estimator. The LM statistic is based on the restricted estimates.

Newey and West (1987b) have devised a counterpart to this set of test statistics for the GMM estimator. The Wald statistic is computed identically, using the results of GMM estimation rather than maximum likelihood. That is, in (13–47), we would use the unrestricted GMM estimator of $\boldsymbol{\theta}$. The appropriate asymptotic covariance matrix is that in (13–45), which might be based on (13–42) or (13–43). Either way, the computation is exactly the same. The counterpart to the LR statistic is the difference in the values of q in (13–40). It is necessary to use the same $\mathbf{W}$ matrix in both restricted and unrestricted estimators. Since the unrestricted estimator is consistent under both H_0 and H_1, a consistent, unrestricted estimator of $\boldsymbol{\theta}$ is used to compute $\mathbf{W}$. Then q is minimized without restrictions to obtain q_1 and subject to the restrictions to obtain q_0. The statistic is then just

$(q_0 - q_1)$.[17] Since we are using the same $\mathbf{W}$ in both cases, this is necessarily nonnegative. Finally, the counterpart to the LM statistic would be

$$\mathrm{LM_{GMM}} = [\mathbf{m}(\mathbf{c}_0)'\mathbf{W}^{-1}\mathbf{A}(\mathbf{c}_0)]\mathrm{Est.Asy.Var}[\mathbf{c}_0][\mathbf{m}(\mathbf{c}_0)'\mathbf{W}^{-1}\mathbf{A}(\mathbf{c}_0)]'.$$

The logic of this LM statistic is the same as that for the MLE. The derivatives of the criterion, q, in (13–40) are

$$\boldsymbol{\alpha} = \frac{\partial q}{\partial \boldsymbol{\theta}} = 2\mathbf{G}(\boldsymbol{\theta})'\mathbf{W}^{-1}\mathbf{m}(\boldsymbol{\theta}).$$

The LM statistic, $\mathrm{LM_{GMM}}$, is a Wald statistic for testing the hypothesis that this vector equals zero under the restrictions of the null hypothesis. From our earlier results, we would have

$$\mathrm{Var}[\boldsymbol{\alpha}] = 4\mathbf{G}(\boldsymbol{\theta})'\mathbf{W}^{-1}\,\mathrm{Var}[\mathbf{m}(\boldsymbol{\theta})]\mathbf{W}^{-1}\,\mathbf{G}(\boldsymbol{\theta}).$$

The variance of $\mathbf{m}(\boldsymbol{\theta})$ is given after (13–40). In the present notation, it would be

$$\mathrm{Var}[\mathbf{m}(\boldsymbol{\theta})] = \mathbf{G}(\boldsymbol{\theta})'\mathbf{W}^{-1}\,\mathbf{G}(\boldsymbol{\theta}).$$

The Wald statistic would be

$$\mathrm{Wald} = \boldsymbol{\alpha}'(\mathrm{Var}[\boldsymbol{\alpha}])^{-1}\,\boldsymbol{\alpha}.$$

If we insert $\mathbf{c}_0$ and interpret the parts as we have earlier, this produces $\mathrm{LM_{GMM}}$.[18]

EXERCISES

1. What is the covariance matrix of the GLS estimator and the difference between it and the OLS estimator?

$$\mathrm{Cov}[\hat{\boldsymbol{\beta}}, \hat{\boldsymbol{\beta}} - \mathbf{b}],$$

where

$$\hat{\boldsymbol{\beta}} = (\mathbf{X}'\boldsymbol{\Omega}^{-1}\mathbf{X})^{-1}\mathbf{X}'\boldsymbol{\Omega}^{-1}\mathbf{y},$$

and

$$\mathbf{b} = (\mathbf{X}'\mathbf{X})^{-1}\mathbf{X}'\mathbf{y}.$$

The result plays a pivotal role in the development of specification tests in Hausman (1978).

2. For the Poisson model of Exercise 4 in Chapter 10, show that the maximum likelihood estimator is the GLS estimator. Show that the variances you derived in parts (a)

---

[17] Newey and West label this the D test.

[18] Throughout this entire discussion, we have suppressed a normalizing constant, n. Newey and West's results for these statistics all involve multiplication by n, whereas ours do not. The difference can be traced back to their definition of $\mathbf{V}_T$ in (2.6) on page 781. Their entire set of derivations is couched in terms of a matrix $\mathbf{V}_T$ which is the asymptotic covariance matrix of $\sqrt{n}\,\mathbf{m}(\boldsymbol{\theta})$ in our notation. The difference is inconsequential in that they and we reach the identical answers for the test statistics listed above. However, there is a minor error in their paper which does have implications for our results. In the paragraph after their (2.7), they state that $\mathbf{Q}^{-1}$ is the asymptotic covariance matrix of the GMM estimator, $\boldsymbol{\theta}$. In their terms, it is the asymptotic covariance matrix of $\sqrt{T}(\hat{\boldsymbol{\theta}} - \boldsymbol{\theta})$. The implications for our results would be in the covariance matrix in (13–45). If we adhered strictly to the Newey–West definition, the matrix in (13–45) would be multiplied by n, which would be incorrect. This becomes obvious if $\boldsymbol{\Omega} = \sigma^2\mathbf{I}$ and $\hat{\mathbf{X}} = \mathbf{Z}$, which would correspond to least squares in the classical regression model.

and (b) are those in (13–5) and (13–15). (Note that this is an unusual case in that the GLS estimator is fully efficient even though the disturbance variances involve the parameters of the regression.)

3. This and the next two exercises are based on the test statistic usually used to test a set of J linear restrictions in the generalized regression model:

$$F[J, n - K] = \frac{(\mathbf{R}\hat{\boldsymbol{\beta}} - \mathbf{q})'[\mathbf{R}(\mathbf{X}'\boldsymbol{\Omega}^{-1}\mathbf{X})^{-1}\mathbf{R}']^{-1}(\mathbf{R}\hat{\boldsymbol{\beta}} - \mathbf{q})/J}{(\mathbf{y} - \mathbf{X}\hat{\boldsymbol{\beta}})'\boldsymbol{\Omega}^{-1}(\mathbf{y} - \mathbf{X}\hat{\boldsymbol{\beta}})/(n - K)},$$

where $\hat{\boldsymbol{\beta}}$ is the GLS estimator. Show that if $\boldsymbol{\Omega}$ is known and the disturbances are normally distributed, this statistic is exactly distributed as F with J and $n - K$ degrees of freedom. What assumptions about the regressors are needed to reach this conclusion? Need they be nonstochastic?

4. Now suppose that the disturbances are not normally distributed, though $\boldsymbol{\Omega}$ is still known. Proceeding along the lines of the proof in Section 10.3.4, show that the previous statistic is asymptotically distributed as $(1/J)$ times a chi-squared variable with J degrees of freedom. (**Hint:** The transformed model of (13–12) satisfies the assumptions of the theorem in Chapter 10.) Conclude that in the generalized regression model, the Wald statistic,

$$W = (\mathbf{R}\hat{\boldsymbol{\beta}} - \mathbf{q})'\{\mathbf{R}(\text{Est.Var}[\hat{\boldsymbol{\beta}}])\mathbf{R}'\}^{-1}(\mathbf{R}\hat{\boldsymbol{\beta}} - \mathbf{q}),$$

tends asymptotically to a chi-squared statistic with J degrees of freedom, regardless of the distribution of the disturbances, so long as the data are otherwise well behaved. Note that in a finite sample the true distribution may be approximated with an $F[J, n - K]$ distribution. It is a bit ambiguous, however, to interpret this as implying that the statistic is asymptotically distributed as F with J and $n - K$ degrees of freedom, as the limiting distribution used to obtain our result is the chi-squared, not the F. In this instance, the $F[J, n - K]$ is a random variable that tends asymptotically to the chi-squared variate.

5. Finally, suppose that $\boldsymbol{\Omega}$ must be estimated but that assumptions (13–27) and (13–28) are met by the estimator. What changes are required in the development of the previous problem?

6. An intriguing result is the following:

> In the generalized regression model, if the K columns of $\mathbf{X}$ are characteristic vectors of $\boldsymbol{\Omega}$, then ordinary least squares and generalized least squares are identical.

(The result is actually a bit broader; $\mathbf{X}$ may be any linear combination of exactly K characteristic vectors.)
(a) Prove the result directly, using matrix algebra.
(b) Prove that if $\mathbf{X}$ contains a constant term and if the remaining columns are in deviation form (so that the column sum is zero), the model of Example 13.1 is one of these cases. (The seemingly unrelated regressions model with identical regressor matrices, which is discussed in Chapter 17, is another.)

7. In the generalized regression model, suppose that $\boldsymbol{\Omega}$ is known.
(a) What is the covariance matrix of the OLS and GLS estimators of $\boldsymbol{\beta}$?
(b) What is the covariance matrix of the OLS residual vector, $\mathbf{e} = \mathbf{y} - \mathbf{Xb}$?
(c) What is the covariance matrix of the GLS residual vector, $\hat{\boldsymbol{\varepsilon}} = \mathbf{y} - \mathbf{X}\hat{\boldsymbol{\beta}}$?
(d) What is the covariance matrix of the OLS and GLS residual vectors?

8. Derive a general expression for the expected value of s^2, the OLS estimator of σ^2, in the context of the generalized regression model.

9. Suppose that y has the pdf

$$f(y|x) = \left[\frac{1}{\beta'x}\right]e^{-y/(\beta'x)}, \qquad y > 0.$$

Then $E[y|x] = \beta'x$ and $\text{Var}[y|x] = (\beta'x)^2$. For this model, prove that GLS and MLE are the same, even though this distribution, like the one in Exercise 2, involves the same parameters in the conditional mean function and the disturbance variance.

10. Consider estimation of σ^2 in the generalized regression model. There is a fundamental ambiguity in regard to this "parameter," as it is merely a scaling of $E[\varepsilon\varepsilon'] = \sigma^2\Omega$. Since both components are unknown, σ^2 cannot be regarded as an estimable parameter until some scaling of Ω is assumed to remove the indeterminacy. The most convenient assumption is

$$\text{tr}(\Omega) = n.$$

The classical regression model in which $\Omega = I$ is one such case, so this provides a useful benchmark. Note that the second example in the Introduction embodies this assumption. Now consider the estimator $s^2 = e'e/(n - K)$, where e is the vector of least squares residuals.

(a) Prove that the exact expectation of s^2 is

$$E[s^2] = \frac{n\sigma^2}{n - K} - \frac{\sigma^2\text{tr}[\{X'X/(n - K)\}^{-1}\{X'\Omega X/(n - K)\}]}{n - K},$$

so that s^2 is biased. (**Hint:** As always, $e = M\varepsilon$. To obtain the expectation, use the same method as in Chapter 6.)

(b) Prove that if the assumptions in (13–6) hold,

$$\lim_{n\to\infty} E[s^2] = \sigma^2.$$

(c) To consider the issue of consistency, prove that

$$\text{plim } s^2 = \text{plim}\left(\frac{1}{n - K}\right)\sum_i \varepsilon_i^2.$$

[**Hint:** Expand $e'e/(n - K) = \varepsilon'M\varepsilon/(n - K)$.] What are the exact mean and variance of the statistic on the right-hand side? Under what conditions is plim $s^2 = \sigma^2$?

14

Heteroscedasticity

14.1. Introduction

If the disturbance variance is not constant across observations, the regression is **heteroscedastic.** In this case,

$$\text{Var}(\varepsilon_i) = \sigma_i^2, \qquad i = 1, \ldots, n.$$

We continue to assume that the disturbances are pairwise uncorrelated. Thus,

$$E[\varepsilon\varepsilon'] = \sigma^2\Omega = \begin{bmatrix} \sigma_1^2 & 0 & 0 & \cdots & 0 \\ 0 & \sigma_2^2 & 0 & \cdots & 0 \\ & & \vdots & & \\ 0 & 0 & 0 & \cdots & \sigma_n^2 \end{bmatrix}.$$

It will sometimes prove useful to write

$$\sigma_i^2 = \sigma^2\omega_i.$$

In any case, this is an arbitrary scaling. Thus, we shall use the normalization

$$\text{tr}(\Omega) = \sum_i \omega_i = n.$$

This makes the classical regression with homoscedastic disturbances a simple special case with $\omega_i = 1$. Intuitively, one might think of the ωs as weights that are scaled in such a way as to reflect only the variety in the disturbance variances. The scale factor, σ^2, then provides the overall scaling for the model of the disturbance process.

Heteroscedasticity arises in numerous applications, primarily in the analysis of cross-section data. For example, even after accounting for differences in firm sizes, we expect to observe greater variation in the profits of large firms than in those of small ones. The variance of profits might also depend upon product diversification, research and development expenditure, and industry characteristics, and thus might also vary across firms of similar sizes. In analyzing family spending patterns, we find that there is greater variation in expenditure on certain commodity groups among high-income families than low ones due to the greater discretion allowed by higher incomes.[1] Heteroscedasticity is sometimes a consequence of data aggregation. In Section 9.4, we found that the appropriate model for grouped data included a disturbance whose variance was σ^2/n_g, where n_g is the num-

---

[1] Prais and Houthakker (1955).

ber of data points in the gth group. When we analyze group means, the greater precision of an average based on a larger sample implies that the disturbance variance in the regression model will vary inversely with the group size.

EXAMPLE 14.1 _____

The data in Table 14.1 give per capita expenditure on public schools and per capita income by state in 1979.

TABLE 14.1

State	Exp.	Income	State	Exp.	Income	State	Exp.	Income
Ala.	275	6247	Alaska	821	10851	Ariz.	339	7374
Ark.	275	6183	Calif.	387	8850	Colo.	452	8001
Conn.	531	8914	Del.	424	8604	D.C.	428	10022
Fla.	316	7505	Ga.	265	6700	Hawaii	403	8380
Idaho	304	6813	Ill.	437	8745	Ind.	345	7696
Iowa	431	7873	Kans.	355	8001	Ky.	260	6615
La.	316	6640	Maine	327	6333	Md.	427	8306
Mass.	427	8063	Mich.	466	8442	Minn.	477	7847
Miss.	259	5736	Mo.	274	7342	Mont.	433	7051
Nebr.	294	7391	Nev.	359	9032	N.H.	279	7277
N.J.	423	8818	N. Mex.	388	6505	N.Y.	447	8267
N.C.	335	6607	N. Dak.	311	7478	Ohio	322	7812
Okla.	320	6951	Oreg.	397	7839	Pa.	412	7733
R.I.	342	7526	S.C.	315	6242	S. Dak.	321	6841
Tenn.	268	6489	Tex.	315	7697	Utah	417	6622
Vt.	353	6541	Va.	356	7624	Wash.	415	8450
W. Va.	320	6456	Wis.	Missing	7597	Wyo.	500	9096

Source: Data from the U.S. Department of Commerce (1979, p. 157).

Least squares regression of spending on a constant, per capita income and the square of per capita income produces the results given in Table 14.2, with the estimated standard errors given in parentheses. (Income is scaled by 10^{-4} in these and all subsequent calculations.)

TABLE 14.2 Ordinary Least Squares Results

	Constant	Income	Income^2
Coefficient	832.91	−1834.2	1587.04
Standard error	(327.3)	(829.0)	(591.1)
t ratio	2.545	−2.213	3.057
	$R^2 = 0.65534$		
	$s^2 = 3212.46$		

Individually, the coefficients appear to be statistically significant different from zero by the usual t test. The joint test based on $F = [R^2/2]/[1 - R^2)/47] = 44.68$ suggests that the coefficients are jointly significant as well. (The 1 percent critical value is 5.09.) A plot

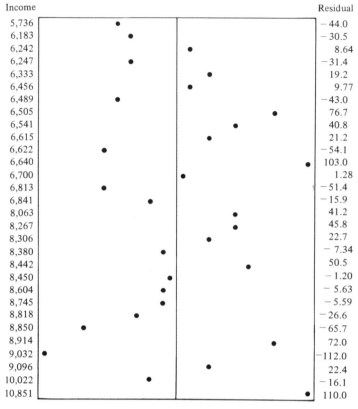

FIGURE 14.1 Plot of residuals against income.

of the residuals against income for the 15 highest and 15 lowest values of income suggests that the disturbances in this regression are somewhat heteroscedastic (Figure 14.1).

14.2. Ordinary Least Squares Estimation

The results of Section 13.2 specialize for a heteroscedastic regression. Therefore, it follows immediately that

   1. $\mathbf{b} = (\mathbf{X'X})^{-1}\mathbf{X'y}$ is unbiased.

If the disturbances are normally distributed,

   2. Conditioned on $\mathbf{X}$, $\mathbf{b}$ is normally distributed with

$$E[\mathbf{b}] = \boldsymbol{\beta}$$

   and

$$\text{Var}[\mathbf{b}] = \frac{\sigma^2}{n}\left(\frac{\mathbf{X'X}}{n}\right)^{-1}\left(\frac{\mathbf{X'\Omega X}}{n}\right)\left(\frac{\mathbf{X'X}}{n}\right)^{-1}$$

$$= \sigma^2(\mathbf{X'X})^{-1}\left(\sum_i \omega_i \mathbf{x}_i \mathbf{x}_i'\right)(\mathbf{X'X})^{-1}.$$

[See (13–3) to (13–5).] Assuming, as usual, that the regressors are well behaved, so that $(\mathbf{X}'\mathbf{X}/n)^{-1}$ converges to a positive definite matrix, we find that the mean square consistency of $\mathbf{b}$ depends on the limiting behavior of the matrix

$$\mathbf{Q}_n^* = \frac{\mathbf{X}'\boldsymbol{\Omega}\mathbf{X}}{n} = \frac{1}{n}\sum_i \omega_i \mathbf{x}_i \mathbf{x}_i'. \tag{14–1}$$

If $\mathbf{Q}_n^*$ converges to a positive definite matrix as $n \to \infty$, $\mathbf{b}$ will converge to $\boldsymbol{\beta}$ in mean square. Under most circumstances, if ω_i is finite for all i, we would expect this to be true. Note that $\mathbf{Q}_n^*$ is a weighted sum of the squares and cross-products of $\mathbf{x}$ with weights ω_i/n, which sum to one. We have already assumed that another weighted sum, $\mathbf{X}'\mathbf{X}/n$, in which the weights are $1/n$, converges to a positive definite matrix, so it would be surprising if $\mathbf{Q}_n^*$ did not converge as well. In most cases, we would expect that

3. plim $\mathbf{b} = \boldsymbol{\beta}$, that is, $\mathbf{b}$ is consistent for $\boldsymbol{\beta}$.

In addition, if the assumptions needed to ensure consistency are met, we can easily show that the least squares estimator is asymptotically normally distributed. The proof in Section 10.3.2 applies directly simply by defining $\mathbf{Q}_i$ to be $\omega_i\mathbf{x}_i\mathbf{x}_i'$ instead of $\mathbf{x}_i\mathbf{x}_i'$. If the ω_i's are not dominated by any particular element, the proof is identical. We conclude, then, that

4. $\mathbf{b} \overset{a}{\to} N\left[\boldsymbol{\beta}, \dfrac{\sigma^2}{n}\mathbf{Q}^{-1}\mathbf{Q}^*\mathbf{Q}^{-1}\right]$.

where

$$\mathbf{Q} = \text{plim } \frac{1}{n}\mathbf{X}'\mathbf{X}$$

and

$$\mathbf{Q}^* = \text{plim } \mathbf{Q}_n^*.$$

14.2.1. Inefficiency of Least Squares

It follows from our earlier results that $\mathbf{b}$ is inefficient relative to the GLS estimator, though by how much depends on the setting.

EXAMPLE 14.2 Inefficiency of Ordinary Least Squares _____

Consider a very simple model,

$$y_i = \beta x_i + \varepsilon_i$$
$$\text{Var}[\varepsilon_i] = \sigma^2 x_i^2,$$

and assume that y and x are measured as deviations from their means. The variances of the OLS and GLS estimators of β are

$$\text{Var}[b] = \sigma^2[\mathbf{X}'\mathbf{X}]^{-1}[\mathbf{X}'\boldsymbol{\Omega}\mathbf{X}][\mathbf{X}'\mathbf{X}]^{-1} = \sigma^2\frac{\Sigma_i x_i^4}{(\Sigma_i x_i^2)^2}$$

and

$$\text{Var}[\hat{\beta}] = \sigma^2[\mathbf{X}'\boldsymbol{\Omega}^{-1}\mathbf{X}]^{-1} = \frac{\sigma^2}{n}.$$

The relative (in)efficiency of OLS is

$$k = \frac{n\Sigma_i x_i^4}{(\Sigma x_i^2)^2} = \frac{[\Sigma_i x_i^4/n]}{[\Sigma_i x_i^2/n]^2}. \tag{14–2}$$

This ratio must be greater than one. Let z_i equal x_i^2. Then

$$k = \frac{(1/n)\Sigma_i z_i^2}{[(1/n)\Sigma_i z_i]^2} = \frac{(1/n)\Sigma_i z_i^2}{\bar{z}^2}.$$

But

$$\frac{1}{n}\sum_i z_i^2 = \frac{1}{n}\sum_i (z_i - \bar{z})^2 + \bar{z}^2,$$

so

$$k = \frac{(1/n)\Sigma_i(z_i - \bar{z})^2}{\bar{z}^2} + 1 > 1.$$

Therefore, in this model, ordinary least squares is never as efficient as generalized least squares.

Suppose that the x's are drawn from a distribution with zero mean and finite fourth moment. Then, by applying the Slutsky theorem and Theorem 4.3 [with (4–20)], we obtain

$$\text{plim } k = \frac{E[x_i^4]}{E[x_i^2]^2} = \frac{\mu_4}{\sigma_x^4}.$$

This is the standardized measure of kurtosis that was discussed in Chapter 3 and Section 10.5.4. Its value depends on the distribution of x_i; it is three for the normal distribution. Theoretically, k can take any value greater than one, but for economic data, it is typically between two and four.[2] This example would suggest that the gain in efficiency from GLS over OLS can be substantial. A properly constructed confidence interval based on the OLS estimates would be over 70 percent wider than one based on GLS.

14.2.2. The Estimated Covariance Matrix of b

If the type of heteroscedasticity is known with certainty, the ordinary least squares estimator is undesirable; we should use generalized least squares instead. However, the precise form of the heteroscedasticity is often unknown. In that case, generalized least squares is not usable, and we may need to salvage what we can from the results of ordinary least squares.

The conventionally estimated variance matrix for the least squares estimator, $\sigma^2(\mathbf{X}'\mathbf{X})^{-1}$, is inappropriate; the appropriate matrix is $\sigma^2(\mathbf{X}'\mathbf{X})^{-1}(\mathbf{X}'\mathbf{\Omega}\mathbf{X})(\mathbf{X}'\mathbf{X})^{-1}$. It is unlikely that these two would coincide, so the usual estimators of the standard errors are likely to be erroneous. In this section, we consider how erroneous the conventional estimator is likely to be.

---

[2] Some examples: The logs of capital and labor in the example used in Chapter 7 have $k = 2.39$ and 2.64; the same variables for the data of Example 11.5 have $k = 2.72$ and 3.15; the kurtosis of the income data in Example 14.1 is 3.40.

As usual,

$$s^2 = \frac{\mathbf{e'e}}{n-K} = \frac{\boldsymbol{\varepsilon'}\mathbf{M}\boldsymbol{\varepsilon}}{n-K},$$

where

$$\mathbf{M} = \mathbf{I} - \mathbf{X}(\mathbf{X'X})^{-1}\mathbf{X'}.$$

Expanding this, we obtain

$$s^2 = \frac{\boldsymbol{\varepsilon'}\boldsymbol{\varepsilon}}{n-K} - \frac{\boldsymbol{\varepsilon'}\mathbf{X}(\mathbf{X'X})^{-1}\mathbf{X'}\boldsymbol{\varepsilon}}{n-K}. \tag{14-3}$$

Taking the two parts separately yields

$$E\left[\frac{\boldsymbol{\varepsilon'}\boldsymbol{\varepsilon}}{n-K}\right] = \frac{\text{tr}E[\boldsymbol{\varepsilon}\boldsymbol{\varepsilon'}]}{n-K} = \frac{n\sigma^2}{n-K}. \tag{14-4}$$

[We have used the scaling, $\text{tr}(\boldsymbol{\Omega}) = n$.] In addition,

$$E\left[\frac{\boldsymbol{\varepsilon'}\mathbf{X}(\mathbf{X'X})^{-1}\mathbf{X'}\boldsymbol{\varepsilon}}{n-K}\right] = \frac{\text{tr}[E[(\mathbf{X'X})^{-1}\mathbf{X'}\boldsymbol{\varepsilon}\boldsymbol{\varepsilon'}\mathbf{X}]]}{n-K}$$

$$= \frac{\text{tr}\left[\sigma^2\left(\frac{\mathbf{X'X}}{n}\right)^{-1}\left(\frac{\mathbf{X'}\boldsymbol{\Omega}\mathbf{X}}{n}\right)\right]}{n-K} \tag{14-5}$$

$$= \frac{\sigma^2}{n-K}\text{tr}\left[\left(\frac{\mathbf{X'X}}{n}\right)^{-1}\mathbf{Q}_n^*\right],$$

where $\mathbf{Q}_n^*$ is defined in (14–1). As $n \to \infty$, the term in (14–4) will converge to σ^2. The term in (14–5) will converge to zero if $\mathbf{b}$ is consistent, as both matrices in the product are finite. Therefore,

If $\mathbf{b}$ is consistent, $\lim_{n\to\infty} E[s^2] = \sigma^2$.

It can also be shown—we leave it as an exercise—that if the fourth moment of every disturbance is finite and all of our other assumptions are met,

$$\lim_{n\to\infty} \text{Var}\left[\frac{\mathbf{e'e}}{n-K}\right] = \lim_{n\to\infty} \text{Var}\left[\frac{\boldsymbol{\varepsilon'}\boldsymbol{\varepsilon}}{n-K}\right] = 0.$$

This implies, therefore, that

If plim $\mathbf{b} = \boldsymbol{\beta}$, then plim $s^2 = \sigma^2$.

Before proceeding, it is useful to pursue this result. The normalization $\text{tr}(\boldsymbol{\Omega}) = n$ implies that

$$\sigma^2 = \overline{\sigma}^2 = \frac{1}{n}\sum_i \sigma_i^2$$

and

$$\omega_i = \frac{\sigma_i^2}{\overline{\sigma}^2}.$$

Therefore, our previous convergence result implies that the least squares estimator, s^2, converges to plim $\overline{\sigma}^2$, that is, the probability limit of the average variance of the disturbances, *assuming that this probability limit exists*. Thus, some further assumption about these variances is necessary in order to obtain the result. For example, note the particular assumption that is needed in Example 14.2. (For another application, see Exercise 7 in Chapter 16.)

The difference between the conventional estimator and the appropriate covariance matrix for **b** is

$$\text{Est. Var}[\mathbf{b}] - \text{Var}[\mathbf{b}] = s^2(\mathbf{X'X})^{-1} - \sigma^2(\mathbf{X'X})^{-1}(\mathbf{X'\Omega X})(\mathbf{X'X})^{-1}.$$

In a large sample, this is approximately equal to

$$\frac{\sigma^2}{n}\left(\frac{\mathbf{X'X}}{n}\right)^{-1}\left[\frac{\mathbf{X'X}}{n} - \frac{\mathbf{X'\Omega X}}{n}\right]\left(\frac{\mathbf{X'X}}{n}\right)^{-1}.$$

The difference between the two matrices hinges upon

$$\Delta = \frac{\mathbf{X'X}}{n} - \frac{\mathbf{X'\Omega X}}{n}$$

$$= \sum_i \left(\frac{1}{n}\right)\mathbf{x}_i\mathbf{x}_i' - \sum_i \left(\frac{\omega_i}{n}\right)\mathbf{x}_i\mathbf{x}_i', \tag{14-6}$$

where $\mathbf{x}_i'$ is the ith row of $\mathbf{X}$. These are two weighted averages of the matrices $\mathbf{S}_i = \mathbf{x}_i\mathbf{x}_i'$, using weights $1/n$ for the first term and ω_i/n for the second. The scaling $\text{tr}(\mathbf{\Omega}) = n$ implies that $\Sigma_i(\omega_i/n) = 1$. Whether the weighted average based on ω_i/n differs much from the one using $1/n$ depends on the weights. If the weights are related to the values in $\mathbf{x}_i$, the difference can be considerable. However, if the weights are uncorrelated with $\mathbf{x}_i\mathbf{x}_i'$, the weighted average will tend to equal the unweighted average.[3]

Therefore, the comparison rests on whether the heteroscedasticity is related to any of x_k or $x_j \cdot x_k$. The conclusion is that, in general, *if the heteroscedasticity is not correlated with the variables in the model, then, at least in large samples, the ordinary least squares computations, while not the optimal way to use the data, will not be misleading.*

EXAMPLE 14.3

In the heteroscedastic regression of Example 13.2, if the observations are grouped in the subsamples in a way that is unrelated to the variables in **X,** then the usual OLS estimator of Var[**b**] will, at least in large samples, provide a reliable estimate of the appropriate covariance matrix. It is worth remembering, however, that the least squares estimator will be inefficient, the more so the larger is the difference between the variances of the two groups.[4]

The preceding is a useful result, but we should not be overly optimistic. First, it remains true that ordinary least squares is demonstrably inefficient. Second, if the primary assumption of the analysis—that the heteroscedasticity is unrelated to the variables in the model, is incorrect—then the conventional standard errors may be quite far from the appropriate values.

---

[3] Suppose, for example, that **X** contains a single column, and that both x_i and ω_i are independent and identically distributed random variables. Then $\mathbf{x'x}/n$ converges to $E[\mathbf{x}_i^2]$, while $\mathbf{x'\Omega x}/n$ converges to $\text{Cov}[\omega_i, x_i^2] + E[\omega_i]E[x_i^2]$. $E[\omega_i] = 1$, so if ω and x^2 are uncorrelated, the sums have the same probability limit. An analogous argument is used earlier.

[4] Some general results, including analysis of the properties of the estimator based on estimated variances, are given in Taylor (1977).

14.2.3. Estimating the Appropriate Covariance Matrix for Ordinary Least Squares

It is clear from the preceding that heteroscedasticity has some potentially serious implications for inferences based on the results of least squares. However, the application of more appropriate estimation techniques requires a detailed formulation of Ω. It may well be that the form of the heteroscedasticity is unknown. White (1980) has shown that it is still possible to obtain an appropriate estimator for the variance of the least squares estimator, even if the heteroscedasticity is related to the variables in $\mathbf{X}$.

The covariance matrix of $\mathbf{b}$ is $(\mathbf{X'X})^{-1}[\mathbf{X'}(\sigma^2\Omega)\mathbf{X}](\mathbf{X'X})^{-1}$. It would appear that in order to compute an estimate of this matrix, we need an estimate of $\sigma^2\Omega$, which is unavailable. But what is actually required is an estimate of

$$\Sigma = \frac{\sigma^2\mathbf{X'}\Omega\mathbf{X}}{n} = \frac{1}{n}\sum_i \sigma_i^2\mathbf{x}_i\mathbf{x}_i'. \qquad (14\text{--}7)$$

White (1980b) shows that under very general conditions, the matrix

$$\mathbf{S}_0 = \frac{1}{n}\sum_i e_i^2\mathbf{x}_i\mathbf{x}_i', \qquad (14\text{--}8)$$

where e_i is the ith least squares residual, is a consistent estimator of Σ.[5] Therefore,

$$\text{Est. Var}[\mathbf{b}] = n(\mathbf{X'X})^{-1}\mathbf{S}_0(\mathbf{X'X})^{-1} \qquad (14\text{--}9)$$

can be used as an estimate of the true variance of the least squares estimator.

This is an extremely important and useful result.[6] It implies that without actually specifying the type of heteroscedasticity, we can still make appropriate inferences based on the results of least squares. This is especially useful if we are unsure of the precise nature of the heteroscedasticity (which is probably most of the time).

EXAMPLE 14.4

If the disturbances in the regression of Example 14.1 are heteroscedastic, as Figure 14.1 suggests, the ordinary least squares standard errors should be biased. Using the White estimator for the variance matrix of the least squares estimators produces the results given in Table 14.3. The corrected standard errors are considerably larger than the conventionally computed values. Indeed, neither of the slope coefficients appears to be statistically significant after the correction. The joint test of their significance can no longer be carried

TABLE 14.3

	Constant	Income	Income^2
Coefficient	832.91	−1834.2	1587.04
OLS standard error	(327.3)	(829.0)	(519.1)
White SE	(460.9)	(1243.0)	(830.0)
t ratio	1.807	−1.476	1.912

[5] See also Eicker (1967), Horn et al. (1975), and MacKinnon and White (1985).

[6] Further discussion and some refinements may be found in Cragg (1982). Cragg shows how White's observation can be extended to devise an estimator that improves on the efficiency of ordinary least squares.

out with the F test used in Example 14.1, as it relies on homoscedasticity. We can, however, use a Wald test. The statistic is

$$W = (\mathbf{Rb})'\{\mathbf{R}(\text{Est. } \text{Var}[\mathbf{b}])\mathbf{R}'\}^{-1}(\mathbf{Rb}),$$

where

$$\mathbf{R} = \begin{bmatrix} 0 & 1 & 0 \\ 0 & 0 & 1 \end{bmatrix}$$

and the covariance matrix is the White estimator. The statistic is asymptotically distributed as chi-squared with degrees of freedom equal to the number of slopes (here, two). (We use the last two elements of $\mathbf{b}$ and the lower 2×2 submatrix of the estimate of Var[$\mathbf{b}$] for the test.) Using our previous results, we obtain $W = 49.5355$, which is highly significant. The conclusion would be that, as in cases of multicollinearity, the regressors jointly explain a significant amount of variation in expenditure, but that the individual affects are obscured. Of course, income and income squared cannot vary independently, so this is not surprising.

14.3. Testing for Heteroscedasticity

Heteroscedasticity poses potentially severe problems for inferences based on least squares. However, one can rarely be certain that the data are heteroscedastic and, unfortunately, what form the heteroscedasticity takes if they are. As such, it is useful to be able to test for homoscedasticity and, if necessary, modify our estimation procedures accordingly.[7] Several types of tests have been suggested. They can be roughly grouped in descending order in terms of their generality and, as might be expected, in ascending order in terms of their power.[8]

Most of the tests for heteroscedasticity are based on the following strategy: Ordinary least squares is a consistent estimator of $\boldsymbol{\beta}$ even in the presence of heteroscedasticity. As such, the ordinary least squares residuals will mimic, albeit imperfectly because of sampling variability, the heteroscedasticity of the true disturbances. Therefore, tests designed to detect heteroscedasticity will, in most cases, be applied to the ordinary least squares residuals.

14.3.1. White's General Test

To formulate most of the available tests, it is necessary to specify, at least in rough terms, the nature of the heteroscedasticity. It would be desirable to be able to test a general hypothesis of the form

$$H_0: \sigma_i^2 = \sigma^2 \quad \text{for all } i,$$

$$H_1: \text{Not } H_0.$$

---

[7] In Section 8.5, we considered the problems of pretest estimators. In the current context, the issue is the possibility that a preliminary test for heteroscedasticity will incorrectly lead us to use weighted least squares or fail to alert us to heteroscedasticity and lead us improperly to use ordinary least squares. The situation is rather more favorable here, as both estimators are consistent in both settings. Some limited results for the case of heteroscedasticity are given by Ohtani and Toyoda (1980). Their results suggest that it is best to test first for heteroscedasticity rather than merely to assume that it is present.

[8] A recent study that examines the power of several tests for heteroscedasticity is Ali and Giacotto (1984).

In view of our earlier finding on the difficulty of estimation in a model with n unknown parameters, this is rather ambitious. Nonetheless, such a test has been devised by White (1980b). The correct covariance matrix for the least squares estimator is

$$\text{Var}[\mathbf{b}] = \sigma^2[\mathbf{X'X}]^{-1}[\mathbf{X'\Omega X}][\mathbf{X'X}]^{-1}, \qquad (14\text{--}10)$$

which, as we have seen, can be estimated by

$$\text{Est.Var}[\mathbf{b}] = [\mathbf{X'X}]^{-1}\left[\sum_i e_i^2 \mathbf{x}_i \mathbf{x}_i'\right][\mathbf{X'X}]^{-1}. \qquad (14\text{--}11)$$

The conventional estimator is

$$\mathbf{V} = s^2[\mathbf{X'X}]^{-1}. \qquad (14\text{--}12)$$

If there is no heteroscedasticity, $(14\text{--}12)$ will give a consistent estimator of $\text{Var}[\mathbf{b}]$, while if there is, it will not. White has devised a statistical test based on this observation. A simple operational version of his test is carried out by obtaining nR^2 in the regression of e_i^2 on a constant and all unique variables in $\mathbf{x} \otimes \mathbf{x}$. The statistic is asymptotically distributed as chi-squared with $P - 1$ degrees of freedom, where P is the number of regressors in the regression, not including the constant.

EXAMPLE 14.5 _____

For the expenditure data of Example 14.1, the regression of the squares of the least squares residuals on a constant, income, and income squared, cubed, and to the fourth power produces an R^2 of 0.42314. The chi-squared statistic is, therefore, $50(0.42314) = 21.157$, which is highly significant. The 95 percent critical value for chi-squared [3] is 7.81.

_____

The White test is extremely general. In order to carry it out, we need not make any specific assumptions about the nature of the heteroscedasticity. Although this is a virtue, it is, at the same time, a potentially serious shortcoming. The test may reveal heteroscedasticity, but it may instead simply identify some other specification error (such as the omission of x^2 from a simple regression).[9] Except in the context of a specific problem, little can be said about the power of this test; it may be very low against some alternatives. In addition, unlike some of the other tests we shall discuss, the White test is _nonconstructive_. If we reject the hypothesis of homoscedasticity, the result of the test gives no indication of what to do next.

14.3.2. The Goldfeld–Quandt Test

By narrowing our focus somewhat, we can obtain a more powerful test. Two tests that are relatively general are the Goldfeld–Quandt (1965) test and the Breusch–Pagan (1979) Lagrange multiplier test.

For the Goldfeld–Quandt test, we assume that the observations can be divided into two groups in such a way that under the hypothesis of homoscedasticity, the disturbance variances would be the same in the two groups, while under the alternative, the disturbance variances would differ systematically. The most favorable case for this test would be the groupwise heteroscedastic model of Section 14.3.4 and Example 14.9 or a model such

_____

[9] Thursby (1982) considers this issue in detail.

as $\sigma_i^2 = \sigma^2 x_i^2$ for some variable, x. By ranking the observations based on this x, we can separate the observations into those with high and low variances. The test is applied by dividing the sample into two groups with n_1 and n_2 observations. In order to obtain statistically independent variance estimators, the regression is then estimated separately with the two sets of observations. The test statistic is

$$F[n_1 - K, n_2 - K] = \frac{\mathbf{e}_1'\mathbf{e}_1}{\mathbf{e}_2'\mathbf{e}_2},$$

where we assume that the disturbance variance is larger in the first sample. (If not, reverse the subscripts.) Under the null hypothesis of homoscedasticity, this has an F distribution with $n_1 - K$ and $n_2 - K$ degrees of freedom. The sample value can be referred to the standard F table to carry out the test, with a large value leading to rejection of the null hypothesis.

In order to increase the power of the test, Goldfeld and Quandt suggest that a number of observations in the middle of the sample be omitted. However, the more observations are dropped, the smaller will be the degrees of freedom for estimation in each group, which will tend to diminish the power of the test. As a consequence, the choice of how many central observations to drop is largely subjective. Evidence by Harvey and Phillips (1974) suggests that no more than a third of the observations should be dropped. If the disturbances are normally distributed, the Goldfeld–Quandt statistic is exactly distributed as F under the null hypothesis, and the nominal size of the test is correct. If not, the F distribution is inappropriate and some alternative method with known large-sample properties, such as White's test, is called for.

EXAMPLE 14.6 Goldfeld–Quandt Test _____

We sort the expenditure data of Example 14.1 on the basis of income and then fit separate regressions for observations 1–17 and 34–51 (omitting the 49th). The sums of squared residuals in the two regressions are 27,096.50 and 52,685.18, so the test statistic is

$$F[14, 14] = \frac{52,685.18}{27,096.50}$$

$$= 1.944.$$

The 5 percent critical value from the F table is 2.49, so we would not reject the hypothesis of homoscedasticity at this level of significance on the basis of this test. Based on a 25/25 split of the sample, the sums of squares are 44,598.68 and 85,526.35, giving an $F[22, 22]$ of 1.918. The 5 percent critical value is 2.048, so this is insignificant as well.

14.3.3. The Breusch–Pagan/Godfrey Test

The Goldfeld–Quandt test has been found to be reasonably powerful when we are able to identify correctly the variable to use in the sample separation. However, this requirement does limit its generality. For example, several of the models we will consider allow the disturbance variance to vary with a set of regressors. [See (14–18) to (14–23).] Breusch and Pagan[10] have devised a Lagrange multiplier test of the hypothesis that $\sigma_i^2 = \sigma^2 f(\alpha_0 + \boldsymbol{\alpha}'\mathbf{z}_i)$, where $\mathbf{z}$ is a vector of independent variables. The model is homoscedastic if $\boldsymbol{\alpha} = \mathbf{0}$.

[10] Op.cit.

The test can be carried out with a simple regression,

$$\text{LM} = \tfrac{1}{2} \text{ explained sum of squares} \tag{14-13}$$

$$\text{in the regression of } \frac{e_i^2}{\mathbf{e}'\mathbf{e}/n} \text{ on } \mathbf{z}.$$

For computation purposes, let $\mathbf{Z}$ be the $n \times (P + 1)$ matrix of observations on $(1, \mathbf{z}_i)$ and let $\mathbf{g}$ be the vector of observations on $g_i = e_i^2/(\mathbf{e}'\mathbf{e}/n)$. Then

$$\text{LM} = \tfrac{1}{2}(\mathbf{g}'\mathbf{Z}(\mathbf{Z}'\mathbf{Z})^{-1}\mathbf{Z}'\mathbf{g} - n).$$

Under the null hypothesis of homoscedasticity, LM is asymptotically distributed as chi-squared with degrees of freedom equal to the number of variables in $\mathbf{z}$. This test can be applied to a variety of models, including, for example, those examined in (14–18) to (14–23).[11]

It has been argued that the Breusch–Pagan Lagrange multiplier test is quite sensitive to the assumption of normality. Koenkar (1981) and Koenkar and Bassett (1982) suggest that the computation of LM be based on a more robust estimator of the variance of ε_i^2,

$$V = \frac{1}{n} \sum_i \left(e_i^2 - \frac{\mathbf{e}'\mathbf{e}}{n} \right)^2.$$

The variance of ε_i^2 is not necessarily equal to $2\sigma^4$ if ε_i is not normally distributed. Let $\mathbf{u}$ equal $(e_1^2, e_2^2, \ldots, e_n^2)$ and $\mathbf{i}$ be an $n \times 1$ column of ones. Then $\bar{u} = \mathbf{e}'\mathbf{e}/n$. With this change, the computation becomes

$$\text{LM} = \left(\frac{1}{V} \right)(\mathbf{u} - \bar{u}\mathbf{i})'\mathbf{Z}(\mathbf{Z}'\mathbf{Z})^{-1}\mathbf{Z}'(\mathbf{u} - \bar{u}\mathbf{i}).$$

Under normality, this modified statistic will have the same asymptotic distribution as the Breusch–Pagan statistic, but absent normality, there is some evidence that it provides a more powerful test. Waldman (1983) has shown that if the variables in $\mathbf{z}$ are the same as those used for the White test described earlier, the two tests are algebraically the same.

EXAMPLE 14.7

For the school spending data, the Breusch–Pagan Lagrange multiplier statistic and the corrected version of Koenkar and Basset are 18.912 and 7.916, respectively.[12] These are both statistically significant. The results thus far are mixed. Most of the tests strongly suggest that the disturbance is heteroscedastic, with the Goldfeld–Quandt test standing as an exception.

14.3.4. Testing for Groupwise Heteroscedasticity

The more specific we can be about the form of the heteroscedasticity, the more powerful a test we can devise. For example, for the groupwise heteroscedasticity model of Example 14.9, under normality the likelihood ratio test will be a most powerful consistent test. The log-likelihood function, assuming homoscedasticity, is

$$\ln L_0 = -\frac{n}{2}(\ln(2\pi) + \ln \sigma^2) - \frac{1}{2\sigma^2} \sum_i \varepsilon_i^2,$$

---

[11] The model $\sigma_i^2 = \sigma^2 \exp(\boldsymbol{\alpha}'\mathbf{z}_i)$ is one of these cases. In analyzing this model specifically, Harvey (1976) derived the same test statistic.

[12] Waldman's result does not apply here because $\mathbf{z}$ does not contain the third or fourth powers of income.

where $n = \Sigma_g n_g$ is the total number of observations. Under the alternative hypothesis of heteroscedasticity across G groups,

$$\ln L_1 = -\frac{n}{2}\ln(2\pi) - \frac{1}{2}\sum_g n_g \ln \sigma_g^2 - \frac{1}{2}\sum_g \left(\frac{1}{\sigma_g^2}\sum_i \varepsilon_{ig}^2\right).$$

The maximum likelihood estimators of σ^2 and σ_g^2 are

$$s^2 = \frac{\mathbf{e'e}}{n} \quad \text{and} \quad s_g^2 = \frac{\mathbf{e_g'e_g}}{n_g},$$

respectively. The maximum likelihood estimator of $\boldsymbol{\beta}$ in Example 13.2 is to be used for the slope vector.[13] If we evaluate $\ln L_0$ and $\ln L_1$ at these estimates, the likelihood ratio test statistic for homoscedasticity is

$$-2(\ln L_0 - \ln L_1) = n \ln s^2 - \sum_g n_g \ln s_g^2.$$

Under the null hypothesis, the statistic is asymptotically distributed as chi-squared with $G - 1$ degrees of freedom.

14.3.5. Tests Based on Regressions—Glesjer's Test

Section 14.5 considers three specific formulations in the class of models encompassed by the Lagrange multiplier test:

1. $\text{Var}[\varepsilon_i] = \sigma^2[\boldsymbol{\alpha}'\mathbf{z}_i]$.
2. $\text{Var}[\varepsilon_i] = \sigma^2[\boldsymbol{\alpha}'\mathbf{z}_i]^2$.
3. $\text{Var}[\varepsilon_i] = \sigma^2\exp[\boldsymbol{\alpha}'\mathbf{z}_i]$.

In each case, a preliminary regression is computed to estimate $\boldsymbol{\alpha}$ for use in an FGLS estimator of $\boldsymbol{\beta}$. A joint test of the hypothesis that the slopes are all zero in each preceding case would be equivalent to a test of homoscedasticity. In particular, let w_i be $e_i^2, |e_i|$, or $\ln|e_i|$. A Wald statistic can be used in each model to carry out the test. This would be

$$W = \mathbf{a'}\{\text{Var}[\mathbf{a}]\}^{-1}\mathbf{a}.$$

Under the null hypothesis of homoscedasticity, W is asymptotically distributed as chi-squared with P degrees of freedom, where P is the number of variables in $\mathbf{z}$, excluding the constant term. The appropriate variance matrix to use will differ in the three models; however, an asymptotically valid expedient would be to use the White estimator in (14–9) (which will now involve the fourth powers of the residuals).[14] Each of these tests is likely to be more powerful than an omnibus test such as White's or Breusch–Pagan's *in the specific context of its regression model*.

EXAMPLE 14.8

The preceding Wald statistics for the three specifications given, based on White's covariance matrix, are 9.692, 5.678, and 11.096. The critical value from the table of chi-squared with two degrees of freedom (for income and income squared) is 5.99.

---

[13] It has been suggested that for convenience, we may use the OLS slope vectors within each group instead. If the sample is large enough, this will be valid. But in a small sample, if the information that the slope vector is the same in all groups is not used, the power of the test is likely to be reduced.

[14] See Fomby et al. (1984, pp. 176–187). Harvey (1976) derives an explicit expression for Var[a] for the model in Example 14.15.

14.4. Generalized Least Squares When Ω Is Known

Having tested for and found evidence of heteroscedasticity, the logical next step is to revise the estimation technique to account for it. The GLS estimator is

$$\hat{\beta} = (X'\Omega^{-1}X)^{-1}X'\Omega^{-1}y.$$

Consider the most general case,

$$\text{Var}[\varepsilon_i] = \sigma_i^2 = \sigma^2 \omega_i.$$

Then

$$\Omega = \begin{bmatrix} \omega_1 & 0 & 0 & \cdots & 0 \\ 0 & \omega_2 & 0 & \cdots & 0 \\ & & \vdots & & \\ 0 & 0 & 0 & \cdots & \omega_n \end{bmatrix}.$$

so Ω^{-1} is a diagonal matrix whose ith diagonal element is $1/\omega_i$. The GLS estimator is obtained by regressing

$$Py = \begin{bmatrix} y_1/\sqrt{\omega_1} \\ y_2/\sqrt{\omega_2} \\ \vdots \\ y_n/\sqrt{\omega_n} \end{bmatrix} \quad \text{on} \quad PX = \begin{bmatrix} x_1/\sqrt{\omega_1} \\ x_2\sqrt{\omega_2} \\ \vdots \\ x_n/\sqrt{\omega_n} \end{bmatrix}.$$

Applying ordinary least squares to the transformed model, we obtain the **weighted least squares (WLS)** estimator.

$$\hat{\beta} = \left[\sum_i w_i x_i x_i' \right]^{-1} \left[\sum_i w_i x_i y_i \right],$$

where

$$w_i = \frac{1}{\omega_i}. \quad 15$$

The logic of the computation is that observations with smaller variances receive a larger weight in the computations of the sums and, therefore, have greater influence in the estimates obtained.

EXAMPLE 14.9 Groupwise Heteroscedasticity

Consider again the groupwise heteroscedastic regression model of Example 13.2. Assume that the variances are known. The GLS estimator is

$$\hat{\beta} = \left[\sum_g \left(\frac{1}{\sigma_g^2} \right) X_g' X_g \right]^{-1} \left[\sum_g \left(\frac{1}{\sigma_g^2} \right) X_g' y_g \right].$$

---

[15] The weights are often denoted $w_i = 1/\sigma_i^2$. This is consistent with the equivalent $\hat{\beta} = [X'(\sigma^2\Omega)^{-1}X]^{-1}X'(\sigma^2\Omega)^{-1}y$. The σ^2's cancel, leaving the expression given previously.

Since $\mathbf{X}_g'\mathbf{y}_g = \mathbf{X}_g'\mathbf{X}_g\mathbf{b}_g$, where $\mathbf{b}_g$ is the OLS estimator in the gth subset of observations,

$$\hat{\boldsymbol{\beta}} = \left[\sum_g \left(\frac{1}{\sigma_g^2} \right) \mathbf{X}_g'\mathbf{X}_g \right]^{-1} \left[\sum_g \left(\frac{1}{\sigma_g^2} \right) \mathbf{X}_g'\mathbf{X}_g\mathbf{b}_g \right]$$

$$= \left[\sum_g \mathbf{V}_g \right]^{-1} \left[\sum_g \mathbf{V}_g\mathbf{b}_g \right].$$

This is a matrix weighted average of the G least squares estimators. The weighting matrices are $\mathbf{W}_g = \left[\sum_g (\mathrm{Var}(\mathbf{b}_g))^{-1} \right]^{-1} \left[\mathrm{Var}(\mathbf{b}_g) \right]^{-1}$. The estimator with the smaller variance matrix therefore receives the larger weight.

Suppose, in addition, that $\mathbf{X}_g$ is the same in every group. This might occur in repeated sampling of experimental data. With a common $\mathbf{X}$ matrix, the GLS estimator reduces to

$$\hat{\boldsymbol{\beta}} = \sum_g w_g\mathbf{b}_g,$$

where

$$w_g = \frac{1/\sigma_g^2}{\sum_g 1/\sigma_g^2}.$$

Once again, the weights are larger for the estimators with the smaller variances.

A common specification is that the variance is proportional to one of the regressors or its square. Our earlier example of family expenditures is one in which the relevant variable is usually income. Similarly, in studies of firm profits, the dominant variable is typically assumed to be firm size. If

$$\sigma_i^2 = \sigma^2 x_{ik}^2,$$

the transformed regression model for GLS is

$$\frac{y}{x_k} = \beta_k + \beta_1 \left[\frac{x_1}{x_k} \right] + \beta_2 \left[\frac{x_2}{x_k} \right] + \cdots + \frac{\varepsilon}{x_k}. \tag{14–14}$$

If the variance is proportional to x_k instead of x_k^2, the weight applied to each observation is $1/\sqrt{x_k}$ instead of $1/x_k$.

EXAMPLE 14.10

Weighted least squares estimates of the model in (14–14) are given in Table 14.4. Estimated standard errors are shown in parentheses.

TABLE 14.4 WLS Results

	Constant	Income	Income^2
Least squares	832.91	−1834.20	1587.04
	(327.3)	(829.0)	(519.1)
$\mathrm{Var}(\varepsilon) = \sigma^2$ income	746.36	−1612.25	1447.46
	(328.2)	(844.8)	(537.7)
$\mathrm{Var}(\varepsilon) = \sigma^2$ income^2	664.58	−1399.28	1311.35
	(333.6)	(872.1)	(563.7)

In (14–14), the coefficient on x_k becomes the constant term. But if the variance is proportional to any power of x_k other than two, the transformed model will no longer contain a constant, and we encounter the problem of interpreting R^2 mentioned earlier. For example, no conclusion should be drawn if the R^2 in the regression of y/z on $1/z$ and x/z is higher than that in the regression of y on a constant and x for any z, including x. The good fit of the weighted regression might be due to the presence of $1/z$ on both sides of the equality.

14.5. Estimation When Ω Contains Unknown Parameters

The general form of the heteroscedastic regression model has too many parameters to estimate by ordinary methods. Typically, the model is restricted by formulating $\sigma^2\Omega$ as a function of a few parameters, as in $\sigma_i^2 = \sigma^2 x_i^\alpha$ or $\sigma_i^2 = \sigma^2[\alpha'\mathbf{x}_i]^2$. GLS based on a consistent estimate of Ω is asymptotically equivalent to GLS, and FGLS based on a maximum likelihood estimate of Ω is the maximum likelihood estimator if Ω does not contain any elements of $\boldsymbol{\beta}$. As in the general case, however, the new problem introduced is that we must first find consistent estimates of the unknown parameters in Ω. Two methods are typically used for models of heteroscedasticity, two-step GLS and maximum likelihood.

14.5.1. Two-Step Estimation

For the heteroscedastic regression model, the GLS estimator is

$$\hat{\boldsymbol{\beta}} = \left[\sum_i \left(\frac{1}{\sigma_i^2}\right)\mathbf{x}_i\mathbf{x}_i'\right]^{-1}\left[\sum_i \left(\frac{1}{\sigma_i^2}\right)\mathbf{x}_i y_i\right].$$

The two-step estimators are computed by first obtaining estimates $\hat{\sigma}_i^2$, usually by some function of least squares residuals, and then

$$\hat{\hat{\boldsymbol{\beta}}} = \left[\sum_i \left(\frac{1}{\hat{\sigma}_i^2}\right)\mathbf{x}_i\mathbf{x}_i'\right]^{-1}\left[\sum_i \left(\frac{1}{\hat{\sigma}_i^2}\right)\mathbf{x}_i y_i\right].$$

The OLS estimates of $\boldsymbol{\beta}$, while inefficient, are still consistent. As such, the least squares residuals,

$$e_i = y_i - \mathbf{x}_i'\mathbf{b}$$

$$= y_i - \mathbf{x}_i'\boldsymbol{\beta} - \mathbf{x}_i'(\mathbf{b} - \boldsymbol{\beta}) \tag{14–15}$$

$$= \varepsilon_i + v_i,$$

have the same limiting distribution as the true disturbances, ε_i. For the true ε_i's, $E[\varepsilon_i^2] = \sigma_i^2$. We can form a regression,

$$\varepsilon_i^2 = \sigma_i^2 + u_i, \tag{14–16}$$

where u_i is the difference between ε_i^2 and its expectation. For the least squares residual,

$$e_i^2 = \varepsilon_i^2 + (\mathbf{x}_i'(\mathbf{b} - \boldsymbol{\beta}))^2 - 2\varepsilon_i\mathbf{x}_i'(\mathbf{b} - \boldsymbol{\beta}).$$

The latter two terms will be negligible asymptotically, so that, at least approximately,[16]

$$e_i^2 = \sigma_i^2 + v_i. \tag{14-17}$$

A general procedure suggested by this is to treat the variance function as a regression model and use the squares of the least squares residuals as the dependent variable to estimate the parameters. If $\mathrm{Var}(\varepsilon_i) = \sigma_i^2(\boldsymbol{\alpha}, \mathbf{z}_i)$, the (possibly nonlinear) regression of the squared residuals on $\mathbf{z}$ will provide a consistent estimate of $\boldsymbol{\alpha}$.[17] With estimates of the unknown parameters in $\boldsymbol{\Omega}$ in hand, we may then use FGLS.

To take a particularly straightforward case, suppose that

$$\sigma_i^2 = \boldsymbol{\alpha}'\mathbf{z}_i.^{[18]}$$

or

$$e_i^2 \simeq \boldsymbol{\alpha}'\mathbf{z}_i + v_i. \tag{14-18}$$

This is not a classical regression model; in a finite sample, v_i has a nonzero mean, is heteroscedastic, and is correlated across observations because each v_i is constructed from the same estimate of $\boldsymbol{\beta}$. However, as shown by Amemiya, the first and third of these difficulties are absent in large samples—v_i has a zero mean and is nonautocorrelated—so we can expect the ordinary least squares estimator of $\boldsymbol{\alpha}$ to be consistent. That is all that is required for the efficient estimation of $\boldsymbol{\beta}$ by FGLS using $\boldsymbol{\Omega}(\hat{\boldsymbol{\alpha}})$.

All of the general results obtained earlier apply directly. The small-sample properties of such an estimator are generally unknown. Because v_i is heteroscedastic, the OLS estimator of $\boldsymbol{\alpha}$ is inefficient. A more efficient estimator could be obtained in some cases.[19] The degree to which this would improve the sampling properties of the FGLS estimator remains to be determined. Asymptotically, it makes no difference, but the finite-sample properties remain uncertain.

EXAMPLE 14.11

In applying the preceding to the school expenditure data of Example 14.1, we find, first, that least squares regression of the squared residuals on a constant, income, and income squared produces the results shown in Table 14.5. The large difference between the OLS and White estimators of the standard errors is to be expected, given the heteroscedasticity in v_i. These estimates are then used to compute the elements of $\boldsymbol{\Omega}$.[20] We then obtain the FGLS estimates in Table 14.6.

TABLE 14.5 OLS Regression Using the Squared OLS Residuals

	Constant	**Income**	**Income^2**
Coefficient	59,218.80	−161,960	113,663
Standard error	(22,790)	(58,190)	(36,440)
White's SE	(28,170)	(77,000)	(52,225)

[16] Formal analysis may be found in Amemiya (1985).

[17] Jobson and Fuller (1980) prove a somewhat more general version.

[18] This case is analyzed at length in Amemiya (1985, pp. 203–207, and 1977a).

[19] See Fomby et al. (1984, pp. 177–186) and Amemiya (1985).

[20] This particular specification, unfortunately, does not preclude negative variances. For these data, none of the predicted variances were negative.

TABLE 14.6 Generalized Least Squares
Based on $\text{Var}[\varepsilon_i] = \sigma^2(\alpha'z_i)$

	Constant	**Income**	**Income^2**
Coefficient	709.05	−1506.40	1374.15
Standard error	(451.9)	(1199.0)	(790.8)

The preceding general results have been extended to other functional forms, most commonly

$$\text{Var}[\varepsilon_i] = \sigma^2(\alpha'\mathbf{z}_i)^2, \tag{14–19}$$

$$\text{Var}[\varepsilon_i] = \sigma^2\exp(\alpha'\mathbf{z}_i), \tag{14–20}$$

where $\mathbf{z}$ is a set of independent variables that may or may not coincide with $\mathbf{x}$.[21] In (14–19), the standard deviation, rather than the variance, is a linear function of the exogenous variables. In this case, a regression of the absolute values of the residuals on $\mathbf{z}$ provides the estimates of α required to compute the FGLS estimator.[22] To estimate α in (14–20), we would regress $\ln(e^2)$ on a constant and $\mathbf{z}$. (See Example 14.15.)

A special case of (14–19) is a model in which the variance is proportional to the square of the mean:

$$y_i = \mathbf{x}_i'\boldsymbol{\beta} + \varepsilon_i,$$
$$\text{Var}[\varepsilon_i] = \sigma^2[\mathbf{x}_i'\boldsymbol{\beta}]^2. \tag{14–21}$$

This differs from the earlier models in that no secondary regression of the residuals on $\mathbf{x}$ is required to estimate the parameters of the variance. We can use the fitted values from the least squares regression (or, if necessary, their absolute values) as the weights for weighted least squares. However, for this case, FGLS is not fully efficient, as $\boldsymbol{\beta}$ appears in Ω as well as the regression.[23]

EXAMPLE 14.12

Continuing our earlier example, weighted least squares using the absolute values of the fitted values from the first regression produces the results given in Table 14.7.

TABLE 14.7 WLS with the Variance
Proportional to the Square of the Mean

	Constant	**Income**	**Income^2**
Coefficient	59.08	−1195.15	1172.22
Standard error	(371.0)	(981.2)	(642.7)

[21] An empirical study employing both of these models is Rutemiller and Bowers (1968).

[22] The estimator was devised by Glesjer (1969). Harvey (1976) shows that this estimator is consistent for $c\alpha$, where c is a constant that depends on the distribution of ε_i. This implies that the matrix Ω is consistently estimated only up to the scale factor, c^2. Since this will fall out of the GLS estimator anyway, the scaling is of no consequence. Additional discussion may be found in Amemiya (1985).

[23] See Theil (1971), Prais and Houthakker (1955), and Amemiya (1973a). Amemiya examines maximum likelihood estimation in a model in which FGLS is efficient in spite of this complication.

In model (14–20), if the variables in $\mathbf{z}$ are logs, the model is equivalent to

$$\sigma_i^2 = \sigma^2 \prod_m \mathbf{z}_{im}^{\alpha_m}.$$

A special case, with a single variable, is

$$\sigma_i^2 = \sigma^2 z_i^{\alpha}. \tag{14–22}$$

If $\alpha = 0$, the disturbance is homoscedastic.[24] The models in Example 14.10 are special cases with α equal to one and two. For this model, the regression used to estimate the variances is

$$\ln e_i^2 \simeq \ln \sigma^2 + \boldsymbol{\alpha}'\mathbf{z}_i + v_i. \tag{14–23}$$

EXAMPLE 14.13

We use (14–23) to specify the variance of the disturbance in Example 14.1. The regression of the log of the squared residual on a constant, income, and income squared is given in Table 14.8.

TABLE 14.8 Regression of $\ln e^2$ on a Constant, Income, Income²

	Constant	**Income**	**Income²**
Coefficient	21.858	−44.277	30.863
Standard error	(16.04)	(40.63)	(25.44)

Then the WLS regression, where the estimated variances are the exponents of the fitted values from the previous regression, is shown in Table 14.9. With this specification, the estimated standard errors of the coefficients have become quite large. However, as before, although neither coefficient is statistically significant by the usual test, the Wald statistic for testing their joint significance is 39.291, which far exceeds the tabled critical value of 5.99 for a size of 5 percent.

TABLE 14.9 WLS Regression Based on $\ln \sigma_i^2 = \ln \sigma^2 + \Sigma_m \alpha_m z_{im}$

	Constant	**Income**	**Income²**
Coefficient	488.43	−912.69	980.71
Standard error	(529.1)	(1423.0)	(950.3)

14.5.2. Maximum Likelihood Estimation

The log-likelihood function for a sample of normally distributed observations would be

$$\ln L = -\frac{n}{2}\ln(2\pi) - \frac{1}{2}\sum_i\left[\ln \sigma_i^2 + \frac{1}{\sigma_i^2}(y_i - \boldsymbol{\beta}'\mathbf{x}_i)^2\right]. \tag{14–24}$$

This can, in principle, be maximized directly, for example, using one of the methods discussed in Chapter 12. This is likely to be rather involved for most very general models. But if the variance function is relatively uncomplicated, a simple search procedure may simplify things considerably.

---

[24] See Park (1966).

EXAMPLE 14.14

Consider maximum likelihood estimation of the model in (14–22).[25] In this case, where z_i is income,

$$\sigma_i^2 = \sigma^2 z_i^\alpha$$

involves only a single new parameter whose value will probably fall in a reasonably small range, say, zero to three. For this model,

$$\ln L = -\frac{n}{2}[\ln(2\pi) + \ln \sigma^2] - \frac{\alpha}{2} \sum_i \ln z_i - \frac{1}{2\sigma^2} \sum_i \frac{\varepsilon_i^2}{z_i^\alpha}$$

$$\frac{\partial \ln L}{\partial \boldsymbol{\beta}} = \sum_i \mathbf{x}_i \frac{\varepsilon_i}{\sigma^2 z_i^\alpha}$$

$$\frac{\partial \ln L}{\partial \sigma^2} = -\frac{n}{2\sigma^2} + \frac{1}{2\sigma^4} \sum_i \frac{\varepsilon_i^2}{z_i^\alpha} \qquad (14\text{--}25)$$

$$\frac{\partial \ln L}{\partial \alpha} = -\frac{1}{2} \sum_i \ln z_i + \frac{1}{2\sigma^2} \sum_i \frac{\varepsilon_i^2 \ln z_i}{z_i^\alpha}.$$

For a given value of α, we estimate $\boldsymbol{\beta}$ and σ^2 by generalized least squares, using, as weights, z_i^α. The maximum of the likelihood function can be found by searching over values of α and choosing the one that, with the associated values of $\boldsymbol{\beta}$ and σ^2, maximizes the likelihood function.

TABLE 14.10

α	$\ln L$
0.0	-271.2698
0.5	-270.3565
1.0	-269.6020
1.5	-269.0048
2.0	-268.5618
2.5	-268.2684
3.0	-268.1186
3.1	-268.1053
3.2	-268.0974
3.3	-268.0948
3.4	-268.0975
3.5	-268.1055

For the school spending data, the values of the log likelihood for various values of α are as listed in Table 14.10. (Normally, one would do a more precise search or use an iterative technique such as the one discussed in Example 14.15 to estimate α. The maximizer is $\alpha = 3.2948$.) Denoting the full parameter vector by $\boldsymbol{\gamma}$, we use

$$\left(-E\left[\frac{\partial^2 \ln L}{\partial \boldsymbol{\gamma} \, \partial \boldsymbol{\gamma}'}\right]\right)^{-1} = \begin{bmatrix} (1/\sigma^2)\Sigma_i \mathbf{x}_i \mathbf{x}_i'/z_i^\alpha & \mathbf{0} & \mathbf{0} \\ \mathbf{0}' & n/2\sigma^4 & (1/(2\sigma^2))\Sigma_i \ln z_i \\ \mathbf{0}' & (1/(2\sigma^2))\Sigma_i \ln z_i & (1/2)\Sigma_i(\ln z_i)^2 \end{bmatrix}^{-1}$$

[25] An empirical study using this model is Lahiri and Egy (1981).

to estimate the asymptotic covariance matrix for the maximum likelihood estimator. The sample estimate is

$$
\begin{bmatrix}
112{,}606 \\
-298{,}867 & 798{,}495 \\
198{,}404 & -523{,}996 & 346{,}735 \\
0 & 0 & 0 & 9{,}959{,}705 \\
0 & 0 & 0 & 4{,}269.91 & 2.24049.
\end{bmatrix}
$$

The square roots of the diagonal elements give the estimated asymptotic standard errors. The full set of maximum likelihood estimates is given in Table 14.11.

TABLE 14.11

	Estimate	Standard Error	t ratio
Constant	560.72	335.6	1.67
Income	-1124.18	893.6	-1.26
Income^2	1132.18	588.5	1.92
σ^2	6749.71	3155.9	2.14
α	3.3	1.497	2.20

We now consider more general models of heteroscedasticity. For simplicity, let

$$
\sigma_i^2 = \sigma^2 f_i(\boldsymbol{\theta}), \tag{14–26}
$$

where $\boldsymbol{\theta}$ is the vector of unknown parameters in $\boldsymbol{\Omega}$ and $f_i(\boldsymbol{\theta})$ is indexed by i to indicate that it is a function of $\mathbf{z}_i$. Assume, as well, that no elements of $\boldsymbol{\beta}$ appear in $\boldsymbol{\theta}$. The log-likelihood function becomes

$$
\ln L = -\frac{n}{2}[\ln(2\pi) + \ln \sigma^2] - \frac{1}{2}\sum_i \ln f_i(\boldsymbol{\theta}) - \frac{1}{2\sigma^2}\sum_i \left[\frac{1}{f_i(\boldsymbol{\theta})}\right](y_i - \boldsymbol{\beta}'\mathbf{x}_i)^2. \tag{14–27}
$$

For convenience in what follows, substitute ε_i for $(y_i - \boldsymbol{\beta}'\mathbf{x}_i)$, denote $f_i(\boldsymbol{\theta})$ as just f_i and denote the vector of derivatives, $\partial f_i(\boldsymbol{\theta})/\partial\boldsymbol{\theta}$, as $\mathbf{g}_i$. Then the derivatives of the log-likelihood function are

$$
\frac{\partial \ln L}{\partial \boldsymbol{\beta}} = \sum_i \mathbf{x}_i \frac{\varepsilon_i}{\sigma^2 f_i}
$$

$$
\frac{\partial \ln L}{\partial \sigma^2} = -\frac{n}{2\sigma^2} + \frac{1}{2\sigma^4}\sum_i \frac{\varepsilon_i^2}{f_i} \tag{14–28}
$$

$$
\frac{\partial \ln L}{\partial \boldsymbol{\theta}} = -\frac{1}{2}\sum_i \mathbf{g}_i \frac{1}{f_i} + \frac{1}{2\sigma^2}\sum_i \mathbf{g}_i \frac{\varepsilon_i^2}{f_i^2}
$$

$$
= \frac{1}{2}\sum_i \left(\frac{\varepsilon_i^2}{\sigma^2 f_i} - 1\right)\frac{1}{f_i}\mathbf{g}_i.
$$

Since $E[\varepsilon_i] = 0$ and $E[\varepsilon_i^2] = \sigma^2 f_i$, it is clear that all derivatives have expectation zero, as required. The maximum likelihood estimators are those values of $\boldsymbol{\beta}$, σ^2, and $\boldsymbol{\theta}$ that simultaneously equate these derivatives to zero. The equations are generally highly non-linear and will often require an iterative solution.

Note that the necessary conditions are identical to those for generalized least squares if θ is known. Likewise, for a given value of θ, the necessary condition for σ^2 gives the familiar prescription, $1/n$ times the normalized sum of squared residuals. At the same time, conditioned on current values of β and σ^2, the third set of first-order conditions is a set of nonlinear equations whose solution will depend on the problem at hand.

Let $\mathbf{G}$ be the $n \times M$ matrix whose ith row is $\partial f_i / \partial \theta'$, and let $\mathbf{i}$ be an $n \times 1$ column vector of ones. From (14–26), Ω is a diagonal matrix with ith diagonal element equal to f_i. The asymptotic covariance matrix for the maximum likelihood estimator in this model is

$$
\left(-E\left[\frac{\partial^2 \ln L}{\partial \gamma\, \partial \gamma'} \right] \right)^{-1} =
\begin{bmatrix}
(1/\sigma^2)\mathbf{X}'\Omega^{-1}\mathbf{X} & \mathbf{0} & \mathbf{0} \\
\mathbf{0}' & n/2\sigma^4 & (1/(2\sigma^2))\mathbf{i}'\Omega^{-1}\mathbf{G} \\
\mathbf{0}' & (1/(2\sigma^2))\mathbf{G}'\Omega^{-1}\mathbf{i} & (1/2)\mathbf{G}'\Omega^{-2}\mathbf{G}
\end{bmatrix}^{-1} ,
$$
$$(14\text{–}29)$$

where $\gamma' = [\beta', \sigma^2, \theta']$. (The proof is considered in the exercises.) For computational purposes, the Berndt et al. estimator,[26]

$$
\hat{\mathbf{V}} = \left[\sum_i \hat{\mathbf{d}}_i \hat{\mathbf{d}}_i' \right]^{-1}
$$

where

$$
\mathbf{d}_i =
\begin{bmatrix}
\mathbf{x}_i \dfrac{\varepsilon_i}{\sigma^2 f_i} \\[2ex]
\dfrac{1}{2\sigma^2}\left(\dfrac{\varepsilon_i^2}{\sigma^2 f_i} - 1 \right) \\[2ex]
\dfrac{1}{2 f_i}\left(\dfrac{\varepsilon_i^2}{\sigma^2 f_i} - 1 \right)\mathbf{g}_i
\end{bmatrix} ,
$$
$$(14\text{–}30)$$

may be easier to compute than the Hessian. Both estimators are valid asymptotically.

A second method of maximizing the log likelihood is the procedure proposed by Oberhofer and Kmenta (1974). Solving the full set of likelihood equations simultaneously may be extremely difficult. But, as we have seen, for given values of the variance parameters, the solutions for β and σ^2 are the GLS estimators. It may also be possible to solve the first-order conditions for θ for a given set of values for β and σ^2 relatively straightforwardly. In this model, this "zigzag" procedure will be a valid means of finding maximum likelihood estimates.

EXAMPLE 14.15 Multiplicative Heteroscedasticity[27]

Suppose that $\mathbf{q}_i$ is a set of variables and

$$
\sigma_i^2 = \sigma^2 \exp(\alpha' \mathbf{q}_i).
$$

This is a general model that includes several special cases, including the model in Example 14.14, in which $q_i = \ln z_i$.[28] As Godfrey suggests, there is a useful simplification of

---

[26] See Section 4.5.2, (4–52).

[27] This model is examined at length by Harvey (1976).

[28] See Judge et al. (1985, pp. 439–441), Harvey (1976), and Just and Pope (1978).

the formulation. Let $\mathbf{z}_i = [1, \mathbf{q}_i]$ and $\boldsymbol{\gamma} = [\ln \sigma^2, \boldsymbol{\alpha}]$. Then we can write the model as simply

$$\sigma_i^2 = \exp(\boldsymbol{\gamma}'\mathbf{z}_i). \tag{14–31}$$

Once the full parameter vector is estimated, $\exp(\gamma_1)$ provides the estimator of σ^2.[29]
The log likelihood is

$$
\begin{aligned}
\ln L &= -\frac{n}{2} \ln(2\pi) - \frac{1}{2} \sum_i \ln \sigma_i^2 - \frac{1}{2} \sum_i \frac{\varepsilon_i^2}{\sigma_i^2} \\
&= -\frac{n}{2} \ln(2\pi) - \frac{1}{2} \sum_i \boldsymbol{\gamma}'\mathbf{z}_i - \frac{1}{2} \sum_i \frac{\varepsilon_i^2}{\exp(\boldsymbol{\gamma}'\mathbf{z}_i)}.
\end{aligned}
\tag{14–32}
$$

The likelihood equations are

$$\frac{\partial \ln L}{\partial \boldsymbol{\beta}} = \sum_i \mathbf{x}_i \frac{\varepsilon_i}{\exp(\boldsymbol{\gamma}'\mathbf{z}_i)} = \mathbf{0} = \mathbf{X}'\boldsymbol{\Omega}^{-1}\boldsymbol{\varepsilon}$$

and

$$\frac{\partial \ln L}{\partial \boldsymbol{\gamma}} = \frac{1}{2} \sum_i \mathbf{z}_i \left(\frac{\varepsilon_i^2}{\exp(\boldsymbol{\gamma}'\mathbf{z}_i)} - 1 \right) = \mathbf{0}. \tag{14–33}$$

For this model, the method of scoring turns out to be a particularly convenient way to maximize the log-likelihood function. The terms in the Hessian are

$$\frac{\partial^2 \ln L}{\partial \boldsymbol{\beta}\, \partial \boldsymbol{\beta}'} = -\sum_i \frac{1}{\exp(\boldsymbol{\gamma}'\mathbf{z}_i)} \mathbf{x}_i\mathbf{x}_i' = -\mathbf{X}'\boldsymbol{\Omega}^{-1}\mathbf{X}$$

$$\frac{\partial^2 \ln L}{\partial \boldsymbol{\beta}\, \partial \boldsymbol{\gamma}'} = -\sum_i \frac{\varepsilon_i}{\exp(\boldsymbol{\gamma}'\mathbf{z}_i)} \mathbf{x}_i\mathbf{z}_i' \tag{14–34}$$

$$\frac{\partial^2 \ln L}{\partial \boldsymbol{\gamma}\, \partial \boldsymbol{\gamma}'} = -\frac{1}{2} \sum_i \frac{\varepsilon_i^2}{\exp(\boldsymbol{\gamma}'\mathbf{z}_i)} \mathbf{z}_i\mathbf{z}_i'.$$

The expected value of $\partial^2 \ln L/\partial\boldsymbol{\beta}\, \partial\boldsymbol{\gamma}'$ is $\mathbf{0}$ since $E[\varepsilon_i] = 0$. The expected value of the fraction in $\partial^2 \ln L/\partial\boldsymbol{\gamma}\, \partial\boldsymbol{\gamma}'$ is $E[\varepsilon_i^2/\sigma_i^2] = 1$. Let $\boldsymbol{\delta} = [\boldsymbol{\beta}, \boldsymbol{\gamma}]$. Then

$$-E\left(\frac{\partial^2 \ln L}{\partial \boldsymbol{\delta}\, \partial \boldsymbol{\delta}'} \right) = \begin{bmatrix} \mathbf{X}'\boldsymbol{\Omega}^{-1}\mathbf{X} & \mathbf{0}' \\ \mathbf{0} & \frac{1}{2}\mathbf{Z}'\mathbf{Z} \end{bmatrix} = -\mathbf{H}.$$

The scoring method is

$$\boldsymbol{\delta}_{t+1} = \boldsymbol{\delta}_t - \mathbf{H}_t^{-1}\mathbf{g}_t,$$

where $\boldsymbol{\delta}_t$ (i.e., $\boldsymbol{\beta}_t$, $\boldsymbol{\gamma}_t$, and $\boldsymbol{\Omega}_t$) is the estimate at iteration t, $\mathbf{g}_t$ is the two-part vector of first derivatives, $[\partial \ln L/\partial\boldsymbol{\beta}_t, \partial \ln L/\partial\boldsymbol{\gamma}_t]$ and $\mathbf{H}_t$ is partitioned likewise. Since $\mathbf{H}_t$ is block diagonal, the iteration can be written as separate equations:

$$
\begin{aligned}
\boldsymbol{\beta}_{t+1} &= \boldsymbol{\beta}_t + (\mathbf{X}'\boldsymbol{\Omega}_t^{-1}\mathbf{X})^{-1}(\mathbf{X}'\boldsymbol{\Omega}_t^{-1}\boldsymbol{\varepsilon}_t) \\
&= \boldsymbol{\beta}_t + (\mathbf{X}'\boldsymbol{\Omega}_t^{-1}\mathbf{X})^{-1}\mathbf{X}'\boldsymbol{\Omega}_t^{-1}(\mathbf{y} - \mathbf{X}\boldsymbol{\beta}_t) \\
&= (\mathbf{X}'\boldsymbol{\Omega}_t^{-1}\mathbf{X})^{-1}\mathbf{X}'\boldsymbol{\Omega}_t^{-1}\mathbf{y} \quad \text{(of course).}
\end{aligned}
$$

---

[29] This uses the invariance result for maximum likelihood estimation. See Section 4.5.1.

Therefore, the updated coefficient vector, $\boldsymbol{\beta}_{t+1}$, is computed by FGLS using the previously computed estimate of $\boldsymbol{\gamma}$ to compute $\boldsymbol{\Omega}$. We use the same approach for $\boldsymbol{\gamma}$:

$$\boldsymbol{\gamma}_{t+1} = \boldsymbol{\gamma}_t + 2(\mathbf{Z}'\mathbf{Z})^{-1} \frac{1}{2} \sum_i \mathbf{z}_i \left(\frac{\varepsilon_i^2}{\exp(\boldsymbol{\gamma}'\mathbf{z}_i)} - 1 \right). \tag{14-35}$$

The 2 and $\frac{1}{2}$ cancel. The updated value of $\boldsymbol{\gamma}$ is computed by updating the old one with the vector of slopes in the least squares regression of $[\varepsilon_i^2/\exp(\boldsymbol{\gamma}'\mathbf{z}_i) - 1]$ on $\mathbf{z}$. Note that the correction is $2(\mathbf{Z}'\mathbf{Z})^{-1}\mathbf{Z}'(\partial \ln L/\partial\boldsymbol{\gamma})$, so convergence occurs when the derivative is zero.

The remaining detail is to determine the starting value for the iteration. Since any consistent estimator will do, the simplest procedure is to use OLS for $\boldsymbol{\beta}$ and the slopes in a regression of the logs of the squares of the least squares residuals on $\mathbf{z}_i$ for $\boldsymbol{\gamma}$. Harvey (1976) shows that this will produce an inconsistent estimator of $\gamma_1 = \ln \sigma^2$, but the inconsistency can be corrected just by adding 1.2704 to the value obtained.[30] Thereafter, the iteration is simply:

1. Estimate the disturbance variances, σ_i^2, with $\exp(\boldsymbol{\gamma}_t'\mathbf{z}_i)$.
2. Compute $\boldsymbol{\beta}_{t+1}$ by FGLS.[31]
3. Update $\boldsymbol{\gamma}_t$ using the regression shown in (14–35).
4. Compute $\mathbf{d}_{t+1} = [\boldsymbol{\beta}_{t+1}, \boldsymbol{\gamma}_{t+1}] - [\boldsymbol{\beta}_t, \boldsymbol{\gamma}_t]$. If $\mathbf{d}_t$ is large, return to step 1.

If $\mathbf{d}_{t+1}$ at step 4 is sufficiently small, exit the iteration. The asymptotic covariance matrix is simply $-\mathbf{H}^{-1}$, which is block diagonal with blocks

$$\text{Asy.Var}[\hat{\boldsymbol{\beta}}_{\text{ML}}] = (\mathbf{X}'\boldsymbol{\Omega}^{-1}\mathbf{X})^{-1}$$
$$\text{Asy.Var}[\hat{\boldsymbol{\gamma}}_{\text{ML}}] = 2(\mathbf{Z}'\mathbf{Z})^{-1}. \tag{14-36}$$

If desired, $\hat{\sigma}^2 = \exp(\hat{\gamma}_1)$. The asymptotic variance would be $[\exp(\gamma_1)]^2 \, \text{Asy.Var}[\hat{\gamma}_{1\text{ML}}]$.

14.6. General Conclusions

It is rarely possible to be certain about the nature of the heteroscedasticity in a regression model. In one respect, this is only a minor problem. The weighted least squares estimator,

$$\hat{\boldsymbol{\beta}} = \left[\sum_i w_i \mathbf{x}_i \mathbf{x}_i' \right]^{-1} \sum_i w_i \mathbf{x}_i y_i,$$

is consistent regardless of the weights used, as long as the weights are uncorrelated with the disturbances. Note the similarity of the estimates in Table 14.12, which summarizes the estimators discussed earlier. The effect is even more striking in the set of estimates of

$$\gamma = \frac{\partial \text{spending}}{\partial \text{income}} = \beta_2 + 2\beta_3 \text{income},$$

which is computed at the mean income of 7608 for each model.

But using the wrong set of weights has two other consequences which may be less benign. First, the improperly weighted least squares estimator is inefficient. This might be

---

[30] He also presents a correction for the asymptotic covariance matrix for this first step estimator of $\boldsymbol{\gamma}$.

[31] The two-step estimator obtained by stopping here would be fully efficient if the starting value for $\boldsymbol{\gamma}$ were consistent. But it would not be the maximum likelihood estimator.

TABLE 14.12

	Constant	Income	Income^2	γ
Ordinary least squares				
(1)	832.91	-1834.2	1587.04	580.818
	(327.3)	(829.0)	(519.1)	
Weighted least squares				
Var$[\varepsilon_i] = \sigma^2$Income$_i$				
(2)	560.72	-1124.18	1132.43	598.925
	(335.6)	(893.6)	(588.5)	
Var$[\varepsilon_i] = \sigma^2$Income$_i^2$				
(3)	644.58	-1399.28	1311.35	596.217
	(333.6)	(872.1)	(563.7)	
Generalized least squares based on Var$[\varepsilon_i] = \boldsymbol{\alpha}'\mathbf{z}_i$				
(4)	709.05	-1506.40	1374.15	584.661
	(451.9)	(1199.0)	(790.8)	
Weighted least squares with the variance proportional to				
the square of the mean				
(5)	591.08	-1195.15	1172.22	588.631
	(371.0)	(981.2)	(642.7)	
Weighted least squares regression based on				
ln $\sigma_i^2 = $ ln $\sigma^2 + \Sigma_m \alpha_m z_{im}$				
(6)	488.43	-912.69	980.71	579.668
	(529.1)	(1423.0)	(950.3)	

a moot point if the correct weights are unknown, but the GLS standard errors will also be incorrect. The asymptotic covariance matrix of the estimator

$$\hat{\boldsymbol{\beta}} = [\mathbf{X}'\mathbf{V}^{-1}\mathbf{X}]^{-1}\mathbf{X}'\mathbf{V}^{-1}\mathbf{y},$$

is

$$\text{Asy.Var}[\hat{\boldsymbol{\beta}}] = [\mathbf{X}'\mathbf{V}^{-1}\mathbf{X}]^{-1}\mathbf{X}'\mathbf{V}^{-1}\boldsymbol{\Omega}\mathbf{V}^{-1}\mathbf{X}[\mathbf{X}'\mathbf{V}^{-1}\mathbf{X}]^{-1}.$$

This may or may not resemble the usual estimator, which would be the matrix in brackets. This underscores the usefulness of the White estimator in (14–9).

Finally, if the form of the heteroscedasticity is known but involves unknown parameters, it remains uncertain whether FGLS corrections are better than OLS. Asymptotically, the comparison is clear, but in small or moderate-sized samples, the additional variation incorporated by the estimated variance parameters may offset the gains to GLS.

EXERCISES

1. Suppose that the regression model is

$$y_i = \mu + \varepsilon_i,$$

where

$$E[\varepsilon_i | x_i] = 0, \quad \text{but } \text{Var}[\varepsilon_i | x_i] = \sigma^2 x_i^2, \quad x_i > 0.$$

(a) Given a sample of observations on y_i and x_i, what is the most efficient estimator of μ? What is its variance?

(b) What is the OLS estimator of μ, and what is the variance of the ordinary least squares estimator?

(c) Prove that the estimator in part (a) is at least as efficient as the estimator in part (b).

2. For the model in the previous exercise, what is the probability limit of the following?

$$s^2 = \frac{1}{n-1} \sum_i (y_i - \bar{y})^2.$$

Note that this is the least squares estimate of the residual variance. It is also n times the conventional estimator of the variance of the OLS estimator,

$$\text{Est. Var}[\bar{y}] = s^2(\mathbf{X}'\mathbf{X})^{-1} = \frac{s^2}{n}.$$

How does this compare to the true value you found in part (b) of Exercise 1? Does the conventional estimator produce the correct estimate of the true asymptotic variance of the least squares estimator?

3. Two samples of 50 observations each produce the following moment matrices. (In each case, $\mathbf{X}$ is a constant and one variable.)

	Sample 1	Sample 2
$\mathbf{X}'\mathbf{X}$	$\begin{bmatrix} 50 & 300 \\ 300 & 2100 \end{bmatrix}$	$\begin{bmatrix} 50 & 300 \\ 300 & 2100 \end{bmatrix}$
$\mathbf{y}'\mathbf{X}$	$[300 \quad 2000]$	$[300 \quad 2200]$
$\mathbf{y}'\mathbf{y}$	2100	2800

(a) Compute the least squares regression coefficients and the residual variances, s^2, for each data set. Compute the R^2 for each regression.

(b) Compute the OLS estimate of the coefficient vector, assuming that the coefficients and disturbance variances are the same in the two regressions. Also, compute the estimate of the asymptotic covariance matrix of the estimate.

(c) Test the hypothesis that the variances in the two regressions are the same without assuming that the coefficients are the same in the two regressions.

(d) Compute the two-step FGLS estimator of the coefficients in the regressions, assuming that the constant and slope are the same in both regressions. Compute the estimate of the covariance matrix and compare it to the result of part (b).

4. Using the data in the previous exercise, use the Oberhofer–Kmenta method to compute the maximum likelihood estimate of the common coefficient vector.

5. This exercise is based on the data set on p. 410.
   (a) Compute the ordinary least squares regression of Y on a constant, X_1, and X_2. Be sure to compute the conventional estimator of the asymptotic covariance matrix of the OLS estimator as well.
   (b) Compute the White estimator of the appropriate asymptotic covariance matrix for the OLS estimates. [See (14–9).]
   (c) Test for the presence of heteroscedasticity, using White's general test. Do your results suggest the nature of the heteroscedasticity?
   (d) Use the Breusch–Pagan Lagrange multiplier test to test for heteroscedasticity.
   (e) Sort the data keying on X_1, and use the Goldfeld–Quandt test to test for heteroscedasticity. Repeat the procedure, using X_2. What do you find?
   (f) Use one of Glesjer's tests to test for heteroscedasticity.

			50 Observations on Y					
−1.42	2.75	2.10	−5.08	1.49	1.00	0.16	−1.11	1.66
−0.26	−4.87	5.94	2.21	−6.87	0.90	1.61	2.11	−3.82
−0.62	7.01	26.14	7.39	0.79	1.93	1.97	−23.17	−2.52
−1.26	−0.15	3.41	−5.45	1.31	1.52	2.04	3.00	6.31
5.51	−15.22	−1.47	−1.48	6.66	1.78	2.62	−5.16	−4.71
−0.35	−0.48	1.24	0.69	1.91				

			50 Observations on X_1					
−1.65	1.48	0.77	0.67	0.68	0.23	−0.40	−1.13	0.15
−0.63	0.34	0.35	0.79	0.77	−1.04	0.28	0.58	−0.41
−1.78	1.25	0.22	1.25	−0.12	0.66	1.06	−0.66	−1.18
−0.80	−1.32	0.16	1.06	−0.60	0.79	0.86	2.04	−0.51
0.02	0.33	−1.99	0.70	−0.17	0.33	0.48	1.90	−0.18
−0.18	−1.62	0.39	0.17	1.02				

			50 Observations on X_2					
−0.67	0.70	0.32	2.88	−0.19	−1.28	−2.72	−0.70	−1.55
−0.74	−1.87	1.56	0.37	−2.07	1.20	0.26	−1.34	−2.10
0.61	2.32	4.38	2.16	1.51	0.30	−0.17	7.82	−1.15
1.77	2.92	−1.94	2.09	1.50	−0.46	0.19	−0.39	1.54
1.87	−3.45	−.88	−1.53	1.42	−2.70	1.77	−1.89	−1.85
2.01	1.26	−2.02	1.91	−2.23				

6. Using the data of Exercise 5, reestimate the parameters, using a two-step FGLS estimator. Try (14–19), (14–20), and (14–21). Which one appears to be most appropriate?

7. For the model in Exercise 1, suppose that ε is normally distributed, with mean zero and variance $\sigma^2(1 + (\gamma x)^2)$. Show that σ^2 and γ^2 can be consistently estimated by a regression of the least squares residuals on a constant and x^2. Is this estimator efficient?

8. Derive the log-likelihood function, first-order conditions for maximization, and information matrix for the model

$$y_i = \boldsymbol{\beta}'\mathbf{x}_i + \varepsilon_i.$$

$$\varepsilon_i \sim N[0, \sigma^2(\boldsymbol{\gamma}'\mathbf{z}_i)^2].$$

9. For the model of (14–26) to (14–29), prove the result in (14–29). (**Hints:** Remember that the only stochastic components of the derivatives are ε and ε^2. For all derivatives except $\partial^2 \ln L/\partial\boldsymbol{\theta}\,\partial\boldsymbol{\theta}'$, just differentiate and take expected values. Then write sums involving $1/f_i$ in terms of $\boldsymbol{\Omega}^{-1}$. For the remaining term, simplify the expressions by letting $c_i = [\varepsilon_i^2/(\sigma^2 f_i)] - 1]$ and $\mathbf{r}_i = \mathbf{g}_i/f_i$. $E[c_i] = 0$ and $\mathbf{r}_i$ is nonstochastic. Use $\partial \ln L/\partial\boldsymbol{\theta} = \frac{1}{2}\Sigma_i\, c_i\mathbf{r}_i$. Now, differentiate, collect terms, and take expected values.

10. In Example 14.14, it is noted that the initial estimator of γ_1, the constant term in the regression of $\ln e_i^2$ on a constant and $\mathbf{z}_i$ is inconsistent by the amount 1.2704. Harvey points out that if the purpose of this initial regression is only to obtain starting values for the iterations, then the correction is not necessary. Explain why this would be the case.

15

Autocorrelated Disturbances

15.1. Introduction

Heteroscedasticity is most commonly associated with cross-section data. In a time-series setting, the more common problem is autocorrelation, or serial correlation of the disturbances across periods. Consider, for example, the plot of the least squares residuals in the following example.

EXAMPLE 15.1

The data listed in Table 15.1 are used to fit an investment equation. GNP and gross private domestic investment are in nominal terms in billions of dollars. The price index is the implicit price deflator for GNP. The interest rate is the average yearly discount rate

TABLE 15.1

Year	GNP	Investment	Price Index	Interest Rate
1963	596.7	90.9	0.7167	3.23
1964	637.7	97.4	0.7277	3.55
1965	691.1	113.5	0.7436	4.04
1966	756.0	125.7	0.7676	4.50
1967	799.6	122.8	0.7906	4.19
1968	873.4	133.3	0.8254	5.16
1969	944.0	149.3	0.8679	5.87
1970	992.7	144.2	0.9145	5.95
1971	1077.6	166.4	0.9601	4.88
1972	1185.9	195.0	1.0000	4.50
1973	1326.4	229.8	1.0575	6.44
1974	1434.2	228.7	1.1508	7.83
1975	1549.2	206.1	1.2579	6.25
1976	1718.0	257.9	1.3234	5.50
1977	1918.3	324.1	1.4005	5.46
1978	2163.9	386.6	1.5042	7.46
1979	2417.8	423.0	1.6342	10.28
1980	2631.7	401.9	1.7842	11.77
1981	2954.1	474.9	1.9514	13.42
1982	3073.0	414.5	2.0688	11.02

Source: Data from the *Economic Report of the President*, U.S. Government Printing Office, Washington, D.C., 1984.

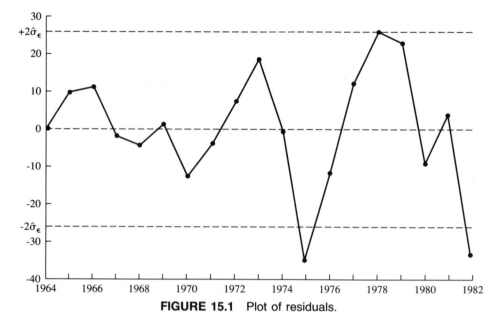

FIGURE 15.1 Plot of residuals.

charged by the New York Federal Reserve Bank. Variables used in the regressions reported in the examples to follow are real GNP and real investment, obtained by dividing the nominal figures by the price index. An approximation to the real interest rate is obtained by subtracting the rate of change in the price index from the discount rate.

Least squares regression of real investment on real GNP and the real interest rate produces the results given in Table 15.2.

TABLE 15.2

Variable	Coefficient	Standard Error
Constant	-12.5336	24.920
Real Interest	-1.00144	2.369
Real GNP	0.16914	0.02057
	$R^2 = 0.81406$	

A plot of residuals is shown in Figure 15.1. The pattern in the residuals suggests that knowledge of the sign of a residual in one period is a fair indicator of the sign of the residual in the next period. This suggests that the effect of a given disturbance is carried, at least in part, across periods.

One explanation for autocorrelation is that the factors omitted from the time-series regression, like those included, are correlated across periods. Of course, this may be due to serial correlation in factors that should be in the regression model. Still, even after accounting for this possibility, it is reasonable to model most time series data as having some serial correlation. A second source of autocorrelation is the manner in which some published statistics are produced. For example, in seasonally adjusting variables such as the CPI and GNP, government agencies build autocorrelation into series that might otherwise be uncorrelated.

EXAMPLE 15.2 _____

Suppose that x_t, $t = 1, \ldots, T$ is a random sample from a distribution with mean zero and variance σ^2.[1] Then $\text{Cov}[x_t, x_s] = 0$ if $t \neq s$. Let z_t be a "seasonally adjusted" series such that

$$z_t = \sum_{s=0}^{11} w_s x_{t-s},$$

where w_s is a monthly weight. Then

$$\text{Cov}[z_t, z_{t-s}] = w_0 w_s \sigma^2$$

for $s = 0, 1, \ldots, 11$ and zero for s greater than 11. The original series is uncorrelated, but the adjustment induces autocorrelation of 11 periods' duration.

_____

The problems for estimation and inference caused by autocorrelation are similar to (though, unfortunately, more involved than) those caused by heteroscedasticity. As before, least squares is inefficient and inference based on the least squares estimates is adversely affected. Depending on the underlying process, however GLS and FGLS estimators can be devised that circumvent these problems. We should emphasize that the models we shall examine here are quite far removed from the classical regression. The exact or small-sample properties of the estimators are rarely known, and only their asymptotic properties have been derived.

15.2. The Analysis of Time-Series Data

The analysis of autocorrelation in disturbances brings us into the realm of time-series analysis. Time-series analysis requires some revision of the interpretation of both data generation and sampling that we have maintained thus far.

A time-series model will typically describe the path of a variable y_t in terms of contemporaneous (and perhaps lagged) factors $\mathbf{x}_t$, disturbances (or innovations in the parlance of the recent work on this subject), ε_t, and its own past, $y_{t-1}, \ldots$. For example,

$$y_t = \beta_1 + \beta_2 x_t + \beta_3 y_{t-1} + \varepsilon_t.$$

The time series is a single occurrence of a random event. For example, the yearly series on real output in the United States from 1945 to 1990 is a single realization of a process GNP_t. The entire history over this period constitutes a realization of the process. At least in economics, the process could not be repeated. There is no counterpart to repeated sampling in a cross section. Nonetheless, were circumstances different at the end of World War II, the observed history *could* have been different. In principle, a completely different realization of the entire series might have occurred.

The properties of y_t as a random variable in a cross section are straightforward and are conveniently summarized in a statement about its mean and variance or the probability distribution generating y_t. The statement is less obvious here. It is common to assume that

_____

[1] Since this chapter deals exclusively with time-series data, we shall use the t index for observations and T for the sample size throughout.

disturbances are generated independently from one period to the next, with the familiar assumptions

$$E[\varepsilon_t] = 0,$$

$$\text{Var}[\varepsilon_t] = \sigma^2,$$

and

$$\text{Cov}[\varepsilon_t, \varepsilon_s] = 0 \quad \text{for } t \neq s.$$

In the current context, the distribution of ε_t is said to be **covariance stationary** or **weakly stationary.** Thus, while the substantive notion of "random sampling" must be extended for the time series ε_t, the mathematical results based on that notion apply here. It can be said that ε_t is generated by a process whose mean and variance are not changing over time.[2] As such, by the method we will discuss in this chapter, we could, at least in principle, obtain sample information and use it to characterize the distribution of ε_t. Could the same be said of y_t? There is an obvious difference between the series ε_t and y_t; observations on y_t at different points in time are necessarily correlated. Suppose that the y_t series *is* weakly stationary and x_t is nonstochastic.[3] Then we could say the following:

$$\text{Var}[y_t] = \beta_3^2 \text{Var}[y_{t-1}] + \text{Var}[\varepsilon_t]$$

or

$$\gamma_0 = \beta_3^2 \gamma_0 + \sigma^2$$

or

$$\gamma_0 = \frac{\sigma^2}{1 - \beta_3^2}.$$

Thus, γ_0, the variance of y_t, is a fixed characteristic of the process generating y_t. Note how the stationarity assumption, which apparently includes $|\beta_3| < 1$, has been used. The assumption that $|\beta_3| < 1$ is needed to ensure a finite and positive variance.[4]

Alternatively, consider simply repeated substitution of lagged values into the expression for y_t,

$$y_t = \beta_1 + \beta_2 x_t + \beta_3(\beta_1 + \beta_2 x_{t-1} + \beta_3 y_{t-2} + \varepsilon_{t-1}) + \varepsilon_t, \quad (15\text{--}1)$$

and so on. We see that, in fact, the current y_t is an accumulation of the entire history of x_t and ε_t. So if we wish to characterize the distribution of y_t, we might do so in terms of sums of random variables. By continuing to substitute for y_{t-2}, then y_{t-3}, . . . in (15–1), we obtain

$$y_t = \sum_{i=0}^{\infty} \beta_3^i(\beta_1 + \beta_2 x_{t-i} + \varepsilon_{t-i}).$$

[2] Stationarity could be extended to "strong stationarity" by asserting that the *distribution* is not changing over time. This would strictly validate results based on a "random sampling" assumption. But the assumption of strong stationarity is not necessary for what we do here, so we will not take this additional step.

[3] Whether x_t is regarded as stochastic or nonstochastic, as we saw in Chapter 10, is immaterial to large sample estimation and inference results. The former probably makes more sense. For the present, it is convenient to do the analysis conditionally on x_t, as if it were nonstochastic.

[4] There is an explosion of articles in the current literature in macroeconometrics on cases in which $\beta_3 = 1$ (or counterparts in different models). For example, two recent surveys of "unit roots" in economic time series, Nerlove and Diebold (1990) and Campbell and Perron (1991), cite between them over 200 sources. We will return to this subject in Chapter 19.

By this construction,

$$\text{Var}[y_t] = \sum_{i=0}^{\infty} (\beta_3^i)^2 \, \text{Var}[\varepsilon_{t-i}]$$

$$= \sigma^2 \sum_{i=0}^{\infty} \beta_3^{2i}$$

$$= \frac{\sigma^2}{1 - \beta_3^2}.$$

Once again, the stationarity assumption, $|\beta_3| < 1$, is necessary.

Do sums that reach back into the infinite past make any sense? We might view the process as having begun generating data at some remote, effectively "infinite" past. As long as distant observations become progressively less important, the extension to an infinite past is merely a mathematical convenience. The diminishing importance of past observations is implied by $|\beta_3| < 1$. Notice that, not coincidentally, this is the same requirement as that needed to solve for γ_0 in the preceding paragraph. A second possibility is to assume that the *observation* of *this* time series begins at some time 0 [with (x_0, ε_0) called the **initial conditions**], by which time the underlying process has reached a state such that the mean and variance of y_t are not (or are no longer) changing over time. The mathematics are slightly different, but this leads to the same characterization of the random process generating y_t. In fact, the same weak stationarity assumption ensures both of them.

Except in very special cases, we would expect all of the elements in the T component random vector $(y_1, \ldots, y_T)$ to be correlated. In this instance, said correlation is called "autocorrelation." As such, the results pertaining to estimation with independent or uncorrelated observations which we used in the previous chapters are no longer relevant. In point of fact, we have a sample of but one observation on the multivariate random variable $[y_t, t = 1, \ldots, T]$. There is a counterpart to the cross-sectional notion of parameter estimation, but only under assumptions (e.g., weak stationarity) which establish that parameters in the familiar sense even exist. Even with stationarity, it will emerge that for estimation and inference, none of our earlier finite sample results are usable. Consistency and asymptotic normality of estimators are somewhat more difficult to establish in time series settings because results that require independent observations, such as the central limit theorems, are no longer usable. Nonetheless, counterparts to our earlier results have been established for most of the estimation problems we will consider in this and Chapters 18 and 19. Where necessary, we will just invoke them with a minimum of derivation.[5]

15.3. Disturbance Processes

15.3.1. Characteristics of Disturbance Processes

In the usual time-series setting, the disturbances are assumed to be homoscedastic, but correlated across observations, so that

$$E[\boldsymbol{\varepsilon}\boldsymbol{\varepsilon}'] = \sigma^2 \boldsymbol{\Omega},$$

---

[5] See Section 10.4 for a discussion of the results of Mann and Wald (1943).

where $\sigma^2 \boldsymbol{\Omega}$ is a full, positive definite matrix with a constant $\sigma^2 = \mathrm{Var}[\varepsilon_t]$ on the diagonal. As will be clear in the following discussion, we shall also assume that $\boldsymbol{\Omega}_{ts}$ is a function of $|t - s|$, but not of t or s alone. This is a **stationarity** assumption. (See the preceding section.) It implies that the covariance between observations t and s is a function only of $|t - s|$, the distance apart in time of the observations. We define the **autocovariances,**

$$\mathrm{Cov}[\varepsilon_t, \varepsilon_{t-s}] = \mathrm{Cov}[\varepsilon_{t+s}, \varepsilon_t] = \gamma_s.$$

Note that $\sigma^2 = \gamma_0$. The correlation between ε_t and ε_{t-s} is their **autocorrelation,**

$$\mathrm{Corr}[\varepsilon_t, \varepsilon_{t-s}] = \frac{\mathrm{Cov}[\varepsilon_t, \varepsilon_{t-s}]}{\sqrt{\mathrm{Var}[\varepsilon_t]\,\mathrm{Var}[\varepsilon_{t-s}]}} = \frac{\gamma_s}{\gamma_0} = \rho_s.$$

We can then write

$$E[\boldsymbol{\varepsilon}\boldsymbol{\varepsilon}'] = \gamma_0 \mathbf{R},$$

where $\mathbf{R}$ is an **autocorrelation matrix:**

$$\mathbf{R}_{ts} = \frac{\gamma_{|t-s|}}{\gamma_0}.$$

Different types of processes imply different patterns in $\mathbf{R}$. For example, the most frequently analyzed process is a **first-order autoregression** or AR(1) process,

$$\varepsilon_t = \rho \varepsilon_{t-1} + u_t,$$

for which we will verify that $\rho_s = \rho^s$. Higher-order **autoregressive processes** of the form

$$\varepsilon_t = \theta_1 \varepsilon_{t-1} + \theta_2 \varepsilon_{t-2} + \cdots + \theta_p \varepsilon_{t-p} + u_t$$

imply more involved patterns, including, for some values of the parameters, cyclical behavior of the autocorrelations.[6] Autoregressions are structured so that the influence of a given disturbance fades as it recedes into the more distant past but vanishes only asymptotically. For example, for the AR(1), $\mathrm{Cov}[\varepsilon_t, \varepsilon_{t-s}]$ is never zero, but does become negligible if $|\rho|$ is less than one. *Moving average* processes such as the one in Example 15.2, conversely, have a short memory. For the MA(1) process,

$$\varepsilon_t = u_t - \lambda u_{t-1},$$

the memory in the process is only one period:

$$\gamma_0 = \sigma_u^2(1 + \lambda^2),$$
$$\gamma_1 = -\lambda \sigma_u^2,$$

but

$$\gamma_k = 0 \qquad \text{if } k > 1.$$

The memory in the MA(11) process of Example 15.2 is 11 periods.

15.3.2. AR(1) Disturbances

Time-series processes such as the ones listed here can be characterized by their order, the values of their parameters, and the behavior of their autocorrelations.[7] We shall consider

---

[6] This is considered in more detail in Chapter 18.

[7] See Box and Jenkins (1984) for an authoritative study.

various forms at different points. The received empirical literature is overwhelmingly dominated by the AR(1) model. This is partly a matter of convenience. Processes more involved than this model are usually extremely difficult to analyze.[8] However, there is a more practical reason. It is very optimistic to expect to know precisely the correct form of the appropriate model for the disturbance in any given situation. The first-order autoregression has withstood the test of time and experimentation as a reasonable *model* for underlying processes that probably, in truth, are impenetrably complex. It is sometimes argued that models can be improved by more elaborate disturbance processes (we shall examine some of these in Chapter 18), but there is often a *je ne sais quoi* flavor to this exercise. The results are often highly sensitive to the specification chosen, and, in general, it is the data rather than an underlying theory that lead to the choice of the model, which is risky at best. As such, most researchers choose the simpler expedient of the AR(1) model in most cases.

The first-order autoregressive disturbance, or AR(1) process, is represented in the **autoregressive form** as

$$\varepsilon_t = \rho \varepsilon_{t-1} + u_t, \tag{15-2}$$

where

$$E[u_t] = 0,$$

$$E[u_t^2] = \sigma_u^2,$$

and

$$\text{Cov}[u_t, u_s] = 0 \quad \text{if } t \neq s.$$

By repeated substitution, we have

$$\varepsilon_t = u_t + \rho u_{t-1} + \rho^2 u_{t-2} + \cdots. \tag{15-3}$$

From the preceding **moving average form,** it is evident that each disturbance, ε_t, embodies the entire past history of the u's, with the most recent observations receiving greater weight than those in the distant past. Depending on the sign of ρ, the series will exhibit clusters of positive and then negative observations or, if ρ is negative, regular oscillations of sign.[9]

Since the successive values of u_t are uncorrelated, the variance of ε_t is the variance of the right-hand side of (15–3):

$$\text{Var}[\varepsilon_t] = \sigma_u^2 + \rho^2 \sigma_u^2 + \rho^4 \sigma_u^2 + \cdots. \tag{15-4}$$

In order to proceed, a restriction must be placed on ρ,

$$|\rho| < 1, \tag{15-5}$$

because otherwise (15–4) must explode. This is the stationarity assumption discussed earlier. With (15–5), which implies that $\lim_{s \to \infty} \rho^s = 0$,

$$E[\varepsilon_t] = 0$$

---

[8] The literature on time series and autocorrelation is voluminous and enormously complex. For example, the bibliography in Judge et al. (1985) on the latter subject alone runs to 13 pages.

[9] Unless the data have been first differenced or otherwise manipulated in an unusual fashion, the case of negative autocorrelation is normally not relevant to economic data.

and

$$\text{Var}[\varepsilon_t] = \frac{\sigma_u^2}{1 - \rho^2} \tag{15-6}$$

$$= \sigma_\varepsilon^2.$$

With the stationarity assumption, there is an easier way to obtain the variance:

$$\text{Var}[\varepsilon_t] = \rho^2 \text{Var}[\varepsilon_{t-1}] + \sigma_u^2,$$

as $\text{Cov}[u_t, \varepsilon_s] = 0$ if $t > s$. With stationarity, $\text{Var}[\varepsilon_{t-1}] = \text{Var}[\varepsilon_t]$, which implies (15–6). Proceeding in the same fashion,

$$\begin{aligned}
\text{Cov}[\varepsilon_t, \varepsilon_{t-1}] &= E[\varepsilon_t \varepsilon_{t-1}] \\
&= E[\varepsilon_{t-1}(\rho \varepsilon_{t-1} + u_t)] \\
&= \rho \text{Var}[\varepsilon_{t-1}] \\
&= \frac{\rho \sigma_u^2}{1 - \rho^2}.
\end{aligned} \tag{15-7}$$

By repeated substitution in (15–2), we see that for any s,

$$\varepsilon_t = \rho^s \varepsilon_{t-s} + \sum_{i=0}^{s-1} \rho^i u_{t-i}$$

(e.g., $\varepsilon_t = \rho^3 \varepsilon_{t-3} + \rho^2 u_{t-2} + \rho u_{t-1} + u_t$). Therefore, since ε_s is not correlated with any u_t for which $t > s$ (i.e., any subsequent u_t), it follows that

$$\text{Cov}[\varepsilon_t, \varepsilon_{t-s}] = E[\varepsilon_t \varepsilon_{t-s}] = \frac{\rho^s \sigma_u^2}{1 - \rho^2}. \tag{15-8}$$

Dividing by $\gamma_0 = \sigma_u^2/(1 - \rho^2)$ provides the autocorrelations,

$$\text{Corr}[\varepsilon_t, \varepsilon_{t-s}] = \rho_s = \rho^s. \tag{15-9}$$

With the stationarity assumption, the autocorrelations fade over time. Depending on the sign of ρ, they will either be declining in geometric progression or alternating in sign if ρ is negative. Collecting terms, we have

$$\sigma^2 \Omega = \frac{\sigma_u^2}{1 - \rho^2} \begin{bmatrix} 1 & \rho & \rho^2 & \rho^3 & \cdots & \rho^{T-1} \\ \rho & 1 & \rho & \rho^2 & \cdots & \rho^{T-2} \\ \rho^2 & \rho & 1 & \rho & \cdots & \rho^{T-3} \\ & & & \vdots & & \rho \ \vdots \\ \rho^{T-1} & \rho^{T-2} & & & \cdots & 1 \end{bmatrix}. \tag{15-10}$$

15.4. Least Squares Estimation

Since Ω is not equal to $\mathbf{I}$, the now familiar problems will apply to least squares estimation. In general, least squares will continue to be unbiased; the earlier general proof includes autocorrelated disturbances. Whether least squares is consistent or not depends, as before, on the matrix

$$\mathbf{Q}_T^* = \frac{1}{T} \mathbf{X}' \Omega \mathbf{X}.$$

If this matrix converges to a matrix of finite elements, then, by our earlier reasoning, OLS is mean square consistent. We can expand this as

$$\mathbf{Q}_T^* = \frac{1}{T} \sum_t \sum_s \rho_{|t-s|}[\mathbf{x}_t \mathbf{x}_s' + \mathbf{x}_s \mathbf{x}_t'], \qquad (15\text{--}11)$$

where $\mathbf{x}_t'$ and $\mathbf{x}_s'$ are rows of $\mathbf{X}$ and $\rho_{|t-s|}$ is the autocorrelation between ε_t and ε_s. Sufficient conditions for this matrix to converge are that the regressors be well behaved and the correlations between disturbances die off reasonably rapidly as the observations become further apart in time. For example, if the disturbances follow the AR(1) process described earlier, $\rho_k = \rho^k$ and $\mathbf{Q}_T^*$ will converge to a positive definite matrix $\mathbf{Q}^*$ as $T \to \infty$.

Asymptotic normality of least squares is extremely difficult to establish for the general model, due, once again, to the complexity of (15–11). The results of Amemiya (1985), Mann and Wald (1943), and Anderson (1971) noted in Chapter 13 do carry over to most of the familiar types of autocorrelated disturbances, so we shall assume that their analyses include the cases we examine here. We conclude, then, that ordinary least squares continues to be unbiased, consistent, asymptotically normally distributed, and, as before, inefficient.

15.4.1. OLS Estimation with Lagged Dependent Variables

There is an important exception to the results in the preceding paragraph. If the regression contains any lagged values of the dependent variable, least squares will no longer be unbiased or consistent. To take the simplest case, suppose that

$$y_t = \beta y_{t-1} + \varepsilon_t$$
$$\varepsilon_t = \rho \varepsilon_{t-1} + u_t. \qquad (15\text{--}12)$$

In this model, the regressor and the disturbance are correlated:

$$\mathrm{Cov}[y_{t-1}, \varepsilon_t] = \mathrm{Cov}[y_{t-1}, \rho \varepsilon_{t-1} + u_t]$$
$$= \rho\, \mathrm{Cov}[y_{t-1}, \varepsilon_{t-1}]$$
$$= \rho\, \mathrm{Cov}[y_t, \varepsilon_t]$$

since the process is stationary and u_t is uncorrelated with everything that precedes it. Continuing yields

$$\rho\, \mathrm{Cov}[y_t, \varepsilon_t] = \rho\, \mathrm{Cov}[\beta y_{t-1} + \varepsilon_t, \varepsilon_t]$$
$$= \rho\{\beta\, \mathrm{Cov}[y_{t-1}, \varepsilon_t] + \mathrm{Cov}[\varepsilon_t, \varepsilon_t]\}$$
$$= \rho\{\beta\, \mathrm{Cov}[y_{t-1}, \varepsilon_t] + \mathrm{Var}[\varepsilon_t]\}.$$

Therefore,

$$\mathrm{Cov}[y_{t-1}, \varepsilon_t] = \beta\rho\, \mathrm{Cov}[y_{t-1}, \varepsilon_t] + \rho\, \mathrm{Var}[\varepsilon_t]$$
$$= \frac{\rho \sigma_u^2}{(1 - \beta\rho)(1 - \rho^2)}. \qquad (15\text{--}13)$$

(Note that this *is* zero if ρ is zero, regardless of β. This result is consistent with the observation that as long as the regressor is asymptotically uncorrelated with the disturbance, ordinary least squares is consistent even if the regressor is stochastic.) For the least squares estimator, we can use the general result

$$\text{plim } b = \beta + \frac{\text{Cov}[y_{t-1}, \varepsilon_t]}{\text{Var}[y_t]}. \tag{15–14}$$

But

$$\text{Var}[y_t] = \beta^2 \, \text{Var}[y_{t-1}] + \text{Var}[\varepsilon_t] + 2\beta \, \text{Cov}[y_{t-1}, \varepsilon_t].$$

Since the process is stationary, $\text{Var}[y_t] = \text{Var}[y_{t-1}]$. $\text{Var}[\varepsilon_t]$ is given in (15–6), while $\text{Cov}[y_{t-1}, \varepsilon_t]$ is given in (15–13). Collecting terms, we have

$$\text{Var}[y_t] = \frac{\sigma_u^2(1 + \beta\rho)}{(1 - \rho^2)(1 - \beta^2)(1 - \beta\rho)},$$

so

$$\text{plim } b = \beta + \frac{\rho(1 - \beta^2)}{1 + \beta\rho}. \tag{15–15}$$

Therefore, least squares is inconsistent unless ρ equals zero.

15.4.2. Efficiency of Least Squares

Since the model with autocorrelated disturbances is a generalized regression model, we should expect least squares to be inefficient. There are, however, few general results on how inefficient it is because knowledge of both the disturbance process and the process generating $\mathbf{X}$ is required. A few useful cases have been examined in detail.

First, suppose that the model is

$$\begin{aligned} y_t &= \beta x_t + \varepsilon_t, \\ \varepsilon_t &= \rho\varepsilon_{t-1} + u_t, \end{aligned} \tag{15–16}$$

and x_t is also generated by an AR(1) process,

$$x_t = \delta x_{t-1} + v_t.$$

For convenience, let

$$\text{Var}[x_t] = \frac{\text{Var}[v_t]}{1 - \delta^2} \quad \text{and} \quad \text{Var}[\varepsilon_t] = \frac{\sigma_u^2}{1 - \rho^2}$$

$$= \sigma_x^2 \qquad\qquad\qquad = \sigma_\varepsilon^2.$$

With $\boldsymbol{\Omega}$ given in (15–10),

$$\frac{1}{T}\mathbf{x}'\boldsymbol{\Omega}\mathbf{x} = \frac{\sum_{1}^{T} x_t^2}{T} + 2\rho\frac{\sum_{2}^{T} x_t x_{t-1}}{T} + 2\rho^2\frac{\sum_{3}^{T} x_t x_{t-2}}{T} + \cdots + 2\rho^{T-1}\frac{x_1 x_T}{T}. \tag{15–17}$$

The autocovariances of x are σ_x^2, $\delta\sigma_x^2$, $\delta^2\sigma_x^2$, and so on. If T is large enough, the leading sums in (15–17) will approximate these, while if $|\delta| < 1$, the latter terms will be negligible. So if T is large enough,

$$\frac{1}{T}\mathbf{x'\Omega x} \simeq \sigma_x^2 + 2\rho\delta\sigma_x^2 + 2\rho^2\delta^2\sigma_x^2 + \cdots$$

$$= 2\sigma_x^2 \left(\sum_{i=0}^{\infty} (\rho\delta)^i \right) - \sigma_x^2$$

$$= \left(\frac{2\sigma_x^2}{1 - \rho\delta} \right) - \sigma_x^2$$

$$= \frac{\sigma_x^2(1 + \rho\delta)}{1 - \rho\delta}.$$

Collecting terms, we find that

$$\text{Var}[b] = \frac{\sigma_\varepsilon^2}{T} \left[\frac{\mathbf{x'x}}{T} \right]^{-1} \left[\frac{\mathbf{x'\Omega x}}{T} \right] \left[\frac{\mathbf{x'x}}{T} \right]^{-1}$$

is approximately

$$\text{Var}[b] \simeq \frac{\sigma_\varepsilon^2(1 + \rho\delta)}{T\sigma_x^2(1 - \rho\delta)}. \tag{15-18}$$

The variance of the GLS estimator is

$$\text{Var}[\hat{\beta}] = \left(\frac{\sigma_\varepsilon^2}{T} \right) \left[\frac{\mathbf{x'\Omega^{-1}x}}{T} \right]^{-1},$$

for which we require

$$\mathbf{\Omega^{-1}} = \frac{1}{1 - \rho^2} \begin{bmatrix} 1 & -\rho & 0 & 0 & 0 & \cdots & \cdots & 0 \\ -\rho & 1+\rho^2 & -\rho & 0 & 0 & \cdots & \cdots & 0 \\ 0 & -\rho & 1+\rho^2 & -\rho & 0 & \cdots & \cdots & 0 \\ & & & \vdots & & & & \\ 0 & 0 & 0 & 0 & \cdots & -\rho & 1+\rho^2 & -\rho \\ 0 & 0 & 0 & 0 & \cdots & 0 & -\rho & 1 \end{bmatrix}. \tag{15-19}$$

Then

$$\text{Var}[\hat{\beta}] = \frac{\sigma_\varepsilon^2}{T} \left[\frac{1}{1-\rho^2} \left((1+\rho^2)\frac{\sum_{t=1}^{T} x_t^2}{T} - \rho^2\frac{x_1^2 + x_T^2}{T} - 2\rho\frac{\sum_{t=2}^{T} x_t x_{t-1}}{T} \right) \right]^{-1}.$$

If the sample is large, the *end effect*, $(x_1^2 + x_T^2)/T$, will be negligible, so that

$$\text{Var}[\hat{\beta}] \simeq \frac{\sigma_\varepsilon^2(1 - \rho^2)}{T\sigma_x^2(1 + \rho^2 - 2\rho\delta)}. \tag{15-20}$$

The (in)efficiency of least squares relative to GLS is, therefore, approximately

$$\frac{\text{Var}[b]}{\text{Var}[\hat{\beta}]} = \frac{(1 + \rho\delta)/(1 - \rho\delta)}{(1 - \rho^2)/(1 + \rho^2 - 2\rho\delta)}. \tag{15-21}$$

Values of the ratio are given in Table 15.3. The function is not monotonic in δ, but clearly, the least favorable cases are those with large values of ρ for any given δ. The efficiency of least squares relative to generalized least squares falls to less than 10 percent if ρ is close to one.

TABLE 15.3 Efficiency Ratio: Var[OLS]/Var[GLS]

	ρ						
δ	**−0.9**	**−0.6**	**−0.3**	**0.0**	**0.3**	**0.6**	**0.9**
−0.9	9.53	1.46	1.05	1.00	1.03	1.14	1.90
−0.6	12.86	2.13	1.15	1.00	1.11	1.53	4.54
−0.3	11.63	2.25	1.30	1.00	1.17	1.87	7.11
0.0	9.53	2.12	1.20	1.00	1.20	2.13	9.53
0.3	7.11	1.87	1.17	1.00	1.20	2.25	11.64
0.6	4.54	1.53	1.11	1.00	1.15	2.12	12.86
0.9	1.90	1.14	1.03	1.00	1.05	1.46	9.53

The preceding discussion gives a rather pessimistic conclusion, but it is derived under somewhat narrow assumptions. For models that involve relatively slowly changing variables, such as macroeconomic flows like consumption or output, the loss of efficiency in using least squares might not be quite so severe as this result suggests.[10]

15.4.3. Estimating the Variance of the Least Squares Estimator

As usual, $s^2(\mathbf{X'X})^{-1}$ is an inappropriate estimator of $\sigma^2(\mathbf{X'X})^{-1}(\mathbf{X'\Omega X})(\mathbf{X'X})^{-1}$, both because s^2 is a biased estimator of σ^2 and because the matrix is incorrect. With regard to σ^2, the analysis of Section 14.2.2 concerning heteroscedasticity is in general terms, and includes the current case as well. Thus, it is shown there that s^2 is a biased but consistent estimator of σ^2. Asymptotically, therefore, the difference between the estimated variance and the true variance of least squares hinges on the two matrices. For the model in (15–16),

$$\frac{(\mathbf{x'x}/T)^{-1}}{(\mathbf{x'x}/T)^{-1}(\mathbf{x'\Omega x}/T)(\mathbf{x'x}/T)^{-1}} \approx \frac{1 - \rho\delta}{1 + \rho\delta}. \tag{15–22}$$

If ρ and δ have the same sign, the ratio is less than 1. Since, in most economic time series, the autocorrelation is positive, this would seem to be the norm. As such, the standard errors conventionally *estimated* by least squares are likely to be too small.

In view of this situation, if one is going to use least squares, it is desirable to have an appropriate estimator of the covariance matrix of the least squares estimator. There are two approaches. If the form of the autocorrelation is known, one can estimate the parameters of $\mathbf{\Omega}$ directly and compute a consistent estimator. Of course, if so, it would be more sensible to use generalized least squares instead and not waste the sample information on an inefficient estimator. The second approach parallels the use of the White estimator for heteroscedasticity. Suppose that the form of the autocorrelation is unknown. Then a direct estimator of $\mathbf{\Omega}$ or $\mathbf{\Omega}(\boldsymbol{\theta})$ is not available. The problem in this setting is estimation of

$$\mathbf{\Sigma} = \frac{1}{T} \sum_t \sum_s \rho_{|t-s|}[\mathbf{x}_t\mathbf{x}_s' + \mathbf{x}_s\mathbf{x}_t']. \tag{15–23}$$

Following White's suggestion for heteroscedasticity,[11] Newey and West (1987) have devised an estimator for autocorrelated disturbances with an unspecified structure:

$$S_* = S_0 + \frac{1}{T} \sum_{j=1}^{L} \sum_{t=j+1}^{T} w_j e_t e_{t-j}(\mathbf{x}_t\mathbf{x}_{t-j}' + \mathbf{x}_{t-j}\mathbf{x}_t'), \tag{15–24}$$

---

[10] See Judge et al. (1982, p. 280).

[11] See Section 14.2.3.

where S_0 is the White estimator in (14–9) and

$$w_j = 1 - \frac{j}{L+1}. \tag{15-25}$$

The result is surprisingly simple and relatively easy to implement. There is a final problem to be solved. It must be determined a priori how large L should be in order that autocorrelations at lags greater than L are small enough to ignore. For a moving average process, this can be expected to be a relatively small number. However, for autoregressive processes or mixtures, the autocorrelations are never zero, and the researcher must make a judgment as to how far back it is necessary to go. Unfortunately, the result is not so crisp as the White estimator for heteroscedasticity.

EXAMPLE 15.3

Using the investment data of Example 15.1, we find that the Newey–West estimator of the variance matrix of least squares based on $L = 4$ yields the results listed in Table 15.4.

TABLE 15.4

Variable	OLS Estimate	OLS SE	Corrected SE
Constant	−12.5336	24.92	18.96
Real interest	−1.00144	2.369	3.342
Real GNP	0.16914	0.02057	0.01675

15.5. Testing for Autocorrelation

15.5.1. The Durbin–Watson Test

Most of the available tests for autocorrelation are based on the principle that if the true disturbances are autocorrelated, this will be revealed through the autocorrelations of the least squares residuals. By far the most widely used test is the Durbin–Watson test.[12] The test statistic is

$$d = \frac{\sum\limits_{t=2}^{T} (e_t - e_{t-1})^2}{\sum\limits_{t=1}^{T} e_t^2}. \tag{15-26}$$

The statistic is closely related to the sample autocorrelation:

$$d = 2(1 - r) + \frac{e_1^2 + e_T^2}{\sum\limits_{t=1}^{T} e_t^2}.$$

If the sample is reasonably large, the last term will be negligible, leaving

$$d \simeq 2(1 - r). \tag{15-27}$$

[12] Durbin and Watson (1950, 1951).

Values of d that differ significantly from two suggest autocorrelation of the disturbances. For testing for positive autocorrelation, the procedure would be to

$$\text{Reject } H_0\text{: } \rho = 0 \qquad \text{if } d < d_*,$$

where d_* is the appropriate critical value for the distribution of d under H_0. (A test for negative autocorrelation can be based on $4 - d$.)

A serious shortcoming of the Durbin–Watson test is that the exact distribution of d depends on the data matrix. Durbin and Watson have provided a partial solution to this problem. They show that the true distribution of d lies between that of two other statistics, d_l (the lower bound) and d_u (the upper bound), such that the 5 percent critical value for the true distribution of d must lie to the right of that of d_l and to the left of that of d_u. The usefulness of the result is that the distributions of d_l and d_u depend only on T and K, and their 5 percent and 1 percent critical values have been tabulated.[13] Therefore, the test that may be carried out is

$$\text{Do not reject } H_0 \qquad \text{if } d > d_{*u},$$

$$\text{Reject } H_0 \qquad \text{if } d \le d_{*l}.$$

No conclusion is drawn if $d_{*l} \le d \le d_{*u}$. An analogous test has been derived for quarterly data and fourth-order autocorrelation [see (15–39)] by Wallis (1972) based on

$$d_4 = \frac{\displaystyle\sum_{t=5}^{T} (e_t - e_{t-4})^2}{\displaystyle\sum_{t=1}^{T} e_t^2}. \tag{15–28}$$

Tables of the bounding distributions are given by Wallis.

EXAMPLE 15.4

The Durbin–Watson statistic for the investment equation is 1.3215. The 5 percent critical values from the Savin–White (1977) tables are 1.074 and 1.536. Since the sample value falls in the inconclusive region, further analysis is called for.

The inconclusive region in the Durbin–Watson tables is a troubling problem. This area can be rather wide. For example, for $T = 19$ and $K = 3$ (i.e., our particular problem), the inconclusive region encompasses values of ρ from 0.218 to 0.463 (using $1 - d/2$). A great deal of research has been devoted to narrowing or eliminating this region. One approach is to deal specifically with certain kinds of regressors. For example, the critical values in the tables assume that the regression contains a constant term. If not, d_{*l} may be replaced with d_{*m}, where d_{*m} is greater than d_{*l}.[14] King (1981) presents an alternative set of bounds for regressions with quarterly seasonal dummy variables. Giles and King (1978) present corresponding modifications for the Wallis test.

One could argue, on grounds of conservatism, that d_{*u} should always be used as the critical value. Failing to account for autocorrelation when it is present is almost surely worse than accounting for it when it is not. If the data are slowly changing, the correct critical value is more likely than not to be close to d_{*u}.[15] It is possible to calculate the

---

[13] See Savin and White (1977) or the appendix at the end of this book.

[14] See Farebrother (1980).

[15] See, for example, Theil and Nagar (1961) and Hannan and Terrell (1966).

correct percentage point for d for the particular data set, but this requires specialized software and is likely to be rather difficult. A number of authors have attempted to derive approximations to the appropriate critical values for the Durbin–Watson test. One that has been found to be quite accurate is also due to Durbin and Watson (1971).

The Durbin–Watson statistic can be written as

$$d = \frac{e'Ae}{e'e},$$

where

$$A = \begin{bmatrix} 1 & -1 & 0 & 0 & \cdots & 0 \\ -1 & 2 & -1 & 0 & \cdots & 0 \\ 0 & -1 & 2 & -1 & \cdots & 0 \\ 0 & 0 & \cdots & -1 & 2 & -1 \\ 0 & 0 & 0 & \cdots & -1 & 1 \end{bmatrix}. \tag{15-29}$$

Since $e = M\varepsilon$, where $M = I - X(X'X)^{-1}X'$,

$$d = \frac{(\varepsilon/\sigma)'MAM(\varepsilon/\sigma)}{(\varepsilon/\sigma)'M(\varepsilon/\sigma)}. \tag{15-30}$$

The exact distribution of this statistic depends on X. The approach is to approximate the true critical value, using

$$\hat{d}_* = a + bd_{*u},$$

where a and b are determined from

$$E[d] = a + bE[d_u],$$
$$\text{Var}[d] = b^2\text{Var}[d_u]. \tag{15-31}$$

The expectations and variances are computed using the characteristic roots of A:

$$E[d_u] = \frac{1}{n} \sum_{j=K+1}^{T} \theta_j = \bar{\theta},$$
$$\text{Var}[d_u] = \frac{2}{n(n+2)} \left[\sum_{j=K+1}^{T} \theta_j^2 - n\bar{\theta}^2 \right], \tag{15-32}$$

where $n = T - K$. We use the $T - K$ largest roots of A. Then $E[d]$ and $\text{Var}[d]$ are computed in the same manner, using the n nonzero characteristic roots of MAM.[16]

EXAMPLE 15.5

For our investment data, the characteristic roots, λ, of MAM are the following:

3.95633	3.87667	3.74689	3.55003	3.32671	3.08085
2.69580	2.48651	2.10701	1.81835	1.48363	1.18083
0.897094	0.644495	0.398000	0.209969	and three zeros.	

---

[16] The characteristic roots of A are $\theta_i = 2 - 2\cos[\pi(i-1)/T]$, which can easily be computed. But if T is even moderately large, the calculation of the characteristic roots of MAM, which is a $T \times T$ matrix, are likely to be quite burdensome, assuming that the necessary software is available at all. An alternative calculation based only on $K \times K$ matrices is given in Judge et al. (1982, pp. 468–469).

The 18 nonzero characteristic roots, θ, of **A** are the following:

3.97272	3.89163	3.75895	3.57828	3.35456	3.09390
2.80339	2.49097	2.16516	1.83484	1.50903	1.19661
0.906104	0.645437	0.421719	0.241052	0.108366	0.0272774

(The last is always zero.) Inserting these roots in the preceding equations gives $b = 0.9984689$ and $a = -0.0221681$. Therefore, the approximate value for d_* is 1.5115. This is consistent with our earlier observation in Example 15.4. Since the Durbin–Watson statistic for the regression is 1.3215, we would reject the hypothesis of no autocorrelation. Note that 1.3215 is squarely in the inconclusive region.

15.5.2. Other Testing Procedures

The Durbin–Watson test has been found to be quite powerful when compared to others for AR(1) processes. The test is not limited to testing for AR(1) disturbances, however. Regardless of the stochastic process,

$$\text{plim } d = 2 - 2\rho_1$$

where

$$\rho_1 = \text{Corr}[\varepsilon_t, \varepsilon_{t-1}].$$

Aside from the difficulty of the inconclusive region, however, there are two problems. First, it is strictly correct only when **X** is nonstochastic. Second, if the process is not an AR(1), ρ_1 may not be truly indicative of the pattern of autocorrelation.[17] Two alternative tests that are less restrictive have been devised.

The Breusch (1978)–Godfrey (1978b) test is a Lagrange multiplier test of

$$H_0: \text{No autocorrelation,}$$

versus

$$H_1: \varepsilon_t = \text{AR}(P) \quad \text{or} \quad \varepsilon_t = \text{MA}(P).$$

The same test is used for either structure. Operationally, the test can be carried out simply by regressing the ordinary least squares residuals, e_t, on $\mathbf{x}_t, e_{t-1}, \ldots, e_{t-P}$ (filling in missing values for lagged residuals with zeros) and referring TR^2 to the tabled critical value for the chi-squared distribution with P degrees of freedom. Since $\mathbf{X}'\mathbf{e} = \mathbf{0}$, the test is equivalent to regressing e_t on the part of the lagged residuals that is unexplained by **X**. There is, therefore, a compelling logic to it; if any fit is found, it is due to correlation between the current and lagged residuals. The test is a joint test of the first P autocorrelations of ε_t, not just the first.

An alternative though quite similar test is due to Box and Pierce. The Q test is carried out by referring

$$Q = T \sum_{j=1}^{L} r_j^2, \tag{15–33}$$

[17] See Example 15.6.

where

$$r_j = \frac{\sum\limits_{t=j+1}^{T} e_t e_{t-j}}{\sum\limits_{t=1}^{T} e_t^2}$$

to the critical values of the chi-squared table with L degrees of freedom. A refinement suggested by Ljung and Box (1979) is

$$Q' = T(T + 2) \sum_{j=1}^{L} \frac{r_j^2}{T - j}. \qquad (15\text{--}33')$$

This test has also been found to be reasonably powerful; however, it and the Breusch–Godfrey test have been criticized for the difficulty with the choice of L. It is worth noting that this problem of determining the depth of the lag to consider in these models of autocorrelation has reappeared at various points in our work here and pervades this literature.

EXAMPLE 15.6 _____

The regression of the current residual on a constant, real GNP, the real interest rate, and four lags of the residual produces

$$e_t = -0.9840 - 0.000273\text{GNP} + 4.781\text{i} \qquad T = 19$$
$$(17.57) \quad (0.01451) \qquad\quad (2.080) \qquad R^2 = 0.6352$$

$$-0.387e_{t-1} - 0.285e_{t-2} - 0.837e_{t-3} - 0.640e_{t-4}$$
$$(0.308) \qquad (0.325) \qquad (0.342) \qquad (0.372)$$

The Breusch–Godfrey statistic is, thus, 12.068. The 5 percent critical value for the chi-squared distribution with four degrees of freedom is 9.488. The 1 percent critical value is 13.277. Therefore, the null hypothesis would be rejected at a significance level of 5 percent. The first four autocorrelations for the least squares residuals are

$$r_1 = 0.2507$$

$$r_2 = -0.2752$$

$$r_3 = -0.6605$$

$$r_4 = -0.3699$$

The Box–Pierce Q statistic is 13.5219, while the Ljung–Box statistic is 17.6895. Both are statistically significant at the 1 percent level. Both of these tests suggest that the insignificance of the Durbin–Watson test results from the fact that a significant autocorrelation appears at lag 3 but not at lag 1. Unfortunately, there is nothing in the construction of the data that would imply such a pattern of strong negative autocorrelation at lag 3. The small-sample size (19 observations) does imply that these results should be interpreted with caution.

The essential difference between the Godfrey–Breusch and the Box–Pierce tests is the use of partial correlations (controlling for $\mathbf{X}$ and the other variables) in the former and simple correlations in the latter. Under the hypothesis, there is no autocorrelation in ε_t, and no correlation between $\mathbf{x}_t$ and ε_s in any event, so the two tests are asymptotically equivalent.

15.5.3. Testing in the Presence of Lagged Dependent Variables

The Durbin–Watson test is not likely to be valid when there is a lagged dependent variable in the equation.[18] The statistic will usually be biased toward a finding of no autocorrelation. Three alternatives have been devised.

The two tests described in the previous section can be used whether or not the regression contains a lagged dependent variable. As a simple alternative to the standard test, Durbin (1970) has derived a Lagrange multiplier test that is unaffected by the lagged dependent variable. The test may be carried out by referring

$$h = \left(1 - \frac{d}{2}\right) \sqrt{\frac{T}{1 - Ts_c^2}}, \tag{15-34}$$

where s_c^2 is the estimated variance of the least squares regression coefficient on y_{t-1}, to the standard normal tables. Large values of h lead to rejection of H_0. The test has the virtues that it can be used even if the regression contains additional lags of y_t, and it can be computed using the standard results from the initial regression without any further regressions. However, if $s_c^2 > 1/T$, it cannot be computed. An alternative is to regress e_t on $\mathbf{x}_t$, y_{t-1}, . . . , e_{t-1}, and any additional lags that are appropriate for e_t, and then testing the joint significance of the coefficient(s) on the lagged residual(s) with the standard F test. This is, of course, a modification of the Breusch–Godfrey test. Under H_0, the coefficients on the remaining variables will be zero, so the tests are the same asymptotically.

15.6. Efficient Estimation When Ω Is Known

15.6.1. Generalized Least Squares

If the parameters of Ω are known, the GLS estimator,

$$\hat{\boldsymbol{\beta}} = [\mathbf{X}'\Omega^{-1}\mathbf{X}]^{-1}[\mathbf{X}'\Omega^{-1}\mathbf{y}],$$

and its sampling variance,

$$\text{Var}[\hat{\boldsymbol{\beta}}] = \sigma_\varepsilon^2 [\mathbf{X}'\Omega^{-1}\mathbf{X}]^{-1},$$

can be computed directly. For the AR(1) process,

$$\Omega^{-1/2} = \mathbf{P} = \begin{bmatrix} \sqrt{1-\rho^2} & 0 & 0 & 0 & \cdots & 0 & 0 \\ -\rho & 1 & 0 & 0 & \cdots & 0 & 0 \\ 0 & -\rho & 0 & 0 & \cdots & 0 & 0 \\ & & & \vdots & & & \\ 0 & 0 & 0 & 0 & \cdots & -\rho & 1 \end{bmatrix}, \tag{15-35}$$

so the data for the transformed model are

$$\mathbf{y}_* = \begin{bmatrix} \sqrt{1-\rho^2}\,y_1 \\ y_2 - \rho y_1 \\ y_3 - \rho y_2 \\ \vdots \\ y_T - \rho y_{T-1} \end{bmatrix}, \qquad \mathbf{X}_* = \begin{bmatrix} \sqrt{1-\rho^2}\,\mathbf{x}_1 \\ \mathbf{x}_2 - \rho\mathbf{x}_1 \\ \mathbf{x}_3 - \rho\mathbf{x}_2 \\ \vdots \\ \mathbf{x}_T - \rho\mathbf{x}_{T-1} \end{bmatrix}. \tag{15-36}$$

---

[18] This issue has been studied by Nerlove and Wallis (1966), Durbin (1970), and Dezhbaksh (1990).

(These transformations are sometimes labeled *quasi-differences* or *pseudo-differences*.) Note that in the transformed model, every observation except the first contains a constant term. What was the column of ones in $\mathbf{X}$ is transformed to $[\sqrt{1 - \rho^2}, 1 - \rho, 1 - \rho, \ldots]$. Therefore, if the sample is relatively small, the problems noted earlier with measures of fit will reappear.

The variance of the transformed disturbance is

$$\text{Var}[\varepsilon_t - \rho\varepsilon_{t-1}] = \text{Var}[u_t] = \sigma_u^2.$$

[The variance of the first disturbance is also σ_u^2; see (15–6).]

Corresponding results have been derived for higher-order autoregressive processes. For the AR(2) model,

$$\varepsilon_t = \theta_1\varepsilon_{t-1} + \theta_2\varepsilon_{t-2} + u_t, \tag{15–37}$$

the transformed data for generalized least squares are obtained by

$$\mathbf{z}_{*_1} = \left[\frac{(1 + \theta_2)[(1 - \theta_2)^2 - \theta_1^2]}{1 - \theta_2} \right]^{1/2} \mathbf{z}_1,$$

$$\mathbf{z}_{*_2} = (1 - \theta_2^2)^{1/2}\mathbf{z}_2 - \frac{\theta_1(1 - \theta_1^2)^{1/2}}{1 - \theta_2}\mathbf{z}_1, \tag{15–38}$$

$$\mathbf{z}_{*_t} = \mathbf{z}_t - \theta_1\mathbf{z}_{t-1} - \theta_2\mathbf{z}_{t-2} \qquad t > 2,$$

where $\mathbf{z}$ is used for y_t or $\mathbf{x}_t$. The transformation becomes progressively more complex for higher-order processes.[19]

Note that in both the AR(1) and AR(2) models, the transformation to y_* and $\mathbf{X}_*$ involves "starting values" for the processes that depend only on the first one or two observations. We can view the process as having begun in the infinite past. However, since the sample contains only T observations, it is convenient to treat the first one or two (or P) observations as shown and consider them as "initial values." Whether we view the process as having begun at time $t = 1$ or in the infinite past is ultimately immaterial in regard to the asymptotic properties of our estimators. However, as we shall see, what we do with the initial values in a finite sample can make a substantial difference.

Higher-order MA processes and mixtures of AR and MA processes can be estimated by approximations to GLS.[20] (Full GLS is not well worked out for very many processes involving MA disturbances.) One would have to ask, however, how such a process might arise in the first place. Nicholls et al. (1975) describe some instances in which MA(1) disturbances might be expected, but as a general rule, they do not arise naturally. In the widely studied case of adjustment models that we examine in Chapter 18, the model does have an MA(1) disturbance, but it also contains a lagged dependent variable. As such, none of the apparatus developed earlier is applicable. The upshot is that MA and ARMA (mixtures of AR and MA) disturbances in econometric models should be applied with circumspection. A particular type of higher-order AR model has been advocated by Wallis (1972). In particular, for quarterly data, he suggests that the model

$$\varepsilon_t = \rho\varepsilon_{t-4} + u_t \tag{15–39}$$

is more appropriate than, say, an AR(1) model, because random effects are more likely to be correlated with the corresponding previous season than with the immediately preceding

---

[19] See Box and Jenkins (1984) and Fuller (1976).

[20] See, for example, Kmenta (1986, pp. 326–328) and Greenberg and Webster (1983) for moving average models.

season. This process has a distinctive pattern of autocorrelations:

$$\text{Cov}[\varepsilon_t, \varepsilon_{t-i}] = \sigma_u^2 \frac{\rho^{i/4}}{1 - \rho^2}, \qquad i = 0, 4, 8, \ldots$$

$$= 0 \text{ otherwise.}$$

Full GLS for this model is obtained using

$$\mathbf{x}_{*_t} = \sqrt{1 - \rho^2}\mathbf{z}_t, \qquad t = 1, 2, 3, 4,$$

$$= \mathbf{z}_t - \rho\mathbf{z}_{t-4}, \qquad t > 4.$$

15.6.2. Maximum Likelihood Estimation

If the parameters of the disturbance process are known, GLS and maximum likelihood estimation for the AR(1) model are equivalent. In order to obtain the likelihood function for normally distributed disturbances, we make use of

$$f(y_1, y_2, \ldots y_T) = f(y_1)f(y_2|y_1)f(y_3|y_2)\cdots f(y_T|y_{T-1}).$$

Based on (15–36), we find that the transformed regression is

$$y_t^* = \boldsymbol{\beta}'\mathbf{x}_t^* + u_t,$$

so that in terms of the original data,

$$y_1 = \boldsymbol{\beta}'\mathbf{x}_1 + \frac{u_1}{\sqrt{1 - \rho^2}}$$

and

$$y_t|y_{t-1} = \rho y_{t-1} + \boldsymbol{\beta}'\mathbf{x}_t - \rho\boldsymbol{\beta}'\mathbf{x}_{t-1} + u_t$$

for $t = 2, \ldots, T$. For the first observation, we use the change of variable formula from Section 3.5 to obtain

$$f(y_1) = |\sqrt{(1 - \rho^2)}|f_{u_1}\{\sqrt{(1 - \rho^2)}(y_1 - \boldsymbol{\beta}'\mathbf{x}_1)\}$$

$$= (1 - \rho^2)^{1/2}(2\pi\sigma^2)^{-1/2}e^{-[(1 - \rho^2)/(2\sigma_u^2)](y_1 - \boldsymbol{\beta}'\mathbf{x}_1)^2}.$$

The log-likelihood function is

$$\ln L = \ln f(y_1) + \sum_{t=2}^{T} \ln f(y_t|y_{t-1})$$

$$= -\frac{1}{2}[\ln(2\pi) + \ln \sigma_u^2 - \ln(1 - \rho^2)] - \frac{1 - \rho^2}{2\sigma_u^2}(y_1 - \boldsymbol{\beta}'\mathbf{x}_1)^2$$

$$- \frac{T - 1}{2}(\ln(2\pi) + \ln \sigma_u^2) \qquad\qquad (15\text{–}40)$$

$$- \frac{1}{2\sigma_u^2}\sum_{t=2}^{T} [(y_t - \rho y_{t-1}) - \boldsymbol{\beta}'(\mathbf{x}_t - \rho\mathbf{x}_{t-1})]^2$$

$$= -\frac{T}{2}[\ln(2\pi) + \ln \sigma_u^2] + \frac{1}{2}\ln(1 - \rho^2) - \frac{1}{2\sigma_u^2}\sum_{t=1}^{T} [y_{*_t} - \boldsymbol{\beta}'\mathbf{x}_{*_t}]^2.$$

The sum of squares term is the residual sum of squares from the transformed, classical regression model in (15–36). *If ρ is known, the solution is least squares for $\boldsymbol{\beta}$ and σ^2, as usual, which is the GLS solution given in* (15–36). The derivatives of the log likelihood for a known Ω were found earlier and apply here. The information matrix is

$$\mathbf{I}(\boldsymbol{\beta},\ \sigma_u^2) = \begin{bmatrix} (1/\sigma_u^2)(\mathbf{X}'\Omega^{-1}\mathbf{X}) & \mathbf{0} \\ \mathbf{0}' & T/2\sigma_u^4 \end{bmatrix}.$$

15.7. Estimation When Ω Is Unknown

15.7.1. AR(1) Disturbances

For an unknown Ω, there is, if anything, an embarrassment of riches of FGLS estimators. All have the same asymptotic properties, as we saw earlier for the general case, as long as the first-round estimators are consistent. But there is considerable variation in their small-sample properties.

Once again, the AR(1) model is the one most widely used and studied. The most common procedure is to begin FGLS with a natural estimator of ρ, the autocorrelation of the residuals. Since **b** is consistent, we can use

$$r = \frac{\displaystyle\sum_{t=2}^{T} e_t e_{t-1}}{\displaystyle\sum_{t=2}^{T} e_t^2}. \tag{15–41}$$

Two of the many other modifications that have been suggested are Theil's estimator.[21]

$$r^* = \left[\frac{T-K}{T-1}\right] r$$

and

$$r^{**} = 1 - \frac{d}{2},$$

where d is the Durbin–Watson statistic for testing the hypothesis that ρ equals zero.[22] The estimator suggested by Durbin (1960) is the coefficient on y_{t-1} in the least squares regression

$$y_t = \rho y_{t-1} + \boldsymbol{\beta}'\mathbf{x}_t - (\rho\boldsymbol{\beta})'\mathbf{x}_{t-1} + u_t. \tag{15–42}$$

(The coefficients are computed ignoring the constraint.) All of these are consistent estimators of ρ. Since ρ must be in the range minus one to one, another possibility is to search over this range and choose the value of ρ that leads to the smallest sum of squares.[23]

For the second step of FGLS, there are two possibilities:

1. *Full FGLS.* This is the Prais–Winsten (1954) estimator.
2. *FGLS omitting the first observation.* This was first suggested by Cochrane and Orcutt (1949).

---

[21] Theil (1971, p. 254).

[22] See, for example, Johnston (1984, p. 324).

[23] See Hildreth and Lu (1960).

In a large sample, the two are likely to be the same. However, the typical economic time series is not particularly long, and which one is chosen may make a great deal of difference. The question is not merely one of different numerical values. The efficiency of the FGLS estimator can be very adversely affected by discarding the initial observation(s) if the sample is relatively small and the regressors have a trend, which is common in economic data.[24]

It is possible to iterate these estimators to convergence. Since the estimator is efficient at every iteration, nothing is gained asymptotically by doing so. Moreover, unlike the heteroscedastic model, iterating when there is autocorrelation does not secure the maximum likelihood estimator. The iterated FGLS estimator does not account for the term $(\frac{1}{2}) \ln(1 - \rho^2)$ in the log-likelihood function [see (15–40)]. None of the estimators discussed thus far satisfy $\partial \ln L/\partial \rho = 0$ for the current estimates of $\boldsymbol{\beta}$ and σ_u^2.

Full maximum likelihood estimators can be obtained by maximizing the log likelihood in (15–40) with respect to $\boldsymbol{\beta}$, σ^2, and ρ. Apart from the constant term, the log-likelihood function may be written

$$\ln L = -\frac{\mathbf{u'u}}{2\sigma_u^2} + \frac{1}{2} \ln(1 - \rho^2) - \frac{T}{2} \ln \sigma_u^2 \qquad (15\text{–}43)$$

(where, as before, the first observation is computed differently from the others). The likelihood equations can be derived from (15–40) and (15–43). From (15–43),

$$\frac{\partial \ln L}{\partial \boldsymbol{\beta}} = \frac{1}{\sigma_u^2} \sum_{t=1}^{T} u_t \mathbf{x}_{*_t},$$

where

$$u_1 = \sqrt{(1 - \rho^2)}(y_1 - \boldsymbol{\beta}'\mathbf{x}_1),$$

$$u_t = (y_t - \rho y_{t-1}) - \boldsymbol{\beta}'(\mathbf{x}_t - \rho \mathbf{x}_{t-1}) \qquad \text{for } t = 2, \dots, T.$$

[Note that $\mathbf{x}_{*_1} = \sqrt{1 - \rho^2}\mathbf{x}_1$ and $\mathbf{x}_{*_t} = (\mathbf{x}_t - \rho \mathbf{x}_{t-1})$.] Also, from (15–43), we have

$$\frac{\partial \ln L}{\partial \sigma_u^2} = -\frac{T}{2\sigma_u^2} + \frac{1}{2\sigma_u^4} \sum_{t=1}^{T} u_t^2.$$

Turning now to the first part of (15–40), we find that

$$\frac{\partial \ln L}{\partial \rho} = \frac{1}{\sigma_u^2} \sum_{t=2}^{T} u_t \varepsilon_{t-1} + \frac{\rho \varepsilon_1^2}{\sigma_u^2} - \frac{\rho}{1 - \rho^2},$$

where $\varepsilon_t = y_t - \boldsymbol{\beta}'\mathbf{x}_t$. For a given value of ρ, the maximum likelihood estimates of $\boldsymbol{\beta}$ and σ_u^2 are the usual ones, GLS and the mean squared residual using the transformed data. The problem is estimation of ρ. One possibility is to search the range $-1 < \rho < 1$ for the value that with the implied estimates of the other parameters, maximizes $\ln L$. This is analogous to the Hildreth–Lu estimator.[25] Beach and MacKinnon (1978a) argue that this is a very inefficient way to do the search and have devised a much faster algorithm.

[24] See Maeshiro (1979), Poirier (1978a), and Park and Mitchell (1980).

[25] An improvement on this is provided by Hildreth and Dent (1974).

The components of the information matrix are derived from

$$\frac{\partial^2 \ln L}{\partial \boldsymbol{\beta} \, \partial \boldsymbol{\beta}'} = -\frac{1}{\sigma_u^2} \sum_{t=1}^{T} \mathbf{x}_{*_t} \mathbf{x}_{*_t}' = -\frac{1}{\sigma_u^2} \mathbf{X}' \boldsymbol{\Omega}^{-1} \mathbf{X},$$

$$\frac{\partial^2 \ln L}{\partial \boldsymbol{\beta} \, \partial \sigma_u^2} = -\frac{1}{\sigma_u^4} \sum_{t=1}^{T} u_t \mathbf{x}_{*_t},$$

$$\frac{\partial^2 \ln L}{\partial \boldsymbol{\beta} \, \partial \rho} = \frac{1}{\sigma_u^2} \sum_{t=1}^{T} u_t \left(\frac{\partial \mathbf{x}_{*_t}}{\partial \rho} \right),$$

$$\frac{\partial^2 \ln L}{\partial (\sigma_u^2)^2} = \frac{T}{2\sigma_u^4} - \frac{1}{\sigma_u^6} \sum_{t=1}^{T} u_t^2,$$

$$\frac{\partial^2 \ln L}{\partial \rho \, \partial \sigma_u^2} = -\frac{1}{\sigma_u^4} \left(\sum_{t=2}^{T} u_t \varepsilon_{t-1} + \rho \varepsilon_1^2 \right),$$

$$\frac{\partial^2 \ln L}{\partial \rho^2} = -\frac{1}{\sigma_u^2} \sum_{t=2}^{T} \varepsilon_{t-1}^2 + \frac{\varepsilon_1^2}{\sigma_u^2} + \frac{1 + \rho^2}{(1 - \rho^2)^2}$$

(using $u_t = \varepsilon_t - \rho \varepsilon_{t-1}$). Taking the negative of the expected values produces the information matrix

$$\mathbf{I}(\boldsymbol{\beta}, \sigma_u^2, \rho) = \begin{bmatrix} \dfrac{1}{\sigma_u^2} \mathbf{X}' \boldsymbol{\Omega}^{-1} \mathbf{X} & \mathbf{0} & \mathbf{0} \\ \mathbf{0}' & \dfrac{T}{2\sigma_u^4} & \dfrac{\rho}{\sigma_u^2(1 - \rho^2)} \\ \mathbf{0}' & \dfrac{\rho}{\sigma_u^2(1 - \rho^2)} & \dfrac{T - 2}{1 - \rho^2} - \dfrac{1 + \rho^2}{(1 - \rho^2)^2} \end{bmatrix}.$$

The off-diagonal elements at the lower right result from the treatment of the first observation. If this observation is omitted, the calculations simplify a bit. Note that the other terms in the block are sums of $T - 1$ observations, so these "end effects" will be negligible asymptotically. Once again, their importance may be greater in a finite sample. Omitting the first observation produces the common approximation

$$\mathbf{I}(\boldsymbol{\beta}, \sigma_u^2, \rho) = \begin{bmatrix} \dfrac{1}{\sigma_u^2} \mathbf{X}' \boldsymbol{\Omega}^{-1} \mathbf{X} & \mathbf{0} & \mathbf{0} \\ \mathbf{0}' & \dfrac{T}{2\sigma_u^4} & 0 \\ \mathbf{0}' & 0 & \dfrac{T - 1}{1 - \rho^2} \end{bmatrix}. \tag{15--44}$$

It is common to drop the first observation from the previous calculations, arguing that it will be negligible asymptotically. Alternatively, one might do the analysis *conditionally* on the first observation (which appears unavoidably in the preceding sums.) From the point of view of the asymptotic properties of the estimators, it is certainly true that the first observation is inconsequential. But it must be remembered that the typical time series is not very long, and the numerical answers one obtains with and without explicit treatment of the first observation may be quite different. In such a case, the evidence suggests that retention is preferable.[26]

All of the foregoing estimators have the same asymptotic properties. The available evidence on their small-sample properties comes from Monte Carlo studies and is, unfortunately, only suggestive. Griliches and Rao (1969) find evidence that if the sample is relatively small and ρ is not particularly large, say, less than 0.3, least squares is as good as or better than FGLS. The problem is the additional variation introduced into the sampling variance by the variance of r (which increases or decreases). A second fairly firm conclusion is that it can be far worse to omit the first observation than to keep it.[27] Beyond these, the results are rather mixed. Maximum likelihood seems to perform well in general, but the Prais–Winsten estimator is evidently nearly as efficient.

EXAMPLE 15.7

The various estimators described earlier give rather different results for the investment data of Example 15.1. First, some different estimates of ρ are given in Table 15.5. Estimates of the regression parameters are shown in Table 15.6.

TABLE 15.5

r	0.3392
$1 - d/2$	0.3393
Theil	0.3015
Theil–Nagar	0.3735 $[T^2(1 - d/2) + K^2/(T^2 - K^2)]^a$
Durbin	0.6385

[a]From Theil and Nagar (1961).

TABLE 15.6 Parameter Estimates. Standard Errors in Parentheses.

Estimator	Constant	GNP	Interest	ρ
OLS	−12.5336	0.16914	−1.00144	0
	(24.92)	(0.02057)	(2.369)	
Prais–Winsten				
Two-step	−15.6551	0.17073	−0.70394	0.3392
	(33.76)	(0.02791)	(2.816)	
Iterated	−15.673	0.17075	−0.70462	0.3527
(two iterations)	(33.84)	(0.02796)	(2.817)	
Cochrane–Orcutt				
Two-step	−18.3567	0.17286	−0.80775	0.3392
	(44.83)	(0.03633)	(3.102)	
Iterated	−18.3567	0.17286	−0.80775	0.3559
(two iterations)	(44.83)	(0.03633)	(3.102)	
Maximum likelihood	−14.4989	0.17006	−0.82422	0.27996
	(31.56)	(0.02608)	(2.718)	
Durbin	−26.787	0.21351	0.38499	0.6385
	(32.53)	(0.07050)	(3.824)	
Hildreth–Lu	−14.887	0.17029	−0.78936	0.3000
	(32.47)	(0.02681)	(2.754)	

[26]See, for example, Maeshiro (1979) and Poirier (1978a).

[27]See Harvey and McAvinchey (1979).

There are some distinctive results in Table 15.6. First, it would appear that the OLS standard errors are considerably biased downward. Second, comparing the Cochrane–Orcutt estimates to the Prais–Winsten estimates, the loss of efficiency from discarding the initial observation is substantial. Obtaining the maximum likelihood estimates by the method of Beach and MacKinnon required only three function evaluations, which is only one more than the iterated two-step estimators.

15.7.2. AR(2) Disturbances

Maximum likelihood procedures for most other disturbance processes are exceedingly complex. Beach and MacKinnon (1978b) have derived an algorithm for AR(2) disturbances. For higher-order autoregressive models, maximum likelihood estimation is presently impractical, but the two-step estimators can easily be extended. For models of the form

$$\varepsilon_t = \theta_1 \varepsilon_{t-1} + \theta_2 \varepsilon_{t-2} + \cdots + \theta_P \varepsilon_{t-P} + u_t, \tag{15–45}$$

a simple approach for estimation of the autoregressive parameters is to use either of the following methods:

1. An analog of Durbin's method. Regress y_t on $y_{t-1}, \ldots, y_{t-p}$, $\mathbf{x}$, $\mathbf{x}_{t-1}, \ldots$, and $\mathbf{x}_{t-P}$. The slopes on the lagged values of y give consistent estimates of the autoregressive parameters. If there are many regressors, this may involve an excessive number of variables.
2. By regressing e_t on $e_{t-1}, \ldots, e_{t-P}$, we also obtain consistent estimates of the autoregressive parameters.

With the estimates of $\theta_1, \ldots, \theta_P$ in hand, the Cochrane–Orcutt estimator can be obtained. If the model is an AR(2), the full FGLS procedure should be used instead.[28] The least squares computations for the transformed data provide (at least asymptotically) the appropriate estimates of σ^2 and the covariance matrix of $\hat{\boldsymbol{\beta}}$. As before, iteration is possible but brings no gains in efficiency.

15.7.3. Estimation with a Lagged Dependent Variable

In Section 15.4.1, we considered the problem of estimation by least squares when the model contains both autocorrelation and lagged dependent variable(s). Since the OLS estimator is inconsistent, the residuals on which an estimator of ρ would be based are likewise inconsistent. Therefore $\hat{\rho}$ will be inconsistent as well. The consequence is that the FGLS estimators described earlier are not usable in this case. There is, however, an alternative way to proceed, based on the method of instrumental variables.

The method of instrumental variables was introduced in Section 9.5.3 in the context of measurement error in the classical regression model. To review, the general problem is that in the model

$$\mathbf{y} = \mathbf{X}\boldsymbol{\beta} + \boldsymbol{\varepsilon},$$

if

$$\text{plim}\, \frac{1}{T}\mathbf{X}'\boldsymbol{\varepsilon} \neq \mathbf{0},$$

---

[28] Fuller (1976) gives expressions for general autoregressive processes, but these are rather cumbersome and are not yet in wide use.

the least squares estimator is not consistent. A consistent estimator is

$$\mathbf{b}_{\text{IV}} = (\mathbf{Z}'\mathbf{X})^{-1}(\mathbf{Z}'\mathbf{y}),$$

where $\mathbf{Z}$ is a set of K variables chosen such that

$$\text{plim} \, \frac{1}{T}\mathbf{Z}'\boldsymbol{\varepsilon} = \mathbf{0}$$

but

$$\text{plim} \, \frac{1}{T}\mathbf{Z}'\mathbf{X} \neq \mathbf{0}.$$

For the purpose of consistency only, any such set of $\mathbf{z}$'s will suffice. The relevance of that fact here is that the obstacle to consistent FGLS is, at least for the present, the lack of a consistent estimator of ρ. By using the technique of instrumental variables, we may estimate $\boldsymbol{\beta}$ consistently, then estimate ρ, and proceed.

Hatanaka (1974) has devised an efficient two-step estimator based on this principle. To put the estimator in the current context, we consider estimation of the model

$$y_t = \boldsymbol{\beta}'\mathbf{x}_t + \gamma y_{t-1} + \varepsilon_t,$$

$$\varepsilon_t = \rho\varepsilon_{t-1} + u_t.$$

In order to get to the second step of FGLS, we require consistent estimates of the slope parameters. These can be obtained using an IV estimator, where the column of $\mathbf{Z}$ corresponding to y_{t-1} is the only one that need be different from that of $\mathbf{X}$. An appropriate instrument can be obtained by using the fitted values in the regression of y_t on $\mathbf{x}_t$ and $\mathbf{x}_{t-1}$.[29] The residuals from this regression are then used to construct

$$\hat{\rho} = \frac{\displaystyle\sum_{t=3}^{T} \hat{\varepsilon}_t\hat{\varepsilon}_{t-1}}{\displaystyle\sum_{t=3}^{T} \hat{\varepsilon}_t^2},$$

where

$$\hat{\varepsilon}_t = y_t - \mathbf{b}_{\text{IV}}'\mathbf{x}_t - c_{\text{IV}}y_{t-1}.$$

FGLS estimates may now be computed by regressing

$$y_{*_t} = y_t - \hat{\rho}y_{t-1}$$

on

$$\mathbf{x}_{*_t} = \mathbf{x}_t - \hat{\rho}\mathbf{x}_{t-1},$$

$$y_{*_{t-1}} = y_{t-1} - \hat{\rho}y_{t-2},$$

and

$$\hat{\varepsilon}_{t-1} = y_{t-1} - \mathbf{b}_{\text{IV}}'\mathbf{x}_{t-1} - c_{\text{IV}}y_{t-2}.$$

Let d be the coefficient on $\hat{\varepsilon}_{t-1}$ in this regression. The efficient estimator of ρ is

$$\hat{\hat{\rho}} = \hat{\rho} + d.$$

Appropriate asymptotic standard errors for the estimators, including $\hat{\hat{\rho}}$, are obtained from the $s^2[\mathbf{X}_*'\mathbf{X}_*]^{-1}$ computed at the second step. Hatanaka shows that these estimates are asymptotically equivalent to maximum likelihood estimates.

---

[29] One might use additional lags of $\mathbf{x}$ at this stage, perhaps to improve the small-sample properties of the estimator. Asymptotically, it is immaterial.

15.8. Forecasting in the Presence of Autocorrelation

For purposes of forecasting, we refer first to the transformed model,

$$y_{*_t} = \boldsymbol{\beta}'\mathbf{x}_{*_t} + \varepsilon_{*_t}.$$

Suppose that the process generating ε_t is an AR(1), and ρ is known. Since this is a classical regression model, the results of Chapter 6 may be used directly. The optimal forecast of $y^0_{*_{T+1}}$, given $\mathbf{x}^0_{T+1}$ and $\mathbf{x}_T$ (i.e., $\mathbf{x}^0_{*_{T+1}}$), is

$$\hat{y}^0_{*_{T+1}} = \hat{\boldsymbol{\beta}}'\mathbf{x}^0_{*_{T+1}}.$$

Disassembling $\hat{y}^0_{*_{T+1}}$, we find

$$\hat{y}^0_{T+1} - \rho y_T = \hat{\boldsymbol{\beta}}'\mathbf{x}^0_{T+1} - \rho\hat{\boldsymbol{\beta}}'\mathbf{x}_T$$

or

$$\begin{aligned}
\hat{y}^0_{T+1} &= \hat{\boldsymbol{\beta}}'\mathbf{x}^0_{T+1} + \rho(y_T - \hat{\boldsymbol{\beta}}'\mathbf{x}_T) \\
&= \hat{\boldsymbol{\beta}}'\mathbf{x}^0_{T+1} + \rho e_T.
\end{aligned} \tag{15–46}$$

Thus, we carry forward a proportion ρ of the estimated disturbance in the preceding period. This can be justified by reference to

$$E[\varepsilon_{T+1}\,|\,\varepsilon_T] = \rho\varepsilon_T.$$

It can also be shown that to forecast n periods ahead, we would use

$$\hat{y}^0_{T+n} = \hat{\boldsymbol{\beta}}'\mathbf{x}^0_{T+n} + \rho^n e_t. \tag{15–47}$$

The extension to higher-order autoregressions is direct. For a second-order model, for example,

$$\hat{y}^0_{T+n} = \hat{\boldsymbol{\beta}}'\mathbf{x}^0_{T+n} + \theta_1 e_{T+n-1} + \theta_2 e_{T+n-2}. \tag{15–48}$$

For residuals that are outside the sample period, we use the recursion

$$\hat{e}_s = \theta_1\hat{e}_{s-1} + \theta_2\hat{e}_{s-2}, \tag{15–49}$$

beginning with the last two residuals within the sample.

Moving average models are somewhat simpler, as the autocorrelation lasts for only one period. For an MA(1) model, for the first postsample period,

$$\hat{y}^0_{T+1} = \hat{\boldsymbol{\beta}}'\mathbf{x}^0_{T+1} + \hat{\varepsilon}_{T+1},$$

where

$$\hat{\varepsilon}_{T+1} = \hat{u}_{T+1} - \lambda\hat{u}_T.$$

Therefore, a forecast of ε_{T+1} will use all previous residuals. One way to proceed is to accumulate $\hat{\varepsilon}_{T+1}$ from the recursion

$$\hat{u}_t = \hat{\varepsilon}_t + \lambda\hat{u}_{t-1}$$

with $\hat{u}_{T+1} = \hat{u}_0 = 0$ and $\hat{\varepsilon}_t = (y_t - \hat{\boldsymbol{\beta}}'\mathbf{x}_t)$. After the first postsample period, $\hat{\varepsilon}_{T+n} = \hat{u}_{T+n} - \lambda\hat{u}_{T+n-1} = 0$.

If the parameters of the disturbance process are known, the variances for the forecast errors can be computed using the results of Chapter 6. For an AR(1) disturbance, the estimated variance would be

$$s_f^2 = \hat{\sigma}_\varepsilon^2[1 + (\mathbf{x}_t - \rho\mathbf{x}_{t-1})'\{\text{Est. Var}[\hat{\boldsymbol{\beta}}]\}(\mathbf{x}_t - \rho\mathbf{x}_{t-1})]. \tag{15–50}$$

For a higher-order process, it is only necessary to modify the calculation of $\mathbf{x}_{*_t}$ accordingly. The forecast variances for an MA(1) process are somewhat more involved. Details may be found in Judge et al. (1985). If the parameters of the disturbance process, ρ, λ, θ_j, and so on, are estimated as well, the forecast variance will be greater. For an AR(1) model, the necessary correction to the forecast variance of the n-period-ahead forecast error is $\hat{\sigma}_\varepsilon^2 n^2 \rho^{2(n-1)}/T$. [For a one-period-ahead forecast, this merely adds a term, $1/T$, in the brackets in (15–50).] Higher-order AR and MA processes are analyzed in Baille (1979). Finally, if the regressors are stochastic, the expressions become more complex by another order of magnitude.

If ρ is known, (15–47) provides the best linear unbiased forecast of y_{t+1}.[30] If, however, ρ must be estimated, this assessment must be modified. There is information about ε_{t+1} embodied in e_t. However, having to estimate ρ implies that some or all of the value of this information is offset by the variation introduced into the forecast by including the stochastic component $\hat{\rho} e_t$.[31] Whether (15–47) is preferable to the obvious expedient, $\hat{y}_{T+n}^0 = \hat{\boldsymbol{\beta}}' \mathbf{x}_{T+n}^0$, in a small sample when ρ is estimated remains to be settled.

For computational purposes, Pagan and Nicholls (1984) have extended Salkever's augmented regression (Section 6.8.1) to models of autocorrelation. The augmented regression for forecasting T^0 periods ahead, based on $\mathbf{X}^0$, would use

$$\tilde{\mathbf{X}} = \begin{bmatrix} \mathbf{X} & \mathbf{0} & & & \\ \mathbf{x}_{T+1}^0 & 1 & 0 & 0 & \cdots \\ \mathbf{x}_{T+2}^0 & \rho & 1 & 0 & \cdots \\ \mathbf{x}_{T+3}^0 & \rho^2 & \rho & 1 & \cdots \end{bmatrix}, \qquad \tilde{\mathbf{y}} = \begin{bmatrix} \mathbf{y} \\ \mathbf{y}^0 \end{bmatrix}.$$

etc.

The authors have obtained general expressions for higher-order models and for mixtures of AR and MA models. There are two drawbacks, however. First, the unknown ρ must be replaced with the sample estimate. This is simple in principle. But it presents a practical difficulty not present in Salkever's computations. The classical regression is done in a single pass, so $\tilde{\mathbf{X}}$ and $\tilde{\mathbf{y}}$ can be constructed before the computations are begun. Pagan and Nicholls' augmented regressors must be constructed *after* the initial least squares regression. Most software does not relinquish control once the estimation of a model with autocorrelated disturbances is begun until all computations are finished. The second difficulty, also not present in Salkever's formulation, is that this augmented regression requires $\mathbf{y}^0$. Therefore, it can be used only for within-sample purposes (or for model validation based on partitioning of the sample).

15.9. Autoregressive Conditional Heteroscedasticity

Heteroscedasticity is usually associated with cross-sectional data, while time series are typically studied in the context of homoscedastic processes. In analyses of macroeconomic data, Engle (1982, 1983) and Cragg (1982) have found evidence that for some phenomena the disturbance variances in time-series models are less stable than usually assumed.

Engle's results suggest that in analyzing models of inflation, large and small forecast errors appear to occur in clusters, suggesting a form of heteroscedasticity in which the

---

[30] See Goldberger (1962).

[31] See Baille (1979).

variance of the forecast error depends on the size of the preceding disturbance. He has suggested the **AutoRegressive, Conditionally Heteroscedastic,** or **ARCH,** model as an alternative to the usual time-series process. A simple version of his model is

$$y_t = \boldsymbol{\beta}'\mathbf{x}_t + \varepsilon_t$$

$$\varepsilon_t = u_t[\alpha_0 + \alpha_1\varepsilon_{t-1}^2]^{1/2}, \tag{15-51}$$

where u_t is standard normal.[32] It follows that

$$E[\varepsilon_t | \varepsilon_{t-1}] = 0,$$

so

$$E[\varepsilon_t] = 0 \quad \text{and} \quad E[y_t] = \boldsymbol{\beta}'\mathbf{x}_t.$$

Also,

$$
\begin{aligned}
\text{Var}[\varepsilon_t | \varepsilon_{t-1}] &= E[\varepsilon_t^2 | \varepsilon_{t-1}] \\
&= E[u_t^2][\alpha_0 + \alpha_1\varepsilon_{t-1}^2] \\
&= \alpha_0 + \alpha_1\varepsilon_{t-1}^2 \\
&= \text{Var}[y_t | y_{t-1}].
\end{aligned}
$$

Conditional on ε_{t-1}, ε_t is heteroscedastic. The *unconditional* variance of ε_t is[33]

$$
\begin{aligned}
\text{Var}[\varepsilon_t] &= E[\text{Var}[\varepsilon_t | \varepsilon_{t-1}]] \\
&= \alpha_0 + \alpha_1 E[\varepsilon_{t-1}^2] \\
&= \alpha_0 + \alpha_1\text{Var}[\varepsilon_{t-1}].
\end{aligned}
$$

If the process generating the disturbances is **variance stationary,**[34] the unconditional variance is unchanging over time. Then,

$$
\begin{aligned}
\text{Var}[\varepsilon_t] &= \text{Var}[\varepsilon_{t-1}] \\
&= \alpha_0 + \alpha_1\text{Var}[\varepsilon_{t-1}] \tag{15-52} \\
&= \frac{\alpha_0}{1 - \alpha_1}.
\end{aligned}
$$

Therefore, the model obeys the classical assumptions, and ordinary least squares is the most efficient *linear* estimator of $\boldsymbol{\beta}$.

But there is a more efficient *nonlinear* estimator. The log-likelihood function for this model is given by Engle (1982). Conditioned on starting values y_0 and $\mathbf{x}_0$, the log likelihood for observations $t = 1, \ldots, T$ is

$$\ln L = -\frac{1}{2}\sum_{t=1}^{T}\ln(\alpha_0 + \alpha_1\varepsilon_{t-1}^2) - \frac{1}{2}\sum_{t=1}^{T}\frac{\varepsilon_t^2}{\alpha_0 + \alpha_1\varepsilon_{t-1}^2}, \tag{15-53}$$

where

$$\varepsilon_t = y_t - \boldsymbol{\beta}'\mathbf{x}_t.$$

---

[32] The assumption that u_t has unit variance is not a restriction. The scaling implied by any other variance would be absorbed by the other parameters.

[33] We are using the variance decomposition in (3–70). The variance of $E[\varepsilon_t | \varepsilon_{t-1}]$ is zero.

[34] We shall treat this concept in more detail in Chapter 19.

Maximization of ln L may be done by conventional methods. However, a simpler, four-step FGLS estimator is available.[35] Let the sample consist of y_t and $\mathbf{x}_t$ for $t = 0, 1, \ldots , T$, including the initial values.

1. Regress $\mathbf{y}$ on $\mathbf{X}$, using least squares and all available observations to obtain $\mathbf{b}$ and $\mathbf{e}$.
2. Regress e_t^2 on a constant and e_{t-1}^2 to obtain initial estimates of α_0 and α_1, using the T observations $t = 1, \ldots , T$. Notice that this is the same procedure we have used in several other FGLS procedures to estimate the variance parameters consistently. Denote the 2×1 estimated vector as $[a_0, a_1]' = \mathbf{a}$.
3. Compute $f_t = a_0 + a_1 e_{t-1}^2$ for $t = 1, \ldots , T$. Then compute the asymptotically efficient estimate

$$\hat{\alpha} = \mathbf{a} + \mathbf{d}_\alpha,$$

where $\mathbf{d}_\alpha$ is the least squares coefficient vector in the regression of $[(e_t^2/f_t) - 1]$ on $(1/f_t)$ and (e_{t-1}^2/f_t). The asymptotic covariance matrix for $\hat{\alpha}$ is $2(\mathbf{Z}'\mathbf{Z})^{-1}$, where $\mathbf{Z}$ is the regressor matrix in this regression.[36]
4. Recompute f_t, using $\hat{\alpha}$; then, for observations $t = 1, \ldots , T - 1$, compute

$$r_t = \left[\frac{1}{f_t} + 2\left(\frac{\hat{\alpha}_1 e_t}{f_{t+1}} \right)^2 \right]^{1/2}$$

and

$$s_t = \frac{1}{f_t} - \frac{\hat{\alpha}_1}{f_{t+1}} \left(\frac{e_{t+1}^2}{f_{t+1}} - 1 \right).$$

Compute the estimate

$$\hat{\boldsymbol{\beta}} = \mathbf{b} + \mathbf{d}_\beta,$$

where $\mathbf{d}_\beta$ is the least squares coefficient vector in the regression of $e_t s_t / r_t$ on $\mathbf{x}_t r_t$. The asymptotic covariance matrix for $\hat{\boldsymbol{\beta}}$ is $(\mathbf{W}'\mathbf{W})^{-1}$, where $\mathbf{W}$ is the regressor matrix used in this regression.

This procedure is asymptotically equivalent to maximum likelihood. It is possible to iterate by returning to step 2 with new residuals calculated after step 4, but this brings no gains in efficiency and does not draw the procedure to the true maximum likelihood estimate. (Step 2 is not the solution to the likelihood equation for $\boldsymbol{\alpha}$.) One possible refinement of the model would be to add further lags in the ARCH process. The modification of the estimation process is minor; the regression in step 2 and the computation of f_t are extended by adding the additional lags of e^2.[37]

EXAMPLE 15.8 ARCH Process for the Rate of Inflation _____

The annual percentage rate of increase in the U.S. Consumer Price Index by year from 1940 to 1986 is listed in Table 15.7.

We shall use these data and the four-step method outlined earlier to fit the ARCH model:

$$\Delta p_t = \beta_1 + \beta_2 \, \Delta p_{t-1} + \varepsilon_t$$

$$\varepsilon_t = u_t [\alpha_0 + \alpha_1 \varepsilon_{t-1}^2]^{1/2}.$$

[35] See Engle (1982) and Judge et al. (1985, pp. 441–444).

[36] This procedure is based on the method of scoring. Note the similarity of this step to the analogous step in Example 14.15.

[37] See Bollerslev (1986) and Chapter 19 for a discussion and some further generalizations.

TABLE 15.7

1940	1.0	1950	5.8	1960	1.5	1970	5.5	1980	12.4
1941	9.7	1951	5.9	1961	0.7	1971	3.4	1981	8.9
1942	9.3	1952	0.9	1962	1.2	1972	3.4	1982	3.9
1943	3.2	1953	0.6	1963	1.6	1973	8.8	1983	3.8
1944	2.1	1954	−0.5	1964	1.2	1974	12.2	1984	4.0
1945	2.3	1955	0.4	1965	1.9	1975	7.0	1985	3.8
1946	18.2	1956	2.9	1966	3.4	1976	4.8	1986	1.1
1947	9.0	1957	3.0	1967	3.0	1977	6.8		
1948	2.7	1958	1.8	1968	4.7	1978	9.0		
1949	−1.8	1959	1.5	1969	6.1	1979	13.3		

Source: Data from the 1987 *Economic Report of the President*, p. 312.

Where appropriate, standard errors are given in parentheses below the estimates.

1. Regression of Δp_t on a constant and Δp_{t-1} for 1941–1986:

$$\Delta p_t = 2.34625 + 0.4968 \ \Delta p_{t-1}$$
$$(0.8082) \quad (0.1307).$$

2. Regression of the squared residual on a constant and the lagged squared residual:

$$e_t^2 = 12.0453 - 0.031778 e_{t-1}^2$$

$$R^2 = 0.0014, \qquad T = 45.$$

3. The correction to be applied to the preceding estimates is

$$\mathbf{d}_\alpha = [-0.02867, \quad 0.0019644],$$

which gives $\hat{\boldsymbol{\alpha}}$. Then

$$e_t^2 = 12.0166 \ - \ 0.029814 e_{t-1}^2$$
$$(2.6248) - (0.03662).$$

4. The correction to the parameters, and updated values are

$$\mathbf{d}_\beta = [-0.105687, \quad -0.031742]$$

$$\Delta p_t = \quad 2.45193 + 0.46508 \Delta p_{t-1}$$
$$(0.7923) + (0.1248)$$

The change that results from estimating according to the ARCH model is relatively small—compare step 4 to step 1. This was to be expected in view of the insignificant results at step 3.

Engle also presents a Lagrange multiplier test for the ARCH process against the null hypothesis that the disturbance is conditionally homoscedastic. The statistic is T times the R^2 in the regression at step 2. This is asymptotically distributed as chi-squared with one degree of freedom. For the inflation data used in the example, the chi-squared value is 0.0468., which is far from statistically significant.

The recent literature contains a wealth of extensions to Engel's ARCH model. The extension to P lags,

$$\text{Var}[\varepsilon_t | \varepsilon_{t-1}, \ \varepsilon_{t-2}, \ \ldots, \ \varepsilon_{t-P}] = \sigma_t^2$$

where

$$\sigma_t^2 = \alpha^0 + \alpha_1 \varepsilon_{t-1}^2 + \alpha^2 \varepsilon_{t-2}^2 + \cdots + \alpha^P \varepsilon_{t-P}^2$$

requires only a minor change in steps 3 and 4 of the previous method. More recent studies, beginning with Bollerslev (1986), have used the generalized ARCH (or GARCH) model,

$$\sigma_t^2 = \alpha^0 + \alpha^1 \varepsilon_{t-1}^2 + \delta \sigma_{t-1}^2.$$

This model is considered in detail in Section 19.7.

EXERCISES

1. Does first differencing reduce autocorrelation? Consider the models

$$y_t = \boldsymbol{\beta}' \mathbf{x}_t + \varepsilon_t,$$

where

$$\varepsilon_t = \rho \varepsilon_{t-1} + u_t$$

and

$$\varepsilon_t = u_t - \lambda u_{t-1}.$$

Compare the autocorrelation of ε_t in the original model to that of v_t in

$$y_t - y_{t-1} = \boldsymbol{\beta}'(\mathbf{x}_t - \mathbf{x}_{t-1}) + v_t,$$

where

$$v_t = \varepsilon_t - \varepsilon_{t-1}.$$

2. Derive the disturbance covariance matrix for the model

$$y_t = \boldsymbol{\beta}' \mathbf{x}_t + \varepsilon_t,$$

$$\varepsilon_t = \rho \varepsilon_{t-1} + u_t - \lambda u_{t-1}.$$

What parameter is estimated by the regression of the OLS residuals on their lagged values?

3. A least squares regression based on 24 observations produces the following results:

$$y_t = 0.3 + 1.21 x_t \qquad R^2 = 0.982$$
$$\quad (0.1) \quad (0.2) \qquad \text{D-W} = 1.31.$$

Test the hypothesis that the disturbances are not autocorrelated.

4. It can be shown in the regression model

$$y_t = \beta y_{t-1} + \varepsilon_t,$$

$$\varepsilon_t = \rho \varepsilon_{t-1} + u_t,$$

that

$$\text{plim } r = \frac{\beta \rho (\beta + \rho)}{1 + \beta \rho},$$

where

$$r = \frac{\displaystyle\sum_{t=2}^{T} e_t e_{t-1}}{\displaystyle\sum_{t=2}^{T} e_t^2}.$$

Use this result to show that

$$\text{plim} \; \frac{r}{b} = \beta\rho,$$

$$\text{plim} \; b + r = \beta + \rho,$$

where b is the OLS estimator of β. If you were given only the ordinary least squares regression results and the Durbin–Watson statistic, could you estimate β and ρ? If so, how? If not, why not?

5. The appendix to Chapter 20 contains data for 1953 to 1984 on (among other variables) gross private domestic investment (I) and corporate profits (P). Estimate the efficiency ratio (15–21) for OLS estimation using the model

$$I_t = \alpha + \beta P_t + \varepsilon_t,$$

assuming that corporate profits satisfy the assumption made in that derivation.

6. Using the data and model of the previous problem, compute and plot the ordinary least squares residuals. Obtain the first and second autocorrelations of the OLS residuals. Now compute the FGLS estimator, assuming that the disturbances are an AR(1) process. Use the Prais–Winsten estimator and then the Cochrane–Orcutt estimator. What differences do you observe? To estimate ρ, use any of the estimators discussed in the text.

7. The following regression is obtained by ordinary least squares, using 21 observations. (Estimated asymptotic standard errors are shown in parentheses.)

$$y_t = 1.3 + 0.97y_{t-1} + 2.31x_t, \qquad \text{D-W} = 1.21.$$
$$\quad (0.3) \quad (0.18) \qquad (1.04)$$

Test for the presence of autocorrelation in the disturbances.

8. It is commonly asserted that the Durbin–Watson statistic is appropriate only for testing for first-order autoregressive disturbances. What combination of the coefficients of the model is estimated by the Durbin–Watson statistic in each of the following cases: AR(1), AR(2), MA(1).? In each case, assume that the regression model does not contain a lagged dependent variable. Comment on the impact on your results of relaxing this assumption.

16

Models That Use Both Cross-Section and Time-Series Data

16.1. Introduction

Data sets that combine time series and cross sections are common in economics. For example, the published statistics of the OECD contain numerous series of economic aggregates observed yearly for many countries. Recently constructed *longitudinal* data sets contain observations on thousands of individuals or families, each observed at several points in time. Some empirical studies have analyzed time series data on several firms, states, or industries simultaneously. These data sets provide a rich source of information about the economy. However, modeling in this setting calls for some quite complex stochastic specifications. In this chapter and the next, we survey the most commonly used techniques for time-series—cross-section data analyses.

16.2. Time-Series–Cross-Section Data

Many studies have analyzed data observed across countries or firms in which the number of cross-sectional units is relatively small and the number of time periods is (potentially) relatively large. The data set in Example 16.1 is an example, with five firms each observed for 20 years. In this setting, we can emphasize time series analysis. The data sets are typically "long" enough that we may study the disturbance terms in the context of stochastic processes. Heteroscedasticity is the effect of different processes applying to different cross-sectional units. The "narrow width" (i.e., smallness of the number of cross sections) of some of these data sets is not a serious concern.

Many recent studies have analyzed panel, or longitudinal, data sets. Two very famous ones are the National Longitudinal Survey of Labor Market Experience (NLS) and the Michigan Panel Study of Income Dynamics (PSID). In these data sets, very large cross sections, consisting of thousands of micro units, are followed through time. But the number of periods is often quite small. The PSID, for example, is a study of roughly 6000 families and 15,000 individuals who have been interviewed periodically from 1968 to the present. Another group of intensively studied panel data sets is those from the negative income tax experiments of the early 1970s, in which thousands of families were followed for 8 or 13 quarters. Constructing long, evenly spaced time series in this context would be prohibitively expensive, but for the purposes for which these data are typically used, this is unnecessary. Time effects are often viewed as "transitions" or discrete changes of state. They are typically modeled as specific to the period in which they occur and are not carried across periods within a cross-sectional unit.[1] Panel data sets are more oriented toward cross-section analyses; they are wide but typically short. Heterogeneity across units is an integral part—indeed, often the central focus—of the analysis.

EXAMPLE 16.1 Investment Data

Tables 16.1 to 16.3 are part of the data used in a classic study of investment demand,[2] and are typical of the kinds of data that we would include in our first category. The data consist of time series of 20 yearly observations for 5 firms (of 10 in the original study) and 3 variables:

$$I_t = \text{gross investment,}$$

$$F_t = \text{market value of the firm at the end of the previous year,}$$

$$C_t = \text{value of the stock of plant and equipment at the end of the previous year.}$$

TABLE 16.1[a]

	General Motors			Chrysler		
	I_t	F_t	C_t	I_t	F_t	C_t
1935	317.6	3078.5	2.8	40.29	417.5	10.5
1936	391.8	4661.7	52.6	72.76	837.8	10.2
1937	410.6	5387.1	156.9	66.26	883.9	34.7
1938	257.7	2792.2	209.2	51.60	437.9	51.8
1939	330.8	4313.2	203.4	52.41	679.7	64.3
1940	461.2	4643.9	207.2	69.41	727.8	67.1
1941	512.0	4551.2	255.2	68.35	643.6	75.2
1942	448.0	3244.1	303.7	46.80	410.9	71.4
1943	499.6	4053.7	264.1	47.40	588.4	67.1
1944	547.5	4379.3	201.6	59.57	698.4	60.5
1945	561.2	4840.9	265.0	88.78	846.4	54.6
1946	688.1	4900.9	402.2	74.12	893.8	84.8
1947	568.9	3526.5	761.5	62.68	579.0	96.8
1948	529.2	3254.7	922.4	89.36	694.6	110.2
1949	555.1	3700.2	1020.1	78.98	590.3	147.4
1950	642.9	3755.6	1099.0	100.66	693.5	163.2
1951	755.9	4833.0	1207.7	160.62	809.0	203.5
1952	891.2	4924.9	1430.5	145.00	727.0	290.6
1953	1304.4	6241.7	1777.3	174.93	1001.5	346.1
1954	1486.7	5593.6	2226.3	172.49	703.2	414.9

[a] I = gross investment, from *Moody's Industrial Manual* and Annual Reports of Corporations; F = value of the firm, from *Bank and Quotation Record* and *Moody's Industrial Manual*; and C = stock of plant and equipment, from *Survey of Current Business*.

---

[1] This has not prevented theorists from devising autocorrelation models applicable to panel data sets. See, for example, Lee (1978a). As a practical matter, however, the empirical literature in this field has tended to concentrate on the less intricate models. Time series modeling of the sort discussed in the previous chapter is somewhat unusual in the analysis of longitudinal data.

[2] Grunfeld (1958) and Grunfeld and Griliches (1960). The data were also used in Boot and deWitt (1960).

TABLE 16.2[a]

	General Electric			Westinghouse		
	I_t	F_t	C_t	I_t	F_t	C_t
1935	33.1	1170.6	97.8	12.93	191.5	1.8
1936	45.0	2015.8	104.4	25.90	516.0	0.8
1937	77.2	2803.3	118.0	35.05	729.0	7.4
1938	44.6	2039.7	156.2	22.89	560.4	18.1
1939	48.1	2256.2	172.6	18.84	519.9	23.5
1940	74.4	2132.2	186.6	28.57	628.5	26.5
1941	113.0	1834.1	220.9	48.51	537.1	36.2
1942	91.9	1588.0	287.8	43.34	561.2	60.8
1943	61.3	1749.4	319.9	37.02	617.2	84.4
1944	56.8	1687.2	321.3	37.81	626.7	91.2
1945	93.6	2007.7	319.6	39.27	737.2	92.4
1946	159.9	2208.3	346.0	53.46	760.5	86.0
1947	147.2	1656.7	456.4	55.56	581.4	111.1
1948	146.3	1604.4	543.4	49.56	662.3	130.6
1949	98.3	1431.8	618.3	32.04	583.8	141.8
1950	93.5	1610.5	647.4	32.24	635.2	136.7
1951	135.2	1819.4	671.3	54.38	723.8	129.7
1952	157.3	2079.7	726.1	71.78	864.1	145.5
1953	179.5	2371.6	800.3	90.08	1193.5	174.8
1954	189.6	2759.9	888.9	68.60	1188.9	213.5

[a]See the footnote to Table 16.1.

TABLE 16.3[a]

	U.S. Steel		
	I_t	F_t	C_t
1935	209.9	1362.4	53.8
1936	355.3	1807.1	50.5
1937	469.9	2676.3	118.1
1938	262.3	1801.9	260.2
1939	230.4	1957.3	312.7
1940	261.6	2202.9	254.2
1941	472.8	2380.5	261.4
1942	445.6	2168.6	298.7
1943	361.6	1985.1	301.8
1944	288.2	1813.9	279.1
1945	258.7	1850.2	213.8
1946	420.3	2067.7	232.6
1947	420.5	1796.7	264.8
1948	494.5	1625.8	306.9
1949	405.1	1667.0	351.1
1950	418.8	1677.4	357.8
1951	588.2	2289.5	342.1
1952	645.2	2159.4	444.2
1953	641.0	2031.3	623.6
1954	459.3	2115.5	669.7

[a]See the footnote to Table 16.1.

The variables F_t and I_t reflect anticipated profit and the expected amount of replacement investment required.[3]

The model to be estimated with these data is

$$I_{it} = \beta_1 + \beta_2 F_{it} + \beta_3 C_{it} + \varepsilon_{it}. \tag{16-1}$$

In the models we shall examine in this chapter, the data set consists of n cross-sectional units, denoted $i = 1, \ldots, n$, observed at each of T time periods, $t = 1, \ldots, T$.[4] We have a total of nT observations. Discussion of asymptotic properties will be couched in terms of $n \to \infty$ and/or $T \to \infty$. Which, if either, applies will make a difference in a particular context, and we will have to be specific in each case we examine. In the next section, the asymptotic results we obtain are with respect to $T \to \infty$. We assume that n is fixed, except where specifically noted otherwise.

16.3. Models of Several Time Series

The basic framework for this analysis is the generalized regression model:

$$y_{it} = \boldsymbol{\beta}' \mathbf{x}_{it} + \varepsilon_{it}. \tag{16-2}$$

It is useful to collect the n time series,

$$\mathbf{y}_i = \mathbf{X}_i \boldsymbol{\beta} + \boldsymbol{\varepsilon}_i,$$

so that

$$\begin{bmatrix} \mathbf{y}_1 \\ \mathbf{y}_2 \\ \vdots \\ \mathbf{y}_n \end{bmatrix} = \begin{bmatrix} \mathbf{X}_1 \\ \mathbf{X}_2 \\ \vdots \\ \mathbf{X}_n \end{bmatrix} \boldsymbol{\beta} + \begin{bmatrix} \boldsymbol{\varepsilon}_1 \\ \boldsymbol{\varepsilon}_2 \\ \vdots \\ \boldsymbol{\varepsilon}_n \end{bmatrix}. \tag{16-3}$$

Each submatrix or subvector has T observations. In general terms,

$$V = E[\boldsymbol{\varepsilon}\boldsymbol{\varepsilon}'] = \begin{bmatrix} \sigma_{11}\boldsymbol{\Omega}_{11} & \sigma_{12}\boldsymbol{\Omega}_{12} & \cdots & \sigma_{1n}\boldsymbol{\Omega}_{1n} \\ \sigma_{21}\boldsymbol{\Omega}_{21} & \sigma_{22}\boldsymbol{\Omega}_{22} & \cdots & \sigma_{2n}\boldsymbol{\Omega}_{2n} \\ & & \vdots & \\ \sigma_{n1}\boldsymbol{\Omega}_{n1} & \sigma_{n2}\boldsymbol{\Omega}_{n2} & \cdots & \sigma_{nn}\boldsymbol{\Omega}_{nn} \end{bmatrix} \tag{16-4}$$

For the present, we assume that the parameter vector $\boldsymbol{\beta}$ is the same for all i. A variety of models are obtained by varying the structure of $\mathbf{V}$.

The classical regression model specifies that

$$E[\varepsilon_{it}] = 0,$$

$$\text{Var}[\varepsilon_{it}] = \sigma^2,$$

$$\text{Cov}[\varepsilon_{it}, \varepsilon_{js}] = 0 \qquad \text{if } t \neq s \text{ or } i \neq j.$$

---

[3] In the original study, the authors used the notation F_{t-1} and C_{t-1}. In order to avoid possible conflicts with the usual subscripting conventions used here, we have used the preceding notation instead.

[4] The requirement that each unit be observed the same number of periods is not necessary for much of this analysis.

Then

$$\mathbf{V} = \begin{bmatrix} \sigma^2\mathbf{I} & \mathbf{0} & \cdots & \mathbf{0} \\ \mathbf{0} & \sigma^2\mathbf{I} & \cdots & \mathbf{0} \\ & & \vdots & \\ \mathbf{0} & \mathbf{0} & \cdots & \sigma^2\mathbf{I} \end{bmatrix}. \tag{16-5}$$

We can also stack the data in the pooled regression model in

$$\mathbf{y} = \mathbf{X}\boldsymbol{\beta} + \boldsymbol{\varepsilon}.$$

For this simple model, the GLS estimator reduces to pooled ordinary least squares.

EXAMPLE 16.2 Classical Regression —————————————————————————

By pooling all 100 observations and estimating the coefficients by ordinary least squares, we obtain

$$I_t = -48.0297 + 0.105085F_t + 0.305366C_t,$$
$$(21.16) \quad (0.01121) \quad (0.04285)$$

$$R^2 = 0.77886, \quad \hat{\sigma}^2 = 15708.84, \quad \text{log likelihood} = -677.398.$$

In this and the following examples, estimated standard errors for the parameter estimates are shown in parentheses. To make them comparable to the results below, the variance estimate and estimated standard errors are based on $\mathbf{e}'\mathbf{e}/(nT)$. There is no degrees of freedom correction.

16.3.1. Cross-Sectional Heteroscedasticity

The pooled regression model of (16–5) and Example 16.2 implies a number of restrictions on $\mathbf{V}$. Examination of the data in the example suggests that the variance will be quite different in the five time series. If this were a cross-country comparison, we would expect tremendous variation in the scales of all variables in the model. We can relax the classical assumption by allowing σ^2 to vary across i. This results in the groupwise heteroscedastic model of Section 14.3.4:

$$\mathbf{V} = \begin{bmatrix} \sigma_1^2\mathbf{I} & \mathbf{0} & \cdots & \mathbf{0} \\ \mathbf{0} & \sigma_2^2\mathbf{I} & \cdots & \mathbf{0} \\ & & \vdots & \\ \mathbf{0} & \mathbf{0} & \cdots & \sigma_n^2\mathbf{I} \end{bmatrix}. \tag{16-6}$$

The GLS estimator, as we saw earlier, is

$$\hat{\boldsymbol{\beta}} = [\mathbf{X}'\mathbf{V}^{-1}\mathbf{X}]^{-1}[\mathbf{X}'\mathbf{V}^{-1}\mathbf{y}]$$

$$= \left[\sum_{i=1}^{n} \frac{1}{\sigma_i^2}\mathbf{X}_i'\mathbf{X}_i\right]^{-1}\left[\sum_{i=1}^{n} \frac{1}{\sigma_i^2}\mathbf{X}_i'\mathbf{y}_i\right].$$

Of course, the disturbance variances, σ_i^2, will rarely be known, so an alternative estimator will be required. The estimation procedure can be either two-step FGLS or, if maximum likelihood estimates are required, iterated two-step estimation.

EXAMPLE 16.3 Testing and Estimation with Groupwise Heteroscedasticity _____

Using the OLS parameter estimates, we obtain the estimates of σ_i^2 listed in Table 16.4. These estimates suggest that the variance differs substantially across firms. We can use any of three possible tests for heteroscedasticity.

TABLE 16.4 Residual Variances

General Motors (GM)	9,410.91
Chrysler (CH)	755.85
General Electric (GE)	34,288.89
Westinghouse (WE)	633.42
U.S. Steel (US)	33,455.51
Pooled	15,708.84

The Lagrange multiplier test is probably the most convenient test, since it does not require another regression after the pooled least squares regression. The log-likelihood function and its derivatives for the sample *without the restriction of equal variances* are

$$\ln L = -\frac{nT}{2}\ln(2\pi) - \frac{T}{2}\sum_i \ln \sigma_i^2 - \frac{1}{2}\sum_i \frac{\varepsilon_i'\varepsilon_i}{\sigma_i^2},$$

$$\frac{\partial \ln L}{\partial \boldsymbol{\beta}} = \sum_i \frac{1}{\sigma_i^2}\mathbf{X}_i'(\mathbf{y}_i - \mathbf{X}_i\boldsymbol{\beta}) = \sum_i \frac{1}{\sigma_i^2}\mathbf{X}_i'\boldsymbol{\varepsilon}_i,$$

$$\frac{\partial \ln L}{\partial \sigma_i^2} = \frac{-T}{2\sigma_i^2} + \frac{1}{2\sigma_i^4}\varepsilon_i'\varepsilon_i, \qquad i = 1, \ldots, n,$$

$$\frac{\partial^2 \ln L}{\partial \boldsymbol{\beta} \, \partial \boldsymbol{\beta}'} = -\sum_i \frac{1}{\sigma_i^2}\mathbf{X}_i'\mathbf{X}_i,$$

$$\frac{\partial^2 \ln L}{\partial(\sigma_i^2)^2} = \frac{T}{2\sigma_i^4} - \frac{\varepsilon_i'\varepsilon_i}{\sigma_i^6}, \qquad i = 1, \ldots, n,$$

$$\frac{\partial^2 \ln L}{\partial \boldsymbol{\beta} \, \partial \sigma_i^2} = -\sum_i \frac{1}{\sigma_i^4}\mathbf{X}_i'\boldsymbol{\varepsilon}_i, \qquad i = 1, \ldots, n.$$

Under the null hypothesis of equal variances, the first derivatives are

$$\mathbf{g} = \begin{bmatrix} \partial \ln L/\partial \boldsymbol{\beta} \\ \partial \ln L/\partial \sigma_i^2 \end{bmatrix} = \begin{bmatrix} (1/\sigma^2)\Sigma_i\mathbf{X}_i'\boldsymbol{\varepsilon}_i \\ -T/(2\sigma^2) + \boldsymbol{\varepsilon}_i'\boldsymbol{\varepsilon}_i/(2\sigma^4) \end{bmatrix}$$

and the negative of the expected second derivatives matrix is

$$\mathbf{H}(\boldsymbol{\beta},\sigma^2) = \begin{bmatrix} (1/\sigma^2)\mathbf{X}'\mathbf{X} & \mathbf{0} \\ \mathbf{0}' & (T/(2\sigma^4))\mathbf{I} \end{bmatrix}.$$

It is convenient to rewrite

$$\frac{\partial \ln L}{\partial \sigma_i^2} = \frac{T}{2\sigma^2}\left[\frac{\hat{\sigma}_i^2}{\sigma^2} - 1\right],$$

where $\hat{\sigma}_i^2$ is the ith unit-specific estimate of σ^2. The restricted maximum likelihood estimator of $\boldsymbol{\beta}$ is the pooled ordinary least squares estimator. At this restricted estimator, under the null hypothesis, $\partial \ln L / \partial \boldsymbol{\beta} = \mathbf{0}$, as these are the OLS normal equations. The restricted maximum likelihood estimator of the common σ^2 is

$$s^2 = \frac{\mathbf{e}'\mathbf{e}}{nT}$$

$$= \frac{\Sigma_i \mathbf{e}_i' \mathbf{e}_i}{nT}$$

$$= \frac{1}{n} \sum_i s_i^2.$$

It is a simple average of the n consistent estimators. With this in hand, the Lagrange multiplier statistic, $\mathbf{g}'\mathbf{H}^{-1}\mathbf{g}$ (computed at the pooled OLS estimates), reduces to

$$\text{LM} = \sum_i \left[\frac{T}{2s^2} \left(\frac{s_i^2}{s^2} - 1 \right) \right]^2 \left[\frac{2s^4}{T} \right]$$

$$= \frac{T}{2} \sum_i \left[\frac{s_i^2}{s^2} - 1 \right]^2.$$

The statistic has n degrees of freedom. Based on the preceding least squares results, LM = 46.63, which is highly significant.

The Lagrange multiplier statistic is simple to compute and asymptotically equivalent to a likelihood ratio test. It does assume normality. If this is not feasible, White's general test[5] is an alternative. To use White's test, we regress the squared OLS residual on a constant, F, C, F^2, C^2, and FC. The R^2 in this regression is 0.36854, so the chi-squared statistic is $(nT)R^2 = 36.854$, with five degrees of freedom. The 1 percent critical value from the table is 15.056, so we can reject the hypothesis of homoscedasticity on the basis of this test.

We can also carry out an approximate likelihood ratio test (these are not the maximum likelihood estimators), using the test statistic in Section 14.3.4. The appropriate likelihood ratio statistic is

$$-2 \ln \lambda = (nT) \ln \hat{\sigma}^2 - \sum_i T \ln \hat{\sigma}_i^2,$$

where

$$\hat{\sigma}^2 = \frac{\mathbf{e}'\mathbf{e}}{nT} \quad \text{and} \quad \hat{\sigma}_i^2 = \frac{\mathbf{e}_i' \mathbf{e}_i}{T},$$

with all residuals computed using the maximum likelihood estimators. This chi-squared statistic has $n - 1$ degrees of freedom. (Iterated FGLS can be used to compute them.) If only least squares results are available, s^2 and s_i^2 may be used, possibly with some loss of power in small samples. For these data,

$$\chi^2 = 100 \ln s^2 - \sum_i 20 \ln s_i^2 = 104.415.$$

This far exceeds the tabled critical value.

---

[5] See Section 14.3.1.

TABLE 16.5

	FGLS		ML	
$\hat{\beta}_1$	-36.2537	(6.1244)	-23.2583	(4.815)
$\hat{\beta}_2$	0.09499	(0.007409)	0.0943499	(0.006283)
$\hat{\beta}_3$	0.337813	(0.030225)	0.333702	(0.02204)
Log likelihood	—		-616.941	

Variances $\hat{\sigma}_{ii}$

GM	8,612.15	8,657.87
CH	409.19	175.80
GE	36,563.24	4,0211.13
WE	777.97	1,241.01
US	32,902.83	29,824.92

We proceed to reestimate the regression, allowing for heteroscedasticity. The two estimators, FGLS and MLE, are given in Table 16.5.

The likelihood ratio statistic for a test of homoscedasticity based on the MLEs is 120.914, which is extremely significant. With the unrestricted estimates, as an alternative test procedure, we may use the Wald statistic. If we assume normality, the asymptotic variance of each variance estimator is $2\sigma_i^4/T$, and the variances are asymptotically uncorrelated. Therefore, the Wald statistic to test the hypothesis of a common variance, σ^2, would be

$$W = \sum_i (s_i^2 - \sigma^2)^2 \left(\frac{2\sigma_i^4}{T}\right)^{-1}.$$

Using s_i^2 to estimate σ_i^2 produces the sample statistic

$$W = \frac{T}{2} \sum_i \left(\frac{\sigma^2}{s_i^2} - 1\right)^2.$$

Note the similarity to the Lagrange multiplier statistic. The estimator of the common variance can be the pooled estimator from the first least squares regression or the total sum of squared GLS residuals divided by nT. Using the FGLS estimates above and the pooled OLS estimator for σ^2, the Wald statistic is 17,676.32. We observe the common occurrence of an extremely large Wald test statistic. (Based on the sum of squared GLS residuals, $\hat{\sigma}^2 = 15,853.08$ and $W = 18,012.86$.)

If the assumption of normally distributed disturbances is inappropriate, then neither the Lagrange multiplier nor the likelihood ratio tests are usable. Moreover, the Wald statistic defined above is also incorrect, since it is the normality assumption which provides $(2\sigma_i^4/T)$ as $\mathrm{Var}[s_i^2]$. It remains possible to construct a usable Wald statistic as follows: Under the null hypothesis of constant variance, σ^2, the Wald statistic is

$$W = \sum_i \frac{(s_i^2 - \sigma^2)^2}{\mathrm{Var}[s_i^2]}.$$

If the hypothesis is correct,

$$W \xrightarrow{d} \chi^2[n].$$

By hypothesis,

$$\mathrm{plim}\ s^2 = \sigma^2,$$

where s^2 is the disturbance variance estimator from the pooled regression. (For our example, this is 15,708.84. See Example 16.2 and Table 16.4.) The statistic obtained by substituting s^2 for σ^2 in W has the same limiting chi-squared distribution. This is identical to the earlier definition, but we must now reconsider $\text{Var}[s_i^2]$. Since

$$s_i^2 = \frac{1}{T} \sum_t e_{it}^2,$$

it is a sample moment, and at the same time, a mean of T observations. As such, we may use the results of Section 4.6.2 to estimate $\text{Var}[s_i^2]$. In particular, we can use

$$V_i = \frac{1}{T} \frac{1}{T-1} \sum_t (e_{it}^2 - s_i^2)^2.$$

The modified Wald statistic is then

$$W' = \sum_i \frac{(s_i^2 - s^2)^2}{V_i},$$

For our investment data, the values of s_i^2 are given in Table 16.5. The five estimated variances based on residuals computed with the FGLS estimates in Table 16.5 are

$$\mathbf{V} = [8.3931 \times 10^6, 18,688., 3.366 \times 10^7, 1.0456 \times 10^5, 4.9012 \times 10^7].$$

The value for W' using these values is 14,681.3, which leads us to the same conclusion.

Returning to the least squares estimators, we should expect the OLS standard errors to be incorrect, given our findings. There are two possible corrections we can use, the White estimator and direct computation of the appropriate asymptotic covariance matrix. These give the results shown in Table 16.6.

TABLE 16.6

Coefficient	OLS SE	White	Correct
−48.0297	21.15	15.02	14.20
0.105085	0.01121	0.009146	0.009065
0.305366	0.04285	0.05911	0.040947

16.3.2. Cross-Sectional Correlation

In the example data, we have two automobile producers, two major suppliers to the electric utility industry, and one major supplier to all four of the others, U.S. Steel. It is very likely that the macroeconomic factors that affect these firms affect all of them to varying degrees. For the auto industry, the fates of GM and Chrysler are obviously tied both to the economy as a whole and to factors that are specific to the two firms. As such, it would seem reasonable to allow correlation of the disturbances across firms. The extension of the model for cross-sectional correlation is

$$E[\boldsymbol{\varepsilon}_i \boldsymbol{\varepsilon}_j'] = \sigma_{ij} \mathbf{I}.$$

We continue to assume that observations are uncorrelated across time. With this generalization, we obtain

$$\mathbf{V} = \begin{bmatrix} \sigma_{11}\mathbf{I} & \sigma_{12}\mathbf{I} & \cdots & \sigma_{1n}\mathbf{I} \\ \sigma_{21}\mathbf{I} & \sigma_{22}\mathbf{I} & \cdots & \sigma_{2n}\mathbf{I} \\ & \vdots & & \\ \sigma_{n1}\mathbf{I} & \sigma_{n2}\mathbf{I} & \cdots & \sigma_{nn}\mathbf{I} \end{bmatrix}. \tag{16-7}$$

This model can also be estimated either by FGLS or MLE by iterating. As before, at step 1, we use OLS to obtain $\mathbf{b}$ and $\mathbf{e}_i$. A consistent estimate of σ_{ij} can be obtained using the least squares residuals in

$$s_{ij} = \frac{\mathbf{e}_i'\mathbf{e}_j}{T}. \tag{16–8}$$

Some treatments use $T - K$ instead of T in the denominator of s_{ij}.[6] There is no problem created by doing so, but we should note that the resulting estimator is not unbiased regardless. With s_{ij} in hand, FGLS may be computed using $[\mathbf{X}'\hat{\mathbf{V}}^{-1}\mathbf{X}]^{-1}[\mathbf{X}'\hat{\mathbf{V}}^{-1}\mathbf{y}]$, where $\mathbf{X}$ and $\mathbf{y}$ are the stacked data matrices in (16–3).

Once again, in practical terms, this is a formidable computation. However, as before, things are simpler than they appear. $\mathbf{V}$ can be written as

$$\mathbf{V} = \mathbf{\Sigma} \otimes \mathbf{I}, \tag{16–9}$$

where $\mathbf{\Sigma}$ is an $n \times n$ matrix, so

$$\mathbf{V}^{-1} = \mathbf{\Sigma}^{-1} \otimes \mathbf{I}. \tag{16–10}$$

Let σ^{ij} denote the ijth element of $\mathbf{\Sigma}^{-1}$. Then

$$\mathbf{V}^{-1} = \begin{bmatrix} \sigma^{11}\mathbf{I} & \sigma^{12}\mathbf{I} & \cdots & \sigma^{1n}\mathbf{I} \\ \sigma^{21}\mathbf{I} & \sigma^{22}\mathbf{I} & \cdots & \sigma^{2n}\mathbf{I} \\ & & \vdots & \\ \sigma^{n1}\mathbf{I} & \sigma^{n2}\mathbf{I} & \cdots & \sigma^{nn}\mathbf{I} \end{bmatrix}.$$

The usefulness of this is that

$$\mathbf{X}'\mathbf{V}^{-1}\mathbf{X} = \sum_i \sum_j \sigma^{ij}\mathbf{X}_i'\mathbf{X}_j$$

and

$$\mathbf{X}'\mathbf{V}^{-1}\mathbf{y} = \sum_i \sum_j \sigma^{ij}\mathbf{X}_i'\mathbf{y}_j,$$

so

$$\hat{\boldsymbol{\beta}} = \left[\sum_i \sum_j \sigma^{ij}\mathbf{X}_i'\mathbf{X}_j \right]^{-1} \left[\sum_i \sum_j \sigma^{ij}\mathbf{X}_i'\mathbf{y}_j \right]. \tag{16–11}$$

Therefore, to compute the FGLS estimators for this model, we first compute the full set of sample moments, $\mathbf{y}_i'\mathbf{y}_j$, $\mathbf{X}_i'\mathbf{X}_j$, and $\mathbf{X}_i'\mathbf{y}_j$, for all pairs of cross-sectional units. Maximum likelihood estimates can be obtained by iterating to convergence between

$$\hat{\hat{\boldsymbol{\beta}}} = [\mathbf{X}'\hat{\mathbf{V}}^{-1}\mathbf{X}]^{-1}[\mathbf{X}'\hat{\mathbf{V}}^{-1}\mathbf{y}]$$

and

$$s_{ij} = \frac{[\mathbf{y}_i'\mathbf{y}_j + \hat{\hat{\boldsymbol{\beta}}}'\mathbf{X}_i'\mathbf{X}_j\hat{\hat{\boldsymbol{\beta}}} - \hat{\hat{\boldsymbol{\beta}}}'\mathbf{X}_i'\mathbf{y}_j - \hat{\hat{\boldsymbol{\beta}}}'\mathbf{X}_j'\mathbf{y}_i]}{T}. \tag{16–12}$$

The computations are simple, using basic matrix algebra. Hypothesis tests about $\boldsymbol{\beta}$ may be done using the usual results. The appropriate asymptotic covariance matrix is the inverse matrix in brackets in (16–11).[7]

---

[6] See, for example, Kmenta (1986, p. 620). Elsewhere, for example, in Fomby et al. (1984, p. 327), T is used instead.

[7] For programming purposes, it is useful to note that these are all matrices of small orders, whereas the general formulation involves an $nT \times nT$ matrix.

EXAMPLE 16.4 Testing and Estimation with Groupwise Heteroscedasticity and Cross-Sectional Correlation

For the investment data, the FGLS and maximum likelihood estimates are listed in Table 16.7.

TABLE 16.7

	β_1	β_2	β_3
FGLS	−30.281	0.094127	0.34057
	(5.589)	(0.006836)	(0.02683)
MLE	11.503	0.051921	0.31909
	(2.470)	(0.004274)	(0.01572)
	Log likelihood = −520.27		

The estimated covariance matrix for the disturbances based on the FGLS estimates, with correlations placed in parentheses above the diagonal for purposes of the display, is given in Table 16.8.[8] Note that the disturbance variances have changed dramatically. This is due in large part to the quite large off-diagonal elements. It is noteworthy that in spite of the great changes in Σ, the parameter estimates have not changed much from the earlier ones.

TABLE 16.8

	GM	CH	GE	WE	US
GM	8,466.464	(−0.216)	(−0.152)	(−0.330)	(0.015)
CH	−323.7408	265.1038	(−0.501)	(−0.152)	(0.578)
GE	−2,755.097	−1,602.251	38,591.00	(0.809)	(−0.819)
WE	−941.3622	−76.33833	4,929.060	961.5490	(−0.552)
US	260.1078	1,665.469	−28,514.58	−3,029.154	31,365.40

For testing the hypothesis that the off-diagonal elements of Σ are zero, that is, that there is no correlation across firms, there are two approaches. If we have obtained maximum likelihood estimates, we can use a likelihood ratio test. This test is based on the statistic

$$\lambda_{LR} = T\left(\sum_i \ln \hat{\sigma}_i^2 - \ln|\hat{\Sigma}|\right), \tag{16-13}$$

where $\hat{\sigma}_i^2$ are the estimates of σ_i^2 obtained from iterating the groupwise heteroscedastic treatment (see Example 16.3) and $\hat{\Sigma}$ is the maximum likelihood estimator in the unrestricted model, that is, this example. The large-sample distribution of the statistic is chi-squared with $n(n-1)/2$ degrees of freedom. The Lagrange multiplier test developed by Breusch and Pagan (1980) provides an alternative. The general form of the statistic is

$$\lambda_{LM} = T \sum_{i=2}^{M} \sum_{j=1}^{i-1} r_{ij}^2, \tag{16-14}$$

---

[8] The estimate of Σ computed with the MLEs as well as the implied correlations are somewhat different. The results of the hypothesis tests are the same.

where r_{ij}^2 is the ijth residual correlation coefficient. If every firm had a different parameter vector, then, firm by firm, ordinary least squares would be efficient (and MLE), and we would compute r_{ij} from the OLS residuals. However, here we are assuming only a single parameter vector. Therefore, the strictly appropriate basis for computing the correlations is the residuals from the iterated estimator in the groupwise heteroscedastic model, that is, the same residuals used to compute $\hat{\sigma}_i^2$ in Table 16.5. An asymptotically valid approximation to the test can be based on the FGLS residuals instead. The two test statistics based on the results given previously are

$$\lambda_{LR} = 20(42.264 - 37.838) = 88.52$$

(the MLE of Σ is not shown) and

$$\lambda_{LM} = 51.315$$

based on the FGLS estimates given in Table 16.5. Using the MLEs, $\lambda_{LM} = 43.491$. For 10 degrees of freedom, the critical value from the chi-squared table is 23.21, so both results lead to rejection of the hypothesis of a diagonal Σ. We conclude that the simple heteroscedastic model is not general enough for these data.

Postscript. We shall examine the effect of assuming that all five firms have the same parameters in Chapter 17. For now, we note that one of the effects is to inflate the disturbance correlations. When the Lagrange multiplier statistic is recomputed with firm-by-firm separate regressions, the statistic falls to 29.04, which is still significant, but far less than what we found earlier.

16.3.3. Autocorrelation

The preceding discussion dealt with heteroscedasticity and cross-sectional correlation. Through a simple modification of the procedures, it is possible to relax the assumption of nonautocorrelation as well.

Before proceeding, we note that problems are introduced by models that contain lagged dependent variables. These are the same ones we encountered in Chapter 15, and the remedies discussed there will apply here. In addition, because of the Jacobian term in the log-likelihood function pertaining to the initial observation(s), iterated FGLS will no longer give maximum likelihood estimates. Therefore, in what follows, we shall not iterate the FGLS estimators. In many settings, this is likely to be an important consideration, as the typical time series is relatively short. It is possible, however, to scan the admissible range of the autocorrelation parameters for the maximum likelihood estimators. Lastly, at various points, variance estimators are computed using $\mathbf{e}'\mathbf{e}/T$. One could use the degrees of freedom, $T - K$, instead. Either is appropriate, and the asymptotic properties are the same for both. However, because this is not a classical regression model, the degrees of freedom correction does not bring about an unbiased estimator.

It is simplest to begin with the assumption that

$$\text{Corr}[\varepsilon_{it}, \varepsilon_{js}] = 0 \qquad \text{if } i \neq j.$$

That is, the disturbances between cross-sectional units are uncorrelated. Now we can take the approach of Chapter 15 to allow for autocorrelation within the cross-sectional units. Suppose that, for each i,

$$E[\boldsymbol{\varepsilon}_i\boldsymbol{\varepsilon}_i'] = \sigma_i^2\boldsymbol{\Omega}_i,$$

where $\boldsymbol{\Omega}_i$ is an autocorrelation matrix. With our earlier assumption, this produces

$$
\mathbf{V} = \begin{bmatrix} \sigma_1^2\boldsymbol{\Omega}_1 & \mathbf{0} & \cdots & \mathbf{0} \\ \mathbf{0} & \sigma_2^2\boldsymbol{\Omega}_2 & \cdots & \mathbf{0} \\ & & \vdots & \\ \mathbf{0} & \mathbf{0} & & \sigma_n^2\boldsymbol{\Omega}_n \end{bmatrix}. \tag{16-15}
$$

The AR(1) model is the simplest to formulate. Generalizations along the lines discussed in Chapter 15 would be cumbersome but straightforward. Consider, in general, then, the model

$$
\varepsilon_{it} = \rho_i \varepsilon_{it-1} + u_{it}
$$

$$
\text{Var}[\varepsilon_{it}] = \sigma_i^2 = \frac{\sigma_{ui}^2}{1 - \rho_i^2}. \tag{16-16}
$$

For FGLS estimation of the model, suppose that r_i is a consistent estimate of ρ_i. Then, if we take each time series $[\mathbf{y}_i, \mathbf{X}_i]$ separately, we can transform the data using the Prais–Winsten transformation,

$$
\mathbf{y}_{*_i} = \begin{bmatrix} \sqrt{1 - r_i^2}\, y_{i1} \\ y_{i2} - r_i y_{i1} \\ y_{i3} - r_i y_{i2} \\ \vdots \\ y_{iT} - r_i y_{iT-1} \end{bmatrix}, \qquad \mathbf{X}_{*_i} = \begin{bmatrix} \sqrt{1 - r_i^2}\, \mathbf{x}_{i1} \\ \mathbf{x}_{i2} - r_i \mathbf{x}_{i1} \\ \mathbf{x}_{i3} - r_i \mathbf{x}_{i2} \\ \vdots \\ \mathbf{x}_{iT} - r_i \mathbf{x}_{iT-1} \end{bmatrix}. \tag{16-17}
$$

In terms of the transformed data, $\mathbf{y}_{*_i}$ and $\mathbf{X}_{*_i}$, the model is now only heteroscedastic; the transformation has removed the autocorrelation. As such, the groupwise heteroscedastic model of Section 16.3.1 applies to the transformed data. We may use weighted least squares, as described earlier. This requires a second least squares estimate. The first regression produces initial estimates of ρ_i. The transformed data are then used in a second least squares regression to obtain consistent estimates,

$$
\hat{\sigma}_{ui}^2 = \frac{\mathbf{e}_{*_i}' \mathbf{e}_{*_i}}{T}. \tag{16-18}
$$

With these estimates in hand, we may proceed to the calculation of the heteroscedastic regression. If needed, the computational procedure given in the preceding note can be used. At the end of the calculation, the moment matrix used in the last regression gives the correct asymptotic covariance matrix for $\hat{\hat{\boldsymbol{\beta}}}$. If desired, a consistent estimate of $\sigma_{\varepsilon i}^2$ is obtained using

$$
\hat{\sigma}_{\varepsilon i}^2 = \frac{\hat{\sigma}_{ui}^2}{1 - r_i^2}. \tag{16-19}
$$

The remaining question is how to obtain the initial estimates, r_i. There are two possible structures to consider.

If the disturbances have a common stochastic process, with the same ρ_i, $\boldsymbol{\Omega}_i = \boldsymbol{\Omega}$ for all i. Three possible estimators of the common ρ, all of which are consistent, are

$$
\bar{r} = \frac{1}{n} \sum_i r_i,
$$

$$
r = \frac{\displaystyle\sum_i \sum_t e_{it} e_{it-1}}{\displaystyle\sum_i \sum_t e_{it}^2}. \tag{16-20}
$$

and

$$r^* = \text{sample Corr}[e_{i,t-1}, e_{it}].$$

Note that the first is an average of consistent but inefficient estimates.[9] The components r_i in $\bar{r}$ may be any of the estimators in Section 15.7.1 derived from the individual units. Since asymptotically each estimate has a variance of $(1 - \rho_i^2)/T$, a more efficient weighting would use the reciprocals of the variances, leading to

$$\bar{\bar{r}} = \sum_i w_i r_i,$$

$$w_i = \frac{1/(1 - r_i^2)}{\sum_i 1/(1 - r_i^2)}. \tag{16-21}$$

Since FGLS based on any of these estimators is asymptotically efficient, the choice of which to use is arbitrary. The small-sample properties are likely to be different, however.

The assumption of a common ρ is a restriction on the model, but not so severe a restriction as homoscedasticity. In Example 16.5, we shall see that the estimated autocorrelations of the first three firms are quite similar. Also, if the time series are short, this may be a necessary restriction in order to bring enough information to bear on the estimation of ρ to produce a reasonable estimate of $\boldsymbol{\beta}$. Once again, the relevance is to the small-sample properties. If the time series are very short, it may be preferable to impose the restriction of a common ρ, even if it is violated in the population, in order to improve the small-sample performance of the estimator $\hat{\boldsymbol{\beta}}$.[10]

If the processes are different across observational units, each time series may be analyzed separately. Any of the estimators described in Chapter 15 may be used; once again, the objective is consistency of the estimator. We note, both for this case and the previous one, that if there are lagged dependent variables in the model, the original least squares estimates will not yield consistent estimates of ρ_i. Instrumental variables or the method of Hatanaka may be used instead.

Last, one may wish to allow for cross-sectional correlation across units. Example 16.4 strongly suggests that this is appropriate for our investment data. The preceding has a natural generalization. If we assume that

$$\text{Cov}[u_{it}, u_{jt}] = \sigma_{uij},$$

we obtain the model of Section 16.3.2 in which the off-diagonal blocks of $\mathbf{V}$, $\sigma_{ij}\mathbf{I}$, are replaced by

$$\boldsymbol{\Omega}_{ij} = \frac{\sigma_{uij}}{1 - \rho_i\rho_j} \begin{bmatrix} 1 & \rho_j & \rho_j^2 & \cdots & \rho_j^{T-1} \\ \rho_i & 1 & \rho_j & \cdots & \rho_j^{T-2} \\ \rho_i^2 & \rho_i & 1 & \cdots & \rho_j^{T-3} \\ & & & \vdots & \\ \rho_i^{T-1} & \rho_i^{T-2} & \rho_i^{T-3} & \cdots & 1 \end{bmatrix}. \tag{16-22}$$

For estimation of this model, the technique of the preceding section needs only to be extended to the model of cross-sectional correlation in the obvious fashion. Initial

---

[9]The consistency of $\bar{r}$ follows from the consistency of r_i in the dimension T, not from convergence in the dimension of n. An average of a fixed number of consistent estimators will be consistent, even if they are correlated. We continue to take n as fixed in this section.

[10]This is a point at which increasing n can play a role in the asymptotic properties of the estimates. Suppose that T is fixed and relatively small. Then, if $n \rightarrow \infty$, all of the estimators of ρ will still be consistent.

estimates of ρ_i are required, as before. The Prais–Winsten transformation renders all of the blocks in $\mathbf{V}$ diagonal. Therefore, the model of cross-sectional correlation in Section 16.3.2 applies to the transformed data. The method of estimation described there may be used directly. Once again, the GLS moment matrix obtained at the last iteration (or the first, if no iterations are performed) provides the asymptotic covariance matrix for $\hat{\boldsymbol{\beta}}$. Estimates of $\sigma_{\varepsilon ij}$ can be obtained from the least squares residual covariances obtained from the transformed data:

$$\hat{\sigma}_{\varepsilon ij} = \frac{\hat{\sigma}_{uij}}{1 - r_i r_j}, \tag{16–23}$$

where

$$\hat{\sigma}_{uij} = \frac{\mathbf{e}'_{*i} \mathbf{e}_{*j}}{T}.$$

EXAMPLE 16.5

We now allow for different AR(1) processes for each firm. From the initial least squares estimates, the firm-specific autocorrelations and estimated variances of u_{it} and ε_{it} based on the transformed data are given in Table 16.9. The FGLS parameter estimates based on the transformed data are as shown in Table 16.10. Finally, the estimates are recomputed using the full model with cross-sectional covariances, giving the results shown in Table 16.11. The estimated variances using these estimates follow in Table 16.12.

TABLE 16.9

	Firm				
Estimate	**GM**	**CH**	**GE**	**WE**	**US**
r	0.47792	0.79364	0.90456	0.60208	0.86840
s_{ui}^2	5792.1	453.57	11,330.0	381.59	12,444.51
$s_{\varepsilon i}^2$	7506.68	1225.45	62,330.4	598.58	50,611.8

TABLE 16.10

	$\hat{\hat{\beta}}_1$	$\hat{\hat{\beta}}_2$	$\hat{\hat{\beta}}_3$
FGLS	−37.447	0.09128	0.35000
	(7.393)	(0.007721)	(0.03283)

TABLE 16.11

	$\hat{\hat{\beta}}_1$	$\hat{\hat{\beta}}_2$	$\hat{\hat{\beta}}_3$
FGLS	−35.523	0.09064	0.34777
	(7.288)	(0.007724)	(0.03184)

TABLE 16.12

	\multicolumn{5}{c}{Firm}				
	GM	**CH**	**GE**	**WE**	**US**
s_{ui}^2	6166.08	368.182	10,908.4	399.729	12,851.18
$s_{\varepsilon i}^2$	7991.3	994.74	60,011.0	627.03	52,266.0
r_{uiuj} (cross-sectional correlations)					
CH	0.065	—	—	—	—
GE	−0.160	−0.321	—	—	—
WE	−0.378	−0.057	0.518	—	—
US	0.041	0.198	−0.646	−0.202	—

16.3.4. A Random Coefficients Model

Thus far, the model $\mathbf{y}_i = \mathbf{X}_i\boldsymbol{\beta} + \boldsymbol{\varepsilon}_i$ has been analyzed within the familiar limits of heteroscedasticity and autocorrelation. Although the models in Sections 16.3.2 and 16.3.3 allow considerable flexibility, they do entail the not entirely plausible assumption that there is no parameter variation across firms (i.e., across the cross-sectional units). A fully general approach would combine all of the machinery of the previous sections with a model that allows $\boldsymbol{\beta}$ to vary across firms. We shall examine just such a model in Chapter 17.

In an interesting (albeit fairly short) branch of literature, a number of authors have suggested that parameter heterogeneity can be reasonably viewed as due to stochastic variation.[11] Suppose that we write

$$\mathbf{y}_i = \mathbf{X}_i\boldsymbol{\beta}_i + \boldsymbol{\varepsilon}_i,$$

where

$$\boldsymbol{\beta}_i = \boldsymbol{\beta} + \mathbf{v}_i,$$
$$E[\mathbf{v}_i] = \mathbf{0}, \tag{16-24}$$

and

$$E[\mathbf{v}_i\mathbf{v}_i'] = \boldsymbol{\Gamma}.$$

Assume for now that there is no autocorrelation or cross-sectional correlation of the sort examined in the previous section. Then the $\boldsymbol{\beta}_i$ applying to a particular cross-sectional unit is the outcome of a random process with mean vector $\boldsymbol{\beta}$ and covariance matrix $\boldsymbol{\Gamma}$. Combining terms, we obtain the model

$$\mathbf{y}_i = \mathbf{X}_i\boldsymbol{\beta} + (\boldsymbol{\varepsilon}_i + \mathbf{X}_i\mathbf{v}_i)$$
$$= \mathbf{X}_i\boldsymbol{\beta} + \mathbf{w}_i, \tag{16-25}$$

where

$$E[\mathbf{w}_i] = \mathbf{0}$$

and

$$E[\mathbf{w}_i\mathbf{w}_i'] = \sigma_i^2\mathbf{I} + \mathbf{X}_i\boldsymbol{\Gamma}\mathbf{X}_i'$$
$$= \boldsymbol{\Pi}_i.$$

[11] The most widely cited studies are Hildreth and Houck (1968), Swamy (1970, 1971, 1974), and Hsiao (1975).

This model fits directly into our earlier framework of groupwise heteroscedasticity (although the matrix algebra is a bit more weighty). For the full sample of observations,

$$
\mathbf{V} = \begin{bmatrix} \mathbf{\Pi}_1 & \mathbf{0} & \mathbf{0} & \cdots & \mathbf{0} \\ \mathbf{0} & \mathbf{\Pi}_2 & \mathbf{0} & \cdots & \mathbf{0} \\ & & \vdots & & \\ \mathbf{0} & \mathbf{0} & \mathbf{0} & & \mathbf{\Pi}_n \end{bmatrix}.
$$

For purposes of estimation, let $\mathbf{b}_i$ be the ith ordinary least squares coefficient vector, and let $\mathbf{V}_i + \mathbf{\Gamma} = (\mathbf{X}_i'\mathbf{X}_i)^{-1}\mathbf{X}_i'\mathbf{\Pi}_i\mathbf{X}_i(\mathbf{X}_i'\mathbf{X}_i)^{-1}$ be the covariance matrix of $\mathbf{b}_i$ [see (13–5)], where

$$
\mathbf{V}_i = \sigma_i^2[\mathbf{X}_i'\mathbf{X}_i]^{-1}. \tag{16–26}
$$

It can be shown[12] that the GLS estimator in this groupwise heteroscedastic model may be written

$$
\hat{\boldsymbol{\beta}} = \sum_i \mathbf{W}_i \mathbf{b}_i, \tag{16–27}
$$

where

$$
\mathbf{W}_i = \left\{ \sum_{i=1}^n [\mathbf{\Gamma} + \mathbf{V}_i]^{-1} \right\}^{-1} [\mathbf{\Gamma} + \mathbf{V}_i]^{-1}.
$$

This result shows (once again) the intuitive property that the GLS estimator is a matrix weighted average of the OLS estimators. (As in all such cases, $\Sigma_i \mathbf{W}_i = \mathbf{I}$.) The asymptotic covariance matrix for $\hat{\boldsymbol{\beta}}$ is the inverse matrix in braces in the previous expression.

The obstacle to the application of (16–27) is the unknown parameters in $\mathbf{\Gamma}$ and $\mathbf{V}_i$. Swamy (1971) has suggested a two-step approach. As always, it begins with ordinary least squares. Let $\mathbf{b}_i$ be the group specific OLS coefficient vector, and let $\hat{\mathbf{V}}_i$ be the sample covariance matrix, $s_i^2(\mathbf{X}_i'\mathbf{X}_i)^{-1}$, where $s_i^2 = \mathbf{e}_i'\mathbf{e}_i/(T - K)$. Let

$$
\overline{\mathbf{b}} = \frac{1}{n}\sum_i \mathbf{b}_i. \tag{16–28}
$$

Then,

$$
\hat{\mathbf{\Gamma}} = \mathbf{G} = \frac{1}{n-1}\left(\sum_i \mathbf{b}_i\mathbf{b}_i' - n\overline{\mathbf{b}}\overline{\mathbf{b}}' \right) - \frac{1}{n}\sum_i \hat{\mathbf{V}}_i. \tag{16–29}
$$

A potential problem (which appears in our data) is that $\mathbf{G}$ may not be positive definite. The two matrices in $\mathbf{G}$ are of order 1 and $1/(nT)$. Therefore, in terms of the large-sample behavior of $\mathbf{G}$, the second matrix will be negligible. Swamy suggests various fixups for a non-positive definite $\mathbf{G}$, but a simple and asymptotically valid expedient is simply to drop the second part.[13]

---

[12] This uses a result due to Rao (1965, p. 29).

[13] We should note that $\mathbf{G}$ is not a matrix that converges to $\mathbf{0}$ asymptotically. It is the estimator of the variance of the process generating $\boldsymbol{\beta}_i$, not of a sampling distribution of an estimator.

EXAMPLE 16.6 A Random Coefficients Model for Investment

For our investment data, least squares for the five firms produces the estimates given in Table 16.13. (The last estimate, $\widetilde{\mathbf{b}}$, is an alternative weighted average of the OLS estimates that is discussed in Examples 16.7 and 16.8.) As noted, $\widehat{\boldsymbol{\Gamma}}$ in (16–29) is not positive definite. Using the simpler version, we obtain for the FGLS random coefficients estimator,

$$\widehat{\boldsymbol{\beta}} = [-23.5836 \ (34.55), \ 0.080765 \ (0.02508), \ 0.283988 \ (0.06779)].$$

TABLE 16.13

	β_1		β_2		β_3	
GM	−149.782	(105.8)	0.11928	(0.02583)	0.37145	(0.03707)
CH	−9.9563	(31.37)	0.02655	(0.01557)	0.15169	(0.02570)
GE	−30.3685	(157.0)	0.15657	(0.07889)	0.42386	(0.1552)
WE	−6.18995	(13.51)	0.07795	(0.01997)	0.31572	(0.0288)
US	−0.50938	(8.015)	0.05289	(0.01571)	0.09241	(0.05610)
$\underline{\mathbf{b}}$	−39.3613		0.086649		0.271026	
$\overline{\mathbf{b}}$	−2.05809		0.05372		0.21136	

Finally, for comparison, the FGLS estimates from the least restrictive model of the previous section were

$$\text{FGLS} = [-35.523(7.288), \ 0.09064 \ (0.007,24), \ 0.34777 \ (0.03184)].$$

The standard errors of the random coefficient estimators are quite a bit larger than those of the FGLS estimator. This is to be expected. The variation of the estimates across firms is explicitly accounted for in the variance of the random coefficients model, while it is not in the generalized regression.

The FGLS procedure estimates the mean vector of the random process generating $\boldsymbol{\beta}_i$. It may be useful to produce predictions of the individual parameter vectors as well. A best linear predictor for $\boldsymbol{\beta}_i$ would be

$$\begin{aligned}
\widehat{\boldsymbol{\beta}}_i &= [\boldsymbol{\Gamma}^{-1} + \mathbf{V}_i^{-1}][\boldsymbol{\Gamma}^{-1}\widehat{\boldsymbol{\beta}} + \mathbf{V}_i^{-1}\mathbf{b}_i] \\
&= \mathbf{A}_i\widehat{\boldsymbol{\beta}} + [\mathbf{I} - \mathbf{A}_i]\mathbf{b}_i,
\end{aligned} \qquad (16\text{--}30)$$

once again, a matrix weighted average.[14] In this case, the weights are the inverses of the variance matrices of $\widehat{\boldsymbol{\beta}}_i$ and $\mathbf{b}_i$. The forecast is made feasible by inserting our estimates $\mathbf{G}$ and $\widehat{\mathbf{V}}_i$.

EXAMPLE 16.7

The forecasts and the OLS estimates for the investment data are listed in Table 16.14.

It has been suggested that a test of the random coefficients model can be based on the differences between the OLS estimates equation by equation and a weighted average of the OLS estimates. The test statistic suggested by Swamy (1971) is

$$\chi^2 = \sum_i [\mathbf{b}_i - \overline{\overline{\mathbf{b}}}]'\widehat{\mathbf{V}}_i^{-1}[\mathbf{b}_i - \overline{\overline{\mathbf{b}}}], \qquad (16\text{--}31)$$

---

[14] See Lee and Griffiths (1979).

TABLE 16.14

	β_1		β_2		β_3	
	OLS	**Predicted**	**OLS**	**Predicted**	**OLS**	**Predicted**
GM	-149.782	-71.629	0.11928	0.10278	0.37145	0.36785
CH	-9.9563	-12.033	0.02655	0.02794	0.15169	0.15083
GE	-30.3685	-27.706	0.15657	0.14776	0.42386	0.45133
WE	-6.18995	-9.8193	0.07795	0.08424	0.31572	0.30922
US	-0.50938	3.2695	0.05289	0.04111	0.09241	0.14072

where

$$\widetilde{\overline{\mathbf{b}}} = \left[\sum_i \hat{\mathbf{V}}_i^{-1}\right]^{-1} \sum_i \hat{\mathbf{V}}_i^{-1}\mathbf{b}_i.$$

The statistic is asymptotically distributed as chi-squared with $K(n-1)$ degrees of freedom under the null hypothesis of parameter constancy. It can be shown[15] that the statistic is algebraically the same as the standard F statistic for testing

$$H_0: \boldsymbol{\beta}_1 = \boldsymbol{\beta}_2 = \cdots = \boldsymbol{\beta}_n$$

in the generalized model

$$\begin{bmatrix} \mathbf{y}_1 \\ \mathbf{y}_2 \\ \vdots \\ \mathbf{y}_n \end{bmatrix} = \begin{bmatrix} \mathbf{X}_1 & \mathbf{0} & \cdots & \mathbf{0} \\ \mathbf{0} & \mathbf{X}_2 & \cdots & \mathbf{0} \\ & & \vdots & \\ \mathbf{0} & \mathbf{0} & \cdots & \mathbf{X}_n \end{bmatrix} \begin{bmatrix} \boldsymbol{\beta}_1 \\ \boldsymbol{\beta}_2 \\ \vdots \\ \boldsymbol{\beta}_n \end{bmatrix} + \begin{bmatrix} \boldsymbol{\varepsilon}_1 \\ \boldsymbol{\varepsilon}_2 \\ \vdots \\ \boldsymbol{\varepsilon}_n \end{bmatrix}$$

$$E[\boldsymbol{\varepsilon}_i\boldsymbol{\varepsilon}_j'] = \sigma_i^2\mathbf{I} \qquad \text{if } i = j \text{ and } [\mathbf{0}] \text{ if not.}$$

Which method is more convenient will depend on the format of the data and the available software.

EXAMPLE 16.8 ───

For the investment data, the weighted average estimator, $\widetilde{\mathbf{b}}$, is given in Example 16.6. The chi-squared test statistic, with 12 degrees of freedom, is 603.99. This is statistically significant by any measure. Consequently, we would reject the hypothesis of parameter constancy (again).

This test is not strictly a test for the random coefficients model. It can be construed as such, but also simply as a test of constancy of the parameter vector across classical regression models. This raises an interesting question that reappears at various points in this literature. If the coefficients are found to differ across units, should we attribute this to random variation or to fixed parameters that simply are different? Unfortunately, the same data are consistent with both hypotheses. Conditioned on the data we have actually observed, it is little more than a matter of interpretation whether we attribute heterogeneity to random or fixed effects.

---

[15] See Johnston (1984, p. 415).

16.3.5. Summary

The preceding sections have suggested a variety of different specifications of the generalized regression model. Which ones apply in a given situation depends on the setting. Homoscedasticity will depend on the nature of the data and will often be directly observable at the outset. Uncorrelatedness across the cross-sectional units is a strong assumption, particularly in view of the fact that the model assigns the same parameter vector to all units. Autocorrelation is a qualitatively different property. Although it does appear to arise naturally in time-series data, one would want to look carefully at the data before assuming that it is present.

The properties of all of these estimators depend on an increase in T, so they are generally not well suited to the types of data sets described in the next section. The various models, in increasing order of their generality, produced the estimates for our sample data shown in Table 16.15.

Moving down the columns, we see that the gains in efficiency that result from relaxing the constraints in $\mathbf{V}$ are clearly visible in the first three models. Not surprisingly, the standard errors rise noticeably with the introduction of autocorrelation in the fourth model. The disturbance variance that previously contained only contemporaneous variation now reflects the retention of lagged effects and their attendant variation in the current disturbance. This suggests that one might want to exercise some caution in extending a model to this level of generality. Nonautocorrelation is a testable restriction, and it is clear that there is some benefit to be gained if it is not present. (Of course, neglecting it when it *is* present is probably even worse.) The reduction in the standard errors of the estimates from the fourth to the fifth models reflects the same gain present in the difference between the second and third models. Allowing the off-diagonal elements of the contemporaneous disturbance covariance matrix to be nonzero introduces a large amount of new information into the estimator. Finally, the random coefficients model undoes some of the alleged efficiencies of the previous models by apportioning some of the cross-unit variation to the parameters instead of putting all of it in the disturbances.

Figure 16.1 is a plot of the residuals from the FGLS regression based on the least restrictive specification (the next to last one in Table 16.15). The figure is particularly revealing. Not only does it show quite clearly the groupwise heteroscedasticity induced by

TABLE 16.15

	Parameter		
Model	β_1	β_2	β_3
Classical regression	−48.030	0.10508	0.30534
	(21.16)	(0.01121)	(0.04285)
Groupwise heteroscedastic	−36.254	0.09499	0.33781
	(6.124)	(0.0074)	(0.0302)
Groupwise heteroscedastic and	−30.281	0.09412	0.34057
cross-sectionally correlated	(5.589)	(0.0068)	(0.0268)
Groupwise heteroscedastic,	−37.447	0.09128	0.35000
cross-sectionally correlated,	(7.393)	(0.0077)	(0.0328)
and within-group autocorrelated			
Groupwise heteroscedastic,	−35.523	0.09064	0.34777
cross-sectionally correlated,	(7.288)	(0.0077)	(0.0318)
within- and between-group			
autocorrelated			
Random coefficients	−23.484	0.08077	0.28399
	(34.55)	(0.0251)	(0.0678)

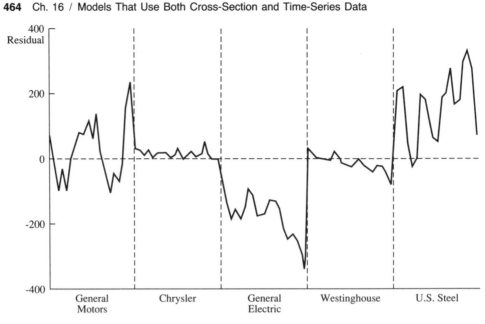

FIGURE 16.1

this model, but the autocorrelation of the residuals is also clearly visible. It is also clear that assuming that the same coefficient vector applies to all firms induces quite a serious misspecification for GE and U.S. Steel. We will return to this issue in Chapter 17.

16.4. Longitudinal Data

The analysis of panel or longitudinal data is the subject of one of the most active and innovative bodies of literature in econometrics. This is partly because panel data provide such a rich environment for the development of estimation techniques and theoretical results. In more practical terms, however, researchers have been able to use time-series cross-sectional data to examine issues that could not be studied in either cross-sectional or time-series settings alone. Two examples are as follows:

1. In a widely cited study of labor supply, Ben-Porath (1973) observes that at a certain point in time, in a cohort of women, 50 percent may appear to be working. It is ambiguous whether this finding implies that, in this cohort, one-half of the women on average will be working or that the same one-half will be working in every period. These have very different implications for policy and for the interpretation of any statistical results. Cross-sectional data alone will not shed any light on the question.

2. A long-standing problem in the analysis of production functions has been the inability to separate economies of scale and technological change. Cross-sectional data provide information only about the former, while time-series data muddle the two effects, with no prospect of separation. It is common, for example, to assume constant returns to scale in order to reveal the technical change.[16] Of course, this

---

[16] In a classic study of this issue, Solow (1957) states: "From time series of $\dot{Q}/Q$, w_K, $\dot{K}/K$, w_L and $\dot{L}/L$ or their discrete year-to-year analogues, we could estimate $\dot{A}/A$ and thence $A(t)$ itself. Actually an amusing thing happens here. Nothing has been said so far about returns to scale. But if all factor inputs are classified either as K or L, then the available figures always show w_K and w_L adding up to one. Since we have assumed that factors are paid their marginal products, this amounts to assuming the hypothesis of Euler's theorem. The calculus being what it is, we might just as well assume the conclusion, namely, that F is homogeneous of degree one."

assumes away the problem. A study by Greene (1983) examines the cost of electric power generation for a large number of firms, each observed in each of several years. The basic model, for the ith firm in year t,

$$\text{Cost}_{it} = C(Y_{it}, P_{it}, t),$$

where Y is output and $\mathbf{p}$ is a vector of factor prices, provides estimates of the rate of technological change,

$$\delta_t = \frac{-d \ln C}{dt}$$

and economies of scale,

$$\text{e.s.}_{it} = \frac{1}{d \ln C / d \ln Y_{it}} - 1.^{17}$$

In principle, the methods of Section 16.3 can be applied to longitudinal data sets. However, in the typical panel, there are a large number of cross-sectional units and only a few periods. Thus, the time-series methods discussed earlier may be somewhat problematic. Recent work has generally concentrated on models better suited to these short and wide data sets. The techniques are focused on cross-sectional variation, or heterogeneity. In this section, we shall examine the two most widely used models.

16.4.1. A Basic Model of Heterogeneity

The basic framework for this discussion is a regression model of the form

$$y_{it} = \alpha_i + \boldsymbol{\beta}'\mathbf{x}_{it} + \varepsilon_{it}. \tag{16-32}$$

There are K regressors in $\mathbf{x}_{it}$, *not including the constant term*. The **individual effect** is α_i, which is taken to be constant over time, t, and specific to the individual cross-sectional unit, i. As it stands, this is a classical regression model. In particular, if we take the α_is to be the same across units, ordinary least squares provides consistent and efficient estimates of α and $\boldsymbol{\beta}$.

EXAMPLE 16.9 Cost Function _____

The data in Table 16.16 are taken from the study by Greene described earlier. Output in millions of kilowatt-hours and total generation cost in millions of dollars, consisting of fuel, labor, and capital costs, are observed for six firms in each of 4 years. For purposes of the example, we fit the simple regression

$$\ln C_{it} = \alpha + \beta \ln Y_{it} + \varepsilon_{it}.$$

Least squares regression produces

$$\ln C = -4.17478 + 0.887987 \ln Y \qquad R^2 = 0.9707$$
$$(0.2769) \quad\;\; (0.0329) \qquad\quad s^2 = 0.04614.$$

---

[17] Different measures of economies of scale are used in different studies. For the one given, there are economies of scale if e.s.$_{it}$ is positive, constant returns to scale if it is zero, and diseconomies of scale if it is negative.

TABLE 16.16

Firm		t = 1 1955	t = 2 1960	t = 3 1965	t = 4 1970
		\multicolumn{4}{c}{Time}			

Firm		t = 1 1955	t = 2 1960	t = 3 1965	t = 4 1970
$i = 1$	Cost	3.154	4.271	4.584	5.849
	Output	214	419	588	1,025
$i = 2$	Cost	3.859	5.535	8.127	10.966
	Output	696	811	1,640	2,506
$i = 3$	Cost	19.035	26.041	32.444	41.180
	Output	3,202	4,802	5,821	9,275
$i = 4$	Cost	35.229	51.111	61.045	77.885
	Output	5,668	7,612	10,206	13,702
$i = 5$	Cost	33.154	40.044	43.125	57.727
	Output	6,000	8,222	8,484	10,004
$i = 6$	Cost	73.050	98.846	138.88	191.56
	Output	11,796	15,551	27,218	30,958

16.4.2. Fixed Effects

A common formulation of the model assumes that differences across units can be captured in differences in the constant term.[18] Thus, in (16–32), each α_i is an unknown parameter to be estimated. Let $\mathbf{y}_i$ and $\mathbf{X}_i$ be the T observations for the ith unit, and let $\boldsymbol{\varepsilon}_i$ be the associated $T \times 1$ vector of disturbances. Then, we may write (16–32) as

$$\mathbf{y}_i = \mathbf{i}\alpha_i + \mathbf{X}_i\boldsymbol{\beta} + \boldsymbol{\varepsilon}_i.$$

Collecting these, we have

$$\begin{bmatrix} \mathbf{y}_1 \\ \mathbf{y}_2 \\ \vdots \\ \mathbf{y}_n \end{bmatrix} = \begin{bmatrix} \mathbf{i} & \mathbf{0} & \cdots & \mathbf{0} \\ \mathbf{0} & \mathbf{i} & \cdots & \mathbf{0} \\ & & \vdots & \\ \mathbf{0} & \mathbf{0} & \cdots & \mathbf{i} \end{bmatrix} \begin{bmatrix} \alpha_1 \\ \alpha_2 \\ \vdots \\ \alpha_n \end{bmatrix} + \begin{bmatrix} \mathbf{X}_1 \\ \mathbf{X}_2 \\ \vdots \\ \mathbf{X}_n \end{bmatrix} \boldsymbol{\beta} + \begin{bmatrix} \boldsymbol{\varepsilon}_1 \\ \boldsymbol{\varepsilon}_2 \\ \vdots \\ \boldsymbol{\varepsilon}_n \end{bmatrix} \tag{16–33}$$

or

$$\mathbf{y} = [\mathbf{d}_1, \mathbf{d}_2 \cdots \mathbf{d}_n \quad \mathbf{X}] \begin{bmatrix} \boldsymbol{\alpha} \\ \boldsymbol{\beta} \end{bmatrix} + \boldsymbol{\varepsilon},$$

where $\mathbf{d}_i$ is a dummy variable indicating the ith unit. Let the $nT \times n$ matrix $\mathbf{D} = [\mathbf{d}_1, \mathbf{d}_2, \ldots, \mathbf{d}_n]$. Then, assembling all nT rows gives

$$\mathbf{y} = \mathbf{D}\boldsymbol{\alpha} + \mathbf{X}\boldsymbol{\beta} + \boldsymbol{\varepsilon}. \tag{16–34}$$

This is usually referred to as the *least squares dummy variable* (*LSDV*) model.

This is a classical regression model, so no new results are needed to analyze it. If n is small enough, the model can be estimated by ordinary least squares with K regressors in $\mathbf{X}$ and n columns in $\mathbf{D}$, as a multiple regression with $n + K$ parameters. Of course, if n is thousands, as is typical, this is likely to exceed the storage capabilities of any computer.

---

[18] It is also possible to allow the slopes to vary across i, but this introduces some new methodological issues, as well as considerable complexity in the calculations. A recent study on the topic is Cornwell and Schmidt (1984). Also, the assumption of a fixed T is only for convenience. The more general case in which T_i varies across units is considered in the exercises and in Greene (1991).

But, as we found in Chapter 8, there is an easier way to proceed. Using familiar results for a partitioned regression,[19] we write the OLS estimator of $\boldsymbol{\beta}$ as

$$\mathbf{b} = [\mathbf{X}'\mathbf{M}_d\mathbf{X}]^{-1}[\mathbf{X}'\mathbf{M}_d\mathbf{y}], \qquad (16\text{--}35)$$

where

$$\mathbf{M}_d = \mathbf{I} - \mathbf{D}(\mathbf{D}'\mathbf{D})^{-1}\mathbf{D}'.$$

This amounts to a least squares regression using the transformed data, $\mathbf{X}_* = \mathbf{M}_d\mathbf{X}$ and $\mathbf{y}_* = \mathbf{M}_d\mathbf{y}$. The structure of $\mathbf{D}$ is particularly convenient; its columns are orthogonal, so

$$\mathbf{M}_d = \begin{bmatrix} \mathbf{M}^0 & \mathbf{0} & \mathbf{0} & \cdots & \mathbf{0} \\ \mathbf{0} & \mathbf{M}^0 & \mathbf{0} & \cdots & \mathbf{0} \\ & & \vdots & & \\ \mathbf{0} & \mathbf{0} & \mathbf{0} & \cdots & \mathbf{M}^0 \end{bmatrix}.$$

Each matrix on the diagonal is

$$\mathbf{M}^0 = \mathbf{I}_T - \frac{1}{T}\mathbf{i}\mathbf{i}'.$$

Premultiplying any $T \times 1$ *vector*, $\mathbf{z}_i$, by $\mathbf{M}^0$ creates $\mathbf{M}^0\mathbf{z}_i = \mathbf{z}_i - \bar{z}\mathbf{i}$. (Note that the mean is taken over only the T observations for unit i.) Therefore, the regression of $\mathbf{M}_d\mathbf{y}$ on $\mathbf{M}_d\mathbf{X}$ is equivalent to the regression of $[y_{it} - \bar{y}_{i.}]$ on $[\mathbf{x}_{it} - \bar{\mathbf{x}}_{i.}]$, where $\bar{\mathbf{x}}_{i.}$ is the $K \times 1$ vector of means of $\mathbf{x}_{it}$ over the T observations. The dummy variable coefficients can be recovered from the other normal equation in the partitioned regression:

$$\mathbf{D}'\mathbf{D}\mathbf{a} + \mathbf{D}'\mathbf{X}\mathbf{b} = \mathbf{D}'\mathbf{y}$$

or $\qquad\qquad\qquad\qquad\qquad\qquad\qquad\qquad\qquad\qquad\qquad (16\text{--}36)$

$$\mathbf{a} = [\mathbf{D}'\mathbf{D}]^{-1}\mathbf{D}'(\mathbf{y} - \mathbf{X}\mathbf{b}).$$

This implies that for each i,

$$a_i = \text{the mean residual in the } i\text{th group.} \qquad (16\text{--}37)$$

Alternatively,

$$a_i = \bar{y}_{i.} - \mathbf{b}'\bar{\mathbf{x}}_{i.}.$$

The appropriate estimator of the variance matrix for $\mathbf{b}$ is

$$\text{Var}[\mathbf{b}] = s^2[\mathbf{X}'\mathbf{M}_d\mathbf{X}]^{-1}, \qquad (16\text{--}38)$$

which uses the usual second moment matrix with $\mathbf{x}$s, now expressed as deviations from their respective unit means. The disturbance variance estimator is

$$s^2 = \frac{\displaystyle\sum_i \sum_t (y_{it} - a_i - \mathbf{b}'\mathbf{x}_{it})^2}{nT - n - K}.$$

The itth residual is

$$\begin{aligned} e_{it} &= y_{it} - a_i - \mathbf{b}'\mathbf{x}_{it} \\ &= y_{it} - (\bar{y}_{i.} - \mathbf{b}'\bar{\mathbf{x}}_{i.}) - \mathbf{b}'\mathbf{x}_{it} \\ &= (y_{it} - \bar{y}_{i.}) - \mathbf{b}'(\mathbf{x}_{it} - \bar{\mathbf{x}}_{i.}). \end{aligned}$$

---

[19] See Section 6.3.4.

Thus, the numerator in s^2 is exactly the sum of squared residuals from the regression in (16–35). But most computer programs will use $nT - K$ for the denominator in computing s^2, so a correction will be necessary. For the individual effects,

$$\text{Var}[a_i] = \frac{\sigma^2}{T} + \bar{\mathbf{x}}'_{i.}\text{Var}[\mathbf{b}]\bar{\mathbf{x}}_{i.} \qquad (16\text{–}39)$$

so a simple estimator based on s^2 can be computed.

The usual t-ratio for a_i implies a test of the hypothesis that α_i equals zero. But typically this is not a useful hypothesis to test in a regression context. If we are interested in differences across groups, we can test the hypothesis that the constant terms are all equal with an F test. Under the null hypothesis, the efficient estimator is pooled least squares. The F ratio used for the test is

$$F(n - 1, nT - n - K) = \frac{(R_u^2 - R_p^2)/(n - 1)}{(1 - R_u^2)/(nT - n - K)}, \qquad (16\text{–}40)$$

where u indicates the unrestricted model and p indicates the pooled or restricted model with only a single overall constant term. (The sums of squared residuals may be used instead if that is more convenient.) It may be more convenient to estimate the model with an overall constant and $n - 1$ dummy variables instead. The other results will be unchanged, and, rather than estimate α_i, each dummy variable coefficient will be an estimate of $\alpha_i - \alpha_1$. The F test that the coefficients on the $n - 1$ dummy variables are zero is identical to the one above. It is important to keep in mind that although the statistical results are the same, the interpretation of the dummy variable coefficients in the two formulations is different.[20]

EXAMPLE 16.10 Cost Function with Firm Effects _____

Least squares estimation of the model in Example 16.9 with individual firm dummy variables produces

$$\ln C = \underset{(0.06113)}{0.674279} \ln Y \qquad \begin{array}{l} R^2 = 0.9924 \\ s^2 = 0.0155 \end{array}$$

$$\underset{(0.3828)}{-2.69353d_1} - \underset{(0.4396)}{2.9117d_2} - \underset{(0.5287)}{2.4400d_3}$$

$$\underset{(0.5588)}{-2.13449d_4} - \underset{(0.5532)}{2.3108d_5} - \underset{(0.6081)}{1.9035d_6}$$

$$F[5, 17] = \frac{(0.9924 - 0.9707)/5}{(1 - 0.9924)/17} = 9.708.$$

The 1 percent critical value from the F table is 4.34, so the hypothesis that the firm effects are the same is rejected at the 1 percent significance level.

_____

The least squares dummy variable approach can be extended to include a time-specific effect as well. The extended model is

$$y_{it} = \alpha_i + \gamma_t + \boldsymbol{\beta}'\mathbf{x}_{it} + \varepsilon_{it}. \qquad (16\text{–}41)$$

This model is obtained from the preceding one by the inclusion of an additional $T - 1$ dummy variables. (One of the time effects must be dropped to avoid perfect collinearity.)

_____

[20] For a discussion of the differences, see Suits (1984).

If the number of variables is too large to handle by ordinary regression, this can also be estimated by using the partitioned regression. Least squares estimates of the slopes are obtained by regression of

$$y_{*_{it}} = y_{it} - \bar{y}_{i.} - \bar{y}_{.t} + \bar{\bar{y}} \qquad (16\text{--}42)$$

on

$$\mathbf{x}_{*_{it}} = \mathbf{x}_{it} - \bar{\mathbf{x}}_{i.} - \bar{\mathbf{x}}_{.t} + \bar{\bar{\mathbf{x}}},$$

where

$$\bar{y}_{.t} = \frac{1}{n} \sum_i y_{it}$$

and

$$\bar{\bar{y}} = \frac{1}{nT} \sum_i \sum_t y_{it},$$

and likewise for $\bar{\mathbf{x}}_{.t}$ and $\bar{\bar{\mathbf{x}}}$. The dummy variable coefficients can be recovered from the normal equations as

$$a_i = (\bar{y}_{i.} - \bar{\bar{y}}) - \mathbf{b}'(\bar{\mathbf{x}}_{i.} - \bar{\bar{\mathbf{x}}}),$$
$$c_t = (\bar{y}_{.t} - \bar{\bar{y}}) - \mathbf{b}'(\bar{\mathbf{x}}_{.t} - \bar{\bar{\mathbf{x}}}). \qquad (16\text{--}43)$$

(If one of n or T is small and the other is large, it will usually be simpler just to treat the smaller set as an ordinary set of variables and apply the previous results to the one-way fixed effects model defined by the larger set.) Although more general, this model is rarely used in practice. There are two reasons. First, the cost in terms of degrees of freedom is often not justified. Second, in those instances in which a model of the timewise evolution of the disturbance is desired, a more general model than the dummy variable formulation is usually used.

16.4.3. Random Effects

The fixed effects model is a reasonable approach when we can be confident that the differences between units can be viewed as parametric shifts of the regression function. This model might be viewed as applying only to the cross-sectional units in the study, not to additional ones outside the sample. For example, an intercountry comparison may well include the full set of countries for which it is reasonable to assume that the model is constant. Likewise, in Greene's study cited earlier, the sample of 114 firms was nearly exhaustive of the investor-owned utilities in the United States. In other settings, it might be more appropriate to view individual specific constant terms as randomly distributed across cross-sectional units. This would be appropriate if we believed that sampled cross-sectional units were drawn from a large population. It would certainly be the case for the longitudinal data sets listed in the Introduction.[21]

Consider, then, a reformulation of the model

$$y_{it} = \alpha + \boldsymbol{\beta}'\mathbf{x}_{it} + u_i + \varepsilon_{it}, \qquad (16\text{--}44)$$

where there are K regressors in addition to the constant term. The component u_i is the random disturbance characterizing the ith observation and is constant through time. In the

---

[21] This is not a hard and fast distinction; it is purely heuristic. We shall return to this issue later.

analysis of families, we can view them as the collection of factors not in the regression that are specific to that family. We assume further that

$$E[\varepsilon_{it}] = E[u_i] = 0,$$

$$E[\varepsilon_{it}^2] = \sigma_\varepsilon^2,$$

$$E[u_i^2] = \sigma_u^2,$$

$$E[\varepsilon_{it} u_j] = 0 \qquad \text{for all } i, t, \text{ and } j$$

$$E[\varepsilon_{it} \varepsilon_{js}] = 0 \qquad \text{if } t \neq s \text{ or } i \neq j,$$

$$E[u_i u_j] = 0 \qquad \text{if } i \neq j.$$

$$(16–45)$$

As before, it is useful to view the formulation of the model in blocks of T observations for observations i, $\mathbf{y}_i$, $\mathbf{X}_i$, $u_i\mathbf{i}$, and $\boldsymbol{\varepsilon}_i$. For these T observations, let

$$w_{it} = \varepsilon_{it} + u_i$$

and

$$\mathbf{w}_i = [w_{i1}, w_{i2}, \ldots, w_{iT}]'.$$

Then

$$E[w_{it}^2] = \sigma_\varepsilon^2 + \sigma_u^2,$$

$$E[w_{it} w_{is}] = \sigma_u^2.$$

For the T observations for unit i, let $\boldsymbol{\Omega} = E[\mathbf{w}_i \mathbf{w}_i']$. Then

$$\boldsymbol{\Omega} = \begin{bmatrix} \sigma_\varepsilon^2 + \sigma_u^2 & \sigma_u^2 & \sigma_u^2 & \cdots & \sigma_u^2 \\ \sigma_u^2 & \sigma_\varepsilon^2 + \sigma_u^2 & \sigma_u^2 & \cdots & \sigma_u^2 \\ & & \vdots & & \\ \sigma_u^2 & \sigma_u^2 & \sigma_u^2 & & \sigma_\varepsilon^2 + \sigma_u^2 \end{bmatrix} \qquad (16–46)$$

$$= \sigma_\varepsilon^2 \mathbf{I} + \sigma_u^2 \mathbf{i}\mathbf{i}',$$

where $\mathbf{i}$ is a $T \times 1$ column vector of ones. Since observations i and j are independent, the disturbance covariance for the full nT observations is

$$\mathbf{V} = \begin{bmatrix} \boldsymbol{\Omega} & \mathbf{0} & \mathbf{0} & \mathbf{0} \\ \mathbf{0} & \boldsymbol{\Omega} & \mathbf{0} & \mathbf{0} \\ & & \vdots & \\ \mathbf{0} & \mathbf{0} & \mathbf{0} & \boldsymbol{\Omega} \end{bmatrix} = \mathbf{I} \otimes \boldsymbol{\Omega}. \qquad (16–47)$$

This matrix has a particularly simple structure.

16.4.3a. Generalized Least Squares. For generalized least squares, we require $\mathbf{V}^{-1/2} = \mathbf{I} \otimes \boldsymbol{\Omega}^{-1/2}$. Therefore, we need only find $\boldsymbol{\Omega}^{-1/2}$, which is

$$\boldsymbol{\Omega}^{-1/2} = \mathbf{I} - \frac{\theta}{T} \mathbf{i}\mathbf{i}',$$

where

$$\theta = 1 - \frac{\sigma_\varepsilon}{(T\sigma_u^2 + \sigma_\varepsilon^2)^{1/2}}.$$

The transformation of $\mathbf{y}_i$ and $\mathbf{X}_i$ for GLS is, therefore,

$$\boldsymbol{\Omega}^{-1/2}\mathbf{y}_i = \begin{bmatrix} y_{i1} - \theta\bar{y}_{i.} \\ y_{i2} - \theta\bar{y}_{i.} \\ \vdots \\ y_{iT} - \theta\bar{y}_{i.} \end{bmatrix}, \tag{16-48}$$

and likewise for the rows of $\mathbf{X}_i.$ [22] For the data set as a whole, generalized least squares is computed by the regression of these partial deviations in y_{it} on the same transformations of x_{it}. Note the similarity of this procedure to the computation in the LSDV model, which has $\theta = 1$.

An alternative formulation of the GLS estimator is illuminating. We could formulate the regression model in three ways: First, the original formulation is

$$y_{it} = \alpha + \boldsymbol{\beta}'\mathbf{x}_{it} + \varepsilon_{it} + u_i. \tag{16-49a}$$

In terms of deviations from the unit means,

$$y_{it} - \bar{y}_{i.} = \boldsymbol{\beta}'(\mathbf{x}_{it} - \bar{\mathbf{x}}_{i.}) + \varepsilon_{it} - \bar{\varepsilon}_{i.}, \tag{16-49b}$$

while in terms of the unit means,

$$\bar{y}_{i.} = \alpha + \boldsymbol{\beta}'\bar{\mathbf{x}}_{i.} + \bar{\varepsilon}_{i.} + u_i. \tag{16-49c}$$

All three are generalized regression models, and, in principle, all three could be estimated, at least consistently if not efficiently, by ordinary least squares. [Note that (16–49c) involves only n observations.] Consider, then, the matrices of sums of squares and cross-products that would be used in each case, where we focus only on estimation of $\boldsymbol{\beta}$. In (16–49a), the moments would be about the overall means, $\bar{\bar{y}}$ and $\bar{\bar{\mathbf{x}}}$, and we would use the *total* sums of squares and cross-products,

$$\mathbf{S}_{xx}^t = \sum_i \sum_t (\mathbf{x}_{it} - \bar{\bar{\mathbf{x}}})(\mathbf{x}_{it} - \bar{\bar{\mathbf{x}}})'$$

and

$$\mathbf{S}_{xy}^t = \sum_i \sum_t (\mathbf{x}_{it} - \bar{\bar{\mathbf{x}}})(y_{it} - \bar{\bar{y}}).$$

(The use of the superscript t indicates "total" and is unrelated to the time subscript.) For (16–49b), since the data are in deviations already, the means of $(y_{it} - \bar{y}_{i.})$ and $(\mathbf{x}_{it} - \bar{\mathbf{x}}_{i.})$ are zero. The moment matrices are the *within-units* sums of squares and cross-products,

$$\mathbf{S}_{xx}^w = \sum_i \sum_t (\mathbf{x}_{it} - \bar{\mathbf{x}}_{i.})(\mathbf{x}_{it} - \bar{\mathbf{x}}_{i.})'$$

and

$$\mathbf{S}_{xy}^w = \sum_i \sum_t (\mathbf{x}_{it} - \bar{\mathbf{x}}_{i.})(y_{it} - \bar{y}_{i.}).$$

Finally, for (16–49c), the mean of unit means is the overall mean. The moment matrices are the *between-units* sums of squares and cross-products,

$$\mathbf{S}_{xx}^b = \sum_i T(\bar{\mathbf{x}}_{i.} - \bar{\bar{\mathbf{x}}})(\bar{\mathbf{x}}_{i.} - \bar{\bar{\mathbf{x}}})'$$

---

[22] This is a special case of the more general model treated in Nerlove (1971b).

and

$$S_{xy}^b = \sum_i T(\bar{\mathbf{x}}_{i.} - \bar{\bar{\mathbf{x}}})(\bar{y}_{i.} - \bar{\bar{y}}).$$

It is easy to verify that

$$S_{xx}^t = S_{xx}^w + S_{xx}^b$$

and

$$S_{xy}^t = S_{xy}^w + S_{xy}^b.$$

There are, therefore, three possible least squares estimators of $\boldsymbol{\beta}$ corresponding to the decomposition. The least squares estimator is

$$\begin{aligned}
\mathbf{b}^t &= [S_{xx}^t]^{-1}S_{xy}^t \\
&= [S_{xx}^w + S_{xx}^b]^{-1}[S_{xy}^w + S_{xy}^b].
\end{aligned} \tag{16-50}$$

The *within-units* estimator is

$$\mathbf{b}^w = [S_{xx}^w]^{-1}S_{xy}^w. \tag{16-51}$$

This is the LSDV estimator computed earlier. [See (16–35).] An alternative estimator would be the *between-units* estimator,

$$\mathbf{b}^b = [S_{xx}^b]^{-1}S_{xy}^b. \tag{16-52}$$

This is the least squares estimator of (16–49c) based on the n sets of groups means. From the preceding expressions (and familiar previous results),

$$S_{xy}^w = S_{xx}^w \mathbf{b}^w$$

and

$$S_{xy}^b = S_{xx}^b \mathbf{b}^b.$$

Inserting these in (16–50), we see that the OLS estimator is a matrix weighted average of the within- and between-units estimators:

$$\mathbf{b}^t = \mathbf{F}^w \mathbf{b}^w + \mathbf{F}^b \mathbf{b}^b, \tag{16-53}$$

where

$$\mathbf{F}^w = [S_{xx}^w + S_{xx}^b]^{-1}S_{xx}^w = \mathbf{I} - \mathbf{F}^b.$$

EXAMPLE 16.11

The OLS estimator for the cost data is given in Example 16.9. The LSDV estimator in Example 16.10 is the within-units estimator. For the six firms, the unit means are as listed in Table 16.17.

TABLE 16.17 Firm Means

Firm	ln Cost	ln Output
1	1.47234	6.17826
2	1.88787	7.11813
3	3.35085	8.58816
4	3.99068	9.08403
5	3.75274	8.99269
6	4.76838	9.89485
Overall	3.20381	8.30935

The three estimators for the slope are

$$b^t = 0.887987,$$

$$b^w = 0.674279,$$

$$b^b = 0.911073.$$

The weighting for the two estimators can be derived from

$$b^t = mb^w + (1 - m)b^b,$$

so

$$m = \frac{b^t - b^b}{b^w - b^b} = 0.09749.$$

Most of variation is between units. The data were chosen to include wide variation in output across firms, so this is not surprising. The steady but undramatic growth of the firms that provides the within-units variation is small compared to the differences across firms.

It can be shown that the GLS estimator is, likewise, a matrix weighted average of the within- and between-units estimators:

$$\hat{\boldsymbol{\beta}} = \hat{\mathbf{F}}^w \mathbf{b}^w + (\mathbf{I} - \hat{\mathbf{F}}^w)\mathbf{b}^b,^{[23]} \tag{16–54}$$

where

$$\hat{\mathbf{F}}^w = [\mathbf{S}_{xx}^w + \lambda \mathbf{S}_{xx}^b]^{-1} \mathbf{S}_{xx}^w,$$

$$\lambda = \frac{\sigma_\varepsilon^2}{\sigma_\varepsilon^2 + T\sigma_u^2} = (1 - \theta)^2.$$

To the extent that λ differs from one, we see that the inefficiency of least squares will follow from an inefficient weighting of the two least squares estimators. In particular, compared to generalized least squares, ordinary least squares places too much weight on the between-units variation. It includes it all in the variation in $\mathbf{X}$, rather than apportioning some of it to random variation across groups attributable to the variation in u_i across units.

There are some polar cases to consider. If λ equals one, generalized least squares is ordinary least squares. This would occur if σ_u^2 were zero, in which case a classical regression model would apply. If λ equals zero, the estimator is the dummy variable estimator we used in the fixed effects setting. There are two possibilities. If σ_ε^2 were zero, all variation across units would be due to the different u_i's, which, because they are constant across time, would be equivalent to the dummy variables we used in the fixed-effects model. The question of whether they were fixed or random would then become moot. They are the only source of variation across units once the regression is accounted for. The other case is $T \to \infty$. We can view it this way: If $T \to \infty$, the unobserved u_i becomes observable. Take the T observations for the ith unit. Our estimator of $[\alpha, \boldsymbol{\beta}]$ is consistent in the dimensions T or n. Therefore,

$$y_{it} - \alpha - \boldsymbol{\beta}' \mathbf{x}_{it} = u_i - \varepsilon_{it}$$

---

[23] An alternative form of this expression, in which the weighting matrices are proportional to the variance matrices of the two estimators, is given by Judge et al. (1985).

is observable. The individual means will provide

$$\bar{y}_{i.} - \alpha - \boldsymbol{\beta}'\bar{\mathbf{x}}_{i.} = u_i + \bar{\varepsilon}_{i.}.$$

But $\bar{\varepsilon}_{i.}$ converges to zero, which reveals u_i to us. Therefore, if T goes to infinity, u_i becomes the d_i we used earlier. (The fact that it is not 1 is immaterial; it is nonzero only for unit i.)

16.4.3b. Feasible Generalized Least Squares When Ω Is Unknown. If the variance components are known, generalized least squares can be computed without much difficulty. Of course, this is not likely, so, as usual, we must first estimate the disturbance variances and then use an FGLS procedure. A heuristic approach to estimation of the components is as follows:

$$y_{it} = \alpha + \boldsymbol{\beta}'\mathbf{x}_{it} + \varepsilon_{it} + u_i$$

and

$$\bar{y}_{i.} = \alpha + \boldsymbol{\beta}'\bar{\mathbf{x}}_{i.} + \bar{\varepsilon}_{i.} + u_i. \tag{16-55}$$

Therefore, deviations from the unit means remove the heterogeneity:

$$y_{it} - \bar{y}_{i.} = \boldsymbol{\beta}'[\mathbf{x}_{it} - \bar{\mathbf{x}}_{i.}] + [\varepsilon_{it} - \bar{\varepsilon}_{i.}]. \tag{16-56}$$

Since

$$E\left[\sum_t (\varepsilon_{it} - \bar{\varepsilon}_{i.})^2\right] = (T-1)\sigma_\varepsilon^2,$$

if $\boldsymbol{\beta}$ were observed, an unbiased estimator of σ_ε^2 based on T observations in unit i would be

$$\hat{\sigma}_{\varepsilon i}^2 = \frac{1}{T-1} \sum_t (\varepsilon_{it} - \bar{\varepsilon}_{i.})^2. \tag{16-57}$$

Since $\boldsymbol{\beta}$ must be estimated—we use the LSDV estimator in (16–35)—we make the usual degrees of freedom correction and use

$$s_{ei}^2 = \frac{\sum_t (e_{it} - \bar{e}_{i.})^2}{T-K-1}. \tag{16-58}$$

We have n such estimators, so we average them to obtain

$$\bar{s}_e^2 = \frac{1}{n} \sum_i s_{ei}^2$$

$$= \frac{1}{n} \sum_i \frac{\sum_t (e_{it} - \bar{e}_{i.})^2}{T-K-1} \tag{16-59}$$

$$= \frac{1}{nT - nK - n} \sum_i \sum_t (e_{it} - \bar{e}_{i.})^2.$$

The degrees of freedom correction in $\bar{s}_e^2$ is excessive, as it assumes that α and $\boldsymbol{\beta}$ are reestimated for each i. The estimated parameters are the n means $\bar{y}_{i.}$ and the K slopes.

Therefore, we propose the unbiased estimator

$$\hat{\sigma}_\varepsilon^2 = \frac{\sum_i \sum_t (e_{it} - \bar{e}_{i.})^2}{(nT - n - K)}.^{24} \tag{16-60}$$

For convenience, it is worth noting that this is just the variance estimator in the LSDV model in (16-60), appropriately corrected for degrees of freedom. The n means,

$$\varepsilon_{**_i} = \bar{y}_{i.} - \alpha - \boldsymbol{\beta}'\bar{\mathbf{x}}_{i.} \tag{16-61}$$
$$= \bar{\varepsilon}_{i.} + u_i,$$

are independent and have variance

$$\mathrm{Var}[\varepsilon_{**_i}] = \sigma_{**}^2 = \frac{\sigma_\varepsilon^2}{T} + \sigma_u^2.$$

Incorporating the degrees of freedom correction for the estimate of $\boldsymbol{\beta}$ in the group means least squares regression of (16–55), we can use

$$\hat{\sigma}_{**}^2 = \frac{\mathbf{e}'_{**}\mathbf{e}_{**}}{n - K} \tag{16-62}$$

as an unbiased estimator of $\sigma_\varepsilon^2/T + \sigma_u^2$. This suggests the estimator

$$\hat{\sigma}_u^2 = \hat{\sigma}_{**}^2 - \frac{\hat{\sigma}_\varepsilon^2}{T}. \tag{16-63}$$

The estimator in (16–63) is unbiased but could be negative in a finite sample. Alternative estimators have been proposed.[25] Indeed, since we only require a consistent estimator of σ_u^2, *any* consistent estimate of $\boldsymbol{\beta}$ could be used in (16–62), including the original pooled OLS estimator. However, such a finding might cast some doubt on the appropriateness of the model, and before proceeding in this fashion, one might do well to reconsider the random effects specification.

There is a remaining complication. If there are any regressors that do not vary within the groups, the LSDV estimator cannot be computed. For example, in a model of family income or labor supply, one of the regressors might be a dummy variable for location, family structure, or living arrangement. Any of these could be perfectly collinear with the fixed effect for that family, which would prevent computation of the LSDV estimator. In this case it is still possible to estimate the random effects variance components. Once again, let [a, **b**] be any consistent estimator of [α, $\boldsymbol{\beta}$], for example the ordinary least squares estimator. Then, using all nT residuals,

$$\frac{\mathrm{plim}\ \mathbf{e}'\mathbf{e}}{nT} = \sigma_\varepsilon^2 + \sigma_u^2.$$

Now, using the n group means, (16–62) is still usable for estimation. This provides two moment equations in the two unknown variance terms. As before, this can produce a negative estimate of σ_u^2 which, once again, calls the specification of the model into question.

---

[24] A formal proof of this proposition may be found in Maddala (1971) or in Judge et al. (1985, p. 551).

[25] See, for example, Wallace and Hussain (1969), Maddala (1971), Fuller and Battese (1974), and Amemiya (1971).

Breusch and Pagan (1980) have devised a Lagrange multiplier test for the random effects model based on the OLS residuals. For

$$H_0: \sigma_u^2 = 0 \qquad (\text{or } \text{Corr}[w_{it}, w_{is}] = 0),$$

$$H_1: \sigma_u^2 \neq 0,$$

the test statistic is

$$LM = \frac{nT}{2(T-1)} \left[\frac{\sum_i \left(\sum_t e_{it} \right)^2}{\sum_i \sum_t e_{it}^2} - 1 \right]^2. \qquad (16\text{--}64)$$

Under the null hypothesis, LM is distributed as chi-squared with one degree of freedom. A useful shortcut for computing LM is as follows: Let **D** be the matrix of dummy variables defined in (16–33), and let **e** be the OLS residual vector. Then

$$LM = \frac{nT}{2(T-1)} \left[\frac{\mathbf{e'DD'e}}{\mathbf{e'e}} - 1 \right]^2. \qquad (16\text{--}65)$$

EXAMPLE 16.12

The least squares estimates for the cost data are given in Example 16.9. Based on the OLS residuals, we obtain a Lagrange multiplier test statistic of

$$\frac{6(4)}{2(4-1)} \left[\frac{2.24522}{1.01520} - 1 \right]^2 = 5.87185.$$

The 5 percent and 1 percent critical values from the chi-squared distribution with one degree of freedom are 3.842 and 6.635, so the statistic is significant at the 5 percent level of significance but not at the 1 percent level. The evidence in favor of the error components model is present, but not compelling.

With the variance estimators in hand, FGLS can be used to estimate the parameters of the model. All of our earlier results for FGLS estimators apply here. It would also be possible to obtain the maximum likelihood estimator.[26] The likelihood function is complicated, but as we have seen repeatedly, the MLE of $\boldsymbol{\beta}$ will be GLS based on the maximum likelihood estimators of the variance components. It can be shown that the MLEs of σ_ε^2 and σ_u^2 are the unbiased estimators shown earlier, *without* their degrees of freedom corrections.[27] This model satisfies the requirements for the Oberhofer–Kmenta algorithm, so we could also use the iterated FGLS procedure to obtain the MLEs if desired. The initial consistent estimates could be based on least squares residuals. Still other estimators have been proposed. None will have better asymptotic properties than the MLE or FGLS estimators, but they may outperform them in a finite sample.[28]

[26] See Hsiao (1986).

[27] See Berzeg (1979).

[28] See Maddala and Mount (1973).

EXAMPLE 16.13 _____

To compute the FGLS estimator, we require estimates of the variance components. As noted earlier, the unbiased estimator of σ_ε^2 is the residual variance estimator in the within-units (LSDV) regression. Thus,

$$\hat{\sigma}_\varepsilon^2 = \frac{0.264062}{17} = 0.015531.$$

The unit means are given in Example 16.11. The residual sum of squares in the unit means regression is 0.135202, so

$$\overbrace{\frac{\sigma_\varepsilon^2}{T} + \sigma_u^2} = \frac{0.135202}{4} = 0.033801.$$

Therefore,

$$\hat{\sigma}_u^2 = 0.033801 - \frac{0.015531}{4} = 0.0299178.$$

For purposes of FGLS,

$$\hat{\theta} = 1 - \left[\frac{0.015531}{4(0.033801)}\right]^{1/2} = 0.661074.$$

Finally, the FGLS regression produces

$$\ln C_{it} - \hat{\theta}\,\overline{\ln C_{i.}} = -3.41310 + \underset{(0.3615)}{} 0.796321\,(\ln Y_{it} - \hat{\theta}\,\overline{\ln Y_{i.}}).$$
$$\phantom{\ln C_{it} - \hat{\theta}\,\overline{\ln C_{i.}} = -3.41310 + }(0.3615)\quad(0.04256)$$

It is instructive to compare these to the OLS results we obtained earlier:

$$\ln C = -4.17478 + 0.887987\,\ln Y.$$
$$(0.2769)\quad(0.0329)$$

The FGLS constant term is an estimate of $\alpha(1 - \theta)$, so the implied estimate of the constant term would be -10.0703.[29] Recall that we derived the implicit weighting between the within- and between-units estimators for OLS:

$$0.887987 = 0.09749b^w + 0.90251b^b,$$

where

$$b^w = 0.674279$$

and

$$b^b = 0.911073.$$

To do likewise for the FGLS estimator, we require the decomposition of the variance of $\ln Y$, which is

$$S_{xx}^t = 42.63166,$$

$$S_{xx}^b = 38.4754,$$

$$S_{xx}^w = 4.15626.$$

---

[29] The estimate of θ is a function of two moments of the residuals. The constant in the regression is also a sample moment [see the equations preceding (5–25)]. Therefore, the results of Section 4.6.2 could be used to estimate the standard error of $a/(1 - \hat{\theta})$.

The weighting to be used would be

$$w_{GLS} = \frac{S_{xx}^w}{S_{xx}^w + (1 - \hat{\theta})^2 S_{xx}^b} = 0.4846.$$

Therefore, for the FGLS estimator,

$$0.796321 = 0.4846 b^w + 0.5154 b^b.$$

As expected, the weight attached to the between-units estimator is lower when we use FGLS.

None of the desirable properties of the estimators in the random effects model rely on T going to infinity.[30] Indeed, T is likely to be quite small. The maximum likelihood estimator of σ_ε^2 is exactly equal to an average of n estimators, each based on the T observations for unit i. [See (16–59).] Each component in this average is, in principle, consistent. That is, its variance is of order $1/T$ or smaller. Since T is small, this may be relatively large; however, each term provides some information about the parameter. The average over the n cross-sectional units has a variance of order $1/(nT)$, which will go to zero if n increases, even if we regard T as fixed. The conclusion to draw is that nothing in this treatment relies on T growing large. Although it can be shown that some consistency results will follow for T increasing, the typical panel data set is based on data sets for which it does not make sense to assume that T increases without bound or, in some cases, at all.[31] As a general proposition, it is necessary to take some care in devising estimators whose properties hinge on whether T is large or not. The widely used conventional ones we have discussed here do not, but we have not exhausted the possibilities.

The LSDV model *does* rely on T increasing for consistency. To see this, we use the partitioned regression. The slopes are

$$\mathbf{b} = [\mathbf{X}'\mathbf{M}_d\mathbf{X}]^{-1}[\mathbf{X}'\mathbf{M}_d\mathbf{y}].$$

Since $\mathbf{X}$ is $nT \times K$, as long as the inverted moment matrix converges to a zero matrix, $\mathbf{b}$ is consistent as long as either n or T increases without bound. But the dummy variable coefficients are

$$a_i = \bar{y}_{i.} - \mathbf{b}'\bar{\mathbf{x}}_{i.}$$

$$= \frac{1}{T} \sum_t e_{it}.$$

We have already seen that $\mathbf{b}$ is consistent. Suppose, for the present, that $\bar{\mathbf{x}}_{i.} = \mathbf{0}$. Then $\text{Var}[a_i] = \text{Var}[y_{it}]/T$. Therefore, unless $T \to \infty$, the estimates of the unit-specific effects are not consistent. (They are, however, best linear unbiased.) This is worth bearing in mind when analyzing data sets for which T is fixed and there is no intention to replicate the study, and no logical argument that would justify the claim that it could have been replicated in principle.

The random effects model was developed by Balestra and Nerlove (1966). Their formulation included a time-specific component as well as the individual effect:

$$y_{it} = \alpha + \boldsymbol{\beta}'\mathbf{x}_{it} + \varepsilon_{it} + u_i + v_t.$$

---

[30] See Nickell (1981).

[31] In this connection, Chamberlain (1983) has provided some innovative treatments of panel data that, in fact, take T as given in the model and that base consistency results solely on n increasing. Some additional results for dynamic models are given by Bhargava and Sargan (1988).

The extended formulation is rather complicated analytically. In Balestra and Nerlove's study, it was made even more so by the presence of a lagged dependent variable that causes all of the problems discussed earlier in our discussion of autocorrelation. A full set of results for this extended model, including a method for handling the lagged dependent variable, has been developed.[32] However, the full model is rarely used. Most studies limit the model to the individual effects and, if needed, model the time effects in some other fashion.[33]

16.4.4. Fixed or Random Effects?

At various points, we have made the distinction between fixed and random effects models. An inevitable question is, which should be used? It has been suggested that the distinction between fixed and random effects models is an erroneous interpretation. Mundlak (1978) argues that we should always treat the individual effects as random. The fixed effects model is simply analyzed conditionally on the effects present in the observed sample. One can argue that certain institutional factors or characteristics of the data argue for one or the other, but, unfortunately, this approach does not always provide much guidance. From a purely practical standpoint, the dummy variable approach is costly in terms of degrees of freedom lost, and in a wide, longitudinal data set, the random effects model has some intuitive appeal. On the other hand, the fixed effects approach has one considerable virtue. There is no justification for treating the individual effects as uncorrelated with the other regressors, as is assumed in the random effects model. The random effects treatment, therefore, may suffer from the inconsistency due to omitted variables.[34]

It is possible to test for orthogonality of the random effects and the regressors. The specification test devised by Hausman (1978)[35] has the same format as that for the errors in variables model discussed in Section 9.5.6. It is based on the idea that under the hypothesis of no correlation, both OLS in the LSDV model and GLS are consistent, but OLS is inefficient,[36] while under the alternative, OLS is consistent, but GLS is not. Therefore, under the null hypothesis, the two estimates should not differ systematically, and a test can be based on the difference. The other essential ingredient for the test is the variance of the difference vector, $[\mathbf{b} - \hat{\boldsymbol{\beta}}]$;

$$\text{Var}[\mathbf{b} - \hat{\boldsymbol{\beta}}] = \text{Var}[\mathbf{b}] + \text{Var}[\hat{\boldsymbol{\beta}}] - \text{Cov}[\mathbf{b}, \hat{\boldsymbol{\beta}}] - \text{Cov}[\mathbf{b}, \hat{\boldsymbol{\beta}}]'. \qquad (16\text{--}66)$$

Hausman's essential result is that *the covariance of an efficient estimator with its difference from an inefficient estimator, is zero*. This implies that

$$\text{Cov}[(\mathbf{b} - \hat{\boldsymbol{\beta}}), \hat{\boldsymbol{\beta}}] = \text{Cov}[\mathbf{b}, \hat{\boldsymbol{\beta}}] - \text{Var}[\hat{\boldsymbol{\beta}}] = \mathbf{0},$$

or that

$$\text{Cov}[\mathbf{b}, \hat{\boldsymbol{\beta}}] = \text{Var}[\hat{\boldsymbol{\beta}}].$$

Inserting this in (16–66) produces the required variance matrix for the test,

$$\text{Var}[\mathbf{b} - \hat{\boldsymbol{\beta}}] = \text{Var}[\mathbf{b}] - \text{Var}[\hat{\boldsymbol{\beta}}] = \boldsymbol{\Sigma}. \qquad (16\text{--}67)$$

---

[32] See Balestra and Nerlove (1966), Fomby et al. (1984), Judge et al. (1985), Hsiao (1986), Anderson and Hsiao (1982), and Nerlove (1971a).

[33] See Macurdy (1982) and Beggs (1986).

[34] See Hausman and Taylor (1981) and Chamberlain (1978).

[35] Related results are given by Baltagi (1986).

[36] Referring to the GLS matrix weighted average given earlier, we see that the efficient weight uses θ, while OLS sets $\theta = 1$.

The chi-squared test is based on the Wald criterion:

$$W = \chi^2[K] = [\mathbf{b} - \hat{\boldsymbol{\beta}}]'\hat{\boldsymbol{\Sigma}}^{-1}[\mathbf{b} - \hat{\boldsymbol{\beta}}]. \tag{16-68}$$

For $\hat{\boldsymbol{\Sigma}}$, we use the estimated variance matrices of the slope estimator in the LSDV model and the estimated variance matrix in the random effects model, excluding the constant term. Under the null hypothesis, W is asymptotically distributed as chi-squared with K degrees of freedom.

EXAMPLE 16.14

For the cost function example, the test is based on a single coefficient, so it simplifies to

$$W = \frac{(b - \hat{\beta})^2}{\text{Var}[b] - \text{Var}[\hat{\beta}]},$$

which is asymptotically distributed as chi-squared with one degree of freedom. Alternatively, the square root of this statistic may be referred to the standard normal table.
  From Examples 16.10 and 16.13, we have

$$W = \frac{(0.674279 - 0.796321)^2}{0.06113^2 - 0.04256^2} = 7.735$$

The hypothesis that the individual effects are uncorrelated with log Y should be rejected.

EXERCISES

1. The model

$$\begin{bmatrix} \mathbf{y}_1 \\ \mathbf{y}_2 \end{bmatrix} = \begin{bmatrix} \mathbf{x}_1 \\ \mathbf{x}_2 \end{bmatrix} \beta + \begin{bmatrix} \boldsymbol{\varepsilon}_1 \\ \boldsymbol{\varepsilon}_2 \end{bmatrix}$$

satisfies the groupwise heteroscedastic regression model of (16–3) and (16–6). All variables have zero means. The following sample second moment matrix is obtained from a sample of 20 observations:

$$\begin{array}{c c} & \begin{array}{cccc} y_1 & y_2 & x_1 & x_2 \end{array} \\ \begin{array}{c} y_1 \\ y_2 \\ x_1 \\ x_2 \end{array} & \begin{bmatrix} 20 & 6 & 4 & 3 \\ 6 & 10 & 3 & 6 \\ 4 & 3 & 5 & 2 \\ 3 & 6 & 2 & 10 \end{bmatrix}. \end{array}$$

(a) Compute the two separate OLS estimates of β, their sampling variances, the estimates of σ_1^2 and σ_2^2, and the R^2s in the two regressions.
(b) Carry out the Lagrange multiplier test of the hypothesis that $\sigma_1^2 = \sigma_2^2$.
(c) Compute the two-step FGLS estimate of β and an estimate of its sampling variance. Test the hypothesis that β equals one.
(d) Carry out the Wald test of equal disturbance variances.
(e) Compute the maximum likelihood estimates of β, σ_1^2, and σ_2^2 by iterating the FGLS estimates to convergence.
(f) Carry out a likelihood ratio test of equal disturbance variances.
(g) Compute the two-step FGLS estimate of β, assuming that the model in (16–7) applies. [That is, allow for cross-sectional correlation.] Compare your results to those of part (c).

2. Suppose that in the model of Section 16.3.1, $\mathbf{X}_i$ is the same for all i. What is the generalized least squares estimator of $\boldsymbol{\beta}$? How would you compute the estimator if it were necessary to estimate σ_i^2?

3. Repeat Exercise 2 for the model of Section 16.3.2.

4. The following table presents a hypothetical panel of data:

	$i = 1$		$i = 2$		$i = 3$	
t	y	x	y	x	y	x
1	30.27	24.31	38.71	28.35	37.03	21.16
2	35.59	28.47	29.74	27.38	43.82	26.76
3	17.90	23.74	11.29	12.74	37.12	22.21
4	44.90	25.44	26.17	21.08	24.34	19.02
5	37.58	20.80	5.85	14.02	26.15	18.64
6	23.15	10.55	29.01	20.43	26.01	18.97
7	30.53	18.40	30.38	28.13	29.64	21.35
8	39.90	25.40	36.03	21.78	30.25	21.34
9	20.44	13.57	37.90	25.65	25.41	15.86
10	36.85	25.60	33.90	11.66	26.04	13.28

(a) Estimate the groupwise heteroscedastic model of Section 16.3.1. Include an estimate of the asymptotic variance of the slope estimator. Use a two-step procedure, basing the FGLS estimator at the second step on residuals from the pooled least squares regression.

(b) Carry out the Wald, Lagrange multiplier, and likelihood ratio tests of the hypothesis that the variances are all equal. For the likelihood ratio test, use the FGLS estimates.

(c) Carry out a Lagrange multiplier test of the hypothesis that the disturbances are uncorrelated across individuals.

5. The following is a panel of data on investment (y) and profit (x) for $n = 3$ firms over $T = 10$ periods:

	$i = 1$		$i = 2$		$i = 3$	
t	y	x	y	x	y	x
1	13.32	12.85	20.30	22.93	8.85	8.65
2	26.30	25.69	17.47	17.96	19.60	16.55
3	2.62	5.48	9.31	9.16	3.87	1.47
4	14.94	13.79	18.01	18.73	24.19	24.91
5	15.80	15.41	7.63	11.31	3.99	5.01
6	12.20	12.59	19.84	21.15	5.73	8.34
7	14.93	16.64	13.76	16.13	26.68	22.70
8	29.82	26.45	10.00	11.61	11.49	8.36
9	20.32	19.64	19.51	19.55	18.49	15.44
10	4.77	5.43	18.32	17.06	20.84	17.87

(a) Pool the data and compute the least squares regression coefficients of the model

$$y_{it} = \alpha + \beta x_{it} + \varepsilon_{it}.$$

(b) Estimate the fixed effects model of (16–33), and then test the hypothesis that the constant term is the same for all three firms.

(c) Estimate the random effects model of (16–44), and then carry out the Lagrange multiplier test of the hypothesis that the classical model without the common effect applies.

(d) Carry out Hausman's specification test for the random versus the fixed model.

6. Suppose that the model of (16–33) is formulated with an overall constant term and $n - 1$ dummy variables (dropping, say, the last one). Investigate the effect that this has on the set of dummy variable coefficients and on the least squares estimates of the slopes.

7. Derive the log-likelihood function for the model in (16–44), assuming that ε_{it} and u_i are normally distributed. [**Hints:** Write the log-likelihood function as

$$\ln L = \sum_{i=1}^{n} \ln L_i,$$

where $\ln L_i$ is the log-likelihood function for the T observations in group i. These T observations are joint normally distributed, with the covariance matrix given in (16–46). The log likelihood is the sum of the logs of the joint normal densities of the n sets of T observations,

$$\varepsilon_{it} + u_i = y_{it} - \alpha - \boldsymbol{\beta}' \mathbf{x}_{it}.$$

This will involve the inverse and determinant of $\boldsymbol{\Omega}$. Use (2–66) to prove that

$$\boldsymbol{\Omega}^{-1} = \frac{1}{\sigma_\varepsilon^2} \left[\mathbf{I} - \frac{\sigma_u^2}{\sigma_\varepsilon^2 + T\sigma_u^2} \mathbf{ii}' \right].$$

To find the determinant, use the product of the characteristic roots. Note first that

$$\left| \sigma_\varepsilon^2 \mathbf{I} + \sigma_u^2 \mathbf{ii}' \right| = (\sigma_\varepsilon^2)^T \left| \mathbf{I} + \frac{\sigma_u^2}{\sigma_\varepsilon^2} \mathbf{ii}' \right|.$$

The roots are determined by

$$\left[\mathbf{I} + \frac{\sigma_u^2}{\sigma_\varepsilon^2} \mathbf{ii}' \right] \mathbf{c} = \lambda \mathbf{c}$$

or

$$\frac{\sigma_\varepsilon^2}{\sigma_u^2} \mathbf{ii}' \mathbf{c} = (\lambda - 1) \mathbf{c}.$$

Any vector whose elements sum to zero is a solution. There are $T - 1$ such independent vectors, so $T - 1$ characteristic roots are $(\lambda - 1) = 0$ or $\lambda = 1$. Premultiply the expression by $\mathbf{i}'$ to obtain the remaining characteristic root. (Remember to add 1 to the result.) Now collect terms to obtain the log likelihood.]

8. *Unbalanced design for random effects:* Suppose that the random effects model of Section 16.4.3 is to be estimated with a panel in which the groups have different numbers of observations. Let T_i be the number of observations in group i.

(a) Show that the pooled least squares estimator in (16–44) is unbiased and consistent in spite of this complication.

(b) Show that the estimator in (16–60) based on the pooled least squares estimator of $\boldsymbol{\beta}$ (or, for that matter, *any* consistent estimator of $\boldsymbol{\beta}$) is a consistent estimator of σ_ε^2.

(c) The group mean regression in (16–61) is heteroscedastic. Investigate the properties of the residual variance estimator. [**Hints:** For large-sample results, rely on $n \to \infty$, not T_i. Take T_i as potentially small and fixed for each i. This set of results will parallel the discussion of Section 14.2.2. What will you require to assert that the estimator based on (16–60) and (16–62),

$$\hat{\sigma}_u = \hat{\sigma}_{**}^2 - Q\hat{\sigma}_\varepsilon^2,$$

where

$$Q = \left(\frac{1}{n}\right)\left(\frac{1}{T_1} + \frac{1}{T_2} + \cdots + \frac{1}{T_n}\right),$$

is a consistent estimator of σ_u^2?]

(d) What change is needed in (16–48) in order to implement an FGLS estimator? [*Note:* The term $(nT)/(2(T-1))$ in (16–64) must be replaced with $(\Sigma_i T_i)^2/(2\Sigma_i T_i(T_i - 1))$.]

9. In estimating the random effects model, if $K + 1$ is greater than n, the group means regression cannot be computed. Comment on the suggestion that in this event, we use a generalized inverse by dropping enough columns (variables) to produce a nonsingular moment matrix and then using the sum of squared residuals from this regression.

10. What are the probability limits of $(1/n)$LM, where LM is defined in (16–64) under the null hypotheses that $\sigma_u^2 = 0$ and under the alternative that $\sigma_u^2 \neq 0$?

11. The text proposes two possible residuals to use in the estimation of σ_{**}^2 in (16–62): the least squares coefficient vector, including the constant term in the group means regression, and the full slope vector, including the constant term, in the pooled least squares estimator. Comment on the third alternative, $\bar{e}_{i.} = \bar{y}_{i.} - a_i - \mathbf{b}'\bar{\mathbf{x}}_{i.}$, based on the LSDV estimators.

12. *A two-way fixed-effects model:* Suppose that the fixed-effects model is modified to include a time-specific dummy variable, as well as an individual-specific variable. Then

$$y_{it} = \alpha_i + \gamma_t + \boldsymbol{\beta}'\mathbf{x}_{it} + \varepsilon_{it}.$$

At every observation, the individual- and time-specific dummy variables sum to one, so there are some redundant coefficients. The discussion following (16–41) shows one way to remove the redundancy. Another useful way to do this is to include an overall constant and to drop one of the time-specific *and* one of the time-dummy variables. The model is, thus,

$$y_{it} = \delta + (\alpha_i - \alpha_1) + (\gamma_t - \gamma_1) + \boldsymbol{\beta}'\mathbf{x}_{it} + \varepsilon_{it}.$$

(Note that the respective time- or individual-specific variable is zero when t or i equals one.) Ordinary least squares estimates of β can be obtained by regression of

$$y_{it} - \bar{y}_{i.} - \bar{y}_{.t} + \bar{\bar{y}}$$

on

$$\mathbf{x}_{it} - \bar{\mathbf{x}}_{i.} - \bar{\mathbf{x}}_{.t} + \bar{\bar{\mathbf{x}}}$$

Then $(\alpha_i - \alpha_1)$ and $(\gamma_t - \gamma_1)$ are estimated using the expressions in (16–43), while $d = \bar{\bar{y}} - \mathbf{b}'\bar{\bar{\mathbf{x}}}$. Using the following data, estimate the full set of coefficients for the least squares dummy variable model:

	$t = 1$	$t = 2$	$t = 3$	$t = 4$	$t = 5$	$t = 6$	$t = 7$	$t = 8$	$t = 9$	$t = 10$
					$i = 1$					
y	21.7	10.9	33.5	22.0	17.6	16.1	19.0	18.1	14.9	23.2
x_1	26.4	17.3	23.8	17.6	26.2	21.1	17.5	22.9	22.9	14.9
x_2	5.79	2.60	8.36	5.50	5.26	1.03	3.11	4.87	3.79	7.24
					$i = 2$					
y	21.8	21.0	33.8	18.0	12.2	30.0	21.7	24.9	21.9	23.6
x_1	19.6	22.8	27.8	14.0	11.4	16.0	28.8	16.8	11.8	18.6
x_2	3.36	1.59	6.19	3.75	1.59	9.87	1.31	5.42	6.32	5.35
					$i = 3$					
y	25.2	41.9	31.3	27.8	13.2	27.9	33.3	20.5	16.7	20.7
x_1	13.4	29.7	21.6	25.1	14.1	24.1	10.5	22.1	17.0	20.5
x_2	9.57	9.62	6.61	7.24	1.64	5.99	9.00	1.75	1.74	1.82
					$i = 4$					
y	15.3	25.9	21.9	15.5	16.7	26.1	34.8	22.6	29.0	37.1
x_1	14.2	18.0	29.9	14.1	18.4	20.1	27.6	27.4	28.5	28.6
x_2	4.09	9.56	2.18	5.43	6.33	8.27	9.16	5.24	7.92	9.63

Test the hypotheses that (1) the "period" effects are all zero, (2) the "group" effects are all zero, and (3) both period and group effects are zero. Use an F test in each case.

13. *Two-way random-effects model:* We modify the random-effects model by the addition of a time-specific disturbance. Thus,

$$y_{it} = \alpha + \beta'x_{it} + \varepsilon_{it} + u_i + v_t,$$

where

$$E[\varepsilon_{it}] = E[u_i] = E[v_t] = 0,$$

$$E[\varepsilon_{it}u_j] = E[\varepsilon_{it}v_s] = E[u_iv_t] = 0 \qquad \text{for all } i, j, t, s,$$

$$\text{Var}[\varepsilon_{it}] = \sigma_\varepsilon^2, \qquad \text{Cov}[\varepsilon_{it},\varepsilon_{js}] = 0 \qquad \text{for all } i, j, t, s,$$

$$\text{Var}[u_i] = \sigma_u^2, \qquad \text{Cov}[u_i,u_j] = 0 \qquad \text{for all } i, j,$$

$$\text{Var}[v_t] = \sigma_v^2, \qquad \text{Cov}[v_t,v_s] = 0 \qquad \text{for all } t, s.$$

Write out the full covariance matrix for a data set with $n = 2$ and $T = 2$.

14. *Estimation of the full random effects model:* Fuller and Battese (1974) have developed a method of FGLS estimation of the two-way random-effects model.[37] Let

$$s_{i.}^2 = \text{residual variance in the regression of group means of } y_{it} \text{ on a constant and the group means of } x_{it}. \text{ (This is } n \text{ observations.)}$$

$$s_{.t}^2 = \text{residual variance in the regression of period means of } y_{it} \text{ on a constant and the period means of } x_{it}. \text{ (This is } T \text{ observations.)}$$

[37] See also Judge et al. (1985, pp. 530–536).

s_d^2 = residual variance in the full dummy variable regression with both individual- and time-specific dummies. This can be computed using the method described in Exercise 12.

The following notation is that of Judge et al. (1985, p. 534). Using the three preceding regressions, we can show that

$$(n - K - 1)s_{i.}^2 \text{ estimates } \sigma_1^2 = \sigma_\varepsilon^2 + T\sigma_u^2,$$

$$(T - K - 1)s_{.t}^2 \text{ estimates } \sigma_2^2 = \sigma_\varepsilon^2 + n\sigma_v^2,$$

$$s_d^2 \text{ estimates } \sigma_\varepsilon^2.$$

Then

$$(n - K - 1)s_{i.}^2 + (T - K - 1)s_{.t}^2 - s_d^2 \text{ estimates } \sigma_3^2 = \sigma_\varepsilon^2 + T\sigma_u^2 + n\sigma_v^2.$$

Let

$$\theta_1 = 1 - \frac{\sigma_\varepsilon}{\sigma_1},$$

$$\theta_2 = 1 - \frac{\sigma_\varepsilon}{\sigma_2},$$

$$\theta_3 = \theta_1 + \theta_2 - 1 + \frac{\sigma_\varepsilon}{\sigma_3}.$$

Generalized least squares is equivalent to ordinary least squares regression of

$$y_{it}^* = y_{it} - \theta_1 \bar{y}_{i.} - \theta_2 \bar{y}_{.t} + \theta_3 \bar{\bar{y}}$$

on

$$\mathbf{x}_{it}^* = \mathbf{x}_{it} - \theta_1 \bar{\mathbf{x}}_{i.} - \theta_2 \bar{\mathbf{x}}_{.t} + \theta_3 \bar{\bar{\mathbf{x}}},$$

where $\mathbf{x}_{it}^*$ includes the constant term. This provides efficient estimates of the coefficients of the model. The usual estimator of the asymptotic covariance matrix of the estimated coefficient vector is appropriate. The sample estimates of θ_1, θ_2, and θ_3 are used when their population counterparts are unknown.

(a) Using the data from Exercise 12, estimate the parameters of the two-way random effects model. [**Hint:** The variance estimators based on the group means lead to negative estimates of the variance components. But as shown in Problem 11, (16–62) can be based on any consistent estimator of the slopes. Use the pooled ordinary least squares estimates instead.]

(b) The extension of the Lagrange multiplier statistic of (16–64) to this model is

$$LM = \frac{nT}{2} \left[\frac{1}{T - 1} \left[\frac{\sum_i \left(\sum_t e_{it} \right)^2}{\sum_i \sum_t e_{it}^2} - 1 \right]^2 + \frac{1}{n - 1} \left[\frac{\sum_t \left(\sum_i e_{it} \right)^2}{\sum_i \sum_t e_{it}^2} - 1 \right]^2 \right].$$

This statistic is asymptotically distributed as chi-squared with two degrees of freedom. Carry out the Lagrange multiplier test of the two-way random effects model.

15. Describe how to estimate the model in (16–44) with the additional specification

$$\varepsilon_{it} = \rho \varepsilon_{i,t-1} + w_{it}, \qquad |\rho| < 1.$$

CHAPTER 17

Systems of Regression Equations

17.1. Introduction

There are many settings in which the models of the previous chapters apply to a group of related variables. In these contexts, it makes sense to consider the several models jointly. Some examples follow.

1. In the Grunfeld–Boot and de Witt investment model of Chapter 16, we have a set of firms each of which makes investment decisions based on variables that reflect anticipated profit and replacement of the capital stock. We specified

$$I_{it} = \beta_1 + \beta_2 F_{it} + \beta_3 C_{it} + \varepsilon_{it}.$$

Whether the parameter vector should be the same for all firms is a question that we shall study in this chapter. But the disturbances in the investment equations certainly include factors that are common to all of the firms, such as the perceived general health of the economy, as well as factors that are specific to the particular firm or industry. We discovered in our examples that considerable efficiency was gained by estimating the equations jointly (with the assumed common parameter vector) as a generalized regression. The hypothesis that the disturbances of the five companies were contemporaneously uncorrelated was strongly rejected by both likelihood ratio and Lagrange multiplier tests in Example 16.4.

2. The capital asset pricing model of finance stipulates that for a given security,

$$r_{it} - r_{ft} = \alpha_i + \beta_i(r_{mt} - r_{ft}) + \varepsilon_{it},$$

where r_{it} is the return over period t on security i, r_{ft} is the return on a risk-free security, r_{mt} is the market return, and β_i is that security's beta coefficient. The disturbances are obviously correlated across securities. The knowledge that the return on security i exceeds the risk-free rate by a given amount gives some information about the excess return of security j, at least for some js. It will be useful to estimate the previous M equations jointly rather than to ignore this connection.

3. In a model of production, the optimization conditions of economic theory imply that if a firm faces a set of factor prices $\mathbf{p}$, its set of cost-minimizing factor demands for producing output Y will be a set of equations of the form $x_m = f_m(Y, \mathbf{p})$. Cast in the form of an econometric model, we have

$$x_1 = f_1(Y, \mathbf{p} : \boldsymbol{\theta}) + \varepsilon_1$$
$$x_2 = f_2(Y, \mathbf{p} : \boldsymbol{\theta}) + \varepsilon_2$$
$$\vdots$$
$$x_M = f_M(Y, \mathbf{p} : \boldsymbol{\theta}) + \varepsilon_M.$$

Once again, the disturbances should be correlated. In addition, the same parameters of the production technology will enter all of the demand equations, so the set of equations has cross-equation restrictions. Estimating the equations separately will waste the information that the same set of parameters appears in all of the equations.

All of these examples have a common multiple equation structure, which we may write as

$$
\begin{aligned}
\mathbf{y}_1 &= \mathbf{X}_1\boldsymbol{\beta}_1 + \boldsymbol{\varepsilon}_1 \\
\mathbf{y}_2 &= \mathbf{X}_2\boldsymbol{\beta}_2 + \boldsymbol{\varepsilon}_2 \\
&\;\;\vdots \\
\mathbf{y}_M &= \mathbf{X}_M\boldsymbol{\beta}_M + \boldsymbol{\varepsilon}_M.
\end{aligned}
\tag{17-1}
$$

There are M equations and T observations in the sample of data used to estimate them.[1] The three examples embody different types of constraints across equations and different structures of the disturbances. However, a basic set of principles will apply to all of them.

17.2. The Seemingly Unrelated Regressions Model

All of the preceding examples and several of the models in Chapter 16 can be written in the form

$$
\mathbf{y}_m = \mathbf{X}_m\boldsymbol{\beta}_m + \boldsymbol{\varepsilon}_m, \; m = 1, \ldots, M,
\tag{17-2}
$$

where

$$
\boldsymbol{\varepsilon} = [\boldsymbol{\varepsilon}_1', \, \boldsymbol{\varepsilon}_2', \, \ldots, \, \boldsymbol{\varepsilon}_M']'
$$

has

$$
E[\boldsymbol{\varepsilon}] = \mathbf{0}
$$

and

$$
E[\boldsymbol{\varepsilon}\boldsymbol{\varepsilon}'] = \mathbf{V}.
$$

We assume that a total of T observations are used in estimating the parameters of the M equations. Each equation involves K_m regressors, for a total of $K = \Sigma_m K_m$. The data are assumed to be well behaved, as described in Chapter 10, and we shall not treat the issue separately here. For the present, we also assume that disturbances are uncorrelated across observations. Therefore,

$$
E[\varepsilon_{mt}\varepsilon_{ns}] = \sigma_{mn} \qquad \text{if } t = s \text{ and } 0 \text{ otherwise.}
$$

For present purposes, we use the subscript n to indicate the nth equation in the system, rather than the nth observation in a sample of n, as in previous chapters. The subscript m is used throughout to indicate the mth equation. The disturbance formulation is, therefore,

$$
E[\boldsymbol{\varepsilon}_m\boldsymbol{\varepsilon}_n'] = \sigma_{mn}\mathbf{I}_T
$$

or

$$
E[\boldsymbol{\varepsilon}\boldsymbol{\varepsilon}'] = \mathbf{V} =
\begin{bmatrix}
\sigma_{11}\mathbf{I} & \sigma_{12}\mathbf{I} & \cdots & \sigma_{1M}\mathbf{I} \\
\sigma_{21}\mathbf{I} & \sigma_{22}\mathbf{I} & \cdots & \sigma_{2M}\mathbf{I} \\
& & \vdots & \\
\sigma_{M1}\mathbf{I} & \sigma_{M2}\mathbf{I} & \cdots & \sigma_{MM}\mathbf{I}
\end{bmatrix}.
\tag{17-3}
$$

[1] The use of T is not necessarily meant to imply any connection to time series. For instance, in example 3, the data might be cross-sectional.

17.2.1. Generalized Least Squares

Each equation is, by itself, a classical regression. Therefore, the parameters could be estimated consistently, if not efficiently, by ordinary least squares. The generalized regression model applies to the stacked regression,

$$
\begin{bmatrix} y_1 \\ y_2 \\ \vdots \\ y_M \end{bmatrix} = \begin{bmatrix} X_1 & 0 & \cdots & 0 \\ 0 & X_2 & \cdots & 0 \\ & & & \vdots \\ 0 & 0 & \cdots & X_M \end{bmatrix} \begin{bmatrix} \beta_1 \\ \beta_2 \\ \vdots \\ \beta_M \end{bmatrix} + \begin{bmatrix} \varepsilon_1 \\ \varepsilon_2 \\ \vdots \\ \varepsilon_M \end{bmatrix} \tag{17-4}
$$

$$
= X\beta + \varepsilon.
$$

Therefore, the efficient estimator is generalized least squares. The model has a particularly convenient form. For the tth observation, the $M \times M$ covariance matrix of the disturbances is

$$
\Sigma = \begin{bmatrix} \sigma_{11} & \sigma_{12} & \cdots & \sigma_{1M} \\ \sigma_{21} & \sigma_{22} & \cdots & \sigma_{2M} \\ & & \vdots & \\ \sigma_{M1} & \sigma_{M2} & \cdots & \sigma_{MM} \end{bmatrix}, \tag{17-5}
$$

so, in (17–3),

$$
V = \Sigma \otimes I \tag{17-6}
$$

and

$$
V^{-1} = \Sigma^{-1} \otimes I. \tag{17-7}
$$

Denoting the ijth element of Σ^{-1} by σ^{ij}, we find that the GLS estimator is

$$
\hat{\beta} = [X'V^{-1}X]^{-1}X'V^{-1}y
$$

$$
= [X'(\Sigma^{-1} \otimes I)X]^{-1}X'(\Sigma^{-1} \otimes I)y
$$

$$
= \begin{bmatrix} \sigma^{11}X_1'X_1 & \sigma^{12}X_1'X_2 & \cdots & \sigma^{1M}X_1'X_M \\ \sigma^{21}X_2'X_1 & \sigma^{22}X_2'X_2 & \cdots & \sigma^{2M}X_2'X_M \\ & & \vdots & \\ \sigma^{M1}X_M'X_1 & \sigma^{M2}X_M'X_2 & \cdots & \sigma^{MM}X_M'X_M \end{bmatrix}^{-1} \begin{bmatrix} \Sigma_m\sigma^{1m}X_1'y_m \\ \Sigma_m\sigma^{2m}X_2'y_m \\ \vdots \\ \Sigma_m\sigma^{Mm}X_M'y_m \end{bmatrix}. \tag{17-8}
$$

The asymptotic covariance matrix for the GLS estimator is the inverse matrix in (17–8). All of the results of Chapter 13 carry over to this model.

This is obviously different from ordinary least squares. At this point, however, the equations are linked only by their disturbances—hence the name *seemingly unrelated regressions model*—so it is interesting to ask just how much efficiency is gained by using generalized least squares instead of ordinary least squares. Dwivedi and Srivastava (1978) have analyzed some special cases in detail.

1. If the equations are actually unrelated, that is, $\sigma_{mn} = 0$, there is obviously no payoff to GLS. Indeed, GLS is OLS.
2. If the equations have identical explanatory variables, that is, $X_m = X_n$, it can be shown (we leave it as an exercise) that OLS and GLS are identical.[2]

---

[2] An intriguing result, albeit probably of negligible practical significance, is that the result also applies if the Xs are all nonsingular, and not necessarily identical, linear combinations of the same set of variables.

3. If the regressors in one block of equations are a subset of those in another, GLS brings no efficiency gain in estimation of the smaller equations.[3]

In the more general case, with unrestricted correlation of the disturbances and different regressors in the equations, the results are complicated and dependent on the data. Two propositions that apply generally are as follows:

1. The greater the correlation of the disturbances, the greater the efficiency gain accruing to GLS.
2. The less correlation there is between the $\mathbf{X}$ matrices, the greater is the gain in using GLS.

17.2.2. Feasible Generalized Least Squares

The preceding discussion assumes that $\boldsymbol{\Sigma}$ is known, which, as usual, is rarely the case. FGLS estimators have been devised, however.[4] The least squares residuals may be used (of course) to estimate consistently the elements of $\boldsymbol{\Sigma}$ with

$$\hat{\sigma}_{mn} = s_{mn} = \frac{\mathbf{e}'_m \mathbf{e}_n}{T}. \qquad (17\text{--}9)$$

The consistency of s_{mn} follows from that of $\mathbf{b}_m$. A degrees of freedom correction in the divisor is occasionally suggested.[5] Two possibilities are

$$s^*_{mn} = \frac{\mathbf{e}'_m \mathbf{e}_n}{[(T - K_m)(T - K_n)]^{1/2}}$$

and

$$s^{**}_{mn} = \frac{\mathbf{e}'_m \mathbf{e}_n}{T - \max(K_m, K_n)}.$$

The second is unbiased only if m equals n or K_m equals K_n, while the first is unbiased only if m equals n. Whether unbiasedness of the estimate of $\boldsymbol{\Sigma}$ used for FGLS is a virtue here is uncertain.[6] The asymptotic properties of $\hat{\hat{\boldsymbol{\beta}}}$ do not rely on an unbiased estimator of $\boldsymbol{\Sigma}$; all of our results from Chapter 13 for FGLS estimators carry over to this model, with no modification. It is worth noting that the matrix $\hat{\boldsymbol{\Sigma}}$ based on the second correction is not necessarily positive definite. If the sample is large, it will be, but then the degrees of freedom correction is moot anyway. How the different estimators will behave in small samples is another question. Precise results are available only for some special cases, though suggestive results have been obtained in Monte Carlo studies.[7] We shall use (17–9) in what follows. With

$$\mathbf{S} = \begin{bmatrix} s_{11} & s_{12} & \cdots & s_{1M} \\ s_{21} & s_{22} & \cdots & s_{2M} \\ & & \vdots & \\ s_{M1} & s_{M2} & \cdots & s_{MM} \end{bmatrix} \qquad (17\text{--}10)$$

---

[3] We shall examine one such model in detail later. The result was analyzed by Goldberger (1970) and later by Revankar (1974) and Conniffe (1982a).

[4] See Zellner (1962) and Zellner and Huang (1962).

[5] See, for example, Theil (1971, p. 321) and Judge et al. (1985, p. 469).

[6] Kakwani's (1967) result applies to all three; the FGLS estimator of $\boldsymbol{\beta}$ is unbiased regardless of which divisor is used.

[7] Zellner (1963), Kmenta and Gilbert (1968), Conniffe (1982b), and Revankar (1974).

in hand, FGLS can proceed as usual. Iterated FGLS will be maximum likelihood if it is based on (17–9).

Goodness of fit measures for the system have been devised. For instance, McElroy (1977) suggested the systemwide measure

$$R_*^2 = 1 - \frac{\hat{\boldsymbol{\varepsilon}}' \hat{\mathbf{V}}^{-1} \hat{\boldsymbol{\varepsilon}}}{\Sigma_m \Sigma_n \hat{\sigma}^{mn}[\Sigma_t(y_{mt} - \bar{y}_m)(y_{nt} - \bar{y}_n)]} \tag{17–11}$$

where $\hat{}$ indicates the FGLS estimate. The measure is bounded by zero and one and is related to the F statistic used to test the hypothesis that all of the slopes in the model are zero. Fit measures in this context have all of the shortcomings discussed in Chapter 13. An additional problem for this model is that overall fit measures such as (17–11) will obscure the variation in fit across equations. For the investment example, using the FGLS residuals for the model in Table 16.7, McElroy's measure gives a value of $1 - 100/648.94$, or 0.846. But a look at Figure 16.1 shows that this apparently good overall fit is an aggregate of mediocre fits for Chrysler and Westinghouse and obviously terrible fits for GM, GE, and U.S. Steel. Indeed, the conventional measure $1 - \mathbf{e}'\mathbf{e}/\mathbf{y}'\mathbf{M}^0\mathbf{y}$ for GE based on the same FGLS residuals is -16.7!

It might be desirable to compare the fit of the unrestricted model, with separate coefficient vectors by firm, with the restricted one in Chapter 16. The computation in (17–11) with the FGLS residuals based on the seemingly unrelated regression estimates in Table 17.1 below gives a value of 0.871, which appears to be an unimpressive improvement in the fit of the model. But a comparison of the residual plot in Figure 17.1 with that in Figure 16.1 shows that, on the contrary, the fit of the model has improved dramatically. The upshot is that while a fit measure for the system might have some virtue as a descriptive measure, it should be used with care.

The value of exactly $MT = 100$ for the numerator for R_*^2 might seem odd. But combining (17–7) and (17–9), we see that since the matrix $\hat{\mathbf{V}}$ in (17–11) is computed using $\hat{\boldsymbol{\varepsilon}}$, the quantity in the numerator is nothing more than

$$T \sum_m \sum_n \hat{\sigma}^{mn} \hat{\sigma}_{mn} = T \times \text{tr}(\hat{\boldsymbol{\Sigma}}^{-1} \hat{\boldsymbol{\Sigma}}) = T \times \text{tr}(\mathbf{I}_M) = MT.$$

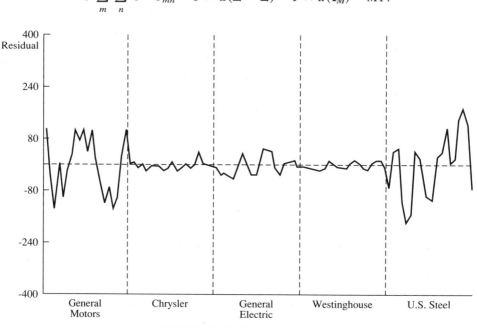

FIGURE 17.1   Residual plot.

(Further discussion of this result appears in Section 17.2.3b.) The denominator can also be simplified in a way that facilitates the computation. By the same logic as above, the double sum in the denominator is

$$T \sum_m \sum_n \hat{\sigma}^{mn} s_{yy,mn} = T \times \text{tr}(\hat{\Sigma}^{-1} \mathbf{S}_{yy}),$$

where

$$[\mathbf{S}_{yy}]_{mn} = \frac{1}{T} \sum_t (y_{mt} - \bar{y}_m)(y_{nt} - \bar{y}_n).$$

Combining all of these, we get

$$R_*^2 = 1 - \frac{M}{\text{tr}(\hat{\Sigma}^{-1} \mathbf{S}_{yy})}.$$

The advantage of this formulation is that it involves $M \times M$ matrices, which are typically quite small, while $\hat{\mathbf{V}}$ in (17–11) is $MT \times MT$. In our case, M equals 5, but MT equals 100.

For testing a hypothesis about $\boldsymbol{\beta}$, a statistic analogous to the F ratio in multiple regression analysis is

$$F[J, MT - K] = \frac{(\mathbf{R}\hat{\boldsymbol{\beta}} - \mathbf{q})'[\mathbf{R}(\mathbf{X}'\mathbf{V}^{-1}\mathbf{X})^{-1}\mathbf{R}']^{-1}(\mathbf{R}\hat{\boldsymbol{\beta}} - \mathbf{q})/J}{\hat{\boldsymbol{\varepsilon}}'\mathbf{V}^{-1}\hat{\boldsymbol{\varepsilon}}/(MT - K)} \qquad (17\text{–}12)$$

The computation requires the unknown $\mathbf{V}$. If we insert the FGLS estimate, $\hat{\mathbf{V}}$ based on (17–9), and use the result that the denominator converges to 1, the statistic will behave the same as

$$\hat{F} = \frac{1}{J}(\mathbf{R}\hat{\hat{\boldsymbol{\beta}}} - \mathbf{q})'[\mathbf{R} \ \text{V}\hat{\text{a}}\text{r}[\hat{\hat{\boldsymbol{\beta}}}]\mathbf{R}']^{-1}(\mathbf{R}\hat{\hat{\boldsymbol{\beta}}} - \mathbf{q}). \qquad (17\text{–}13)$$

This can be referred to the standard F table. Because it uses the estimated $\boldsymbol{\Sigma}$, the F distribution is only asymptotically valid. In general, the statistic $F[J, n]$ converges to $1/J$ times chi-squared (J) as $n \to \infty$. Therefore, an alternative test statistic that is asymptotically distributed as chi-squared with J degrees of freedom is

$$J\hat{F} = (\mathbf{R}\hat{\hat{\boldsymbol{\beta}}} - \mathbf{q})'[\mathbf{R} \ \text{V}\hat{\text{a}}\text{r}[\hat{\hat{\boldsymbol{\beta}}}]\mathbf{R}']^{-1}(\mathbf{R}\hat{\hat{\boldsymbol{\beta}}} - \mathbf{q}). \qquad (17\text{–}14)$$

This can be recognized as a Wald statistic that measures the distance between $\mathbf{R}\hat{\hat{\boldsymbol{\beta}}}$ and $\mathbf{q}$. Both statistics are valid asymptotically, but (17–13) may perform better in a small or moderately sized sample.[8] Once again, the divisor used in computing $\hat{\sigma}_{ij}$ will make a difference, and there is no general rule.

EXAMPLE 17.1

By relaxing the constraint that all five firms have the same parameter vector in Example 16.4, we obtain a five-equation, seemingly unrelated regressions model. The FGLS estimates for the system are given in Table 17.1, where we have included the equality constrained estimator of Example 16.4 for comparison, as well as the ordinary least squares estimates of the GM equation. The variables are the constant term, F and C, respectively.

---

[8] See Judge et al. (1985, p. 476).

TABLE 17.1 Parameter Estimates (Standard Errors in Parentheses)

GM	CH	GE	WE	US	Pooled	GM by OLS
			Seemingly Unrelated Regressions			
−162.36	0.5043	−22.439	1.0889	85.423	−30.281	−149.78
(89.46)	(11.51)	(25.52)	(6.259)	(111.9)	(5.589)	(105.8)
0.12049	0.06955	0.03729	0.05701	0.1015	0.09413	0.11928
(0.0216)	(0.0169)	(0.0123)	(0.0114)	(0.0547)	(0.00684)	(0.0258)
0.38275	0.3086	0.13078	0.0415	0.3999	0.3406	0.37145
(0.0328)	(0.0259)	(0.0221)	(0.0412)	(0.1278)	(0.0268)	(0.0371)

Residual Covariance Matrix

	GM	CH	GE	WE	US
GM	7216.04	(−0.299)	(0.269)	(0.257)	(−0.330)
CH	−313.70	152.85	(0.006)	(0.238)	(0.384)
GE	605.34	2.0474	700.46	(0.777)	(0.482)
WE	129.89	16.661	200.32	94.912	(0.699)
US	−2686.5	455.09	1224.4	652.72	9188.2

The correlations of the GLS residuals are given above the diagonal in Table 17.1. It is worth noting that the assumption of equal-parameter vectors appears to have seriously distorted the earlier estimated correlations. A comparison with Table 16.8 shows that the elements in $\hat{\boldsymbol{\Sigma}}$ are drastically inflated by the imposition of the constraint, as are the correlations across equations.

The F statistic for testing the hypothesis of equal-parameter vectors in all five equations is 1550.03 with 12 and $(100 - 15)$ degrees of freedom. This is obviously larger than the tabled critical value, so the hypothesis of parameter homogeneity should be rejected. We might have expected this result in view of the dramatic reduction in the diagonal elements of $\hat{\boldsymbol{\Sigma}}$ compared to those of Example 16.4.

It may also be of interest to test whether $\boldsymbol{\Sigma}$ is a diagonal matrix. Two possible approaches were described in Example 16.4 [see (16–13) and (16–14).] The unrestricted model is the one we are using here, while the restricted model is the groupwise heteroscedastic model of Chapter 16, without the restriction of equal-parameter vectors. As such, the restricted model reduces to separate regression models, estimable by ordinary least squares. The likelihood ratio statistic would be

$$\lambda_{\mathrm{LR}} = T\left[\sum_m \ln s_m^2 - \ln|\hat{\boldsymbol{\Sigma}}|\right], \tag{17-15}$$

where s_m^2 is $\mathbf{e}_m'\mathbf{e}_m/T$ from the individual least squares regressions and $\hat{\boldsymbol{\Sigma}}$ is the maximum likelihood estimate of $\boldsymbol{\Sigma}$. This statistic is asymptotically distributed as chi-squared with $M(M - 1)/2$ degrees of freedom.

The alternative suggested by Breusch and Pagan (1980) is the Lagrange multiplier statistic,

$$\lambda_{\mathrm{LM}} = T\sum_{m=2}^{M}\sum_{n=1}^{m-1} r_{mn}^2, \tag{17-16}$$

where r_{mn}^2 is the estimated correlation, $s_{mn}/[s_{mm}s_{nn}]^{1/2}$. Note the similarity of this to the Box–Pierce statistic we encountered in Chapter 15. Asymptotically, this statistic is also distributed as chi-squared with $M(M - 1)/2$ degrees of freedom. This test has the advantage that it does not require computation of the maximum likelihood estimator of Σ, since it is based on the OLS residuals.

EXAMPLE 17.2

The sample correlations of the ordinary least squares residuals are shown below the diagonal in Table 17.2. For comparison, the estimates of the correlations using the FGLS estimator of β are shown above the diagonal. Based on the OLS results, the Lagrange multiplier statistic is 29.046, with 10 degrees of freedom. The 1 percent critical value is 23.209, so the hypothesis that Σ is diagonal can be rejected.

TABLE 17.2

	GM	GE	US	CH	WE
GM	—	0.269	−0.329	−0.298	0.157
US	0.279	—	0.483	0.006	0.777
GE	−0.278	0.373	—	0.384	0.699
CH	−0.273	−0.068	0.362	—	0.138
WE	0.158	0.729	0.615	0.115	—

17.2.3. Maximum Likelihood Estimation

17.2.3a. Iterated FGLS. The Oberhofer–Kmenta (1974) conditions are met for the seemingly unrelated regressions model, so maximum likelihood estimates can be obtained by iterating the FGLS procedure. We note, once again, that this presumes the use of (17–9) for estimation of σ_{ij} at each iteration. It is worth noting that maximum likelihood enjoys no advantages over FGLS in its asymptotic properties. Whether it would be preferable in a small sample is an open question whose answer will depend, unfortunately, on the particular data set.

EXAMPLE 17.3

The maximum likelihood estimates of the parameters estimated by FGLS in Example 17.1 are given in Table 17.3. As might be expected, the differences are not substantial. The estimates are, in fact, not radically different from the ordinary least squares estimates. But they are very different from the values in Table 16.7.

17.2.3b. Direct Maximum Likelihood Estimation. By simply inserting the special form of V in the log-likelihood function for the generalized regression model in (13–19), we can consider direct maximization instead of iterated FGLS. It is useful, however, to reexamine the model in a somewhat different formulation. This alternative construction of the likelihood function appears in many other related models in a number of literatures.

Consider one observation on each of the M dependent variables and their associated regressors. We wish to arrange this observation horizontally instead of vertically. The model for this observation can be written

$$[y_1 \quad y_2 \quad \cdots \quad y_M]_t = [\mathbf{x}_t^*]'[\boldsymbol{\pi}_1 \quad \boldsymbol{\pi}_2 \quad \cdots \quad \boldsymbol{\pi}_M] + [\varepsilon_1 \quad \varepsilon_2 \quad \cdots \quad \varepsilon_M]_t, \quad (17\text{–}17)$$

where $\mathbf{x}_t^*$ is the full set of all K different independent variables that appear in the model. The parameter matrix then has one column for each equation, but the columns are not the

TABLE 17.3 Parameter Estimates (Standard Errors in Parentheses)

	GM	**CH**	**GE**	**WE**	**US**
Constant	−173.218	2.39111	−16.6623	4.37312	136.969
	(84.30)	(11.63)	(24.96)	(6.018)	(94.8)
F	0.122040	0.06741	0.0371	0.05397	0.08865
	(0.02025)	(0.01709)	(0.01177)	(0.0103)	(0.04542)
C	0.38914	0.30520	0.11723	0.026930	0.31246
	(0.03185)	(0.02606)	(0.02173)	(0.03708)	(0.118)

Residual Covariance Matrix

	GM	**CH**	**GE**	**WE**	**US**
GM	7307.30				
CH	−330.55	155.08			
GE	550.27	11.429	741.22		
WE	118.83	18.376	220.33	103.13	
US	−2879.10	463.21	1408.11	734.83	9671.4

same as $\boldsymbol{\beta}_m$ in (17–2) unless every variable happens to appear in every equation. Otherwise, the ith equation will have a number of zeros in it, imposing an **exclusion restriction.**

EXAMPLE 17.4

Consider the GM and GE equations from the Boot–de Witt data we have used in the previous examples. The tth observation would be

$$[I_g \quad I_e] = [1 \quad F_g \quad C_g \quad F_e \quad C_e] \begin{bmatrix} \alpha_g & \alpha_e \\ \beta_{1g} & 0 \\ \beta_{2g} & 0 \\ 0 & \beta_{1e} \\ 0 & \beta_{2e} \end{bmatrix} + [\varepsilon_g \quad \varepsilon_e].$$

This is one observation. Let $\boldsymbol{\varepsilon}_t$ be the vector of M disturbances for this observation arranged, for now, in a column. Then, $E[\boldsymbol{\varepsilon}_t\boldsymbol{\varepsilon}_t'] = \boldsymbol{\Sigma}.$ The log of the joint normal density of these M disturbances is

$$\ln L_t = -\frac{M}{2}\ln(2\pi) - \frac{1}{2}\ln|\boldsymbol{\Sigma}| - \frac{1}{2}\boldsymbol{\varepsilon}_t'\boldsymbol{\Sigma}^{-1}\boldsymbol{\varepsilon}_t. \tag{17–18}$$

The log likelihood for a sample of T joint observations is the sum of these over t:

$$\ln L = \sum_t \ln L_t$$

$$= -\frac{MT}{2}\ln(2\pi) - \frac{T}{2}\ln|\boldsymbol{\Sigma}| - \frac{1}{2}\sum_{t=1}^{T} \boldsymbol{\varepsilon}_t'\boldsymbol{\Sigma}^{-1}\boldsymbol{\varepsilon}_t. \tag{17–19}$$

Denote the *mn*th element of $\boldsymbol{\Sigma}^{-1}$ as σ^{mn}. Then

$$\boldsymbol{\varepsilon}_t'\boldsymbol{\Sigma}^{-1}\boldsymbol{\varepsilon}_t = \sum_{m=1}^{M}\sum_{n=1}^{M}\varepsilon_{tm}\varepsilon_{tn}\sigma^{mn}.$$

Summing these over T observations, we have

$$\sum_{t=1}^{T}\boldsymbol{\varepsilon}_t'\boldsymbol{\Sigma}^{-1}\boldsymbol{\varepsilon}_t = \sum_{t=1}^{T}\sum_{m=1}^{M}\sum_{n=1}^{M}\varepsilon_{tm}\varepsilon_{tn}\sigma^{mn}.$$

Now reverse the order of summation and move σ^{mn} outside to obtain

$$\sum_{t=1}^{T}\boldsymbol{\varepsilon}_t'\boldsymbol{\Sigma}^{-1}\boldsymbol{\varepsilon}_t = \sum_{m=1}^{M}\sum_{n=1}^{M}\sigma^{mn}\sum_{t=1}^{T}\varepsilon_{tm}\varepsilon_{tn}.$$

The innermost sum, $\sum_{t=1}^{T}\varepsilon_{tm}\varepsilon_{tn}$, is T times the *mn*th element of $\mathbf{W}$, where

$$\mathbf{W}_{mn} = \frac{1}{T}\sum_{t=1}^{T}\varepsilon_{tm}\varepsilon_{tn}.$$

Since this uses actual disturbances, $E[\mathbf{W}_{mn}] = \sigma_{mn}$; $\mathbf{W}$ is the $M \times M$ matrix we would use to estimate $\boldsymbol{\Sigma}$ if the εs were actually observed. Returning to the derivation, we have, therefore,

$$\sum_{t=1}^{T}\boldsymbol{\varepsilon}_t'\boldsymbol{\Sigma}^{-1}\boldsymbol{\varepsilon}_t = T\sum_{m=1}^{M}\sum_{n=1}^{M}\sigma^{mn}\mathbf{W}_{mn}.$$

Finally, the *m*th diagonal element of the matrix product $\boldsymbol{\Sigma}^{-1}\mathbf{W}$ is $\sum_n\sigma^{mn}\mathbf{W}_{mn}$. The preceding sum is T times the sum of these, which is T times the trace of the product. Therefore,

$$\sum_{t=1}^{T}\boldsymbol{\varepsilon}_t'\boldsymbol{\Sigma}^{-1}\boldsymbol{\varepsilon}_t = T\ \text{tr}(\boldsymbol{\Sigma}^{-1}\mathbf{W}). \tag{17--20}$$

Inserting this in the log likelihood, we have

$$\ln L = -\frac{MT}{2}\ln(2\pi) - \frac{T}{2}\ln|\boldsymbol{\Sigma}| - \frac{T}{2}\text{tr}(\boldsymbol{\Sigma}^{-1}\mathbf{W}). \tag{17--21}$$

This is a particularly simple and useful formulation. Recall that $\mathbf{W}$ is the matrix of residual sums of squares and cross-products. We now consider maximum likelihood estimation of parameters of a model.

It has been shown[9] that

$$\frac{\partial \ln L}{\partial \boldsymbol{\Sigma}} = -\frac{T}{2}\boldsymbol{\Sigma}^{-1}(\boldsymbol{\Sigma} - \mathbf{W})\boldsymbol{\Sigma}^{-1}. \tag{17--22}$$

Equating this to a zero matrix, we see that given the maximum likelihood estimates of the slope parameters, the maximum likelihood estimator of $\boldsymbol{\Sigma}$ is $\mathbf{W}$, the matrix of mean residual sums of squares and cross-products, that is, the matrix we have used for FGLS. (Notice that there is no correction for degrees of freedom; $\partial \ln L/\partial \boldsymbol{\Sigma} = \mathbf{0}$ implies (17--9).)

---

[9] See, for example, Joreskog (1973).

We also know that because this is a generalized regression model, the maximum likelihood estimator of the parameter matrix, [**B**], must be equivalent to the FGLS estimator we discussed earlier.[10] It is useful to go a step further. If we insert our solution for $\boldsymbol{\Sigma}$ in the likelihood function, we obtain the **concentrated log likelihood,**

$$\ln L_c = -\frac{MT}{2}(1 + \ln(2\pi)) - \frac{T}{2}\ln|\mathbf{W}|. \tag{17–23}$$

We have shown, therefore, that the criterion for choosing the maximum likelihood estimator of $\boldsymbol{\beta}$ is

$$\hat{\boldsymbol{\beta}}_{ML} = \text{Min}_\beta \frac{1}{2}\ln|\mathbf{W}| \tag{17–24}$$

subject to the exclusion restrictions. This is an important result that reappears in many other models and settings. This minimization must be done subject to the constraints in the parameter matrix. In our two-equation example, there are two blocks of zeros in the parameter matrix. These must be present in the MLE as well.[11]

This maximization problem is particularly simple to solve using Newton's method. To construct the gradient of the log-likelihood, let

$$\boldsymbol{\Pi} = [\boldsymbol{\pi}_1 \quad \boldsymbol{\pi}_2 \quad \cdots \quad \boldsymbol{\pi}_M].$$

So $\boldsymbol{\Pi}$ is a $K \times M$ parameter matrix (which usually contains many zeros). Then

$$\ln L_c = -\frac{MT}{2}(1 + \ln(2\pi)) - \frac{T}{2}\ln|\mathbf{W}|,$$

where

$$\mathbf{W} = \frac{1}{T}(\mathbf{Y} - \mathbf{X}\boldsymbol{\Pi})'(\mathbf{Y} - \mathbf{X}\boldsymbol{\Pi}).$$

The matrix of derivatives is

$$\frac{\partial \ln L_c}{\partial \boldsymbol{\Pi}} = \mathbf{X}'\mathbf{W}^{-1}(\mathbf{Y} - \mathbf{X}\boldsymbol{\Pi}).$$

To construct the appropriate vector, just extract the elements that correspond to nonzero elements of $\boldsymbol{\Pi}$, columnwise, and arrange them in a column vector. The Hessian is

$$\frac{\partial^2 \ln L_c}{\partial \pi_{km} \partial \pi_{ln}} = -\mathbf{W}^{mn}[(\mathbf{X}'\mathbf{X})^{-1}]_{kl}.$$

These are then arranged in a matrix that corresponds to the column vector of derivatives. Then Newton's method can be used to maximize the log likelihood. As we saw earlier, iterated FGLS can also be used to compute the MLE. One advantage of this method is that it is particularly fast. The first and second derivatives are, after a small amount of manipulation, functions only of $\mathbf{Y}'\mathbf{Y}/T$, $\mathbf{X}'\mathbf{X}/T$, and $\mathbf{X}'\mathbf{Y}/T$. This means that the amount of computation needed is independent of the sample size once the moments are computed. Second, the log-likelihood function is globally concave, so this method normally con-

---

[10] This establishes the Oberhofer–Kmenta conditions.

[11] The estimate of $\boldsymbol{\beta}$ is the set of nonzero elements in the parameter matrix in (17–17).

verges after only a few iterations. Finally, it is particularly simple to impose the sort of cross-equation equality constraints which arise in demand systems with this method. Joreskog (1973) provides details.

The results of Chapter 13 apply here, so we need not rederive the information matrix to obtain the correct asymptotic covariance matrix for the maximum likelihood estimates. They are the ones given earlier for GLS. It would rarely be used, but, if needed, the asymptotic covariance matrix for the maximum likelihood estimator of Σ is (with the elements stacked in an $M^2 \times 1$ vector)

$$\text{Asy.Var}[\hat{\Sigma}_{ML}] = \frac{2}{T}\Sigma \otimes \Sigma. \tag{17-25}$$

This can be estimated with $(2/T)\mathbf{W} \otimes \mathbf{W}$. It can be used, for example, to test the hypothesis that Σ is diagonal.

The likelihood ratio statistic is an alternative to the F statistic discussed earlier for testing hypotheses about $\boldsymbol{\beta}$. The likelihood ratio statistic is

$$\lambda = -2(\ln L_r - \ln L_u) = T(\ln|\mathbf{W}_r| - \ln|\mathbf{W}_u|), \tag{17-26}$$

where $\mathbf{W}_r$ and $\mathbf{W}_u$ are the residual sums of squares and cross-product matrices using the constrained and unconstrained estimators, respectively. The likelihood ratio statistic is asymptotically distributed as chi-squared with degrees of freedom equal to the number of restrictions.

EXAMPLE 17.5 _____

The log determinant of the unrestricted maximum likelihood estimator of Σ given in Example 17.4 is 31.71986. The log likelihood is, therefore,

$$L_u = -\frac{20(5)}{2}(\ln(2\pi) + 1) - \frac{20}{2}31.71986$$

$$= -459.0925.$$

The restricted model with equal-parameter vectors and correlation across equations is discussed in Section 16.3.2, and the restricted MLEs are given in Example 16.4. (The MLE of Σ is not shown there.) The log determinant for the constrained model is 37.838. The log likelihood for the constrained model is, therefore, -520.27. The likelihood ratio test statistic is 122.36. The 1 percent critical value from the chi-squared distribution with 12 degrees of freedom is 26.217, so the hypothesis of homogeneity is (once again) rejected.

17.2.4. Autocorrelation

The seemingly unrelated regressions model can be extended to allow for autocorrelation in the same fashion as in Chapter 16. To reiterate, suppose that

$$\mathbf{y}_m = \mathbf{X}_m\boldsymbol{\beta}_m + \boldsymbol{\varepsilon}_m,$$

$$\varepsilon_{mt} = \rho_m\varepsilon_{m,t-1} + u_{mt},$$

where u_{mt} is uncorrelated across observations. This will imply that the blocks in $\mathbf{V}$, instead of $\sigma_{mn}\mathbf{I}$, are $\sigma_{mn}\boldsymbol{\Omega}_{mn}$, where $\boldsymbol{\Omega}_{mn}$ is given in (16–22).

The treatment shown by Parks (1967) is the one we used earlier.[12] This calls for a three-step approach:

1. Estimate each equation in the system by ordinary least squares. Use any of the consistent estimators of ρ described in Chapter 15. For that equation, transform the data by the Prais–Winsten transformation to remove the autocorrelation.[13] Note that there will not be a constant term in the transformed data, as there will be a column with $(1 - r_m^2)^{1/2}$ as the first observation and $(1 - r_m)$ for the remainder.

2. Using the transformed data, use ordinary least squares once more to estimate Σ.

3. Use FGLS based on the estimated Σ and the transformed data.

There is no benefit to iteration. The estimator is efficient at every step, and iteration does not produce a maximum likelihood estimator. After the last step, Σ should be reestimated with the GLS estimates. The estimated covariance matrix for $\boldsymbol{\varepsilon}$ can then be reconstructed using

$$\hat{\sigma}_{mn}(\varepsilon) = \frac{\hat{\sigma}_{mn}}{1 - r_m r_n}. \tag{17-27}$$

EXAMPLE 17.6

Table 17.4 is a list of the autocorrelation-corrected estimates of the model of Example 17.1. The Durbin–Watson statistics for the five data sets given here, with the exception of

TABLE 17.4

	GM	CH	GE	WE	US
Durbin–Watson	0.9375	1.984	1.0721	1.413	0.9091
Autocorrelation	0.531	0.008	0.463	0.294	0.545

Residual Covariance Matrix $[\hat{\sigma}_{mn}/(1 - r_m r_n)]$

	GM	CH	GE	WE	US
GM	6679.5				
CH	−220.97	151.96			
GE	483.79	43.7891	684.59		
WE	88.373	19.964	190.37	92.788	
US	−1381.6	342.89	1484.10	676.88	8638.1

Parameter Estimates (Standard Errors in Parentheses)

	GM	CH	GE	WE	US
β_1	−51.337	−0.4536	−24.913	4.7091	14.0207
	(80.62)	(11.86)	(25.67)	(6.510)	(96.49)
β_2	0.094038	0.06847	0.04271	0.05091	0.16415
	(0.01733)	(0.0174)	(0.01134)	(0.01060)	(0.0386)
β_3	0.40723	0.32041	0.10954	0.04284	0.2006
	(0.04261)	(0.0258)	(0.03012)	(0.04127)	(0.1428)

[12] Guilkey (1974) and Guilkey and Schmidt (1973) present an alternative treatment based on $\boldsymbol{\varepsilon}_t = \mathbf{R}\boldsymbol{\varepsilon}_{t-1} + \mathbf{u}_t$, where $\boldsymbol{\varepsilon}_t$ is the $M \times 1$ vector of disturbances at time t and $\mathbf{R}$ is a correlation matrix.

[13] There is a complication with the first observation, which is not treated quite correctly by this procedure. For details, see Judge et al. (1985, pp. 486–489). The strictly correct (and quite cumbersome) results are for the true GLS estimator, which assumes a known $\boldsymbol{\Omega}$. It is unlikely that in a finite sample anything is lost by using the Prais–Winsten procedure with the estimated $\boldsymbol{\Omega}$. One suggestion has been to use the Cochrane–Orcutt procedure and drop the first observation. But in a small sample, the cost of discarding the first observation is almost surely greater than that of neglecting to account properly for the correlation of the first disturbance with the other first disturbances. It is an issue that merits further study.

Chrysler, strongly suggest that there is, indeed, autocorrelation in the disturbances. The differences between these and the uncorrected estimates given earlier are sometimes relatively large, as might be expected, given the fairly high autocorrelation and small sample size. The smaller diagonal elements in the disturbance covariance matrix compared to those of Example 17.1 reflect the improved fit brought about by introducing the lagged variables into the equation.

17.3. Systems of Demand Equations—Singular Systems

Most of the recent applications of the multivariate regression model[14] have been in the context of systems of demand equations, either commodity demands or factor demands in studies of production.

EXAMPLE 17.7

Stone's expenditure system[15] based on a set of logarithmic commodity demand equations, income Y, and commodity prices p_n is

$$\ln q_m = \alpha_m + \eta_m \ln\!\left(\frac{Y}{P}\right) + \sum_n \eta^*_{mn}\ln\!\left(\frac{p_n}{P}\right),$$

where P is a generalized (share-weighted) price index, η_m is an income elasticity, and η^*_{mn} is a compensated price elasticity. We can interpret this as the demand equation in real expenditure and real prices. The resulting set of equations constitutes an econometric model in the form of a set of seemingly unrelated regressions. In estimation, we must account for a number of restrictions including homogeneity of degree one in income, $\Sigma_m \eta_m = 1$, and symmetry of the matrix of compensated price elasticities, $\eta^*_{mn} = \eta^*_{nm}$.

Other examples include the systems of factor demands and factor cost shares from production, which we shall consider again later. In principle, each of these is merely a particular application of the model of the previous section. But some special problems arise in these settings. First, the parameters of the systems are generally constrained across equations. That is, the unconstrained model is inconsistent with the underlying theory.[16] The numerous constraints in the system of demand equations presented earlier give an example. A second intrinsic feature of many of these models is that the disturbance covariance matrix, $\boldsymbol{\Sigma}$, is singular.

---

[14] Note the distinction between the multi*variate* or multiple-equation model discussed here and the *multiple* regression model introduced in Chapter 6.

[15] A very readable survey of the estimation of systems of commodity demands is Deaton and Muellbauer (1980b). The example discussed here is taken from their Chapter 3 and the references to Stone's (1954a,b) work cited therein. A counterpart for production function modeling is Chambers (1988).

[16] This does not imply that the theoretical restrictions are not testable or that the unrestricted model cannot be estimated. However, sometimes the meaning of the model is ambiguous without the restrictions. Statistically rejecting the restrictions implied by the theory, which were used to derive the econometric model in the first place, can put us in a rather uncomfortable position. For example, in a study of utility functions, Christensen et al. (1975), after rejecting the cross-equation symmetry of a set of commodity demands, stated: "With this conclusion we can terminate the test sequence, since these results invalidate the theory of demand" (p. 380).

EXAMPLE 17.8 Cobb–Douglas Cost Function ——————————————

Consider a Cobb–Douglas production function,

$$Y = \alpha_0 \prod_m x_m^{\alpha_m}. \tag{17–28}$$

Profit maximization calls for the firm to maximize output for a given cost level, C (or minimize costs for a given output, Y). The Lagrangean for the maximization problem is

$$\Lambda = \alpha_0 \prod_m x_m^{\alpha_m} + \lambda(C - \mathbf{p}'\mathbf{x}),$$

where $\mathbf{p}$ is the vector of M factor prices. The necessary conditions for maximizing this are

$$\frac{\partial \Lambda}{\partial x_m} = \frac{\alpha_m Y}{x_m} - \lambda p_m = 0,$$

$$\frac{\partial \Lambda}{\partial \lambda} = C - \mathbf{p}'\mathbf{x} = 0.$$

The joint solution provides $x_m(Y, \mathbf{p})$ and $\lambda(Y, \mathbf{p})$. The total cost of production is

$$\sum_m p_m x_m = \sum_m \frac{\alpha_m Y}{\lambda}.$$

The cost share allocated to the mth factor is

$$\frac{p_m x_m}{\sum_m p_m x_m} = \frac{\alpha_m}{\sum_m \alpha_m} = \beta_m. \tag{17–29}$$

This provides the basis for a multivariate regression model. The full model is[17]

$$\ln C = \beta_0 + \beta_y \ln Y + \sum_m \beta_m \ln p_m + \varepsilon_c,$$

$$s_1 = \beta_1 + \varepsilon_1$$
$$s_2 = \beta_2 + \varepsilon_2 \tag{17–30}$$
$$\vdots$$
$$s_M = \beta_M + \varepsilon_M.$$

By construction,

$$\sum_m \beta_m = 1$$

and $$\tag{17–31}$$

$$\sum_m s_m = 1.$$

---

[17] We leave as an exercise the derivation of β_0, which is a mixture of all of the parameters and β_y, which equals $1/\sum_m \alpha_m$.

The cost shares will also sum identically to one in the data. It follows, therefore, that

$$\sum_m \varepsilon_m = 0$$

at every data point, so the system is singular. For the moment, ignore the cost function. Let the $M \times 1$ disturbance vector from the shares be

$$\varepsilon = [\varepsilon_1, \varepsilon_2, \ldots, \varepsilon_M]'.$$

Since

$$\varepsilon' i = 0 \qquad \text{(where } i \text{ is a column of ones),}$$

it follows that

$$E[\varepsilon\varepsilon' i] = \Sigma i = 0.$$

This implies that Σ is singular. Therefore, the methods of the previous sections cannot be used here. (You should verify that the *sample* covariance matrix of the OLS residuals will also be singular.)

The solution to the singularity problem appears to be to drop one of the equations, estimate the remainder, and solve for the last parameter from the other $M - 1$. The constraint in (17–31) is that the cost function must be homogeneous of degree one in the prices, a theoretical necessity. If we impose the constraint

$$\beta_M = 1 - \beta_1 - \beta_2 - \cdots - \beta_{M-1}, \tag{17–32}$$

the system is reduced to a nonsingular one:

$$\ln\left(\frac{C}{p_M}\right) = \beta_0 + \beta_y \ln Y + \sum_{m=1}^{M-1} \beta_m \ln\left(\frac{p_m}{p_M}\right) + \varepsilon_c,$$

$$s_1 = \beta_1 + \varepsilon_1$$

$$s_2 = \beta_2 + \varepsilon_2$$

$$\vdots$$

$$s_{M-1} = \beta_{M-1} + \varepsilon_{M-1}.$$

This system provides estimates of β_0, β_y, and $\beta_1, \ldots, \beta_{M-1}$. The last parameter is estimated using (17–32).

In principle, it is immaterial which factor is chosen as the numeraire. Unfortunately, the FGLS parameter estimates in the now nonsingular system will depend on which one is chosen. Invariance is achieved by using maximum likelihood estimates instead of FGLS.[18] These can be obtained by iterating FGLS or by direct maximum likelihood estimation.[19]

EXAMPLE 17.9

Nerlove's (1963) study of the electric power industry described in Example 8.3 provides an example of the preceding Cobb–Douglas cost function model. His ordinary least squares estimates of the parameters were listed in the earlier example. Among the results are (unfortunately) a negative capital coefficient in three of the six regressions. Nerlove

---

[18] The invariance result is proved in Barten (1969).

[19] Some additional results on the method are given by Revankar (1976).

also found that the simple Cobb–Douglas model did not adequately account for the relationship between output and average cost. Christensen and Greene (1976) further analyzed the Nerlove data and augmented the data set with cost share data in order to estimate the complete demand system. Table 17.5 lists 20 of Nerlove's 145 observations with Christensen and Greene's cost share data. Cost is the total cost of generation in millions of dollars, output is in millions of kilowatt-hours, the capital price is an index of construction costs, the wage rate is in dollars per hour for production and maintenance, the fuel price is an index of the cost per BTU of fuel purchased by the firms, and the data reflect the 1955 costs of production.

TABLE 17.5.   Cost Function Data

Firm	Cost	Output	Pk	Pl	Pf	Sk	Sl	Sf
1	0.423	39	164	2.30	23.6	0.4137	0.1702	0.4161
2	1.130	130	176	1.82	38.9	0.2779	0.1712	0.5509
3	1.565	197	183	2.19	29.1	0.4151	0.0692	0.5157
4	2.382	338	163	1.85	24.6	0.4799	0.0616	0.4585
5	4.580	484	176	1.75	42.8	0.2828	0.1009	0.6163
6	5.535	719	174	1.70	26.9	0.4946	0.0703	0.4351
7	6.754	984	158	1.70	26.9	0.2435	0.1083	0.6482
8	7.743	1,122	162	2.19	29.1	0.3744	0.0977	0.5279
9	8.488	1,215	164	2.19	29.1	0.4390	0.0695	0.4915
10	10.879	1,649	177	2.32	31.9	0.3991	0.0974	0.5035
11	15.437	2,028	163	2.11	24.4	0.3989	0.0808	0.5203
12	12.905	2,341	183	2.04	20.7	0.4165	0.0945	0.4890
13	11.320	2,870	167	1.76	10.3	0.5822	0.1333	0.2845
14	19.035	3,202	170	2.30	23.6	0.4974	0.0983	0.4043
15	29.845	4,764	195	2.19	29.1	0.3530	0.1328	0.5142
16	21.988	5,283	159	2.04	20.7	0.4491	0.0630	0.4879
17	40.594	7,193	162	2.12	28.6	0.3550	0.0729	0.5721
18	33.354	7,886	178	1.61	17.8	0.5835	0.0587	0.3578
19	67.120	11,477	151	2.24	26.5	0.3458	0.0670	0.5872
20	119.939	16,719	162	2.30	23.6	0.4340	0.0906	0.4754

The regression estimates are given in Table 17.6.

TABLE 17.6.   Regression Estimates (Standard Errors in Parentheses)

	Ordinary Least Squares				Multivariate Regression			
β_0	−6.512	(1.03)	−6.380	(1.01)	−8.192	(0.148)	−7.114	(0.444)
β_y	0.9044	(0.021)	0.6959	(0.156)	0.9173	(0.019)	0.5975	(0.131)
β_{yy}	—		0.01543	(0.011)	—		0.02250	(0.0095)
β_k	−0.08659	(0.229)	−0.1911	(0.237)	0.4108	(0.019)	0.4118	(0.0194)
β_l	0.4802	(0.231)	0.3492	(0.245)	0.0958	(0.007)	0.0957	(0.007)
β_f	0.4332	(0.117)	0.4597	(0.116)	0.4934	(0.019)	0.4926	(0.018)
R^2	0.9931		0.9939		—		—	
Log $|\mathbf{W}|$	—		—		−15.874		−16.049	

Least squares estimates of the Cobb–Douglas cost function are given in the first column.[20] As expected, the coefficient on capital is negative. In view of the fact that β_m =

[20] Results based on Nerlove's full data set are given in Example 8.3.

$\beta_y \partial \ln Y / \partial \ln x_m$, that is, a positive multiple of the output elasticity of the mth factor, this is a troubling finding. The third column gives the maximum likelihood estimates obtained in the constrained system. Two things to note are the dramatically smaller standard errors and the now positive (and reasonable) estimate of the capital coefficient. The estimates of economies of scale in the basic Cobb–Douglas model are $1/\beta_y = 1.11$ (column 1) and 1.05 (column 3), which suggests some increasing returns to scale. However, Nerlove had found evidence that at extremely large firm sizes, economies of scale diminished and eventually disappeared. In order to account for this (essentially a classical U-shaped average cost curve), he appended a quadratic term in log output in the cost function. The single equation and maximum likelihood multivariate regression estimates are given in the second and fourth columns.

17.4. Flexible Functional Forms— Translog Cost Function

The literatures on production and cost and on utility and demand have evolved in several directions. In the area of models of producer behavior, the classic paper by Arrow et al. (1961) called into question the inherent restriction of the Cobb–Douglas model that all elasticities of factor substitution are equal to one. Researchers have since developed numerous flexible functions that allow substitution to be unrestricted (i.e., not even constant).[21] Similar strands of literature have appeared in the analysis of commodity demands.[22] In this section, we examine in detail a model of production.

Suppose that production is characterized by a production function,

$$Y = f(\mathbf{x}).$$

The solution to the problem of minimizing the cost of producing a specified output rate given a set of factor prices produces the cost-minimizing set of factor demands

$$x_m = x_m(Y, \mathbf{p}).$$

The total cost of production is given by the cost function,

$$C = \sum_m p_m x_m(Y, \mathbf{p}) = C(Y, \mathbf{p}). \tag{17–33}$$

If there are constant returns to scale, it can be shown that

$$C = Yc(\mathbf{p}) \tag{17–34}$$

or

$$\frac{C}{Y} = c(\mathbf{p}),$$

[21] See, in particular, Berndt and Christensen (1972). Two useful surveys of the topic are Jorgenson (1983) and Diewert (1974).

[22] See, for example, Christensen et al. (1975) and two surveys, Deaton and Muellbauer (1980b) and Deaton (1983). Berndt (1990) contains many useful results.

where $c(\mathbf{p})$ is the unit or average cost function.[23] The cost-minimizing factor demands are obtained by applying Shephard's (1970) lemma, which states that if $C(Y, \mathbf{p})$ gives the minimum total cost of production, then the cost-minimizing set of factor demands is given by

$$x_m^* = \frac{\partial C(Y, \mathbf{p})}{\partial p_m}$$

$$= \frac{Y \partial c(\mathbf{p})}{\partial p_m}. \tag{17-35}$$

Alternatively, by differentiating logarithmically, we obtain the cost-minimizing factor cost shares:

$$s_m = \frac{\partial \ln C(Y, \mathbf{p})}{\partial \ln p_m}$$

$$= \frac{p_m x_m}{C}. \tag{17-36}$$

With constant returns to scale, $\ln C(Y, \mathbf{p}) = \ln Y + \ln c(\mathbf{p})$, so

$$s_m = \frac{\partial \ln c(\mathbf{p})}{\partial \ln p_m}. \tag{17-37}$$

In many empirical studies, the objects of estimation are the elasticities of factor substitution and the own price elasticities of demand. These are given by

$$\theta_{mn} = \frac{c(\partial^2 c / \partial p_m \, \partial p_n)}{(\partial c / \partial p_m)(\partial c / \partial p_n)}$$

and

$$\eta_{mm} = s_m \theta_{mm}.$$

By suitably parameterizing the cost function (17–34) and the cost shares (17–37), we obtain an M or $M + 1$ equation econometric model that can be used to estimate these quantities.[24]

The translog function is the most frequently used flexible function in empirical work.[25] By expanding $\ln c(\mathbf{p})$ in a second-order Taylor series about the point $\ln \mathbf{p} = \mathbf{0}$, we obtain

$$\ln c \simeq \beta_0 + \sum_m \left(\frac{\partial \ln c}{\partial \ln p_m} \right) \ln p_m + \frac{1}{2} \sum_m \sum_n \left(\frac{\partial^2 \ln c}{\partial \ln p_m \, \partial \ln p_n} \right) \ln p_m \ln p_n, \tag{17-38}$$

---

[23] The Cobb–Douglas function of the previous section gives an illustration. The restriction of constant returns to scale is $\beta_y = 1$, which is equivalent to $C = Yc(\mathbf{p})$. Nerlove's more general version of the cost function allows nonconstant returns to scale. See Christensen and Greene (1976) and Diewert (1974) for some of the formalities of the cost function and its relationship to the structure of production.

[24] The cost function is only one of several approaches to this study. See Jorgenson (1983) for a discussion.

[25] The function was developed as a means of approximating the CES production function by Kmenta (1967) and was introduced formally in a series of papers by Berndt, Christensen, Jorgenson, and Lau, including Berndt and Christensen (1972) and Christensen et al. (1973). The literature has produced something of a competition in the development of exotic functional forms. However, the translog function has remained the most popular, and by one account, Guilkey et al. (1983) is the most reliable of several available alternatives.

where all derivatives are evaluated at the expansion point. If we identify these derivatives as coefficients and impose the symmetry of the cross-price derivatives, the cost function becomes

$$\ln c = \beta_0 + \beta_1 \ln p_1 + \cdots + \beta_M \ln p_M$$

$$+ \frac{\delta_{11}(\ln p_1)^2}{2}$$

$$+ \delta_{12} \ln p_1 \ln p_2 + \frac{\delta_{22}(\ln p_2)^2}{2} \qquad (17\text{--}39)$$

$$+ \qquad \vdots$$

$$+ \cdots \qquad + \frac{\delta_{MM}(\ln p_M)^2}{2}.$$

This is the transcendental logarithmic, or translog, cost function. If δ_{mn} equals zero, it reduces to the Cobb–Douglas function we looked at earlier. The cost shares are given by

$$s_1 = \frac{\partial \ln c}{\partial \ln p_1} = \beta_1 + \delta_{11} \ln p_1 + \delta_{12} \ln p_2 + \cdots + \delta_{1M} \ln p_M,$$

$$s_2 = \frac{\partial \ln c}{\partial \ln p_2} = \beta_2 + \delta_{12} \ln p_1 + \delta_{22} \ln p_2 + \cdots + \delta_{2M} \ln p_M, \qquad (17\text{--}40)$$

$$\vdots$$

$$s_M = \frac{\partial \ln c}{\partial \ln p_M} = \beta_M + \delta_{1M} \ln p_1 + \delta_{2M} \ln p_2 + \cdots + \delta_{MM} \ln p_M.$$

The cost shares must sum to 1, which requires, in addition to the symmetry restrictions already imposed,

$$\beta_1 + \beta_2 + \cdots + \beta_M = 1,$$

$$\sum_m \delta_{mn} = 0 \qquad \text{(column sums equal zero)}, \qquad (17\text{--}41)$$

$$\sum_n \delta_{mn} = 0 \qquad \text{(row sums equal zero)}.$$

The system of share equations provides a seemingly unrelated regressions model that can be used to estimate the parameters of the model.[26] To make the model operational, we must impose the restrictions in (17–41) and solve the problem of singularity of the disturbance covariance matrix of the share equations. The first is accomplished by dividing the first $M - 1$ prices by the Mth, thus eliminating the last term in each row and column of the parameter matrix. As in the Cobb–Douglas model, we obtain a nonsingular system by dropping the Mth share equation. We compute maximum likelihood estimates of the parameters in order to ensure invariance with respect to the choice of which share equation

---

[26] The cost function may be included if desired. This will provide an estimate of β_0 but is otherwise inessential. However, absent the assumption of constant returns to scale, the cost function will contain parameters of interest that do not appear in the share equations. As such, one would want to include it in the model. See Christensen and Greene (1976) for an example.

we drop. For the translog cost function, the elasticities of substitution are particularly simple to compute once the parameters have been estimated.

$$\theta_{mn} = \frac{\delta_{mn} + s_m s_n}{s_m s_n},$$

$$\theta_{mm} = \frac{\delta_{mm} + s_m(s_m - 1)}{s_m^2}.$$

(17–42)

These will differ at every data point. It is common to compute them at some central point such as the means of the data.[27]

EXAMPLE 17.10 A Cost Function for U.S. Manufacturing ————————

A number of recent studies utilizing the translog methodology have used a four-factor model, with capital, K, labor, L, energy, E, and materials, M, the factors of production.

TABLE 17.7

Year	Total Input Cost[a]	Cost Shares				Input Prices			
		K	L	E	M	P_k	P_1	P_e	P_m
1947	182.373	0.05107	0.24727	0.04253	0.65913	1.00000	1.00000	1.00000	1.00000
1948	183.161	0.05817	0.27716	0.05127	0.61340	1.00270	1.15457	1.30258	1.05525
1949	186.533	0.04602	0.25911	0.05075	0.64411	0.74371	1.15584	1.19663	1.06225
1950	221.710	0.04991	0.24794	0.04606	0.65609	0.92497	1.23535	1.21442	1.12430
1951	255.945	0.05039	0.25487	0.04482	0.64992	1.04877	1.33784	1.25179	1.21694
1952	264.699	0.04916	0.26655	0.04460	0.63969	0.99744	1.37949	1.27919	1.19961
1953	291.160	0.04728	0.26832	0.04369	0.64071	1.00653	1.43458	1.27505	1.19044
1954	274.457	0.05635	0.27167	0.04787	0.62411	1.08757	1.45362	1.30356	1.20612
1955	308.908	0.05258	0.26465	0.04517	0.63760	1.10315	1.51120	1.34277	1.23835
1956	328.286	0.04604	0.26880	0.04576	0.63940	0.99606	1.58186	1.37154	1.29336
1957	338.633	0.05033	0.27184	0.04820	0.62962	1.06321	1.64641	1.38010	1.30703
1958	323.318	0.06015	0.27283	0.04836	0.61866	1.15619	1.67389	1.39338	1.32699
1959	358.435	0.06185	0.27303	0.04563	0.61948	1.30758	1.73430	1.36756	1.30774
1960	366.251	0.05788	0.27738	0.04585	0.61889	1.25413	1.78280	1.38025	1.33946
1961	366.162	0.05903	0.27839	0.04640	0.61617	1.26328	1.81977	1.37630	1.34319
1962	390.668	0.05578	0.28280	0.04530	0.61613	1.26525	1.88531	1.37689	1.34745
1963	412.188	0.05601	0.27968	0.04470	0.61962	1.32294	1.93379	1.34737	1.33143
1964	433.768	0.05452	0.28343	0.04392	0.61814	1.32798	2.00998	1.38969	1.35197
1965	474.969	0.05467	0.27996	0.04114	0.62423	1.40659	2.05539	1.38635	1.37542
1966	521.291	0.05460	0.28363	0.04014	0.62163	1.45100	2.13441	1.40102	1.41878
1967	540.941	0.05443	0.28646	0.04074	0.61837	1.38617	2.20616	1.39197	1.42428
1968	585.447	0.05758	0.28883	0.03971	0.61388	1.49901	2.33869	1.43388	1.43481
1969	630.450	0.05410	0.29031	0.03963	0.61597	1.44957	2.46412	1.46481	1.53356
1970	623.466	0.05255	0.29755	0.04348	0.60642	1.32464	2.60532	1.45907	1.54758
1971	658.235	0.04675	0.28905	0.04479	0.61940	1.20177	2.76025	1.64689	1.54978

Source: E. Berndt and D. Wood, "Technology, Prices, and the Derived Demand for Energy," *Review of Economics and Statistics,* 57, 1975, pp. 376–384.

[a]Billions of current dollars.

———

[27]They will also be highly nonlinear functions of the parameters and the data. A method of computing asymptotic standard errors for the estimated elasticities is presented in Anderson and Thursby (1986).

TABLE 17.8. Parameter Estimates
(Standard Errors in Parentheses)

β_K	0.05803	(0.00138)	δ_{KM}	−0.02649	(0.01030)
β_L	0.2549	(0.00214)	δ_{LL}	0.07111	(0.00675)
β_E	0.04725	(0.00101)	δ_{LE}	−0.01068	(0.00301)
β_M	0.6398	(0.00354)	δ_{LM}	−0.05823	(0.01130)
δ_{KK}	0.03484	(0.00585)	δ_{EE}	−0.00087	(0.00326)
δ_{KL}	−0.002192	(0.00399)	δ_{EM}	0.01771	(0.00778)
δ_{KE}	−0.006159	(0.00360)	δ_{MM}	0.06702	(0.02477)

Berndt and Wood (1975) have estimated a translog cost function for the U.S. manufacturing sector. The three factor shares used to estimate the model are

$$s_K = \beta_K + \delta_{KK} \ln\left(\frac{p_K}{p_M}\right) + \delta_{KL} \ln\left(\frac{p_L}{p_M}\right) + \delta_{KE} \ln\left(\frac{p_E}{p_M}\right),$$

$$s_L = \beta_L + \delta_{KL} \ln\left(\frac{p_K}{p_M}\right) + \delta_{LL} \ln\left(\frac{p_L}{p_M}\right) + \delta_{LE} \ln\left(\frac{p_E}{p_M}\right),$$

$$s_E = \beta_E + \delta_{KE} \ln\left(\frac{p_K}{p_M}\right) + \delta_{LE} \ln\left(\frac{p_L}{p_M}\right) + \delta_{EE} \ln\left(\frac{p_E}{p_M}\right).$$

Berndt and Wood's data are reproduced in Table 17.7. Maximum likelihood estimates of the full set of parameters are given in Table 17.8.[28]

The implied estimates of the elasticities of substitution and demand for 1959 (the central year in the data) are derived in Table 17.9 using the fitted cost shares. The departure from the Cobb–Douglas model with unit elasticities is substantial. For example, the results suggest almost no substitutability between energy and labor[29] and some complementarity between capital and energy.

TABLE 17.9

	Capital	Labor	Energy	Materials
Cost shares for 1959				
Fitted share	0.05713	0.27451	0.044192	0.62416
Actual share	0.06185	0.27303	0.04563	0.61948
Implied elasticities of substitution				
Capital	−5.828			
Labor	0.8602	−1.699		
Energy	−1.440	0.1196	−22.07	
Materials	0.2572	0.6602	1.642	−0.4302
Implied own price elasticities				
	−0.3330	−0.4666	−0.9755	−0.2685

[28] These are not the same as those reported by Berndt and Wood. In order to purge their data of possible correlation with the disturbances, they first regressed the prices on 10 exogenous macroeconomic variables, such as U.S. population, government purchases of labor services, real exports of durable goods, and U.S. tangible capital stock, and then based their analysis on the fitted values. The estimates given here are, in general, quite close to those given by Berndt and Wood. For example, their estimates of the first five parameters are 0.0564, 0.2539, 0.0442, 0.6455, and 0.0254.

[29] Berndt and Wood's estimate of θ_{EL} for 1959 is 0.64.

EXERCISES

1. A sample of 100 observations produces the following sample data:

$$\bar{y}_1 = 1 \qquad \bar{y}_2 = 2$$
$$\mathbf{y}_1'\mathbf{y}_1 = 150 \qquad \mathbf{y}_2'\mathbf{y}_2 = 550$$
$$\mathbf{y}_1'\mathbf{y}_2 = 260.$$

The underlying bivariate regression model is

$$y_1 = \mu + \varepsilon_1,$$
$$y_2 = \mu + \varepsilon_2.$$

(a) Compute the OLS estimate of μ, and estimate the sampling variance of this estimator.

(b) Compute the FGLS estimate of μ and the sampling variance of your estimator.

2. Consider estimation of the following two-equation model:

$$y_1 = \beta_1 \quad + \varepsilon_1,$$
$$y_2 = \beta_2 x + \varepsilon_2.$$

A sample of 50 observations produces the following moment matrix:

$$
\begin{array}{c c}
 & \begin{array}{cccc} 1 & y_1 & y_2 & x \end{array} \\
\begin{array}{c} 1 \\ y_1 \\ y_2 \\ x \end{array} &
\left[\begin{array}{cccc}
50 & & & \\
150 & 500 & & \\
50 & 40 & 90 & \\
100 & 60 & 50 & 100
\end{array} \right].
\end{array}
$$

(a) Write the explicit formula for the GLS estimator of $[\beta_1, \beta_2]$. What is the asymptotic covariance matrix of the estimator?

(b) Derive the OLS estimator and its sampling variance in this model.

(c) Obtain the OLS estimates of β_1 and β_2, and estimate the sampling covariance matrix of the two estimates. Use n instead of $(n - 1)$ as the divisor to compute the estimates of the disturbance variances.

(d) Compute the FGLS estimates of β_1 and β_2 and the estimated sampling covariance matrix.

(e) Test the hypothesis that $\beta_2 = 1$.

3. The model

$$y_1 = \beta_1 x_1 + \varepsilon_1,$$
$$y_2 = \beta_2 x_2 + \varepsilon_2,$$

satisfies all of the assumptions of the classical multivariate regression model. All variables have zero means. The following sample second moment matrix is obtained from a sample of 20 observations:

$$
\begin{array}{c c}
 & \begin{array}{cccc} y_1 & y_2 & x_1 & x_2 \end{array} \\
\begin{array}{c} y_1 \\ y_2 \\ x_1 \\ x_2 \end{array} &
\left[\begin{array}{cccc}
20 & 6 & 4 & 3 \\
6 & 10 & 3 & 6 \\
4 & 3 & 5 & 2 \\
3 & 6 & 2 & 10
\end{array} \right].
\end{array}
$$

(*Note:* These are the data from Exercise 1 in Chapter 16.)

(a) Compute the FGLS estimates of β_1 and β_2.

(b) Test the hypothesis that $\beta_1 = \beta_2$.

(c) Compute the maximum likelihood estimates of the model parameters.

(d) Use the likelihood ratio test to test the hypothesis in part (b).

4. Prove that in the model

$$\mathbf{y}_1 = \mathbf{X}_1\boldsymbol{\beta}_1 + \boldsymbol{\varepsilon}_1,$$

$$\mathbf{y}_2 = \mathbf{X}_2\boldsymbol{\beta}_2 + \boldsymbol{\varepsilon}_2,$$

generalized least squares is equivalent to equation-by-equation ordinary least squares if $\mathbf{X}_1 = \mathbf{X}_2$. Does your result hold if it is also known that $\boldsymbol{\beta}_1 = \boldsymbol{\beta}_2$?

5. Consider the two-equation system

$$y_1 = \beta_1 x_1 \qquad\qquad + \varepsilon_1$$

$$y_2 = \qquad \beta_2 x_2 + \beta_3 x_3 + \varepsilon_2.$$

Assume that the disturbance variances and covariance are known. Now suppose that the analyst of this model applies GLS, but erroneously omits x_3 from the second equation. What effect does this specification error have on the consistency of the estimator of β_1?

6. Consider the system

$$y_1 = \alpha_1 + \beta x + \varepsilon_1$$

$$y_2 = \alpha_2 \qquad + \varepsilon_2.$$

The disturbances are freely correlated. Prove that GLS applied to the system leads to the OLS estimates of α_1 and α_2 but to a mixture of the least squares slopes in the regressions of y_1 and y_2 on x as the estimator of β. What is the mixture? To simplify the algebra, assume (with no loss of generality) that $\bar{x} = 0$.

7. For the model

$$y_1 = \alpha_1 + \beta x + \varepsilon_1$$

$$y_2 = \alpha_2 \qquad + \varepsilon_2$$

$$y_3 = \alpha_3 \qquad + \varepsilon_3$$

assume that $y_{i2} + y_{i3} = 1$ at every observation. Prove that the sample covariance matrix of the least squares residuals from the three equations will be singular, thereby precluding computation of the FGLS estimator. How could you proceed in this case?

8. Continuing the analysis of Section 17.4.1, we find that a translog cost function for one output and three factor inputs that does not impose constant returns to scale is

$$\ln C = \alpha + \beta_1 \ln p_1 + \beta_2 \ln p_2 + \beta_2 \ln p_3$$

$$+ \delta_{11} \frac{\ln^2 p_1}{2} + \delta_{12} \ln p_1 \ln p_2 + \delta_{13} \ln p_1 \ln p_3$$

$$+ \delta_{22} \frac{\ln^2 p_2}{2} + \delta_{23} \ln p_2 \ln p_3$$

$$+ \delta_{33} \frac{\ln^2 p_3}{2}$$

$$+ \gamma_{y1} \ln Y \ln p_1 + \gamma_{y2} \ln Y \ln p_2 + \gamma_{y3} \ln Y \ln p_3$$

$$+ \beta_y \ln Y + \beta_{yy} \frac{\ln^2 Y}{2} + \varepsilon_c.$$

The factor share equations are

$$S_1 = \beta_1 + \delta_{11} \ln p_1 + \delta_{12} \ln p_2 + \delta_{13} \ln p_3 + \gamma_{y1} \ln Y + \varepsilon_1,$$

$$S_2 = \beta_2 + \delta_{12} \ln p_1 + \delta_{22} \ln p_2 + \delta_{23} \ln p_3 + \gamma_{y2} \ln Y + \varepsilon_2,$$

$$S_3 = \beta_3 + \delta_{13} \ln p_1 + \delta_{23} \ln p_2 + \delta_{33} \ln p_3 + \gamma_{y3} \ln Y + \varepsilon_3.$$

[See Christensen and Greene (1976) for analysis of this model.]

(a) The three factor shares must add identically to 1. What restrictions does this place on the model parameters?

(b) Show that the adding-up condition in (17–41) can be imposed directly on the model by specifying the translog model in (C/p_3), (p_1/p_3), and (p_2/p_3) and dropping the third share equation. (See Example 17.10.) Notice that this reduces the number of free parameters in the model to 10.

(c) Continuing part (b), the model as specified, with the symmetry and equality restrictions, has 15 parameters. By imposing the constraints, you reduce this number to 10 in the estimating equations. How would you obtain estimates of the parameters not estimated directly?

The remaining parts of this exercise require specialized software. The **TSP, LIMDEP, Shazam,** or **ET** programs noted in the Preface are four that could be used. All estimation is to be done using the data in Example 17.9.

(d) Estimate each of the three equations you obtained in part (b) by ordinary least squares. Do the estimates appear to satisfy the cross-equation equality and symmetry restrictions implied by the theory?

(e) Using the data in Example 17.9, estimate the full system of three equations (cost and the two independent shares), imposing the symmetry and cross-equation equality constraints.

(f) Using your parameter estimates, compute the estimates of the elasticities in (17–42) at the means of the variables.

(g) Use a likelihood ratio statistic to test the joint hypothesis that $\gamma_{yi} = 0$, $i = 1, 2, 3$. [(**Hint:** Just drop the relevant variables from the model.)]

18

Regressions with Lagged Variables

18.1. Introduction

With the exceptions of autocorrelation and the possibly deleterious effects of lagged dependent variables on ordinary least squares, the models considered thus far have given only a very limited role to time as an influencing factor. In this and the next chapter, we consider a number of models and topics in which time and relationships through time play an explicit part in the formulation. We begin with a discussion of *distributed lag models*. These are models that specifically include as independent variables earlier as well as contemporaneous values of the regressors. It is also in this context that lagged values of the dependent variable appear as a consequence of the theoretical basis of the model rather than as a computational means of removing autocorrelation. In Sections 18.2 to 18.5 we discuss in detail three types of distributed lag models: unrestricted finite lag models, polynomial lag models, and the geometric lag model. These do not nearly exhaust the list of available models. But this discussion will present the elements that are common to estimation of most types of distributed lag models. In Section 18.6 we describe a very general dynamic model that encompasses many types of distributed lag models, as well as many of the extensions and more formal macroeconomic models for time-series data that are presented in Chapter 19.[1]

18.2. Distributed Lag Models

Many events have effects that persist over time, and an appropriate model will include lagged variables.

EXAMPLE 18.1 The Demand for Energy

In the typical household, electricity, heating fuels, and gasoline are demanded not for their own sake but for use in appliances, furnaces, and cars. The household's accumulated energy using "capital stock" is determined by income, habits, and past prices of fuels. Consequently, in any period, the household's demand for energy, Q_t, is a function of the current price, P_t, which influences how intensively the stock of equipment, K_t, is used,

---

[1] Basic sources to consider on the subject of distributed lag models are Griliches (1967), Dhrymes (1971), Nerlove (1972), Hendry et al. (1984), and Harvey (1990).

and income, Y_t, and past prices, which have influenced the size and composition of the stock. A simple structural model of these effects might be

Demand: $Q_t = \alpha + \beta P_t + \gamma K_t + u_t,$

Equipment: $K_t = \theta_0 + \theta_1 P_{t-1} + \theta_2 P_{t-2} + \cdots + \delta Y_t + v_t.$

Inserting the second equation in the first produces a **distributed lag model,**

$$Q_t = \alpha + \beta P_t + \gamma(\theta_0 + \theta_1 P_{t-1} + \theta_2 P_{t-2} + \cdots + \delta Y_t) + u_t + \gamma v_t$$

$$= \alpha_0 + \alpha_1 Y_t + \beta_0 P_t + \beta_1 P_{t-1} + \beta_2 P_{t-2} + \cdots + \varepsilon_t.$$

When the price of energy changes, its immediate impact will be to cause households to use their equipment less intensively. But it takes time to replace that equipment, so the full effect of a price change will not be felt for some time thereafter.

18.2.1. Lagged Effects in a Regression Model

A general form of distributed lag model is

$$y_t = \alpha + \sum_{i=0}^{\infty} \beta_i x_{t-i} + \varepsilon_t. \tag{18-1}$$

In this model a one-time change in x_t at any point in time will affect $E[y_s]$ in every period thereafter. When it is believed that the duration of the lagged effects is extremely long, for example, in the analysis of monetary policy, *infinite lag* models that have effects that gradually fade over time are quite common. But models are often constructed in which changes in x cease to have any influence after a fairly small number of periods. We shall consider these *finite lag* models first.[2]

Marginal effects in the classical regression model are one-time events. The response of y to a change in x is assumed to be immediate and to be complete at the end of the period of measurement. In a distributed lag model, the counterpart to a marginal effect is the effect of a one-time change in x_t on the equilibrium of y_t. If the level of x_t has been unchanged for many periods prior to t, the equilibrium value of $E[y_t]$ (assuming that it exists) will be

$$\bar{y} = \alpha + \sum_{i=0}^{\infty} \beta_i \bar{x}$$

$$= \alpha + \bar{x} \sum_{i=0}^{\infty} \beta_i, \tag{18-2}$$

where $\bar{x}$ is the permanent value of x_i. For this to be finite, we require that

$$\left| \sum_{i=0}^{\infty} \beta_i \right| < \infty.$$

Consider the effect of a unit change in $\bar{x}$ occurring in period s. To focus ideas, consider the earlier example of consumers' demand for electricity, and suppose that x_t is the unit price.

---

[2] As in Section 15.2, the formulation of a model with infinite lags is not meant to imply that lagged effects from the infinite past are necessarily of substance in the current period. This is just a convenient representation of a model in which lagged effects are very persistent and fade only gradually over time.

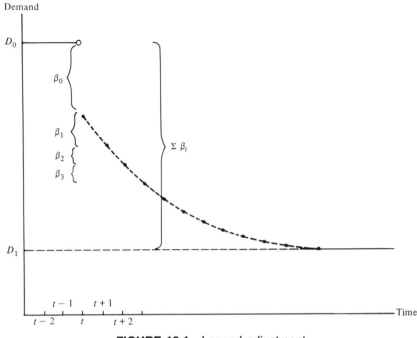

FIGURE 18.1 Lagged adjustment.

Prior to the oil shock, demand had reached an equilibrium consistent with accumulated habits, experience with stable real prices, and the accumulated stocks of appliances. Now suppose that the price, x, rises from $\bar{x}$ to $\bar{x} + 1$ in period s. The path to the new equilibrium might appear as shown in Figure 18.1. The short-run effect is that which occurs in the same period as the change in x. This is β_0 in the figure.

Definition. β_0 = **impact multiplier**
= **short-run multiplier.**

The difference between the old equilibrium, D_0, and the new one, D_1, is the sum of the individual period effects. The **long-run multiplier** is this total effect.

Definition. $\beta = \Sigma_{i=0}^{\infty} \beta_i = $ **equilibrium multiplier.**

Since the lag coefficients are regression coefficients, their scale is determined by the scales of the variables in the model. As such, it is often useful to define

$$\textbf{Lag weights: } w_i = \frac{\beta_i}{\displaystyle\sum_{i=0}^{\infty} \beta_i}, \qquad (18\text{–}3)$$

and to rewrite the model as

$$y_t = \alpha + \beta \sum_{i=0}^{\infty} w_i x_{t-i} + \varepsilon_t. \qquad (18\text{–}4)$$

Two useful statistics, based on the lag weights, that characterize the period of adjustment to a new equilibrium are the

$$\textbf{median lag} = q^* \qquad \text{such that} \quad \sum_{i=0}^{q^*-1} w_i = 0.5 \qquad (18\text{–}5)$$

and

$$\text{mean lag} = \sum_{i=0}^{\infty} i w_i.^{3} \tag{18-6}$$

18.2.2. The Lag and Difference Operators

A convenient device for manipulating lagged variables is the lag operator,

$$Lx_t = x_{t-1}.$$

It follows that

$$L(Lx_t) = L^2 x_t = x_{t-2}.$$

Thus

$$L^p x_t = x_{t-p}$$

and

$$L^q(L^p x_t) = L^{p+q} x_t = x_{t-p-q}.$$

By convention,

$$L^0 x_t = 1 x_t = x_t.$$

A related operation is the first difference,

$$\Delta x_t = x_t - x_{t-1}.$$

Obviously,

$$\Delta x_t = (1 - L)x_t.$$

These two operations can be usefully combined, for example, as in

$$\Delta^2 x_t = (1 - L)^2 x_t$$
$$= (1 - 2L + L^2)x_t$$
$$= x_t - 2x_{t-1} + x_{t-2}.$$

Note that

$$(1 - L)^2 x_t = (1 - L)(1 - L)x_t$$
$$= (1 - L)(x_t - x_{t-1})$$
$$= (x_t - x_{t-1}) - (x_{t-1} - x_{t-2}).$$

The distributed lag model can be written

$$y_t = \alpha + \sum_{i=0}^{\infty} \beta_i L^i x_t + \varepsilon_t$$
$$= \alpha + B(L)x_t + \varepsilon_t, \tag{18-7}$$

---

[3] If the lag coefficients do not all have the same sign, these results may not be meaningful. In some contexts, lag coefficients with different signs may be taken as an indication that there is a flaw in the specification of the model.

where $B(L)$ is a polynomial in L,

$$B(L) = \beta_0 + \beta_1 L + \beta_2 L^2 + \cdots.$$

Two useful results are

$$B(1) = \beta_0 1^0 + \beta_1 1^1 + \beta_2 1^2 + \cdots$$
$$= \text{long-run multiplier} \tag{18-8}$$

and

$$B'(1) = \left.\frac{dB(L)}{dL}\right|_{L=1} = \sum_{i=0}^{\infty} i\beta_i,$$

so that

$$\frac{B'(1)}{B(1)} = \text{mean lag.} \tag{18-9}$$

18.3. Unrestricted Finite Distributed Lag Models

An unrestricted finite distributed lag model would be specified as

$$y_t = \alpha + \sum_{i=0}^{q} \beta_i x_{t-i} + \varepsilon_t. \tag{18-10}$$

For the present, we assume that x_t satisfies the conditions discussed in Section 10.4. The assumption that there are no other regressors is just a convenience. We also assume that ε_t is distributed with mean zero and variance σ_ε^2. Unstructured models such as this, with long but finite lags, have been used in many macroeconomic analyses.[4]

If the lag length, q, is known, (18–10) is a classical regression model. Aside from questions about the properties of the independent variables, the usual estimation results apply.[5] Unfortunately, the appropriate length of the lag is rarely, if ever, known, so one must undertake a specification search, with all its pitfalls. Worse yet, least squares is likely to be rather ineffective, as (1) the typical time series is fairly short, so (18–10) will consume an excessive number of degrees of freedom; (2) ε_t will usually be serially correlated; and (3) multicollinearity is likely to be quite severe.

Various procedures have been suggested for determining the appropriate lag length. The adjusted R^2, $\bar{R}^2$ [see (6–40)], is one possibility. Another commonly used fit measure is **Akaike's** (1973) **information criterion (AIC),**

$$\text{AIC}(q) = \ln\frac{\mathbf{e}'\mathbf{e}}{T} + \frac{2q}{T}. \tag{18-11}$$

If some maximum, Q, is known, $q \le Q$ can be chosen to minimize $\text{AIC}(q)$. $\text{AIC}(q)$ is similar in spirit to $\bar{R}^2$ in that it rewards good fit but penalizes the loss of degrees of freedom.[6] An alternative approach, also based on a known Q, is to do sequential F tests

[4] See, for example, Sims (1972) and the spate of subsequent related studies.

[5] The question of whether the regressors are well behaved or not becomes particularly pertinent in this setting, especially if one or more of them happen to be lagged values of the dependent variable. In what follows, we shall assume that the Grenander conditions discussed in Chapter 10 are met. We thus assume that the usual asymptotic results for the classical or generalized regression model will hold.

[6] For further discussion and some alternative measures, see Geweke and Meese (1981), Amemiya (1985, pp. 146–147), and Judge et al. (1985, pp. 353–355).

TABLE 18.1 Money, Output, and Price Deflator Data

	Nominal GNP				M1				Implicit Price Deflator			
	I	II	III	IV	I	II	III	IV	I	II	III	IV
1950	267.6	277.1	294.8	306.3	110.20	111.75	112.95	113.93	56.04	56.21	56.41	56.67
1951	320.4	328.3	335.0	339.2	115.08	116.19	117.76	119.89	56.77	57.01	56.99	57.58
1952	341.9	342.1	347.8	360.0	121.31	122.37	123.64	124.72	57.58	57.57	57.92	58.58
1953	366.1	369.4	368.4	363.1	125.33	126.05	126.22	126.37	58.76	58.80	59.00	58.74
1954	362.5	362.3	366.7	375.6	126.54	127.18	128.38	129.72	59.38	59.58	59.45	59.77
1955	388.2	396.2	404.8	411.0	131.07	131.88	132.40	132.64	60.27	60.65	61.03	61.40
1956	412.8	418.4	423.5	432.1	133.11	133.38	133.48	134.09	61.91	62.43	63.13	63.69
1957	440.2	442.3	449.4	444.0	134.29	134.36	134.26	133.48	64.40	64.65	65.28	65.37
1958	436.8	440.7	453.9	467.0	133.72	135.22	136.64	138.48	65.63	65.79	66.17	66.47
1959	477.0	490.6	489.0	495.0	140.35	141.75	142.23	141.20	67.04	67.55	67.81	68.00
1960	506.9	506.3	508.0	504.8	140.83	140.83	142.00	141.98	68.44	68.56	68.86	68.96
1961	508.2	519.2	528.2	542.6	142.85	143.88	144.90	146.18	68.88	69.22	69.54	69.65
1962	554.2	562.7	568.9	574.3	147.18	147.95	147.90	148.93	70.23	70.48	70.62	71.08
1963	582.0	590.7	601.8	612.4	150.45	151.93	153.38	154.80	71.41	71.46	71.66	72.17
1964	625.3	634.0	642.8	648.8	155.85	157.20	159.75	161.63	72.36	72.57	72.97	73.16
1965	668.8	681.7	696.4	717.2	162.90	163.90	166.05	169.10	73.77	74.13	74.56	74.96
1966	738.5	750.0	760.6	774.9	171.95	172.98	172.80	173.33	75.71	76.58	76.99	77.75
1967	780.7	788.6	805.7	823.3	175.25	178.10	181.93	184.73	78.27	78.53	79.28	80.13
1968	841.2	867.2	884.9	900.3	187.15	190.63	194.30	198.55	81.15	82.14	82.84	83.99
1969	921.2	937.4	955.3	962.0	201.73	203.18	204.18	206.10	84.97	86.10	87.49	88.62
1970	972.0	986.3	1003.6	1009.0	207.90	209.78	212.78	216.08	89.89	91.07	91.79	93.03
1971	1049.3	1068.9	1086.6	1105.8	220.28	225.25	228.45	230.70	94.40	95.70	96.52	97.39
1972	1142.4	1171.7	1196.1	1233.5	235.60	239.38	244.55	250.70	98.72	99.42	100.25	101.54
1973	1283.5	1307.6	1337.7	1376.7	254.80	258.40	261.03	264.68	102.95	104.75	106.53	108.74
1974	1387.7	1423.8	1451.6	1473.8	268.77	271.23	273.73	276.73	110.72	113.48	116.42	119.79
1975	1479.8	1516.7	1578.5	1621.8	278.75	283.80	288.13	290.88	122.88	124.44	126.68	128.99
1976	1672.0	1698.6	1729.0	1772.5	295.18	299.53	303.35	309.35	130.12	131.30	132.89	134.99
1977	1834.8	1895.1	1954.4	1988.9	316.55	321.80	327.60	334.80	136.80	139.01	141.03	143.24
1978	2031.7	2139.5	2202.5	2281.6	341.13	348.70	335.45	361.38	145.12	148.89	152.02	155.38
1979	2335.5	2377.9	2454.8	2502.9	367.08	376.10	384.58	388.38	158.60	161.85	165.12	168.05
1980	2572.9	2578.8	2639.1	2736.0	394.30	390.00	405.50	416.10	171.94	176.46	180.24	185.13
1981	2875.8	2918.0	3009.3	3027.9	420.90	429.30	432.60	437.50	190.01	193.03	197.70	201.69
1982	3026.0	3061.2	3080.1	3109.6	448.80	451.30	458.20	475.70	203.98	206.77	208.53	210.27
1983	3173.8	3267.0	3346.6	3431.7	490.90	505.20	517.20	523.40	212.87	214.25	215.89	218.21

Source: Data from Gordon (1986, Appendix); compiled by R. Gordon and N. Balke.

on the last $Q - q$ coefficients, stopping when the test rejects the hypothesis that the coefficients are jointly zero. Each of these criteria has flaws and virtues. The AIC criterion, for example, retains a positive probability of leading to overfitting even as $T \to \infty$. It does, however, avoid the inference problems of sequential estimators. The sequential F tests require successive revision of the significance levels to be appropriate, but do have a statistical underpinning.[7]

EXAMPLE 18.2 Finite Unstructured Distributed Lag Models

''Does Money Matter?'' The literature received is ambivalent on whether or not the available evidence suggests that a change in the money stock ultimately leads to a change in output.[8] In this example we estimate a distributed lag model for changes in M1 and changes in real GNP.

Table 18.1 presents quarterly data on M1, nominal GNP, and the implicit price deflator for GNP from 1950 to 1983. We first fit the distributed lag model,

$$\ln Y_t = \alpha + \sum_{i=0}^{8} \beta_i \ln M_{t-i} + \varepsilon_t,$$

where Y_t is nominal GNP divided by the price index (i.e., real GNP). OLS produces the results in Table 18.2. (Asymptotic t ratios are given in parentheses below the coefficients.)

TABLE 18.2   Distributed Lag Model in Logs

β_0	β_1	β_2	β_3	β_4	β_5	β_6	β_7	β_8
1.82	0.292	−0.216	0.050	0.194	0.003	−0.422	−0.228	−0.934
(2.3)	(0.28)	(−0.20)	(0.05)	(0.18)	(0.01)	(−0.39)	(−0.21)	(−1.1)

$R^2 = 0.9293$, $s = 0.0846$,   D–W $= 0.0501$, $r = 0.975$

The extremely low t ratios and the very high F statistic (1711.2) suggest a problem of multicollinearity. The Durbin–Watson statistic also suggests a considerable amount of autocorrelation. The data were, therefore, first differenced to obtain the following results.[9] The model finally estimated is

$$\Delta \ln Y_t = \alpha + \sum_{i=0}^{8} \beta_i(\Delta \ln M_{t-i}) + \varepsilon_t.$$

(What is the implication of the nonzero constant term in this model?) Results for various lag lengths are given in Table 18.3. Observations for 1952.II through 1983.IV are used in all regressions. t Ratios for the estimates are given in parentheses below the estimated coefficients.

There is no obvious interpretation of the persistent negative weights at lags of four, five, and six quarters. It is intriguing to note that in their much more extensive study, which included several other variables in the regression, used levels instead of logarithms,

[7] See Pagano and Hartley (1981) and Trivedi and Pagan (1979).

[8] See, for example, the recent survey by Blanchard (1987). An interesting empirical study is Schmidt and Waud (1973).

[9] Further motivation for using first differences is discussed in Chapter 19.

TABLE 18.3 Unrestricted Distributed Lags

Lag	8	7	6	5	4	3	2	1	0
R^2	0.4881	0.4069	0.3241	0.1652	0.1384	0.1318	0.1131	0.1114	0.1106
$\bar{R}^2$	0.4487	0.3667	0.2783	0.1234	0.1027	0.1033	0.0914	0.0971	0.1037
AIC[a]	1134.	1293.	1451.	1764.	1792.	1805.	1788.	1763.	1737.
D–W	1.534	1.417	1.764	2.072	1.919	1.872	1.853	1.857	1.853
Sum	−0.108	0.054	−0.109	0.191	0.318	0.432	0.487	0.452	0.418
Wald[b]	0.393	0.091	0.354	0.954	2.899	6.060	8.968	9.796	15.573
$t-0$	0.410	0.373	0.474	0.456	0.419	0.416	0.400	0.415	0.418
	(4.43)	(3.77)	(4.66)	(4.06)	(3.73)	(3.68)	(3.59)	(3.88)	(3.94)
$t-1$	0.281	0.178	0.187	0.097	0.092	0.059	0.033	0.037	
	(3.03)	(0.85)	(1.83)	(0.87)	(0.81)	(0.53)	(0.31)	(0.34)	
$t-2$	0.094	0.093	0.137	0.128	0.101	0.054	0.054		
	(1.04)	(0.95)	(1.33)	(1.13)	(0.88)	(0.48)	(0.48)		
$t-3$	0.045	0.008	0.008	−0.568	−0.101	−0.098			
	(0.49)	(0.08)	(0.07)	(−0.50)	(−0.89)	(−0.85)			
$t-4$	−0.157	−0.151	−0.095	−0.203	−0.193				
	(−1.68)	(−1.52)	(−0.91)	(−1.79)	(−1.68)				
$t-5$	−0.288	−0.332	−0.258	−0.230					
	(−3.03)	(−3.28)	(−2.43)	(−1.96)					
$t-6$	−0.463	−0.536	−0.561						
	(−4.89)	(−5.34)	(−5.29)						
$t-7$	0.692	0.422							
	(4.03)	(4.06)							
$t-8$	−0.421								
	(−4.31)								

[a]Multiplied by 10^7.
[b]Wald = Sum^2/Est. Var[Sum]. The 5% critical value is 3.84.

518

and used data from a different period, Schmidt and Waud (1973) found negative weights at lags of five and six quarters in regressions of nominal GNP on money. The long-run multiplier displays an intriguing pattern. The results suggest that there is no long-run response of the growth of real output to changes in the growth of the money stock. The short-term response is substantial, but in the long run, the results are reversed by the substantial negative effects at the longer lags. The Wald statistics given in Table 18.3 are consistent with this pattern. If the number of lags included in the model exceeds four, the long-run response drops convincingly toward zero.

18.4. Polynomial Distributed Lag Models

In some settings, the necessary lag length may be extremely long. In principle, this merely extends (18–10), but the problem of multicollinearity is likely to become quite severe, especially in macroeconomic data. In such cases it is common to impose some structure on the lag distribution, in effect reducing the number of parameters in the model. A model that is quite popular is the **polynomial distributed lag,** or *Almon* (1965) *lag*. The polynomial lag model is based on an assumption that the true distribution of lag coefficients can be well approximated by a polynomial of fairly low order,

$$\beta_i = \alpha_0 + \alpha_1 i + \alpha_2 i^2 + \cdots + \alpha_p i^p, \qquad i = 0, \ldots, q > p.[10] \qquad (18\text{–}12)$$

Figure 18.2 shows the principle. The order of the polynomial, p, is usually taken to be quite low, rarely exceeding three or four.[11]

In addition to the $p + 1$ parameters of the polynomial, there are two unknowns to be determined: the length of the lag structure, q, and the degree of the polynomial, p. We

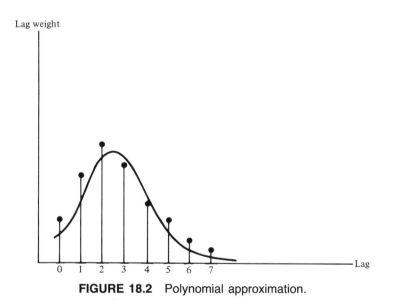

FIGURE 18.2 Polynomial approximation.

---

[10] The original formulation in terms of Lagrangean polynomials is considerably more complex but produces the same results.

[11] See Amemiya and Morimune (1974).

shall return to these later and, for the present, take them as given. After substituting (18–12) in (18–10) and collecting terms, the model can be written

$$
\begin{aligned}
y_t = \alpha &+ \alpha_0(x_t + x_{t-1} + x_{t-2} + x_{t-3} + \cdots + x_{t-q}) \\
&+ \alpha_1(x_{t-1} + 2x_{t-2} + 3x_{t-3} + \cdots + qx_{t-q}) \\
&+ \alpha_2(x_{t-1} + 4x_{t-2} + 9x_{t-3} + \cdots + q^2x_{t-q}) \\
&+ \qquad\qquad\qquad \vdots \\
&+ \alpha_p(x_{t-1} + 2^p x_{t-2} + 3^p x_{t-3} + \cdots + q^p x_{t-q}) \\
&+ \varepsilon_t \\
= \alpha &+ \alpha_0 z_{t0} + \alpha_1 z_{t1} + \alpha_2 z_{t2} + \cdots + \alpha_p z_{tp} + \varepsilon_t.
\end{aligned}
\tag{18–13}
$$

Each z_j is a linear combination of x and the q lagged variables. We can collect the relationships in (18–13) in $\boldsymbol{\beta} = \mathbf{H}\boldsymbol{\alpha}$, where

$$
\mathbf{H} =
\begin{bmatrix}
1 & 0 & 0 & \cdots & 0 \\
1 & 1 & 1 & \cdots & 1 \\
1 & 2 & 4 & \cdots & 2^p \\
1 & 3 & 9 & & 3^p \\
\vdots & & & & \\
1 & q & q^2 & \cdots & q^p
\end{bmatrix},
\tag{18–14}
$$

and write the full model as

$$
\begin{aligned}
\mathbf{y} &= \mathbf{XH}\boldsymbol{\alpha} + \boldsymbol{\varepsilon} \\
&= \mathbf{Z}\boldsymbol{\alpha} + \boldsymbol{\varepsilon}.
\end{aligned}
\tag{18–15}
$$

In this formulation, the model can be estimated by OLS or FGLS if the disturbances are autocorrelated. Once again, this is a classical regression model, so no new tools are required. After

$$
\hat{\boldsymbol{\alpha}} = [\mathbf{Z}'\mathbf{Z}]^{-1}\mathbf{Z}'\mathbf{y}
\tag{18–16}
$$

has been computed, estimates of the distributed lag coefficients may be recovered using

$$
\hat{\boldsymbol{\beta}} = \mathbf{H}\hat{\boldsymbol{\alpha}}.
\tag{18–17}
$$

Asymptotic standard errors may be obtained using

$$
\hat{\mathrm{Var}}[\hat{\boldsymbol{\beta}}] = \mathbf{H}\{\hat{\mathrm{Var}}[\hat{\boldsymbol{\alpha}}]\}\mathbf{H}' = s^2\mathbf{H}[\mathbf{Z}'\mathbf{Z}]^{-1}\mathbf{H}'.
\tag{18–18}
$$

It is suggested occasionally that the lag distribution should be "tied down" at its endpoints by imposing $\beta_{-1} = 0$ and $\beta_{q+1} = 0$.[12] Normally, it is inadvisable to impose these restrictions. The model does not pertain to the coefficients outside the interval

---

[12]The implied restrictions are
$$
\beta_{-1} = \alpha_0 - \alpha_1 + \alpha_2 - \cdots = 0
$$
and
$$
\beta_{q+1} = \alpha_0 + \alpha_1(q + 1) + \alpha_2(q + 1)^2 + \cdots = 0.
$$

$[0, \ldots, q]$, so the restrictions are not justifiable on theoretical grounds. But, more important, the endpoint restrictions will constrain all the coefficients in the model, not just the head and tail, in ways that might not be desirable.[13]

EXAMPLE 18.3 Polynomial Distributed Lag Models

In her pioneering study, Almon (1965) estimated a polynomial lag model for the relationship between appropriations and capital expenditure for "all manufacturing" and a large number of specific industries. The aggregate data used for this study are listed in Table 18.4.[14]

TABLE 18.4 Capital Appropriations Data (Millions of Dollars)

	Expenditures				Appropriations			
	I	**II**	**III**	**IV**	**I**	**II**	**III**	**IV**
1953	2072	2077	2078	2043	1660	1926	2181	1897
1954	2062	2067	1964	1981	1695	1705	1731	2151
1955	1914	1991	2129	2309	2556	3152	3763	3903
1956	2614	2896	3058	3309	3912	3571	3199	3262
1957	3446	3466	3435	3183	3476	2993	2262	2011
1958	2697	2338	2140	2012	1511	1631	1990	1993
1959	2071	2192	2240	2421	2520	2804	2919	3024
1960	2639	2733	2721	2640	2725	2321	2131	2552
1961	2513	2448	2429	2516	2234	2282	2533	2517

Almon's regressions were computed using a fourth-order polynomial and lags extending back for seven periods. She also included seasonal dummy variables whose four coefficients were constrained to sum to zero and imposed both endpoint restrictions noted earlier. The results of several regressions are reported in Table 18.5.[15] The maximum likelihood estimates were obtained using Beach and MacKinnon's (1978) method for AR(1) disturbances. For brevity, only the overall test statistics are reported.

Note the similarity of the polynomial lag coefficients to the unrestricted least-squares estimates. The F test of the restrictions implied by the polynomial model is far from significant by any standard. (There are three restrictions in the lag model and two additional restrictions for the endpoint constraints.) Figure 18.3 shows the three lag distributions estimated by least squares. In principle, the sum of the lag coefficients should be 1 if all appropriations ultimately become expenditures within the length of time of the longest lag. Our results come quite close to this. (Almon's estimate of the long-run multiplier for this model was 0.922. She attributed the discrepancy to cancellations of past appropriations.)

---

[13] See Schmidt and Waud (1973).

[14] The original study used quarterly data for 1953 to 1961. Longer series (through 1967) for the same variables may be found in Maddala (1977, p. 370) and Judge et al. (1982, p. 734) (through 1974). Those wishing to extend these results to more recent data sets might consider these sources and the original, National Industrial Conference Board, "Survey of Capital Appropriations," *Conference Board Business Record*, various years.

[15] The OLS results for the polynomial lag with $\beta_{-1} = \beta_8 = 0$ do not match those reported by Almon. It was not possible to reproduce her results with these data.

TABLE 18.5 Polynomial Distributed Lag Models

	Unrestricted Model		Polynomial Lag		Polynomial Lag with $\beta_{-1} = \beta_8 = 0$	
	OLS	**MLE**	**OLS**	**MLE**	**OLS**	**MLE**
Qtr.I	−2.97	1.01	−6.98	−5.95	−13.30	−7.96
Qtr.II	−5.54	−.51	−8.76	−3.00	−7.02	−3.36
Qtr.III	−23.31	−14.81	−15.70	−6.41	−7.63	−4.16
Qtr.IV	31.84	14.31	31.44	15.36	27.95	15.48
$t - 0$	0.040	0.065	0.027	0.059	0.087	0.090
$t - 1$	0.110	0.090	0.144	0.131	0.123	0.133
$t - 2$	0.189	0.199	0.182	0.169	0.134	0.147
$t - 3$	0.223	0.218	0.165	0.170	0.137	0.148
$t - 4$	0.070	0.092	0.122	0.141	0.139	0.143
$t - 5$	0.064	0.074	0.085	0.102	0.139	0.134
$t - 6$	0.139	0.140	0.088	0.085	0.129	0.115
$t - 7$	0.146	0.113	0.168	0.133	0.092	0.076
Sum	0.981	0.991	0.981	0.990	0.980	0.986
R^2	0.9189	—	0.9177	—	0.9142	—
$F[q - p, 27]$			0.1331		0.3129	
D–W	0.406	—	0.445	—	0.445	—
ln L	—	−168.22	—	−169.49	—	−169.87

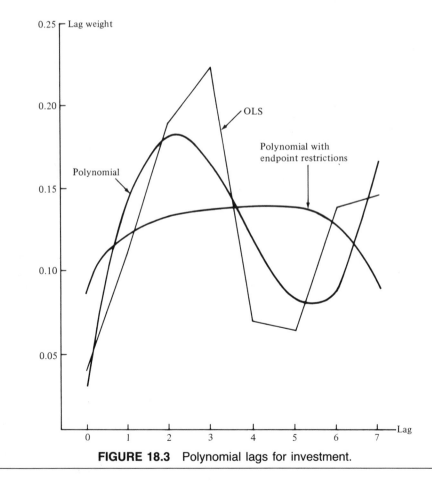

FIGURE 18.3 Polynomial lags for investment.

18.4.1. Estimation by Restricted Least Squares

If there are q lags in the model, the polynomial lag model imposes $q - p$ constraints on the parameters. A pth-order polynomial lag structure implies the constraints

$$(1 - L)^{p+1}\beta_i = 0.^{16}$$

For example, for a third-order polynomial, the restrictions would be

$$\beta_0 - 4\beta_1 + 6\beta_2 - 4\beta_3 + \beta_4 = 0,$$

$$\beta_1 - 4\beta_2 + 6\beta_3 - 4\beta_4 + \beta_5 = 0,$$

and so on. Thus the polynomial distributed lag model can also be estimated using constrained least squares. Ignoring for the moment any other parameters (such as the constant term) that might appear in the model, the restrictions of the polynomial lag model may be written in the form

$$\mathbf{R}\beta = \mathbf{0}.$$

The elements in $\mathbf{R}$ can be obtained from Pascal's triangle,

$$
\begin{array}{ccccccccc}
 & & & & 1 & & & & \\
 & & & 1 & & -1 & & & \\
 & & 1 & & -2 & & 1 & & \\
 & 1 & & -3 & & 3 & & -1 & \\
1 & & -4 & & 6 & & -4 & & 1 \\
 & & & & \vdots & & & &
\end{array}
$$

and so on. Each value is the sum of the two nearest values above it, while the signs in each row alternate beginning with positive. For a pth-order polynomial, the relevant row is the $(p + 1)$st. Then the $(q - p) \times (q + 1)$ matrix for the restrictions is

$$\mathbf{R} = \begin{bmatrix} \mathbf{r}' & 0 & 0 & \cdots & 0 \\ 0 & \mathbf{r}' & 0 & \cdots & \\ & & \vdots & & \\ 0 & 0 & 0 & \cdots & \mathbf{r}' \end{bmatrix},^{17}$$

where $\mathbf{r}'$ is the appropriate row from Pascal's triangle.

There are two practical advantages to this approach. First, if the maximum lag length is known, the entire analysis of the polynomial lags may be based on the single unrestricted regression involving the full set of lagged variables. Second, considerable rounding error can accumulate in calculation of the "scrambled variables" in (18–13), while the restricted regression is computed with the full precision of least squares. In a relatively low order polynomial, the problem will be insignificant. But for higher-order models, particularly if the data are highly collinear, the differences can be quite large.[18]

18.4.2. Determining the Degree of the Polynomial

If the appropriate lag length, q, is known, determining the right degree for the polynomial becomes a problem of testing nested hypotheses. It helps to note, first, that if we use a q-degree polynomial when the maximum lag is q, then $\mathbf{H}$ is square, and we simply have

---

[16] See, for example, Fomby et al. (1984, pp. 375–377).

[17] If there are additional variables in the model, $\mathbf{R}$ will contain corresponding columns of zeros.

[18] See Cooper (1972).

$\alpha = H^{-1}\beta$. As a consequence, the $q + 1$ OLS estimates (including the coefficient on x_t) will fit exactly on the qth-order polynomial. The polynomial lag model thus places no restrictions on the coefficients. Successively lower-order polynomials do impose restrictions. A sequential testing procedure may be used by beginning with a high-order polynomial, say p^*—absent any knowledge about p^*, we might use $p^* = q$—and reducing its degree by one in successive regressions.[19] At each step, the F statistic for testing a polynomial of degree p against one of degree p^* is

$$F[p^* - p, T - p^* - 1] = \frac{[e'e\,|p - e'e|\,p^*]/(p^* - p)}{e'e|p^*/(T - p^* - 1)}. \tag{18-19}$$

The denominator degrees of freedom is reduced if there are other coefficients, such as a constant term, in the model. The appropriate degree of the polynomial is assumed to be the lowest p for which the statistic in (18–19) is less than the appropriate critical value from the F table. It must be remembered, though, that at each step except the first, the true significance level differs from the nominal one because of the probability of a type 2 error at the previous step. Trivedi and Pagan[20] suggest that the appropriate significance level at the jth step is

$$\alpha_j' = 1 - (1 - \alpha_1)(1 - \alpha_2) \cdots (1 - \alpha_j). \tag{18-20}$$

If, as would be common, the same nominal significance level is used at each step, the true significance level would be

$$\alpha_j' = 1 - (1 - \alpha)^j.$$

For example, at the usual 5 percent significance level, we would have 5 percent, 9.75 percent, 14.26 percent, and so on, for the sequential tests. The practical implication is that at successively lower levels, we should require progressively higher F statistics to reject the restrictions at the same true significance level.

18.4.3. Determining the Lag Length

If the lag length is unknown, the problem of inference is compounded.[21] One possible procedure would be first to determine the lag length using the OLS or GLS estimates and the procedures described in the preceding section. Once the maximum lag is determined, we may then employ the method just described to determine the appropriate degree of the polynomial. Unfortunately, unless the test statistics are overwhelming, a large amount of caution must be exercised. The true significance levels in these tests remains to be derived, and the true distribution of the resulting estimator is unknown.

There has been extensive analysis of the consequences of misspecifying the lag length and order of the polynomial in the polynomial lag model. The generalities are what intuition would suggest. Assuming that there is a true polynomial and lag length, fitting a polynomial of insufficient order is equivalent to imposing invalid restrictions.[22] Overfitting the polynomial would lead only to inefficiency, since if the lag coefficients lie on a polynomial of order p, they will also lie on one of order $p + 1$, $p + 2$, and so on. The consequences of misspecifying the lag length are somewhat more complicated. Underesti-

---

[19] See Godfrey and Poskitt (1975).

[20] Trivedi and Pagan (1979).

[21] Frost (1975).

[22] This assumption may be a bit optimistic. See Schmidt and Sickles (1975).

mating the lag length leads to the familiar results. However, overfitting the lag may not be so harmless here. In an unrestricted model, the zero coefficients on superfluous variables would be consistently estimated by least squares. However, if we force the coefficients to lie on a polynomial, the restriction may force a coefficient that is truly zero to be nonzero in the model.[23]

18.5. The Geometric Lag Model

Estimation of the unrestricted model of (18–10) will be difficult at best. The polynomial lag model reduces the problem, but it has some troubling limitations. Finding the right degree for the polynomial and the appropriate lag length presents difficult inference problems. The infinite lag model is often preferable, but obviously, some restrictions have to be placed on the parameters in order to make it estimable. These considerations have led researchers to formulate compact parametric models that allow infinite lags, but require only a small number of parameters.

The similarity of the lag weights in a distributed lag model [see (18–3)] to discrete probabilities has suggested a number of formulations. The geometric lag model,

$$w_i = (1 - \lambda)\lambda^i, \qquad 0 \le \lambda < 1, \tag{18–21}$$

and the Gamma lag model,[24]

$$w_i = (i + 1)^\gamma \lambda^i, \qquad 0 \le \lambda < 1, \quad 0 < \gamma < 1, \tag{18–22}$$

shown in Figure 18.4 are two examples of infinite lag models. Both models incorporate infinite lags but assign arbitrarily small weights to the distant past. The geometric lag model is by far the most popular distributed lag model in the empirical literature, so we will examine it in detail.

---

[23] See, for example, Schmidt and Waud (1973), Trivedi and Pagan (1979), Hendry et al. (1984), and Schmidt and Sickles (1975) for extensive discussion.

[24] Tsurumi (1971), Theil and Stern (1960), and Schmidt (1974).

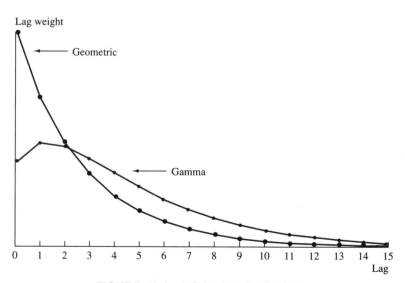

FIGURE 18.4   Infinite lag distributions.

The geometric lag model is

$$\beta_i = \beta(1 - \lambda)\lambda^i. \tag{18-23}$$

Thus

$$y_t = \alpha + \beta \sum_{i=0}^{\infty} (1 - \lambda)\lambda^i x_{t-i} + \varepsilon_t. \tag{18-24}$$

The polynomial in the lag operator in this model would be

$$B(L) = (1 - \lambda)(1 + \lambda L + \lambda^2 L^2 + \lambda^3 L^3 + \cdots). \tag{18-25}$$

This is an infinite series, so there is some question as to whether it will converge or not. If $|\lambda| < 1$, we may write (18–25) as

$$B(L) = \frac{(1 - \lambda)}{1 - \lambda L}.$$

The mean lag is

$$\overline{w} = \frac{B'(1)}{B(1)}$$

$$= \frac{\lambda}{1 - \lambda}. \tag{18-26}$$

The median lag is q^* such that

$$\sum_{i=0}^{q^*-1} w_i = 0.5. \tag{18-27}$$

We can solve for q^* by using the result that

$$\sum_{i=0}^{q} \lambda^i = \frac{1 - \lambda^{q+1}}{1 - \lambda}.$$

Thus

$$q^* = \frac{\ln 0.5}{\ln \lambda}.$$

The impact multiplier is $\beta(1 - \lambda)$. The long-run multiplier is

$$\beta(1 - \lambda) \sum_{i=0}^{\infty} \lambda^i = \beta.$$

As in (18–2), the equilibrium value of y_t would be obtained by fixing x_t at $\overline{x}$ in (18–24). Thus

$$\overline{y} = \alpha + \beta\overline{x}. \tag{18-28}$$

18.5.1. Economic Models with Geometric Lags

There are many cases in which the distributed lag is a model of the accumulation of information. The formation of expectations is an example. In these instances, intuition suggests that the most recent past will receive the greatest weight in the process, and the influence of past observations will fade uniformly with the passage of time. The geometric lag model is a commonly used tool for these settings.

Initially, the model was associated with Koyck's (1954) study of investment. It also arises naturally in two familiar economic frameworks: models of expectations and models of partial adjustment. The **adaptive expectations** model consists of a regression equation,

$$y_t = \alpha + \beta x_t^* + \varepsilon_t \tag{18-29}$$

in the expectations variable, x_t^*, and a mechanism for the formation of the expectation based on the current observation, x_t;

$$x_t^* - x_{t-1}^* = (1 - \lambda)(x_t - x_{t-1}^*). \tag{18-30}$$

One example is a demand equation based on an expected price. The expectation would be revised after observing the current outcome. A more intuitively appealing, equivalent form might be

$$x_t^* = \lambda x_{t-1}^* + (1 - \lambda)x_t. \tag{18-31}$$

Thus the currently formed expectation is a weighted average of the previous expectation and the most recent observation. The parameter λ is the adjustment coefficient. If λ equals 1, the current datum is ignored and expectations are never revised. A value of zero characterizes a strict pragmatist. The model can be "solved" by writing (18–31) as

$$x_t^* = \lambda L x_t^* + (1 - \lambda)x_t$$

or

$$
\begin{aligned}
x_t^* &= \frac{1 - \lambda}{1 - \lambda L} x_t \\
&= (1 - \lambda)[x_t + \lambda x_{t-1} + \lambda^2 x_{t-2} + \cdots].
\end{aligned}
\tag{18-32}
$$

Inserting (18–32) in (18–29) leads to a regression with geometrically declining weights,

$$y_t = \alpha + \beta(1 - \lambda)[x_t + \lambda x_{t-1} + \lambda^2 x_{t-2} + \cdots] + \varepsilon_t. \tag{18-33}$$

(In this form, it would probably provide a suitable model for Example 18.1.)

It may be reasonable to treat ε_t in (18–33) as a spherical, serially independent disturbance, which makes (18–33) a classical regression. If, instead, ε_t is autocorrelated, it will be necessary to adapt a method of FGLS. In either case, the primary obstacle to estimation will be the infinite number of regressors.

The model in (18–33) is called the **moving average (MA)** form. It is also called the **distributed lag** form. The **autoregressive (AR)** form is an alternative that is often useful. We insert (18–32) in (18–29) to obtain

$$y_t = \alpha + \beta \left[\frac{1 - \lambda}{1 - \lambda L} \right] x_t + \varepsilon_t,$$

multiply through by $(1 - \lambda L)$, and collect terms in

$$y_t = \alpha(1 - \lambda) + \lambda y_{t-1} + \beta(1 - \lambda)x_t + (\varepsilon_t - \lambda \varepsilon_{t-1}). \tag{18-34}$$

The autoregressive form is commonly used in demand equations. If the variables are in logarithms, the short-run elasticity is $\beta(1 - \lambda)$ and the long-run elasticity is β. But for the (serious) complication of a lagged dependent variable appearing with an autocorrelated disturbance, the parameters could be estimated by OLS or two-step GLS. Unfortunately, without some special assumptions, neither of these methods will provide consistent estimates.

The primary equation of the **partial adjustment** model describes the *desired* level of y_t:

$$y_t^* = \alpha + \beta x_t. \tag{18-35}$$

For example, this might describe a rule for the optimal inventory level as a function of sales. The adjustment of the actual level is a proportion of the difference between this period's desired level and last period's actual level:

$$y_t - y_{t-1} = (1 - \lambda)(y_t^* - y_{t-1}) + \varepsilon_t. \tag{18-36}$$

In the alternative form,

$$y_t = (1 - \lambda)y_t^* + \lambda y_{t-1} + \varepsilon_t,$$

the actual current level is a weighted average of the desired level and last period's actual level. The adjustment parameter reflects the degree to which the input variable, x_t, will be incorporated in y_t. To continue the example, $\lambda = 0$ would reflect a fixed-inventory policy, while $\lambda = 1$ would make desired inventory a function only of current sales.

Inserting (18–35) in (18–36) and rearranging terms produces the autoregressive form,

$$y_t = \alpha(1 - \lambda) + \lambda y_{t-1} + \beta(1 - \lambda)x_t + \varepsilon_t. \tag{18-37}$$

[Note the similarity to (18–34).] Alternatively, we may write (18–37) as

$$y_t(1 - \lambda L) = \alpha(1 - \lambda) + \beta(1 - \lambda)x_t + \varepsilon_t.$$

Dividing both sides by $(1 - \lambda L)$ and expanding produces the moving average form,

$$y_t = \alpha + \beta(1 - \lambda) \sum_{i=0}^{\infty} \lambda^i x_{t-i} + \sum_{i=0}^{\infty} \lambda^i \varepsilon_{t-i}. \tag{18-38}$$

The infinite moving average disturbance can be written as u_t, where

$$u_t = \lambda u_{t-1} + \varepsilon_t. \tag{18-39}$$

Therefore, the moving average form of the partial adjustment model has an AR(1) disturbance with the same parameter as the lag weights. Note again that apart from the disturbance, the MA form of the partial adjustment model in (18–38) is the same as that of the adaptive expectations model in (18–33).

18.5.2. Stochastic Specifications in the Geometric Lag Models

The most efficient means of estimating the parameters of the geometric lag model will depend on the stochastic specification of the structural disturbance, ε_t. Two possibilities are usually considered:

1. *White noise:* ε_t is homoscedastic and not autocorrelated.
2. *AR(1):* $\varepsilon_t = \rho \varepsilon_{t-1} + u_t$, where u_t is white noise.

There are, of course, any number of other possibilities, but these two dominate the applications.

The model can be estimated in either the moving average or the autoregressive form. Estimation of the autoregressive form is usually simpler, since it involves a linear regression. On the other hand, estimation of the moving average form will, in general, be preferable because it is more robust to misspecification of autocorrelation of the disturbance.[25] This might provide a useful test of the specification, since we should obtain the

---

[25] See Maddala and Rao (1971).

same estimates either way, apart from sampling variation. The best estimation method depends on which form is estimated and whether or not the disturbances are autocorrelated. For the MA form of the model, we shall use nonlinear least squares. The best estimator for the AR forms of the models is instrumental variables. In each case, a correction may be needed to accommodate autocorrelation.

18.5.3. Estimating the Moving Average Form of the Geometric Lag Model

The MA form of the geometric lag model is most convenient for the adaptive expectations model. If ε_t in (18–29) is white noise, the resulting MA form in (18–33) is a classical regression model (apart from its infinite number of regressors). Similarly, if ε_t in (18–29) is autocorrelated, (18–33) can, in principle, be estimated using the methods described in Chapter 15. We consider these two possibilities in turn with reference to the adaptive expectations model. We shall then consider the partial adjustment model.

18.5.3a. Uncorrelated Disturbances. We may write (18–24) as

$$
\begin{aligned}
y_t &= \alpha + \beta(1 - \lambda) \sum_{i=0}^{\infty} \lambda^i x_{t-i} + \varepsilon_t \\
&= \alpha + \beta(1 - \lambda)(x_t + \lambda x_{t-1} + \cdots + \lambda^{t-1} x_1) \\
&\quad + \beta(1 - \lambda)\lambda^t(x_0 + \lambda x_{-1} + \cdots) + \varepsilon_t.
\end{aligned}
\tag{18–40}
$$

The third term is

$$
\mu^0 = E[y_0 - \alpha].
$$

If we treat this *truncation remainder* as an unknown parameter, the model becomes

$$
y_t = \alpha + \beta(1 - \lambda)x_t^* + \lambda^t \mu^0 + \varepsilon_t,
$$

where

$$
x_t^* = x_t + \lambda x_{t-1} + \cdots + \lambda^{t-1} x_1.
\tag{18–41}
$$

The log likelihood for normally distributed disturbances in this nonlinear regression model is

$$
\ln L(\alpha, \beta, \lambda, \mu^0, \sigma_\varepsilon^2) = -\frac{T}{2}[\ln(2\pi) + \ln \sigma_\varepsilon^2] - \frac{1}{2\sigma_\varepsilon^2} \sum_t \varepsilon_t^2,
\tag{18–42}
$$

where

$$
\varepsilon_t = y_t - \alpha - \beta(1 - \lambda)x_t^* - \mu^0 \lambda^t.
$$

Maximum likelihood estimates can be obtained by nonlinear least squares.[26] The maximum likelihood estimator of σ_ε^2 is the familiar one,

$$
\hat{\sigma}_\varepsilon^2 = \frac{1}{T} \sum_t \hat{\varepsilon}_t^2.
\tag{18–43}
$$

[26] See Dhrymes (1969). Without normality, the nonlinear least squares estimator would remain consistent but might not be efficient. One difference would be that the asymptotic variance of the estimator of σ_ε^2 might not be $2\sigma_\varepsilon^4/T$. Instead of $2s^4/T$, we could use $(1/T^2)\Sigma_t(e_t^2 - s^2)^2$. (See Section 4.6.2.) The rest of the asymptotic covariance matrix in (19–45) is the same as (11–13) for the nonlinear least squares estimator.

For a given value of λ, estimates of α, $\theta = \beta(1 - \lambda)$, and μ^0 can be obtained by a *linear* regression of y_t on a constant, x_t^*, and λ^t. Since λ is between zero and 1, the estimates can be computed by searching over values of λ between zero and 1 and choosing as the set of estimates those associated with the value of λ that produces the smallest sum of squared residuals. In practice, x_t^* may be computed by the recursion

$$x_1^* = x_1$$
$$x_t^* = x_t + \lambda x_{t-1}^*, \qquad t = 2, \ldots, T. \tag{18-44}$$

The estimates of the standard errors of the parameters may be based on the inverse of the information matrix,

$$\mathbf{I}(\alpha, \theta, \mu^0, \lambda, \sigma_\varepsilon^2) = \frac{1}{\sigma_\varepsilon^2} \begin{bmatrix} T \\ \Sigma_t x_t^* & \Sigma_t x_t^{*2} \\ \Sigma_t \lambda^t & \Sigma_t \lambda^t x_t^* & \Sigma_t (\lambda^t)^2 \\ \Sigma_t \Delta_t & \Sigma_t \Delta_t x_t^* & \Sigma_t \Delta_t \lambda^t & \Sigma_t \Delta_t^2 \\ 0 & 0 & 0 & 0 & T/(2\sigma_\varepsilon^2) \end{bmatrix}, \tag{18-45}$$

where

$$\Delta_t = \frac{\partial(\theta x_t^* + \mu^0 \lambda^t)}{\partial \lambda} \tag{18-46}$$
$$= \theta \frac{\partial x_t^*}{\partial \lambda} + \mu^0 t \lambda^{t-1}.$$

The sample values of $\partial x_t^*/\partial \lambda$ may also be computed by a recursion. Using (18–44), we obtain

$$\frac{\partial x_1^*}{\partial \lambda} = 0$$
$$\frac{\partial x_2^*}{\partial \lambda} = x_1 \tag{18-47}$$

and

$$\frac{\partial x_t^*}{\partial \lambda} = \lambda \frac{\partial x_{t-1}^*}{\partial \lambda} + x_{t-1}^*, \qquad t = 3, \ldots, T. \tag{18-48}$$

Finally,

$$\hat{\beta} = \frac{\hat{\theta}}{1 - \hat{\lambda}}. \tag{18-49}$$

The asymptotic standard error of this estimate may be estimated with

$$\widehat{\mathrm{Var}}[\hat{\beta}] \approx \left(\frac{\partial \hat{\beta}}{\partial \hat{\theta}}\right)^2 \widehat{\mathrm{Var}}[\hat{\theta}] + \left(\frac{\partial \hat{\beta}}{\partial \hat{\lambda}}\right)^2 \widehat{\mathrm{Var}}[\hat{\lambda}] + 2\left(\frac{\partial \hat{\beta}}{\partial \hat{\theta}}\right)\left(\frac{\partial \hat{\beta}}{\partial \hat{\lambda}}\right) \widehat{\mathrm{Cov}}[\hat{\theta}, \hat{\lambda}].[27] \tag{18-50}$$

There is a question as to whether one need even bother with the truncation remainder. Asymptotically, it makes no difference. As $T \to \infty$, the column of values λ^t will be

---

[27] See Section 4.4.4 and Theorem 4.5.

predominately zeros.[28] Nonetheless, there is some evidence that it can make a considerable difference in a small sample. The available results suggest that it is better to keep the truncation remainder than to omit it.[29]

18.5.3b. Autocorrelated Disturbances. If the disturbance in (18–24) is autocorrelated, with

$$\varepsilon_t = \rho \varepsilon_{t-1} + u_t,$$

the preceding may be applied to the transformed model,

$$[y_t - \rho y_{t-1}] = \alpha(1 - \rho) + \theta[x_t^* - \rho x_{t-1}^*] + \mu^0[\lambda^t - \rho\lambda^{t-1}] + [\varepsilon_t - \rho\varepsilon_{t-1}].$$
$$(18\text{–}51)$$

For a given value of ρ, we would use the method of the earlier paragraphs. A method for finding the full set of parameters would be a two-dimensional search over values of λ from zero to 1 and over ρ from -1 to 1. The pair that with the associated least squares estimates of the other parameters produces the smallest sum of squared deviations gives the maximum likelihood estimates.[30] The inverse of the information matrix provides an estimate of the asymptotic covariance matrix of the estimates. In (18–52), the operator δ is used to indicate the partial difference, as in $\delta x_t^* = x_t^* - \rho x_{t-1}^*$. The information matrix is

$$
\mathbf{I}\begin{bmatrix} \alpha \\ \theta \\ \mu^0 \\ \lambda \\ \sigma_\varepsilon^2 \\ \rho \end{bmatrix} = \frac{1}{\sigma_u^2}\begin{bmatrix} T(1-\rho) \\ \Sigma_t\, \delta x_t^* & \Sigma_t(\delta x_t^*)^2 \\ \Sigma_t\, \delta\lambda^t & \Sigma_t\, \delta\lambda^t\delta x_t^* & \Sigma_t(\delta\lambda^t)^2 \\ \Sigma_t\, \delta\Delta_t & \Sigma_t\, \delta\Delta_t\, \delta x_t^* & \Sigma_t\, \delta\Delta_t\delta\lambda^t & \Sigma_t(\delta\Delta_t)^2 \\ 0 & 0 & 0 & 0 & T/(2\sigma_u^2) \\ 0 & 0 & 0 & 0 & 0 & T\sigma_u^2/(1-\rho^2) \end{bmatrix}
$$
$$(18\text{–}52)$$

EXAMPLE 18.4 Consumption Function

In a widely cited study, Zellner and Geisel (1970) applied the foregoing results to estimation of a consumption function,

$$C_t = \beta Y_t^* + \varepsilon_t$$

where C_t is consumption and Y_t^* is normal real income. Normal income satisfies the adjustment model,

$$Y_t^* = (1 - \lambda)Y_t + \lambda Y_{t-1}^*.$$

From (18–32), we obtain

$$Y_t^* = (1 - \lambda)(Y_t + \lambda Y_{t-1} + \lambda^2 Y_{t-2} + \cdots),$$

which, when inserted in the consumption function, produces the geometric lag model. This differs from the earlier treatment in the absence of a constant term. The authors estimated the model using quarterly data on U.S. consumption and disposable personal income for the years 1947 to 1960.[31] In this example we reestimate the model using more

---

[28] Consequently, $\hat{\mu}^0$ is not consistent.

[29] See, Schmidt (1975), Pesaran (1973), and Maddala and Rao (1971).

[30] This analysis is conditioned on the first observation. See Chapter 15 for an analysis of the unconditional approach.

[31] Their data are listed in Griliches et al. (1962).

TABLE 18.6 Consumption and Income Data

	Consumption				Disposable Income			
	I	**II**	**III**	**IV**	**I**	**II**	**III**	**IV**
1953	362.8	364.6	363.6	362.6	395.5	401.0	399.7	400.2
1954	363.5	366.2	371.8	378.6	399.7	397.3	403.8	411.8
1955	385.2	392.2	396.4	402.6	414.7	423.8	430.8	437.6
1956	403.2	403.9	405.1	409.3	441.2	444.7	446.6	452.7
1957	411.7	412.4	415.2	416.0	452.6	455.4	457.9	456.0
1958	411.0	414.7	420.9	425.2	452.1	455.1	464.6	471.3
1959	424.1	439.7	443.3	444.6	474.5	482.2	479.0	483.1
1960	448.1	454.1	452.7	453.2	487.8	490.7	491.0	488.8
1961	454.0	459.9	461.4	470.3	493.4	500.7	505.5	514.8
1962	474.5	479.8	483.7	490.0	519.5	523.9	526.7	529.0
1963	493.1	497.4	503.9	507.5	533.3	538.9	544.4	552.5
1964	516.6	525.6	534.3	535.3	563.6	579.4	586.4	593.0
1965	546.0	550.7	559.2	573.9	599.7	607.8	623.6	634.6
1966	581.2	582.3	588.6	590.5	639.7	642.0	649.2	700.7
1967	594.8	602.4	605.2	608.2	665.0	671.3	676.5	682.0
1968	620.7	629.9	642.3	644.7	690.4	701.9	703.6	708.7
1969	651.9	656.2	659.6	663.9	710.4	717.0	730.1	733.2
1970	667.4	670.5	676.5	673.9	737.1	752.6	759.7	756.1
1971	687.0	693.3	698.2	708.6	771.3	779.7	781.0	785.5
1972	718.6	731.1	741.3	757.1	791.7	798.5	842.2	838.1
1973	768.8	766.3	769.7	766.7	855.0	862.1	868.0	873.4
1974	761.2	764.1	769.4	756.5	859.9	859.7	859.7	851.1
1975	763.3	775.6	785.4	793.3	845.1	891.3	878.4	884.9
1976	809.9	817.1	826.5	838.9	899.3	904.1	908.8	914.9
1977	851.7	858.0	867.3	880.4	919.6	934.1	951.9	965.9
1978	883.8	901.1	908.6	919.2	973.5	982.6	994.2	1005.0
1979	921.2	919.5	930.9	938.6	1011.1	1011.8	1019.7	1020.2
1980	938.3	919.6	929.4	940.0	1025.9	1011.8	1019.3	1030.2
1981	950.2	949.1	955.7	946.8	1044.0	1041.0	1058.4	1056.0
1982	953.7	958.9	964.2	976.3	1052.8	1054.7	1057.7	1067.5
1983	982.5	1006.2	1015.6	1032.4	1073.3	1082.2	1102.1	1124.4
1984	1044.1	1064.2	1065.9	1075.4	1147.8	1165.3	1176.7	1186.9

Source: Data from the National Income and Product Accounts, U.S. Department of Commerce, Bureau of Economic Analysis, *Survey of Current Business: Business Statistics, 1984,* Washington, D.C., 1984, pp. 205, 212, and 221. The data are normalized to 1972 dollars, using the implicit price deflator for personal consumption.

recent data and then compare our results to those of Zellner and Geisel. Table 18.6 lists quarterly data for real consumption and real disposable income for the years 1953 to 1984.

For the model with uncorrelated disturbances, the search over the values of λ produced the results shown in Table 18.7. The global minimum occurs at $\lambda = 0.25$. The full set of results based on $\hat{\lambda} = 0.25$ is shown in Table 18.8. It is useful to compare the implied lag coefficients to those obtained by unrestricted OLS. For the first three periods, the OLS estimates are 0.668, 0.203, and 0.037.[32] The corresponding values for the geometric lag model are $\beta(1 - \lambda) = 0.862$, $\beta(1 - \lambda)\lambda = 0.171$, and $\beta(1 - \lambda)\lambda^2 = 0.043$.

In their study, Zellner and Geisel found two minima of the sum of squares function, a local minimum at $[\lambda, \beta] = [0.45, 0.937]$ and the global minimum at $[0.96, 1.129]$. The

---

[32] After three periods, the OLS estimates become small and negative.

TABLE 18.7

λ	$e'e$	$\beta(1 - \lambda)$	μ^0	λ	$e'e$	$\beta(1 - \lambda)$	μ^0
0.05	11,284	0.86191	438.37	0.40	11,180	0.54718	365.48
0.10	11,114	0.81695	397.38	0.45	11,428	0.50222	364.05
0.15	10,991	0.77199	383.62	0.50	11,775	0.45725	362.85
0.20	10,915	0.72703	376.64	0.55	12,240	0.41228	361.83
0.21	10,906	0.71804	375.63	0.60	12,850	0.36730	360.97
0.22	10,899	0.70905	374.71	0.65	13,632	0.32231	360.28
0.23	10,894	0.70006	373.86	0.70	14,623	0.27732	359.78
0.24	10,891	0.69105	373.08	0.75	15,856	0.23232	359.48
0.25	10,890	0.68207	372.36	0.80	17,380	0.18732	359.36
0.26	10,892	0.67308	371.69	0.85	19,324	0.14232	359.32
0.30	10,922	0.63711	369.41	0.90	22,375	0.09736	359.14
0.35	11,015	0.59215	367.21	0.95	30,033	0.05252	359.31

TABLE 18.8

Parameter	Estimate	Standard Error
β	0.9094	0.00369
λ	0.25	0.0901
μ^0	364.13	36.33
σ_ε^2	85.08	7.52
$\lambda/(1 - \lambda)$	0.3333	0.1602

optimal value of β is implausible on theoretical grounds. The authors attributed the result to possible inadequacies of the model or the data. With the more recent data, $\hat{\beta}$ is between zero and 1 as expected and the likelihood function has a single maximum. The Durbin–Watson statistic based on the nonlinear least squares residuals is 0.5960. While the Durbin–Watson tables are not quite appropriate because this is not a linear regression model with nonstochastic regressors, a value this small is nonetheless compelling. The estimated autocorrelation given in Table 18.9 is 0.87. Zellner and Geisel's estimate of the same parameter is 0.69. Thus there is considerable evidence of autocorrelation in both data sets.

A two-dimensional search over λ and ρ produced the results shown in Table 18.9; we present both our results and those of Zellner and Geisel for comparison. The estimate of σ_ε^2 is $\hat{\sigma}_u^2/(1 - \hat{\rho}^2)$. The standard errors for σ_ε^2 and $\hat{\lambda}/(1 - \hat{\lambda})$ are estimated using the formula for the variance of a nonlinear function. Note the similarity of the estimates of λ and β for the two data sets.

TABLE 18.9

Parameter	Estimate	Std. Error	Zellner and Geisel Estimate	Zellner and Geisel Std. Error
λ	0.64	0.0080	0.66	0.085
β	0.9205	0.0451	0.94	0.46
μ^0	368.31	30.54	—	—
σ_u^2	26.58	2.359	8.07	—
ρ	0.87	0.044	0.69	0.076
σ_ε^2	110.24	16.24	—	—
$\lambda/(1 - \lambda)$	1.78	0.062	1.94	0.735

18.5.3c. Estimating the MA Form of the Partial Adjustment Model. The MA form of the partial adjustment model given in (18–38) and (18–39) is exactly the second case we looked at in (18–51) with the additional restriction that $\rho = \lambda$. Let us see what becomes of the nonlinear least squares estimator if we impose this restriction. Referring to (18–51), it is immediately apparent that the truncation remainder vanishes. In addition, in (18–44), if $\lambda = \rho$, then $(x_t^* - \rho x_{t-1}^*)$ equals x_t. This implies that the estimating equation (18–51) is

$$y_t - \lambda y_{t-1} = \alpha(1 - \lambda) + \theta x_t + u_t$$

or

$$y_t = \alpha(1 - \lambda) + \beta(1 - \lambda)x_t + \lambda y_{t-1} + u_t. \qquad (18\text{–}51')$$

Therefore, in the partial adjustment model with uncorrelated disturbances, efficient estimates of $\alpha(1 - \lambda)$, $\beta(1 - \lambda)$, and λ are obtained by linear least squares regression of y_t on a constant, x_t, and y_{t-1}. The results of Section 10.4 apply directly.

18.5.4. Estimating the Autoregressive Form of the Geometric Lag Model

The autoregressive model is

$$y_t = \alpha(1 - \lambda) + \beta(1 - \lambda)x_t + \lambda y_{t-1} + \varepsilon_t. \qquad (18\text{–}53)$$

The lagged dependent variable removes this model from the classical regression framework. Depending on the formulation of ε_t, the estimation may be further complicated by autocorrelation. For example, in the adaptive expectations model, the disturbance in this form is $\varepsilon_t - \lambda \varepsilon_{t-1}$. As we saw in Section 15.4.1, autocorrelation in the presence of a lagged dependent variable renders the usual two-step procedures ineffective, as the estimates at the first step are inconsistent.[33] The autoregressive form of the geometric model is best suited to estimation of the partial adjustment model. Thus, consistent with the earlier treatment, we analyze this model first, then return to the adaptive expectations model.

18.5.4a. Uncorrelated Disturbances. Even if ε_t is not serially correlated, the classical assumption that ε_t is uncorrelated with $z_s = [1, x_s, y_{s-1}]$ *for all t and s* is violated. Since y_t embodies all *previous* values y_s, it follows that every ε_t is correlated with every *subsequent* y_s. The correlation does fade with increasing separation in time, however, with the consequence that despite this complication and its stochastic regressor, (18–53) may be treated as a classical regression, at least asymptotically. The requirements

$$|\lambda| < 1$$

and

$$\text{plim } \frac{1}{T} \sum_t \begin{bmatrix} 1 \\ x_t \\ y_{t-1} \end{bmatrix} [1, x_t, y_{t-1}] = \mathbf{Q}, \qquad (18\text{–}54)$$

where $\mathbf{Q}$ is a positive definite matrix, are sufficient to ensure that the OLS estimates retain their desirable *asymptotic* properties. (The exact finite sample properties are largely un-

---

[33]For some overviews, see, for example, Grether and Maddala (1973) and Dhrymes (1969 and 1971).

known.[34]) As we saw earlier, OLS is the asymptotically efficient estimator for the partial adjustment model, assuming that the disturbance in (18–36) is not autocorrelated.

18.5.4b. Autocorrelated Disturbances—Instrumental Variables.

If ε_t is autocorrelated, OLS estimates based on (18–53) are biased and inconsistent. (See Section 15.4.1 for a derivation of the precise result when there is no regressor.) There are, however, several ways to obtain consistent estimates.

The method of instrumental variables was introduced in Section 9.5.3 in connection with the errors-in-variables problem, and used in Section 15.7.3 for precisely the problem facing us here. To reiterate, let

$$\mathbf{X} = [\mathbf{i}, \mathbf{x}, \mathbf{y}_{-1}].$$

The problem is that

$$\text{plim} \, \frac{1}{T} \, \mathbf{X}'\boldsymbol{\varepsilon} \neq \mathbf{0}.$$

The instrumental variable estimator of the parameter vector $\boldsymbol{\theta}$,

$$\hat{\boldsymbol{\theta}}_{\text{IV}} = (\mathbf{Z}'\mathbf{X})^{-1}\mathbf{Z}'\mathbf{y},$$

will be consistent and asymptotically normally distributed as

$$\hat{\boldsymbol{\theta}}_{\text{IV}} \overset{a}{\to} N[\boldsymbol{\theta}, \sigma_\varepsilon^2 (\mathbf{Z}'\mathbf{X})^{-1}(\mathbf{Z}'\mathbf{Z})(\mathbf{X}'\mathbf{Z})^{-1}], \qquad (18\text{–}55)$$

provided that the matrix of instrumental variables satisfies the two requirements

$$\text{plim} \, \frac{1}{T} \, \mathbf{Z}'\boldsymbol{\varepsilon} = \mathbf{0}$$

and

$$\text{plim} \, \frac{1}{T} \, \mathbf{Z}'\mathbf{X} \neq \mathbf{0}. \qquad (18\text{–}56)$$

The constant and $\mathbf{x}$ can serve as their own instruments. A frequent choice for the instrumental variable for y_{t-1} is x_{t-1},[35] leading to

$$\mathbf{Z} = [\mathbf{i}, \mathbf{x}, \mathbf{x}_{-1}].$$

It is useful to note at this point that if the instrumental variables satisfy (18–56), $\hat{\boldsymbol{\theta}}_{\text{IV}}$ is consistent *regardless of the type of autocorrelation in ε.*

18.5.4c. Autoregressive Disturbances—Hatanaka's Estimator and the Maximum Likelihood Estimator.

Although the IV estimator is consistent, it is generally inefficient. Hatanaka (1976) showed that a second-round estimator using the IV estimator at the first step would have the same asymptotic properties as the maximum likelihood estimator for normally distributed AR(1) disturbances. (However, he did raise some questions about the small sample performance of the estimator.) The procedure, detailed in Section 15.7.3, is as follows:

1. Use the IV estimator to estimate the parameters, then compute $\hat{\rho}$ using the residuals.
2. Regress $y_t - \hat{\rho}y_{t-1}$ on a constant, $x_t - \hat{\rho}x_{t-1}$, $y_{t-1} - \hat{\rho}y_{t-2}$, and $\hat{u}_{t-1}$.

---

[34] Doran and Griffiths (1978). See also Schmidt (1976, pp. 96–101).

[35] Liviatan (1963).

The appropriate asymptotic covariance matrix is the conventional estimator computed at step 2.

For normally distributed disturbances, we may also compute a maximum likelihood estimator. If $\varepsilon_t = \rho\varepsilon_{t-1} + u_t$,

$$u_t = (y_t - \rho y_{t-1}) - \alpha(1 - \lambda)(1 - \rho) - \beta(1 - \lambda)(x_t - \rho x_{t-1}) - \lambda(y_{t-1} - \rho y_{t-2}). \tag{18–57}$$

Conditioned on the initial observations, the estimates that minimize the sum of squares provide the maximum likelihood estimates. For a given value of ρ, this requires only a linear regression of δy_t on a constant, δx_t and δy_{t-1}. [We use $\delta x_t = x_t - \rho x_{t-1}$. See (18–52).] Since the OLS estimates are inconsistent, the Cochrane–Orcutt method will not necessarily produce a consistent estimate, even if it is iterated.[36] A simple expedient is to scan the range of $-1 < \rho < 1$ for the value that produces the global minimum of $\Sigma_t\, u_t^2$. Alternatively, if the process is begun with a consistent estimator of ρ, such as the IV estimator, the second step (and subsequent) estimators will have the desirable properties of maximum likelihood estimators. Standard errors for the maximum likelihood estimates of $[\alpha(1 - \lambda), \beta(1 - \lambda), \lambda, \rho, \sigma_u^2]$ may be obtained from the inverse of the estimate of the information matrix,[37]

$$
\mathbf{I}\begin{bmatrix} \alpha' \\ \theta \\ \lambda \\ \rho \\ \sigma_u^2 \end{bmatrix} = \frac{1}{\sigma_u^2}\begin{bmatrix} T(1 - \rho)^2 \\ (1 - \rho)\,\Sigma_t\,\delta x_t & \Sigma_t(\delta x_t)^2 \\ (1 - \rho)\,\Sigma_t\,\delta y_{t-1} & \Sigma_t\,\delta x_t \delta y_{t-1} & \Sigma_t(\delta y_{t-1})^2 \\ 0 & 0 & T\sigma_u^2/(1 - \lambda) & T\sigma_u^2/(1 - \rho^2) \\ 0 & 0 & 0 & 0 & T/(2\sigma_u^2) \end{bmatrix}
$$
$$\tag{18–58}$$

where $\alpha' = \alpha(1 - \lambda)$. Standard errors for the individual estimates of α and β are computed using the result for the variance of a nonlinear function. [See (18–49) and (18–50).]

18.5.4d. MA Disturbances—The Adaptive Expectations Model.

The AR form of the adaptive expectations model is

$$y_t = \alpha(1 - \lambda) + \beta(1 - \lambda)x_t + \lambda y_{t-1} + (\varepsilon_t - \lambda\varepsilon_{t-1}). \tag{18–59}$$

This AR form has an MA(1) disturbance with the same parameter as the adjustment equation. Consistent estimates can be obtained by using the method of instrumental variables. As we saw earlier, efficient estimates can be computed by using the MA form and the truncation remainder. [See (18–42) and the subsequent discussion.] The (only apparently) messy case, in which, in addition, $\varepsilon_t = \rho\varepsilon_{t-1} + u_t$, is exactly the model in (18–51). In either case, no new results are needed. The upshot is that *efficient* estimates of the AR form with a moving average error are obtained simply by reverting back to the MA form.

---

[36] Betancourt and Kelejian (1981) and Fomby and Guilkey (1983).

[37] The counterpart to the 4,3 element in Johnston (1984, p. 367) is in error. It is obtained here as $TE[(-\partial u_t/\partial\lambda)(-\partial u_t/\partial\rho)]$. We use (19–57) to find $-\partial u_t/\partial\lambda = y_{t-1} - \rho y_{t-2}$ and $u_t = \varepsilon_t - \rho\varepsilon_{t-1}$ to obtain $-\partial u_t/\partial\rho = \varepsilon_{t-1}$. Now write (19–53) as $y_s = \alpha + \beta(1 - \lambda)x_s/(1 - \lambda L)$ for $s = t - 1$ and $t - 2$. Therefore, $E[\varepsilon_{t-1}y_{t-1}] = \sigma_\varepsilon^2/(1 - \lambda)$ and $\rho E[\varepsilon_{t-1}y_{t-2}] = \rho^2\sigma_\varepsilon^2/(1 - \lambda)$. Combining terms and imposing $\sigma_\varepsilon^2 = \sigma_u^2/(1 - \rho^2)$ leads to the previous result. For $\partial u_t/\partial\lambda$, note that $\alpha(1 - \lambda)$ and $\beta(1 - \lambda)$ are free parameters.

EXAMPLE 18.5 Estimates of the AR Form _____

Using the techniques described earlier, we obtain the estimates in Table 18.10 for the autoregressive form of the consumption function. Estimated asymptotic standard errors are given in parentheses. The grid search produced a single minimum of the sum of squared deviations. The sum of squares declined monotonically from 5384 at $\rho = -0.5$ to the minimum of 3500.04 at $\rho = 0.27$, then increased monotonically to 4735 at $\rho = 0.9$.

TABLE 18.10

	Least Squares	Instrumental Variables	Hatanaka Two-Step	AR(1) with Grid Search	Zellner–Geisel
$\beta(1 - \lambda)$	0.1767 (0.0451)	0.4651 (0.1115)	0.2863 (0.0560)	0.2423 (0.0498)	0.321 —
λ	0.8119 (0.0502)	0.4913 (0.1240)	0.6901 (0.0623)	0.7386 (0.0555)	0.66 (0.085)
β	0.9394 (0.0148)	0.9142 (0.0122)	0.9238 (0.0078)	0.9269 (0.0067)	0.94 (0.46)
$\dfrac{\lambda}{1 - \lambda}$	4.32 (1.419)	0.966 (0.4791)	2.27 (0.6487)	2.83 (0.8122)	1.94 (0.74)
ρ	0 —	0 —	0.3869 (0.0805)	0.27 (0.0861)	0.69 (0.076)
$\dfrac{e'e}{T}$	29.26	31.41	28.38	27.78	—

18.5.5. Disturbance Specifications in the Geometric Lag Model

The preceding discussion has analyzed numerous combinations of model formulation (adaptive expectation or partial adjustment), stochastic specification of the structural disturbance [white noise, AR(1)], and estimating equation (MA or AR form). Given the number of possibilities, it might appear that one could merely pick one off the shelf and estimate the model with whatever form seems simplest to use (or produces the most agreeable results). It is worth emphasizing that, particularly in the MA form, the answers one will obtain depend crucially on the stochastic assumption. For example, Table 18.11

TABLE 18.11 Estimates of Lag Coefficients

Lag:	0	1	2
MA form			
OLS	0.671	0.199	0.038
Nonlinear OLS	0.682	0.171	0.043
Nonlinear GLS	0.320	0.211	0.139
AR form			
OLS	0.177	0.144	0.117
Inst. variable	0.465	0.228	0.112
Hatanaka	0.286	0.197	0.136
Grid search	0.242	0.178	0.132

gives the implied estimates of the first three lag coefficients for the several estimators computed in Examples 18.4 and 18.5. Such wide disparity might seem a bit surprising in a data set in which the R^2 in the simplest regression (C_t on Y_t) exceeds 0.998.

The residuals should be examined carefully to ascertain the appropriate stochastic specification. It is useful to note that for this purpose we have two robust estimators of the parameters. For the MA form, the nonlinear least squares estimator is consistent regardless of the form of autocorrelation. Similarly, in the AR form, the instrumental variables estimator is robust to different types of disturbances. We thus have two ways to obtain a set of usable residuals for the analysis.

18.6. Dynamic Regression Models

The polynomial lag model has the attractive feature that it allows a great deal of flexibility in the shape of the lag distribution. In contrast, the geometric lag model imposes a declining pattern of the lag weights that might be inconsistent with the data. However, unlike the geometric lag model, the polynomial model truncates the distribution at an arbitrarily chosen point and requires an estimate of the degree of the polynomial. Many alternatives to these two popular functional forms have been devised that combine the desirable features of both models.[38] A very general specification that has proved useful in recent applications is Jorgenson's (1966) *rational lag model,* or, in more recent literature, the **autoregressive distributed lag (ARDL)** model,

$$y_t = \mu + \frac{B(L)}{C(L)} x_i + \varepsilon_t. \tag{18–60}$$

$B(L)$ and $C(L)$ are polynomials in the lag operator.[39] The ratio of two polynomials in the lag operator can produce essentially any desired shape of the lag distribution with relatively few parameters. The autoregressive form is

$$C(L)y_t = \alpha + B(L)x_t + C(L)\varepsilon_t. \tag{18–61}$$

In this form, the model has lagged dependent and independent variables and a moving average (MA) disturbance. For example, if both $B(L)$ and $C(L)$ are quadratic, then

$$y_t = \mu + \frac{\beta_0 + \beta_1 L + \beta_2 L^2}{1 - \gamma_1 L - \gamma_2 L^2} x_t + \varepsilon_t,$$

or

$$y_t = \mu(1 - \gamma_1 - \gamma_2) + \beta_0 x_t + \beta_1 x_{t-1} + \beta_2 x_{t-2} +$$
$$\gamma_1 y_{t-1} + \gamma_2 y_{t-2} + \varepsilon_t - \gamma_1 \varepsilon_{t-1} - \gamma_2 \varepsilon_{t-2}.^{[40]}$$

---

[38] The sources mentioned in Section 18.1 provide extensive summaries. Maddala (1977) also provides a concise catalog with many useful observations on the mechanics of estimation. There is a bit of gadgetry in some of the proposed lag distributions, but unfortunately, economic theory is usually silent on what a lag distribution should look like. The data themselves and the resourcefulness of the analyst often provide most of the guidance.

[39] We could add additional independent variables, each with its own lag structure. But that would add notation without changing the essential character of the model. Our assumption of only a single regressor is purely for convenience.

[40] Note that the leading coefficient in $C(L)$ is normalized to 1. This is necessary because the two polynomials could each be multiplied by the same constant without changing the dynamic model. To remove the indeterminacy, γ_0 is set equal to 1. The result is nothing more than to eliminate an unknown coefficient on the dependent variable in the regression.

In (18–61), the same lag structure is applied to ε_t and y_t. This is an unnecessary and sometimes undesirable restriction on the model. A much more general, flexible model is obtained by allowing the disturbance to have a dynamic structure of its own. The resulting model is

$$C(L)y_t = \alpha + B(L)x_t + D(L)\varepsilon_t, \tag{18–62}$$

where $\alpha = \mu C(1)$. This is known as an ARMAX model.[41] An important special case is the ARMA model, which is an ARMAX model with no regressor:

$$y_t = \alpha + \gamma_1 y_{t-1} + \gamma_2 y_{t-2} + \cdots + \gamma_p y_{t-p} + \varepsilon_t - \theta_1 \varepsilon_{t-1} - \cdots - \theta_q \varepsilon_{t-q}. \tag{18–63}$$

The conventional notation ARMA(p, q) or ARMAX(p, q) indicates the number of lagged terms in the AR part, $C(L)y_t$, and MA part, $D(L)\varepsilon_t$, respectively. The example given earlier is an ARMAX(2, 2) model. ARMAX and ARMA models are pervasive in the analysis of time series. For the present, we will continue to analyze them in the context of dynamic regression models. Alternative uses and interpretations are considered in Chapter 19.

Before continuing, it is useful to make some simplifications. The disturbance, ε_t, in (18–62) is taken to be a serially uncorrelated, constant variance random variable. That is, we have not allowed for the possibility of autoregressive disturbances of the sort that have appeared repeatedly in previous models. In fact, no generality has been lost, since we may assume that if the original disturbances were subject to autoregression, (18–62) is the result of partial differencing which has removed that part of the disturbance process. Second, even allowing for more than one exogenous variable, as long as $B(L)$ has a finite number of terms for each, the exogenous part of the model could simply be written as

$$\sum_i B_i(L)x_{ti} = \boldsymbol{\beta}' \mathbf{x}_t$$

for some set of unknown coefficients and contemporaneous and lagged values x_{si}. Finally, the variables in the model, y_t and x_t, could themselves have been differenced one or more times.[42] (See Example 18.6 below.) As such, a quite general formulation of the ARMAX model is

$$y_t = \mu + \gamma_1 y_{t-1} + \cdots + \gamma_p y_{t-p} + \boldsymbol{\beta}' \mathbf{x}_t + \varepsilon_t - \theta_1 \varepsilon_{t-1} - \cdots - \varepsilon_{t-q}. \tag{18–64}$$

What appears to be a simple modification of the basic ARMA model produces a dynamic model of considerable generality.[43]

18.6.1. Nonlinear Least Squares Estimation of ARIMA and ARMAX Models

If there are no moving average terms in (18–64), it is a linear regression model with stochastic regressors. The results of Mann and Wald (1943) and the discussion of Section 10.4 apply. The parameter vector,

$$\boldsymbol{\phi} = [\mu, \gamma_1, \ldots, \gamma_p, \beta_1, \ldots, \beta_K]',$$

---

[41] It is also known as a transfer function. Functions of this sort have been used extensively in engineering applications. In that context, x_t represents the **impulse** and what we have identified as the distributed lag coefficients are the **impulse response characteristics.** Harvey (1990) contains extensive discussion and numerous examples of transfer functions and ARMAX models.

[42] This produces an *ARIMA model,* which is developed further in Chapter 19.

[43] Extensive analysis of the many special cases appears in Granger and Watson (1984), Hendry et al. (1984), and Harvey (1990).

may be estimated consistently by ordinary least squares regression of y_t on

$$\mathbf{z}_t = [1, y_{t-1}, y_{t-2}, \ldots, y_{t-p}, \mathbf{x}_t']'.$$

(Recall that $\mathbf{x}_t$ may also contain lagged values of exogenous variables.) The OLS estimator in this setting would be asymptotically normally distributed with asymptotic covariance matrix

$$\text{Asy.Var}[\hat{\boldsymbol{\phi}}] = \frac{1}{T-p} \, \text{plim} \, \sigma_\varepsilon^2 \left(\frac{\mathbf{Z}'\mathbf{Z}}{T-p} \right)^{-1}$$

The disturbance variance, σ_ε^2, may be estimated residually as usual, since

$$\text{plim} \, \frac{1}{T-p} \sum_{t=p+1}^{T} \hat{\varepsilon}_t^2 = \sigma_\varepsilon^2.$$

Under the Mann and Wald conditions, *ordinary, linear least squares* estimation and inference procedures are valid asymptotically. Henceforth, we assume that this is the case.

When there are moving average disturbances, the model becomes nonlinear. In this case, the *nonlinear least squares* estimator will be consistent and asymptotically normally distributed. If ε_t is assumed to be normally distributed, nonlinear least squares, conditioned on the initial observations, will also be maximum likelihood. As such, least squares will also be efficient. It should be noted that *ordinary* least squares applied to (18–64) will not even be consistent. The model contains both lagged dependent variables and autocorrelation.[44] The sum of squares to be minimized is

$$S(\mu, \boldsymbol{\gamma}, \boldsymbol{\beta}, \boldsymbol{\theta}) = S(\boldsymbol{\phi}) = \sum_t \varepsilon_t^2.$$

Details on the nonlinear least squares procedure are given in the Appendix to this chapter. After the parameters have been estimated, the variance estimator is

$$\hat{\sigma}_\varepsilon^2 = \frac{1}{T-p-1-K-q} \sum_{t=p+q+1}^{T} \hat{\varepsilon}_t^2$$

where

$$\hat{\varepsilon}_t = y_t - \hat{\gamma}_1 y_{t-1} - \cdots - \hat{\gamma}_p y_{t-p} - \hat{\mu} - \hat{\boldsymbol{\beta}}' \mathbf{x}_t + \hat{\theta}_1 \hat{\varepsilon}_{t-1} + \cdots \hat{\theta}_q \hat{\varepsilon}_{t-q}. \quad (18\text{–}65)$$

The estimated asymptotic covariance matrix for the parameter estimates is

$$\text{Est.Asy.Var}[\hat{\boldsymbol{\phi}}] = \hat{\sigma}_\varepsilon^2 (\hat{\mathbf{G}}'\hat{\mathbf{G}})^{-1},$$

where $\mathbf{G}$ is the $(T - p - q) \times (1 + K + p + q)$ matrix of derivatives of the residuals with respect to the parameters. [This is (11–13).] The matrix is the sum of squares and cross products computed at the last iteration.[45]

---

[44] See Section 15.4.1.

[45] Harvey (1990, pp. 207–210) provides further discussion of the estimation problem for this model. With normally distributed disturbances, the estimator described here is an "approximate MLE," conditioned on the initial observations. Normality may be a bit much to ask for, but the properties of nonlinear least squares may be claimed in any event.

EXAMPLE 18.6 ARMAX Model

To continue Example 18.2, we will analyze the ARMAX (ARIMAX?) model

$$\Delta \ln \frac{GNP_t}{P_t} = \mu + \beta_0(\Delta \ln M1_t) + \beta_1(\Delta \ln M1_{t-1}) + \beta_2(\Delta \ln M1_{t-2})$$

$$+ \gamma_1 \Delta \ln \frac{GNP_{t-1}}{P_{t-1}} + \gamma_2 \Delta \ln \frac{GNP_{t-2}}{P_{t-2}} + \varepsilon_t - \theta_1\varepsilon_{t-1}.$$

We will use this model to analyze the effect of changes in the rate of growth of M1 on the growth of real output. Nonlinear least squares estimates of the parameters are given in Table 18.12.

TABLE 18.12 Estimated ARMAX Model

Data: Quarterly, 1950.I to 1983.IV. $T = 136$.
Estimated standard errors are given in parentheses.

μ	0.0006120 (0.002744)	0.0025929 (0.002028)	0.0028985 (0.002257)	0.00084058 (0.002272)
β_0	0.43340 (0.1101)	0.40402 (0.1130)	0.38842 (0.1146)	0.43841 (0.1121)
β_1	−0.05886 (0.1836)	0.020130 (0.1090)	0.021563 (0.1106)	0.0039259 (0.1136)
β_2	−0.03004 (0.1161)	0.057865 (0.1128)	0.057369 (0.1151)	−0.050821 (0.1173)
γ_1	0.25568 (0.3562)	—	—	0.11871 (0.08313)
γ_2	0.16953 (0.0945)	—	—	0.21789 (0.08270)
θ_1	−0.16379 (0.3689)	0.091266 (0.08746)	—	—
σ_ε	0.012900	0.013214	0.013414	0.012878
$e'e$	0.021967	0.023047	0.023753	0.021891

Using a likelihood ratio statistic, we find that the two lagged values of the output variable are jointly significant, both with the moving average term,

$$LR_{ma} = 132 \ln \frac{0.013214^2}{0.012900^2} = 6.349$$

or without,

$$LR = 132 \ln \frac{0.013414^2}{0.012878^2} = 10.765.$$

The 5 percent critical value from the chi-squared distribution is 5.99. The corresponding F statistics defined in (11–46) are 3.072 and 5.017, while the critical value from the table is 3.09. The moving average term is not significant; the asymptotic t ratio is only −0.444

with the lagged dependent variables and 1.043 without them. It remains to be seen whether the model suggests that changes in the growth rate of M1 ultimately translate into changes in the growth of output. We pursue that in Example 18.7.

18.6.2. Computation of the Lag Weights in the ARMAX Model

The lag coefficients on $x_t, x_{t-1}, \ldots$ in the model in (18–64) are the individual terms in the ratio of polynomials. We denote these as

$$\alpha_0, \alpha_1, \alpha_2, \ldots = \text{the coefficient on } 1, L, L^2, \ldots \text{ in } B(L)/C(L). \quad (18\text{–}66)$$

A convenient way to compute these lag coefficients is to write the left-hand side of (18–66) as $A(L)$ and note that (18–66) implies that $A(L)C(L) = B(L)$. So we can just equate coefficients. Example 18.7 demonstrates the procedure.

EXAMPLE 18.7 Lag Weights in a Rational Lag Model _____

The systematic part of the model in Example 18.6 is

$$y_t = \mu + \gamma_1 y_{t-1} + \gamma_2 y_{t-2} + \beta_0 x_t + \beta_1 x_{t-1} + \beta_2 x_{t-2}.^{46}$$

The lag coefficients are given by the equality

$$(\alpha_0 + \alpha_1 L + \alpha_2 L^2 + \cdots)(1 - \gamma_1 L - \gamma_2 L^2) = (\beta_0 + \beta_1 L + \beta_2 L^2).$$

Note that $A(L)$ is an infinite polynomial. Thus, the lag coefficients are

$\quad 1: \quad \alpha_0 = \beta_0.$ (This will always be the case.)

$\quad L: \quad -\alpha_0 \gamma_1 + \alpha_1 = \beta_1 \text{ or } \alpha_1 = \beta_1 + \alpha_0 \gamma_1,$

$\quad L^2: \quad -\alpha_0 \gamma_2 - \alpha_1 \gamma_1 + \alpha_2 = \beta_2, \text{ or } \alpha_2 = \beta_2 + \alpha_0 \gamma_2 + \alpha_1 \gamma_1,$

$\quad L^3: \quad -\alpha_1 \gamma_2 - \alpha_2 \gamma_1 + \alpha_3 = 0, \text{ or } \alpha_3 = \alpha_2 \gamma_1 + \alpha_1 \gamma_0,$

$\quad L^4: \quad -\alpha_2 \gamma_2 - \alpha_3 \gamma_1 + \alpha_4 = 0,$

and so on. Notice that from the fourth term onward, the series follows the recursion

$$\alpha_k = \gamma_1 \alpha_{k-1} + \gamma_2 \alpha_{k-2}. \quad (18\text{–}67)$$

The general result is that after a few initial terms which involve the lag coefficients in $B(L)$, the series of lag weights will follow the same difference equation that the lagged values of y_t follow in the autoregressive part of the model. Thus, the lag coefficients are calculated using a simple recursion. For the most general model in Table 18.12, the first four terms are 0.4334, 0.0520, 0.0567, and 0.0001. Thereafter, the coefficients are essentially zero.

The long-run effect in a rational lag model is $\Sigma_{i=0}^{\infty} \alpha_i$. This is easy to compute, since it is simply

$$\sum_{i=0}^{\infty} \alpha_i = \frac{B(1)}{C(1)}. \quad (18\text{–}68)$$

For the four models listed in Table 18.12, (18–65) gives 0.5993, 0.48199, 0.46735, and 0.59016, respectively.

---

[46] The dynamic characteristics of the systematic part of the equation are unrelated to ε_t or any moving average terms, so we have omitted that part of the model.

The results obtained with this model are similar to those in Table 18.3. But the long-run multiplier estimated here is persistently closer to 0.5, as opposed to the near-zero values found for the unrestricted models with longer lags. The difference is that despite its more general structure, the dynamic model estimated in this example more nearly resembles the geometric lag model than does the unrestricted model. With only two lagged values, this model still forces the lag coefficients to converge to zero, in this case, fairly rapidly.

18.6.3. Stability of a Dynamic Equation

In the geometric lag model, we found that a stability condition $|\lambda| < 1$, was necessary for the model to be well behaved. [Similarly, in the AR(1) model for the disturbance in (18–39) or (18–51), the autocorrelation parameter, ρ, must be restricted to $-1 < \rho < 1$ for the same reason.] The dynamic model in (18–63) must also be restricted, but in ways that are less obvious. Consider once again the question of whether there exists an equilibrium value of y_t.

In (18–60), suppose that x_t is fixed at some value, $\bar{x}$, and the disturbances, ε_t, are fixed at their expectation of zero. Would y_t converge to an equilibrium? The relevant dynamic equation is

$$y_t = \bar{\alpha} + \gamma_1 y_{t-1} + \gamma_2 y_{t-1} + \cdots + \gamma_p y_{t-p},$$

where $\bar{\alpha} = \mu + B(1)\bar{x}$. Whether this converges or explodes depends on the coefficients. If so, the equilibrium is

$$\bar{y} = \frac{\mu + B(1)\bar{x}}{C(1)} = \frac{\bar{\alpha}}{C(1)}.$$

Note that this exactly is what appears in (18–2), where $C(L) = 1$, and in (18–28), where $B(L) = \beta$ and $C(L) = 1 - \lambda L$.

Stability of a dynamic equation hinges on the **characteristic equation** for the autoregressive part of the model. The roots of the characteristic equation,

$$C(z) = 1 - \gamma_1 z - \gamma_2 z^2 - \cdots - \gamma_p z^p = 0,$$

must be greater than 1 in absolute value for the model to be stable. To take a simple example, the characteristic equation for the first-order models we have examined thus far is

$$C(z) = 1 - \lambda z = 0.$$

This single root of this equation is $z = 1/\lambda$, which is greater than 1 in absolute value if $|\lambda|$ is less than 1. The roots of a more general characteristic equation are the reciprocals of the characteristic roots of the matrix

$$\mathbf{C} = \begin{bmatrix} \gamma_1 & \gamma_2 & \gamma_3 & \cdots & \gamma_{p-1} & \gamma_p \\ 1 & 0 & 0 & \cdots & 0 & 0 \\ 0 & 1 & 0 & \cdots & 0 & 0 \\ 0 & 0 & 1 & \cdots & 0 & 0 \\ & & & \vdots & 0 & 0 \\ 0 & 0 & 0 & \cdots & 1 & 0 \end{bmatrix}$$

Since the matrix is asymmetric, its roots may include complex pairs. The reciprocal of the complex number $a + bi$ is $a/M - (b/M)i$, where $M = a^2 + b^2$ and $i^2 = -1$.

It is useful to examine the role of the matrix $\mathbf{C}$ in a dynamic equation. The **univariate autoregression,**

$$y_t = \mu + \gamma_1 y_{t-1} + \gamma_2 y_{t-2} + \cdots + \gamma_p Y_{t-p},$$

can be augmented with the $p - 1$ equations

$$y_{t-1} = y_{t-1},$$

$$y_{t-2} = y_{t-2},$$

and so on, to give a **vector autoregression,**

$$\mathbf{y}_t = \boldsymbol{\mu} + \mathbf{C}\mathbf{y}_{t-1},$$

where $\mathbf{y}_t$ has p elements and $\boldsymbol{\mu} = (\mu, 0, 0, \ldots)'$. Now, by successive substitution, we obtain

$$\mathbf{y}_t = \boldsymbol{\mu} + \mathbf{C}\boldsymbol{\mu} + \mathbf{C}^2\boldsymbol{\mu} + \cdots,$$

which may or may not converge. Write $\mathbf{C}$ in the spectral form $\mathbf{C} = \mathbf{P}\boldsymbol{\Lambda}\mathbf{Q}$, where $\mathbf{Q}\mathbf{P} = \mathbf{I}$ and $\boldsymbol{\Lambda}$ is a diagonal matrix of the characteristic roots. (Note that the characteristic vectors in $\mathbf{P}$ are also complex.) We then obtain

$$\mathbf{y}_t = \left[\sum_{i=0}^{\infty} \mathbf{P}\boldsymbol{\Lambda}^i\mathbf{Q}\right]\boldsymbol{\mu}.$$

If all of the roots of $\mathbf{C}$ are finite, this will converge to the equilibrium

$$\mathbf{y}_{\infty} = (\mathbf{I} - \mathbf{C})^{-1}\boldsymbol{\mu}.$$

Nonexplosion of the powers of the roots of $\mathbf{C}$ is equivalent to $|\lambda_p| < 1$, or $|1/\lambda_p| > 1$, which was our original requirement. Note, finally, that since $\boldsymbol{\mu}$ is a multiple of the first column of $\mathbf{I}_p$, it must be the case that each element in the first column of $(\mathbf{I} - \mathbf{C})^{-1}$ is the same. At equilibrium, we must have $y_t = y_{t-1} = \cdots = y_{\infty}$.

EXAMPLE 18.8 _____

For the first model given in Table 18.12, the roots of the characteristic equation are both real, 1.789 and -3.297, and larger than 1, so the model is stable. The roots also give information about the path of y_t to its equilibrium. See Section 20.6 for details.

18.6.4. Forecasting

Thus far we have treated the ARMAX model essentially as an extension of the rational lag model. In that context, primary interest centers on the lag weights in the ARDL model.[47] Another use of the model is for forecasting.[48]

Conditioned on the full set of information available up to time T and on forecasts of the exogenous variables, $\mathbf{x}$, the l period ahead forecast of y_t would be

$$\hat{y}_{T+l|T} = \mu + \boldsymbol{\beta}'\mathbf{x}_{T+l} + \gamma_1\hat{y}_{T+l-1|T} + \gamma_2\hat{y}_{T+l-2|T} + \cdots + \hat{\varepsilon}_{T+l|T} - \theta_1\hat{\varepsilon}_{T+l-1|T} - \cdots$$

Disturbances past the sample period, $\varepsilon_{T+1}, \ldots$ are replaced with their expectation of zero. The sequence of within-sample disturbances can be generated recursively using (18–65) and q initial values of zero. The forecasts will require $(q - l + 1)$ forecasted disturbances at the end of the sample period for $\hat{y}_{T+l|T}$. The forecasts, themselves, are

---

[47] See Harvey (1990, Chapter 7).

[48] Extensive analysis may be found in Harvey (1990) and Mills (1990).

based on observed values of y_t for the last p values in the sample and the forecasted lagged values when $T + l$ extends beyond $T + p$.

If the data have been differenced before estimation, the series must be reintegrated to produce a forecast of y_{T+l}. For example, if the first difference has been taken, then

$$\hat{y}_{T+l|T} = \hat{y}_{T+l-1|T} + \Delta\hat{y}_{T+l|T}$$

For second and higher differences, the operation must be repeated.

The expected squared forecast error can be derived by reverting back to the moving average form of the model. Thus,

$$y_{T+l|T} = \frac{\mu + \beta' \mathbf{x}_{T+l|T}}{C(L)} + \frac{D(L)}{C(L)} \varepsilon_t.$$

We may proceed in the same fashion as in Example 18.6 to derive Ψ_j, the coefficients on L^j in $[D(L)/C(L)]\varepsilon_t$;

$$(1 + \Psi_1 L + \Psi_2 L^2 + \cdots)(1 - \gamma_1 L - \gamma_2 L^2 - \cdots - \gamma_p L^p) =$$
$$(1 - \theta_1 L - \theta_2 L^2 - \cdots - \theta_q L^q).$$

Then the expected square forecast error is

$$\text{MSE}(\hat{y}_{T+l|T}) = \sigma_\varepsilon^2(1 + \Psi_1^2 + \cdots + \Psi_{l-1}^2). \tag{18–69}$$

The number of nonzero terms increases with the number of periods ahead for which the forecast is made.

The preceding takes the parameters as known. Obviously, this is not going to hold in practice. Unfortunately, except in the simplest cases, the precise form of the MSE which accounts for the sampling variability of the parameter estimates remains to be derived. Harvey (1990, pp. 215–216 and 254) suggests that the contribution of the parameter estimates to the forecast variance is $O(1/T)$, and that of the forecasted disturbances, themselves, is $O(1)$. Thus, if T is relatively large, the variance of the parameter estimates could be ignored. Of course, the typical time-series setting involves a relatively small T, so this advice may be a bit optimistic. One possibility could be to revert back to the ARDL form of the model and use the familiar form of the forecast variance given in (6–42):

$$\text{MSE}(\hat{y}_{T+l|T}) = \sigma_\varepsilon^2(1 + \Psi_1^2 + \cdots + \Psi_{l-1}^2) + \mathbf{z}^{0'}\{\text{Est.Var}[\hat{\mu}, \hat{\gamma}, \hat{\beta}]\}\mathbf{z}^0$$

and

$$\mathbf{z}^0 = [1, \hat{y}_{T+l-1|T}, \ldots, \mathbf{x}_{T+l}].$$

Since the disturbances and the regressors in this model are correlated, the decomposition above neglects a covariance term that might be substantial. It is not obvious whether ignoring the parameter variation or using what might be an erroneous approximation is the poorer option in this setting. On the other hand, it is unambiguous that the correct variance to use would be understated by (18–66).

Appendix: Nonlinear Least Squares Estimation

Nonlinear least squares estimates of the dynamic regression model can be obtained as follows: The iteration is based on the Gauss–Newton method.[49] The sum of squares to be minimized is

$$S(\mu, \gamma, \beta, \theta) = S(\phi) = \sum_t \varepsilon_t^2.$$

---

[49] See Section 11.2.2. Note that the ARMA model is a special case in which there is no exogenous variable. Thus, there is no need to consider ARMA models separately from ARMAX models.

The iteration is

$$\hat{\phi}^{s+1} = \hat{\phi}^s - [\mathbf{G}_s'\mathbf{G}_s]^{-1}\mathbf{G}_s'\hat{\epsilon}_s,$$

where $\mathbf{G}_s$ is a $(T - p - q) \times (1 + p + K + q)$ matrix of derivatives of the residuals with respect to the parameters. The derivatives are computed as follows:

$$\frac{\partial \epsilon_t}{\partial \mu} = 1 - \theta_1 \left(\frac{\partial \epsilon_{t-1}}{\partial \mu}\right) - \cdots \theta_q \left(\frac{\partial \epsilon_{t-q}}{\partial \mu}\right),$$

$$\frac{\partial \epsilon_t}{\partial \gamma_i} = y_{t-i} - \theta_1 \left(\frac{\partial \epsilon_{t-1}}{\partial \gamma_i}\right) - \cdots \theta_q \left(\frac{\partial \epsilon_{t-q}}{\partial \gamma_i}\right), \qquad i = 1, \ldots, p,$$

$$\frac{\partial \epsilon_t}{\partial \beta_k} = x_{tk} - \theta_1 \left(\frac{\partial \epsilon_{t-1}}{\partial \beta_k}\right) - \cdots \theta_q \left(\frac{\partial \epsilon_{t-q}}{\partial \beta_k}\right), \qquad k = 1, \ldots, K,$$

$$\frac{\partial \epsilon_t}{\partial \theta_j} = \epsilon_{t-j} - \theta_1 \left(\frac{\partial \epsilon_{t-1}}{\partial \theta_j}\right) - \cdots \theta_q \left(\frac{\partial \epsilon_{t-q}}{\partial \theta_j}\right), \qquad j = 1, \ldots, q.$$

These are difference equations that can be computed recursively after initializing ϵ_t and the derivatives with q zeros. In a matrix format we would have

$$\mathbf{G}_{\mu,t} = \left[\frac{\partial \epsilon_{t-s}}{\partial \mu}\right], \qquad s = 1, \ldots, q \quad (1 \times q),$$

$$\mathbf{G}_{\gamma,t} = \left[\frac{\partial \epsilon_{t-s}}{\partial \gamma}\right], \qquad s = 1, \ldots, q \quad (p \times q),$$

$$\mathbf{G}_{\beta,t} = \left[\frac{\partial \epsilon_{t-s}}{\partial \beta}\right], \qquad s = 1, \ldots, q \quad (K \times q),$$

$$\mathbf{G}_{\theta,t} = \left[\frac{\partial \epsilon_{t-s}}{\partial \theta}\right], \qquad s = 1, \ldots, q \quad (q \times q),$$

Then the tth row of $\mathbf{G}_s$ is

$$\mathbf{g}_s^{(t)} = \left[\left(\frac{\partial \epsilon_t}{\partial \mu}\right), \left(\frac{\partial \epsilon_t}{\partial \gamma'}\right), \left(\frac{\partial \epsilon_t}{\partial \beta'}\right), \left(\frac{\partial \epsilon_t}{\partial \theta'}\right)\right],$$

where

$$\frac{\partial \epsilon_t}{\partial \mu} = 1 - \mathbf{G}_{\mu,t}\boldsymbol{\theta},$$

$$\frac{\partial \epsilon_t}{\partial \gamma} = \mathbf{y}_{\text{lags}} - \mathbf{G}_{\gamma,t}\boldsymbol{\theta},$$

$$\frac{\partial \epsilon_t}{\partial \beta} = \mathbf{x}_t - \mathbf{G}_{\beta,t}\boldsymbol{\theta},$$

$$\frac{\partial \epsilon_t}{\partial \theta} = \boldsymbol{\epsilon}_{\text{lags}} - \mathbf{G}_{\theta,t}\boldsymbol{\theta}.$$

Consistent starting values for the iterations can be computed as follows: OLS does not provide consistent estimates of any of the parameters. But an instrumental variables estimator can be employed using lagged values of the exogenous variables, $\mathbf{x}_t$, as instruments for $[y_{t-1}, \ldots, y_{t-p}]$. Constructing initial values for $[\theta_1, \ldots, \theta_q]$ is a bit involved.

Box and Jenkins (1984) suggest the following method of moments estimation procedure, which can be based on the residuals from the instrumental variable estimator:

1. Let c_i, $i = 0, 1, \ldots, q$, be the sample covariances of e_t and e_{t-i}. (These are *autocovariances*.) Start with $\boldsymbol{\theta} = 0$.
2. Compute $s^2 = c_0/(1 + \boldsymbol{\theta}'\boldsymbol{\theta})$.
3. For $i = q, q - 1, \ldots, 1$ (working backward), compute $\theta_i = c_i/s^2 - \sum_{j=1}^{q-i} \theta_j \theta_{j+i}$.
4. Check for convergence based on the change from the last iteration. If so, exit; otherwise, return to step 2.

This method need not converge. The estimates may diverge, in which case the specification of the model becomes suspect. Overfitting, that is, specifying too many moving average terms, can lead to this condition.

EXERCISES

1. Obtain the mean lag and the long- and short-run multipliers for the following distributed lag models:
   (a) $y_t = 0.55(0.02x_t + 0.15x_{t-1} + 0.43x_{t-2} + 0.23x_{t-3} + 0.17x_{t-4}) + \varepsilon_t$.
   (b) The model in Exercise 5.
   (c) The model in Exercise 8. (Do for either x or z.)

2. Explain how to estimate the parameters of the following model:

$$y_t = \alpha + \beta x_t + \gamma y_{t-1} + \delta y_{t-2} + \varepsilon_t,$$

$$\varepsilon_t = \rho \varepsilon_{t-1} + u_t.$$

Is there any problem with ordinary least squares? Using the method you have described, fit the previous model to the data in Table 18.6. Report your results.

3. Show how to estimate a polynomial distributed lag model with lags of six periods and a third-order polynomial, using restricted least squares.

4. Using the data in the appendix to Chapter 20, fit a polynomial distributed lag model of the form

$$\text{investment}_t = \alpha + \beta \sum_i \delta_i \text{ profit}_{t-i} + \varepsilon_t.$$

Attempt to determine the appropriate lag length and polynomial degree, using the methods discussed in the text.

5. Expand the rational lag model

$$y_t = \frac{0.6 + 2L}{1 - 0.6L + 0.5L^2} x_t + \varepsilon_t.$$

What are the coefficients on x_t, x_{t-1}, x_{t-2}, x_{t-3}, and x_{t-4}?

6. Suppose that the model of Exercise 5 were respecified as

$$y_t = \alpha + \frac{\beta + \gamma L}{1 - \delta_1 L + \delta_2 L^2} x_t + \varepsilon_t.$$

Describe a method of estimating the parameters. Is ordinary least squares consistent?

7. Derive equation (18–45).

8. Describe how to estimate the parameters of the model

$$y_t = \alpha + \beta \frac{x_t}{1 - \gamma L} + \delta \frac{z_t}{1 - \phi L} + \varepsilon_t,$$

where ε_t is a serially uncorrelated, homoscedastic, classical disturbance.

CHAPTER 19

Time-Series Models

19.1. Introduction

In this chapter we introduce some of the tools employed in the analysis of time-series data.[1] Section 19.2 describes stationary stochastic processes. We first encountered this body of theory in Chapters 15 and 18, where we discovered that certain assumptions were required in order to ascribe familiar properties to a time series of data. We continue that discussion by defining several characteristics of time-series data. The recent literature in macroeconometrics has seen an explosion of studies of nonstationary time series. Nonstationarity mandates a revision of the standard inference tools we have used thus far. In Sections 19.3 to 19.6 on unit roots and cointegration we consider the analysis of certain types of nonstationary stochastic processes and discuss some of the appropriate tools. Section 19.7 on GARCH models extends the time-series models of Section 19.2 to the regression variance.

Some of the concepts to be discussed here were introduced in Section 15.2. This section also contains a broad introduction to the nature of time-series processes. It will be useful to review that material before proceeding with the rest of the chapter. In addition, Section 10.4, in which we discuss regressions with stochastic regressors and the important theorem of Mann and Wald, is directly relevant to the material of this chapter. Finally, Sections 18.6.1 on estimation and 18.6.3 on stability of dynamic models will be especially useful for this chapter.

19.2. Stationary Stochastic Processes

Univariate time-series models describe the behavior of a variable in terms of its own past values. Consider, for example, the autoregressive disturbance models introduced in Chapter 15,

$$\varepsilon_t = \rho \varepsilon_{t-1} + u_t. \tag{19-1}$$

---

[1] Each of the topics discussed here is the subject of a vast literature with articles and book-length treatments at all levels. For example, two recent survey papers on the subject of unit roots in economic time-series data, Nerlove and Diebold (1990) and Campbell and Perron (1991), cite between them over 200 basic sources on the subject, most of them written in the last five years. Useful references on the subjects of this chapter are Box and Jenkins (1984), Judge et al. (1985), Mills (1990), Granger and Newbold (1977), Granger and Watson (1984), Hendry et al. (1984) , Geweke (1984), and especially, Harvey (1989) and (1990). There are also many survey style and pedagogical articles on these subjects. The aforementioned paper by Nerlove and Diebold is a useful tour guide through some of the most recent literature.

Long experience has validated this as a useful description of the noise in many time-series regression models. Autoregressive disturbances are generally the residual variation in a regression model built up from what may be an elaborate underlying theory,

$$y_t = \boldsymbol{\beta}'\mathbf{x}_t + \varepsilon_t.$$

The theory usually stops short of stating what enters the disturbance. But the presumption that some time-series process generates the variables specifically included in the model, $\mathbf{x}_t$, should extend equally to those variables that have been excluded. Note, for example, the symmetric approach to modeling x_t and ε_t in Section 15.4.2.

Occasionally, statistical evidence is convincing that a more intricate process is at work in the disturbance. Perhaps a second-order autoregression,

$$\varepsilon_t = \rho_1\varepsilon_{t-1} + \rho_2\varepsilon_{t-2} + u_t, \tag{19-2}$$

better explains the movement in time of the disturbances in the regression. The model may not arise naturally from an underlying behavioral theory. But in the face of certain kinds of statistical evidence, one might conclude that the more elaborate model would be preferable.[2]

In a time-series setting, a tight economic theory that explains the variation in a variable may be hard to come by. But a model that describes the behavior of a variable (or a set of variables) in terms of past values may well prove quite satisfactory.[3]

19.2.1. Autoregressive–Moving Average Processes

The variable y_t in the model

$$y_t = \mu + \gamma y_{t-1} + \varepsilon_t \tag{19-3}$$

is said to be *autoregressive* (or self-regressive) because under certain assumptions,

$$E[y_t|y_{t-1}] = \mu + \gamma y_{t-1}.$$

A more general, pth-order autoregression or AR(p) process would be written

$$y_t = \mu + \gamma_1 y_{t-1} + \gamma_2 y_{t-2} + \cdots + \gamma_p y_{t-p} + \varepsilon_t. \tag{19-4}$$

The analogy to the classical regression is clear. Consider the specification

$$y_t = \mu + \varepsilon_t - \theta\varepsilon_{t-1}.$$

By writing

$$y_t = \mu + (1 - \theta L)\varepsilon_t$$

or

$$\frac{y_t}{1 - \theta L} = \frac{\mu}{1 - \theta} + \varepsilon_t,^4 \tag{19-5}$$

---

[2] For example, the estimates of u_t computed after a correction for first-order autocorrelation may well fail tests of randomness such as the Durbin–Watson test.

[3] This exercise is not necessarily atheoretical. An autoregressive model may arise as the reduced form of an economic model involving several equations and quite explicitly stated relationships. Example 20.2 considers one such case in detail.

[4] The lag operator is discussed in Section 18.2.2. Since μ is a constant, $\mu/(1 - \theta L) = \mu + \theta\mu + \theta^2\mu + \cdots = \mu/(1 - \theta)$. The lag operator may be set equal to 1 when it operates on a constant.

we find that

$$y_t = \frac{\mu}{1 - \theta} + \theta y_{t-1} + \theta^2 y_{t-2} + \cdots + \varepsilon_t.$$

Once again, the effect is to represent y_t as a function of its own past values.

An extremely general model that encompasses both of the cases above is the **autoregressive moving average,** or ARMA(p, q) model,

$$y_t = \mu + \gamma_1 y_{t-1} + \gamma_2 y_{t-2} + \cdots + \gamma_p y_{t-p} + \varepsilon_t - \theta_1 \varepsilon_{t-1} - \cdots - \theta_q \varepsilon_{t-q}.$$

(19–6)

Note the convention that the ARMA(p, q) process has p autoregressive (lagged dependent variable) terms and q lagged moving average terms.

The disturbances, ε_t, are labeled the **innovations** in the model. The term is fitting insofar as the only new information that enters the processes shown above are the innovations that appear in each period. Consider, then, the AR(1) process,

$$y_t = \mu + \gamma y_{t-1} + \varepsilon_t.$$

(19–7)

Either by successive substitution or by just using the lag operator, we obtain

$$y_t(1 - \gamma L) = \mu + \varepsilon_t$$

or

$$y_t = \frac{\mu}{1 - \gamma} + \sum_{i=0}^{\infty} \gamma^i \varepsilon_{t-i}.^5$$

(19–8)

Therefore, the observed series is a particular type of aggregation of the history of the innovations. The moving average, MA(q), model,

$$y_t = \mu + \varepsilon_t - \theta_1 \varepsilon_{t-1} - \cdots - \theta_q \varepsilon_{t-q},$$

(19–9)

is yet another, particularly simple form of aggregation in that only information from the q most recent periods is retained. (See, for example, Example 15.2.) The general result is that time-series processes can be viewed either as regressions on lagged values with additive disturbances or as aggregations of a history of innovations. They differ from one to the next in the form of that aggregation.

More involved processes can be similarly represented in either an autoregressive or moving average form. (We will turn to the mathematical requirements in the next section.) Consider, for example, the ARMA(2, 1) process

$$y_t = \mu + \gamma_1 y_{t-1} + \gamma_2 y_{t-2} + \varepsilon_t - \theta \varepsilon_{t-1}.$$

Assuming that $|\theta| < 1$, this can also be written

$$\varepsilon_t = \sum_{i=0}^{\infty} \theta^i (y_{t-i} - \mu - \gamma_1 y_{t-i-1} - \gamma_2 y_{t-i-2}).$$

After some tedious manipulation, this produces

$$y_t = \frac{-\mu}{1 - \theta} + \sum_{i=1}^{\infty} \pi_i y_{t-i} + \varepsilon_t,$$

---

[5] See Section 15.2 for discussion of models with infinite lag structures.

where

$$\pi_1 = \gamma_1 - \theta \quad \text{and} \quad \pi_j = -(\theta^j - \gamma_1\theta^{j-1} - \gamma_2\theta^{j-2}), \qquad j = 2, 3, \ldots$$
$$(19\text{--}10)$$

Alternatively, by similar (yet more tedious) manipulation, we would be able to write

$$y_t = \frac{\mu}{1 - \gamma_1 - \gamma_2} + \sum_{i=0}^{\infty} \delta_i \varepsilon_{t-i}.$$

In each case, the weights, π_i in the autoregressive form and δ_i in the moving average form, are complicated functions of the original parameters. But, nonetheless, each is just an alternative representation of the same-time series process that produces the current value of y_t.

The autoregressive model in (19–4) is of the sort discussed in Section 10.4; it is a linear regression model with stochastic regressors. The parameters can be estimated consistently and, with normality of ε_t, efficiently by ordinary least squares. With moving average terms, as in (19–6), the model becomes nonlinear. The ARMA model is a special case of the ARMAX model discussed in Section 18.6. The nonlinear least squares procedure described in Section 18.6.1 and the Appendix to Chapter 18 extend directly to this model.

19.2.2. Vector Autoregressions

The preceding can be extended to sets of variables. In the most general case, we would have

$$\mathbf{y}_t = \boldsymbol{\mu} + \boldsymbol{\Gamma}_1\mathbf{y}_{t-1} + \cdots + \boldsymbol{\Gamma}_p\mathbf{y}_{t-p} + \boldsymbol{\varepsilon}_t + \boldsymbol{\Theta}_1\boldsymbol{\varepsilon}_{t-1} + \cdots + \boldsymbol{\Theta}_q\boldsymbol{\varepsilon}_{t-q},$$

where $\mathbf{y}_t$ and $\boldsymbol{\varepsilon}_t$ are $M \times 1$ vectors of random variables, $\boldsymbol{\mu}$ is the mean vector, and $\boldsymbol{\Gamma}_1, \ldots, \boldsymbol{\Gamma}_p$ and $\boldsymbol{\Theta}_1, \ldots, \boldsymbol{\Theta}_q$ are $M \times M$ parameter matrices. In principle, $\boldsymbol{\Theta}_1, \ldots, \boldsymbol{\Theta}_q$ are unrestricted. This produces a **vector ARMA** model,[6] Applications in econometrics have typically been based on simpler models without moving average terms. The resulting model,

$$\mathbf{y}_t = \boldsymbol{\mu} + \boldsymbol{\Gamma}_1\mathbf{y}_{t-1} + \cdots + \boldsymbol{\Gamma}_p\mathbf{y}_{t-p} + \boldsymbol{\varepsilon}_t, \qquad (19\text{--}11)$$

is a **vector autoregression,** or **VAR.** The individual equations are

$$y_{it} = \mu_i + \sum_{j=1}^{p} (\boldsymbol{\Gamma}_j)_{i1} y_{1,t-j} + \sum_{j=1}^{p} (\boldsymbol{\Gamma}_j)_{i2} y_{2,t-j} + \cdots + \sum_{j=1}^{p} (\boldsymbol{\Gamma}_j)_{ip} y_{p,t-j} + \varepsilon_{it},$$

where $(\boldsymbol{\Gamma}_j)_{im}$ indicates the imth element of $\boldsymbol{\Gamma}_j$.

In the form of (19–11), that is, without autocorrelation of the disturbances, VARs are particularly simple to estimate. Although the equation system can be exceedingly large, it is, in fact, a seemingly unrelated regressions model with identical regressors. As such, the equations should be estimated separately by ordinary least squares.[7] The disturbance covariance matrix can then be estimated with average sums of squares or cross products of the least squares residuals. [See (17–9).] The proliferation of parameters in VARs is often

---

[6] See Box and Tiao (1981).

[7] See Section 17.2.1.

cited as a major disadvantage of their use. Consider, for example, a VAR involving five variables and five lags. Each Γ has 25 unconstrained elements, and there are five of them, for 125 free parameters, plus any others in μ. On the other hand, each single equation has only 25 parameters, and at least given sufficient degrees of freedom—there's the rub—a linear regression with 25 parameters is simple work even for a PC. Moreover, applications rarely involve even as many as four variables, so the model size issue may well be exaggerated.

VARs have been used primarily in macroeconomics. It was argued by some authors[8] that unrestricted VARs would do a better job of forecasting than structural multiple equations. This view would have to be purely empirical, however. One could argue that, as long as μ includes the (truly) relevant exogenous variables, the VAR is simply an overfit reduced form of some simultaneous equations model. The overfitting results from the possible inclusion of more lags than would be appropriate in the original model. (See Section 20.6 for a detailed examination of one such model.) On the other hand, one of the virtues of the VAR (it is argued) is that it obviates a decision as to what contemporaneous variables are exogenous; it has only lagged variables on the right-hand side.

Another common use of VARs has been in testing for causality between variables. Causality in the sense defined by Granger (1969) and Sims (1980) is inferred when lagged values of a variable, say x_t, have explanatory power in a regression of a variable y_t on lagged values of y_t and x_t. The VAR can be used to test the hypothesis.[9] Tests of the restrictions can be based on simple F tests in the single equations of the VAR model. The fact that the unrestricted equations have identical regressors means that these tests can be based on the results of simple OLS estimates.

There is a complication in these causality tests. The VAR is an article of faith. There is no theory behind the formulation. As such, the causality tests are predicated on a model which may, in fact be missing either intervening variables or additional lagged effects that should be present but are not. For the first of these, the problem is that a finding of causal effects might equally well result from the omission of a variable that is correlated with both (or all) of the left-hand-side variables. The second shortcoming is more tractable if one is willing to assume normality for the disturbances. Let S be the $M \times M$ residual covariance matrix based on a lag length of p and let S^* be its counterpart when there are $p + 1$ lags. Then the likelihood ratio statistic in (17–26), which would be

$$\lambda = T(\ln |S| - \ln |S^*|),$$

can be used to test the hypothesis that $\Gamma_{p+1} = 0$. The statistic would have a limiting chi-squared distribution with M^2 degrees of freedom. In principle, one might base a specification search for the right lag length on this calculation. The procedure would be to test up from $p = 1$ until addition of the last parameter matrix does not lead to a significant improvement in the fit. The same caution that underlies (18–20) would apply here; one would have to adjust the significance level at each step.

VARs have recently appeared in the microeconometrics literature as well. Chamberlain (1983) suggested that a useful approach to the analysis of panel data (see Section 16.4) would be to treat each period's observation as a separate equation. For the case of $T = 2$, we would have

$$y_{i1} = \alpha_i + \beta' x_{i1} + \varepsilon_{i1}$$

$$y_{i2} = \alpha_i + \beta' x_{i2} + \varepsilon_{i2}$$

---

[8] See, for example, Litterman (1979).

[9] See Geweke et al. (1983) as well as Sims (1980).

where i indexes individuals and α_i are unobserved individual effects. This produces a multivariate regression, to which Chamberlain added restrictions related to the individual effects. Holtz-Eakin et al.'s (1988) approach is to specify the equation as

$$y_{it} = \alpha_{0t} + \sum_{l=1}^{m} \alpha_{lt} y_{i,t-l} + \sum_{l=1}^{m} \delta_{lt} x_{i,t-l} + \Psi_t f_i + u_{it}.$$

In their study, y_{it} is hours worked by individual i in period t and x_{it} is the individual's wage in that period. A second equation for earnings is specified with lagged values of hours and earnings on the right-hand side. The individual, unobserved effects are f_i. This model is similar to the VAR in (19–11), but differs in several ways, as well. The number of periods is quite small (14 yearly observations for each individual), but there are nearly 1000 individuals. The dynamic equation is specified for a specific period, however, so the relevant sample size in each case is n, not T. Also, the number of lags in the model used is relatively small; the authors fixed it at 3. They thus have a two-equation VAR containing 12 unknown parameters, six in each equation. The authors used the model to analyze causality, measurement error, and parameter stability, that is, constancy of α_{it} and δ_{lt} across time.

19.2.3. Stationarity and Invertibility

At several points in the preceding, we have alluded to the notion of stationarity. In Section 15.2 we characterized an AR(1) disturbance process,

$$\varepsilon_t = \rho \varepsilon_{t-1} + u_t,$$

as stationary if $|\rho| < 1$. With that restriction, and the assumptions that $E[u_t] = $ zero, $\text{Var}[u_t] = \sigma_u^2$, and $\text{Cov}[u_t, u_s] = $ zero if $t \neq s$, we were able to show that

$$E[\varepsilon_t] = 0 \qquad \text{for all } t,$$

$$\text{Var}[\varepsilon_t] = \frac{\sigma_u^2}{1 - \rho^2}, \tag{19–12}$$

$$\text{Cov}[\varepsilon_t, \varepsilon_s] = \frac{\rho^{|t-s|} \sigma_u^2}{1 - \rho^2}.$$

Without the assumption about ρ, we found that the variance of ε_t would be infinite.

In the following, we use ε_t to denote the innovations in the process. The ARMA(p, q) process will be denoted as in (19–6). Henceforth, ε_t is assumed to be a **white noise process,** that is, one with zero mean, constant variance, σ_ε^2, and zero covariances at all lags.

Definition. A stochastic process, y_t, is **weakly stationary,** or **covariance stationary** if it satisfies the following requirements:

1. $E[y_t]$ is independent of t.
2. $\text{Var}[y_t]$ is a constant, independent of t.
3. $\text{Cov}[y_t, y_s]$ is a function of $t - s$, but not of t or s.

The third requirement is that the covariation between observations in the series is a function only of how far apart they are in time, not the time at which they occur. These properties clearly hold for the AR(1) process immediately above. Whether they apply for the other models we have examined remains to be seen.

We define the **autocovariance at lag k** as

$$\lambda_k = \text{Cov}[y_t, y_{t-k}].$$

Note that

$$\lambda_{-k} = \text{Cov}[y_t, y_{t+k}] = \lambda_k.$$

Stationarity implies that autocovariances are a function of k, but not of t. For example, in (19–12), we see that the autocovariances of the AR(1) process,

$$y_t = \mu + \gamma y_{t-1} + \varepsilon_t,$$

are

$$\text{Cov}[y_t, y_{t-k}] = \frac{\gamma^k \sigma_\varepsilon^2}{1 - \gamma^2}, \qquad k = 0, 1, \ldots \tag{19–13}$$

If $|\gamma| < 1$, this process is stationary.

For the MA(1) process,

$$y_t = \mu + \varepsilon_t - \theta \varepsilon_{t-1},$$

$$E[y_t] = \mu + E[\varepsilon_t] - \theta E[\varepsilon_{t-1}] = \mu,$$

$$\text{Var}[y_t] = (1 + \theta^2)\sigma_\varepsilon^2$$

$$\text{Cov}[y_t, y_{t-1}] = -\theta \sigma_\varepsilon^2$$

$$\text{Cov}[y_t, y_{t-k}] = 0 \qquad \text{for all } k > 1.$$

For any MA(q) series,

$$y_t = \mu + \varepsilon_t - \theta_1 \varepsilon_{t-1} - \cdots - \theta_q \varepsilon_{t-q},$$

$$E[y_t] = \mu + E[\varepsilon_t] + \theta_1 E[\varepsilon_{t-1}] + \cdots + \theta_q E[\varepsilon_{t-q}] = \mu, \tag{19–14}$$

$$\text{Var}[y_t] = (1 + \theta_1^2 + \cdots + \theta_q^2)\sigma_\varepsilon^2,$$

$$\text{Cov}[y_t, y_{t-1}] = -(\theta_1 \theta_2 + \theta_2 \theta_3 + \cdots + \theta_{q-1} \theta_q)\sigma_\varepsilon^2,$$

and so on, until

$$\text{Cov}[y_t, y_{t-q}] = -\theta_1 \theta_q \sigma_\varepsilon^2.$$

For lags greater than q, the autocovariances are zero. It follows, therefore, that finite moving average process is stationary regardless of the values of the parameters.

For the AR(1) process, the stationarity requirement is that $|\gamma| < 1$. This, in turn, implies that the variance of the moving average representation in (19–8) is finite. Consider the AR(2) process,

$$y_t = \mu + \gamma_1 y_{t-1} + \gamma_2 y_{t-2} + \varepsilon_t.$$

Write this as

$$C(L)y_t = \mu + \varepsilon_t,$$

where

$$C(L) = 1 - \gamma_1 L - \gamma_2 L^2.$$

Then, if it is possible,

$$y_t = [C(L)]^{-1}(\mu + \varepsilon_t).$$

Whether the inversion of the polynomial in the lag operator leads to a convergent series obviously depends on the values of γ_1 and γ_2. If so, the moving average representation will be

$$y_t = \sum_{i=0}^{\infty} \pi_i(\mu + \varepsilon_{t-i})$$

so that

$$\text{Var}[y_t] = \sum_{i=0}^{\infty} \pi_i^2 \sigma_\varepsilon^2.$$

Whether this is finite depends on whether the series of π_is is exploding or converging. For the AR(2) case, the series converges if (1) $|\gamma_2| < 1$; (2) $\gamma_1 + \gamma_2 < 1$; and (3) $\gamma_2 - \gamma_1 < 1$.[10]

For the more general case, convergence requires that the roots of the **characteristic equation,**

$$C(z) = 1 - \gamma_1 z - \gamma_2 z^2 - \cdots - \gamma_p z^p = 0,$$

have modulus greater than 1.[11] The general result is that the autoregressive process is stationary if the roots of the characteristic equation are greater than 1 or "lie outside the unit circle."[12] It follows that if a stochastic process is stationary, it has an infinite moving average representation (and, if not, it does not). The AR(1) process is the simplest case. The characteristic polynomial is

$$C(z) = 1 - \gamma z = 0,$$

and its single root is $1/\gamma$. This lies outside the unit circle if $|\gamma| < 1$, which we saw earlier.

Finally, consider the inversion of the moving average process in (19–9) and (19–10). Whether this is possible depends on the coefficients in $D(L)$ in the same fashion that stationarity hinges on the coefficients in $C(L)$. This counterpart to stationarity of an autoregressive process is called **invertibility.** In order for it to be possible to invert a moving average process to produce an autoregressive representation, the roots of $D(L) = 0$ must be outside the unit circle. Notice, for example, that in (19–5), the inversion of the moving average process is possible only if $|\theta| < 1$. Since the characteristic equation for the MA(1) process is $1 - \theta L = 0$, the root is $1/\theta$, which must be larger than 1.

If the roots of the characteristic equation of a moving average process all lie outside the unit circle, the series is said to be invertible. Note that invertibility has no bearing on the stationarity of a process. All moving average processes with finite coefficients are stationary. Whether an ARMA process is stationary or not depends only on the AR part of the model.

---

[10] This restricts (γ_1, γ_2) to a triangle with points at $(-1, 2)$, $(-1, -2)$, and $(1, 0)$.

[11] The roots may be complex. The characteristic equation is discussed in Section 18.6.3.

[12] The roots are of the form $a \pm bi$, where $i = \sqrt{-1}$. The unit circle refers to the two-dimensional set of values of a and b defined by $a^2 + b^2 = 1$.

19.2.4. Autocorrelations of a Stationary Process

The function

$$\lambda_k = \text{Cov}[y_t, y_{t-k}]$$

is called the autocovariance function of the process y_t. The **autocorrelation function,** or ACF, is obtained by dividing by the variance, λ_0, to obtain

$$\rho_k = \frac{\lambda_k}{\lambda_0}, \qquad -1 \le \rho_k \le 1.$$

For a stationary process, the ACF will be a function of k and the parameters of the process. The ACF is a useful device for describing a time-series process, in much the way that the moments are used to describe the distribution of a random variable. The sample counterpart to the ACF is the **correlogram,**

$$r_k = \frac{\displaystyle\sum_{t=k+1}^{T} (y_t - \bar{y})(y_{t-k} - \bar{y})/[T - (k + 1)]}{\displaystyle\sum_{t=1}^{T} (y_t - \bar{y})^2/(T - 1)}. \tag{19-15}$$

A plot of r_k against k provides a description of a process, and can be used to help discern what type of process is generating the data. Techniques for using the ACF, and a companion function, the **partial autocorrelation function,** or PACF, are the subjects of a library of "how to" books on the subject of "identification" of time series, that is, determining from the sample statistics the form of ARMA model that underlies the observed data. The partial autocorrelation of y_t and y_{t-k} is the least squares regression coefficient on y_{t-k} in a regression of y_t on a constant and k lagged values of y_t. This is computed for a number of lags, $k = 1, \ldots, K$. Thus, it is the correlation of y_t and y_{t-k}, after "partialing out" the influence of the intervening lags. (See Section 6.3.5 for further discussion of partial correlations and partial regression coefficients.) We see from (19–4) and, for example, (19–13) that an AR process will have an ACF that tapers off but exactly p nonzero PACs. From (19–5) and (19–14) we see the reverse for MA processes. ARMA processes are mixtures, so their ACFs and PACFs are also.[13]

One of the characteristics of a stationary stochastic process is an autocorrelation function that eventually tapers off to zero. The AR(1) process provides the simplest example, since

$$\rho_k = \gamma^k.$$

This is a geometric series that declines monotonically with positive or alternative signs. For higher-order autoregressive series, the autocorrelations may decline monotonically or may progress in the fashion of a damped sine wave.[14]

There are diagnostic tests based on the ACF which are used to discern whether a time series appears to be nonautocorrelated.[15] The Box–Pierce (1970) statistic,

$$Q = T \sum_{k=1}^{p} r_k^2,$$

---

[13] Box and Jenkins (1984) and Mills (1990) give numerous examples. The "identification" of time series from ACFs and PACFs is one of the intriguing mixtures of art and science in econometrics.

[14] The behavior is a function of the roots of the characteristic equation. This aspect is discussed further in Section 20.6 and, especially, 20.6.3.

[15] The Durbin–Watson test discussed in Section 15.5.1 is one of these.

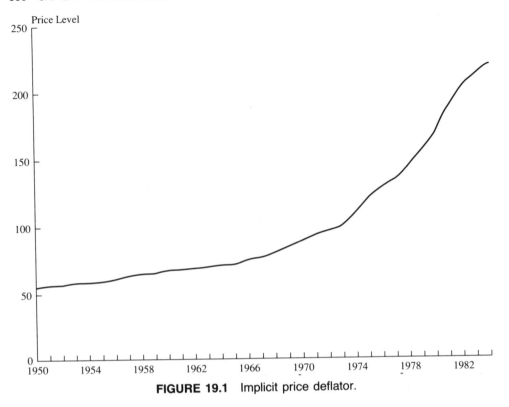

FIGURE 19.1 Implicit price deflator.

is commonly used to test whether a series is white noise. Under the null hypothesis that it is, Q is asymptotically distributed as chi-squared with p degrees of freedom. A refinement that appears to have better finite sample properties is the Box–Ljung (1978) statistic,

$$Q' = T(T + 2) \sum_{k=1}^{p} \frac{r_k^2}{T - k}.$$

The asymptotic distribution of Q' is the same as that of Q.[16]

EXAMPLE 19.1 Autocorrelation Function

The first 15 autocorrelations of the GNP deflator series used in Example 18.2 (see Table 18.1) are shown in Figure 19.1. The autocorrelations of the original series show the signature of a strongly trended, nonstationary series. The first difference also exhibits nonstationarity, as the autocorrelations are still very large and rising after a lag of 15 periods. The second difference shows fairly substantial negative autocorrelation, but behaves as one would expect a stationary series to behave. Intuition might suggest that further differencing would reduce the autocorrelation further, but this would be incorrect. We leave as an exercise to show that, in fact, for values of γ less than about 0.5, first differencing of an AR(1) process actually increases autocorrelation.

---

[16]There is some disagreement about the appropriateness of Q and Q' for testing model adequacy in this context. [See Maddala (1992, pp. 540–542).] The argument is essentially the same as that against using the Durbin–Watson statistic in the presence of lagged dependent variables. See Section 15.3.

19.3. Integrated Processes and Differencing

A process which figures prominently in recent work is the *random walk,*

$$y_t = \mu + y_{t-1} + \varepsilon_t.$$

By direct substitution,

$$y_t = \sum_{i=0}^{\infty} (\mu + \varepsilon_{t-i}).$$

That is, y_t is the simple sum of what will eventually be an infinite number of random variables, possibly with nonzero mean. If the innovations are being generated by the same zero-mean, constant variance distribution, the variance of y_t would obviously be infinite. As such, the random walk is clearly a nonstationary process, even if μ equals zero. On the other hand, the first difference of y_t,

$$z_t = y_t - y_{t-1} = \mu + \varepsilon_t,$$

is simply the innovation plus the mean, which we have already assumed is stationary.

The series y_t is said to be **integrated of order one,** denoted $I(1)$, because taking a first difference produces a stationary process. A series is integrated of order d, denoted $I(d)$, if the series becomes stationary after being first differenced d times. A further generalization of the ARMA model discussed in Section 19.2.1 would be the assumption that it applies not to y_t but to the differenced variable

$$z_t = (1 - L)^d y_t = \Delta^d y_t.$$

The resulting model is denoted an **autoregressive integrated moving average** model, or ARIMA (p, d, q).[17] In full, the model would be

$$\Delta^d y_t = \mu + \gamma_1 \Delta^d y_{t-1} + \gamma_2 \Delta^d y_{t-2} + \cdots + \gamma_p \Delta^d y_{t-p} + \varepsilon_t - \theta_1 \varepsilon_{t-1} - \cdots - \theta_q \varepsilon_{t-q}$$

where

$$\Delta y_t = y_t - y_{t-1} = (1 - L)y_t. \tag{19--16}$$

This may be written compactly as

$$C(L)[(1 - L)^d y_t] = \mu + D(L)\varepsilon_t, \tag{19--17}$$

where $C(L)$ and $D(L)$ are the polynomials in the lag operator and $(1 - L)^d y_t = \Delta^d y_t$ is the dth difference of y_t.

An $I(1)$ series in its raw (undifferenced) form is constantly growing. Most macroeconomic flows and stocks that relate to population size, such as output or employment, are $I(1)$. The nominal GNP series in Table 18.1 is an example. An $I(2)$ series is growing at an ever-increasing rate. The price-level data in Table 18.1 and shown below appear to be $I(2)$. But series that are $I(3)$ or greater are extremely unusual. Among the few manifestly $I(3)$ series that could be listed, one would find, for example, the money stocks or price levels in hyperinflationary economies such as interwar Germany or Hungary after World War II.

---

[17] There are yet further refinements one might consider, for example, removing seasonal effects from z_t by further differencing by quarter or month. Further discussion is given in Harvey (1990) and Davidson and MacKinnon (1993). For simplicity, we will not pursue these additional modifications.

EXAMPLE 19.2 Integrated Series _____

The variables in Tables 18.1 and 18.6 are strongly trended, so the mean is changing over time. Figure 19.2, 19.3, and 19.4 plot the GNP Deflator series in Table 18.1 and its first and second differences. The original series and first differences are obviously non-stationary.

_____

19.4. Random Walks, Trends, and Spurious Regressions

In a seminal paper, Granger and Newbold (1974) argued that researchers had not paid sufficient attention to the warning of very high autocorrelation in the residuals from conventional regression models. Among their conclusions were that macroeconomic data, as a rule, were integrated and that in regressions involving the levels of such data, the standard significance tests were usually misleading. The conventional t and F tests would tend to reject the hypothesis of no relationship when, in fact, there might be none. The general result at the center of these findings is that the regression of one random walk on another is virtually certain to produce a significant relationship, even if the two are, in fact, independent. Among their extreme conclusions, Granger and Newbold suggested that researchers use a critical t value of 11.2 rather than the standard normal value of 1.96 to assess the significance of a coefficient estimate. Phillips (1986) takes strong issue with this conclusion. Based on a more general model and on an analytical rather than a Monte Carlo approach, he suggests that the normalized statistic $t_\beta/\sqrt{T}$ be used for testing purposes rather than t_β itself. For the 50 observations used by Granger and Newbold, the

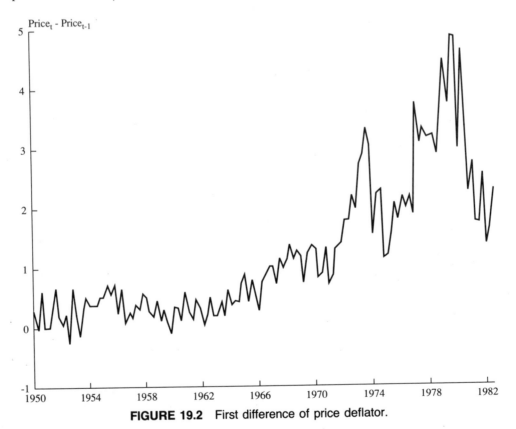

FIGURE 19.2 First difference of price deflator.

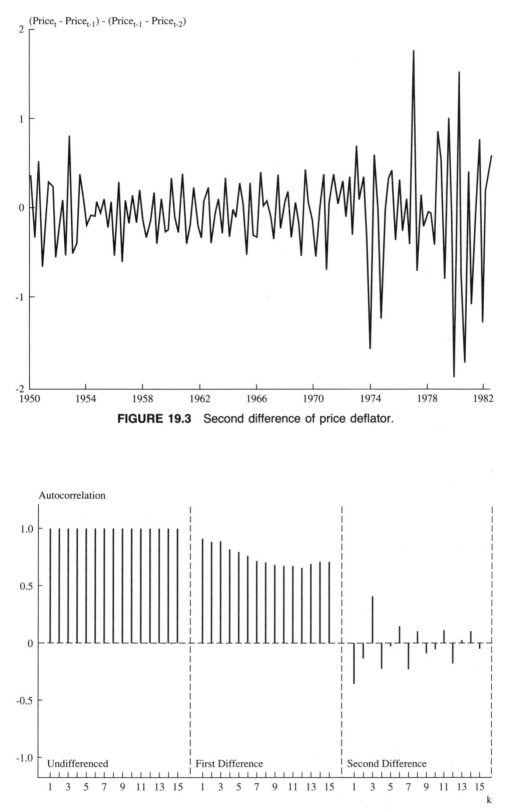

FIGURE 19.3   Second difference of price deflator.

FIGURE 19.4   Autocorrelations.

appropriate critical value would be close to 15! If anything, Granger and Newbold were too optimistic.

The **random walk with drift**

$$z_t = \mu + z_{t-1} + u_t, \tag{19–18}$$

and the **trend stationary process,**

$$z_t = \mu + \beta t + u_t, \tag{19–19}$$

where, in both cases, u_t is a white noise process, appear to be reasonable characterizations of many macroeconomic time series.[18] Clearly both of these will produce strongly trended, nonstationary series,[19] so it is not surprising that regressions involving such variables almost always produce significant relationships. The strong correlation would seem to be a consequence of the underlying trend, whether or not there really is any regression at work. But Granger and Newbold went a step further. The intuition is less clear if there is a pure **random walk** at work,

$$z_t = z_{t-1} + u_t, \tag{19–20}$$

but even here, they found that regression "relationships" appear to persist even in unrelated series.

Each of these three series is characterized by a **unit root.** In each case, the **data generating process** (DGP) can be written

$$(1 - L)z_t = \alpha + v_t, \tag{19–21}$$

where $\alpha = \mu$, β, and 0, and v_t is a stationary process, respectively. Thus, the characteristic equation has a single root equal to 1; hence the name. The upshot of Granger and Newbold's and Phillips's findings is that the use of data characterized by unit roots has the potential to lead to serious errors in inferences.

In all three settings, the case for first differencing or detrending is compelling. On the other hand, it is not going to be immediately obvious which is the correct way to proceed— the data are strongly trended in all three cases—and taking the incorrect approach will not necessarily improve matters. For example, first differencing in (19–18) or (19–20) produces a white noise series, but first differencing in (19–19) trades the trend for autocorrelation in the form of an MA(1) process. On the other hand, detrending, that is, computing the residuals from a regression on time, is obviously counterproductive in (19–18) and (19–20), even though the regression of z_t on a trend will appear to be significant for the reasons we have been discussing, whereas detrending in (19–19) appears to be the right approach.[20] Since none of these approaches are likely to be obviously preferable at the outset, some means of choosing is necessary. Considering nesting all three models in a single equation,

$$z_t = \mu + \beta t + z_{t-1} + u_t.$$

---

[18] The analysis to follow has been extended to more general disturbance process, but that complicates matters substantially. In this case, in fact, our assumption does cost considerable generality, but the extension is beyond the scope of our work. Some references on the subject are Phillips and Perron (1988) and Davidson and MacKinnon (1993).

[19] The constant term, μ, produces the trend in the random walk with drift. For convenience, suppose that the process starts at time zero. Then $z_t = \Sigma_{s=0}^{t} (\mu + u_t) = \mu t + \Sigma_{s=0}^{t} u_t$. Thus, z_t consists of a trend plus the sum of the innovations. The result is a variable with increasing variance around a linear trend.

[20] See Nelson and Kang (1981, 1984).

Now, subtract z_{t-1} from both sides of the equation and introduce the artificial parameter, γ:

$$z_t - z_{t-1} = \mu(1 - \gamma) + \beta\gamma + \beta(1 - \gamma)t + (\gamma - 1)z_{t-1} + u_t,$$
$$= \alpha_0 + \alpha_1 t + (\gamma - 1)z_{t-1}. \tag{19-22}$$

where, by hypothesis, $\gamma = 1$. Equation (19–22) provides the basis for a variety of tests for unit roots in economic data. In principle, a test of the hypothesis that $\gamma - 1$ equals zero gives confirmation of the random walk with drift, since if γ equals 1 (and α_1 equals zero), (19–24) results. If $\gamma - 1$ is less than zero, the evidence favors the trend stationary (or some other) model, and detrending (or some alternative) is the preferable approach. The practical difficulty is that standard inference procedures based on least squares and the familiar test statistics are not valid in this setting. The issue is discussed in the next section.

19.5. Unit Roots in Economic Data

The implications of unit roots in macroeconomic data are, at least potentially, profound. If a structural variable, such as real output, is truly $I(1)$, shocks to it will have permanent effects. If confirmed, this observation would mandate some rather serious reconsiderations of the analysis of macroeconomic policy. For example, the argument that monetary policy could have transitory effects on real output (which seems to be consistent with our regressions in Chapter 18) would vanish.[21] The literature is not without its skeptics, however. This result rests on a razor's edge. While the literature is thick with tests that have failed to reject the hypothesis that $\gamma = 1$, many have also not rejected the hypothesis that $\gamma \geq 0.95$, and at 0.95 (or, even at 0.99), the entire issue becomes moot.[22] Choi (1990), for example, suggests that the formulation of the commonly used augmented Dickey–Fuller test discussed below would be distorted by the presence of moving average components in the innovations.

Consider the simple AR(1) model with zero-mean, white noise innovations,

$$y_t = \gamma y_{t-1} + \varepsilon_t.$$

The downward bias of the least squares estimator when γ approaches 1 has been widely documented.[23] However, for $|\gamma| < 1$, the least squares estimator,

$$c = \frac{\displaystyle\sum_{t=2}^{T} y_t y_{t-1}}{\displaystyle\sum_{t=2}^{T} y_{t-1}^2},$$

does have

$$\text{plim } c = \gamma$$

and

$$\sqrt{T}(c - \gamma) \overset{d}{\to} N[0, 1 - \gamma^2].$$

---

[21] The observation seems to have touched off a bit of a feeding frenzy in the literature, as the 1980s saw the appearance of literally hundreds of studies, both theoretical and applied, of unit roots in economic data. An important example is Nelson and Plosser (1982).

[22] A large number of issues are raised in Maddala (1992, pp. 582–588).

[23] See, for example, Evans and Savin (1981, 1984).

Does the result hold up if $\gamma = 1$? The case is called the unit root case, since in the ARMA representation, $C(L)y_t = \varepsilon_t$, the characteristic equation, $1 - \gamma z = 0$, has one root equal to 1. The fact that the asymptotic variance appears to go to zero should raise suspicions. The literature on the question dates back to Mann and Wald (1943) and Rubin (1950). But for econometric purposes, the literature has a focal point at the celebrated papers of Dickey and Fuller (1979, 1981). They showed that if γ equals 1, then

$$T(c - \gamma) \overset{d}{\to} v$$

where v is a random variable with finite variance, and, in finite samples,

$$E[c] < 1.$$

There are two important implications in the Dickey–Fuller results. The first and obvious one is that the estimator of γ is biased downward if γ equals 1. The second is that the OLS estimate of c converges to its probability limit more rapidly than the estimators we are accustomed to. That is, the variance of c under the null hypothesis is $O(1/T^2)$, not $O(1/T)$. It turns out that the implications of this finding for regressions with trended data are considerable.

We have already observed that in some cases, differencing or detrending is required to achieve stationarity of a series. Suppose, though, that the AR(1) model above is fit to an $I(1)$ series, despite that fact. The upshot of the preceding is that the conventional measures will tend to hide the true value of γ; the sample estimate is biased downward and by dint of the very small *true* sampling variance, the conventional t test will tend, incorrectly, to reject the hypothesis that $\gamma = 1$. The practical solution to this problem devised by Dickey and Fuller was to derive, through Monte Carlo methods, an appropriate set of critical values for testing the hypothesis that γ equals 1 in an AR(1) regression when there truly is a unit root. The hypothesis may be carried out with a conventional t test, but with a revised set of critical values. A few of the values from the Dickey–Fuller tables are reproduced in Table 19.1. They also present values for testing for a unit root in the modified regressions

$$y_t = \mu + \gamma y_{t-1} + \varepsilon_t$$

and

$$y_t = \mu + \beta t + \gamma y_{t-1} + \varepsilon_t.$$

A convenient reformulation of the $I(1)$ model is

$$\Delta y_t = \mu + \gamma^* y_{t-1} + \varepsilon_t,$$

where

$$\gamma^* = \gamma - 1.$$

With this formulation, the Dickey–Fuller test for a unit root is carried out by testing the hypothesis that γ^* equals zero. The standard t statistic,

$$\frac{c^*}{\{\text{Est.Var}[c^*]\}^{1/2}},$$

is then referred to the Dickey–Fuller tables. The *augmented Dickey–Fuller test* is the same one as above, carried out in the context of the model

$$\Delta y_t = \mu + \gamma^* y_{t-1} + \sum_{j=1}^{p-1} \phi_j \Delta y_{t-j} + \varepsilon_t,$$

TABLE 19.1 Critical Values for the Dickey–Fuller Test

	Sample Size			
	25	**50**	**100**	**∞**
F ratio (D-F)[a]	7.24	6.73	6.49	6.25
F ratio (standard)	3.42	3.20	3.10	3.00
AR model[b]				
0.01	−2.66	−2.62	−2.60	−2.58
0.025	−2.26	−2.25	−2.24	−2.23
0.975	1.70	1.66	1.64	1.62
0.99	2.16	2.08	2.03	2.00
AR model with constant				
0.01	−3.75	−3.58	−3.51	−3.43
0.025	−3.333	−3.22	−3.17	−3.12
0.975	0.34	0.29	0.26	0.23
0.99	0.72	0.66	0.63	0.60
AR model with constant and time trend				
0.01	−4.38	−4.15	−4.04	−3.96
0.025	−3.95	−3.80	−3.69	−3.66
0.975	−0.50	−0.58	−0.62	−0.66
0.99	−0.15	−0.15	−0.28	−0.33

[a] From Dickey and Fuller (1981, p. 1063). Degrees of freedom are 2 and $T - p - 3$.
[b] From Fuller (1976, p. 373).

where

$$\phi_j = - \sum_{k=j+1}^{p} \gamma_k$$

and

$$\gamma^* = \left(\sum_{i=1}^{p} \gamma_i \right) - 1.$$

The advantage of this formulation is that it can accommodate higher-order autoregressive moving average processes in ε_t. The unit root test is carried out as before, against $\gamma^* = 0$.[24] The failure to reject the unit root produces the AR($p - 1$) model in the first differences. For a model with a time trend,

$$\Delta y_t = \mu + \beta t + \gamma^* y_{t-1} + \sum_{j=1}^{p-1} \phi_j \, \Delta y_{t-j} + \varepsilon_t,$$

the test is carried out by testing the joint hypothesis that $\beta = \gamma^* = 0$. Dickey and Fuller (1981) present counterparts to the critical *F* statistics for testing the hypothesis.

EXAMPLE 19.3 Test for a Unit Root

In their 1981 paper, Dickey and Fuller apply their methodology to a model for the log of a quarterly series on output, the Federal Reserve Board Production Index. The model used is

$$y_t = \mu + \beta t + \gamma y_{t-1} + \phi(y_{t-1} - y_{t-2}) + \varepsilon_t.$$

[24] It is easily verified that one of the roots of the characteristic polynomial is $1/(\gamma_1 + \gamma_2 + \cdots + \gamma_p)$.

The test is carried out by testing the joint hypothesis that both β and γ^* are zero in the model

$$y_t - y_{t-1} = \mu + \beta t + \gamma^* y_{t-1} + \phi(y_{t-1} - y_{t-2}) + \varepsilon_t.$$

We will replicate the study with our data on real GNP from Table 18.1. Recall, for our examples, $y_t = \ln(GNP_t/P_t)$. To begin, the simple AR(1) regression produces

$$y_t - y_{t-1} = \underset{(2.984)}{0.026313} - \underset{(-2.023)}{0.0078336 y_{t-1}}.$$

Asymptotic t ratios are given in parentheses. Based on the conventional critical point of -1.96, we would reject the hypothesis of a unit root. But the value from Table 19.1 for 134 observations would be roughly -3.17. So the hypothesis of a unit root is decidedly not rejected. The augmented regressions produce

$$y_t - y_{t-1} = \underset{(3.368)}{0.18348} + \underset{(2.987)}{0.00081864 t} - \underset{(-3.177)}{0.10349 y_{t-1}} + \underset{(2.091)}{0.17534(y_{t-1} - y_{t-2})},$$
$$R^2 = 0.1106678$$

and

$$y_t - y_{t-1} = \underset{(4.930)}{0.0072184} + \underset{(1.922)}{0.16366(y_{t-1} - y_{t-2})}, \qquad R^2 = 0.02722884.$$

The sample is observations 1950.4 to 1983.4.

$$F = \frac{(0.1106678 - 0.02722884)/2}{(1 - 0.1106678)/(134 - 4)} = 6.098.$$

The F statistic is larger than the conventional critical value of 3.10, but less than the Dickey–Fuller value of 6.49. Therefore, once again, we do not reject the hypothesis of a unit root in the process generating the log of real GNP. You might recall in Example 18.2 our initial results suggested that first differences appeared to be called for.

Recent literature on this subject has produced a hunt for unit roots in published data [e.g., Plosser and Nelson (1982)] and numerous extensions of the methodology. Convenient summaries are Nerlove and Diebold (1990) and Campbell and Perron (1991). The extensions include regressions with polynomials in time (Ouliaris et al., 1989) and splines in time (Perron, 1990). The extension to models with regressors of a general nature is complicated because the distribution of the standard test statistics is a function of the right-hand-side variables. Some useful results on the subject are in Phillips (1986).

19.6. Cointegration and Error Correction

In the *fully specified* regression model,

$$y_t = \beta x_t + \varepsilon_t,$$

there is a presumption that the disturbances, ε_t, are a white noise series.[25] By implication, then, the series ε_t is a stationary series. But this cannot be true if y_t and x_t are integrated of different orders. Thus, there must be some kind of inconsistency in the model. Intuitively, the regression specifies that the difference between y_t and x_t, $y_t - \beta x_t$, is varying ran-

---

[25] That is, if there is autocorrelation in the model, it has been removed through an appropriate transformation.

domly around some fixed level, with a fixed variance. But if x_t and y_t are integrated of different orders, they must be drifting apart, so this cannot be correct. For example, the regression of an $I(2)$ series on an $I(1)$ series would have a variable that is growing at an increasing rate being made a function of one that is growing at a constant rate. As such, the distance between them would have to be increasing with time, not varying randomly.

Generally, if two series are integrated to different orders, linear combinations of them will be integrated to the higher of the two orders. For example, in a regression of y_t, which is $I(1)$ on an x_t that is $I(0)$, the linear combination

$$e_t = y_t - bx_t$$

will be $I(1)$, regardless of b (that is, not just for the OLS slope, but for any b). On the other hand, if the two series are both $I(1)$, there may be a β such that

$$\varepsilon_t = y_t - \beta x_t$$

is $I(0)$. Intuitively, if the two series are both $I(1)$, this difference between them might be stable around a fixed mean. The implication would be that the series are drifting upward together at roughly the same rate. Two series that satisfy this requirement are said to be **cointegrated** and the vector $[1, -\beta]$ (or any multiple of it) is a **cointegrating vector.** In such a case, we can distinguish between a long-run relationship between y_t and x_t, that is, the manner in which the two variables drift upward together, and the short-run dynamics, that is, the relationship between deviations of y_t from its long-run trend and deviations of x_t from its long-run trend. If this is the case, clearly we must temper the conclusion of the preceding section. First differencing of the data would come at a cost, since it must obscure the long-run relationship between y_t and x_t. Studies of cointegration and error correction models, for example, Engle and Granger (1987), are concerned with methods of estimation that preserve the information about both forms of covariation.

Engle and Granger (1987) suggested a two-step approach to modeling cointegrated processes.[26] The first step involves fitting the long-run relationship in levels (despite the earlier warnings), by least squares.[27] The hypothesis of cointegration can then be tested by applying the Dickey–Fuller test to the residuals from the regression.[28] If the residuals fail the test, the series are taken not to be cointegrated, and the specification would have to be reconsidered. Otherwise, at a second step, use the residuals from the static regression as an **error correction** term in the dynamic, first-difference regression. One can then ''test down'' to find a parsimonious structure. (If this process is used for several iterations, one might give some thought to the problems of sequential estimation discussed in Section 8.5, with all of the other problems!)

EXAMPLE 19.4 Cointegration

Continuing the earlier examples of real GNP and M1, we have, for the regression in levels,

$$\ln\frac{GNP_t}{P_t} = \underset{(-15.177)}{-1.4505} + \underset{(38.877)}{0.69909}\ln M1_t, \quad R^2 = 0.92924, \quad r_e = 0.98867,$$

$$D - W = 0.02265.$$

---

[26] See Harvey (1990, p. 295).

[27] Since this regression involves variables with unit roots, the conventional inference results may still require modification. Stock (1987) and Banerjee et al. (1986) consider the statistical issues in the estimation of **cointegrating vectors.**

[28] An adjustment to the Dickey–Fuller test which accounts for the fact that the residuals are estimates of the true disturbances is given by Sargan and Bhargava (1983).

Notice that the Durbin–Watson statistic is close to zero. The residuals are nearly a random walk. The Dickey–Fuller test for the residuals is based on the regression

$$e_t - e_{t-1} = -0.00001957 - \underset{(-1.831)}{0.00002518 e_{t-1}}$$

The slope on e_{t-1} is not even significant by the conventional measure, so we conclude that real ln GNP and ln M1 are not cointegrated.

19.7. Generalized Autoregressive Conditional Heteroscedasticity

The ARCH model discussed in Section 15.9 has proven to be useful in studying a variety of macroeconomic phenomena, including the volatility of inflation (Coulson and Roberts, 1985), the term structure of interest rates (Engle et al., 1985), and foreign exchange markets (Domowitz and Hakkio, 1985), to name a few.[29] The common element in these studies is the observation of clusters of small and large regression residuals, which cannot be described adequately by conventional regression models. To reiterate, the ARCH(1) model is

$$y_t = \boldsymbol{\beta}' \mathbf{x}_t + \varepsilon_t,$$

$$\varepsilon_t | \varepsilon_{t-1} \sim N[0, \sigma_t^2], \tag{19-23}$$

$$\sigma_t^2 = \alpha_0 + \alpha_1 \varepsilon_{t-1}^2.$$

If $|\alpha_1| < 1$, then unconditionally,

$$\varepsilon_t \sim N\left[0, \frac{\alpha_0}{1 - \alpha_1}\right].$$

OLS is still the best *linear* unbiased estimator, but the *nonlinear* GLS estimator discussed in Section 15.9 is more efficient. Most empirical studies, for example, Engle and Kraft (1983), have used the more general ARCH(q) model,

$$\sigma_t^2 = \alpha_0 + \alpha_1 \varepsilon_{t-1}^2 + \alpha_2 \varepsilon_{t-1}^2 + \cdots + \alpha_q \varepsilon_{t-q}^2. \tag{19-24}$$

The ARCH(q) process in (19–24) is an *MA* process as discussed in Section 19.2.1, and much of the analysis of the model parallels that set of results. [Once again, see Engle (1982).] This section will generalize the ARCH(q) model, as suggested by Bollerslev (1986), in the direction of the ARMA models of Section 19.2.1. The discussion will parallel his development, although a large number of details are omitted for brevity. The reader is referred to his paper for the background and some of the less critical details. In addition, the discussion to follow will draw heavily on Example 14.15, so it may be helpful to review that example and Section 15.9 before proceeding.[30]

---

[29] Engle and Rothschild (1992) give an up-to-date survey of this literature.

[30] As have most areas in time-series econometrics, the line of literature on GARCH models has progressed rapidly in recent years and will surely continue to do so. We have presented Bollerslev's model in some detail, despite many recent extensions, not only to introduce the topic as a bridge to the literature, but also because it provides a convenient and interesting setting in which to discuss several related topics: for example, double length regression and pseudo-maximum likelihood estimation.

The model of generalized autoregressive conditional heteroscedasticity (GARCH) is defined as follows: The underlying regression is the usual one in (19–23). *Conditioned on an information set at time t,* denoted ψ_t, the distribution of the disturbance is assumed to be

$$\varepsilon_t | \psi_t \sim N[0, \sigma_t^2],$$

where the conditional variance is

$$\sigma_t^2 = \alpha_0 + \alpha_1 \varepsilon_{t-1}^2 + \alpha_2 \varepsilon_{t-2}^2 + \cdots + \alpha_q \varepsilon_{t-q}^2 + \delta_1 \sigma_{t-1}^2 + \delta_2 \sigma_{t-2}^2 + \cdots + \delta_p \sigma_{t-p}^2.^{[31]}$$
$$(19\text{–}25)$$

Define

$$\mathbf{z}_t = [1, \varepsilon_{t-1}^2, \varepsilon_{t-2}^2, \ldots, \varepsilon_{t-q}^2, \sigma_{t-1}^2, \sigma_{t-2}^2, \ldots, \sigma_{t-p}^2]'$$

and

$$\boldsymbol{\gamma} = [\alpha_0, \alpha_1, \ldots, \alpha_q, \delta_1, \delta_2, \ldots, \delta_p]' = [\boldsymbol{\alpha}', \boldsymbol{\delta}']'.$$

Then,

$$\sigma_t^2 = \boldsymbol{\gamma}' \mathbf{z}_t.$$

Notice that the conditional variance is defined by an ARMA(p, q) process in the innovations ε_t^2, exactly as in Section 19.2.1. The difference here is that the *mean* of the random variable of interest, y_t is described completely by a heteroscedastic, but otherwise ordinary regression model. The *conditional variance,* however, evolves over time in what might be a very complicated manner, depending on the parameter values and on p and q. The model in (19–25) is a GARCH(p, q) model, where p refers, as before, to the order of the autoregressive part. As Bollerslev demonstrates with an example, the virtue of this approach is that a GARCH model with a small number of terms appears to perform as well as or better than an ARCH model with many.

The stationarity conditions discussed in Section 19.2.3 are important in this context to ensure that the moments of the normal distribution are finite. The reason is that higher moments of the normal distribution are finite powers of the variance. A normal distribution with variance σ_t^2 has fourth moment $3\sigma_t^4$, sixth moment is $15\sigma_t^6$, and so on. (The precise relationship of the even moments of the normal distribution to the variance is given in Exercise 14 of Chapter 4.) Simply ensuring that σ_t^2 is stable does not ensure that higher powers are as well.[32] Bollerslev presents a useful figure that shows the conditions needed to ensure stability for moments up to order 12 for a GARCH(1, 1) model and gives some additional discussion. For example, for a GARCH(1, 1) process, in order for the fourth moment to exist, $3\alpha_1^2 + 2\alpha_1\delta_1 + \delta_1^2$ must be less than 1.

It is convenient to write (19–25) in terms of polynomials in the lag operator in the format of (19–7):

$$\sigma_t^2 = \alpha_0 + A(L)\varepsilon_t^2 + D(L)\sigma_t^2.$$

---

[31] We have changed Bollerslev's notation slightly so as not to conflict with our previous presentation. He used β instead of our δ and b instead of our β in (19–23).

[32] The conditions cannot be imposed a priori. In fact, there is no nonzero set of parameters that guarantees stability of *all* moments, even though the normal distribution has finite moments of all orders. As such, the normality assumption must be viewed as an approximation. See Section 19.7.2.

As we saw in Section 19.2.2, the stationarity condition for such an equation is that the roots of the characteristic equation, $1 - D(z) = 0$, must lie outside the unit circle. For the present, we will assume that this is the case for the model we are considering and that $A(1) + D(1) < 1$. [This is stronger than the assumption needed to ensure stationarity in a higher-order autoregressive model; that would depend only on $D(L)$.] The implication is that the GARCH process is covariance stationary with $E[\varepsilon_t] = 0$ (unconditionally), $\text{Var}[\varepsilon_t] = \alpha_0/[1 - A(1) - D(1)]$, and $\text{Cov}[\varepsilon_t, \varepsilon_s] = 0$ for all $t \neq s$. This means that unconditionally the model is the classical regression model that we examined in Chapter 6.

The usefulness of this specification is that it allows the variance to evolve over time in a way that is much more general than the simple specification examined in Section 15.9. The comparison between simple finite distributed lag models and the dynamic regression model discussed in Chapter 18 is analogous. For the example discussed in his paper, Bollerslev reports that although Engle and Kraft's (1983) ARCH(8) model for the rate of inflation in the GNP deflator appears to remove all ARCH effects, a closer look reveals GARCH effects at several lags. By fitting a GARCH(1, 1) model to the same data, Bollerslev finds that the ARCH effects out to the same eight-period lag as fit by Engle and Kraft and his observed GARCH effects are all satisfactorily accounted for.

19.7.1. Maximum Likelihood Estimation of the GARCH Model

Bollerslev describes a method of estimation based on the BHHH algorithm. (See Section 12.5.[33]) As he shows, the method is relatively simple, although with the line search and first derivative method that he suggests, it probably involves more computation and more iterations than necessary. Following the suggestions of Harvey (1976), it turns out that there is a simpler way to estimate the GARCH model that is also very illuminating. It shows how this model is actually very similar to the more conventional model of multiplicative heteroscedasticity that we examined in Example 14.15. This is also essentially the technique used in Section 15.9, although we will simplify that presentation a bit here.

For normally distributed disturbances, the log likelihood for a sample of T observations is

$$\ln L = \sum_t -\frac{1}{2}\left[\ln(2\pi) + \ln \sigma_t^2 + \frac{\varepsilon_t^2}{\sigma_t^2}\right]$$

$$= \sum_t \ln f_t(\boldsymbol{\theta}) = \sum_t l_t(\boldsymbol{\theta}),^{[34]}$$

where

$$\varepsilon_t = y_t - \boldsymbol{\beta}'\mathbf{x}_t$$

and

$$\boldsymbol{\theta} = (\boldsymbol{\beta}', \boldsymbol{\alpha}', \boldsymbol{\delta}')' = (\boldsymbol{\beta}', \boldsymbol{\gamma}')'.$$

---

[33] The BHHH algorithm is a variable metric algorithm similar to the DFP method discussed in Section 12.5. The weighting matrix used in the algorithm is the BHHH estimator of the asymptotic covariance matrix of the parameters based on the current estimates.

[34] There are three minor errors in Bollerslev's derivation that we note here to avoid the apparent inconsistencies. In his (22), $\frac{1}{2}h_t$ should be $\frac{1}{2}h_t^{-1}$. In (23), $-2h_t^{-2}$ should be $-h_t^{-2}$. In (28), $h\ \partial h/\partial\omega$ should, in each case, be $(1/h)\ \partial h/\partial\omega$. [In his (8), $\alpha_0\alpha_1$ should be $\alpha_0 + \alpha_1$, but this has no implications for our derivation.]

For convenience, we will examine derivatives of l_t. Derivatives of $\ln L$ are obtained by summation. The first derivatives with respect to the variance parameters are

$$\frac{\partial l_t}{\partial \boldsymbol{\gamma}} = -\frac{1}{2}\left[\frac{1}{\sigma_t^2} - \frac{\varepsilon_t^2}{(\sigma_t^2)^2}\right]\frac{\partial \sigma_t^2}{\partial \boldsymbol{\gamma}}$$

$$= \frac{1}{2}\left(\frac{1}{\sigma_t^2}\right)\frac{\partial \sigma_t^2}{\partial \boldsymbol{\gamma}}\left(\frac{\varepsilon_t^2}{\sigma_t^2} - 1\right) \qquad (19\text{--}26)$$

$$= \frac{1}{2}\left(\frac{1}{\sigma_t^2}\right)\mathbf{g}_t v_t.$$

Note that $E[v_t] = 0$. Using the notation defined above, we have

$$\frac{\partial^2 l_t}{\partial \boldsymbol{\gamma}\,\partial \boldsymbol{\gamma}'} = \frac{1}{2}v_t\left\{\frac{\partial[(1/\sigma_t^2)\mathbf{g}_t]}{\partial \boldsymbol{\gamma}'}\right\} + \frac{1}{2}\left(\frac{1}{\sigma_t^2}\right)\mathbf{g}_t\left\{\frac{\partial[(\varepsilon_t^2/\sigma_t^2) - 1]}{\partial \boldsymbol{\gamma}'}\right\}$$

$$= \frac{1}{2}v_t\left\{\frac{\partial[(1/\sigma_t^2)\mathbf{g}_t]}{\partial \boldsymbol{\gamma}'}\right\} - \frac{1}{2}\left(\frac{\mathbf{g}_t}{\sigma_t^2}\right)\left(\frac{\mathbf{g}_t}{\sigma_t^2}\right)'\frac{\varepsilon_t^2}{\sigma_t^2}. \qquad (19\text{--}27)$$

We will return to the computation of the derivatives, $\mathbf{g}_t$, later. Suppose, for now, that there are no regression parameters. Newton's method for estimating the variance parameters would be

$$\hat{\boldsymbol{\gamma}}^{i+1} = \hat{\boldsymbol{\gamma}}^i - \mathbf{H}^{-1}\mathbf{g},$$

where $\mathbf{H}$ indicates the Hessian and $\mathbf{g}$ is the first derivatives vector. Following Harvey's suggestion (see Example 14.15), we will use the method of scoring instead. To do this we make use of $E[v_t] = 0$ and $E[\varepsilon_t^2/\sigma_t^2] = 1$. After taking expectations in (19–27), the iteration reduces to

$$\hat{\boldsymbol{\gamma}}^{i+1} = \hat{\boldsymbol{\gamma}}^i + \left[\sum_t \frac{1}{2}\left(\frac{\mathbf{g}_t}{\sigma_t^2}\right)\left(\frac{\mathbf{g}_t}{\sigma_t^2}\right)'\right]^{-1}\left[\sum_t \frac{1}{2}\left(\frac{\mathbf{g}_t}{\sigma_t^2}\right)v_t\right].$$

Notice that this is exactly equation (14–35). For this part of the iteration, we would obtain the update for the estimate of the variance parameters as the vector of slopes in a linear regression of $v_{*t} = (1/\sqrt{2})v_t$ on regressors $\mathbf{w}_{*t} = (1/\sqrt{2})\mathbf{g}_t/\sigma_t^2$. That is,

$$\hat{\boldsymbol{\gamma}}^{i+1} = \hat{\boldsymbol{\gamma}}^i + [\mathbf{W}_*'\mathbf{W}_*]^{-1}\mathbf{W}_*'\mathbf{v}_*,$$

$$= \hat{\boldsymbol{\gamma}}^i + [\mathbf{W}_*'\mathbf{W}_*]^{-1}\left(\frac{\partial \ln L}{\partial \boldsymbol{\gamma}}\right), \qquad (19\text{--}28)$$

where row t of $\mathbf{W}_*$ is $\mathbf{w}_{*t}'$. As in Example 14.15, the iteration has converged when the slope vector is zero, which happens when the first derivative vector is zero. When the iterations are complete, the estimated asymptotic covariance matrix is simply

$$\text{Est.Asy.Var}[\hat{\boldsymbol{\gamma}}] = [\hat{\mathbf{W}}_*'\hat{\mathbf{W}}_*]^{-1}$$

based on the estimated parameters. Note that this matrix is close to, but not quite the same as the BHHH estimator. It is instructive to make the difference explicit. From the derivation above,

$$\mathbf{W}_*'\mathbf{W}_* = \sum_t \left[\left(\frac{1}{\sqrt{2}}\right)\frac{\mathbf{g}_t}{\sigma_t^2}\right]\left[\left(\frac{1}{\sqrt{2}}\right)\frac{\mathbf{g}_t}{\sigma_t^2}\right]' \qquad (19\text{--}29)$$

From the first derivatives in (19–26), the BHHH estimator would be the inverse of

$$\mathbf{B'B} = \sum_t v_t^2 \left[\frac{1}{2}\frac{\mathbf{g}_t}{\sigma_t^2}\right]\left[\frac{1}{2}\frac{\mathbf{g}_t}{\sigma_t^2}\right]'. \tag{19–30}$$

But $E[v_t^2] = 2$, so the expectations of these two matrices are the same.

The usefulness of the derivation just given is that $E[\partial^2 \ln L/\partial\boldsymbol{\gamma}\,\partial\boldsymbol{\beta}']$ is, in fact, zero. Since the expected Hessian is block diagonal, applying the method of scoring to the full parameter vector can proceed in two parts, exactly as it did in Example 14.15 for the multiplicative heteroscedasticity model. That is, the updates for the mean and variance parameter vectors can be computed separately.

Consider, then, the slope parameters, $\boldsymbol{\beta}$. The relevant first derivative is

$$\frac{\partial l_t}{\partial\boldsymbol{\beta}} = \frac{\varepsilon_t \mathbf{x}_t}{\sigma_t^2} + \frac{1}{2}\left(\frac{1}{\sigma_t^2}\right)v_t\left(\frac{\partial\sigma_t^2}{\partial\boldsymbol{\beta}}\right). \tag{19–31}$$

For convenience, denote $\partial\sigma_t^2/\partial\boldsymbol{\beta}$ as $\mathbf{d}_t$. Then the second derivatives are

$$\frac{\partial^2 l_t}{\partial\boldsymbol{\beta}\,\partial\boldsymbol{\beta}'} = -\left(\frac{1}{\sigma_t^2}\right)\mathbf{x}_t\mathbf{x}_t' - \left(\frac{1}{\sigma_t^2}\right)^2 \varepsilon_t\mathbf{x}_t\mathbf{d}_t'$$

$$-\frac{1}{2}\left(\frac{1}{\sigma_t^2}\right)^2 v_t\mathbf{d}_t\mathbf{d}_t' + \frac{1}{2}\left(\frac{1}{\sigma_t^2}\right)v_t\frac{\partial\mathbf{d}_t}{\partial\boldsymbol{\beta}'} + \frac{1}{2}\left(\frac{1}{\sigma_t^2}\right)\mathbf{d}_t\frac{\partial v_t}{\partial\boldsymbol{\beta}'}. \tag{19–32}$$

Recall that $v_t = (\varepsilon_t^2/\sigma_t^2) - 1$, so

$$\frac{\partial v_t}{\partial\boldsymbol{\beta}'} = -2\left(\frac{1}{\sigma_t^2}\right)\varepsilon_t\mathbf{x}_t' - \left(\frac{1}{\sigma_t^2}\right)\left(\frac{\varepsilon_t^2}{\sigma_t^2}\right)\mathbf{d}_t'.$$

Since $\mathbf{d}_t$ is not a function of current innovations, and $E(\varepsilon_t) = E(v_t) = 0$, only the first term in (19–32) and the second term in $\partial v_t/\partial\boldsymbol{\beta}'$ have nonzero expectation (conditioned on ψ_t). Also, $E[\varepsilon_t^2/\sigma_t^2] = 1$. Collecting terms, we are left with

$$E\left[\frac{\partial^2 l_t}{\partial\boldsymbol{\beta}\,\partial\boldsymbol{\beta}'}\right] = -\left(\frac{1}{\sigma_t^2}\right)\mathbf{x}_t\mathbf{x}_t' - \frac{1}{2}\left(\frac{1}{\sigma_t^2}\right)^2\mathbf{d}_t\mathbf{d}_t'.$$

The same type of modified scoring method as used earlier produces the iteration

$$\hat{\boldsymbol{\beta}}^{i+1} = \hat{\boldsymbol{\beta}}^i + \left[\sum_t \frac{\mathbf{x}_t\mathbf{x}_t'}{\sigma_t^2} + \frac{1}{2}\left(\frac{\mathbf{d}_t}{\sigma_t^2}\right)\left(\frac{\mathbf{d}_t}{\sigma_t^2}\right)'\right]^{-1}\left[\sum_t \frac{\mathbf{x}_t\varepsilon_t}{\sigma_t^2} + \frac{1}{2}\left(\frac{\mathbf{d}_t}{\sigma_t^2}\right)v_t\right]$$

$$= \hat{\boldsymbol{\beta}}^i + \left[\sum_t \frac{\mathbf{x}_t\mathbf{x}_t'}{\sigma_t^2} + \frac{1}{2}\left(\frac{\mathbf{d}_t}{\sigma_t^2}\right)\left(\frac{\mathbf{d}_t}{\sigma_t^2}\right)'\right]^{-1}\frac{\partial \ln L}{\partial\boldsymbol{\beta}} \tag{19–33}$$

$$= \hat{\boldsymbol{\beta}}^i + \mathbf{h}^i.$$

This has been referred to as a **double-length regression**. [See Orme (1990) and Davidson and MacKinnon (1993, Chapter 14).] The update vector, $\mathbf{h}^i$, is the vector of slopes in an augmented, or double-length generalized regression,

$$\mathbf{h}^i = [\mathbf{C}'\boldsymbol{\Omega}^{-1}\mathbf{C}]^{-1}[\mathbf{C}'\boldsymbol{\Omega}^{-1}\mathbf{a}], \tag{19–34}$$

where $\mathbf{C}$ is a $2T \times K$ matrix whose first T rows are the $\mathbf{X}$ from the original regression model and whose next T rows are $(1/\sqrt{2})\mathbf{d}_t/\sigma_t^2$, $t = 1, \ldots, T$; $\mathbf{a}$ is a $2T \times 1$ vector whose first T elements are ε_t and whose next T elements are $(1/\sqrt{2})v_t$, $t = 1, \ldots, T$; and $\boldsymbol{\Omega}$ is a diagonal matrix with $1/\sigma_t^2$ in positions $1, \ldots, T$ and ones below observation

T. At convergence, $[\mathbf{C}'\mathbf{\Omega}^{-1}\mathbf{C}]^{-1}$ provides the asymptotic covariance matrix for the MLE. The resemblance to the familiar result for the generalized regression model is striking, but note that this is based on the double-length regression.

It remains to formulate the computation of $\mathbf{g}_t$ and $\mathbf{d}_t$. These are as follows:

$$\frac{\partial \sigma_t^2}{\partial \boldsymbol{\gamma}} = \mathbf{g}_t = \mathbf{z}_t + \sum_{i=1}^{p} \delta_i \mathbf{g}_{t-i}.$$

[Recall that $\mathbf{z}_t$ is defined after (19–25).] Starting values are needed to begin this recursion. Bollerslev suggests that the presample variances and squared disturbances be estimated with $s^2 = \mathbf{e}'\mathbf{e}/T$, which would be based on the current parameter estimates. Therefore,

$$\mathbf{z}_0 = \mathbf{z}_{-1} = \cdots = [1, s^2, s^2, \ldots].$$

The derivative may be written as

$$\mathbf{g}_t = \mathbf{z}_t + \mathbf{G}_t\boldsymbol{\delta}$$

where $\mathbf{G}_t$ is a $(1 + q + p) \times p$ matrix whose p columns are, at observation t, the p previous observations on $\mathbf{g}$. It is now necessary to estimate the presample values of $\mathbf{g}_t$. If the GARCH process were at a constant value (defined by $\mathbf{z}_0$) for many periods prior to the sample, then $\mathbf{g}$, being a sum of previous $\mathbf{z}$'s, would be also. By substitution, we would have

$$\mathbf{g}_0 = \mathbf{z}_0 + \delta_1 \mathbf{g}_0 + \delta_2 \mathbf{g}_0 + \cdots + \delta_p \mathbf{z}_0,$$

or

$$\mathbf{g}_0 = \frac{1}{1 - \delta_1 - \delta_2 - \cdots - \delta_p}\mathbf{z}_0 = \frac{1}{1 - D(1)}\mathbf{z}_0.$$

The earlier values would be the same. Any presample columns in $\mathbf{G}_t$ can be set equal to $\mathbf{g}_0$. As the summation progresses, columns are shifted rightward in $\mathbf{G}_t$ with the leftmost one replaced at the end of the computation with the current value of $\mathbf{g}_t$ obtained, in anticipation of the next observation. A similar procedure can be used to compute

$$\frac{\partial \sigma_t^2}{\partial \boldsymbol{\beta}} = \mathbf{d}_t = -2\sum_{j=1}^{q} \alpha_j \mathbf{x}_{t-j}\varepsilon_{t-j} + \sum_{j=1}^{p} \delta_j \mathbf{d}_{t-j}.$$

$$= \mathbf{E}_t\boldsymbol{\alpha} + \mathbf{D}_t\boldsymbol{\delta}. \tag{19–35}$$

$\mathbf{E}_t$ is a $K \times q$ matrix whose jth column is $-2\mathbf{x}_{t-j}\varepsilon_{t-j}$ and $\mathbf{D}_t$ is a $(1 + q + p) \times p$ matrix whose p columns are the p previous observations on $\mathbf{d}_t$. The matrices $\mathbf{E}_t$ and $\mathbf{D}_t$ can be computed in a summation in the same fashion as $\mathbf{G}_t$ shown earlier. This recursion is simpler to initialize, since presample values of ε_t may be set to their expectation of zero. Thus, any presample columns in $\mathbf{E}_t$ and $\mathbf{D}_t$ can be filled with columns of zeros.

The iteration is done simply by computing the update vectors to the current parameters as defined above. The only important consideration is that to apply the scoring method, the estimates of $\boldsymbol{\beta}$ and $\boldsymbol{\gamma}$ are updated simultaneously. That is, one does not use the updated estimate of $\boldsymbol{\gamma}$ in (19–28) to update the weights for the GLS regression to compute the new $\boldsymbol{\beta}$ in (19–34). The same estimates (the results of the prior iteration) are used on the right-hand sides of both (19–28) and (19–33). The remaining problem is to obtain starting values for the iterations. One obvious choice is $\mathbf{b}$, the OLS estimator, for $\boldsymbol{\beta}$, $\mathbf{e}'\mathbf{e}/T = s^2$ for α_0 and zero for all of the remaining parameters. The OLS slope vector will be consistent under all specifications. A useful alternative in this context would be to start $\boldsymbol{\alpha}$ at the vector of slopes in the least squares regression of e_t^2, the squared OLS residual, on a constant and q lagged values.[35] As discussed below, an LM test for the presence of GARCH effects is then a by-product of the first iteration. In principle, the updated result of the first iteration is an **efficient two-step estimator** of all the parameters. But having gone to the full effort to set up the iterations, nothing is gained by not iterating to convergence. One virtue of allowing the procedure to iterate to convergence is that the resulting log-likelihood function can be used in likelihood ratio tests.

19.7.2. Pseudo-Maximum Likelihood Estimation

We now consider an implication of nonnormality of the disturbances. If the assumption of normality is weakened to only

$$E[\varepsilon_t | \psi_t] = 0,$$

$$E\left[\frac{\varepsilon_t^2}{\sigma_t^2} \middle| \psi_t\right] = 1,$$

and

$$E\left[\frac{\varepsilon_t^4}{\sigma_t^4} \middle| \psi_t\right] = \kappa, \qquad \text{a finite value,}$$

where σ_t^2 is as defined earlier, the normal log-likelihood function is inappropriate. In this case, the nonlinear (ordinary or weighted) least squares estimator would have the properties discussed in Chapter 11. However, it would be more difficult to compute than the MLE discussed earlier. It has been shown [see White (1982c) and Weiss (1982)] that the *pseudo-MLE* obtained by maximizing the same log likelihood as if it were correct produces a consistent estimator despite the misspecification.[36] However, the asymptotic covariance matrices for the parameter estimates must be adjusted.

The general result for cases such as this one [see Gourieroux et al. (1984)] is that the appropriate asymptotic covariance matrix for the pseudo-MLE of a parameter vector $\boldsymbol{\theta}$ would be

$$\text{Asy.Var}[\hat{\boldsymbol{\theta}}] = \mathbf{H}^{-1}\mathbf{F}\mathbf{H}^{-1} \tag{19–36}$$

where

$$\mathbf{H} = -E\left[\frac{\partial^2 \ln L}{\partial \boldsymbol{\theta} \, \partial \boldsymbol{\theta}'}\right]$$

and

$$\mathbf{F} = E\left[\left(\frac{\partial \ln L}{\partial \boldsymbol{\theta}}\right)\left(\frac{\partial \ln L}{\partial \boldsymbol{\theta}}\right)'\right]$$

(that is, the BHHH estimator), and $\ln L$ is the utilized but inappropriate log-likelihood function. For present purposes, $\mathbf{H}$ and $\mathbf{F}$ are still block diagonal, so we can treat the mean

---

[35] A test for the presence of q ARCH effects against none can be carried out by carrying TR^2 from this regression into a table of critical values for the chi-squared distribution. But in the presence of GARCH effects, this procedure loses its validity.

[36] White (1982c) gives some additional requirements for the true underlying density of ε_t. Gourieroux et al. (1984) also consider the issue. Under the assumptions given, the expectations of the matrices in (19–27) and (19–32) remain the same as under normality. The consistency and asymptotic normality of the pseudo-MLE can be argued under the logic of GMM estimators.

and variance parameters separately. In addition, $E[v_t]$ is still zero, so the second derivative terms in both blocks are quite simple. (The parts involving $\partial^2 \sigma_t^2 / \partial \gamma \, \partial \gamma'$ and $\partial^2 \sigma_t^2 / \partial \boldsymbol{\beta} \, \partial \boldsymbol{\beta}'$ fall out of the expectation.) Taking expectations and inserting the parts produces the corrected asymptotic covariance matrix for the variance parameters:

$$\text{Asy.Var.}[\hat{\boldsymbol{\gamma}}_{\text{qmle}}] = [\mathbf{W}'_* \mathbf{W}_*]^{-1} \mathbf{B}' \mathbf{B} [\mathbf{W}'_* \mathbf{W}_*]^{-1},$$

where the matrices are defined in (19–29) and (19–30). For the slope parameters, the adjusted asymptotic covariance matrix would be

$$\text{Asy.Var.}[\hat{\boldsymbol{\beta}}_{\text{qmle}}] = [\mathbf{C}' \boldsymbol{\Omega}^{-1} \mathbf{C}]^{-1} \left[\sum_t \mathbf{b}_t \mathbf{b}'_t \right] [\mathbf{C}' \boldsymbol{\Omega}^{-1} \mathbf{C}]^{-1},$$

where the outer matrix is defined in (19–34) and, from the first derivatives given in (19–29),

$$\mathbf{b}_t = \frac{\mathbf{x}_t \varepsilon_t}{\sigma_t^2} + \frac{1}{2} \left(\frac{v_t}{\sigma_t^2} \right) \mathbf{d}_t$$

and $\mathbf{d}_t$ is defined after (19–29) and in (19–35).

19.7.3. Testing for GARCH Effects

The preceding development appears fairly complicated. In fact, it is not, since at each step, nothing more than a linear least squares regression is required. The intricate part of the computation is setting up the derivatives. On the other hand, it does take a fair amount of programming to get this far.[37] As Bollerslev suggests, it might be useful to test for GARCH effects first.

The simplest approach is to examine the squares of the least squares residuals. The autocorrelations of the squares of the residuals provide evidence about ARCH effects. An LM test of ARCH(q) against the hypothesis of no ARCH effects [ARCH(0), the classical model] can be carried out by computing $\chi^2 = TR^2$ in the regression of $\mathbf{e}_t^2$ on a constant and q lagged values. The statistic has a limiting chi-squared distribution with q degrees of freedom. Values larger than the critical table value give evidence of the presence of ARCH (or GARCH) effects.

Bollerslev suggests a Lagrange multiplier statistic which is, in fact, surprisingly simple to compute. The LM test for GARCH(p, 0) against GARCH(p, q) can be carried out by referring T times the R^2 in the linear regression defined in (19–28) to the chi-squared critical value with q degrees of freedom. Note that this is precisely the statistic used in Section 15.9 for testing ARCH(1) against ARCH(0). There is, unfortunately, an indeterminacy in this test procedure. The test for ARCH(q) against GARCH(p, q) is exactly the same as that for ARCH(q) against ARCH($p + q$). For carrying out the test, one can use as starting values a set of estimates that includes $\boldsymbol{\delta} = \mathbf{0}$ and any consistent estimates for $\boldsymbol{\beta}$ and $\boldsymbol{\alpha}$. Then, TR^2 for the regression at the initial iteration provides the test statistic.[38]

A number of recent papers have questioned the use of test statistics based solely on normality. Woolridge (1991) is a useful summary with several examples.

---

[37] Since this procedure is available as a preprogrammed procedure in TSP (Hall, 1982), RATS (VAR Econometrics), and LIMDEP (Greene, 1991), among others, this warning might itself be overstated.

[38] Bollerslev argues that in view of the complexity of the computations involved in estimating the GARCH model, it is useful to have a test for GARCH effects. However, this is a case (as are many other maximum likelihood problems) in which the apparatus for carrying out the test is the same as that for estimating the model. Having computed the LM statistic for GARCH effects, one can proceed to estimate the model just by allowing the program to iterate to convergence. There is no additional cost beyond waiting for the answer.

19.7.4. An Example

Bollerslev reports the results of a study of the implicit price deflator for GNP done by Engle and Kraft (1983) using an ARCH(8) model and his extension of it based on a GARCH(1, 1) model. Table 19.2 reports three sets of estimates for the model

$$\pi_t = \beta_0 + \beta_1 \pi_{t-1} + \beta_2 \pi_{t-2} + \beta_3 \pi_{t-3} + \beta_4 \pi_{t-4} + \varepsilon_t,$$

where

$$\pi_t = 100 \ln \frac{P_t}{P_{t-1}}.$$

The data used in the regressions are quarterly observations on the implicit price deflator for GNP from 1948.II to 1983.IV.

The first set of results are obtained by ordinary least squares. The least squares residuals give no evidence of autocorrelation out to lag 10, but the squares of the residuals show significant autocorrelations at lags of 1, 3, 7, 9, and 10. The LM test statistics for ARCH(1), ARCH(4), and ARCH(8) are all highly significant.

The declining linear lag model specified by Engle and Kraft (1983) is shown second. Note that there is a linear restriction in the model, the eight terms in the ARCH part of the model are actually functions of a single parameter. The values decline linearly from 0.179 to 0.022. The normalized residuals, e_t/σ_t, from the ARCH(8) model show, again, no evidence of autocorrelation, nor do their squares. The linear restriction of the linear lag model on the unrestricted ARCH(8) model appears not to be significant; the χ^2 value is 8.87, while the 95 percentile for the chi-squared distribution with seven degrees of freedom is 14.01. The ARCH(8) model therefore appears to have accounted adequately for the lagged effects in the conditional variance. But the LM test statistic for the inclusion of σ_{t-1}^2 in the conditional variance is 4.57, which is significant at the 5 percent level.

The third set of estimates is for the GARCH(1, 1) model. The normalized residuals and their squares once again appear to be nonautocorrelated to lags of 10 periods. The LM test statistic for the additional ARCH terms, both singly and linearly restricted, is insignificant, as is the LM test statistic for another GARCH term in the model. [Recall, though, there is an equivalence in these tests, for example for GARCH(1, 2) and GARCH(2, 1).] On this basis, the specification appears to be adequate.

TABLE 19.2. Estimated Models of Inflation[a]

	Constant	π_{t-1}	π_{t-2}	π_{t-3}	π_{t-4}
Classical model	0.240	0.552	0.177	0.232	−0.209
	(0.080)	(0.083)	(0.089)	(0.090)	(0.080)
	$\sigma^2 = 0.282$				
	(0.034)				
ARCH(8)	0.138	0.423	0.222	0.377	−0.175
	(0.059)	(0.081)	(0.108)	(0.078)	(0.104)
	$\sigma_t^2 = 0.058 + 0.808 \sum_{i=1}^{8} \left(\frac{9-i}{36}\right) \varepsilon_{t-i}^2$				
	(0.033) (0.265)				
GARCH(1, 1)	0.151	0.433	0.229	0.349	−0.162
	(0.060)	(0.081)	(0.110)	(0.077)	(0.104)
	$\sigma_t^2 = 0.007 + 0.135 \varepsilon_{t-1}^2 + 0.829 \sigma_{t-1}^2$				
	(0.006) (0.070) (0.068)				

[a] Asymptotic standard errors are given in parentheses.

Plots of the actual inflation rate and asymptotic confidence intervals for the one-step-ahead forecast errors are given in Bollerslev's paper for the predictions of the model estimated by least squares and by the GARCH(1, 1) model. The clear pattern is that in periods of very volatile inflation (the late 1940s and early to mid-1950s), the simple least squares regression is a visibly better predictor. The effect is reversed in the more stable period of the late 1950s to early 1970s.

EXERCISE

Data on the implicit price deflator for GNP for 1950.I to 1983.IV are given in Table 18.1. Repeat the analysis of Section 19.7.4 using this subset of Engle and Kraft's data.

CHAPTER 20

Simultaneous Equations Models

20.1. Introduction

Most of our work thus far has been in the context of single-equation models. But, even a cursory look through almost any economics textbook shows that much of the theory is built upon sets, or *systems,* of relationships. Familiar examples include market equilibrium, models of the macroeconomy, and sets of factor or commodity demand equations. Whether one's interest is only in a particular part of the system or in the system as a whole, the interaction of the variables in the model will have important implications for both interpretation and estimation of the model's equations. The implications of simultaneity for econometric estimation were recognized long before the apparatus discussed in this chapter was developed.[1] The subsequent research in the subject, continuing to the present, is perhaps the most extensive in econometrics.[2]

   This chapter considers the issues that arise in interpreting and estimating multiple-equations models. Section 20.2 describes the general framework used for analyzing systems of simultaneous equations and presents some examples. Most of the discussion of these models centers on problems of estimation. But, before estimation can even be considered, the fundamental question of whether the parameters of interest in the model are even estimable must be resolved. This problem of identification is discussed in Section 20.3. Section 20.4 then discusses methods of estimation. Section 20.5 is concerned with specification tests. In Section 20.6 the special characteristics of dynamic models are examined.

20.2. Fundamental Issues in Simultaneous Equations Models

In this section we describe the basic terminology and statistical issues in the analysis of simultaneous-equations models. We begin with some simple examples and then present a general framework.

---

[1] See, for example, Working (1926) and Haavelmo (1943).

[2] The literature on simultaneous-equations models is enormous and continually expanding. Even constructing a complete and current bibliography is a considerable undertaking. Three recent surveys in the *Handbook of Econometrics,* Vol. I (Griliches and Intrilligator, 1983) by C. Hsiao on identification, J. Hausman on specification and estimation, and P. Phillips on small-sample properties of estimators provide a good overview of the literature. Other extensive sources include Judge et al. (1985) and Fomby et al. (1984). The latter half of Schmidt (1976) contains many useful theorems and results.

20.2.1. Illustrative Systems of Equations

A familiar example of a system of simultaneous equations is a model of market equilibrium, consisting of the following:

$$\textbf{Demand equation:} \qquad q_d = \alpha_1 p + \alpha_2 y + \varepsilon_d,$$

$$\textbf{Supply equation:} \qquad q_s = \beta_1 p \qquad\qquad + \varepsilon_s,$$

$$\textbf{Equilibrium condition:} \quad q_d = q_s = q.$$

These are **structural equations** in that they are derived from theory and each purports to describe a particular aspect of the economy.[3] Since the model is one of the joint determination of price and quantity, they are labeled **jointly dependent** or **endogenous** variables. Income, y, is assumed to be determined outside of the model, which makes it **exogenous.** The disturbances are added to the usual textbook description to obtain an **econometric model.** All three equations are needed to determine the equilibrium price and quantity, so the system is **interdependent.** Finally, since an equilibrium solution for price and quantity in terms of income and the disturbances is, indeed, implied (unless α_1 equals β_1), the system is said to be a **complete system of equations.**

Suppose that interest centers on estimating the demand elasticity, α_1. For simplicity, assume that ε_d and ε_s are well-behaved, classical disturbances with

$$E[\varepsilon_{dt}] = E[\varepsilon_{st}] = 0,$$
$$E[\varepsilon_{dt}^2] = \sigma_d^2, \qquad E[\varepsilon_{st}^2] = \sigma_s^2, \qquad E[\varepsilon_{dt}\varepsilon_{st}] = 0,$$

and

$$E[\varepsilon_{dt}y_t] = E[\varepsilon_{st}y_t] = 0.$$

All variables are mutually uncorrelated with observations at different time periods. Price, quantity, and income are measured in logarithms in deviations from their sample means. Solving the equations for p and q in terms of y, ε_d, and ε_s produces the **reduced form** of the model,

$$p = \frac{\alpha_2 y}{\beta_1 - \alpha_1} + \frac{\varepsilon_d - \varepsilon_s}{\beta_1 - \alpha_1} = \pi_1 y + v_1,$$

$$q = \frac{\beta_1 \alpha_2 y}{\beta_1 - \alpha_1} + \frac{\beta_1 \varepsilon_d - \alpha_1 \varepsilon_s}{\beta_1 - \alpha_1} = \pi_2 y + v_2. \tag{20-1}$$

(Note the "completeness" requirement that α_1 not equal β_1.)

It follows that $\text{Cov}[p, \varepsilon_d] = \sigma_d^2/(\beta_1 - \alpha_1)$, so the demand equation does not satisfy the assumptions of the classical regression model. The price elasticity cannot be consistently estimated by least squares regression of q on y and p. This result is characteristic of simultaneous-equations models. Because the endogenous variables are all correlated with the disturbances, least squares estimates of the parameters of equations with endogenous variables on the right-hand side are inconsistent.[4]

Suppose that we have a sample of T observations on p, q, and y, such that

$$\text{plim} \, \frac{1}{T} \, \mathbf{y}'\mathbf{y} = \sigma_y^2.$$

---

[3] The distinction between **structural** and **nonstructural** models is sometimes drawn on this basis. See, for example, Cooley and LeRoy (1985).

[4] This failure of least squares is sometimes labeled **simultaneous-equations bias.**

Since least squares is inconsistent, we might instead use an **instrumental variable estimator.**[5] The only variable in the system that is not correlated with the disturbances is y. Consider, then, the IV estimator, $\hat{\beta}_1 = \mathbf{q}'\mathbf{y}/\mathbf{p}'\mathbf{y}$. This estimator has

$$\text{plim } \hat{\beta}_1 = \text{plim } \frac{\mathbf{q}'\mathbf{y}/T}{\mathbf{p}'\mathbf{y}/T} = \frac{\beta_1\alpha_2/(\beta_1 - \alpha_1)}{\alpha_2/(\beta_1 - \alpha_1)} = \beta_1.$$

Evidently, the parameter of the supply curve can be estimated by using an instrumental variable estimator. There are two useful arrangements of this result. First, from (20–1), we see that

$$\hat{\beta}_1 = \frac{p_{11}}{p_{12}} = \frac{\text{slope in the regression of } q \text{ on } y}{\text{slope in the regression of } p \text{ on } y}.$$

Thus, the estimator is the ratio of the OLS estimates of π_1 and π_2. This technique is labeled **indirect least squares.** Second, in the least squares regression of $\mathbf{p}$ on $\mathbf{y}$, the predicted values are

$$\hat{\mathbf{p}} = \left(\frac{\mathbf{p}'\mathbf{y}}{\mathbf{y}'\mathbf{y}}\right)\mathbf{y}.$$

It follows that in the instrumental variable regression the instrument is $\hat{\mathbf{p}}$. That is,

$$\hat{\beta}_1 = \frac{\hat{\mathbf{p}}'\mathbf{q}}{\hat{\mathbf{p}}'\mathbf{p}}.$$

Finally, since $\hat{\mathbf{p}}'\mathbf{p} = \hat{\mathbf{p}}'\hat{\mathbf{p}}$, $\hat{\beta}_1$ is also the slope in a regression of q on these predicted values. This interpretation defines the **two-stage least squares estimator.**

EXAMPLE 20.1 Supply Equation for Agricultural Goods

Yearly data on price and quantity for the U.S. agricultural sector and real per capita disposable income for U.S. consumers for the years 1960 to 1986 are listed in the appendix to this chapter. Ordinary least squares regression of Q on P produces

$$\hat{Q} = 54.13 + 0.4195P.$$

The instrumental variable estimator suggested earlier produces

$$\hat{Q} = 46.93 + 0.5038P,$$

a 20.1 percent difference in the estimated slope.

It would be desirable to use a similar device to estimate the parameters of the demand equation. But, unfortunately, we have exhausted the information in the sample. Not only does least squares fail to estimate the demand equation but, without some further assumptions, the sample contains no other information that can be used. This example illustrates the **problem of identification** alluded to in Section 20.1.

A second example is the following simple model of income determination.

EXAMPLE 20.2. A Small Macroeconomic Model

(Consumption) $\quad c_t = \alpha_0 + \alpha_1 y_t + \alpha_2 c_{t-1} + \varepsilon_{t1},$

(Investment) $\quad i_t = \beta_0 + \beta_1 r_t + \beta_2(y_t - y_{t-1}) + \varepsilon_{t2},$

(Demand) $\quad y_t = c_t + i_t + g_t.$

[5] See Sections 9.5.3 and 18.5.4b if this is not familiar.

The model contains the autoregressive consumption function we examined in Section 18.5, an investment equation based on interest and the growth in output, and an equilibrium condition. The model determines the values of the three endogenous variables, c_t, i_t, and y_t. This is a **dynamic model.** In addition to the exogenous variables, r_t and g_t, it contains two **predetermined variables,** c_{t-1} and y_{t-1}. These are obviously not exogenous, but, as regards the current values of the endogenous variables, may be regarded as having already been determined. The deciding factor is whether or not they are uncorrelated with the correct disturbances, which we might assume. The reduced form of this model is

$$Ac_t = \alpha_0(1 - \beta_2) + \beta_0\alpha_1 + \alpha_1\beta_1 r_t + \alpha_1 g_t$$
$$+ \alpha_2(1 - \beta_2)c_{t-1} - \alpha_1\beta_2 y_{t-1} + (1 - \beta_2)\varepsilon_{t1} + \alpha_1\varepsilon_{t2},$$

$$Ai_t = \alpha_0\beta_2 + \beta_0(1 - \alpha_1) + \beta_1(1 - \alpha_1)r_t + \beta_2 g_t$$
$$+ \alpha_2\beta_2 c_{t-1} - \beta_2(1 - \alpha_1)y_{t-1} + \beta_2\varepsilon_{t1} + (1 - \alpha_1)\varepsilon_{t2},$$

$$Ay_t = \alpha_0 + \beta_0 + \beta_1 r_t + g_t + \alpha_2 c_{t-1} - \beta_2 y_{t-1} + \varepsilon_{t1} + \varepsilon_{t2},$$

where

$$A = 1 - \alpha_1 - \beta_2.$$

Note that the reduced form preserves the equilibrium condition.

The distinction between endogenous and exogenous variables in econometric models is occasionally controversial. In a model of supply and demand, there is little question as to what is and what is not determined within the market. But in macroeconomic models the issue is much more ambiguous. To take a common example, the estimation of consumption functions by least squares, as we did in Chapter 18, is usually treated as a respectable enterprise, in spite of the fact that most macroeconomic models (including the examples given here) depart from a consumption function in which income is endogenous. Nonetheless, the distinction is crucial. *The completeness of the system requires that the number of equations equal the number of endogenous variables.* We observe that, as a general rule, it is not possible to estimate the parameters of incomplete systems.

The preceding two models illustrate systems in which there are **behavioral equations** and **equilibrium conditions.** The latter are distinct in that even in an econometric model, they have no disturbances. Another model, which illustrates nearly all of the concepts to be discussed in this chapter, is shown in the next example.

EXAMPLE 20.3 Klein's Model I

A widely used example of a simultaneous equations model of the economy is Klein's (1950) *Model I.* The model may be written

$$C_t = \alpha_0 + \alpha_1 P_t + \alpha_2 P_{t-1} + \alpha_3(W_t^p + W_t^g) + \varepsilon_{1t} \quad \text{(consumption)},$$

$$I_t = \beta_0 + \beta_1 P_t + \beta_2 P_{t-1} + \beta_3 K_{t-1} \qquad + \varepsilon_{2t} \quad \text{(investment)},$$

$$W_t^p = \gamma_0 + \gamma_1 X_t + \gamma_2 X_{t-1} + \gamma_3 A_t \qquad + \varepsilon_{3t} \quad \text{(private wages)},$$

$$X_t = C_t + I_t + G_t \qquad\qquad \text{(equilibrium demand)},$$

$$P_t = X_t - T_t - W_t^p \qquad\qquad \text{(private profits)},$$

$$K_t = K_{t-1} + I_t \qquad\qquad \text{(capital stock)}.$$

The endogenous variables are each on the left-hand side of an equation and labeled on the right. The exogenous variables are G = government nonwage spending, T = indirect business taxes plus net exports, W^g = government wage bill, A = time trend measured as years from 1931, and the constant term. There are also three predetermined variables: the lagged values of the capital stock, private profits, and total demand. The model contains three behavioral equations, an equilibrium condition and two accounting identities. This model provides an excellent example of a small, dynamic model of the economy. It has also been widely used as a test ground for simultaneous-equations estimators. Klein estimated the parameters using data for 1921 to 1941. The data are listed in the appendix.

20.2.2. A General Notation for Simultaneous Equations Models

The **structural form** of the model is[6]

$$
\gamma_{11} y_{t1} + \gamma_{21} y_{t2} + \cdots + \gamma_{M1} y_{tM} + \beta_{11} x_{t1} + \cdots + \beta_{K1} x_{tK} = \varepsilon_{t1}
$$

$$
\gamma_{12} y_{t1} + \gamma_{22} y_{t2} + \cdots + \gamma_{M2} y_{tM} + \beta_{12} x_{t1} + \cdots + \beta_{K2} x_{tK} = \varepsilon_{t2}
$$

$$
\vdots \tag{20-2}
$$

$$
\gamma_{1M} y_{t1} + \gamma_{2M} y_{t2} + \cdots + \gamma_{MM} y_{tM} + \beta_{1M} x_{t1} + \cdots + \beta_{KM} x_{tK} = \varepsilon_{tM}.
$$

There are M equations and M endogenous variables, denoted $y_1, \ldots y_M$. There are K exogenous variables, $x_1, \ldots x_K$, which may include predetermined values of $y_1, \ldots y_M$ as well. The first element of $\mathbf{x}_t$ will usually be the constant, 1. Finally, $\varepsilon_{t1}, \ldots, \varepsilon_{tM}$ are the **structural disturbances.** The subscript, t, will be used to index observations, $t = 1, \ldots, T$.

In matrix terms, the system may be written

$$
[y_1 \quad y_2 \quad \cdots \quad y_M]_t
\begin{bmatrix}
\gamma_{11} & \gamma_{12} & \cdots & \gamma_{1M} \\
\gamma_{21} & \gamma_{22} & \cdots & \gamma_{2M} \\
& & \vdots & \\
\gamma_{M1} & \gamma_{M2} & \cdots & \gamma_{MM}
\end{bmatrix}
+ [x_1 \quad x_2 \quad \cdots \quad x_K]_t
\begin{bmatrix}
\beta_{11} & \beta_{12} & \cdots & \beta_{1M} \\
\beta_{21} & \beta_{22} & \cdots & \beta_{2M} \\
& & \vdots & \\
\beta_{K1} & \beta_{K2} & \cdots & \beta_{KM}
\end{bmatrix}
$$

$$
= [\varepsilon_1 \quad \varepsilon_2 \quad \cdots \quad \varepsilon_M]_t
$$

or

$$
\mathbf{y}_t' \mathbf{\Gamma} + \mathbf{x}_t' \mathbf{B} = \boldsymbol{\varepsilon}_t'.
$$

Each column of the parameter matrices is the vector of coefficients in a particular equation, while each row applies to a specific variable.

The underlying theory will imply a number of restrictions on $\mathbf{\Gamma}$ and $\mathbf{B}$. One of the variables in each equation is labeled the *dependent* variable, so that its coefficient in the model will be 1. Thus, there will be at least one "1" in each column of $\mathbf{\Gamma}$. If there are any identities, the corresponding columns of $\mathbf{\Gamma}$ and $\mathbf{B}$ will be completely known, and there will be no disturbance for that equation. Since not all variables appear in all equations, some of the parameters will be zero. The theory may also impose other types of restrictions on the parameter matrices.

A special case of the preceding is worth noting before we proceed. If $\mathbf{\Gamma}$ is an upper triangular matrix, the system is said to be **triangular.** In this case, the model is of the form

$$
y_{t1} = f_1(\mathbf{x}_t) + \varepsilon_{t1}
$$

$$
y_{t2} = f_2(y_{t1}, \mathbf{x}_t) + \varepsilon_{t2}
$$

$$
\vdots
$$

$$
y_{tM} = f_M(y_{t1}, y_{t2}, \ldots, y_{t,M-1} \mathbf{x}_t) + \varepsilon_{tM}.
$$

---

[6] For the present, it is convenient to ignore the special nature of lagged endogenous variables and treat them the same as the strictly exogenous variables.

The joint determination of the variables in this model is *recursive*. The first is completely determined by the exogenous factors. Then, given the first, the second is likewise determined, and so on. The temporal aspects of some processes in the economy suggest this form of model.

EXAMPLE 20.4 Cobweb Model

The cobweb model of market equilibrium may be written

$$Q_t = \alpha_0 + \alpha_1 P_{t-1} + \varepsilon_{1t} \qquad \text{(supply)},$$

$$P_t = \beta_0 + \beta_1 Q_t + \varepsilon_{2t} \qquad \text{(inverse demand)}.$$

The quantity supplied to the market is determined by last year's price, a bygone. Supply in the current period is perfectly inelastic. Demand responds to the usual forces and determines an equilibrium price, which feeds into next year's supply.

In essence, the endogenous variables are determined in turn, each one depending on the values of the logically preceding ones. Users of spreadsheet programs and those who fill out their own tax returns will recognize other familiar examples of recursive systems.

The solution of the system of equations determining $\mathbf{y}_t$ in terms of $\mathbf{x}_t$ and $\boldsymbol{\varepsilon}_t$ is the **reduced form** of the model,

$$\mathbf{y}_t' = -\mathbf{x}_t'\mathbf{B}\boldsymbol{\Gamma}^{-1} + \boldsymbol{\varepsilon}_t'\boldsymbol{\Gamma}^{-1}$$

$$= \mathbf{x}_t'\boldsymbol{\Pi} + \mathbf{v}_t'$$

$$= [x_1 \quad x_2 \quad \cdots \quad x_K]_t \begin{bmatrix} \pi_{11} & \pi_{12} & \cdots & \pi_{1M} \\ \pi_{21} & \pi_{22} & \cdots & \pi_{2M} \\ & & \vdots & \\ \pi_{K1} & \pi_{K2} & \cdots & \pi_{KM} \end{bmatrix} + [v_1 \quad \cdots \quad v_M]_t$$

where

$$\boldsymbol{\Pi} = -\mathbf{B}\boldsymbol{\Gamma}^{-1}$$

and

$$\mathbf{v}_t' = \boldsymbol{\varepsilon}_t'\boldsymbol{\Gamma}^{-1}.$$

In order for this solution to exist, the model must satisfy the

Completeness condition: $\boldsymbol{\Gamma}$ is nonsingular.

EXAMPLE 20.5 Structure and Reduced Form

For the small model in Example 20.2,

$$\mathbf{y}' = [c, i, y], \qquad \mathbf{x}' = [1, r, g, c_{-1}, y_{-1}]$$

$$\boldsymbol{\Gamma} = \begin{bmatrix} 1 & 0 & -1 \\ 0 & 1 & -1 \\ -\alpha_1 & -\beta_2 & 1 \end{bmatrix}, \qquad \mathbf{B} = \begin{bmatrix} -\alpha_0 & -\beta_0 & 0 \\ 0 & -\beta_1 & 0 \\ 0 & 0 & -1 \\ -\alpha_2 & 0 & 0 \\ 0 & \beta_2 & 0 \end{bmatrix}$$

$$\mathbf{\Gamma}^{-1} = \frac{1}{1 - \alpha_1 - \beta_2} \begin{bmatrix} 1 - \beta_2 & \beta_2 & 1 \\ \alpha_1 & 1 - \alpha_1 & 1 \\ \alpha_1 & \beta_2 & 1 \end{bmatrix}$$

$$\mathbf{\Pi}' = \frac{1}{1 - \alpha_1 - \beta_2} \begin{bmatrix} \alpha_0(1 - \beta_2 + \beta_0\alpha_1) & \alpha_1\beta_1 & \alpha_1 & \alpha_2(1 - \beta_2) & -\beta_2\alpha_1 \\ \alpha_0\beta_2 + \beta_0(1 - \alpha_1) & \beta_1(1 - \alpha_1) & \beta_2 & \alpha_2\beta_2 & -\beta_2(1 - \alpha_1) \\ \alpha_0 + \beta_0 & \beta_1 & 1 & \alpha_2 & -\beta_2 \end{bmatrix}$$

The completeness condition is that α_1 and β_2 do not sum to one.

The structural disturbances are assumed to be randomly drawn from an M-variate distribution with

$$E[\boldsymbol{\varepsilon}_t] = \mathbf{0} \qquad \text{and} \qquad E[\boldsymbol{\varepsilon}_t\boldsymbol{\varepsilon}_t'] = \boldsymbol{\Sigma}.$$

For the present, we assume that

$$E[\boldsymbol{\varepsilon}_t\boldsymbol{\varepsilon}_s'] = \mathbf{0} \qquad \text{for all } t \neq s.$$

Later, we will drop this assumption in order to allow for autocorrelation. It will occasionally be useful to assume that ε_t has a multivariate normal distribution, but we shall postpone this assumption until it becomes necessary. It may be convenient to retain the identities without disturbances as separate equations. If so, one way to proceed with the stochastic specification is to place rows and columns of zeros in the appropriate places in $\boldsymbol{\Sigma}$.

It follows that the **reduced-form disturbances,**

$$\mathbf{v}_t' = \boldsymbol{\varepsilon}_t'\mathbf{\Gamma}^{-1}$$

have

$$E[\mathbf{v}_t] = (\mathbf{\Gamma}^{-1})'\mathbf{0} = \mathbf{0},$$

$$E[\mathbf{v}_t\mathbf{v}_t'] = (\mathbf{\Gamma}^{-1})'\boldsymbol{\Sigma}\mathbf{\Gamma}^{-1} = \boldsymbol{\Omega}.$$

This implies that

$$\boldsymbol{\Sigma} = \mathbf{\Gamma}'\boldsymbol{\Omega}\mathbf{\Gamma}.$$

The preceding formulation describes the model as it applies to an observation $[\mathbf{y}', \mathbf{x}', \boldsymbol{\varepsilon}']_t$ at a particular point in time or in a cross section. In a sample of data, each joint observation will be one row in a data matrix,

$$[\mathbf{Y} \quad \mathbf{X} \quad \mathbf{E}] = \begin{bmatrix} \mathbf{y}_1' & \mathbf{x}_1' & \boldsymbol{\varepsilon}_1' \\ \mathbf{y}_2' & \mathbf{x}_2' & \boldsymbol{\varepsilon}_2' \\ \vdots & & \\ \mathbf{y}_T' & \mathbf{x}_T' & \boldsymbol{\varepsilon}_T' \end{bmatrix}.$$

In terms of the full set of T observations, the structure is

$$\mathbf{Y}\mathbf{\Gamma} + \mathbf{X}\mathbf{B} = \mathbf{E},$$

with

$$E[\mathbf{E}] = \mathbf{0} \qquad \text{and} \qquad E\left[\frac{\mathbf{E}'\mathbf{E}}{T}\right] = \boldsymbol{\Sigma}.$$

Under general conditions, we can strengthen this to

$$\text{plim} \left[\frac{\mathbf{E}'\mathbf{E}}{T} \right] = \boldsymbol{\Sigma}.$$

An important assumption, comparable to the one made in Chapter 10 for the classical regression model, is

$$\text{plim} \frac{\mathbf{X}'\mathbf{X}}{T} = \mathbf{Q}, \qquad \text{a finite positive definite matrix.}[7] \qquad (20\text{--}3)$$

We also assume that

$$\text{plim} \frac{\mathbf{X}'\mathbf{E}}{T} = \mathbf{0}. \qquad (20\text{--}4)$$

This is what distinguishes the predetermined from the endogenous variables.

The reduced form is

$$\mathbf{Y} = \mathbf{X}\boldsymbol{\Pi} + \mathbf{V},$$

where

$$\mathbf{V} = \mathbf{E}\boldsymbol{\Gamma}^{-1}.$$

With the earlier assumptions, we also have

$$\text{plim} \frac{\mathbf{V}'\mathbf{V}}{T} = (\boldsymbol{\Gamma}^{-1})'\boldsymbol{\Sigma}\boldsymbol{\Gamma}^{-1} = \boldsymbol{\Omega},$$

$$\text{plim} \frac{\mathbf{Y}'\mathbf{Y}}{T} = \boldsymbol{\Pi}'\mathbf{Q}\boldsymbol{\Pi} + \boldsymbol{\Omega},$$

$$\text{plim} \frac{\mathbf{X}'\mathbf{V}}{T} = \mathbf{0}, \qquad\qquad (20\text{--}5)$$

$$\text{plim} \frac{\mathbf{X}'\mathbf{Y}}{T} = \mathbf{Q}\boldsymbol{\Pi}.$$

20.3. The Problem of Identification

Solving the problem to be considered here, the identification problem, logically precedes estimation. We ask at this point whether there is *any* way to obtain estimates of the parameters of the model. We have in hand a certain amount of information upon which to base any inference about its underlying structure. If more than one theory is consistent with the same "data," they are said to be **observationally equivalent,** and there is no way of distinguishing them. The structure is said to be *unidentified.*[8]

EXAMPLE 20.6 Observational Equivalence

The *observed* data consist of the market outcomes shown in Figure 20.1a. We have no knowledge of the conditions of supply and demand beyond our belief that the data repre-

---

[7] The time trend is, once again, an important exception. The conditions required for **X** to be well behaved are discussed in Section 10.3. If **X** contains lagged dependent variables, the results of Mann and Wald (1943) will be required. Schmidt (1976) gives some additional results.

[8] A useful survey of this issue is Hsiao (1983).

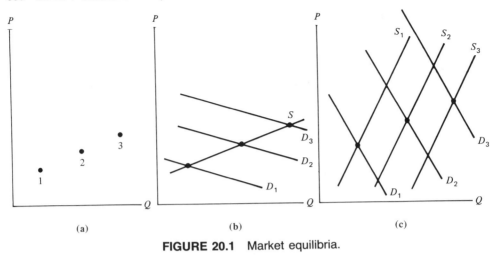

FIGURE 20.1 Market equilibria.

sent *equilibria*. Unfortunately, Figure 20.1b and c both show *structures*, that is, true underlying supply and demand curves, which are consistent with the data in Figure 20.1a. With only the data in Figure 20.1a, we have no way of determining which of theories 20.1b or c is the right one. Thus, the structure underlying the data in Figure 20.1a is unidentified.[9] To suggest where our discussion is headed, suppose that we add to the preceding the known fact that the conditions of supply were unchanged during the period over which the data were drawn. This rules out 20.1c and identifies 20.1b as the correct structure. Note how this scenario relates to the first example in Section 20.2.1 and to the discussion following Example 20.1.

The identification problem is not one of sampling properties or the size of the sample. To focus ideas, it is even useful to suppose that we have at hand an infinite-sized sample of observations on the variables in the model. Now, with this and our prior theory, what information do we have?

In the reduced form,

$$\mathbf{y}_t' = \mathbf{x}_t'\mathbf{\Pi} + \mathbf{v}_t', \qquad E[\mathbf{v}_t\mathbf{v}_t'] = \mathbf{\Omega},$$

the predetermined variables are uncorrelated with the disturbances. Thus, we can "observe"

$$\text{plim } \frac{\mathbf{X}'\mathbf{X}}{T} = \mathbf{Q} \qquad \text{[assumed; see (20–3)]},$$

$$\text{plim } \frac{\mathbf{X}'\mathbf{Y}}{T} = \text{plim } \frac{\mathbf{X}'(\mathbf{X}\mathbf{\Pi} + \mathbf{V})}{T} = \mathbf{Q}\mathbf{\Pi},$$

$$\text{plim } \frac{\mathbf{Y}'\mathbf{Y}}{T} = \text{plim } \frac{(\mathbf{\Pi}'\mathbf{X}' + \mathbf{V}')(\mathbf{X}\mathbf{\Pi} + \mathbf{V})}{T} = \mathbf{\Pi}'\mathbf{Q}\mathbf{\Pi} + \mathbf{\Omega}.$$

Therefore, $\mathbf{\Pi}$, the matrix of reduced-form coefficients, is observable:

$$\mathbf{\Pi} = \left[\text{plim}\left(\frac{\mathbf{X}'\mathbf{X}}{T}\right)\right]^{-1}\left[\text{plim}\left(\frac{\mathbf{X}'\mathbf{Y}}{T}\right)\right].$$

---

[9]This example paraphrases the classic argument of Working (1926).

This is simply the equation-by-equation least squares regression of $\mathbf{Y}$ on $\mathbf{X}$. Since $\mathbf{\Pi}$ is observable, $\mathbf{\Omega}$ is also:

$$\mathbf{\Omega} = \text{plim } \frac{\mathbf{Y'Y}}{T} - \text{plim}\left[\frac{\mathbf{Y'X}}{T}\right]\left[\frac{\mathbf{X'X}}{T}\right]^{-1}\left[\frac{\mathbf{X'Y}}{T}\right].$$

This should be recognizable as the matrix of least squares residual variances and covariances. Therefore,

> $\mathbf{\Pi}$ and $\mathbf{\Omega}$ can be estimated consistently by
> ordinary least squares regression of $\mathbf{Y}$ on $\mathbf{X}$.

The information in hand, therefore, consists of $\mathbf{\Pi}$, $\mathbf{\Omega}$, and whatever other nonsample information we have about the structure.[10]

Now, can we deduce the structural parameters from the reduced form? Consider the following example:

EXAMPLE 20.7 Identification

Consider a market in which q is quantity of Q, p is price, and z is the price of Z, a related good. We assume that z enters both the supply and demand equations. For example, Z might be a crop that is purchased by consumers and that will be grown by farmers instead of Q if its price rises enough relative to p. Thus, we would expect $\alpha_2 > 0$ and $\beta_2 < 0$.

$$q_d = \alpha_0 + \alpha_1 p + \alpha_2 z + \varepsilon_1 \quad \text{(demand)},$$

$$q_s = \beta_0 + \beta_1 p + \beta_2 z + \varepsilon_2 \quad \text{(supply)},$$

$$q_d = q_s = q \qquad\qquad \text{(equilibrium)}.$$

The reduced form is

$$q = \frac{\alpha_1\beta_0 - \alpha_0\beta_1}{\alpha_1 - \beta_1} + \frac{\alpha_1\beta_2 - \alpha_2\beta_1}{\alpha_1 - \beta_1}z + \frac{\alpha_1\varepsilon_2 - \alpha_2\varepsilon_1}{\alpha_1 - \beta_1}$$

$$= \pi_{11} + \pi_{21}z + v_q,$$

$$p = \frac{\beta_0 - \alpha_0}{\alpha_1 - \beta_1} + \frac{\beta_2 - \alpha_2}{\alpha_1 - \beta_1}z + \frac{\varepsilon_2 - \varepsilon_1}{\alpha_1 - \beta_1}$$

$$= \pi_{12} + \pi_{22}z + v_p.$$

With only four reduced form coefficients and six structural parameters, it is obvious that there will not be a solution. Suppose, though, that it is known that $\beta_2 = 0$ (farmers do not substitute the alternative crop for this one). Then the solution for β_1 is π_{22}/π_{21}. After a bit of manipulation, we also obtain $\beta_0 = \pi_{11} - \pi_{12}\pi_{22}/\pi_{21}$. The restriction identifies the supply parameters. Unfortunately, this is as far as we can go.

The correspondence between the structural and reduced-form parameters is the relationships

$$\mathbf{\Pi} = -\mathbf{B\Gamma}^{-1} \quad \text{and} \quad \mathbf{\Omega} = E[\mathbf{vv'}] = (\mathbf{\Gamma}^{-1})'\mathbf{\Sigma\Gamma}^{-1}.$$

---

[10] We have not necessarily shown that this is *all* of the information in the sample. In general, we observe the conditional distribution, $f(\mathbf{y}_t | \mathbf{x}_t)$, which constitutes the likelihood for the reduced form. With normally distributed disturbances, this is a function of $\mathbf{\Pi}$, $\mathbf{\Omega}$. (See Section 20.4.5b.) With other distributions, other or higher moments of the variables might provide additional information. See, for example, Goldberger (1964, p. 311), Hausman (1983, pp. 402–403), and, esp., Riersol (1950).

If $\boldsymbol{\Gamma}$ were known, we could deduce $\mathbf{B}$ as $-\boldsymbol{\Pi}\boldsymbol{\Gamma}$ and $\boldsymbol{\Sigma}$ and $\boldsymbol{\Gamma}'\boldsymbol{\Omega}\boldsymbol{\Gamma}$. It would appear, therefore, that our problem boils down to obtaining $\boldsymbol{\Gamma}$. This makes sense. If $\boldsymbol{\Gamma}$ were known, we could rewrite (20–2), collecting the endogenous variables times their respective coefficients on the left-hand side of a regression, and estimate the remaining unknown coefficients on the predetermined variables by ordinary least squares.[11]

Suppose that the true structure is $[\boldsymbol{\Gamma}, \mathbf{B}, \boldsymbol{\Sigma}]$. Now consider an imposter,

$$\mathbf{y}'\tilde{\boldsymbol{\Gamma}} + \mathbf{x}'\tilde{\mathbf{B}} = \tilde{\boldsymbol{\varepsilon}}',$$

obtained by postmultiplying the first structure by some nonsingular matrix, $\mathbf{F}$. Thus,

$$\tilde{\boldsymbol{\Gamma}} = \boldsymbol{\Gamma}\mathbf{F}, \quad \tilde{\mathbf{B}} = \mathbf{B}\mathbf{F} \qquad \text{and} \qquad \tilde{\boldsymbol{\varepsilon}}' = \boldsymbol{\varepsilon}'\mathbf{F}.$$

The reduced form that corresponds to this structure is

$$\tilde{\boldsymbol{\Pi}} = -\tilde{\mathbf{B}}\tilde{\boldsymbol{\Gamma}}^{-1} = \mathbf{B}\mathbf{F}\mathbf{F}^{-1}\boldsymbol{\Gamma}^{-1} = \boldsymbol{\Pi},$$

and, in the same fashion, $\tilde{\boldsymbol{\Omega}} = \boldsymbol{\Omega}$. The false structure looks just like the true one, at least in terms of the information we have. Statistically, there is no way we can tell them apart. The structures are observationally equivalent.

Since $\mathbf{F}$ was chosen arbitrarily, we conclude that *any* nonsingular transformation of the original structure has the same reduced form. Any reason for optimism that we might have had should be abandoned. As the model stands, there is no means by which the structural parameters can be deduced from the reduced form. The practical implication is that if the only information that we have is the reduced-form parameters, then the model is not estimable. So how were we able to identify the models in the earlier examples? The answer is: by bringing to bear our nonsample information, namely our theoretical restrictions. Look once again at Example 20.7. Before formalizing the notion, it is useful to consider another example.

EXAMPLE 20.8 An Identified Model

Suppose that in the earlier example income, y, rather than z, appears in the demand equation. The revised model is

$$\begin{aligned}
q &= \alpha_0 + \alpha_1 p + \quad\; \alpha_2 y + \varepsilon_1, \\
q &= \beta_0 + \beta_1 p + \beta_2 z \quad\;\; + \varepsilon_2.
\end{aligned}$$

The structure is now

$$[q \quad p]\begin{bmatrix} 1 & 1 \\ -\alpha_1 & -\beta_1 \end{bmatrix} + [1 \quad y \quad z]\begin{bmatrix} -\alpha_0 & -\beta_0 \\ -\alpha_2 & 0 \\ 0 & -\beta_2 \end{bmatrix} = [\varepsilon_1 \quad \varepsilon_2].$$

The reduced form is

$$[q \quad p] = [1 \quad y \quad z]\begin{bmatrix} (\alpha_1\beta_0 - \alpha_0\beta_1)/\Delta & (\beta_0 - \alpha_0)/\Delta \\ -\alpha_2\beta_1/\Delta & -\alpha_2/\Delta \\ \alpha_1\beta_2/\Delta & \beta_2/\Delta \end{bmatrix} + [v_1 \quad v_2]$$

where

$$\Delta = (\alpha_1 - \beta_1).$$

---

[11] This is precisely the approach of the LIML estimator. See Section 20.4.4c.

Every false structure has the same reduced form. But in the coefficient matrix,

$$\tilde{\mathbf{B}} = \mathbf{BF} = \begin{bmatrix} \alpha_0 f_{11} + \beta_0 f_{12} & \alpha_0 f_{12} + \beta_0 f_{22} \\ \alpha_3 f_{11} & \alpha_3 f_{12} \\ \beta_2 f_{21} & \beta_2 f_{22} \end{bmatrix},$$

if f_{12} is not zero, the imposter will have income appearing in the supply equation, which our theory has ruled out. Likewise, if f_{21} is not zero, z will appear in the demand equation, which is also ruled out by our theory. Thus, while all false structures have the same reduced form as the true one, the only one that is consistent with our theory (i.e., is **admissible**) and has coefficients of 1 on q in both equations (examine $\mathbf{\Gamma F}$) is $\mathbf{F} = \mathbf{I}$. This just produces the original structure.

The unique solutions for the structural parameters in terms of the reduced form parameters are

$$\alpha_0 = \pi_{11} - \pi_{12}\left(\frac{\pi_{31}}{\pi_{32}}\right), \qquad \beta_0 = \pi_{11} - \pi_{12}\left(\frac{\pi_{21}}{\pi_{22}}\right),$$

$$\alpha_1 = \frac{\pi_{31}}{\pi_{32}}, \qquad \beta_1 = \frac{\pi_{21}}{\pi_{22}},$$

$$\alpha_2 = \pi_{22}\left(\frac{\pi_{21}}{\pi_{22}} - \frac{\pi_{31}}{\pi_{32}}\right), \qquad \beta_2 = \pi_{32}\left(\frac{\pi_{31}}{\pi_{32}} - \frac{\pi_{21}}{\pi_{22}}\right).$$

The preceding discussion has considered two equivalent methods of establishing identifiability. If it is possible to deduce the structural parameters from the known reduced-form parameters, the model is identified. Alternatively, if it can be shown that no false structure is admissible, that is, satisfies the theoretical restrictions, then the model is identified.[12]

20.3.1. The Rank and Order Conditions for Identification

It is useful to summarize what we have determined thus far. The unknown structural parameters consist of

$$\mathbf{\Gamma} = \text{an } M \times M \text{ nonsingular matrix,}$$

$$\mathbf{B} = \text{a } K \times M \text{ parameter matrix,}$$

$$\mathbf{\Sigma} = \text{an } M \times M \text{ symmetric positive definite matrix.}$$

The known, reduced-form parameters are

$$\mathbf{\Pi} = \text{the } K \times M \text{ reduced-form coefficients}$$

$$\mathbf{\Omega} = \text{the } M \times M \text{ reduced-form covariance matrix.}$$

Simply counting parameters in the structure and reduced forms yields an excess of

$$l = M^2 + KM + \frac{M(M+1)}{2} - KM - \frac{M(M+1)}{2}$$

$$= M^2,$$

which is, as might be expected from the earlier results, the number of unknown elements in $\mathbf{\Gamma}$. Without further information, identification is clearly impossible. The additional information comes in several forms.

[12] For other interpretations, see Amemiya (1985, p. 230) and Gabrielsen (1978).

1. *Normalizations*. In each equation, one variable has a coefficient of one. This normalization is a necessary scaling of the equation that is logically equivalent to putting one variable on the left-hand side of a regression. For purposes of identification (and some estimation methods), the choice among the endogenous variables is arbitrary. But at the time the model is formulated, each equation will usually have some natural dependent variable. The normalization does not identify the dependent variable in any formal or causal sense. For example, in a model of supply and demand, both the "demand" equation, $Q = f(P, \mathbf{x})$, and the "inverse demand" equation, $P = g(Q, \mathbf{x})$, are appropriate specifications of the relationship between price and quantity. We note, though, the following:

> With the normalizations there are $M(M - 1)$, not M^2, undetermined values in $\boldsymbol{\Gamma}$, and this many indeterminacies in the model to be resolved through nonsample information.

2. *Identities*. In some models, variable definitions or equilibrium conditions imply that all of the coefficients in a particular equation are known. In the preceding market example, there are three equations, but the third is the equilibrium condition $Q_d = Q_s$. Klein's Model I (Example 20.3) contains six equations, including two accounting identities and the equilibrium condition. There is no question of identification with respect to identities. They may be carried as additional equations in the model, as we do with Klein's Model I in several later examples, or built into the model a priori, as is typical in models of supply and demand.

The substantive nonsample information that will be used in identifying the model will consist of the following:

3. *Exclusions*. The omission of variables from an equation places zeros in $\mathbf{B}$ and $\boldsymbol{\Gamma}$. In the previous example, the exclusion of income from the supply equation served to identify its parameters.

4. *Linear restrictions*. Restrictions on the structural parameters may also serve to rule out false structures. For example, a long-standing problem in the estimation of production models using time series data is the inability to disentangle the effects of economies of scale from those of technological change. In some treatments, the solution is to assume that there are constant returns to scale, thereby identifying the effects due to technological change.[13]

5. *Restrictions on the disturbance covariance matrix*. In the identification of a model, these are similar to restrictions on the slope parameters. For example, if the previous market model were to apply to a microeconomic setting, it would probably be reasonable to assume that the structural disturbances in the supply and demand equations are uncorrelated. Example 20.12 shows a case in which a covariance restriction identifies an otherwise unidentified model.

6. *Nonlinearities*. In many models, the variables and/or the parameters enter nonlinearly. For example, a variable may appear in both levels and logarithms. Or there may be nonlinear restrictions on the coefficients. Although this will usually greatly complicate the analysis, nonlinearities can aid in identification. Exercise 4 considers such a case.

---

[13] See Section 16.4 and footnote 16 in Chapter 16.

TABLE 20.1 Components of Equation j
(Dependent Variable $= y_j$)

	Endogenous Variables	**Exogenous Variables**
Included	$\mathbf{Y}_j = M_j$ variables	$\mathbf{x}_j = K_j$ variables
Excluded	$\mathbf{Y}_j^* = M_j^*$ variables	$\mathbf{x}_j^* = K_j^*$ variables

To formalize the identification criteria, we require a notation for a single equation. The coefficients of the jth equation are contained in the jth columns of $\boldsymbol{\Gamma}$ and $\mathbf{B}$. The jth equation is

$$\mathbf{y}'\boldsymbol{\Gamma}_j + \mathbf{x}'\mathbf{B}_j = \varepsilon_j. \tag{20-6}$$

(For convenience, we have dropped the observation subscript.) In this equation, we know that (1) one of the elements in $\boldsymbol{\Gamma}_j$ is one and (2) some variables that appear elsewhere in the model are excluded from this equation. Table 20.1 defines the notation used to incorporate these restrictions in (20–6).

The number of equations is $M_j + M_j^* + 1 = M$.
The number of exogenous variables is $K_j + K_j^* = K$.
The coefficient on y_j in equation j is one.
*'s will always be associated with excluded variables.

Equation j may be written

$$\mathbf{y}_j = \mathbf{Y}_j'\boldsymbol{\gamma}_j + \mathbf{Y}_j^{*\prime}\boldsymbol{\gamma}_j^* + \mathbf{x}_j'\boldsymbol{\beta}_j + \mathbf{x}_j^{*\prime}\boldsymbol{\beta}_j^* + \varepsilon_j$$

The exclusions imply that $\boldsymbol{\gamma}_j^* = \mathbf{0}$ and $\boldsymbol{\beta}_j^* = \mathbf{0}$. Thus,

$$\boldsymbol{\Gamma}_j' = [1 \quad -\boldsymbol{\gamma}_j' \quad \mathbf{0}'] \qquad \text{and} \qquad \mathbf{B}_j' = [-\boldsymbol{\beta}_j' \quad \mathbf{0}'].$$

(Note the sign convention.)

For this equation, we partition the reduced-form coefficient matrix in the same fashion:

$$[\mathbf{y}_j \quad \mathbf{Y}_j' \quad \mathbf{Y}_j^{*\prime}] = [\mathbf{x}_j' \quad \mathbf{x}_j^{*\prime}] \begin{array}{c} (1) \quad (M_j) \quad (M_j^*) \\ \begin{bmatrix} \boldsymbol{\pi}_j & \boldsymbol{\Pi}_j & \overline{\boldsymbol{\Pi}}_j \\ \boldsymbol{\pi}_j^* & \boldsymbol{\Pi}_j^* & \overline{\boldsymbol{\Pi}}_j^* \end{bmatrix} \end{array} + [\mathbf{v}_j \quad \mathbf{V}_j' \quad \mathbf{V}_j^{*\prime}] \begin{array}{l} [K_j \text{ rows}] \\ {}[K_j^* \text{ rows}] \end{array} \tag{20-7}$$

The reduced-form coefficient matrix is

$$\boldsymbol{\Pi} = -\mathbf{B}\boldsymbol{\Gamma}^{-1},$$

which implies that

$$\boldsymbol{\Pi}\boldsymbol{\Gamma} = -\mathbf{B}.$$

The jth column of this matrix equation applies to the jth equation,

$$\boldsymbol{\Pi}\boldsymbol{\Gamma}_j = -\mathbf{B}_j.$$

Inserting the parts from Table 20.1 yields

$$\begin{bmatrix} \boldsymbol{\pi}_j & \boldsymbol{\Pi}_j & \overline{\boldsymbol{\Pi}}_j \\ \boldsymbol{\pi}_j^* & \boldsymbol{\Pi}_j^* & \overline{\boldsymbol{\Pi}}_j^* \end{bmatrix} \begin{bmatrix} 1 \\ -\boldsymbol{\gamma}_j \\ \mathbf{0} \end{bmatrix} = \begin{bmatrix} \boldsymbol{\beta}_j \\ \mathbf{0} \end{bmatrix}.$$

Now extract the two subequations,

$$\boldsymbol{\pi}_j - \underline{\mathbf{\Pi}}_j\boldsymbol{\gamma}_j = \boldsymbol{\beta}_j \qquad (K_j \text{ equations}) \tag{20--8}$$

$$\boldsymbol{\pi}_j^* - \mathbf{\Pi}_j^*\boldsymbol{\gamma}_j = \mathbf{0} \qquad (K_j^* \text{ equations}). \tag{20--9}$$
$$\quad(1)\quad(M_j)$$

The solution for **B** in terms of **Γ** that we observed at the beginning of this discussion is in (20–8). Equation (20–9) may be written

$$\mathbf{\Pi}_j^*\boldsymbol{\gamma}_j = \boldsymbol{\pi}_j^*. \tag{20--10}$$

This is K_j^* equations in M_j unknowns. If they can be solved for $\boldsymbol{\gamma}_j$, (20–8) gives the solution for $\boldsymbol{\beta}_j$ and the equation is identified. In order for there to be a solution, there must be at least as many equations as unknowns, which leads to the following condition.

Order Condition for Identification of Equation j

$$K_j^* \geq M_j. \tag{20--11}$$

The number of exogenous variables excluded from equation j must be at least as large as the number of endogenous variables included in equation j.

The order condition is only a counting rule. It is a necessary, but not sufficient condition for identification. It ensures that (20–10) has at least one solution, but it does not ensure that it has only one solution. The sufficient condition for uniqueness follows.

Rank Condition for Identification

$$\text{rank}[\boldsymbol{\pi}_j^*, \mathbf{\Pi}_j^*] = \text{rank}[\mathbf{\Pi}_j^*] = M_j.$$

This imposes a restriction on a submatrix of the reduced-form coefficient matrix.

The rank condition ensures that there is one solution for the structural parameters given the reduced-form parameters. Our alternative approach to the identification problem was to use the prior restrictions on **[Γ, B]** to eliminate all false structures. An equivalent condition based on this approach is simpler to apply and has more intuitive appeal. We first rearrange the structural coefficients in the matrix

$$\mathbf{A} = \begin{bmatrix} \mathbf{\Gamma} \\ \mathbf{B} \end{bmatrix} = \begin{bmatrix} 1 & \mathbf{A}_1 \\ -\boldsymbol{\gamma}_j & \mathbf{A}_2 \\ \mathbf{0} & \mathbf{A}_3 \\ -\boldsymbol{\beta}_j & \mathbf{A}_4 \\ \mathbf{0} & \mathbf{A}_5 \end{bmatrix} = [\mathbf{a}_j \quad \mathbf{A}_j]. \tag{20--12}$$

The jth column in a false structure **[ΓF, BF]** (i.e., the imposter for our equation j) would be **[Γf$_j$, Bf$_j$]**, where $\mathbf{f}_j$ is the jth column of **F**. This new jth equation is to be built up as a linear combination of the old one and the other equations in the model. Thus, partitioning as previously,

$$\tilde{\mathbf{a}}_j = \begin{bmatrix} 1 & \mathbf{A}_1 \\ -\boldsymbol{\gamma}_j & \mathbf{A}_2 \\ \mathbf{0} & \mathbf{A}_3 \\ -\boldsymbol{\beta}_j & \mathbf{A}_4 \\ \mathbf{0} & \mathbf{A}_5 \end{bmatrix} \begin{bmatrix} f^0 \\ \mathbf{f}^1 \end{bmatrix} = \begin{bmatrix} 1 \\ \tilde{\boldsymbol{\gamma}}_j \\ \mathbf{0} \\ \tilde{\boldsymbol{\beta}}_j \\ \mathbf{0} \end{bmatrix}.$$

If this hybrid is to have the same variables as the original, it must have nonzero elements in the same places, which can be ensured by taking $f^0 = 1$, and zeroes in the same positions as the original a_j. Extracting the third and fifth rows, if $\tilde{a}_j$ is to be admissible, it must meet the requirement

$$\begin{bmatrix} A_3 \\ A_5 \end{bmatrix} f^1 = 0.$$

This is not possible if the preceding $(M_j^* + K_j^*) \times (M - 1)$ matrix has full column rank, so we have the equivalent rank condition,

$$\text{rank} \begin{bmatrix} A_3 \\ A_5 \end{bmatrix} = M - 1.$$

The corresponding order condition is that the preceding matrix have at least as many rows as columns. Thus $M_j^* + K_j^* \geq M - 1$. But since $M = M_j + M_j^* + 1$, this is the same as the order condition in (20–11). The equivalence of the two rank conditions is pursued in the exercises.

The preceding provides a simple method for checking the rank and order conditions. We need only arrange the structural parameters in a tableau and examine the relevant submatrices one at a time; A_3 and A_5 are the structural coefficients in the other equations on the variables that are excluded from equation j.

EXAMPLE 20.9 Rank and Order Conditions

The structural coefficients in the model of Example 20.7 may be written in the preceding form as

	q	p	1	z
Demand	1	$-\alpha_1$	$-\alpha_0$	$-\alpha_2$
Supply	1	$-\beta_1$	$-\beta_0$	$-\beta_2$

Neither A_3 nor A_5 has any rows, so $[A_3', A_5']$ cannot have rank $M - 1 = 1$. Neither equation is identified. The alternative in Example 20.8 is

	q	p	1	y	z
Demand	1	$-\alpha_1$	$-\alpha_0$	$-\alpha_2$	0
Supply	1	$-\beta_1$	$-\beta_0$	0	$-\beta_2$

For the demand equation,

$$[A_3', A_5'] = -\beta_2,$$

which has rank $M - 1 = 1$ unless $\beta_2 = 0$. The supply equation is also identified unless $\alpha_2 = 0$. Now suppose that z appears in the demand equation but not in the supply equation. Then the structure is

	q	p	1	y	z
Demand	1	$-\alpha_1$	$-\alpha_0$	$-\alpha_2$	$-\alpha_3$
Supply	1	$-\beta_1$	$-\beta_0$	0	0

For the demand equation, $[A_3', A_5']$ has no rows, so the equation is not identified. But, for the supply equation,

$$[A_3', A_5'] = [-\alpha_2 \quad -\alpha_3],$$

which has rank one, so the supply equation is identified. This example illustrates the possibility that a model may be *partially identified*.

There is a rule of thumb that is sometimes useful in checking the rank and order conditions of a model:

> If every equation has its own predetermined
> variable, the entire model is identified.

The proof is simple and is left as an exercise. For a final example, we consider a somewhat larger model.

EXAMPLE 20.10 Identification of Klein's Model I

The structural coefficients in the consumption function of Klein's Model I (transposed and multiplied by minus one for convenience) are listed in Table 20.2.

TABLE 20.2

	C	I	W^p	X	P	K	1	W^g	G	T	A	P_{-1}	K_{-1}	X_{-1}
C	-1	0	α_3	0	α_1	0	α_0	α_3	0	0	0	α_2	0	0
I	0	-1	0	0	β_1	0	β_0	0	0	0	0	β_2	β_3	0
W^p	0	0	-1	γ_1	0	0	γ_0	0	0	0	γ_3	0	0	γ_2
X	1	1	0	-1	0	0	0	0	1	0	0	0	0	0
P	0	0	-1	1	-1	0	0	0	0	-1	0	0	0	0
K	0	1	0	0	0	-1	0	0	0	0	0	0	1	0

Identification requires that the matrix shown in Table 20.3 have rank five. None of the columns marked by x's can be formed as linear combinations of the others, so the rank condition is met. Verification of the rank and order conditions for the other two equations is left as an exercise.

TABLE 20.3

Eq.	$\mathbf{A}_3'$			$\mathbf{A}_5'$				
	I	X	K	G	T	A	K_{-1}	X_{-1}
I	-1	0	0	0	0	0	β_3	0
Wp	0	γ_1	0	0	0	γ_3	0	γ_2
X	1	-1	0	1	-1	0	0	0
P	0	1	0	0	0	0	0	0
X	1	0	-1	0	0	0	1	0
	x	x		x	x	x		

It is unusual for a model to pass the order but not the rank condition. (But see Example 20.13 for a case in the literature.) Generally, either the conditions are obvious or the model is so large and has so many predetermined variables that the conditions are met trivially. In practice, for a small model it is simple to check both conditions. For a large model, frequently only the order condition is verified. We distinguish three cases:

1. *Underidentified.* $K_j^* < M_j$ or rank condition fails.
2. *Exactly identified.* $K_j^* = M_j$ and rank condition is met.
3. *Overidentified.* $K_j^* > M_j$ and rank condition is met.

20.3.2. Identification Through Nonsample Information

The rank and order conditions given in the preceding section apply to identification of an equation through **exclusion restrictions.** Intuition might suggest that other types of nonsample information should be equally useful in securing identification. To take a specific example, suppose that in Example 20.7, it is known that β_2 equals 2, not 0. The second equation could then be written as

$$\mathbf{q}_d - 2\mathbf{z} = \mathbf{q}_d^* = \beta_0 + \beta_1\mathbf{p} + \beta_j^*\mathbf{z} + \varepsilon_2.$$

But we know that $\beta_j^* = 0$, so the supply equation is identified by this restriction. (This is exactly the case examined at the end of that example.) As this example suggests, a linear restriction on the parameters *within* an equation is, for identification purposes, essentially the same as an exclusion.[14] By an appropriate manipulation, that is, by "solving out" the restriction, we can turn the restriction into one more exclusion. A general formulation for identification of an equation which treats exclusions the same as any other type of linear restriction on the parameters is as follows:[15] Let

$$\mathbf{\Phi}_j = \text{matrix with one row for each restriction and one}$$
$$\text{column for each parameter in the equation.}$$

That is, $\mathbf{\Phi}_j$ has the same number of columns, $M + K$, as $\mathbf{A}$ in (20–12) has rows. Each row in $\mathbf{\Phi}_j$ is the coefficient in a linear restriction, and the restrictions that apply to equation j are

$$\mathbf{\Phi}_j \begin{bmatrix} \mathbf{\Gamma}_j \\ \mathbf{B}_j \end{bmatrix} = \mathbf{c}_j, \qquad \text{a vector of constants. [See (20–6).]}$$

Then the rank condition for identification with restrictions is

$$\text{rank}(\mathbf{\Phi}_j\mathbf{A}_j) = M - 1,$$

where $\mathbf{A}_j$ is defined in (20–12). The order condition that emerges is

$$n_j \geq M - 1,$$

where n_j is the total number of restrictions. Since $M - 1 = M_j + M_j^*$ and n_j is the number of exclusions plus r_j, the number of additional restrictions, this condition is equivalent to

$$r_j + K_j^* + M_j^* \geq M_j + M_j^*,$$

or

$$r_j + K_j^* \geq M_j.$$

This is the same as (20–11) save for the addition of the number of restrictions, which is the result suggested above.

The rows of $\mathbf{\Phi}_j$ that correspond to simple exclusions just have a 1 in the position corresponding to the appropriate coefficient. By multiplying it out, you can see that if the only restrictions are exclusions, then

$$
\mathbf{\Phi}_j = \begin{array}{ccccc}
1 & M_j & M_j^* & K_j & K_j^* \\
0 & 0 & \mathbf{I} & 0 & 0 \\
0 & 0 & 0 & 0 & \mathbf{I}
\end{array}
\begin{array}{c}
\\ M_j^* \\ K_j^*
\end{array}
$$

and we get exactly the same result as before.

---

[14] The analysis is much more complicated if the restrictions are *across* equations, that is, involve the parameters in more than one equation. Kelly (1975) contains a number of results and examples.

[15] See Fisher (1976).

EXAMPLE 20.11 Identification with Linear Restrictions ———————

We verified in Example 20.10 that the consumption function in Klein's Model I is identified using only the exclusion restrictions. But there is also a linear restriction in the equation. The coefficients on W^p and W^g are equal. Using the ordering of the variables in Example 20.10, this would add a row $\phi_9 = [0, 0, 1, 0, 0, 0, 0, -1, 0, 0, 0, 0, 0, 0]$. The resulting tableau in Table 20.3 would have another column, $[0, -1, 0, -1, 0]'$. Of course, since the equation is already identified, the restriction is superfluous.

———————————————

The observant reader will have noticed that no mention of Σ is made in the preceding discussion. To this point, that is because all of the information contained by Ω is used in the estimation of Σ—for given Γ, the relationship between Ω and Σ is one-to-one. Recall that $\Sigma = \Gamma'\Omega\Gamma$. But if restrictions are placed on Σ, there is more information in Ω than is needed for estimation of Σ. This is useful because the excess information can be used, instead, to help infer the elements in Γ. A useful case is that of zero covariances across the disturbances.[16] Once again, it is most convenient to consider this case in terms of a false structure. In particular, if the structure is $[\Gamma, B, \Sigma]$, a false structure would have parameters

$$[\tilde{\Gamma}, \tilde{B}, \tilde{\Sigma}] = [\Gamma F, BF, F'\Sigma F].$$

If any of the elements in Σ are zero, in order to be admissible, the false structure must preserve those restrictions. For example, suppose that we specify that $\sigma_{12} = 0$. Then it must also be true that $\tilde{\sigma}_{12} = f_1'\Sigma f_2 = 0$, where f_1 and f_2 are columns of F. As such, there is a restriction on F that may identify the model.

EXAMPLE 20.12 The Fully Recursive Model ———————

The fully recursive model is an important special case of the preceding result. A triangular model is

$$y_1 = \beta_1'x + \varepsilon_1$$
$$y_2 = \gamma_{12}y_1 + \beta_2'x + \varepsilon_2$$
$$\vdots$$
$$y_M = \gamma_{1M}y_1 + \gamma_{2M}y_2 + \cdots + \gamma_{M-1,M}y_{M-1} + \beta_M'x + \varepsilon_M.$$

We place no restrictions on B. The first equation is identified, since it is already in reduced form. But for any of the others, linear combinations of it and the ones above it involve the same variables. Thus, we conclude that *without some identifying restrictions, only the parameters of the first equation in a triangular system are identified.* But suppose that Σ is diagonal. Then the entire model is identified, as we now prove. As usual, we attempt to find a false structure that satisfies the restrictions of the model.

The jth column of F, f_j, is the coefficients in a linear combination of the equations that will be an imposter for equation j. Many f_j's are already precluded.

1. f_1 must be the first column of an identity matrix. The first equation is identified and normalized on y_1.
2. In all remaining columns of F, all elements below the diagonal must be zero, since an equation can only involve the y's in it or the equations above it.

———————————————

[16]More general cases are discussed in Hausman (1983) and Judge et al. (1985).

Unfortunately, without further restrictions, any upper triangular $\mathbf{F}$ is an admissible transformation. But with a diagonal $\boldsymbol{\Sigma}$, we have more information. Consider the second column. Since $\bar{\boldsymbol{\Sigma}}$ must be diagonal, $\mathbf{f}_1'\boldsymbol{\Sigma}\mathbf{f}_2 = 0$. But given $\mathbf{f}_1$ above,

$$\mathbf{f}_1'\boldsymbol{\Sigma}\mathbf{f}_2 = \sigma_{11}f_{12} = 0,$$

so $f_{12} = 0$. The second column of $\mathbf{F}$ is now complete and is equal to the second column of $\mathbf{I}$. Continuing in the same manner, we find that

$$\mathbf{f}_1'\boldsymbol{\Sigma}\mathbf{f}_3 = 0 \qquad \text{and} \qquad \mathbf{f}_2'\boldsymbol{\Sigma}\mathbf{f}_3 = 0$$

will suffice to establish that $\mathbf{f}_3$ is the third column of $\mathbf{I}$. In this fashion, it can be shown that the only admissible $\mathbf{F}$ is $\mathbf{F} = \mathbf{I}$, which was to be shown.

With $\boldsymbol{\Gamma}$ upper triangular, $M(M - 1)/2$ unknown parameters remained. That is exactly the number of restrictions placed on $\boldsymbol{\Sigma}$ when it was assumed to be diagonal.

Another even more complex problem arises in models that are nonlinear in the endogenous variables. They arise fairly frequently, for example, in models in which variables appear both in levels and in logarithms, and in macroeconomic models in which the price level and real and nominal variables all appear. For some reasonably general cases, a number of results have been obtained.[17] A very useful, simple result has been obtained for the common case in which the model involves the endogenous variables and nonlinear functions of them that each involve a single variable.[18] For these models, the fundamental rank condition,

$$\text{rank}[\boldsymbol{\Phi}\mathbf{A}] = M - 1,$$

is extended by simply adding the nonlinear functions to the system as additional endogenous variables (but without increasing the number of equations). The following example illustrates the use of this criterion.

EXAMPLE 20.13 A Model of Industry Structure

The following model of industry structure and performance was estimated by Strickland and Weiss (1976). Note that the square of the endogenous variable, C, appears in the first equation.

$$\frac{A}{S} = \alpha_0 + \alpha_1 M + \alpha_2\left(\frac{Cd}{S}\right) + \alpha_3 C + \alpha_4 C^2 + \alpha_5 Gr + \alpha_6 D + \varepsilon_1,$$

$$C = \beta_0 + \beta_1\left(\frac{A}{S}\right) + \beta_2\left(\frac{MES}{S}\right) + \varepsilon_2,$$

$$M = \gamma_0 + \gamma_1\left(\frac{K}{S}\right) + \gamma_2 Gr + \gamma_3 C + \gamma_4 Gd + \gamma_5\left(\frac{A}{S}\right) + \gamma_6\left(\frac{MES}{S}\right) + \varepsilon_3.$$

A = advertising	M = price cost margin
S = industry sales	D = durable goods industry (0/1)
C = concentration	Gr = industry growth rate
Cd = consumer demand	K = capital stock
MES = efficient scale	Gd = geographic dispersion.

---

[17] See Brown (1983).

[18] See Fisher (1976, pp. 127–167, especially pp. 147–148).

TABLE 20.4

	Γ				B						
	A/S	C	C²	M	l	Cd/S	Gr	D	MES/S	K/S	Gd
Advt.	-1	α_3	α_4	α_1	α_0	α_2	α_5	α_6	0	0	0
Conc.	β_1	-1	0	0	β_0	0	0	0	β_2	0	0
Margin	γ_5	γ_3	0	-1	γ_0	0	γ_2	0	γ_6	γ_1	γ_4

Since the only restrictions are exclusions, we may use the rule rank $[\mathbf{A}'_3, \mathbf{A}'_5] = M - 1$ discussed in the first part of this section. The augmented coefficient matrix (with all signs reversed) is shown in Table 20.4. Identification of the first equation requires

$$[\mathbf{A}'_3, \mathbf{A}'_5] = \begin{bmatrix} \beta_2 & 0 & 0 \\ \gamma_6 & \gamma_1 & \gamma_4 \end{bmatrix}$$

to have rank two, which it does unless $\beta_2 = 0$. Thus, the first equation is identified by the presence of the scale variable in the second equation. It is easily seen that the second equation is overidentified. But for the third,

$$[\mathbf{A}'_3, \mathbf{A}'_5] = \begin{bmatrix} \alpha_4 & \alpha_2 & \alpha_6 \\ 0 & 0 & 0 \end{bmatrix}(!),$$

which has rank one, not two. The third equation is not identified. It passes the order condition but fails the rank condition.[19]

20.4. Methods of Estimation

It is possible to estimate the reduced-form parameters, $\mathbf{\Pi}$ and $\mathbf{\Omega}$, consistently by ordinary least squares. But except for forecasting $\mathbf{y}$ given $\mathbf{x}$, these are generally not the parameters of interest; $\mathbf{\Gamma}$, $\mathbf{B}$, and $\mathbf{\Sigma}$ are. Ordinary least squares (OLS) estimates of the structural parameters are inconsistent, ostensibly because the included endogenous variables in each equation are correlated with the disturbances. Still, it is at least of passing interest to examine what, in particular, is estimated by ordinary least squares, particularly in view of its widespread use (in spite of its inconsistency). Since the proof of identification was based on solving for $\mathbf{\Gamma}$, $\mathbf{B}$, and $\mathbf{\Sigma}$ from $\mathbf{\Pi}$ and $\mathbf{\Omega}$, one way to proceed is to apply our finding to the sample estimates, $\mathbf{P}$ and $\mathbf{W}$. This **indirect least squares approach** is feasible but inefficient. Worse, there will usually be more than one possible estimator, and no obvious means of choosing among them. There are two approaches for direct estimation, both based on the principle of instrumental variables. It is possible to estimate each equation separately, using a **limited information** estimator. But the same principle that suggests that joint estimation brings efficiency gains in the seemingly unrelated regressions setting is at work here, so we shall also consider **full information** or system methods of estimation.

---

[19] The failure of the third equation is obvious on inspection. There is no variable in the second equation that is not in the third. The reader who has already studied this topic may wonder at this point how the authors were able to obtain their two-stage least squares estimates of this equation. This question is considered in Section 20.4.4e.

20.4.1. Ordinary Least Squares and Triangular Systems

For all T observations, the nonzero terms in the jth equation are

$$y_j = \mathbf{Y}_j \boldsymbol{\gamma}_j + \mathbf{X}_j \boldsymbol{\beta}_j + \boldsymbol{\varepsilon}_j$$
$$= \mathbf{Z}_j \boldsymbol{\delta}_j + \boldsymbol{\varepsilon}_j.$$

The M reduced-form equations are

$$\mathbf{Y} = \mathbf{X}\mathbf{\Pi} + \mathbf{V}.$$

For the included endogenous variables, $\mathbf{Y}_j$, the reduced forms are the M_j appropriate columns of $\mathbf{\Pi}$ and $\mathbf{V}$, written

$$\mathbf{Y}_j = \mathbf{X}\mathbf{\Pi}_j + \mathbf{V}_j. \tag{20-13}$$

[Note that $\mathbf{\Pi}_j$ is the middle part of $\mathbf{\Pi}$ shown in (20–7).] Likewise, $\mathbf{V}_j$ is M_j columns of $\mathbf{V} = \mathbf{E}\mathbf{\Gamma}^{-1}$. The least squares estimator is

$$\mathbf{d}_j = [\mathbf{Z}_j'\mathbf{Z}_j]^{-1}\mathbf{Z}_j'\mathbf{y}_j$$
$$= \boldsymbol{\delta}_j + \begin{bmatrix} \mathbf{Y}_j'\mathbf{Y}_j & \mathbf{Y}_j'\mathbf{X}_j \\ \mathbf{X}_j'\mathbf{Y}_j & \mathbf{X}_j'\mathbf{X}_j \end{bmatrix}^{-1} \begin{bmatrix} \mathbf{Y}_j'\boldsymbol{\varepsilon}_j \\ \mathbf{X}_j'\boldsymbol{\varepsilon}_j \end{bmatrix}.$$

None of the terms in the inverse matrix converge to $\mathbf{0}$. Although $\mathrm{plim}(1/T)\mathbf{X}_j'\boldsymbol{\varepsilon}_j = \mathbf{0}$,

$$\mathrm{plim}\, \frac{\mathbf{Y}_j'\boldsymbol{\varepsilon}_j}{T} = \underline{\boldsymbol{\omega}}_j - \mathbf{\Omega}_{jj}\boldsymbol{\gamma}_j,$$

where $\underline{\boldsymbol{\omega}}_j$ and $\mathbf{\Omega}_{jj}$ are parts of $\mathbf{\Omega}$. [See the equation before (20–24).]

To show this, first note that since $\mathbf{V} = \mathbf{E}\mathbf{\Gamma}^{-1}$, $\mathbf{E} = \mathbf{V}\mathbf{\Gamma}$. Thus, $\boldsymbol{\varepsilon}_j = \mathbf{V}\mathbf{\Gamma}_j$, where $\mathbf{\Gamma}_j$ is the jth column of $\mathbf{\Gamma}$. This is $(1, -\boldsymbol{\gamma}_j', \mathbf{0}')'$. [See the equation preceding (20–8).] Thus, $\mathrm{plim}(\mathbf{Y}_j'\boldsymbol{\varepsilon}_t/T) = \mathrm{plim}(\mathbf{V}_j'\mathbf{V}\mathbf{\Gamma}_j/T) = \mathrm{plim}(\mathbf{V}_j'\mathbf{V}/T)\mathbf{\Gamma}_j$. The first matrix is the second row of the partitioning of $\mathbf{\Omega}$ which is given in the equation preceding (20–24). Then, $[\underline{\boldsymbol{\omega}}_j\ \mathbf{\Omega}_{jj}](1, -\boldsymbol{\gamma}_j', \mathbf{0}')' = \underline{\boldsymbol{\omega}}_j - \mathbf{\Omega}_{jj}\boldsymbol{\gamma}_j$, which is the result given above. Therefore, both parts of $\mathbf{d}_j$ are inconsistent.

EXAMPLE 20.14 Regression Function

The model of Example 20.7 is

$$q = \alpha_1 p + \alpha_2 z + \varepsilon_1 \quad \text{(demand)},$$
$$q = \beta_1 p + \beta_2 z + \varepsilon_2 \quad \text{(supply)}.$$

The reduced form is

$$q = \frac{\alpha_1\beta_2 - \alpha_2\beta_1}{\alpha_1 - \beta_1} z + v_1 = \pi_1 z + v_1,$$

$$p = \frac{\beta_2 - \alpha_2}{\alpha_1 - \beta_1} z + v_2 = \pi_2 z + v_2.$$

It is convenient to assume that $\mathrm{Var}(z) = \Sigma_{zz} = 1$. Based on this, we may derive the quantities.

$$\mathrm{Var}[q] = \pi_1^2 + \omega_{11} \qquad \mathrm{Cov}[q, z] = \pi_1,$$

$$\mathrm{Var}[p] = \pi_2^2 + \omega_{22} \qquad \mathrm{Cov}[p, z] = \pi_2,$$

$$\mathrm{Cov}[q, p] = \pi_1\pi_2 + \omega_{12}.$$

If we compute the OLS regression of q on p and z, using a sample of observations, the slope vector, $\mathbf{d}$, will estimate

$$\text{plim} \begin{bmatrix} \mathbf{p'p}/T & \mathbf{p'z}/T \\ \mathbf{z'p}/T & \mathbf{z'z}/T \end{bmatrix}^{-1} \begin{bmatrix} \mathbf{p'q}/T \\ \mathbf{z'q}/T \end{bmatrix} = \begin{bmatrix} \text{Var}[p] & \text{Cov}[p, z] \\ \text{Cov}[z, p] & \text{Var}[z] \end{bmatrix}^{-1} \begin{bmatrix} \text{Cov}[p, q] \\ \text{Cov}[z, q] \end{bmatrix}.$$

After some tedious algebra (including the computation of $\mathbf{\Omega} = (\mathbf{\Gamma}^{-1})'\mathbf{\Sigma}\mathbf{\Gamma}^{-1}$), this reduces to

$$\text{plim } \mathbf{d} = \theta \begin{bmatrix} \alpha_1 \\ \alpha_2 \end{bmatrix} + (1 - \theta) \begin{bmatrix} \beta_1 \\ \beta_2 \end{bmatrix},$$

where

$$\theta = \frac{\sigma_{11} - \sigma_{12}}{\sigma_{11} + \sigma_{22} - 2\sigma_{12}}.$$

Therefore, least squares estimates a mixture of the supply and demand curves, where the weights are proportional to the sources of variation.

The preceding example illustrates a general result. The least squares estimates are inconsistent estimates of a structural equation precisely because they are consistent estimates of a mixture of all of the equations in the model.[20]

An intuitively appealing form of simultaneous equations model is the **triangular system,**

$$(1) \quad y_1 = \mathbf{x'}\boldsymbol{\beta}_1 \qquad\qquad\qquad\quad + \varepsilon_1,$$

$$(2) \quad y_2 = \mathbf{x'}\boldsymbol{\beta}_2 + \gamma_{12}y_1 \qquad\qquad + \varepsilon_2,$$

$$(3) \quad y_3 = \mathbf{x'}\boldsymbol{\beta}_3 + \gamma_{13}y_1 + \gamma_{23}y_2 + \varepsilon_3,$$

and so on. If $\mathbf{\Gamma}$ is upper triangular and $\mathbf{\Sigma}$ is diagonal, so that the disturbances are uncorrelated, the system is a **fully recursive model.** (No restrictions are placed on $\mathbf{B}$.) It is easy to see that in this case the entire system may be estimated consistently (and, as we shall show later, efficiently) by ordinary least squares. The first equation is a classical regression model. In the second equation, $\text{Cov}(y_1, \varepsilon_2) = \text{Cov}(\mathbf{x'}\boldsymbol{\beta}_1 + \varepsilon_1, \varepsilon_2) = 0$, so it too may be estimated by ordinary least squares. Proceeding in the same fashion to (3), it is clear that y_1 and ε_3 are uncorrelated. Likewise, if we substitute (1) in (2) and then the result for y_2 in (3), we find that y_2 is also uncorrelated with ε_3. Continuing in this way, we find that in every equation the full set of right-hand variables is uncorrelated with the respective disturbance. The result is that *the fully recursive model may be consistently estimated using equation-by-equation ordinary least squares.*

In the more general case, in which $\mathbf{\Sigma}$ is not diagonal, the preceding argument does not apply. Consistent and efficient estimates can be obtained using the methods to be discussed below. This model does have an interesting feature, however. Although *ordinary least squares is inconsistent, generalized least squares estimation of the entire system, in the manner of the seemingly unrelated regressions model, ignoring the simultaneity,* produces both consistent and efficient estimates.[21] If $\mathbf{\Sigma}$ must be estimated, which will

---

[20] The distinction between structures and regressions, or conditional mean functions that we have explored here, is the subject of some interesting commentary in the literature. See, for example, Working (1926), Haavelmo (1943), and Waugh (1961). Waugh argued for the use of least squares, offering as justification the example in which hog farmers would be interested in knowing the expected price given a year's output.

[21] This intriguing result is due to Lahiri and Schmidt (1978).

almost always be the case, Lahiri and Schmidt find that full efficiency in estimation requires an *efficient* estimate of $\boldsymbol{\Sigma}$. This is in contrast to the seemingly unrelated regressions model, which requires only a *consistent* estimate of $\boldsymbol{\Sigma}$. (See Section 17.2.2.) Iterating via the Oberhofer and Kmenta (1974) method produces the desired estimates. (See Section 17.2.3a.)

20.4.2. Indirect Least Squares

In obtaining the rank and order conditions for identification, we implicitly defined an estimator for the structural parameters. For the jth equation,

$$\boldsymbol{\pi}_j - \underline{\boldsymbol{\Pi}}_j \boldsymbol{\gamma}_j = \boldsymbol{\beta}_j \qquad (K_j \text{ equations}),$$

$$\boldsymbol{\pi}_j^* - \boldsymbol{\Pi}_j^* \boldsymbol{\gamma}_j = \mathbf{0} \qquad (K_j^* \text{ equations}).$$

(20–14)

By analogy, then, if $\mathbf{P}$ is the OLS estimate of $\boldsymbol{\Pi}$, the ILS estimator of $\boldsymbol{\beta}_j$ would be

$$\mathbf{b}_j = \mathbf{p}_j - \underline{\mathbf{P}}_j \mathbf{c}_j.$$

It remains to find $\mathbf{c}_j$, the indirect least squares (ILS) estimator of $\boldsymbol{\gamma}_j$. In the second equation, there are K_j^* equations and M_j unknown parameters to be determined. There are three possibilities:

1. $K_j^* < M_j$. Then the equation is unidentified, and no solution can be obtained.
2. $K_j^* = M_j$. The equation is exactly identified. In this case, we may compute

$$\mathbf{c}_j = [\mathbf{P}_j^*]^{-1} \mathbf{p}_j^*.$$

3. $K_j^* > M_j$. The equation is overidentified. There is more than one solution.

20.4.3. Estimation by Instrumental Variables

In the next several sections, we will discuss various methods of consistent and efficient estimation. As will be evident quite soon, there is a surprisingly long menu of choices. It is a useful result that all of the methods in general use can be placed under the umbrella of **instrumental variable (IV) estimators.**

Returning to the structural form, we first consider direct estimation of the jth equation,

$$\mathbf{y}_j = \mathbf{Y}_j \boldsymbol{\gamma}_j + \mathbf{X}_j \boldsymbol{\beta}_j + \boldsymbol{\varepsilon}_j$$

$$= \mathbf{Z}_j \boldsymbol{\delta}_j + \boldsymbol{\varepsilon}_j.$$

As we saw above, OLS estimates of $\boldsymbol{\delta}_j$ are inconsistent because of the correlation of $\mathbf{Z}_j$ and $\boldsymbol{\varepsilon}_j$. A general method of obtaining consistent estimates is the method of instrumental variables. Let $\mathbf{W}_j$ be a $T \times (M_j + K_j)$ matrix that satisfies the requirements for an IV estimator,

$$\text{plim } \frac{\mathbf{W}_j' \mathbf{Z}_j}{T} = \boldsymbol{\Sigma}_{wz} = \text{a finite nonsingular matrix,} \qquad (20\text{–}15a)$$

$$\text{plim } \frac{\mathbf{W}_j' \boldsymbol{\varepsilon}_j}{T} = \mathbf{0}, \qquad (20\text{–}15b)$$

$$\text{plim } \frac{\mathbf{W}_j' \mathbf{W}_j}{T} = \boldsymbol{\Sigma}_{ww} = \text{a positive definite matrix.} \qquad (20\text{–}15c)$$

Then the IV estimator,

$$\hat{\boldsymbol{\delta}}_{j,\text{IV}} = [\mathbf{W}_j'\mathbf{Z}_j]^{-1}\mathbf{W}_j'\mathbf{y}_j,$$

will be consistent and have asymptotic covariance matrix

$$\text{Asy.Var}[\hat{\boldsymbol{\delta}}_{j,\text{IV}}] = \frac{\sigma_{jj}}{T}\text{plim}\left[\frac{\mathbf{W}_j'\mathbf{Z}_j}{T}\right]^{-1}\left[\frac{\mathbf{W}_j'\mathbf{W}_j}{T}\right]\left[\frac{\mathbf{Z}_j'\mathbf{W}_j}{T}\right]^{-1}$$

$$= \frac{\sigma_{jj}}{T}[\boldsymbol{\Sigma}_{wz}^{-1}\boldsymbol{\Sigma}_{ww}\boldsymbol{\Sigma}_{zw}^{-1}]. \tag{20-16}$$

A consistent estimate of σ_{jj} is obtained using

$$\hat{\sigma}_{jj} = \frac{(\mathbf{Y}_j - \mathbf{Z}_j\hat{\boldsymbol{\delta}}_{j,\text{IV}})'(\mathbf{Y}_j - \mathbf{Z}_j\hat{\boldsymbol{\delta}}_{j,\text{IV}})}{T}. \tag{20-17}$$

This is the familiar sum of squares of the estimated disturbances. A degrees of freedom correction for the denominator, $T - M_j - K_j$, is sometimes suggested. Asymptotically, the correction is immaterial. Whether it is beneficial in a small sample remains to be settled. The resultant estimator is not unbiased in any event, as it would be in the classical regression model. (Only) in the interest of simplicity, we shall omit the degrees of freedom correction in what follows.

The various estimators that have been developed for simultaneous-equations models are all IV estimators. They differ in the choice of instruments and in whether the equations are estimated one at a time or jointly. We divide them into two classes, **limited information** or **full information,** on this basis.

20.4.4. Single-Equation Instrumental Variable Methods

Estimation of the system one equation at a time has the benefit of computational simplicity. But because these methods neglect information contained in the other equations, they are labeled *limited-information methods*.

20.4.4a. Estimating an Exactly Identified Equation. A useful departure point is an exactly identified equation. Identification of equation j requires that K_j^*, the number of excluded exogenous variables, be at least as large as M_j, the number of included endogenous variables in $\mathbf{Y}_j$. If the equation is exactly identified, $K_j^* = M_j$. Consider, then, the IV estimator based on

$$\mathbf{W}_j = [\mathbf{X}_j^* \ \mathbf{X}_j] = \mathbf{X}.$$

There is an excluded exogenous variable available to serve as an instrument for each included endogenous variable. The estimator is

$$\hat{\boldsymbol{\delta}}_{j,\text{ILS}} = [\mathbf{X}'\mathbf{Z}_j]^{-1}\mathbf{X}'\mathbf{y}_j = \begin{bmatrix} \mathbf{c}_j \\ \mathbf{b}_j \end{bmatrix}. \tag{20-18}$$

This is the ILS estimator. The estimated reduced form is

$$\mathbf{P} = (\mathbf{X}'\mathbf{X})^{-1}\mathbf{X}'[\mathbf{y}_j \ \mathbf{Y}_j \ \mathbf{Y}_j^*].$$

We do not require the last M_j^* columns. For the remainder, after premultiplying by $\mathbf{X}'\mathbf{X}$ and partitioning $\mathbf{X}$ as $\mathbf{W}_j$ as shown above, we have

$$\begin{bmatrix} \mathbf{X}_j^{*'}\mathbf{X}_j^* & \mathbf{X}_j^{*'}\mathbf{X}_j \\ \mathbf{X}_j'\mathbf{X}_j^* & \mathbf{X}_j'\mathbf{X}_j \end{bmatrix}\begin{bmatrix} \mathbf{p}_j^* & \mathbf{P}_j^* \\ \mathbf{p}_j & \underline{\mathbf{P}}_j \end{bmatrix} = \begin{bmatrix} \mathbf{X}_j^{*'}\mathbf{y}_j & \mathbf{X}_j^{*'}\mathbf{Y}_j \\ \mathbf{X}_j'\mathbf{y}_j & \mathbf{X}_j'\mathbf{Y}_j \end{bmatrix}. \tag{20-19}$$

Recall the equations that defined the ILS estimator (20–14). Using $\mathbf{P}$ instead,

$$\begin{bmatrix} \mathbf{p}_j^* & \mathbf{P}_j^* \\ \mathbf{p}_j & \mathbf{P}_j \end{bmatrix}\begin{bmatrix} 1 \\ -\mathbf{c}_j \end{bmatrix} = \begin{bmatrix} \mathbf{0} \\ \mathbf{b}_j \end{bmatrix}.$$

Postmultiplying both sides of (20–19) by $[1 \quad -\mathbf{c}_j']'$ produces

$$\begin{bmatrix} \mathbf{X}_j^{*\prime}\mathbf{X}_j^* & \mathbf{X}_j^{*\prime}\mathbf{X}_j \\ \mathbf{X}_j'\mathbf{X}_j^* & \mathbf{X}_j'\mathbf{X}_j \end{bmatrix}\begin{bmatrix} \mathbf{0} \\ \mathbf{b}_j \end{bmatrix} = \begin{bmatrix} \mathbf{X}_j^{*\prime}\mathbf{y}_j & \mathbf{X}_j^{*\prime}\mathbf{Y}_j \\ \mathbf{X}_j'\mathbf{y}_j & \mathbf{X}_j'\mathbf{Y}_j \end{bmatrix}\begin{bmatrix} 1 \\ -\mathbf{c}_j \end{bmatrix}.$$

Upon collecting terms, this defines the ILS estimator according to the equations

$$\begin{bmatrix} \mathbf{X}_j^{*\prime}\mathbf{X}_j & \mathbf{X}_j^{*\prime}\mathbf{Y}_j \\ \mathbf{X}_j'\mathbf{X}_j & \mathbf{X}_j'\mathbf{Y}_j \end{bmatrix}\begin{bmatrix} \mathbf{b}_j \\ \mathbf{c}_j \end{bmatrix} = \begin{bmatrix} \mathbf{X}_j^{*\prime}\mathbf{y}_j \\ \mathbf{X}_j'\mathbf{y}_j \end{bmatrix}.$$

By premultiplying (20–18) by $\mathbf{X}'\mathbf{Z}_j$, we obtain exactly this expression, so the two are equivalent. To reiterate the result, for an exactly identified equation, we may obtain consistent estimates by using the excluded exogenous variables as instruments for the included endogenous variables. The appropriate asymptotic covariance matrix can be computed using (20–16) and (20–17).

20.4.4b. Two-Stage Least Squares. For the exactly identified equation, ILS provides a consistent (and, we shall show, efficient) estimate. In the usual case, however, the equation to be estimated will be overidentified, so $\mathbf{X}'\mathbf{Z}_j$ will have more rows than columns and cannot be inverted. As such, the ILS/IV estimator cannot be used. The method of two-stage least squares is the usual alternative.[22]

Since we have an excess of exogenous variables in $\mathbf{X}_j^*$ to choose from, it might make sense just to choose M_j from the set. Indeed, you can easily show that we could just use any M_j independent linear combinations of them,

$$\hat{\mathbf{Y}} = \mathbf{X}_j^*\mathbf{D}, \tag{20–20}$$

for some matrix $\mathbf{D}$ with full column rank. A natural candidate would be the predicted values from a set of regressions of the variables in $\mathbf{Y}_j$ on $\mathbf{X}_j^*$. We leave as an exercise the proof that this would provide a consistent estimator. However, it would not be efficient. In our discussion of IV estimators in Section 9.5.3, we obtained the qualitative result that the greater the correlation of the instruments with the included variables, the smaller the asymptotic variance matrix. Now from the reduced form (20–13), we know that $\mathbf{Y}_j = \mathbf{X}\mathbf{\Pi}_j + \mathbf{V}_j$, so, by regressing $\mathbf{Y}_j$ only on a subset of the x's, we neglect the information about $\mathbf{Y}_j$ contained in the remainder. The **two-stage least squares (2SLS)** method consists of using as the instruments for $\mathbf{Y}_j$ the predicted values in a regression of $\mathbf{Y}_j$ on *all* of the x's:

$$\hat{\mathbf{Y}}_j = \mathbf{X}[(\mathbf{X}'\mathbf{X})^{-1}\mathbf{X}'\mathbf{Y}_j] = \mathbf{X}\mathbf{P}_j.$$

(It can be shown that this is the most efficient IV estimator that can be formed using only the columns of $\mathbf{X}$.) Note the emulation of $E[\mathbf{Y}_j] = \mathbf{X}\mathbf{\Pi}_j$ in the result. The 2SLS estimator is, thus,

$$\hat{\boldsymbol{\delta}}_{j,\text{2SLS}} = \begin{bmatrix} \hat{\mathbf{Y}}_j'\mathbf{Y}_j & \hat{\mathbf{Y}}_j'\mathbf{X}_j \\ \mathbf{X}_j'\mathbf{Y}_j & \mathbf{X}_j'\mathbf{X}_j \end{bmatrix}^{-1}\begin{bmatrix} \hat{\mathbf{Y}}_j'\mathbf{y}_j \\ \mathbf{X}_j'\mathbf{y}_j \end{bmatrix}. \tag{20–21}$$

---

[22] Since this method leads to indirect least squares if the equation is exactly identified, the two cases need not be considered separately.

Before proceeding, it is important to emphasize the role of the identification condition in this result. In the matrix $[\hat{\mathbf{Y}}_j, \mathbf{X}_j]$, which has $M_j + K_j$ columns, all columns are linear functions of the K columns of $\mathbf{X}$. There exist, at most, K linearly independent combinations of the columns of $\mathbf{X}$. If the equation is not identified, $M_j + K_j$ is greater than K, and $[\hat{\mathbf{Y}}_j, \mathbf{X}_j]$ will not have full column rank. In this case, the 2SLS estimator cannot be computed. If, however, the order condition but not the rank condition is met, then although the 2SLS estimator can be computed, it is not a consistent estimator. See Example 20.13 for a case in point.

There are a few useful simplifications. First, since

$$\mathbf{X}(\mathbf{X}'\mathbf{X})^{-1}\mathbf{X}' = (\mathbf{I} - \mathbf{M})$$

is idempotent,

$$\hat{\mathbf{Y}}_j'\mathbf{Y}_j = \hat{\mathbf{Y}}_j'\hat{\mathbf{Y}}_j.$$

Second,

$$\mathbf{X}_j'\mathbf{X}(\mathbf{X}'\mathbf{X})^{-1}\mathbf{X}' = \mathbf{X}_j',$$

implies

$$\mathbf{X}_j'\mathbf{Y}_j = \mathbf{X}_j'\hat{\mathbf{Y}}_j.$$

Thus, (20–21) can also be written

$$\hat{\boldsymbol{\delta}}_{j,2\text{SLS}} = \begin{bmatrix} \hat{\mathbf{Y}}_j'\hat{\mathbf{Y}}_j & \hat{\mathbf{Y}}_j'\mathbf{X}_j \\ \mathbf{X}_j'\hat{\mathbf{Y}}_j & \mathbf{X}_j'\mathbf{X}_j \end{bmatrix}^{-1} \begin{bmatrix} \hat{\mathbf{Y}}_j'\mathbf{y}_j \\ \mathbf{X}_j'\mathbf{y}_j \end{bmatrix}. \tag{20–22}$$

The 2SLS estimator is obtained by ordinary least squares regression of $\mathbf{y}_j$ on $\hat{\mathbf{Y}}_j$ and $\mathbf{X}_j$. Thus, the name stems from the two regressions in the procedure:

1. *Stage 1*. Obtain the ordinary least squares predictions from regression of $\mathbf{Y}_j$ on $\mathbf{X}$.
2. *Stage 2*. Estimate $\boldsymbol{\delta}_j$ by ordinary least squares regression of $\mathbf{y}_j$ on $\hat{\mathbf{Y}}_j$ and $\mathbf{X}_j$.

A direct proof of the consistency of the 2SLS estimator requires only that we establish that it is a valid IV estimator. For (20–15a) we require

$$\text{plim} \begin{bmatrix} \hat{\mathbf{Y}}_j'\mathbf{Y}_j/T & \hat{\mathbf{Y}}_j'\mathbf{X}_j/T \\ \mathbf{X}_j'\mathbf{Y}_j/T & \mathbf{X}_j'\mathbf{X}_j/T \end{bmatrix} = \text{plim} \begin{bmatrix} \mathbf{P}_j'\mathbf{X}'(\mathbf{X}\mathbf{\Pi}_j + \mathbf{V}_j)/T & \mathbf{P}_j'\mathbf{X}'\mathbf{X}/T \\ \mathbf{X}_j'(\mathbf{X}\mathbf{\Pi}_j + \mathbf{V}_j)/T & \mathbf{X}_j'\mathbf{X}_j/T \end{bmatrix}$$

to be a finite nonsingular matrix. We have used (20–13) for $\mathbf{Y}_j$. This is a continuous function of $\mathbf{P}_j$, which has plim $\mathbf{P}_j = \mathbf{\Pi}_j$. The Slutsky theorem thus allows us to substitute $\mathbf{\Pi}_j$ for $\mathbf{P}_j$ in the probability limit. That the parts converge to a finite matrix follows from (20–3) and (20–5). It will be nonsingular if $\mathbf{\Pi}_j$ has full column rank, which, in turn, will be true if the equation is identified.[23] For (20–15b), we require

$$\text{plim}\frac{1}{T}\begin{bmatrix} \hat{\mathbf{Y}}_j'\boldsymbol{\varepsilon}_j \\ \mathbf{X}_j'\boldsymbol{\varepsilon}_j \end{bmatrix} = \begin{bmatrix} \mathbf{0} \\ \mathbf{0} \end{bmatrix}.$$

The second part is assumed in (20–4). For the first, by direct substitution,

$$\text{plim}\frac{1}{T}\hat{\mathbf{Y}}_j'\mathbf{X}(\mathbf{X}'\mathbf{X})^{-1}\mathbf{X}'\boldsymbol{\varepsilon}_j = \text{plim}\left(\frac{\mathbf{Y}_j'\mathbf{X}}{T}\right)\left(\frac{\mathbf{X}'\mathbf{X}}{T}\right)^{-1}\left(\frac{\mathbf{X}'\boldsymbol{\varepsilon}_j}{T}\right).$$

The third part on the right converges to zero, while the other two converge to finite matrices, which confirms the result. Since $\hat{\boldsymbol{\delta}}_{j,2\text{SLS}}$ is an IV estimator, we can appeal to the

---

[23] Schmidt (1976, pp. 150–151) provides a proof of this result.

earlier results for the asymptotic distribution. A proof of asymptotic efficiency requires the establishment of the benchmark, which we shall do in the discussion of the MLE. Finally, by a (rather involved) application of the central limit theorem, it can be shown that if the data are well behaved, the two-stage least squares estimator is asymptotically normally distributed.

As a final shortcut that is useful for programming purposes, we note that if $\mathbf{X}_j$ is regressed on $\mathbf{X}$, a perfect fit is obtained, so $\hat{\mathbf{X}}_j = \mathbf{X}_j$. Using the idempotent matrix $(\mathbf{I} - \mathbf{M})$, we can thus write (20–22) as

$$\hat{\boldsymbol{\delta}}_{j,2\mathrm{SLS}} = \begin{bmatrix} \mathbf{Y}_j'(\mathbf{I} - \mathbf{M})\mathbf{Y}_j & \mathbf{Y}_j'(\mathbf{I} - \mathbf{M})\mathbf{X}_j \\ \mathbf{X}_j'(\mathbf{I} - \mathbf{M})\mathbf{Y}_j & \mathbf{X}_j'(\mathbf{I} - \mathbf{M})\mathbf{X}_j \end{bmatrix}^{-1} \begin{bmatrix} \mathbf{Y}_j'(\mathbf{I} - \mathbf{M})\mathbf{y}_j \\ \mathbf{X}_j'(\mathbf{I} - \mathbf{M})\mathbf{y}_j \end{bmatrix}.$$

Thus,

$$\begin{aligned} \hat{\boldsymbol{\delta}}_{j,2\mathrm{SLS}} &= [\hat{\mathbf{Z}}_j'\hat{\mathbf{Z}}_j]^{-1}\hat{\mathbf{Z}}_j'\mathbf{y}_j \\ &= [(\mathbf{Z}_j'\mathbf{X})(\mathbf{X}'\mathbf{X})^{-1}(\mathbf{X}'\mathbf{Z}_j)]^{-1}(\mathbf{Z}_j'\mathbf{X})(\mathbf{X}'\mathbf{X})^{-1}\mathbf{X}'\mathbf{y}_j, \end{aligned} \tag{20–23}$$

where all columns of $\hat{\mathbf{Z}}_j'$ are obtained as predictions in a regression of the corresponding column of $\mathbf{Z}_j$ on $\mathbf{X}$. This also results in a useful simplification of the estimated asymptotic covariance matrix,

$$\mathrm{Est.Asy.Var}[\hat{\boldsymbol{\delta}}_{j,2\mathrm{SLS}}] = \hat{\sigma}_{jj}[\hat{\mathbf{Z}}_j'\hat{\mathbf{Z}}_j]^{-1}.$$

It is important to note that σ_{jj} is estimated by

$$\hat{\sigma}_{jj} = \frac{(\mathbf{y}_j - \mathbf{Z}_j\hat{\boldsymbol{\delta}}_j)'(\mathbf{y}_j - \mathbf{Z}_j\hat{\boldsymbol{\delta}}_j)}{T},$$

using the original data, not $\hat{\mathbf{Z}}_j$.

It can also be shown that 2SLS applied to an exactly identified equation is the same as ILS. If the equation is exactly identified, $\mathbf{Z}_j'\mathbf{X}$ is square and has an inverse. Thus, the inverse in brackets in (20–23) may be expanded to obtain

$$\hat{\boldsymbol{\delta}}_{2\mathrm{SLS}} = (\mathbf{X}'\mathbf{Z}_j)^{-1}(\mathbf{X}'\mathbf{X})(\mathbf{Z}_j'\mathbf{X})^{-1}(\mathbf{Z}_j'\mathbf{X})(\mathbf{X}'\mathbf{X})^{-1}\mathbf{X}'\mathbf{y}_j.$$

Eliminating the products of inverses leaves *(for the exactly identified case only)*

$$\hat{\boldsymbol{\delta}}_{j,2\mathrm{SLS}} = (\mathbf{X}'\mathbf{Z}_j)^{-1}\mathbf{X}'\mathbf{y}_j,$$

which is (20–18).

20.4.4c. Limited Information Maximum Likelihood.

The **limited information maximum likelihood (LIML) estimator** is based on a single equation. With normally distributed disturbances, LIML is efficient among single-equation estimators. To construct the log-likelihood function for the jth equation, we consider the joint distribution of the endogenous variables, $\mathbf{y}_j$ and $\mathbf{Y}_j$. The reduced form for these $M_j + 1$ variables is

$$[\mathbf{y}_j \quad \mathbf{Y}_j] = [\mathbf{X}_j \quad \mathbf{X}_j^*]\begin{bmatrix} \boldsymbol{\pi}_j & \boldsymbol{\Pi}_j \\ \boldsymbol{\pi}_j^* & \boldsymbol{\Pi}_j^* \end{bmatrix} + [\mathbf{v}_j \quad \mathbf{V}_j]$$

or

$$\mathbf{Y}_j^0 = \mathbf{X}\boldsymbol{\Pi}_j^0 + \mathbf{V}_j^0.$$

The $(M_j + 1) \times (M_j + 1)$ reduced-form covariance matrix is

$$\boldsymbol{\Omega}_j^0 = \begin{bmatrix} \omega_{jj} & \boldsymbol{\omega}_j' \\ \underline{\boldsymbol{\omega}}_j & \boldsymbol{\Omega}_{jj} \end{bmatrix}.$$

The log of the joint density is, therefore,

$$\ln L_j^0 = -\frac{T}{2}[(M_j + 1)\ln(2\pi) + \ln|\boldsymbol{\Omega}_j^0|] - \frac{1}{2}\sum_t [\mathbf{Y}_{jt}^0 - \mathbf{x}_t'\boldsymbol{\Pi}_j^0]'(\boldsymbol{\Omega}_j^0)^{-1}[\mathbf{Y}_{jt}^0 - \mathbf{x}_t'\boldsymbol{\Pi}_j^0].$$

$$(20\text{--}24)$$

The LIML estimator maximizes this log likelihood, subject to the constraints that relate the structure to the reduced form,

$$\boldsymbol{\pi}_j - \underline{\boldsymbol{\Pi}}_j\boldsymbol{\gamma}_j = \boldsymbol{\beta}_j,$$

$$\boldsymbol{\pi}_j^* - \underline{\boldsymbol{\Pi}}_j^*\boldsymbol{\gamma}_j = \mathbf{0}.$$

$$(20\text{--}25)$$

The first of these just shows how to obtain $\boldsymbol{\beta}_j$ given $\boldsymbol{\gamma}_j$. The second shows the restrictions on $\boldsymbol{\Pi}$. There are three cases to consider:

1. The equation is unidentified. No estimation is possible.
2. The equation is exactly identified. There are no restrictions: $\boldsymbol{\gamma}_j = \boldsymbol{\Pi}_j^{*-1}\boldsymbol{\pi}_j^*$.
3. The equation is overidentified. The restrictions in (20–25) are substantive.

Absent any restrictions, (20–24) is the log-likelihood function for the seemingly unrelated regressions model analyzed in Chapter 17. As such, since all equations have the same regressors, ordinary least squares, equation by equation, is consistent and efficient. Before proceeding, therefore, we obtain the following useful result:

> If the equation is exactly identified, the LIML
> estimator is the ILS estimator. Moreover, it is
> also equal to the 2SLS, as was proved earlier.

If the equation is overidentified, the likelihood function is to be maximized with respect to all of its unknown parameters. The analytical solution to the resulting problem is extremely lengthy and involved. Fortunately, this is one of those unusual cases in which the practical application is far simpler than the formal solution.[24]

The LIML, or **least variance ratio** estimator, can be computed as follows: Let

$$\mathbf{W}_j^0 = \mathbf{E}_j^{0\prime}\mathbf{E}_j^0,$$

where

$$\mathbf{E}_j^0 = \mathbf{M}_j\mathbf{Y}_j^0 = [\mathbf{I} - \mathbf{X}_j(\mathbf{X}_j'\mathbf{X}_j)^{-1}\mathbf{X}_j']\mathbf{Y}_j^0.$$

Each column of $\mathbf{E}_j^0$ is a set of least squares residuals in the regression of the corresponding column of $\mathbf{Y}_j^0$ on $\mathbf{X}_j$, that is, the exogenous variables that appear in the jth equation. Thus, $\mathbf{W}_j^0$ is the matrix of sums of squares and cross products of these residuals. Define

$$\mathbf{W}_j^1 = \mathbf{E}_j^{1\prime}\mathbf{E}_j^1 = \mathbf{Y}_j^{0\prime}[\mathbf{I} - \mathbf{X}(\mathbf{X}'\mathbf{X})^{-1}\mathbf{X}']\mathbf{Y}_j^0. \qquad (20\text{--}26)$$

That is, $\mathbf{W}_j^1$ is defined like $\mathbf{W}_j^0$ except that the regressions are on all of the x's in the model, not just the ones in the jth equation. Let

$$\lambda_1 = \text{smallest characteristic root of } (\mathbf{W}_j^1)^{-1}\mathbf{W}_j^0. \qquad (20\text{--}27)$$

This is an asymmetric matrix, but all of the roots are real and greater than or equal to 1.[25] Depending on the available software, it may be more convenient to obtain the identical smallest root of the symmetric matrix

$$\mathbf{D} = (\mathbf{W}_j^1)^{-1/2}\mathbf{W}_j^0(\mathbf{W}_j^1)^{-1/2}.$$

---

[24] See Theil (1971, Appendix). The least variance ratio estimator is derived in Johnston (1984). The LIML estimator was derived by Anderson and Rubin (1949, 1950).

[25] A proof appears in Schmidt (1976, pp. 173–174).

Now partition $\mathbf{W}_j^0$:

$$\mathbf{W}_j^0 = \begin{bmatrix} w_{jj}^0 & \mathbf{w}_j^{0\prime} \\ \mathbf{w}_j^0 & \mathbf{W}_{jj}^0 \end{bmatrix}$$

corresponding to $[\mathbf{y}_j, \mathbf{Y}_j]$, and partition $\mathbf{W}_j^1$ likewise. Then, with these parts in hand,

$$\hat{\boldsymbol{\gamma}}_{j,\text{LIML}} = [\mathbf{W}_{jj}^0 - \lambda_1 \mathbf{W}_{jj}^1]^{-1}(\mathbf{w}_j^0 - \lambda_1 \mathbf{w}_j^1) \tag{20–28}$$

and

$$\hat{\boldsymbol{\beta}}_{j,\text{LIML}} = [\mathbf{X}_j'\mathbf{X}_j]^{-1}\mathbf{X}_j'(\mathbf{y}_j - \mathbf{Y}_j\hat{\boldsymbol{\gamma}}_{j,\text{LIML}}).$$

Note that $\boldsymbol{\beta}_j$ is estimated by a simple least squares regression. The asymptotic covariance matrix for the LIML estimator is identical to that for the 2SLS estimator.[26] The implication is that with normally distributed disturbances, 2SLS is fully efficient. If the equation is exactly identified, it can be shown that $\lambda_1 = 1$, which leads to the ILS estimator.

Note, finally, that the LIML estimator is a method of moments estimator and a function of sufficient statistics. (See Section 4.6.1.)

EXAMPLE 20.15 LIML Estimation of Klein's Consumption Function

For the consumption function in Klein's model I,

$$\mathbf{X}_c = [1, P_{-1}] \quad \text{and} \quad \mathbf{X} = [1, G, T, A, W^g, P_{-1}, K_{-1}, X_{-1}].$$

The included endogenous variables are

$$\mathbf{Y}_c^0 = [C \quad P \quad (W^p + W^g)].$$

The residual sums of squares and cross-product matrices in the regressions of $\mathbf{Y}_c^0$ on $\mathbf{X}_c$ and $\mathbf{X}$ are

$$\mathbf{W}_c^0 = \begin{bmatrix} 541.16 & & \\ 123.82 & 145.49 & \\ 672.21 & 120.26 & 758.59 \end{bmatrix}, \quad \mathbf{W}_c^1 = \begin{bmatrix} 58.099 & & \\ 58.628 & 61.950 & \\ 43.661 & 41.576 & 40.072 \end{bmatrix}.$$

Using (2–105), we obtain

$$(\mathbf{W}_c^1)^{-1/2} = \begin{bmatrix} 0.785645 & & \\ -0.490974 & 0.523609 & \\ -0.266918 & 0.053884 & 0.355695 \end{bmatrix}.$$

The characteristic roots of $(\mathbf{W}_c^1)^{-1/2}\mathbf{W}_c^0(\mathbf{W}_c^1)^{-1/2}$ are 186.161, 7.61756, and 1.49874. Using (20–28), we obtain

$$\hat{\boldsymbol{\gamma}}_c = [-.2225, \quad 0.8226].$$

Finally, the least squares regression of

$$y_c^0 = C + 0.2225P - 0.8226(W^p + W^g)$$

on 1 and P_{-1} produces estimates of 17.477 and 0.396027. (Note that the coefficient on P has the wrong sign. The full information maximum likelihood estimator does also.)

---

[26] This is proved by showing that both estimators are members of the "k class" of estimators, all of which have the same asymptotic covariance matrix. Details are given in Theil (1971) and Schmidt (1976).

There is another approach to the computation of the LIML estimator. For the endogenous variables in equation j, we have $M_j + 1$ equations

$$\mathbf{y}_j = \mathbf{Y}_j\boldsymbol{\gamma}_j + \mathbf{X}_j\boldsymbol{\beta}_j + \boldsymbol{\varepsilon}_j,$$
$$\mathbf{Y}_j = \mathbf{X}\boldsymbol{\Pi}_j^0 \qquad + \mathbf{V}_j.$$

Pagan (1979) has shown that the LIML estimator may be computed by treating the preceding as a seemingly unrelated regressions model, ignoring both the constraints on the reduced form and the correlation between $\mathbf{Y}_j$ and $\boldsymbol{\varepsilon}_j$, and using the iterative GLS method discussed in Chapter 17.[27]

20.4.4d. Two-Stage Least Squares with Autocorrelation.
If the equation being estimated does not contain any lagged endogenous variables, the treatment of autocorrelation is a simple extension of the methods of Chapter 15. Suppose that the autocorrelation is a first-order autoregression,

$$\varepsilon_{t,j} = \rho_j\varepsilon_{t-1,j} + u_{t,j}.$$

In the absence of lagged endogenous variables, the problems caused by autocorrelation concern efficiency and the inappropriateness of the usual estimators of the standard errors of the estimates, not consistency. Making the usual transformation, we have

$$y_{t,j} - \rho_j y_{t-1,j} = (\mathbf{Y}'_{t,j} - \rho_j\mathbf{Y}'_{t-1,j})\boldsymbol{\gamma}_j + (\mathbf{x}'_{t,j} - \rho_j\mathbf{x}'_{t-1,j})\boldsymbol{\beta}_j + u_{t,j}. \qquad (20\text{--}29)$$

If ρ_j were known, the simultaneous-equations estimation problem would carry over in the familiar fashion to this modified equation. A consistent estimate of ρ_j can be obtained by using

$$\hat{\rho}_j = \frac{\sum_t \hat{\varepsilon}_{t,j}\hat{\varepsilon}_{t-1,j}}{\sum_t \hat{\varepsilon}_{t,j}^2}. \qquad (20\text{--}30)$$

where $\hat{\varepsilon}_{t,j}$ is an estimated disturbance based on any consistent estimate of $\boldsymbol{\delta}_j$. The obvious choice is the 2SLS estimator. With $\hat{\rho}_j$ in hand, (20–29) can be estimated by an IV estimator. The asymptotic properties of the resulting estimator are the same as if the true ρ_j were used, so the only issue remaining concerns the choice of the instrumental variables. Since only $\mathbf{Y}_{t,j}$ is correlated with $u_{t,j}$, a consistent estimator is obtained by using $\hat{\mathbf{Y}}_j = \mathbf{X}\mathbf{P}_j$ as usual.[28] The model may be estimated by a three-step procedure:

1. Estimate $\boldsymbol{\Pi}$ with $(\mathbf{X}'\mathbf{X})^{-1}\mathbf{X}'\mathbf{Y}$ and compute $\hat{\mathbf{Y}}_j = \mathbf{X}\mathbf{P}_j$.
2. Compute $\hat{\boldsymbol{\delta}}_j$ using 2SLS; then estimate ρ_j as shown earlier.
3. Using $\hat{\mathbf{Y}}_{t,j}$ based on $\mathbf{x}_t$, compute FGLS estimates based on the modified structural equation (20–29).

It is also possible to iterate step 3, but the benefit of doing so remains to be verified. Asymptotically, it makes no difference, since the estimator is efficient at the first repetition.

---

[27] For Klein's Model I, this procedure took over 80 iterations to converge for the consumption function and over 100 for the investment equation. In view of the rather small number of computations that succeed the extraction of the smallest root, the iterative SURE procedure is rather inefficient. See, as well, Hausman (1983, p. 426).

[28] The restricted set of instruments is a practical simplification. As suggested by (20–29), full efficiency requires the full set of instruments, $\mathbf{y}_{t-1}$, $\mathbf{x}_t$, and $\mathbf{x}_{t-1}$. See Sargan (1961) and Fair (1972). Fair also considers higher-order autocorrelation. Fomby et al. (1984, pp. 582–583) and our first edition incorrectly claim full efficiency for the IV estimator based on $\mathbf{X}\mathbf{P}_j$.

If the equation contains lagged endogenous variables, neither the reduced-form estimates at the first step nor $\hat{\rho}_j$ at the second will be consistent. By repeating the transformation of (20–29), we see that in terms of temporally uncorrelated disturbances, the full reduced form includes $\mathbf{x}_t$, $\mathbf{x}_{t-1}$, $\mathbf{Y}_{t-1}$, and $\mathbf{Y}_{t-2}$, which is likely to be an inordinately large number of variables.[29] With a moderately sized sample, it may even be impossible to compute the estimated reduced form. But at the first step, we only require a consistent estimate of ρ, not an efficient one. A simple expedient is to treat the lagged endogenous variables as if they were current endogenous variables, and include only the current and lagged values of the strictly exogenous variables among the predetermined variables at step 1. The regression at step 2, then, is consistent but not efficient. A consistent set of residuals is produced that can be used in (20–30) to compute $\hat{\rho}$. FGLS estimates based on this $\hat{\rho}$ and the "purged" endogenous variables, $\hat{\mathbf{Y}}_j$ and $\hat{\mathbf{Y}}_{-1,j}$, are then computed at step 3.

Step 3 almost surely brings gains in asymptotic efficiency, though, as always, the issue as regards a small sample is less clear. We should note, though, that even with normally distributed disturbances, the estimator is not fully efficient for two reasons. First, as suggested by Sargan (1961), full efficiency would require an estimate of the full reduced form.[30] Second, unlike the previous case, this estimator requires an efficient estimator of ρ. This can be achieved by iterating over ρ at step 3. Another approach that is also fully efficient involves an extension of Hatanaka's method.[31]

20.4.4e. Two-Stage Least Squares in Models that Are Nonlinear in Variables.
The analysis of simultaneous equations becomes considerably more complicated when the equations are nonlinear. Amemiya presents a general treatment of nonlinear models.[32] A case that is broad enough to include many practical applications is the one analyzed by Kelejian (1971),

$$\mathbf{y}_j = \gamma_{1j}\mathbf{f}_{1j}(\mathbf{y}, \mathbf{x}) + \gamma_{2j}\mathbf{f}_{2j}(\mathbf{y}, \mathbf{x}) + \cdots + \mathbf{X}_j\boldsymbol{\beta}_j + \boldsymbol{\varepsilon}_j.\text{[33]}$$

This is the direct extension of (8–4). Ordinary least squares will be inconsistent for the same reasons as before, but an IV estimator, if one can be devised, should have the usual properties. Because of the nonlinearity, it may not be possible to solve for the reduced-form equations (assuming that they exist), $h_{ij}(\mathbf{x}) = E[f_{ij}\,|\,\mathbf{x}]$. Kelejian shows that 2SLS based on a Taylor series approximation to h_{ij}, using linear terms, higher powers, and cross-products of the variables in $\mathbf{x}$, will be consistent. The analysis of 2SLS presented earlier, then, applies to the $\hat{\mathbf{Z}}_j$ consisting of $[\hat{\mathbf{f}}_{1j}, \hat{\mathbf{f}}_{2j}, \ldots, \mathbf{X}_j]$.[34]

EXAMPLE 20.16 Nonlinear Two-Stage Least Squares _____

The model of Example 20.13 contains three endogenous variables, A/S, C, and M. The first equation also involves C^2. Fitted values for 2SLS were obtained by regressing all four endogenous functions on a constant, the exogenous variables and their squares, and

---

[29] Fair (1970).

[30] See, as well, Fair (1972).

[31] See Section 15.7.3 and Hatanaka (1976).

[32] Amemiya (1985, pp. 245–265).

[33] 2SLS for models which are nonlinear in the parameters is discussed in Chapter 13 in connection with GMM estimators.

[34] The alternative approach of directly computing fitted values for $\mathbf{y}$ appears to be inconsistent. See Kelejian (1971) and Goldfeld and Quandt (1968).

all distinct cross-products. A much larger nonlinear model (42 equations in total, including 16 behavioral equations) was estimated by Rice and Smith (1977). They used linear approximations for the reduced forms.

In a linear model, if an equation fails the order condition, it cannot be estimated by 2SLS. This is not true of Kelejian's approach, however, since taking higher powers of the regressors creates many more linearly independent instrumental variables. If an equation in a linear model fails the rank condition but not the order condition, the 2SLS estimates can be computed in a finite sample but will fail to exist asymptotically because $\mathbf{X}\Pi_j$ will have short rank. Unfortunately, to the extent that Kelejian's approximation never exactly equals the true reduced form unless it happens to be the polynomial in $\mathbf{x}$ (unlikely), this built-in control need not be present, even asymptotically. As such, there is an interesting (and open) question of just what is estimated by the estimator if the model is not identified. Thus, as we saw earlier, although the model in Example 20.13 is unidentified, computation of Kelejian's 2SLS estimator appears to be routine. The upshot, of course, is that one should ensure that the model is identified before embarking on the estimation step.

20.4.5. System Methods of Estimation

We may formulate the full system of equations as

$$
\begin{bmatrix} \mathbf{y}_1 \\ \mathbf{y}_2 \\ \vdots \\ \mathbf{y}_M \end{bmatrix} = \begin{bmatrix} \mathbf{Z}_1 & \mathbf{0} & \cdots & \mathbf{0} \\ \mathbf{0} & \mathbf{Z}_2 & \cdots & \mathbf{0} \\ \vdots & \vdots & \vdots & \vdots \\ \mathbf{0} & \mathbf{0} & \cdots & \mathbf{Z}_M \end{bmatrix} \begin{bmatrix} \delta_1 \\ \delta_2 \\ \vdots \\ \delta_M \end{bmatrix} + \begin{bmatrix} \varepsilon_1 \\ \varepsilon_2 \\ \vdots \\ \varepsilon_M \end{bmatrix}
$$

or

$$
\mathbf{y} = \mathbf{Z}\delta + \varepsilon,
$$

where

$$
E[\varepsilon] = \mathbf{0}
$$

and

$$
E[\varepsilon\varepsilon'] = \overline{\Sigma} = \begin{bmatrix} \sigma_{11}\mathbf{I} & \sigma_{12}\mathbf{I} & \cdots & \sigma_{1M}\mathbf{I} \\ \sigma_{21}\mathbf{I} & \sigma_{22}\mathbf{I} & \cdots & \sigma_{2M}\mathbf{I} \\ & & & \\ \sigma_{M1}\mathbf{I} & \sigma_{M2}\mathbf{I} & \cdots & \sigma_{MM}\mathbf{I} \end{bmatrix} = \Sigma \otimes \mathbf{I}.
$$

The least squares estimator,

$$
\mathbf{d} = [\mathbf{Z}'\mathbf{Z}]^{-1}\mathbf{Z}'\mathbf{y},
$$

which is equation-by-equation ordinary least squares, is inconsistent. But even if ordinary least squares were consistent, we know from our results for the seemingly unrelated regressions model that it would be inefficient compared to an estimator that makes use of the cross-equation correlations of the disturbances. For the first issue, we turn once again to an IV estimator. For the second, as we did in Chapter 17, we use a generalized least squares approach. Thus, assuming that $\overline{\mathbf{W}}$ satisfies the requirements for an IV estimator, a consistent though inefficient estimator would be

$$
\hat{\delta}_{IV} = [\overline{\mathbf{W}}'\mathbf{Z}]^{-1}\overline{\mathbf{W}}'\mathbf{y}.
$$

Analogous to the seemingly unrelated regressions model, a more efficient estimator would be based on the generalized least squares principle,

$$\hat{\boldsymbol{\delta}}_{IV,GLS} = [\overline{\mathbf{W}}'(\boldsymbol{\Sigma}^{-1} \otimes \mathbf{I})\mathbf{Z}]^{-1}\overline{\mathbf{W}}'(\boldsymbol{\Sigma}^{-1} \otimes \mathbf{I})\mathbf{y}$$

or

$$\hat{\boldsymbol{\delta}}_{IV,GLS} = \begin{bmatrix} \sigma^{11}\mathbf{W}_1'\mathbf{Z}_1 & \sigma^{12}\mathbf{W}_1'\mathbf{Z}_2 & \cdots & \sigma^{1M}\mathbf{W}_1'\mathbf{Z}_M \\ \sigma^{21}\mathbf{W}_2'\mathbf{Z}_1 & \sigma^{22}\mathbf{W}_2'\mathbf{Z}_2 & \cdots & \sigma^{2M}\mathbf{W}_2'\mathbf{Z}_M \\ & & \vdots & \\ \sigma^{M1}\mathbf{W}_M'\mathbf{Z}_1 & \sigma^{M2}\mathbf{W}_M'\mathbf{Z}_2 & \cdots & \sigma^{MM}\mathbf{W}_M'\mathbf{Z}_M \end{bmatrix}^{-1} \begin{bmatrix} \Sigma_j\sigma^{1j}\mathbf{W}_1'\mathbf{y}_j \\ \Sigma_j\sigma^{2j}\mathbf{W}_2'\mathbf{y}_j \\ \vdots \\ \Sigma_j\sigma^{Mj}\mathbf{W}_M'\mathbf{y}_j \end{bmatrix}.$$

Two techniques are generally used for joint estimation of the entire system of equations: three-stage least squares and maximum likelihood.

20.4.5a. Three-Stage Least Squares. Consider the IV estimator formed from

$$\overline{\mathbf{W}} = \hat{\mathbf{Z}} = \begin{bmatrix} \mathbf{X}(\mathbf{X}'\mathbf{X})^{-1}\mathbf{X}'\mathbf{Z}_1 & \mathbf{0} & \cdots & \mathbf{0} \\ \mathbf{0} & \mathbf{X}(\mathbf{X}'\mathbf{X})^{-1}\mathbf{X}'\mathbf{Z}_2 & \cdots & \mathbf{0} \\ & & \vdots & \\ \mathbf{0} & \mathbf{0} & & \mathbf{X}(\mathbf{X}'\mathbf{X})^{-1}\mathbf{X}'\mathbf{Z}_M \end{bmatrix}$$

$$= \begin{bmatrix} \hat{\mathbf{Z}}_1 & \mathbf{0} & \cdots & \mathbf{0} \\ \mathbf{0} & \hat{\mathbf{Z}}_2 & \cdots & \mathbf{0} \\ & & \vdots & \\ \mathbf{0} & \mathbf{0} & \cdots & \hat{\mathbf{Z}}_M \end{bmatrix}.$$

The IV estimator

$$\hat{\boldsymbol{\delta}}_{IV} = [\hat{\mathbf{Z}}'\mathbf{Z}]^{-1}\hat{\mathbf{Z}}'\mathbf{y}$$

is nothing more than equation-by-equation 2SLS. We have already established the consistency of 2SLS. However, by analogy with the seemingly unrelated regressions model of Chapter 17, we would expect this estimator to be less efficient than a GLS estimator. A natural candidate would be

$$\hat{\boldsymbol{\delta}}_{3SLS} = [\hat{\mathbf{Z}}'(\boldsymbol{\Sigma}^{-1} \otimes \mathbf{I})\mathbf{Z}]^{-1}\hat{\mathbf{Z}}'(\boldsymbol{\Sigma}^{-1} \otimes \mathbf{I})\mathbf{y}.$$

In order for this to be a valid IV estimator, we must establish that

$$\text{plim } \frac{1}{T} \hat{\mathbf{Z}}'(\boldsymbol{\Sigma}^{-1} \otimes \mathbf{I})\boldsymbol{\varepsilon} = \mathbf{0}.$$

This is M sets of equations of the form

$$\text{plim } \frac{1}{T} \sum_j \sigma^{ij}\hat{\mathbf{Z}}_j'\boldsymbol{\varepsilon}_j = \mathbf{0}.$$

Each is the sum of vectors all of which converge to zero, as we saw in the development of the 2SLS estimator. The second requirement, that

$$\text{plim } \frac{1}{T} \hat{\mathbf{Z}}'(\boldsymbol{\Sigma} \otimes \mathbf{I})\mathbf{Z} \neq \mathbf{0}$$

and that the matrix be nonsingular can be established along the lines of its counterpart for 2SLS. Identification of every equation by the rank condition is sufficient.[35]

---

[35] A formal proof is given by Schmidt (1976, pp. 205–207).

Once again using the idempotency of $\mathbf{I} - \mathbf{M}$, we may also interpret this as a GLS estimator of the form

$$\hat{\boldsymbol{\delta}}_{3SLS} = [\hat{\mathbf{Z}}'(\boldsymbol{\Sigma}^{-1} \otimes \mathbf{I})\hat{\mathbf{Z}}]^{-1}\hat{\mathbf{Z}}'(\boldsymbol{\Sigma}^{-1} \otimes \mathbf{I})\mathbf{y}. \tag{20-31}$$

The appropriate asymptotic covariance matrix for the estimator is

$$\text{Asy.Var}[\hat{\boldsymbol{\delta}}_{3SLS}] = [\overline{\mathbf{Z}}'(\boldsymbol{\Sigma}^{-1} \otimes \mathbf{I})\overline{\mathbf{Z}}]^{-1}, \tag{20-32}$$

where $\overline{\mathbf{Z}} = \text{diag}[\mathbf{XII}_j, \mathbf{X}_j]$. This would be estimated with the inverse matrix in (20–31).

Using sample data, we find that $\overline{\mathbf{Z}}$ may be estimated with $\hat{\mathbf{Z}}$. The remaining difficulty is to obtain an estimate of $\boldsymbol{\Sigma}$. In estimation of the multivariate regression model, for efficient estimation (that remains to be shown), any consistent estimate of $\boldsymbol{\Sigma}$ will do. The designers of the 3SLS method, Zellner and Theil (1962), suggest the natural choice arising out of the two-stage least estimates. The **three-stage least squares (3SLS) estimator** is thus defined as follows:

1. Estimate $\mathbf{II}$ by ordinary least squares and compute $\hat{\mathbf{Y}}_j$ for each equation.
2. Compute $\hat{\boldsymbol{\delta}}_{j,2SLS}$ for each equation; then

$$\hat{\sigma}_{ij} = \frac{(\mathbf{y}_i - \mathbf{Z}_i\hat{\boldsymbol{\delta}}_i)'(\mathbf{y}_j - \mathbf{Z}_j\hat{\boldsymbol{\delta}}_j)}{T}.$$

3. Compute the GLS estimator according to (20–31) and an estimate of the asymptotic covariance matrix according to (20–32), using $\hat{\mathbf{Z}}$ and $\hat{\boldsymbol{\Sigma}}$.

It is also possible to iterate the 3SLS computation. However, unlike the seemingly unrelated regressions estimator, this does not provide the maximum likelihood estimator, nor does it improve the asymptotic efficiency.

By showing that the 3SLS estimator satisfies the requirements for an IV estimator, we have established its consistency. The question of asymptotic efficiency remains. Now it can be shown that among all IV estimators that use only the sample information embodied in the system, 3SLS is asymptotically efficient.[36] For normally distributed disturbances, it can be also shown that 3SLS has the same asymptotic distribution as the full-information maximum likelihood estimator, which is asymptotically efficient among all estimators. A direct proof based on the information matrix is possible, but we shall take a much simpler route by simply exploiting a handy result due to Hausman in the next section.

20.4.5b. Full-Information Maximum Likelihood. Because of their simplicity and asymptotic efficiency, 2SLS and 3SLS are used almost exclusively (when ordinary least squares is not used) for the estimation of simultaneous-equations models. Nonetheless, it is occasionally useful to obtain maximum likelihood estimates directly. The **full-information maximum likelihood (FIML) estimator** is based on the entire system of equations. With normally distributed disturbances, FIML is efficient among all estimators.

The FIML estimator treats all equations and all parameters jointly. To formulate the appropriate log-likelihood function, we begin with the reduced form,

$$\mathbf{Y} = \mathbf{XII} + \mathbf{V},$$

where each row of $\mathbf{V}$ is assumed to be multivariate normally distributed, with mean $\mathbf{0}$ and covariance matrix, $E[\mathbf{v}_t\mathbf{v}_t'] = \boldsymbol{\Omega}$. The log likelihood for this model is precisely that of the

---

[36] See Schmidt (1976) for a proof of its efficiency relative to 2SLS.

seemingly unrelated regressions model of Chapter 17. For the moment, we can ignore the relationship between the structural and reduced-form parameters. Thus, from (17–21),

$$\ln L = -\frac{T}{2}[M \ln(2\pi) + \ln|\mathbf{\Omega}| + tr(\mathbf{\Omega}^{-1}\mathbf{W})], \qquad (20\text{–}33)$$

where

$$\mathbf{W}_{ij} = \frac{(\mathbf{y}_i - \mathbf{X}\boldsymbol{\pi}_i^0)'(\mathbf{y}_j - \mathbf{X}\boldsymbol{\pi}_j^0)}{T}$$

and

$$\boldsymbol{\pi}_j^0 = j\text{th column of } \mathbf{\Pi}.$$

This is to be maximized subject to all of the restrictions imposed by the structure. Make the substitutions

$$\mathbf{\Pi} = -\mathbf{B}\mathbf{\Gamma}^{-1} \qquad \text{and} \qquad \mathbf{\Omega} = (\mathbf{\Gamma}^{-1})'\boldsymbol{\Sigma}\mathbf{\Gamma}^{-1},$$

so that

$$\mathbf{\Omega}^{-1} = \mathbf{\Gamma}\boldsymbol{\Sigma}^{-1}\mathbf{\Gamma}'.$$

Thus,

$$\ln L = -\frac{MT}{2} \ln (2\pi) - \frac{T}{2} \ln|(\mathbf{\Gamma}^{-1})'\boldsymbol{\Sigma}\mathbf{\Gamma}^{-1}|$$

$$-\frac{T}{2}tr\left(\frac{\mathbf{\Gamma}\boldsymbol{\Sigma}^{-1}\mathbf{\Gamma}'(\mathbf{Y} + \mathbf{X}\mathbf{B}\mathbf{\Gamma}^{-1})'(\mathbf{Y} + \mathbf{X}\mathbf{B}\mathbf{\Gamma}^{-1})}{T}\right).$$

This can be simplified. First,

$$-\frac{T}{2} \ln|(\mathbf{\Gamma}^{-1})'\boldsymbol{\Sigma}\mathbf{\Gamma}^{-1}| = -\frac{T}{2} \ln|\boldsymbol{\Sigma}| + T \ln|\mathbf{\Gamma}|.$$

Second, $\mathbf{\Gamma}'(\mathbf{Y} + \mathbf{X}\mathbf{B}\mathbf{\Gamma}^{-1})' = \mathbf{\Gamma}'\mathbf{Y}' + \mathbf{B}'\mathbf{X}'$. By permuting $\mathbf{\Gamma}$ from the beginning to the end of the trace and collecting terms,

$$tr(\mathbf{\Omega}^{-1}\mathbf{W}) = tr\left[\frac{\boldsymbol{\Sigma}^{-1}(\mathbf{Y}\mathbf{\Gamma} + \mathbf{X}\mathbf{B})'(\mathbf{Y}\mathbf{\Gamma} + \mathbf{X}\mathbf{B})}{T}\right].$$

Therefore, the log likelihood is

$$\ln L = -\frac{MT}{2} \ln (2\pi) + T \ln|\mathbf{\Gamma}| - \frac{T}{2}tr(\boldsymbol{\Sigma}^{-1}\mathbf{S}),$$

where

$$s_{ij} = \frac{(\mathbf{Y}\mathbf{\Gamma}_i + \mathbf{X}\mathbf{B}_i)'(\mathbf{Y}\mathbf{\Gamma}_j + \mathbf{X}\mathbf{B}_j)}{T}.$$

[In terms of nonzero parameters, s_{ij} is $\hat{\sigma}_{ij}$ of (20–17).]

In maximizing $\ln L$, it is necessary to impose all of the additional restrictions on the structure. It is useful, therefore, to note that the trace may be written in the form

$$tr(\boldsymbol{\Sigma}^{-1}\mathbf{S}) = \frac{\Sigma_i\Sigma_j\sigma^{ij}(\mathbf{y}_i - \mathbf{Y}_i\boldsymbol{\gamma}_i - \mathbf{X}_i\boldsymbol{\beta}_i)'(\mathbf{y}_j - \mathbf{Y}_j\boldsymbol{\gamma}_j - \mathbf{X}_j\boldsymbol{\beta}_j)}{T}. \qquad (20\text{–}34)$$

Maximizing ln L subject to the exclusions in (20–34) and any other restrictions, if necessary produces the FIML estimator. This has all of the desirable asymptotic properties of maximum likelihood estimators and, therefore, is asymptotically efficient among estimators of the simultaneous-equations model. The asymptotic covariance matrix for the FIML estimator is the same as that for the 3SLS estimator.

A useful interpretation of the FIML estimator is provided by Hausman (1975, 1983). He shows that the FIML estimator of $\boldsymbol{\delta}$ is a fixed point in the equation

$$\hat{\boldsymbol{\delta}}_{\text{FIML}} = [\hat{\mathbf{Z}}(\hat{\boldsymbol{\delta}})'(\hat{\boldsymbol{\Sigma}}^{-1} \otimes \mathbf{I})\mathbf{Z}]^{-1}[\hat{\mathbf{Z}}(\hat{\boldsymbol{\delta}})'(\hat{\boldsymbol{\Sigma}}^{-1} \otimes \mathbf{I})\mathbf{y}] = [\hat{\bar{\mathbf{Z}}}'\mathbf{Z}]^{-1}\hat{\bar{\mathbf{Z}}}'\mathbf{y},$$

where

$$\hat{\mathbf{Z}}(\hat{\boldsymbol{\delta}})'(\hat{\boldsymbol{\Sigma}}^{-1} \otimes \mathbf{I}) = \begin{bmatrix} \hat{\sigma}^{11}\hat{\mathbf{Z}}_1 & \hat{\sigma}^{12}\hat{\mathbf{Z}}_1 & \cdots & \hat{\sigma}^{1M}\hat{\mathbf{Z}}_1 \\ \hat{\sigma}^{21}\hat{\mathbf{Z}}_2 & \hat{\sigma}^{22}\hat{\mathbf{Z}}_2 & \cdots & \hat{\sigma}^{2M}\hat{\mathbf{Z}}_2 \\ & & & \\ \hat{\sigma}^{M1}\hat{\mathbf{Z}}_M & \hat{\sigma}^{M2}\hat{\mathbf{Z}}_M & \cdots & \hat{\sigma}^{MM}\hat{\mathbf{Z}}_M \end{bmatrix}' = \hat{\bar{\mathbf{Z}}}'$$

and

$$\hat{\mathbf{Z}}_j = [\mathbf{X}\hat{\boldsymbol{\Pi}}_j \quad \mathbf{X}_j].$$

$\hat{\boldsymbol{\Pi}}$ is computed from the structural estimates

$$\hat{\boldsymbol{\Pi}}_j = M_j \text{ columns of } -\hat{\mathbf{B}}\hat{\boldsymbol{\Gamma}}^{-1}$$

and

$$\hat{\sigma}_{ij} = \frac{(\mathbf{y}_i - \mathbf{Z}_i\hat{\boldsymbol{\delta}}_i)'(\mathbf{y}_j - \mathbf{Z}_j\hat{\boldsymbol{\delta}}_j)}{T},$$

$$\hat{\sigma}^{ij} = (\hat{\boldsymbol{\Sigma}}^{-1})_{ij}.$$

This result implies that the FIML estimator is also an IV estimator. The asymptotic covariance matrix for the FIML estimator follows directly from its form as an IV estimator. Since this is the same as that of the 3SLS estimator, we conclude that with normally distributed disturbances, 3SLS has the same asymptotic distribution as maximum likelihood. The practical usefulness of this important result has not gone unnoticed by practitioners. The 3SLS estimator is far easier to compute than the FIML estimator. The benefit in computational cost comes at no cost in asymptotic efficiency.

Finally, there are two special cases worth noting. First, for the fully recursive model,

1. $\boldsymbol{\Gamma}$ is upper triangular, with ones on the diagonal. Therefore, $|\boldsymbol{\Gamma}| = 1$ and $\ln|\boldsymbol{\Gamma}| = 0$.
2. $\boldsymbol{\Sigma}$ is diagonal, so $\ln|\boldsymbol{\Sigma}| = \Sigma_j \ln \sigma_{jj}$ and the trace in the exponent becomes

$$\text{tr}(\boldsymbol{\Sigma}^{-1}\mathbf{S}) = \sum_j \frac{1}{\sigma_{jj}} \frac{(\mathbf{y}_j - \mathbf{Y}_j\boldsymbol{\gamma}_j - \mathbf{X}_j\boldsymbol{\beta}_j)'(\mathbf{y}_j - \mathbf{Y}_j\boldsymbol{\gamma}_j - \mathbf{X}_j\boldsymbol{\beta}_j)}{T}.$$

The log likelihood reduces to $\ln L = \Sigma_{j=1}^{M} \ln L_j$, where

$$\ln L_j = -\frac{T}{2}[\ln(2\pi) + \ln \sigma_{jj}] - \frac{1}{2\sigma_{jj}}(\mathbf{y}_j - \mathbf{Y}_j\boldsymbol{\gamma}_j - \mathbf{X}_j\boldsymbol{\beta}_j)'(\mathbf{y}_j - \mathbf{Y}_j\boldsymbol{\gamma}_j - \mathbf{X}_j\boldsymbol{\beta}_j).$$

Therefore, the FIML estimator for this model is just equation-by-equation least squares. We found earlier that ordinary least squares was consistent in this setting. We now find that it is asymptotically efficient as well.

TABLE 20.5 Estimates of Klein's Model I (Estimated Asymptotic Standard Errors in Parentheses)

	Limited-Information Estimates				Full-Information Estimates			
		2SLS				3SLS		
C	16.6	0.017	0.216	0.810	16.4	0.125	0.163	0.790
	(1.32)	(0.118)	(0.107)	(0.040)	(1.30)	(0.108)	(0.100)	(0.033)
I	20.3	0.150	0.616	−0.158	28.2	−0.013	0.756	−0.195
	(7.54)	(0.173)	(0.162)	(0.036)	(6.79)	(0.162)	(0.153)	(0.038)
Wp	1.50	0.439	0.147	0.130	1.80	0.400	0.181	0.150
	(1.15)	(0.036)	(0.039)	(0.029)	(1.12)	(0.032)	(0.034)	(0.028)
		LIML				FIML		
C	17.5	−0.222	0.396	0.823	17.8	−0.214	0.351	0.853
	(1.93)	(0.212)	(0.182)	(0.058)	(2.12)	(0.96)	(0.101)	(0.047)
I	22.6	0.075	0.680	−0.168	17.2	0.130	0.613	−0.136
	(6.89)	(0.275)	(0.205)	(0.049)	(6.47)	(0.137)	(0.140)	(0.038)
Wp	1.53	0.434	0.151	0.132	1.41	0.498	0.087	0.403
	(1.08)	(0.057)	(0.141)	(0.169)	(0.943)	(0.018)	(0.015)	(0.021)
		OLS				I3SLS		
C	16.2	0.193	0.090	0.796	16.6	0.165	0.177	0.766
	(1.30)	(0.091)	(0.091)	(0.040)	(1.22)	(0.096)	(0.090)	(0.035)
I	10.1	0.480	0.333	−0.112	42.9	−0.356	1.01	−0.260
	(5.47)	(0.097)	(0.101)	(0.027)	(10.6)	(0.260)	(0.249)	(0.051)
Wp	1.48	0.439	0.146	0.130	2.62	0.375	0.194	0.168
	(1.27)	(0.032)	(0.037)	(0.032)	(1.20)	(0.031)	(0.032)	(0.029)

The second case is that of the exactly identified model. If every equation is exactly identified, there is a one-to-one correspondence between $[\Gamma, B]$ and $[\Pi]$. Since Π is unrestricted in the exactly identified case, FIML is obtained by estimating Π by OLS. Without going further, we may simply appeal to the general invariance result of MLEs. In an exactly identified model, ILS is also the FIML estimator.

20.4.6. Comparison of Methods

The preceding has described a large number of estimators for simultaneous-equations models. For practical purposes, it is appropriate to consider which is to be preferred. As an example, Table 20.5 presents limited- and full-information estimates for Klein's Model I based on the original data for 1921 to 1941. (For those who wish to update these results, the appendix to this chapter contains yearly data from 1953 to 1984 on the variables in Klein's Model I, as well as several other macroeconomic variables.)

EXAMPLE 20.17 Estimates of Klein's Model I _____

It might seem, in light of the entire discussion, that one of the structural estimators, which have been described previously, should always be preferred to ordinary least squares, which, alone among the estimators considered here, is inconsistent. Unfortunately, the issue is not so clear. First, it is often found that the OLS estimator is surprisingly close to the structural estimator. It can be shown that at least in some cases, OLS has a smaller variance about its mean than does 2SLS about its mean, leading to the possibility that OLS might be more precise in a mean squared error sense.[37] But this result must be tempered by the finding that the OLS standard errors are, in all likelihood, not useful for inference purposes.[38] In spite of this, OLS appears to be the most frequently used estimator. Obviously this discussion is relevant only to finite samples. Asymptotically, 2SLS must dominate OLS and, in a correctly specified model, any full-information estimator must dominate any limited-information one. The finite-sample properties are of crucial importance. Most of what we know is asymptotic properties, but nearly all applications are based on rather small or moderate-sized samples.

Intuition would surely suggest that systems methods, 3SLS and FIML, are to be preferred to single-equation methods, 2SLS and LIML. Indeed, since the advantage is so transparent, why would one ever choose a single-equation estimator? The proper analogy is to the use of single-equation OLS versus GLS in the SURE model of Chapter 17. An obvious practical consideration is the computational simplicity of the single-equation methods. But the current state of available software has all but eliminated this advantage. However, several related aspects make the choice less clear-cut.

Although the systems methods are asymptotically better, they have two problems. First, any specification error in the structure of the model will be propagated throughout the system by 3SLS or FIML. The limited-information estimators will, by and large, confine a problem to the particular equation in which it appears. Second, in the same fashion as the SURE model, the finite-sample variation of the estimated covariance matrix is transmitted throughout the system. Thus, the finite-sample variance of 3SLS may well be as large as or larger than that of 2SLS. Although they are only estimates, the previous results for Klein's Model I give a striking example. The upshot would appear to be that the advantage of the systems estimators in finite samples may be more modest than the asymptotic results would suggest. Monte Carlo studies of the issue have tended to reach the same conclusion.[39]

Since asymptotic comparisons are unambiguous, the remaining considerations are based primarily on small-sample behavior. Unfortunately, there are few usable general results. What results there are come from two sources: extensive analysis of very small models and Monte Carlo studies.[40] In the main, these studies tend to reinforce what intuition would suggest.

20.5. Specification Tests

In a strident criticism of structural estimation, Liu (1960) argued that all simultaneous-equations models of the economy were truly unidentified and that only reduced forms could be estimated. While his criticisms may have been exaggerated (and never gained wide acceptance), modelers have been interested in testing the restrictions that overidentify an econometric model.

The first procedure for testing the overidentifying restrictions in a model was developed by Anderson and Rubin (1950). Their likelihood ratio test statistic is a by-product of LIML estimation:

$$\text{LR} = \chi^2[K_j^* - M_j] = T(\lambda_j - 1),$$

---

[37] See Goldberger (1964, pp. 359–360).

[38] Cragg (1967).

[39] See Cragg (1967) and the many related studies listed by Judge et al. (1985, pp. 646–653).

[40] See, for example, Greenberg and Webster (1983, pp. 243–280) and Phillips (1983).

where λ_j is the root used to find the LIML estimator. [See (20–27).] The statistic is asymptotically distributed as chi-squared with degrees of freedom equal to the number of overidentifying restrictions. A large value is taken as evidence that there are exogenous variables in the model that have been inappropriately omitted from the equation being examined. If the equation is exactly identified, $K_j^* - M_j = 0$, but, at the same time, the root will be one. In later work, Basmann (1960) found that the Anderson–Rubin statistic rejected the null hypothesis too often. He suggested two alternatives. First,

$$F'[K_j^* - M_j, T - K] = \frac{T - K}{K_j^* - M_j}(\lambda_j' - 1),$$

where

$$\lambda_j' = \frac{\hat{\gamma}_{j,2\mathrm{sls}}^{0'}\mathbf{W}_j^0\hat{\gamma}_{j,2\mathrm{sls}}^{0}}{\hat{\gamma}_{j,2\mathrm{sls}}^{0'}\mathbf{W}_j^1\hat{\gamma}_{j,2\mathrm{sls}}^{0}}$$

$$\hat{\gamma}_{j,2\mathrm{sls}}^{0'} = [1, -\hat{\gamma}_{j,2\mathrm{sls}}].$$

[If the LIML estimator is used instead of 2SLS, this gives the λ_j in (20–27).] The matrices $\mathbf{W}_j^0$ and $\mathbf{W}_j^1$ are defined in (20–26). Second, he suggested computing F' at the LIML estimator. Both are approximately normally distributed as $F[K_j^* - M_j, T - K]$ under the null hypothesis of exact identification. An alternative based on the Lagrange multiplier principle was proposed by Hausman (1983, p. 433). Operationally, the test requires only the calculation of TR^2, where the R^2 is the uncentered R^2 in the regression of

$$\hat{\varepsilon}_j = \mathbf{y}_j - \mathbf{Z}_j\hat{\delta}_j$$

on all of the predetermined variables in the model. The estimated parameters may be computed using 2SLS, LIML, or any other *efficient* limited-information estimator. The statistic is asymptotically distributed as chi-squared with $K_j^* - M_j$ degrees of freedom.

Finally, a systemwide statistic may be based on the restrictions imposed on $\mathbf{\Pi}$ by the structure. If the entire system is exactly identified, the reduced form estimated by OLS is fully efficient. If not, an efficient estimate of $\mathbf{\Pi}$ that embodies the restrictions is $\hat{\mathbf{\Pi}} = -\hat{\mathbf{B}}\hat{\mathbf{\Gamma}}^{-1}$, where the latter are *any efficient full-information estimators* (say, 3SLS or FIML). The log likelihood for the reduced form is given in (20–33). By concentrating over $\mathbf{\Omega}$, we obtain, at the maximum,

$$\ln L = -\frac{MT}{2}(1 + \ln 2\pi) - \frac{T}{2}\ln|\mathbf{W}|,$$

where

$$\mathbf{W} = \frac{1}{T}(\mathbf{Y} - \mathbf{X}\hat{\mathbf{\Pi}})'(\mathbf{Y} - \mathbf{X}\hat{\mathbf{\Pi}}).^{41}$$

Therefore, the likelihood ratio statistic based on the two estimators of $\mathbf{\Pi}$ is simply

$$\mathrm{LR} = -2(\ln L_r - \ln L_u) = T(\ln|\mathbf{W}_{\mathrm{FI}}| - \ln|\mathbf{W}_{\mathrm{OLS}}|).$$

This statistic is asymptotically distributed as chi-squared with degrees of freedom equal to the total number of overidentifying restrictions:

$$d = \sum_j (K_j^* - M_j).$$

---

[41] For a system containing identities, $\mathbf{W}$ is computed by assembling $\hat{\mathbf{\Pi}}$ for the full system first and then discarding columns corresponding to the identities. Doing the same for $\mathbf{Y}$, we then compute $\mathbf{W} = (\mathbf{Y}'\mathbf{Y} - \mathbf{Y}'\mathbf{X}\hat{\mathbf{\Pi}} - \hat{\mathbf{\Pi}}'\mathbf{X}'\mathbf{Y} + \hat{\mathbf{\Pi}}'\mathbf{X}'\mathbf{X}\hat{\mathbf{\Pi}})/T$.

EXAMPLE 20.18. Testing Overidentifying Restrictions ————————

For Klein's Model I, the test statistics for the overidentifying restrictions for the three equations are given in Table 20.6. The likelihood ratio statistic for the entire system is 77.441. Critical values for the chi-squared and F distributions are listed in Table 20.7. There are 21 observations used to estimate the model and 8 predetermined variables. The overidentifying restrictions for the wage equation are rejected by all single-equation tests. There are two possibilities. The equation may well be misspecified. Or, as Liu suggests, in a dynamic model, if there is autocorrelation of the disturbances, the treatment of lagged endogenous variables as if they were exogenous is a specification error.

TABLE 20.6   Test Statistics

	λ	λ'	LR	TR^2	F	F'	$K_j^* - M_j$
Consumption	1.499	1.716	9.98	8.77	1.08	1.55	2
Investment	1.086	1.095	1.72	1.81	0.223	0.247	3
Wages	2.466	2.469	29.3	12.49	3.81	3.82	3

TABLE 20.7   Critical Values

	$F[2, 13]$	$F[3, 13]$	$\chi^2[2]$	$\chi^2[3]$	$\chi^2[8]$
5%	3.81	3.41	5.99	7.82	15.51
1%	6.70	5.74	9.21	11.34	22.09

Another specification error occurs if the variables assumed to be exogenous in the system are not, in fact, uncorrelated with the structural disturbances. Since all of the asymptotic properties claimed earlier rest on this assumption, this specification error would be quite serious. Several authors have studied this issue.[42] The specification test devised by Hausman that we used in Section 9.5.5 in the errors in variables model and Section 16.4.4 in analyzing cross-section/time-series models provides a method of testing for exogeneity in a simultaneous-equations model. Suppose that the variable x^* is in question. The test is based on the existence of two estimators, say $\hat{\delta}$ and $\hat{\delta}^*$, such that

Under H_0: (x^* is exogenous), both $\hat{\delta}$ and $\hat{\delta}^*$ are consistent
and $\hat{\delta}^*$ is asymptotically efficient.

Under H_1: (x^* is endogenous), $\hat{\delta}$ is consistent, but $\hat{\delta}^*$ is
inconsistent.

Hausman bases his version of the test on $\hat{\delta}$ being the 2SLS estimator and $\hat{\delta}^*$ being the 3SLS estimator. A shortcoming of the procedure is that it requires an arbitrary choice of some equation that does not contain x^* for the test. For instance, in the next example, to pursue the finding of Example 20.18, we consider the exogeneity of X_{-1} in the third equation of Klein's Model I. To apply this test, we must use one of the other two equations.

A single-equation version of the test has been devised by Spencer and Berk (1981). We now suppose that x^* appears in equation j, so that

$$y_j = Y_j\gamma_j + X_j\beta_j + x^*\theta + \varepsilon_j$$
$$= [Y_j \quad X_j \quad x^*]\delta_j + \varepsilon_j.$$

[42]Wu (1973), Durbin (1954), Hausman (1978), and Nakamura and Nakamura (1981).

Then $\hat{\boldsymbol{\delta}}^*$ is the 2SLS estimator, treating x^* as an exogenous variable in the system, while $\hat{\boldsymbol{\delta}}$ is the IV estimator based on regressing $\mathbf{y}_j$ on $\hat{\mathbf{Y}}_j$, $\mathbf{X}_j$, and $\hat{x}^*$, where the least squares fitted values are based on all of the remaining exogenous variables, excluding x^*. The test statistic is then

$$w = (\hat{\boldsymbol{\delta}}^* - \hat{\boldsymbol{\delta}})\{\text{Est.Var}[\hat{\boldsymbol{\delta}}] - \text{Est.Var}[\hat{\boldsymbol{\delta}}^*]\}^{-1}(\hat{\boldsymbol{\delta}}^* - \hat{\boldsymbol{\delta}}). \tag{20-35}$$

This is the Wald statistic based on the difference of the two estimators. The statistic has one degree of freedom. (The extension to a set of variables is direct.)

EXAMPLE 20.19 Exogeneity Test

The previous example suggested a specification problem in the third equation of Klein's Model I. To pursue that finding, we now apply the preceding to test the exogeneity of X_{-1}. This is roughly equivalent to a test of autocorrelation, albeit a bit indirect (and probably not too powerful), since if the disturbances are autocorrelated, lagged endogenous variables may no longer be treated as predetermined. The two estimated parameter vectors are

$$\boldsymbol{\delta}^* = [1.5003, \quad 0.43886, \quad 0.14667, \quad 0.13040] \qquad (\text{i.e., 2SLS})$$

and

$$\hat{\boldsymbol{\delta}} = [1.2524, \quad 0.42277, \quad 0.167614, \quad 0.13062].$$

Using the Wald criterion, the chi-squared statistic is 1.3977. Thus, the hypothesis (such as it is) is not rejected.

20.6. Properties of Dynamic Models

Models with lagged endogenous variables may be viewed as generalizations of the autoregressive distributed lag models we examined in Chapter 18. In these models, the entire previous time path of the exogenous variables and disturbances, not just their current values, determines the current value of the dependent variables. As we saw earlier, the intrinsic dynamic properties of the autoregressive model, such as stability and the existence of an equilibrium value, are embodied in their autoregressive parameters. In this section, we extend the analysis of Section 18.6.3 to multiple equations. As before, we are interested in long- and short-run multipliers, stability properties, and simulated time paths of the dependent variables.

20.6.1. Dynamic Models and Their Multipliers

The structural form of a dynamic model is

$$\mathbf{y}_t'\boldsymbol{\Gamma} + \mathbf{x}_t'\mathbf{B} + \mathbf{y}_{t-1}'\boldsymbol{\Phi} = \boldsymbol{\varepsilon}_t'.^{43} \tag{20-36}$$

The reduced form is

$$\mathbf{y}_t' = \mathbf{x}_t'\boldsymbol{\Pi} + \mathbf{y}_{t-1}'\boldsymbol{\Delta} + \mathbf{v}_t',$$

---

[43] The model may also contain lagged exogenous variables but, for present purposes, these need not be treated separately. If there are additional lags of the endogenous variables in the model, it can still be written in the preceding form by using an extension of the technique detailed in Section 18.6.3. No generality is lost by assuming that only one lagged value of $\mathbf{y}_t$ appears in the model.

where

$$\Pi = -B\Gamma^{-1}$$

and

$$\Delta = -\Phi\Gamma^{-1}.$$

EXAMPLE 20.20

The 2SLS estimates of the structure and reduced form of Klein's Model I are given in Table 20.8. (Only the nonzero rows of $\hat{\Phi}$ and $\hat{\Delta}$ are shown.)

From the reduced form,

$$\frac{\partial y_{t,m}}{\partial x_{t,k}} = \Pi_{km}.$$

The short-run effects are the coefficients on the current x's, so Π is the matrix of **impact multipliers**. By substituting for y_{t-1} in (20–36), we obtain

$$y_t' = x_t'\Pi + x_{t-1}'\Pi\Delta + y_{t-2}'\Delta^2 + (v_t' + v_{t-1}'\Delta^2).$$

Continuing this for the full t periods, we obtain

$$y_t' = \sum_{s=0}^{t-1} [x_{t-s}'\Pi\Delta^s] + y_0'\Delta^t + \sum_{s=0}^{t-1} v_{t-s}'\Delta^s. \tag{20–37}$$

TABLE 20.8   Coefficient Matrices

	Variable	\multicolumn{6}{c}{Equation}

	Variable	C	I	W^p	X	P	K
	C	1	0	0	−1	0	0
	I	0	1	0	−1	0	−1
$\hat{\Gamma} =$	W^p	−0.810	0	1	0	1	0
	X	0	0	−0.439	1	−1	0
	P	−0.017	−0.15	0	0	1	0
	K	0	0	0	0	0	1
	1	−16.555	−20.278	−1.5	0	0	0
	W^g	−0.810	0	0	0	0	0
$\hat{B} =$	T	0	0	0	0	1	0
	G	0	0	0	−1	0	0
	t	0	0	−0.13	0	0	0
	X_{-1}	0	0	−0.147	0	0	0
$\hat{\Phi} =$	P_{-1}	−0.216	−0.616	0	0	0	0
	K_{-1}	0	0.158	0	0	0	−1
	1	42.80	25.83	31.63	68.63	37.00	25.83
	W^g	1.35	0.124	0.646	1.47	0.825	0.125
$\hat{\Pi} =$	T	−0.128	−0.176	−0.133	−0.303	−1.17	−0.176
	G	0.663	0.153	0.797	1.82	1.02	0.153
	t	0.159	−0.007	0.197	0.152	−0.045	−0.007
	X_{-1}	0.179	−0.008	0.222	0.172	−0.051	−0.008
$\hat{\Delta} =$	P_{-1}	0.767	0.743	0.663	1.511	0.848	0.743
	K_{-1}	−0.105	−0.182	−0.125	−0.287	−0.161	0.818

This shows how the **initial conditions, y_0**, and the subsequent time path of the exogenous variables and disturbances completely determine the current values of the endogenous variables. The coefficient matrices in the bracketed sum are the **dynamic multipliers,**

$$\frac{\partial y_{t,m}}{\partial x_{t-s,k}} = (\mathbf{\Pi\Delta}^s)_{km}.$$

The **cumulated multipliers** are obtained by adding the matrices of dynamic multipliers. If we let s go to infinity in (20–37), we obtain the **final form** of the model,[44]

$$\mathbf{y}_t' = \sum_{s=0}^{\infty} [\mathbf{x}_{t-s}'\mathbf{\Pi\Delta}^s] + \sum_{s=0}^{\infty} [\mathbf{v}_{t-s}'\mathbf{\Delta}^s].$$

This is analogous to the moving average form of the distributed lag model in (18–33).

Assume for the present that $\lim_{t \to \infty}\mathbf{\Delta}^t = \mathbf{0}$. Then the matrix of cumulated multipliers in the final form is

$$\mathbf{\Pi}[\mathbf{I} + \mathbf{\Delta} + \mathbf{\Delta}^2 + \cdots] = \mathbf{\Pi}[\mathbf{I} - \mathbf{\Delta}]^{-1}.$$

These coefficient matrices are the long-run or **equilibrium multipliers.** Analogous to our single-equation case, we can also obtain the cumulated multipliers for s periods as

$$\text{Cumulated multipliers} = \mathbf{\Pi}[\mathbf{I} - \mathbf{\Delta}]^{-1}[\mathbf{I} - \mathbf{\Delta}^s].$$

Suppose that the values of $\mathbf{x}$ were permanently fixed at $\bar{\mathbf{x}}$. Then the final form shows that if there are no disturbances, the equilibrium value of $\mathbf{y}_t$ would be

$$\bar{\mathbf{y}} = \sum_{s=0}^{\infty} [\bar{\mathbf{x}}\mathbf{\Pi\Delta}^s]$$

$$= \bar{\mathbf{x}} \sum_{s=0}^{\infty} \mathbf{\Pi\Delta}^s \tag{20–38}$$

$$= \bar{\mathbf{x}}\mathbf{\Pi}[\mathbf{I} - \mathbf{\Delta}]^{-1}.$$

Therefore, the equilibrium multipliers are

$$\frac{\partial \bar{y}_m}{\partial \bar{x}_k} = [\mathbf{\Pi}(\mathbf{I} - \mathbf{\Delta})^{-1}]_{km}.$$

Some examples will now be shown for Klein's Model I.

EXAMPLE 20.21 Dynamic Multipliers

For a particular variable or group of variables, the various multipliers are submatrices of the multiplier matrices. The dynamic multipliers for the fiscal policy variables, T and G, corresponding to the estimates in Example 20.20, are given in Table 20.9 for several lags.[45]

---

[44] In some treatments, (20–37) is labeled the final form instead. Both forms eliminate the lagged values of the dependent variables from the current value. The dependence of the first form on the initial values may be simpler to interpret.

[45] A method of computing asymptotic standard errors for the estimates of the dynamic multipliers is given by Schmidt (1973).

TABLE 20.9. Dynamic Multipliers

	Taxes				Spending			
	Investment		Output		Investment		Output	
Lag	**Period**	**Cum.**	**Period**	**Cum.**	**Period**	**Cum.**	**Period**	**Cum.**
0	−0.760	−0.760	−1.30	−1.30	0.153	0.153	1.82	1.82
1	−0.834	−1.59	−1.74	−3.04	0.715	0.868	1.06	2.88
2	−0.507	−2.10	−1.27	−4.31	0.383	1.25	1.01	3.89
3	−0.122	−2.22	−0.502	−4.81	0.061	1.31	0.334	4.22
4	0.192	−2.03	0.198	−4.61	−0.184	1.13	−0.225	4.00
5	0.388	−1.64	0.682	−3.93	−0.328	0.800	−0.590	3.41
6	0.462	−1.18	0.914	−3.02	−0.374	0.426	−0.748	2.66
7	0.434	−0.749	0.921	−2.10	−0.342	0.084	−0.731	1.93
8	0.338	−0.411	0.764	−1.33	−0.258	−0.174	−0.591	1.34
9	0.210	−0.201	0.519	−0.814	−0.154	−0.328	−0.387	0.952
10	0.082	−0.119	0.253	−0.561	−0.052	−0.380	−0.173	0.779
11	−0.023	−0.142	0.019	−0.542	0.030	−0.350	0.009	0.788
12	−0.095	−0.237	−0.152	−0.694	0.083	−0.267	0.138	0.926
13	−0.129	−0.366	−0.247	−0.941	0.106	−0.161	0.206	1.13
14	−0.131	−0.497	−0.271	−1.21	0.104	−0.057	0.218	1.35
15	−0.109	−0.606	−0.241	−1.45	0.085	0.028	0.189	1.54
16	−0.075	−0.681	−0.178	−1.63	0.056	0.084	0.134	1.67
17	−0.037	−0.718	−0.101	−1.73	0.025	0.109	0.072	1.75
18	−0.003	−0.721	−0.023	−1.76	−0.007	0.102	0.015	1.76
19	0.021	−0.700	0.028	−1.73	−0.019	0.083	−0.028	1.73
20	0.035	−0.665	0.064	−1.67	−0.029	0.054	−0.054	1.68
∞	0	0	0	−1.48	0	0	0	2.10

The model has the interesting feature that the long-run multipliers of both policy variables for investment are both zero. This is intrinsic to the model. We shall return to this point in the later discussion of equilibrium. The estimated long-run *balanced-budget multiplier* for equal increases in spending and taxes (an anachronism?) is $2.10 + (-1.48) = 0.62$.

20.6.2. Stability

It remains to be shown that the matrix of multipliers in the final form converges. In order for the analysis to proceed, it is necessary for the matrix Δ^t to converge to a zero matrix. Although Δ is not a symmetric matrix, it will still have a spectral decomposition of the form

$$\Delta = C\Lambda C^{-1}, \qquad (20\text{–}39)$$

where Λ is a diagonal matrix containing the characteristic roots of Δ and each column of C is a right characteristic vector,

$$\Delta c_m = \lambda_m c_m. \qquad (20\text{–}40)$$

Since Δ is not symmetric, the elements of Λ (and C) may be complex. Nonetheless, (2–105) continues to hold:

$$\Delta^2 = C\Lambda C^{-1}C\Lambda C^{-1} = C\Lambda^2 C^{-1}$$

and

$$\Delta^t = C\Lambda^t C^{-1}. \tag{20-41}$$

It is apparent that whether or not Δ^t vanishes as $t \to \infty$ depends on its characteristic roots. The condition is $|\lambda_m| < 1$. For the case of a complex root,

$$|\lambda_m| = |a + bi| = \sqrt{a^2 + b^2}.$$

For a given model, the stability may be established by examining the largest or **dominant root.** Since it is ultimately a function of the sample estimates of the parameters, the estimate of the dominant root of the model is a sample statistic for which an estimate of its asymptotic sampling variance can be computed.[46]

With many endogenous variables in the model but only a few lagged variables, Δ is a large but sparse matrix. Finding the characteristic roots of large, asymmetric matrices is a rather complex computation problem (although there exists specialized software for doing so). There is a way to make the problem a bit more compact. To put this in the context of an example, in Klein's Model I, Δ is 6×6, but with three rows of zeros, it has only rank three and three nonzero roots. The following partitioning is useful. Let y_{t1} be the set of endogenous variables that appear in both current and lagged form, and let y_{t2} be those that appear only in current form. Then the model may be written

$$[y'_{t1} \quad y'_{t2}] = x'_t[\Pi_1 \quad \Pi_2] + [y'_{t-1,1} y'_{t-1,2}]\begin{bmatrix} \Delta_1 & \Delta_2 \\ 0 & 0 \end{bmatrix} + [v'_{t1} v'_{t2}]. \tag{20-42}$$

The characteristic roots of Δ are defined by the characteristic polynomial, $|\Delta - \lambda I| = 0$. For the partitioned model, this is

$$\begin{vmatrix} \Delta_1 - \lambda I & \Delta_2 \\ 0 & -\lambda I \end{vmatrix} = 0.$$

We may use (2-72) to obtain

$$|\Delta - \lambda I| = (-\lambda)^{M_2}|\Delta_1 - \lambda I| = 0,$$

where M_2 is the number of variables in y_2. Consequently, we need only concern ourselves with the submatrix of Δ that defines explicit autoregressions. The part of the reduced form defined by

$$y'_{t2} = x'_t\Pi_2 + y'_{t-1,1}\Delta_2$$

is not directly relevant.

EXAMPLE 20.22 Model Stability

For the 2SLS estimates of Klein's Model I, the relevant submatrix of $\hat{\Delta}$ is

$$\hat{\Delta}_1 = \begin{matrix} & X & P & K & \\ & \begin{bmatrix} 0.172 & -0.051 & -0.008 \\ 1.511 & 0.848 & 0.743 \\ -0.287 & -0.161 & 0.818 \end{bmatrix} & \begin{matrix} X_{-1} \\ P_{-1} \\ K_{-1} \end{matrix} \end{matrix}$$

The characteristic roots of this matrix are 0.2995 and the complex pair $0.7692 \pm 0.3494i$. The moduli of the complex roots are 0.8448, so we conclude that the model is stable.

---

[46] The computations are detailed in Theil and Boot (1962). An alternative approach is given by Kmenta and Oberhofer (1973). Schmidt (1974d) shows that (as might be expected) the Theil–Boot formula based on the reduced form and the Oberhofer–Kmenta formula based on the structural form give the same result.

20.6.3. Adjustment to Equilibrium

The adjustment of a dynamic model to an equilibrium involves the following conceptual experiment: We assume that the exogenous variables, $\mathbf{x}_t$, have been fixed at a level, $\overline{\mathbf{x}}$, for a long enough time that the endogenous variables have fully adjusted to their equilibrium, $\overline{\mathbf{y}}$ [defined in (20–38)]. In some arbitrarily chosen period, labeled period 0, an exogenous one-time shock hits the system, so that in period $t = 0$, $\mathbf{x}_t = \mathbf{x}_0 \neq \overline{\mathbf{x}}$. Thereafter, $\mathbf{x}_t$ returns to its former value, $\overline{\mathbf{x}}$, and $\mathbf{x}_t = \overline{\mathbf{x}}$ for all $t > 0$. We know from the expression for the final form that, if disturbed, $\mathbf{y}_t$ will ultimately return to the equilibrium. That is ensured by the stability condition. Here we consider the time path of the adjustment. Since our only concern at this point is with the exogenous shock, we will ignore the disturbances in the analysis.

At time 0,

$$\mathbf{y}_0' = \mathbf{x}_0'\mathbf{\Pi} + \mathbf{y}_{-1}'\mathbf{\Delta}.$$

But prior to time 0, the system was in equilibrium, so

$$\mathbf{y}_0' = \mathbf{x}_0'\mathbf{\Pi} + \overline{\mathbf{y}}'\mathbf{\Delta}.$$

The initial displacement due to the shock to $\overline{\mathbf{x}}$ is

$$\mathbf{y}_0' - \overline{\mathbf{y}}' = \mathbf{x}_0'\mathbf{\Pi} - \overline{\mathbf{y}}'(\mathbf{I} - \mathbf{\Delta}).$$

Substituting $\overline{\mathbf{x}}'\mathbf{\Pi} = \overline{\mathbf{y}}'(\mathbf{I} - \mathbf{\Delta})$ produces

$$\mathbf{y}_0' - \overline{\mathbf{y}}' = (\mathbf{x}_0' - \overline{\mathbf{x}})'\mathbf{\Pi}. \tag{20–43}$$

As might be expected, the initial displacement is determined entirely by the exogenous shock occurring in that period. Since $\mathbf{x}_t = \overline{\mathbf{x}}$ after period 0, (20–37) implies that

$$\mathbf{y}_t' = \sum_{s=0}^{t-1} \overline{\mathbf{x}}'\mathbf{\Pi}\mathbf{\Delta}^s + \mathbf{y}_0'\mathbf{\Delta}^t$$

$$= \overline{\mathbf{x}}'\mathbf{\Pi}(\mathbf{I} - \mathbf{\Delta})^{-1}(\mathbf{I} - \mathbf{\Delta}^t) + \mathbf{y}_0'\mathbf{\Delta}^t$$

$$= \overline{\mathbf{y}}' - \overline{\mathbf{y}}'\mathbf{\Delta}^t + \mathbf{y}_0'\mathbf{\Delta}^t$$

$$= \overline{\mathbf{y}}' + (\mathbf{y}_0' - \overline{\mathbf{y}}')\mathbf{\Delta}^t.$$

Thus, the entire time path is a function of the initial displacement. By inserting (20–43), we see that

$$\mathbf{y}_t' = \overline{\mathbf{y}}' + (\mathbf{x}_0' - \overline{\mathbf{x}})'\mathbf{\Pi}\mathbf{\Delta}^t. \tag{20–44}$$

Since $\lim_{t\to\infty} \mathbf{\Delta}^t = \mathbf{0}$, this defines the path back to the equilibrium subsequent to the exogenous shock $(\mathbf{x}_0 - \overline{\mathbf{x}})$. The stability condition imposed on $\mathbf{\Delta}$ ensures that if the system is disturbed at some point by a one-time shock, barring further shocks or disturbances, it will return to its equilibrium. Since $\mathbf{y}_0$, $\overline{\mathbf{x}}$, $\mathbf{x}_0$, and $\mathbf{\Pi}$ are fixed for all time, the shape of the path is completely determined by the behavior of $\mathbf{\Delta}^t$, which we now examine.

In the preceding section, in (20–39) to (20–42), we used the characteristic roots of $\mathbf{\Delta}$ to infer the (lack of) stability of the model. The spectral decomposition of $\mathbf{\Delta}^t$ given in (20–41) may be written

$$\mathbf{\Delta}^t = \sum_{m=1}^{M} \lambda_m^t \mathbf{c}_m \mathbf{d}_m',$$

where c_m is the mth column of C and d'_m is the mth row of C^{-1}.[47] Inserting this in (20-44), we have

$$(y_t - \bar{y})' = [(x_0 - \bar{x})'\Pi] \sum_{m=1}^{M} \lambda_m^t c_m d'_m$$

$$= \sum_{m=1}^{M} \lambda_m^t [(x_0 - \bar{x})'\Pi c_m d'_m] = \sum_{m=1}^{M} \lambda_m^t g_m.$$

(Note that this may involve fewer than M terms, since some of the roots may be zero. For Klein's Model I, $M = 6$, but there are only three nonzero roots.) Since g_m depends only on the initial conditions and the parameters of the model, the behavior of the time path of $(y_t - \bar{y})$ is completely determined by Λ^t. In each period, the deviation from the equilibrium is a sum of M terms of powers of λ_m times a constant. (Each variable has its own set of constants.) The terms in the sum behave as follows:

λ_m real > 0, λ_m^t adds a damped exponential term,

λ_m real < 0, λ_m^t adds a damped sawtooth term,

λ_m complex, λ_m^t adds a damped sinusoidal term.

If we write the complex root $\lambda_m = a + bi$ in polar form,

$$\lambda = A[\cos B + i \sin B]$$

where

$$A = [a^2 + b^2]^{1/2}$$

and

$$B = \arccos \frac{a}{A} \quad \text{(in radians)},$$

the sinusoidal components each have amplitude A^t and period $2\pi/B$.[48]

EXAMPLE 20.23 Adjustment of Klein's Model I

We start the model at the conditions of the last data point, 1941. The initial and equilibrium values for the six endogenous variables are given in Table 20.10. The equilibrium is based on $W^g = 8.5$, $G = 13.8$, $T = 11.6$, and $A = 10$.) The equilibrium of zero for investment might seem a bit peculiar. But note that the model imposes $K_t - K_{t-1} = I_t$, and both K and I are endogenous. If K_t is in equilibrium, there is no investment. The path to the new equilibrium for the six endogenous variables is shown in Table 20.11.

TABLE 20.10

	C	I	W^p	X	P	K
Initial	69.7	4.9	53.3	88.4	23.5	209.4
Equilibrium	70.5	0	52.2	84.3	20.5	227.7

---

[47] See Section 2.7.9.

[48] Goldberger (1964, p. 378).

TABLE 20.11 Deviations from Equilibrium

Year	C	I	W_p	X	P	K
1941	−0.5	4.9	1.1	4.1	3.0	−18.3
1942	5.0	5.5	5.2	10.5	5.3	−12.8
1943	7.3	6.2	7.4	13.5	6.0	−6.6
1944	7.7	5.6	7.8	13.3	5.5	−1.0
1945	6.7	4.2	6.7	10.8	4.1	3.1
1946	4.8	2.4	4.8	7.2	2.5	5.5
1947	2.6	0.8	2.5	3.4	0.8	6.3
1948	0.6	−0.6	0.5	0.0	−0.5	5.7
1949	−1.0	−1.4	−1.0	−2.4	−1.3	4.3
1950	−1.9	−1.8	−2.0	−3.7	−1.7	2.6
1951	−2.2	−1.7	−2.3	−3.9	−1.7	0.9
1952	−2.1	−1.4	−2.1	−3.4	−1.4	−0.5
1953	−1.6	−0.9	−1.6	−2.5	−0.9	−1.4
1954	−1.0	−0.4	−1.0	−1.4	−0.4	−1.8
1955	−0.4	0.0	−0.3	−0.3	0.0	−1.8
1956	0.1	0.3	0.2	0.5	0.3	−1.4
1957	0.5	0.5	0.5	1.0	0.5	−0.9
1958	0.6	0.5	0.6	1.1	0.5	−0.4
1959	0.6	0.4	0.6	1.1	0.4	0.0
1960	0.5	0.3	0.5	0.8	0.3	0.3
1961	0.4	0.2	0.3	0.5	0.2	0.5
1962	0.2	0.0	0.2	0.2	0.0	0.5
1963	0.0	0.0	0.0	0.0	−0.0	0.5
1964	−0.1	−0.1	−0.1	−0.2	−0.1	0.3
1965	−0.2	−0.1	−0.2	−0.3	−0.1	0.2
1966	−0.2	−0.1	−0.2	−0.3	−0.1	0.0
1967	−0.2	−0.1	−0.2	−0.3	−0.1	−0.0
1968	−0.1	−0.0	−0.1	−0.2	0.0	−0.1
1969	0.0	0.0	0.0	0.0	0.0	−0.2
1970	0.0	0.0	0.0	0.0	0.0	−0.1
1971	0.0	0.0	0.0	0.0	0.0	−0.1
1972	0.0	0.0	0.0	0.0	0.0	0.0

Note the cyclical behavior in Table 20.11. The complex roots are $0.8448[\cos 0.4263 \pm i \sin 0.4263]$. The period for the oscillations is, thus, $2\pi/0.4263 = 14.73$.

EXERCISES

1. Consider the following two-equation model:

$$y_1 = \gamma_1 y_2 + \beta_{11} x_1 + \beta_{21} x_2 + \beta_{31} x_3 + \varepsilon_1,$$

$$y_2 = \gamma_2 y_1 + \beta_{12} x_1 + \beta_{22} x_2 + \beta_{32} x_3 + \varepsilon_1.$$

(a) Verify that, as stated, neither equation is identified.

(b) Establish whether or not the following restrictions are sufficient to identify (or partially identify) the model:

(1) $\beta_{21} = \beta_{32} = 0$,
(2) $\beta_{12} = \beta_{22} = 0$,
(3) $\gamma_1 = 0$,
(4) $\gamma_1 = \gamma_2$ and $\beta_{32} = 0$,
(5) $\sigma_{12} = 0$ and $\beta_{31} = 0$,
(6) $\gamma_1 = 0$ and $\sigma_{12} = 0$,
(7) $\beta_{21} + \beta_{22} = 1$,
(8) $\sigma_{12} = 0$, $\beta_{21} = \beta_{22} = \beta_{31} = \beta_{32} = 0$,
(9) $\sigma_{12} = 0$, $\beta_{11} = \beta_{21} = \beta_{22} = \beta_{31} = \beta_{32} = 0$.

2. Verify the rank and order conditions for identification of the second and third behavioral equations in Klein's Model I. (**Hint:** See Example 20.10.)

3. Check the identifiability of the parameters of the following model:

$$[y_1 \quad y_2 \quad y_3 \quad y_4] \begin{bmatrix} 1 & \gamma_{12} & 0 & 0 \\ \gamma_{21} & 1 & \gamma_{23} & \gamma_{24} \\ 0 & \gamma_{32} & 1 & \gamma_{34} \\ \gamma_{41} & \gamma_{42} & 0 & 1 \end{bmatrix}$$

$$+ [x_1 \quad x_2 \quad x_3 \quad x_4 \quad x_5] \begin{bmatrix} 0 & \beta_{12} & \beta_{13} & \beta_{14} \\ \beta_{21} & 1 & 0 & \beta_{24} \\ \beta_{31} & \beta_{32} & \beta_{33} & 0 \\ 0 & 0 & \beta_{43} & \beta_{44} \\ 0 & \beta_{52} & 0 & 0 \end{bmatrix}$$

$$= [\varepsilon_1 \quad \varepsilon_2 \quad \varepsilon_3 \quad \varepsilon_4].$$

4. Examine the identifiability of the following supply and demand model:

$$\ln Q = \beta_0 + \beta_1 \ln P + \beta_2 \ln \text{income} + \varepsilon_1 \quad \text{(demand)},$$

$$Q = \gamma_0 + \gamma_1 P \qquad + \gamma_2 \text{ input cost} + \varepsilon_2 \quad \text{(supply)}.$$

5. Obtain the reduced form for the model in Exercise 1 under each of the assumptions made in parts (a) and (b1), (b6), and (b9).

6. The following model is specified:

$$y_1 = \gamma_1 y_2 + \beta_{11} x_1 \qquad + \varepsilon_1,$$

$$y_2 = \gamma_2 y_1 + \beta_{22} x_2 + \beta_{32} x_3 + \varepsilon_2.$$

All variables are measured as deviations from their means. The sample of 25 observations produces the following matrix of sums of squares and cross-products:

	y_1	y_2	x_1	x_2	x_3
y_1	20	6	4	3	5
y_2	6	10	3	6	7
x_1	4	3	5	2	3
x_2	3	6	2	10	8
x_3	5	7	3	8	15

(a) Estimate the two equations by OLS.

(b) Estimate the parameters of the two equations by 2SLS. Also, estimate the asymptotic covariance matrix of the 2SLS estimates.

(c) Obtain the LIML estimates of the parameters of the first equation.

(d) Estimate the two equations by 3SLS.

(e) Estimate the reduced-form coefficient matrix by OLS and indirectly by using your structural estimates from part (b).

7. For the model

$$y_1 = \gamma_1 y_2 + \beta_{11} x_1 + \beta_{21} x_2 + \varepsilon_1,$$

$$y_2 = \gamma_2 y_1 + \beta_{32} x_3 + \beta_{42} x_4 + \varepsilon_2,$$

show that there are two restrictions on the reduced-form coefficients. Describe a procedure for estimating the model while incorporating the restrictions.

8. Show that (20–20) produces a consistent estimate for any $\mathbf{D}$ with rank M_j.

9. An updated version of Klein's Model I was estimated with the data in the appendix to this chapter. Using the 2SLS estimates, the relevant submatrix of $\mathbf{\Delta}$ [see (20–42)] is

$$\mathbf{\Delta}_1 = \begin{bmatrix} -0.1899 & -0.9471 & -0.8991 \\ 0 & 1.0287 & 0 \\ -0.0656 & -0.0791 & 0.0952 \end{bmatrix}$$

Is the model stable?

10. Prove that

$$\operatorname{plim} \frac{\mathbf{Y}_j' \boldsymbol{\varepsilon}_j}{T} = \underline{\boldsymbol{\omega}}_j - \boldsymbol{\Omega}_{jj} \boldsymbol{\gamma}_j.$$

11. Prove that an underidentified equation cannot be estimated by 2SLS.

12. The full set of data necessary for updating Klein's Model I is given in Table 20.12 in the appendix to this chapter.

(a) Reestimate the three structural equations of Klein's Model I, using 2SLS and the 1953–1984 data.

(b) Reestimate the system, using 3SLS.

(c) Compare your results to those obtained in the text for the earlier period.

Appendix: Yearly Data on the U.S. Economy

The data used to estimate Klein's Model I are listed in Table 20.12. Variable definitions are given in Example 20.3. All estimates are computed using the 1921–1941 data because of the lagged values of P and X.

The data used for the updated version of Klein's Model I are listed in Tables 20.13–20.16. Several other variables are also listed for those who wish to estimate different specifications or alternative models. For constructing more extensive data sets, the data sources also contain quarterly data on these and numerous other variables.[49] All flow variables (e.g., consumption, investment, imports) are seasonally adjusted annual rates in constant (1972) dollars. The variables in the tables are as follows:

---

[49] A pitfall to avoid: The data in the national income and product accounts are annual rates. Thus, direct application of $K_t = K_{t-1} + I_t$ overestimates the capital stock by a factor of almost four. The investment series must be converted to a quarterly rate.

TABLE 20.12 Data for Klein's Model I

Year	C	P	W^p	I	K_{-1}	X	W^g	G	T
1920	39.8	12.7	28.8	2.7	180.1	44.9	2.2	2.4	3.4
1921	41.9	12.4	25.5	−0.2	182.8	45.6	2.7	3.9	7.7
1922	45.0	16.9	29.3	1.9	182.6	50.1	2.9	3.2	3.9
1923	49.2	18.4	34.1	5.2	184.5	57.2	2.9	2.8	4.7
1924	50.6	19.4	33.9	3.0	189.7	57.1	3.1	3.5	3.8
1925	52.6	20.1	35.4	5.1	192.7	61.0	3.2	3.3	5.5
1926	55.1	19.6	37.4	5.6	197.8	64.0	3.3	3.3	7.0
1927	56.2	19.8	37.9	4.2	203.4	64.4	3.6	4.0	6.7
1928	57.3	21.1	39.2	3.0	207.6	64.5	3.7	4.2	4.2
1929	57.8	21.7	41.3	5.1	210.6	67.0	4.0	4.1	4.0
1930	55.0	15.6	37.9	1.0	215.7	61.2	4.2	5.2	7.7
1931	50.9	11.4	34.5	−3.4	216.7	53.4	4.8	5.9	7.5
1932	45.6	7.0	29.0	−6.2	213.3	44.3	5.3	4.9	8.3
1933	46.5	11.2	28.5	−5.1	207.1	45.1	5.6	3.7	5.4
1934	48.7	12.3	30.6	−3.0	202.0	49.7	6.0	4.0	6.8
1935	51.3	14.0	33.2	−1.3	199.0	54.4	6.1	4.4	7.2
1936	57.7	17.6	36.8	2.1	197.7	62.7	7.4	2.9	8.3
1937	58.7	17.3	41.0	2.0	199.8	65.0	6.7	4.3	6.7
1938	57.5	15.3	38.2	−1.9	201.8	60.9	7.7	5.3	7.4
1939	61.6	19.0	41.6	1.3	199.9	69.5	7.8	6.6	8.9
1940	65.0	21.1	45.0	3.3	201.2	75.7	8.0	7.4	9.6
1941	69.7	23.5	53.3	4.9	204.5	88.4	8.5	13.8	11.6

TABLE 20.13

	P^c	P^g	C	Y^d	**GNP**	G	T
1953	63.2	58.8	363.4	399.1	623.6	114.7	19.0
1954	63.7	59.6	370.0	403.6	616.1	96.1	17.0
1955	64.4	60.8	394.1	427.0	657.5	88.2	18.1
1956	65.6	62.8	405.4	446.5	671.6	86.8	18.5
1957	67.8	64.9	413.8	455.2	683.8	90.6	18.8
1958	69.2	66.0	418.0	461.0	680.9	93.4	18.0
1959	70.6	67.6	440.4	479.3	721.7	91.4	18.6
1960	71.9	68.7	452.0	489.6	737.2	90.4	20.1
1961	72.6	69.3	461.4	503.9	756.6	95.3	20.2
1962	73.7	70.6	482.0	524.8	800.3	102.8	21.5
1963	74.8	71.7	500.5	542.7	832.5	101.8	22.6
1964	75.9	72.8	528.0	580.5	876.4	100.2	22.5
1965	77.2	74.4	557.5	616.3	929.3	100.3	22.5
1966	79.4	76.7	585.7	647.0	984.8	112.6	20.7
1967	81.4	79.1	602.7	673.1	1011.4	125.1	21.0
1968	84.6	82.5	634.4	701.4	1058.1	128.1	21.8
1969	88.4	86.8	657.9	722.7	1087.6	121.8	21.7
1970	92.5	91.5	672.1	751.7	1085.6	110.6	21.1
1971	96.5	96.0	696.8	779.1	1122.4	103.7	21.1
1972	100.0	100.0	737.1	810.3	1185.9	101.7	19.9
1973	105.7	105.8	767.9	865.2	1254.3	95.9	19.9
1974	116.4	115.1	762.8	857.7	1246.3	96.6	18.9
1975	125.3	125.8	779.4	874.8	1231.6	97.4	11.3
1976	131.7	132.3	823.1	906.9	1298.2	96.8	17.7
1977	139.3	140.0	864.3	943.3	1369.7	100.4	17.8
1978	149.1	150.4	903.2	988.6	1438.6	100.3	18.7
1979	162.5	163.4	927.6	1015.5	1479.4	102.1	18.4
1980	179.0	178.4	931.8	1021.7	1475.0	106.4	22.8
1981	194.5	195.6	950.5	1049.7	1512.2	110.3	31.3
1982	206.0	207.8	963.3	1058.5	1480.0	117.0	24.1
1983	213.6	215.3	1009.2	1095.5	1534.7	116.2	24.3
1984	220.4	223.4	1062.4	1169.1	1639.3	122.5	24.8

Source: With two exceptions, all data have been obtained from the U.S. Department of Commerce, Bureau of Economic Analysis, *Business Statistics 1984,* Supplement to the *Survey of Current Business.* The exceptions are M1, K_{1952}, and r, which were obtained from Gordon (1986), and T, which was obtained from various issues of the *Survey of Current Business.*

TABLE 20.14

	M1	**K**	**I**	**P**	**E**	**M**	**r**
1953	125.99	655.7	85.3	70.0	26.6	21.8	2.52
1954	127.95	738.8	83.1	65.0	27.8	20.9	1.59
1955	132.00	842.6	103.8	80.9	30.7	23.4	2.19
1956	133.51	945.2	102.6	79.0	35.3	25.2	3.31
1957	134.10	1042.2	97.0	74.1	38.0	26.1	3.82
1958	136.02	1129.7	87.5	63.4	33.2	27.6	2.47
1959	141.38	1237.7	108.0	77.8	33.8	31.1	3.96
1960	141.41	1342.4	104.7	72.5	38.4	30.7	3.85
1961	144.45	1446.3	103.9	71.7	39.3	30.9	2.96
1962	147.99	1563.9	117.6	77.9	41.8	34.3	3.26
1963	152.64	1689.0	125.1	83.2	44.8	35.4	3.56
1964	158.61	1822.0	133.0	91.4	50.3	37.5	3.96
1965	165.49	1973.9	151.9	103.8	51.7	41.6	4.38
1966	172.76	2136.9	163.0	108.1	54.4	47.9	5.55
1967	180.00	2291.8	154.9	100.8	56.7	51.3	5.11
1968	192.66	2453.4	161.6	107.2	61.2	59.3	5.90
1969	203.79	2624.8	171.4	99.9	65.0	64.1	7.83
1970	211.63	2783.3	158.5	82.4	70.5	66.6	7.71
1971	226.17	2957.2	173.9	90.4	71.0	69.3	5.11
1972	242.56	3152.2	195.0	100.6	77.5	76.7	4.73
1973	259.73	3369.7	217.5	118.8	97.3	81.8	8.15
1974	272.61	3565.2	195.5	118.8	108.5	80.7	9.84
1975	285.39	3720.0	154.8	105.0	103.5	71.4	6.32
1976	301.85	3904.5	184.5	125.7	110.1	84.7	5.34
1977	325.19	4118.7	214.2	139.0	112.9	90.9	5.61
1978	351.66	4355.4	236.7	152.3	126.7	102.7	7.99
1979	379.03	4591.7	236.3	154.6	146.2	109.0	10.91
1980	401.48	4800.2	208.5	131.5	159.1	108.8	12.29
1981	430.08	5031.1	230.9	113.1	160.2	116.4	14.76
1982	458.50	5225.4	194.3	79.6	147.6	118.0	11.89
1983	509.18	5446.4	221.0	94.4	139.5	126.9	8.81
1984	547.30	5736.3	289.9	105.5	146.0	161.1	10.16

TABLE 20.15

	W^g	W^p	W	X	U
1953	49.6	429.5	479.1	578.2	3.9
1954	47.2	427.0	474.1	556.1	4.1
1955	45.9	448.6	494.4	593.4	4.0
1956	45.6	461.8	507.4	604.9	4.1
1957	45.8	474.6	520.4	613.3	4.3
1958	44.5	478.5	523.0	604.5	6.9
1959	44.5	501.5	546.0	642.5	5.5
1960	45.2	517.0	562.2	654.8	5.5
1961	46.2	530.9	577.1	669.0	6.7
1962	48.3	562.2	610.5	699.9	5.5
1963	48.2	582.8	631.0	736.8	5.7
1964	48.5	611.6	660.1	774.0	5.2
1965	48.7	644.8	693.5	819.8	4.5
1966	53.0	686.0	739.0	867.8	3.8
1967	57.2	709.1	766.3	888.1	3.8
1968	58.0	739.0	797.0	926.0	3.6
1969	58.2	772.2	830.4	954.0	3.5
1970	55.2	786.3	841.5	965.1	4.9
1971	52.5	812.0	864.5	976.1	5.9
1972	50.1	864.0	914.1	1034.6	5.6
1973	48.2	910.0	958.2	1096.8	4.9
1974	48.5	896.6	945.1	1082.7	5.6
1975	48.4	899.0	947.4	1063.7	8.5
1976	48.5	938.0	986.5	1129.8	7.7
1977	48.6	995.4	1044.0	1200.8	7.1
1978	49.3	1043.9	1093.2	1264.2	6.1
1979	49.0	1081.2	1130.2	1303.2	5.8
1980	49.6	1093.2	1142.8	1297.0	7.1
1981	50.0	1141.1	1191.1	1335.5	7.6
1982	50.5	1150.0	1200.5	1304.2	9.7
1983	51.3	1189.0	1240.3	1359.0	9.6
1984	51.9	1277.5	1329.4	1459.7	7.5

TABLE 20.16

Year	Output	Price Index	Land Value	Input Cost	CPI	Income
1960	72	51	24	46	88.7	6,036
1961	70	52	25	46	89.6	6,113
1962	71	54	26	47	90.6	6,271
1963	74	55	27	47	91.7	6,378
1964	72	55	29	47	92.9	6,727
1965	76	53	31	48	94.5	7,027
1966	73	55	33	50	97.2	7,280
1967	77	52	35	50	100.0	7,513
1968	79	52	38	50	104.2	7,728
1969	80	50	40	52	109.8	7,891
1970	77	52	42	54	116.3	8,134
1971	86	56	43	57	121.3	8,322
1972	87	60	47	61	125.3	8,562
1973	92	91	53	73	133.1	9,042
1974	84	117	66	83	147.7	8,867
1975	93	105	75	91	161.2	8,944
1976	92	102	86	97	170.5	9,175
1977	100	100	100	100	181.5	9,381
1978	102	105	109	108	195.4	9,735
1979	113	116	125	125	217.4	9,829
1980	101	125	145	138	246.8	9,722
1981	117	134	158	148	272.4	9,769
1982	117	121	157	150	289.1	9,725
1983	88	128	148	153	298.4	9,930
1984	111	139	146	155	311.1	10,421
1985	117	120	128	151	322.2	10,563
1986	108	106	112	146	328.4	10,780

Source: Economic Report of the President, 1987.

P^c = implicit price deflator for personal consumption (1972 = 100)

P^g = implicit price deflator for GNP (1972 = 100)

C = personal consumption, total

Y^d = disposal personal income

GNP = gross national product

G = federal government nonwage spending

T = indirect business taxes

M1 = money stock

I = gross private domestic investment

K = capital stock = $K_{-1} + I$; $K_{1952} = 655.7$

P = corporate profits

E = exports

M = imports

r = 6-month commercial paper rate

X = total product = $C + I + G + X - M$

W^g = federal government compensation of employees

W^p = private wages = $X - P - W^g$

W = total wages = $W^p + W^g$

U = civilian rate of unemployment

The data used for estimating the model of the agricultural sector are listed in Table 20.16. Output, the agricultural price, land values, input costs, and the consumer price index are all index numbers. Income is real (1982) per capita disposable income. Some variables not used in the text are listed for readers who are interested in estimating different forms of the model.

CHAPTER 21

Models with Discrete Dependent Variables

21.1. Introduction

There are many settings in which the phenomenon we seek to model is discrete rather than continuous. Consider, for example, modeling labor force participation, the decision of whether or not to make a major purchase, or the decision of which candidate to vote for in an election. For the first of these, intuition would suggest that factors such as age, education, marital status, number of children, and other economic factors would be relevant in explaining whether an individual chooses to seek work or not in a given period. But something is obviously lacking if this is treated as the same sort of regression model we used to analyze consumption or the costs of production. In this chapter, we shall examine a variety of what have come to be known as *qualitative response* (*QR*) models. There are numerous different types that apply in different situations. What they have in common is that they are models in which the dependent variable is a discrete outcome, such as a "yes or no" decision, so that conventional regression methods are inappropriate.

This chapter is a lengthy but far from complete survey of topics in estimating QR models. Almost none of these models can be estimated with linear regression methods. Therefore, readers interested in the mechanics of estimation may want to review the material in Chapter 12 before continuing. In nearly all cases, the method of estimation is maximum likelihood. The various properties of maximum likelihood estimators were discussed in Chapter 4. We shall assume throughout this chapter that the necessary conditions behind the optimality properties of maximum likelihood estimators are met and, therefore, will not derive or establish these properties specifically for the QR models. Detailed proofs for most of these models can be found in surveys by Amemiya (1981), McFadden (1984), Maddala (1983), and Dhrymes (1984).

21.2. Discrete Choice Models

The general class of models we shall consider are those for which the dependent variable takes values 0, 1, 2, . . . In a few cases, the values will themselves be meaningful, as in the following:

1. Number of patents: $y = 0, 1, 2, . . .$ These are *count* data.

But in most of the cases we shall study, the values taken by the dependent variable are merely a coding for some qualitative outcome. Some examples are as follows:

2. Labor force participation: We equate "no" with zero and "yes" with one. These are qualitative choices. The zero/one coding is a mere convenience.

3. Opinions of a certain type of legislation: Let zero represent "strongly opposed," one "opposed," two "neutral," three "support," and four "strongly support." These are *rankings,* and the values chosen are not quantitative but merely an ordering. The difference between the outcomes represented by one and zero is not necessarily the same as that between two and one.

4. The occupational field chosen by an individual: Let zero be clerk, one engineer, two lawyer, three politician, and so on. These are merely categories, giving neither a ranking nor a count.

5. A consumer chooses among several shopping areas in deciding where to shop on a given day. This has the same characteristics as example 4 but, as we shall see, the appropriate model is a bit different.

None of these situations lend themselves readily to regression analysis. Nonetheless, in each case, we can construct models that link the decision or outcome to a set of factors, at least in the spirit of regression. Our approach will be to analyze each of them in the general framework of probability models:

$$\text{Prob}(\text{event } j \text{ occurs}) = \text{Prob}(Y = j) = F[\text{relevant effects: parameters}]. \quad (21\text{--}1)$$

It is convenient for our purposes to group the models into two broad categories, binomial and multinomial, depending on whether the outcome is the choice between two or more than two alternatives. The great majority of recent empirical work in economics has used binomial models. As such, most of the material of this chapter will be devoted to them. The multinomial cases involve some new issues but are, for the most part, extensions of the binomial models. Within the multinomial models, we further divide the settings into unordered outcomes, such as those in examples 4 and 5, and ordered outcomes, such as those in examples 1 and 3. The latter have some of the familiar characteristics of regression models but involve some new complications as well. They are considered in Section 21.8.

21.3. Models for Binary Choice

Models for explaining a binary (0/1) dependent variable typically arise in two contexts. In many cases, the analyst is essentially interested in a regression model in the same spirit as the models of Chapters 5 to 17. With data on the variable of interest and a set of covariates, the analyst is interested in specifying a relationship between the former and the latter, more or less along the lines of the models we have already studied. The example of voting behavior is typical. In other cases, the binary choice model arises in the context of a formal regression model in which the nature of the data observed dictate the special treatment of a binary choice model. In a model of the demand for tickets for a sporting event, in which the variable of interest is number of tickets, it could happen that the observation consists only of whether ($Y = 1$) or not ($Y = 0$) the sports facility was filled to capacity. It will generally turn out that the models and techniques used in both cases are the same. Nonetheless, it is useful to examine both of them.

21.3.1. The Regression Approach

To focus ideas, consider a model of labor force participation.[1] The respondent either works or seeks work ($Y = 1$) or doesn't ($Y = 0$) in the period in which our survey is

---

[1] Models for qualitative dependent variables can now be found in most disciplines in economics. However, their most frequent use is in labor economics in the analysis of microlevel data sets.

taken. We believe that a set of factors, such as age, marital status, education, work history, and so on, gathered in a vector, $\mathbf{x}$, explain the decision, so that

$$\text{Prob}(Y = 1) = F(\boldsymbol{\beta}'\mathbf{x})$$
$$\text{Prob}(Y = 0) = 1 - F(\boldsymbol{\beta}'\mathbf{x}). \tag{21-2}$$

The set of parameters $\boldsymbol{\beta}$ reflect the impact of changes in $\mathbf{x}$ on the probability. For example, among the factors that might interest us is the marginal effect of marital status on the probability of labor force participation. The problem at this point is to devise a suitable model for the right-hand side of the equation.

One possibility is a linear regression,

$$F(\mathbf{x}, \boldsymbol{\beta}) = \boldsymbol{\beta}'\mathbf{x}.$$

Since $E[y] = F(\mathbf{x}, \boldsymbol{\beta})$, we can construct the regression model,

$$y = E[y] + (y - E[y])$$
$$= \boldsymbol{\beta}'\mathbf{x} + \varepsilon. \tag{21-3}$$

But the **linear probability model** has a number of shortcomings. A minor complication is presented by the fact that ε is heteroscedastic in a way that depends on $\boldsymbol{\beta}$. Since $\boldsymbol{\beta}'\mathbf{x} + \varepsilon$ must equal zero or one, ε equals either $-\boldsymbol{\beta}'\mathbf{x}$ or $1 - \boldsymbol{\beta}'\mathbf{x}$, with probabilities $1 - F$ and F, respectively. Thus, you can easily show that

$$\text{Var}[\varepsilon] = \boldsymbol{\beta}'\mathbf{x}(1 - \boldsymbol{\beta}'\mathbf{x}). \tag{21-4}$$

Of course, absent any other problems, we could manage this with an FGLS estimator in the fashion of Chapter 14. For our purposes, though, a more serious flaw is that without some ad hoc tinkering with the disturbances, we cannot be assured that the predictions from this model will truly look like probabilities. We cannot constrain $\boldsymbol{\beta}'\mathbf{x}$ to the zero–one interval. This produces both nonsense probabilities and negative variances. In view of this, and given the ready availability of convenient software for estimation, the linear model is becoming less frequently used except as a basis for comparison to some other more appropriate models.[2]

Our requirement, then, is a model that will produce predictions consistent with the underlying theory in (21–1). For a given regressor vector, we would expect

$$\lim_{\boldsymbol{\beta}'\mathbf{x} \to +\infty} \text{Prob}(Y = 1) = 1,$$

and

$$\lim_{\boldsymbol{\beta}'\mathbf{x} \to -\infty} \text{Prob}(Y = 1) = 0. \tag{21-5}$$

See Figure 21.1. In principle, any proper, continuous probability distribution defined over the real line will suffice. The normal distribution has been used in many analyses, giving rise to the **probit** model,

$$\text{Prob}(Y = 1) = \int_{-\infty}^{\boldsymbol{\beta}'\mathbf{x}} \phi(t) \, dt.$$
$$= \Phi(\boldsymbol{\beta}'\mathbf{x}). \tag{21-6}$$

---

[2] The linear model is not beyond redemption. Aldrich and Nelson (1984) analyze the properties of the model at length. Judge et al. (1985) and Fomby et al. (1984) give interesting discussions of the ways we may modify the model to force internal consistency. But the fixes are sample dependent, and the resulting estimator, such as it is, may have no known sampling properties. Additional discussion of weighted least squares appears in Amemiya (1977b) and Mullahy (1990). Finally, its shortcomings notwithstanding, the linear probability model is applied by Caudill (1988) and Heckman and MaCurdy (1985).

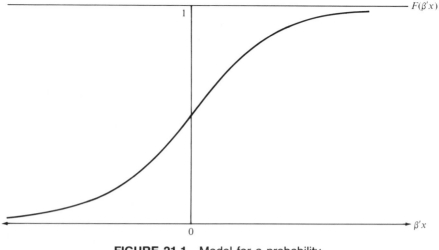

FIGURE 21.1   Model for a probability.

The function $\Phi(.)$ is a commonly used notation for the standard normal distribution. Partly because of its mathematical convenience, the logistic distribution,

$$
\text{Prob}(Y = 1) = \frac{e^{\boldsymbol{\beta'x}}}{1 + e^{\boldsymbol{\beta'x}}}
$$
$$
= \Lambda(\boldsymbol{\beta'x}),
$$

$(21\text{--}7)$

has also been used in many applications. We shall use the notation $\Lambda(.)$ to indicate the logistic cumulative distribution function. This model is called the **logit** model for reasons we shall discuss in the next section. Other distributions have been suggested,[3] but in econometric applications the probit and logit models have been used almost exclusively.

The question of which distribution to use is a natural one. The logistic distribution is similar to the normal except in the tails, which are considerably heavier. (It more closely resembles a t distribution with seven degrees of freedom.) Therefore, for intermediate values of $\boldsymbol{\beta'x}$ (say, between -1.2 and $+1.2$), the two distributions tend to give similar probabilities. The logistic distribution tends to give larger probabilities to $y = 0$ when $\boldsymbol{\beta'x}$ is extremely small (and smaller probabilities to $y = 0$ when $\boldsymbol{\beta'x}$ is very large) than the normal distribution. It is difficult to provide practical generalities on this basis, however, since they would require knowledge of $\boldsymbol{\beta}$. However, we should expect different predictions from the two models if our sample contains (1) very few responses (Y's equal to one) or very few nonresponses (Y's equal to zero) and (2) very wide variation in an important independent variable, particularly if (1) is also true. There are practical reasons for favoring one or the other in some cases for mathematical convenience, but it is difficult to justify the choice of one distribution or another on theoretical grounds. Amemiya (1981) discusses a number of related issues, but as a general proposition, the question is unresolved. In most applications, it seems not to make much difference.

The probability model is a regression:

$$
E[y] = 0[1 - F(\boldsymbol{\beta'x})] + 1[F(\boldsymbol{\beta'x})]
$$
$$
= F(\boldsymbol{\beta'x})
$$

$(21\text{--}8)$

[3] See, for example, Maddala (1983, pp. 27–32) and Aldrich and Nelson (1984).

Whatever distribution is used, it is important to note that the parameters of the model, like those of any nonlinear regression model, are not necessarily the marginal effects we are accustomed to analyzing. In general,

$$\frac{\partial E[y]}{\partial \mathbf{x}} = \left\{ \frac{dF(\boldsymbol{\beta}'\mathbf{x})}{d(\boldsymbol{\beta}'\mathbf{x})} \right\} \boldsymbol{\beta}$$

$$= f(\boldsymbol{\beta}'\mathbf{x})\boldsymbol{\beta}, \tag{21-9}$$

where $f(.)$ is the density function that corresponds to the cumulative distribution, $F(.)$. For the normal distribution, this is

$$\frac{\partial E[y]}{\partial \mathbf{x}} = \phi(\boldsymbol{\beta}'\mathbf{x})\boldsymbol{\beta}, \tag{21-10}$$

where $\phi(t)$ is the standard normal density. For the logistic distribution,

$$\frac{d\Lambda[\boldsymbol{\beta}'\mathbf{x}]}{d(\boldsymbol{\beta}'\mathbf{x})} = \frac{e^{\boldsymbol{\beta}'\mathbf{x}}}{(1 + e^{\boldsymbol{\beta}'\mathbf{x}})^2}$$

$$= \Lambda(\boldsymbol{\beta}'\mathbf{x})(1 - \Lambda(\boldsymbol{\beta}'\mathbf{x})), \tag{21-11}$$

which is particularly convenient. Thus, in the logit model,

$$\frac{\partial E[y]}{\partial \mathbf{x}} = \Lambda(\boldsymbol{\beta}'\mathbf{x})(1 - \Lambda(\boldsymbol{\beta}'\mathbf{x}))\boldsymbol{\beta}. \tag{21-12}$$

It is obvious that these will vary with the values of $\mathbf{x}$. In interpreting the estimated model, it will be useful to calculate this at, say, the means of the regressors and, where necessary, other pertinent values. For convenience, it is worth noting that the same scale factor applies to all of the slopes in the model.

EXAMPLE 21.1 Probability Models

The data listed in Table 21.1 were used by Spector and Mazzeo (1980) to analyze the effectiveness of a new method of teaching economics. The "dependent variable" for the

TABLE 21.1 Data Used to Study Program Effectiveness

Obs.	GPA	TUCE	PSI	GRADE	Obs.	GPA	TUCE	PSI	GRADE
1	2.66	20	0	0	17	2.75	25	0	0
2	2.89	22	0	0	18	2.83	19	0	0
3	3.28	24	0	0	19	3.12	23	1	0
4	2.92	12	0	0	20	3.16	25	1	1
5	4.00	21	0	1	21	2.06	22	1	0
6	2.86	17	0	0	22	3.62	28	1	1
7	2.76	17	0	0	23	2.89	14	1	0
8	2.87	21	0	0	24	3.51	26	1	0
9	3.03	25	0	0	25	3.54	24	1	1
10	3.92	29	0	1	26	2.83	27	1	1
11	2.63	20	0	0	27	3.39	17	1	1
12	3.32	23	0	0	28	2.67	24	1	0
13	3.57	23	0	0	29	3.65	21	1	1
14	3.26	25	0	1	30	4.00	23	1	1
15	3.53	26	0	0	31	3.10	21	1	0
16	2.74	19	0	0	32	2.39	19	1	1

TABLE 21.2 Estimated Probability Models

Variable	Linear		Logistic		Probit		Weibull	
	Coeff.	**Slope**	**Coeff.**	**Slope**	**Coeff.**	**Slope**	**Coeff.**	**Slope**
Constant	-1.498	—	-13.021	—	-7.452	—	-10.631	—
GPA	0.464	0.464	2.826	0.534	1.626	0.533	2.293	0.477
TUCE	0.010	0.010	0.095	0.018	0.052	0.017	0.041	0.009
PSI	0.379	0.379	2.379	0.449	1.426	0.468	1.562	0.325
$f(\boldsymbol{\beta}'\mathbf{x})$	1.000		0.189		0.328		0.208	

study is GRADE, an indicator of whether students' grades on an examination improved after exposure to PSI, a new method of teaching economics. The other variables are GPA, the grade point average; TUCE, the score on a pretest which indicates entering knowledge of the material; and PSI, a binary variable indicator of whether the student was exposed to the new teaching method.

Table 21.2 presents four sets of parameter estimates. The slope parameters and derivatives were computed for four probability models: linear, probit, logit, and Weibull. The Weibull distribution is an asymmetric distribution with CDF

$$\text{Prob(GRADE} = 1) = 1 - \exp(-\exp(\boldsymbol{\beta}'\mathbf{x})).$$

The last three sets of estimates are computed by maximizing the appropriate log-likelihood function. Estimation is discussed in the next section, so standard errors are not presented here. The scale factor given in the last row is the density function evaluated at the means of the variables. Also, note that the slope given for PSI is the derivative, not the change in the function with PSI changed from 0 to 1 with other variables held constant.

If one looked only at the coefficient estimates, it would be natural to conclude that the four models had produced radically different estimates. But a comparison of the columns of slopes shows that this is clearly wrong. The models are very similar; in fact, the logit and probit model results are nearly identical.

These data are only moderately unbalanced between 0's and 1's for the dependent variable (21 and 11). As such, we might expect similar results for the probit and logit models. One indicator is a comparison of the coefficients. In view of the different variances of the distributions, 1 for the normal and $\pi^2/3$ for the logistic, we might expect to obtain comparable estimates by multiplying the probit coefficients by $\pi/\sqrt{3} \approx 1.8$. Amemiya (1981) found, through trial and error, that scaling by 1.6, instead produced better results. This proportionality result is frequently cited. The result in (21–9) may help to explain the finding. The index $\boldsymbol{\beta}'\mathbf{x}$ is not the random variable. (See Section 21.3.2.) The marginal effect in the probit model for, say, x_k is $\phi(\boldsymbol{\beta}_p'\mathbf{x})\beta_{pk}$, while that for the logit is $\Lambda(1 - \Lambda)\beta_{lk}$. (The subscripts p and l are for probit and logit.) Amemiya suggests that his approximation works best at the center of the distribution, where $F = 0.5$, or $\boldsymbol{\beta}'\mathbf{x} = 0$ for either distribution. Suppose it is. Then $\phi(0) = 0.3989$ and $\Lambda(0)(1 - \Lambda(0)) = 0.25$. If the marginal effects are to be the same, then $0.3989\beta_{pk} = 0.25\beta_{lk}$, or $\beta_{lk} = 1.6\beta_{pk}$, which is the regularity observed by Amemiya. Note, though, as we depart from the center of the distribution, that the relationship will move away from 1.6. Since the logistic density descends more slowly than the normal, for unbalanced samples such as ours, the ratio of the logit coefficients to the probit coefficients will tend to be larger than 1.6. The ratio for the ones in Table 21.2 are closer to 1.7 than 1.6.

The computation of the derivatives of the conditional mean function is useful when the variable in question is continuous. But most applications contain at least one dummy variable, for which partial derivatives or marginal effects may not be meaningful. It turns out that the marginal effects suggested in (21–9) generally produce a reasonable approximation to the change in the probability that Y equals 1 at a point such as the regressor means. But at the same time, we can analyze the effect of the dummy variable on the whole distribution by computing $\text{Prob}(Y = 1)$ over the range of $\boldsymbol{\beta}'\mathbf{x}$ (using the sample estimates) and with the two values of the binary variable. Example 21.2 and Figure 21.2 illustrate for the probit model of Example 21.1.

EXAMPLE 21.2

Using the coefficients from the probit model in Table 21.2, we have the following probabilities as a function of GPA, at the mean of TUCE:

$$\text{PSI} = 0: \text{Prob}(\text{GRADE} = 1) = \Phi(-7.45 + 1.62\text{GPA} + 0.052(21.938))\qquad)$$

$$\text{PSI} = 1: \text{Prob}(\text{GRADE} = 1) = \Phi(-7.45 + 1.62\text{GPA} + 0.052(21.938) + 1.4263)$$

Figure 21.2 shows these two functions plotted over the range of GRADE observed in the sample, 2.0 to 4.0. The effect of PSI on the probabilities is substantial. The marginal effect of PSI is the difference between the two functions, which ranges from only about 0.06 at GPA = 2 to about 0.50 at GPA of 3.5. This shows that the probability that a student's grade will increase after exposure to PSI is far greater for students with high GPAs than for those with low GPAs. At the sample mean of GPA of 3.117, the effect of PSI on the probability is 0.465. The simple derivative calculation of (21–9) is given in Table 21.2; the estimate is 0.468. But, of course, this does not show the wide range of differences displayed in Figure 21.2.

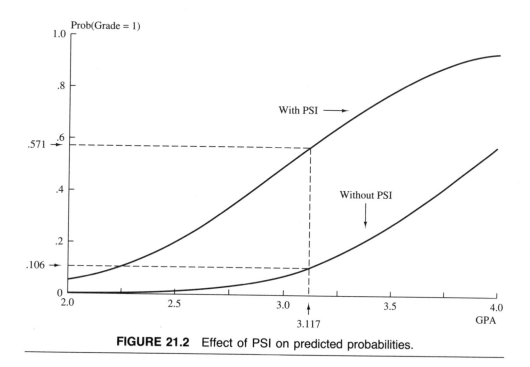

FIGURE 21.2 Effect of PSI on predicted probabilities.

21.3.2. Index Function and Random Utility Models

Discrete dependent-variable models are often cast in the form of *index function models*. We view the outcome of a discrete choice as a reflection of an underlying regression. As an often cited example, consider the decision to make a large purchase. The theory states that the consumer makes a marginal benefit–marginal cost calculation. Since marginal benefit is obviously not observable, we model the difference between benefit and cost as an unobserved variable, y^*, such that

$$y^* = \boldsymbol{\beta}'\mathbf{x} + \varepsilon.$$

We assume that ε has a standard logistic or a normal distribution with mean zero and variance one. We do not observe the net benefit of the purchase, only whether it is made or not. Therefore, our observation is

$$y = 1 \quad \text{if } y^* > 0,$$

$$y = 0 \quad \text{if } y^* \leq 0.$$

In this formulation, $\boldsymbol{\beta}'\mathbf{x}$ is called the *index function*.

Two aspects of this construction merit our attention. First, the assumption of unit variance is an innocent normalization. Suppose that we assume that the variance is σ^2 instead and likewise multiply the coefficients by σ^2. Our observed data will be unchanged; y is zero or one, depending only on the sign of y^*, not on its scale. Second, the assumption of zero for the threshold is likewise innocent if the model contains a constant term.[4] Now the probability that $y = 1$ is

$$\text{Prob}(y^* > 0) = \text{Prob}(\boldsymbol{\beta}'\mathbf{x} + \varepsilon > 0)$$

$$= \text{Prob}(\varepsilon > -\boldsymbol{\beta}'\mathbf{x}).$$

If the distribution is symmetric, as are the normal and logistic,

$$\text{Prob}(y^* > 0) = \text{Prob}(\varepsilon < \boldsymbol{\beta}'\mathbf{x})$$

$$= F(\boldsymbol{\beta}'\mathbf{x}).$$

This, therefore, provides an underlying structural model for our probability.

EXAMPLE 21.3 Structural Equations for a Probit Model

Nakosteen and Zimmer (1980) analyze a model of migration based on the following structure:[5]

For individual, i, the market wage they can earn at their present location is

$$y_p^* = \boldsymbol{\beta}'\mathbf{x}_p + \varepsilon_p.$$

Variables in the equation include age, sex, race, growth in employment, and growth in per capita income. If the individual migrates to a new location, his market wage would be

$$y_m^* = \boldsymbol{\gamma}'\mathbf{x}_m + \varepsilon_m$$

---

[4] Unless there is some compelling reason, binomial probability models should not be estimated without constant terms.

[5] A number of other studies have also used variants of this basic formulation. Some important examples are Willis and Rosen (1979) and Robinson and Tomes (1982). The study by Tunali examined in Example 21.8 is another example.

However, migration entails costs that are related both to the individual and to the labor market,

$$C^* = \boldsymbol{\alpha}'\mathbf{z} + u.$$

Costs of moving are related to whether the individual is self-employed and whether the individual recently changed their industry of employment. The individual migrates if the benefit, $y_m^* - y_p^*$, is greater than the cost, C^*. The net benefit of moving is

$$
\begin{aligned}
M^* &= y_m^* - y_p^* - C^* \\
&= \boldsymbol{\gamma}'\mathbf{x}_m - \boldsymbol{\beta}'\mathbf{x}_p - \boldsymbol{\alpha}'\mathbf{z} + (\varepsilon_m - \varepsilon_p - u) \\
&= \boldsymbol{\delta}'\mathbf{w} + \varepsilon.
\end{aligned}
$$

We could use an ordinary regression but for the fact that M^* is unobservable. The individual either moves or does not. After the fact, we observe only y_m^* if the individual has moved or y_p^* if he or she has not. But we do observe that $M = 1$ for a move and $M = 0$ for no move. If the disturbances are normally distributed, this produces the probit model we analyzed earlier. Logistic disturbances produce the logit model instead.

An alternative interpretation of data on individual choices is provided by the *random utility* model. Suppose that, in the Nakosteen–Zimmer framework, y_m and y_p represent the individual's utility of two choices, which we might denote U^a and U^b. For another example, U^a might be the utility of rental housing and U^b that of home ownership. The observed choice between the two reveals which one provides the greater utility, but not the unobservable utilities. Hence, the observed indicator equals one if $U^a > U^b$ and zero if $U^a \leq U^b$.

21.4. Estimation and Inference in Binary Choice Models

With the exception of the linear probability model, estimation of binary choice models is usually based on the method of maximum likelihood. Each observation is treated as a single draw from a Bernoulli distribution (binomial with one draw). The model with success probability $F(\boldsymbol{\beta}'\mathbf{x})$ and independent observations leads to the joint probability, or likelihood function,

$$\text{Prob}(Y_1 = y_1, Y_2 = y_2, \ldots, Y_n = y_n) = \prod_{y_i=0} [1 - F(\boldsymbol{\beta}'\mathbf{x}_i)] \prod_{y_i=1} F(\boldsymbol{\beta}'\mathbf{x}_i). \quad (21\text{–}13)$$

This can be conveniently written as

$$L = \prod_i [F(\boldsymbol{\beta}'\mathbf{x}_i)]^{y_i}[1 - F(\boldsymbol{\beta}'\mathbf{x}_i)]^{1-y_i}. \quad (21\text{–}14)$$

This is the likelihood for a sample of n observations. Taking logs, we obtain

$$\ln L = \sum_i [y_i \ln F(\boldsymbol{\beta}'\mathbf{x}_i) + (1 - y_i) \ln(1 - F(\boldsymbol{\beta}'\mathbf{x}_i))].^6 \quad (21\text{–}15)$$

---

[6] If the distribution is symmetric, as the normal and logistic are, then $1 - F(\boldsymbol{\beta}'\mathbf{x}) = F(-\boldsymbol{\beta}'\mathbf{x})$. Then there is a further simplification. Let $q = 2y - 1$. Then $\ln L = \Sigma_i \ln F(q_i \, \boldsymbol{\beta}'\mathbf{x}_i)$.

The first-order conditions for maximization require

$$\frac{\partial \ln L}{\partial \boldsymbol{\beta}} = \sum_i \left[\frac{y_i f_i}{F_i} + (1 - y_i)\frac{-f_i}{(1 - F_i)} \right] \mathbf{x}_i = \mathbf{0}. \tag{21-16}$$

[In (21–16) and later, we will use the subscript i to indicate that the function has an argument $\boldsymbol{\beta}'\mathbf{x}_i$.] The choice of a particular form for F_i leads to the empirical model.

Unless we are using the linear probability model, the equations in (21–16) will be nonlinear and require an iterative solution. But both of the models we have looked at thus far are relatively straightforward to analyze. For the logit model, by inserting (21–7) and (21–11) in (21–16), we get, after a bit of manipulation, the necessary conditions

$$\frac{\partial \ln L}{\partial \boldsymbol{\beta}} = \sum_i (y_i - \Lambda_i)\mathbf{x}_i = \mathbf{0}. \tag{21-17}$$

Note that if $\mathbf{x}_i$ contains a constant term, the first-order conditions imply that the average of the predicted probabilities must equal the proportion of ones in the sample. This also bears some similarity to the least squares normal equations if we view the term $y_i - \Lambda_i$ as a residual.[7] For the normal distribution, the log likelihood is

$$\ln L = \sum_{y_i=0} \ln(1 - \Phi_i) + \sum_{y_i=1} \ln \Phi_i. \tag{21-18}$$

The first-order conditions for maximizing L are

$$\frac{\partial \ln L}{\partial \boldsymbol{\beta}} = \sum_{y_i=0} \frac{-\phi_i}{1 - \Phi_i} \mathbf{x}_i + \sum_{y_i=1} \frac{\phi_i}{\Phi_i} \mathbf{x}_i. \tag{21-19}$$

For both models, Newton's method is a straightforward way to compute the parameter estimates. The actual second derivatives for the logit model are quite simple based on (21–17):

$$\mathbf{H} = \frac{\partial^2 \ln L}{\partial \boldsymbol{\beta} \, \partial \boldsymbol{\beta}'} = -\sum_i \Lambda_i(1 - \Lambda_i)\mathbf{x}_i\mathbf{x}_i'. \tag{21-20}$$

Since the second derivatives do not involve the random variable, y_i, Newton's method is also the method of scoring for the logit model. Note that the Hessian is always negative definite, so the log likelihood is globally concave. Newton's method will usually converge to the maximum of the log likelihood in just a few iterations unless the data are especially badly conditioned.

The computation is slightly more involved for the probit model. A useful simplification is obtained by defining

$$\lambda_i = \lambda_{0i} = \frac{-\phi_i}{1 - \Phi_i} \qquad \text{if } y_i = 0$$

and

$$\lambda_i = \lambda_{1i} = \frac{\phi_i}{\Phi_i} \qquad \text{if } y_i = 1. \tag{21-21}$$

---

[7] The same result holds for the linear probability model. Although regularly observed in practice, the result has not been verified for the probit model. A general result for the distributions for which the mean predicted probability will equal the sample proportion is given in Hein (1987).

With this variable, the first derivative is simply

$$\frac{\partial \ln L}{\partial \boldsymbol{\beta}} = \sum_i \lambda_i \mathbf{x}_i. \tag{21-22}$$

The second derivative can be obtained by using the result

$$\frac{d\phi(z)}{dz} = -z\phi(z).$$

Then

$$\mathbf{H} = \frac{\partial^2 \ln L}{\partial \boldsymbol{\beta} \, \partial \boldsymbol{\beta}'} = -\sum_i \lambda_i(\lambda_i + \boldsymbol{\beta}'\mathbf{x}_i)\mathbf{x}_i\mathbf{x}_i'. \tag{21-23}$$

This is also negative definite for all values of $\boldsymbol{\beta}$. The proof is less obvious than for the logit model.[8] For present purposes it suffices to note that the scalar part in the summation is $1 - \text{Var}[\varepsilon \,|\, \varepsilon < \boldsymbol{\beta}'\mathbf{x}]$ when $y = 1$, and $1 - \text{Var}[\varepsilon \,|\, \varepsilon > -\boldsymbol{\beta}'\mathbf{x}]$ when $y = 0$. In both cases the variance is between 0 and 1, so the complement is as well.[9]

The asymptotic covariance matrix for the maximum likelihood estimator can be estimated by using the inverse of the Hessian evaluated at the maximum likelihood estimates. There are also two other estimators available. The Berndt, Hall, Hall, and Hausman estimator [see (4–52) and (11–25) for an example] would be

$$\mathbf{B} = \sum_i g_i^2 \mathbf{x}_i \, \mathbf{x}_i',$$

where $g_i = (y_i - \Lambda_i)$ for the logit model [see (21–17)] and $g_i = \lambda_i$ for the probit model [see (21–22)]. The third estimator would be based on the expected value of the Hessian. As we saw earlier, the Hessian for the logit model does not involve y_i, so $\mathbf{H} = E[\mathbf{H}]$. But, because λ_i is a function of y_i [see (21–21)], this is not true for the probit model. Amemiya (1981) showed that for the probit model,

$$E\left[\frac{\partial^2 \ln L}{\partial \boldsymbol{\beta} \, \partial \boldsymbol{\beta}'}\right]_{\text{probit}} = \sum_i \lambda_{0i} \, \lambda_{i1} \, \mathbf{x}_i\mathbf{x}_i'. \tag{21-24}$$

Once again, the scalar part of the expression is always negative [see (21–21)]. The estimate of the asymptotic covariance matrix for the maximum likelihood estimates is then the negative inverse of whichever matrix is used to estimate the expected Hessian. Since the actual Hessian is generally used for the iterations, this is the usual choice. As we shall see below, though, for certain hypothesis tests, the BHHH estimator is a more convenient choice.

The predicted probabilities, $F(\hat{\boldsymbol{\beta}}'\mathbf{x}) = \hat{F}$, and the estimated marginal effects, $f(\hat{\boldsymbol{\beta}}'\mathbf{x}) \times \hat{\boldsymbol{\beta}} = \hat{f}\hat{\boldsymbol{\beta}}$, are nonlinear functions of the parameter estimates. To compute standard errors, we can use the linear approximation approach discussed in Chapter 4. For the predicted probabilities,

$$\text{Asy.Var}[\hat{F}] = \left(\frac{\partial \hat{F}}{\partial \hat{\boldsymbol{\beta}}}\right)' \mathbf{V} \left(\frac{\partial \hat{F}}{\partial \hat{\boldsymbol{\beta}}}\right),$$

where

$$\mathbf{V} = \text{Asy.Var}[\hat{\boldsymbol{\beta}}].$$

---

[8] See, for example, Amemiya (1985, pp. 273–274) and Maddala (1983, p. 63).

[9] See Johnson and Kotz (1971) and Heckman (1979). We will make repeated use of this result in Chapter 22.

The estimated asymptotic variance matrix of $\hat{\boldsymbol{\beta}}$ can be any of the three described earlier. Let $z = \mathbf{x}'\hat{\boldsymbol{\beta}}$. Then the derivative vector is

$$\frac{\partial \hat{F}}{\partial \hat{\boldsymbol{\beta}}} = \left(\frac{d\hat{F}}{dz}\right)\left(\frac{\partial z}{\partial \hat{\boldsymbol{\beta}}}\right) = \hat{f}\mathbf{x}.$$

Combining terms gives

$$\text{Asy.Var}[\hat{F}] = \hat{f}^2 \mathbf{x}'\mathbf{V}\mathbf{x}.$$

This depends, of course, on the particular $\mathbf{x}$ vector used.

For the marginal effects, let $\hat{\boldsymbol{\gamma}} = \hat{f}\hat{\boldsymbol{\beta}}$. Then,

$$\text{Asy.Var}[\hat{\boldsymbol{\gamma}}] = \left[\frac{\partial \hat{\boldsymbol{\gamma}}}{\partial \hat{\boldsymbol{\beta}}'}\right]\mathbf{V}\left[\frac{\partial \hat{\boldsymbol{\gamma}}}{\partial \hat{\boldsymbol{\beta}}'}\right]'.$$

The matrix of the derivatives is

$$\hat{f}\left(\frac{\partial \hat{\boldsymbol{\beta}}}{\partial \hat{\boldsymbol{\beta}}'}\right) + \boldsymbol{\beta}\left(\frac{d\hat{f}}{dz}\right)\left(\frac{\partial z}{\partial \hat{\boldsymbol{\beta}}'}\right) = \hat{f}\mathbf{I} + \left(\frac{d\hat{f}}{dz}\right)\hat{\boldsymbol{\beta}}\mathbf{x}'.$$

For the probit model, $df/dz = -z\phi$, so

$$\text{Asy.Var}[\hat{\boldsymbol{\gamma}}] = \phi^2[\mathbf{I} - (\boldsymbol{\beta}'\mathbf{x})\boldsymbol{\beta}\mathbf{x}']\mathbf{V}[\mathbf{I} - (\boldsymbol{\beta}'\mathbf{x})\boldsymbol{\beta}\mathbf{x}']' \qquad (21\text{--}25)$$

For the logit model, $\hat{f} = \hat{\Lambda}(1 - \hat{\Lambda})$, so

$$\frac{d\hat{f}}{dz} = (1 - 2\hat{\Lambda})\left(\frac{d\hat{\Lambda}}{dz}\right) = (1 - 2\hat{\Lambda})\hat{\Lambda}(1 - \hat{\Lambda}).$$

Collecting terms, we obtain

$$\text{Asy.Var}[\hat{\boldsymbol{\gamma}}] = (\hat{\Lambda}(1 - \hat{\Lambda}))^2[\mathbf{I} + (1 - 2\hat{\Lambda})\hat{\boldsymbol{\beta}}\mathbf{x}']\mathbf{V}[\mathbf{I} + (1 - 2\hat{\Lambda})\hat{\boldsymbol{\beta}}\mathbf{x}']'. \quad (21\text{--}26)$$

As before, the value obtained will depend on the $\mathbf{x}$ vector used.[10]

EXAMPLE 21.4 Estimates of Logit and Probit Models

Table 21.3 presents the estimated coefficients and marginal effects for the probit and logit models in Table 21.2. In both cases, the asymptotic covariance matrix is computed from the negative inverse of the actual Hessian of the log likelihood.

TABLE 21.3 Estimated Coefficients and Standard Errors (Standard Errors in Parentheses)

Variable	Logistic				Probit			
	Coeff.	t ratio	Slope	t ratio	Coeff.	t ratio	Slope	t ratio
Constant	−13.021	−2.640	—	—	−7.452	−2.930	—	—
	(4.931)				(2.542)			
GPA	2.826	2.238	0.534	2.252	1.626	2.343	0.533	1.761
	(1.263)		(0.237)		(0.694)		(0.303)	
TUCE	0.095	0.672	0.018	0.685	0.052	0.617	0.017	0.587
	(0.142)		(0.026)		(0.084)		(0.029)	
PSI	2.379	2.234	0.449	2.284	1.426	2.397	0.468	1.695
	(2.234)		(0.197)		(0.595)		(0.276)	

[10] For an application, see the study by Cecchetti discussed in Example 21.9.

For testing hypotheses about the coefficients, the full menu of procedures is available. The simplest method for a single restriction would be based on the usual t tests, using the standard errors from the information matrix. Using the normal distribution of the estimator, we would use the standard normal table rather than the t table for critical points. For more involved restrictions, it is possible to use the Wald test. For a set of restrictions $\mathbf{R}\boldsymbol{\beta} = \mathbf{q}$, the statistic is

$$W = (\mathbf{R}\hat{\boldsymbol{\beta}} - \mathbf{q})'\{\mathbf{R}(\text{Est.Asy.Var}[\hat{\boldsymbol{\beta}}])\mathbf{R}'\}^{-1}(\mathbf{R}\hat{\boldsymbol{\beta}} - \mathbf{q}).$$

EXAMPLE 21.5 Wald Test for a Subset of Coefficients

For testing the hypothesis that a subset of the coefficients, say the last L, are zero, the Wald statistic uses

$$\mathbf{R} = [\mathbf{0}\,|\,\mathbf{I}_L]$$

and $\mathbf{q} = \mathbf{0}$. Collecting terms, we find that the statistic is

$$W = \hat{\boldsymbol{\beta}}'_L\mathbf{V}_L^{-1}\hat{\boldsymbol{\beta}}_L, \tag{21–27}$$

where the subscript L indicates the subvector or submatrix corresponding to the L variables and $\mathbf{V}$ is the estimated asymptotic covariance matrix of $\hat{\boldsymbol{\beta}}$.

Likelihood ratio and Lagrange multiplier statistics can also be computed. The likelihood ratio statistic is

$$\text{LR} = -2[\ln \hat{L}_r - \ln \hat{L}],$$

where $\hat{L}_r$ and $\hat{L}$ are the log-likelihood functions evaluated at the unrestricted and restricted estimates, respectively. A common test, which is similar to the F test that all of the slopes in a regression are zero, is the likelihood ratio test that all of the slope coefficients in the probit or logit model are zero. For this test, the constant term remains unrestricted. In this case, the restricted log likelihood is the same for both probit and logit models,

$$\ln L_0 = n[P \ln P + (1 - P) \ln(1 - P)] \tag{21–28}$$

where P is the proportion of the observations that have dependent variable equal to 1.

EXAMPLE 21.6 Restricted Log Likelihoods

For the Spector and Mazzeo data, $P = 11/32$, so the restricted log likelihood is -20.5917. The unrestricted log likelihoods for the probit and logit models are -12.819 and -12.890, respectively. The chi-squared statistics are therefore 15.546 for the probit model and 15.404 for the logit model. With 3 degrees of freedom, the critical value from the chi-squared table is 7.815, so the joint hypothesis that the coefficients on GPA, TUCE, and PSI are all zero is rejected.

It might be tempting to use the likelihood ratio test to choose between the probit and logit models. But there is no restriction involved, and the test is not valid for this purpose. To underscore the point, there is nothing in its construction to prevent the chi-squared statistic for this "test" from being negative.

The Lagrange multiplier test statistic is $\text{LM} = \mathbf{g}'\mathbf{V}\mathbf{g}$, where $\mathbf{g}$ is the first derivatives of the unrestricted model evaluated at the restricted parameter vector and $\mathbf{V}$ is any of the three estimators of the asymptotic covariance matrix of the maximum likelihood estimator. Davidson and MacKinnon (1984) find evidence that $E[\mathbf{H}]$ is the best of the three estimators to use, which gives

$$\text{LM} = \left(\sum_i g_i \mathbf{x}_i\right)' \left\{\sum_i E[h_i]\mathbf{x}_i\mathbf{x}_i'\right\}^{-1} \left(\sum_i g_i\mathbf{x}_i\right), \tag{21-29}$$

where

$$h_i = d^2 \ln F_i/d(\boldsymbol{\beta}'\mathbf{x}_i)^2.$$

For the logit model, when the hypothesis is that all of the slopes are zero,

$$\text{LM} = nR^2,$$

where R^2 is the uncentered coefficient of determination in the regression of $(y_i - P)$ on $\mathbf{x}_i$ and P is the proportion of ones in the sample. All of the statistics listed here are asymptotically equivalent, and are asymptotically distributed as chi-squared with degrees of freedom equal to the number of restrictions being tested. We consider some examples below.

21.4.1. Specification Tests in Binary Choice Models

In the classical regression model, we considered two important specification problems, the effect of omitted variables and the effect of heteroscedasticity. In the classical model, $\mathbf{y} = \mathbf{X}_1\boldsymbol{\beta}_1 + \mathbf{X}_2\boldsymbol{\beta}_2 + \boldsymbol{\varepsilon}$, when least squares estimates $\mathbf{b}_1$ are computed omitting $\mathbf{X}_2$,

$$E[\mathbf{b}_1] = \boldsymbol{\beta}_1 + [\mathbf{X}_1'\mathbf{X}_1]^{-1}\mathbf{X}_1'\mathbf{X}_2\boldsymbol{\beta}_2.$$

Unless $\mathbf{X}_1$ and $\mathbf{X}_2$ are orthogonal, $\mathbf{b}_1$ is biased. If we ignore heteroscedasticity, although the least squares estimator is still unbiased and consistent, it is inefficient and the usual estimate of its sampling covariance matrix is inappropriate. Yatchew and Griliches (1984) have examined these same issues in the setting of the probit and logit models. Their general results are far more pessimistic. In the context of a binary choice model, they find the following:

1. If x_2 is omitted from a model containing x_1 and x_2,

$$\text{plim } \hat{\beta}_1 = c_1\beta_1 + c_2\beta_2,$$

where c_1 and c_2 are complicated functions of the unknown parameters. The implication is that even if the omitted variable is uncorrelated with the included one, the coefficient on the included variable will be inconsistent.

2. If the disturbances in the underlying regression are heteroscedastic, the maximum likelihood estimators are inconsistent and the variance matrix is inappropriate.

The second result is particularly troubling in view of the fact that the probit model is most often used with microeconomic data, which are frequently heteroscedastic.

Any of the three methods of hypothesis testing can be used to analyze these specification problems. The Lagrange multiplier test has the advantage that it can be carried out using the estimates from the restricted model, which sometimes brings a large saving in computational effort. This is especially true for the test for heteroscedasticity.[11]

To reiterate, the Lagrange multiplier statistic is computed as follows: Let the null hypothesis, H_0, be a specification of the model, and let H_1 be the alternative. For exam-

---

[11] The results in this section are based on Davidson and MacKinnon (1984) and Engle (1984). A recent symposium on the subject of specification tests in discrete choice models is Blundell (1987).

ple, H_0 might specify that only variables $\mathbf{x}_1$ appear in the model, while H_1 might specify that $\mathbf{x}_2$ appears in the model as well. The statistic is

$$\text{LM} = \mathbf{g}_0' \mathbf{V}_0^{-1} \mathbf{g}_0,$$

where $\mathbf{g}_0$ is the vector of derivatives of the log likelihood as specified by H_1, but evaluated at the maximum likelihood estimator of the parameters assuming that H_0 is true, and $\mathbf{V}_0^{-1}$ is any of the three consistent estimators of the variance matrix of the maximum likelihood estimator under H_1, also computed using the maximum likelihood estimators based on H_0. The statistic is asymptotically distributed as chi-squared with degrees of freedom equal to the number of restrictions.

21.4.1a. Testing for Omitted Variables. The hypothesis to be tested is

$$
\begin{aligned}
H_0 &: y^* = \boldsymbol{\beta}_1' \mathbf{x}_1 + \qquad\quad + \varepsilon, \\
H_1 &: y^* = \boldsymbol{\beta}_1' \mathbf{x}_1 + \boldsymbol{\beta}_2' \mathbf{x}_2 + \varepsilon,
\end{aligned}
\tag{21-30}
$$

so the test is of the hypothesis that $\boldsymbol{\beta}_2 = \mathbf{0}$. Examples 21.5 and 21.6 show how to carry out the Wald and LR tests. The Lagrange multiplier test would be carried out as follows:

1. Estimate the model in H_0 by maximum likelihood. The restricted coefficient vector is $[\hat{\boldsymbol{\beta}}, \mathbf{0}]$.
2. Let $\mathbf{x}$ be the compound vector, $[\mathbf{x}_1, \mathbf{x}_2]$.

The statistic is then computed according to (21–29). It is possible to show that this is equivalent to nR^2 in the regression of

$$
r_i = y_i \left[\frac{1 - F_i}{F_i} \right]^{1/2} + (y_i - 1) \left[\frac{F_i}{1 - F_i} \right]^{1/2}
\tag{21-31}
$$

on

$$
\mathbf{x}_i^* = \frac{f_i}{[F_i(1 - F_i)]^{1/2}} \mathbf{x}_i.
$$

Given the simplicity of (21–29) the appeal of this solution may be largely aesthetic. It is noteworthy, though, that in this case as in many others, the Lagrange multiplier is the coefficient of determination in a regression.[12]

21.4.1b. Testing for Heteroscedasticity. We use the general formulation analyzed by Harvey (1976),

$$\text{Var}[\varepsilon] = [\exp(\boldsymbol{\gamma}' \mathbf{z})]^2 .[13]$$

As noted by Davidson and MacKinnon, this test is not well suited to the logit model, so we will derive it specifically for the probit model. The model is

$$
\begin{aligned}
y^* &= \boldsymbol{\beta}' \mathbf{x} + \varepsilon, \\
\text{Var}[\varepsilon] &= [e^{\boldsymbol{\gamma}' \mathbf{z}}]^2
\end{aligned}
\tag{21-32}
$$

The log likelihood is

$$
\ln L = \sum_i y_i \ln F\left(\frac{\boldsymbol{\beta}' \mathbf{x}_i}{\exp(\boldsymbol{\gamma}' \mathbf{z}_i)} \right) + (1 - y_i) \ln \left[1 - F\left(\frac{\boldsymbol{\beta}' \mathbf{x}_i}{\exp(\boldsymbol{\gamma}' \mathbf{z}_i)} \right) \right].
\tag{21-33}
$$

---

[12] The denominator in R^2 is *uncentered*.

[13] See Example 14.15.

In order to be able to estimate all of the parameters, z cannot have a constant term. The derivatives are

$$\frac{\partial \ln L}{\partial \boldsymbol{\beta}} = \sum_i \left[\frac{f_i(y_i - F_i)}{F_i(1 - F_i)}\right] \exp(-\boldsymbol{\gamma}'\mathbf{z}_i)\mathbf{x}_i,$$

$$\frac{\partial \ln L}{\partial \boldsymbol{\gamma}} = \sum_i \left[\frac{f_i(y_i - F_i)}{F_i(1 - F_i)}\right] \exp(-\boldsymbol{\gamma}'\mathbf{z}_i)\mathbf{z}_i(-\boldsymbol{\beta}'\mathbf{x}_i).^{14}$$

(21–34)

This is a difficult log likelihood to maximize. But if the model is estimated assuming that $\boldsymbol{\gamma} = \mathbf{0}$, we can easily test for homoscedasticity. Let

$$\mathbf{w}_i = \left[\begin{array}{c} \mathbf{x}_i \\ (-\hat{\boldsymbol{\beta}}'\mathbf{x}_i)\mathbf{z}_i \end{array}\right]$$

(21–35)

computed at the maximum likelihood estimator, assuming that $\boldsymbol{\gamma} = \mathbf{0}$. Then (21–29) can be used as usual for the Lagrange multiplier statistic.

Davidson and MacKinnon carried out a Monte Carlo study to examine the true sizes and power functions of these tests. As might be expected, the test for omitted variables is relatively powerful. However, the test for heteroscedasticity may well pick up some other form of misspecification, including perhaps the simple omission of $\mathbf{z}$ from the index function, so its power may be problematic. It is perhaps not surprising that the same problem arose earlier in our tests for heteroscedasticity in the linear regression model.

EXAMPLE 21.7 Probit Model with Heteroscedasticity

Table 21.4 presents estimates of the probit model of the earlier examples, now with a correction for heteroscedasticity of the form

$$\text{Var}[\varepsilon_i] = \exp(\gamma \text{GPA}_i).$$

The three tests for homoscedasticity give

$$\text{LR} = -2[-12.045 - (-12.819)] = 1.55$$

$$\text{LM} = 1.106 \text{ based on BHHH estimator}$$

$$\text{Wald} = \frac{(-1.1920)^2}{1.054^2} = 1.279.$$

TABLE 21.4 Estimated Coefficients

		Estimate	Std. Error	Estimate	Std. Error
Constant	β_1	−7.452	2.542	−0.2203	0.7074
GPA	β_2	1.626	0.694	0.0540	0.1726
TUCE	β_3	0.052	0.084	0.000749	0.00338
PSI	β_4	1.426	0.595	0.02686	0.0978
GPA	γ	0.000	—	−1.1920	1.054
Log L		−12.819		−12.045	

---

[14] See Knapp and Seaks (1992) for an application.

None of these are larger than the critical chi-squared value of 3.84, so the hypothesis that γ equals 0 is not rejected. The very large standard errors and small coefficients suggest that the assumption of heteroscedasticity leads to a considerable distortion of the results. But this is deceiving. For the model with heteroscedasticity,

$$\frac{\partial \text{Prob}(Y = 1)}{\partial x_k} = \left[\frac{\phi \boldsymbol{\beta}' \mathbf{x}}{\exp(\boldsymbol{\gamma}' \mathbf{z})} \right] \times \frac{\beta_k}{\exp(\boldsymbol{\gamma}' \mathbf{z})}.$$

For the model here, the means of the variables are [1.0, 3.117, 21.3, 0.4375]. The variable in $\mathbf{z}$ is GPA, with mean 3.117. Using the coefficient estimates given in Table 21.4, we obtain a marginal effect of 0.5367. The counterpart for the model without heteroscedasticity is given in Table 21.3; it is 0.533. So the marginal effect of GPA is nearly identical. We leave as an exercise the comparison for the other two variables.

21.4.2. Measuring Goodness of Fit

There have been many attempts to derive fit measures for the QR models.[15] At a minimum, one would want to report the maximized value of the log-likelihood function, $\ln L$. Since the hypothesis that all of the slopes in the model are zero is often interesting, the log likelihood computed with only a constant term, $\ln L_0$ [see (21–28)] should also be reported. An analog to the R^2 in a conventional regression model is the likelihood ratio index,

$$\text{LRI} = 1 - \ln L / \ln L_0.$$

The measure has an intuitive appeal in that it is bounded by zero and 1. If all of the slope coefficients are zero, it equals zero. There is no way to make LRI equal 1, although one can come close. If F_i is always 1 when y equals 1 and zero when y equals zero, then $\ln L$ equals zero (the log of 1) and LRI equals 1. It has been suggested that this finding is indicative of a ''perfect fit'' and that LRI increases as the fit of the model improves. Unfortunately, values between zero and 1 have no natural interpretation. If F_i is a proper pdf, then even with many regressors, the model cannot fit perfectly unless $\boldsymbol{\beta}' \mathbf{x}$ explodes to $+\infty$ or $-\infty$. As a practical matter, this does happen. But, when it does, this is indicative of a flaw in the model, not a good fit.

> If one of the regressors contains a value, say x^*, such that whenever this x is greater than x^*, y equals 1, and vice versa, and whenever this x is less than x^*, y equals zero, and vice versa, then the model will be a perfect predictor. This also holds if the sign of $\boldsymbol{\beta}' \mathbf{x}$ gives a perfect predictor of y for some $\boldsymbol{\beta}$.[16]

For example, careless researchers sometimes include as regressors dummy variables that are identical, or nearly so, to the dependent variable. In this case, the maximization procedure will break down precisely because $\boldsymbol{\beta}' \mathbf{x}$ is exploding during the iterations. Of course, this is not at all what we had in mind for a good fit.

A useful summary of the predictive ability of the model is a 2×2 table of the hits and misses of a prediction rule.

$$\hat{y} = 1 \qquad \text{if } \hat{F} > F^* \text{ and 0 otherwise.} \qquad (21\text{–}36)$$

---

[15] See, for example, Cragg and Uhler (1970), Amemiya (1981), Maddala (1983), McFadden (1974), and Zavoina and McElvey (1975).

[16] See McFadden (1984). If this condition holds, gradient methods *will* find that $\boldsymbol{\beta}$.

The usual threshold value is 0.5, under the logic that we predict a 1 if the model says a 1 is more likely than a 0. However, it is important not to place too much emphasis on this measure of goodness of fit. Consider, for example, the naive predictor

$$\hat{y} = 1 \text{ if } P > 0.5 \text{ and } 0 \text{ otherwise,} \qquad (21\text{--}37)$$

where P is the proportion of ones in the sample. This rule will always predict correctly $100P$ percent of the observations, which means that the naive model does not have zero fit. In fact, if the proportion of ones in the sample is very high, it is possible to construct examples in which the second model will generate more correct predictions than the first! Once again, this is not a flaw in the model; it is a flaw in the fit measure.[17]

A second consideration is that 0.5, although the usual choice, may not be a very good value to use for the threshold. If the sample is relatively unbalanced, that is, has many more 1s than zeros, or vice versa, then by this prediction rule, it might never predict a 1 (or zero). To consider an example, suppose that in a sample of 10,000 observations, only 1000 have $Y = 1$. We know that the average predicted probability in the sample will be 0.10. As such, it may require an extreme configuration of regressors even to produce an F of 0.2, to say nothing of 0.5. In such a setting, the prediction rule may fail every time to predict when $Y = 1$. The obvious adjustment is to reduce F^*. Of course, this comes at a cost. In general, any prediction rule of the form in (21–36) will make two types of errors. It will incorrectly classify 0s as 1s and 1s as 0s. In practice, these errors need not be symmetric in the costs that result. For example, in a credit scoring model [see Boyes et al. (1989)], incorrectly classifying an applicant as a bad risk represents a missed opportunity, while incorrectly classifying a bad risk as good could lead to real and substantial costs. Changing F^* will always reduce the probability of one type of error while increasing the probability of the other. There is no correct answer as to the best value to choose. It depends on the setting and on the criterion function upon which the prediction rule depends.

EXAMPLE 21.8

Tunali (1986) estimated a probit model in a study of migration, subsequent remigration, and earnings for a large sample of observations of male members of households in Turkey. Among his results, he reports the following summary for a probit model:

		Predicted		
		$D = 0$	$D = 1$	Total
	$D = 0$	471	16	487
Actual	$D = 1$	183	20	203
	Total	654	36	690

The estimated model is highly significant, with a likelihood ratio test of the hypothesis that the coefficients (16 of them) are zero based on a chi-squared value of 69 with 16 degrees of freedom.[18] The model predicts 491 of 690, or 71.2 percent, of the observations correctly, though the likelihood ratio index is only 0.083. A naive model, which always predicts that $y = 0$ because $P < 0.5$, predicts 487 of 690, or 70.6 percent, of the observations correctly. This is hardly suggestive of no fit. The maximum likelihood estimator

---

[17]See Amemiya (1981).

[18]This actually understates slightly the significance of his model, as the preceding predictions are based on a bivariate model. However, the likelihood ratio test fails to reject the hypothesis that a univariate model applies.

produces several significant influences on the probability but makes only four more correct predictions than the naive predictor.[19]

The likelihood ratio index is obviously related to the likelihood ratio statistic for testing the hypothesis that the coefficient vector is zero. Other similar fit measures have been proposed. Although they are suggestive, whether they have any relationship to maximizing any type of fit in the more familiar sense is a question that needs to be studied. The maximum likelihood estimator is *not* chosen in order to maximize a fitting criterion based on prediction of y, as it is in the classical regression (which maximizes R^2). It is chosen to maximize the joint density of the observed dependent variables. It remains an interesting question for research whether fitting y well or obtaining good parameter estimates is a preferable estimation criterion. Evidently, they are not necessarily compatible.

21.4.3. Analysis of Proportions Data

Data for the analysis of binary responses will be in one of two forms. The data we have considered thus far are *individual;* each observation consists of $[y_i, \mathbf{x}_i]$, the actual response of an individual and associated regressor vector. *Grouped* data usually consist of counts or proportions. Grouped data are obtained by observing the response of n_i individuals, all of whom have the same $\mathbf{x}_i$. The observed dependent variable will consist of the proportion, P_i, of the n_i individuals, *ij*, who respond with $y_{ij} = 1$. An observation is thus $[n_i, P_i, \mathbf{x}_i]$, $i = 1, \ldots, N$. Election data are typical.[20] In the grouped data setting, it is possible to use regression methods as well as maximum likelihood procedures to analyze the relationship between P_i and $\mathbf{x}_i$. The observation P_i is an estimate of the population $\pi_i = F(\boldsymbol{\beta}'\mathbf{x}_i)$. If we treat this as a simple problem in sampling from a Bernoulli population, then, from basic statistics,

$$P_i = \mathrm{F}(\boldsymbol{\beta}'\mathbf{x}_i) + \varepsilon_i = \pi_i + \varepsilon_i,$$

where

$$E[\varepsilon_i] = 0, \qquad \mathrm{Var}[\varepsilon_i] = \frac{\pi_i(1 - \pi_i)}{n_i}. \tag{21-38}$$

This heteroscedastic regression format suggests that the parameters could be estimated by a nonlinear weighted least squares regression. But there is a simpler way to proceed. Since the function $F(\boldsymbol{\beta}'\mathbf{x}_i)$ is strictly monotonic, it has an inverse. (See Figure 21.1.) Consider, then, a Taylor series approximation to this function around the point $\varepsilon_i = 0$:

$$F^{-1}(P_i) = F^{-1}(\pi_i + \varepsilon_i) \approx F^{-1}(\pi_i) + \left[\frac{dF^{-1}(\pi_i)}{d\pi_i} \right] \varepsilon_i.$$

But

$$F^{-1}(\pi_i) = \boldsymbol{\beta}'\mathbf{x}_i$$

and

$$\frac{dF^{-1}(\pi_i)}{d\pi_1} = \frac{1}{dF(\pi_i)/d\pi_i} = \frac{1}{f(\pi_i)},$$

---

[19] It is also noteworthy that nearly all of the correct predictions of the maximum likelihood estimator are the zeroes. It hits only 10 percent of the 1's in the sample.

[20] The earliest work on probit modeling involved applications of grouped data in laboratory experiments. Each observation consisted of n_i subjects receiving dosage x_i of some treatment, such as an insecticide, and a proportion P_i "responding" to the treatment, usually by dying. Finney (1971) and Cox (1970) are useful and important surveys of this literature.

so

$$F^{-1}(P_i) \approx \boldsymbol{\beta}'\mathbf{x}_i + \frac{\varepsilon_i}{f_i}.$$

This produces a heteroscedastic linear regression,

$$F^{-1}(P_i) = z_i = \boldsymbol{\beta}'\mathbf{x}_i + u_i,$$

where

$$E[u_i] = 0 \qquad \text{and} \qquad \text{Var}[u_i] = \frac{F_i(1 - F_i)}{n_i f_i^2}. \tag{21-39}$$

The inverse function for the logistic model is particularly easy to obtain; if

$$P_i = \frac{\exp(\boldsymbol{\beta}'\mathbf{x}_i)}{1 + \exp(\boldsymbol{\beta}'\mathbf{x}_i)}$$

then

$$\ln\left(\frac{P_i}{1 - P_i}\right) = \boldsymbol{\beta}'\mathbf{x}_i.$$

This function is called the **logit** of P_i, hence the name "logit" model. For the normal distribution, the inverse function, $\Phi^{-1}(P_i)$, called the **normit** of P_i, must be approximated. The usual approach is a ratio of polynomials.[21]

Weighted least squares regression based on (21–39) produces the **minimum chi-squared estimates** of $\boldsymbol{\beta}$. Since the weights are functions of the unknown parameters, a two-step procedure is called for. As always, simple least squares at the first step produces consistent but inefficient estimates. Then the weights,

$$w_i = \left[\frac{n_i \phi_i^2}{\Phi_i(1 - \Phi_i)}\right]^{1/2}$$

for the probit model and

$$w_i = [n_i \Lambda_i(1 - \Lambda_i)]^{1/2}$$

based on the first step estimates can be used for weighted least squares.[22] It has been shown that this estimator has the same properties as the maximum likelihood estimator. [See Amemiya (1985), pp. 275–280).]

Two complications arise in practice. The familiar result in (21–38) suggests that when the proportion is based on a large population, the variance of the estimator can be exceedingly low. This will resurface in implausibly low standard errors and high t ratios in the minimum chi-squared regression. Unfortunately, that is a consequence of the model.[23] The same result will emerge in maximum likelihood estimates based on proportions data. For grouped data, the log likelihood is

$$\ln L = \sum_i n_i[P_i \ln F(\boldsymbol{\beta}'\mathbf{x}_i) + (1 - P_i) \ln(1 - F(\boldsymbol{\beta}'\mathbf{x}_i))].$$

---

[21] See Abramovitz and Stegun (1971). The function Normit + 5 is called the **probit** of P_i. The term dates from the early days of this analysis, when the avoidance of negative numbers was a simplification with considerable payoff.

[22] Simply using P_i and $f(F^{-1}(P_i))$ might seem to be a simple expedient in computing the weights. But this would be analogous to using y_i^2 instead of an estimate of σ_i^2 in a heteroscedastic regression. Fitted probabilities and, for the probit model, densities should be based on a consistent set of parameter values.

[23] Whether the proportion should, in fact, be considered as a single observation from a distribution of proportions is a question that arises in all of these cases. It is unambiguous in the bioassay cases noted earlier. But the issue is less clear with election data, especially since in these cases, the n_i will represent most if not all of the potential respondents in location i rather than a random sample of respondents.

Second, both the MLE and FGLS estimators break down if any of the proportions are zero or 1. A number of ad hoc patches have been suggested; the one that seems to be most widely used is just to add or subtract a small constant, say 0.001, from the observed value when it is zero or 1.

21.5. Recent Developments

Qualitative response models have been a growth industry in econometrics. The recent literature, particularly in the area of panel data analysis, has produced a number of new techniques.

21.5.1. Fixed and Random Effects Models for Panel Data

The structural probit model for a panel of data would be written

$$y_{it}^* = \beta' \mathbf{x}_{it} + u_{it}, \qquad u_{it} \sim N[0, 1],$$

$$y_{it} = 1 \qquad \text{if } y_{it}^* > 0, \text{ and } 0 \text{ otherwise.}$$

If the u_{it}s are taken to be independent standard normal variables, then the panel nature of the data is irrelevant, and the methods of the previous sections would apply. It has been found that the probit model does not lend itself at all to the fixed effects treatment ($u_{it} = \alpha_i$) of Chapter 16. There is no feasible way to remove the heterogeneity, and with large numbers of cross-sectional units, estimation of the α_i's is intractible. Some progress has been made on a *random effects* specification. Ideally, we would like to specify that u_{it} and u_{is} are freely correlated (within a group, but not across groups). This will involve computing joint probabilities from a T variate normal distribution, which is problematic. (We will return to this issue in Section 21.6.) An alternative, "limited information" approach based on the GMM estimation method has been suggested by Avery, Hansen, and Hotz (1981). A specification, which has the same structure as the random effects model of Chapter 16 has been devised by Butler and Moffitt (1982). They show that the random effects model can be estimated using only one-dimensional standard normal integrals. The Butler and Moffitt approach has been criticized for the restriction of equal correlation across periods. But it does have the compelling virtue that the model can be efficiently estimated even with fairly large T using conventional computational methods. [See Greene (1991, pp. 438–440).]

In contrast to the probit model, the logit model does lend itself to a *fixed effects* treatment (but not a random effects specification). A fixed effects logit model that accounts for the heterogeneity is

$$\text{Prob}(y_{it} = 1) = \frac{e^{\alpha_i + \beta' \mathbf{x}_{it}}}{1 + e^{\alpha_i + \beta' \mathbf{x}_{it}}}.$$

In this nonlinear model, it is not possible to sweep out the heterogeneity by taking differences or deviations from group means.[24] Chamberlain (1980) has suggested a different

---

[24] In addition, even if it is possible to estimate the parameters, any desirable properties for the estimated individual effects, α_i, will depend on increasing T, which will not make sense in the typical panel. This will be particularly problematic for maximum likelihood estimators, whose only desirable properties are asymptotic. The solution, as Chamberlain suggests, is to remove the heterogeneity by some other means, and thereby finesse the problem of estimating the α_is.

approach to estimating this model with data sets with large n and small T.[25] His suggestion, which was infeasible for the probit model, is that we consider the set of T observations for unit i as a group. The unconditional likelihood for the nT observations is

$$L = \prod_i \prod_t (F_{it})^{y_{it}} (1 - F_{it})^{1-y_{it}}.$$

Chamberlain suggests, instead, that we maximize the conditional likelihood function,

$$L^c = \prod_i \text{Prob}\left(Y_{i1} = y_{i1}, Y_{i2} = y_{i2}, \ldots, Y_{iT} = y_{iT} \bigg| \sum_t y_{it}\right).$$

That is, the likelihood for each set of T observations is conditioned on the number of 1's in the set. It is useful to consider an example. Suppose that the sample consists of a large number of cross-sectional units, each observed in two periods, 1 and 2. The unconditional likelihood is

$$L = \prod_i \text{Prob}(Y_{i1} = y_{i1}) \, \text{Prob}(Y_{i2} = y_{i2}).$$

(The observations are independent, so the likelihood function is the product of the probabilities.) For each pair of observations, we have the possibilities:

1. $y_{i1} = 0$ and $y_{i2} = 0$. $\text{Prob}(0, 0 \,|\, \text{sum} = 0) = 1$.
2. $y_{i1} = 1$ and $y_{i2} = 1$. $\text{Prob}(1, 1 \,|\, \text{sum} = 2) = 1$.

The ith term in L^c for either of these is just 1, so they contribute nothing to the conditional likelihood function. When we take logs, these terms (and these observations) will drop out. But suppose that $y_{i1} = 0$ and $y_{i2} = 1$. Then,

$$\textbf{3. } \text{Prob}(0, 1 \,|\, \text{sum} = 1) = \frac{\text{Prob}(0, 1 \textit{ and } \text{sum} = 1)}{\text{Prob}(\text{sum} = 1)}$$

$$= \frac{\text{Prob}(0, 1)}{\text{Prob}(0, 1) + \text{Prob}(1, 0)}.$$

(The fourth probability would be obtained similarly.) Therefore, for this pair of observations, the conditional probability is

$$\frac{\dfrac{1}{1 + e^{\alpha_i + \boldsymbol{\beta}' \mathbf{x}_{i1}}} \dfrac{e^{\alpha_i + \boldsymbol{\beta}' \mathbf{x}_{i2}}}{1 + e^{\alpha_i + \boldsymbol{\beta}' \mathbf{x}_{i2}}}}{\dfrac{1}{1 + e^{\alpha_i + \boldsymbol{\beta}' \mathbf{x}_{i1}}} \dfrac{e^{\alpha_i + \boldsymbol{\beta}' \mathbf{x}_{i2}}}{1 + e^{\alpha_i + \boldsymbol{\beta}' \mathbf{x}_{i2}}} + \dfrac{e^{\alpha_i + \boldsymbol{\beta}' \mathbf{x}_{i1}}}{1 + e^{\alpha_i + \boldsymbol{\beta}' \mathbf{x}_{i1}}} \dfrac{1}{1 + e^{\alpha_i + \boldsymbol{\beta}' \mathbf{x}_{i2}}}} = \frac{e^{\boldsymbol{\beta}' \mathbf{x}_{i2}}}{e^{\boldsymbol{\beta}' \mathbf{x}_{i1}} + e^{\boldsymbol{\beta}' \mathbf{x}_{i2}}}.$$

By conditioning on the sum of the two observations, we have been able to remove the heterogeneity. Therefore, we can construct the conditional likelihood function as the product of these terms for the pairs of observations for which the two observations are $(0, 1)$. Pairs of observations with one and zero are included analogously. The product of the terms such as the preceding, for those observation sets for which the sum is not zero or T, constitutes the conditional likelihood. Maximization of the resulting function is straightforward and may be done by conventional methods.

---

[25] In principle, his technique is not limited to small T. But the amount of computation rises geometrically with T, and becomes excessive for T larger than about 10.

As in the linear regression model, it is of some interest to test whether there is, indeed, heterogeneity. With homogeneity ($\alpha_i = \alpha$), there is no unusual problem, and the model can be estimated, as usual, as a logit model. However, it is not possible to test the hypothesis using the likelihood ratio test, because the two likelihoods are not comparable. (The conditional likelihood is based on a restricted data set.) None of the usual tests of restrictions can be used because the individual effects are never actually estimated. However, Hausman's (1978) specification test is a natural one to use here. Under the null hypothesis of homogeneity, both Chamberlain's conditional maximum likelihood estimator (CMLE) and the usual maximum likelihood estimator are consistent, but Chamberlain's is inefficient. (It fails to use the information that $\alpha_i = \alpha$, and it may not use all of the data.) Under the alternative hypothesis, the unconditional maximum likelihood estimator is inconsistent, while Chamberlain's estimator is consistent and efficient. The Hausman test can be based on the chi-squared statistic

$$\chi^2 = (\hat{\boldsymbol{\beta}}_{\text{CML}} - \hat{\boldsymbol{\beta}}_{\text{ML}})'(\text{Var}[\text{CML}] - \text{Var}[\text{ML}])^{-1}(\hat{\boldsymbol{\beta}}_{\text{CML}} - \hat{\boldsymbol{\beta}}_{\text{ML}}).$$

The estimated variance matrices are those computed for the two maximum likelihood estimators. For the maximum likelihood estimator, the row and column corresponding to the constant term are dropped. A large value will cast doubt on the hypothesis of homogeneity. (There are K degrees of freedom for the test.) It is possible that the variance matrix for the maximum likelihood estimator will be larger than that for the conditional maximum likelihood estimator. If so, the difference matrix in brackets is assumed to be a zero matrix, and the chi-squared statistic is therefore zero.

EXAMPLE 21.9

Cecchetti (1986) applied Chamberlain's model in a study of the frequency of the price changes for a sample of 38 magazines observed over a 27-year period. The constant term for each magazine was allowed to change every 3 years, implying a total of 318 free parameters. The data were analyzed in 9-year subperiods, so a cross-section unit in our earlier notation consists of $T = 3$ periods. Since a price change could occur in any period, the sums of y_{it} were zero, one, two, or three. The model included as regressors (1) the time since the last price change, (2) inflation since the last price change, (3) the size of the last price change, (4) current inflation, (5) industry sales growth, and (6) a measure of sales volatility. The most important determinants of the probability of a price change were found to be (1), (2), and (5). In none of Cecchetti's models was the Hausman statistic less than 40, indicating that the data did exhibit heterogeneity.

21.5.2. Semiparametric Estimation

In his survey of qualitative response models, Amemiya (1981) reports the following widely cited approximations for the linear probability (LP) model: Over the range of probabilities of 30 to 70 percent,

$$\hat{\beta}_{\text{LP}} \approx 0.4\beta_{\text{probit}} \quad \text{for the slopes}$$

$$\hat{\beta}_{\text{LP}} \approx 0.25\beta_{\text{logit}} \quad \text{for the slopes.}[26]$$

Aside from confirming our intuition that least squares approximates the nonlinear model and providing a quick comparison for the three models involved, the practical usefulness

---

[26] An additional 0.5 is added for the constant term in both models.

of the formula is somewhat limited. Still, it is a striking result.[27] A recent series of studies has focused on reasons why the least squares estimates should be proportional to the probit and logit estimates. A related question concerns the problems associated with assuming that a probit model applies when, in fact, a logit model is appropriate, or vice versa.[28] The approximation would seem to suggest that with this type of misspecification, we would, once again, obtain a scaled version of the correct coefficient vector. (Amemiya also reports the widely observed relationship $\hat{\beta}_{logit} = 1.6\hat{\beta}_{probit}$, which follows from the results above.)

Greene (1983a), building on Goldberger (1981), finds that if the probit model is correctly specified and if the regressors are themselves joint normally distributed, that the probability limit of the least squares estimator is a multiple of the true coefficient vector.[29] Greene's result is useful only for the same purpose as Amemiya's quick correction of OLS. Multivariate normality is obviously inconsistent with most applications. For example, nearly all applications include at least one dummy variable. However, Cheung and Goldberger (1984) have shown that much weaker conditions than joint normality will achieve the same proportionality result. For a probit model, they require only that $E[\mathbf{x}|y^*]$ be linear in y^*. Several authors have built on these observations to pursue the issue of what circumstances will lead to proportionality results such as these. Stoker (1986) has extended them to a very wide class of models that goes well beyond those of Cheung and Goldberger. Curiously enough, Stoker's results rule out dummy variables, but it is those for which the proportionality result seems to be most robust.[30]

21.5.3. Nonparametric Estimation—The Maximum Score Estimator

In Section 21.4.2 we discussed the issue of prediction rules for the probit and logit models. In contrast to the linear regression model, estimation of these binary choice models is not based on a fitting rule, such as the sum of squared residuals, which is related to the fit of the model to the data. The maximum score estimator[31] is based on a fitting rule,

$$\text{Maximize}_{\boldsymbol{\beta}} \ S_{N\alpha}(\boldsymbol{\beta}) = \frac{1}{n} \sum_i [z_i - (1 - 2\alpha) \ \text{sgn}(\boldsymbol{\beta}'\mathbf{x}_i)].$$

The parameter α is a preset quantile, and $z_i = 2y_i - 1$. (So $z = -1$ if $y = 0$.) If α is set to $\frac{1}{2}$, then the maximum score estimator chooses the $\boldsymbol{\beta}$ to maximize the number of times that the prediction has the same sign as z. This matches our prediction rule in (21–36) with $F^* = 0.5$. So for $\alpha = 0.5$, maximum score attempts to maximize the number of correct predictions. Since the sign of $\boldsymbol{\beta}'\mathbf{x}$ is the same for all positive multiples of $\boldsymbol{\beta}$, the estimator is computed subject to the constraint that $\boldsymbol{\beta}'\boldsymbol{\beta} = 1$.

Since there is no log-likelihood function underlying the fitting criterion, there is no information matrix to provide a method of obtaining standard errors for the estimates. A method that is used to provide at least some idea of the sampling variability of the

---

[27] This does not imply that it is useful to report 2.5 times the linear probability estimates with the probit estimates for comparability. The linear probability estimates are already in the form of marginal effects, while the probit coefficients must be scaled *downward*. If the sample proportion happens to be close to 0.5, the right scale factor will be roughly $\phi[\Phi^{-1}(0.5)] = 0.3989$. But the density falls rapidly as P moves away from 0.5.

[28] See Ruud (1986) and Gourieroux et al. (1987).

[29] The scale factor is estimable with the sample data, so under these assumptions, a method of moments estimator is available.

[30] See Greene (1983a).

[31] See Manski (1975, 1985, 1986) and Manski and Thompson (1986).

estimator is called **bootstrapping.** The method proceeds as follows: After the set of coefficients, b_0, is computed, M randomly drawn samples of T observations are drawn from the original data set *with replacement. T* may be less than or equal to n, the sample size. With each such sample, the maximum score estimator is recomputed, giving b_m. Then the **mean squared deviation matrix**

$$\mathbf{MSD(b)} = \frac{1}{M} \sum_m (\mathbf{b}_m - \mathbf{b}_0)(\mathbf{b}_m - \mathbf{b}_0)'$$

is computed. The authors of the technique emphasize that this is not a covariance matrix.[32]

EXAMPLE 21.10 The Maximum Score Estimator

Table 21.5 presents maximum score estimates for Spector and Mazzeo's GRADE model. Note that they are quite far removed from the probit estimates. Of course, there is no meaningful comparison of the coefficients, since the maximum score estimates are not the slopes of a conditional mean function. Surprisingly enough, the maximum score approach does not predict the dependent variable as well as the probit model. The relevant score for the two estimators are also given in the table. The probit model correctly classifies four observations with $Y = 1$ that are misclassified by the maximum score estimator.

TABLE 21.5   Maximum Score Estimator

		Maximum Score			Probit	
		Estimate	**Mean Sq. Dev.**		**Estimate**	**Std. Error**
Constant	β_1	0.3534	0.7886		-7.4522	2.5420
GPA	β_2	0.9142	0.8558		1.6260	0.6939
TUCE	β_3	-0.1696	0.1623		0.05173	0.08389
PSI	β_4	-0.1029	0.7007		1.4264	0.5950

		Fitted				Fitted	
		0	1			0	1
Actual	0	18	3	Actual	0	18	3
	1	7	4		1	3	8

Nonparametric approaches such as this have the virtue that they do not make a possibly erroneous assumption about the underlying distribution. On the other hand, as seen in the example, this is no guarantee that the estimator will outperform the fully parametric estimator. One additional practical consideration is that nonparametric estimators such as this are very computation intensive. At present, the maximum score estimator is not useable for more than roughly 15 coefficients and perhaps 1500 to 2000 observations.[33]

---

[32] Note that we are not yet agreed that b_0 even converges to a meaningful coefficient vector, since no underlying probability distribution as such as been assumed. Once it is agreed that there is an underlying regression function at work, then a meaningful set of asymptotic results, including consistency can be developed. Manski et al. (op. cit.) and Kim and Pollard (1990) present a number of results. Even so, it has been shown that the bootstrap MSD matrix is useful for little more than descriptive purposes.

[33] Communication from C. Manski to the author. The maximum score estimator has been implemented by Manski and Thompson (1986) and Greene (1991).

21.6. Bivariate and Multivariate Probit Models

In Chapter 17, we analyzed a number of different multiple-equation extensions of the classical and generalized regression. A natural extension of the probit model would be to allow more than one equation, with correlated disturbances, in the same spirit as the seemingly unrelated regressions model. The general specification for a two-equation model would be

$$y_1^* = \boldsymbol{\beta}_1' \mathbf{x}_1 + \varepsilon_1, \qquad y_1 = 1 \text{ if } y_1^* > 0, \ 0 \text{ otherwise,}$$

$$y_2^* = \boldsymbol{\beta}_2' \mathbf{x}_2 + \varepsilon_2, \qquad y_2 = 1 \text{ if } y_2^* > 0, \ 0 \text{ otherwise,}$$

$$E[\varepsilon_1] = E[\varepsilon_2] = 0, \tag{21-40}$$

$$\text{Var}[\varepsilon_1] = \text{Var}[\varepsilon_2] = 1,$$

$$\text{Cov}[\varepsilon_1, \varepsilon_2] = \rho.$$

EXAMPLE 21.11 _____

Greene (1984) reports estimates of a model of voter behavior in two decisions, whether to send at least one child to public school and whether to vote in favor of a school budget.[34] Regressors in the model were "income," "taxes" = property taxes paid, and "years" of residence in the community. The results in Table 21.6 were obtained using 95 observations.

TABLE 21.6

	Single Equation		Bivariate
Public school			
Constant	−4.972	(3.996)	−4.764 (4.009)
Income	0.1537	(0.4495)	0.1149 (0.5958)
Taxes	0.6440	(0.5654)	0.6699 (0.7226)
School budget			
Constant	−0.6862	(4.009)	−0.3066 (3.850)
Income	0.9961	(0.4404)	0.9895 (0.4863)
Taxes	−1.2646	(0.5672)	−1.3080 (0.6748)
Years	−0.01644	(0.0147)	−0.0176 (0.0136)
ρ	0.0		0.317 (0.2303)
Log likelihood	−40.0830 + −58.5006		−97.4117

21.6.1. Maximum Likelihood Estimation

To construct the log likelihood, we will use a useful shorthand. Let

$$q_{i1} = 2y_{i1} - 1$$

and

$$q_{i2} = 2y_{i2} - 1.$$

_____

[34] Data for the study are given in Pindyck and Rubinfeld (1981) and Rubinfeld (1977).

Thus, $q_{ij} = 1$ if $y_{ij} = 1$ and -1 if $y_{ij} = 0$ for $j = 1$ and 2. The bivariate normal cdf is

$$\text{Prob}(X_1 < x_1, X_2 < x_2) = \int_{-\infty}^{x_2} \int_{-\infty}^{x_1} \phi_2(z_1, z_2, \rho) \, dz_1 \, dz_2,$$

which we denote $\Phi_2(x_1, x_2, \rho)$. The density (which was given in Chapter 3) is

$$\phi_2(x_1, x_2, \rho) = \frac{e^{-(1/2)(x_1^2 + x_2^2 - 2\rho x_1 x_2)/(1 - \rho^2)}}{2\pi(1 - \rho^2)^{1/2}}.$$

Now let

$$z_{i1} = \boldsymbol{\beta}_1' \mathbf{x}_{i1}, \qquad w_{i1} = q_{i1} z_{i1},$$

$$z_{i2} = \boldsymbol{\beta}_2' \mathbf{x}_{i2}, \qquad w_{i2} = q_{i2} z_{i_2},$$

$$\rho_{i*} = q_{i1} q_{i2} \rho.$$

Note the notational convention. The subscript 2 is used to indicate the bivariate normal density, ϕ_2 and cdf, Φ_2. In all other cases, the subscript 2 indicates the variables in the second equation in (21–40). As before, ϕ and Φ without subscripts denote the univariate density and cdf.

The probabilities that enter the likelihood function are

$$\text{Prob}(Y_1 = y_{i1}, Y_2 = y_{i2}) = \Phi_2(w_{i1}, w_{i2}, \rho_{i*}).$$

This accounts for all of the necessary sign changes needed to compute probabilities for ys equal to zero and one. Thus,

$$\ln L = \sum_i \ln \Phi_2(w_{i1}, w_{i2}, \rho_{i*}).^{[35]} \qquad (21\text{–}41)$$

The derivatives of the log likelihood then reduce to

$$\frac{\partial \ln L}{\partial \boldsymbol{\beta}_1} = \sum_i \left(\frac{q_{i1} g_{i1}}{\Phi_2} \right) \mathbf{x}_{i1}$$

$$\frac{\partial \ln L}{\partial \boldsymbol{\beta}_2} = \sum_i \left(\frac{q_{i2} g_{i2}}{\Phi_2} \right) \mathbf{x}_{i2} \qquad (21\text{–}42)$$

$$\frac{\partial \ln L}{\partial \rho} = \sum_i \frac{q_{i1} q_{i2} \phi_2}{\Phi_2},$$

where

$$g_{i1} = \phi(w_{i1}) \Phi \left[\frac{w_{i2} - \rho_{i*} w_{i1}}{(1 - \rho_{i*}^2)^{1/2}} \right],$$

$$g_{i2} = \phi(w_{i2}) \Phi \left[\frac{w_{i1} - \rho_{i*} w_{i2}}{(1 - \rho_{i*}^2)^{1/2}} \right]. \qquad (21\text{–}43)$$

Note that the derivatives are functions of the univariate normal distribution and are, therefore, simple to compute.[36] The derivative with respect to ρ is also surprisingly

---

[35] To avoid further ambiguity, the observation subscript will be omitted from $\Phi_2 = \Phi_2(w_{i1}, w_{i2}, \rho_{i*})$ and from $\phi_2 = \phi_2(w_{i1}, w_{i2}, \rho_{i*})$.

[36] This suggests that a trivariate model could be estimated, since the derivatives of the trivariate normal distribution are functions of the bivariate normal integrals. In obtaining the parameters, gradient methods need not actually compute the log-likelihood function. The function itself is needed only for hypothesis testing. A study that uses this result is Hausman and Wise (1978).

simple. Before considering the Hessian, it is useful to note what becomes of the preceding if $\rho = 0$. For $\partial \ln L / \partial \boldsymbol{\beta}_1$, if $\rho = \rho_{i*} = 0$, g_{i1} reduces to $\phi(w_{i1})\Phi(w_{i2})$, ϕ_2 is $\phi(w_{i1})\phi(w_{i2})$, and $\Phi_2 = \Phi(w_{i1})\Phi(w_{i2})$. Inserting these in (21–42) with q_{i1} and q_{i2} produces (21–19). Since $\Phi_2 = \Phi(w_{i1})\Phi(w_{i2})$ is not a function of ρ, $\partial \ln L / \partial \rho$ is zero.

The maximum likelihood estimates are obtained by simultaneously setting the three derivatives to zero. The second derivatives are relatively straightforward but tedious. Some simplifications are useful. Let

$$\delta_i = \frac{1}{\sqrt{1 - \rho_{i*}^2}},$$

$$v_{i1} = \delta_i(w_{i2} - \rho_{i*}w_{i1}), \qquad \text{so} \qquad g_{i1} = \phi(w_{i1})\Phi(v_{i1}),$$

$$v_{i2} = \delta_i(w_{i1} - \rho_{i*}w_{i2}), \qquad \text{so} \qquad g_{i2} = \phi(w_{i2})\Phi(v_{i2}).$$

By multiplying it out, you can show that

$$\delta_i\phi(w_{i1})\phi(v_{i1}) = \delta_i\phi(w_{i2})\phi(v_{i2}) = \phi_2.$$

Then

$$\frac{\partial^2 \ln L}{\partial \boldsymbol{\beta}_1 \, \partial \boldsymbol{\beta}_1'} = \sum_i \mathbf{x}_{i1}\mathbf{x}_{i1}' \left[\frac{-w_{i1}g_{i1}}{\Phi_2} - \frac{\rho_{i*}\phi_2}{\Phi_2} - \frac{g_{i1}^2}{\Phi_2^2} \right],$$

$$\frac{\partial^2 \ln L}{\partial \boldsymbol{\beta}_1 \, \partial \boldsymbol{\beta}_2'} = \sum_i q_{i1}q_{i2}\mathbf{x}_{i1}\mathbf{x}_{i2}' \left[\frac{\phi_2}{\Phi_2} - \frac{g_{i1}g_{i2}}{\Phi_2^2} \right],$$

$$\frac{\partial^2 \ln L}{\partial \boldsymbol{\beta}_1 \, \partial \rho} = \sum_i q_{i2}\mathbf{x}_{i1} \frac{\phi_2}{\Phi_2} \left[\rho_{i*}\delta_i v_{i1} - w_{i1} - \frac{g_{i1}}{\Phi_2} \right],$$

$$\frac{\partial^2 \ln L}{\partial \rho^2} = \sum_i \frac{\phi_2}{\Phi_2} \left[\delta_i^2\rho_{i*}(1 - \mathbf{w}_i'\mathbf{R}_i^{-1}\mathbf{w}_i) + \delta_i w_{i1}w_{i2} - \frac{\phi_2}{\Phi_2} \right],$$

where $\mathbf{w}_i'\mathbf{R}_i^{-1}\mathbf{w}_i = \delta_i^2(w_{i1}^2 + w_{i2}^2 - 2\rho_{i*}w_{i1}w_{i2})$. (For $\boldsymbol{\beta}_2$, change the subscripts in $\partial^2 \ln L / \partial \boldsymbol{\beta}_1 \, \partial \boldsymbol{\beta}_1'$ and $\partial^2 \ln L / \partial \boldsymbol{\beta}_1 \partial \rho$ accordingly.) The complexity of the second derivatives for this model makes it an excellent candidate for the Berndt et al. estimator of the variance matrix of the maximum likelihood estimator.

Even though it is (almost) impossible to estimate higher-dimensional models, it is possible to test for correlation among the equations. The Lagrange multiplier test is a natural device in this setting. Under the null hypothesis that ρ equals zero, the model consists of independent probit equations, which can be estimated separately. Moreover, in the multivariate model, all of the bivariate (or multivariate) densities and probabilities factor into the products of the marginals if the correlations are zero. This makes construction of the test statistic a simple matter of manipulating the results of the independent probits. The Lagrange multiplier statistic for testing $H_0 : \rho = 0$ in a bivariate probit model is[37]

$$\text{LM} = \frac{g^2}{h},$$

---

[37] This is derived in Kiefer (1982).

where

$$g = \sum_i q_{i1} q_{i2} \frac{\phi(w_{i1})\phi(w_{i2})}{\Phi(w_{i1})\Phi(w_{i2})}$$

and

$$h = \sum_i \frac{[\phi(w_{i1})\phi(w_{i2})]^2}{\Phi(w_{i1})\Phi(-w_{i1})\Phi(w_{i2})\Phi(-w_{i2})}.$$

EXAMPLE 21.12

Continuing the preceding example, we find that there are three ways in which we may test the hypothesis that ρ equals zero. A simple t test is equivalent to the Wald test. The square of the t ratio is the Wald statistic. Under the null hypothesis, the log likelihood is the sum of the log likelihoods for the two independent probits. The Lagrange multiplier statistic is computed as shown earlier, using only the two independent probits. The results are

Wald statistic:	1.8947,
Likelihood ratio:	2.3438,
Lagrange multiplier:	2.0581.

All three statistics suggest that the hypothesis that ρ equals zero cannot be rejected.

21.6.2. Extensions

21.6.2a. A Multivariate Probit Model. In principle, a multivariate model would extend (21–40) to more than two outcome variables just by adding equations. The practical obstacle to such an extension is the evaluation of higher order multivariate normal integrals. Some progress has been made on trivariate integration, but existing results are not sufficient to allow accurate and efficient evaluation for more than two variables in a sample of even moderate size.

An altogether different approach has recently shown some potential. Lerman and Manski (1981) suggested that one might approximate multivariate normal probabilities by random sampling. For example, to approximate $\text{Prob}(Y_1 > 1, Y_2 < 3, Y_3 < -1 \mid \rho_{12}, \rho_{13}, \rho_{23})$, we would simply draw random observations from this trivariate distribution and count the number of observations that meet the inequality.[38] In order to obtain an accurate estimate of the probability, a quite large number of draws is required. But McFadden (1989) pointed out that for purposes of maximum likelihood estimation, accurate evaluation of probabilities is not the problem that needs to be solved. One can view the computation of the log likelihood and its derivatives as a problem of estimating a mean. That is, in (21–41) and (21–42), the same problem arises if we divide by n. The idea is that even though the individual terms in the average might be in error, if the error has mean zero, it will average out in the summation. The insight is, then, that if we can obtain probability estimates which only err randomly both positively and negatively, it may be possible to obtain an estimate of the log likelihood and its derivatives which is

---

[38] Sampling from the standard normal distribution is straightforward, using, say, the inverse probability transform method. To obtain a draw from $N_M[\mathbf{0}, \boldsymbol{\Sigma}]$, we would obtain an $M \times 1$ vector of independent draws from the standard normal. Denote this as $\mathbf{x}$. With this in hand, $\boldsymbol{\Sigma}^{1/2}\mathbf{x} = \mathbf{z}$ is a multivariate draw from the desired distribution.

reasonably close to the one that would result from actually computing the integral. The important result, from a practical standpoint, is that it does not take inordinately large numbers of random draws to achieve this. The upshot would be that the evaluation of multivariate normal integrals may ultimately cease to be the obstacle to the estimation of models based on the multivariate normal distribution.[39]

21.6.2b. A Model with Censoring. There are situations in which the observed variables in the bivariate probit model are censored in one way or another. For example, in an evaluation of credit scoring models, Boyes et al. (1989) analyzed data generated by the following rule:

$y_1 = 1$ if individual i defaults on a loan, 0 otherwise

$y_2 = 1$ if the individual is granted a loan, 0 otherwise.

For a given individual, y_1 is not observed unless y_2 equals 1. Thus, there are three types of observations in the sample with unconditional probabilities:[40]

$$y_2 = 0: \quad \text{Prob}(Y_2 = 0) = 1 - \Phi(\boldsymbol{\beta}_2' \mathbf{x}_2)$$

$$y_1 = 0, \ y_2 = 1: \quad \text{Prob}(y_1 = 0, \ y_2 = 1) = \Phi_2[-\boldsymbol{\beta}_1' \mathbf{x}_1, \ \boldsymbol{\beta}_2' \mathbf{x}_2, \ -\rho]$$

$$y_1 = 1, \ y_2 = 1: \quad \text{Prob}(y_1 = 1, \ y_2 = 1) = \Phi_2[\boldsymbol{\beta}_1' \mathbf{x}_1, \ \boldsymbol{\beta}_2' \mathbf{x}_2, \ \rho].$$

The log-likelihood function is based on these probabilities.[41]

21.7. Models for Multiple Choices

Some recent studies of multiple-choice settings include the following:

1. Hensher (1986), McFadden (1974), and many others have analyzed the travel mode of urban commuters.
2. Schmidt and Strauss (1975a, 1975b) and Boskin (1974) have analyzed occupational choice among multiple alternatives.
3. Terza (1985a) has studied the assignment of bond ratings to corporate bonds as a choice among multiple alternatives.

These are all distinct from the multivariate probit model we examined earlier. In that setting, there were several decisions, each between two alternatives. Here there is a single decision among two or more alternatives. We will examine two broad types of choice sets, *ordered* and *unordered*. The choice among means of getting to work, by car, bus, train, or bicycle, is clearly unordered. However, a bond rating is, by design, a ranking—that is its purpose. As we shall see, quite different techniques are used for the two types of models.

21.7.1. Unordered Multiple Choices

Unordered-choice models can be motivated by a random utility model. For the ith consumer faced with J choices, suppose that the utility of choice j is

$$U_{ij} = \boldsymbol{\beta}' \mathbf{z}_{ij} + \varepsilon_{ij}.$$

[39] Recent papers which propose improved methods of simulating probabilities include Pakes and Pollard (1989) and, especially, Börsch-Supan and Hajivassilou (1992).

[40] The model was first proposed by Wynand and van Praag (1981).

[41] Extensions of the bivariate probit model to other types of censoring are discussed in Poirier (1980) and Abowd and Farber (1982).

If the consumer makes choice j in particular, we assume that U_{ij} is the maximum among the J utilities. Hence, the statistical model is driven by the probability that choice j is made, which is

$$\text{Prob}(U_{ij} > U_{ik}) \qquad \text{for all other } k \neq j.$$

The model is made operational by a particular choice of distribution for the disturbances. As before, two models have been considered, logit and probit. Because of the need to evaluate multiple integrals of the normal distribution, the probit model has found rather limited use in this setting. Let Y_i be a random variable indicating the choice made. McFadden (1973) has shown that if (and only if) the J disturbances are independent and identically distributed with Weibull distribution,

$$F(\varepsilon_{ij}) = \exp(e^{-\varepsilon_{ij}}),$$

then

$$\text{Prob}(Y_i = j) = \frac{e^{\beta' z_{ij}}}{\sum_j e^{\beta' z_{ij}}}. \tag{21-44}$$

This leads to what is called the *conditional logit model*.[42]

Utility depends on x_{ij}, which includes aspects specific to the individual as well as to the choices. It is useful to distinguish them. Let $z_{ij} = [x_{ij}, w_i]$. Then x_{ij} varies across the choices and possibly across the individuals as well. (The components of x_{ij} are typically called the **attributes** of the choices.) But w_i contains the characteristics of the individual and is, therefore, the same for all choices. If we incorporate this in the model, (21-44) becomes

$$\text{Prob}(Y_i = j) = \frac{e^{\beta' z_{ij} + \alpha' w_i}}{\sum_j e^{\beta' z_{ij} + \alpha' w_i}}.$$

Terms that do not vary across alternatives, that is, those specific to the individual, fall out of the probability. Evidently, if the model is to allow individual specific effects, it must be modified. One method is to create a set of dummy variables for the choices and multiply each of them by the common **w.** We then allow the coefficient to vary across the choices instead of the characteristics.

EXAMPLE 21.13

A model of shopping center choice by individuals might specify that the choice depends on attributes of the shopping centers such as number of stores and distance from the central business district, both of which are the same for all individuals, and income, which varies across individuals. Suppose that there were three choices. The three regressor vectors would be as follows:

Choice 1: Stores Distance Income   0   0

Choice 2: Stores Distance   0   Income   0

Choice 3: Stores Distance   0   0   Income

---

[42] It is occasionally labeled the *multinomial logit model,* but this conflicts with the usual name for the model discussed in the next section, which differs slightly.

The data sets typically analyzed by economists do not contain mixtures of individual- and choice-specific attributes. Such data would be far too costly to gather for most purposes. When they do, the preceding framework can be used. For the present, it is useful to examine the two types of data separately and consider aspects of the model that are specific to the two types of applications.

21.7.1a. The Multinomial Logit Model. To set up the model that applies when data are individual specific, it will help to consider an example.

EXAMPLE 21.14 _____

Schmidt and Strauss (1975a, 1975b) estimated a model of occupational choice based on a sample of 1000 observations drawn from the Public Use Samples for three years, 1960, 1967, and 1970. For each sample, the data for each individual in the sample consist of the following:

1. *Occupation:* 1 = menial, 2 = blue collar, 3 = craft, 4 = white collar, 5 = professional.
2. *Regressors:* Constant, Education, Experience, Race, Sex.

Schmidt and Strauss coded the outcomes 1, 2, 3, 4, and 5. For consistency with our earlier models, we will relabel them 0, 1, 2, 3, and 4. The model for occupational choice is, then,

$$\text{Prob}(Y_i = j) = \frac{e^{\beta_j' \mathbf{x}_i}}{\sum_{k=0}^{4} e^{\beta_k' \mathbf{x}_i}}. \tag{21-45}$$

_____

The model in (21–45) is the **multinomial logit model.**[43] The estimated equations provide a set of probabilities for the $J + 1$ choices for a decision maker with characteristics $\mathbf{x}_i$. Before proceeding, we must remove an indeterminacy in the model. If we define $\boldsymbol{\beta}_j^* = \boldsymbol{\beta}_j + \mathbf{q}$ for any nonzero vector $\mathbf{q}$, the identical set of probabilities result, as the terms involving $\mathbf{q}$ all drop out. A convenient normalization that solves the problem is to assume that $\boldsymbol{\beta}_0 = \mathbf{0}$. The probabilities are, therefore,

$$\text{Prob}(Y = j) = \frac{e^{\beta_j' \mathbf{x}_i}}{1 + \sum_{k=1}^{J} e^{\beta_k' \mathbf{x}_i}} \qquad \text{for } j = 1, 2, \ldots, J.$$

$$\tag{21-46}$$

$$\text{Prob}(Y = 0) = \frac{1}{1 + \sum_{k=1}^{J} e^{\beta_k' \mathbf{x}_i}}.$$

The binomial model examined in Section 21.4 is now the special case with $J = 1$.

The coefficients in this model are difficult to interpret. By differentiating (21–46), we find that the marginal effects of the regressors on the probabilities are

$$\frac{\partial P_j}{\partial \mathbf{x}_i} = P_j \left[\boldsymbol{\beta}_j - \sum_k P_k \boldsymbol{\beta}_k \right]. \tag{21-47}$$

---

[43] Nerlove and Press (1973).

These can be computed from the parameter estimates. Standard errors can be estimated using the results of the last section but are likely to be exceedingly complex.[44] The model implies that we can compute J log-odds ratios

$$\ln\left[\frac{P_{ij}}{P_{i0}}\right] = \boldsymbol{\beta}_j'\mathbf{x}_i.$$

We could normalize on any other probability as well and obtain

$$\ln\left[\frac{P_{ij}}{P_{ik}}\right] = \mathbf{x}_i'(\boldsymbol{\beta}_j - \boldsymbol{\beta}_k).$$

From the point of view of estimation, it is useful that the odds ratio, P_j/P_k, does not depend on the other choices. This follows from the independence of disturbances in the original model. From a behavioral viewpoint, this is not so attractive. We shall return to this problem later.

Estimation of the multinomial logit model is straightforward. Newton's method will normally find a solution very readily unless the data are badly conditioned. The log likelihood can be derived by defining, for each individual, $d_{ij} = 1$ if alternative j is chosen by individual i, and 0 if not, for the $J + 1$ possible outcomes. Then, for each i, one and only one of the d_{ij}'s is one. The log likelihood is a generalization of that for the binomial probit or logit model:

$$\ln L = \sum_i \sum_{j=0}^J d_{ij} \ln \text{Prob}(Y_i = j).$$

The derivatives have the characteristically simple form

$$\frac{\partial \ln L}{\partial \boldsymbol{\beta}_j} = \sum_i [d_{ij} - P_{ij}]\mathbf{x}_i \qquad \text{for } j = 1, \ldots, J.$$

The exact second derivatives matrix has J^2 blocks, each $K \times K$.

The jth diagonal block is $\qquad \sum_i - P_{ij}(1 - P_{ij})\mathbf{x}_i\mathbf{x}_i'.$

The jkth off-diagonal block is $\qquad \sum_i (P_{ij}P_{ik})\mathbf{x}_i\mathbf{x}_i'.$

Since the Hessian does not involve d_{ij}, these are the expected values, and Newton's method is equivalent to the method of scoring. The Berndt et al. method can be used instead by summing the outer products of the first derivatives. However, this will rarely be an improvement because of the very simple form and global concavity of the log likelihood. It is worth noting that the number of parameters in this model proliferates with the number of choices. This is unfortunate, as the typical cross section sometimes involves a fairly large number of regressors.

Finding adequate fit measures in this setting presents the same difficulties as in the binomial models. As before, it is useful to report the log likelihood. The hypothesis that

---

[44] The literature contains relatively few studies in which the marginal effects and *their* standard errors are presented. The usual focus is on the coefficient estimates. Equation (21–47) suggests that there is at least some potential for confusion. Note, for example, that for any particular x_k, $\partial P_j/\partial x_k$ need not have the same sign as β_{jk}. See Greene (1991, pp. 478–485).

all of the slope coefficients are zero is simple to test *if the regressor vector includes a constant term*. If so, the restricted log likelihood is

$$\ln L_0 = \sum_{j=0}^{J} n_j \ln P_j,$$

where P_j is the sample proportion of observations that make choice j. If desired, the likelihood ratio index can also be reported. A useful table will give a listing of hits and misses of the prediction rule "predict $Y_i = j$ if P_j is the maximum of the predicted probabilities."[45]

21.7.1b. The Conditional Logit Model. When the data consist of choice-specific attributes instead of individual-specific characteristics, the appropriate model is

$$\text{Prob}(Y_i = j) = \frac{e^{\beta' z_{ij}}}{\sum_J e^{\beta' z_{ij}}}. \tag{21–48}$$

Here, we let $j = 1, 2, \ldots, J$ for a total of J alternatives. The model is otherwise essentially the same as the multinomial logit. However, even more care will be required in interpreting the parameters. Once again, an example will help to focus ideas.

EXAMPLE 21.15 _____

Hensher (1986) estimated a model of mode choice for urban travel for a sample of Sydney commuters. The four choices were Car/Driver (C/D), Car/Passenger, Train, and Bus. For a basic model, the attributes were (1) a Car/Driver dummy, (2) a Car/Passenger dummy, (3) a Train dummy, (4) In-Vehicle Time (in minutes), (5) Waiting Time (in minutes), (6) Walking Time (in minutes), (7) In-Vehicle Costs, (8) Parking Cost, (9) Number of Household Business Vehicles Required, and (10) Percentage of Travel Cost Covered by a Nonhousehold Source [(9) and (10) for C/D only]. The sample consists of 1455 observations. A summary of the data is given in Table 21.7.

TABLE 21.7 Summary Statistics for Model Structure

	In-Veh. Cost	In-Veh. Time	Walk Time	Wait Time	Number Choosing
C/D	64.56	28.65	0.76	0.15	953
C/P	4.37	28.32	0.71	2.89	78
Train	98.23	43.84	10.50	8.37	279
Bus	81.61	38.15	7.47	7.11	145

C/D only: Parking cost = 26.59
            Household business vehicles = 0.186
            Percent travel cost paid for = 17.58

Source: Hensher (1986, p. 14). Standard deviations given by Hensher are omitted.

---

[45] Unfortunately, it is common for this rule to predict all observations with the same value in an unbalanced sample or a model with little explanatory power.

Hensher reports the results listed in Table 21.8.

TABLE 21.8 Parameter Estimates (*t* Values in Parentheses)

(1)	0.8973	(4.86)	(2)	−2.2154 (−10.36)
(3)	1.3286	(9.10)	(4)	−0.0227 (−4.70)
(5)	−0.1336 (−6.68)		(6)	−0.0672 (−5.44)
(7)	−0.0063 (−5.03)		(8)	−0.0086 (−5.05)
(9)	0.4524	(1.83)	(10)	0.0119 (3.71)

Log likelihood at $\beta = 0$ = −2017.1
Log likelihood (sample shares) = −1426.6
Log likelihood at convergence = −598.2

At the sample means given here, the four predicted probabilities and predicted frequencies are given in Table 21.9.

TABLE 21.9

	C/D	C/P	Train	Bus
Probability	0.88625	0.03799	0.01390	0.06186
Predicted N	1290	55	20	90
Actual N	953	78	279	145

Elasticities of Probabilities
with Respect to In-vehicle Cost

	Attribute Level of:			
Mode	C/D	C/P	Train	Bus
CD	−0.077	0.253	0.253	0.253
CP	0.002	−0.013	0.002	0.002
Train	0.098	0.098	−0.231	0.098
Bus	0.042	0.042	0.042	−0.292

In this model, the coefficients are not directly tied to the marginal effects. The marginal effects for continuous variables can be obtained by differentiating (21–48) with respect to **x** to obtain

$$\frac{\partial P_j}{\partial \mathbf{x}_j} = P_j(1 - P_j)\boldsymbol{\beta},$$

$$\frac{\partial P_j}{\partial \mathbf{x}_k} = -P_j P_k \boldsymbol{\beta}.$$

(To avoid cluttering the notation, we have dropped the observation subscript.) It is clear that through its presence in P_j and P_k, every attribute set $\mathbf{x}_j$ affects all of the probabilities.

Hensher suggests that one might prefer to report elasticities of the probabilities. These would be

$$\frac{\partial \ln P_j}{\partial \ln x_{jm}} = \beta_m x_{jm}(1 - P_j),$$

$$\frac{\partial \ln P_j}{\partial \ln x_{km}} = -\beta_m x_{km} P_j.$$

Since there is no ambiguity about the scale of the probability itself, whether one should report the derivatives or the elasticities is largely a matter of taste. Some of Hensher's elasticity estimates are presented in the previous example.

Estimation of the conditional logit model is simplest by Newton's method or the method of scoring. The log likelihood is the same as for the multinomial logit model. Once again, we define $d_{ij} = 1$ if $Y_i = j$ and 0 otherwise. Then

$$\ln L = \sum_i d_{ij} \ln \text{Prob}(d_{ij} = 1).$$

Because of the simple form of L, the gradient and Hessian have particularly convenient forms:

$$\frac{\partial \ln L}{\partial \boldsymbol{\beta}} = \sum_i \sum_j P_{ij}(\mathbf{x}_{ij} - \bar{\mathbf{x}}_i)$$

$$\frac{\partial^2 \ln L}{\partial \boldsymbol{\beta} \, \partial \boldsymbol{\beta}'} = -\sum_i \sum_j P_{ij}(\mathbf{x}_{ij} - \bar{\mathbf{x}}_i)(\mathbf{x}_{ij} - \bar{\mathbf{x}}_i)',$$

where

$$\bar{\mathbf{x}}_i = \sum_j P_{ij} \mathbf{x}_{ij}.$$

Once again, Newton's method and the method of scoring are equivalent and should converge readily. In this setting, the size of the estimation problem is independent of the number of choices. It is feasible to estimate a model for up to 100 or more alternatives. (Whether it is reasonable to model consumer choices with this many alternatives is a different question.) A data set constructed with more than a few choices is likely to be quite cumbersome. In this context, it is the data that proliferate with the number of choices, and far faster than the number of parameters did in the previous model. Every new choice added to the set adds a new row to the data set for every observation. For the example, the four-outcome model requires $4 \times 1455 = 5820$ rows. Adding only one more alternative would add another 1455 rows of data.

The usual problems of fit measures appear here. The log-likelihood ratio and tabulation of actual versus predicted choices will be useful. There are two possible constrained log likelihoods. Since the model cannot contain a constant term, the constraint $\boldsymbol{\beta} = \mathbf{0}$ renders all probabilities equal to $1/J$. The constrained log likelihood for this constraint is then $L_0 = -n \ln J$. Of course, it is unlikely that this hypothesis would fail to be rejected. Alternatively, we could fit the model with only the $J - 1$ choice-specific dummy variables. This makes the constrained log likelihood the same as in the multinomial logit model, $\ln L_0^* = \Sigma_j n_j \ln P_j$.

21.7.1c. The Independence of Irrelevant Alternatives.

We noted earlier that the odds ratios in the multinomial logit or conditional logit models are independent of the other alternatives. This is a convenient property as regards estimation, but it is not a particularly appealing restriction to place on consumer behavior. The property of the logit model whereby P_j/P_k is independent of the remaining probabilities is termed the **independence of irrelevant alternatives.** An example of the problem is suggested by Hensher's data. The model allocates 89 percent of the passengers to cars as drivers. Thus, the odds ratio between cars as drivers and buses is 0.89/0.06, or about 14.8 to 1. Suppose that we differentiate by type of car, domestic and foreign, and it happens to be an even split. We might expect the 89 percent of the population who drive to work to divide themselves evenly and the others to continue as they did before. Unfortunately, if they do, the odds between each car type and bus will fall to 7.4 to 1. In order to preserve the 14.8 to 1 odds ratio between cars and buses, half of the bus riders will be switched either to the train or to cars as passengers.

The independence assumption follows from the initial assumption that the disturbances are independent. Two tests have been developed for testing the validity of the assumption. Hausman and McFadden (1984) suggest that if a subset of the choice set truly is irrelevant, omitting it from the model altogether will not change parameter estimates systematically. Inclusion of these choices will be inefficient but will not lead to inconsistency. But if the remaining odds ratios are not truly independent of these alternatives, the parameter estimates obtained when these choices are eliminated will be inconsistent. This is the usual basis for Hausman's specification test. The statistic is

$$\chi^2 = (\hat{\boldsymbol{\beta}}_s - \hat{\boldsymbol{\beta}}_f)'[\hat{\mathbf{V}}_s - \hat{\mathbf{V}}_f]^{-1}(\hat{\boldsymbol{\beta}}_s - \hat{\boldsymbol{\beta}}_f),$$

where s indicates the estimators based on the restricted subset, f indicates the estimator based on the full set of choices, and $\hat{\mathbf{V}}_s - \hat{\mathbf{V}}_f$ are the respective estimates of the asymptotic covariance matrices. The statistic is asymptotically distributed as chi-squared with K degrees of freedom.[46]

EXAMPLE 21.16

In Example 21.15, are the odds ratios C/D to Bus and C/D to Train really independent of the presence of the C/P alternative? To use the Hausman test, we would eliminate choice 2, C/P, from the choice set and estimate a three-choice model. Since 78 respondents chose this mode, we would lose 78 observations. In addition, for every data vector left in the sample, the second attribute, which is the C/P dummy, would always be zero. Thus, this parameter could not be estimated. We would drop this variable. The test would be based on the two estimators of the nine remaining parameters.

If the independence of irrelevant alternatives test fails, an alternative to the multinomial logit model may be needed. The natural alternative is a multivariate probit model:

$$U_j = \boldsymbol{\beta}'\mathbf{x}_j + \varepsilon_j, \qquad j = 1, \ldots J.$$
$$[\varepsilon_1, \varepsilon_2, \ldots, \varepsilon_J] \sim N[\mathbf{0}, \boldsymbol{\Sigma}].$$

We had considered this model earlier but found that as a general model of consumer choice, its failing was the practical difficulty of computing the multinormal integral. Hausman and Wise (1978) point out that for a model of consumer choice, the probit model may not be so impractical as it might seem. First, for J choices, the comparisons implicit in $U_j > U_k$ for $k \neq j$ involve the $J - 1$ differences, $\varepsilon_j - \varepsilon_k$. Thus, starting with a J-dimensional problem, we need only consider $J - 1$ order probabilities. Second, as we saw

[46] McFadden (1987) shows how this hypothesis can also be tested using a Lagrange multiplier test.

earlier, the derivatives of the L-variate normal distribution involve only $L-1$ variate probabilities. It is not necessary to compute the log-likelihood function in order to maximize it, only its derivatives. Therefore, to come to a concrete example, a model with four choices requires only the evaluation of bivariate normal integrals, which is well within the received technology.

21.7.2. Ordered Data

Some multinomial-choice variables are inherently ordered. Examples that have appeared in the literature are the following:

1. Bond ratings.
2. Results of taste tests.
3. Opinion surveys.
4. The assignment of military personnel to job classifications by skill level.
5. Voting outcomes on certain programs.
6. The level of insurance coverage taken by a consumer: none, part, or full.
7. Employment: unemployed, part time, or full time.

In each of these cases, although the outcome is discrete, the multinomial logit or probit models would fail to account for the ordinal nature of the dependent variable.[47] However, ordinary regression analysis would err in the opposite direction. Take the outcome of an opinion survey. If the responses are coded 0, 1, 2, 3, or 4, linear regression would treat the difference between a 4 and a 3 the same as that between a 3 and a 2, while in fact they are only a ranking.

The ordered probit and logit models have come into fairly wide use as a framework for analyzing such responses (Zavoina and McElvey, 1975). The model is built around a latent regression in the same manner as the binomial probit model. We begin with

$$y^* = \boldsymbol{\beta}'\mathbf{x} + \varepsilon.$$

As usual, y^* is unobserved. What we do observe is

$$
\begin{aligned}
y &= 0 && \text{if } y^* \leq 0,\\
&= 1 && \text{if } 0 < y^* \leq \mu_1,\\
&= 2 && \text{if } \mu_1 < y^* \leq \mu_2,\\
&\ \ \vdots\\
&= J && \text{if } \mu_{J-1} \leq y^*.
\end{aligned}
$$

This is a form of censoring. The μ's are unknown parameters to be estimated with $\boldsymbol{\beta}$. Consider, for example, an opinion survey. The respondents have their own intensity of feelings, which depends on certain measurable factors, $\mathbf{x}$, and certain unobservable factors, ε. In principle, they could respond to the questionnaire with their own y^* if asked to do so. Given only, say, five possible answers, they choose the cell that most closely represents their own feelings on the question.

---

[47] In two recent papers, Beggs et al. (1981) and Hausman and Ruud (1986), the authors have begun to explore the possibility of using a richer specification of the logit model when respondents provide their rankings of the full set of alternatives in addition to the identity of the most preferred choice. This application falls somewhere between the conditional logit model and the ones we shall discuss here, in that rather than provide a single choice among J either unordered or ordered alternatives, the consumer chooses one of the $J!$ possible orderings of the set of unordered alternatives.

As before, we assume that ε is normally distributed across observations. For the same reasons as in the binomial probit model (which is the special case of $J = 1$), we normalize the mean and variance of ε to zero and one. (The model can also be estimated with a logistically distributed disturbance. This is a trivial modification of the formulation and appears to make virtually no difference in practice.) With the normal distribution, we have the following probabilities:

$$\text{Prob}(y = 0) = \Phi(-\boldsymbol{\beta}'\mathbf{x}),$$

$$\text{Prob}(y = 1) = \Phi(\mu_1 - \boldsymbol{\beta}'\mathbf{x}) - \Phi(-\boldsymbol{\beta}'\mathbf{x}),$$

$$\text{Prob}(y = 2) = \Phi(\mu_2 - \boldsymbol{\beta}'\mathbf{x}) - \Phi(\mu_1 - \boldsymbol{\beta}'\mathbf{x}),$$

$$\vdots$$

$$\text{Prob}(y = J) = 1 - \Phi(\mu_{J-1} - \boldsymbol{\beta}'\mathbf{x}).$$

In order for all of the probabilities to be positive, we must have

$$0 < \mu_1 < \mu_2 < \cdots < \mu_{J-1}.$$

Figure 21.3 shows the implications of the structure. It is evident that this is a generalization of the probit model we looked at earlier. The log-likelihood function and its derivatives can be obtained readily, and optimization can be done by the usual means.

As usual, the marginal effects of the regressors, $\mathbf{x}$, on the probabilities are not equal to the coefficients. It is helpful to consider a simple example. Suppose that there are three categories. This implies only one unknown threshold parameter. The three probabilities are

$$\text{Prob}(y = 0) = 1 - \Phi(\boldsymbol{\beta}'\mathbf{x}),$$

$$\text{Prob}(y = 1) = \Phi(\mu - \boldsymbol{\beta}'\mathbf{x}) - \Phi(-\boldsymbol{\beta}'\mathbf{x}),$$

$$\text{Prob}(y = 2) = 1 - \Phi(\mu - \boldsymbol{\beta}'\mathbf{x}).$$

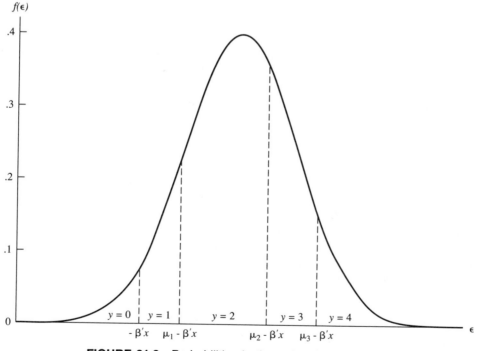

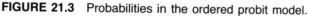

FIGURE 21.3 Probabilities in the ordered probit model.

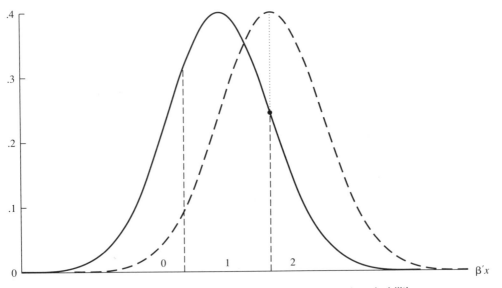

FIGURE 21.4 Effects of change in x on predicted probabilities.

For the three probabilities, the marginal effects of changes in the regressors are

$$\frac{\partial\ \text{Prob}(y = 0)}{\partial\mathbf{x}} = -\phi(\boldsymbol{\beta}'\mathbf{x})\boldsymbol{\beta},$$

$$\frac{\partial\ \text{Prob}(y = 1)}{\partial\mathbf{x}} = (\phi(-\boldsymbol{\beta}'\mathbf{x}) - \phi(\mu - \boldsymbol{\beta}'\mathbf{x}))\boldsymbol{\beta},$$

$$\frac{\partial\ \text{Prob}(y = 2)}{\partial\mathbf{x}} = \phi(\mu - \boldsymbol{\beta}'\mathbf{x})\boldsymbol{\beta}.$$

Figure 21.4 illustrates the effect. The probability distributions of y and y^* are shown in the solid curve. Increasing one of the **x**'s while holding $\boldsymbol{\beta}$ and μ constant is equivalent to shifting the distribution slightly to the right, which is shown as the dashed curve. The effect of the shift is unambiguously to shift some mass out of the leftmost cell. Assuming that $\boldsymbol{\beta}$ is positive (for this **x**), this means that $\text{Prob}(y = 0)$ must decline. Alternatively, from the previous expression, it is obvious that the derivative of $\text{Prob}(y = 0)$ has the opposite sign from $\boldsymbol{\beta}$. By a similar logic, the change in $\text{Prob}(y = 2)$ [or $\text{Prob}(y = J)$ in the general case] must have the same sign as $\boldsymbol{\beta}$. Assuming that the particular $\boldsymbol{\beta}$ is positive, we are shifting some probability into the rightmost cell. But what happens to the middle cell is ambiguous. It depends on the two densities. In the general case, relative to the signs of the coefficients, only the signs of the changes in $\text{Prob}(y = 0)$ and $\text{Prob}(y = J)$ are unambiguous! The upshot is that we must be very careful in interpreting the coefficients in this model. This is the least obvious of all of the models we have considered. Indeed, without a fair amount of extra calculation, it is quite unclear how the coefficients in the ordered probit model should be interpreted.[48]

---

[48] This point seems uniformly to be overlooked in the received literature. Authors routinely report coefficients and t ratios, occasionally with some commentary about significant effects, but rarely suggest upon what or in what direction those effects are exerted.

EXAMPLE 21.17 Rating Assignments _____

Marcus and Greene (1985) estimated an ordered probit model for the job assignments of new Navy recruits. The Navy attempts to direct recruits into job classifications in which they will be most productive. The broad classifications the authors analyzed were technical jobs with three clearly ranked skill ratings: "medium skilled," "highly skilled," and "nuclear qualified/highly skilled." Since the assignment is partly based on the Navy's own assessment and needs and partly on factors specific to the individual, an ordered probit model was used with the following determinants: (1) ENSPE = a dummy variable indicating that the individual entered the Navy with an "A school" (technical training) guarantee, (2) EDMA = educational level of the entrant's mother, (3) AFQT = score on the Air Force Qualifying Test, (4) EDYRS = years of education completed by the trainee, (5) MARR = a dummy variable indicating that the individual was married at the time of enlistment, and (6) AGEAT = trainee's age at the time of enlistment. The sample size was 5641. The results are reported in Table 21.10. The extremely large t ratio on the AFQT score is to be expected, since it is a primary sorting device used to assign job classifications. In order to obtain the marginal effects of the continuous variables, we require the standard normal density evaluated at $-\beta'\overline{x} = -0.8479$ and $\mu - \beta'\overline{x} = 0.9421$. The predicted probabilities are $\Phi(-0.8479) = 0.198$, $\Phi(0.9421) - \Phi(-0.8479) = 0.628$, and $1 - \Phi(0.9421) = 0.173$. (The actual frequencies were 0.25, 0.52, and 0.23.) The two densities are $\phi(-0.8479) = 0.278$ and $\phi(0.9421) = 0.255$. Therefore, the derivatives of the three probabilities with respect to AFQT, for example, are:

$$\frac{\partial P_0}{\partial \text{AFQT}} = (-0.278)0.039 \qquad = -0.01084,$$

$$\frac{\partial P_1}{\partial \text{AFQT}} = (0.278 - 0.255)0.039 = 0.0009,$$

$$\frac{\partial P_2}{\partial \text{AFQT}} = 0.255(0.039) \qquad = 0.00995.$$

Note that the marginal effects sum to zero; this follows from the requirement that the probabilities add to one. This approach is not appropriate for evaluating the effect of a dummy variable. We can analyze a dummy variable by comparing the probabilities that result when the variable takes its two different values with those that occur with the other variables held at their sample means. For example, for the MARR variable, we have the results given in Table 21.11.

TABLE 21.10

Variable	Estimate	t ratio	Mean of Variable
Constant	−4.34	—	—
ENSPA	0.057	1.7	0.66
EDMA	0.007	0.8	12.1
AFQT	0.039	39.9	71.2
EDYRS	0.190	8.7	12.1
MARR	−0.48	−9.0	0.08
AGEAT	0.0015	0.1	18.8
μ	1.79	80.8	—

TABLE 21.11

	$-\hat{\beta}'\mathbf{x}$	$\hat{\mu} - \hat{\beta}'\mathbf{x}$	Prob($y = 0$)	Prob($y = 1$)	Prob($y = 2$)
MARR = 0	−0.8863	0.9037	0.187	0.629	0.184
MARR = 1	−0.4063	1.3837	0.342	0.574	0.084
Change			0.155	−0.055	−0.100

21.8. A Poisson Model for Count Data

The data on ship accidents analyzed in Example 8.2 are typical of count data. (They are reproduced in Table 21.12.) In principle, we could analyze them using multiple linear regression, as we did in Example 8.2. But the preponderance of zeroes and small values and the clearly discrete nature of the dependent variable suggest that we could improve on least squares with a model that accounts for these characteristics. The Poisson regression model has been widely used to study such data.

TABLE 21.12

	Ship Type					Year Constructed				Accidents		
	A	B	C	D	E	60–64	65–69	70–74	75–79	Service	Actual	Fitted
1	1	0	0	0	0	1	0	0	0	127	0	3.12
2	1	0	0	0	0	0	1	0	0	63	4	4.63
3	1	0	0	0	0	0	0	1	0	1,095	18	14.70
4	1	0	0	0	0	0	0	0	1	2,244	11	10.54
5	0	1	0	0	0	1	0	0	0	17,176	29	23.05
6	0	1	0	0	0	0	1	0	0	20,370	53	54.38
7	0	1	0	0	0	0	0	1	0	13,099	44	52.85
8	0	1	0	0	0	0	0	0	1	7,117	18	13.71
9	0	0	1	0	0	1	0	0	0	1,179	1	0.55
10	0	0	1	0	0	0	1	0	0	676	1	0.76
11	0	0	1	0	0	0	0	1	0	1,948	2	2.50
12	0	0	1	0	0	0	0	0	1	274	1	1.20
13	0	0	0	1	0	1	0	0	0	251	0	1.44
14	0	0	0	1	0	0	1	0	0	288	0	2.16
15	0	0	0	1	0	0	0	1	0	1,208	11	6.76
16	0	0	0	1	0	0	0	0	1	2,051	4	4.64
17	0	0	0	0	1	1	0	0	0	45	0	1.84
18	0	0	0	0	1	0	1	0	0	789	7	3.06
19	0	0	0	0	1	0	0	1	0	2,161	12	10.19
20	0	0	0	0	1	0	0	0	1	542	1	4.92

EXAMPLE 21.18 _____

The number of accidents for a sample of ships are listed in Table 21.12. The ships are one of five types constructed in one of four periods. Service is an indicator of the amount of service the ship has seen.[49]

---

[49] Data are from McCullagh and Nelder (1983). See Example 8.2 for details.

The Poisson regression model has been used by a number of authors to analyze count data. The model stipulates that each y_i is drawn from a Poisson distribution with parameter λ_i, which is related to the regressors, $\mathbf{x}_i$. The primary equation of the model is

$$\text{Prob}(Y_i = y_i) = \frac{e^{-\lambda_i} \lambda_i^{y_i}}{y_i!}, \qquad y_i = 0, 1, 2, \ldots$$

The most common formulation for λ_i is

$$\ln \lambda_i = \boldsymbol{\beta}' \mathbf{x}_i.$$

It is easily shown that

$$E[y_i | \mathbf{x}_i] = \text{Var}[y_i | \mathbf{x}_i] = \lambda_i$$
$$= e^{\boldsymbol{\beta}' \mathbf{x}_i},$$

so

$$\frac{\partial E[y_i | \mathbf{x}_i]}{\partial \mathbf{x}_i} = \lambda_i \boldsymbol{\beta}.$$

With the parameter estimates in hand, this can be computed using any data vector desired.

In principle, the Poisson model is simply a nonlinear regression. But it is far easier to estimate the parameters with maximum likelihood techniques. The log-likelihood function is

$$\ln L = \sum_i [-\lambda_i + y_i \boldsymbol{\beta}' \mathbf{x}_i - \ln y_i!].$$

The likelihood equations are

$$\frac{\partial \ln L}{\partial \boldsymbol{\beta}} = \sum_i (y_i - \lambda_i) \mathbf{x}_i = \mathbf{0}.$$

The Hessian is

$$\frac{\partial^2 \ln L}{\partial \boldsymbol{\beta} \, \partial \boldsymbol{\beta}'} = -\sum_i \lambda_i \mathbf{x}_i \mathbf{x}_i'.$$

The Hessian is negative definite for all $\mathbf{x}$ and $\boldsymbol{\beta}$. Newton's method is a simple algorithm for this model and will usually converge rapidly. At convergence, $[\sum_i \hat{\lambda}_i \mathbf{x}_i \mathbf{x}_i']^{-1}$ provides an estimate of the asymptotic covariance matrix for the parameter estimates. Given the estimates, the prediction for observation i is $\hat{\lambda}_i$. A standard error for the prediction interval can be formed by using a linear Taylor series approximation. The estimated variance of the prediction will be $\lambda_i^2 \mathbf{x}_i' \mathbf{V} \mathbf{x}_i$, where $\mathbf{V}$ is the estimated asymptotic covariance matrix for $\hat{\boldsymbol{\beta}}$.

EXAMPLE 21.19

A Poisson regression model is shown in Table 21.13.

The hypothesis that the year of construction is not a significant factor in explaining the number of accidents is strongly rejected by the likelihood ratio test.

$$\chi^2 = -2[-69.931 - (-46.799)] = 46.264.$$

TABLE 21.13

	Unrestricted			Restricted
Log likelihood	−46.799			−69.931
Scale factor for slopes	0.11207			0.08540
Restricted (slopes = 0)			−199.899	
log L				
Mean dependent variable			10.85	

Variable	Coefficient	Asy. t ratio	Coefficient	Asy. t ratio
Constant	1.1211	4.0890	2.0433	11.680
Type = B	−0.43206	−0.98213	0.41778	1.2278
Type = C	−1.8946	−3.9455	−1.8960	−3.9509
Type = D	−0.79328	−2.5474	−0.79275	−2.5458
Type = E	−0.51914	−1.8295	−0.50046	−1.7661
65–69	0.40292	1.6845	—	—
70–74	1.4109	6.1860	—	—
75–79	0.91409	3.1294	—	—
Service	0.0001426	4.6418	0.00007340	3.9668

Two modifications of the Poisson model have been explored by economists. There are cases in which a Poisson model would appear to apply, but the data are censored or truncated. (The difference is explored at length in Chapter 22.) For example, consider the answer to a questionnaire which asks "how many trips to the doctor did you make in the last year?" The responses might be 0, 1, 2, 3, or more. These data are censored. Any observation greater than 3 is masked by being labeled a 3. Alternatively, we might consider a setting in which values of zero for the dependent variable were qualitatively different from the other values. For example, if the response variable is the number of trips to a particular recreational facility that were made in the last year, then zero might represent a qualitative decision not to visit the site, whereas values greater than zero represent one's choice of the number of visits to make, given that any visits at all would be made. In such a setting, it might make sense to confine attention to the nonzero observations, thereby truncating the distribution of responses. Models with these characteristics can be handled within the Poisson framework by using the laws of probability to modify the likelihood. For example, in the censoring case, the relevant probabilities that enter the log likelihood are

$$P_i = \text{Prob}(y_i = j) = \frac{e^{-\lambda_i}\lambda_i^j}{j!} \quad \text{if } y_i = 0, 1, 2$$

$$P_i = \text{Prob}(y_i \geq 3) = 1 - \text{Prob}(y_i < 3) \quad \text{if } y_i = 3$$

$$= 1 - (\text{Prob}(y_i = 0) + \text{Prob}(y_i = 1) + \text{Prob}(y_i = 2)).$$

A number of alternative cases are discussed by Terza (1985b), Mullahey (1986), Shaw (1988), Grogger and Carson (1991), Greene (1991), and Lambert (1992).

The Poisson model has been criticized because of its implicit assumption that the variance of y_i equals its mean. A number of extensions of the Poisson model that relax this assumption have been proposed by Hausman et al. (1984), McCullagh and Nelder (1983), and Cameron and Trivedi (1986). Aside from the alternative specifications, a number of authors have devised tests for "overdispersion" within the context of the Poisson model. [See Cameron and Trivedi (1990), Gurmu (1991), Lee (1986).]

EXAMPLE 21.20 Overdispersion in the Poisson Model _____

In their presentation of the data used above, McCullagh and Nelder assert, without evidence, that there is overdispersion in the data. Some of their analysis follows on an assumption that the standard deviation of y_i is 1.3 times the mean. Cameron and Trivedi (1990) offer several different tests for overdispersion. A simple procedure used for testing the hypothesis

$$H_0: \quad \text{Var}[y_i] = E[y_i]$$

$$H_1: \quad \text{Var}[y_i] = E[y_i] + \alpha g(E[y_i])$$

is carried out by regressing

$$z_i = \frac{(y_i - \lambda_i)^2 - \lambda_i}{\lambda_i \sqrt{2}},$$

where λ_i is the predicted value from the regression, on either a constant term or λ_i without a constant term. A simple t test of whether the coefficient is significantly different from zero tests H_0 vs. H_1. For the data above, the t statistics for the two regressions are 1.059 and 0.012, respectively, so we do not reject H_0. But see Example 22.13 for a different approach.

EXERCISES

1. A binomial probability model is to be based on the following index function model:

$$y^* = \alpha + \beta d + \varepsilon,$$

$$y = 1 \qquad \text{if } y^* > 0,$$

$$y = 0 \qquad \text{otherwise.}$$

The only regressor, d, is a dummy variable. The data consist of 100 observations that have the following:

		y	
		0	1
	0	24	28
d			
	1	32	16

Obtain the maximum likelihood estimators of α and β, and estimate the asymptotic standard errors of your estimates. Test the hypothesis that β equals zero by using a Wald test (asymptotic t test) and a likelihood ratio test. Use the probit model and then repeat, using the logit model. Do your results change? (**Hint:** Formulate the log likelihood in terms of α and $\delta = \alpha + \beta$.)

2. Suppose that a linear probability model is to be fit to a set of observations on a dependent variable, y, which takes values zero and one, and a single regressor, x, which varies continuously across observations. Obtain the exact expressions for the least squares slope in the regression in terms of the mean(s) and variance of x, and interpret the result.

3. Given the following data set,

$$
\begin{array}{c|ccccccccccc}
Y & 1 & 0 & 0 & 1 & 1 & 0 & 0 & 1 & 1 & 1, \\
\hline
X & 9 & 2 & 5 & 4 & 6 & 7 & 3 & 5 & 2 & 6, \\
\end{array}
$$

estimate a probit model, and test the hypothesis that X is not influential in determining the probability that Y equals one.

4. Construct the Lagrange multiplier statistic for testing the hypothesis that all of the slopes (but not the constant term) equal zero in the binomial logit model. Prove that the Lagrange multiplier statistic is nR^2 in the regression of $(y_i - P)$ on the x's, where P is the sample proportion of ones.

5. We are interested in the ordered probit model. Our data consist of 250 observations, of which the response are

$$
\begin{array}{c|ccccc}
Y & 0 & 1 & 2 & 3 & 4 \\
\hline
n & 50 & 40 & 45 & 80 & 35 \\
\end{array}
$$

Using the preceding data, obtain maximum likelihood estimates of the unknown parameters of the model. (**Hint:** Consider the probabilities as the unknown parameters.)

6. The following hypothetical data give the participation rates in a particular type of recycling program and the number of trucks purchased for collection by 10 towns in a small mid-Atlantic state:

Town	Trucks	Participation (%)
1	160	11
2	250	74
3	170	8
4	365	87
5	210	62
6	206	83
7	203	48
8	305	84
9	270	71
10	340	79

The town of Eleven is contemplating initiating a recycling program but wishes to achieve a 95 percent rate of participation. Using a probit model for your analysis,
  (a) How many trucks would the town expect to have to purchase in order to achieve their goal? (**Hint:** See Section 21.4.3.) Note that you will use $n_i = 1$.
  (b) If trucks cost $20,000 each, is a goal of 90 percent reachable within a budget of $6.5 million? (That is, should they *expect* to reach the goal?)
  (c) According to your model, what is the marginal value of the 301st truck in terms of the increase in the percentage participation?

7. A data set consists of $n = n_1 + n_2 + n_3$ observations on y and x. For the first n_1 observations, $y = 1$ and $x = 1$. For the next n_2 observations, $y = 0$ and $x = 1$. For the last n_3 observations, $y = 0$ and $x = 0$. Prove that neither (21–15) nor (21–17) has a solution.

8. Data on t = strike duration and x = unanticipated industrial production for a number of strikes in each of 9 years are given in Table 22.7. Use the Poisson regression model discussed in Section 21.8 to determine whether x is a significant determinant of the *number of strikes* in a given year.

CHAPTER 22

Limited Dependent Variable and Duration Models

22.1. Introduction

This chapter is concerned with truncation and censoring.[1] The effect of truncation occurs when sample data are drawn from a subset of a larger population of interest. For example, studies of income based on incomes above or below some poverty line may be of limited usefulness for inference about the whole population. This is essentially a characteristic of the distribution from which the sample data are drawn. Censoring is a more common problem in recent studies. To continue the example, suppose that instead of being unobserved, incomes below the poverty line are reported as if they were *at* the poverty line. The censoring of a range of values of the variable of interest introduces a distortion into conventional statistical results similar to that of truncation. Unlike truncation, however, censoring is essentially a defect in the sample data. Presumably, if they were not censored, the data would be a representative sample from the population of interest.

This chapter will discuss four broad topics: truncation, censoring, a form of truncation called the *sample selection problem,* and a class of models called *duration models.* Although most empirical work in the first three involves censoring rather than truncation, we will study the simpler model of truncation first. It provides most of the theoretical tools we need to analyze models of censoring and sample selection. The fourth topic, on models of duration—when will a spell of unemployment or a strike end?—could reasonably stand alone. It does in countless articles and a library of books. We include our introduction to this subject in this chapter because in most applications, duration modeling involves censored data and it is thus convenient to treat duration here (and because we are nearing the end of our survey and yet another chapter seems unwarranted).

22.2. Truncation

In this section, we are concerned with inferring the characteristics of a population from a sample drawn from a restricted part of that population.

---

[1] Four recent surveys of these topics are Dhrymes (1984), Maddala (1983, 1984), and Amemiya (1984). The last is part of a symposium on censored and truncated regression models.

EXAMPLE 22.1 _____

"The typical 'upper affluent American' . . . makes \$142,000 per year. . . . The people surveyed had household of income of at least \$100,000."[2] Does this statistic tell us anything about the "typical American"? As it stands, probably not (popular impressions notwithstanding). The article goes on to state, "If you're in that category, pat yourself on the back—only 2 percent of American households make the grade, according to the survey."

_____

22.2.1. Truncated Distributions

For our purposes, a truncated distribution is the part of an untruncated distribution that is above or below some specified value. For instance, in Example 22.1, we are given a characteristic of the distribution of incomes above \$100,000. This is, of course, only a part of the full distribution.

THEOREM 22.1. DENSITY OF A TRUNCATED RANDOM VARIABLE: *If a continuous random variable, x, has pdf f(x) and a is a constant,*

$$f(x \mid x > a) = \frac{f(x)}{\text{Prob}(x > a)}.\,[3]$$

The proof follows from the definition of conditional probability. This amounts to scaling the density so that it integrates to one over the range above a.

EXAMPLE 22.2 _____

If x has a uniform distribution, $U(0, 1)$,

$$f(x) = 1, \qquad 0 \le x \le 1.$$

For truncation at $x = \frac{1}{3}$,

$$f\left(x \mid x > \frac{1}{3}\right) = \frac{f(x)}{\text{Prob}(x > \frac{1}{3})}$$

$$= \frac{1}{\left(\frac{2}{3}\right)}$$

$$= \tfrac{3}{2}, \qquad \tfrac{1}{3} < x \le 1.$$

_____

Most recent applications use the **truncated normal distribution.** If x has a normal distribution with mean μ and standard deviation σ,

$$\text{Prob}(x > a) = 1 - \Phi\left(\frac{a - \mu}{\sigma}\right)$$

$$= 1 - \Phi(\alpha),$$

---

[2]*New York Post* (1987).

[3]The case of truncation from above instead of below is handled in an analogous fashion and does not require any new results.

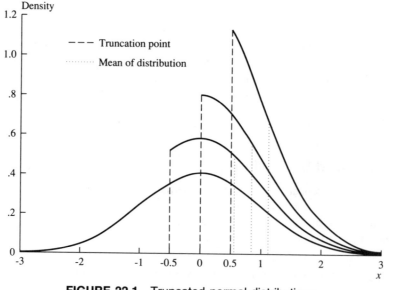

FIGURE 22.1 Truncated normal distributions.

where

$$\alpha = \frac{a - \mu}{\sigma}$$

and $\Phi(.)$ is the standard normal cdf.

The truncated normal distribution is, then,

$$f(x|x > a) = \frac{f(x)}{1 - \Phi(\alpha)}$$

$$= \frac{(2\pi\sigma^2)^{-1/2}e^{-(x-\mu)^2/(2\sigma^2)}}{1 - \Phi(\alpha)}$$

$$= \frac{(1/\sigma)\phi((x - \mu)/\sigma)}{1 - \Phi(\alpha)},$$

where $\phi(.)$ is the standard normal pdf. The **truncated standard normal distribution,** with $\mu = 0$ and $\sigma = 1$, is illustrated for $a = -0.5$, 0, and 0.5 in Figure 22.1. For convenience in what follows, we shall call a random variable whose distribution is truncated a **truncated random variable.**

22.2.2. Moments of Truncated Distributions

We are usually interested in the mean and variance of the truncated random variable. These would be obtained in the usual fashion:

$$E[x|x > a] = \int_a^\infty xf(x|x > a)dx$$

for the mean, and likewise for the variance.

EXAMPLE 22.3

For the uniformly distributed random variable in Example 22.2,

$$E[x \,|\, x > \tfrac{1}{3}] = \int_{1/3}^{1} x(\tfrac{3}{2}) dx = \tfrac{2}{3}.$$

For a variable distributed uniformly between L and U, the variance is $(U - L)^2/12$. Thus,

$$\mathrm{Var}[x \,|\, x > \tfrac{1}{3}] = \tfrac{1}{27}.$$

The mean and variance of the untruncated distribution are $\tfrac{1}{2}$ and $\tfrac{1}{12}$, respectively.

Example 22.3 illustrates two results.

1. If the truncation is from below, the mean of the truncated variable is greater than the mean of the original one. If the truncation is from above, the mean of the truncated variable is smaller than the mean of the original one.
2. Truncation reduces the variance compared to the variance in the untruncated distribution.

Henceforth, we shall use the terms **truncated mean** and **truncated variance** to refer to the mean and variance in the truncated distribution.

For the truncated normal distribution, we have the following theorem:[4]

THEOREM 22.2. MOMENTS OF THE TRUNCATED NORMAL DISTRIBUTION: *If $x \sim N[\mu, \sigma^2]$ and a is a constant,*

$$E[x \,|\, \text{truncation}] = \mu + \sigma\lambda(\alpha) \tag{22-1}$$

$$\mathrm{Var}[x \,|\, \text{truncation}] = \sigma^2(1 - \delta(\alpha)), \tag{22-2}$$

where $\alpha = (a - \mu)/\sigma$ and

$$\lambda(\alpha) = \frac{\phi(\alpha)}{1 - \Phi(\alpha)} \qquad \text{if truncation is } x > a, \tag{22-3a}$$

$$\lambda(\alpha) = \frac{-\phi(\alpha)}{\Phi(\alpha)} \qquad \text{if truncation is } x < a, \tag{22-3b}$$

$$\delta(\alpha) = \lambda(\alpha)(\lambda(\alpha) - \alpha). \tag{22-4}$$

An important result is

$$0 < \delta(\alpha) < 1, \qquad \text{for all values of } \alpha.$$

This implies (2) earlier. A result that we will use at several points below is

$$\frac{d\phi(\alpha)}{d\alpha} = -\alpha\phi(\alpha).$$

The function $\lambda(\alpha)$ is called the **inverse Mills ratio.** The function (22–3a) is also the **hazard function** for the distribution. The mean of the truncated standard normal distribution as a function of the truncation point is shown in Figure 22.2. A useful way to view truncation is in terms of the probability that x is less than a, which we shall call the **degree of truncation.** This is an increasing function of a. As this probability rises, a greater proportion of the distribution is being discarded, and the mean rises accordingly. Figure 22.3 shows the relationship between $E[x \,|\, x > a]$ and $\mathrm{Prob}[x > a]$ for the standard normal distribution.

[4] Details may be found in Johnson and Kotz (1970, p. 81).

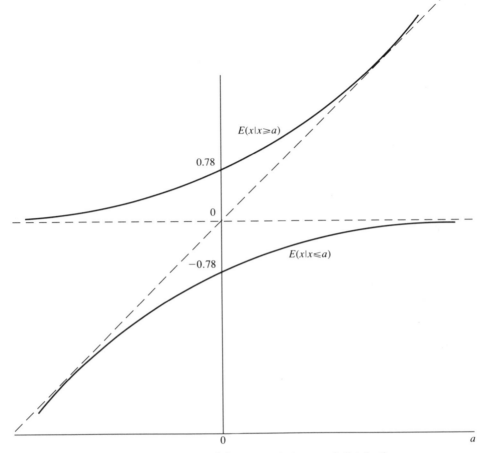

FIGURE 22.2 Mean of the truncated normal distribution.

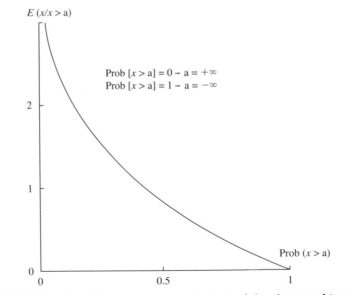

FIGURE 22.3 Conditional mean as a function of the degree of truncation.

EXAMPLE 22.4

Continuing Example 22.1, since the degree of truncation in the sample is 98 percent, the $142,000 is probably quite far from the mean in the full population.

Suppose that incomes in the population are lognormally distributed.[5] Then the log of income has a normal distribution with, say, mean μ and standard deviation σ. Let $y = \ln x$. Two useful numbers for this example are $\ln 100 = 4.605$ and $\ln 142 = 4.956$. Suppose that the survey is large enough for us to treat the sample average as the true mean. The article states that

$$E[y|y > 4.605] = 4.956.$$

It also tells us that $\text{Prob}[y > 4.605] = 0.02$. From Theorem 22.2,

$$E[y|y > 4.605] = \mu + \frac{\sigma\phi(\alpha)}{1 - \Phi(\alpha)},$$

where

$$\alpha = \frac{4.605 - \mu}{\sigma}.$$

But we know that $\Phi(\alpha) = 0.98$, so $\alpha = \Phi^{-1}(0.98) = 2.054$. Continuing, then,

$$\text{(a)} \quad 2.054\sigma = 4.605 - \mu.$$

In addition, given $\alpha = 2.054$, $\phi(\alpha) = \phi(2.054) = 0.0484$. From (22–1), then,

$$4.956 = \mu + \sigma\left(\frac{0.0484}{0.02}\right)$$

or

$$\text{(b)} \quad 4.956 = \mu + 2.420\sigma.$$

The solutions to (a) and (b) are

$$\mu = 2.635 \quad \text{and} \quad \sigma = 0.959.$$

To obtain the mean income, we use the result

$$\text{If } z \sim N[\mu, \sigma^2], \quad E[e^z] = e^{\mu + \sigma^2/2}.$$

Inserting our values for μ and σ gives $E[z] = \$22,087$.[6]

22.2.3. The Truncated Regression Model

In the model of the earlier examples, we now assume that

$$\mu = \boldsymbol{\beta}'\mathbf{x}_i,$$

the deterministic part of the classical regression model. Then

$$y_i = \boldsymbol{\beta}'\mathbf{x}_i + \varepsilon_i,$$

where

$$\varepsilon_i \sim N[0, \sigma^2],$$

---

[5] See Section 3.4.4.

[6] The 1987 *Statistical Abstract of the United States* lists average household income across all groups for the United States as about $25,000.

so that

$$y_i \mid \mathbf{x}_i \sim N[\boldsymbol{\beta}'\mathbf{x}_i, \, \sigma^2].$$

We are interested in the distribution of y_i given that y_i is greater than the truncation point, a. This is precisely the model described in Theorem 22.2. It follows that

$$E[y_i \mid y_i > a] = \boldsymbol{\beta}'\mathbf{x}_i + \sigma \frac{\phi((a - \boldsymbol{\beta}'\mathbf{x}_i)/\sigma)}{1 - \Phi((a - \boldsymbol{\beta}'\mathbf{x}_i)\sigma)}. \tag{22-5}$$

The conditional mean is therefore a nonlinear function of $\mathbf{x}$ and $\boldsymbol{\beta}$.

The marginal effects in this model *in the subpopulation* can be obtained by writing

$$E[y_i \mid y_i > a] = \boldsymbol{\beta}'\mathbf{x} + \sigma\lambda(\alpha_i), \tag{22-6}$$

where now $\alpha_i = (a - \boldsymbol{\beta}'\mathbf{x}_i)/\sigma$. Then

$$\frac{\partial E[y \mid y > a]}{\partial \mathbf{x}} = \boldsymbol{\beta} + \sigma\left(\frac{d\lambda_i}{d\alpha_i}\right)\frac{\partial \alpha_i}{\partial \mathbf{x}}$$

$$= \boldsymbol{\beta} + \sigma(\lambda_i^2 - \alpha_i\lambda_i)\left(-\frac{\boldsymbol{\beta}}{\sigma}\right) \tag{22-7}$$

$$= \boldsymbol{\beta}(1 - \lambda_i^2 + \alpha_i\lambda_i)$$

$$= \boldsymbol{\beta}(1 - \delta(\alpha_i)).$$

Note the appearance of the truncated variance. Since the truncated variance is between zero and one, we conclude that for every element of $\mathbf{x}$, the marginal effect is less than the corresponding coefficient. There is a similar attenuation of the variance. In the subpopulation $y_i > a$, the regression variance is not σ^2 but

$$\text{Var}[y_i \mid y_i > a] = \sigma^2(1 - \delta(\alpha_i)).$$

Whether the marginal effect in (22-7) or the coefficient $\boldsymbol{\beta}$ itself is of interest depends on the intended inferences of the study. If the analysis is to be confined to the subpopulation, (22-7) is of interest. However, if the study is intended to extend to the entire population, it is the coefficients $\boldsymbol{\beta}$ that are actually of interest.

EXAMPLE 22.5 _____

Hausman and Wise (1977) estimated an earnings equation for low-income families.[7] The truncation in their model is from above, with thresholds at poverty levels defined as a function of family size. Their model links the log of earnings to education, a score on an intelligence test, a union membership dummy variable, the number of months in vocational training, a dummy variable equal to one if the individual reported having an illness that limited the ability to work, and age. The assumption implicit in the model is that there is a linear equation connecting these variables in the full population that we seek to study, using data drawn from the subpopulation of people with incomes below the poverty levels. The discussion of the estimates in the article appears to indicate particular attention to the group from which the sample is drawn, not the population at large. (A set of estimates is presented in Example 22.6.)

_____

[7]A similar set of results is presented in Crawford (1975).

22.2.3a. Least Squares Estimation. We now consider estimation of the parameters of the truncated regression. One's first inclination might be to use ordinary least squares. For the subpopulation from which the data are drawn, we could write (22-6) in the form

$$y_i | y_i > a = E[y_i | y_i > a] + u_i$$
$$= \boldsymbol{\beta}' \mathbf{x}_i + \sigma \lambda_i + u_i, \tag{22-8}$$

where u_i is y_i minus its conditional expectation. By construction, u_i has a zero mean, but it is heteroscedastic,

$$\text{Var}[u_i] = \sigma^2 (1 - \lambda_i^2 + \lambda_i \alpha_i),$$

which is a function of $\mathbf{x}_i$. If we estimate (22-8) by ordinary least squares regression of $\mathbf{y}$ on $\mathbf{X}$, we have omitted a variable, the nonlinear term λ_i. All of the biases that arise because of an omitted variable can be expected.

Without some knowledge of the distribution of $\mathbf{x}$, it is not possible to determine how serious the bias is likely to be. A result obtained by Cheung and Goldberger (1984) is broadly suggestive. If $E[\mathbf{x}|y]$ in the full population is a linear function of y, then

$$\text{plim } \mathbf{b} = \boldsymbol{\beta}\tau$$

for some proportionality constant, τ. This is consistent with the widely observed (albeit rather rough) proportionality relationship between least squares estimates of this model and consistent maximum likelihood estimates.[8] The proportionality result appears to be quite general. In applications, it is usually found that, compared to consistent maximum likelihood estimates, the OLS estimates are biased toward zero. (See Example 22.6.)

22.2.3b. Maximum Likelihood Estimation. As specified in Theorem 22.1,

$$f(y_i) = \frac{\dfrac{1}{\sigma} \phi((y_i - \boldsymbol{\beta}'\mathbf{x}_i)/\sigma)}{1 - \Phi((a - \boldsymbol{\beta}'\mathbf{x}_i)/\sigma)}.$$

The log likelihood is the sum of logs of these densities,

$$\ln L = -\frac{n}{2}(\ln(2\pi) + \ln \sigma^2) - \frac{1}{2\sigma^2} \sum_i (y_i - \boldsymbol{\beta}'\mathbf{x}_i)^2 \tag{22-9}$$

$$- \sum_i \ln\left[1 - \Phi\left(\frac{a - \boldsymbol{\beta}'\mathbf{x}_i}{\sigma}\right)\right].$$

Maximization, while rather involved because of the extreme nonlinearity of the function, is straightforward in principle using the methods of Chapter 12. After a small amount of manipulation, the necessary conditions for maximizing (22-9) reduce to

$$\frac{\partial \ln L}{\partial \boldsymbol{\beta}} = \sum_i \left[\frac{y_i - \boldsymbol{\beta}'\mathbf{x}_i}{\sigma^2} - \frac{\lambda_i}{\sigma}\right]\mathbf{x}_i = \mathbf{0},$$

$$\frac{\partial \ln L}{\partial \sigma^2} = \sum_i \left[-\frac{1}{2\sigma^2} + \frac{(y_i - \boldsymbol{\beta}'\mathbf{x}_i)^2}{2\sigma^4} - \frac{\alpha_i \lambda_i}{2\sigma^2}\right] = 0, \tag{22-10}$$

---

[8] See, as well, the appendix in Hausman and Wise (1977) and Greene (1983b).

where

$$\alpha_i = \frac{a - \boldsymbol{\beta}'\mathbf{x}_i}{\sigma}$$

and

$$\lambda_i = \frac{\phi(\alpha_i)}{1 - \Phi(\alpha_i)}.$$

The Hessian for this model is quite involved. [See Olsen (1978) for a simplification.] Hausman and Wise suggest using the Berndt et al. estimator during the iterations and to obtain the standard errors instead. This involves summing the outer product of the vectors in (22–10) which are written by individual observation to suggest the computation involved.[9]

EXAMPLE 22.6

Hausman and Wise report the estimates listed in Table 22.1 for the study described in the previous example. Standard errors are given in parentheses. The authors used 684 observations. The marginal effects are computed using (22–7), with an assumed income cutoff of $5002. In the study, this was used for a family of four. The scale factor is 0.2456. Since the dependent variable is measured in logarithms, the effects are given in percentages. (The authors did not present these marginal effects.)

TABLE 22.1

	Least Squares	Maximum Likelihood	Mean of X	Marginal Effect (%)
Constant	8.2030	9.1023	1.00	
	(0.0910)	(0.0255)		
Education	0.0095	0.0146	8.76	0.36
	(0.0057)	(0.0070)		
IQ	0.0016	0.0061	33.5	0.14
	(0.0016)	(0.0048)		
Training	0.0022	0.0065	3.27	0.14
	(0.0016)	(0.0031)		
Union	0.0900	0.2463	0.56	
	(0.0305)	(0.0887)		
Illness	−0.0761	−0.2259	0.21	
	(0.0378)	(0.1069)		
Age	−0.0030	−0.0162	36.7	−0.39
	(0.0018)	(0.0053)		
σ	0.391	0.618	$\sigma_{y|x} = 0.306$	

The authors note, for example, that "If we interpret the coefficient on education as the rate of return to a year of education, we find that it is quite low, approximately 1.6 percent" (p. 926). (The coefficient 0.0165 is reported for a model with a different specification for the age variable.) The surrounding discussion is obviously directed at low-income people in the sample, for which, in view of (22–7), their observation rather understates the case. Their estimate of the return to a year of education *for the low-income people in their sample* is closer to about 0.4 percent.

---

[9] In fact, Olsen's results make Newton's method and the actual Hessian a preferable approach. This is detailed in Section 22.3.3.

22.3. Censored Data

A very common problem in microeconomic data is censoring of the dependent variable. When the dependent variable is censored, values in a certain range are all transformed to (or reported as) a single value.[10]

EXAMPLE 22.7 _____

We are interested in the number of tickets *demanded* for events at a certain arena. Our only measure is the number actually *sold*. However, whenever an event sells out, we know that the actual number demanded is larger than the number sold. The number of tickets demanded is censored when it is transformed to obtain the number sold.

Some other examples that have appeared in the empirical literature are as follows:[11]

1. Household purchases of durable goods.[12]
2. The number of extramarital affairs.[13]
3. The number of hours worked by a woman in the labor force.[14]
4. The number of arrests after release from prison.[15]
5. Household expenditure on various commodity groups.[16]

Each of these studies analyzes a dependent variable that is zero for a significant fraction of the observations. Conventional regression methods fail to account for the qualitative difference between *limit* (zero) observations and *nonlimit* (continuous) observations.

22.3.1. The Censored Normal Distribution

The relevant distribution theory for a censored variable is similar to that for a truncated one. Once again, we focus on the normal distribution, as nearly all of the received work has been based on an assumption of normality. We also assume that the censoring point is zero, though this is only a convenient normalization.

In a truncated distribution, only the part of distribution above $y = 0$ is relevant to our computations. To make the distribution integrate to one, we scale it up by the probability that an observation in the untruncated population falls in the range that interests us. When data are censored, the distribution *that applies to the sample data* is a mixture of discrete and continuous distributions. Figure 22.4 shows the effects.

To analyze this distribution, we define a new random variable, y, transformed from the original one, y^*, by

$$y = 0 \qquad \text{if } y^* \leq 0,$$
$$y = y^* \qquad \text{if } y^* > 0.$$

---

[10] See, for example, Section 21.8 for an application in a discrete choice model.

[11] More extensive listings may be found in Amemiya (1984) and Maddala (1983).

[12] Tobin (1958).

[13] Fair (1977, 1978).

[14] Quester and Greene (1982).

[15] Witte (1980).

[16] Jarque (1987).

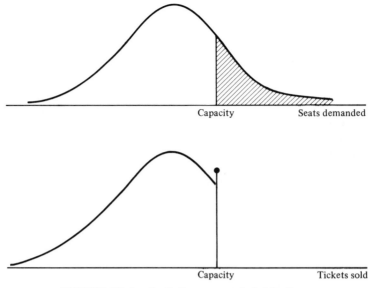

FIGURE 22.4 Partially censored distribution.

The distribution that applies if $y^* \sim N[\mu, \sigma^2]$ is

$$\text{Prob}(y = 0) = \text{Prob}(y^* \leq 0)$$

$$= \Phi\left(-\frac{\mu}{\sigma}\right)$$

$$= 1 - \Phi\left(\frac{\mu}{\sigma}\right)$$

and if $y^* > 0$, y has the density of y^*.

This distribution is a mixture of discrete and continuous parts. The total probability is one, as required, but instead of scaling the second part, we simply assign the full probability in the censored region to the censoring point, in this case, zero.

THEOREM 22.3. MOMENTS OF THE CENSORED NORMAL VARIABLE: *If $y^* \sim N[\mu, \sigma^2]$ and $y = a$ if $y^* \leq a$ else $y = y^*$ then*

$$E[y] = \Phi a + (1 - \Phi)(\mu + \sigma\lambda)$$

and

$$\text{Var}[y] = \sigma^2(1 - \Phi)[(1 - \delta) + (\alpha - \lambda)^2\Phi],$$

where $\Phi[(a - \mu)/\sigma] = \Phi(\alpha) = \text{Prob}(y^* \leq a) = \Phi$, $\lambda = \phi/(1 - \Phi)$ *and* $\delta = \lambda^2 - \lambda\alpha$.

Proof:

$$E[y] = \text{Prob}(y = a) \times E[y|y = a] + \text{Prob}(y > a) \times E[y|y > a]$$

$$= \text{Prob}(y^* \leq a) \times a + \text{Prob}(y^* > a) \times E[y^*|y^* > a]$$

$$= \Phi a + (1 - \Phi)(\mu + \sigma\lambda) \qquad \text{using Theorem 22.2.}$$

For the variance, we use a counterpart to the decomposition in (3–70), that is, $\text{Var}[y] = E[\text{conditional variance}] + \text{Var}[\text{conditional mean}]$, and Theorem 22.2.

$$E[\text{conditional variance}] = \Phi\text{Var}[y\,|\,y = a] + (1 - \Phi)\,\text{Var}[y\,|\,y > a]$$
$$= \Phi 0 + (1 - \Phi)\,\text{Var}[y^*\,|\,y^* > a] = (1 - \Phi)\sigma^2(1 - \delta).$$

$$\text{Var}[\text{conditional mean}] = \Phi\{a - E[y]\}^2 + (1 - \Phi)\{E[y\,|\,y > a] - E[y]\}^2$$
$$= \Phi\{a - \Phi a - (1 - \Phi)(\mu + \sigma\lambda)\}^2 +$$
$$(1 - \Phi)\{(\mu + \sigma\lambda) - \Phi a - (1 - \Phi)(\mu + \sigma\lambda)\}^2$$
$$= \Phi\{(1 - \Phi)(a - \mu - \sigma\lambda)\}^2 + (1 - \Phi)\{\Phi(a - \mu - \sigma\lambda)\}^2.$$

In the second term, a squared -1 has been dropped. Substitute $a - \mu = \sigma\alpha$ and collect terms to obtain

$$\text{Var}[\text{conditional mean}] = \{\Phi(1 - \Phi)^2 + (1 - \Phi)\Phi^2\}\sigma^2(\alpha - \lambda)^2$$
$$= \Phi(1 - \Phi)\sigma^2(\alpha - \lambda)^2.$$

Finally, the sum is

$$\text{Var}[y] = \sigma^2(1 - \Phi)[(1 - \delta) + (\alpha - \lambda)^2\Phi].$$

For the special case of $a = 0$, the mean simplifies to

$$E[y\,|\,a = 0] = \Phi\left(\frac{\mu}{\sigma}\right)(\mu + \sigma\lambda), \qquad \text{where } \lambda = \frac{\phi(\mu/\sigma)}{\Phi(\mu/\sigma)}.$$

For censoring of the upper part of the distribution instead of the lower, it is only necessary to reverse the role of Φ and $1 - \Phi$ and redefine λ as in Theorem 22.2.

EXAMPLE 22.8

To continue Example 22.7, suppose that the arena in question has 20,000 seats and, in a recent season, sold out 25 percent of the time. If the average attendance, including sell-outs, was 18,000, what are the mean and standard deviation of the demand for seats? According to Theorem 22.3, the 18,000 is an estimate of

$$E[\text{Sales}] = 20,000(1 - \Phi) + [\mu + \sigma\lambda]\Phi.$$

Since this is censoring from above, rather than below,

$$\lambda = \frac{-\phi(\alpha)}{\Phi(\alpha)}.$$

The argument of Φ, ϕ, and λ is

$$\alpha = \frac{20,000 - \mu}{\sigma}.$$

If 25 percent of the events are sellouts, $\Phi = 0.75$. Inverting the standard normal at 0.75 gives $\alpha = 0.675$. In addition, if $\alpha = 0.675$, then $-\phi(0.675)/0.75 = \lambda = -0.424$. This provides a pair of equations in μ and σ,

$$18,000 = 0.25(20,000) + 0.75(\mu - 0.424\sigma)$$

and

$$0.675\sigma = 20,000 - \mu.$$

The solutions are $\sigma = 2426$ and $\mu = 18,362$.

For comparison, suppose that we were told that the mean of 18,000 applies only to the events that were *not* sold out and that, on average, the arena sells out 25 percent of the time. Now our estimates would be obtained from the equations

$$18{,}000 = \mu - 0.424\sigma$$

and

$$0.675\sigma = 20{,}000 - \mu.$$

The solutions are $\sigma = 1820$ and $\mu = 18{,}772$.

22.3.2. The Censored Regression Model—Tobit Analysis

The regression model based on the preceding discussion is referred to as the **censored regression model** or the **tobit model**.[17] The regression is obtained by making the mean in the preceding correspond to a classical regression model. The general formulation is usually given in terms of an index function,

$$y_i^* = \boldsymbol{\beta}'\mathbf{x}_i + \varepsilon_i,$$
$$y_i = 0 \quad \text{if } y_i^* \le 0, \qquad\qquad (22\text{--}11)$$
$$y_i = y_i^* \quad \text{if } y_i^* > 0.$$

There are potentially three conditional mean functions to consider, depending on the purpose of the study. For the index variable, sometimes called the *latent variable, $E[y_i^*]$* is $\boldsymbol{\beta}'\mathbf{x}_i$. However, if the data are always censored, this will usually not be useful. Consistent with Theorem 22.3, for an observation randomly drawn from the population, which may or may not be censored,

$$E[y_i\,|\,\mathbf{x}_i] = \Phi\!\left(\frac{\boldsymbol{\beta}'\mathbf{x}_i}{\sigma}\right)(\boldsymbol{\beta}'\mathbf{x}_i + \sigma\lambda_i),$$

where

$$\lambda_i = \frac{\phi(\boldsymbol{\beta}'\mathbf{x}_i/\sigma)}{\Phi(\boldsymbol{\beta}'\mathbf{x}_i/\sigma)}. \qquad\qquad (22\text{--}12)$$

Finally, if we intend to confine our attention to uncensored observations, the results of the previous section apply.[18] It is an unresolved question which of these functions should be used for computing predicted values from this model. Intuition suggests that $E[y_i\,|\,\mathbf{x}_i]$ is correct, but authors differ on this point. For the setting in Example 22.8, for predicting the number of tickets sold, say, in order to plan for an upcoming event, the censored mean is obviously the relevant quantity. On the other hand, if the objective is to study the need for a new facility, the mean of the latent variable, y_i^*, would be more interesting.

There are differences in the marginal effects in the models as well. For the index variable,

$$\frac{\partial E[y_i^*\,|\,\mathbf{x}_i]}{\partial \mathbf{x}_i} = \boldsymbol{\beta}.$$

[17] This is in reference to Tobin (1958), where the model was first proposed.

[18] This does not mean that limit observations should be discarded, since this just produces the truncated regression setting. This is no more amenable to least squares than the censored data model.

But for y, given the censoring, the marginal effect is only

$$\frac{\partial E[y_i|\mathbf{x}_i]}{\partial \mathbf{x}_i} = \boldsymbol{\beta}\Phi\left(\frac{\boldsymbol{\beta}'\mathbf{x}_i}{\sigma}\right).^{19}$$

Once again, which one is relevant depends on the purpose of the estimates.

McDonald and Moffitt (1980) suggested a useful decomposition of $\partial E[y_i|\mathbf{x}_i]/\partial \mathbf{x}_i$,

$$\frac{\partial E[y_i|\mathbf{x}_i]}{\partial \mathbf{x}_i} = \boldsymbol{\beta} \times [\Phi_i(1 - \lambda_i(\alpha_i + \lambda_i)) + \phi_i(\alpha_i + \lambda_i)],$$

where

$$\Phi_i = \Phi(\boldsymbol{\beta}'\mathbf{x}_i/\sigma) = \Phi(\alpha_i)$$

and

$$\lambda_i = \phi_i/\Phi_i.$$

Taking the two parts separately, this decomposes the slope vector into

$$\frac{\partial E[y_i|\mathbf{x}_i]}{\partial \mathbf{x}_i} = \text{Prob}[y_i^* > 0]\,\frac{\partial E[y_i^*|\mathbf{x}_i, y_i^* > 0]}{\partial \mathbf{x}_i} + E[y_i^*|\mathbf{x}_i, y_i^* > 0]\,\frac{\partial \text{Prob}[y_i^* > 0]}{\partial \mathbf{x}_i}$$

Thus, a change in $\mathbf{x}_i$ has two effects. It effects the conditional mean of y_i^* in the positive part of the distribution, and it affects the probability that the observation will fall in that part of the distribution.

EXAMPLE 22.9

In the study of the number of hours worked in a survey year by a large sample of wives, Quester and Greene (1982) were interested in whether wives whose marriages were statistically more likely to dissolve hedged against that possibility by spending, on average, more time working.[20] They reported the Tobit estimates given in Table 22.2. The last figure in the table implies that a very large proportion of the women surveyed reported zero hours, so least squares regression would be inappropriate.

The figures in parentheses are the ratio of the coefficient estimate to the estimated asymptotic standard error. The dependent variable is hours worked in the survey year. "Small kids" is a dummy variable indicating whether there were children in the household. The "Education difference" and "Relative wage" variables compare husband and wife on these two dimensions. The wage rate used for wives was predicted using a previously estimated regression model and is thus available for all individuals, whether working or not. "Second marriage" is a dummy variable. Divorce probabilities were produced by a large microsimulation model presented in another study.[21] The variables used here were dummy variables indicating "Mean" if the predicted probability was between 0.01 and 0.03 and "High" if it was greater than 0.03. The "slopes" are the marginal effects described earlier.

---

[19] The result that the marginal effect is obtained by scaling the parameters by the probability in the uncensored region carries over to more general settings, as well. Rosett and Nelson (1975) and Nakamura and Nakamura (1983) consider a model with censoring on both ends of the distribution. For a model in which values of y^* less than or equal to a are reported as a and values greater than or equal to b are reported as b, $\partial E[y_i|\mathbf{x}_i]/\partial \mathbf{x}_i = \boldsymbol{\beta} \times \text{Prob}(a \le y_i^* \le b) = \boldsymbol{\beta}[\Phi((b - \boldsymbol{\beta}'\mathbf{x}_i)/\sigma) - \Phi((a - \boldsymbol{\beta}'\mathbf{x}_i)/\sigma)]$.

[20] In a not completely unrelated study done at roughly the same time, Fair (1978) applied the Tobit model to a study of the allocation of leisure time between spouse and paramour.

[21] Orcutt et al. (1976).

TABLE 22.2 Tobit Estimates of an Hours-Worked Equation

	White Wives		Black Wives	
	Coefficient	**Slope**	**Coefficient**	**Slope**
Constant	−1803.13		−2753.87	
	(−8.64)		(−9.68)	
Small kids	−1324.84	−385.89	−824.19	−376.53
	(−19.78)		(−10.14)	
Education	−48.08	−14.00	22.59	10.32
difference	(−4.77)		(1.96)	
Relative	312.07	90.90	286.39	130.93
wage	(5.71)		(3.32)	
Second	175.85	51.51	25.33	11.57
marriage	(3.47)		(0.41)	
Mean divorce	417.39	121.58	481.02	219.75
probability	(6.52)		(5.28)	
High divorce	670.22	195.22	578.66	264.36
probability	(8.40)		(5.33)	
σ	1559	618	1511	826
Sample size	7459		2798	
Proportion working	0.29		0.46	

Note the marginal effects compared to the tobit coefficients. Likewise, the estimate of σ is quite misleading as an estimate of the standard deviation of hours worked.

The effects of the divorce probability variables were as expected, and were quite large. One of the questions raised in connection with this study was whether the divorce probabilities could reasonably be treated as independent variables. It might be that for these individuals, the number of hours worked was a significant determinant of the probability.

22.3.3. Estimation

Estimation of this model is very similar to that of truncated regression. In practical terms, the tobit model has become so routine, and been incorporated in so many computer packages, that in spite of formidable obstacles in years past, estimation is now essentially on the level of ordinary regression.[22]

The log likelihood for the censored regression model is

$$\ln L = \sum_{y_i > 0} -\tfrac{1}{2}\left[\ln(2\pi) + \ln \sigma^2 + \frac{(y_i - \boldsymbol{\beta}'\mathbf{x}_i)^2}{\sigma^2}\right] + \sum_{y_i = 0} \ln\left[1 - \Phi\left(\frac{\boldsymbol{\beta}'\mathbf{x}_i}{\sigma}\right)\right]. \quad (22\text{--}13)$$

The two parts correspond to the classical regression for the nonlimit observations and the relevant probabilities for the limit observations. This is a nonstandard type of likelihood, since it is a mixture of discrete and continuous distributions. In a seminal paper, Amemiya (1973b) showed that despite the complications, proceeding in the usual fashion to maximize $\ln L$ would produce an estimator with all of the usual desirable properties assumed for MLEs.

[22] See Hall (1984).

The log-likelihood function is still fairly involved, but a considerable simplification is achieved by using Olsen's (1978) reparameterization. Let $\gamma = \beta/\sigma$ and $\theta = 1/\sigma$. Then the log likelihood is

$$\ln L = \sum_{y_i > 0} -\tfrac{1}{2}[\ln(2\pi) - \ln \theta^2 + (\theta y_i - \gamma' \mathbf{x}_i)^2] + \sum_{y_i = 0} \ln[1 - \Phi(\gamma' \mathbf{x}_i)].$$

Aside from its much simpler structure, this form has the virtue that the Hessian is always negative definite. As such, Newton's method is simple to use, and usually converges quickly. After convergence, the original parameters can be recovered using $\sigma = 1/\theta$ and $\beta = \gamma/\theta$. The asymptotic covariance matrix for these estimates can be obtained from that for the estimates of $[\gamma, \theta]$ using

$$\text{Asy.Var}[\beta, \sigma] = \mathbf{J} \, \text{Asy.Var}[\gamma, \theta] \mathbf{J}'$$

where

$$\mathbf{J} = \begin{bmatrix} \partial\beta/\partial\gamma' & \partial\beta/\partial\theta \\ \partial\sigma/\partial\gamma' & \partial\sigma/\partial\theta \end{bmatrix} = \begin{bmatrix} (1/\theta)\mathbf{I} & (-1/\theta^2)\gamma \\ \mathbf{0}' & -1/\theta^2 \end{bmatrix}.$$

Researchers often compute ordinary least squares estimates despite their inconsistency. Almost without exception, it is found that the OLS estimates are smaller in absolute value than the MLEs. A striking empirical regularity is that the maximum likelihood estimates can often be approximated by dividing the OLS estimates by the proportion of nonlimit observations in the sample.[23]

Although ordinary least squares is demonstrably inconsistent in this setting, a number of consistent alternatives to maximum likelihood estimation have been proposed. One possibility is to apply nonlinear least squares to the conditional mean function of either the tobit model using the full sample or to the truncated regression using only the nonlimit observations.[24] A second possibility is to use Heckman's two-step correction to ordinary least squares, which is described in Section 22.4.[25]

EXAMPLE 22.10 Least Squares Versus Maximum Likelihood _____

For their second regression in Example 22.9, Quester and Greene also obtained the least squares results listed in Table 22.3.

The marginal effects in the model are obtained by scaling the maximum likelihood estimates by $\hat{\Phi} = 0.4568 = \Phi(\hat{\beta}'\bar{\mathbf{x}}/\hat{\sigma})$. The scale factor for the least squares estimates is $1/P$, where P is the proportion of nonlimit observations in the sample, 0.4601. There are two things to note. First, as expected, the scaled least squares coefficients closely resemble the consistent maximum likelihood estimates. Second, the marginal effects estimated for the tobit model rather closely resemble the least squares estimates. We recall the discussion of nonlinear regression models in Chapter 11. The slopes of the highly nonlinear conditional mean function in this model appear to be approximated rather well by the OLS estimates.

---

[23] This is explored further in Greene (1980b), Goldberger (1981), and Cheung and Goldberger (1984).

[24] See Amemiya (1985, Chap. 10).

[25] See Heckman (1979), Wales and Woodland (1980), Greene (1981), Stapleton and Young (1981), Paarsch (1984), and Nelson (1984).

TABLE 22.3

Variable	MLE	Marginal Effect	Least Squares	Scaled Least Squares
Small kids	−824.19	−376.53	−352.63	−766.59
Education difference	22.59	10.32	11.47	24.93
Relative wage	286.39	130.93	123.95	269.46
Second marriage	25.33	11.57	13.14	28.57
Mean divorce probability	481.02	219.75	219.22	476.57
High divorce probability	578.66	264.36	244.17	530.80

22.3.4. Some Issues in Specification

Two issues that commonly arise in microeconomic data, heteroscedasticity and nonnormality, have been analyzed at length in the Tobit setting.[26]

22.3.4a. Heteroscedasticity. Maddala and Nelson (1975), Hurd (1979), Arabmazar and Schmidt (1982a, 1982b), and Brown and Moffitt (1982) all have varying degrees of pessimism regarding how inconsistent the maximum likelihood estimator will be when heteroscedasticity occurs. Not surprisingly, the degree of censoring is the primary determinant. Unfortunately, all of the analyses have been carried out in the setting of very specific models, for example, involving only a single dummy variable or one with groupwise heteroscedasticity, so the primary lesson is the very general conclusion that heteroscedasticity emerges as an obviously serious problem.

One can approach the heteroscedasticity problem directly. Petersen and Waldman (1981) present the computations needed to estimate a tobit model with heteroscedasticity of several types. Replacing σ with σ_i in the log-likelihood function and including σ_i^2 in the summations produces the needed generality. Specification of a particular model for σ_i provides the empirical model for estimation.

EXAMPLE 22.11 _____

Petersen and Waldman analyzed the volume of short interest in a cross section of common stocks. The regressors included a measure of the market component of heterogeneous expectations as measured by the firm's *BETA* coefficient; a company-specific measure of heterogeneous expectations, *NONMARKET*; the *NUMBER* of analysts making earnings forecasts for the company; the number of common shares to be issued for the acquisition of another firm, *MERGER*; and a dummy variable for the existence of *OPTION*s. They report the results listed in Table 22.4 for a model in which the variance is assumed to be of the form $\sigma_i^2 = \exp(\boldsymbol{\alpha}'\mathbf{x}_i)$. The values in parentheses are the ratio of the coefficient to the estimated asymptotic standard error.

---

[26]Two recent symposia that contain numerous results on these subjects are Blundell (1987) and Duncan (1986b).

TABLE 22.4 Estimates of a Tobit Model

	Homoscedastic	Heteroscedastic	
	β	β	α
Constant	−18.28	−4.11	−0.47
	(5.10)	(3.28)	(0.60)
BETA	10.97	2.22	1.20
	(3.61)	(2.00)	(1.81)
NONMARKET	0.65	0.12	0.08
	(7.41)	(1.90)	(7.55)
NUMBER	0.75	0.33	0.15
	(5.74)	(4.50)	(4.58)
MERGER	0.50	0.24	0.06
	(5.90)	(3.00)	(4.17)
OPTION	2.56	2.96	0.83
	(1.51)	(2.99)	(1.70)
Log L	−547.30	−466.27	
Sample size	200	200	

The effect of heteroscedasticity on the estimates is extremely large. A test of the hypothesis that $\alpha = 0$ (except for the constant term) can be based on the likelihood ratio statistic. For these results, the statistic is $-2(-547.3 - (-466.27)) = 162.06$. This is asymptotically distributed as chi-squared with five degrees of freedom. The sample value exceeds the critical value in the table, so the hypothesis can be rejected.

In the preceding example, we carried out a likelihood ratio test against the hypothesis of homoscedasticity. It would be desirable to be able to carry out the test without having to estimate the unrestricted model. A Lagrange multiplier test can be used for that purpose. Consider the heteroscedastic tobit model in which we specify that

$$\sigma_i^2 = \sigma^2 e^{\alpha' \mathbf{w}_i}.$$

This is a fairly general model that includes many familiar ones as special cases. The null hypothesis of homoscedasticity is $\alpha = 0$. After some algebra, the necessary conditions for maximization of the log likelihood *under the null hypothesis* reduce to the following, in which subscripts are used to indicate partial differentiation of the log likelihood:

$$\ln L_\beta = \sum_i a_i \mathbf{x}_i,$$

$$\ln L_{\sigma^2} = \sum_i b_i,$$

$$\ln L_\alpha = \sum_i \sigma^2 b_i \mathbf{w}_i,$$

where z_i is 1 if y_i is positive and 0 otherwise,

$$a_i = z_i \left(\frac{\varepsilon_i}{\sigma^2} \right) + \frac{(1 - z_i)(-\phi_i/(1 - \Phi_i))}{\sigma}$$

and

$$b_i = \frac{z_i(\varepsilon_i^2/\sigma^2 - 1)}{2\sigma^2} + \frac{(1 - z_i)(\boldsymbol{\beta}'\mathbf{x}_i\phi_i/(1 - \Phi_i))}{2\sigma^3}.$$

The sums are taken over all observations, and all functions involving unknown parameters (ε, ϕ, $\boldsymbol{\beta}'\mathbf{x}_i$, etc.) are evaluated at the restricted (homoscedastic) maximum likelihood estimates. To construct the Lagrange multiplier statistic, we use the Berndt et al. estimator for the information matrix. Under the null hypothesis, at the maximum likelihood estimates, L_β and L_{σ^2} are both zero. Therefore, the statistic can be computed as

$$\mathrm{LM} = \ln L_\alpha' \mathbf{Q}_{\alpha\alpha'} \ln L_\alpha,$$

where $\ln L_\alpha$ is as above and $\mathbf{Q}_{\alpha\alpha'}$ is the lower right block in

$$\mathbf{Q} = \left[\sum_i \begin{bmatrix} a_i^2 \mathbf{x}_i \mathbf{x}_i' & a_i b_i \mathbf{x}_i & \sigma^2 a_i b_i \mathbf{x}_i \mathbf{w}_i' \\ a_i b_i \mathbf{x}_i' & b_i^2 & \sigma^2 b_i^2 \mathbf{w}_i' \\ \sigma^2 a_i b_i \mathbf{w}_i \mathbf{x}_i' & \sigma^2 b_i^2 \mathbf{w}_i & \sigma^4 b_i^2 \mathbf{w}_i \mathbf{w}_i' \end{bmatrix} \right]^{-1}$$

Unfortunately, this does not reduce to an elegant nR^2, as it would in the classical regression model. (If there were no limit observations, it would reduce to the Breusch–Pagan statistic discussed in Chapter 14.) But given the maximum likelihood estimates of the tobit model coefficients, it is quite simple to compute. The statistic is asymptotically distributed as chi-squared with degrees of freedom equal to the number of variables in $\mathbf{w}_i$.

22.3.4b. Misspecification of Prob[y* < 0]. In an early study in this literature, Cragg(1971) proposed a somewhat more general model in which the probability of a limit observation is independent of the regression model for the nonlimit data. One can imagine, for instance, the decision on whether or not to purchase a car as being different from the decision on how much to spend on the car, having decided to buy one. A related problem raised by Fin and Schmidt (1984) is that in the tobit model, a variable that increases the probability of an observation being a nonlimit observation also increases the mean of the variable. They cite as an example loss due to fire in buildings. Older buildings might be more likely to have fires, so that $\partial \mathrm{Prob}[y_i > 0]/\partial \mathrm{age}_i > 0$, but, because of the greater value of newer buildings, incur smaller losses when they do, so that $\partial E[y_i | y_i > 0]/\partial \mathrm{age}_i < 0$. This would require the coefficient on age to have different signs in the two functions. This is impossible in the tobit model because they are the same coefficient.

A more general model that accomodates these objections is

1. Decision equation:

$$\mathrm{Prob}[y_i^* > 0] = \Phi(\boldsymbol{\lambda}'\mathbf{x}_i), \qquad z_i = 1 \text{ if } y_i^* > 0,$$
$$\mathrm{Prob}[y_i^* \leq 0] = 1 - \Phi(\boldsymbol{\lambda}'\mathbf{x}_i), \qquad z_i = 0 \text{ if } y_i^* \leq 0.$$

2. Regression equation for nonlimit observations:

$$E[y_i | z_i = 1] = \boldsymbol{\beta}'\mathbf{x}_i + \sigma\lambda_i,$$

according to Theorem 21.2.

This is a combination of the truncated regression model of Section 22.2 and the univariate probit model of Chapter 21, which suggests a method of analyzing it. The tobit model of this section arises if $\boldsymbol{\lambda} = \boldsymbol{\beta}/\sigma$. The parameters of the decision equation can be estimated independently using the truncated regression model of Section 22.2

Fin and Schmidt considered testing the restriction of the tobit model. Based only on the tobit model, they devised a Lagrange multiplier statistic that, while a bit cumbersome algebraically, can be computed without great difficulty. If one is able to estimate the truncated regression model, the tobit model, and the probit model separately, there is a simpler way to test the hypothesis. The tobit log-likelihood is the sum of the log-likelihoods for the truncated regression and probit models. [To show this, add and subtract $\Sigma_{y_i=1}\ln\Phi(\boldsymbol{\beta}'\mathbf{x}_i/\sigma)$ in (22–13). This produces (22–9) for the truncated regression model plus (21–15) for the probit model.] Therefore, a likelihood ratio statistic can be computed using

$$\lambda = -2[\ln L_T - (\ln L_P + \ln L_{TR})],$$

where

L_T = likelihood for the tobit model in (22–13), with the same coefficients,
L_P = likelihood for the probit model in (21–15), fit separately,
L_{TR} = likelihood for the truncated regression model in (22–9), fit separately.

22.3.4c. Nonnormality.
Nonnormality is an especially difficult problem in this setting. It has been shown that if the underlying disturbances are not normally distributed, the usual estimator is inconsistent. Research is ongoing both on alternative estimators and on methods for testing for this type of misspecification.[27]

One approach to the estimation is use an alternative distribution. Kalbfleisch and Prentice[28] present a unifying treatment that includes several distributions such as the exponential, lognormal, and Weibull. (Their primary focus is on survival analysis in a medical statistics setting. This is an interesting convergence of the techniques in very different disciplines.) Of course, assuming some other specific distribution does not necessarily solve the problem and may make it worse. A preferable alternative would be to devise an estimator that is robust to changes in the distribution. Powell's (1981) least absolute deviations estimator appears to offer some promise. The main drawback to its use is its computational complexity. Research on robust methods is ongoing.[29]

Although estimation in the nonnormal case is quite difficult, testing for this failure of the model is worthwhile in order to assess the estimates obtained by the conventional methods. Among the tests that have been developed are Lagrange multiplier tests[30] and Hausman tests. The latter were developed by Nelson (1981). In the usual case, to employ a Hausman test, we require an estimator that is consistent and efficient under the null hypothesis but inconsistent under the alternative—the tobit estimator with normality—and an estimator that is consistent under both hypotheses but inefficient under the null hypothesis. For estimation of $\boldsymbol{\beta}$, this requires a robust estimator of $\boldsymbol{\beta}$, which restores the difficulties of the previous paragraph. However, Nelson simplifies the problem by considering, instead of $\boldsymbol{\beta}$, Prob[$y > 0$] from the marginal distribution of y and $E[(1/n)\mathbf{X}'\mathbf{y}]$, both of which can be estimated using sample moments. More recent results on conditional moment tests are considered in the next section.

22.3.4d. Conditional Moment Tests—An Introduction.
A spate of recent studies has shown how to use *conditional moment restrictions* both for estimation and specifica-

---

[27] See Duncan (1983, 1986b), Goldberger (1983), and Fernandez (1986). We will examine one of the tests more closely in the next section.

[28] Kalbfleisch and Prentice (1980).

[29] See Duncan (1986a, 1986b) for a symposium on the subject and Amemiya (1984).

[30] Bera et al. (1982).

tion testing.[31] The first of these is the GMM method of estimation discussed in Section 13.5. The second is a general methodology for testing hypotheses that has proved useful in a wide variety of settings. The logic of the conditional moment (CM) test is as follows: The model specification implies that certain moment restrictions will hold in the population from which the data were drawn. If the specification is correct, the sample data should mimic the implied relationships. For example, in the classical regression model, the assumption of homoscedasticity implies that the disturbance variance is independent of the regressors. As such,

$$E\{\mathbf{x}_i[(y_i - \boldsymbol{\beta}'\mathbf{x}_i)^2 - \sigma^2]\} = E[\mathbf{x}_i(\varepsilon_i^2 - \sigma^2)] = \mathbf{0}.$$

If, on the other hand, the regression is heteroscedastic in a way that depends on $\mathbf{x}_i$, then this covariance will not be zero. If the hypothesis of homoscedasticity is correct, then we would expect the sample counterpart to the moment condition,

$$\mathbf{r} = \frac{1}{n} \sum_i \mathbf{x}_i(e_i^2 - s^2),$$

where e_i is the OLS residual, to be close to zero. (This is the basis of Breusch and Pagan's LM test for homoscedasticity. See Section 14.3.3.) The practical problems to be solved are (1) to formulate suitable moment conditions that do correspond to the hypothesis test—this is usually straightforward, (2) to devise the appropriate sample counterpart— this may not be so simple, as we shall see below, and (3) to devise a suitable measure of closeness to zero of the sample moment estimator. The last of these will be in the framework of the Wald statistics that we have examined at various points in this book.[32] So the problem will be to devise the appropriate covariance matrix for the sample moments.

Pagan and Vella (1989) have devised a set of specification tests for the tobit model based on this principle.[33] We will consider three:

1. The variables $\mathbf{z}$ have not been erroneously omitted from the model.
2. The disturbances in the model are homoscedastic.
3. The underlying disturbances in the model are normally distributed.

For the third of these, we will take the standard approach of examining the third and fourth moments, which for the normal distribution are 0 and $3\sigma^4$, respectively.[34] The underlying motivation for the tests can be made with reference to the regression part of the tobit model in (22–11),

$$y_i^* = \boldsymbol{\beta}'\mathbf{x}_i + \varepsilon_i.$$

Neglecting for the moment that we only observe y_i^* subject to the censoring, the three hypotheses imply the following expectations:

(1) $E[\mathbf{z}_i(y_i - \boldsymbol{\beta}'\mathbf{x}_i)] = \mathbf{0},$

(2) $E\{\mathbf{z}_i[(y_i - \boldsymbol{\beta}'\mathbf{x}_i)^2 - \sigma^2]\} = \mathbf{0},$

(3) $E[(y_i - \boldsymbol{\beta}'\mathbf{x}_i)^3] = 0 \quad$ and $\quad E[(y_i - \boldsymbol{\beta}'\mathbf{x}_i)^4 - 3\sigma^4] = 0.$

---

[31] Developing specification tests for the Tobit model has been a popular enterprise. A sampling of the received literature includes Nelson (1980), Bera et al. (1982), Chesher and Irish (1987), (Chesher et al., 1985), Gourieroux et al., (1984, 1987), Newey (1986), Rivers and Vuong (1988), Horowitz and Newman (1989), and Pagan and Vella (1989). Newey (1985a, 1985b) are useful references on the general subject of conditional moment testing. More general treatments of specification testing are Godfrey (1988) and Ruud (1984).

[32] See Section 4.8.3, especially Section 4.8.3b.

[33] Their survey is quite general and includes other models, specifications, and estimation methods. We will consider only the simplest cases here. The reader is referred to their paper for formal presentation of these results.

[34] See Example 4.26 and Section 10.5.4.

In (1), the variables in $\mathbf{z}_i$ would be one or more variables not already in the model. We are interested in assessing whether they should be or not. In (2), presumably, though not necessarily, $\mathbf{z}_i$ would be the regressors in the model. For the present, we will assume that y^* is observed directly, without censoring. That is, we will construct the CM tests for the classical linear regression model. Then we will go back to the necessary step and make the modification needed to account for the censoring of the dependent variable.

The sample counterparts to the moment restrictions in (1) to (3) are

$$\mathbf{r}_1 = \frac{1}{n}\sum_i \mathbf{z}_i e_i, \text{ where } e_i = y_i - \mathbf{b}'\mathbf{x}_i \text{ and } \mathbf{b} = (\mathbf{X}'\mathbf{X})^{-1}\mathbf{X}'\mathbf{y},$$

$$\mathbf{r}_2 = \frac{1}{n}\sum_i \mathbf{z}_i(e_i^2 - s^2), \text{ where } s^2 = \frac{\mathbf{e}'\mathbf{e}}{n},$$

$$\mathbf{r}_3 = \frac{1}{n}\sum_i \begin{bmatrix} e_i^3 \\ e_i^4 - 3s^4 \end{bmatrix}.$$

Note that in each case, the moment can be written as

$$\mathbf{r}_j = \frac{1}{n}\sum_i \mathbf{m}_i(y_i, \mathbf{x}_i, \mathbf{z}_i, \hat{\boldsymbol{\beta}}, \hat{\sigma}) = \frac{1}{n}\sum_i \hat{\mathbf{m}}_i. \tag{22-14}$$

The hypothesis is that $E[\mathbf{m}_i] = E[\mathbf{r}] = \mathbf{0}$. With random sampling, consistency of the parameter estimates, and the assumption of the null hypothesis, the central limit theorem (Theorem 4.4) applies, so

$$\sqrt{n}\mathbf{r}_j \xrightarrow{d} N[\mathbf{0}, \boldsymbol{\Sigma}]$$

for some covariance matrix $\boldsymbol{\Sigma}$ that we have yet to estimate. Given an estimate of $\boldsymbol{\Sigma}$, it follows that the Wald statistic,

$$n\mathbf{r}_j'\hat{\boldsymbol{\Sigma}}^{-1}\mathbf{r}_j \xrightarrow{d} \text{chi-squared}[J], \tag{22-15}$$

where the degrees of freedom, J, is the number of moment restrictions being tested. (This statistic is discussed in Section 10.3.4.) Thus, the statistic can be referred to the chi-squared table.

It remains to determine the estimator of $\boldsymbol{\Sigma}$. The full derivation of $\boldsymbol{\Sigma}$ is fairly complicated. [See Pagan and Vella (1989, pp. S32–S33).] But when the vector of parameter estimates is a maximum likelihood estimate, as it would be for the least squares estimator with normally distributed disturbances, a surprisingly simple estimator can be used. In order to set the stage for the tobit model, we will present this in general terms rather than specifically for the classical linear regression model. Suppose, then, that the parameter vector used to compute the moments above is obtained by solving the equations

$$\sum_i \mathbf{d}(y_i, \mathbf{x}_i, \hat{\boldsymbol{\theta}}) = \sum_i \hat{\mathbf{d}}_i = \mathbf{0}, \tag{22-16}$$

where $\hat{\boldsymbol{\theta}}$ is the estimated parameter vector [e.g., $(\hat{\boldsymbol{\beta}}, \hat{\sigma})$]. For the linear regression model, that would be the normal equations,

$$\mathbf{X}'\mathbf{e} = \sum_i \mathbf{x}_i(y_i - \mathbf{b}'\mathbf{x}_i) = \mathbf{0}.$$

Let the matrix $\mathbf{D}$ be the $n \times K$ matrix with ith row equal to $\hat{\mathbf{d}}'_i$. Let $\mathbf{M}$ be the $n \times J$ matrix whose ith row is $\hat{\mathbf{m}}'_i$ [see (22–14)]. Pagan and Vella show that for maximum likelihood estimators, $\boldsymbol{\Sigma}$ can be estimated using

$$\mathbf{S} = \frac{1}{n}(\mathbf{M'M} - \mathbf{M'D}(\mathbf{D'D})^{-1}\mathbf{D'M}).^{35}$$ (22–17)

This looks like an involved matrix computation, but it is simple with any regression program. Each element of $\mathbf{S}$ is the mean square or cross product of the least squares residuals in a linear regression of a column of $\mathbf{M}$ on the variables in $\mathbf{D}$. That is, $\mathbf{S}$ is exactly the matrix in (17–9) and (17–10).[36] Therefore, the operational version of the statistic is

$$C = n\mathbf{r}'_j \mathbf{S}^{-1} \mathbf{r}_j,$$ (22–18)

which, once again, is referred to the appropriate critical value in the chi-squared table. This provides a joint test that all of the moment conditions are satisfied simultaneously. An individual test of just one of the moment restrictions in isolation can be computed even more easily. For testing one of the L conditions, say the ℓth one,

the test can be carried out by a simple t test of whether the constant term is zero in a linear regression of the ℓth column of $\mathbf{M}$ on a constant term and all of the columns of $\mathbf{D}$.

In fact, the test statistic in (22–18) could also be obtained by stacking the J columns of $\mathbf{M}$ and treating the L equations as a seemingly unrelated regressions model with $(\mathbf{i}, \mathbf{D})$ as the (identical) regressors in each equation, and then testing the joint hypothesis that all of the constant terms are zero.

EXAMPLE 22.12 Testing for Heteroscedasticity in the Linear Regression Model

Suppose that the linear model is specified as

$$y_i = \beta_1 + \beta_2 x_i + \beta_3 z_i + \varepsilon_i.$$

To test whether

$$E[z_i^2(\varepsilon_i^2 - \sigma^2)] = 0,$$

we linearly regress $z_i^2(e_i^2 - s^2)$ on a constant, e_i, $x_i e_i$, and $z_i e_i$. A standard t test of whether the constant term in this regression is zero carries out the test. To test the hypothesis that there is no heteroscedasticity with respect to both x and z, we would regress both x and z on $[1, e_i, x_i e_i, z_i e_i]$, and collect the two columns of residuals in $\mathbf{V}$. Then $\mathbf{S} = (1/n)\mathbf{V'V}$. The moment vector would be

$$\mathbf{r} = \frac{1}{n} \sum_i \begin{bmatrix} x_i \\ z_i \end{bmatrix}(e_i^2 - s^2).$$

---

[35] It might be tempting just to use $(1/n)\mathbf{M'M}$. This would be incorrect, as $\mathbf{S}$ accounts for the fact that $\mathbf{M}$ is a function of the estimated parameter vector which is converging to its probability limit at the same rate as the sample moments are converging to theirs.

[36] If the estimator is not an MLE, estimation of $\boldsymbol{\Sigma}$ is more involved, but also straightforward using basic matrix algebra. The advantage of (22–17) is that it involves simple sums of variables that have already been computed in order to obtain $\hat{\boldsymbol{\theta}}$ and $\mathbf{r}_j$.

With the preceding in place, the extension to the tobit model is relatively simple. We reconsider the model definition in (22–11) and the log-likelihood function in (22–13). Define $q_{i1} = 1$ if $y_i > 0$ and 0 otherwise and $q_{i0} = 1 - q_{i1}$, so $q_{i0} = 1$ if $y_i = 0$. To save some notation, define

$$A_i = \frac{\boldsymbol{\beta}'\mathbf{x}_i}{\sigma},$$

$$\lambda_i = \frac{\phi(A_i)}{1 - \Phi(A_i)} = \frac{\phi_i}{1 - \Phi_i}.$$

With these in hand, the derivatives of the log-likelihood function in (22–13) are

$$\frac{\partial \ln L}{\partial \boldsymbol{\beta}} = \sum_i \mathbf{x}_i\left[q_{1i}\frac{e_i}{\sigma^2} - q_{0i}\frac{\lambda_i}{\sigma}\right],$$

$$\frac{\partial \ln L}{\partial \sigma} = \sum_i \left[q_{1i}\left(\frac{e_i^2}{\sigma^2} - 1\right)\sigma + q_{i0}\frac{\lambda_i A_i}{\sigma}\right].$$

The maximum likelihood estimator of $[\boldsymbol{\beta}, \sigma]$ is found by simultaneously equating these to **0**. If we combine these two into a single vector, we obtain the definitional equations for our estimator. That is, the maximum likelihood estimator is found by setting

$$\frac{\partial \ln L}{\partial [\boldsymbol{\beta}', \sigma]'} = \sum_i \mathbf{d}_i = \mathbf{0},$$

so this gives us the matrix **D** for our tests. The rows of **D** are the individual terms in the derivative vector of the log likelihood.

The moment conditions are a little more involved because of the censoring. For the positive observations, we observe y^*, so the observations in **M** can be the same as for the classical regression model, that is,

(1) $\mathbf{m}_i = \mathbf{z}_i(y_i - \boldsymbol{\beta}'\mathbf{x}_i),$

(2) $\mathbf{m}_i = \mathbf{z}_i[(y_i - \boldsymbol{\beta}'\mathbf{x}_i)^2 - \sigma^2],$

(3) $\mathbf{m}_i = [(y_i - \boldsymbol{\beta}'\mathbf{x}_i)^3, (y_i - \boldsymbol{\beta}'\mathbf{x}_i)^4 - 3\sigma^4]'.$

For the limit observations, these are replaced with their expected values, conditioned on $y = 0$ (i.e., on $y^* \le 0$). In order to construct these, note, first, that $y^* \le 0$ implies $\boldsymbol{\beta}'\mathbf{x}_i + \varepsilon_i \le 0$, or $\varepsilon_i \le -\boldsymbol{\beta}'\mathbf{x}$. Then

(1) $\mathbf{m}_i = \mathbf{z}_i E[(y_i^* - \boldsymbol{\beta}'\mathbf{x}_i)|y = 0] = (\boldsymbol{\beta}'\mathbf{x}_i - \sigma\lambda_i) - \boldsymbol{\beta}'\mathbf{x}_i = -\sigma\lambda_i.$

See (22–3b). Note that $\alpha = (0 - \boldsymbol{\beta}'\mathbf{x}_i)/\sigma$ and that $\Phi(-t) = 1 - \Phi(t)$.

(2) $\mathbf{m}_i = \mathbf{z}_i E[(y_i^* - \boldsymbol{\beta}'\mathbf{x}_i)^2 - \sigma^2|y = 0] = \mathbf{z}_i[\sigma^2(1 + A_i\lambda_i) - \sigma^2] = \mathbf{z}_i[\sigma^2 A_i\lambda_i].$

Note that $E[\varepsilon_i^2|y = 0]$ is not the variance, since the mean is not zero. See (22–2) and (22–4). For the third and fourth moments, we simply reproduce Pagan and Vella's results. [See also Greene (1991, p. 594).]

(3) $\mathbf{m}_i = \begin{bmatrix} -\sigma^3\lambda_i(2 + A_i^2) \\ \sigma^4\lambda_i(3A_i + A_i^3) \end{bmatrix}.$

These are the remaining terms needed to compute **M**. Thereafter, the test is exactly the same as before.

Conditional moment specifications provide a rich source of information about a model and its consistency with the observed data. Pagan and Vella provide numerous other examples.

EXAMPLE 22.13 Overdispersion in the Poisson Regression Model

In Example 21.20, we tested the hypothesis of overdispersion in the Poisson regression model. The hypothesis that $\text{Var}[y_i] = E[y_i]$ could not be rejected on the basis of a test that, essentially, formulated the alternative as $\text{Var}[y_i] = E[y_i] + g(E[y_i])$. That is a very specific type of overdispersion. Now we will consider the more general hypothesis that $\text{Var}[y_i]$ is completely given by $E[y_i]$. The alternative is that the variance is systematically related to the regressors in a way that is not completely accounted for by $E[y_i]$. Formally, we have

$$E[y_i] = \exp(\boldsymbol{\beta}'\mathbf{x}_i) = \lambda_i.$$

(Note the notational conflict. This is not the same λ_i as used above, but it is the standard notation for the mean of the Poisson regression.) The null hypothesis is that $\text{Var}[y_i] = \lambda_i$. The moment restriction is

$$E\{\mathbf{z}_i[(y_i - \lambda_i)^2 - \lambda_i]\} = \mathbf{0}.$$

To carry out the test, we do the following:

1. Compute the Poisson regression by maximum likelihood.
2. Compute

$$\mathbf{r} = \frac{1}{n} \sum_i \mathbf{z}_i[(y_i - \hat{\lambda}_i)^2 - \hat{\lambda}_i].$$

based on the maximum likelihood estimates.

The vector $\mathbf{z}$ omits the constant term in $\mathbf{x}_i$. This defines $\mathbf{M}$.

3. The rows of $\mathbf{D}$ are $\mathbf{x}_i'(y_i - \lambda_i)$, computed using the MLEs.
4. Compute $\mathbf{S} = \frac{1}{20}[\mathbf{M}'\mathbf{M} - \mathbf{M}'\mathbf{D}(\mathbf{D}'\mathbf{D})^{-1}\mathbf{D}'\mathbf{M}]$.
5. $C = 20\mathbf{r}'\mathbf{S}^{-1}\mathbf{r} = 18.931$. There are 8 degrees of freedom.

The 5 percent critical value from the chi-squared table is 15.50732. So the hypothesis is rejected. This conflicts with the Cameron and Trivedi result we found earlier. But this test is much more general, since the form of overdispersion is not specified here. That may explain the difference. Note that this affirms McCullagh and Nelder's conjecture.

22.4. Selection—Incidental Truncation

The topic of sample selection, or *incidental truncation,* has been the subject of an enormous recent literature, both theoretical and applied.[37] This analysis combines both of the previous topics.

EXAMPLE 22.14 Incidental Truncation

In the high-income survey discussed in Examples 22.1 and 22.4, respondents were also included in the survey if their net worth, not including their homes, was at least $500,000.

---

[37] The four surveys noted in the Introduction provide fairly extensive, though far from exhaustive, lists of the studies. Recent studies that suggest the likely direction of future development are Heckman (1990), Manski (1989, 1990), and Newey et al. (1990).

Suppose that the survey of incomes was based *only* on people whose net worth was at least $500,000. This is a form of truncation, but not quite the same as in Section 22.2. This selection criterion does not necessarily exclude individuals whose incomes at the time might be quite low. Still, one would expect that, on average, individuals with a high net worth would have a high income as well. Thus, the average income in this subpopulation would, in all likelihood, also be misleading as an indication of the income of the typical American. The data in such a survey would be incidentally truncated, or nonrandomly selected.

Recent econometric studies of nonrandom sampling have analyzed the deleterious effects of sample selection on the properties of conventional estimators such as least squares; have produced a variety of alternative estimation techniques; and, in the process, have yielded a rich crop of empirical models. In some cases, the analysis has led to a reinterpretation of earlier results.

22.4.1. Incidental Truncation in a Bivariate Distribution

Suppose that y and z have a bivariate distribution with correlation ρ. We are interested in the distribution of y given that z exceeds a particular value. Intuition suggests that if y and z are positively correlated, the truncation of z should push the distribution of y to the right. As before, we are interested in (1) the form of the incidentally truncated distribution and (2) the mean and variance of the incidentally truncated random variable. Since it has dominated the empirical literature, we will focus on the bivariate normal distribution.[38]

The truncated *joint* density of y and z is

$$f(y, z \mid z > a) = \frac{f(y, z)}{\text{Prob}(z > a)}.$$

To obtain the incidentally truncated marginal density for y, we would then integrate z out of this expression.

The moments of the incidentally truncated normal distribution are given in Theorem 22.4.[39]

THEOREM 22.4. MOMENTS OF THE INCIDENTALLY TRUNCATED BIVARIATE NORMAL DISTRIBUTION: *If y and z have a bivariate normal distribution with means μ_y and μ_z, standard deviations σ_y and σ_z, and correlation ρ, then*

$$E[y \mid z > a] = \mu_y + \rho \sigma_y \lambda(\alpha_z)$$
$$\text{Var}[y \mid z > a] = \sigma_y^2 (1 - \rho^2 \delta(\alpha_z)),$$

(22–19)

where

$$\alpha_z = \frac{a - \mu_z}{\sigma_z},$$

$$\lambda(\alpha_z) = \frac{\phi(\alpha_z)}{1 - \Phi(\alpha_z)},$$

$$\delta(\alpha_z) = \lambda(\alpha_z)(\lambda(\alpha_z) - \alpha_z).$$

---

[38] We will reconsider the issue of the normality assumption in Section 22.4.5.

[39] Much more general forms of the result that apply to multivariate distributions are given in Johnson and Kotz (1974). See also Maddala (1983, pp. 266–267).

Note that the expressions involving z are precisely analogous to the moments of the truncated distribution of x given in Theorem 22.2. If the truncation is $z < a$, we make the replacement

$$\lambda(\alpha_z) = \frac{-\phi(\alpha_z)}{\Phi(\alpha_z)}.$$

As expected, the truncated mean is pushed in the direction of the correlation if the truncation is from below and in the opposite direction if it is from above. In addition, the incidental truncation reduces the variance, as both $\delta(\alpha)$ and ρ^2 are between zero and one. However, as might be expected, the variance is reduced less by incidental truncation than by direct truncation.

22.4.2. Regression in a Model of Selection

To motivate a regression model that corresponds to the results in Theorem 22.4, we consider two examples.

EXAMPLE 22.15 A Model of Labor Supply ─────────────────────────────

A simple model of female labor supply that has been examined in many studies consists of two equations:[40]

1. *Wage equation:* The difference between a person's *market wage,* what they could command in the labor market, and their *reservation wage,* the wage rate necessary to make them choose to participate in the labor market, is a function of characteristics such as age and education, as well as, for example, number of children and where they live.
2. *Hours equation:* The desired number of labor hours supplied depends on the wage, home characteristics such as whether there are small children present, marital status (see Example 22.9), and so on.

The problem of truncation surfaces when we account for the fact that the second equation describes desired hours, but an actual figure is observed only if the individual is working. We infer from this that the market wage exceeds the reservation wage. Thus, the hours variable in the second equation is incidentally truncated.

EXAMPLE 22.16 A Migration Model ──────────────────────────────────

Example 21.3 presents a model of migration analyzed by Nakosteen and Zimmer. That model fits precisely into the framework described earlier. Briefly, the equations of the model are

$$\text{Net benefit of moving:} \quad M_i^* = \boldsymbol{\gamma}'\mathbf{w}_i + u_i,$$

$$\text{Income if moves:} \quad I_{i1} = \boldsymbol{\beta}_1'\mathbf{x}_{i1} + \varepsilon_{i1},$$

$$\text{Income if stays:} \quad I_{i0} = \boldsymbol{\beta}_0'\mathbf{x}_{i0} + \varepsilon_{i0}.$$

One of the components of the net benefit is the market wage individuals could achieve if they move, compared to what they could obtain if they stay. Therefore, among the determinants of the net benefit are factors that also affect the income received in either place.

───────────────────────────────

[40] See, for example, Heckman (1976). This strand of literature begins with an exchange by Gronau (1974) and Lewis (1974).

An analysis of income in a sample of migrants must account for the incidental truncation of the mover's income on a positive net benefit. Likewise, the income of the stayer is incidentally truncated on a nonpositive net benefit. The model implies an income after moving for all observations, but we observe it only for those who actually do move.

To put the preceding examples in a general framework, let the equation that determines the sample selection be

$$z_i^* = \boldsymbol{\gamma}'\mathbf{w}_i + u_i$$

and let the equation of primary interest be

$$y = \boldsymbol{\beta}'\mathbf{x}_i + \varepsilon_i.$$

The sample rule is that y_i is observed only when z_i^* is greater than zero. Suppose, as well, that ε_i and u_i have a bivariate normal distribution with zero means and correlation ρ. Then we may insert these in Theorem 22.4 to obtain the model *that applies to the observations in our sample:*

$$E[y_i|y_i \text{ is observed}] = E[y_i|z_i^* > 0]$$
$$= E[y_i|u_i > -\boldsymbol{\gamma}'\mathbf{w}_i]$$
$$= \boldsymbol{\beta}'\mathbf{x}_i + E[\varepsilon_i|u_i > -\boldsymbol{\gamma}'\mathbf{w}_i]$$
$$= \boldsymbol{\beta}'\mathbf{x}_i + \rho\sigma_\varepsilon\lambda_i(\alpha_u)$$
$$= \boldsymbol{\beta}'\mathbf{x}_i + \beta_\lambda\lambda_i(\alpha_u),$$

where

$$\alpha_u = \frac{-\boldsymbol{\gamma}'\mathbf{w}_i}{\sigma_u}$$

and

$$\lambda(\alpha) = \frac{\phi(\boldsymbol{\gamma}'\mathbf{w}_i/\sigma_u)}{\Phi(\boldsymbol{\gamma}'\mathbf{w}_i/\sigma_u)}.$$

So

$$y_i|z_i^* > 0 = \boldsymbol{\beta}'\mathbf{x}_i + \beta_\lambda\lambda_i(\alpha_u) + v_i.$$

Least squares regression using the observed data—for instance, OLS regression of hours on its determinants, using only data for women who are working—produces inconsistent estimates of $\boldsymbol{\beta}$. Once again, we can view the problem as an omitted variable. Least squares regression of y on $\mathbf{x}$ *and* λ would produce consistent estimates, but if λ is omitted, the specification error of an omitted variable is committed. Note, finally, that the second part of Theorem 22.4 implies that even if λ were observed, least squares would be inefficient. The disturbance, v, is heteroscedastic.

The marginal effect of the regressors on y_i *in the observed sample* consists of two components. There is the direct effect on the mean of y_i, which is $\boldsymbol{\beta}$. In addition, for a particular independent variable, if it appears in the probability that z_i^* is positive, it will influence y_i through its presence in λ_i. The full effect of changes in a regressor that appears in both $\mathbf{x}_i$ and $\mathbf{w}_i$ on y is

$$\frac{\partial E[y_i|z_i^* > 0]}{\partial x_{ik}} = \beta_k - \gamma_k\left(\frac{\rho\sigma_\varepsilon}{\sigma_u}\right)\delta_i(\alpha_u),$$

where

$$\delta_i = \lambda_i^2 + \alpha_i\lambda_i.^{41}$$

Suppose that ρ is positive and $E[y_i]$ is greater when z_i^* is positive than when it is negative. Since $0 < \delta_i < 1$, the additional term serves to reduce the marginal effect. The change in the probability affects the mean of y_i in that the mean in the group $z_i^* > 0$ is higher. The second term in the derivative compensates for this effect, leaving only the marginal effect of a change *given that $z_i^* \geq 0$ to begin with*. Consider Example 22.16, and suppose that education affects both the probability of migration and the income in either state. If we suppose that the income of migrants is higher than that of otherwise identical people who do not migrate, the marginal effect of education has two parts, one due to its influence in increasing the probability of the individual's entering a higher income group and one due to its influence on income within the group. As such, the coefficient on age in the regression overstates the marginal effect of the education of migrants and understates it for nonmigrants. The sizes of the various parts depend on the setting. It is quite possible that the magnitude, sign, and statistical significance of the effect might all be different from those of the estimate of $\boldsymbol{\beta}$, a point that appears frequently to be overlooked in empirical studies.

In most cases, the selection variable z^* is not observed. Rather, we observe only its sign. To consider our two examples, we typically observe only whether a woman is working or not working, or whether an individual migrated or not. We can infer the sign of z^*, but not its magnitude, from such information. Since there is no information on the scale of z^*, the disturbance variance in the selection equation cannot be estimated. (We encountered this problem in Chapter 21 in connection with the probit model.) Thus, we reformulate the model as follows:

Selection Mechanism

$$z_i^* = \boldsymbol{\gamma}'\mathbf{w}_i + u_i,$$

$$z_i = 1 \qquad \text{if } z_i^* > 0,$$

$$z_i = 0 \qquad \text{if } z_i^* \leq 0,$$

$$\text{Prob}(z_i = 1) = \Phi(\boldsymbol{\gamma}'\mathbf{w}_i),$$

$$\text{Prob}(z_i = 0) = 1 - \Phi(\boldsymbol{\gamma}'\mathbf{w}_i).$$

Regression Model

$$y_i = \boldsymbol{\beta}'\mathbf{x}_i + \varepsilon_i, \qquad \text{observed only if } z_i = 1,$$

$$(u_i, \varepsilon_i) \sim \text{bivariate normal } [0, 0, 1, \sigma_\varepsilon, \rho].$$

Suppose that, as in many of these studies, z_i and $\mathbf{w}_i$ are observed for a random sample of individuals, but y_i is observed only when $z_i = 1$. This is precisely the model we examined earlier, with

$$E[y_i | z_i = 1] = \boldsymbol{\beta}'\mathbf{x} + \rho\sigma_\varepsilon\lambda(\boldsymbol{\gamma}'\mathbf{w}).$$

---

[41] We have reversed the sign of α_u in (22–19) since $a = 0$, and $\alpha = \boldsymbol{\gamma}'\mathbf{w}/\sigma_u$ is somewhat more convenient. Also, as such, $\partial\lambda/\partial\alpha = -\delta$.

22.4.3. Estimation

The parameters of the sample selection model can be estimated by maximum likelihood. However, this is quite cumbersome, and an alternative procedure due to Heckman (1979) is usually used instead. Heckman's two-step estimation procedure is as follows:

1. Estimate the probit equation by maximum likelihood to obtain estimates of $\boldsymbol{\gamma}$. For each observation in the selected sample compute

$$\hat{\lambda}_i = \frac{\phi(\hat{\boldsymbol{\gamma}}'\mathbf{w}_i)}{\Phi(\hat{\boldsymbol{\gamma}}'\mathbf{w}_i)}.$$

We shall also require

$$\hat{\delta}_i = \hat{\lambda}_i(\hat{\lambda}_i + \hat{\boldsymbol{\gamma}}'\mathbf{w}_i).$$

2. Estimate $\boldsymbol{\beta}$ and $\beta_\lambda = \rho\sigma_\varepsilon$ by least squares regression of y on $\mathbf{x}$ and $\hat{\lambda}$.

EXAMPLE 22.17 The Migration Model Continued _____

Nakosteen and Zimmer (1980) applied the model of Example 22.16 to a sample of 9223 individuals with data for 2 years (1971 and 1973) sampled from the Social Security Administration's Continuous Work History Sample. Over the period, 1078 individuals migrated and the remaining 8145 did not. The independent variables in the migration equation were as follows:

$$SE = \text{self-employment dummy variable; 1 if yes,}$$

$$\Delta EMP = \text{rate of growth of state employment,}$$

$$\Delta PCI = \text{growth of state per capita income,}$$

$$AGE, RACE \text{ (nonwhite = 1), } SEX \text{ (female = 1),}$$

$$\Delta SIC = 1 \text{ if individual changes industry.}$$

The earnings equations included ΔSIC and SE. The authors reported the results given in Table 22.5. The figures in parentheses are asymptotic t ratios.

TABLE 22.5

	Migration	Migrant Earnings	Nonmigrant Earnings
Constant	−1.509	9.041	8.593
SE	−0.708	−4.104	−4.161
	(−5.72)	(−9.54)	(−57.71)
ΔEMP	−1.488	—	—
	(−2.60)		
ΔPCI	1.455	—	—
	(3.14)		
AGE	−0.008	—	—
	(−5.29)		
RACE	−0.065	—	—
	(−1.17)		
SEX	−0.082	—	—
	(−2.14)		
ΔSIC	0.948	−0.790	−0.927
	(24.15)	(−2.24)	(−9.35)
λ	—	0.212	.863
		(0.50)	(2.84)

It is also possible to obtain consistent estimates of the individual parameters ρ and σ_ε. At each observation, the true variance of the disturbance would be

$$\sigma_i^2 = \sigma_\varepsilon^2(1 - \rho^2\delta_i).$$

The average variance for the sample would converge to

$$\text{plim} \frac{1}{n} \sum_i \sigma_i^2 = \sigma_\varepsilon^2 - \sigma_\varepsilon^2\rho^2\overline{\delta}.$$

This is what is estimated by the least squares residual variance, $\mathbf{e}'\mathbf{e}/n$. For the square of the coefficient on λ, we have

$$\text{plim} \, b_\lambda^2 = \rho^2\sigma_\varepsilon^2,$$

while based on the probit results, we have

$$\text{plim} \frac{1}{n} \sum_i \hat{\delta}_i = \overline{\delta}.$$

Then we can obtain a consistent estimator of σ_ε^2 using

$$\hat{\sigma}_\varepsilon^2 = \frac{\mathbf{e}'\mathbf{e}}{n} + \overline{\delta}b_\lambda^2.$$

Finally, an estimate of ρ^2 is obtained as

$$\hat{\rho}^2 = \frac{b_\lambda^2}{\hat{\sigma}_\varepsilon^2}.$$

This provides a complete set of estimates of the model's parameters.[42]

In order to test hypotheses, an estimate of the asymptotic covariance matrix of $[\mathbf{b}', b_\lambda]$ is needed. We have two problems to contend with. First, we can see in Theorem 22.4 that the disturbance term in

$$(y_i|z_i = 1) = \boldsymbol{\beta}'\mathbf{x}_i + \rho\sigma_\varepsilon\lambda_i + v_i \tag{22-20}$$

is heteroscedastic:

$$\text{Var}[v_i] = \sigma_\varepsilon^2(1 - \rho^2\delta_i).$$

Suppose that we assume for the moment that λ and δ are known (i.e., we do not have to estimate $\boldsymbol{\gamma}$). For convenience, let $\mathbf{x}_i^* = [\mathbf{x}_i, \lambda_i]$ and let $\mathbf{b}^*$ be the least squares coefficient vector in the regression of y on $\mathbf{x}^*$ in the selected data. Then, using the appropriate form of the variance of ordinary least squares in a heteroscedastic model, from Chapter 14, we would have to estimate

$$\text{Var}[\mathbf{b}^*] = \sigma_\varepsilon^2[\mathbf{X}_*'\mathbf{X}_*]^{-1}\left[\sum_i (1 - \rho^2\delta_i)\mathbf{x}_i^*\mathbf{x}_i^{*'}\right][\mathbf{X}_*'\mathbf{X}_*]^{-1}$$

$$= \sigma_\varepsilon^2[\mathbf{X}_*'\mathbf{X}_*]^{-1}[\mathbf{X}_*'(\mathbf{I} - \rho^2\boldsymbol{\Delta})\mathbf{X}_*][\mathbf{X}_*'\mathbf{X}_*]^{-1},$$

where $\mathbf{I} - \rho^2\boldsymbol{\Delta}$ is a diagonal matrix with $(1 - \rho^2\delta_i)$ on the diagonal. Without any other complications, this could be computed fairly easily using $\mathbf{X}$, the sample estimates of σ_ε^2 and ρ^2, and the assumed known values of λ_i and δ_i.

---

[42]Note that $\hat{\rho}^2$ is not a sample correlation and, as such, is not limited to [0, 1]. See Greene (1981) for discussion.

The parameters in $\boldsymbol{\gamma}$ do have to be estimated using the probit equation. Rewrite (22–20) as

$$(y_i|z_i = 1) = \boldsymbol{\beta}'\mathbf{x}_i + \beta_\lambda \lambda_i + v_i + \beta_\lambda(\hat{\lambda}_i - \lambda_i).$$

In this form, we see that in the preceding expression, we have ignored both an additional source of variation in the compound disturbance and correlation across observations; the same estimate of $\boldsymbol{\gamma}$ is used to compute $\hat{\lambda}$ for every observation. Heckman has shown that the earlier variance matrix can be appropriately corrected by adding a term inside the brackets,

$$\mathbf{Q} = \hat{\rho}^2(\mathbf{X}'_*\boldsymbol{\Delta}\mathbf{W}) \text{ Est. Var}[\hat{\boldsymbol{\gamma}}](\mathbf{W}'\boldsymbol{\Delta}\mathbf{X}_*) = \hat{\rho}^2\mathbf{F}\hat{\mathbf{V}}\mathbf{F}',$$

where $\hat{\mathbf{V}} = \text{Est.Asy.Var}[\hat{\boldsymbol{\gamma}}]$, the estimator of the asymptotic covariance of the probit coefficients. Any of the estimators in (21–20) to (21–24) may be used to compute $\hat{\mathbf{V}}$. The complete expression is

$$\text{Var}[\mathbf{b}, b_\lambda] = \hat{\sigma}_\varepsilon^2[\mathbf{X}'_*\mathbf{X}_*]^{-1}[\mathbf{X}'_*(\mathbf{I} - \hat{\rho}^2\boldsymbol{\Delta})\mathbf{X}_* + \mathbf{Q}][\mathbf{X}'_*\mathbf{X}_*]^{-1}.^{[43]}$$

22.4.4. Treatment Effects

The basic model of selectivity outlined earlier has been extended in an impressive variety of directions.[44] An interesting application that has found wide use is the measurement of treatment effects and program effectiveness.

An earnings equation that accounts for the value of a college education is

$$\text{Earnings}_i = \boldsymbol{\beta}'\mathbf{x}_i + \delta C_i + \varepsilon_i,$$

where C_i is a dummy variable indicating whether or not the individual attended college. The same format has been used in any number of other analyses of programs, experiments, and treatments. The question is, does δ measure the value of a college education (assuming that the rest of the regression model is correctly specified)? The answer is no if the typical individual who chooses to go to college would have relatively high earnings whether or not he or she went to college. The problem is one of self-selection. If our observation is correct, least squares estimates of δ will actually overestimate the treatment effect. The same observation applies to estimates of the treatment effects in other settings in which the individuals themselves decide whether or not they will receive the treatment.

To put this in a more familiar context, suppose that we model program participation (e.g., whether or not the individual goes to college) as

$$C_i^* = \boldsymbol{\gamma}'\mathbf{w}_i + u_i$$

$$C_i = 1 \quad \text{if } C_i^* > 0, \text{ 0 otherwise.}$$

We also suppose that, consistent with our previous conjecture, u_i and ε_i are correlated. Coupled with our earnings equation, we find that

$$E[y_i|C_i = 1] = \boldsymbol{\beta}'\mathbf{x}_i + \delta + E[\varepsilon_i|C_i = 1]$$

$$\quad\quad (22-21)$$

$$= \boldsymbol{\beta}'\mathbf{x}_i + \delta + \rho\sigma_\varepsilon\lambda(\boldsymbol{\gamma}'\mathbf{w}_i)$$

once again. Evidently, a viable strategy for estimating this model is to use the two-step estimator discussed earlier. The net result will be a different estimate of δ that will account

---

[43] This formulation is derived in Greene (1981).

[44] For a survey, see Maddala (1983).

for the self-selected nature of program participation. For nonparticipants, the counterpart to (22–21) is

$$E[y_i | C_i = 0] = \boldsymbol{\beta}' \mathbf{x}_i + \rho \sigma_\varepsilon \left[\frac{-\phi(\boldsymbol{\gamma}' \mathbf{w}_i)}{1 - \Phi(\boldsymbol{\gamma}' \mathbf{w}_i)} \right].$$

The difference in expected earnings between participants and nonparticipants is, then,

$$E[y_i | C_i = 1] - E[y_i | C_i = 0] = \delta + \rho \sigma_\varepsilon \left[\frac{\phi_i}{\Phi_i (1 - \Phi_i)} \right].$$

If the selectivity correction, λ_i is omitted from the least squares regression, this difference is what is estimated by the least squares coefficient on the treatment dummy variable. But since (by assumption) all terms are positive, we see that least squares overestimates the treatment effect. Note, finally, that simply estimating separate equations for participants and nonparticipants does not solve the problem. In fact, this would be equivalent to estimating the two regressions of Example 22.16 by least squares, which, as we have seen, would lead to inconsistent estimates of both sets of parameters.

There are many variations of this model in the recent empirical literature. They have been applied to the analysis of education,[45] the Head Start program,[46] and a host of other settings.[47] This is a particularly important strand of literature, as the use of dummy variable models to analyze treatment effects and program participation has a long history in empirical economics. This analysis has called into question the interpretation of a number of received studies.

22.4.5. The Normality Assumption

Recent research has cast some skepticism on the selection model based on the normal distribution. [See Goldberger (1983) for an early salvo in this literature.] Among the findings are that the parameter estimates are surprisingly sensitive to the distributional assumption that underlies the model. Of course, this in itself does not invalidate the normality assumption, but it does call its generality into question. On the other hand, the received evidence is compelling that sample selection, in the abstract, raises serious problems, distributional questions aside. The most recent literature, for example Duncan (1986b), Manski (1989, 1990), and Heckman (1990), has suggested some promising approaches based on robust and nonparametric estimators. These obviously have the virtue of greater generality. Unfortunately, the cost is that these approaches generally are quite limited in the breadth of the models they can accommodate. That is, one might gain the robustness of a nonparametric estimator at the cost of being unable to make use of the rich set of accompanying variables usually present in the panels to which selectivity models are often applied. For example, the nonparametric bounds approach of Manski (1990) is defined for two regressors. Other methods [e.g., Duncan (1986b)] allow more elaborate specification. The upshot is that the issue remains unsettled. For better or worse, the empirical literature on the subject continues to be dominated by Heckman's original model built around the joint normal distribution.

[45] Willis and Rosen (1979).

[46] Goldberger (1972b).

[47] A useful summary of the issues is Barnow et al. (1981). See also Maddala (1983) for a long list of applications. A related application is the switching regression model. See, for example, Quandt (1982, 1988).

22.5. Models for Duration Data[48]

Intuition might suggest that the longer a strike persists, the more likely it is that it will end within, say, the next week. Or is it? It seems equally plausible to suggest that the longer a strike has lasted, the more difficult must be the problems that led to it in the first place, and hence the *less* likely it is that it will end in the next short time interval. A similar kind of reasoning could be applied to spells of unemployment or the interval between conceptions. In each of these cases, it is not only the duration of the event, per se, which is interesting, but also the likelihood that the event will end in "the next period" given that it has lasted as long as it has.

The analysis of duration data comes fairly recently to the economics literature. Analysis of the length of *time until failure* has interested engineers for decades. For example, the models discussed below were applied to the durability of electric and electronic components long before economists discovered their usefulness. Likewise, the analysis of *survival times,* for example, the length of survival after the diagnosis of a disease or after an operation such as a heart transplant, has long been a staple of biomedical research. Social scientists have recently applied the same body of techniques to strike duration, length of unemployment spells, intervals between conception, time until business failure, length of time between arrests, length of time from purchase until a warranty claim is made, intervals between purchases, and so on.

This section will give a brief introduction to the econometric analysis of duration data. As usual, we will restrict our attention to a few straightforward, relatively uncomplicated techniques and applications, primarily to introduce terms and concepts. The reader can then wade into the literature to find the extensions and variations. We will concentrate primarily on what are known as parametric models. These apply familiar inference techniques and provide a convenient departure point. Alternative approaches are considered at the end of the discussion.

22.5.1. Duration Data

The variable of interest in the analysis of duration is the length of time that elapses from the beginning of some event either until its end or until the measurement is taken, which may precede termination. Observations will typically consist of a cross section of durations, $t_1, t_2, \ldots, t_n$. The process being observed may have begun at different points in calendar time. For example, the strike duration data examined below are drawn from nine different years.

Censoring is a pervasive and usually unavoidable problem in the analysis of duration data. The common cause is that the measurement is made while the process is ongoing. An obvious example can be drawn from medical research. Consider analyzing the survival times of heart transplant patients. Although the beginning times may be known with precision, at the time of the measurement, observations on any individuals who are still alive are necessarily censored. Likewise, samples of spells of unemployment drawn from surveys will probably include some individuals who are unemployed at the time the survey is taken. For these individuals, duration, or survival, is at least the observed t_i, but

---

[48] Analysis of duration is a fairly new, but rapidly growing area in econometrics. There are a large number of highly technical articles, but relatively few accessible sources for the uninitiated. A particularly useful introductory survey is Kiefer (1988), upon which we have drawn heavily for this section. Other useful sources are Kalbfleisch and Prentice (1980), Heckman and Singer (1984a), and Lancaster (1990).

not equal to it. Estimation must account for the censored nature of the data for the same reasons as considered in Section 22.3. The consequences of ignoring censoring in duration data are not unlike those which arise in regression analysis.

In a conventional regression model that characterizes the conditional mean and variance of a distribution, the regressors can be taken as fixed characteristics at the point in time or for the individual for which the measurement is taken. When measuring duration, the observation is implicitly on a process that has been under way for a length of time, $[0, t)$. If the analysis is conditioned on a set of covariates (the counterparts to regressors) $\mathbf{x}_t$, the duration is implicitly a function of the entire time path of the variables $\mathbf{x}(t)$, $t = [0, t)$, which may have changed during the interval. For example, the observed duration of employment in a job may be a function of the individual's rank in the firm. But, their rank may well have changed several times between the time they were hired and when the observation was made. As such, observed rank at the end of the job tenure is not necessarily a complete description of the individual's rank *while they were employed*. Likewise, marital status, family size, and amount of education are all variables that can change during the duration of unemployment, and which one would like to account for in the duration model. The treatment of *time varying covariates* is a considerable complication.[49]

22.5.2. A Regression-like Approach—Parametric Models of Duration

We'll use the term "spell" as a catchall for the different duration variables we might measure. Spell length is represented by the random variable T. A simple approach to duration analysis would be to apply regression analysis to the sample of observed spells. By this device, we could characterize the expected duration, perhaps conditioned on a set of covariates whose values were measured at the end of the period. We could also assume that conditioned on an $\mathbf{x}$ which has remained fixed from $T = 0$ to $T = t$, t has a normal distribution, as we commonly do in regression. We could then characterize the probability distribution of observed duration times. But normality turns out not to be particularly attractive in this setting for a number of reasons, not least of which is that duration is positive by construction, while a normally distributed variable can take negative values. (*Log*normality turns out to be a palatable alternative, but it is only one among a long roster of contenders.)

22.5.2a. Theoretical Background. Suppose that the random variable T has a continuous probability distribution, $f(t)$, where t is a realization of T. The cumulative probability is

$$F(t) = \int_0^t f(s) \, ds = \text{Prob}(T \le t).$$

We will usually be more interested in the probability that the spell is of length *at least t*, which is given by the *survival function*,

$$S(t) = 1 - F(t) = \text{Prob}(T \ge t).$$

Consider the question raised in the introduction, which is, given that the spell has lasted until time t, what is the probability that it will end in the next short interval of time, say Δ? This is

$$l(t, \Delta) = \text{Prob}(t \le T \le t + \Delta \,|\, T \ge t).$$

---

[49] See Petersen (1986) for one approach to this problem.

A useful function for characterizing this aspect of the distribution is the *hazard rate,*

$$\lambda(t) = \lim_{\Delta \to 0} \frac{\text{Prob}(t \le T \le t + \Delta \,|\, T \ge t)}{\Delta}$$

$$= \lim_{\Delta \to 0} \frac{F(t + \Delta) - F(t)}{\Delta S(t)}$$

$$= \frac{f(t)}{S(t)}.$$

Roughly, the hazard rate is the rate at which spells are completed after duration t, given that they last at least until t. As such, the hazard function gives an answer to our original question.

Given the way our question was posed at the outset, we might prefer to model the hazard function rather than the density, the CDF, or the survival function. Clearly, all four functions are related. The hazard function is

$$\lambda(t) = \frac{-d \ln S(t)}{dt}$$

and

$$f(t) = S(t)\lambda(t).$$

Another useful function is the **integrated hazard function**

$$\Lambda(t) = \int_0^t \lambda(t) \; dt,$$

for which

$$S(t) = e^{-\Lambda(t)},$$

so

$$\Lambda(t) = -\ln S(t).$$

22.5.2b. Models of the Hazard Rate. For present purposes, the hazard function is more interesting than the survival rate or the density. Indeed, based on the results above, one might consider modeling the hazard function directly, rather than the survival function, then, for purposes of estimation, integrating backward to obtain the density. For example, the base case for many analyses is a hazard rate that does not vary over time. That is, $\lambda(t)$ is a constant, λ. This is characteristic of a process that has no memory; the *conditional* probability of "failure" in a given short interval is the same regardless of when the observation is made. Thus.

$$\lambda(t) = \lambda.$$

From the earlier definition, we obtain the simple differential equation,

$$\frac{-d \ln S(t)}{dt} = \lambda.$$

The solution is

$$\ln S(t) = k - \lambda t,$$

or

$$S(t) = Ke^{-\lambda t},$$

TABLE 22.6 Some Survival Distributions[a]

Distribution	Hazard Function, $\lambda(t)$	Survival Function, $S(t)$
Exponential	λ,	$S(t) = e^{-\lambda t}$
Weibull	$\lambda p(\lambda t)^{p-1}$,	$S(t) = e^{-(\lambda t)^p}$
Lognormal	$f(t) = (p/t)\phi(p \ln (\lambda t))$	$S(t) = \Phi(-p \ln (\lambda t))$
	($\ln t$ is normally distributed with mean $-\ln \lambda$ and standard deviation $1/p$.)	
Log-logistic	$\lambda(t) = \lambda p(\lambda t)^{p-1}/[1 + (\lambda t)^p]$,	$S(t) = 1/[1 + (\lambda t)^p]$
	($\ln t$ has a logistic distribution with mean $-\ln \lambda$ and variance $\pi^2/(3p^2)$.)	

[a] These formulations differ slightly from Kiefer's. His formulation of the Weibull hazard is $\lambda(t) = \gamma p t^{p-1}$, so his γ corresponds to our λ^p. We follow the convention of Kalbfleisch and Prentice (1980).

where K is the constant of integration. The condition that $S(0) = 1$ implies that $K = 1$, and the solution is

$$S(t) = e^{-\lambda t}.$$

This is the exponential distribution, which has been used to model the time until failure of electronic components, precisely because of the memoryless property of the distribution. Estimation of λ is simple, since with an exponential distribution, $E[t] = 1/\lambda$. The maximum likelihood estimate of λ would be $1/\bar{t}$.

A natural extension might be to model the hazard rate as a linear function, $\lambda(t) = \alpha + \beta t$. Then, $\Lambda(t) = \alpha t + \frac{1}{2}\beta t^2$ and $f(t) = \lambda(t)S(t) = \lambda(t) \exp(-\Lambda(t))$.[50] With an observed sample of durations, estimation of α and β is, at least in principle, a straightforward problem in maximum likelihood. [Kennan (1985) used a similar approach.]

A distribution whose hazard function slopes upward is said to have *positive duration dependence*. For such distributions, the likelihood of failure at time t, conditional upon duration up to time t, is increasing in t. The opposite case is that of decreasing hazard or *negative duration dependence*. Our question in the introduction about whether the strike is more or less likely to end at time t given that it has lasted until time t can be framed in terms of positive or negative duration dependence. The assumed distribution has a considerable bearing on the answer. If one is unsure at the outset of the analysis whether the data can be characterized by positive or negative duration dependence, it is counterproductive to assume a distribution that displays one characteristic or the other over the entire range of t. Thus, the exponential distribution and our suggested extension could be problematic.

The literature contains a cornucopia of choices for duration models, including normal, inverse normal [inverse Gaussian; see Lancaster (1990)], lognormal, F, gamma, Weibull (which is a popular choice), and many others.[51] To illustrate the differences, we will examine a few of the simpler ones. Table 22.6 lists the hazard functions and survival functions for four commonly used distributions.

All of these are distributions for a nonnegative random variable. Their hazard functions display very different behaviors. The hazard function for the exponential distribution is constant, that for the Weibull is monotonically increasing or decreasing depending on p, and the hazards for lognormal and log-logistic distributions first increase, then decrease. Which among these or the many alternatives is likely to be best in any application is uncertain.

[50] To avoid a negative hazard function, one might depart from $\lambda(t) = \exp(g(t, \boldsymbol{\theta}))$, where $\boldsymbol{\theta}$ is the vector of parameters to be estimated.

[51] Three sources that contain numerous specifications are Kalbfleisch and Prentice (1980), Cox and Oakes (1985), and Lancaster (1990).

22.5.2c. Maximum Likelihood Estimation. The parameters λ and p of these models can be estimated by maximum likelihood. For observed duration data, $t_1, t_2, \ldots, t_n$, the log-likelihood function can be formulated and maximized in the ways we have become familiar with in earlier chapters. Censored observations can be incorporated exactly as in Section 22.3 for the Tobit model. [See (22–13).] As such,

$$\ln L = \Sigma_{\text{uncensored observations}} \ln f(t\,|\,\theta) + \Sigma_{\text{censored observations}} \ln S(t\,|\,\theta),$$

where $\theta = (\lambda, p)$. For some distributions, it is convenient to formulate the log-likelihood function in terms of $f(t) = \lambda(t)S(t)$, so that

$$\ln L = \Sigma_{\text{uncensored observations}} \lambda(t\,|\,\theta) + \Sigma_{\text{all observations}} \ln S(t\,|\,\theta).$$

Inference about the parameters can be done in the usual way. Either the BHHH estimator or actual second derivatives can be used to estimate asymptotic standard errors for the estimates.[52]

EXAMPLE 22.18 Log-Linear Survival Models for Strike Duration _____

The strike duration data given in Kennan (1985, pp. 14–16) have become a familiar standard for the demonstration of hazard models. Table 22.7 lists the durations in days of 62 strikes that commenced in June of the years 1968 to 1976. Each involved at least 1000 workers and began at the expiration or reopening of a contract. Kennan reported the actual duration. In his survey, Kiefer, using the same observations we use below, censored the data at 80 days in order to demonstrate the effects of censoring. We have kept the data in their original form; the interested reader is referred to Kiefer for further analysis of the censoring problem.[53] The variable x reported with the strike duration data is a measure of unanticipated aggregate industrial production net of seasonal and trend components. It is computed as the residual in a regression of the log of industrial production in manufacturing on time, time squared, and monthly dummy variables.

TABLE 22.7   Strike Duration Data

Year	x	Strike Durations (days)										
1968	0.01138	7	9	13	14	26	29	52	130			
1969	0.02299	9	37	41	49	52	119					
1970	−0.03957	3	17	19	28	72	99	104	114	152	153	216
1971	−0.05467	15	61	98								
1972	0.00535	2	25	85								
1973	0.07427	3	10									
1974	0.06450	1	2	3	3	3	4	8	11	22		
		23	27	32	33	35	43	43	44	100		
1975	−0.10443	5	49									
1976	−0.00700	2	12	12	21	21	27	38	42	117		

---

[52] The transformation $w = p(\ln t + \ln \lambda)$ for these distributions greatly facilitates maximum likelihood estimation. For example, for the Weibull model, by defining $w = p(\ln t + \ln \lambda)$, we obtain the very simple density $f(w) = \exp(w - \exp(w))$. Therefore, by using $\ln t$ instead of t, we greatly simplify the log-likelihood function. Details for these and several other distributions may be found in Kalbfleisch and Prentice (1980, pp. 56–60). The Weibull distribution is examined in detail below.

[53] Our statistical results are nearly the same as Kiefer's despite the censoring.

TABLE 22.8 Estimated Duration Models (Estimated Standard Errors in Parentheses)

	λ	p	**Median Duration**
Exponential	0.02344	1.00000	29.571
	(0.00279)	(0.00000)	(3.5224)
Weibull	0.02439	0.92083	27.54275
	(0.00354)	(0.11086)	(3.9969)
Log-logistic	0.04153	1.33148	24.07853
	(0.00707)	(0.17201)	(4.10188)
Lognormal	0.04514	0.77206	22.15175
	(0.00806)	(0.08865)	(3.95395)

Parameter estimates for the four duration models are given in Table 22.8. The estimate of the median of the survival distribution is obtained by solving the equation $S(t) = 0.5$. For example, for the Weibull model,

$$S(M) = 0.5 = e^{-(\lambda M)^p}$$

or

$$M = \frac{1}{\lambda} (\ln 2)^{1/p}.$$

For the exponential model, $p = 1$. For the lognormal and log-logistic models, $M = 1/\lambda$. The delta method is then used to estimate the standard error of this function of the parameter estimates. (See Section 4.4.4.) All of these distributions are skewed to the right. As such, $E[t]$ is greater than the median. For the exponential and Weibull models, $E[t] = [1/\lambda]^p$; for the normal, $E[t] = (1/\lambda)[\exp(1/p^2)]^{1/2}$. The implied hazard functions are shown in Figure 22.5.

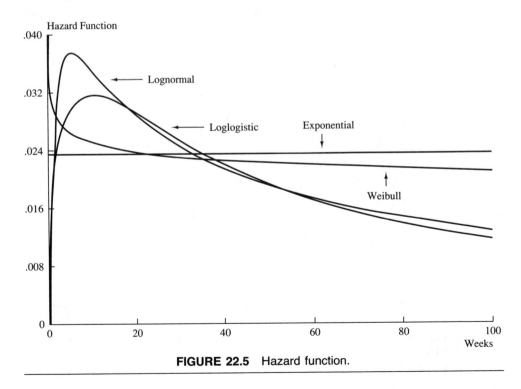

FIGURE 22.5 Hazard function.

22.5.2d. Exogenous Variables. One limitation of the models given above is that external factors are not given a role in the survival distribution. The addition of "covariates" to duration models is fairly straightforward, although the interpretation of the coefficients in the model is less so. Consider, for example, the Weibull model. (The extension to other distributions will be direct.) Let

$$\lambda_i = e^{-\boldsymbol{\beta}'\mathbf{x}_i},$$

where $\mathbf{x}_i$ is a constant term and a set of variables which are assumed not to change from time $T = 0$ to the "failure time," $T = t$. Making λ a function of a set of regressors is equivalent to changing the units of measurement on the time axis. For this reason, these models are sometimes called "accelerated failure time" models. Note, as well, that in all of the models listed (and generally), the regressors do not bear on the question of duration dependence, which is a function of p. Let

$$\sigma = \frac{1}{p},$$

$$\delta_i = \begin{cases} 1 & \text{if the spell is completed} \\ 0 & \text{if it is censored,} \end{cases}$$

$$w_i = p \ln (\lambda_i t_i) = \frac{\ln t_i - \boldsymbol{\beta}'\mathbf{x}_i}{\sigma}.$$

By making the change of variable, we find that

$$f(w_i) = \left(\frac{1}{\sigma}\right) \exp(w_i - e^{w_i})$$

$$S(w_i) = \exp(-e^{w_i}).$$

The log likelihood is

$$\ln L = \sum_i [\delta_i \ln f(w_i) + (1 - \delta_i) \ln S(w_i)],$$

which reduces to

$$\ln L = \sum_i [\delta_i(w_i - \ln \sigma) - e^{w_i}].$$

(Many other distributions, including the others in Table 22.6, simplify in the same way.) The derivatives are obtained by using $\partial w_i/\partial \sigma = -w_i/\sigma$ and $\partial w_i/\partial \boldsymbol{\beta} = -\mathbf{x}_i/\sigma$. These can be equated to zero using the methods described in Chapter 12. The individual terms can also be used to form the BHHH estimator of the asymptotic covariance matrix for the estimates.[54] The Hessian is also simple to derive, so Newton's method could be used instead.[55]

Note that the hazard function generally depends on t, p, and $\mathbf{x}$. The sign of the estimated coefficient suggests the direction of the effect of the variable on the hazard function when the hazard is monotonic. But in those cases, such as the log-logistic, in which the

---

[54] Note that the log-likelihood function has the same form as that for the Tobit model in Section 22.3. By just reinterpreting the nonlimit observations in a Tobit setting, we can, therefore, use this framework to apply a wide range of distributions to the Tobit model. [See Greene (1991) and references given therein.]

[55] See Kalbfleisch and Prentice (1980) for numerous other examples.

hazard is nonmonotonic, even this may be ambiguous. The magnitudes of the effects may also be difficult to interpret in terms of the hazard function. But in a few cases, we do get a regression-like interpretation. In the Weibull and exponential models, $E[t|\mathbf{x}_i] = \exp(p\boldsymbol{\beta}'\mathbf{x}_i)$, while for the log-normal and log-logistic models, $E[\ln t|\mathbf{x}_i] = \boldsymbol{\beta}'\mathbf{x}_i$. In these cases, β_k is the derivative (or a multiple of the derivative) of this conditional mean. Other cases are discussed by Kiefer (1988) and Kalbfleisch and Prentice (1980).

EXAMPLE 22.19 Weibull Model with a Covariate

With the industrial production variable included as a covariate, the estimated Weibull model is

$$-\ln \lambda = \begin{array}{cc} 3.7772 & - \quad 9.3515x, \\ (0.1394) & (2.973) \end{array} \qquad \begin{array}{c} p = 1.00288 \\ (0.1217), \end{array}$$

$$\text{Median strike length} = 27.35 \ (3.667) \text{ days}, \qquad E[t] = 39.83 \text{ days}.$$

Note that the Weibull model is now almost identical to the exponential model ($p = 1$). Since the hazard conditioned on x is approximately equal to λ_i, it follows that the hazard function is increasing in "unexpected" industrial production. A 1 percent increase in x leads to a 9.35 percent increase in λ, which since $p \approx 1$, translates into a 9.35 percent decrease in the median strike length, or about 2.6 days. (Note, $M = \ln 2/\lambda$.)

22.5.2e. Specification Analysis. There is no direct counterpart to the set of regression residuals with which to assess the validity of the specification of the duration model. The coefficients themselves can be analyzed with the familiar trinity of tests that we have used previously for analyzing maximum likelihood estimates. In most parametric models of duration, maximum likelihood estimation is fairly routine, so the choice among Wald, Lagrange multiplier, or likelihood ratio tests can be based on convenience. But an assessment of the overall specification of the model is more difficult. The integrated hazard function provides one useful measure. Regardless of the specification, under the hypothesis of the model, the sample of observations on $S(t|\theta)$, computed at the true parameter values, will have a uniform distribution. This is an application of the fundamental probability transform: Let $F(t)$ denote the CDF of t and let $z = F(t)$. Then $t = F^{-1}(z)$, and the CDF of z is $F(z) = F(F^{-1}(z)) = z$, which is the CDF of the standard uniform distribution. If $F(t) \sim U(0, 1)$, so is $S(t) = 1 - F(t)$. As such, one possible check on the specification of the model would be to see if the sample of estimated survival rates computed from the model looks like a sample from the uniform distribution. The usual approach is to use, instead, the

$$\text{generalized residual} = \varepsilon = \Lambda(t|\boldsymbol{\theta}) = -\ln S(t|\boldsymbol{\theta}).$$

This transformation of a $U(0, 1)$ variable will have CDF

$$F(\varepsilon) = 1 - e^{-\varepsilon},$$

which is the CDF of an exponential variable with parameter $\lambda = 1$. With this in hand, a rough check on the specification of the model can be done by examining the moments of the generalized residuals. The theoretical values for the unit exponential distribution, in the absence of censoring, based on $E[\varepsilon^r] = r!$, would be 1, 1, 2, and 9 for the mean and the next three central moments. The first is imposed by the maximization of the log likelihood, but the other moment restrictions could be tested, for example using the methods in Section 22.3.4c. The conditional moment test is derived in general terms in Kiefer (1985b) and Sharma (1989). The precise test procedure for our Weibull model, based on Pagan and Vella's (1989) results (see Section 22.3.4c), is detailed in Jaggia (1991).

EXAMPLE 22.20 A Conditional Moment Test for the Weibull Distribution _____

The generalized residuals for the Weibull model are

$$e_i = [\exp(-\hat{\boldsymbol{\beta}}'\mathbf{x}_i)t_i]^{\hat{p}}.$$

The sample mean is 1.0 as expected. The theoretical moments which we can use for a specification test are

$$\mu_2' = E[\varepsilon^2] = 2$$

$$\mu_3' = E[\varepsilon^3] = 6$$

$$\mu_4' = E[\varepsilon^4] = 24$$

$$\mu_*' = E[\ln \varepsilon] = \Psi(1) = -0.5772.$$

Jaggia suggests two tests, one based on μ_2' and μ_*', and one based on μ_2', μ_3', and μ_4'. Both tests are based on Pagan and Vella's results for conditional moment tests. The test statistic is

$$\chi^2[2 \text{ or } 3] = \mathbf{i}'\mathbf{M}(\mathbf{M}'\mathbf{M} - \mathbf{M}'\mathbf{D}(\mathbf{D}'\mathbf{D})^{-1}\mathbf{D}'\mathbf{M})^{-1}\mathbf{M}'\mathbf{i},$$

where

$\mathbf{i} = n \times 1$ column of 1s ($n = 62$),

$\mathbf{M} = n \times J$ matrix whose ith row is the individual term in the moment.

For the first test, the sample moment is

$$\mathbf{m} = \frac{1}{62} \sum_i \begin{bmatrix} e_i^2 - 2 \\ \ln e_i - \Psi(1) \end{bmatrix}.$$

The transpose of the ith term is the ith row in $\mathbf{M}$. For the second test, the ith row in $\mathbf{M}$ is

$$\mathbf{M}^i = [e_i^2 - 2, \ e_i^3 - 6, \ e_i^4 - 24].$$

The matrix $(\mathbf{D}'\mathbf{D})^{-1}$ is the estimator of the asymptotic covariance matrix of the parameter estimators. For the Weibull model, the parameters are $\boldsymbol{\theta}' = [\beta_1, \beta_2, p]$. The estimates are given in Example 22.19. This is the BHHH estimator of the asymptotic covariance matrix. The log likelihood is given in Section 22.5.2d. The derivatives of the individual terms in $\ln L = \Sigma_i \ln f_i$ are

$$\frac{\partial \ln f_i}{\partial \boldsymbol{\theta}'} = \frac{1}{\sigma} \begin{bmatrix} \mathbf{x}_i(e_i^{w_i} - \delta_i) - \mathbf{0} \\ w_i(e_i^{w_i} - \delta_i) - \delta_i \end{bmatrix}'.$$

This gives the ith row of $\mathbf{D}$. The values of the two test statistics are 50.2285 and 60.6528. The critical values from the chi-squared table are 5.99 for the first and 7.82 for the second, so these results cast doubt on the specification of the Weibull model. (Jaggia reaches the same conclusion using all 566 of Kennan's observations.)

Other approaches to specification analysis are suggested by Kiefer (1985a, 1988), Lancaster and Chesher (1985), Chesher et al. (1985), Lawless (1982), and Lancaster (1990).

22.5.2f. Heterogeneity. The problem of heterogeneity in duration models can be viewed essentially as the result of an incomplete specification. Individual specific covariates are intended to incorporate observation specific effects. But if the model specification is incomplete, and systematic individual differences in the distribution remain after the observed effects are accounted for, then inference based on the improperly specified model is likely to be problematic. We have already encountered several settings in which the possibility of heterogeneity mandated a change in the model specification; the fixed and random effects regression, logit, and probit models all incorporate observation-specific effects. Indeed, all of the failures of the linear regression model discussed in the preceding chapters can be interpreted as a consequence of heterogeneity arising from an incomplete specification.

There are a number of ways of extending duration models to account for heterogeneity. The strictly nonparametric approach of the Kaplan–Meier estimator is largely immune to the problem, but it is also rather limited in how much information can be culled from it. One direct approach is to model heterogeneity in the parametric model. Suppose that we posit a survival function conditioned on the individual specific effect, v_i. We treat the survival function as $S(t_i|v_i)$. Then add to that a model for the unobserved heterogeneity, $f(v_i)$. (Note that this is a counterpart to the incorporation of a disturbance in a regression model.) Then

$$S(t) = E_v[S(t|v)]$$

$$= \int_v f(v)S(t|v) \, dv.$$

The gamma distribution is frequently used for this purpose.[56] Consider, for example, using this device to incorporate heterogeneity into the Weibull model we used earlier. As is typical, we assume that v has a gamma distribution with mean 1 and variance $\theta = 1/k$. Then

$$f(v) = \frac{k^k}{\Gamma(k)} e^{-kv} v^{k-1}$$

and

$$S(t|v) = e^{-(v\lambda t)^p}.$$

After a bit of manipulation, we obtain the unconditional distribution,

$$S(t) = \int_0^\infty f(v)S(t|v) \, dv = [1 + \theta(\lambda t)^p]^{-1/\theta}.$$

The limiting value, with $\theta = 0$, is the Weibull survival model, so $\theta = 0$ corresponds to $\text{Var}[v] = 0$, or no heterogeneity.[57] The hazard function for this model is

$$\lambda(t) = \lambda p(\lambda t)^{p-1}[S(t)]^\theta,$$

which shows the relationship to the Weibull model.

This is a common approach to parametric modeling of heterogeneity. In an important paper on this subject, Heckman and Singer (1984b) argued that this approach tends to overparameterize the survival distribution and can lead to rather serious errors in inference. They gave some dramatic examples to make the point. They also expressed some

---

[56] See, for example, Hausman et al. (1984), who use it to incorporate heterogeneity in the Poisson regression model.

[57] For the strike data analyzed earlier, the maximum likelihood estimate of θ is 0.0004, which suggests that at least in the context of the Weibull model, heterogeneity does not appear to be a problem.

concern that researchers tend to choose the distribution of heterogeneity more on the basis of mathematical convenience than on any sensible economic basis.

22.5.3. Other Approaches

The parametric models are attractive for their simplicity. But by imposing as much structure on the data as they do, the models may distort the estimated hazard rates. It may be that a more accurate representation can be obtained by imposing fewer restrictions.

The Kaplan–Meier **product limit estimator** is a strictly empirical approach to survival and hazard function estimation. Assume that the observations on duration are sorted in ascending order, so $t_1 \leq t_2$, and so on, and for now, that no observations are censored. Suppose, as well, that there are K distinct survival times in the data, denoted T_k; K will equal n unless there are ties. Let n_k denote the number of individuals whose observed duration is at least T_k. The set of individuals whose duration is at least T_k is called the *risk set* at this duration. (We borrow, once again, from biostatistics, where the risk set is those individuals still "at risk" at time T_k). Thus, n_k is the size of the risk set at time T_k. Let h_k denote the number of observed spells completed at time T_k. An empirical estimate of the survivor function would be

$$\widehat{S}(T) = \frac{n_k - h_k}{n}.$$

The estimator of the hazard rate is

$$\widehat{\lambda}(T_k) = \frac{h_k}{n_k}.$$

Corrections are necessary for observations that are censored. Lawless (1982), Kalbfleisch and Prentice (1980), Kiefer (1988), and Greene (1991) give details.

EXAMPLE 22.21 _____

The estimates of $\lambda(t)$ and $S(t)$ are tabulated in Kiefer (1988, p. 658). Figures 22.6 and 22.7 show the estimated survival and hazard functions.

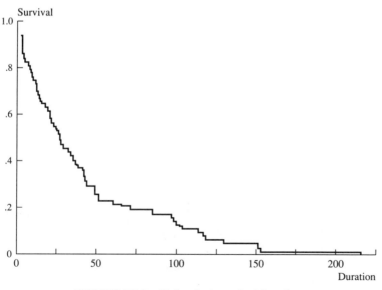

FIGURE 22.6 Estimated survival function.

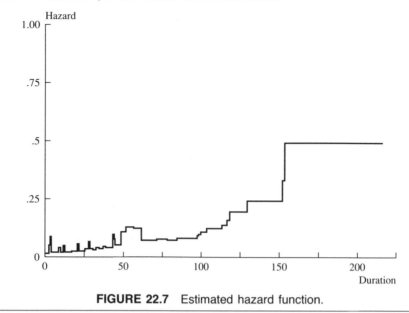

FIGURE 22.7 Estimated hazard function.

Cox's (1972) approach to the *proportional hazard model* is another popular method of analyzing the effect of covariates on the hazard rate. The model specifies that

$$\lambda(t_i) = e^{-\beta' x_i}\lambda_0(t_i).$$

The function λ_0 is the "baseline" hazard. In principle, this is a parameter for each observation which must be estimated. Cox's partial likelihood estimator provides a method of estimating β without requiring estimation of λ_0. The estimator is somewhat similar to Chamberlain's estimator for the logit model with panel data in that a conditioning operation is used to remove the heterogeneity. (See Section 21.5.1.) Hausman and Han (1990) and Meyer (1988) have devised other "semiparametric" specifications for hazard models.

EXAMPLE 22.22 _____

The proportional hazard model does not have a constant term. (The baseline hazard is an individual specific constant.) For the strike data, the estimate of β is -9.0726, with an estimated standard error of 3.225. This is very similar to the estimate obtained for the Weibull model in Example 22.19.

EXERCISES

1. The following 20 observations are drawn from a censored normal distribution:

3.8396	7.2040	0.00000	0.00000	4.4132	8.0230
5.7971	7.0828	0.00000	0.80260	13.0670	4.3211
0.00000	8.6801	5.4571	0.00000	8.1021	0.00000
1.2526	5.6016				

The applicable model is

$$y_i^* = \mu + \varepsilon_i$$

$$y_i = y_i^* \qquad \text{if } \mu + \varepsilon_i > 0, \ 0 \text{ otherwise.}$$

$$\varepsilon_i \sim N[0, \sigma^2].$$

All exercises in this section are based on the preceding. The OLS estimator of μ in the context of this tobit model is simply the sample mean. Compute the mean of all 20 observations. Would you expect this estimator to over- or underestimate μ? If we consider only the nonzero observations, the truncated regression model applies. The sample mean of the nonlimit observations is the least squares estimator in this context. Compute it and then comment on whether this should be an overestimate or an underestimate of the true mean.

2. We now consider the tobit model that applies to the full data set.
   (a) Formulate the log likelihood for this very simple Tobit model.
   (b) Reformulate the log likelihood in terms of $\theta = 1/\sigma$ and $\gamma = \mu/\sigma$. Then derive the necessary conditions for maximizing the log likelihood with respect to θ and γ.
   (c) Discuss how you would obtain the values of θ and γ to solve the problem in part (b).
   (d) Obtain the maximum likelihood estimators of μ and σ.

3. Using only the nonlimit observations, repeat Exercise 2 in the context of the truncated regression model.

4. Estimate μ and σ by using the method of moments estimator outlined in Example 22.4. Compare your results to those in the previous exercises.

5. Continuing to use the data in Exercise 1, consider once again only the nonzero observations. Suppose that the sampling mechanism is as follows: y^* and another normally distributed random variable, z, have population correlation 0.7. The two variables, y^* and z, are sampled jointly. When z is greater than zero, y is reported. When z is less than zero, both z and y are discarded. Exactly 35 draws were required in order to obtain the preceding sample. Estimate μ and σ. (**Hint:**   Use Theorem 22.4.)

Appendix Tables

TABLE 1. Cumulative Normal Distribution; Table Entry Is Prob($Z \leq z$)

z	.00	.01	.02	.03	.04	.05	.06	.07	.08	.09
0.0	.5000	.5040	.5080	.5120	.5160	.5199	.5239	.5279	.5319	.5359
0.1	.5398	.5438	.5478	.5517	.5557	.5596	.5636	.5675	.5714	.5753
0.2	.5793	.5832	.5871	.5910	.5948	.5987	.6026	.6064	.6103	.6141
0.3	.6179	.6217	.6255	.6293	.6331	.6368	.6406	.6443	.6480	.6517
0.4	.6554	.6591	.6628	.6664	.6700	.6736	.6772	.6808	.6844	.6879
0.5	.6915	.6950	.6985	.7019	.7054	.7088	.7123	.7157	.7190	.7224
0.6	.7257	.7291	.7324	.7357	.7389	.7422	.7454	.7486	.7517	.7549
0.7	.7580	.7611	.7642	.7673	.7704	.7734	.7764	.7794	.7823	.7852
0.8	.7881	.7910	.7939	.7967	.7995	.8023	.8051	.8078	.8106	.8133
0.9	.8159	.8186	.8212	.8238	.8264	.8289	.8315	.8340	.8365	.8389
1.0	.8413	.8438	.8461	.8485	.8508	.8531	.8554	.8577	.8599	.8621
1.1	.8643	.8665	.8686	.8708	.8729	.8749	.8770	.8790	.8810	.8830
1.2	.8849	.8869	.8888	.8907	.8925	.8944	.8962	.8980	.8997	.9015
1.3	.9032	.9049	.9066	.9082	.9099	.9115	.9131	.9147	.9162	.9177
1.4	.9192	.9207	.9222	.9236	.9251	.9265	.9279	.9292	.9306	.9319
1.5	.9332	.9345	.9357	.9370	.9382	.9394	.9406	.9418	.9429	.9441
1.6	.9452	.9463	.9474	.9484	.9495	.9505	.9515	.9525	.9535	.9545
1.7	.9554	.9564	.9573	.9582	.9591	.9599	.9608	.9616	.9625	.9633
1.8	.9641	.9649	.9656	.9664	.9671	.9678	.9686	.9693	.9699	.9706
1.9	.9713	.9719	.9726	.9732	.9738	.9744	.9750	.9756	.9761	.9767
2.0	.9772	.9778	.9783	.9788	.9793	.9798	.9803	.9808	.9812	.9817
2.1	.9821	.9826	.9830	.9834	.9838	.9842	.9846	.9850	.9854	.9857
2.2	.9861	.9864	.9868	.9871	.9875	.9878	.9881	.9884	.9887	.9890
2.3	.9893	.9896	.9898	.9901	.9904	.9906	.9909	.9911	.9913	.9916
2.4	.9918	.9920	.9922	.9925	.9927	.9929	.9931	.9932	.9934	.9936
2.5	.9938	.9940	.9941	.9943	.9945	.9946	.9948	.9949	.9951	.9952
2.6	.9953	.9955	.9956	.9957	.9959	.9960	.9961	.9962	.9963	.9964
2.7	.9965	.9966	.9967	.9968	.9969	.9970	.9971	.9972	.9973	.9974
2.8	.9974	.9975	.9976	.9977	.9977	.9978	.9979	.9979	.9980	.9981
2.9	.9981	.9982	.9982	.9983	.9984	.9984	.9985	.9985	.9986	.9986
3.0	.9987	.9987	.9987	.9988	.9988	.9989	.9989	.9989	.9990	.9990
3.1	.9990	.9991	.9991	.9991	.9992	.9992	.9992	.9992	.9993	.9993
3.2	.9993	.9993	.9994	.9994	.9994	.9994	.9994	.9995	.9995	.9995
3.3	.9995	.9995	.9995	.9996	.9996	.9996	.9996	.9996	.9996	.9997
3.4	.9997	.9997	.9997	.9997	.9997	.9997	.9997	.9997	.9997	.9998

TABLE 2. Ordinates of the Standard Normal Density; Table Entry Is $f(z)$

z	.00	.01	.02	.03	.04	.05	.06	.07	.08	.09
0.0	.3989	.3989	.3989	.3988	.3986	.3984	.3982	.3980	.3977	.3973
0.1	.3970	.3965	.3961	.3956	.3951	.3945	.3939	.3932	.3925	.3918
0.2	.3910	.3902	.3894	.3885	.3876	.3867	.3857	.3847	.3836	.3825
0.3	.3814	.3802	.3790	.3778	.3765	.3752	.3739	.3725	.3712	.3697
0.4	.3683	.3668	.3653	.3637	.3621	.3605	.3589	.3572	.3555	.3538
0.5	.3521	.3503	.3485	.3467	.3448	.3429	.3410	.3391	.3372	.3352
0.6	.3332	.3312	.3292	.3271	.3251	.3230	.3209	.3187	.3166	.3144
0.7	.3123	.3101	.3079	.3056	.3034	.3011	.2989	.2966	.2943	.2920
0.8	.2897	.2874	.2850	.2827	.2803	.2780	.2756	.2732	.2709	.2685
0.9	.2661	.2637	.2613	.2589	.2565	.2541	.2516	.2492	.2468	.2444
1.0	.2420	.2396	.2371	.2347	.2323	.2299	.2275	.2251	.2227	.2203
1.1	.2179	.2155	.2131	.2107	.2083	.2059	.2036	.2012	.1989	.1965
1.2	.1942	.1919	.1895	.1872	.1849	.1826	.1804	.1781	.1758	.1736
1.3	.1714	.1691	.1669	.1647	.1626	.1604	.1582	.1561	.1539	.1518
1.4	.1497	.1476	.1456	.1435	.1415	.1394	.1374	.1354	.1334	.1315
1.5	.1295	.1276	.1257	.1238	.1219	.1200	.1182	.1163	.1145	.1127
1.6	.1109	.1092	.1074	.1057	.1040	.1023	.1006	.0989	.0973	.0957
1.7	.0940	.0925	.0909	.0893	.0878	.0863	.0848	.0833	.0818	.0804
1.8	.0790	.0775	.0761	.0748	.0734	.0721	.0707	.0694	.0681	.0669
1.9	.0656	.0644	.0632	.0620	.0608	.0596	.0584	.0573	.0562	.0551
2.0	.0540	.0529	.0519	.0508	.0498	.0488	.0478	.0468	.0459	.0449
2.1	.0440	.0431	.0422	.0413	.0404	.0396	.0387	.0379	.0371	.0363
2.2	.0355	.0347	.0339	.0332	.0325	.0317	.0310	.0303	.0297	.0290
2.3	.0283	.0277	.0270	.0264	.0258	.0252	.0246	.0241	.0235	.0229
2.4	.0224	.0219	.0213	.0208	.0203	.0198	.0194	.0189	.0184	.0180
2.5	.0175	.0171	.0167	.0163	.0158	.0154	.0151	.0147	.0143	.0139
2.6	.0136	.0132	.0129	.0126	.0122	.0119	.0116	.0113	.0110	.0107
2.7	.0104	.0101	.0099	.0096	.0093	.0091	.0088	.0086	.0084	.0081
2.8	.0079	.0077	.0075	.0073	.0071	.0069	.0067	.0065	.0063	.0061
2.9	.0060	.0058	.0056	.0055	.0053	.0051	.0050	.0048	.0047	.0046
3.0	.0044	.0043	.0042	.0040	.0039	.0038	.0037	.0036	.0035	.0034
3.1	.0033	.0032	.0031	.0030	.0029	.0028	.0027	.0026	.0025	.0025
3.2	.0024	.0023	.0022	.0022	.0021	.0020	.0020	.0019	.0018	.0018
3.3	.0017	.0017	.0016	.0016	.0015	.0015	.0014	.0014	.0013	.0013
3.4	.0012	.0012	.0012	.0011	.0011	.0010	.0010	.0010	.0009	.0009

TABLE 3. Percentiles of the Student's *t* Distribution;
Table Entry Is *x* Such That Prob($t_n \leq x$) = *P*

$\dfrac{P}{n}$	.750	.900	.950	.975	.990	.995
1	1.000	3.078	6.314	12.71	31.82	63.66
2	0.817	1.886	2.920	4.303	6.965	9.925
3	0.766	1.638	2.354	3.182	4.541	5.841
4	0.741	1.533	2.132	2.777	3.747	4.604
5	0.727	1.476	2.015	2.571	3.365	4.032
6	0.718	1.440	1.943	2.447	3.143	3.708
7	0.711	1.415	1.895	2.365	2.998	3.500
8	0.706	1.397	1.860	2.306	2.897	3.355
9	0.703	1.383	1.833	2.262	2.822	3.250
10	0.700	1.372	1.813	2.228	2.764	3.169
11	0.698	1.363	1.796	2.201	2.718	3.106
12	0.696	1.356	1.782	2.179	2.681	3.055
13	0.694	1.350	1.771	2.161	2.650	3.012
14	0.693	1.345	1.762	2.145	2.624	2.977
15	0.691	1.341	1.753	2.132	2.602	2.947
16	0.691	1.337	1.746	2.120	2.584	2.921
17	0.689	1.333	1.740	2.110	2.567	2.898
18	0.688	1.330	1.734	2.101	2.552	2.879
19	0.688	1.328	1.729	2.093	2.539	2.861
20	0.687	1.326	1.725	2.086	2.528	2.845
21	0.687	1.323	1.721	2.080	2.518	2.831
22	0.686	1.321	1.717	2.074	2.508	2.819
23	0.686	1.319	1.714	2.069	2.500	2.807
24	0.686	1.318	1.711	2.064	2.492	2.797
25	0.685	1.316	1.708	2.060	2.485	2.787
26	0.684	1.315	1.706	2.056	2.479	2.779
27	0.684	1.314	1.704	2.052	2.473	2.771
28	0.683	1.313	1.701	2.048	2.467	2.763
29	0.683	1.311	1.699	2.045	2.462	2.756
30	0.683	1.311	1.697	2.042	2.457	2.750
35	0.682	1.307	1.690	2.030	2.438	2.724
40	0.681	1.303	1.684	2.021	2.423	2.705
45	0.680	1.301	1.680	2.014	2.412	2.690
50	0.680	1.299	1.676	2.009	2.403	2.678
60	0.679	1.296	1.671	2.000	2.390	2.660
70	0.679	1.294	1.667	1.994	2.381	2.648
80	0.679	1.292	1.664	1.990	2.374	2.639
90	0.678	1.291	1.662	1.987	2.368	2.632
100	0.677	1.290	1.660	1.984	2.364	2.626
∞	0.674	1.282	1.645	1.960	2.326	2.576

TABLE 4. Percentiles of the Chi-Squared Distribution; Table Entry Is c Such That $\text{Prob}(\chi_n^2 \leq c) = P$

n \ P	.005	.010	.025	.050	.100	.250	.500	.750	.900	.950	.975	.990	.995
1	.00004	.0002	.001	.004	0.02	0.10	0.46	1.32	2.71	3.84	5.02	6.63	7.89
2	0.01	0.02	0.05	0.10	0.21	0.58	1.39	2.77	4.61	5.99	7.38	9.21	10.60
3	0.07	0.12	0.22	0.35	0.59	1.21	2.37	4.11	6.25	7.82	9.35	11.34	12.84
4	0.21	0.30	0.49	0.71	1.06	1.92	3.36	5.39	7.78	9.49	11.14	13.28	14.86
5	0.41	0.56	0.83	1.15	1.61	2.68	4.35	6.63	9.24	11.07	12.83	15.09	16.75
6	0.68	0.87	1.24	1.64	2.21	3.46	5.35	7.84	10.64	12.59	14.45	16.81	18.55
7	0.99	1.24	1.69	2.17	2.83	4.25	6.35	9.04	12.02	14.07	16.01	18.48	20.28
8	1.35	1.65	2.18	2.73	3.49	5.07	7.34	10.22	13.36	15.51	17.54	20.09	21.96
9	1.74	2.09	2.70	3.33	4.17	5.90	8.34	11.39	14.68	16.92	19.02	21.67	23.59
10	2.16	2.56	3.25	3.94	4.87	6.74	9.34	12.55	15.99	18.31	20.48	23.21	25.19
11	2.60	3.05	3.82	4.57	5.58	7.59	10.34	13.70	17.28	19.68	21.92	24.72	26.76
12	3.07	3.57	4.40	5.23	6.30	8.44	11.34	14.85	18.55	21.03	23.34	26.22	28.30
13	3.57	4.11	5.01	5.89	7.04	9.30	12.34	15.98	19.81	22.36	24.74	27.69	29.82
14	4.07	4.66	5.63	6.57	7.79	10.17	13.34	17.12	21.07	23.69	26.12	29.14	31.32
15	4.60	5.23	6.26	7.26	8.55	11.04	14.34	18.25	22.31	25.00	27.49	30.58	32.80
16	5.14	5.81	6.91	7.96	9.31	11.91	15.34	19.37	23.54	26.30	28.85	32.00	34.27
17	5.70	6.41	7.57	8.67	10.09	12.79	16.34	20.49	24.77	27.59	30.19	33.41	35.72
18	6.26	7.01	8.23	9.39	10.86	13.68	17.34	21.61	25.99	28.87	31.53	34.81	37.16
19	6.84	7.63	8.91	10.12	11.65	14.56	18.34	22.72	27.20	30.14	32.85	36.19	38.58
20	7.43	8.26	9.59	10.85	12.44	15.45	19.34	23.83	28.41	31.41	34.17	37.57	40.00
21	8.03	8.90	10.28	11.59	13.24	16.35	20.34	24.93	29.62	32.67	35.48	38.93	41.40
22	8.64	9.54	10.98	12.34	14.04	17.24	21.34	26.04	30.81	33.93	36.78	40.29	42.80
23	9.26	10.20	11.69	13.09	14.85	18.14	22.34	27.14	32.01	35.17	38.08	41.64	44.18
24	9.89	10.86	12.40	13.85	15.66	19.04	23.34	28.24	33.20	36.42	39.37	42.98	45.56
25	10.52	11.52	13.12	14.61	16.47	19.94	24.34	29.34	34.38	37.65	40.65	44.32	46.93
26	11.16	12.20	13.84	15.38	17.29	20.84	25.34	30.44	35.56	38.89	41.92	45.64	48.29
27	11.81	12.88	14.57	16.15	18.11	21.75	26.34	31.53	36.74	40.11	43.19	46.96	49.65
28	12.46	13.56	15.31	16.93	18.94	22.66	27.34	32.62	37.92	41.34	44.46	48.28	50.99
29	13.12	14.26	16.05	17.71	19.77	23.57	28.34	33.71	39.09	42.56	45.72	49.59	52.34

n \ P	.005	.010	.025	.050	.100	.250	.500	.750	.900	.950	.975	.990	.995
30	13.79	14.95	16.79	18.49	20.60	24.48	29.34	34.80	40.26	43.77	46.98	50.89	53.67
31	13.70	15.04	17.11	19.01	21.31	25.46	30.50	36.00	41.33	44.70	47.73	51.38	53.94
32	14.37	15.74	17.87	19.80	22.15	26.37	31.50	37.08	42.49	45.91	48.98	52.67	55.26
33	15.05	16.45	18.62	20.59	22.99	27.29	32.50	38.17	43.65	47.12	50.22	53.96	56.59
34	15.73	17.16	19.38	21.39	23.83	28.21	33.50	39.25	44.81	48.32	51.46	55.25	57.90
35	16.42	17.88	20.14	22.19	24.68	29.13	34.50	40.33	45.97	49.52	52.70	56.53	59.21
36	17.11	18.60	20.91	22.99	25.52	30.05	35.50	41.41	47.12	50.71	53.94	57.81	60.52
37	17.81	19.33	21.68	23.80	26.37	30.97	36.50	42.49	48.27	51.91	55.17	59.08	61.83
38	18.51	20.06	22.45	24.61	27.22	31.89	37.50	43.57	49.42	53.10	56.39	60.35	63.13
39	19.22	20.79	23.22	25.42	28.08	32.81	38.50	44.65	50.57	54.29	57.62	61.62	64.42
40	19.92	21.53	24.00	26.23	28.93	33.73	39.50	45.72	51.71	55.47	58.84	62.88	65.71
41	20.64	22.27	24.78	27.05	29.79	34.66	40.50	46.80	52.86	56.66	60.06	64.14	67.00
42	21.35	23.01	25.57	27.87	30.65	35.58	41.50	47.87	54.00	57.84	61.28	65.40	68.29
43	22.07	23.76	26.35	28.69	31.51	36.51	42.50	48.95	55.14	59.02	62.49	66.65	69.57
44	22.79	24.51	27.14	29.51	32.37	37.44	43.50	50.02	56.27	60.19	63.70	67.91	70.84
45	23.52	25.26	27.93	30.34	33.23	38.37	44.50	51.09	57.41	61.37	64.91	69.15	72.12
46	24.25	26.02	28.72	31.16	34.10	39.29	45.50	52.16	58.55	62.54	66.12	70.40	73.39
47	24.98	26.77	29.52	31.99	34.96	40.22	46.50	53.23	59.68	63.72	67.32	71.64	74.66
48	25.71	27.53	30.32	32.82	35.83	41.15	47.50	54.30	60.81	64.89	68.53	72.88	75.92
49	26.45	28.30	31.12	33.65	36.70	42.08	48.50	55.37	61.94	66.05	69.73	74.12	77.19
50	27.19	29.06	31.92	34.49	37.57	43.02	49.50	56.44	63.07	67.22	70.92	75.35	78.45

TABLE 5. 95th Percentiles of the F Distribution; Table Entry Is f Such That $\text{Prob}(F_{n_1,n_2} \leq f) = 0.95$

n_1 = Degrees of Freedom for the Numerator

n_2	1	2	3	4	5	6	7	8	9	10	12	15	20	30	40	50	60	∞
1	161.	200.	216.	225.	230.	234.	237.	239.	241.	242.	244.	246.	248.	250.	251.	251.	252.	254.
2	18.5	19.0	19.2	19.2	19.3	19.3	19.4	19.4	19.4	19.4	19.4	19.4	19.5	19.5	19.5	19.5	19.5	19.5
3	10.1	9.55	9.28	9.12	9.01	8.94	8.89	8.85	8.81	8.79	8.74	8.70	8.66	8.62	8.59	8.58	8.57	8.53
4	7.71	6.94	6.59	6.39	6.26	6.16	6.09	6.04	6.00	5.97	5.91	5.86	5.80	5.75	5.72	5.70	5.69	5.63
5	6.61	5.79	5.41	5.19	5.05	4.95	4.88	4.82	4.77	4.74	4.68	4.62	4.56	4.50	4.46	4.44	4.43	4.37
6	5.99	5.14	4.76	4.53	4.39	4.28	4.21	4.15	4.10	4.06	4.00	3.94	3.88	3.81	3.78	3.75	3.74	3.67
7	5.59	4.74	4.35	4.12	3.97	3.87	3.79	3.73	3.68	3.64	3.58	3.51	3.45	3.38	3.34	3.32	3.31	3.23
8	5.32	4.46	4.07	3.84	3.69	3.58	3.50	3.44	3.39	3.35	3.28	3.22	3.15	3.08	3.04	3.02	3.01	2.93
9	5.12	4.26	3.86	3.63	3.48	3.37	3.29	3.23	3.18	3.14	3.07	3.01	2.94	2.86	2.83	2.80	2.79	2.71
10	4.96	4.10	3.71	3.48	3.33	3.22	3.14	3.07	3.02	2.98	2.91	2.85	2.78	2.70	2.66	2.64	2.62	2.54
11	4.84	3.98	3.59	3.36	3.20	3.10	3.01	2.95	2.90	2.85	2.79	2.72	2.65	2.57	2.53	2.51	2.49	2.40
12	4.75	3.89	3.49	3.26	3.11	3.00	2.91	2.85	2.80	2.75	2.69	2.62	2.54	2.47	2.43	2.40	2.39	2.30
13	4.67	3.81	3.41	3.18	3.03	2.92	2.83	2.77	2.72	2.67	2.60	2.53	2.46	2.38	2.34	2.31	2.30	2.21
14	4.60	3.74	3.34	3.11	2.96	2.85	2.77	2.70	2.65	2.60	2.54	2.46	2.39	2.31	2.27	2.24	2.22	2.13
15	4.54	3.68	3.29	3.06	2.90	2.79	2.71	2.64	2.59	2.54	2.48	2.40	2.33	2.25	2.21	2.18	2.16	2.07
16	4.49	3.63	3.24	3.01	2.85	2.74	2.66	2.59	2.54	2.49	2.43	2.35	2.28	2.19	2.15	2.12	2.11	2.01
17	4.45	3.59	3.20	2.97	2.81	2.70	2.62	2.55	2.50	2.45	2.38	2.31	2.23	2.15	2.10	2.08	2.06	1.96
18	4.41	3.56	3.16	2.93	2.77	2.66	2.58	2.51	2.46	2.41	2.34	2.27	2.19	2.11	2.06	2.04	2.02	1.92
19	4.38	3.52	3.13	2.90	2.74	2.63	2.54	2.48	2.42	2.38	2.31	2.24	2.16	2.07	2.03	2.00	1.98	1.88
20	4.35	3.49	3.10	2.87	2.71	2.60	2.52	2.45	2.39	2.35	2.28	2.20	2.13	2.04	1.99	1.97	1.95	1.84
21	4.32	3.47	3.07	2.84	2.69	2.57	2.49	2.42	2.37	2.32	2.25	2.18	2.10	2.01	1.97	1.94	1.92	1.81
22	4.30	3.44	3.05	2.82	2.66	2.55	2.46	2.40	2.34	2.30	2.23	2.15	2.07	1.99	1.94	1.91	1.89	1.78
23	4.28	3.42	3.03	2.80	2.64	2.53	2.44	2.38	2.32	2.28	2.20	2.13	2.05	1.96	1.91	1.89	1.87	1.76
24	4.26	3.40	3.01	2.78	2.62	2.51	2.42	2.36	2.30	2.26	2.18	2.11	2.03	1.94	1.89	1.86	1.84	1.73
25	4.24	3.39	2.99	2.76	2.60	2.49	2.41	2.34	2.28	2.24	2.17	2.09	2.01	1.92	1.87	1.84	1.82	1.71
26	4.23	3.37	2.98	2.74	2.59	2.48	2.39	2.32	2.27	2.22	2.15	2.07	1.99	1.90	1.85	1.82	1.80	1.70
27	4.22	3.36	2.96	2.73	2.57	2.46	2.37	2.31	2.25	2.21	2.13	2.06	1.97	1.89	1.84	1.81	1.79	1.68

n_1 = Degrees of Freedom for the Numerator

n_2	1	2	3	4	5	6	7	8	9	10	12	15	20	30	40	50	60	∞
28	4.20	3.34	2.95	2.72	2.56	2.45	2.36	2.29	2.24	2.19	2.12	2.04	1.96	1.87	1.82	1.79	1.77	1.66
29	4.18	3.33	2.94	2.70	2.55	2.43	2.35	2.28	2.22	2.18	2.11	2.03	1.95	1.86	1.81	1.78	1.75	1.65
30	4.17	3.32	2.92	2.69	2.53	2.42	2.34	2.27	2.21	2.17	2.09	2.02	1.93	1.84	1.79	1.76	1.74	1.62
35	4.12	3.27	2.88	2.64	2.49	2.37	2.29	2.22	2.16	2.12	2.04	1.96	1.88	1.79	1.74	1.70	1.68	1.57
40	4.08	3.23	2.84	2.61	2.45	2.34	2.25	2.18	2.13	2.08	2.00	1.92	1.84	1.75	1.69	1.66	1.64	1.51
45	4.06	3.21	2.81	2.58	2.42	2.31	2.22	2.15	2.10	2.05	1.98	1.90	1.81	1.71	1.66	1.63	1.60	1.48
50	4.05	3.18	2.79	2.56	2.40	2.29	2.20	2.13	2.07	2.03	1.95	1.87	1.79	1.69	1.63	1.60	1.58	1.45
60	4.00	3.15	2.76	2.53	2.37	2.26	2.17	2.10	2.04	1.99	1.92	1.84	1.75	1.65	1.60	1.56	1.54	1.39
70	3.98	3.13	2.74	2.50	2.35	2.23	2.14	2.07	2.02	1.97	1.89	1.81	1.72	1.62	1.57	1.53	1.51	1.36
80	3.96	3.11	2.72	2.49	2.33	2.22	2.13	2.06	2.00	1.95	1.88	1.79	1.70	1.60	1.55	1.51	1.48	1.34
90	3.95	3.10	2.71	2.47	2.32	2.20	2.11	2.04	1.99	1.94	1.86	1.78	1.69	1.59	1.53	1.49	1.47	1.32
100	3.94	3.09	2.70	2.46	2.31	2.19	2.10	2.03	1.98	1.93	1.85	1.77	1.68	1.57	1.52	1.48	1.45	1.30
∞	3.84	3.00	2.60	2.37	2.21	2.10	2.01	1.94	1.88	1.83	1.75	1.67	1.57	1.46	1.39	1.34	1.31	1.00

TABLE 6. 99th Percentiles of the F Distribution; Table Entry Is f Such That $\mathrm{Prob}(F_{n_1,n_2} \le f) = 0.99$

n_1 = Degrees of Freedom for the Numerator

n_2	1	2	3	4	5	6	7	8	9	10	12	15	20	30	40	50	60	∞
1	4052	5000	5403	5625	5724	5859	5928	5982	6023	6056	6106	6157	6209	6261	6287	6302	6313	6366
2	98.5	99.0	99.2	99.3	99.3	99.3	99.4	99.4	99.4	99.4	99.4	99.4	99.5	99.5	99.5	99.5	99.5	99.5
3	34.1	30.8	29.5	28.7	28.2	27.9	27.7	27.5	27.3	27.2	27.1	26.9	26.7	26.5	26.4	26.4	26.3	26.1
4	21.2	18.0	16.7	16.0	15.5	15.2	15.0	14.8	14.7	14.6	14.4	14.2	14.0	13.8	13.8	13.7	13.6	13.5
5	16.3	13.3	12.1	11.4	11.0	10.6	10.5	10.3	10.2	10.1	9.89	9.72	9.55	9.38	9.29	9.24	9.20	9.02
6	13.7	10.9	9.78	9.15	8.75	8.47	8.26	8.10	7.98	7.88	7.72	7.56	7.40	7.23	7.14	7.09	7.06	6.88
7	12.2	9.55	8.45	7.85	7.46	7.19	6.99	6.84	6.72	6.62	6.47	6.31	6.16	5.99	5.91	5.86	5.82	5.65
8	11.3	8.65	7.59	7.01	6.63	6.37	6.18	6.03	5.91	5.81	5.67	5.52	5.36	5.20	5.12	5.07	5.03	4.86
9	10.6	8.02	6.99	6.42	6.06	5.80	5.61	5.47	5.35	5.26	5.11	4.96	4.81	4.65	4.57	4.52	4.48	4.31
10	10.0	7.56	6.55	6.00	5.64	5.39	5.20	5.06	4.94	4.85	4.71	4.56	4.41	4.25	4.17	4.12	4.08	3.91
11	9.65	7.21	6.22	5.67	5.32	5.07	4.89	4.74	4.63	4.54	4.40	4.25	4.10	3.94	3.86	3.81	3.78	3.60
12	9.33	6.93	5.95	5.41	5.06	4.82	4.64	4.50	4.39	4.30	4.16	4.01	3.86	3.70	3.62	3.57	3.54	3.36
13	9.07	6.70	5.74	5.21	4.86	4.62	4.44	4.30	4.19	4.10	3.96	3.82	3.67	3.51	3.43	3.38	3.34	3.17
14	8.86	6.51	5.56	5.04	4.69	4.46	4.28	4.14	4.03	3.94	3.80	3.66	3.51	3.35	3.27	3.22	3.18	3.00
15	8.68	6.36	5.42	4.89	4.56	4.32	4.14	4.01	3.90	3.81	3.67	3.52	3.37	3.22	3.13	3.08	3.05	2.87
16	8.53	6.23	5.29	4.77	4.44	4.20	4.03	3.89	3.78	3.69	3.55	3.41	3.26	3.10	3.02	2.97	2.93	2.75
17	8.40	6.11	5.18	4.67	4.34	4.10	3.93	3.79	3.68	3.59	3.46	3.31	3.16	3.00	2.92	2.87	2.84	2.65
18	8.29	6.01	5.09	4.58	4.25	4.01	3.84	3.71	3.60	3.51	3.37	3.23	3.08	2.92	2.84	2.79	2.75	2.57
19	8.19	5.93	5.01	4.50	4.17	3.94	3.77	3.63	3.52	3.43	3.30	3.15	3.00	2.85	2.76	2.71	2.68	2.49
20	8.10	5.85	4.94	4.43	4.10	3.87	3.70	3.57	3.46	3.37	3.23	3.09	2.94	2.78	2.70	2.64	2.61	2.42
21	8.02	5.78	4.88	4.37	4.04	3.81	3.64	3.51	3.40	3.31	3.17	3.03	2.88	2.72	2.64	2.58	2.55	2.36
22	7.95	5.72	4.82	4.31	3.99	3.76	3.59	3.45	3.35	3.26	3.12	2.98	2.83	2.67	2.58	2.53	2.50	2.31
23	7.88	5.66	4.76	4.26	3.94	3.71	3.54	3.41	3.30	3.21	3.08	2.93	2.78	2.62	2.54	2.48	2.45	2.26
24	7.82	5.61	4.72	4.22	3.90	3.67	3.50	3.36	3.26	3.17	3.03	2.89	2.74	2.58	2.49	2.44	2.40	2.21
25	7.77	5.57	4.68	4.18	3.86	3.63	3.46	3.32	3.22	3.13	2.99	2.85	2.70	2.54	2.45	2.40	2.36	2.17
26	7.72	5.53	4.64	4.14	3.82	3.59	3.42	3.29	3.18	3.10	2.96	2.82	2.66	2.50	2.42	2.36	2.33	2.13
27	7.68	5.49	4.60	4.11	3.79	3.56	3.39	3.26	3.15	3.06	2.93	2.78	2.63	2.47	2.38	2.33	2.29	2.10

n_1 = Degrees of Freedom for the Numerator

n_2	1	2	3	4	5	6	7	8	9	10	12	15	20	30	40	50	60	∞
28	7.64	5.45	4.57	4.07	3.75	3.53	3.36	3.23	3.12	3.03	2.90	2.75	2.60	2.44	2.35	2.30	2.26	2.06
29	7.60	5.42	4.54	4.04	3.73	3.50	3.33	3.20	3.09	3.01	2.87	2.73	2.58	2.41	2.33	2.27	2.24	2.03
30	7.56	5.39	4.51	4.02	3.70	3.47	3.31	3.17	3.07	2.98	2.84	2.70	2.55	2.39	2.30	2.25	2.21	2.01
35	7.41	5.27	4.40	3.91	3.59	3.37	3.20	3.07	2.96	2.88	2.74	2.60	2.45	2.28	2.19	2.14	2.10	1.91
40	7.31	5.18	4.31	3.83	3.51	3.29	3.12	2.99	2.89	2.80	2.67	2.52	2.37	2.20	2.12	2.06	2.02	1.81
45	7.23	5.11	4.25	3.77	3.46	3.23	3.07	2.94	2.83	2.74	2.61	2.47	2.31	2.15	2.06	2.00	1.96	1.75
50	7.17	5.06	4.20	3.72	3.41	3.19	3.02	2.89	2.79	2.70	2.56	2.42	2.27	2.10	2.01	1.95	1.91	1.68
60	7.08	4.98	4.13	3.65	3.34	3.12	2.95	2.82	2.72	2.63	2.50	2.35	2.20	2.03	1.94	1.88	1.84	1.60
70	7.01	4.92	4.07	3.60	3.29	3.07	2.91	2.78	2.67	2.59	2.45	2.31	2.15	1.98	1.89	1.83	1.79	1.53
80	6.96	4.88	4.04	3.56	3.26	3.04	2.87	2.74	2.64	2.55	2.42	2.27	2.12	1.94	1.85	1.79	1.75	1.49
90	6.93	4.85	4.01	3.54	3.23	3.01	2.85	2.72	2.61	2.53	2.39	2.25	2.09	1.92	1.82	1.76	1.72	1.48
100	6.90	4.82	3.98	3.51	3.21	2.99	2.82	2.70	2.59	2.50	2.37	2.22	2.07	1.89	1.80	1.74	1.69	1.43
∞	6.63	4.61	3.78	3.32	3.02	2.80	2.64	2.51	2.41	2.32	2.18	2.04	1.88	1.70	1.57	1.51	1.46	1.00

TABLE 7a. Durbin–Watson Statistic: 1 Percent Significance Points of d_L and d_U[a]

n	k'=1 dL	dU	k'=2 dL	dU	k'=3 dL	dU	k'=4 dL	dU	k'=5 dL	dU	k'=6 dL	dU	k'=7 dL	dU	k'=8 dL	dU	k'=9 dL	dU	k'=10 dL	dU
6	0.390	1.142	—	—																
7	0.435	1.036	0.294	1.676																
8	0.497	1.003	0.345	1.489	0.229	2.102														
9	0.554	0.998	0.408	1.389	0.279	1.875	0.183	2.433												
10	0.604	1.001	0.466	1.333	0.340	1.733	0.230	2.193	0.150	2.690										
11	0.653	1.010	0.519	1.297	0.396	1.640	0.286	2.030	0.193	2.453	0.124	2.892								
12	0.697	1.023	0.569	1.274	0.449	1.575	0.339	1.913	0.244	2.280	0.164	2.665	0.105	3.053						
13	0.738	1.038	0.616	1.261	0.499	1.526	0.391	1.826	0.294	2.150	0.211	2.490	0.140	2.838	0.090	3.182				
14	0.776	1.054	0.660	1.254	0.547	1.490	0.441	1.757	0.343	2.049	0.257	2.354	0.183	2.667	0.122	2.981	0.078	3.287		
15	0.811	1.070	0.700	1.252	0.591	1.464	0.488	1.704	0.391	1.967	0.303	2.244	0.226	2.530	0.161	2.817	0.107	3.101	0.068	3.374
16	0.844	1.086	0.737	1.252	0.633	1.446	0.532	1.663	0.437	1.900	0.349	2.153	0.269	2.416	0.200	2.681	0.142	2.944	0.094	3.201
17	0.874	1.102	0.772	1.255	0.672	1.432	0.574	1.630	0.480	1.847	0.393	2.078	0.313	2.319	0.241	2.566	0.179	2.811	0.127	3.053
18	0.902	1.118	0.805	1.259	0.708	1.422	0.613	1.604	0.522	1.803	0.435	2.015	0.355	2.238	0.282	2.467	0.216	2.697	0.160	2.925
19	0.928	1.132	0.835	1.265	0.742	1.415	0.650	1.584	0.561	1.767	0.476	1.963	0.396	2.169	0.322	2.381	0.255	2.597	0.196	2.813
20	0.952	1.147	0.863	1.271	0.773	1.411	0.685	1.567	0.598	1.737	0.515	1.918	0.436	2.110	0.362	2.308	0.294	2.510	0.232	2.714
21	0.975	1.161	0.890	1.277	0.803	1.408	0.718	1.554	0.633	1.712	0.552	1.881	0.474	2.059	0.400	2.244	0.331	2.434	0.268	2.625
22	0.997	1.174	0.914	1.284	0.831	1.407	0.748	1.543	0.667	1.691	0.587	1.849	0.510	2.015	0.437	2.188	0.368	2.367	0.304	2.548
23	1.018	1.187	0.938	1.291	0.858	1.407	0.777	1.534	0.698	1.673	0.620	1.821	0.545	1.977	0.473	2.140	0.404	2.308	0.340	2.479
24	1.037	1.199	0.960	1.298	0.882	1.407	0.805	1.528	0.728	1.658	0.652	1.797	0.578	1.944	0.507	2.097	0.439	2.255	0.375	2.417
25	1.055	1.211	0.981	1.305	0.906	1.409	0.831	1.523	0.756	1.645	0.682	1.766	0.610	1.915	0.540	2.059	0.473	2.209	0.409	2.362
26	1.072	1.222	1.001	1.312	0.928	1.411	0.855	1.518	0.783	1.635	0.711	1.759	0.640	1.889	0.572	2.026	0.505	2.168	0.441	2.313
27	1.089	1.233	1.019	1.319	0.949	1.413	0.878	1.515	0.808	1.626	0.738	1.743	0.669	1.867	0.602	1.997	0.536	2.131	0.473	2.269
28	1.104	1.244	1.037	1.325	0.969	1.415	0.900	1.513	0.832	1.618	0.764	1.729	0.696	1.847	0.630	1.970	0.566	2.098	0.504	2.229
29	1.119	1.254	1.054	1.332	0.988	1.418	0.921	1.512	0.855	1.611	0.788	1.718	0.723	1.830	0.658	1.947	0.595	2.068	0.533	2.193
30	1.133	1.263	1.070	1.339	1.006	1.421	0.941	1.511	0.877	1.606	0.812	1.707	0.748	1.814	0.684	1.925	0.622	2.041	0.562	2.160
31	1.147	1.273	1.085	1.345	1.023	1.425	0.960	1.510	0.897	1.601	0.834	1.698	0.772	1.800	0.710	1.906	0.649	2.017	0.589	2.131
32	1.160	1.282	1.100	1.352	1.040	1.428	0.979	1.510	0.917	1.597	0.856	1.690	0.794	1.788	0.734	1.889	0.674	1.995	0.615	2.104
33	1.172	1.291	1.114	1.358	1.055	1.432	0.996	1.510	0.936	1.594	0.876	1.683	0.816	1.776	0.757	1.874	0.698	1.975	0.641	2.080
34	1.184	1.299	1.128	1.364	1.070	1.435	1.012	1.511	0.954	1.591	0.896	1.677	0.837	1.766	0.779	1.860	0.722	1.957	0.665	2.057
35	1.195	1.307	1.140	1.370	1.085	1.439	1.028	1.512	0.971	1.589	0.914	1.671	0.857	1.757	0.800	1.847	0.744	1.940	0.689	2.037
36	1.206	1.315	1.153	1.376	1.098	1.442	1.043	1.513	0.988	1.588	0.932	1.666	0.877	1.749	0.821	1.836	0.766	1.925	0.711	2.018
37	1.217	1.323	1.165	1.382	1.112	1.446	1.058	1.514	1.004	1.586	0.950	1.662	0.895	1.742	0.841	1.825	0.787	1.911	0.733	2.001

n	k'=1 dL	k'=1 dU	k'=2 dL	k'=2 dU	k'=3 dL	k'=3 dU	k'=4 dL	k'=4 dU	k'=5 dL	k'=5 dU	k'=6 dL	k'=6 dU	k'=7 dL	k'=7 dU	k'=8 dL	k'=8 dU	k'=9 dL	k'=9 dU	k'=10 dL	k'=10 dU
38	1.227	1.330	1.176	1.388	1.124	1.449	1.072	1.515	1.019	1.585	0.966	1.658	0.913	1.735	0.860	1.816	0.807	1.899	0.754	1.985
39	1.237	1.337	1.187	1.393	1.137	1.453	1.085	1.517	1.034	1.584	0.982	1.655	0.930	1.729	0.878	1.807	0.826	1.887	0.774	1.970
40	1.246	1.344	1.198	1.398	1.148	1.457	1.098	1.518	1.048	1.584	0.997	1.652	0.946	1.724	0.895	1.799	0.844	1.876	0.789	1.956
45	1.288	1.376	1.245	1.423	1.201	1.474	1.156	1.528	1.111	1.584	1.065	1.643	1.019	1.704	0.974	1.768	0.927	1.834	0.881	1.902
50	1.324	1.403	1.285	1.446	1.245	1.491	1.205	1.538	1.164	1.587	1.123	1.639	1.081	1.692	1.039	1.748	0.997	1.805	0.955	1.864
55	1.356	1.427	1.320	1.466	1.284	1.506	1.247	1.548	1.209	1.592	1.172	1.638	1.134	1.685	1.095	1.734	1.057	1.785	1.018	1.837
60	1.383	1.449	1.350	1.484	1.317	1.520	1.283	1.558	1.249	1.598	1.214	1.639	1.179	1.682	1.144	1.726	1.108	1.771	1.072	1.817
65	1.407	1.468	1.377	1.500	1.346	1.534	1.315	1.568	1.283	1.604	1.251	1.642	1.218	1.680	1.186	1.720	1.153	1.761	1.120	1.802
70	1.429	1.485	1.400	1.515	1.372	1.546	1.343	1.578	1.313	1.611	1.283	1.645	1.253	1.680	1.223	1.716	1.192	1.754	1.162	1.792
75	1.448	1.501	1.422	1.529	1.395	1.557	1.368	1.587	1.340	1.617	1.313	1.646	1.284	1.682	1.256	1.716	1.227	1.746	1.199	1.785
80	1.466	1.515	1.441	1.541	1.416	1.568	1.390	1.595	1.364	1.624	1.338	1.653	1.312	1.683	1.285	1.714	1.259	1.745	1.232	1.777
85	1.482	1.528	1.458	1.553	1.435	1.578	1.411	1.603	1.386	1.630	1.362	1.657	1.337	1.685	1.312	1.714	1.287	1.743	1.262	1.773
90	1.496	1.540	1.474	1.563	1.452	1.587	1.429	1.611	1.406	1.636	1.383	1.661	1.360	1.687	1.336	1.714	1.312	1.741	1.288	1.769
95	1.510	1.552	1.489	1.573	1.468	1.596	1.446	1.618	1.425	1.642	1.403	1.666	1.381	1.690	1.358	1.715	1.336	1.741	1.313	1.767
100	1.522	1.562	1.503	1.583	1.482	1.604	1.462	1.625	1.441	1.647	1.421	1.670	1.400	1.693	1.378	1.717	1.357	1.741	1.335	1.765
150	1.611	1.637	1.598	1.651	1.584	1.665	1.571	1.679	1.557	1.693	1.543	1.708	1.530	1.722	1.515	1.737	1.501	1.752	1.486	1.767
200	1.664	1.684	1.653	1.693	1.643	1.704	1.633	1.715	1.623	1.725	1.613	1.735	1.603	1.746	1.592	1.575	1.582	1.768	1.571	1.779

n	k'=11 dL	k'=11 dU	k'=12 dL	k'=12 dU	k'=13 dL	k'=13 dU	k'=14 dL	k'=14 dU	k'=15 dL	k'=15 dU	k'=16 dL	k'=16 dU	k'=17 dL	k'=17 dU	k'=18 dL	k'=18 dU	k'=19 dL	k'=19 dU	k'=20 dL	k'=20 dU
16	0.060	3.446	—	—	—	—	—	—	—	—	—	—	—	—	—	—	—	—	—	—
17	0.084	3.286	0.053	3.506	—	—	—	—	—	—	—	—	—	—	—	—	—	—	—	—
18	0.113	3.146	0.075	3.358	0.047	3.557	—	—	—	—	—	—	—	—	—	—	—	—	—	—
19	0.145	3.023	0.102	3.227	0.067	3.420	0.043	3.601	—	—	—	—	—	—	—	—	—	—	—	—
20	0.178	2.914	0.131	3.109	0.092	3.297	0.061	3.474	0.038	3.639	—	—	—	—	—	—	—	—	—	—
21	0.212	2.817	0.162	3.004	0.119	3.185	0.084	3.358	0.055	3.521	0.035	3.671	—	—	—	—	—	—	—	—
22	0.246	2.729	0.194	2.909	0.148	3.084	0.109	3.252	0.077	3.412	0.050	3.562	0.032	3.700	—	—	—	—	—	—
23	0.281	2.651	0.227	2.822	0.178	2.991	0.136	3.155	0.100	3.311	0.070	3.459	0.046	3.597	0.029	3.725	—	—	—	—
24	0.315	2.580	0.260	2.744	0.209	2.906	0.165	3.065	0.125	3.218	0.092	3.363	0.065	3.501	0.043	3.629	0.027	3.747	—	—

Source: N. E. Savin and K. J. White, "The Durbin–Watson Test for Serial Correlation with Extreme Sample Sizes of Many Regressors," *Econometrica*, 45(8), Nov. 1977, pp. 1992–1995.

[a] k' is the number of regressors excluding the intercept.

TABLE 7a. Durbin–Watson Statistic: 1 Percent Significance Points of dL and dU[a]

	$k' = 11$		$k' = 12$		$k' = 13$		$k' = 14$		$k' = 15$		$k' = 16$		$k' = 17$		$k' = 18$		$k' = 19$		$k' = 20$	
n	dL	dU	dL	dU	dL	dU	dL	dU	dL	dU	dL	dU	dL	dU	dL	dU	dL	dU	dL	dU
25	0.348	2.517	0.292	2.674	0.240	2.829	0.194	2.982	0.152	3.131	0.116	3.274	0.085	3.410	0.060	3.538	0.039	3.657	0.025	3.766
26	0.381	2.460	0.324	2.610	0.272	2.758	0.224	2.906	0.180	3.050	0.141	3.191	0.107	3.325	0.079	3.452	0.055	3.572	0.036	3.682
27	0.413	2.409	0.356	2.552	0.303	2.694	0.253	2.836	0.208	2.976	0.167	3.113	0.131	3.245	0.100	3.371	0.073	3.490	0.051	3.602
28	0.444	2.363	0.387	2.499	0.333	2.635	0.283	2.772	0.237	2.907	0.194	3.040	0.156	3.169	0.122	3.294	0.093	3.412	0.068	3.524
29	0.474	2.321	0.417	2.451	0.363	2.582	0.313	2.713	0.266	2.843	0.222	2.972	0.182	3.098	0.146	3.220	0.114	3.338	0.087	3.450
30	0.503	2.283	0.447	2.407	0.393	2.533	0.342	2.659	0.294	2.785	0.249	2.909	0.208	3.032	0.171	3.152	0.137	3.267	0.107	3.379
31	0.531	2.248	0.475	2.367	0.422	2.487	0.371	2.609	0.322	2.730	0.277	2.851	0.234	2.970	0.196	3.087	0.160	3.201	0.128	3.311
32	0.558	2.216	0.503	2.330	0.450	2.446	0.399	2.563	0.350	2.680	0.304	2.797	0.261	2.912	0.221	3.026	0.184	3.137	0.151	3.246
33	0.585	2.187	0.530	2.296	0.477	2.408	0.426	2.520	0.377	2.633	0.331	2.746	0.287	2.858	0.246	2.969	0.209	3.078	0.174	3.184
34	0.610	2.160	0.556	2.266	0.503	2.373	0.452	2.481	0.404	2.590	0.357	2.699	0.313	2.808	0.272	2.915	0.233	3.022	0.197	3.126
35	0.634	2.136	0.581	2.237	0.529	2.340	0.478	2.444	0.430	2.550	0.383	2.655	0.339	2.761	0.297	2.865	0.257	2.969	0.221	3.071
36	0.658	2.113	0.605	2.210	0.554	2.310	0.504	2.410	0.455	2.512	0.409	2.614	0.364	2.717	0.322	2.818	0.282	2.919	0.244	3.019
37	0.680	2.092	0.628	2.186	0.578	2.282	0.528	2.379	0.480	2.477	0.434	2.576	0.389	2.675	0.347	2.774	0.306	2.872	0.268	2.969
38	0.702	2.073	0.651	2.164	0.601	2.256	0.552	2.350	0.504	2.445	0.458	2.540	0.414	2.637	0.371	2.733	0.330	2.828	0.291	2.923
39	0.723	2.055	0.673	2.143	0.623	2.232	0.575	2.323	0.528	2.414	0.482	2.507	0.438	2.600	0.395	2.694	0.354	2.787	0.315	2.879
40	0.744	2.039	0.694	2.123	0.645	2.210	0.597	2.297	0.551	2.386	0.505	2.476	0.461	2.566	0.418	2.657	0.377	2.748	0.338	2.838
45	0.835	1.972	0.790	2.044	0.744	2.118	0.700	2.193	0.655	2.269	0.612	2.346	0.570	2.424	0.528	2.503	0.488	2.582	0.448	2.661
50	0.913	1.925	0.871	1.987	0.829	2.051	0.787	2.116	0.746	2.182	0.705	2.250	0.665	2.318	0.625	2.387	0.586	2.456	0.548	2.526
55	0.979	1.891	0.940	1.945	0.902	2.002	0.863	2.059	0.825	2.117	0.786	2.176	0.748	2.237	0.711	2.298	0.674	2.359	0.637	2.421
60	1.037	1.865	1.001	1.914	0.965	1.964	0.929	2.015	0.893	2.067	0.857	2.120	0.822	2.173	0.786	2.227	0.751	2.283	0.716	2.338
65	1.087	1.845	1.053	1.889	1.020	1.934	0.986	1.980	0.953	2.027	0.919	2.075	0.886	2.123	0.852	2.172	0.819	2.221	0.786	2.272
70	1.131	1.831	1.099	1.870	1.068	1.911	1.037	1.953	1.005	1.995	0.974	2.038	0.943	2.082	0.911	2.127	0.880	2.172	0.849	2.217
75	1.170	1.819	1.141	1.856	1.111	1.893	1.082	1.931	1.052	1.970	1.023	2.009	0.993	2.049	0.964	2.090	0.934	2.131	0.905	2.172
80	1.205	1.810	1.177	1.844	1.150	1.878	1.122	1.913	1.094	1.949	1.066	1.984	1.039	2.022	1.011	2.057	0.983	2.097	0.955	2.135
85	1.236	1.803	1.210	1.834	1.184	1.866	1.158	1.898	1.132	1.931	1.106	1.965	1.080	1.999	1.053	2.033	1.027	2.068	1.000	2.104
90	1.264	1.798	1.240	1.827	1.215	1.856	1.191	1.886	1.166	1.917	1.141	1.948	1.116	1.979	1.091	2.012	1.066	2.044	1.041	2.077
95	1.290	1.793	1.267	1.821	1.244	1.848	1.221	1.876	1.197	1.905	1.174	1.934	1.150	1.963	1.126	1.993	1.102	2.023	1.079	2.054
100	1.314	1.790	1.292	1.816	1.270	1.841	1.248	1.868	1.225	1.895	1.203	1.922	1.181	1.949	1.158	1.977	1.136	2.006	1.113	2.034
150	1.473	1.783	1.458	1.799	1.444	1.814	1.429	1.830	1.414	1.847	1.400	1.863	1.385	1.880	1.370	1.897	1.355	1.913	1.340	1.931
200	1.561	1.791	1.550	1.801	1.539	1.813	1.528	1.824	1.518	1.836	1.507	1.847	1.495	1.860	1.484	1.871	1.474	1.883	1.462	1.896

Source: N. E. Savin and K. J. White, "The Durbin–Watson Test for Serial Correlation with Extreme Sample Sizes of Many Regressors," *Econometrica*, 45(8), Nov. 1977, pp. 1992–1995.

[a] k' is the number of regressors excluding the intercept.

TABLE 7b. Durbin–Watson Statistic: 5 Percent Significance of Points of dL and dU[a]

	$k'=1$		$k'=2$		$k'=3$		$k'=4$		$k'=5$		$k'=6$		$k'=7$		$k'=8$		$k'=9$		$k'=10$	
n	dL	dU	dL	dU	dL	dU	dL	dU	dL	dU	dL	dU	dL	dU	dL	dU	dL	dU	dL	dU
6	0.610	1.400	—	—	—	—	—	—	—	—	—	—	—	—	—	—	—	—	—	—
7	0.700	1.356	0.467	1.896	—	—	—	—	—	—	—	—	—	—	—	—	—	—	—	—
8	0.763	1.332	0.559	1.777	0.368	2.287	—	—	—	—	—	—	—	—	—	—	—	—	—	—
9	0.824	1.320	0.629	1.699	0.455	2.128	0.296	2.588	—	—	—	—	—	—	—	—	—	—	—	—
10	0.879	1.320	0.697	1.641	0.525	2.016	0.376	2.414	0.243	2.822	—	—	—	—	—	—	—	—	—	—
11	0.927	1.324	0.758	1.604	0.595	1.928	0.444	2.283	0.316	2.645	0.203	3.005	—	—	—	—	—	—	—	—
12	0.971	1.331	0.812	1.579	0.658	1.864	0.512	2.177	0.379	2.506	0.268	2.832	0.171	3.149	—	—	—	—	—	—
13	1.010	1.340	0.861	1.562	0.715	1.816	0.574	2.094	0.445	2.390	0.328	2.692	0.230	2.985	0.147	3.266	—	—	—	—
14	1.045	1.350	0.905	1.551	0.767	1.779	0.632	2.030	0.505	2.296	0.389	2.572	0.286	2.848	0.200	3.111	0.127	3.360	—	—
15	1.077	1.361	0.946	1.543	0.814	1.750	0.685	1.977	0.562	2.220	0.447	2.472	0.343	2.727	0.251	2.979	0.175	3.216	0.111	3.438
16	1.106	1.371	0.982	1.539	0.857	1.728	0.734	1.935	0.615	2.157	0.502	2.388	0.398	2.624	0.304	2.860	0.222	3.090	0.155	3.304
17	1.133	1.381	1.015	1.536	0.897	1.710	0.779	1.900	0.664	2.104	0.554	2.318	0.451	2.537	0.356	2.757	0.272	2.975	0.198	3.184
18	1.158	1.391	1.046	1.535	0.933	1.696	0.820	1.872	0.710	2.060	0.603	2.257	0.502	2.461	0.407	2.667	0.321	2.873	0.244	3.073
19	1.180	1.401	1.074	1.536	0.967	1.685	0.859	1.848	0.752	2.023	0.649	2.206	0.459	2.396	0.456	2.589	0.369	2.783	0.290	2.974
20	1.201	1.411	1.100	1.537	0.998	1.676	0.894	1.828	0.792	1.991	0.692	2.162	0.595	2.339	0.502	2.521	0.416	2.704	0.336	2.885
21	1.221	1.420	1.125	1.538	1.026	1.669	0.927	1.812	0.829	1.964	0.732	2.124	0.637	2.290	0.547	2.460	0.461	2.633	0.380	2.806
22	1.239	1.429	1.147	1.541	1.053	1.664	0.958	1.797	0.863	1.940	0.769	2.090	0.677	2.246	0.588	2.407	0.504	2.571	0.424	2.734
23	1.257	1.437	1.168	1.543	1.078	1.660	0.986	1.785	0.895	1.920	0.804	2.061	0.715	2.208	0.628	2.360	0.545	2.514	0.465	2.670
24	1.273	1.446	1.188	1.546	1.101	1.656	1.013	1.775	0.925	1.902	0.837	2.035	0.751	2.174	0.666	2.318	0.584	2.464	0.506	2.613
25	1.288	1.454	1.206	1.550	1.123	1.654	1.038	1.767	0.953	1.886	0.868	2.012	0.784	2.144	0.702	2.280	0.621	2.419	0.544	2.560
26	1.302	1.461	1.224	1.553	1.143	1.652	1.062	1.759	0.979	1.873	0.897	1.992	0.816	2.117	0.735	2.246	0.657	2.379	0.581	2.513
27	1.316	1.469	1.240	1.556	1.162	1.651	1.084	1.753	1.004	1.861	0.925	1.974	0.845	2.093	0.767	2.216	0.691	2.342	0.616	2.470
28	1.328	1.476	1.255	1.560	1.181	1.650	1.104	1.747	1.028	1.850	0.951	1.958	0.874	2.071	0.798	2.188	0.723	2.309	0.650	2.431
29	1.341	1.483	1.270	1.563	1.198	1.650	1.124	1.743	1.050	1.841	0.975	1.944	0.900	2.052	0.826	2.164	0.753	2.278	0.682	2.396
30	1.352	1.489	1.284	1.567	1.214	1.650	1.143	1.739	1.071	1.833	0.998	1.931	0.926	2.034	0.854	2.141	0.782	2.251	0.712	2.363
31	1.363	1.496	1.297	1.570	1.229	1.650	1.160	1.735	1.090	1.825	1.020	1.920	0.950	2.018	0.879	2.120	0.810	2.226	0.741	2.333
32	1.373	1.502	1.309	1.574	1.244	1.650	1.177	1.732	1.109	1.819	1.041	1.909	0.972	2.004	0.904	2.102	0.836	2.203	0.769	2.306
33	1.383	1.508	1.321	1.577	1.258	1.651	1.193	1.730	1.127	1.813	1.061	1.900	0.994	1.991	0.927	2.085	0.861	2.181	0.795	2.281
34	1.393	1.514	1.333	1.580	1.271	1.652	1.208	1.728	1.144	1.808	1.080	1.891	1.015	1.979	0.950	2.069	0.885	2.162	0.821	2.257
35	1.402	1.519	1.343	1.584	1.283	1.653	1.222	1.726	1.160	1.803	1.097	1.884	1.034	1.967	0.971	2.054	0.908	2.144	0.845	2.236
36	1.411	1.525	1.354	1.587	1.295	1.654	1.236	1.724	1.175	1.799	1.114	1.877	1.053	1.957	0.991	2.041	0.930	2.127	0.868	2.216
37	1.419	1.530	1.364	1.590	1.307	1.655	1.249	1.723	1.190	1.795	1.131	1.870	1.071	1.948	1.011	2.029	0.951	2.112	0.891	2.198

n	$k'=1$		$k'=2$		$k'=3$		$k'=4$		$k'=5$		$k'=6$		$k'=7$		$k'=8$		$k'=9$		$k'=10$	
	dL	dU	dL	dU	dL	dU	dL	dU	dL	dU	dL	dU	dL	dU	dL	dU	dL	dU	dL	dU
38	1.427	1.535	1.373	1.594	1.318	1.656	1.261	1.722	1.204	1.792	1.146	1.864	1.088	1.939	1.029	2.017	0.970	2.098	0.912	2.180
39	1.435	1.540	1.382	1.597	1.328	1.658	1.273	1.722	1.218	1.789	1.161	1.859	1.104	1.932	1.047	2.007	0.990	2.085	0.932	2.164
40	1.442	1.544	1.391	1.600	1.338	1.659	1.285	1.721	1.230	1.786	1.175	1.854	1.120	1.924	1.064	1.997	1.008	2.072	0.945	2.149
45	1.475	1.566	1.430	1.615	1.383	1.666	1.336	1.720	1.287	1.776	1.238	1.835	1.189	1.895	1.139	1.958	1.089	2.002	1.038	2.088
50	1.503	1.585	1.462	1.628	1.421	1.674	1.378	1.721	1.355	1.771	1.291	1.822	1.246	1.875	1.201	1.930	1.156	1.986	1.110	2.044
55	1.528	1.601	1.490	1.641	1.452	1.681	1.414	1.724	1.374	1.768	1.334	1.814	1.294	1.861	1.253	1.909	1.212	1.959	1.170	2.010
60	1.549	1.616	1.514	1.652	1.480	1.689	1.444	1.727	1.408	1.767	1.372	1.808	1.335	1.850	1.298	1.894	1.260	1.939	1.222	1.984
65	1.567	1.629	1.536	1.662	1.503	1.696	1.471	1.731	1.438	1.767	1.404	1.805	1.370	1.843	1.336	1.882	1.301	1.923	1.266	1.964
70	1.583	1.641	1.554	1.672	1.525	1.703	1.494	1.735	1.464	1.768	1.433	1.802	1.401	1.837	1.369	1.873	1.337	1.910	1.305	1.948
75	1.598	1.652	1.571	1.680	1.543	1.709	1.515	1.739	1.487	1.770	1.458	1.801	1.428	1.834	1.399	1.867	1.369	1.901	1.339	1.935
80	1.611	1.662	1.586	1.688	1.560	1.715	1.534	1.743	1.507	1.772	1.480	1.801	1.453	1.831	1.425	1.861	1.397	1.893	1.369	1.925
85	1.624	1.671	1.600	1.696	1.575	1.721	1.550	1.747	1.525	1.774	1.500	1.801	1.474	1.829	1.448	1.857	1.422	1.886	1.396	1.916
90	1.635	1.679	1.612	1.703	1.589	1.726	1.566	1.751	1.542	1.776	1.518	1.801	1.494	1.827	1.469	1.854	1.445	1.881	1.420	1.909
95	1.645	1.687	1.623	1.709	1.602	1.732	1.579	1.755	1.557	1.778	1.535	1.802	1.512	1.827	1.489	1.852	1.465	1.877	1.442	1.903
100	1.654	1.694	1.634	1.715	1.613	1.736	1.592	1.758	1.571	1.780	1.550	1.803	1.528	1.826	1.506	1.850	1.484	1.874	1.462	1.898
150	1.720	1.746	1.706	1.760	1.693	1.774	1.679	1.788	1.665	1.802	1.651	1.817	1.637	1.832	1.622	1.847	1.608	1.862	1.594	1.877
200	1.758	1.778	1.748	1.789	1.738	1.799	1.728	1.810	1.718	1.820	1.707	1.831	1.697	1.841	1.686	1.852	1.675	1.863	1.665	1.874

n	$k'=11$		$k'=12$		$k'=13$		$k'=14$		$k'=15$		$k'=16$		$k'=17$		$k'=18$		$k'=19$		$k'=20$	
	dL	dU	dL	dU	dL	dU	dL	dU	dL	dU	dL	dU	dL	dU	dL	dU	dL	dU	dL	dU
16	0.098	3.503	—	—	—	—	—	—	—	—	—	—	—	—	—	—	—	—	—	—
17	0.138	3.378	0.087	3.557	—	—	—	—	—	—	—	—	—	—	—	—	—	—	—	—
18	0.177	3.265	0.123	3.441	0.078	3.603	—	—	—	—	—	—	—	—	—	—	—	—	—	—
19	0.220	3.159	0.160	3.335	0.111	3.496	0.070	3.642	—	—	—	—	—	—	—	—	—	—	—	—
20	0.263	3.063	0.200	3.234	0.145	3.395	0.100	3.542	0.063	3.676	—	—	—	—	—	—	—	—	—	—
21	0.307	2.976	0.240	3.141	0.182	3.300	0.132	3.448	0.091	3.583	0.058	3.705	—	—	—	—	—	—	—	—
22	0.349	2.897	0.281	3.057	0.220	3.211	0.166	3.358	0.120	3.495	0.083	3.619	0.052	3.731	—	—	—	—	—	—
23	0.391	2.826	0.322	2.979	0.259	3.128	0.202	3.272	0.153	3.409	0.110	3.535	0.076	3.650	0.048	3.753	—	—	—	—
24	0.431	2.761	0.362	2.908	0.297	3.053	0.239	3.193	0.186	3.327	0.141	3.454	0.101	3.572	0.070	3.678	0.044	3.773	—	—

Source: N. E. Savin and K. J. White, "The Durbin–Watson Test for Serial Correlation with Extreme Sample Sizes of Many Regressors," *Econometrica*, 45(8), Nov. 1977, pp. 1992–1995.

[a] k' is the number of regressors excluding the intercept.

TABLE 7b. Durbin–Watson Statistic: 5 Percent Significance of Points of dL and dU^a

n	$k'=11$ dL	dU	$k'=12$ dL	dU	$k'=13$ dL	dU	$k'=14$ dL	dU	$k'=15$ dL	dU	$k'=16$ dL	dU	$k'=17$ dL	dU	$k'=18$ dL	dU	$k'=19$ dL	dU	$k'=20$ dL	dU
25	0.470	2.702	0.400	2.844	0.335	2.983	0.275	3.119	0.221	3.251	0.172	3.376	0.130	4.494	0.094	3.604	0.065	3.702	0.041	3.790
26	0.508	2.649	0.438	2.784	0.373	2.919	0.312	3.051	0.256	3.179	0.205	3.303	0.160	3.420	0.120	3.531	0.087	3.632	0.060	3.724
27	0.544	2.600	0.475	2.730	0.409	2.859	0.348	2.987	0.291	3.112	0.238	3.233	0.191	3.349	0.149	3.460	0.112	3.563	0.081	3.658
28	0.578	2.555	0.510	2.680	0.445	2.805	0.383	2.928	0.325	3.050	0.271	3.168	0.222	3.283	0.178	3.392	0.138	3.495	0.104	3.592
29	0.612	2.515	0.544	2.634	0.479	2.755	0.418	2.874	0.359	2.992	0.305	3.107	0.254	3.219	0.208	3.327	0.166	3.431	0.129	3.528
30	0.643	2.477	0.577	2.592	0.512	2.708	0.451	2.823	0.392	2.937	0.337	3.050	0.286	3.160	0.238	3.266	0.195	3.368	0.156	3.465
31	0.674	2.443	0.608	2.553	0.545	2.665	0.484	2.776	0.425	2.887	0.370	2.996	0.317	3.103	0.269	3.208	0.224	3.309	0.183	3.406
32	0.703	2.411	0.638	2.517	0.576	2.625	0.515	2.733	0.457	2.840	0.401	2.946	0.349	3.050	0.299	3.153	0.253	3.252	0.211	3.348
33	0.731	2.382	0.668	2.484	0.606	2.588	0.546	2.692	0.488	2.796	0.432	2.899	0.379	3.000	0.329	3.100	0.283	3.198	0.239	3.293
34	0.758	2.355	0.695	2.454	0.634	2.554	0.575	2.654	0.518	2.754	0.462	2.854	0.409	2.954	0.359	3.051	0.312	3.147	0.267	3.240
35	0.783	2.330	0.722	2.425	0.662	2.521	0.604	2.619	0.547	2.716	0.492	2.813	0.439	2.910	0.388	3.005	0.340	3.099	0.295	3.190
36	0.808	2.306	0.748	2.398	0.689	2.492	0.631	2.586	0.575	2.680	0.520	2.774	0.467	2.868	0.417	2.961	0.369	3.053	0.323	3.142
37	0.831	2.285	0.772	2.374	0.714	2.464	0.657	2.555	0.602	2.646	0.548	2.738	0.495	2.829	0.445	2.920	0.397	3.009	0.351	3.097
38	0.854	2.265	0.796	2.351	0.739	2.438	0.683	2.526	0.628	2.614	0.575	2.703	0.522	2.792	0.472	2.880	0.424	2.968	0.378	3.054
39	0.875	2.246	0.819	2.329	0.763	2.413	0.707	2.499	0.653	2.585	0.600	2.671	0.549	2.757	0.499	2.843	0.451	2.929	0.404	3.013
40	0.896	2.228	0.840	2.309	0.785	2.391	0.731	2.473	0.678	2.557	0.626	2.641	0.575	2.724	0.525	2.808	0.477	2.892	0.430	2.974
45	0.988	2.156	0.938	2.225	0.887	2.296	0.838	2.367	0.788	2.439	0.740	2.512	0.692	2.586	0.644	2.659	0.598	2.733	0.553	2.807
50	1.064	2.103	1.019	2.163	0.973	2.225	0.927	2.287	0.882	2.350	0.836	2.414	0.792	2.479	0.747	2.544	0.703	2.610	0.660	2.675
55	1.129	2.062	1.087	2.116	1.045	2.170	1.003	2.225	0.961	2.281	0.919	2.338	0.877	2.396	0.836	2.454	0.795	2.512	0.754	2.571
60	1.184	2.031	1.145	2.079	1.106	2.127	1.068	2.177	1.029	2.227	0.990	2.278	0.951	2.330	0.913	2.382	0.874	2.434	0.836	2.487
65	1.231	2.006	1.195	2.049	1.160	2.093	1.124	2.138	1.088	2.183	1.052	2.229	1.016	2.276	0.980	2.323	0.944	2.371	0.908	2.419
70	1.272	1.986	1.239	2.026	1.206	2.066	1.172	2.106	1.139	2.148	1.105	2.189	1.072	2.232	1.038	2.275	1.005	2.318	0.971	2.362
75	1.308	1.970	1.277	2.006	1.247	2.043	1.215	2.080	1.184	2.118	1.153	2.156	1.121	2.195	1.090	2.235	1.058	2.275	1.027	2.315
80	1.340	1.957	1.311	1.991	1.283	2.024	1.253	2.059	1.224	2.093	1.195	2.129	1.165	2.165	1.136	2.201	1.106	2.238	1.076	2.275
85	1.369	1.946	1.342	1.977	1.315	2.009	1.287	2.040	1.260	2.073	1.232	2.105	1.205	2.139	1.177	2.172	1.149	2.206	1.121	2.241
90	1.395	1.937	1.369	1.966	1.344	1.995	1.318	2.025	1.292	2.055	1.266	2.085	1.240	2.116	1.213	2.148	1.187	2.179	1.160	2.211
95	1.418	1.929	1.394	1.956	1.370	1.984	1.345	2.012	1.321	2.040	1.296	2.068	1.271	2.097	1.247	2.126	1.222	2.156	1.197	2.186
100	1.434	1.923	1.416	1.948	1.393	1.974	1.371	2.000	1.347	2.026	1.324	2.053	1.301	2.080	1.277	2.108	1.253	2.135	1.229	2.164
150	1.579	1.892	1.564	1.908	1.550	1.924	1.535	1.940	1.519	1.956	1.504	1.972	1.489	1.989	1.474	2.006	1.458	2.023	1.443	2.040
200	1.654	1.885	1.643	1.896	1.632	1.908	1.621	1.919	1.610	1.931	1.599	1.943	1.588	1.955	1.576	1.967	1.565	1.979	1.554	1.991

Source: N. E. Savin and K. J. White, "The Durbin–Watson Test for Serial Correlation with Extreme Sample Sizes of Many Regressors," *Econometrica*, 45(8), Nov. 1977, pp. 1992–1995.

$^a k'$ is the number of regressors excluding the intercept.

TABLE 8 Five Percent Significance Point of $d_{4,L}$ and $d_{4,U}$ for Regressions Without Quarterly Dummy Variables ($k = k' + 1$)

n	$k' = 1$		$k' = 2$		$k' = 3$		$k' = 4$		$k' = 5$	
	$d_{4,L}$	$d_{4,U}$	$d_{4,L}$	$d_{4,U}$	$d_{4,L}$	$d_{4,U}$	$d_{4,L}$	$d_{4,U}$	$d_{4,L}$	$d_{4,U}$
16	0.774	0.982	0.662	1.109	0.549	1.275	0.435	1.381	0.350	1.532
20	0.924	1.102	0.827	1.203	0.728	1.327	0.626	1.428	0.544	1.556
24	1.036	1.189	0.953	1.273	0.867	1.371	0.779	1.459	0.702	1.565
28	1.123	1.257	1.050	1.328	0.975	1.410	0.898	1.487	0.828	1.576
32	1.192	1.311	1.127	1.373	1.061	1.443	0.993	1.511	0.929	1.587
36	1.248	1.355	1.191	1.410	1.131	1.471	1.070	1.532	1.013	1.598
40	1.295	1.392	1.243	1.442	1.190	1.496	1.135	1.550	1.082	1.609
44	1.335	1.423	1.288	1.469	1.239	1.518	1.189	1.567	1.141	1.620
48	1.369	1.451	1.326	1.493	1.281	1.537	1.236	1.582	1.191	1.630
52	1.399	1.475	1.359	1.513	1.318	1.554	1.276	1.595	1.235	1.639
56	1.426	1.496	1.389	1.532	1.351	1.569	1.312	1.608	1.273	1.648
60	1.449	1.515	1.415	1.548	1.379	1.583	1.343	1.619	1.307	1.656
64	1.470	1.532	1.438	1.563	1.405	1.596	1.371	1.629	1.337	1.664
68	1.489	1.548	1.459	1.577	1.427	1.608	1.396	1.639	1.364	1.671
72	1.507	1.562	1.478	1.589	1.448	1.618	1.418	1.648	1.388	1.678
76	1.522	1.574	1.495	1.601	1.467	1.628	1.439	1.656	1.411	1.685
80	1.537	1.586	1.511	1.611	1.484	1.637	1.457	1.663	1.431	1.691
84	1.550	1.597	1.525	1.621	1.500	1.646	1.475	1.671	1.449	1.696
88	1.562	1.607	1.539	1.630	1.515	1.654	1.490	1.677	1.466	1.702
92	1.574	1.617	1.551	1.639	1.528	1.661	1.505	1.684	1.482	1.707
96	1.584	1.626	1.563	1.647	1.541	1.668	1.519	1.690	1.496	1.712
100	1.594	1.634	1.573	1.654	1.552	1.674	1.531	1.695	1.510	1.717

Source: K. F. Wallis, "Testing for Fourth Order Autocorrelation in Quarterly Regression Equations," *Econometrica*, 40(4), July 1972, p. 623.

References

Abowd, J., and H. Farber, "Job Queues and Union Status of Workers," *Industrial and Labor Relations Review,* 35, 1982, pp. 354–367.

Abramovitz, M., and I. Stegun, *Handbook of Mathematical Functions.* New York: Dover Press, 1971.

Adelman, F. and I. Adelman, "The Dynamic Properties of the Klein–Goldberger Model," *Econometrica,* 27, 1959, pp. 596–625.

Afifi, T., and R. Elashoff, "Missing Observations in Multivariate Statistics," *Journal of the American Statistical Association,* 61, 1966, pp. 595–604.

Afifi, T., and R. Elashoff, "Missing Observations in Multivariate Statistics," *Journal of the American Statistical Association,* 62, 1967, pp. 10–29.

Aigner, D., "MSE Dominance of Least Squares with Errors of Observation," *Journal of Econometrics,* 2, 1974, pp. 365–372.

Aigner, D., and A. Goldberger, eds., *Latent Variables in Socioeconomic Models.* Amsterdam: North-Holland, 1977.

Aigner, D., A. Goldberger, and G. Kalton, "On the Explanatory Power of Dummy Variable Regressions," *International Economic Review,* 16(2), 1975, pp. 503–509.

Aigner, D., K. Lovell, and P. Schmidt, "Formulation and Estimation of Stochastic Frontier Production Models," *Journal of Econometrics,* 6, 1977, pp. 21–37.

Aigner, D., C. Hsiao, A. Kapteyn, and T. Wansbeek, "Latent Variable Models in Econometrics," in Z. Griliches and M. Intriligator, eds., *Handbook of Econometrics,* Vol. 3. Amsterdam: North-Holland, 1983.

Aitchison, J., and J. Brown, *The Lognormal Distribution with Special Reference to Its Uses in Economics.* New York: Cambridge University Press, 1969.

Aitken, A., "On Least Squares and Linear Combinations of Observations," *Proceedings of the Royal Statistical Society,* 55, 1935, pp. 42–48.

Akaike, H., "Information Theory and an Extension of the Maximum Likelihood Principle," in B. Petrov and F. Csake, eds., *2nd International Symposium on Information Theory,* Budapest, Akademiai Kiado, 1973.

Albright, R., S. Lerman, and C. Manski, *Report on the Development of an Estimation Program for the Multinomial Probit Model.* Washington, D.C.: Federal Highway Administration, 1977.

Aldrich, J., and F. Nelson, *Linear Probability, Logit, and Probit Models.* Beverly Hills, Calif.: Sage, 1984.

Ali, M., and C. Giaccotto, "A Study of Several New and Existing Tests for Heteroscedasticity in the General Linear Model," *Journal of Econometrics,* 26, 1984, pp. 355–374.

Almon, S., "The Distributed Lag Between Capital Appropriations and Expenditures," *Econometrica,* 33, 1965, pp. 178–196.

Amemiya, T., "The Estimation of Variances in a Variance-Components Model," *International Economic Review,* 12, 1971, pp. 1–13.

Amemiya, T., "Regression Analysis When the Variance of the Dependent Variable Is Proportional to the Square of Its Expectation," *Journal of the American Statistical Association,* 68, 1973a, pp. 928–934.

Amemiya, T., "Regression Analysis When the Dependent Variable Is Truncated Normal," *Econometrica,* 41, 1973b, pp. 997–1016.

Amemiya, T., "A Note on a Heteroscedastic Model," *Journal of Econometrics,* 6, 1977a, pp. 365–370.

Amemiya, T., "Some Theorems in the Linear Probability Model," *International Economic Review,* 18, 1977b, pp. 645–650.

Amemiya, T., "The Estimation of a Simultaneous Equation Generalized Probit Model," *Econometrica,* 46, 1978, pp. 1193–1205.

Amemiya, T., "Selection of Regressors," *International Economic Review,* 21, 1980, pp. 331–354.

Amemiya, T., "Qualitative Response Models: A Survey," *Journal of Economic Literature,* 19, 4, 1981, pp. 481–536.

Amemiya, T., "Tobit Models: A Survey," *Journal of Econometrics,* 24, 1984, pp. 3–63.

Amemiya, T., *Advanced Econometrics.* Cambridge, Mass.: Harvard University Press, 1985.

Amemiya, T., and K. Morimune, "Selecting the Optimal Order of Polynomial in the Almon Distributed Lag," *Review of Economics and Statistics,* 56, 1974, pp. 378–386.

Amemiya, T., and F. Nold, "A Modified Logit Model," *Review of Economics and Statistics,* 57, 1975, pp. 255–257.

Anderson, T., "Maximum Likelihood Estimates for a Multivariate Normal Distribution When Some Observations Are Missing," *Journal of the American Statistical Association,* 52, 1957, pp. 200–203.

Anderson, T., *The Statistical Analysis of Time Series.* New York: Wiley, 1971.

Anderson, T., and C. Hsiao, "Formulation and Estimation of Dynamic Models Using Panel Data," *Journal of Econometrics,* 18, 1982, pp. 67–82.

Anderson, T., and H. Rubin, "Estimation of the Parameters of a Single Equation in a Complete System of Stochastic Equations," *Annals of Mathematical Statistics,* 20, 1949, pp. 46–63.

Anderson, T., and H. Rubin, "The Asymptotic Properties of Estimators of the Parameters of a Single Equation in a Complete System of Stochastic Equations," *Annals of Mathematical Statistics,* 21, 1950, pp. 570–582.

Anderson, R., and J. Thursby, "Confidence Intervals for Elasticity Estimators in Translog Models," *Review of Economics and Statistics,* 68, 1986, pp. 647–657.

Andrews, D., "A Robust Method for Multiple Linear Regression," *Technometrics,* 16, 1974, pp. 523–531.

Aneuryn-Evans, G., and A. Deaton, "Testing Linear Versus Logarithmic Regression Models," *Review of Economics Studies,* 47, 1980, pp. 275–291.

Arabmazar, A., and P. Schmidt, "An Investigation into the Robustness of the Tobit Estimator to Nonnormality," *Econometrica,* 50, 1982a, pp. 1055–1063.

Arabmazar, A., and P. Schmidt, "Further Evidence on the Robustness of the Tobit Estimator to Heteroscedasticity," *Journal of Econometrics,* 17, 1982b, pp. 253–258.

Arrow, K., H. Chenery, B. Minhas, and R. Solow, "Capital–Labor Substitution and Economic Efficiency," *Review of Economics and Statistics,* 45, 1961, pp. 225–247.

Avery, R., "Modeling Monetary Policy as an Unobserved Variable," *Journal of Econometrics,* 10, 1979, pp. 291–311.

Avery, R., L. Hansen, and J. Hotz, "Multiperiod Probit Models and Orthogonality Condition Estimation," *Working Paper 62-80-81,* Department of Economics, Carnegie Mellon University, 1981.

Baille, R., "The Asymptotic Mean Squared Error of Multistep Prediction from the Regression Model with Autoregressive Errors," *Journal of the American Statistical Association,* 74, 1979, pp. 175–184.

Balestra, P., "A Note on the Exact Transformation Associated with the First-Order Moving Average Process," *Journal of Econometrics,* 14, 1980, pp. 381–394.

Balestra, P., and M. Nerlove, "Pooling Cross Section and Time Series Data in the Estimation of a Dynamic Model: The Demand for Natural Gas," *Econometrica,* 34, 1966, pp. 585–612.

Baltagi, B., "Pooling Under Misspecification, Some Monte Carlo Evidence on the Kmenta and Error Components Techniques," *Econometric Theory,* 2, 1986, pp. 429–441.

Banerjee, A., J. Dolado, D. Hendry, and G. Smith, "Exploring Equilibrium Relationships in Econometrics Through Static Models: Some Monte Carlo Evidence," *Oxford Bulletin of Economics and Statistics,* 48, 1986, pp. 253–277.

Barnow, B., G. Cain, and A. Goldberger, "Issues in the Analysis of Selectivity Bias," in E. Stromsdorfer and G. Farkas, eds., *Evaluation Studies Review Annual,* Vol. 5. Beverly Hills, Calif.: Sage, 1981.

Barro, R., "Unanticipated Money, Output and the Price Level in the U.S.," *Journal of Political Economy,* 67, 1977, pp. 549–580.

Barten, A., "Maximum Likelihood Estimation of a Complete System of Demand Equations," *European Economic Review,* 1, Fall 1969, pp. 7–73.

Bartlett, M., "Properties of Sufficiency and Statistical Tests," *Proceedings of the Royal Statistical Society, Series A,* 160, 1937, pp. 268–282.

Basmann, R., "A Generalized Classical Method of Linear Estimation of Coefficients in a Structural Equation," *Econometrica,* 25, 1957, pp. 77–83.

Basmann, R., "On Finite Sample Distributions of Generalized Classical Linear Identifiability Test Statistics," *Journal of the American Statistical Association,* 55, 1960, pp. 650–659.

Bazaraa, M., and C. Shetty, *Nonlinear Programming—Theory and Algorithms.* New York: Wiley, 1979.

Beach, C., and J. MacKinnon, "A Maximum Likelihood Procedure for Regression with Autocorrelated Errors," *Econometrica,* 46, 1978a, pp. 51–58.

Beach, J., and J. MacKinnon, "Full Maximum Likelihood Estimation of Second Order Autoregressive Error Models," *Journal of Econometrics,* 7, 1978b, pp. 187–198.

Beggs, J., "Time Series Analysis in Pooled Cross Sections," *Econometric Theory,* 2, 1986, pp. 331–349.

Beggs, J., "A Simple Model for Heterogeneity in Binary Logit Models," *Economics Letters,* 27, 1988, pp. 245–249.

Beggs, S., S. Cardell, and J. Hausman, "Assessing the Potential Demand for Electric Cars," *Journal of Econometrics,* 17, 1981, pp. 19–20.

Bellman, R., *Introduction to Matrix Analysis.* New York: McGraw-Hill, 1970.

Belsley, D., "On the Efficient Computation of the Nonlinear Full-Information Maximum

Likelihood Estimator," *Technical Report 5*, Vol. II, Center for Computational Research in Economics and Management Science, Cambridge, Mass., 1980.

Belsley, D., *Conditioning Diagnostics, Collinearity, and Weak Data in Regression*. New York: Wiley, 1991.

Belsley, D., E. Kuh, and R. Welsch, *Regression Diagnostics: Identifying Influential Data and Sources of Collinearity*. New York: Wiley, 1980.

Ben-Porath, Y., "Labor Force Participation Rates and Labor Supply," *Journal of Political Economy*, 81, 1973, pp. 697–704.

Bera, A., C. Jarque, "Model Specification Tests: A Simultaneous Approach," *Journal of Econometrics*, 20, 1980a, pp. 59–82.

Bera, A., and C. Jarque, "Efficient Tests for Normality, Heteroscedasticity, and Serial Independence of Regression Residuals," *Economics Letters*, 6, 1980b, pp. 255–259.

Bera, A., C. Jarque, and L. Lee, "Testing for the Normality Assumption in Limited Dependent Variable Models," mimeo, Department of Economics, University of Minnesota, 1982.

Berndt, E., *The Practice of Econometrics*. Reading, Mass.: Addison-Wesley, 1990.

Berndt, E., and L. Christensen, "The Translog Function and the Substitution of Equipment, Structures, and Labor in U.S. Manufacturing, 1929–1968," *Journal of Econometrics*, 1, 1972, pp. 81–114.

Berndt, E., and E. Savin, "Conflict Among Criteria for Testing Hypotheses in the Multivariate Linear Regression Model," *Econometrica*, 45, 1977, pp. 1263–1277.

Berndt, E., and D. Wood, "Technology, Prices, and the Derived Demand for Energy," *Review of Economics and Statistics*, 57, 1975, pp. 376–384.

Berndt, E., B. Hall, R. Hall, and J. Hausman, "Estimation and Inference in Nonlinear Structural Models," *Annals of Economic and Social Measurement*, 3/4, 1974, pp. 653–665.

Berzeg, K., "The Error Components Model: Conditions for the Existence of Maximum Likelihood Estimates," *Journal of Econometrics*, 10, 1979, pp. 99–102.

Betancourt, R., and H. Kelejian, "Lagged Endogenous Variables and the Cochrane–Orcutt Procedure," *Econometrica*, 49, 1981, pp. 1073–1078.

Beveridge, S., and C. Nelson, "A New Approach to Decomposition of Economic Time Series into Permanent and Transitory Components with Particular Attention to Measurement of the Business Cycle," *Journal of Monetary Economics*, 7, 1981, pp. 151–174.

Bhargava, A., and J. Sargan, "Estimating Dynamic Random Effects Models from Panel Data Covering Short Periods," *Econometrica*, 51, 1981, pp. 221–236.

Blackley, R., J. Follain, and J. Ondrich, "Box–Cox Estimation of Hedonic Models: How Serious Is the Iterative OLS Variance Bias?" *Review of Economics and Statistics*, 66, 1984, pp. 348–353.

Blanchard, O., "Why Does Money Affect Output? A Survey," *Working Paper 2285*, National Bureau of Economic Research, Cambridge, 1987.

Blundell, R., ed., "Specification Testing in Limited and Discrete Dependent Variable Models," *Journal of Econometrics*, 34, 1/2, 1987.

Bock, M., T. Yancey, and G. Judge, "The Statistical Consequences of Preliminary Test Estimators in Regression," *Journal of the American Statistical Association*, 68, 1972, pp. 109–116.

Bollerslev, T., "Generalized Autoregressive Conditional Heteroscedasticity," *Journal of Econometrics*, 31, 1986, pp. 307–327.

Boot, J., and G. deWitt, "Investment Demand: An Empirical Contribution to the Aggregation Problem," *International Economic Review*, 1, 1960, pp. 3–30.

Börsch-Supan, A., and V. Hajivassilou, "Smooth Unbiased Multivariate Probability Simulators for Maximum Likelihood Estimation of Limited Dependent Variable Models," *Cowles Foundation Discussion Paper,* Yale University, 1990; forthcoming, *Journal of Econometrics, 1992.*

Boskin, M., "A Conditional Logit Model of Occupational Choice," *Journal of Political Economy,* 82, 1974, pp. 389–398.

Bowden, R., "The Theory of Parametric Identification," *Econometrica,* 41, 1973, pp. 1069–1074.

Box, G., and D. Cox, "An Analysis of Transformations," *Journal of the Royal Statistical Society, Series B,* 1964, pp. 211–264.

Box, G., and G. Jenkins, *Time Series Analysis: Forecasting and Control,* 2nd ed. San Francisco: Holden-Day, 1984.

Box, G., and D. Pierce, "Distribution of Residual Autocorrelations in Autoregressive Moving Average Time Series Models," *Journal of the American Statistical Association,* 65, 1970, pp. 1509–1526.

Box, G., and G. Tiao, "Modelling Multiple Time Series with Applications," *Journal of the American Statistical Association,* 76, 1981, pp. 802–816.

Boyes, W., D. Hoffman, and S. Low, "An Econometric Analysis of the Bank Credit Scoring Problem," *Journal of Econometrics,* 40, 1989, pp. 3–14.

Breusch, T., "Testing for Autocorrelation in Dynamic Linear Models," *Australian Economic Papers,* 17, 1978, pp. 334–355.

Breusch, T., and A. Pagan, "A Simple Test for Heteroscedasticity and Random Coefficient Variation," *Econometrica,* 47, 1979, pp. 1287–1294.

Breusch, T., and A. Pagan, "The LM Test and Its Applications to Model Specification in Econometrics," *Review of Economics Studies,* 47, 1980, pp. 239–254.

Bridge, J., *Applied Econometrics.* Amsterdam: North-Holland, 1971.

Brown, R., "The Identification Problem in Systems Nonlinear in the Variables," *Econometrica,* 51, 1983, pp. 175–196.

Brown, C., and Moffitt, R., "The Effect of Ignoring Heteroscedasticity on Estimates of the Tobit Model," mimeo, University of Maryland, Department of Economics, June 1982.

Brown, R., J. Durbin, and J. Evans, "Techniques for Testing the Constancy of Regression Relationships over Time," *Journal of the Royal Statistical Society, Series B,* 37, 1975, pp. 149–172.

Brundy, J., and D. Jorgenson, "Consistent and Efficient Estimation of Systems of Simultaneous Equations by Means of Instrumental Variables," *Review of Economics and Statistics,* 53, 1971, pp. 207–224.

Brundy, J., and D. Jorgenson, "Consistent and Efficient Estimation of Systems of Simultaneous Equations by Means of Instrumental Variables," in P. Zarembka, ed., *Frontiers in Econometrics.* New York: Academic Press, 1974.

Burmeister, E., and K. Wall, "Kalman Filtering Estimation of Unobserved Rational Expectations with an Application to the German Hyperinflation," *Journal of Econometrics,* 20, 1982, pp. 255–284.

Buse, A., "Goodness of Fit in Generalized Least Squares Estimation," *The American Statistician,* 27, 1973, pp. 106–108.

Buse, A., "The Likelihood Ratio, Wald, and Lagrange Multiplier Tests: An Expository Note," *The American Statistician,* 36, 1982, pp. 153–157.

Butler, J., and R. Moffitt, "A Computationally Efficient Quadrature Procedure for the One Factor Multinomial Probit Model," *Econometrica,* 50, 1982, pp. 761–764.

Cameron, A., and P. Trivedi, "Econometric Models Based on Count Data: Comparisons and Applications of Some Estimators and Tests," *Journal of Applied Econometrics,* 1, 1986, pp. 29–54.

Cameron, A., and P. Trivedi, "Regression Based Tests for Overdispersion in the Poisson Model," *Journal of Econometrics,* 46, 1990, pp. 347–364.

Campbell, J., and P. Perron, "Pitfalls and Opportunities: What Macroeconomists Should Know About Unit Roots," *National Bureau of Economic Research, Macroeconomics Conference,* Cambridge, February 1991.

Catsiapis, G., and C. Robinson, "Sample Selection Bias with Multiple Selection Rules: An Application to Student Aid Grants," *Journal of Econometrics,* 18, 1982, pp. 351–368.

Caudill, S., "An Advantage of the Linear Probability Model over Probit or Logit," *Oxford Bulletin of Economics and Statistics,* 50, 1988, pp. 425–427.

Caves, D., L. Christensen, and M. Trethaway, "Flexible Cost Functions for Multiproduct firms," *Review of Economics and Statistics,* 62, 1980, pp. 477–481.

Cecchetti, S., "The Frequency of Price Adjustment: A Study of the Newsstand Prices of Magazines," *Journal of Econometrics,* 31, 1986, pp. 255–274.

Chamberlain, G., "Omitted Variable Bias in Panel Data: Estimating the Returns to Schooling," *Annales de L'Insee,* 30/31, 1978, pp. 49–82.

Chamberlain, G., "Analysis of Covariance with Qualitative Data," *Review of Economic Studies,* 47, 1980, pp. 225–238.

Chamberlain, G., "Multivariate Regression Models for Panel Data," *Journal of Econometrics,* 18, 1982, pp. 5–46.

Chamberlain, G., "Panel Data," in Z. Griliches and M. Intriligator, eds., *Handbook of Econometrics.* Amsterdam: North-Holland 1983.

Chamberlain, G., "Asymptotic Efficiency in Semi-parametric Models with Censoring," *Journal of Econometrics,* 32, 1986, pp. 189–218.

Chamberlain, G., "Asymptotic Efficiency in Estimation with Conditional Moment Restrictions," *Journal of Econometrics,* 34, 1987, pp. 305–334.

Chamberlain, G., and Z. Griliches, "Unobservables with a Variance Components Structure: Ability, Schooling, and the Economic Success of Brothers," *International Economic Review,* 16, 1975, pp. 422–450.

Chambers, R., *Applied Production Analysis: A Dual Approach.* New York: Cambridge University Press, 1988.

Chatfield, C., *The Analysis of Time Series: Theory and Practice.* London: Chapman & Hall, 1975.

Chemical Rubber Company, *Standard Mathematical Tables.* Cleveland, Ohio: CRC Press, 1972.

Chen, C., "The EM Approach to the Multiple Indicators and Multiple Causes Model via the Estimation of the Latent Variable," *Journal of the American Statistical Association,* 76, 1981, pp. 704–708.

Chesher, A., and M. Irish, "Residual Analysis in the Grouped Data and Censored Normal Linear Model," *Journal of Econometrics,* 34, 1987, pp. 33–62.

Chesher, A., T. Lancaster, and M. Irish, "On Detecting the Failure of Distributional Assumptions," *Annales de L'Insee,* 59/60, 1985, pp. 7–44.

Cheung, C., and A. Goldberger, "Proportional Projections in Limited Dependent Variable Models," *Econometrica,* 52, 1984, pp. 531–534.

Chow, G., "Tests of Equality Between Sets of Coefficients in Two Linear Regressions," *Econometrica,* 28, 1960, pp. 591–605.

Christensen, L., and W. Greene, "Economies of Scale in U.S. Electric Power Generation," *Journal of Political Economy,* 84, 1976, pp. 655–676.

Christensen, L., and M. Manser, "Estimating U.S. Consumer Preferences for Meat with a Flexible Utility Function," *Journal of Econometrics,* 5, 1977, pp. 37–53.

Christensen, L., D. Jorgenson, and L. Lau, "Transcendental Logarithmic Production Frontiers," *Review of Economics and Statistics,* 55, 1973, pp. 28–45.

Christensen, L., D. Jorgenson, and L. Lau, "Transcendental Logarithmic Utility Functions," *American Economic Review,* 65, 1975, pp. 367–383.

Clark, C., "The Greatest of a Finite Set of Random Variables," *Operations Research,* 9, 1961, pp. 145–162.

Clark, C., *Mathematical Bioeconomics.* New York: Wiley, 1971.

Cochrane, D., and G. Orcutt, "Application of Least Squares Regression to Relationships Containing Autocorrelated Error Terms," *Journal of the American Statistical Association,* 44, 1949, pp. 32–61.

Conniffe, D., "Covariance Analysis and Seemingly Unrelated Regression Equations," *The American Statistician,* 36, 1982a, pp. 169–171.

Conniffe, D., "A Note on Seemingly Unrelated Regressions," *Econometrica,* 50, 1982b, pp. 229–233.

Conway, D., and H. Roberts, "Reverse Regression, Fairness and Employment Discrimination," *Journal of Business and Economic Statistics,* 1, 1, 1983, pp. 75–85.

Cooley, T., and S. LeRoy, "Atheoretical Macroeconomics: A Critique," *Journal of Monetary Economics,* 16, 1985, pp. 283–308.

Cooley, T., and E. Prescott, "An Adaptive Regression Model," *International Economic Review,* 14, 1973a, pp. 364–371.

Cooley, T., and E. Prescott, "Varying Parameter Regression: A Theory and Some Applications," *Annals of Economic and Social Measurement,* 2/4, 1973b, pp. 463–473.

Cooper, P., "Two Approaches to Polynomial Distributed Lag Estimation," *The American Statistician,* 26, 1972, pp. 32–35.

Cornwell, C., and P. Schmidt, "Models for which the MLE and Conditional MLE Coincide," *Empirical Economics,* 17, 1991, pp. 67–75.

Coulson, N., and R. Robins, "Aggregate Economic Activity and the Variance of Inflation: Another Look," *Economics Letters,* 17, 1985, pp. 71–75.

Council of Economic Advisors, *Economic Report of the President, 1987.* Washington, D.C.: U.S. Government Printing Office, 1987.

Cox, D., "Tests of Separate Families of Hypotheses," in *Proceedings of the 4th Berkeley Symposium on Mathematical Statistics and Probability,* Vol. 1. Berkeley, Calif.: University of California Press, 1961.

Cox, D., "Further Results on Tests of Separate Families of Hypotheses," *Journal of the Royal Statistical Society, Series B,* 24, 1962, pp. 406–424.

Cox, D., *Analysis of Binary Data.* London: Methuen, 1970.

Cox, D., "Regression Models and Life Tables," *Journal of the Royal Statistical Society, Series B,* 34, 1972, pp. 187–220.

Cox, D., and D. Oakes, *Analysis of Survival Data.* New York: Chapman & Hall, 1985.

Cragg, J., "On the Relative Small-Sample Properties of Several Structural-Equation Estimators," *Econometrica,* 35, 1967, pp. 89–110.

Cragg, J., "Some Statistical Models for Limited Dependent Variables with Application to the Demand for Durable Goods," *Econometrica,* 39, 1971, pp. 829–844.

Cragg, J., "Estimation and Testing in Time Series Regression Models with Heteroscedastic Disturbances," *Journal of Econometrics,* 20, 1982, pp. 135–157.

Cragg, J., "More Efficient Estimation in the Presence of Heteroscedasticity of Unknown Form," *Econometrica,* 51, 1983, pp. 751–763.

Cragg, J., and R. Uhler, "The Demand for Automobiles," *Canadian Journal of Economics*, 3, 1970, pp. 386–406.

Cramer, J. S., "Efficient Grouping, Regression and Correlation in Engel Curve Analysis," *Journal of the American Statistical Association*, 59, 1964, pp. 233–250.

Crawford, D., "Estimating Earnings Functions from Truncated Samples," *Discussion Paper 287-75*, Institute for Research on Poverty, University of Wisconsin, 1975.

Cumby, R., J. Huizinga, and M. Obstfeld, "Two-Step, Two Stage Least Squares Estimation in Models with Rational Expectations," *Journal of Econometrics*, 21, 1983, pp. 333–355.

Dadkah, K. M., "Confidence Interval Predictions for Logarithmic Models," *Review of Economics and Statistics*, 77, 1984, pp. 527–528.

Daganzo, C., F. Bouthelier, and Y. Sheffi, "Multinomial Probit and Qualitative Choice—A Computationally Efficient Algorithm," *Transportation Science*, 11, 1977, pp. 338–358.

Davidson, J., and J. Mackinnon, *Estimation and Inference in Econometrics*, New York: Oxford University Press, 1993.

Davidson, R., and J. MacKinnon, "Several Tests for Model Specification in the Presence of Alternative Hypotheses," *Econometrica*, 49, 1981, pp. 781–793.

Davidson, R., and J. MacKinnon, "Small Sample Properties of Alternative Forms of the Lagrange Multiplier Test," *Economics Letters*, 12, 1983, pp. 269–275.

Davidson, R., and J. MacKinnon, "Convenient Specification Tests for Logit and Probit Models," *Journal of Econometrics*, 25, 1984, pp. 241–262.

Davidson, R., and J. MacKinnon, "Testing Linear and Loglinear Regressions Against Box–Cox Alternatives," *Canadian Journal of Economics*, 18, 1985, pp. 499–517.

Deaton, A., "Demand Analysis," in Z. Griliches and M. Intriligator, eds., *Handbook of Econometrics*. Amsterdam: North-Holland 1983.

Deaton, A., and J. Muellbauer, "An Almost Ideal Demand System," *American Economic Review*, 70, 1980a, pp. 312–326.

Deaton, A., and J. Muellbauer, *Economics and Consumer Behavior*. New York: Cambridge University Press, 1980b.

Dempster, A., N. Laird, and D. Rubin, "Maximum Likelihood Estimation from Incomplete Data via the EM Algorithm," *Journal of the Royal Statistical Society, Series B*, 39, 1977, pp. 1–38.

Desai, M., *Applied Econometrics*. New York: McGraw-Hill, 1976.

Dewald, W., J. Thursby, and R. Anderson, "Replication in Empirical Economics: The *Journal of Money, Credit, and Banking* Project," *American Economic Review*, 76, 1986, pp. 587–603.

Dezhbaksh, H., "The Inappropriate Use of Serial Correlation Tests in Dynamic Linear Models, *Review of Economics and Statistics*, 72, 1990, pp. 126–132.

Dhrymes, P., "Efficient Estimation of Distributed Lags with Autocorrelated Errors," *International Economic Review*, 10, 1969, pp. 47–67.

Dhrymes, P., *Distributed Lags: Problems of Estimation and Formulation*, San Francisco: Holden-Day, 1971.

Dhrymes, P., "Restricted and Unrestricted Reduced Forms: Asymptotic Distribution and Relative Efficiency," *Econometrica*, 41, 1973, pp. 119–134.

Dhrymes, P., *Mathematics for Econometrics*, Needham, Mass.: Springer-Verlag, 1974.

Dhrymes, P., "Limited Dependent Variables," in Z. Griliches and M. Intriligator, eds., *Handbook of Econometrics*, Vol. 2. Amsterdam: North-Holland, 1984.

Dickey, D., and W. Fuller, "Distribution of the Estimators for Autoregressive Time

Series with a Unit Root," *Journal of the American Statistical Association,* 74, 1979, pp. 427–431.

Dickey, D., and W. Fuller, "Likelihood Ratio Tests for Autoregressive Time Series with a Unit Root," *Econometrica,* 49, 1981, pp. 1057–1072.

Diewert, E., "Applications of Duality Theory," in M. Intriligator and D. Kendrick, eds., *Frontiers in Quantitative Economics.* Amsterdam: North-Holland, 1974.

Domowitz, I., and C. Hakkio, "Conditional Variance and the Risk Premium in the Foreign Exchange Market," *Journal of International Economics,* 19, 1985, pp. 47–66.

Don, F., and J. Magnus, "On the Unbiasedness of the Iterated GLS Estimator," *Communications in Statistics,* 1980, pp. 519–527.

Doran, H., and W. Griffiths, "Inconsistency of the OLS Estimator of the Partial Adjustment—Adaptive Expectations Model," *Journal of Econometrics,* 6, 1978, pp. 133–146.

Draper, N., and D. Cox, "On Distributions and Their Transformation to Normality," *Journal of the Royal Statistical Society, Series B,* 31, 1969, pp. 472–476.

Draper, N., and H. Smith, *Applied Regression Analysis.* New York: Wiley, 1980.

Duncan, G., "Sample Selectivity as a Proxy Variable Problem: On the Use and Misuse of Gaussian Selectivity Corrections," *Research in Labor Economics,* Supplement 2, 1983, pp. 333–345.

Duncan, G., "A Semiparametric Censored Regression Estimator," *Journal of Econometrics,* 31, 1986a, pp. 5–34.

Duncan, G., ed., "Continuous/Discrete Econometric Models with Unspecified Error Distribution," *Journal of Econometrics,* 32, 1, 1986b.

Durbin, J., "Errors in Variables," *Review of the International Statistical Institute,* 22, 1954, pp. 23–32.

Durbin, J., "Estimation of Parameters in Time-Series Regression Models," *Journal of the Royal Statistical Society, Series B,* 22, 1960, pp. 139–153.

Durbin, J., "Testing for Serial Correlation in Least Squares Regression When Some of the Regressors Are Lagged Dependent Variables," *Econometrica,* 38, 1970, pp. 410–421.

Durbin, J., and G. Watson, "Testing for Serial Correlation in Least Squares Regression—I," *Biometrika,* 37, 1950, pp. 409–428.

Durbin, J., and G. Watson, "Testing for Serial Correlation in Least Squares Regression—II," *Biometrika,* 38, 1951, pp. 159–178.

Durbin, J., and G. Watson, "Testing for Serial Correlation in Least Squares Regression—III," *Biometrika,* 58, 1971, pp. 1–42.

Dwivedi, T., and K. Srivastava, "Optimality of Least Squares in the Seemingly Unrelated Regressions Model," *Journal of Econometrics,* 7, 1978, pp. 391–395.

Edlefson, L., and S. Jones, *Gauss.* Kent, Wash.: Aptech Systems, 1985.

Eicker, F., "Limit Theorems for Regression with Unequal and Dependent Errors," in L. LeCam and J. Neyman, eds., *Proceedings of the 5th Berkeley Symposium on Mathematical Statistics and Probability.* Berkeley, Calif.: University of California Press, 1967, pp. 59–82.

Engle, R., "Estimating Structural Models of Seasonality," in A. Zellner, ed., *Seasonal Analysis of Time Series.* Washington, D.C.: U.S. Bureau of the Census, 1978, pp. 281–308.

Engle, R., "Autoregressive Conditional Heteroscedasticity with Estimates of the Variance of United Kingdom Inflations," *Econometrica,* 50, 1982, pp. 987–1008.

Engle, R., "Estimates of the Variance of U.S. Inflation Based on the ARCH Model," *Journal of Money, Credit, and Banking,* 15, 1983, pp. 286–301.

Engle, R., "Wald, Likelihood Ratio, and Lagrange Multiplier Tests in Econometrics," in Z. Griliches and M. Intriligator, eds., *Handbook of Econometrics,* Vol. 2. Amsterdam: North-Holland, 1984.

Engle, R., and C. Granger, "Co-integration and Error Correction: Representation, Estimation and Testing," *Econometrica,* 35, 1987, pp. 251–276.

Engle, R., and D. Kraft, "Multiperiod Forecast Error Variances of Inflation Estimated From ARCH Models," in A. Zellner, ed., *Applied Time Series Analysis of Economic Data.* Washington D.C.: Bureau of the Census, 1983.

Engle, R., D. Lilien, and R. Robins, "Estimation of Time Varying Risk Premiums in the Term Structure," University of California, San Diego, Department of Economics, Discussion paper 85-17, 1985.

Engle, R., D. Lilien, and R. Robins, "Estimating Time Varying Risk Premia in the Term Structure: The ARCH-M Model," *Econometrica,* 55, 1987, pp. 391–407.

Engle, R., and M. Rothschild, "ARCH Models in Finance," *Journal of Econometrics, 52, 1/2,* 1992.

Engle, R., and M. Watson, "A One Factor Multivariate Time Series Model, of Metropolitan Wage Rates," *Journal of the American Statistical Association,* 76, 1981, pp. 774–781.

Evans, G., and Savin, N., "Testing for Unit Roots: I," *Econometrica,* 49, 1981, pp. 753–779.

Evans, G., and Savin, N., "Testing for Unit Roots: II," *Econometrica,* 52, 1984, pp. 1241–1269.

Even, W., "Testing Exogeneity in a Probit Model," *Economics Letters,* 26, 1988, pp. 125–128.

Fair, R., "The Estimation of Simultaneous Equations Models with Lagged Endogenous Variables and First Order Serially Correlated Errors," *Econometrica,* 38, 1970, pp. 507–516.

Fair, R., "Efficient Estimation of Simultaneous Equations with Autoregressive Errors by Instrumental Variables," *Review of Economics and Statistics,* 54, 1972, pp. 444–449.

Fair, R., "A Note on Computation of the Tobit Estimator," *Econometrica,* 45, 1977, pp. 1723–1727.

Fair, R., "A Theory of Extramarital Affairs," *Journal of Political Economy,* 86, 1978, pp. 45–61.

Fair, R., *Specification and Analysis of Macroeconomic Models.* Cambridge: Harvard University Press, 1984.

Fair, R., and D. Jaffee, "Methods of Estimation for Markets in Disequilibrium," *Econometrica,* 40, 1972, pp. 497–514.

Farebrother, R. "The Durbin–Watson Test for Serial Correlation When There Is No Intercept in the Regression," *Econometrica,* 48, 1980, pp. 1553–1563.

Farrar, D., and R. Glauber, "Multicollinearity in Regression Analysis: The Problem Revisited," *Review of Economics and Statistics,* 49, 1967, pp. 92–107.

Feldstein, M., "The Error of Forecast in Econometric Models When the Forecast-Period Exogenous Variables Are Stochastic," *Econometrica,* 39, 1971, pp. 55–60.

Feldstein, M., "Multicollinearity and the MSE of Alternative Estimators," *Econometrica,* 41, 1973, pp. 337–346.

Fernandez, L., "Nonparametric Maximum Likelihood Estimation of Censored Regression Models," *Journal of Econometrics,* 32, 1986, pp. 35–57.

Fin, T., and P. Schmidt, "A Test of the Tobit Specification Against an Alternative Suggested by Cragg," *Review of Economics and Statistics,* 66, 1984, pp. 174–177.

Finney, D., *Probit Analysis*. Cambridge: Cambridge University Press, 1971.

Fisher, F., "Tests of Equality Between Sets of Coefficients in Two Linear Regressions: An Expository Note," *Econometrica,* 28, 1970, pp. 361–366.

Fisher, F., *The Identification Problem in Econometrics*. New York: R. E. Krieger, 1976.

Fletcher, R., *Practical Methods of Optimization*. New York: Wiley, 1980.

Fomby, T., and D. Guilkey, "An Examination of Two-Step Estimators for Models with Lagged Dependent Variables and Autocorrelated Errors," *Jounral of Econometrics,* 22, 1983, pp. 291–300.

Fomby, T., C. Hill, and S. Johnson, "An Optimal Property of Principal Components in the Context of Restricted Least Squares," *Journal of the American Statistical Association,* 73, 1978, pp. 191–193.

Fomby, T., C. Hill, and S. Johnson, *Advanced Econometric Methods*. Needham, Mass.: Springer-Verlag, 1984.

Forsund, F., K. Lovell, and P. Schmidt, "A Survey of Frontier Production Functions and of Their Relationship to Efficiency Measurement," *Journal of Econometrics,* 13, 1980, pp. 5–25.

Friedman, M., *A Theory of the Consumption Function*. Princeton, N.J.: Princeton University Press, 1957.

Frisch, R., "Editorial," *Econometrica,* 1, 1933, pp. 1–4.

Frisch, R., and F. Waugh, "Partial Time Regressions as Compared with Individual Trends," *Econometrica,* 1, 1933, pp. 387–401.

Frost, P., "Some Properties of the Almon Lag Technique When One Searches for Degree of Polynomial and Lag," *Journal of the American Statistical Association,* 70, 1975, pp. 606–612.

Fuller, W., *Introduction to Statistical Time Series*. New York: Wiley, 1976.

Fuller, W., and G. Battese, "Estimation of Linear Models with Crossed-Error Structure," *Journal of Econometrics,* 2, 1974, pp. 67–78.

Gabrielsen, A., "Consistency and Identifiability," *Journal of Econometrics,* 8, 1978, pp. 261–263.

Galpin, J., and D. Hawkins, "The Use of Recursive Residuals in Checking Model Fit in Linear Regression," *American Statistician,* 38, 1984, pp. 94–105.

Garber, S., and S. Klepper, "Extending the Classical Normal Errors in Variables Model," *Econometrica,* 48, 1980, pp. 1541–1546.

Garber, S., and D. Poirier, "The Determinants of Aerospace Profit Rates," *Southern Economic Journal,* 41, 1974, pp. 228–238.

Gaver, K., and M. Geisel, "Discriminating Among Alternative Models: Bayesian and Non-Bayesian Methods," in P. Zarembka, ed., *Frontiers in Econometrics*. New York: Academic Press, 1974.

Geweke, J., "Inference and Causality in Econometric Time Series Models," in Z. Griliches and M. Intriligator, eds., *Handbook of Econometrics*, Vol. 2. Amsterdam: North-Holland, 1984.

Geweke, J., and R. Meese, "Estimating Regression Models of Finite but Unknown Order," *International Economic Review,* 22, 1981, pp. 55–70.

Giles, D., and M. King, "Fourth Order Autocorrelation: Further Significance Points for the Wallis Test," *Journal of Econometrics,* 8, 1978, pp. 255–259.

Glesjer, H., "A New Test for Heteroscedasticity," *Journal of the American Statistical Association,* 64, 1969, pp. 316–323.

Godfrey, L., "Testing for Multiplicative Heteroscedasticity," *Journal of Econometrics,* 8, 1978a, pp. 227–236.

Godfrey, L., "Testing Against General Autoregressive and Moving Average Error Models When the Regressors Include Lagged Dependent Variables," *Econometrica,* 46, 1978b, pp. 1293–1302.

Godfrey, L., *Misspecification Tests in Econometrics,* Cambridge: Cambridge University Press, 1988.

Godfrey, L., and M. Wickens, "Testing Linear and Log-Linear Regressions for Functional Form," Review of Economic Studies, 48, 1981, pp. 487–496.

Godfrey, L., and D. Poskitt, "Testing the Restrictions of the Almon Lag Technique," *Journal of the American Statistical Association,* 70, 1975, pp. 105–108.

Goldberger, A., *Impact Multipliers and Dynamic Properties of the Klein–Goldberger Model.* Amsterdam: North-Holland, 1959.

Goldberger, A., "Best Linear Unbiased Prediction in the Generalized Regression Model," *Journal of the American Statistical Association,* 57, 1962, pp. 369–375.

Goldberger, A., *Econometric Theory.* New York: Wiley, 1964.

Goldberger, A., "Estimation of a Regression Coefficient Matrix Containing a Block of Zeroes," *Paper 7002,* University of Wisconsin, SSRI, EME, 1970.

Goldberger, A., "Econometrics and Psychometrics: A Survey of Commonalities," *Biometrika,* 36, 1971, pp. 83–107.

Goldberger, A., "Maximum Likelihood Estimation of Regressions Containing Unobservable Independent Variables," *International Economic Review,* 13, 1972a, pp. 1–15.

Goldberger, A., "Selection Bias in Evaluating Treatment Effects: Some Formal Illustrations," *Discussion Paper 123-72,* Institute for Research on Poverty, University of Wisconsin–Madison, 1972b.

Goldberger, A., "Linear Regression After Selection," *Journal of Econometrics,* 15, 1981, pp. 357–366.

Goldberger, A., "Abnormal Selection Bias," in S. Karlin, T. Amemiya, and L. Goodman, eds., *Studies in Econometrics, Time Series, and Multivariate Statistics.* New York: Academic Press, 1983.

Goldberger, A., "One-Sided and Inequality Tests for a Pair of Means," *Paper 8629,* Social Science Research Institute, University of Wisconsin–Madison, 1986.

Goldberger, A., *A Course in Econometrics.* Cambridge, Mass.: Harvard University Press, 1990.

Goldfeld, S., "The Demand for Money Revisited," *Brookings Papers on Economic Activity,* Vol. 3. Washington, D.C.: Brookings Institution, 1973.

Goldfeld, S., and R. Quandt, "Some Tests for Homoscedasticity," *Journal of the American Statistical Association,* 60, 1965, pp. 539–547.

Goldfeld, S., and R. Quandt, "Nonlinear Simultaneous Equations: Estimation and Prediction," *International Economic Review,* 9, 1968, pp. 113–136.

Goldfeld, S., and R. Quandt, *Nonlinear Methods in Econometrics.* Amsterdam: North-Holland, 1971.

Goldfeld, S., and R. Quandt, "GQOPT: A Package for Numerical Optimization of Functions," Department of Economics, Princeton University, 1972.

Goldfeld, S., R. Quandt, and H. Trotter, "Maximization by Quadratic Hill Climbing," *Econometrica,* 1966, pp. 541–551.

Goodwin, B., "A Simplified Approach to Estimating Simultaneous-Equation Tobit Models," mimeo, Department of Agricultural Economics, Kansas State University, June 1991.

Gordon, R., ed., *The American Business Cycle.* Chicago: National Bureau of Economic Research, 1986.

Gourieroux, C., A. Monfort, and A. Trognon, "Pseudo Maximum Likelihood Methods: Applications to Poisson Models," *Econometrica,* 52, 1984, pp. 701–720.

Gourieroux, C., A. Monfort, E. Renault, and A. Trognon, "Generalized Residuals," *Journal of Econometrics,* 34, 1987, pp. 5–32.

Granger, C., *Forecasting in Business and Economics.* New York: Academic Press, 1980.

Granger, C., "Investigating Causal Relations by Econometric Models and Cross-Spectral Methods," *Econometrica,* 37, 1969, pp. 424–438.

Granger, C., and P. Newbold, "Spurious Regressions in Econometrics," *Journal of Econometrics,* 2, 1974, pp. 111–120.

Granger, C., and P. Newbold, *Forecasting Economic Time Series.* New York: Academic Press, 1977.

Granger, C., and M. Watson, "Time Series and Spectral Methods in Econometrics," in Z. Griliches and M. Intriligator, eds., *Handbook of Econometrics,* Vol. 2, Chapter 17. Amsterdam: North-Holland, 1984.

Greenberg, E., and C. Webster, *Advanced Econometrics: A Bridge to the Literature.* New York: Wiley, 1983.

Greene, W., "Maximum Likelihood Estimation of Econometric Frontier Functions," *Journal of Econometrics,* 13, 1980a, pp. 27–56.

Greene, W., "On the Asymptotic Bias of the Ordinary Least Squares Estimator of the Tobit Model," *Econometrica,* 48, 1980b, pp. 505–514.

Greene, W., "Sample Selection Bias as a Specification Error: Comment," *Econometrica,* 49, 1981, pp. 795–798.

Greene, W., "Estimation of Limited Dependent Variable Models by Ordinary Least Squares and the Method of Moments," *Journal of Econometrics,* 21, 1983a, pp. 195–212.

Greene, W., "Simultaneous Estimation of Factor Substitution, Economics of Scale, and Non-neutral Technical Change," in A. Dogramaci, ed. *Econometric Analyses of Productivity.* Boston: Kluwer-Nijoff, 1983b.

Greene, W., "Estimation of the Correlation Coefficient in a Bivariate Probit Model Using the Method of Moments," *Economics Letters,* 16, 1984, pp. 285–291.

Greene, W., *LIMDEP, Version 6.0: User's Manual.* Bellport, N.Y.: Econometric Software, 1991.

Greene, W., and T. Seaks, "The Restricted Least Squares Estimator: A Pedagogical Note," *Review of Economics and Statistics,* 73, 1991, pp. 563–567.

Greenstadt, J., "On the Relative Efficiencies of Gradient Methods," *Mathematics of Computation,* 1967, pp. 360–367.

Grether, D., and G. Maddala, "Errors in Variables and Serially Correlated Disturbances in Distributed Lag Models," *Econometrica,* 41, 1973, pp. 255–262.

Griliches, Z., "Hybrid Corn: An Exploration in the Economics of Technological Change," *Econometrica,* 25, 1957, pp. 501–522.

Griliches, Z., "A Note on Serial Correlation Bias in Estimates of Distributed Lags," *Econometrica,* 26, 1961a, pp. 65–73.

Griliches, Z., "Hedonic Price Indexes for Automobiles: An Econometric Analysis of Quality Change," *Government Price Statistics, Hearings,* U.S. Congress, Joint Economic Committee, January 24, 1961b.

Griliches, Z., "Distributed Lags: A Survey," *Econometrica,* 35, 1967, pp. 16–49.

Griliches, Z., "Economic Data Issues," in Z. Griliches and M. Intriligator, eds., *Handbook of Econometrics,* Vol. 3. Amsterdam: North-Holland, 1986.

Griliches, Z., and J. Hausman, "Errors in Variables in Panel Data," *Journal of Econometrics,* 31, 1986, pp. 93–118.

Griliches, Z., and P. Rao, "Small Sample Properties of Several Two Stage Regression

Methods in the Context of Autocorrelated Errors," *Journal of the American Statistical Association*, 64, 1969, pp. 253–272.

Griliches, Z., G. Maddala, R. Lucas, and N. Wallace, "Notes on Estimated Aggregate Quarterly Consumption Functions," *Econometrica*, 30, 1962, pp. 491–500.

Grogger, J., "A Simple Test for Exogeneity in Probit, Logit, and Poisson Regression Models," *Economics Letters*, 33, 1990, pp. 329–332.

Grogger, J., and R. Carson, "Models for Truncated Counts," *Journal of Applied Econometrics*, 6, 1991, pp. 225–238.

Gronau, R., "Wage Comparisons: A Selectivity Bias," and Lewis, H., "Comments on Selectivity Biases in Wage Comparisons," *Journal of Political Economy*, 82, 1974, pp. 1119–1155.

Grunfeld, Y., "The Determinants of Corporate Investment," unpublished Ph.D. thesis, Department of Economics, University of Chicago, 1958.

Grunfeld, Y., and Z. Griliches, "Is Aggregation Necessarily Bad?" *Review of Economics and Statistics*, 42, 1960, pp. 1–13.

Guilkey, D., "Alternative Tests for a First-Order Vector Autoregressive Error Specification," *Journal of Econometrics*, 2, 1974, pp. 95–104.

Guilkey, D., and P. Schmidt, "Estimation of Seemingly Unrelated Regressions with Vector Autoregressive Errors," *Journal of the American Statistical Association*, 1973, pp. 642–647.

Guilkey, D., and P. Schmidt, "Extended Tabulations for Dickey–Fuller Tests," *Economics Letters*, 31, 1989, pp. 355–358.

Guilkey, D., K. Lovell, and R. Sickles, "A Comparison of the Performance of Three Flexible Functional Forms," *International Economic Review*, 24, 1983, pp. 591–616.

Gurmu, S., "Tests for Detecting Overdispersion in the Positive Poisson Regression Model," *Journal of Business and Economic Statistics*, 9, 1991, pp. 215–222.

Haavelmo, T., "The Statistical Implications of a System of Simultaneous Equations," *Econometrica*, 11, 1943, pp. 1–12.

Hadley, G., *Linear Algebra*. Reading, Mass.: Addison-Wesley, 1961.

Haitovsky, Y., "Missing Data in Regression Analysis," *Journal of the Royal Statistical Society, Series B*, 1968, pp. 67–82.

Hall, B., *TSP Version 4.0 Reference Manual*. Stanford, Calif.: TSP International, 1982.

Hall, B., "Software for the Computation of Tobit Model Estimates," *Journal of Econometrics*, 24, 1984, pp. 215–222.

Hamilton, J., "A Standard Error for the Estimated State Vector of a State-Space Model," *Journal of Econometrics*, 33, 1986, pp. 387–398.

Hannan, E., and R. Terrell, "Testing for Serial Correlation After Least Squares Regression," *Econometrica*, 1966, pp. 646–660.

Hansen, L., "Large Sample Properties of Generalized Method of Moments Estimators," *Econometrica*, 50, 1982, pp. 1029–1054.

Hansen, L., and K. Singleton, "Efficient Estimation of Asset Pricing Models with Moving Average Errors," mimeo, Department of Economics, Carnegie-Mellon University, 1988.

Hartley, M., "The Tobit and Probit Models: Maximum Likelihood Estimation by OLS," *Working Paper 375*, State University of New York, Buffalo, Department of Economics, 1976.

Harvey, A., "Estimation of Parameters in a Heteroscedastic Regression Model," presented at the *European Meetings of the Econometric Society*, Grenoble, 1974.

Harvey, A., "Estimating Regression Models with Multiplicative Heteroscedasticity," *Econometrica*, 44, 1976, pp. 461–465.

Jorgenson, D., "Econometric Methods for Modeling Producer Behavior," in Z. Griliches and M. Intriligator, *Handbook of Econometrics*, Vol. 3. Amsterdam: North-Holland, 1983.

Judge, G., and M. Bock, *The Statistical Implications of Pre-test and Stein Rule Estimators in Econometrics*. Amsterdam: North-Holland, 1978.

Judge, G., and M. Bock, "Biased Estimation," in Z. Griliches and M. Intrilligator, eds., *Handbook of Econometrics*, Vol. 1. Amsterdam: North-Holland, 1983.

Judge, G., and T. Yancey, "Sampling Properties of an Inequality Restricted Estimator," *Economics Letters*, 4, 1981, pp. 327–333.

Judge, G., C. Hill, W. Griffiths, T. Lee, and H. Lutkepol, *An Introduction to the Theory and Practice of Econometrics*. New York: Wiley, 1982.

Judge, G., C. Hill, W. Griffiths, T. Lee, *The Theory and Practice of Econometrics*. New York: Wiley, 1985.

Just, R., and R. Pope, "Stochastic Specification of Production Functions and Economic Implications," *Journal of Econometrics*, 7, 1978, pp. 67–86.

Kakwani, N., "The Unbiasedness of Zellner's Seemingly Unrelated Regression Equation Estimators," *Journal of the American Statistical Association*, 62, 1967, pp. 141–142.

Kalbfleisch, J., and R. Prentice, *The Statistical Analysis of Failure Time Data*. New York: Wiley, 1980.

Kalman, R., "A New Approach to Linear Filtering and Prediction Problems," *Journal of Basic Engineering, Transactions ASME, Series D*, 82, 1960, pp. 35–45.

Kamlich, R., and S. Polachek, "Discrimination: Fact or Fiction? An Examination Using an Alternative Approach," *Southern Economic Journal*, October 1982, pp. 450–461.

...jian, H., "Missing Observations in Multivariate Regression—Efficiency of a First Order Method," *Journal of the American Statistical Association*, 64, 1969, pp. 1609–1616.

...H., "Two-State Least Squares and Econometric Systems Linear in Parameters but Nonlinear in the Endogenous Variables," *Journal of the American Statistical Association*, 66, 1971, pp. 373–374.

...H., and I. Prucha, "Independent or Uncorrelated Disturbances in Linear Regression: An Illustration of the Difference," *Economics Letters*, 19, 1985, ...35–38.

...inear Cross Equation Constraints and the Identification Problem," *Econometrica*, 43, 1975, pp. 125–140.

...d A. Stuart, *The Advanced Theory of Statistics*, Vol. 2. London: Charles ...1961.

...A. Stuart, *The Advanced Theory of Statistics*, Vol. 1, *Distribution* ...ondon: Charles Griffin, 1969.

...Duration of Contract Strikes in U.S. Manufacturing," *Journal of* ..., 28, 1985, pp. 5–28.

...al Theory of Employment, Interest, and Money*. New York: Har-...nd Jovanovich, 1936.

...e of Sample Separation Information," *Econometrica*, 47, 1979,

...Fixed Effects Models for Time Series of Cross-Sections with ...oral Covariance," *Journal of Econometrics*, 14, 1980,

...endence in Multivariate Probit Models," *Biometrika*, 69,

Harvey, A., *Forecasting, Structural Time Series Models and the Kalman Filter*. New York: Cambridge University Press, 1989.

Harvey, A., *The Econometric Analysis of Time Series*, 2nd ed. Cambridge, Mass.: MIT Press, 1990.

Harvey, A., and G. Collier, "Testing for Functional Misspecification in Regression Analysis," *Journal of Econometrics*, 6, 1977, pp. 103–119.

Harvey, A., and I. McAvinchey, "On the Relative Efficiency of Various Estimators of Regression Models with Moving Average Disturbances," in E. Charatsis, ed., *Proceedings of the Econometric Society European Meetings*, Athens, 1979. Amsterdam: North-Holland, 1981.

Harvey, A., and G. Phillips, "A Comparison of the Power of Some Tests for Heteroscedasticity in the General Linear Model," *Journal of Econometrics*, 2, 1974, pp. 307–316.

Harvey, A., and G. Phillips, "Testing for Heteroscedasticity in Simultaneous Equations Models," *Journal of Econometrics*, 11, 1981, pp. 311–340.

Hatanaka, M., "An Efficient Estimator for the Dynamic Adjustment Model with Autocorrelated Errors," *Journal of Econometrics*, 2, 1974, pp. 199–220.

Hatanaka, M., "Several Efficient Two-Step Estimators for the Dynamic Simultaneous Equations Model with Autoregressive Disturbances," *Journal of Econometrics*, 4, 1976, pp. 189–204.

Hausman, J., "An Instrumental Variable Approach to Full-Information Estimators for Linear and Certain Nonlinear Models," *Econometrica*, 43, 1975, pp. 727–738.

Hausman, J., "Specification Tests in Econometrics," *Econometrica*, 46, 1978, pp. 1251–1271.

Hausman, J., "Specification and Estimation of Simultaneous Equations Models," in Z. Griliches and M. Intriligator, eds., *Handbook of Econometrics*. Amsterdam: North-Holland, 1983.

Hausman, J., and A. Han, "Flexible Parametric Estimation of Duration and Competing Risk Models," *Journal of Applied Econometrics*, 5, 1990, pp. 1–28.

Hausman, J., and McFadden, D., "A Specification Test for the Multinomial Logit Model," *Econometrica*, 52, 1984, pp. 1219–1240.

Hausman, J., and P. Ruud, "Specifying and Testing Econometric Models for Rank Ordered Data with an Application to the Demand for Mobile and Portable Telephones," *Working Paper 8605*, University of California, Berkeley, Department of Economics, 1986.

Hausman, J., and W. Taylor, "Panel Data and Unobservable Individual Effects," *Econometrica*, 49, 1981, pp. 1377–1398.

Hausman, J., and D. Wise, "Social Experimentation, Truncated Distributions, and Efficient Estimation," *Econometrica*, 45, 1977, pp. 919–938.

Hausman, J., and D. Wise, "A Conditional Probit Model for Qualitative Choice: Discrete Decisions Recognizing Interdependence and Heterogeneous Preferences," *Econometrica*, 46, 1978, pp. 403–426.

Hausman, J., B. Hall, and Z. Griliches, "Economic Models for Count Data with an Application to the Patents–R&D Relationship," *Econometrica*, 52, 1984, pp. 909–938.

Heckman, J., "The Common Structure of Statistical Models of Truncation, Sample Selection, and Limited Dependent Variables and a Simple Estimator for Such Models," *Annals of Economic and Social Measurement*, 5, 1976, pp. 475–492.

Heckman, J., "Dummy Endogenous Variables in a Simultaneous Equation System," *Econometrica*, 46, 1978, pp. 931–959.

Heckman, J., "Sample Selection Bias as a Specification Error," *Econometrica*, 47, 1979, pp. 153–161.

Heckman, J., "Varieties of Selection Bias," *American Economic Review*, 80, 1990, pp. 313–318.

Heckman, J., and T. MaCurdy, "A Simultaneous Equations Linear Probability Model," *Canadian Journal of Economics*, 18, 1985, pp. 28–37.

Heckman, J., and B. Singer, "Econometric Duration Analysis," *Journal of Econometrics*, 24, 1984a, pp. 63–132.

Heckman, J., and B. Singer, "A Method for Minimizing the Impact of Distributional Assumptions in Econometric Models for Duration Data," *Econometrica*, 52, 1984b, pp. 271–320.

Heckman, J., and B. Singer, eds., "Econometric Analysis of Longitudinal Data," *Journal of Econometrics*, 32, 1985.

Heckman, J., and R. Willis, "A Beta-Logistic Model for the Analysis of Sequential Labor Force Participation by Married Women," *Working Paper 112*, Chicago: National Bureau of Economic Research, November 1975.

Heckman, J., and Willis, R., "Estimation of a Stochastic Model of Reproduction: An Econometric Approach," in N. Terleckyj, ed., *Household Production and Consumption*. New York: National Bureau of Economic Research, 1976.

Hein, D., "Predicted and Actual Frequencies in Binomial Response Models," *Economics Letters*, 23, 1987, pp. 104–107.

Hendry, D., "Econometrics: Alchemy or Science?" *Economica*, 47, 1980, pp. 387–406.

Hendry, D., and J. Richard, "On the Formulation of Empirical Models in Dynamic Econometrics," *Journal of Econometrics*, 20, 1982, pp. 193–220.

Hendry, D., A. Pagan, and J. Sargan, "Dynamic Specification," in Z. Griliches and M. Intriligator, eds., *Handbook of Econometrics*, Vol. 2. Amsterdam: North-Holland, 1984.

Hensher, D., "Simultaneous Estimation of Hierarchical Logit Mode Choice Models," *Working Paper 24*, MacQuarie University, School of Economic and Financial Studies, 1986.

Hildebrand, G., and T. Liu, *Manufacturing Production Functions in the United States*. Ithaca, N.Y.: Cornell University Press, 1957.

Hildreth, C., and W. Dent, "An Adjusted Maximum Likelihood Estimator," in W. Saelkert, ed., *Econometrics and Economic Theory: Essays in Honor of Jan Tinbergen*. London: Macmillan, 1974, pp. 3–25.

Hildreth, C., and C. Houck, "Some Estimators for a Linear Model with Random Coefficients," *Journal of the American Statistical Association*, 63, 1968, pp. 584–595.

Hildreth, C., and J. Lu, "Demand Relations with Autocorrelated Disturbances," *Technical Bulletin 276*, Michigan State University Agricultural Experiment Station, 1960.

Hite, S., *Women and Love*. New York: Alfred A. Knopf, 1987.

Hoerl, A., and R. Kennard, "Ridge Regression: Biased Estimation for Nonorthogonal Problems," *Technometrics*, 12, 1970, pp. 69–82.

Holtz-Eakin, D., "Testing for Individual Effects," *Journal of Econometrics*, 39, 1988b, pp. 297–309.

Holtz-Eakin, D., W. Newey, and H. Rosen, "Estimating Vector Autoregressions with Panel Data," *Econometrica*, 56, 6, 1988, pp. 1371–1395.

Horn, D., A. Horn, and G. Duncan, "Estimating Heteroscedastic Variances in Linear Models," *Journal of the American Statistical Association*, 70, 1975, pp. 380–385.

Horowitz, J., and G. Neumann, "Specification Testing in Censored Regression Models," *Journal of Applied Econometrics*, 4(S), 1989, pp. S35–S60.

Hsiao, C., "Some Estimation Methods for a Random Coefficient Model," *Econometrica*, 43, 1975, pp. 305–325.

Hsiao, C., "Identification," in Z. Griliches and M. Intriligator, eds., *Handbook of Econometrics*. Amsterdam: North-Holland, 1983.

Hsiao, C., "Benefits and Limitations of Panel Data," *Econometric Reviews*, 4(1), 1985, pp. 121–174.

Hsiao, C., *Analysis of Panel Data*. New York: Cambridge University Press, 1986.

Hurd, M., "Estimation in Truncated Samples When There Is Heteroscedasticity," *Journal of Econometrics*, 11, 1979, pp. 247–258.

Husby, R., "A Nonlinear Consumption Function Estimated from Time Series and Cross Section Data," *Review of Economics and Statistics*, 53, 1971, pp. 76–79.

Jaggia, S., "Tests of Moment Restrictions in Parametric Duration Models," *Economics Letters*, 37, 1991, pp. 35–38.

James, W., and C. Stein, "Estimation with Quadratic Loss," in J. Neyman, ed., *Proceedings of the 4th Berkeley Symposium on Mathematical Statistics and Probability*, Vol. 1. Berkeley, Calif.: University of California Press, 1961, pp. 36–379.

Jarque, C., "An Application of LDV Models to Household Expenditure Analysis Mexico," *Journal of Econometrics*, 36, 1987, pp. 31–54.

Jayatissa, W., "Tests of Equality Between Sets of Coefficients in Two Linear sions When Disturbances Variances Are Unequal," *Econometrica*, pp. 1291–1292.

Jennrich, R. I., "The Asymptotic Properties of Nonlinear Least Squares," *Annals of Statistics*, 2, 1969, pp. 633–643.

Jobson, J., and W. Fuller, "Least Squares Estimation When the Covariance Parameter Vector Are Functionally Related," *Journal of the American Statistical Association*, 75, 1980, pp. 176–181.

Johnson, N., and S. Kotz, *Distributions in Statistics—Continuous Distributions*, Vol. 2. New York: Wiley, 1970.

Johnson, N., and S. Kotz, *Distributions in Statistics—Discrete Distributions*. Wiley, 1971.

Johnson, N., and S. Kotz, *Distributions in Statistics—Continuous Distributions*. New York: Wiley, 1974.

Johnston, J., *Econometric Methods*. New York: McGraw-Hill,

Jones, R., "Maximum Likelihood Fitting of ARIMA Observations," *Technometrics*, 22, 19

Joreskog, K., "A General Method for Estimation in A. Goldberger and O. Duncan, Sciences. New York: Academic

Joreskog, K., and A. Goldberger, "Est Multiple Causes of a Single cal Association, 70, 1975

Joreskog, G., and Gruvaeus, G Several Variables," Services, 1970.

Joreskog, K., and D. Sor Resources, 1981.

Jorgenson, D., "Rational Di 149.

Kiefer, N., "Econometric Analysis of Duration Data," *Journal of Econometrics,* 28, 1, 1985a.

Kiefer, N., "Specification Diagnostics Based on Laguerre Alternatives for Econometric Models of Duration," *Journal of Econometrics,* 28, 1985b, pp. 135–154.

Kiefer, N., "Economic Duration Data and Hazard Functions," *Journal of Economic Literature,* 26, 1988, pp. 646–679.

Kiefer, N., and M. Salmon, "Testing Normality in Econometric Models," *Economics Letters,* 11, 1983, pp. 123–128.

Kim, H., and J. Pollard, "Cube Root Asymptotics," *Annals of Statistics,* March 1990, pp. 191–219.

King, B., "Market and Industry Factors in Stock Price Behavior," *Journal of Business,* 39, 1966, pp. 139–168.

King, M., "The Durbin–Watson Test for Serial Correlation: Bounds for Regressions with Trend and/or Seasonal Dummy Variables," *Econometrica,* 49, 1981, pp. 1571–1581.

Klein, L., *Economic Fluctuations in the United States 1921–1941.* New York: Wiley, 1950.

Klein, L., *An Introduction to Econometrics.* Englewood Cliffs, N.J.: Prentice Hall, 1962.

Klepper, S., and E. Leamer, "Consistent Sets of Estimates for Regressions with Errors in All Variables," *Econometrica,* 52, 1983, pp. 163–184.

Kloek, T., and Y. Haitovsky, eds., "Competing Statistical Paradigms in Econometrics," *Journal of Econometrics,* 37, 1, 1988.

Kmenta, J., "On Estimation of the CES Production Function," *International Economic Review,* 8, 1967, pp. 180–189.

Kmenta, J., *Elements of Econometrics.* New York: Macmillan, 1986.

Kmenta, J., and R. Gilbert, "Small Sample Properties of Alternative Estimators of Seemingly Unrelated Regressions," *Journal of the American Statistical Association,* 63, 1968, pp. 1180–1200.

Kmenta, J., and W. Oberhofer, "Estimation of Standard Errors of the Characteristic Roots of a Dynamic Econometric Model," *Econometrica,* 41, 1973, pp. 171–177.

Knapp, L., and T. Seaks, "An Analysis of the Probability of Default on Federally Guaranteed Student Loans," *Review of Economics and Statistics,* 74, 1992, forthcoming.

Kobiyashi, M., "A Bounds Test of Equality Between Sets of Coefficients in Two Linear Regressions When Distrubance Variances Are Unequal," *Journal of the American Statistical Association,* 81, 1986, pp. 510–514.

Koenkar, R., "A Note on Studentizing a Test for Heteroscedasticity," *Journal of Econometrics,* 17, 1981, pp. 107–112.

Koenkar, R., and G. Bassett, "Regression Quantiles," *Econometrica,* 46, 1978, pp. 107–112.

Koenkar, R., and G. Bassett, "Robust Tests for Heteroscedasticity Based on Regression Quantiles," *Econometrica,* 50, 1982, pp. 43–61.

Kosobud, R., "A Note on a Problem Caused by the Assignment of Missing Data in Sample Surveys," *Econometrica,* 31, 1963, pp. 562–563.

Koyck, L., *Distributed Lags and Investment Analysis.* Amsterdam: North-Holland, 1954.

Lahiri, K., and D. Egy, "Joint Estimation and Testing for Functional Form and Heteroscedasticity," *Journal of Econometrics,* 15, 1981, pp. 299–307.

Lahiri, K., and P. Schmidt, "On the Estimation of Triangular Structural Systems," *Econometrica,* 46, 1978, pp. 1217–1221.

Lambert, D., "Zero-Inflated Poisson Regression, With an Application to Defects in Manufacturing," *Technometrics,* 34, 1, 1992, pp. 1–14.

Lancaster, T., "A Stochastic Model for the Duration of a Strike," *Journal of the Royal Statistical Society, Series B,* 135, part 2, 1972, pp. 257–271.

Lancaster, T., "Econometric Models for the Duration of Unemployment," *Econometrica,* 47, 1974, pp. 939–956.

Lancaster, T., "Generalized Residuals and Heterogeneous Duration Models: With Applications to the Weibull Model," *Journal of Econometrics,* 28, 1985, pp. 155–169.

Lancaster, T., *The Analysis of Transition Data.* New York: Cambridge University Press, 1990.

Lancaster, T., and A. Chesher, "Residual Tests and Plots with a Job Matching Illustration," *Annales de L'Insee,* 59/60, 1985, pp. 47–70.

Lawless, J., *Statistical Models and Methods for Lifetime Data.* New York: Wiley, 1982.

Leamer, E., *Specification Searches: Ad Hoc Inferences with Nonexperimental Data.* New York: Wiley, 1978.

Leamer, E., "Let's Take the Con Out of Econometrics," *American Economic Review,* 73, 1983, pp. 31–43.

Leamer, E., and H. Leonard, "Reporting the Fragility of Regression Estimates," *Review of Economics and Statistics,* 64, 1983, pp. 306–317.

Lee, L., "Estimation of Error Components Model with ARMA(p, q) Time Component—An Exact GLS Approach," *Paper 78-104,* University of Minnesota, Center for Economics Research, 1978a.

Lee, L., "Unionism and Wage Rates: A Simultaneous Equation Model with Qualitative and Limited Dependent Variables," *International Economic Review,* 19, 1978b, pp. 415–433.

Lee, L., "Specification Tests for Poisson Regression Models," *International Economic Review,* 27, 1986, pp. 689–706.

Lee, L., and W. Griffiths, "The Prior Likelihood and Best Linear Unbiased Prediction in Stochastic Coefficient Linear Models," *Paper 1,* University of New England Working Papers in Econometrics and Applied Statistics, 1979.

Lerman, R., and C. Manski, "On the Use of Simulated Frequencies to Approximate Choice Probabilities," in C. Manski and D. McFadden, eds., *Structural Analysis of Discrete Data with Econometric Applications.* Cambridge, Mass.: MIT Press, 1981.

Levi, M., "Errors in the Variables in the Presence of Correctly Measured Variables," *Econometrica,* 41, 1973, pp. 985–986.

Lewis, H., "Comments on Selectivity Biases in Wage Comparisons," *Journal of Political Economy,* 82, 1974, pp. 1119–1155.

Leyden, D., "Modified Quadratic Hill-Climbing with SAS/IML," *Computer Science in Economics and Management,* 4, 1991, pp. 15–31.

Litterman, R., "Techniques of Forecasting Using Vector Autoregressions," Federal Reserve Bank of Minneapolis, Working Paper Number 15, 1979.

Litterman, R., "Forecasting with Bayesian Bector Autoregressions—Five Years of Experience," *Journal of Business and Economic Statistics,* 4, 1986, pp. 25–38.

Liu, T., "Underidentification, Structural Estimation, and Forecasting," *Econometrica,* 28, 1960, pp. 855–865.

Liviatan, N., "Consistent Estimation of Distributed Lags," *International Economic Review,* 4, 1963, pp. 44–52.

Ljung, G., and G. Box, "On a Measure of Lack of Fit in Time Series Models," *Biometrika,* 66, 1979, pp. 265–270.

Lluch, C., and R. Williams, "Consumer Demand Systems and Aggregate Consumption in the U.S.A.: An Application of the Extended Linear Expenditure System," *Canadian Journal of Economics,* 8, 1974, pp. 49–66.

Longley, J., "An Appraisal of Least Squares Programs from the Point of the User," *Journal of the American Statistical Association,* 62, 1967, pp. 819–841.

MacKinnon, J., and H. White, "Some Heteroscedasticity Consistent Covariance Matrix Estimators with Improved Finite Sample Properties," *Journal of Econometrics,* 19, 1985, pp. 305–325.

MacKinnon, J., H. White, and R. Davidson, "Tests for Model Specification in the Presence of Alternative Hypotheses; Some Further Results," *Journal of Econometrics,* 21, 1983, pp. 53–70.

Macurdy, T., "The Use of Time Series Processes to Model the Error Structure of Earnings in a Longitudinal Data Analysis," *Journal of Econometrics,* 18, 1982, pp. 83–114.

Maddala, G., "The Use of Variance Components Models in Pooling Cross Section and Time Series Data," *Econometrica,* 39, 1971, pp. 341–358.

Maddala, G., *Econometrics.* New York: McGraw-Hill, 1977.

Maddala, G., *Limited Dependent and Qualitative Variables in Econometrics.* New York: Cambridge University Press, 1983.

Maddala, G., "Disequilibrium, Self-Selection, and Switching Models," in Z. Griliches and M. Intriligator, eds., *Handbook of Econometrics.* Amsterdam: North-Holland, 1984.

Maddala, G., *Introduction to Econometrics,* 2nd ed., New York: Macmillan, 1992.

Maddala, G., and T. Mount, "A Comparative Study of Alternative Estimators for Variance Component Models," *Journal of the American Statistical Association,* 68, 1973, pp. 324–328.

Maddala, G., and F. Nelson, "Specification Errors in Limited Dependent Variable Models," *Working Paper 96,* National Bureau of Economic Research, Cambridge, 1975.

Maddala, G., and A. Rao, "Maximum Likelihood Estimation of Solow's and Jorgenson's Distributed Lag Models," *Review of Economics and Statistics,* 53, 1971, pp. 80–88.

Maddala, G., and A. Rao, "Tests for Serial Correlation in Regression Models with Lagged Dependent Variables and Serially Correlated Errors," *Econometrica,* 41, 1976, pp. 761–774.

Maeshiro, A., "On the Retention of the First Observations in Serial Correlation Adjustment of Regression Models," *International Economic Review,* 20, 1979, pp. 259–265.

Magnus, J., "Maximum Likelihood Estimation of the Generalized Regression Model with Unknown Parameters in the Disturbance Covariance Matrix," *Journal of Econometrics,* 7, 1978, pp. 281–312.

Magnus, J., and H. Neudecker, *Matrix Differential Calculus with Applications in Statistics and Econometrics,* New York: Wiley, 1988.

Malinvaud, E., *Statistical Methods of Econometrics.* Amsterdam: North-Holland, 1970.

Mann, H., and A. Wald, "On the Statistical Treatment of Linear Stochastic Difference Equations," *Econometrica,* 11, 1943, pp. 173–220.

Manski, C., "The Maximum Score Estimator of the Stochastic Utility Model of Choice," *Journal of Econometrics,* 3, 1975, pp. 313–333.

Manski, C., "Semiparametric Analysis of Discrete Response: Asymptotic Properties of the Maximum Score Estimator," *Journal of Econometrics,* 27, 1985, pp. 313–333.

Manski, C., "Operational Characteristics of the Maximum Score Estimator," *Journal of Econometrics,* 32, 1986, pp. 85–100.

Manski, C., "Anatomy of the Selection Problem," *Journal of Human Resources,* 24, 1989, pp. 343–360.

Manski, C., "Nonparametric Bounds on Treatment Effects," *American Economic Review,* 80, 1990, pp. 319–323.

Manski, C., and D. McFadden, *Structural Analysis of Discrete Data with Econometric Applications.* Cambridge, Mass.: MIT Press, 1981.

Manski, C., and S. Thompson, "MSCORE: A Program for Maximum Score Estimation of Linear Quantile Regressions from Binary Response Data," mimeo, University of Wisconsin, Madison, Department of Economics, 1986.

Manski, C., and S. Thompson, "Estimation of Best Predictors of Binary Response," *Journal of Econometrics,* 40, 1989, pp. 97–124.

Marcus, A., and W. Greene, "The Determinants of Rating Assignment and Performance," *Working Paper CRC528,* Center for Naval Analyses, 1985.

Mazodier, P., ed., *Annales de L'Insee,* 30/31, 1978.

McAleer, M., G. Fisher, and P. Volker, "Separate Misspecified Regressions and the U.S. Long-Run Demand for Money Function," *Review of Economics and Statistics,* 64, 1982, pp. 572–583.

McAleer, M., A. Pagan, and P. Volker, "What Will Take the Con Out of Econometrics?" *American Economic Review,* 75, 1985, pp. 293–307.

McCallum, B., "Relative Asymptotic Bias from Errors of Omission and Measurement," *Econometrica,* 40, 1972, pp. 757–758.

McCullagh, P., and J. Nelder, *Generalized Linear Models.* New York: Chapman & Hall, 1983.

McDonald, J., and R. Moffitt, "The Uses of Tobit Analysis," *Review of Economics and Statistics,* 62, 1980, pp. 318–321.

McElroy, M., "Goodness of Fit for Seemingly Unrelated Regressions: Glahn's $R^2_{y \cdot x}$ and Hooper's $\bar{r}^2$," *Journal of Econometrics,* 6, 1977, pp. 381–387.

McFadden, D., "Conditional Logit Analysis of Qualitative Choice Behavior," in P. Zarembka, ed., *Frontiers in Econometrics.* New York: Academic Press, 1973.

McFadden, D., "The Measurement of Urban Travel Demand," *Journal of Public Economics,* 3, 1974, pp. 303–328.

McFadden, D., "Econometric Analysis of Qualitative Response Models," in Z. Griliches and M. Intriligator, eds., *Handbook of Econometrics,* Vol. 2. Amsterdam: North-Holland, 1984.

McFadden, D., "Regression Based Specification Tests for the Multinomial Logit Model," *Journal of Econometrics,* 34, 1987, pp. 63–82.

McFadden, D., "A Method of Simulated Moments for Estimation of Discrete Response Models Without Numerical Integration," *Econometrica,* 57, 1989, pp. 995–1026.

McFadden, D., and W. Newey, "Asymptotic Properties of Nonlinear Estimators," mimeo, Department of Economics, MIT, 1988.

Meyer, B., "Semiparametric Estimation of Hazard Models," Northwestern University, Department of Economics, 1988.

Mills, T., *Time Series Techniques for Economists.* New York: Cambridge University Press, 1990.

Mood, A., F. Graybill, and D. Boes, *Introduction to the Theory of Statistics.* New York: McGraw-Hill, 1974.

Mullahey, J., "Specification and Testing of Some Modified Count Data Models," *Journal of Econometrics,* 33, 1986, pp. 341–365.

Mullahey, J., "Weighted Least Squares Estimation of the Linear Probability Model, Revisited," *Economics Letters,* 32, 1990, pp. 35–41.

Mundlak, Y., "On the Pooling of Time Series and Cross Sectional Data," *Econometrica,* 46, 1978, pp. 69–86.

Nakamura, A., and M. Nakamura, "On the Relationships Among Several Specification Error Tests Presented by Durbin, Wu, and Hausman," *Econometrica,* 49, 1981, pp. 1583–1588.

Nakamura, A., and M. Nakamura, "Part-Time and Full Time Work Behavior of Married Women: A Model with a Doubly Truncated Dependent Variable," *Canadian Journal of Economics,* 1983, pp. 201–218.

Nakosteen, R., and M. Zimmer, "Migration and Income: The Question of Self-Selection," *Southern Economic Journal,* 46, 1980, pp. 840–851.

Nelson, F., "Censored Regression Models with Unobserved Censoring Thresholds," *Journal of Econometrics,* 6, 1977, pp. 309–327.

Nelson, F., "A Test for Misspecification in the Censored Normal Model," *Econometrica,* 48, 1980, pp. 1317–1329.

Nelson, F., "Efficiency of the Two-Step Estimator for Models with Endogenous Sample Selection," *Journal of Econometrics,* 24, 1984, pp. 181–196.

Nelson, C., and H. Kang, "Pitfalls in the Use of Time as an Explanatory Variable in Regression," *Journal of Business and Economic Statistics,* 2, 1984, pp. 73–82.

Nelson, C., and H. Kang, "Spurious Periodicity in Inappropriately Detrended Time Series," *Econometrica,* 49, 1981, pp. 741–751.

Nelson, C., and C. Plosser, "Trends and Random Walks in Macroeconomic Time Series: Some Evidence and Implications," *Journal of Monetary Economics,* 10, 1982, pp. 139–162.

Nerlove, M., "Returns to Scale in Electricity Supply," in C. Christ, ed., *Measurement in Economics: Studies in Mathematical Economics and Econometrics in Memory of Yehuda Grunfeld.* Stanford, Calif.: Stanford University Press, 1963.

Nerlove, M., "Further Evidence on the Estimation of Dynamic Relations from a Time Series of Cross Sections," *Econometrica,* 39, 1971a, pp. 359–382.

Nerlove, M., "A Note on Error Components Models," *Econometrica,* 39, 1971b, pp. 383–396.

Nerlove, M., "Lags in Economic Behavior," *Econometrica,* 40, 1972, pp. 221–251.

Nerlove, M., and F. Diebold, "Unit Roots in Economic Time Series: A Selective Survey," in T. Bewley, ed., *Advances in Econometrics,* Vol. 8. New York: JAI Press, 1990.

Nerlove, M., and S. Press, "Univariate and Multivariate Log-Linear and Logistic Models," *RAND—R1306-EDA/NIH,* Santa Monica, Calif., 1973.

Nerlove, M., and K. Wallis, "Use of the Durbin–Watson Statistic in Inappropriate Situations," *Econometrica,* 34, 1966, pp. 235–238.

New York Post, "America's New Big Wheels of Fortune," May 22, 1987.

Newey, W., "A Method of Moments Interpretation of Sequential Estimators," *Economics Letters,* 14, 1984, pp. 201–206.

Newey, W., "Maximum Likelihood Specification Testing and Conditional Moment Tests," *Econometrica,* 53, 1985a, pp. 1047–1070.

Newey, W., "Generalized Method of Moments Specification Testing," *Journal of Econometrics,* 29, 1985b, pp. 229–256.

Newey, W., "Specification Tests for Distributional Assumptions in the Tobit Model," *Journal of Econometrics,* 34, 1986, pp. 125–146.

Newey, W., and K. West, "A Simple Positive Semi-Definite, Heteroscedasticity and Autocorrelation Consistent Covariance Matrix," *Econometrica,* 55, 1987a, pp. 703–708.

Newey, W., and K. West, "Hypothesis Testing with Efficient Method of Moments Estimation," *International Economic Review,* 28, 1987b, pp. 777–787.

Newey, W., J. Powell, and J. Walker, "Semiparametric Estimation of Selection Models," *American Economic Review,* 80, 1990, pp. 324–328.

Nicholls, D., A. Pagan, and R. Terrell, "The Estimation and Use of Models with Moving Average Disturbance Terms: A Survey," *International Economic Review,* 16, 1975, pp. 113–134.

Nickell, S., "Biases in Dynamic Models with Fixed Effects," *Econometrica,* 49, 1981, pp. 1417–1426.

Norden, R. H., "A Survey of Maximum Likelihood Estimation," *Review of the International Statistical Institute,* 1972, pp. 329–354.

Oberhofer, W., and J. Kmenta, "A General Procedure for Obtaining Maximum Likelihood Estimates in Generalized Regression Models," *Econometrica,* 42, 1974, pp. 579–590.

Ohtani, K., and M. Kobiyashi, "A Bounds Test for Equality Between Sets of Coefficients in 2 Linear Regression Models Under Heteroscedasticity," *Econometric Theory,* 2, 1986, pp. 220–231.

Ohtani, K., and T. Toyoda, "Estimation of Regression Coefficients After a Preliminary Test for Homoscedasticity," *Journal of Econometrics,* 12, 1980, pp. 151–159.

Ohtani, K., and T. Toyoda, "Small Sample Properties of Tests of Equality Between Sets of Coefficients in Two Linear Regressions Under Heteroscedasticity," *International Economic Review,* 26, 1985, pp. 37–44.

Olsen, R., "A Note on the Uniqueness of the Maximum Likelihood Estimator in the Tobit Model," *Econometrica,* 46, 1978, pp. 1211–1215.

Olsen, R., "Approximating a Truncated Normal Regression with the Method of Moments," *Econometrica,* 48, 1980, pp. 1099–1106.

Orcutt, G., S. Caldwell, and R. Wertheimer, *Policy Exploration Through Microanalytic Simulation.* Washington, D.C.: Urban Institute, 1976.

Orme, C., "Double and Triple Length Regressions for the Information Matrix Test and Other Conditional Moment Tests," University of York, UK, Department of Economics, mimeo, 1990.

Ouliaris, S., J. Park, and P. Phillips, "Testing for a Unit Root in the Presence of a Maintained Trend," in B. Raj, ed., *Advances in Econometrics and Modeling.* Needham, Mass.: Kluwer Nijoff, 1989.

Paarsch, H., "A Monte Carlo Comparison of Estimators for Censored Regression Models," *Journal of Econometrics,* 24, 1984, pp. 197–214.

Pagan, A., "Some Consequences of Viewing LIML as an Iterated Aitken Estimator," *Economics Letters,* 3, 1979, pp. 369–372.

Pagan, A., "Econometric Issues in the Analysis of Regressions with Generated Regressors," *International Economic Review,* 25, 1984, pp. 221–247.

Pagan, A., and A. Hall, "Diagnostic Tests as Residual Analysis," *Econometric Reviews,* 2, 1983, pp. 159–218.

Pagan, A., and D. Nicholls, "Estimating Prediction Errors and Their Standard Deviations Using Constructed Variables," *Journal of Econometrics,* 24, 1984, pp. 293–310.

Pagan, A., and F. Vella, "Diagnostic Tests for Models Based on Individual Data: A Survey," *Journal of Applied Econometrics,* 4, Supplement, 1989, pp. S29–S59.

Pagan, A., and M. Wickens, "A Survey of Some Recent Econometric Methods," *The Economic Journal*, 99, 1989, pp. 962–1025.

Pagano, M., and M. Hartley, "On Fitting Distributed Lag Models Subject to Polynomial Restrictions," *Journal of Econometrics*, 16, 1981, pp. 171–198.

Pakes, A., and D. Pollard, "Simulation and the Asymptotics of Optimization Estimators," *Econometrica*, 57, 1989, pp. 1027–1058.

Pal, M., "Consistent Moment Estimators of Regression Coefficients in the Presence of Errors in Variables," *Journal of Econometrics*, 14, 1980, pp. 666–668.

Park, R., "Estimation with Heteroscedastic Error Terms," *Econometrica*, 34, 1966, p. 888.

Park, R., and B. Mitchell, "Estimating the Autocorrelated Error Model with Trended Data," *Journal of Econometrics*, 13, 1980, pp. 185–201.

Parks, R., "Efficient Estimation of a System of Regression Equations When Disturbances Are Both Serially and Contemporaneously Correlated," *Journal of the American Statistical Association*, 62, 1967, pp. 500–509.

Perron, P., "Testing for a Unit Root in a Time Series with a Changing Mean," *Journal of Business and Economic Statistics*, 8, 1990, pp. 153–162.

Pesaran, H., "The Small Sample Problem of Truncation Remainders in the Estimation of Distributed Lag Models with Autocorrelated Errors," *International Economic Review*, 14, 1973b, pp. 120–131.

Pesaran, H., "On the General Problem of Model Selection," *Review of Economic Studies*, 41, 1974, pp. 153–171.

Pesaran, H., and A. Deaton, "Testing Non-nested Nonlinear Regression Models," *Econometrica*, 46, 1978, pp. 677–694.

Pesaran, H., and A. Hall, "A Test of Non-nested Linear Regression Models Subject to Linear Restrictions," *Economics Letters*, 27, 1989, pp. 341–348.

Pesaran, M., "Exact Maximum Likelihood Estimation of a Regression Equation with a First-Order Moving-Average Error," *Review of Economic Studies*, 40, 1973a, pp. 529–536.

Petersen, T., "Fitting Parametric Survival Models with Time Dependent Covariates," *Journal of the Royal Statistical Society, Series C (Applied Statistics)*, 35, 1986, pp. 281–288.

Petersen, D., and D. Waldman, "The Treatment of Heteroscedasticity in the Limited Dependent Variable Model," mimeo, University of North Carolina, Chapel Hill, November 1981.

Phillips, P., "Exact Small Sample Theory in the Simultaneous Equations Model," in Z. Griliches and M. Intriligator, eds., *Handbook of Econometrics*. Amsterdam: North-Holland, 1983.

Phillips, P., "Understanding Spurious Regressions," *Journal of Econometrics*, 33, 1986, pp. 311–340.

Phillips, P., and P. Perron, "Testing for a Unit Root in Time Series Regression," *Biometrika*, 75, 1988, pp. 335–346.

Pindyck, R., and D. Rubinfeld, *Econometric Models and Economic Forecasts*. New York: McGraw-Hill, 1981.

Poirier, D., *The Econometrics of Structural Change*. Amsterdam: North-Holland, 1974.

Poirier, D., "The Effect of the First Observation in Regression Models with First-Order Autoregressive Disturbances," *Applied Statistics*, 27, 1978a, pp. 67–68.

Poirier, D., "The Use of the Box–Cox Transformation in Limited Dependent Variable Models," *Journal of the American Statistical Association*, 73, 1978a, pp. 284–287.

Poirier, D., "Partial Observability in Bivariate Probit Models," *Journal of Econometrics,* 12, 1980, pp. 209–217.

Poirier, D., "Frequentist and Subjectivist Perspectives on the Problems of Model Building in Economics" (with discussion), *Journal of Economic Perspectives,* 2, 1988, pp. 121–144.

Poirier, D., "Bayesian Empirical Studies in Economics and Finance," *Journal of Econometrics,* 49, 1991.

Poirier, D., and A. Melino, "A Note on the Interpretation of Regression Coefficients Within a Class of Truncated Distributions," *Econometrica,* 46, 1978, pp. 1207–1209.

Powell, J., "Least Absolute Deviations Estimation for Censored and Truncated Regression Models," *Technical Report 356,* Stanford University, IMSSS, 1981.

Powell, M., "An Efficient Method for Finding the Minimum of a Function of Several Variables Without Calculating Derivatives," *Computer Journal,* 1964, pp. 165–172.

Prais, S., and H. Houthakker, *The Analysis of Family Budgets.* New York: Cambridge University Press, 1955.

Prais, S., and C. Winsten, "Trend Estimation and Serial Correlation," *Discussion Paper 383,* Cowles Commission, Chicago, 1954.

Quandt, R., "Econometric Disequilibrium Models," *Econometric Reviews,* 1, 1982, pp. 1–63.

Quandt, R., "Computational Problems and Methods," in Z. Griliches and M. Intriligator, eds., *Handbook of Econometrics.* Amsterdam: North-Holland, 1983.

Quandt, R., *The Econometrics of Disequilibrium.* New York: Basil Blackwell, 1988.

Quandt, R., and J. Ramsey, "Estimating Mixtures of Normal Distributions and Switching Regressions," *Journal of the American Statistical Association,* 73, Dec. 1978, pp. 730–738.

Quester, A., and W. Greene, "A State Preference Approach to Wives Labor Supply," *Social Science Quarterly,* 63, 1982, pp. 16–27.

Ramsey, J., "Tests for Specification Errors in Classical Linear Least Squares Regression Analysis," *Journal of the Royal Statistical Statistical Society, Series B,* 31, 1969, pp. 350–371.

Ramsey, J., "Classical Model Selection Through Specification Error Tests," in P. Zarembka, ed., *Frontiers in Econometrics.* New York: Academic Press, 1974.

Ramsey, J., "Perspective and Comment," *Econometric Reviews,* 2, 1983, pp. 241–248.

Rao, C. R., *Linear Statistical Inference and Its Applications.* New York: Wiley, 1965.

Revankar, N., "Some Finite Sample Results in the Context of Two Seemingly Unrelated Regression Equations," *Journal of the American Statistical Association,* 69, 1974, pp. 187–190.

Revankar, N., "Use of Restricted Residuals in SUR Systems: Some Finite Sample Results," *Journal of the American Statistical Association,* 71, 1976, pp. 183–188.

Rice, P., and K. Smith, "An Econometric Model of the Petroleum Industry," *Journal of Econometrics,* 6, 1977, pp. 263–287.

Riersol, O., "Identifiability of a Linear Relation Between Variables Which Are Subject to Error," *Econometrica,* 18, 1950, pp. 375–389.

Rivers, D., and Q. Vuong, "Limited Information Estimators and Exogeneity Tests for Simultaneous Probit Models," *Journal of Econometrics,* 39, 1988, pp. 347–366.

Robinson, C., and N. Tomes, "Self Selection and Interprovincial Migration in Canada," *Canadian Journal of Economics,* 15, 1982, pp. 474–502.

Rosett, R., and F. Nelson, "Estimation of the Two-Limit Probit Regression Model," *Econometrica,* 43, 1975, pp. 141–146.

Rubin, H., "Consistency of Maximum Likelihood Estimators in the Explosive Case," in T. Koopmans, ed., *Statistical Inference in Dynamic Economic Models.* New York: Wiley, 1950.

Rubinfeld, D., "Voting in a Local School Election: A Micro Analysis," *Review of Economics and Statistics,* 59, 1977, pp. 30–42.

Rutemiller, H., and D. Bowers, "Estimation in a Heteroscedastic Regression Model," *Journal of the American Statistical Association,* 63, 1968, pp. 552–557.

Ruud, P., "Specification Errors in Limited Dependent Variable Models," Ph.D. thesis, Department of Economics, Massachusetts Institute of Technology, 1981.

Ruud, P., "Tests of Specification in Econometrics," *Econometric Reviews,* 3, 1984, pp. 211–242.

Ruud, P., "Consistent Estimation of Limited Dependent Variable Models Despite Misspecification of the Distribution," *Journal of Econometrics,* 32, 1986, pp. 157–187.

Salem, D., and T. Mount, "A Convenient Descriptive Model of the Income Distribution," *Econometrica,* 42, 6, 1974, pp. 1115–1128.

Salkever, D., "The Use of Dummy Variables to Compute Predictions, Prediction Errors, and Confidence Intervals," *Journal of Econometrics,* 4, 1976, pp. 393–397.

Sargan, J., "The Maximum Likelihood Estimation of Economic Relationships with Autoregressive Residuals," *Econometrica,* 29, 1961, pp. 414–426.

Sargan, J., and A. Bhargava, "Testing Residuals from Least Squares Regressions for Being Generated by the Gaussian Random Walk," *Econometrica,* 51, 1983, pp. 153–174.

Savin, E., and K. White, "The Durbin–Watson Test for Serial Correlation with Extreme Sample Sizes or Many Regressors," *Econometrica,* 45, 1977, pp. 1989–1996.

Schmidt, P., "The Asymptotic Distribution of Dynamic Multipliers," *Econometrica,* 41, 1973, pp. 161–164.

Schmidt, P., "A Modification of the Almon Distributed Lag," *Journal of the American Statistical Association,* 69, 1974a, pp. 679–681.

Schmidt, P., "An Argument for the Usefulness of the Gamma Distributed Lag Model," *International Economic Review,* 15, 1974b, pp. 246–250.

Schmidt, P., "The Asymptotic Distribution of Forecasts in the Dynamic Simulation of an Econometric Model," *Econometrica,* 42, 1974c, pp. 303–310.

Schmidt, P., "The Algebraic Equivalence of the Oberhofer–Kmenta and Theil–Boot Formulae for the Asymptotic Variance of a Characteristic Root of a Dynamic Econometric Model," *Econometrica,* 42, 1974a, pp. 591–592.

Schmidt, P., "The Small Sample Effects of Various Treatments of Truncation Remainders in the Estimation of Distributed Lag Models," *Review of Economics and Statistics,* 57, 1975, pp. 387–389.

Schmidt, P., *Econometrics.* New York: Marcel Dekker, 1976.

Schmidt, P., "A Note on Dynamic Simulation Forecasts and Stochastic Forecast-Period Exogenous Variables," *Econometrica,* 46, 1978, pp. 1227–1230.

Schmidt, P., "Frontier Production Functions," *Econometric Reviews,* 4(2), 1986, pp. 289–328.

Schmidt, P., and R. Sickles, "On the Efficiency of the Almon Lag Technique," *International Economic Review,* 16, 1975, pp. 792–795.

Schmidt, P., and R. Sickles, "Some Further Evidence on the Use of the Chow Test Under Heteroscedasticity," *Econometrica,* 45, 1977, pp. 1293–1298.

Schmidt, P., and R. Strauss, "The Prediction of Occupation Using Multiple Logit Models," *International Economic Review,* 16, 1975a, pp. 471–486.

Schmidt, P., and R. Strauss, "Estimation of Models with Jointly Dependent Qualitative Variables: A Simultaneous Logit Approach," *Econometrica,* 43, 1975b, pp. 745–755.

Schmidt, P., and R. Waud, "The Almon Lag Technique and the Monetary Versus Fiscal Policy Debate," *Journal of the American Statistical Association,* 68, 1973, pp. 11–19.

Seaks, T., and K. Layson, "Box–Cox Estimation with Standard Econometric Problems," *Review of Economics and Statistics,* 65, 1983, pp. 160–164.

Sharma, S., "Specification Diagnostics for Econometric Models of Duration," mimeo, Department of Economics, University of California at Los Angeles, 1989.

Shaw, D., "'On-Site Samples' Regression Problems of Nonnegative Integers, Truncation, and Endogenous Stratification," *Journal of Econometrics,* 37, 1988, pp. 211–223.

Shephard, R., *The Theory of Cost and Production.* Princeton, N.J.: Princeton University Press, 1970.

Shiller, R., "A Distributed Lag Estimator Derived from Smoothness Priors," *Econometrica,* 41, 1973, pp. 775–778.

Sims, C., "Macroeconomics and Reality," *Econometrica,* 48, 1, 1980, pp. 1–48.

Sims, C., "Money, Income, and Causality," *American Economic Review,* 62, 1972, pp. 540–552.

Smith, R., and R. Blundell, "An Exogeneity Test for a Simultaneous Equation Tobit Model with an Application to Labor Supply," *Econometrica,* 54, 1986, pp. 679–685.

Solow, R., "Technical Change and the Aggregate Production Function," *Review of Economics and Statistics,* 39, 1957, pp. 312–320.

Solow, R., "On a Family of Lag Distributions," *Econometrica,* 28, 1960, pp. 393–406.

Spector, L., and M. Mazzeo, "Probit Analysis and Economic Education," *Journal of Economic Education,* 11, 1980, pp. 37–44.

Spencer, D., and K. Berk, "A Limited Information Specification Test," *Econometrica,* 49, 1981, pp. 1079–1085.

Spitzer, J., "A Fast and Efficient Method for Estimation of Parameters in Models with the Box–Cox Transformation," *Journal of the American Statistical Association,* 77, 1982a, pp. 760–766.

Spitzer, J., "A Primer on Box–Cox Estimation," *Review of Economics and Statistics,* 64, 1982b, pp. 307–313.

Spitzer, J., "Variance Estimates in Models with the Box–Cox Transformation: Implications for Estimation and Hypothesis Testing," *Review of Economics and Statistics,* 66, 1984, pp. 645–652.

Stapleton, D., and D. Young, "Censored Normal Regression with Measurement Error on the Dependent Variable," *Discussion Paper 81-30,* University of British Columbia, Department of Economics, 1981.

Stewart, M., "On Least Squares Estimation When the Dependent Variable Is Grouped," *Review of Economic Studies,* 50, 1983, pp. 141–149.

Stock, J., "Asymptotic Properties of Least Squares Estimators of Cointegrating Vectors," *Econometrica,* 55, 1987, pp. 1035–1056.

Stoker, T., "Consistent Estimation of Scaled Coefficients," *Econometrica,* 54, 1986, pp. 1461–1482.

Stone, R., *The Measurement of Consumers' Expenditure and Behaviour in the United Kingdom, 1920–1938*. Cambridge: Cambridge University Press, 1954a.

Stone, R., "Linear Expenditure Systems and Demand Analysis: An Application to the Pattern of British Demand," *Economic Journal*, 64, 1954b, pp. 511–527.

Strang, G., *Linear Algebra and Its Applications*. New York: Academic Press, 1976.

Strickland, A., and L. Weiss, "Advertising, Concentration, and Price Cost Margins," *Journal of Political Economy*, 84, 1976, pp. 1109–1121.

Stuart, A., and S. Ord, *Kendall's Advanced Theory of Statistics*, New York: Oxford University Press, 1989.

Suits, D., "Dummy Variables: Mechanics vs. Interpretation," *Review of Economics and Statistics*, 66, 1984, pp. 177–180.

Swamy, P., "Efficient Inference in a Random Coefficient Regression Model," *Econometrica*, 38, 1970, pp. 311–323.

Swamy, P., *Statistical Inference in Random Coefficient Regression Models*. New York: Springer-Verlag, 1971.

Swamy, P., "Linear Models with Random Coefficients," in P. Zarembka, ed., *Frontiers in Econometrics*. New York: Academic Press, 1974.

Taylor, L., "Estimation by Minimizing the Sum of Absolute Errors," in P. Zarembka, ed., *Frontiers in Econometrics*. New York: Academic Press, 1974.

Taylor, W., "Smoothness Priors and Stochastic Prior Restrictions in Distributed Lag Estimation," *International Economic Review*, 15, 1974, pp. 803–804.

Taylor, W. E., "Small Sample Properties of a Class of Two Stage Aitken Estimators," *Econometrica*, 45, 1977, pp. 497–508.

Terza, J., "Ordinal Probit: A Generalization," *Communications in Statistics*, 14, 1985a, pp. 1–12.

Terza, J., "A Tobit Type Estimator for the Censored Poisson Regression Model," *Economics Letters*, 18, 1985b, pp. 361–365.

Theil, H., *Economic Forecasts and Policy*. Amsterdam: North-Holland, 1961.

Theil, H., *Principles of Econometrics*. New York: Wiley, 1971.

Theil, H., "Linear Algebra and Matrix Methods in Econometrics," in Z. Griliches and M. Intriligator, eds., *Handbook of Econometrics*, Vol. 1. New York: North-Holland, 1983.

Theil, H., and J. Boot, "The Final Form of Econometric Equation Systems," *Review of the International Statistical Institute*, 30, 1962, pp. 136–152.

Theil, H., and A. Goldberger, "On Pure and Mixed Estimation in Economics," *International Economic Review*, 2, 1961, pp. 65–78.

Theil, H., and A. Nagar, "Testing the Independence of Regression Disturbances," *Journal of the American Statistical Association*, 52, 1961, pp. 793–806.

Theil, H., and R. Stern, "A Simple Unimodal Lag Distribution," *Metroeconomica*, 12, 1960, pp. 111–119.

Thompson, M., "Some Results on the Statistical Properties of an Inequality Constrained Least Squares Estimator in a Linear Model with Two Regressors," *Journal of Econometrics*, 19, 1982, pp. 215–231.

Thursby, J., "Misspecification, Heteroscedasticity, and the Chow and Goldfeld–Quandt Tests," *Review of Economics and Statistics*, 64, 1982, pp. 314–321.

Thursby, J., and P. Schmidt, "Some Properties of Tests for Specification Error in a Linear Regression Model," *Journal of the American Statistical Association*, 72, 1977, pp. 635–641.

Tobin, J., "Estimation of Relationships for Limited Dependent Variables," *Econometrica*, 26, 1958, pp. 24–36.

Toyoda, T., "Use of the Chow Test Under Heteroscedasticity," *Econometrica,* 42, 1974, pp. 601–608.

Toyoda, T., and K. Ohtani, "Testing Equality Between Sets of Coefficients After a Preliminary Test for Equality of Disturbance Variances in Two Linear Regressions," *Journal of Econometrics,* 31, 1986, pp. 67–80.

Trivedi, P., and A. Pagan, "Polynomial Distributed Lags: A Unified Treatment," *Economic Studies Quarterly,* 30, 1979, pp. 37–49.

Tsurumi, H., "A Note on Gamma Distributed Lags," *International Economic Review,* 12, 1971, pp. 317–324.

Tunali, I., "Geographic Mobility, Earnings, and Selectivity: From Theory to Fact—Evidence from Turkey, 1963–1973," Ph.D. thesis, Department of Economics, University of Wisconsin, Madison, 1985.

Tunali, I., "A General Structure for Models of Double Selection and an Application to a Joint Migration/Earnings Process with Remigration," *Research in Labor Economics,* 8, 1986, pp. 235–282.

U.S. Bureau of the Census, *Public Use Samples of Basic Records from the 1970 Census.* Washington, D.C.: U.S. Government Printing Office, 1972.

U.S. Department of Commerce, *Statistical Abstract of the United States.* Washington, D.C.: U.S. Government Printing Office, 1979.

U.S. Department of Commerce, National Income and Product Accounts, BEA, *Survey of Current Business Statistics, 1984.* Washington, D.C.: U.S. Government Printing Office, 1984.

Waldman, D., "A Stationary Point for the Stochastic Frontier Likelihood," *Journal of Econometrics,* 18, 1982, pp. 275–279.

Waldman, D., "A Note on the Algebraic Equivalence of White's Test and a Variant of the Godfrey/Breusch–Pagan Test for Heteroscedasticity," *Economics Letters,* 13, 1983, pp. 197–200.

Wales, T., and A. Woodland, "Sample Selectivity and the Estimation of Labor Supply Functions," *International Economic Review,* 21, 1980, pp. 437–468.

Wallace, T., and V. Ashar, "Sequential Methods in Model Construction," *Review of Economics and Statistics,* 1972, pp. 172–178.

Wallace, T., and A. Hussain, "The Use of Error Components in Combining Cross Section with Time Series Data," *Econometrica,* 37, 1969, pp. 55–72.

Wallace, T., and C. Toro-Vizcarrondo, "Tables for the Mean Squared Error Test for Exact Linear Restrictions in Regression," *Journal of the American Statistical Association,* 1969, pp. 1649–1663.

Wallis, K., "Testing for Fourth Order Autocorrelation in Quarterly Regression Equations," *Econometrica,* 40, 1972, pp. 617–636.

Waugh, F., "The Place of Least Squares in Econometrics," *Econometrica,* 29, 1961, pp. 386–396.

Weiss, A., "Asymptotic Theory for ARCH Models: Stability, Estimation, and Testing," San Diego: University of California, Department of Economics, Discussion Paper 82–36, 1982.

White, H., "Using Least Squares to Approximate Unknown Regression Functions," *International Economic Review,* 21, 1, 1980a, pp. 149–170.

White, H., "A Heteroscedasticity-Consistent Covariance Matrix Estimator and a Direct Test for Heteroscedasticity," *Econometrica,* 48, 1980b, pp. 817–838.

White, H., "Maximum Likelihood Estimation of Misspecified Models," *Econometrica,* 50, 1982a, pp. 1–16.

White, H., ed., "Model Specification," *Journal of Econometrics,* 20, 1, 1982b.

White, H., ed., "Non-nested Models," *Journal of Econometrics,* 21, 1, 1983.

White, H., *Asymptotic Theory for Econometricians.* New York: Academic Press, 1984.

Wickens, M., "A Note on the Use of Proxy Variables," *Econometrica,* 40, 1972, pp. 759–760.

Willis, R., and S. Rosen, "Education and Self-Selection," *Journal of Political Economy,* 87, 1979, pp. S7–S36.

Witte, A., "Estimating an Economic Model of Crime with Individual Data," *Quarterly Journal of Economics,* 94, 1980, pp. 57–84.

Woolridge, J., "An Encompassing Approach to Conditional Mean Tests with Applications to Testing Nonnested Hypotheses," *Journal of Econometrics,* 45, 1990, pp. 331–350.

Woolridge, J., "Specification Testing and Quasi-Maximum Likelihood Estimation," *Journal of Econometrics,* 48, 1/2, 1991, pp. 29–57.

Working, E., "What Do Statistical Demand Curves Show?" *Quarterly Journal of Economics,* 41, 1926, pp. 212–235.

Wu, D., "Alternative Tests of Independence Between Stochastic Regressors and Disturbances," *Econometrica,* 41, 1973, pp. 733–750.

Wynand, P., and B. van Praag, "The Demand for Deductibles in Private Health Insurance: A Probit Model with Sample Selection," *Journal of Econometrics,* 17, 1981, pp. 229–252.

Yatchew, A., and Z. Griliches, "Specification Error in Probit Models," *Review of Economics and Statistics,* 66, 1984, pp. 134–139.

Zarembka, P., "Functional Form in the Demand for Money," *Journal of the American Statistical Association,* 63, 1968, pp. 502–511.

Zarembka, P., "Transformations of Variables in Econometrics," in P. Zarembka, ed., *Frontiers in Econometrics.* Boston: Academic Press, 1974.

Zavoina, R., and W. McElvey, "A Statistical Model for the Analysis of Ordinal Level Dependent Variables," *Journal of Mathematical Sociology,* Summer 1975, pp. 103–120.

Zellner, A., "An Efficient Method of Estimating Seemingly Unrelated Regressions and Tests of Aggregation Bias," *Journal of the American Statistical Association,* 57, 1962, pp. 500–509.

Zellner, A., "Estimators for Seemingly Unrelated Regressions Equations: Some Exact Finite Sample Results," *Journal of the American Statistical Association,* 58, 1963, pp. 977–992.

Zellner, A., ed., *Readings in Economic Statistics and Econometrics.* Boston: Little Brown, 1968.

Zellner, A., "Estimation of Regression Relationships Containing Unobservable Independent Variables," *International Economic Review,* 11, 1970, pp. 441–454.

Zellner, A., *Introduction to Bayesian Inference in Econometrics.* New York: Wiley, 1971.

Zellner, A., "Statistical Theory and Econometrics," in Z. Griliches and M. Intrilligator, eds., *Handbook of Econometrics.* New York: North-Holland, 1983.

Zellner, A., "Bayesian Econometrics," *Econometrica,* 53, 1985, pp. 253–269.

Zellner, A., and M. Geisel, "Analysis of Distributed Lag Models with Application to the Consumption Function," *Econometrica,* 38, 1970, pp. 865–888.

Zellner, A., and D. Huang, "Further Properties of Efficient Estimators for Seemingly Unrelated Regression Equations," *International Economic Review,* 3, 1962, pp. 300–313.

Zellner, A., and N. Revankar, "Generalized Production Functions," *Review of Economic Studies,* 37, 1970, pp. 241–250.

Zellner, A., and H. Theil, "Three Stage Least Squares: Simultaneous Estimation of Simultaneous Equations," *Econometrica,* 30, 1962, pp. 63–68.

AUTHOR INDEX

SUBJECT INDEX